Malaysia

Singapore & Brunei

THE ROUGH GUIDE

Written and researched by
**Charles de Ledesma, Mark Lewis
and Pauline Savage**

THE ROUGH GUIDES

MAP SYMBOLS

━━━	Railway	⌒	Cave
▬▬▬	Motorway	▲	Peak
═══	Road	⋎	Viewpoint
-----	Path	▦	National Park
- - -	Ferry route	✕	Airport
———	Waterway	⚲	Lighthouse
▬ ▬ ▬	Chapter division boundary	⋏	Waterfall
▬▬ ▬▬	International borders	⋓	Marshland
▬▬▬	County boundary	ⓘ	Tourist Office
🏰	Mosque	⊠	Post Office
♠	Buddhist Temple	ℭ	Telephone
♣	Hindu Temple	■	Building
♜	Castle	⊞	Church
∴	Ruins	⊹	Christian Cemetery
ⵟ	Public Gardens	ⵉ	Muslim Cemetery
⛺	Campsite	▦	Park
⌂	Refuge	▨	Pedestrianised area
◉	Hotel/Restaurant		

For Map Index, see p.615

CONTENTS

INTRODUCTION

A t first glance there seems little to link the three countries of **Malaysia**, **Singapore** and **Brunei**, not even geographical proximity. It's almost two thousand kilometres from the northern tip of the Malay peninsula across the azure waters of the South China Sea to the separate Malay state of Sabah, on the northeastern flank of Borneo, the world's third largest island. Bangkok or Jakarta are as close to Kuala Lumpur or Singapore as the Bruneian capital Bandar Seri Begawan; and it's quicker to cross to Indonesian Sumatra from Malaysia's west coast than it is to travel across Malaysia by train from west to east. But all three countries are born of a common history and ethnic composition that links the entire Malay archipelago, from Indonesia to the Phillipines. Each became an important port of call on the trade route between India and China, the two great markets of the early world, and later formed the colonial lynchpins of the Portuguese, Dutch and British empires. However, the nations have only existed in their present form since 1963, when the federation of the eleven peninsular states and the two Borneo territories of Sarawak and Sabah became known as Malaysia. Singapore, an original member of this union, left in 1965 to gain full independence, and Brunei, always content to maintain its own enclave in Borneo, lost its British colonial status in 1984.

Since then, Malaysia, Singapore and Brunei have been united by their economic dominance of Southeast Asia. While the tiny Sultanate of Brunei is locked into a paternalistic regime, using its considerable wealth to guarantee its citizens an enviable standard of living, the city-state of Singapore has long been an icon of free-market profiteering, transformed from a tiny port with no natural resources into one of the world's capitalist giants. Malaysia is the relative newcomer to the scene, publicly declaring itself well on the way to First World status in an ambitious manifesto, whose aim is to double the size of the economy and increase personal income four-fold by the year 2020, massively expanding tourism in the process.

It's not immediately clear to many foreign visitors what they are coming to see, as Malaysia, Singapore and Brunei do not have the grand, ancient ruins of neighbouring Thailand. However, there is a solid **cultural heritage** on show, with traditional architecture and crafts thriving in the rural *kampung* (village) areas and on display in cultural centres and at exhibitions throughout the modern cities. The most dominant cultural force in the region has undoubtedly been that unleashed by the Malay adoption of **Islam** in the fourteenth century, while in Singapore Buddhism has held sway since its foundation. But it's the commitment to religious plurality – most markedly in Malaysia and Singapore – that attracts most interest, often providing startling juxtapositions of mosques, temples and churches. Such diversity is also reflected in the **population**, a blend of indigenous Malays (*bumiputras*), Chinese and Indians, which has spawned a huge variety of annual **festivals** of differing intensity.

Faced with such profuse cultural activity, it's easy to forget the region's astonishing **natural beauty**. With Thailand starting to suffer in parts from tourist overexposure, it

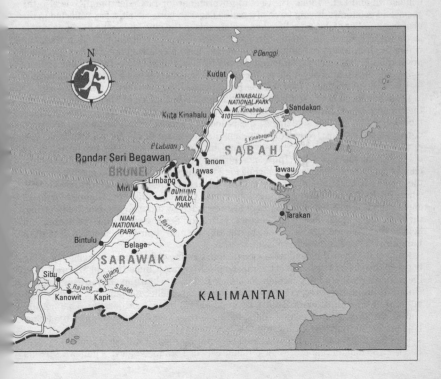

comes as a welcome surprise to discover Malaysia's unspoiled east coast beaches, while the peninsular mainland and the Bornean states contain some of the world's oldest tropical rainforest. The national parks have improved their facilities in recent years and are now among the best organized in the world, providing challenging treks – including that to the peak of Southeast Asia's highest mountain, Sabah's Mount Kinabalu – as well as cave exploration, river-rafting and wildlife-watching opportunities.

Singapore

For many first-time travellers to Asia, **Singapore** is the ideal starting point, providing Western standards of hygiene and comfort, and a dazzling array of consumer items, interlaced with traditional Chinese, Malay and Indian enclaves, themselves shoulder-to-shoulder with the architectural remnants of the state's colonial past. Singapore also rightly holds the title of Asia's gastronomic capital, with snacks at simple hawker stalls, high tea at *Raffles*, the city's most famous hotel, or exquisite Chinese banquets united in their high quality. Most people find that four days or so in the metropolis is enough time to fill shopping bags and empty pockets before moving on to pastures new.

Peninsular Malaysia

Given the distance separating Peninsular Malaysia from the East Malaysian states of Sabah and Sarawak (see below), it's hardly surprising that visitors tend to choose to explore either one or the other. Malaysia's fast-growing capital, **Kuala Lumpur** (or just KL) makes much the same initial impression as does Singapore, with high-rise hotels and air-conditioned shopping malls mitigating the characterful ethnic areas, like Chinatown and Little India. The seat of government for the federation, KL is also the social and economic driving force of a nation eager to better itself, a fact reflected in the growing number of designer bars and restaurants in the city, and in the booming manufacturing industries surrounding it. KL, however, is a city firmly rooted in tradition, where modern Malay executives might always have a cellular phone to hand, but will never miss Friday prayers. Although the city is changing quickly – the sky line appears to be redesigned annually – life on the crowded streets still has a raw, unsophisticated feel, with the markets and food stalls as important as the new banks and businesses.

Less than three hours south of the capital lies the birthplace of Malay civilization and the country's most historic city, **Melaka**, a must on anybody's itinerary. Equally important is the first British settlement, the island of **Penang**, much further up the **west coast**, whose capital, **Georgetown**, retains its fair share of classic colonial buildings, dispersed amongst Malaysia's most vibrant Chinatown. In between the two lie a string of old tin-mining towns, such as **Ipoh** and **Taiping**, which provided the engine of economic change in the nineteenth century, while for a taste of Old England, you need to head for the nearby hill stations of **Fraser's Hill**, **Cameron Highlands** and **Maxwell Hill**, where cooler temperatures and lush countryside provide ample opportunities for walks and a round of golf, exertions traditionally rewarded by a cream tea. North of Penang, there's a more Malay feel to the country, with **Alor Setar** forming the last stronghold before the Thai border. This far north, the premier tourist destination is **Pulau Langkawi**, a popular duty-free island.

Any route down the peninsula's **east coast** is inevitably more relaxing, hopping between the sleepy *kampungs* of the mainland – **Merang**, **Cherating** and **Marang** – and the region's most stunning islands, including **Pulau Perhentian**, **Pulau Redang** and **Pulau Tioman**. However, the coast is not without its intellectual pursuits, most evident in the state capitals of **Kota Bharu**, tucked right up by the northeastern Thai border, and **Kuala Terengganu**, further south, both showcases for the best of Malay traditions, craft production and performing arts.

Crossing the peninsula's mountainous interior by road or rail allows you to venture into the 130-million-year-old tropical rainforests of **Taman Negara**. The park spreads over 4000 square kilometres and although it has become something of a victim of its own success, once away from the main resort area there are enough trails, hill-climbs and salt-lick hides for animal watching, to keep you occupied for weeks. Other interior routes can take in a ride on the **jungle railway**, which links east and west coasts, and visits to the southern **lakes**, which retain communities of indigenous Malays.

East Malaysia and Brunei

The riverine routes into the interior, the remote tribal cultures and some challenging mountain climbing are reason enough to explore the **East Malaysian** states of Sabah and Sarawak. Most approach **Sarawak** from **Kuching**, the old colonial capital, before moving on to the Iban longhouses of the **Batang Ai** river system or to the Bidayuh long-houses close to the Kalimantan border. **Sibu**, much further to the north on the Rejang river, is the starting-point for the most exciting trips, to more authentic Iban longhouses and to those of the Kayan and Kenyah tribes in **Belaga**. In the north of the state, **Gunung Mulu National Park** is the principal destination, its extraordinary razor-sharp limestone needles providing demanding climbing. More remote still are the **Kelabit Highlands**, further to the east, whose rarely explored territories and fresh mountain air bring bountiful rewards for the adventurous.

The abiding reason for a trip to **Sabah** is to conquer the 4101-metre granite peak of **Mount Kinabulu**, set in its own national park, though the capital, Kota Kinabulu – and especially its offshore islands – has its moments, too. Beyond this, the main rewards in visiting Sabah are all to do with its natural riches: turtles, orang utans, proboscis monkeys and hornbills are ubiquitous.

Few travellers venture into **Brunei**, sat between Sabah and Sarawak, perhaps put off by the high transport and accommodation costs. Certainly you'd do better to wait until you reach the East Malaysian states if you intend to visit longhouses, forests or river systems. For those who do pass through, however, there are few more stirring sights than the spectacle of the main mosque in the capital **Bandar Seri Begawan**, towering grandly over the sprawling water village below.

When to go

Temperatures vary little in Malaysia, Singapore and Brunei, constantly hovering around 30°C (22°C in highland areas), while humidity is high all year round. The major distinction in the seasons is marked by the arrival of the **monsoon** (officially termed the "rainy season" to avoid deterring travellers), which affects the east coast of Peninsular Malaysia, the northeastern part of Sabah, Brunei, and the western end of Sarawak from November to February. The peninsula's west coast experiences thunderstorms during the months of April, May and October. The monsoon brings heavy and prolonged down-pours, sometimes lasting two or three hours and prohibiting more or less all activity for the duration – boats to most of the islands in affected areas will not attempt the sea swell during the height of the rainy season. It's worth noting, too, that tropical climates are prone to showers all year round, often occurring in the mid-afternoon, though these short, sheeting downpours clear up as quickly as they arrive. In mountainous areas like the Cameron Highlands, the Kelabit Highlands and any of the hill stations, you may experience more frequent rain as the high peaks gather clouds more or less perma-nently. See the climate chart below for more precise information about temperature and rainfall.

The **best time** to visit is during the first half of the year, between March and July, thereby avoiding the worst of the rains. Arriving just after the monsoon – say, in early March – affords the best of all worlds: an abundant water supply, verdant countryside and bountiful waterfalls. If you brave the heavy showers, the months of January and February are particularly rewarding for **festivals**, boasting two of the best in Chinese New Year and the Hindu celebration of Thaipusam. By sticking to Singapore and the west coast of the peninsula, you not only miss the rains but, coincidentally, find yourself in the most important areas for Chinese and Hindu culture. Arrive in Sabah a little later, in May, and you'll be able to take in the Sabah Fest, a week-long festival of Sabahan culture. In Sarawak, June's Gawai festival is well worth attending, when longhouse doors are flung open for two weeks of rice-harvest merry-making, including dancing, eating, drinking and music-making. Similarly, the pre-monsoon month of September, just around harvest time, is a fruitful time for the Malaysian east coast, where competitions and traditional cultural pursuits are at their most prominent.

CLIMATE CHART

Average daily temperatures (°C, max and min) and monthly rainfall (mm)

	Jan	Feb	March	April	May	June	July	Aug	Sept	Oct	Nov	Dec
Bandar Seri Begawan												
max °C	30	30	31	32	32.5	32	31.5	32	31.5	31.5	31	31
min °C	23	23	23	23.5	23.5	23.5	23.5	23.5	23	23	23	23
rainfall mm	133	63	71	124	218	311	277	256	314	334	296	241
Cameron Highlands												
max °C	21	22	23	23	23	23	22	22	22	22	22	21
min °C	14	14	14	15	15	15	14	15	15	15	15	15
rainfall mm	120	111	198	277	273	137	165	172	241	334	305	202
Kota Bharu												
max °C	29	30	31	32	33	32	32	32	32	31	29	29
min °C	22	23	23	24	24	24	23	23	23	23	23	23
rainfall mm	163	60	99	81	114	132	157	168	195	286	651	603
Kota Kinabalu												
max °C	30	30	31	32	32	31	31	31	31	31	31	31
min °C	23	23	23	24	24	24	24	24	23	23	23	23
rainfall mm	133	63	71	124	218	311	277	256	314	334	296	241
Kuala Lumpur												
max °C	32	33	33	33	33	32	32	32	32	32	31	31
min °C	22	22	23	23	23	23	23	23	23	23	23	23
rainfall mm	159	154	223	276	182	119	120	133	173	258	263	223
Kuching												
max °C	30	30	31	32	33	33	32	33	32	32	31	31
min °C	23	23	23	23	23	23	23	23	23	23	23	23
rainfall mm	683	522	339	286	253	199	199	211	271	326	343	465
Mersing												
max °C	28	29	30	31	32	31	31	31	31	31	29	28
min °C	23	23	23	23	23	23	22	22	22	23	23	23
rainfall mm	319	153	141	12	149	145	17	173	177	207	359	635
Penang												
max °C	32	32	32	32	31	31	31	31	31	31	31	31
min °C	23	23	24	24	24	24	23	23	23	23	23	23
rainfall mm	70	93	141	214	240	170	208	235	341	380	246	107
Singapore												
max °C	31	32	32	32	32	32	31	31	31	31	31	30
min °C	21	22	23	23	23	23	22	22	22	22	22	22
rainfall mm	146	155	182	223	228	151	170	163	200	199	255	258

PART ONE

THE

BASICS

GETTING THERE FROM BRITAIN

Most visitors to the region fly either to Kuala Lumpur (KL) or Singapore. There are regular daily flights to both cities from Britain and the cheapest return tickets start at around £420 in the low season (Jan–June). It's more expensive to reach East Malaysia – Sarawak or Sabah – since it involves a change of planes in KL, though connections are at least very frequent. Direct services are more limited, and even pricier, to Brunei.

For all flights, you're best off booking through an established **discount agent**, which can usually undercut airline prices significantly: there's a list of reliable specialist agents on p.5; or consult the ads in the national Sunday papers (particularly the *Observer* and the *Sunday Times*), London's *Evening Standard* newspaper or *Time Out* magazine, or major regional newspapers and listings magazines, like the Manchester-based *City Life*. It's worth noting that the occasional ludicrously low ad price – £350 to KL – is more often than not a myth, designed to get you to call in the first place. If you are a **student or under 26**, you may be able to get further discounts on flight prices – consult *Campus Travel* or *STA* in the first instance – but for this part of the world, there's little difference between a youth fare and a regular discounted one.

If you're seeing Malaysia or Singapore as part of a longer Southeast Asian trip, then look at discounted flights to Bangkok in Thailand, which can be up to £150 cheaper than to KL; from Bangkok, you can then travel overland by train to

Malaysia and Singapore – see *Getting There From Southeast Asia* (p.14) for all the details. You might also consider a **Round-the-World ticket** (RTW), including KL and Singapore, which start at around £700. There's an increasing number of **package holidays and adventure tours** available, ranging from fly-drive holidays to Malaysia and specialist trekking trips in Sarawak to city-based breaks in Singapore. Although usually not the cheapest way of travelling, these can be worthwhile if you have a specific interest or a tight itinerary.

MALAYSIA

The quickest flights to Malaysia are the **non-stop scheduled services** to Kuala Lumpur **from London** (Heathrow) with either *Malaysia Airlines* (*MAS*) or *British Airways*, a thirteen-hour flight. These, however, can be extremely expensive: the most flexible PEX fare (valid for a minimum of 7 days and a maximum of 6 months, refundable with the payment of a £50 cancellation fee) can run to as much as £899 return in high season (mid-July–Sept), around £100 or so cheaper during the rest of the year. You can buy less expensive scheduled tickets, called Superpex, for around £659–679 return, though these are much more restrictive, valid for only two months and allowing no change to the departure dates and no refund. Add-on fares are also available from other **regional British airports** – *MAS* quotes a total fare of £771–791 on the Manchester–London–KL route, while *STA* charges a flat £60 return to get people from most regional British airports to Heathrow.

Most people, in fact, pay nothing like these prices for a ticket to Malaysia, since several airlines fly **indirectly** to KL, which is considerably cheaper but can take up to eight hours longer – it also, of course, offers the chance of a stopover in another country. Options include *Air India* (via Delhi), *KLM* (via Amsterdam), *Qantas* (via Singapore) and *Aeroflot* (via Moscow and Dubai) – though the latter has probably the worst safety record of any major international airline. Any reliable specialist agent can sell you a ticket on one of these routes, which usually cost around £420–500, though you might find prices higher between June and September. In terms of price, there's little to choose between the airlines.

If you're headed directly for **Sarawak** or **Sabah** you have to get there via KL, connecting with an *MAS* internal flight. Current *MAS* Superpex return fares from London are £724–744 to Kuching, £767–787 to Kota Kinabulu, and the total flight time can vary enormously, depending on what day (and what time of day) you fly. There are up to eight daily flights leaving Kuala Lumpur for Kuching and the best connection adds on another 1 hour 40 minutes to your journey; Kota Kinabulu receives up to nine daily flights from KL, with a best journey time of 2 hours 30 minutes. However, as not all flights from KL to either destination are direct, you could be looking at more like three to fours hours on top of the journey time from London. Although *BA* can quote you a through-fare from Britain to Kuching or Kota Kinabulu, it's prohibitively expensive – it's much cheaper to buy your onward *MAS* ticket in KL. Alternatively, consider buying an *MAS* **Malaysia Pass** – only available in conjunction with an *MAS* return ticket – which can include the flights from KL to Sarawak and Sabah; see *Getting Around*, p.30, for more details.

SINGAPORE

Non-stop scheduled flights to Singapore **from London** Heathrow take thirteen hours, with either *Singapore Airlines, British Airways* or *Qantas*. Again, these scheduled services are relatively expensive with the most flexible PEX tickets going for as much as £899 return in high season (mid-July-Sept). There are cheaper scheduled APEX fares for around £659–679 return, but these carry the usual restrictions – a minimum stay of seven nights in Singapore, maximum of two months and no changes or refunds allowed. *Qantas* do sometimes have some better deals than this; in addition, *Singapore Airlines* makes no extra charge for the first leg **from Manchester**; add-on costs from other **regional British airports** are around £60 return to London.

AIRLINES

Aeroflot, 70 Piccadilly, London W1 (☎0171/355 2233). Usually among the cheapest flights to the region, with one flight a week to KL, two a week to Singapore, both services via Moscow and Dubai. No direct sales to the public, but tickets are available from agents – though some will advise against *Aeroflot* bookings.

Air India, 17 New Bond St, London W1 (☎0171/491 7979). One flight a week to KL (with a six-hour stopover in Delhi) and two extra flights a week via Singapore. Also four direct flights a week to Singapore.

Air Lanka, 22 Regent St, London SW1 (☎0171/930 4688). Flies four times a week to KL via Colombo.

British Airways, 156 Regent St, London W1 (☎0181/897 4000). Three non-stop night flights a week to KL from Manchester, via London Heathrow; one daily non-stop flight a week to Singapore from London, again originating in Manchester.

Finnair, 14 Clifford St, London W1 (☎0171/408 1222). Three flights a week from London to Singapore, via Helsinki.

KLM, 8 Hanover St, London W1 (☎0181/750 9000). Flies via Amsterdam three times a week to KL and once daily to Singapore.

Malaysia Airlines (MAS), 191 Askew Rd, London W12 (☎0181/862 0800). The efficient Malaysian national airline, with one daily non-stop to KL (2 on Sat). Regular connections on to Kuching, Kota Kinabulu and Penang; less frequently to Brunei.

Pakistan International Airways, 1–15 King St, London (☎0171/734 5544). Three flights a week to Singapore, via Karachi.

Qantas, 182 The Strand, London W1 (☎01345/747767). Daily non-stop flights to Singapore; three times a week these flights have connections to KL within two hours of landing. .

Royal Brunei Airlines, Brunei Hall, Norfolk Square, London W2 (☎0171/584 6660). Flies from London Heathrow to Brunei twice a week (Wed & Sat) with short stops in Dubai and Singapore.

Singapore Airlines, 143–147 Regent St, London W1 (☎0181/747 0007). Twice-daily flights to Singapore on the comfortable national carrier, with some immediate connections to KL, Penang and Brunei.

Turkish Airlines, 11 Hanover St, London W1 (☎0171/499 4499). Flies to Singapore three times a week, via Istanbul.

By going to an agent you'll be able to pick up a ticket for much less than this – usually around £420–460 (often a little more in July, August and December), with either Air India (via Delhi), KLM (via Amsterdam), Finnair (via Helsinki), Pakistan International Airways (via Karachi), Turkish Airlines (via Istanbul) or Aeroflot (via Moscow and Dubai; again, the safety warning applies); Pakistan International Airways and Finnair are usually among the cheapest. Most of these indirect services will take around seventeen hours in total to reach Singapore, though the route can take as long as 27 hours.

BRUNEI

The only airline that flies **directly to Brunei** is their national carrier, Royal Brunei Airlines, which flies twice a week **from London** Heathrow to the capital Bandar Seri Begawan, a fourteen-hour flight, with stops in Dubai and Singapore. Fares, even from a discount agent, are high – from £700 return low season to £820 high season – though the tickets are fairly flexible and allow changes and refunds. It's worth noting that flights in July and December are particularly busy. The only way to undercut these prices is to pick up the cheapest possible fare to KL or Singapore and fly on from there with Royal Brunei, Singapore Airlines or

MAS, though the second part of the journey is still going to cost at least another £250 return.

You can also fly from London to Bandar Seri Begawan with MAS, but the connections are poor and involve spending the night in KL. Singapore Airlines flights from London have the better connections, with only a short wait most days in Singapore before catching an onward flight to Brunei. However, both the MAS or Singapore Airlines through-fares to Brunei are very expensive, and rarely worth considering.

ORGANISED TOURS AND PACKAGE HOLIDAYS

There is an increasing number of **organized tours and package holidays** available to both Singapore and Malaysia, and the main operators are listed in the box over the page. For **city breaks**, five nights in Singapore, including flights but with room-only accommodation in a three-star hotel, go for around £600 (£800 in high season), a figure which rises to £800–1000 for two weeks. Standard two-week **packages to Malaysia** usually include nights in KL, Cameron Highlands, Melaka, Penang and Kota Bharu, ending up (or starting) in Singapore, again for a price of just over £1000 in high season, perhaps £150–200 cheaper in winter.

Specialist operators can also arrange itineraries which include jungle-trekking through the rainforest, guided adventure tours in the national parks, and even a ride on the extremely swish *Eastern & Oriental Express* train from Singapore to Bangkok. All these tours tend to be expensive, but may include activities that would be very difficult or impossible to arrange for yourself. Operators like *Explore Worldwide* and *Exodus* usually have competitive prices: *Explore's* "Borneo Adventure" is a two-week trip to Sarawak and Sabah, including visits to a longhouse and various national parks, which costs £1295–1395 depending on the season; *Exodus* offers two- and four-week itineraries in Sabah and Sarawak that run to around £2000; while *MAS*, the Malaysian national airline, can arrange river-rafting trips which start at around

SPECIALIST TOUR OPERATORS

Abercrombie & Kent Travel, Sloane Square House, Holbein Place, London SW1W 8NS (☎0171/730 9600). Experts in compiling top-of-the-range, tailor-made tours, including both city/resort trips and adventure itineraries. Ten-day self-drive tours start at around £1300, while fourteen days in Sarawak and Sabah run to £2500.

Asian Affair Holidays, 142 Regent St, London W1R 7LB (☎0171/439 2601). Upmarket tours to Singapore and Malaysia, staying in high-class hotels and luxury national park lodges – from around £1100 for nine days.

Asia Worldwide, 230 Station Rd, Addlestone, Surrey KT15 2PH (☎01932/820050). City-based holidays in Singapore; fly-drive holidays; trips to Taman Negara, Sarawak, Mount Kinabalu in Sabah; and tours of both west and east coast Malaysia. Recommended, but not budget-priced.

Bales Tours, Bales House, Junction Rd, Dorking, Surrey RH4 3HB (☎01306/76881). Especially recommended for guided tours in Sarawak and Sabah, as well as the £2250 twelve-day "Eastern Oriental" tour from Singapore to Bangkok.

British Airways Holidays, Pacific House, Hazelwick Avenue, Crawley, West Sussex RH10 1NP (☎01293/611611). Five-night city stays in Singapore, KL or Penang for £600–800.

Eastern & Oriental Express, Sea Containers House, 20 Upper Ground, London SE1 (☎0171/928 6000). Tours incorporating one of the most exclusive train journeys in the world (see p.34), but at correspondingly high prices.

Exodus Expeditions, 9 Weir Rd, London SW12 0LT (☎0181/675 5550). Demanding adventure tours in Sabah and Sarawak (no age limit); 16 days starts at £1600, 31 days for around £2000. Their seven-week overland Southeast Asia jaunt (£1150 plus flights) runs along both peninsular Malaysian coasts.

Explore Worldwide, 1 Frederick St, Aldershot, Hants, GU11 1LQ (☎01252/319448). Offers city breaks to Singapore (around £800), but better known for its adventure trips to Sarawak, where a two-week tour, including nights in a longhouse and white-water rafting, runs from £1300–1400.

Hayes & Jarvis, Hayes House, 152 Kings St, London W6 0QU (☎0181/748 5050). Various Malaysian tours including visits to Taman Negara and Gunung Mulu parks.

Kuoni Worldwide, Kuoni House, Dorking, Surrey RH5 4AZ (☎01306/740888). Hotel-based city, peninsular and East Malaysia tours.

Magic Of The Orient, 2 Kingsland Court, Three Bridges Rd, Crawley, West Sussex, RH10 1HL (☎01293/537700). Varied adventure tours in East Malaysia to suit most budgets; specialists in fly-drive packages on the peninsular. Recommended.

MAS, 191 Askew Road, London W12 (☎0181/862 0800). The Malaysian national airline operates seven-day fly-drive holidays from £350 per person, based on two people travelling together, including car and hotels (flight extra). Also arranges trekking trips or six nights/seven days river rafting from £400 per person (flights extra).

Reliance Holidays Asia, 1st floor, Astoria House, 62 Shaftesbury Ave, London W1V 7AA (☎0171/439 2651). Well represented in Malaysia and offering numerous tours of varying length.

Thomas Cook Holidays, PO Box 36, Thorpe Wood, Peterborough PE3 6SB (☎01733/332255). Varied tours to all points in the region – fly-drives, city breaks and beach holidays.

Twickers World, 22 Church St, Twickenham TW1 3NW (☎0181/892 7606). Organizes upmarket tours to East Malaysia's Gunung Mulu and Kinabalu national parks.

World Expeditions, 7 North Rd, Maidenhead, Berks (☎01628/74174). Specialists in small group travel, with the emphasis on meeting indigenous peoples. Prices from £1000 for a two-week trip to Taman Negara or the Sarawak longhouses.

£400 per person for six nights (air fares extra). For more examples of holidays, see the box below for addresses of "Specialist Tour Operators". If you're concerned about cost, you can usually arrange less expensive local tours to all the parks and sights on the ground **in Kuala Lumpur, Sabah and Sarawak** – local tour operators details and prices are given where appropriate in the guide.

Several companies – including *MAS* – also offer **fly-drive** packages to Malaysia and Singapore, with the standard fourteen-day route starting in Singapore and visiting Melaka, Kuala Lumpur, the Cameron Highlands, Penang, Kota Bharu and Kuantan. An itinerary like this costs around £1095, including return flight, the use of a small car and pre-booked accommodation in three-star hotels. Some companies – like *Magic of the Orient* and *Asia Worldwide* – are usually willing to organize a tailor-made fly-drive tour, which gives you the chance to get a little off the beaten track and visit the interior and Taman Negara. Again, two weeks, inclusive of flights, accommodation and car, starts at around £1000 per person.

If you just want to organize renting a car in Malaysia, and not the flights and accommodation, too, see "Getting Around" below for details of car rental.

The cheapest **Round-the-World tickets** through *STA* on *Qantas* start from around £700 in low season (Jan–June & Sept–early Dec) and include three Asian stopovers (Bangkok, Singapore, Hong Kong), but for around £850 you can have up to seven stopovers of your own choosing. Some of the agents listed on p.5 specialize in RTW tickets; remember that you should always confirm onward reservations at every stage. The *Qantas* "Triangle" ticket, for about £630, is a return from London which includes three **Asian stops** – in Bangkok, Singapore and Hong Kong, taken in any order. For students and under-26s, *Campus Travel* has a similar deal for £589 during low season. Another option is an **Open-Jaw** ticket – flying into one airport, say KL, and making your own way overland to Singapore for the return leg. There are occasionally very good deals on a route like this, sometimes as low as £499, though £550–600 is more usual.

The only **courier company** to operate to KL and Singapore is *Polo Express* (☎0181/759 5383). They offer daily flights to both, with maximum stays of two to three weeks, for £375 to Singapore and £399 to KL; one-ways are not available, and you'll also be limited in the amount of luggage you can take.

GETTING THERE FROM IRELAND

There are no non-stop flights from Ireland to Malaysia or Singapore, though both *Singapore Airlines* and *MAS* will quote you through-fares via London (or via Moscow in the case of flights with *Aeroflot*). Students, under-26s and independent travellers should consult *USIT* (see box on p.8 for address) in the first instance, since they can usually offer the best deals.

From Dublin to KL, the cheapest fares with *BA/MAS* range from IR£550–710, depending on the season; there's a IR£20 add-on for the first leg if you're starting from Shannon or Cork. The daily flights **to Singapore** from Dublin, Cork or Shannon with *Aer Lingus/Singapore Airlines* can usually be had for about IR£610 return, though an agent ought to be able to get you a slightly better deal travelling on airlines like *Thai Airways* or even *Aeroflot*, which operates a once-weekly service from Shannon to Singapore, via Moscow,

with fares starting from around IR£540 return. **From Belfast to KL or Singapore**, flights to London are with *BA* or *British Midland* with the

Aer Lingus, 50 Dawson St, Dublin (☎01/899 4747); 46–48 Castle St, Belfast (☎0232/245 151).

British Airways, 60 Dawson St, Dublin (☎01/610666); 9 Fountain Centre, College St, Belfast (☎0232/240 522).

British Midland, Belfast Airport (☎0849/422 888 ext. 4068).

MAS, 20 Upper Merrion St, Dublin (☎01/762131).

Ryanair, 3 Dawson St, Dublin (☎01/677 4422).

Singapore Airlines, 3rd floor, 29 Dawson St, Dublin (☎01/671 0722).

(see "Getting There From Britain" above)

AGENTS AND OPERATORS

Joe Walsh Tours, 8–11 Baggot St, Dublin (☎01/676 7991). Discounted flight agent.

Maxwell's Travel, D'Olivier St, Dublin (☎01/ 677 9479). Only Irish specialist for adventure tours; works in conjunction with *USIT*.

USIT, Aston Quay, O'Connell Bridge, Dublin (☎01/677 8117); 13b College St, Belfast (☎0232/ 324073). Ireland's main outlet for youth and student fares.

onward service by *MAS* or *Singapore Airlines* for a total price of roughly £690–790, depending on the season.

In practice, these prices mean that you're often better off taking advantage of the cheap air fares between Ireland and Britain and picking up an onward flight from London with another airline (see "Getting There From Britain" above). *Aer Lingus, British Midland* or *Ryanair* fly from Dublin to London for around IR£69–89; from Belfast, there are *British Airways* or *British Midland* flights for around £80–100. Any travel agent can sell you a ticket on these routes.

Maxwell's Travel (see below for address) can book you onto one of the **tours** offered by *Explore Worldwide* (see "Getting There From Britain: Specialist Tour Operators" above), and can also arrange city breaks in Singapore (five days; from IR£800) and fly-drive holidays.

GETTING THERE FROM NORTH AMERICA

The cheapest fares and the greatest choice of flights are to Singapore and Kuala Lumpur (KL). Other options include Penang (on the Malaysian west coast), Kuching (in Sarawak), Kota Kinabulu (in Sabah) and Bandar Seri Begawan (in Brunei).

Malaysia and Singapore are roughly halfway around the world from the East Coast, which means that whether you plan on flying east or west you're going to have a long flight with at least one stopover. However, the eastbound (transatlantic) route is more direct because the

usual stopover cities aren't as far out of the way, which makes it quicker – about 21 hours' total travel time – and cheaper. From the West Coast, it's faster to fly westwards (over the Pacific) – Los Angeles to Singapore can be done in as little as nineteen hours – although flying via Europe may not cost that much more, if that suits your itinerary better.

Air fares from North America to Southeast Asia are highest from around early June to late August, and again from early December to early January. All other times are considered low season. The price difference between high season and low season is only about $200 on a typical round-trip fare, but bear in mind that you have to make your reservation further in advance during the high season or you could get stuck paying a higher fare than you'd counted on. Note that flying on weekends ordinarily adds about $100 to the round-trip fare; **price ranges quoted in the sections below assume midweek travel**.

Local **travel agents** should be able to access airlines' up-to-the-minute fares, although in practise they may not have time to thoroughly research all the possibilities – occasionally you'll turn up better deals by calling the **airlines** directly (be sure to ask about seasonal promotions).

Whatever the airlines have on offer, however, there are any number of specialist travel agents which will set out to beat it. These are the outfits

MAJOR ARLINES IN NORTH AMERICA

Aeroflot (☎1-800/995-5555). Flights from several US cities and Montréal to Moscow, with connections to KL and Singapore.

Air Canada (call ☎1-800/555-1212 for local toll-free number). Flights from major Canadian cities to Seoul; agreements with other carriers to KL and Singapore.

Air France (☎1-800/237-2747). Flies to Paris from several US cities, and Montréal and Toronto in Canada, with connections to KL and Singapore.

Air India (☎1-800/223-7776). Flights from New York and Toronto to Delhi, and on to KL and Singapore.

British Airways (☎1-800/247-9297). Flies from major North American cities to London, with connections to KL and Singapore.

Canadian Airlines (call ☎1-800/555-1212 for local toll-free number). Flights from major Canadian cities to Hong Kong; agreements with other carriers to KL and Singapore.

Cathay Pacific (☎1-800/233-2742). Los Angeles, Toronto and Vancouver to Hong Kong, with connections to KL and Singapore.

China Air Lines (☎1-800/334-6787). Los Angeles, San Francisco and New York to Taipei, with connections to KL and Singapore.

Finnair (☎1-800/950-5000). New York to Helsinki, with connections to Singapore.

Garuda Air (☎1-800/342-7832). Los Angeles to KL and Singapore, via Jakarta or Denpasar (Bali).

Japan Air Lines (☎1-800/525-3663). Various US cities, and Vancouver in Canada, to Tokyo; connections to KL and Singapore.

KLM (☎1-800/374-7747; in Canada, ☎1-800/361-5073). Major US and Canadian cities to Amsterdam, with connections to KL and Singapore.

Lufthansa (☎1-800/645-3880). Many US and Canadian cities to Frankfurt, with connections to KL and Singapore.

LOT Polish Airways (☎1-800/223-0593). New York and Chicago to Warsaw, with connections to Singapore.

Malaysia Airlines (☎1-800/421-8641). Los Angeles to KL; connections to Penang, Kuching, Kota Kinabulu, Singapore and Bandar Seri Begawan.

Northwest Airlines (☎1-800/225-2525). Los Angeles, San Francisco, Seattle and Detroit to Singapore, via Tokyo.

Philippine Airlines (☎1-800/435-9725). Los Angeles and San Francisco to Manila, with connections to KL and Singapore.

PIA (Pakistan International Airlines) (☎1-800/221-2552). New York to Karachi/Lahore, with connections to Singapore.

Singapore Airlines (☎1-800/742 3333). New York, Los Angeles, San Francisco and Vancouver to Singapore; connections to KL, Penang, Kuching, Kota Kinabulu and Bandar Seri Begawan.

Thai International (☎1-800/426-5204). Los Angeles to Bangkok, with connections to KL, Penang and Singapore.

United Airlines (☎1-800/538-2929). Major US cities to Hong Kong and Tokyo, and on to Singapore.

---

you'll see advertising in the Sunday newspaper travel sections, and they come in several varieties. **Consolidators** buy up large blocks of tickets to sell on at a discount. They don't normally impose advance purchase requirements (although in busy periods you'll want to book ahead to be sure of getting a seat), but they do often charge very stiff fees for date changes; note also that airlines generally won't alter tickets after they've gone to a consolidator, so you can only make changes through the consolidator. **Discount agents** also wheel and deal in blocks of tickets offloaded by the airlines, but typically offer a range of other travel-related services such as insurance, youth and student ID

cards, car rentals, tours and the like. They tend to be most worthwhile to students and under-26s. **Discount travel clubs**, offering money off air tickets, car rental and the like, are an option if you travel a lot. Most charge annual membership fees.

Don't automatically assume that tickets purchased through a travel specialist will be the cheapest available – once you get a quote, check with the individual airlines and you may be able to turn up an even better deal. Be advised also that the pool of travel companies is swimming with sharks – *never* deal with a company that demands cash up front or refuses to accept payment by credit card.

DISCOUNT AGENTS, CONSOLIDATORS AND TRAVEL CLUBS IN NORTH AMERICA

Council Travel Head Office, 205 E 42nd St, New York, NY 10017 (☎800/743-1823). *Nationwide US student travel organization with branches in San Francisco, Washington DC, Boston, Austin, Seattle, Chicago and Minneapolis.*

Discount Travel International Ives Bldg, 114 Forrest Ave, Suite 205, Narberth, PA 19072 (☎800/334-9294). *Discount travel club.*

Encore Travel Club 4501 Forbes Blvd, Lanham, MD 20706 (☎1-800/444-9800). *Discount travel club.*

Interworld Travel 800 Douglass Rd, Miami, FL 33134 (☎305/443-4929). *Consolidator.*

Moment's Notice 425 Madison Ave, New York, NY 10017 (☎212/486-0503). *Discount travel club.*

STA Travel Main office: 48 East 11th St, New York, NY 10003 (☎800/777-0112; nationwide). *Worldwide specialist in independent travel with branches in the Los Angeles, San Francisco and Boston areas; also offices in KL and Singapore.*

Travel Cuts Main office: 187 College St, Toronto, ON M5T 1P7 (☎416/979-2406). *Canadian student travel organization with branches all over the country.*

Travelers Advantage 3033 S Parker Rd, Suite 900, Aurora, CO 80014 (☎800/548-1116). *Discount travel club.*

Travac Main office: 989 6th Ave, New York NY 10018 (☎800/872-8800). *Consolidator; branch in Orlando.*

Unitravel 1177 N Warson Rd, St Louis, MO 63132 (☎800/325-2222). *Consolidator.*

Worldwide Discount Travel Club 1674 Meridian Ave, Miami Beach, FL 33139 (☎305/534-2082). *Discount travel club.*

MALAYSIA

Malaysia Airlines (MAS) and *Singapore Airlines* operate the only **direct services** between North American and Kuala Lumpur, and also have the only connections to other cities in Malaysia. *MAS*'s only departure point is Los Angeles, with flights from there stopping in either Tokyo or Taipei en route. *Singapore Airlines* flies east out of New York (via Frankfurt or Amsterdam) and west out of LA/San Francisco (via Tokyo, Taipei or Hong Kong) and Vancouver (via Seoul). The airlines can arrange connecting flights from other US or Canadian cities on other carriers, as can any travel agent.

Many other airlines can get you to Malaysia if you don't mind changing planes in their hub city. Heading east, choices include *KLM, Lufthansa, British Airways, Air France, Aeroflot* and *Air India* – or simply hop on any of the dozens of airlines that fly to London and pick up a flight to KL from there. Westbound, *Thai International, China Air Lines, Cathay Pacific, Garuda, Philippines* and *Japan Air Lines* all have connections to KL.

The cheapest fares from **New York to KL** run for about $1200 in the low season, $1350 in the high season. From **Washington, Miami** or **Chicago**, figure on $1300/$1450; from **Houston,**

$1225/$1425; from **Los Angeles**, $1000/$1200; from **San Francisco** or **Seattle**, $1100/$1225; from **Toronto** or **Montréal**, CDN$1275/$1675; and from **Vancouver**, CDN$1200/$1550.

Penang and **Kuching** are common-rated with KL, which means it doesn't cost any extra for the internal connecting flight if you book with *MAS* or *Singapore Airlines* (not so if you buy a discounted ticket through a consolidator). Fares to **Kota Kinabulu** run $100–$150 higher.

If you plan to do much **flying around Malaysia**, consider buying an *MAS* "Malaysia Pass", available only in conjunction with an *MAS* round-trip ticket – see "Getting Around", p.35, for more details.

SINGAPORE

Singapore is one of the world's great air hubs, and competition between the many airlines flying there keeps fares low. It's definitely worth calling around to find the best deal.

Singapore Airlines offers the most frequent departures, with **direct flights** originating in New York (eastbound via Frankfurt or Amsterdam), Los Angeles/San Francisco (westbound via Tokyo, Taipei or Hong Kong) and Vancouver (westbound via Seoul). However, indirect flights on other airlines – or a combination of airlines – might not add much time to your journey, if any, and if you go through a consolidator you might be able to get a free stopover each way. The airlines that fly to Singapore are too numerous to list here: see the airline box below for some of the more noteworthy ones.

From **New York**, you'll be looking at $1175 round-trip in the low season, $1325 in the high season; from **Washington**, **Miami** or **Chicago**, $1275/$1475; from **Houston**, $1200/$1400; from **Los Angeles**, **San Francisco** or **Seattle**, $1000/$1200; from **Toronto** or **Montréal**, CDN$1275/$1675; and from **Vancouver**, CDN$1200/$1550.

BRUNEI

Brunei, on the other hand, is pretty much off the beaten track, and that's reflected in the air fares. Only *MAS* and *Singapore Airlines* fly directly there from North America. You could conceivably pick up a cheap ticket to London, Singapore or KL, and fly on from there with *Royal Brunei Airlines*, *MAS* or *Singapore Airlines* (see "Getting There from Britain" above), but discount agents are unlikely to be able to sell you a ticket for the final leg.

APEX fares with *MAS* and *Singapore* from **New York** are in the $1350/$1525 range; from **Los Angeles**, $1150/$1350; and from **Vancouver**, CDN$1875/$2000.

RTW AND COURIER FLIGHTS

If Malaysia/Singapore is only one stop on a longer journey, you might want to consider buying a **Round-the-World (RTW) ticket**. Some travel agents can sell you an "off-the-shelf" RTW ticket that will have you touching down in about half a dozen cities (Singapore is on many itineraries); other tickets can be tailored to your needs but are apt to be more expensive. Figure on $2200 for a RTW ticket including Southeast Asia and Europe. If you're not planning on going all the way around, but aim to travel in several Asian countries, consider making Hong Kong or Bangkok your first stop; you'll save about $200 over the fare to Singapore or KL and from Bangkok you can travel overland by train to Malaysia and Singapore – see "Getting There From Southeast Asia" (p.14).

Most airlines operating in this part of the world offer so-called **"Circle Pacific"** fares, allowing four (or sometimes more) stopovers in the course of a round trip between North America and Asia or Australasia. However, fares run around $2400 – not very economical unless you have some really obscure stopovers in mind, and plan to travel all the way to the end of the line (say, Perth). Otherwise, you'll probably find it's cheaper to have a discount travel agent put together a ticket with your intended stops.

A further possibility is a **courier flight**, although the hit-or-miss nature of these makes them most suitable for the single traveller with a very flexible schedule. Courier flights to Singapore come up regularly, but most departures are from Los Angeles – figure around $350, maybe less if it's a last-minute deal. Try *Air Courier Association* (☎303/278-8810) or *Now Voyager* (☎212/431-1616).

PACKAGES AND ORGANISED TOURS

Tours in Malaysia and Singapore range from sweaty jungle treks through to five-star city breaks and sightseeing excursions to opulent splendor aboard the *Eastern & Oriental Express* train. Inevitably, these packaged journeys are more expensive and less spontaneous than they would be if done independently, but for the traveller with more money than time they offer a hassle-free experience with a minimum of wasted time.

Including air fare, a one-week vacation is likely to cost at least $1600, and a two-week tour taking in Sarawak and Sabah as well as peninsular Malaysia will cost upwards of $2200. A two-week adventure vacation, involving travel to remote regions, is likely to cost at least $3000. The *Eastern & Oriental* train (see p.34 for more information) is the ultimate in expensive – tours, which invariably throw in several days' worth of luxurious side trips along with the two-night train journey from Singapore to Bangkok, start at $3600. North American operators don't really offer budget tours, although **fly-drive** packages, starting at around $1800, at least allow you to keep costs down by giving you more independence.

Note that your local travel agent should be able to book any tour for you at no additional cost. For a list of North American tour companies, see the box below.

NORTH AMERICAN TOUR OPERATORS

Abercrombie & Kent, 1520 Kensington Rd, Oak Brook, IL 60521 (☎1-800/323-7308). Deluxe tours built around the *Eastern & Oriental Express*.

Adventure Center, 1311 63rd St, Emeryville, CA 94608 (☎1-800/227-8747). Trekking holidays.

Cox & Kings, 511 Lexington Ave, Suite 355, New York, NY 10017 (☎1-800/999-1758). Deluxe sightseeing/wildlife tours.

Creative Adventure Club, PO Box 1918, Costa Mesa, CA 92628 (☎1-800/544-5088). Hiking/nature tours and scuba diving in Sarawak, Sabah and Malaysian peninsula.

Japan & Orient Tours, 3131 Camino del Rio North, Suite 1080, San Diego, CA 92108 (☎1-800/377-1080). Regional tours, KL/Penang/Singapore city breaks, cruises, fly-drives, *E&O Express*.

Journeyworld International, 119 West 57th St, Penthouse N, New York, NY 10019 (☎1-800/635-3900). General Malaysian vacations.

Nature Expeditions International, 474 Wilamette St, Eugene, OR 97440 (☎503/484-6529). Sarawak/Sabah wildlife tours.

Overseas Adventure Travel, 349 Broadway, Cambridge, MA 02139 (☎1-800/221-0814). Trekking in Sarawak and Sabah.

Pacific Bestour, 228 River Vale Rd, River Vale, NJ 07675 (☎1-800/688-3288). Regional tours, Singapore city breaks, *E&O Express*.

Vacationland, 150 Post St, Suite 680, San Francisco, CA 94108 (☎1-800/245-0050). *Malaysia Airlines'* tour arm; extensive range of city breaks, fly-drives, regional tours, sightseeing add-ons, plus golf itineraries.

GETTING THERE FROM AUSTRALASIA

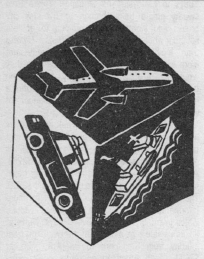

There's a fair amount of choice in flights from Australia or New Zealand to the region, with each country served regularly by its own national airline, *Malasian Airlines* **(MAS)**, *Singapore Airlines* or *Royal Brunei*, as well as by other national carriers.

Many people are planning to see Malaysia and Singapore as part of a longer trip, in which case you'll either be looking at a **Round-the-World** (RTW) ticket or flying somewhere else first – like Thailand or Indonesia – and continuing **overland** from there. Whatever kind of ticket you're after, first call should be one of the **specialist travel agents** listed below, which can fill you in on all the latest deals. If you're a **student or under 26**, you should be able to undercut some of the fares given below; *STA* is a good place to start.

FROM AUSTRALIA

MAS flies twice weekly to Kuala Lumpur, with direct connections on to Singapore and three flights a week on to Brunei. Prices from **eastern Australia** are around AUS$1015 to KL, $1050 to Brunei and $1070 to Singapore. **From Perth**, prices are $850 to KL, $790 to Brunei and $870 to Singapore. A round trip from Sydney with **stopovers** in Singapore, Brunei and Kuala Lumpur costs about $1360.

If you're going with *MAS*, it's worth remembering the **Malaysia Pass**, which allows five single flights within Malaysia, available if booked with the main ticket (see "Getting Around", p.30, for more).

Royal Brunei flies to Singapore or Kuala Lumpur via a stopover in Brunei from **Brisbane** (from $840 to either), **Perth** ($700) and **Darwin**

($790). A round trip from Brisbane with stopovers in Brunei, Singapore and Kuala Lumpur is around $950, or $822 if you make your own way between Singapore and Kuala Lumpur.

Finally, *Singapore Airlines* offers four flights a week to Singapore and Kuala Lumpur; from the east coast it's $910 to Singapore, $940 to Kuala Lumpur; from Perth it's $830 to Singapore, $870 to Kuala Lumpur.

PACKAGES AND CITY BREAKS

For short trips, five-night **packages** in Singapore from eastern Australia go for around $1099 including air fare and twin-share accommodation; or you could have six nights in either Kuala Lumpur ($939), Langkawi island ($949) or Penang ($869); ask at any travel agent. *Qantas* offers similar deals to Singapore, and also has a range of Asian **City Stays** which include flights and hotels in the

---

Note: All **Australian phone numbers** are due to have an extra digit added in the near future.

AIRLINES

Aeroflot, 388 George St, Sydney (☎02/233 7911); no New Zealand office.

Air France, 12 Castlereagh St, Sydney (☎02/233 3277); 57 Fort St, Auckland (☎09/303 1229).

British Airways, 64 Castlereagh St, Sydney (☎02/258 3300); Dilworth Building, corner of Queen St and Customs St, Auckland (☎09/367 7500).

Garuda, 175 Clarence St, Sydney (☎02/334 9900); 120 Albert St, Auckland (☎09/366 1855).

MAS, 388 George St, Sydney (☎02/231 5066 or ☎008/269 998); Floor 12, Swanson Centre, 12–76 Swanson St, Auckland (☎09/373 2741).

Qantas, International Square, Jamison St, Sydney (☎02/957 0111 or 236 3636); Qantas House, 154 Queen St, Auckland (☎09/303 2506).

Royal Brunei, Level 52, MLC Centre, 19 Martin Place, Sydney (☎02/223 1566); no New Zealand office.

Singapore Airlines, 17 Bridge St, Sydney (☎02/236 0111); ground floor, West Plaza Building, corner of Customs St and Albert St, Auckland (☎09/379 3209).

Thai International, 75–77 Pitt St, Sydney (☎02/844 0999 or ☎008/422 020); Kensington Swan Building, 22 Fanshawe St, Auckland (☎09/377 0268).

SPECIALIST AND DISCOUNT AGENTS

Accent on Travel, 545 Queen Street, Brisbane (☎07/832 1777).

Asia and World Travel, corner of George St and Adelaide St, Brisbane (☎07/229 3511).

Asia Specialist Travel, 40 St George Terrace, Perth (☎09/325 5411).

Asia Town and Country Travel, 21 Burwood Highway, Burwood (☎03/808 3233).

Asian Explorer Holidays, 197 Wickham Terrace, Brisbane (☎07/832 4222).

Asian Travel Centre, 126 Russel St, Melbourne (☎03/654 8277).

Budget Travel, PO Box 505, Auckland (☎09/309 4313).

Far East Travel Centre, 50 Margaret St, Sydney (☎02/262 6414).

Flight Centres *Australia*: Circular Quay, Sydney (☎02/241 2422); Bourke St, Melbourne (☎03/650 2899); plus other branches nationwide. *New Zealand*: National Bank Towers, 205–225 Queen St, Auckland (☎09/309 6171); Shop 1M, National

Mutual Arcade, 152 Hereford St, Christchurch (☎09/379 7145); 50–52 Willis St, Wellington (☎04/472 8101); other branches countrywide.

Harvey World Travel, 7 Frederick St, Oatley, NSW (☎02/570 5677); branches across Australia.

JW Asean Travel, Suite 206, 2 Pembroke St, Epping (☎02/868 5199).

Malaysia Tourism, 65 York St, Sydney (☎02/299 4441).

Northern Gateway, 22 Cavenagh St, Darwin (☎089/41 1394).

Singapore Travel, 141 Queen St Mall, Brisbane (☎07/221 4599).

STA Travel *Australia*: 732 Harris St, Ultimo, Sydney (☎02/212 1255); 256 Flinders St, Melbourne (☎03/347 4711); other offices in Townsville and state capitals. *New Zealand*: Traveller's Centre, 10 High St, Auckland (☎09/309 9995); 233 Cuba St, Wellington (☎04/385 0561); 223 High St, Christchurch (☎03/379 9098); other offices in Dunedin, Palmerston North and Hamilton.

price; for example, eight nights in Singapore and Bangkok ($1556), ten nights between Singapore, Hong Kong and Macau ($1949), or thirteen nights in Singapore, Jakarta and Bali ($1920).

FROM NEW ZEALAND

Lowest fares are the twice-weekly flights on *MAS* to Kuala Lumpur (NZ$1174) and *Air France* to Singapore (NZ$971 with a two-night stopover in Noumea, or NZ$1169 direct). A side trip to Brunei from Kuala Lumpur or Singapore is around NZ$520 extra. A **round trip** from Auckland to Singapore, Kuala Lumpur and Brunei with *Air France* is NZ$1990.

RTW AND OVERLAND

A mid-range **Round-the-World** deal is *Qantas* & *British Airways* "Global Explorer" which allows six stopovers wherever these airlines go, costing from A$2299. One route could be Sydney–Jakarta–Singapore/Kuala Lumpur–London–USA. A round trip to Brunei from Kuala Lumpur or Singapore adds an extra $450 to the price.

Thailand isn't a much cheaper starting point for an overland tour; fares on *Thai International*, *Lauda Air*, *Qantas*, *Air France* or *British Airways* begin at around A$900 from eastern Australia, A$820 from Western Australia, and NZ$1550 from Auckland. Coming through **Indonesia**, the cheapest fares are on the weekly *Garuda International* flight from Darwin to Timor (A$330 return), with other services from eastern Australia around A$850 to Denpasar and A$870 to Jakarta. From these, you could island-hop by ferry or plane to Pontianak in west Kalimantan, where it's theoretically possible to travel the 200-odd kilometres overland to Kuching in Sarawak. The border is politically sensitive, however, and you'll definitely need visas in advance. If all else fails, there are daily flights with *Garuda* between Pontianak and Kuching or Singapore.

GETTING THERE FROM SOUTHEAST ASIA

If you are not too restricted by time, it can work out cheaper to get a flight to another Southeast Asian city and then continue your journey from there. Flights to Bangkok can often be particularly good value, and from there, as well as from Jakarta and Hong Kong, there are frequent daily flights to KL, Singapore and other local destinations. It's obviously longer, but cheaper, to travel overland by train from Bangkok – the main line runs down the west coast of Malaysia (for Penang and KL) and ends in Singapore.

There are, of course, other possible routes into either Malaysia or Singapore from Southeast Asia: by ferry, bus or taxi from various southern Thai towns, by sea from points in Sumatra (Indonesia), or by road from Indonesian Kalimantan to Sarawak. There's a round-up below of the most popular border crossings, and details of the routes are included in the text throughout – see the departure information boxes in all the main city accounts.

FROM THAILAND

The most popular way of getting to Malaysia from Thailand is to catch the **train** from Bangkok. Trains leave Bangkok's Hualamphong station (book at least a day in advance from the station ticket office) four times a day for **Hat Yai**, where the line divides. One daily train goes south via the Malaysian border town of Padang Besar (see p.189) and on to Butterworth (p.152) for the Malaysian **west coast route** which continues on to KL (24hr; around £50/US$75 one-way) and Singapore (28hr; £60/US$90 one-way). Two daily trains from Hat Yai follow an **easterly route** to the Thai border town of Sungei Golok, from where it's a short walk to the Malaysian border crossing at Rantau Panjang (see p.132) – from there, you can catch a local bus or taxi the 30km to Kota Bharu – the total journey from Bangkok taking around twenty hours and costing £45/US$70.

There are also frequent **flights from Bangkok** on *Thai Airways International* to KL (10 weekly; one-way £135/US$200), Penang (4 weekly; £105/US$150), Singapore (4 daily; £240/US$360) and Brunei (3 weekly; £220/US$330); but no direct flights to Sarawak or Sabah. **From Phuket**, you can fly to Penang (5 weekly; £45/US$67), KL (3 weekly; £70/US$105) and Singapore (1 daily; £160/US$240); while **from Hat Yai**, there are services to KL (4 weekly; £60/US$90) and Singapore (4 weekly; £150/US$225). Other services from Bangkok are with *MAS* to Kuala Lumpur and Penang.

SOUTHEAST ASIA

0   1000km

Tickets are available from **travel agents** in Bangkok; students and under-26s will probably be able to undercut these prices by booking through STA, which has an office in the *Thai Hotel, 78 Prajathipatai Rd, Banglamphu* (☎02/281 5314); or try *Trade Travel Service, c/o Viengphai Hotel, 42 Thani Rd, Banglamphu* (☎02/281 5788).

By **ferry**, there are scheduled services from the most southwesterly Thai town of **Satun** to the Malaysian west coast towns of Kuala Perlis (boats leave when full; 30min) and Langkawi (3 daily; 1hr). Other options include the ferries from the Thai resort of **Phuket**: once daily to Penang and twice-weekly to Langkawi. The easiest **road access** from Thailand is via the rail junction town of **Hat Yai**, from where buses and share

taxis run regularly to Butterworth and Penang, around a six-hour trip. From the interior Thai town of **Betong** on route 410 there's a road across the border to the Malaysian town of Keroh, which provides access to Butterworth and the west coast; share taxis run along the route. There's also an east coast route from the southeastern Thai town of **Ban Taba**, from where taxi is the only efficient means of transport for the few kilometres to Kota Bharu.

FROM INDONESIA

There are frequent *Garuda* flights from **Jakarta** to either Singapore (1 daily; 3hr) or KL (1 daily; 3hr); as well as services from **Pontianak** to Kuching (1 daily; 1hr) and Singapore, and from

Medan to Penang (1 daily; 20min) and Singapore (3 weekly; 2hr).

There is a **ferry** service four times a week from **Medan** in northern Sumatra to Penang (4hr) and, from **Dumai** further south, a daily service to Melaka (2hr 30min). There are also shorter thirty-minute services twice-daily from **Pulau Batam** in the Riau archipelago (accessible by plane or boat from Sumatra or Jakarta) to either Johor Bahru (p.296) or Singapore; and a minor ferry crossing from **Tanjung Balai** (3 weekly; 45min) to Kukup (see p.295), just to the southwest of JB.

By **road**, it's possible to reach **Sarawak** from Indonesian Kalimantan on various routes, the easiest the nine-hour bus trip from the western city of Pontianak to the border town of Entikong; from here, you cross the border to the Sarawak town of Tebedu (p.350) and then travel onwards to the Sarawak capital, Kuching (p.329) by bus, another four hours away. There's a once-daily *SJS* bus company departure from Pontianak at 6am (around £12/US$18), arriving at the border at 3pm with ample time to catch an onward bus to Kuching. Alternatively, there's a once daily through-bus through to Kuching (£25/US$37) run by the *Damry* company; information and tickets for both departures from the ticket offices at Pontianak bus station at Batu Layang.

Finally, there's a daily **ferry** from Tarakan in eastern Kalimantan to **Tawau** (p.448) in Sabah, which costs around £22/US$33 and takes four hours or so; or more expensive **flights** from Tarakan to Tawau depart three times a week.

FROM HONG KONG

There are non-stop **flights** from Hong Kong to KL on *Cathay Pacific* (1 daily; 3hr) and *MAS* (1 daily; 3hr), and up to six daily flights to Singapore on *Cathay Pacific* and *Singapore Airlines*. Fares aren't particularly good value, but for the best deals, visit one of the following **travel agents** in Hong Kong: *HKFS-STB*, Room 501–509, Trade Square, 681, Cheung Sha Wan Rd, Kowloon (☎725 3983) – agents for *STA*; or *Hong Kong Student Travel*, Room 1021, Star House, Salisbury Rd, Tsim Sha Tsui (☎730 3269).

VISAS AND RED TAPE

Below are detailed the entry requirements for Malaysia, Singapore and Brunei; in most cases visas aren't required for visits of less than three months. If you're unsure about whether or not you require a visa, or any other documentation, your first call should be to the relevant embassy or consulate in your own country, whose main offices are also listed below.

MALAYSIA

British citizens and those of the Republic of Ireland, Australia, New Zealand, Canada, Switzerland and the Netherlands do not need a **visa** to enter Malaysia. Citizens of the United States, most European countries and Japan need visas only for visits of more than three months (which cost US$3); while French nationals require a visa for stays of over one month. All other nationals should contact their local Malaysian embassy for details of visa requirements. **Passports** must be valid for three months beyond your date of departure, and for six months if you're going to Sabah or Sarawak.

On **arrival**, you're stamped in for two months. Should you need to extend your stay, it's a straightforward matter taken care of at immigration department offices in (among other places) Kuala Lumpur (p.109), Penang (p.171) and Johor Bahru (p.296) – though from JB it's simpler just to cross into Singapore and back. In theory, visitors can extend their stay for up to six months in total, although this is subject to the discretion of the official you encounter. In practice, there's rarely a problem with extending your stay to three months.

MALAYSIAN EMBASSIES AND CONSULATES ABROAD

Australia 7 Perth Ave, Yarralumla, Canberra, ACT 2600 (☎06/2731543).

Brunei 437 Kg Pelambayan, jalan Kota Batu, PO Box 2826, Bandar Seri Begawan (☎02/228410).

Canada 60 Boteler St, Ottawa, Ontario K1N 8Y7 (☎613/237 5182).

Indonesia 17 jalan Imam Bonjol, 10310 Jakarta Pusat (☎021/336438).

Ireland No office.

Netherlands Runtenburweg 2, 2517 KE, The Hague (☎070/3506506).

New Zealand 10 Washington Ave, Brooklyn, Wellington (☎4/852439).

Singapore 301 Jervois Rd, Singapore 1024 (☎2350111).

Thailand 35 South Sathorn Rd, Bangkok 10120 (☎02/2861390).

UK 45 Belgrave Square, London SW1X 8QT (☎0171/235 8033).

USA 2401 Massachusetts Ave NW, Washington DC 20008 (☎202/328 2700); Two Grand Central Tower, 140 45th St, 43rd Floor, New York, NY 10017 (☎212/490 2722); 350 Figueroa St, Suite 400, World Trade Centre, Los Angeles, CA 90071 (☎213/621 2991).

Tourists travelling from the peninsula to **East Malaysia** (Sarawak and Sabah) must carry a valid passport and be cleared again by immigration; visitors to Sabah can remain as long as their original two-month stamp is valid; visitors to Sarawak – whether from Sabah or from the mainland – will receive a new, one-month stamp which is rarely extendable. If you start your trip in Sarawak and then fly to the mainland, be sure to go to the immigration office in Kuching (p.342) and have your passport stamped with the usual two-month pass. You'll also need special **travel permits** for certain trips within Sarawak – details are given in the text where applicable.

Malaysia's **duty-free** allowances let you bring in 200 cigarettes, 50 cigars or 250g of tobacco, and wine, spirits or liquor not exceeding

75cl. In addition, no duty is paid on electrical goods, cameras, watches, cosmetics and perfumes. There's no customs clearance for passengers travelling from Singapore or Peninsular Malaysia to East Malaysia, nor for people passing between Sabah and Sarawak.

SINGAPORE

British citizens, and those of the Republic of Ireland, the United States, Canada, Australia and New Zealand don't need a visa to enter Singapore. Nationals of most major European countries and Japan need visas only for stays of over three months. Regulations change from time to time, though, so check with the relevant embassy before departure. Unless you specify how long you intend staying in Singapore, you'll normally be stamped in for fourteen days. Extending for up to three months is possible, at the discretion of the Immigration Department (see p.558 for details); extensions beyond three months are not unknown, but are less common. If you have any problems with extending your stay, there's always the option of taking a bus up to Johor Bahru, across the border in Malaysia, and then coming back in again.

Upon entry from anywhere other than Malaysia (coming from which there are no duty-free restrictions), you can bring in one litre each of spirits, wine and beer duty-free; duty is payable on all tobacco. Other **duty-free** goods in Singapore include electronic and electrical items, cosmetics, cameras, clocks, watches, jewellery, and precious stones and metals.

DRUGS: A WARNING

In Malaysia, Singapore and Brunei, the possession of drugs – hard or soft – carries a hefty prison sentence and trafficking is punishable by the death penalty. If you are caught smuggling drugs into or out of the country, at the very best you are facing a long stretch in a foreign prison; at worst, you could be hanged. This is no idle threat, as the Malaysians have, in the recent past, shown themselves to be prepared to pass the death sentence on Western travellers. The simple answer, of course, is not to have anything to do with drugs in any of these countries; and never agree to carry anything through customs for a third party.

SINGAPOREAN EMBASSIES AND CONSULATES ABROAD

Australia 17 Forster Crescent, Yarralumla, Canberra, ACT 2600 (☎06/273 3944).

Brunei 5th Floor, RBA Plaza, jalan Sultan, Bandar Seri Begawan (☎02/227583).

Canada 1305–999 Hastings St, Vancouver BC V6C 2W2 (☎604/669 5115).

Indonesia Block X/4 Kav No. 2, jalan H.R Rasuna Said, Kuningan, Jakarta 12950 (☎021/520 1489).

Ireland No office.

Malaysia 209 jalan Tun Razak, Kuala Lumpur 50400 (☎03/261 6277).

Netherlands Rotterdam Plaza, Weena 670 3012 CN Rotterdam (☎020/404 2111).

New Zealand 17 Kabul St, Khandallah, Wellington, PO Box 13-140 (☎4/4792076).

Thailand 129 South Sathorn Rd, Bangkok (☎02/2862111).

UK 9 Wilton Crescent, London SW1X 8SA (☎0171/235 8315).

USA 3501 International Place NW, Washington DC, 20008 (☎202/537 3100); 2424 SE Bristol, Suite 320, Santa Ana Heights, CA 92707 (☎714/476 2330).

BRUNEIAN EMBASSIES AND CONSULATES ABROAD

Australia corner of Canberra Ave and Hely St, Griffith Act, PO Box 74, Manuka 2603, Canberra, ACT (☎06/239 6296).

Canada No office; apply to New York office.

Indonesia Wisma Bank Central Asia Building, 8th Floor, jalan Jendral Sudirman, KAV 22-23, Jakarta (☎021/5782180).

Ireland No office.

Malaysia Tingkat 16, Plaza MBF, jalan Ampang, 50450 Kuala Lumpur (☎03/261 2828).

New Zealand No office.

Singapore 7A Tanglin Hill, Singapore 1024 (☎4743393).

Thailand 14th floor Orakarn Building, 26/50 Soi Chitlom Ploenchit Rd, Bangkok 10500 (☎02/515766).

UK 19/20 Belgrave Square, London SW1X 8PG (☎0171/581 0521).

USA Suite 300, 3rd floor, 2600 Virginia Avenue, NW, Washington DC, 20037 (☎202/342 0159); 866 UN Plaza, Room 248, New York, NY 10014 (☎212/838 1600).

BRUNEI

British nationals with the right of abode in the UK, as well as Singaporeans and Malaysians, don't need a visa for visits of up to thirty days; US citizens can stay up to three months without a visa; Canadian, French, Dutch, German, Swedish, Norwegian, Swiss and Belgian citizens can stay for fourteen days without a visa; all other visitors require visas, which can be obtained at local Brunei diplomatic missions (see below) or, failing that, at a British consulate. Visas are normally for two weeks, but renewable in Brunei. Officials may ask to see either an onward ticket, or proof of sufficient funds to cover your stay, when you arrive.

Visitors may bring in 200 cigarettes, 50 cigars or 250 grams of tobacco, and 60ml of perfume; non-Muslims over 17 can also import two quarts of liquor and twelve cans of beer for personal consumption – any alcohol brought into the country must be declared upon arrival.

INSURANCE

Since there are no reciprocal health agreements between Malaysia, Singapore or Brunei and any other country, costs for medical services and hospital care must be borne by the visitor. Consequently, it's essential to arrange travel insurance before you leave, which will cover you for medical expenses incurred, as well as for loss of luggage, cancellation of flights and so on.

If you're going trekking or river rafting in Sabah or Sarawak, check that your policy covers you for outdoor pursuits like this. Always keep receipts for medical treatment and drugs, as they will have to be surrendered to the insurance company in the event of a claim, along with a copy of a police report for any stolen goods.

UK INSURANCE

Insurance is often included if you pay for your trip by credit card. If not, **UK citizens** can ask about policies at any bank or travel agent, or use a policy issued by a specialist travel firm like *Campus Travel* or *STA* (see p.5 for address), or by the low-cost **insurers** *Endsleigh Insurance* (97–107 Southampton Row, London WC1; ☎0171/436 4451) or *Columbus Travel Insurance* (17 Devonshire Square, London EC2; ☎0171/375 0011). Two weeks' cover starts at around £42; a month costs from £50. For trips of up to four months, or if this is one of many short trips in one year, you may be better off with a frequent traveller policy, which offers twelve months of cover for around £100 – details from the companies listed above. Remember that certain activities,

like **scuba diving, mountain climbing** and other dangerous sports, are unlikely to be covered by most policies, although by paying an extra premium of around £25 you can usually get added cover for the period in which these activities are taking place.

AUSTRALIAN INSURANCE

In **Australia**, *CIC Insurance*, offered by *Cover-More Insurance Services* (Level 9, 32 Walker St, North Sydney; ☎02/202 8000; branches in Victoria and Queensland), has some of the widest cover available and can be arranged through most travel agents. It costs from AUS$140 for 31 days.

NORTH AMERICAN INSURANCE

In the US and Canada, insurance tends to be much more expensive, and may offer medical cover only. Before buying a policy, check that you're not already covered by existing insurance plans. **Canadians** are usually covered by their provincial health plans; holders of ISIC cards and some other student/teacher/youth cards are entitled to $3000 worth of accident coverage and sixty days ($100 per diem) of hospital in-patient benefits for the period during which the card is valid. **Students** will often find that their student health coverage extends during the vacations and for one term beyond the date of their last enrollment. Bank and credit cards (particularly *American Express*) often have certain levels of medical or other insurance included, and travel insurance may also be included if you use a major credit or charge card to pay for your trip. **Homeowners' or renters'** insurance often covers theft or loss of documents, money and valuables while overseas, though conditions and maximum amounts vary from company to company.

After exhausting the possibilities above you might want to contact a specialist travel insurance company; your travel agent can usually recommend one. Travel insurance offerings are quite comprehensive, anticipating everything from charter companies going bankrupt to delayed or lost baggage, by way of sundry illnesses and accidents. **Premiums** vary widely, from the very reasonable ones offered primarily through student/youth agencies to those so expensive that the cost for anything more than two months of coverage will probably equal the cost of the worst possible combination of disasters. Note also that very few insurers will arrange on-the-spot payments in the event of a major expense or loss; you will usually be reimbursed only after going home. *Isis* (through travel agencies) charge $50 for fifteen days, $80 for a month, $150 for two months, $190 for three months. Frequent travellers get a good deal from *Travel Assistance International* (☎1-800/821-2828), which charges $200 for a whole year's coverage (90 days maximum per trip).

None of these policies insure against **theft** of anything while overseas. North American travel policies apply only to items **lost** from, or **damaged** in the custody of, an identifiable, responsible third party – hotel porter, airline, luggage consignment, etc. Even in these cases you will have to contact the local police within a certain time limit to have a complete report made out so that your insurer can process the claim. If you are travelling via London it might be better to take out a British policy, available instantly and easily (though making the claim may prove more complicated).

INFORMATION AND MAPS

You can get plenty of information before you leave by calling or writing to the relevant national tourist organizations, which have offices in most foreign countries. Much of the information on Malaysia is fairly general, though you should be able to get hold of good maps and lots of glossy brochures. It tends to be easier to get hold of more specific information on Singapore in advance of your trip, right down to bus timetables and museum opening hours.

For hard information on more remote areas – especially on Sarawak and Sabah – you'll have to wait until you get there, though even in the places themselves you'll often be frustrated by the lack of available information; the MATIC office in KL (p.82) is a good first stop. Specific

tourist office opening hours throughout the region are given in the text where appropriate.

TOURIST OFFICES AND INFORMATION

The **Malaysian Tourism Promotion Board** (MTPB) is the government tourist organization, often referred to as either *Tourism Malaysia* or the *TDC* (Tourism Development Corporation). It operates a **tourist office** in most major towns, usually open Monday to Friday 8am–12.45pm & 2–4.15pm and Saturday 8am–12.45pm; though in the Muslim east coast states these will be closed Thursday afternoon and Friday instead. As a rule, the offices are more than happy to furnish you with glossy brochures and leaflets, organized on a state-by-state basis, but are less helpful for hard information about areas off the beaten track. Best publication is the *Malaysia Travel Planner*, which rounds up all 13 states' attractions as well as listing practical information (like train timetables). In most cases, the offices maintain local accommodation lists, though this doesn't necessarily guarantee any particular standard. There'll always be someone on hand who can speak at least some English. All of Malaysia's **national parks** also have information offices (Taman Negara even has a public library) stocked with maps and leaflets, and staffed by English speakers. Most, however, are badly off for in-depth information, the exceptions being Sarawak's Bako National Park, where photocopied scientific reports are available, and the parks in Sabah, for which extensive fold-out brochures are published by the *Sabah Parks* office (see p.407).

TOURISM MALAYSIA OFFICES ABROAD

Australia 56 William St, Perth, WA 6000 (☎09/481 0400).

Canada 830 Burrard St, Vancouver, BC, V6Z 2K4 (☎604/689 8899).

Ireland No office.

New Zealand No office.

France 29 Rue des Pyramides, 75001 Paris (☎42974171).

Germany Rossmarkt 11, 6000 Frankfurt Am Main (☎069/283782).

Holland c/o *MAS*, Westeringschans 24A, 1017 SG Amsterdam (☎020/6381146).

UK 57 Trafalgar Square, London WC2N 5DU (☎0171/930 7932).

USA 818 West 7th St, Los Angeles, CA 90017 (☎213/689 9702).

STPB OFFICES ABROAD

Australia Westpac Plaza, 60 Margaret St, Sydney 2000 (☎02/2413771).

Canada 175 Bloor Street East, Suite 1112, North Tower, Toronto, Ontario M4W 3R8 (☎416/3239139).

France Centre d'Affaires Le Louvre, 2 Place du Palais-Royal, 75044 Paris (☎01/42971616).

Germany Poststrasse 2-4, D-6000, Frankfurt Am Main (☎069/231456).

Ireland No office.

New Zealand No office.

UK 1st floor, Carrington House, 126–130 Regent St, London W1R 5FE (☎0171/437 0033).

USA 12th floor, 590 Fifth Ave, New York, NY 10036 (☎212/302 4861); 333 N Michigan Ave, Suite 818, Chicago, IL 60601 (☎312/220 0099); 8484 Wilshire Blvd, Suite 510, Beverly Hills CA 90210 (☎213/852 1901).

In Singapore, information is put out by the **Singapore Tourist Promotion Board** (STPB), which has two downtown branches with English-speaking staff and toll-free information lines (see p.479 for details). Each branch has a huge range of handouts, the biggest and best of which is the *Singapore Official Guide*, featuring good cartoon-form maps. You can also pick up the free *Asian Business Press* map, which the STPB endorses.

Brunei barely has a tourist industry, and the only offering from the Economic Development Board (see p.457), which handles tourism, is the lacklustre *Explore Brunei* booklet. For information prior to departure, contact your local Bruneian embassy or consulate.

MAPS

Maps of **Malaysia** are widely available abroad, the best general maps either *Macmillan's* 1:2,000,000 "Malaysia Traveller's Map" or the more detailed *Nelles* 1:650,000 "West Malaysia" (not including Sabah and Sarawak) – both include plans of Singapore and major Malaysian towns. The 1:2,000,000 *Bartholomew* "Singapore & Malaysia World Travel Map" shows the entire region, though check that this (and other maps) is a recent edition - some don't yet show the North–South Highway for example. Better road maps are available once you get there and, if **driving**, you'll want to arm yourself with the free 1:1,000,000 *Road Map of Malaysia*, available from any tourist office. You'll have to buy the excellent *Petronas* "Heritage Mapbook of Peninsular Malaysia", which has 43 double pages showing the Malaysian road system from town to town, with descriptions of all points of interest on the route. In theory, it's available from tourist offices as well as the larger *Petronas* service stations, though, in practice, it can be quite hard to come by.

Good maps of Sarawak and Sabah can be difficult to find, both at home and abroad. For a detailed relief map of **Sarawak**, you'll be hard pressed to find one better than the *Land and Survey Department*'s 1:500,000 issue, available in the bookshop at the Kuching *Holiday Inn* (see *Sarawak*, p.332); the best coverage of **Sabah** is on maps produced by *Nelles*. The **hiking maps** provided by information offices in places like Cameron Highlands and Taman Negara are barely adequate, but they are the best you'll find since there are no proper Ordnance Survey maps of the areas – not available to the general public anyway. If you're following hiking routes marked on sketch maps (including those in this book), it's always wise to ask local advice before setting off.

The best available map of **Singapore** is the 1:22,500 *Nelles* "Singapore"; other maps don't yet include the completed Central Expressway. In

MAP OUTLETS IN THE UK

London

National Map Centre, 22–24 Caxton St, SW1 (☎0171/222 4945).

Stanfords, 12–14 Long Acre, WC2 (☎0171/836 1321).

The Travellers Bookshop, 25 Cecil Court, WC2 (☎0171/836 9132).

Edinburgh

Thomas Nelson and Sons Ltd, 51 York Place, EH1 3JD (☎0131/557 3011).

Glasgow

John Smith and Sons, 57–61 St Vincent St (☎0141/221 7472).

Maps by **mail or phone order** are available from *Stanfords* (☎0171/836 1321).

MAP OUTLETS IN NORTH AMERICA

Chicago

Rand McNally, 444 N Michigan Ave, IL 60611 (☎312/321-1751).

Montréal

Ulysses Travel Bookshop, 4176 St-Denis (☎514/289-0993).

New York

British Travel Bookshop, 551 5th Ave, NY 10176 (☎1-800/448-3039 or ☎212/490-6688).

The Complete Traveler Bookstore, 199 Madison Ave, NY 10016 (☎212/685-9007).

Rand McNally, 150 52nd St, NY 10022 (☎212/758-7488).

Traveler's Bookstore, 22 52nd St, NY 10019 (☎212/664-0995).

San Francisco

The Complete Traveler Bookstore, 3207 Fillmore St, CA 92123 (☎415/923-1511).

Rand McNally, 595 Market St, CA 94105 (☎415/777-3131).

Santa Barbara

Map Link, Inc, 25 East Mason St, CA 93101 (☎805/965-4402).

Seattle

Elliot Bay Book Company, 101 South Main St, WA 98104 (☎206/624-6600).

Toronto

Open Air Books and Maps, 25 Toronto St, M5R 2C1 (☎416/363-0719).

Vancouver

World Wide Books and Maps, 1247 Granville St (☎604/687-3320).

Washington DC

Rand McNally, 1201 Connecticut Ave NW, Washington DC 20036 (☎202/223-6751).

Note: *Rand McNally* now has 24 stores across the US; call ☎1-800/333-0136 (ext 2111) for the address of your nearest store, or for **direct mail** maps.

MAP OUTLETS IN AUSTRALASIA

Adelaide

The Map Shop, 16a Peel St, Adelaide, SA 5000 (☎08/231 2033).

Brisbane

Hema, 239 George St, Brisbane, QLD 4000 (☎07/221 4330).

Melbourne

Bowyangs, 372 Little Bourke St, Melbourne, VIC 3000 (☎03/670 4383).

Sydney

Travel Bookshop, 20 Bridge St, Sydney, NSW 2000 (☎02/241 3554).

Perth

Perth Map Centre, 891 Hay St, Perth, WA 6000 (☎09/322 5733).

Singapore, the *Singapore Street Directory*, from all bookshops, is a must if you're renting a car.

There are few specific maps of **Brunei** available; the coverage on general maps of East Malaysia/Borneo tends to be rather scant. The Bruneian government, however, does produce a map of Bandar Seri Begawan and its environs, which is available free in the capital.

TRAVELLERS WITH DISABILITIES

As you might expect, Singapore is the most accessible of the countries to travellers with disabilities; hefty tax incentives are provided for developers who include access features for the disabled in new buildings. In contrast, Malaysia makes few provisions for its own disabled citizens, a state of affairs that clearly affects the tourist with disabilities.

In both countries, life is made a lot easier if you can afford to pay for more upmarket hotels (which usually have especially adapted elevators) and to shell out for taxis and the odd domestic flight. Similarly, the more expensive international airlines tend to be better equipped to get you there in the first place: *MAS*, *British Airways*, *KLM* and *Qantas* all carry aisle wheelchairs and have at least one toilet adapted for disabled passengers. However, few, if any, tour operators offering holidays in the region accommodate the needs of those with disabilities.

The **Singapore Council of Social Service**, at 11 Penang Lane, Singapore, can provide you with a free copy of *Access Singapore*, a thorough and informative brochure detailing amenities for the disabled in Singapore's hotels, hospitals,

---

CONTACTS FOR TRAVELLERS WITH DISABILITIES

BRITAIN

Holiday Care Service, 2 Old Bank Chambers, Station Rd, Horley, Surrey RH6 9HW (☎01293/774535).
Information on all aspects of travel.

Mobility International, 228 Borough High St, London SE1 1JX (☎0171/403 5688).
Information, access guides, tours and exchange programmes

RADAR, 25 Mortimer St, London W1N 8AB (☎0171/637 5400).
A good source of advice on holidays and travel abroad.

NORTH AMERICA

Information Center for People with Disabilities, Fort Point Place, 27–43 Wormwood St, Boston, MA 02210 (☎617/727-5540).
Clearing house for information, including travel

Jewish Rehabilitation Hospital, 3205 Place Alton Goldbloom, Montréal, Québec H7V 1R2 (☎514/688-9550, ext.226).
Guidebooks and travel information

Kéroul, 4545 ave. Pierre de Coubertin, CP 1000 Station M, Montréal H1V 3R2 (☎512/252-3104).
Travel for mobility-impaired people.

Mobility International USA, Box 10767, Eugene, OR 97440 (☎503/343-1284).
Information, access guides, tours and exchange programmes

Society for the Advancement of Travel for the Handicapped (SATH), 347 5th Ave, New York, NY 10016 (☎212/447-7284).
Information on suitable tour operators and travel agents.

Travel Information Service, Moss Rehabilitation Hospital, 1200 Tabor Rd, Philadelphia, PA 19141 (☎215/456-9600).
Telephone information service and referral.

AUSTRALASIA

Australia
ACROD, PO Box 60, Curtain, ACT 2605 (☎06/682 4333).

Barrier Free Travel, 36 Wheatley St, North Bellingen, NSW 2454 (☎066/551733).

New Zealand
Disabled Persons Assembly, PO Box 10–138, The Terrace, Wellington (☎04/472 2626).

shopping centres, cinemas and banks. Access is improving, slowly, and most hotels now make some provision for disabled guests, though often there will only be one specially designed bedroom in an establishment – always call first for information, and book in plenty of time. Getting around the city is less straightforward: buses are not accessible to wheelchairs and there are no elevators in the MRT system. However, one taxi company, *TIBS* (see p.485 for details), has several cabs big enough to take a wheelchair, and there are acoustic signals at street crossings.

In **Malaysia**, wheelchair users will have a hard time negotiating the uneven pavements in most towns and cities, and will find it difficult to board buses, trains and ferries, none of which have been adapted for wheelchairs. Although most modern hotels in KL and Georgetown have good access, much budget accommodation is located up narrow stairways and presents difficulties for the disabled. Also, do not expect people to respond quickly to requests for help, as strict Muslims particularly avoid bodily contact with non-Muslims as a tenet of their faith.

COSTS, MONEY AND BANKS

Those entering Malaysia from Thailand will find their daily budget remains pretty much unchanged; approaching from Indonesia, on the other hand, costs will take a step up. Once in the region, daily necessities like food, drink and travel are marginally more expensive in Singapore than in Malaysia; over in East Malaysia, room rates tend to be a little higher than on the peninsula, and you'll also find yourself forking out for river trips and nature tours.

Travelling as a couple will help keep costs down, with accommodation and meals working out more economically when shared. The region affords no savings for senior citizens, though an ISIC student card might occasionally pay dividends. However, **bargaining** is *de rigeur* throughout Malaysia and Singapore, especially when shopping or renting a room for the night – it's always worth trying to haggle, though note that you don't bargain for meals. In addition,

most tourist attractions offer discounted entrance fees for **children**, while Malaysia's **public transport network** has a variety of special deals on tickets that help keep costs down (see "Getting Around" for more).

TAKING MONEY ABROAD

The safest and most convenient method of carrying your money is as **travellers' cheques** – either sterling or US dollar cheques are acceptable, though check with your bank before you buy for the latest advice. Available at a small commission from most banks, and from branches of *American Express* and *Thomas Cook*, these can be cashed at Malaysian, Singaporean and Bruneian banks, licensed moneychangers and some hotels, upon presentation of a passport. Some shops will even accept travellers' cheques as cash. Major **credit cards** are widely accepted in the more upmarket hotels, shops and restaurants throughout the region, but beware of the illegal surcharges levied by some establishments – check before you buy something with a card that

---

Each of Malaysia, Singapore and Brunei calls its basic unit of currency the **dollar** (see relevant sections below for more details), written through this book as $. Occasionally, it is neccessary to distinguish between the currencies, in which case the following are used:

M$ = Malaysian dollar.

S$ = Singaporean dollar.

B$ = Bruneian dollar.

US$ = US dollar.

there's no surcharge; if there is, contact your card company and tell them about it. Banks will often **advance cash** against major credit cards; moreover, with *American Express*, *Visa* and *Mastercard*, it's possible to withdraw money from **automatic teller machines** (ATMs) in Singapore and major Malaysian cities – get details from the companies direct before you leave home.

If your funds run out, you can arrange for cash to be transferred from home. **Wiring money** – which can take anything from two to seven working days – incurs a small fee in Southeast Asia and a larger one back home. You'll need, first, to supply your home bank with details of the local branch to which the money should be sent, after which it'll be issued to you upon presentation of some form of ID.

MALAYSIA

Basic food, accommodation and public transport costs in **Peninsular Malaysia** are extremely reasonable and if you're prepared to live frugally – staying in the most spartan lodging houses, roughing it on local transport, and eating and drinking at roadside stalls – it's quite feasible to manage on £8/US\$12 a day. You'll not want to live like this for too long, though, and once you start to treat yourself to a few luxuries, the figures soon add up: an air-conditioned room, a meal at a decent restaurant, and a beer to round off the day could easily bump your **daily budget** up to a more realistic £18/US\$27 a day. From there, the sky's the limit, with Malaysia's plush hotels, swanky restaurants and exclusive nightclubs well capable of emptying even the fullest wallet. You'll find living costs roughly similar in **East Malaysia**, though you can expect room rates to be up to 50 percent more expensive as on the mainland. Moreover, just getting around in Sarawak and Sabah can be fairly expensive, since you'll often have to rent your own transport; there are more details at the beginning of the relevant chapters.

Malaysia's unit of **currency** is the Malaysian **Ringgit**, divided into 100 *sen*. You'll also see the *ringgit* written as "RM", or – as in this book – simply as "\$" (M\$), and often hear it called a "dollar". **Notes** come in M\$1, M\$5, M\$10, M\$20, M\$50, M\$100, M\$500 and M\$1,000 denominations; **coins** are minted in 1 *sen*, 5 *sen*, 10 *sen*, 20 *sen* and 50 *sen* denominations. Also in circulation are M\$1 coins, though these are commemorative issues and are few and far between.

At the time of writing, the **exchange rate** was around M\$3.90 to £1, M\$2.60 to US\$1. It's a realtively stable currency, but more up-to-the-minute rates are posted daily in banks and exchange kiosks, and published in the *New Straits Times*. There is no black market in Malaysia, and no limit to the amount of cash you can take in or out of the country.

Banking hours are generally Monday to Friday 10am–3pm and Saturday 9.30–11.30am, though in the largely Muslim states of Kedah, Perlis, Kelantan and Terengganu, Thursday's hours are 9.30–11.30am and Friday is a holiday.

Major banks represented in Malaysia include the *United Malayan Banking Corporation*, *Maybank*, *Bank Bumiputra*, *Oriental Bank*, *Hong Kong and Shanghai Bank*, and *Standard Chartered*; the *Hong Kong and Shanghai* and the *Oriental* generally offer the best transaction rates. Licensed **moneychangers'** kiosks, found in bigger towns all over the country, tend to open later, until around 6pm, with some opening at weekends, too; some hotels will exchange money at all hours. Exchange rates tend to be more generous at banks, but once you've paid their (often extortionate) commission fees, using a moneychanger often works out cheaper. It's not generally difficult to change money in Sabah or Sarawak, though if you are travelling along a river in the interior for any length of time, it's a wise idea to carry a fair amount of cash, in smallish denominations.

SINGAPORE

As in neighbouring Malaysia, if money is no object, you'll be able to take advantage of hotels, restaurants and shops as sumptuous as any in the world. But equally, with budget dormitory accommodation in plentiful supply, and both food and internal travel cheap in the extreme, you'll find it possible to live on less than £8/US\$12 a day. Upgrading your lodgings to a private room in a guest house, eating in a restaurant and having a beer or two gives a more realistic **daily budget** of £21/US\$32 a day. What's more, once you are housed, fed and watered, Singapore has much of interest that costs nothing at all.

The currency is **Singapore dollars**, written simply as \$ (or – occasionally in this book – S\$ to distinguish it from Malaysian currency) and divided into 100 cents. **Notes** are issued in denominations of \$1, \$2, \$5, \$10, \$20, \$50, \$100,

$500, $1000 and $10,000; **coins** are in denominations of 1, 5, 10, 20 and 50 cents, and $1. The current **exchange rate** is around $2.30 to £1, $1.50 to US$1. Singaporean dollars are not accepted in Malaysia, but are legal tender in Brunei (see below).

Singapore **banking hours** are generally Monday to Friday 10am–3pm and Saturday 11am–1pm, outside of which you'll have to go to a moneychanger in a shopping centre (see p.558 for locations), or to a hotel. **Major banks** represented include the *Overseas Union Bank*, the *United Overseas Bank*, the *OCBC*, the *Development Bank of Singapore*, *Standard Chartered Bank*, *Hong Kong and Shanghai Bank* and *Citibank*; of these, the *OCBC* and the *Overseas Union Bank* usually offer the best rates, while the *Standard Chartered* has a hefty $15 fee for currency transactions. No black market operates in Singapore, nor are there any restrictions on carrying currency in or out of the state.

BRUNEI

Costs for everything except accommodation in Brunei are roughly the same as in Singapore.

However, there's only one budget place to stay in the capital and if you can't get in there, you're looking at around £20/US$30 minimum per night in a hotel, which means an average **daily budget** in Brunei is likely to start at around £25–30/US$37–45. In addition, if you want to see anything of the surrounding countryside, you are dependent on expensive taxis since the public transport network is minimal.

Brunei's currency is the **Brunei dollar**, which is divided into 100 cents; you'll see it written as B$, or simply as $, as in this book (except when there's a need to distinguish it from the other currencies). The Bruneian dollar has **parity with the Singapore dollar** and both are legal tender in either country. Notes come in $1, $5, $10, $50, $100, $500, $1000 and $10,000 denominations; coins come in denominations of 1, 5, 10, 20 and 50 cents.

Brunei **banking hours** are Monday to Friday 9am–3pm and Saturday 9–11am, with **banks** represented in Bandar including the *International Bank of Brunei*, *Citibank*, *Standard Chartered Bank* and the *Overseas Union Bank* – all of which charge a few dollars transaction fee for cashing travellers' cheques.

HEALTH MATTERS

There are no inoculations required for visiting Malaysia, Singapore or Brunei, although the immigration authorities may require proof of a yellow fever vaccination (administered within the last ten years) if you're arriving from an endemic country.

However, it's a wise precaution to visit your doctor no less than four weeks before you leave to check that you are up to date with your **polio**, **typhoid**, **tetanus** and **hepatitis A** inoculations. If you're travelling for a long time, or in rural areas, your doctor may also recommend protection against **Japanese B encephalitis**, **hepatitis B**, **tuberculosis** and **rabies**.

IMMUNIZATION

North Americans will have to pay for these inoculations, available at an **immunization centre** – there's one in every city of any size – or most local clinics.

Most general practitioners in the **UK** have a travel surgery from which you can obtain advice and certain vaccines on prescription, though they may not administer some of the less common immunizations.

For up-to-the-minute information, make an appointment at the **travel clinic** run by the

Hospital for Tropical Diseases at Queen's House, 180–182 Tottenham Court Road, London W1 (Mon–Fri 9am–5pm; ☎0171/636 6099). This also operates a recorded message service on ☎01839/337722 – the code for Malaysia on this message is 87 – which gives hints on hygiene and illness prevention as well as listing appropriate immunizations. A similar service is run by the *British Airways Travel Clinic*, whose main branch at 156 Regent Street, London W1 (Mon–Fri 9am–4.15pm, Sat 10am–4pm; ☎0171/439 9584), can be visited without an appointment; there are also appointment-only branches at 101 Cheapside, London EC2 (☎0171/606 2977) and at the *BA* terminal in London's Victoria Station (☎0171/233 6661). *BA* has an information helpline on ☎01891/224100 and also operates other regional clinics throughout the country (call ☎0171/831 5333 to discover the one nearest to you). All these clinics sell travel-associated **accessories**, including mosquito nets and first-aid kits (if you want to make up your own, see below).

MEDICAL PROBLEMS

The levels of hygiene and medical care in Malaysia and Singapore are higher than in much of the rest of Southeast Asia and with any luck, the most serious thing you'll go down with is a cold or an upset stomach.

A TRAVELLERS' FIRST-AID KIT

Among items you might want to carry with you – especially if you're planning to go trekking (see "Outdoor Pursuits", p.67, for more) – are:

Antiseptic cream.

Plasters/band aids.

Lints and sealed bandages.

Knee supports.

A course of flagyl antibiotics.

Immodium (lomotil) for emergency diarrhoea treatment.

Paracetamol/aspirin (useful for combatting the effects of altitude).

Multi-vitamin and mineral tablets.

Rehydration sachets.

Hypodermic needles and sterilized skin wipes (more for the security of knowing you have them, than any fear that a local hospital would fail to observe basic sanitary precautions).

It's wise, though, to take a few precautions and know about the dangers beforehand. In a tropical climate it's especially important to be vigilant about **personal hygiene**. Wash your hands often, especially before eating, keep all cuts clean, treat them with iodine or antiseptic, and cover them to prevent infection. Be fussier about sharing things like drinks and cigarettes than you might be at home; never share a razor or toothbrush. It is also inadvisable to go around barefoot – and best to wear flip-flop sandals even in the shower. In addition, make sure you eat *enough* – an unfamilar diet may reduce the amount you eat – and **get enough sleep** and rest – it's easy to get run-down if you're on the move a lot, especially in a hot climate.

HEAT PROBLEMS

Travellers unused to tropical climates periodically suffer from **sunburn** and **dehydration**. The easiest way to avoid this is to restrict your exposure to the midday sun, use high-factor sun screens, wear dark glasses to protect your eyes and a hat for your head. You should also drink plenty of water (see below) and, if you do become dehydrated, keep up a regular intake of fluids; weak black tea and clear soups are useful for mineral salts, or a rehydration preparation such as *Dioralyte* also does the trick – the DIY version is a handful of sugar with a good pinch of salt added to a litre of water, which creates roughly the right mineral balance. **Heat stroke** is more serious: it is indicated by a high temperature, dry red skin and a fast pulse and can require hospitalization. To prevent **heat rashes, prickly heat and fungal infections**, use a mild antiseptic soap and dust yourself with prickly heat talcum powder, which you can buy all over Malaysia and Singapore.

STOMACH PROBLEMS: FOOD AND WATER

The most common complaint is a **stomach problem**, which can range from a mild dose of diarrhoea to full-blown dysentery. Since stomach bugs are usually transmitted by contaminated food and water, steer clear of raw vegetables and unpeeled fruit, and stick to freshly cooked foods. How much you pay for a meal is no guarantee of its safety; in fact, food in top hotels has often been hanging around longer than food cooked at roadside stalls. Use your common sense – eat in popular places that look clean, avoid reheated food and be wary of shellfish.

Singapore and Brunei (and in major towns in Sarawak and Sabah), but in rural areas you should buy bottled water, which is available everywhere. If you're going trekking in the national parks, or travelling upriver in Sarawak, you might want to invest in a **water purifier** (see feature below). In addition, drinking excessive amounts of alcohol is a common cause of diarrhoea, and in a tropical climate your tolerance level is likely to be much lower than it would be at home. But however careful you are, spicy or just different food can sometimes upset your system, in which case, try to stick to bland dishes such as rice and noodles and avoid fried food. Ninety-five percent of stomach bugs will be of this unpleasant, but basically unthreatening, type. However, if you notice blood or mucus in your stools, then you may have amoebic or bacillary **dysentery**, in which case you should seek medical help immediately.

MALARIA AND OTHER DISEASES

Although the risk of catching **malaria** in Malaysia, Singapore or Brunei is minimal, if you're planning to travel for a long time or think you might be staying in remote areas, then you should consider protection. Malaria begins with flu-like symptoms, with a fluctuating high fever; it cannot be passed directly from one person to another. The prevention of mosquito bites is the most reliable way to avoid the disease: apply **insect repellent** at regular intervals and sleep with a mosquito net where possible – some places provide these but it is safer to take your own. Mosquito coils (which you light) are very cheap and widely available in shops throughout Malaysia and Singapore. Most doctors will advise the additional use of **malaria tablets** and although they aren't completely effective, taking them can help reduce the symptoms should you develop malaria. You have to start taking them one week before you leave and continue taking them throughout your trip as well as for four weeks when you return; if you don't complete the course, you won't be protected.

It's highly unlikely that you'll catch anything more serious while in Malaysia and Singapore, though long-term travellers may have brought

---

WATER PURIFICATION

Contaminated water is a major cause of sickness due to the presence of micro-organisms which cause diseases such as diarrhoea, gastroenteritis, typhoid, cholera, dysentery, poliomyelitis, hepatitis A, giardiasis and bilharziasis – these can be present even when water looks clean and safe to drink. If you're trekking in the back of beyond, or travelling upriver in deepest Sarawak, all drinking water should be regarded with caution.

Apart from bottled water, there are various methods of **treating water** whether your source is tap water or natural ground water such as a river or stream. **Boiling** is the time-honoured method which will be effective in sterilizing water, although it will not remove unpleasant tastes. A minimum boiling time of five minutes (longer at higher altitudes) is sufficient to kill micro-organisms.

Chemical sterilization can be carried out using either chlorine or iodine tablets or a tincture of iodine liquid. With tablets it is essential to follow the manufacturer's dosage and contact time, whilst, with tincture of iodine, you add a couple of drops to one litre of water and leave to stand for twenty minutes. Iodine tablets are preferred to chlorine as the latter leave an especially unpalatable taste in the water and also are not effective in preventing such diseases as amoebic dysentery and giardiasis. If you are using sterilizing tablets, a **water filter** is useful, not least to improve the taste. However, note that a water filter alone will not remove viruses which, due to their microscopic size, will pass through into the filtered water.

Purification, a two-stage process involving both filtration and sterilization, gives the most complete treatment. Portable water purifiers range in size from units weighing as little as 60 grams which can be slipped into a pocket, to 800 grams for carrying in a backpack. Some of the best water purifiers on the market are made in Britain by **Pre-Mac**; for suppliers contact:

Pre-Mac (Kent) Ltd, 40 Holden Park Rd, Southborough, Tunbridge Wells, Kent TN4 0ER, England (☎01892/534361).

All Water Systems Ltd, 126 Ranelagh, Dublin 6, Ireland (☎496 4598).

Outbound Products, 1580 Zephry Ave, Box 56148, Hayward CA 94545-6148, USA (☎510/ 429-0096).

Outbound Products, 8585 Fraser St, Vancouver, BC V5X 3Y1, Canada (☎604/321-5464).

something with them from elsewhere, so it's important to recognize the early stages of some possible diseases. **Dengue fever** belongs to a family of viruses which are transmitted by the mosquito bite in a similar way to malaria, and tends to occur seasonally and in epidemics. While it is a very common cause of fever and non-specific flu-like symptoms in Southeast Asia, generally speaking the disease is not serious – deaths in adults are very rare. However, the symptoms – severe headache, bone pain (especially of the back), fever and often a fine, red rash over the body – can be serious enough to keep you in bed for a few days. There's no specific treatment, just plenty of rest, adequate fluid intake and painkillers when required.

Typhoid is a lethal disease that is spread by contact with infected water or food. It begins with a headache and a consistently high fever, followed by red spots on the chest and back, dehydration and occasional diarrhoea. If you think you have these symptoms you should seek immediate medical treatment.

Hepatitis is an inflammation of the liver, which may manifest itself as jaundice – a yellow discolouration of the skin and eyes – though extreme tiredness is a common characteristic. While there are many causes of hepatitis (including drug and alcohol abuse), that caused by viruses is most commonly hepatitis A or B, both of which can be prevented by vaccination. A new vaccine, *Havrix*, provides immunity against hepatitis A for up to ten years but requires three expensive doses before protection can be guaranteed. Hepatitis A is one of the most likely infections to be encountered in Asia and is spread via contaminated food and water. Rest, lots of fluids and a total abstinence from alcohol are the major elements in the cure, as well as a simple, bland diet. Hepatitis B is rarer; it is commonly transmitted through infected blood and blood products, so intravenous drug-users, together with those who have had unprotected sex are most at risk.

From time to time, outbreaks of **cholera** are reported in Malaysia; however the vaccine is considered so ineffectual nowadays that there's little point in having it. Cholera is caught by contact with infected water and food, and begins with fever, severe vomiting and diarrheoa, followed by weakness and muscle cramps – seek medical help immediately and watch out for dehydration. **Rabies** is spread by the bite or even the lick of an infected animal – most commonly a

dog or cat. If you suspect that you have been bitten by a rabid animal, wash the wound immediately and thoroughly with antiseptic and seek medical help. Even if you have been inoculated, you'll require further injections.

CUTS, BITES AND STINGS

Wearing protective clothing when swimming, snorkelling or diving can help avoid sunburn and protect against any sea stings. **Sea lice** are the most common hazard, minute creatures causing painful though harmless bites; more dangerous are **jellyfish**, whose stings must be doused with vinegar to deactivate the poison before seeking medical help. **Coral** can also cause nasty cuts and grazes. Any wounds should be cleaned vigorously since retained coral particles are a common cause of prolonged deep infection. After cleaning, make sure you keep the wound as dry as possible until it's properly healed. The only way to avoid well-camouflaged **urchins** and **stone fish** is by not stepping on the sea bed, since even thick-soled shoes don't provide total protection against long, sharp spines. If you do step on one, spines can be removed by softening the skin – although you should try to get a professional to do this.

Jungle trekking presents a few health problems, too. Poisonous **snakes** are rare, but if bitten you must remain absolutely still and calm until help arrives. Meanwhile, get someone to clean and disinfect the wound thoroughly (alcohol will do if nothing else can be found), and apply a bandage with gentle pressure to the affected area. It helps if you can take the dead snake to be identified. Poisonous **spiders** are relatively rare; as with snake bites, keep calm and seek medical help as soon as possible. **Leeches** are a far more common bother and though harmless can, nevertheless, cause an unpleasant sensation. Long trousers and socks can help prevent them attaching themselves to you, but once on your skin they can be hard to remove. Burning them off with a lighter or cigarette is effective, as is rubbing them with alcohol or tobacco juice. See "Outdoor Pursuits", p.67, for more.

TREATMENT: PHARMACIES, DOCTORS AND HOSPITALS

Medical services in Malaysia, Singapore and Brunei are excellent, with staff almost everywhere speaking good English and using up-to-date techniques. Throughout the guide, in the

In a medical **emergency**, dial ☎999 (Malaysia), ☎995 (Singapore) or ☎223366 (Brunei) for an ambulance.

"Listings" sections of major towns, you'll find details of local pharmacists and hospitals; major hospitals are often marked on our maps, too.

In **Malaysia**, there's always a **pharmacy** in main towns, which are well stocked with familar brand name drugs; pharmacists can also recommend products for skin complaints or simple stomach problems, though if you're in any doubt, it always pays to get a proper diagnosis. Opening hours are usually Monday to Saturday 9.30am–7pm (except in Kelantan, Terengganu, Kedah and Perlis states, where Friday and not Sunday is the closing day). Private **clinics** are found even in the smallest towns – your hotel or the local tourist office will be able to recommend a good English-speaking doctor. A visit costs around M$30, not including the cost of any prescribed medication. Don't forget to keep the receipts for insurance claim purposes. Finally, the emergency department of each town's **General Hospital** will see foreigners (usually allowing you to jump the queue) for the token fee of $1, though obviously costs rise rapidly if continued treatment or overnight stays are necessary.

Services in **Singapore** are broadly similar – for the location of Singapore pharmacies and hospitals, turn to p.558.

GETTING AROUND

Public transport in the region is extremely reliable, though not as cheap as in other Southeast Asian countries. Most of your travelling, particularly on the peninsula, will be by bus or long-distance taxi, though the Malaysian train system has its uses, especially on the long haul up the west coast from Singapore and into Thailand. By and large, the roads in Peninsular Malaysia are reasonable and if you're driving, new road construction continues to speed up travel times: the North–South Highway runs the length of the west coast from Johor Bahru to Bukit Kayu Hitam, while the East–West Highway connects Kota Bahru with Penang.

Sabah and Brunei both have their own travel peculiarities – in Sarawak, for instance, you'll be reliant on boats, and occasionally planes, for most long-distance travel; there are more details given below and turn to p.327 (Sarawak), p.405 (Sabah) and p.455 (Brunei) for further information. The main thing to note is that there is no boat service **between Peninsular Malaysia or Singapore and East Malaysia**; consequently, you have to fly from the mainland to Sabah, Sarawak or Brunei. **In Singapore** there's a comprehensive city and island-wide public transport system – all the details are covered on p.480–486.

Many foreigners hitch while in Malaysia, particularly along the east coast, and some consider it to be a valuable way of developing social contact with local people. However, **this guide does not recommend hitching as a means of getting around any part of Malaysia, Singapore or Brunei**, especially since internal transport costs tend to be fairly low.

Details of **specific routes and journey times** between towns are given at the end of each chapter in "Travel Details". Look, too, for the boxed "Leaving" sections in each major town account, which provide useful hints on the most convenient local routes and services.

BUSES

Apart from in Sarawak, the national **bus** network is the easiest and quickest way of getting around Malaysia, with regular services between all major towns. Inter-state destinations are covered by comfortable, air-conditioned **express buses**, stopping only at major points on the route and for refreshment breaks. In addition to the government-run *Ekspress Nasional* and individual state bus companies, a large number of private companies operate services along specific routes; each has an office in the town's bus station where you buy your ticket. The departure time of the company's next bus is usually displayed and since prices are fairly similar on all routes, it matters little which company you opt for. Buses for long-distance routes (those over 3hr) typically leave in clusters in the early morning and late evening, while shorter or more popular routes are served regularly throughout the day. In most cases you can just turn up immediately prior to departure, though on some of the more popular routes – Kuala Lumpur to Penang, or Kuantan to Singapore – it's advisable to **reserve a ticket** in advance, at least a day before at the relevant ticket office (particularly during the major holiday periods of Christmas, Easter and Hari Raya). **Fares** are eminently reasonable: the eight-hour run from KL to Georgetown, for example, costs $18.50; for other fares, see the box below. Many towns and cities have more than one bus station, serving different regions or companies; the text and maps detail where you should go to catch your bus.

Local buses usually, though not always, operate from a separate station. They serve routes within the state and are consequently cheaper, but also slower, less comfortable and without air-conditioning. It's not possible to book a seat – buy your ticket on the bus.

Several buses ply the long-distance routes across **Sabah**, but they are heavily outnumbered by the **minibuses** that buzz around the state, which generally leave from the same terminals. Faster and slightly more expensive than the scheduled bus services, minibuses only leave when jam-packed and are often very uncomfortable as a result – from Kota Kinabulu to Kudat costs around $10, to Sandakan around $15–20. Also prevalent in Sabah are **land cruisers**, outsized jeeps which take only eight passengers and whose fares are priced somewhere between those of a bus and those of a taxi.

Buses in **Sarawak** are only used for getting between Kuching and Bintulu, Sibu and Bintulu, Bintulu and Miri, and from Miri to the Bruneian border. Services (with differing price structures) are either by modern air-con buses or rickety local ones; since part of the route from Sibu to Bintulu is not yet fully paved, the well-sprung air-con buses are more comfortable.

SAMPLE EXPRESS BUS ROUTES AND FARES

All fares are given in Malaysian dollars.

Kuala Lumpur to:

Alor Setar	8hr;	$21
Butterworth	7hr;	$17
Cameron Highlands	4hr;	$10
Ipoh	4hr;	$10
Johor Bahru	7hr;	$17
Kota Bharu	7hr;	$25
Kuala Lipis	3hr;	$8
Kuantan	5hr;	$12
Lumut	5hr 30min;	$13
Melaka	2hr;	$6
Singapore	8hr;	$22

TRAINS

The peninsula's **train** service, operated by *Keretapi Tanah Melayu* (*KTM*), is limited in scope, relatively expensive and extremely slow, making it for the most part an unappealing alternative to the bus. However, it is the only way to reach some of the more interesting places in the interior and there's still a certain thrill in arriving at some of the splendidly solid colonial stations, built when the train was the prime means of transport.

ROUTES AND SERVICES

There are only two main lines through Peninsular Malaysia, both originating in Thailand at the southern town of Hat Yai. The **west coast** route from Thailand via Padang Besar on the Malaysian border runs south through Butterworth (for Penang), Ipoh, Tapah Road (for the Cameron Highlands) and KL, where you usually have to change trains before continuing on to Singapore. Between KL and Singapore the train route splits at **Gemas**, 58km northeast of Melaka, from

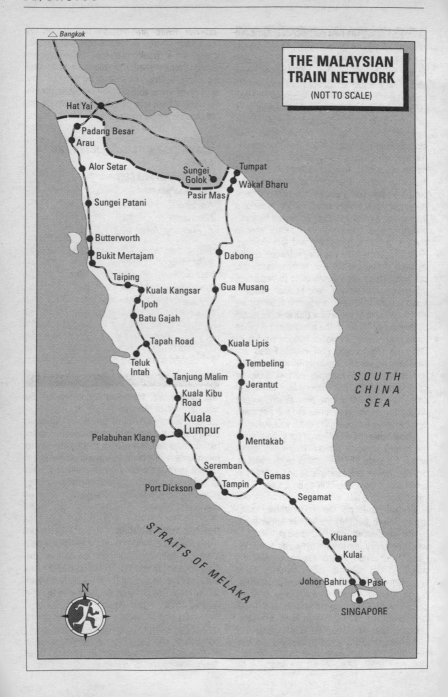

△ Bangkok

**THE MALAYSIAN
TRAIN NETWORK**
(NOT TO SCALE)

Hat Yai

Padang Besar
Arau

Alor Setar

Sungei
Golok

Tumpat

Wakaf Bharu

Pasir Mas

Sungei Patani

Butterworth

Bukit Mertajam

Dabong

Taiping

Kuala Kangsar

Gua Musang

Ipoh

Batu Gajah

Tapah Road

Kuala Lipis

Teluk
Intah

Tembeling

Tanjung Malim

Jerantut

Kuala Kibu
Road

**Kuala
Lumpur**

Pelabuhan Klang

Mentakab

Seremban

Gemas

Tampin

Port Dickson

Segamat

SOUTH
CHINA
SEA

STRAITS OF MELAKA

Kluang

Kulai

Johor Bahru

Pasir

SINGAPORE

N

where a second line runs north through the mountainous interior – a section known as the "**jungle railway**" – via Kuala Lipis and skirting Kota Bharu (nearest station is at Wakaf Bharu) to the northeastern border town of Tumpat. If you want to get to Thailand by train this way, you have to get off at Pasir Mas and catch a bus or taxi to the border crossing at Rantau Panjang, since the Malaysian branch line to the border is no longer used (see p.232 for more details).

East Malaysia's only rail line is the 55-kilometre, narrow-guage link between Kota Kinabalu and Tenom in **Sabah**. The service is slow and jarring, and only really worth following between Beaufort and Tenom, when it traces a dramatic path along sungei Padas; all the details are on p.423.

There are two types of train: **express trains**, running on the west coast line only and stopping at principal stations, and **ordinary trains** (labelled *M* on the timetables), which run on both lines and stop at virtually every station. Where there's a choice, you'll find that the only real difference between them is the speed of the journey, since they both have three classes of travel and a choice of air-con or non-air-con; choosing an express train, however, on a west coast route can knock anything up to three hours off your journey time. You don't need to book in advance for ordinary trains, but you may want to reserve a day or two in advance (which incurs a small charge) on express trains, particularly if you require an overnight berth. This must be done at the station – reservations are not accepted over the phone.

On the **west coast** there are five trains a day between Singapore and KL, and six between KL and Padang Besar; of these, only one is an ordinary train. In addition, there is a once-daily *Kedah Line* service, running between Butterworth and Arau, and one **international express** a day between Butterworth and Bangkok, for which additional charges (see below) apply. Thus to travel from Singapore to Bangkok involves changing at both KL and Butterworth, unless you catch the once-daily **Ekspres Raykat** train (*ER* on the timetable) from Singapore, which stops briefly at KL before continuing on to Butterworth – though you'll still have to wait there until the next day to pick up the Bangkok connection. Two daily services between Kluang and Singapore, and one daily between Gemas and Singapore, augment the west coast schedule. All the trains on the

interior route are ordinary trains, with the exception of the *Tumpat Express* which runs three times weekly between Singapore and Tumpat. There's also a once-daily train from Gemas to Tumpat.

A free **timetable** for the whole country is available from the train station in Kuala Lumpur and other major towns, and details all the services on the various routes; all stations have the departure and arrival times posted near the platform.

TICKETS AND PASSES

Fares vary according to class of travel and type of train; for main routes and prices see the box below. Second-class is usually roomy and comfortable enough for most journeys, and the only real advantage of first-class travel is the air-conditioning, though first-class tickets are almost twice the price. Third-class, although only around half as much as second, is inevitably more crowded, with fewer comforts.

On **overnight sleepers**, there's only first- and second-class available, though you can opt for air-con or non-air-con in second class. A berth on the **international express** between Butterworth and Bangkok (see above) costs $22.60 first-class, from $18.10 in second-class air-con and from $9.10 in non-air-con, depending on whether you want an upper or lower berth; charges for berths on all other overnight trains are marginally higher.

Eurotrain International offers an **Explorer Pass** to all students and people under 30 holding either an *International Student Identity Card* or *IYHF* (hostel) membership card, but you'd have to be prepared to travel almost exclusively by train to get your money's worth. This is valid for unlimited second-class train travel on *KTM* in Peninsular Malaysia and Singapore for 7 (£20/US$32), 14 (£27/US$43) or 21 (£35/US$54) days; the pass includes the cost of seat reservations but not sleeper berth charges; it's also not valid on the Sabah train line. It's available from *Campus Travel* in London (see p.5 for address), or from student-orientated travel agents in Kuala Lumpur and Singapore, where it costs roughly the same in the local currencies.

TRANS-MALAYSIAN ROUTES

Other than the Malaysian journeys, one long-distance route you might consider is the train ride **from Singapore to Bangkok**, which takes a

SAMPLE TRAIN ROUTES AND FARES

All fares are given in Malaysian dollars.	EXPRESS			ORDINARY		
	1st	2nd	3rd	1st	2nd	3rd
Kuala Lumpur to:						
Alor Setar	79.00	39.00	22.00	70.50	30.60	17.40
Butterworth	67.00	34.00	19.00	58.50	25.40	14.40
Gemas	35.00	20.00	11.00	27.00	11.70	6.70
Ipoh	40.00	22.00	12.00	31.50	13.70	7.80
Kuala Lipis	-	-	-	61.50	26.70	15.20
Padang Besar	89.00	44.00	24.00	81.00	35.10	20.00
Taiping	53.00	28.00	16.00	45.00	19.00	11.10
Tapah Road	32.00	19.00	10.00	23.30	10.10	5.80
Tumpat	-	-	-	106.50	46.20	26.20
Singapore	68.00	34.00	19.00	60.00	26.00	14.80
Singapore to:						
Alor Setar	139.00	69.00	37.00	130.50	56.60	32.20
Butterworth	127.00	60.00	34.00	118.50	51.40	29.20
Gemas	43.00	23.00	13.00	34.00	15.00	8.50
Kuala Lipis	-	-	-	67.50	29.30	16.70
Kuala Lumpur	68.00	34.00	19.00	60.00	26.00	14.80
Padang Besar	148.00	69.00	39.00	139.00	60.50	34.40
Tumpat	-	-	-	112.50	48.80	27.70

minimum of fifty hours. While there is only one through-connection from Singapore to Butterworth (the *Ekspres Raykat*; see above), you never usually have to wait longer than an hour in KL to catch an onward service, although unfortunately none of the trains to Butterworth connect conveniently with the international express to Bangkok, involving either an overnight stop in Butterworth or, at best, a six-and-a-half-hour wait. It's a tiring journey done in one go, particularly if you don't book a berth on the overnight leg between Butterworth and Bangkok (see above for charges), but is the quickest way (other than flying) to travel right through Malaysia. **One-way tickets** for the whole route, from Singapore to Bangkok, cost M$206.80 first-class and M$91.70 second-class. though an *Explorer Pass* (see above) is valid on the Malaysian leg of the journey.

Following the same route in considerably more luxury, the **Eastern & Oriental Express** departs every Sunday from Singapore to Bangkok (returning on Wednesdays), stopping at Tampin (for Melaka), Kuala Lumpur, Ipoh and Butterworth; the trip takes 41 hours, includes two nights on the train and costs from M$2900 (£740/US$1110) per person, depending on the type of cabin. **Bookings** can be made at *Eastern & Oriental Express*, Sea Containers House, 20 Upper Ground, London SE1 (☎0171/928 6000); through some of the North American tour operators listed on p.12; in Singapore at *E&O Services*, 05/01 Carlton Building, 90 Cecil St (☎02/323 4390); or in Bangkok through *Sea Tours Co. Ltd*, Room 413/4, 4th floor, Siam Centre, 965 Rama I Rd (☎02/251 4862).

LONG-DISTANCE TAXIS

Most towns have a long-distance taxi rank (usually right next to the express bus station). The four-seater taxis charge fixed-price, per-person fares on long-distance routes throughout the country; you can usually reckon on paying between 50 and 100 percent more than the regular bus fare. Prices are chalked up on a board in the station, so there's no danger of being ripped off – in fact, taxis are generally very reliable and a whole lot quicker than the buses. From Kuala Lumpur you're looking at around $30 to Butterworth, $17 to Ipoh and $35 to Kota Bharu. You'll have to wait until the car has its full complement of four passengers before departure, but in most major towns this should never be more than thirty minutes. More often than not, as a foreigner you'll be pressured to charter the whole car (at four times the one-person fare), making it expensive unless you're in a group.

FERRIES AND BOATS

Ferries sail to all the major islands off Malaysia's east and west coasts, though the traditional **bumboats** – originally used for fishing – are rapidly being replaced by faster, sleeker express models; if you want to experience an old-style bumboat ride, you can still do so in Singapore (p.486). On all ferries, you can buy your ticket in advance from booths at the jetty, though you can usually pay on the boat as well. All the relevant details are given in the text. There's a reduced service to the east coast Perhentian islands and to Redang, Kapas, Tioman and the rest of the Seribuat archipelago between the **monsoon** months of November and February. The only regular **inter-island** connection is between Penang and Langkawi, a daily service taking two hours (p.170); there's a regular catamaran service between **Singapore and Pulau Tioman** (p.481); while boats also run from Malaysian west coast ports to Thailand (see *The West Coast* for details of these).

There are no ferry services across the South China Sea from the peninsula to East Malaysia; you'll have to fly. Once in **Sarawak**, the most usual method of travel is by long, turbo-charged **ekspres** (express) boat along the widespread river systems. These low-lying craft are the lifeline of the people who live along the rivers in the interior and run to a regular timetable – buy your ticket on the boat. Once on the smaller tributaries, travel is by **longboat**, which often turns out to be more expensive since you may have to charter the whole vessel on some routes. For more details on getting around Sarawak by boat, see p.327.

Sabah has no *ekspres* boats, but regular ferries connect Pulau Labuan with Kota Kinabalu, Sipitang and Menumbok on the west coast; details where relevant in the text. In **Brunei**, too, there are occasional boat services of which you

may make use, in particular the speedboat service from the capital, Bandar Seri Begawan, to Bangar and the regular boats from Bandar to Lawas or Limbang in Sarawak and Pulau Labuan in Sabah; see p.459 for all the details.

PLANES

The Malaysian national airline, **MAS**, operates a comprehensive range of domestic flights, though services between major towns on the peninsula are often routed via Kuala Lumpur, making them long-winded and uneconomical. But some routes are definitely worth considering: although expensive, the flight from KL to Langkawi (M$135 one-way) takes just 55 minutes, thus saving a lengthy eleven-hour bus journey followed by an hour's ferry ride.

Special fares offer considerable discounts to tourists. For example, designated **night tourist flights** can reduce the price of a one-way flight between KL and Alor Setar from $113 to $74; similar reductions are available on routes from KL to Kota Bharu, Kota Kinabulu, Kuching and Penang, and from Kota Kinabulu to Johor Bahru. In addition, **one-way** and **return excursion** fares operate between Johor Bahru and Kota Kinabulu, Kuching and Penang, and between KL and Kota Kinabulu, Kuching, Labuan and Miri, representing savings of around 15 percent on the regular one-way fare and 10 percent on the return fare. **Family fares** within Malaysia (but excluding Singapore and Brunei) apply to a return trip made within thirty days: if one family member pays the full fare, the accompanying spouse and/or children get a 25 percent discount. Two types of **group fares** are in operation: between Peninsular Malaysia and East Malaysia and between Sabah and Sarawak, three or more passengers travelling together receive a 50 percent discount; for other routes in Malaysia, a 25 percent discount applies. To qualify, participants must stay between four and thirty days and full payment must be made at least seven days prior to departure. **Blind or disabled** passengers are entitled to a 50 percent discount, with a 25 percent reduction for a companion. There are **no student reductions** for anyone studying outside Malaysia.

One other way to keep internal flight costs down is to buy an *MAS* **Malaysia Pass**, which is only available in conjunction with a *MAS* return ticket from your home country. These cost approximately £60/US$94 for flights within

Peninsular Malaysia, £125/US$194 if you include Sarawak and Sabah, and the passes are valid on a specific pre-booked itinerary for 21 days. The pass is valid for five "sectors", which gives you up to five free flights: from KL to most peninsular destinations counts as one sector. When you buy the pass you must book your first internal connection: you can leave the dates open for the rest of the itinerary, but can't actually change the route once you've bought the pass. See the "Getting There" sections above for details of *MAS* tickets and offices in your own country.

MAS has **booking offices** in every major town and city on the peninsula, as well as in Sarawak, Sabah and Singapore; addresses and phone numbers are given throughout the text.

MAIN ROUTES

The most frequent service is the shuttle **between KL and Singapore**, on either *MAS* or *Singapore Airlines*, with departures every half-hour at peak times for a standard one-way fare of M$119 (S$111); the journey takes 55 minutes. There's also an hourly service **to Penang** (45min;M$104) from KL, and a *Singapore Airlines* service from Singapore (3 daily; S$340 return). In addition, the *MAS* subsidary, *Pelangi Air*, operates Twin-Otter planes to the **islands** of Tioman and Pangkor from Kuala Lumpur, Kuantan and Singapore, as well as to the interior around Taman Negara (see relevant sections for details) – spectacular flights all. The *Singapore Airlines* subsidiary, *SilkAir*, also connects Singapore with Tioman, Langkawi and Kuantan.

Flights to East Malaysia operate mainly out of Kuala Lumpur, with Johor Bahru providing additional services to Kuching and Kota Kinabalu; see "Sarawak practicalities" (p.326) and "Sabah practicalities" (p.404) for more information. Note that flight times from KL to either Kuching or Kota Kinabalu can take longer than you think. Although direct services take roughly 1 hour 40 minutes to Kuching, and 2 hours 30 minutes to Kota Kinaulu, many flights are routed via Johor Bahru, with some Sabah-bound flights then making several more stops in Sarawak on the way. **Within Sarawak and Sabah**, the numerous nineteen-seater Twin-Otter flights help maintain communications with the remote provinces. There are regular rural air services **from Kuching** to most Sarawak towns, **from Kota Kinabalu** to Kudat, Lawas, Limbang, Miri and Sandakan, and **from Lawas** to Ba Kalalan and Limbang, among many others, though the more remote areas are susceptible to delays and cancellations due to weather conditions.

DRIVING AND VEHICLE RENTAL

The condition of the roads in **Peninsular Malaysia** is generally excellent, making driving there a viable prospect for tourists; though not so in **Sabah, Sarawak** and **Brunei** where the roads are rougher and highly susceptible to flash flooding.

On the peninsula, the pristine **North–South Highway** (the only toll road in the country; see below) from Singapore runs nearly 900km up the west coast to the border with Thailand, with **Route 1**, its predecessor, shadowing it virtually all the way. At Kuala Lumpur, **Route 2**, a notorious accident blackspot, cuts through the central region to connect the capital with the east coast town of Kuantan, while much further to the north, the **East–West Highway (Route 4)** traces the Thai border to link Butterworth with Kota Bharu. The mountainous interior is sliced in two by the narrow and winding **Route 8**, which leaves Route 2 roughly 50km from Kuala Lumpur, passing through Kuala Lipis and Kuala Kerai before reaching Kota Bharu. The east coast is served by **Route 3**, a remarkably traffic-free road that begins in Kota Bharu and terminates in Johor Bahru, 700km to the south. As far as **journey times** go, you can reckon on a three-hour journey between Kuala Lumpur and Melaka, and about seven to Penang.

Note that the streets of **major cities** like Kuala Lumpur, Kuantan and Georgetown are particularly traffic-snarled, with confusing one-way systems to boot, not ideal for the disorientated driver.

With main roads so hassle-free, **fly-drive holidays** on the Malaysian peninsula are a popular option. There are several travel agencies (see "Getting There" sections above) which can offer a pre-booked programme from a selection of routes, or a route of your own choosing, which allows you the flexiblilty to wander at will, booking your hotels as you go along.

CAR AND BIKE RENTAL

To **rent a vehicle** in Malaysia, Singapore and Brunei, you must be 23 or over and have held a clean driving licence for at least a year; a national driving licence, particularly if written in English, should be sufficient, though there's no harm in acquiring an International Driving Licence.

The major international **car rental agencies** represented in Malaysia and Singapore are *Avis*, *Budget*, *Hertz* and *National* and you'll find at least one of their offices in each major town and at the airports; there are also a handful of local companies, at which rental costs work out about the same. Useful addresses and phone numbers are given in the accounts of major cities. Note that the international rental agencies need at least two days' notice if you're booking and paying locally, or between three and seven days for a pre-paid booking before you leave your home country (see box above for telephone numbers).

In **Malaysia**, rates begin at around M$135 (£34/US$50) per day for a basic Proton Saga, including unlimited mileage, personal insurance and usually with a collision damage waiver of up to $2000; where this isn't included, an additional charge of around M$15 per day is levied. Rates for periods over three days are better value: a week's rental costs around M$700–800 (£175–200/US$262–300). If you want to take the car into Singapore, a surcharge of US$20 a day applies.

In **Singapore**, rental deals vary according to whether the three percent tax and collision damage waiver is included, but the rate, again for a Proton Saga model, averages around S$130 (£56/US$84) a day, from S$730–830 (£317–360/US$475–540) a week. To take the car into Malaysia incurs a surcharge of S$25 per day. Offices usually require two days notice and a deposit of around S$100, though this can be avoided by pre-booking abroad.

Motorbike rental is much more informal, usually offered by Malaysian guest houses and shops in more touristy areas. You'll probably need to leave your passport as a deposit, but it's unlikely you'll have to show any proof of eligibility – officially you must be over 21 and have an appropriate driving licence. Wearing helmets is compulsory, however. Costs vary from M$15–20 per day, while **bicycles** can be rented for around M$4 a day. For bike rental in Singapore, see p.485.

RULES OF THE ROAD AND OTHER MATTERS

Malaysia, Singapore and Brunei follow the UK system of **driving on the left**: most road signs are internationally recognized, and wearing seat belts in the front is compulsory. One confusing habit that Malaysian drivers have adopted is that they **flash their headlights** when they are claiming the right of way, *not* the other way around, as is common practice in the West.

On highways, the **speed limit** is 100km/hr, and 80km/hr on trunk roads, while in built-up areas it's 50km/hr; you'd be wise to stick religiously to these limits, since speed traps are commonplace and mandatory **fines** are a hefty $200. There are plenty of **garages** throughout Malaysia and Singapore; in any case, the rental agency will supply you with emergency numbers to call in the event of a **breakdown**.

Fuel is readily available in Malaysia and costs just over M$1 (25p/38c) a litre, slightly more in Singapore. The North–South Highway is the only **toll road** – you can reckon on paying approximately M$1 for every 7km travelled.

A DRIVING VOCABULARY

Utara North
Selatan South
Barat West
Timur East
Awas Caution
Ikut Kiri Keep left
Kurangkan Laju Slow down
Jalan Sehala One way
Lencongan Detour
Berhenti Stop
Beri Laluan Give way
Had Laju .../jam Speed limit .../per hour
Dilarang Memotong No Overtaking
Dilarang Melatak Kereta No Parking
Lebuhraya Expressway

Most Malaysian towns have some kind of internal **bus** service and details are given in the text wherever appropriate. Fares are always very cheap even if some of the systems – in places like KL and Georgetown – initially appear absolutely unfathomable to visitors. It's usually easier to jump in a **taxi** and sometimes that's the only way to reach certain local sights. Taxis are always metered, but drivers don't always speak English, so it's not a bad idea to have your destination written down on a piece of paper.

Trishaws (bicycle rickshaws), seating two people, are seen less and less on the streets these days, made redundant by the chaotic traffic systems in most towns. But they are still very much part of the tourist scene in places like Melaka, Penang and Kota Bharu, though in most cases they're not much cheaper than taking a taxi – bargain hard to fix the price in advance. You can expect to pay a minimum of $3 for a short journey, while chartering by the hour can be as much as $15. Taking a **trishaw tour** in Georgetown and Melaka can be a useful introduction to the town and the drivers often provide interesting anecdotal information. Subject to bargaining, these tours usually cost around $20 for an hour's ride. **Singapore** also has trishaws, as well as other methods of getting around – from river trips to helicopter rides; see p.480 for all the details.

ACCOMMODATION

While accommodation in Malaysia and Singapore is not the cheapest in Southeast Asia, in most places you can still get pretty good deals on simple rooms: in Malaysia, double rooms for under M$20 (£5/US$7.50) are common; under S$25 (£11/US$16.50) in Singapore. East Malaysia is more expensive, particularly in Sabah where you'll often pay M$25–30 (£6–7/US$9–10.50) for a very ordinary place, though the longhouses in Sarawak can cost next to nothing.

The very cheapest form of accommodation is in a dormitory bed at a guest house or lodge, but these generally only exist in the more obvious tourist spots – Singapore, Georgetown, Kota Bharu and Cherating. At the other end of the scale, the region's luxury hotels offer a level of comfort and style to rank with any in the world. Prices in these, relatively speaking, aren't too outrageous either, and you have the chance of staying in some of the world's most famous colonial hotels, like the *Raffles* in Singapore and the *E&O* in Georgetown.

At the budget end of the market you'll have to share a bathroom, which in most cases will feature a shower and either a squat or Western-style toilet. Older places, or those in rural areas, sometimes have *mandis* instead of showers, a large basin of cold water which you throw over yourself with a bucket or ladle; it's very bad form to get soap in the basin or, worse still, get in it yourself. While **air-conditioning** is standard in the smarter hotels, some at the budget end also have special, slightly more expensive air-conditioned rooms.

Room rates remain relatively stable throughout the year, though they can rise dramatically during the major holiday periods – Christmas, Easter and Hari Raya; conversely, it's always worth bargaining during the monsoon lull (from November to February). When asking for a room, note that a **"single"** room usually means it will contain one double bed, while a **"double"** has two double beds, a "triple" three, and so on, making most rooms economical for families and groups; baby cots are usually available only in more expensive places.

Local tourist offices can usually **book accommodation** for you, though this is rarely necessary given the choice in most towns. In popular resorts, you'll often be accosted by people at bus or train stations advertising rooms: it's rarely worth going with them (especially since it's hard to turn down the room if you don't like it), although they can be useful in securing you a room in the peak holiday season, saving you a lot of fruitless trudging around.

GUEST HOUSES, HOMESTAYS AND HOSTELS

Mainstay of the travellers' scene in Malaysia and Singapore are the **guest houses**, located in popular tourist areas and usually good places to meet other people and pick up information. They can range from simple beachside A-frame huts to modern multistorey apartment buildings complete with a TV and video room. Their advantage for the single traveller on a tight budget is that almost all offer **dormitory beds**, which can cost as little as M$7–8 a night (S$6–7). There are always basic double rooms available, too, usually with a fan and possibly a mosquito net, and averaging M$15 (S$20). Fierce competition on the Malaysian east coast means that prices there occasionally drop as low as M$10 for a double room, though this is somewhat offset by the pricier huts and chalets on the islands in the south, where you'll be hard pushed to find anything for under M$25.

In certain places – Merang, Cherating and Kota Bharu, especially – **homestay** programmes are available, whereby you stay with a Malaysian family, paying for your bed and board. Fees as well as the facilities are modest – usually no more than M$10 per person per night – and although some people find staying with a family too restrictive, it can be a good way of sampling Malay home cooking and culture. Local tourist offices have details of participants in the scheme.

Official **youth hostels** in Malaysia and Singapore are few and far between, often hopelessly far-flung and no cheaper than dorms and rooms in the guest houses – the rare exceptions are noted in the text. As a rule, it's not worth becoming a *IYHF* member just for the trip to Malaysia or Singapore, though if you're travelling further afield it might pay for itself eventually. Each major town generally also has both a **YMCA** and a **YWCA** which, like the youth

hostels, are rarely conveniently located. Although facilities are better than those at the youth hostels, they cost around M$40 a night, making them poor value compared to the budget hotels.

HOTELS

The cheapest **hotels** in Malaysia and Singapore are usually Chinese-run and cater for a predominantly local clientele. They're generally clean and well kept – though often housed in antiquated buildings – and there's never any need to book in advance: just go to the next place around the corner if your first choice is full. Ordinary rooms go for around M$18 ($25 in Singapore) and are usually divided by thin, partition walls: there'll always be a washbasin, table and ceiling fan, though never a mosquito net; mattresses are usually rock hard. In the better places – often old converted mansions – you may also be treated to beautifully polished wooden floors and antique furniture. You'll often have the choice of air-con rooms as well, though the noisy rattle may not seem worth the extra $10 or so. Showers and toilets (squat-style almost everywhere) are shared and can be pretty basic. The other consideration is the noise level, which can be very considerable since most places are on main streets. A word of **warning**: most of the hotels at the cheaper end of the scale also function as brothels and you should pick and choose carefully, particularly if you're a solo female traveller. Those which use the Malay term *Rumah Persinggahan* usually double as brothels.

If you can't stand the noise in the cheaper places, then the **mid-range hotels** are your only alternative in most towns, though they're rarely better value than a well-kept budget place. The big difference is in the comfort of the mattress – nearly always sprung – and getting your own Western-style bathroom. Prices range from M$40–$150 (S$40–150 in Singapore), and for this you can expect a carpeted room with air-con and TV, and, towards the upper end of the range, a telephone and refridgerator. In these places, too, a genuine distinction is made between single rooms and doubles.

Also in the mid-range category are **Government Rest Houses** (*Rumah Rehat*), which once provided accommodation for visiting colonial officials. These days, a lot of the old buildings have been replaced by more modern constructions and they're mostly privately run, though a genteel atmosphere still remains and they are open to anybody. Facilities, varying from the antiquated to the modern, are generally excellent value: rooms are large and well equipped, usually with a separate lounge area and always with private bathrooms. Each rest house has its own restaurant as well.

Moving to the top of the scale, the **high-class hotels** are as comfortable as you might expect, many employing state-of-the-art facilities. Recently, the trend in Malaysia has been to reflect local traditions with the incorporation of *kampung*-style architecture – low-level timber structures with saddle-shaped roofs and open-sided public areas – though such hotels still feature all the usual trappings, like swimming pools, air conditioning and business facilities. While prices can be as reasonable as M$150 per room (S$200), rates in popular destinations such as Penang can rocket to M$400 and above – though this is still relatively good value compared to hotels of an equivalent standard in London or New York. Having said that, famous hotels, like the *Raffles* in Singapore, can virtually charge what they like. Don't forget that the price quoted by the hotel rarely includes the compulsory 10 percent **service charge** and 5 percent **government tax** (4 percent in Singapore), often signified by "++" (ie, $250++). It is always cheaper to stay at top hotels if you're on a pre-booked package – ask your travel agent if you want to stay at a specific hotel.

LONGHOUSES

Perhaps the most atmospheric type of accommodation in Malaysia is the wood-and-bamboo stilted **longhouse** found only on the rivers in **Sarawak** and **Sabah**. These can house dozens of families, and usually consist of three elevated sections reached by a simple ladder: a long, open verandah is used for jobs like drying rice and washing clothes; behind is a longroom where the families eat, dance, talk and play music and games; further in are the private quarters of each family, usually just one room with an open fire for cooking. Large mats are stored in the rafters and brought down to sleep or sit on. Contemporary longhouses are built increasingly of more durable material like stone and hardwoods, and furnished with corrugated iron roofs, although many built in the traditional manner still exist and some of these are accessible to visitors, too. Most tourists stay at longhouses as part of an organized tour, and these are inevitably more commercial, but if you're interested, it's actually quite easy to travel along the rivers and, with a minimal command of Malay, be directed to communities off the beaten track which seldom see visitors.

Traditionally, there's no charge to stay in a longhouse, though it is good manners to bring **gifts:** writing pads, exercise books, pens and pencils for children make useful offerings. Once there, you can participate in many activities including learning to weave, cook, use a blow-pipe, fish, help in the agricultural plots, and perhaps go out on a wild boar hunt. All the details, including a rundown of longhouse etiquette, are given on p.327 and p.353.

CAMPING

Despite the rural nature of most of Malaysia, there are few official opportunities for **camping**; in any case, guest houses and hotels are inexpensive enough for most pockets. Where there are campsites, they charge around $10 a pitch and facilities are of a very basic nature. If you go trekking in the more remote regions, for example in Endau-Rompin National Park, camping is about your only option, although note that even if you're on an organized trip, equipment is rarely included in the advertised price. In **Singapore**, camping is confined to Pulau Ubin and Pulau Sentosa (see p.487); there are no official campsites in Brunei.

EATING AND DRINKING

One of the best reasons to come in the first place to Malaysia and Singapore (even Brunei, to a lesser extent) is for the food, the countries' cuisines inspired by the heritage of their three main communities, the Malays, Chinese and Indians. From the ubiquitous hawker stalls to the restaurants in world-class hotels, the standard of cooking is extremely high and food everywhere is remarkably good value.

Basic noodle or rice-based meals at a stall will rarely come to more than a few Malaysian or Singaporean dollars and even a full meal with drinks in a reputable restaurant should rarely run to more than M$40 (S$30 in Singapore) – though if you develop a taste for delicacies such as shark's-fin or bird's-nest soup, the sky's the limit. The most renowned culinary centres are Singapore, Georgetown, KL, Melaka and Kota Bharu, although other towns, like Johor Bahru, Ipoh, Kuching and Miri all have their own distinctive dishes.

THE CUISINES

As well as mainstream dishes from the principal ethnic cuisines – Malay, Chinese and Indian – hawker stalls, cafés and restaurants throughout the region serve up a variety of regional dishes that reflect the pattern of immigration over the last five hundred years. The most familar Chinese cooking style is Cantonese, but all over Malaysia and Singapore you can also sample Szechuan, Hokkien, Beijing and other regional Chinese specialities. Indian food splits into northern, southern or Muslim styles of cooking; while even the indigenous Malay cuisine mixes various elements from other Asian cuisines. The main oddity for the visitor is that there is no such thing as specifically Singaporean cuisine – there, and in the former Straits Settlement towns in Malaysia like Georgetown and Melaka, a hybrid cuisine known as Nonya evolved from the mixed-race marriages of early Chinese immigrants amd local Malays. Below are accounts of the different cuisines, while for a rundown of the most popular dishes, turn to the food glossary on pp.46–48.

MALAY FOOD

Surprisingly perhaps, good **Malay** cuisine can be hard to find, with the best cooking often confined to the home; on the positive side, the Malay restaurants that do exist are of a universally high standard, presenting dishes with a loving attention to detail. The cuisine is based on rice, often enriched with *santan* (coconut milk), which is served with a dizzying variety of curries and *sambal*, a condiment comprising pounded chillies blended with *belacan* (shrimp paste), onions and garlic. Other spices which characterize Malay cuisine include ginger and *galangal* (a root-like ginger), coriander, lemon grass and lime leaves.

The most famous **dish** is *satay* – virtually Malaysia's national dish – which is skewers of barbecued meat (chicken, mutton or beef) dipped in spicy peanut sauce. The classic way to sample Malay curries is to eat *nasi campur*, a buffet (usually served at lunchtime) of steamed rice supplemented by any of up to two dozen accompanying dishes, including *lembu* (beef), *kangkong* (greens), fried chicken and fish steaks and curry sauce, and various vegetables. Other popular dishes include *nasi goreng* (mixed fried rice with meat, seafood and vegetables); *rendang* (slow-cooked beef, chicken or mutton in lemon grass and coconut); *lemang* (glutinous rice stuffed into lengths of bamboo); and *kunyit* (rice cooked in turmeric). Pork, of course, is taboo to all Muslims, but it has been married with Malay cooking in Nonya dishes, for which see below. For **breakfast**, the most popular Malay dish is *nasi lemak*, rice cooked in coconut milk and served with *sambal ikan bilis* (tiny crisp-fried anchovies in hot chilli paste), fried peanuts and slices of fried or hard-boiled egg.

Much of the diet of the indigenous groups living in settled communities in **East Malaysia** tends to revolve around standard Malay and Chinese dishes. But in the remoter regions, or at festival times, you may have an opportunity of sampling ethnic cuisine. In Sabah's Klias Peninsula, villagers still produce *ambuyat*, a glue-like, sago starch porridge that's dipped in sauce; or there's the Murut speciality of *jaruk* – raw wild boar, fermented in a bamboo tube, and definitely an acquired taste. Most famous of Sabah's dishes is *hinava*, or raw fish pickled in lime juice. In Sarawak, you're most likely to eat with the Iban or Kelabit, sampling wild boar with jungle ferns and sticky rice.

NONYA FOOD

The earliest Chinese immigrants settled in the Straits Settlements of Melaka, Penang and Singapore and intermarried with local Malays, their descendants – the Peranakans – evolving their own particular culture and cuisine, called **Nonya**, from the name given to women of Straits Chinese families (men were called Babas). There's more information on Peranakan culture on p.54 and p.287.

Typical Nonya **dishes** incorporate elements and ingredients from Chinese, Indonesian and Thai cooking, the end product tending to be spicier than Chinese food. Chicken, fish and seafood forms the backbone of the cuisine, and unlike Malay food, pork is used. Noodles (*mee*) flavoured with chillis, and rich curries made from rice flour and coconut cream, are common. A popular dish is *laksa*, noodles in spicy coconut soup served with seafood and finely chopped beansprouts, lemon grass, pineapple, pepper, lime leaves and chilli; *assam laksa* is the version served in Penang, its fish stock giving it a sharper taste. Other popular Nonya dishes include *ayam buah keluak*, chicken cooked with "black" nuts; *otak-otak*, fish mashed with coconut milk and chilli paste and steamed in a banana leaf; or chicken *kapitan*, a mild curried dish of chicken in coconut milk.

CHINESE FOOD

Chinese food dominates in Singapore and Malaysia, with perhaps only the cooking in Hong Kong reaching a higher standard – fish and seafood is nearly always outstanding, with prawns, crab, squid and a variety of fish on offer almost everywhere. Noodles, too, are ubiquitous, and come in wonderful variations – thin, flat, round, served in soup (wet) or fried (dry).

The dominant style of Chinese cookery is **Cantonese** – as it is in most foreign countries, echoing the pattern of immigration from southern China – but later groups of settlers from **other**

regions of China spread Foochow, Hokkien, Hainanese, Teochow and Szechuan dishes throughout Peninsular Malaysia, East Malaysia and Singapore. Of these, Hokkien and Teochow are the most dominant, especially in Singapore where Hokkien fried *mee* (noodles with pork, prawn and vegetables) and *char kuey teow* (spicy flat noodles mixed with meat, fish and egg) are available almost everywhere. The classic Cantonese lunch is *dim sum* (literally "to touch the heart"), a variety of steamed and fried dumplings served in bamboo baskets in cafés and restaurants. Other popular lunch dishes are Hainan chicken rice (not surprisingly, rice cooked in chicken stock and topped with tender steamed or fried chicken) or rice topped with *char siew* (roast pork); while standard dishes available everywhere include yam basket, a meat-and-vegetable dish cased in a fried yam pastry; chicken in chilli or with cashew nuts; buttered prawns, or prawns served with a sweet and sour sauce; spare ribs; and mixed vegetables with *tofu* (bean curd) and bean sprouts. For something a little more unusual, try a **steamboat**, a Chinese-style fondue filled with boiling stock in which you cook meat, fish, shellfish, eggs and vegetables; or a **claypot** – meat, fish or shellfish cooked over a fire in an earthenware pot.

INDIAN FOOD

In the same way as the Chinese, immigrants from north and south India brought their own cuisines with them, which vary in emphasis and ingredients though all utilize *dhal* (lentils), chutneys, yoghurts and sweet or sour *lassis* (yoghurt drinks); neither north nor south Indians eat beef. North Indian food tends to rely more on meat, especially mutton and chicken, and uses breads – naan, chapatis, parathas and rotis rather than rice to great effect. The most famous style of north Indian cooking is *tandoori* - named after the clay oven in which the food is cooked - and you'll commonly come across tandoori chicken-marinanded in yoghurt and spices and then baked. A favourite **breakfast** is *roti canai* (pancake and dhal) or *roti kaya* (pancake spread with egg and jam).

Southern Indian (and Sri Lankan) food tends to be spicier and more reliant on vegetables. Its staple is the *dosai* (pancake), often served at breakfast time as a *masala dosai*, stuffed with onions, vegetables and chutney, and washed down with *teh tarik*, a sweet, frothy milky tea.

Indian Muslims serve the similar *murtabak*, a grilled *roti* pancake with egg, onion and minced meat.

Many south Indian cafés turn to serving *daun pisang* at lunchtime, usually a vegetarian meal where rice is served on banana leaves and small, replenishable heaps of various vegetable curries are placed alongside; in some places, meat and fish side dishes are on offer, too. It's normal to eat a **banana leaf** meal with your right hand, though restaurants will always have cutlery knocking around if you can't manage. As with the other immigrant cuisines, the Indian food available in Malaysia and Singapore has adapted to Malay tastes and to the availability of ingredients over the years: banana leaf curry, for example, is more widely available in Malaysia and Singapore than in India, while another Malay Indian staple, *mee goreng* – fried egg noodles with spices and chillies – isn't known at all in India.

HAWKERS

To eat inexpensively in Malaysia or Singapore you go to **hawker stalls**, traditionally simple wooden stalls on the roadside, with a few stools to sit at. In Singapore, Kuala Lumpur and some other major cities, the trend is to corral hawker stalls in neat, air-conditioned food centres where you can pick different dishes from a variety of stalls, but in most of Malaysia the old-style stalls still dominate the streets.

Wherever you find the stalls, you don't have to worry too much about **hygiene**: most are scrupulously clean, with the food cooked instantly in front of you. Avoid dishes that look as if they've been standing around for a while, or have been reheated, and you should be fine. The standard of cooking is also very high at most stalls and just because the food produced is cheap doesn't mean it's to be ignored. Politicians and pop stars crowd in with the locals to eat at a cramped hawker's table.

Most hawker stalls serve standard Malay noodle and rice **dishes**, satay and, in many places, more obscure regional delicacies too. The influence of the region's immigrants also means you'll encounter Chinese noodle and seafood dishes, Indian specialities and Indonesian food. At modern food centres, particularly in Singapore, you'll increasingly come across Western food like burgers, and steak and eggs, or even Japanese and Korean food.

Hawker stalls don't have menus, though most have signs in English detailing their specialities; otherwise point at anything you like the look of. When you **order** a dish, make it clear if you want a small, medium or large portion – or else you'll get the biggest and most expensive one. You don't have to sit close to the stall you're patronizing: find a free table, and the vendor will track you down when your food is ready. Meals are paid for when they reach your table.

Most hawker stalls are closed at breakfast time, as Malays tend to eat before they go to work, and Chinese and Indians head for the coffee houses and cafés. Most outdoor stalls open instead at around midday, usually offering the day's *nasi campur* selection; prices are determined by the number of dishes you choose on top of your rice; most stalls (and cafés) charge around $1–1.50 per portion. Hawker stalls usually close well before midnight; any open after this time will be limited to fried noodles and soups. Hawker centres will usually have a hot and cold drinks stall on hand; in Singapore, you'll always be able to get a beer, too.

KEDAI KOPIS

Few streets exist without a **kedai kopi** (a coffee house or café), usually run by Chinese or Indians. Most open at 8am or 9am and closing times vary from 6pm to midnight. Basic Chinese coffee houses serve noodle and rice dishes all day, and feature a decent selection of cakes and cookies. The culinary standard is never spectacularly high, but you're unlikely to spend more than two or three dollars for a filling one-plate meal. Some cafés are a little more adventurous and serve full meals of meat, seafood and vegetables, for which you'll pay from around $5 per person; Malay-run cafés, where you can find them, usually serve a midday spread of *nasi campur* dishes. Indian cafés tend to be a bit livelier and – especially in the Indian quarters of Singapore, Kuala Lumpur, Georgetown and Melaka – decidedly theatrical. Here you can watch the Muslim *mamak* men at work, whose job it is to make the frothy *teh tarik* (tea), by pouring liquid from a height from one vessel into another, and pound and mould the *roti* into an oily, bubble-filled shape.

It's worth noting that the Chinese *kedai kopis* are often the only places you'll be able to get a **beer** in the evening; this is especially true in towns along Malaysia's largely Muslim east coast.

RESTAURANTS

On the whole, proper **restaurants** are either places you go to be seen or to savour particular delicacies found nowhere else, like fish-head curry (a famous Singaporean dish), Chinese specialities like shark's-fin dishes and bird's-nest soup, and high-quality seafood. In many restaurants, the food is not necessarily superior to that served at a good café or hawker stall – you're just paying the (often considerable) extra for air-conditioning and tablecloths. One reason to splash out, though, is to experience a **cultural show** of music and dance, often performed in larger restaurants in the main cities – in Singapore, several of the large Chinese seafood restaurants put on displays. Some of the best of the shows are detailed in the text.

Both Malaysia and Singapore do have a tradition of **haute cuisine**, usually available in new restaurants decorated in traditional *kampung*-style or in the top-notch hotels. All the best hotel-restaurants in Kuala Lumpur, Singapore and Georgetown boast well-known chefs, drawing in the punters with well-recieved French, Thai and Japanese food as well as more local delicacies.

Unless you're in a Muslim restaurant, or anywhere in Brunei, you'll be able to wash down your meal with a glass of cold **beer**; wine is less common, though smarter establishments will normally retain a modest choice. Few **desserts** feature on Southeast Asian restaurant menus, but the region's bounty of tropical **fruit** more than compensates: the glossary on p.48 lists some of the less familiar fruits you may come across.

Tipping is not expected and bills arrive complete with service charge and (in Malaysia

---

VEGETARIANS AND VEGANS

Vegetarians will find specialist Chinese and Indian restaurants in larger towns and cities; the text has details where appropriate. If you're going to more remote areas, things get trickier – the Chinese barely class chicken and pork as meat, and anyway, meat stock forms the basis of many Chinese dishes. It's wise to say "I only eat vegetables" (in Bahasa Malay: *saya hanya makan sayuran*) and steel yourself for a diet of vegetables and rice.

Vegans really have their work cut out: tell your waiter, "I do not eat dairy products or meat" (*saya tidak makanan yang di perbuat dari susu atau daging*) and keep your fingers crossed.

and Singapore) government tax. In the main, restaurants are **open** from 11.30am to 2.30pm and from 6 to 10.30pm, though more basic coffee shops tend to open from 7am to 7pm. Making yourself understood is rarely a problem, and nor is negotiating a **menu**: many are written in English, especially in Singapore.

DRINKING

Tap water is safe to drink in Malaysia and Singapore, though it's wise to stick to bottled water when travelling in rural areas (and in Sarawak and Sabah), widely available for around $2 a litre. Using ice for drinks is generally fine, too, making the huge variety of seasonal **fresh fruit drinks**, available in hawker centres and street corners, even more pleasant; always specify that you want them without sugar, unless you like your fruit juice heavily laced with syrup. Sugar-cane mangles can be found on many street corners, producing a watery, sweet drink that's very cloying yet still manages to be invigorating. The usual range of **soft drinks** is available everywhere for around $1 a can/carton, with the *F&N* and *Yeo* companies providing more unusual flavours, and *Pokka* making cans of decent fruitjuices. Saccharine-filled drinks of fruit juice in boxes with a straw can be handy for journeys, again costing about $1 a piece; soya milk in cartons is another popular local choice.

Tea and coffee are as much national drinks as they are in the West, though you'll often find that sweet condensed milk is added unless you ask for it without (*teh-o* is tea without milk, *kopi-o* for coffee). If you don't like the often overbrewed tea or coffee, most cafés usually have *Milo*, the ubiquitous hot chocolate drink.

ALCOHOLIC DRINKS

Only in Brunei (officially a dry state) and certain places on the east coast of the Malaysian peninsula is drinking **alcohol** outlawed. Elsewhere in Malaysia and Singapore, despite the Muslim influence, alcohol is available in bars, restaurants, Chinese *kedai kopis* and super-markets.

Anchor and *Tiger* **beer** (lager) are locally produced (see p.535 for more) and are probably

the best choice, though you can also get other Western beers, as well as the Chinese *Tsingato* and a variety of stouts (like *Guinness*) – including the Singaporean *ABC*, which is truly horrible. It's best drunk mixed with a *Tiger* beer, which is what you'll see many people doing.

Locally produced **whisky** and **rum** are cheap enough, too, though it's pretty rough stuff and can well do with mixing with Coke. The brandy tends to be better, which is what the local Chinese drink. In the more upmarket restaurants, you can get cocktails and imported **wine**, the latter hideously expensive (at least M$60 a bottle) and often not very good at all. Only on Pulau Langkawi and Sabah's Pulau Labuan, both duty-free islands, can wine be bought from the supermarkets at prices roughly equivalent to the West (approximately M$15 for the least expensive bottle).

WHERE TO DRINK

In **Malaysia**, there is a thriving **bar scene** in KL (mainly in the Golden Triangle) and its modern suburb, Petaling Jaya, popular with fashionable youths and yuppies. Other towns have less of a scene, though in most of the places popular with Western tourists, you'll be able to get a beer in something approaching a bar – otherwise, go to a a Chinese *kedai kopi* for a bottle of beer. Fierce competition keeps **happy hours** a regular feature in most bars (usually daily 5–7pm), bringing the beer down to around M$4.50 a glass, though spirits still remain pricey; look out for "allnight" discounts that appear from time to time. While there are some bars which open all day (11am–11pm), most tend to double as clubs, opening in the evenings until 3 or 4am.

In **Singapore**, bars are much the same, although the variety is even wider, ranging from those run on an English pub theme, featuring occasional guest beers from the UK, through to early evening karaoke bars – all the details are on p.550–552. The more glitzy places often introduce a cover charge (around $8) from 10pm onwards at weekends. Places open from 7pm to midnight, though some also cater for the lunchtime crowd by offering bargain meals.

A FOOD AND DRINK GLOSSARY

Many menus, especially in Singapore, are written in English, but it's worth noting that transliterated spellings are not standardized throughout Malaysia and Singapore – you may well see some of the following dishes written in a variety of ways; we've used the most widely accepted spellings. For a full rundown of the various cuisines available in Malaysia and Singapore, see p.41–43.

NOODLES (*MEE*) AND NOODLE DISHES

Bee hoon Thin rice noodles, like vermicelli; *mee fun* is similar.

Char kuey teow Flat noodles with any combination of prawns, Chinese sausage, fishcake, egg, vegetables and chilli.

Foochow noodles Steamed and served in soy and oyster sauce with spring onions and dried fish.

Hokkien fried mee Yellow noodles fried with pieces of pork, prawn and vegetables.

Kuey teow Flat noodles, comparable to Italian tagliatelle; *hor fun* is similar.

Laksa Noodles, beansprouts, fishcakes and prawns in a spicy coconut soup.

Mee Standard round yellow noodles that look like spaghetti and are made from wheat flour.

Mee goreng Indian fried noodles.

Mee suah Noodles served dry and crispy.

Sar hor fun Flat rice noodles served in a chicken stock soup, to which prawns, fried shallots and beansprouts are added; a speciality in Ipoh.

Wan ton mee Roast pork, noodles and vegetables served in a light soup containing dumplings.

RICE (*NASI*) DISHES

Biriyani Saffron-flavoured rice cooked with chicken, beef or fish; a North Indian speciality.

Claypot Rice topped with meat (as diverse as chicken and turtle), cooked in an earthenware pot over a fire to create a smoky taste.

Daun pisang Malay term for banana leaf curry, a southern Indian meal with chutneys and curries, served on a mound of rice, and presented on a banana leaf with popadums.

Hainan chicken rice Singapore's unofficial national dish: steamed or boiled chicken slices on rice cooked in chicken stock, and served with chicken broth, and chilli and ginger sauce.

Kunyit Rice cooked in tumeric; a side dish.

Lemang Glutinous rice stuffed into lengths of bamboo.

Nasi campur Rice served with an array of meat, fish and vegetable dishes.

Nasi goreng Fried rice with diced meat and vegetables.

Nasi kerabu Purple, green or blue rice with a dash of vegetables, seaweed and grated coconut; a Kota Bharu speciality.

Nasi lemak A Malay classic: *ikan bilis* (fried anchovies), cucumber, peanuts and fried or hard-boiled egg slices served on coconut rice.

Nasi puteh Plain boiled rice.

MEAT, FISH AND BASICS

Ayam	Chicken		*Kepiting*	Crab		*Sup*	Soup
Babi	Pork		*Kambing*	Mutton		*Tahu*	Beancurd
Daging	Beef		*Sayur*	Vegetable		*Telor*	Egg
Ikan	Fish		*Sotong*	Squid		*Udang*	Prawn

GENERAL TERMS

Assam	Sour		*Gula*	Sugar		*Makan*	Food
Garam	Salt		*Istimewa*	Special (as in "today's special")		*Manis*	Sweet
Goreng	Fried		*Kari*	Curry		*Minum*	Drink

OTHER SPECIALITIES

Ayam goreng Malay-style fried chicken.

Ayam percik Barbecued chicken with a creamy coconut sauce; a Kota Bharu speciality.

Bak kut teh Literally "pork bone tea", a Chinese dish of pork ribs in soya sauce, herbs and spices.

Char siew pow Cantonese steamed bun stuffed with roast pork in a sweet sauce.

Chay tow kueh Also known as "carrot cake", this is actually an omelette made with white radish and spring onions.

Congee Rice porridge, cooked in lots of water and eaten with slices of meat and fish; sometimes listed on menus as "porridge".

Coto makassar A meat broth boosted with chunks of rice cake.

Dim sum Chinese titbits – dumplings, rolls, chicken's feet – steamed or fried and served in bamboo baskets.

Dosai Southern Indian pancake, made from ground rice and lentils, and served with *dhal* (lentils) and spicy dips.

Fish-head curry The head of a red snapper (usually), cooked in a spicy curry sauce with tomatoes and okra; a contender for the title of Singapore's most famous dish.

Gado gado Malay/Indonesian salad of lightly cooked vegetables, boiled egg, slices of rice cake and a crunchy peanut sauce.

Ikan bilis Deep-fried anchovies.

Kai pow Similar to *char siew pow*, but chicken and boiled egg.

Kerupuk Crackers.

Murtabak Thick Indian pancake, stuffed with onion, egg and chicken or mutton.

Otak-otak Fish mashed with coconut milk and chilli paste and steamed in a banana leaf; a Nonya dish.

Popiah Chinese spring rolls, filled with peanuts, egg, beanshoots, vegetables and a sweet sauce; sometimes known as *Lumpia*.

Rendang Dry, highly spiced coconut curry with beef, chicken or mutton.

Rojak Indian fritters dipped in chilli and peanut sauce; the Chinese version is a salad of greens, beansprouts, pineapple and cucumber in a peanut-and-prawn paste sauce, similar to *gado gado*.

Roti canai Light, layered Indian pancake served with a thin curry sauce or *dhal*; sometimes called *roti pratha*.

Roti john Simple Indian dish of egg, onion and tomato sauce spread on bread and heated.

Satay Marinated pieces of meat, skewered on small sticks and cooked over charcoal; served with peanut sauce, cucumber and *ketupat* (rice cake).

Sop kambing Spicy Indian mutton soup.

Steamboat Chinese equivalent of the Swiss fondue: raw vegetables, meat or fish and other titbits dunked into a steaming broth until cooked.

Yam basket Sarawak speciality: meat, vegetables and soya bean curd in a fried yam pie crust.

DESSERTS

Bubor cha cha Sweetened coconut milk with pieces of sweet potato, yam and tapioca balls.

Cendol Coconut milk, palm sugar syrup and pea-flour noodles poured over shaved ice.

Es kachang Shaved ice with red beans, cubes of jelly, sweetcorn, rose syrup and evaporated milk.

Pisang goreng Fried banana fritters.

Pisang murtabak Banana pancake.

DRINKS

Air minum Water.

Bir Beer.

Jus Fruit juice.

Kopi Coffee.

Kopi-o Black coffee.

Kopi susu Coffee with milk.

Lassi Sweet or sour yoghurt drink of Indian origin.

Teh Tea.

Teh-o Black tea.

Teh susu Tea with milk.

Teh tarik Sweet, milky tea, poured between two cups to produce a frothy drink.

TROPICAL FRUIT

The more familiar fruits available in Malaysia and Singapore include forty varieties of banana, known locally as *pisang*; coconut (*kelapa*); seven varieties of mango; three types of pineapple (*nanas*); and watermelon (*tembiki*).

Betik Better known as *papaya*, this milky orange-coloured flesh is a rich source of vitamins A and C.

Carambola Also known as *star fruit*, this waxy, pale-green star-shaped fruit is said to be good for high blood pressure; the yellower the fruit, the sweeter its flesh.

Chempedak This smaller version of the *nangka* (see below) is normally deep-fried, enabling the seed, which tastes like new potato, to be eaten too.

Ciku Looks like an apple; varies from yellow to pinkish brown when ripe, with a soft, pulpy flesh.

Durian Malaysia and Singapore's most popular fruit has a greeny-yellow, spiky exterior and grows to the size of a football from March to May, June to August, and November to February. It has thick, yellow-white flesh and an incredibly pungent odour likened to a mixture of mature cheese and caramel.

Guava A green, textured skin and flesh with five times the vitamin C content of orange juice.

Langsat Together with its sister fruit, the *duku*, this looks like a small, round potato, with juicy white flesh which can be anything from sweet to sour.

Longgan Similar to the lychee, this has juicy white flesh and brown seeds.

Mangosteen Available fom June to August and November to January, it has a sweet though slightly acidic flavour. Its smooth rind deepens to a distinctive crimson colour when ripe.

Markisa Known in the West as *passion fruit*, this has purple-brown dimpled skin with a rich flavour; it's a frequent ingredient in drinks.

Nangka This large, pear-shaped fruit, also known as *jackfruit*, grows up to 50cm long and has a greeny-yellow exterior with sweet flesh inside.

Pomelo The pomelo, or *limau bali*, is the largest of all the citrus fruits and looks rather like a grapefruit, though it is slightly drier and has less flavour.

Rambutan The bright red rambutan's soft, spiny exterior has given it its name – *rambut* means "hair" in Malay. Usually about the size of a golf ball, it has a white, opaque fruit of delicate flavour, similar to a lychee.

Salak Teardrop-shaped, the *salak* has a skin like a snake's and a bitter taste.

Zirzat Inside its bumpy, muddy green skin is smooth white flesh like blancmange, hence its other name, *custard apple*; also known as *soursop* (and described by Margaret Brooke, wife of Sarawak's second Rajah, Charles, as "tasting like cotton wool dipped in vinegar and sugar").

COMMUNICATIONS: POST, PHONES AND THE MEDIA

The communications network in Malaysia and Singapore is generally fast and efficient, though you still occasionally experience difficulties in making local phone calls in Malaysia and some of the smaller offshore islands still have no phone network. Mobile phones are in evidence everywhere, and in many remote areas, this can be the only way of keeping in touch.

You can send mail *to* Malaysia, Singapore and Brunei care of the poste restante/general delivery section of the local GPO (see below); when picking up mail, be sure to have the staff check under first names as well as family names – misfiling is common.

POSTAL SERVICES

In **Malaysia**, the postal service is well organized, with mail to and from overseas taking four to seven days to reach its destination. Postcards to anywhere in the world require a 30 *sen* stamp, while aerogrammes cost a uniform 50 *sen;* you can buy stamps in post offices. Packages are expensive to send, with surface/sea mail taking around two months to Europe, longer to the USA, and even air mail taking around a month. There's usually a shop near the post office which will wrap your parcel for $5 or so. Each Malaysian town has a **General Post Office** (GPO) with a **poste restante/general delivery** section, where mail will be held for two months. If you're sending mail there, make sure your surname is in capitals or underlined, and address the letter as follows: name, Poste Restante, GPO, town or city, state (optional). GPOs will also forward mail (for one month), free of charge, if you fill in the appropriate form. Usual post office **opening hours** are Monday to Friday 8am–5pm and Saturday 8am–noon (except for the east coast states, where Friday is closing day).

In **Singapore**, the GPO, housing the poste restante counter, is on Fullerton Road; see p.558 for more details and opening hours. There are other post offices across the state, with usual hours of Monday to Friday 8.30am–5pm and Saturday 8.30am–1pm, though limited, round-the-clock services are available in the GPO lobby and at the *Comcentre* on Killiney Road. Singapore's postal system is predictably efficient, with letters and cards often reaching their destination within three days. Stamps are available at post offices (some have vending machines operating out of hours), and some stationers and hotels. Airmail letters to Europe and the USA rise from 75c, aerogrammes to all destinations cost 35c and postcards cost 30c. You'll find fax and telex facilities in all major post offices, too, while if you want to make up a parcel, *postpacs* (cardboard cartons) are available in varying sizes. Surface mail is the cheapest means of sending a parcel home: a parcel under 10kg costs $43 to the UK, $74 to the USA and $35 to Canada and Australasia; there's a wrapping counter at the GPO.

Post offices in **Brunei** are open Monday to Thursday and Saturday 7.45am–4.30pm; see p.464 for details of the GPO. Some hotels can also provide basic postal facilities. Postcards to anywhere in the world cost 30c, aerogrammes 45c; overseas letters cost 90c for every 10g.

TELEPHONES

For dialling to and from the region, see the box below for all the relevant **dialling code** information. Note that Singapore has no **area codes**; both Malaysia and Brunei do, and they are included in the telephone numbers given throughout the book – omit them if dialling locally. It's also worth pointing out that many businesses in Malaysia and Singapore have **mobile phone numbers** – usually prefixed 011 or 010 – though these are very expensive to call. Finally, you can use your *BT* or *AT&T* **chargecard** in both Malysia and Singapore.

MALAYSIA

The first thing to note about the Malaysian telephone system is that **all the telephone numbers in the country are being changed** as part of a rolling programme. The numbers given throughout this guide were correct at the time of going to press, but some are likely to have changed subsequently; local tourist offices should have up-to-date directories and listings.

There are **public telephone** boxes in most towns in Malaysia; local calls cost just 10 *sen* for an unlimited time. For long-distance calls, it makes sense to use a **card phone**, which are as common as coin-operated phones. There are two companies operating card phones: the ubiquitous *Uniphone* – from whose phones you can make overseas calls – and the government *Kadfon* network (of blue phone boxes), which is less widespread and for domestic calls only. Cards come in denominations of $3 to $50 and can be purchased from *Shell* and *Petronas* service stations and most *7-Eleven* outlets. Before inserting the card, press button *2 and the instructions will appear in English. If your card runs out during the call, press * when you hear the tones to eject the card, and you can insert a new card without losing the connection.

Although there is an international direct-dial (IDD) facility from most phone boxes, you cannot make **collect** (reverse charge) **calls** from them. For these (and for long-distance calls) it's best to go to a **Telekom** office, located in most towns (and detailed in the text throughout), where – if you haven't called collect – you pay the cashier after your call. *Telekom* offices are generaly only open during normal office hours, which can make international calls tricky, though there are 24-hour offices in KL, Penang and Kota Kinabulu.

In Penang and Kota Kinabalu there are also **Home Country Direct** phones – press the appropriate button and you'll be connected with your home operator, who can either arrange a collect call, or debit you; if you're paying, settle your bill with the cashier after the call.

SINGAPORE

Local calls from private phones in Singapore are free; calls from public phones cost 10c for three minutes, with the exception of Changi Airport's free courtesy phones. Singapore has **no area codes** – the only time you'll punch more than seven digits for a local number is if you're dialling a toll-free (☎1800-) number. **Card phones** are taking over from payphones in Singapore: cards, available from the **Comcentre** (see p.559) and post offices, as well as *7-Elevens*, stationers and bookshops, come in denominations rising from $2. **International calls** can be made 24 hours a day from booths at the *Comcentre* and the GPO, and from public phones labelled "Worldphone", using 50c and $1 coins.

Some booths are equipped with **Home Country Direct** phones – see "Malaysia" above for the procedure.. Otherwise, use a card- or credit cardphone – the following numbers will put you through to your home country's operator: UK ☎8004400; USA ☎8000011; Australia ☎8006100; Canada ☎8001000; New Zealand ☎8006400. For directory enquiries, call ☎103 and for IDD information call ☎162.

BRUNEI

Local calls from phone boxes in **Brunei** cost 10c, while calls from private phones are free. International (IDD) calls can be made through hotels, in booths at the *Telekom* office in the capital, or from card phones in shopping centres and other public places. Phone cards rise in value from $10 and up, and can be bought from the *Telekom* office and post offices.

NEWSPAPERS AND MAGAZINES

Malaysia has three daily English-language **newspapers**, another which comes out in the afternoon and a weekly tabloid, all of which are government-owned. *The New Straits Times* – sister to the *Singapore Straits Times* – is a thick broadsheet with blatantly government-slanted

---

PHONING ABROAD

From the UK: dial ☎00 60 (Malaysia), ☎00 65 (Singapore), or ☎00 673 (Brunei) + area code minus first 0 (except Singapore) + number

From the USA: dial ☎011 60 (Malaysia), ☎011 65 (Singapore), or ☎011 673 (Brunei) + area code minus first 0 (except Singapore) + number

FROM MALAYSIA

Dial ☎001 + IDD country code (see below) + area code minus first 0 + subscriber number

FROM SINGAPORE

Dial ☎005 + IDD country code (see below) + area code minus first 0 + subscriber number

FROM BRUNEI

Dial ☎01 + IDD country code (see below) + area code minus first 0 + subscriber number

IDD CODES

Australia ☎61	Canada ☎1	Ireland ☎353
New Zealand ☎64	UK ☎44	USA ☎1

TIME

Malaysia, Singapore and Brunei are 8 hours ahead of GMT, 16 hours ahead of US Pacific Standard Time, 13 ahead of Eastern Standard Time, and 2 hours behind Sydney.

political news and wide arts coverage. *The Business Times* covers finance throughout Southeast Asia, while *The Star* is a news-focused tabloid. The afternoon *Malay Mail* has the most extensive "what's on" sections and the weekly tabloid, *The Sun*, is strong on populist columns about all things Malaysian. *The New Straits Times*, *The Mail* and *The Star* all have Sunday editions as well. There are also Chinese-, Tamil- and Malay-language newspapers and a variety of weekly and monthly **English-language magazines**, the best being the current affairs *Asiaweek* (available worldwide) and *Aliran Monthly*, which treats economic and political issues from a less centralized, more independent perspective.

TV AND RADIO

Two of **Malaysia**'s three **television channels**, *RTM1* and *RTM2*, are broadcast in Malay and are govenment-owned, but they include some material in Chinese. The third station, *TV3*, is run commercially and shows English-language news and documentaries, Chinese kung fu, and Tamil, British and American films and soaps.

In **Singapore**, the *Singapore Broadcasting Company* (*SBC*) screens programmes in English, Chinese, Malay and Tamil on channels 5, 8 and 12 – Channels 5 and 12 feature the most English-language programmes, Channel 8 specializes in Chinese soap operas. Most Singaporean TV sets also receive Malaysia's *RTM1*, *RTM2* and *TV3* channels. **Brunei** has a more limited range. *Radio and Television Brunei* (*RTB*) broadcasts daily on a single channel – many of its programmes are imported, and there's English-language news at 7pm each evening.

The six main Malaysian **radio stations** are also government-run, and include one devoted to pop music, and others broadcasting in Malay, Chinese and Tamil. The *BBC World Service* can be received on shortwave (in Johor, you might be able to pick it up on FM), as can *Voice of America*. In **Singapore**, *SBC* broadcasts four English-language radio shows daily: Radio 1 (90.5FM), an information and music channel; Symphony (92.4FM) featuring classical music; Perfect 10 (98.7FM) playing pop music; and Class (95FM) playing middle of the road hits. There's also a decent pirate radio station operating from Indonesia's Batam island, and BBC World Service (88.9FM) broadcasts 24 hours a day. For locals, there are daily shows in Chinese (95.8FM), Malay (94.2FM) and Tamil (96.8FM). For listings, check in the daily newspapers, or in *8 Days* magazine. In **Brunei**, *RTB* broadcasts two channels a day on the medium wave and FM bands – one in Malay, the other in English and Chinese.

POLICE, TROUBLE AND EMERGENCIES

If you lose something in Malaysia and Singapore, you're more likely to have someone running after you with it than running away. Nevertheless, you shouldn't become complacent – muggings have been known to occur and theft from dormitories by other tourists is a common complaint.

Most people carry their passport, travellers' cheques and other valuables in a concealed money belt, and guest houses and hotels will often have a safety deposit box. Always keep a separate record of the numbers of your traveller's cheques, together with a note of which ones you've cashed. It's probably worth taking a photocopy of the relevant pages of your passport, too, in case it's lost or stolen. In the more remote parts of Sarawak or Sabah there is little crime, and you needn't worry unduly about carrying cash

– in fact, the lack of banks means that you'll probably have to carry more than you might otherwise wish.

It's worth repeating here that it is very unwise to have anything to do with **drugs** of any description in Malaysia and Singapore. The penalties for trafficking drugs in or out of either country are severe in the extreme – foreigners have been executed in the past – and if you are arrested for drugs offences you can expect no mercy and little help from your consular representatives.

MALAYSIA

If you do need to report a crime in Malaysia, head for the nearest police station (marked on our maps and included in the text), where there'll invariably be someone who speaks English –

EMERGENCIES

In an emergency, dial the following numbers:

Malaysia
Police/Ambulance ☎999
Fire Brigade ☎994

Singapore
Police ☎999
Fire Brigade/Ambulance ☎995

Brunei
Police ☎222333
Ambulance ☎223366
Fire Brigade ☎222555

you'll need a copy of the police report for insurance purposes. In many major tourist spots, there are specific **tourist police stations** which are geared up to problems faced by foreign travellers. The police are generally more aloof than in the West, dressed in blue trousers and white short-sleeved shirts, and armed with a small handgun. While you're likely to be excused any minor misdemeanor as a foreigner, it pays to be deferential if caught on the wrong side of the law.

In the predominantly **Muslim** east coast states of Kelantan and Terengganu, restrictions such as "close proximity" between people of the opposite sex and eating in public during daylight hours in the Ramadan month apply to Muslims only, and are customary rather than legal in

nature. However, it's courteous to observe restrictions like this where possible and there's advice throughout the guide on how to avoid giving offence. Lastly, if you're **driving**, watch out for police speed traps – if you're caught speeding there's a spot fine of $200.

SINGAPORE

Singapore is known locally as a "fine city". There's a fine of $500 for smoking in public places such as cinemas, trains, lifts, air-conditioned restaurants and shopping malls, and one of $50 for "jaywalking" – crossing a main road within 50m of a pedestrian crossing or bridge. Littering carries a $1000 fine, with offenders now issued Corrective Work Orders and forced to do litter-picking duty, while eating and drinking on the MRT could cost you $500. Other fines include those for urinating in lifts (legend has it that some lifts are fitted with urine detectors), not flushing a public toilet and chewing gum (which is outlawed in Singapore). It's worth bearing all these offences in mind, since foreigners are not exempt from the various Singaporean punishments – as American Michael Fay discovered early in 1994, when he was given four strokes of the cane for vandalism.

Singapore's **police**, who wear dark blue, keep a fairly low profile, but are polite and helpful when approached. For details of the main police station, and other emergency information, check the relevant sections of "Listings", p.557.

PEOPLES

Largely because of their pivotal position on the maritime trade routes between the Middle East, India and China, the present-day countries of Malaysia, Singapore and Brunei have always been a cultural melting-pot. During the first millenium Malays crossed from present-day Sumatra and Indians arrived from India and Sri Lanka, while later the Chinese migrated from mainland China and Hainan island. But all these traders and settlers arrived to find that the region already contained a gamut of indigenous tribes, first thought to have migrated here around 50,000 years ago, from the Phillipines, which was then connected by a land bridge to Borneo and Southeast

Asia. Indeed, the indigenous tribes which still exist on the peninsula are known as the *orang asli*, Malay for "the first people".

First people they may have been, but the descendants of the various indigenous groups now form a small minority of the overall **populations** of the three countries. Over the last 150 years a massive influx of Chinese and Indian immigrants, escaping poverty, war and revolution, has swelled the population of **Malaysia**, which now stands at nearly 18 million: on the peninsula, the Malays still form the majority of the population at just over 50 percent, the Chinese number nearly 38 percent, Indians 10 percent and the *orang asli* around 1 percent; in Sarawak, on the other hand, the indigenous tribes account for almost 50 percent of the population, the Chinese 30 percent, with the other 20 percent divided amongst Malays and Indians; while in Sabah, the indigenous groups represent around 55 percent, the Chinese 30 percent; with the remainder a mix of Malays, Indians and, latterly, Filiipino immigrants.

Brunei's population of around 260,000 is heavily dominated by Malays, with minorities of Chinese, Indians and indigenous peoples. In **Singapore**, there were only tiny numbers of indigenes left on the island by the time of the arrival of Raffles. They have no modern-day presence in the state and more than three quarters of the 2.8-million strong population are of Chinese extraction, while around 14 percent are Malay, and 7 percent Indian.

THE MALAYS

The **Malays**, a Mongoloid people believed to have originated from the meeting of Central Asians with Pacific islanders, first moved to the west coast of the Malaysian peninsula from Sumatra in early times. Known as *orang laut* (sea people), they sustained an economy built around fishing, boat-building and, in some communities, piracy. Strong in present-day Indonesia during the first millenium, it was the growth in power of the Malay Sultanates from the fifteenth century onwards (see p.565) – coinciding with the arrival of Islam – that established Malays as a force to be reckoned with in the Malay peninsula and in Borneo. They developed an aristocratic tradition, courtly rituals and a social hierarchy (for more on which, see p.285) which have an influence even today. The rulers of the Malaysian states still wield immense social and economic power, reflected in the sharing of the appointment of the *agong*, a pre-eminent Sultan nominated on a five-year cycle. Although it's a purely ceremonial position, the *agong* is seen as the ultimate guardian of Malay Muslim culture and, despite recent legislation to reduce his powers, is still considered to be above the law. The situation is even more pronounced in **Brunei**, to which many Muslim Malay traders fled after the fall of Melaka to the Portuguese in 1511. There, the Sultan is still the supreme ruler (as his descendants have been, on and off, for over 500 years), his powers verging on the autocratic.

Even though Malays have been Muslims since the fifteenth century, the region as a whole is not **fundamentalist** in character. Only in Brunei is alcohol banned, for instance, and while fundamentalist groups do hold sway in the eastern states of Kelantan and Terengganu, their influence is rarely oppressive.

The main contemporary change for Malays in Malaysia was the introduction of the **bumiputra** policy – a Malay word meaning "sons of the soil" – initiated after independence to separate those inhabitants of Peninsular and East Malaysia who had cultural affinities indigenous to the region from those who originated from outside. The policy was designed to make it easier for the Malays, the *orang asli* of the peninsula, and the various Malay-related indigenous groups in Sarawak and Sabah, to compete in economic and educational fields against the Chinese and Indians, who – since the large-scale immigration of the nineteenth century – had traditionally tended to be the higher achievers.

These days, certain **privileges**, mostly financial or status-enhancing, are offered to a *bumiputra* which are not available to the non-*bumiputra*, although in practice these privileges are only fully extended to Muslim Malays. Every Malaysian company must employ a Malay at a senior level and all companies must have at least a 51-percent Malay shareholder profile. Also, Malays get discounts on buying houses and find it much easier to get loans from the *Islamic Bank*, which has by far the closest relationship of any bank with the government. As a consequence, Malays tend to take the top positions in government, state-owned companies and prestigious private firms, and in most spheres of the arts.

Although tensions between Malays and the Chinese have led occasionally to unrest, the worst example being the race riots of 1969, the overall effect of stimulating Malay opportunities, mostly at the expense of the Chinese, seems to have been positive. Some critics have likened the *bumiputra* policy to a form of apartheid, but as long as the modern Malaysian economic miracle continues to enrich the whole community, it's unlikely that those excluded from the policy will complain. The situation is slightly different in **Singapore**, where the policy doesn't hold sway: despite being greatly outnumbered by their Chinese compatriots, Singapore's Malay community appears content to stay south of the causeway and enjoy the state's higher standard of living.

THE CHINESE AND STRAITS CHINESE

Chinese traders began visiting the region in the seventh century, but it was in Melaka in the fifteenth century that the first significant community established itself. However, the ancestors of the majority of Chinese now living in Peninsular Malaysia emigrated from southern China in the nineteenth century to work in the burgeoning tin-mining industry. In Sarawak, Chinese from Foochow, Teochew and Hokkien provinces played an important part in opening up the interior, establishing pepper and rubber plantations along the Rajang river; while in Sabah, Hakka Chinese labourers from Hong Kong were recruited by the *British North Borneo Chartered Company* to plant rubber, and many stayed on forming the base of the Chinese business community there.

Although many Chinese in the peninsula came as labourers, they graduated quickly to shopkeeping and business ventures, both in established towns like Melaka and fast-expanding centres like KL, Penang and Kuching. Chinatowns developed throughout the region, even in Malay strongholds like Kota Bharu and Kuala Terengganu, while **Chinese traditions**, religious festivities, theatre and music became an integral part of a wider Malayan, and later Malaysian, multiracial culture. On the political level, the Malaysian Chinese are well represented in parliament and occupy around a quarter of the current Ministerial positions. By way of contrast, **Chinese Bruneians** are not automatically classed as citizens and suffer a fair amount of discrimination at the hands of the majority Malay population.

Singapore's nineteenth-century trade boom drew large numbers of Cantonese, Teochew and Hakka Chinese traders and labourers, who quickly established a Chinatown on the south bank of the Singapore river. Today, the Chinese account for 78 percent of the state's population and are the most economically successful racial group in Singapore. As the proportion of Singaporean Chinese born on the island increases, the government's efforts to cultivate a feeling of Singaporean national identity are beginning to show signs of working, especially among the younger generation. Consequently, the main difference between the Chinese in Singapore and those in Malaysia is that Singapore's Chinese majority prefers to think of itself simply as Singaporean. Nevertheless, as in Malaysia, they still display their traditional work ethic and spurn none of their cultural heritage.

One of the few examples of regional intermarrying is displayed in the **Peranakan** or "Straits-born Chinese" heritage of Melaka, Singapore and, to a lesser extent, Penang. When male Chinese immigrants settled in these places from the sixteenth century onwards to work as miners or commercial entrepreneurs, they often married local Malay women, whose male offspring were termed "Baba" and the females "Nonya". **Baba-Nonya** society, as it became known, adapted elements from both cultures to create its own traditions: the descendants of these sixteenth-century laisions have a unique culinary and architectural style (for more on which see p.287). Although Baba-Nonyas dress as Malays – the men in stiff-collared tunics and *songkets* and the women in sarongs and fitted, long-sleeved blouses – most follow Chinese Confucianism as their religion and speak a distinct Malay dialect.

THE INDIANS

The second-largest non-*bumiputra* group in Malaysia, the **Indians**, first arrived as traders more than 2000 years ago, although few settled and it wasn't until the early fifteenth century that a small community of Indians (from present-day Tamil Nadu and Sri Lanka) was based in Melaka. But, like the majority of Chinese, the first large wave of Indians – Tamil labourers – arrived in the nineteenth century as indentured workers, to build the roads and railways and to work on the European-run rubber estates. But an embryonic entrepeneurial class from north India soon followed and set up businesses in Penang and Singapore; because most were Muslims, these merchants and traders found it easier to assimilate themselves into the existing Malay community than could the Hindu Tamils.

Although Indians comprise only 10 percent of Malaysia's population (7 percent in Singapore) their impact is felt everywhere. The Hindu festival of Thaipusam (see p.112) is celebrated annually at KL's Batu Caves by upwards of a million people (with a smaller, but still significant celebration in Singapore); the festival of Deepavali is a national holiday; and Indians are increasingly competing with Malays in the arts, and dominate certain professional areas like medicine and law. And then, of course, there is the culinary area – very few Malaysians these days could do without a daily dose of *roti canai*, so much so, that this north Indian snack has been virtually appropriated by Malay and Chinese cafés and hawkers.

Despite this influence, in general Indians are at the bottom of the economic ladder, a situation which has its origins in the colonial system. Even today, many of the Tamils work on private plantations and are unable to reap many of the benefits of Malaysia's economic success. Indians' political voice has also traditionally been weak, although there are signs that a younger generation of political leaders from the two Indian-dominated political parties, the Malaysian Indian Congress and the Indian Progressive Front, are asserting the community's needs more effectively.

THE ORANG ASLI

The **orang asli** – the indigenous peoples of Peninsular Malaysia – mostly belong to three distinct groups, within which various tribes are related either by geography, language or physiological features.

The largest of the groups is the **Senoi** (the *asli* word for person) who number about 40,000. They live in the large, still predominantly forested interior within the states of Perak, Pahang and Kelantan, and divide into two main tribes, the Semiar and the Temiar, which still live a traditional lifestyle, following animist customs in their marriage ceremonies and burial rites. On the whole they follow the practice of shifting cultivation – a regular rotation of jungle-clearance and crop-planting – although goverment resettlement drives have successfully persuaded many to settle and farm just one area.

The **Semang** (or Negritos), of whom there are around 2000, live in the northern areas of the peninsula. They comprise six distinct, if small, tribes, related to each other in appearance – they are mostly dark-skinned and curly haired – and share a traditional nomadic, hunter-gatherer lifestyle. However, most Semang nowadays live in settled communities and work within the cash economy, either as labourers or selling jungle produce in markets. Perhaps the most frequently seen Semang tribe are the Batek, who live in and around Taman Negara.

The third group, the so-called **Aboriginal Malays**, live south of the Kuala Lumpur–Kuantan road. Some of the tribes in this category, like the Jakun who live around Tasek Chini and the Semelais of Tasek Bera, have vigorously retained their animist religion and artistic traditions despite living in permanent villages near Malay communities and working within the regular economy. These are among the easiest of the *orang asli* to approach, since some have obtained employment in the two lakes' tourist industries; others are craftspeople selling their wares from stalls beside the water. See p.222 for more details.

These three main groupings do not represent all the *orang asli* tribes in Malaysia. One, the Lanoh in Perak, are sometimes regarded as Negritos, but their language is closer to that of the Temiar. Another group, the semi-nomadic Che Wong, of whom just a few hundred still survive on the slopes of Gunung Benom in central Pahang, are still dependent on foraging to survive and live in temporary huts made from bamboo and rattan. Two more groups, the Jah Hut of Pahang and the Mah Meri of Selangor, are particularly fine carvers, and it's possible to buy their sculptures at regional craftshops.

The tribes of Tasek Chini and Tasek Bera apart, it's difficult to visit most *orang asli* communities. Many live way off the beaten track and you would need to to go as part of a tour (some operators do visit *orang asli* settlements in Tasek Bera or Endau Rompin National Park). It's most unlikely that visitors would ever chance upon a remote *orang asli* village, though you will sometimes pass tribe members in the national parks or on inaccessible roads in eastern Perak, Pahang and Kelantan. To learn more about the disappearing *asli* culture, the best stop is KL's Orang Asli Museum (see p.113).

SARAWAK'S PEOPLES

In direct contrast to the peninsula, indigenous groups make up a substantial chunk of the population in Sarawak, which is what attracts many visitors there in the first place – see Chapter 6 for all the details. Although the Chinese comprise 29 percent of the state's population and the Malays and Indians around 24 percent together, the remaining 47 percent are made up of various indigenous **Dyak** groups – a word derived from the Malay for "up-country".

The largest Dyak groups are the Iban, Bidayuh, Melanau, Kayan, Kenyah, Kelabit and Penan tribes, all of which have distinct cultures, although most have certain things in common including a lifestyle predominantly based outside towns. Many live in **longhouses** (for more, see p.336) along the rivers or on the sides of hills in the mountainous interior, and maintain a proud cultural legacy which draws on animist religion (see p.58 for more on this), arts and crafts production, jungle skills and a rich tradition of **festivals**. The tribal dances are seldom seen these days, their traditions rapidly being absorbed into wider Malay art forms, but the culturally stronger groups in Sarawak are slowly exerting their distinct identities. The *Ngajat*, a dance traditionally performed by warriors on their return from battle is now more commonly performed in the longhouses, albeit in a milder, truncated form. Spectacular costumes featuring large feathers are worn by the dancers who, arranged in a circle, perform athletic leaps to indicate their virility.

The **Iban**, a stocky, rugged people, make up nearly one-third of Sarawak's population. The Iban originated hundreds of miles south of present-day Sarawak, in the Kapuas valley in Kalimantan, and migrated north in the sixteenth century, coming into conflict with the Kayan and Kenyah tribes and, later, the British, over the next 200 years. Nowadays, Iban longhouse communities are found in the batang Ai river system in the southwest, and along the Rajang, Katibas and Baleh rivers in the interior – though tribe members tend to migrate to Kuching and Miri, looking for work, although most prefer still to base themselves in their longhouses. These are quite accessible, their inhabitants always hospitable and keen to illustrate aspects of their culture like traditional dance, music, textile-weaving, blow-piping, fishing and game-playing. For the Iban, the planting and cultivation of rice – their staple crop – is intimately connected with human existence, a relationship which underpins their animist beliefs. In their time, the Iban were infamous head-hunters and some longhouses are still decorated with authentically collected – then shrunken – heads. These days, though, the tradition of head-hunting has been replaced by that of *berjelai*, or "journey", whereby a young man leaves the community to prove himself in the outside world – returning to their longhouses with television sets, generators and outboard motors, rather than heads. For more details about the Iban, see the feature on p.352–353.

The most southern of Sarawak's indigenous groups are the **Bidayuh** (see p.349 for more), who – unlike most Dyak groups – traditionally lived away from the rivers, building their longhouse on the sides of hills. Culturally, they are similar to the Iban, although in temperament they are much milder and less gregarious, keeping themselves to themselves in their inacccesible homes on Sarawak's mountainous southern border with Kalimantan.

The **Melanau** are a coastal people, living north of Kuching in a region dominated by mangrove swamps. Few roads have been built in this area and not many visitors venture here. Many Melanau, however, now live in towns, preferring the *kampung*--style houses of the Malays to the elegant longhouses of the past. They are expert fishermen and cultivate sago as an alternative to rice. Many Melanau died in the battles that followed when the Iban first migrated northwards, and the survival of their communities owes much to the first White Rajah, James Brooke, who protected them in the last century. He had a soft spot for the Melanau, thinking them the most attractive of the state's ethnic peoples and employing many as boat-builders, labourers and domestic servants.

The **Kelabit** people live on the highland plateau which separates north Sarawak from Kalimantan. Like the Iban, they live in longhouses and maintain a traditional lifestyle, but differ from the other groups in that they are Christian; they were converted just after World War II, during which the highlands had been used by British and Australian forces to launch attacks on the occupying Japanese. The highlands were totally inaccessible before the airstrip at Bario was built; now the area has become popular for hikers, since within a few days' walk of Bario are many longhouses which welcome visitors (see p.394 for more).

The last main group is the semi-nomadic **Penan**, who live in the upper Rajang and Limbang areas of Sarawak in temporary lean-tos or small huts. They rely, like some of the *orang asli* groups in the peninsula, on hunting and gathering and collecting jungle produce for sale in local markets. They also have the lightest pigment of all the ethnic groups of Sarawak, largely because they live within the shade of the forest, rather than on the rivers and in clearings. In recent years the state government has tried to resettle the Penan in small villages, a controversial policy not entirely unconnected with the advance of logging in traditional Penan land, which has caused opposition from the Penan themselves and criticism from international groups. Some tour operators now have itineraries which include visiting Penan communities in the Baram river basin and the primary jungle which slopes away from the Kelabit Highlands.

Most of the other groups in Sarawak fall into the catch-all ethnic classification of **orang ulu** (people of the interior), who inhabit the more remote inland parts of the state, further north than the Iban, along the upper Rajang, Balui and Linau rivers. The most numerous, the **Kayan** and the **Kenyah**, are closely related and in the past often teamed up to defend their lands from the invading Iban. But they also have much in common with their traditional enemy since they are longhouse-dwellers, animists and shifting cultivators. The main difference is the more hierarchial social structure of their communities, with one leader, a *penghulu*, who has immense influence over the other inhabitants of the longhouse. Nowadays, many Kayan are Christians – converted after contact witjh missionaries following World War II – and their longhouses are among the most prosperous in Sarawak. Like the Iban, they maintain a tradition of *berjelai*, and the return of the youths from their wanderings is always an excuse for a big party, at which visitors from abroad or from other longhouses are always welcome. There's more information on both the Kenyah and Kayan on p.368.

SABAH'S PEOPLE

Sabah has a population of around 1.6 million, made up of more than thirty distinct racial groups, between them speaking over eighty different dialects. Most populous of these groups are the **Dusuns**, which account for around a third of Sabah's population. Traditionally agriculturists (the word *Dusun* means "orchard"), the subgroups of the Dusun inhabit the western coastal plains and the interior of the state. These days they are known generically as **Kadazan/Dusuns**, although strictly speaking "Kadazan" refers only to the Dusun of Penampang. Other branches of the Dusun include the Lotud of Tuaran and the Rungus of the Kudat Peninsula, whose convex longhouses are all that remain of the Dusun's

longhouse tradition. Although most Dusun are now Christians, remnants of their animist past are still evident in their culture, most obviously in the harvest festival, or *Pesta Kaamatan*, when their *Bobohizans*, or priestesses, perform rituals to honour the *Bambaazon*, or rice spirit. In the *Samazau* dance – almost the national dance of East Malaysia – the costumes worn are authentically Kadazan. Two rows of men and women dance in a slow, rhythmic movement facing each other, flapping their arms to the pulse of the drum, their hand gestures mimicking the flight of birds. Not to be outdone, the women of the Kwijau community have their own dance, the *Buloh* which features high jumping steps to the percussive sounds of the gong and bamboo.

The mainly Muslim **Bajau** tribe drifted over from the southern Phillippines some two hundred-years ago and now constitutes Sabah's second largest ethnic group, accounting for around 10 percent of the population. Their penchant for piracy quickly earned them the soubriquet "Sea Gypsies", though nowadays they are agriculturists and fishermen, noted for their horsemanship and their rearing of buffaloes. The Bajau live in the northwest of Sabah and occasionally appear on horseback at Kota Belud's *tamu* (or market; see p.427).

Sabah's third sizeable tribe is the **Murut**, which inhabits the area between Keningau and the Sarawak border, in the southwest. Their name means "hill people", though they prefer to be known by their individual tribal names, such as Timugon, Tagal and Nabai. The Murut farm rice and cassava by a system of shifting cultivation and, at times, still hunt using blowpipes and poison darts. Though their head-hunting days are over, they retain other cultural traditions, such as the construction of brightly adorned grave huts to house the graves and belongings of the dead. Another tradition that continues is the consumption at ceremonies of *tapai* or rice wine, drawn from a ceremonial jar using bamboo straws. Although the Murut are now eschewing longhouse life, many villages retain a ceremonial hall, complete with a *lansaran*, or bamboo trampoline, for festive dances and games.

RELIGION, TEMPLES AND SOCIAL CONVENTIONS

Three great religions – Islam, Buddhism and Hinduism – are represented in Malaysia and Singapore, and they play a vital role in the everyday lives of the population. Indeed, some religious festivals, like Muslim Hari Raya and Hindu Thaipusam, have been elevated to such stature that they are among the main cultural events in the regional calendar.

In Malaysia, the vast majority of people are **Muslims**, while in Singapore – where three-quarters of the population are Chinese – **Buddhism** is the main religion. There's a smaller, but no less significant, **Hindu** Indian presence in both countries, while the other chief belief system is **animism**, followed by many of the indigenous ethnic peoples of Malaysia – including the *orang asli* in the peninsular and the various Dyak groups in Sarawak. However, the main tribal group in Sabah, the Kadazan, are **Christian**, as are many of the Kelabit in Sarawak, though this is otherwise a minority religion in much of Malaysia and Singapore, practised primarily by the Eurasian community. The other main feature of religion in the region is that both Islam and Buddhism in Malaysia and Singapore are syncretic adaptations of those practised elsewhere, partly due to the influence of animist elements which over the centuries have been integrated from the indigenous peoples' beliefs.

It's not uncommon to see the **temples** of different creeds happily existing side by side, each providing a social as well as a religious focal point for the corresponding community; in the early days, the temple formed an essential support network for newcomers to Malaysia and Singapore. Architectural traditions mean that the Chinese and Indian temples, built out of brick, have long outlasted the timber Malay mosque, making them the oldest structures you're likely to see in the region.

Although Malaysians and Singaporeans in general are hospitable, friendly and tolerant of visitors, it helps to know about the region's customs and to try to abide by the main rules of **etiquette**. Most are related to tenets of the various religions, though in East Malaysia – especially during stays in a longhouse – you're exposed to more subtle customs to do with status and social behaviour.

ANIMISM

The first principle of **animism** is that everything in nature has a soul or spirit (*semangat*), which inhabits mountains, trees, rocks and lakes, and has to be mollified as it controls the forces of nature. Although many of Malaysia's ethnic groups are now nominally Christian or Muslim, many of their old beliefs and ceremonies still survive. Birds, especially the hornbill, are of particular significance to the Iban and the Kelabit peoples in Sarawak. Many Kelabits depend upon the arrival of migrating flocks to decide when to plant their rice crop, while Iban hunters still interpret sightings of the hornbill and other birds as good or bad omens. In ceremonies, like the Iban male rite-of-passage, a headdress made of hornbill feathers adorns the young man's head.

For the *orang asli* groups in the interior of the peninsula, most of their remaining animist beliefs centre around healing and funereal ceremonies. A sick person, particularly a child, is believed to be invaded by a bad spirit, and drums are played and incantations performed to persuade the spirit to depart. The death of a member of the family is followed by a complex process of burial and re-burial - a procedure which, hopefully, ensures an easy passage for the person's spirit.

An important link between the animism still practised by the tribal groups and Islam is provided by the **bomoh** (medicine man), who can still be found in remote Malay villages performing tasks like calling on the elements to bring rain during droughts or preventing rain from ruining an important ceremony. A central part of the *bomoh's* trade is recitation, often of sections of the Koran, while – like his *orang asli* counterparts – he uses various healing techniques, including herbs, localized burning and chants to cure or ease pain and disease. Although there are still quite a few *bomoh* in Malaysia, they are a vanishing breed, largely because there are fewer younger men willing to continue the tradition.

ISLAM

The first firm foothold **Islam** made in Malaysia was the conversion of Paramesvara, the ruler of Melaka, in the early fifteenth century. The commercial success of Melaka accelerated the process of Islamicization and, one after another, the powerful Malay court rulers took to Islam, adopting the title Sultan ("ruler"), either because of sincere doctrinal conversion or because they took a shrewd view of the practical advantages to be gained by embracing the new faith. On a wider cultural level, too, Islam had great attractions; its revolutionary concepts of equality in subordination to Allah freed people from the feudal Hindu caste system which had previously dominated parts of the region.

With the fall of Melaka in 1511, the migration of Muslim merchants to Brunei strengthened the hold of Islam in the region. The first wave of Islamic missionaries were mostly *Sufis*, the mystical and generally more liberal wing of Islam. Sufi Islam integrated some animist elements and Hindu beliefs: the tradition of pluralist deity worship which is central to Hinduism continued, and accounts for the strong historical and cultural importance of festivals like Deepavali and Thaipusam, where powerful deities are commemorated.

However, in the early nineteenth century the dominance of Sufism declined when a more puritanical Islamic branch, the *Wahabi*, captured Mecca. The return to the Koran's basic teachings became identified with a more militant approach, leading to several *jihads* (holy wars) in Kedah, Kelantan and Terengganu against the Malay rulers' Siamese overlords and, subsequently, the British. The British colonial period inevitably drew Christian missionaries to the region, but they had more success in Borneo than on the peninsula.

Indeed, the British, in a bid to avoid further unrest among the Malays, were restrained in their evangelical efforts and Islam continued to prosper.

Islam in Malaysia today is a mixture of *Sufi* and *Wahabi* elements and as such is relatively liberal. Although most Muslim women wear traditional costume, especially headscarves, very few adopt the veil and some taboos, like not drinking alcohol, are ignored by a growing number of Malays (though public consumption of alcohol is banned in Brunei). There are stricter, more fundamentalist Muslims – in Kelantan the local government is dominated by them – but in general Islam here has a modern outlook, blending a vibrant, practising faith with a business-minded approach.

The most important point of the Islamic year is **Ramadan**, the ninth month of the Muslim lunar calendar, when the majority of Muslims fast from the break of dawn to dusk, and also abstain from drinking and smoking. The reason for the fast is to intensify awareness of the plight of the poor and to identify with the hungry. During Ramadan many hawker stalls sell cakes and fruit, and families often break their fast at the stalls, although the most orthodox Muslim families tend to eat privately during this period. The end of Ramadan is marked by the two-day national holiday, **Hari Raya**, at which point the fast stops and the festivities begin. By tradition, royal palaces (*istanas*) are open over the holiday – usually the only days in the year when they are – and Malay families invite friends and business associates into their houses for food and refreshments.

VISITING A MOSQUE

While only a small proportion of the faithful attend the **mosque** every day, on Friday – the Muslim day of prayer – Malays converge on their nearest mosque (*masjid*), with all employers providing an extended three-hour lunch break to provide time for prayers, lunch and the attendant socializing. In Malaysia, every town, village and hamlet has a mosque, with loudspeakers strapped to the minaret to call the faithful to prayer. The capital city of each state is the site of the *Masjid Negeri*, the state mosque, always more grandiose than its humble regional counterparts - an ostentatious statement of Islam's significance to the Malay people. Designs reflect religious conservatism, and you'll rarely see contemporary mosques varying from the standard square building topped by onion domes and minaret – though there were some notable flirtations with obscure geometrics and fibreglass in the 1960s. Only in Melaka state, where Malaysia's oldest mosques are located, does the architecture become more interesting, revealing unusual Sumatran influences.

Once **at the mosque**, the men wash their hands, feet and faces three times in the outer chambers, before entering the prayer hall to recite sections of the Koran. After this inital period, an Iman will lead prayers and, on occasions, deliver a sermon, where the teachings of Allah will be applied to a contemporary context. Women cannot enter the main prayer hall during prayers and must congregate in a chamber to the side of the hall. Visitors are welcome at certain times (it's always worth checking first with the local tourist office) and must wear acceptable clothing – long trousers and shirt for men, and a long cloak and headdress, which is provided by most mosques, for women. No non-Muslim is allowed to enter a mosque during prayer time or go into the prayer hall at any time, although it's possible to stand just outside and look in.

HINDUISM

Hinduism arrived in Malaysia long before Islam, brought by Indian traders more than a thousand years ago. Its central tenet is the belief that life is a series of rebirths and reincarnations that eventually leads to spiritual release. An individual's progress is determined by *karma*, very much a law of cause and effect, where negative decisions and actions slow up the process of upward reincarnation and positive ones accelerate it. A whole variety of **deities** are worshipped, which on the surface makes Hinduism appear complex, but with only a loose understanding of the *Vedas* – the religion's holy books – the characters and roles of the main gods quickly become apparent. The deities you'll come across most often are the three manifestations of the faith's supreme divine being: Brahma the Creator, Vishnu the Preserver and Shiva the Destroyer.

The earliest Hindu archeological remains are in Kedah (see p.176) and date from the tenth century, although the temples found here indicate a synthesis of Hindu and Buddhist imagery. Although almost all of the region's Hindu past has been obliterated, elements live on in the popular arts like *wayang kulit* (shadow plays), where sacred texts like the *Ramayana* (see below) form the basis of the stories.

There was a Hindu **revival** in the late nineteenth century when immigrants from southern India arrived to work on the Malaysian rubber and palm oil plantations and built temples to house popular idols. The Hindu celebration of Rama's victory – the central theme of the epic *Ramayana* – in time became the national holiday of **Deepavali** (the festival of lights), reflecting the Malaysian policy of religious tolerance, while another Hindu festival, **Thaipusam**, when Lord Subramaniam and elephant-headed Ganesh, the sons of Shiva, are worshipped, has become the single largest religious gathering in the region.

Visitors are welcome in Malaysia and Singapore's Hindu **temples**, and are expected to remove their shoes before entering. Step over the threshold and you enter a veritable Disneyland of colourful gods and fanciful creatures. The style is typically Dravidian (South Indian), as befits the largely Tamil population, with a soaring *gopuram*, or entrance tower, teeming with sculptures and a central courtyard leading to an inner sanctum to the presiding deity. In the temple precinct, there are always busy scenes – incense burning, the application of sandlewood paste, and the *puja* (ritualistic act of worship). However, as most Hindu temples are run by voluntary staff, it's often impossible to find anyone to give you a guided tour of the temples' abundant carvings and sculptures.

CHINESE RELIGIONS

Most visitors will be more aware of the region's **Chinese** religious celebrations than of the Muslim or Hindu ones, largely because the festivals themselves are particularly welcoming of tourists and are often exciting. Most are organized by *kongsis*, or clan houses, which are the cornerstone of all immigrant Chinese communities in Malaysia and Singapore and traditionally provided housing, employment and a social structure for the newly arrived; see p.165 for more.

More so than Islam, Chinese religion shares animist beliefs with the ethnic groups. Chinese pioneers, while opening out the rivers of Sarawak for trade, could understand the beliefs and practices (except the head-hunting!) of the Iban and Melanau tribesmen they were dealing with, partly because they could identify with the animist ideas which were a driving force in their own lives. Malaysian and Singaporean Chinese usually consider themselves either **Buddhist**,

Taoist or **Confucianist**, although in practice they are often a mixture of all three. These different strands in Chinese religion ostensibly lean in very different directions: Confucianism began as a philosophy based on piety, loyalty, humanitarianism and familial devotion, and has transmuted into a set of principles that permeate every aspect of Chinese life; Taoism places animism within a philosophy which propounds unity with nature as its chief tenet; and Buddhism is primarily concerned with the attainment of a state of personal enlightenment, *nirvana*. But in practice, the combination of the three comprises a system of belief which is first and foremost pragmatic. The Chinese use their religion to ease their passage through life, whether in the spheres of work or family, while temples double as social centres, where people meet and exchange views.

CHINESE TEMPLES

The rules of geomancy, or *feng shui* (wind and water), are rigorously applied to the construction of Chinese **temples**, so that the building is placed in such a geographical position as to render it free from evil influences. Visitors wishing to cross the threshold of a temple have to step over a kerb that's intended to trip up evil spirits, and walk through doors painted with fearsome door gods; fronting the doors are two stone lions, whose roars provide yet another defence. Larger temples typically consist of a front entrance hall opening onto a walled-in courtyard, beyond which is the hall of worship, where joss (luck) sticks are burned below images of the deities. The most important and striking element of a Chinese temple is its **roof** – grand, multi-tiered affairs, with low, overhanging eaves, the ridges alive with auspicious creatures such as dragons and phoenixes and, less often, with miniature scenes from traditional Chinese life and legend. Temples are also normally constructed around a framework of huge, lacquered timber beams, adorned with intricately carved warriors, animals and flowers. More figures are moulded onto outer walls, which are dotted with octagonal, heaxagonal or round grille-worked windows. *Feng shui* comes into play again inside the

temple, with auspicious room numbers and sizes, colour and sequence of construction. Elsewhere in the temple grounds, you'll see sizeable ovens, stuffed constantly with paper money, prayer books and other offerings; or a pagoda – a tall, thin tower thought to keep out evil spirits.

Chinese temples, too, play an important part in Chinese community life and many have weekly musical and theatrical performances, which can be enjoyed by visitors as well as locals. Most temples are open from early morning to early evening and devotees go in when they like, to make offerings or to pray; there are no set prayer times. Visitors are welcome and all the larger ones have janitors who will show you round, although only a few speak good English.

SOCIAL CONVENTIONS AND ETIQUETTE

The main **domestic rules** when entering a home are: always take your shoes off; dress modestly – for women that means below-knee length skirts or shorts, a bra and sleeved T-shirts, for men, long trousers; never help yourself to food without first being offered it; and if eating with your hands or chopsticks, avoid using your left hand, which in Islamic culture is considered unclean.

In most respects Malaysia and Brunei are not particularly strict Muslim societies but certain public acts which are quite acceptable in most non-Muslim countries are looked down upon here. Among these are kissing or cuddling, arguing, raising one's voice, pointing, or drinking in public.

Other, more subtle, **points of etiquette** include not touching the head of a Malaysian, Muslim or otherwise, as the head is considered sacred in Eastern culture; and not shaking hands unless the host has offered theirs.

Taking a small present to a Malay home, like flowers, fruit or chocolates, is always appreciated. When travelling to longhouse communities in East Malaysia, or to *orang asli* villages in the peninsula, it's a good idea to bring some little **gifts**, and notebooks and pens for the children will come in useful. For the finer points of longhouse etiquette, see p.353.

FESTIVALS

With so many ethnic groups and religions represented in Malaysia, Singapore and Brunei, you'll be unlucky if your trip doesn't coincide with some sort of festival, either secular or religious. Religious celebrations range from exuberant, family-oriented pageants to blood-curdlingly gory displays of devotion. Secular events might comprise a carnival with a cast of thousands, or just a local market with a few cultural demonstrations laid on. If you're keen to see a major religious festival, it's best to make for a town or city where there is a large population of the particular ethnic group which is celebrating – all the relevant details are given in the list of festivals and events below, and are backed up by special accounts throughout the text.

If you're particularly interested in specifically **Malay festivities**, it's worth noting that in the northeastern Malaysian towns of Kota Bharu and Kuala Terengganu, cultural centres have been established as a platform for traditional Malay pastimes and sports – there's more information in *The East Coast* chapter. **Chinese religious festivals** – in particular, the Festival of Hungry Ghosts – are the best times to catch a free performance of a Chinese opera, or *wayang*, in which characters act out classic Chinese legends, accompanied by crashing cymbals, clanging gongs and stylized singing.

Bear in mind that the major festival periods may play havoc with even the best-planned travel itineraries. Over Ramadan in particular, transport networks and hotel capacity are stretched to their limits, as countless Muslims engage in *balik kampung* – the return to one's home village; Chinese New Year wreaks similar havoc. Some, but by no means all, festivals are also public holidays (when everything closes); check the lists below in "Opening Hours and Public Holidays" for those.

Most of the festivals have **no fixed dates**, but change annually according to the lunar calendar. We've listed rough timings, but for specific dates each year it's a good idea to check with the local tourist office.

A FESTIVAL CALENDAR

JANUARY–FEBRUARY

Perlis Bird Singing Competition Bird-lovers and bird-owners from Malaysia and beyond gather at Kangar to hear the region's most melodious songbirds do battle (early Jan).

Thaiponggal A Tamil thanksgiving festival marking the end of the rainy season and the onset of spring; offerings of food are made at Hindu temples such as Singapore's Sri Srinivasa Perumal Temple on Serangoon Road (mid-Jan).

Procession of Kwong Teck Choon Ong Scores of cultural troupes perform lion dances and operas, and process around Kuching to honour this Chinese deity (Jan).

Chinese New Year Chinese communities spring spectacularly to life, to welcome in the new year. Old debts are settled, friends and relatives visited, and red envelopes (*hong bao*) containing money are given to children; Chinese operas and lion and dragon dance troupes perform in the streets, while ad hoc markets sell sausages and waxed ducks, pussy willow, chrysanthemums and mandarin oranges. Colourful parades of stilt-walkers, lion dancers and floats along Singapore's Orchard Road and through the major towns and cities of west coast Malaysia celebrate the *Chingay* holiday, part of the new year festivities (Jan–Feb).

January–February continued

Chap Goh Mei The fifteenth and climactic day of the Chinese New Year period, and a time for more feasting and firecrackers; women who throw an orange into the sea at this time are supposed to be granted a good husband; the day is known as *Guan Hsiao Chieh* in Sarawak (Feb).

Thaipusam Entranced Hindu penitents carry elaborate steel arches (*kavadi*), attached to their skin by hooks and skewers, to honour Lord Subriaman. The biggest processions are at Kuala Lumpur's Batu Caves and from the Sri Srinivasa Perumal Temple to the Chettiar Hindu Temple in Singapore (Jan/Feb).

Birthday of the Monkey God To celebrate the birthday of one of the most popular deities in the Chinese pantheon, mediums possessed by the Monkey God's spirit pierce themselves with skewers; elsewhere street operas and puppet shows are performed. Make for Singapore's Monkey God Temple on Seng Poh Road, or look out for ad hoc canopies erected near Chinese temples (Feb & Sept).

Regatta Lipa-Lipa *Lipa Lipa* – elegant square-rigged fishing boats – race at Semporna, on Sabah's east coast (Feb).

Brunei National Day The Sultan and 35,000 other Bruneians watch parades and fireworks at the Sultan Hassanal Bolkiah National Stadium, just outside Bandar Seri Begawan; the rest watch on TV (Feb 23).

MARCH–MAY

Ramadan Muslims spend the ninth month of the Islamic calendar fasting in the daytime, and breaking their fasts nightly with delicious Malay sweetmeats served at stalls outside mosques. See *Religion and Social Conventions*, below, for more details (March–April).

Hari Raya Puasa The end of Ramadan, which Muslims celebrate by feasting, and by visiting family and friends; this is the only time the region's royal palaces are open to the public (March–April).

Easter Candle-lit processions held on Good Friday at Christian churches like St Peter's in Melaka and St Joseph's in Singapore (March–April).

Qing Ming Ancestral graves are cleaned and restored, and offerings made by Chinese families at the beginning of the third lunar month – signals the beginning of spring and a new farming year (April).

Vesak Day Saffron-robed monks chant prayers at packed Buddhist temples, and devotees release caged birds to commemorate the Buddha's birth, enlightenment and the attainment of Nirvana (May).

Pesta Kaamatan Celebrated in the villages of Sabah's west coast and interior, the harvest festival of the Kadazan/Dusun people features a ceremony of thanksgiving by a *Bobohizan* (high priestess), followed by lavish festivities; the festival culminates in a major celebration in Kota Kinabalu (May).

Birthday of the Third Prince Entranced mediums cut themselves with swords to honour the birthday of the Buddhist child god Ne Zha; their blood is wiped on much sought-after paper charms. It's a ritual observed at various Chinese temples throughout the region (May).

Sabah Fest A week of events in Kota Kinabalu, offering a chance to experience Sabah's food, handicrafts, dance and music (late May).

Hari Raya Haji An auspicious day for Muslims, who gather at mosques to honour those who have completed the Haj, or pilgrimage to Mecca; goats are sacrificed, and their meat given to the needy (May or July).

JUNE–AUGUST

Yang di-Pertuan Agong's Birthday Festivities are held in KL to celebrate the *Agong*'s birthday – see "Peoples: the Malays" above (June 4).

Malaysia International Kite Festival A showcase of kite-flying and design, held at Tumpat in Kelantan (June).

Gawai Dayak Sarawak's Iban and Bidayuh peoples celebrate the end of harvesting with extravagant longhouse feasts – aim to be in an Iban longhouse on the Rajang river (June).

Singapore Festival of the Arts Biennial celebration of world dance, music, drama and art, utilizing venues around the state (June).

Feast of Saint Peter Melaka's Eurasian community decorate their boats to honour the patron saint of fishermen (June 24).

Dragon Boat Festival Rowing boats, bearing a dragon's head and tail, race in Penang, Melaka, Singapore and Kota Kinabalu, to commemorate a Chinese scholar who drowned himself in protest against political corruption (June–July).

His Majesty the Sultan of Brunei's Birthday Celebrations kick off with a speech by the Sultan on the Padang, and continue for two weeks with parades, lantern processions, traditional sports competitions and fireworks – see local press for details (15 July).

June–August continued

Pesta Rumbia The uses of the *rumbia*, or sago palm, in handicrafts, housing, food and traditional medicines are demonstrated by the villagers of Kuala Penyu, in Sabah (late July).

Kelantan Cultural Week Kelantan citizens celebrate their heritage through cultural performances and handicraft demonstrations; particularly good in Kota Bharu (July–Aug).

Sarawak Extravaganza Kuching hosts a month of arts and crafts shows, street parades, food fairs and traditional games, all celebrating the culture of Sarawak (Aug).

Singapore National Day Singapore's independence is celebrated with a huge show at the National Stadium, featuring military parades and fireworks (Aug 9).

Malaysia National Day Parades in KL, Kuching and Kota Kinabalu to mark the formation of the state of Malaysia (Aug 31).

Festival of the Hungry Ghosts *Yue Lan*; held to appease the souls of the dead released from Purgatory during the seventh lunar month, when Chinese street operas are held, and joss sticks, red candles and paper money burnt outside Chinese homes (late Aug).

SEPTEMBER–DECEMBER

Malaysia Fest Fifteen-day festival in Kuala Lumpur, showcasing the best of Malaysian food, handicrafts and culture (Sept).

Moon Cake Festival Also known as the Mid-Autumn Festival (held on the fifteenth day of the eighth moon), when Chinese people eat and exchange moon cakes (made from sesame and lotus seeds and stuffed with a duck egg) to honour the fall of the Mongol Empire, plotted, so legend has it, by means of messages secreted in cakes. After dark, children parade with gaily coloured lanterns. Chinatowns are the obvious places to view the parades, but Singapore's Chinese Gardens and Kuching's Reservoir Park also have particularly good displays (Sept).

Navarathiri Hindu temples devote nine nights to classical dance and music in honour of the consorts of the Hindu gods, Shiva, Vishnu and Brahma; one reliable venue is Singapore's Chettiar Temple (Sept–Oct).

Thimithi Hindu firewalking ceremony in which devotees prove the strength of their faith by running across a pit of hot coals; best seen at the Sri Mariamman Temple in Singapore (Sept–Nov).

Festival of the Nine Emperor Gods The nine-day sojourn on earth of the Nine Emperor Gods – thought to bring good health and longevity – is celebrated in Singapore at the Kiu Ong Yiah Temple (Upper Serangoon Rd) by Chinese operas and mediums cavorting in the streets (Oct).

Pilgrimage to Kusu Island Locals visit Singapore's Kusu Island in their thousands to pray for good luck and fertility at the Tua Pekong Temple and the island's Muslim shrine (Oct–Nov).

Kota Belud Tamu Besar Sabah's biggest annual market, attended by Bajau tribesmen on horseback, features cultural performances and handicraft demonstrations (Oct–Nov).

Deepavali Hindu festival celebrating the victory of Light over Dark: oil lamps are lit outside homes to attract Lakshmi, the Goddess of Prosperity, and prayers are offered at all temples (Nov).

Christmas Shopping centres in major cities compete to create the most spectacular Christmas decorations (Dec 25).

OPENING HOURS AND PUBLIC HOLIDAYS

Specific opening hours are given throughout the text, but check below for the general opening hours of businesses and offices in Malaysia, Singapore and Brunei. It's worth noting that in Malaysia's more devout Muslim states, Friday – not Sunday – is the day of rest. Businesses and offices close after lunch on Thursday to accommodate this, while goverment offices in Brunei close on Fridays *and* Sundays.

Singapore and Malaysia also share several common **public holidays**, as well as each having their own. Transport becomes a headache on these days, though you're only likely to be really inconvenienced around Chinese New Year (Jan-Feb) and Ramadan (March-April), when hotels are bursting at the seams and restaurants,

banks and shops all close. Local tourist offices can tell you exactly which dates these holidays fall upon annually. In Malaysia, a further complication is that public holidays vary from state to state, depending on each state's religious make-up.

Below, we've listed only the most widely celebrated holidays; in addition, countless localized **state holidays** mark the birthdays of sultans and governors. Don't be surprised to turn up somewhere and find everything closed for the day.

MALAYSIA AND BRUNEI

In **Malaysia**, **shops** are open daily 9.30am–7pm and shopping centres typically open daily 10am–9pm. Government **offices** tend to work Monday

---

PUBLIC HOLIDAYS

For an explanation of the festivities associated with some of the holidays, see "Festivals", above.

SINGAPORE

January 1: New Year's Day	May: Vesak Day
January/February: Chinese New Year (2 days)	May/July: Hari Raya Haji
March/April: Hari Raya Puasa	August 9: National Day
March/April: Good Friday	November: Deepavali
May 1: Labour Day	December 25: Christmas Day

MALAYSIA

January 1: New Year's Day	June 4: Yang di-Pertuan Agong's birthday
February: Thaipusam	June/July: Maal Hijrah (marking Mohammed's journey from Mecca to Medina)
January/February: Chinese New Year (2 days)	
March/April: Hari Raya Puasa	August: Birthday of the Prophet Mohammad
May: Pesta Kaamatan (Sabah only)	August 31: National Day
May 1: Labour Day	November: Deepavali
May/July: Hari Raya Haji	December 25: Christmas Day
June: Gawai Dayak (Sarawak only)	

BRUNEI

January 1: New Year's Day	June 1: Armed Forces' Day
February: Israk Mikraj	May/July: Hari Raya Haji
January/February: Chinese New Year	June/July: First Day of Hijrah
February 23: National Day	July 15: Sultan's Birthday
February/March: First Day of Ramadan	August: Birthday of the prophet Muhammad
March/April: Anniversary of Revelation	December 25: Christmas Day
March/April: Hari Raya	

to Thursday 8am–12.45pm & 2–4.15pm, Friday 8am–12.45pm & 2.45–4.15pm, Saturday 8am–12.45pm; however, in the states of Johor, Kedah, Kelantan, Perlis and Terengannu, on Thursday the hours are 8am–12.45pm and they close on Friday. **Banks** open Monday to Friday 10am–3pm and Saturday 9.30am–1.30pm; as with government offices, Thursday is a half-day and Friday a holiday in the states of Kedah, Perlis, Kelantan and Terengganu. It's impossible to give general opening hours for **temples, mosques and museums** – check the text for specific hours, given where appropriate.

Government offices in **Brunei** open 7.45am–12.15pm & 1.30–4.30pm; except Friday; **shopping centres** daily 10am–10pm; and **banks** Monday to Friday 9am–3pm and Saturday 9–11am.

SINGAPORE

In Singapore, **shopping centres** open daily 10am–10pm; **banks** are sure to open at least Monday to Friday 10am–3pm, Saturday 11am–1pm and sometimes longer; while **offices** generally work Monday to Friday 8.30am–5pm and sometimes on Saturday mornings. In general, Chinese **temples** open daily from 7am to around 6pm, Hindu temples from 6am to noon and 5 to 9pm and **mosques** from 8am to 1pm; specific opening hours for all temples and museums are given in the text.

SHOPPING AND SOUVENIRS

Southeast Asia offers real shopping bargains, with electrical equipment, cameras, clothes, fabrics, tapes and CDs all selling at competitive prices. What's more, the region's ethnic diversity means you'll be spoilt for choice when it comes to souvenirs and handicrafts.

Unless you're in a department store, prices are negotiable, so be prepared to **haggle**. If you're planning to buy something pricey in Singapore – a camera, say, or a stereo – it's a good idea to pay a visit to a fixed-price store and arm yourself with the correct retail price; this way, you'll know if you're being ripped off. Asking for the "best price" is always a good start to negotiations; from there, it's a question of technique, but be realistic – shopkeepers will soon lose interest if you offer an unreasonably low price. Moving towards the door of the shop often pays dividends – it's surprising how often you'll be called back. If you do buy any electrical goods, make sure you get an international **guarantee**, and that it is endorsed by the shop.

Throughout the guide, good buys and bargains are picked out and there are features on the best things to buy in specific regions. Malaysian pastimes throw up some interesting purchases: *wayang kulit* (shadow play) puppets, portraying characters from Hindu legend, are attractive and light to carry; equally colourful but completely impractical if you have to carry them around are the Malaysian kites, which can be several metres long. There's a round-up below of the other main souvenir items you might want to bring back. For specific details of shopping and **shops in Singapore**, see p.556.

FABRICS

The art of producing **batik** cloth originated in Indonesia, but today batik is available across Southeast Asia and supports a thriving industry in Malaysia. Batik is made by applying hot wax to a piece of cloth with either a pen or a copper stamp; when the cloth is dyed, the wax resists the dye and a pattern appears, a process that can be repeated many times to build up colours. Batik is used to create shirts, skirts, bags and hats, as well as traditional **sarongs** – rectangular lengths of cloth wrapped around the waist and legs to form a sort of skirt worn by both males and females. In some of the Malaysian east coast towns, little cottage industries have sprung up enabling tourists to make their own batik clothes; the guide tells you where this is possible.

The exquisite style of fabric known as **songket** is a step up in price from batik; made by handweaving gold and silver thread into plain cloth, *songket* is used to make sarongs, headscarves and the like. The other thing you'll be able to buy in Indian enclaves everywhere is primary coloured silk **sarees** – look in Little India in Singapore and Kuala Lumpur for the best bargains.

METALWORK AND WOODCARVING

Of the wealth of metalwork on offer, **silverware** from Kelantan is among the finest and most intricately designed; it's commonly used to make earrings, brooches and pendants, as well as more substantial pieces. Selangor state is renowned for its **pewter** – a refined blend of tin, antimony and copper, which produces elegant vases, tankards and ornaments. Over in Brunei, the speciality is **brassware** – cannons, kettles (called *kiri*) and gongs – which is decorated with elaborate Islamic motifs.

Natural resources from the forest have traditionally been put to good use, with rattan, cane, wicker and bamboo used to make baskets, bird cages, mats, hats and shoulder bags. **Woodcarving** skills, once employed to decorate the palaces and public buildings of the early sultans, are today used to make less exotic articles such as mirror frames. However, it's still possible to see one of the dynamic **statues** created by the *orang asli* tribes at cultural shows and festivals in Kuala Lumpur and Kuantan. As animists, *orang asli* artists draw upon the natural world - animals, trees, fish, as well as more abstract elements like fire and water – for their imagery. Of particular interest are the **carvings** of the Mah Meri of Selangor which are improvisations on the theme of *moyang*, literally

"ancestor", which is the generic name for all spirit images. Dozens of *moyang*, each representing a different spirit, are incorporated into the Meri's beliefs and inspire the wooden-face sculptures which they carve. Also popular are *topeng*, or face masks.

EAST MALAYSIAN HANDICRAFTS

In East Malaysia, the craft shops of Kota Kinabalu in **Sabah** have a wide variety of ethnic handicrafts native to the state. Most colourful of these are the *tudong duang*, a multicoloured food cover that looks more like a conical hat, and the painstakingly elaborate, beaded necklaces of the Runggus tribe. Also available are the bamboo, rattan and bark haversacks that locals use in the fields. For more unusual mementos, look out for the *sumpitan*, a type of blowpipe, or the *sompoton*, a musical instrument consisting of eight bamboo pipes inserted into a gourd, which sounds like a harmonica.

Sarawak's peoples also produce a wide range of handicrafts using raw materials from the forest, with designs that are inspired by animist beliefs. Unique to Sarawak is *pua kumbu* (in Iban, "blanket"), a textile whose complex designs are created using the *ikat* method of weaving (see p.353 for more details). In longhouses, you may also see blowpipes and tools being made.

OUTDOOR PURSUITS

With some of the oldest tropical rainforest in the world and countless beaches and islands, trekking, snorkelling and scuba diving are common pursuits in Malaysia, while Singapore is only a short step away from these diversions. The more established resorts on the islands of Penang, Langkawi and Tioman offer more elaborate sports such as jet skiing and paragliding, while Cherating (the budget travellers' centre on the east coast), with its exposed, windy bay, is a hot spot for windsurfers. Although all these places and activities are covered in more detail in the relevant chapters, below are some pointers to consider.

If you intend to take up any of these pursuits, check that your travel **insurance policy** covers you (see "Insurance", p.19); and see "Health

Matters" (p.26) for details of any problems you might encounter out in the Malaysian wilds.

SNORKELLING, DIVING AND WINDSURFING

The crystal-clear waters of Malaysia and its abundance of tropical fish and coral make snorkelling and diving a must for any underwater enthusiast. This is particularly true of Sabah's Pulau Sipidan and the peninsula's east coast, where islands like Perhentian, Redang, Kapas and Tioman are turning their natural resources into a lucrative business. **Pulau Tioman** offers the most choice for schools and dive sites – though some damage has already been caused to the coral reefs by overeager visitors. However tempting the coral looks, don't remove it as a souvenir: this can cause irreparable damage and upset the delicate underwater ecosystem.

Most beachside guest houses have **snorkelling equipment** for rent (though flippers are rare) and rates are very reasonable at $10–15 per day – check before you set out that the mask makes a secure seal against your face. **Dive shops** offer courses ranging from a five-day beginners' open water course, typically around M$650, right through to the dive master certificate, a ten-day course costing about M$800. Make sure that the shop is registered with *PADI* (Professional Association of Diving Instructors), and it's a good idea to ascertain the size of the group, as well as that the instructor speaks good English. All equipment and tuition should be included in the price, and it's worth checking the condition of the gear before signing on the dotted line.

Windsurfing has yet to take off in all but the most expensive resorts in Malaysia, with the notable exception of Cherating (p.258). Its large, open bay and shallow water provide near-perfect conditions for the sport and a few local entrepreneurs are catching on by renting out equipment – usually for around M$15 per hour – but don't expect expert coaching.

TREKKING

The majority of **treks**, either on the Malaysian peninsula or in Sarawak and Sabah, require some forethought and preparation. As well as enduring the fierce sun, the tropical climate can unleash torrential rain without any warning, which rapidly affects the condition of trails or the height of a river – what started out as a ten-hour trip can end up taking twice as long. That said, the time of year is not a hugely significant factor when planning a trek. Although the **rainy season** (Nov-Feb) undoubtedly slows your progress on some of the trails, conditions are less humid and the parks and adventure tours not oversubscribed.

Most visitors trek in the large **national parks** to experience the remaining primary jungle and rainforest at first hand. Treks in the parks often require that you go in a group with a **guide**, although it's quite possible to go to most parks on your own and then join a group once there. Costs and conditions vary from park to park: there's a check list of the national parks covered in this guide given below, and each account contains full practical and trekking details. For inexperienced trekkers, Taman Negara is probably the best place to start, boasting the greatest variety of walks; for the more experienced, the parks in Sarawak, especially Gunung Mulu, should offer sufficient challenges for most tastes; the largely inaccessible Endau Rompin park is for serious expedition fiends only. **Tour operators** in your home country (see the various "Getting There" sections), and those based in Kuala Lumpur (p.110), Kuching (p.342), Miri (p.381) and Kota Kinabulu (p.416) are the best places for more information on conditions and options in the parks – Malaysia's tourist offices aren't much help.

Basic **clothing and equipment** for all treks, be they three hours or ten days, should comprise loose cotton trousers and long-sleeved shirts which protect against sun and sharp thorns; good hiking boots, preferably canvas ones which dry out quickly; hats which shield both the front and the back of the head from the sun; and as small and comfortable a rucksack as you can get by with. (Never take all your possessions on a trek if

NATIONAL PARKS: A ROUND-UP

Bako (p.345).
Endau Rompin (p.316).
Gunung Mulu (p.387).
Kinabulu (p.429).
Lambir Hills (p.382).
Niah (p.375).
Similajau (p.374).
Taman Negara (p.194).

CHECKLIST OF TREKKING EQUIPMENT

The check list below is based on staying in hostels and lodges. This may not always be possible and if you plan to camp, you'll need more, not least your own tent (since most tours don't include camping equipment).

ESSENTIALS	CLOTHING AND FOOTWEAR	OTHER USEFUL ITEMS
Backpack	Shirts/T-shirts	Plastic bag (to rainproof your pack)
Sleeping bag	Trousers	
Mosquito net	Skirt/dress (mid-calf length is best)	Candles
Water bottle		Emergency snack food
Toiletries and toilet paper	Woolly sweater	Spare bootlaces
Flashlight	Gloves	Sewing kit
Pocket knife	Rainproof plastic coat or poncho	Small towel
Sunglasses (UV protective)	Cotton hat with brim	Soap powder
Sun block and lip balm	Jacket	Insulation mat
Insect repellent	Trekking boots	Large mug and spoon
Compass	Cotton and woollen socks	Basic first aid kit (see p.27)

you can leave some safely behind.) There's a trekking **equipment checklist** below, which should see you through most of the treks you're likely to undertake in Malaysia.

For many people, the ubiquitous **leech** – whose bite is not actually harmful or painful – is the most irritating aspect to jungle trekking. When there's been a heavy rainfall, you can rely upon the leeches to come out. Always tuck your trousers into your socks and tie your boot laces tight.

The best anti-leech socks are made from calico and can be bought for around $10 from the *Malayan Nature Society*, 485 jalan 5/53, Petaling Jaya, KL (☎03/791 2185). If you find the leeches are getting through, the best remedy is to soak the outside of your socks and your boats in insect repellent, or dampen tobacco and apply it in between your socks and shoes. It's best to get into the habit of checking your feet and legs every twenty minutes or so for bites.

DIRECTORY

AIRPORT TAXES From Malaysia, an airport tax of M$5 is levied on all domestic flights and on flights to Brunei or Singapore, and M$20 on international flights. Singapore charges a S$5 airport tax on flights to Malaysia and Brunei, and S$12 on flights to other countries. Brunei charges B$5 to Malaysia and Singapore, B$12 to other destinations.

CHILDREN The general levels of hygiene in Malaysia, Singapore and Brunei make travelling with children a viable prospect. Asian attitudes towards the young are far more tolerant than they are in the West, though children inevitably attract a great deal of attention, too, which can be both tiring and stressful for the child. Remember also that children dehydrate much more quickly than adults, particularly if they have diarrheoa, so keep up their fluid intake. Everything you might need is readily available, with the exception of fresh milk – though even this can be found in supermarkets. Disposable nappies and powdered milk are easy to find, and the bland Chinese soups and rice dishes are ideal for systems unaccustomed to spicy food. The biggest problem is likely to be in the evening, for only the smartest hotels have a baby-sitting service, though every restaurant or *kedai kopi* will have a highchair. Only upmarket hotels will provide baby cots, though others may be able to rustle something up if given advance warning. However, rooms in the cheaper hotels usually come with an extra bed (see "Accommodation", p.39), for little extra cost. Children under 12 get into most attractions for half-price, and even at the most basic resorts, there'll be a children's playground.

CONTRACEPTIVES Oral contraceptives are available from all pharmacists in Malaysia, Singapore and Brunei, as are spermicidal gels. Condoms are also obtainable.

DUTY-FREE GOODS Duty-free products in Singapore include electronic and electrical goods, cosmetics, cameras, clocks, watches, jewellery, precious stones and metals. Malaysia has no duty on cameras, watches, cosmetics or electronic goods; in addition, perfumes, cigarettes and liquors are duty-free. Pulau Labuan and Pulau Langkawi are both duty-free islands, though neither has a particularly impressive range of products.

ELECTRICITY Mains voltage in Malaysia, Singapore and Brunei is 220 volts, so any equipment which uses 110 volts will need a converter.

GAY AND LESBIAN LIFE Though homosexuality is officially outlawed in Singapore, and punishable by from ten years to life imprisonment, a discrete but thriving scene does exist. In Malaysia, homosexuality is no longer illegal, although the relaxation of the statutes has not led to any significant liberalisation of general attitudes. There is a gay scene in KL, but it's fairly low-key and not especially accessible to visiting tourists. There is no equivalent lesbian scene in Singapore.

LAUNDRY Most towns will have a public launderette, where clothes can be washed cheaply. In addition, some budget hostels have washing machines available for guests for a small charge

or offer a laundry service for around M$7/S$5. Otherwise, small sachets of soap powder (50c) are readily available from general stores if you prefer to hand-wash, though they tend to have a bleaching effect on strongly coloured clothing.

TIME DIFFERENCES Malaysia, Singapore and Brunei are 8 hours ahead of GMT, 16 hours ahead of US Pacific Standard Time, 13 ahead of Eastern Standard Time, and 2 hours behind Sydney.

WOMEN Women in Muslim Malaysia and Brunei have a lower public profile than elsewhere. For the tourist, this manifests itself in the need to dress modestly in conservative and rural areas (particularly in Kelantan and Terengganu) by covering legs and upper arms, though headscarves are not necessary. Most Malay women outside the larger cities dress in long, brightly coloured skirts and headscarves, covering all traces of their limbs, hair and neck – even school children are clothed this way. As a foreigner, there's no need to cover up to this extent – even Chinese women don't adhere to these rules – but it's always wise to respect local customs. In the strictly Muslim areas of Peninsular Malaysia, you should think twice about stripping off and swimming outside resort areas; Muslim women go into the water fully clothed. Muslim women enter the

---

THINGS TO TAKE

A universal electric plug adaptor and a universal sink plug.

A mosquito net.

A sheet sleeping bag.

A small flashlight.

Earplugs (for street noise in hotel rooms).

High-factor sun block.

A pocket alarm clock (for those early morning departures).

An inflatable neck rest, to help you sleep on long journeys.

A multipurpose penknife.

A needle and some thread.

Plastic bags (to sort your baggage, make it easier to pack and unpack, and keep out damp and dust).

Multi-vitamin and mineral tablets.

Suggestions for a general **first-aid kit** are listed on p.27; for **trekking**, see the list on p.69.

mosque by a seperate entrance and worship from behind a screen; non-Muslim woman may be forbidden entrance altogether, though some places allow women inside provided they wear a long cloak (supplied at the door). Sexual harrassment in Malaysia and Singapore is minimal, and certainly no more than you might encounter at home – the level of contact rarely strays beyond the odd whistle or shy giggles. Irritating though it can be, you have to expect some attention both as a foreigner and as a woman, but it's often pure curiosity and your novelty value that attracts, rather than any desire to oppress.

WORKING Unless you've got a prearranged job and a work permit, opportunities for working in Malaysia and Singapore are few and far between. Helping hands are often required in guest houses; wages are low, but often include free board and lodgings. Work is also occasionally available teaching in language schools, though you're far more likely to secure employment if you have a TEFL (Teaching English as a Foreign Language) qualification, or at least some experience in the field.

PART TWO

THE
GUIDE

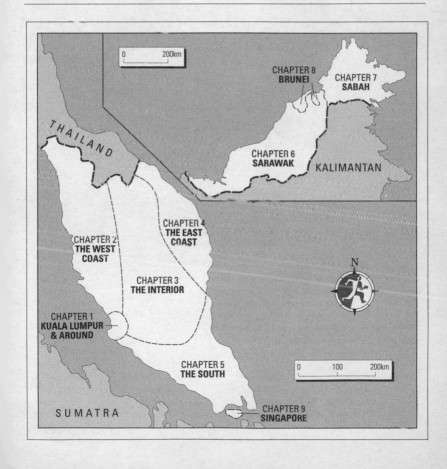

CHAPTER 8
BRUNEI

CHAPTER 7
SABAH

CHAPTER 6
SARAWAK

KALIMANTAN

THAILAND

0   200km

CHAPTER 4
**THE EAST
COAST**

CHAPTER 2
**THE WEST
COAST**

CHAPTER 3
THE INTERIOR

CHAPTER 1
**KUALA LUMPUR
& AROUND**

CHAPTER 5
THE SOUTH

N

0   100   200km

SUMATRA

CHAPTER 9
SINGAPORE

CHAPTER ONE

KUALA LUMPUR AND AROUND

KUALA LUMPUR, or KL as it's known to residents and visitors alike, is the youngest Southeast Asian capital and, these days, the most economically successful after Singapore. Founded as late as the mid-ninetcenth century, signs of growth abound – it's almost impossible to walk through the city without taking detours around vast holes in streets bulging with construction apparatus, while city maps are out of date before the ink's dry. Accordingly, the city is a jigsaw of various periods and styles, the few remaining colonial buildings rubbing shoulders with chic, modern banks designed to look like a traditional Malay house, and other buildings appropriating a futuristic, mega-buck look which wouldn't seem out of place in Hong Kong or New York. But then KL never had a coherent style – the first grand structures around Merdeka Square dating from the 1880s were eccentric mishmashes themselves, British engineers bringing together a zestful conglomeration of Moorish, Moghul, Malay and Victorian architectural elements. You never quite know what's round the next corner – or whether what you saw yesterday will still be in one piece today.

Some people are disappointed by KL. It's neither slow-paced, nor particularly charming, and doesn't have the narrow alleys, bicycles and mahjong games of Melaka or Kota Bharu. Untrammelled development has given it more than its share of featureless buildings, follies and failures, terrible traffic snarl-ups and visible, urban poverty. But on the whole it's a safe and friendly place, where most of the 1.7 million inhabitants are generally eager to please, and there's enough of monumental interest to keep visitors busy for a week at least. The classic tour of KL includes the colonial core around **Merdeka Square** and the enclaves of **Chinatown** and **Little India**, followed either by a trip north up jalan Tunku Abdul Rahman to the warren of plankboard passages known as **Chow Kit Market**, or south to the **Muzium Negara** (National Museum).

But, heading at random in almost any direction is just as rewarding, not least for the contact this brings with KL street life. At the last count, there were 86 **markets** in the city, some, like the wet fish market in between jalan Tun H.S. Lee and jalan Petaling, with entrances you would miss if you blinked at the wrong moment. And everywhere are hawker centres, and soy milk and fresh fruit and juice stalls – the latter to be indulged in frequently, since KL's humidity can fell even the most hardened tropical traveller. You'll soon become aware, too, of the **pollution**, which on certain days hangs above KL in malevolent clouds. The price paid for the city's rapid developent can be best assessed by a trip out to the Klang Valley, west of the city, where craters and half-built structures line the highways, soon to become factories, oil and gas terminals, and timber and rubber processing plants. But despite the building boom, KL still has a fair amount of greenery – it's easy to escape from the heat, pollution, dust and noise to the gentle sanctuary of the **Lake Gardens** and **Lake Titiwangsa**, while the wider expanses of **Templer Park** or the modern hill station of the **Genting Highlands** are both only an hour's bus ride away.

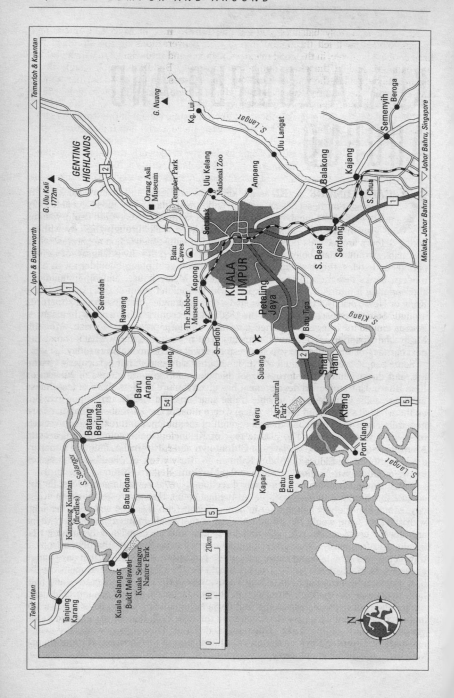

KL's unique, evenly balanced cultural and **ethnic mix** of Malays, Chinese and Indians makes itself felt throughout the city: in conversations on the street, in the variety of food for sale, in the good manners, patience and insouciance to which visitors are exposed, and in the sheer number of mosques, Buddhist temples and Hindu shrines. In particular, the rugged limestone **Batu Caves**, on the city's northern boundary, contain the country's most sacred Hindu shrine, focus of a wild celebration during the annual Thaipusam religous festival.

Kuala Lumpur is also probably the most liberal Islamic capital in the world, its strictures tempered by the influence of Malay *songkets* (headscarfs) and Indian *sarees*, with its citizens found clutching the Koran in one hand and a cellular phone in the other. There is, however, a more traditional side to the city: in the early morning or evening, the sound of the muezzin's call to prayer, *Allah-hu-Akbar*, drifts across from the minarets of the three main mosques, while at Friday lunchtime especially, you can't avoid the thousands of white-robed men converging on the mosques to fulfil their religious duties. Take another look at the architecture, too, and you'll often notice a peculiarly Islamic aesthetic at work in buildings like the Maybank and the Dayabumi Complex, which fuse the modern with the traditional. This is at its most pronounced in KL's most celebrated new building, the Petronas Towers – due, on completion in 1996, to be the tallest building in the world – whose two soaring towers deliberately resemble minarets.

A little history

Kuala Lumpur (Malay for "muddy estuary") was founded in 1857 when the chief of Selangor State, Rajah Abdullah, sent a party of Chinese prospectors upriver to explore the area around the confluence of the Klang and Gombak rivers to see if there were any extractable deposits of tin – a metal that had already brought great wealth to prospectors around the northern town of Ipoh. Although many died from malaria as they hacked through the dense, swampy jungle, the pioneers' reward came with the discovery of rich deposits near Ampang, 6km from the confluence, which grew into a staging post for Chinese labourers who arrived to work in the mines. The first Chinese **towkays** (merchants) set up two secret societies here and fierce competition for the economic spoils soon developed, which boiled over into angry confrontations between rivals, effectively restraining the growth of the settlement until the 1870s. But the arrival of an influential Chinese merchant, **Yap Ah Loy** – who had a fearsome reputation as a secret society boss in mainland China – helped unify the divergent groups. Ah Loy's career was a symbol of the Eldorado lifestyle of the city's early years. Starting out as a minor gangster, he became a local hero when he organized the protests in the Negeri Sembilan miners' rebellion of the mid-1860s (see p.267), on the back of which he invested in gambling dens and tin; by the time he was thirty he had become KL's *Kapitan Cina*, or headman. But the precarious rule of the pioneers was swept rudely aside once the Selangor Civil War had been settled by British gunboat diplomacy, and in 1880 the British Resident of Selangor State, **Frank Swettenham**, took command: KL became the capital of the state and, in 1896, the capital of the Federated Malay States.

Until the 1880s, KL was little more than a shantytown of wooden huts precariously positioned on the edge of the riverbank. Reaching the settlement was a tough job in itself. Small steamers could get within 30km of the town along the Klang river, but from there onwards, the rest of the trip was either by shallow boat or through the roadless jungle. To get to the tin mines was even worse. In his memoirs, *Footprints in Malaya*, Swettenham remembered it being ". . . a twelve-hour effort and very strenuous and unpleasant at that, for there was no discernible path and much of the distance we travelled up to our waste in water. Torn by thorns, poisoned by leech bites and stung by scores of blood-sucking insects, the struggle was one long misery." And yet people were drawn to the town like flies to honey. Early British investors, Malay farmers, Chinese *towkays* and workers and, in the first years of the twentieth century, Indians from Tamil Nadu, all arrived in the search for something better – whether it was work in the tin mines, on surrounding rubber estates or, later, on roads and railway construction.

Swettenham demolished most of the wooden huts and imported British architects from India to design solid, grand edifices, suitable for a new capital. He faced an initial setback in 1881 when fire destroyed all the buildings; rebuilding was slow and the Governor described the sanitary conditions the following year as "pestilential". Nevertheless, by 1887 the city had 500 brick buildings and by the turn of the century eight times that amount; the population grew from 4000 to 40,000, predominantly Chinese, but swollen by the arrival of the Tamils. The seeds of KL's staggering modern growth had been sown.

Development continued steadily in the first quarter of this century, although catastrophic floods in 1926 inspired a major engineering project which straightened the course of the Klang river: confining it within reinforced, raised banks successfully prevented future flooding. By the time the **Japanese invaded** in December 1941, overrunning the British army's positions with devastating speed, the commercial zone around Chinatown had grown to eclipse the original colonial area and the *towkays*, enriched by the rubber boom, were already installed in opulent townhouses along today's jalan Tunku Abdul Rahman and jalan Ampang. Although the Japanese bombed the city, they missed their main targets and little physical damage occurred beyond a general looting of stores and the blowing up of bridges by the retreating British army. But the invasion had a radical psychological impact on each of the ethnic communities represented in the city. The Japanese ingratiated themselves with some of the Malays by suggesting their loyalty would be rewarded with independence after the war, while at the same time inflicting terrible repression on their historic enemies, the Chinese – at least 5000 were killed in the first few weeks of the invasion alone. The Indians also suffered, with thousands sent to Burma to build the infamous railway; very few survived.

At the end of the war, following the **Japanese surrender** in September 1945, the British were once more in charge in the capital, but found they couldn't pick up where they had left off. Nationalistic demands had replaced the Malays' former acceptance of the colonizers, while for some of the Chinese population, identification with Mao's revolution in 1949 led to a desire to see Malaya become a communist state. Although very few incidents actually occurred in KL itself during the Emergency – the guerillas aware that they couldn't actually take the capital – the atmosphere in the city remained tense. Malaysian independence – **Merdeka** – finally came in 1957, but tensions between the Malays and the Chinese later spilled over into race riots in the city in 1969; Tunku Abdul Rahman, the first Prime Minister, was forced to set an agenda for development which aimed to give all Malaysia's ethnic groups an equal slice of the economic cake.

The look of the city changed, too, during this postwar period, with the nineteenth-century buildings which had dominated KL – the Sultan Abdul Samad Building, the Railway Station and other goverment offices – gradually being overshadowed by a plethora of modern developments. Likewise, the interracial hostilities have been transformed in the last twenty years, galvanized into an all-hands-on-deck approach to quicken the pace of economic progress. In recent years the Klang Valley, which runs west from KL to Klang through Petaling Jaya and Shah Alam, has become a thriving industrial zone, feeding the manufacturing sectors of this expansion, while the peripheral towns to the north and south have been converted into residential and industrial satellites.

KUALA LUMPUR

KUALA LUMPUR is constantly being reshaped – the most spectacular example being when the city's second largest hill, south of the centre, was levelled to make way for the new Merdeka Stadium and the earth which was removed then used to fill in the valley below the National Mosque. Clearly, KL has no scruples about rearranging its geography. Appropriately for a city which has always been characterized by a wide variety of architectural styles, new buildings have immediately found their place, with corporate HQs like the Maybank, the Dayabumi and Tabung Haji building, not to mention the new Petronas Towers, set to be the tallest building in the world, adding a modernistic sheen, which Malaysians look upon with pride. But despite the changes to the landscape and architecture over the last twenty years, the centre at least has held onto its particular charms: the tranquillity of Merdeka Square and its colonial surroundings, the commercial zeal of Chinatown, and the silty brown wash of the Klang river. Much of KL's appeal – the markets, the temples and old mosques – is untouched by the new construction muscling in around, though the inevitable by-products of headlong development, such

> The **telephone code** for KL and its environs is ☎03. Note that all Malaysian telephone numbers are being **changed** in a rolling programme lasting several years. Some of the numbers given in this chapter, while correct at the time of going to press, are likely to have changed.

as exhaust and industrial pollution, have grown considerably worse in the last few years. KL now has four times the number of cars joining the multi-lane highways and edging through its narrow streets than it did in 1988.

Orientation

The city centre is quite compact, with the colonial district centred on **Merdeka Square**; close by, across the river and a little to the south, is **Chinatown**, with **Little India** just to its north – these are the two main traditional commercial districts. One of the most prominent (and busiest) of KL's central streets, **jalan Tunku Abdul Rahman** (or jalan TAR), runs due north from Merdeka Square for 2km to **Chow Kit Market**; closer in, west of the square, are the **Lake Gardens**, Parliament House and the National Monument; south, the **Masjid Negara** (National Mosque), the landmark **Railway Station** and the **Muzium Negara** (National Museum).

Everything else of interest in central KL lies to the east of the colonial district. From Merdeka Square, the congested **jalan Tun Perak** leads southeast to the Pudu Raya bus station, 1km further east of which is the **Golden Triangle** – a consumer sector delineated by three main roads, jalan Bukit Bintang, jalan Imbi and jalan Sultan Ismail, which contain most of the city's expensive hotels, modern malls and nightclubs. Just to the north of here, **jalan Ampang** – leading east out of the city – was one of the first streets to be developed at the turn of the century as a residential area for rich tin *towkays* and colonial administrators.

All this is confined within the **jalan Tun Razak** ring road, which encircles the city. Most of what you come to see in KL is inside the ringroad, but there are popular spots just outside in the **suburbs** – like Lake Titiwangsa, the important Thean Hou Temple and the national zoo.

Arrival and information

KL is at the hub of Malaysia's transport systems. It has the main international airport, where you'll have to change if you're flying on to Sarawak or Sabah, while buses from all over Peninsular Malaysia converge on one of four bus stations. The train station even doubles as a sight, a magnificent building fusing Moorish architectural flourishes with a British colonial design. For **departure details** from KL, see "Leaving KL" opposite.

By air

Highly efficient, modern **Subang International Airport** is 30km west of the centre. Bus #47 (every 30min, 6am–9pm; $2) leaves from the bay outside the departure hall, to the left; buy your ticket on board the bus. The journey takes around forty minutes and goes via the Railway Station to the terminus on jalan Sultan Mohammed, opposite the Klang bus station (see below), which is close to Central Market at the southern edge of Chinatown, the main area for budget accommodation. **Taxis** into the centre cost around $22, and you need first to buy a coupon from a clearly visible desk at the right of the departure hall, facing the road, which you present to the driver. You'll doubtless be approached by taxi touts at the airport; stick to the official coupon system or you could find yourself seriously out of pocket.

All the major **car rental** firms have offices at the airport, though if you are seeing Malaysia by car you'd be best advised to pick it up on your last day in KL – driving into and around the downtown areas can take years off your life in one short journey. There are money exchange outlets at the aiport, too, and a tourist office in the arrival hall, where you can pick up a map of the city, and various useful brochures.

By train, bus and taxi

Kuala Lumpur's striking **Railway Station** (see p.90) is on jalan Sultan Hishamuddin, just ten minutes' walk south of Chinatown; the National Art Gallery is opposite and the Muzium Negara another ten minutes' walk further south. There's a good information kiosk (daily 8am–8pm) in the station concourse which has hotel lists and train timetables.

Most long-distance buses arrive at the giant **Pudu Raya** bus station, an island of concrete in the middle of jalan Pudu, just to the east of Chinatown. It looks chaotic, but

---

LEAVING KL

For the addresses and telephone numbers of airlines, foreign consulates, travel agencies and tour operators in KL, see p.109–110.

Airport
The easiest way to get to the airport is to call a taxi from your hotel or lodge, which will cost around $20; taxis flagged down on the street tend not to want to go out that far. Otherwise, bus #47 ($2) leaves from the jalan Sultan Mohammed terminus, opposite Klang bus station, every 30 minutes from 6am–10pm. It's a 40-minute journey – allow for delays in rush hour. For international flight enquiries call: Terminal 2 (☎746 3386 or ☎746 3391); Terminal 3 (☎746 1235); airport office (☎746 5555).

Buses and long-distance taxis
Most **long-distance buses and taxis** leave from inside Pudu Raya bus station (☎230 0145), reached by the footbridge over jalan Pudu. Buses also operate from outside the terminus – you can't miss the hawkers touting places – and although these are legitimate, check when the driver is leaving as he may have to wait for the bus to fill up, which could take a while. Long distance taxi journeys – to destinations like Penang, Melaka and Kuantan – are a good deal, seldom much more than twice the price of the bus, but again the drivers wait for a full car-load before departing.

For some departures you'll need one of the other bus stations: Putra (☎442 9530) by the Putra World Trade Centre for east coast buses; Klang (☎230 7694) on jalan Sultan Mohammed for services west of KL in Selangor State; and Pekeliling (☎112 1250) on jalan Raja Laut for the east coast and interior. For bus route information the *Infoline* (see "Information and Maps" below) is useful.

Trains
The information kiosk in the Railway Station has up-to-date train timetables, or you can phone the Railway Station (☎274 7435) for information and reservations. You must book, preferably at least a day in advance for the night sleeper to Singapore or Butterworth; booking isn't necessary for most other routes. Most of the large hotels can book train tickets for you, but the tourist offices can't.

Ferries
Ferries to Belawan (for Medan) in Sumatra depart two or three times a week from Port Klang, 38km southwest of KL. Take a bus from the Klang bus station on jalan Sultan Mohammed to the port, and see p.000 for the details.

is actually quite an efficient place, with hundreds of buses setting off day and night for most of the main destinations in the peninsula. The buses draw into ground-floor bays, while the ticket offices are on the floor above, along with dozens of stalls selling food, and a left-luggage office. **Long-distance taxis** also arrive at Pudu Raya, on the second floor above the bus ticket offices.

Some buses from the east coast end up instead at **Putra** bus station, a smaller, more modern terminus to the northwest of the city centre, just beside the Putra World Trade Centre. This is handy for the budget hotels on jalan Raja Laut and in the Chow Kit area, but it's quite a way from Chinatown, 2km to the southeast; to head downtown, walk outside the station onto jalan Putra to The Mall shopping centre, from in front of which you can take one of several pink minibuses which run to Central Market on jalan Hang Kasturi – you'll have to ask to make sure you get on the right one.

There are two other bus stations at which you might conceivably arrive. Services from Kuantan or from the interior stop at **Pekeliling** bus station, at the northern end of jalan Raja Laut; from here, too, regular minibuses head south to Chinatown. Finally, the **Klang** bus station on jalan Sultan Mohammed, just south of Central Market, is used by Klang Valley buses to and from Port Klang (where **ferries** arrive from Belawan, in Sumatra, see "Leaving KL" on previous page), Klang, Shah Alam and Kuala Selangor.

Information and maps

As well as the information office in the train station and at the airport, KL is overly endowed with **tourist information centres**, each of which hand out excellent free **maps** listing places to visit and useful telephone numbers. There is also an English-speaking **Infoline** (☎230 0300), worth trying mainly for the long-distance bus timetables. For "what's on" listings, check the "Metro" section in the tabloid *Malay Mail*, which lists concerts, cinema, theatre, clubs, fashion shows and art exhibitions.

The biggest tourist office is **MATIC** (Malaysian Tourist Information Complex) at 109 jalan Ampang (daily 8am–8pm; ☎243 4929), east of the centre close to the junction with jalan Sultan Ismail, a beautiful old colonial building that was originally a tin *towkay*'s house. The main desk here hands out various free city maps and brochures, as well as holding details of accommodation in KL and throughout the country; another desk takes booking for Taman Negara National Park (see p.194). From Monday to Friday cultural shows are held on the first floor – a notice board in the main area broadcasts the latest details.

The **KL Visitors Centre** (daily 8am–8pm; ☎274 6063), at 3 jalan Sultan Hishamuddin, is a little more convenient, to the left of the main entrance to the train station. Perhaps the most extensive selection of brochures is available at the **Tourist Development Corporation** (Mon–Fri 9am–4.30pm; ☎441 1295), Level 2, Putra World Trade Centre on jalan Putra, close to The Mall; while the **KL Tourist Information Centre** (daily 8am–8pm; ☎293 6664), just north of Merdeka Square, where jalan Parlimen cuts away west from jalan TAR, is worth a visit to see the building in which it's housed – a copy of a traditional *Minangkabau* village dwelling (see p.272) – if not for what you can pick up there.

City transport

Most of the the city centre – the colonial district, Chinatown and Little India – is easy to cover on **foot**, though take care; neither cars nor motorbikes can be trusted to stop at traffic lights or pedestrian crossings. In any case, it's inadvisable to walk absolutely everywhere, because you will soon become exhausted by the combined effects of the humidity and the traffic fumes. When you can, either jump on a **bus** – avoiding the rush hour periods (8–10am and 4.15–6pm) if possible – or take a **taxi**. These, altho plentiful and fairly inexpensive, can be tricky to find during rush hour, too, and partic larly during the frequent downpours, when everyone wants to escape the rain quickly.

Buses

KL's **bus** services are comprehensive, quick and inexpensive – for visitors, the down-side is that they're extremely difficult to fathom, because none of the services run in straight lines or seem to start from a particular point.

There are two main types of bus, the standard blue ones and the small pink mini-buses, both of which fill up rapidly. The main depots for the **blue city buses** are the Pudu Raya bus station on jalan Pudu, the jalan Sultan Mohammed terminus (opposite Klang bus station) and lebuh Ampang, on the northern edge of Chinatown. Fares are based on the distance you are travelling and range from 50 *sen* to $2 a journey; all the buses have conductors, so you don't need to have the exact change. There aren't any particular terminals for the **pink minibuses**, but the greatest concentration leaves from jalan Hang Kasturi, directly outside Central Market; on these, there's a flat fare of around 70 *sen*. Services start running at around 6am and operate regularly thoughout the day until midnight.

Taxis

Many visitors depend completely on **taxis** to get around – you'll seldom pay more than $12 for any journey within the city. This is mainly because taxi meters don't clock time while in traffic jams and, as the fares start at $1.50 and rise 10 *sen* for every 300m trav-elled, you've got to be going quite a distance for the price to mount up. However, as KL's traffic is so terrible, it's often faster to get out and walk.

Many of the taxi drivers can't speak English, and some don't know their way around the city, so it's best to carry a map, and have your destination and the name of some main thoroughfares written down. There are numerous taxi ranks around the city, usually situated beside bus stops; it's a good idea to wait on the correct side of the road for the direction you want to go in since taxi drivers often refuse to turn their cab round. Or you can simply flag one down and jump in – and note that bashful visitors will usually be overlooked in the melee. The only place where you can find stationary taxis is at hotels or outside shopping malls, and these invariably charge a more expen-sive flat rate for the journey If you **telephone** for a taxi (see "Listings", p.110, for companies) then an extra $1 is added to the fare.

Accommodation

Accommodation prices in KL are reasonable by international standards, except for the high rates charged in hotels in the Golden Triangle, east of the centre. All the other main areas – Chinatown, Little India, along jalan TAR and around Pudu Raya – contain a wide range of choices, from travellers' hostels and lodges to expensive hotels. You shouldn't need to book in advance unless you're opting for one of the more popular old-style hotels, like the *Colonial* or the *Coliseum*. KL's tourist offices all have accommoda-tion lists, which you can study, though the very cheapest places won't be listed.

Most travellers head for **Chinatown**, though in recent years **Little India** has become a valid alternative, with entrepeneurs opening up both budget and intermedi-ate places to cater for KL's steady increase in visitors. As you'd expect, inexpensive places also proliferate close to the Pudu Raya bus station around **jalan Pudu**, most sited in the very quiet jalan Pudu Lama, just off the main road. Further east, the **Golden Triangle** is where the first-class hotels are situated, alongside fashionable malls and nightclubs. West and north of Little India and Chinatown, the hotels along

stretch of **jalan TAR** include some of the sleaziest and most famous
elds also has a range of good-value accommodation (and a large
th of the city, way beyond walking distance from the centre – there's
te the Central Market on jalan Benteng, or take a taxi.

ACCOMMODATION PRICE CODES

All the places to stay listed in this book have been given one of the following price codes;
for more details, see p.40

① Under $20   ④ $61–100
② $21–40   ⑤ $101–200
③ $41–60   ⑥ $201 and above

Note that all Malaysian telephone numbers are being **changed** in a rolling programme
lasting several years. Some of the numbers given below, while correct at the time of
going to press, are likely to have changed.

Chinatown
All the following lodges, hotels and hostels are marked on the map on p.88–89.

Backpapers Travellers Inn, 60 jalan Sultan (☎238 2473). Centrally located, on the eastern edge of Chinatown, with small, clean single and double rooms, some with air-con, and a dorm. Manager Stephen Chan has added some nice touches like book exchange, games and colour TV. ①.

City Inn Hotel, 11 jalan Sultan (☎238 9190). Mid-range modern hotel, with small, clean air-con rooms with bathroom. ③.

Colonial Hotel, 39–45 jalan Sultan (☎238 0336). Popular, Chinese hotel in a lovely, turn-of-the-century building. The rooms, however, are a bit grubby; there's a communal shower and toilet. ②.

Hotel Furama, Selangor Kompleks, jalan Sultan (☎230 1777). This is a modern air-con hotel with small but comfortable, well-equipped rooms. ③.

Hotel Leng Nam, 165 jalan Tun H.S. Lee (☎230 1489). Beside the Sri Mahamariamman Temple, and close to Chinatown's most picturesque street, jalan Petaling, this traditional Chinese hotel has a great atmosphere. The small rooms come with two large beds; toilets and shower are shared. ①.

Hotel Lok Ann, 113a jalan Petaling (☎238 9544). Neat, modern hotel, with rather charmless, small rooms with full facilities, although better value than others at the same price. ③.

Kuala Lumpur International Youth Hostel, 21 jalan Kampung Attap (☎230 6870). Follow jalan Petaling Street south and cross over a busy road onto Kampung Attap. There are cosy single and double rooms (with shared showers and toilet), dorms, a good café and a laundry service. ①.

Malaysia Hotel, jalan Hang Lekir (☎232 7722). The most expensive hotel in Chinatown and excellent for the price. The deluxe rooms have all the trimmings, while the café is renowned. ④.

Mandarin Hotel, 2–8 jalan Sultan (☎230 3000). Chinatown's largest hotel, with a coffee house, 24-hour room service and even a hair salon and health centre. Rooms are big with full facilities. ④.

Meridien Youth Hostel, 36 jalan Hang Kasturi (☎232 1428). Opposite Central Market, this pokey budget hostel has the cheapest dorm beds in KL, as well as small two- or three-bedded rooms. ①.

Travellers Moon Lodge, 36 jalan Silang (☎230 6601). Just south of jalan Tun Perak, this popular lodge includes a dorm and small two- and three-bedded rooms; prices include breakfast. The management is friendly and has a fine collection of maps, pamphlets and books. ①.

YWCA, 12 jalan Hang Jebat (☎238 3225). This hostel – just east of Chinatown, on a quiet street set back from the main road – is run by nuns and only rents its clean, comfortable singles and doubles to women, couples and families. It's a great deal if you qualify, with a lovely sitting room. ②.

Little India
All the following lodges and hotels are marked on the map on p.96–97.

Champagne Hotel, 141 lorong Bunus, off jalan Masjid India (☎298 6333). This upmarket hotel is popular with the Indian Malaysian elite and offers special deals if you stay for a full week. ③.

Chamtan Hotel, 62 jalan Masjid India (☎293 0144). Smaller than the *Champagne*, but with the same high standard and similar rooms. ③.

Diamond City Lodge, 74b, jalan Masjid India (☎293 2245). This excellent budget lodge, run by the ebullient Mr Ramakrishnan, has a wide range from dorms to twin-bedded rooms with bath. ②.

Empire Hotel, 48b jalan Masjid India (☎293 6890). Cheaper than the better-known *Champagne* and *Chamtan,* this is a very good deal with well-equipped rooms and discounts for longer stays. ②.

Palace Hotel, 46 jalan Masjid India (☎298 6122). Top-of-the-range, with sumptuous, but small, rooms, featuring all mod-cons. ⑤.

Along jalan TAR

All the following lodges and hotels are marked on the map on p.96–97.

Asia Hotel, 69 jalan Haji Hussein (☎292 6077). This long-established hotel has good, small rooms with bath and air-con; its location within Chow Kit Market makes it noisy early in the morning. ④.

Coliseum Hotel, 98 jalan TAR (☎292 6270). KL's most famous old-style hotel. The rooms are cramped and none too clean, but it oozes atmosphere, from the moment you swing through the Western saloon-style door into the bar; the café still serves world-renowned steaks and gravy. ②.

Kowloon Hotel, 142 jalan TAR (☎293 4246). Another (in)famous hotel – in the middle of a small red-light district – with a good coffee house. The good-value rooms are small but fully furnished. ②.

Rex Hotel, 102 jalan (no phone). This none-too-clean Chinese cheapie has unfriendly manageme-ment and no English is spoken – fine, if you like small, shabby rooms with shared facilites. ②.

Tivoli Hotel, 136 jalan TAR (☎292 4108). Another low-budget place overlooking KL's traffic-clogged thoroughfare. Friendlier than the *Rex*, with clean rooms and shared shower and toilet. ②.

Transit Villa, 36 jalan Chow Kit (☎441 0443). Popular with young Malaysians, this friendly, vibrant place is not really set up for travellers, but has facilities ranging from dorms to triples. ①–②.

Around Pudu Raya

All the following lodges and hotels are marked on the map on p.95.

Kawana Tourist Inn, 68 jalan Pudu Lama (☎238 6714). Neat, small rooms in a modern, rather bare place, but extremely good value and only ten minutes' walk from the bus station. ②.

KL City Lodge, 16a jalan Pudu (☎230 5275). Comfortable and convenient in a quiet area – although avoid the rooms at the back which look over the busy jalan Pudu. Choose between dorms and air-con rooms; useful extras include the laundry service and free lockers. ①.

Pudu Raya Hotel, 3rd floor, Pudu Raya Bus Station (☎232 1000). Well positioned for arriving late or leaving town early, but a noisy, polluted area. The rooms are good, small with bath and air-con.②.

Sunrise Travellers Lodge, 89b jalan Pudu Lama (☎230 8878). A very friendly place for travellers, its walls adorned with maps and posters. Accommodation ranges from dorm to three-bedded rooms. ②.

The Golden Triangle

All the following lodges and hotels are marked on the map on p.95.

Concorde Hotel, 2 jalan Sultan Ismail (☎244 2200). The trendiest of the area's hotels, with a *Hard Rock Café* and fashionable boutiques. It has large rooms with full facilities, phone and fridge. ④.

Federal Hotel, 35 jalan Bukit Bintang (☎248 9166). Patronized mostly by Malaysians, this unflashy old hotel with large, comfortable rooms offers some of the best deals in the Golden Triangle. ④.

Hotel Equatorial, jalan Sultan Ismail, opposite the *MAS* building (☎261 7777). Vast 300-room hotel with 400-metre swimming pool and shops. ⑤.

Holiday Inn On The Park, jalan Pinang (☎248 1066). Set back from the noisy street, the large rooms here are furnished and equipped as you'd expect – very well and very comfortably. ⑥.

Hotel Istana, 73 jalan Raja Chulan (☎244 1445). KL's newest luxury hotel with a palace-like decor, tropical plants, swimming pool and a massive ballroom. The rooms are of a high standard, too. ⑥.

Kuala Lumpur Hilton, jalan Sultan Ismail (☎242 2222). Luxurious rooms near the embassies, airlines and commercial district. It hosts concerts, seminars, etc, which are open to everyone. ⑥.

The Lodge, 2 jalan Tengah, off jalan Sultan Ismail (☎242 0122). The cheapest hotel in the area, with motel-style rooms, swimming pool and outdoor restaurant – a good-value deal in the Triangle. ③.

Park Royal Hotel, jalan Imbi, corner of jalan Sultan Ismail (☎242 5588). Undistinguished modern building, but with larger than usual rooms. ⑤.

The Regent, 160 jalan Bukit Bintang (☎241 8000). Easily the city's most expensive and prestigious hotel, with a large swimming pool, massive rooms and immensely luxurious suites. ⑥.

Brickfields

New Winner Hotel, 11 jalan Thambapillai, off jalan Tun Sambanthan (☎273 3766). Average, but quite expensive hotel, aimed at businessmen. The air-con rooms have all the usual facilities. ③–④.

Song Lim Hotel, 167a jalan Abdul Samad (☎274 7393). A much better deal than the *New Winner*, with small well-equipped rooms with bath and air-con. ②.

Quee Ping Hotel, 13–15 jalan Thumbapillai (☎274 3505). New Chinese hotel, whose small, neat rooms have full facilities. ③.

YMCA, 95 jalan Padang Belia (☎274 1439). Best to book ahead for these small but fully equipped rooms. On offer are language lessons, a resources centre, gym, launderette, barber and more. ②.

The city

The **Klang river** divides the city, with the old colonial sector sited on the west bank and Chinatown across on the east bank. South of **Merdeka Square** are many of the city's most impressive buildings and specific tourist sights; to the north and east are the main shopping areas. Two particular places vie for the title of the city's pivotal point. One is where the Klang river joins the Gombak river – the site which gave the city its very name and where was erected the city's oldest Islamic symbol, the **Jame Mosque**. The other, south of the mosque, is the **Central Market**, the epicentre of modern KL.

THE NEW ARCHITECTURE

The construction boom since the 1970s has given Malaysian **architects** untold opportunities both to experiment with new styles and confront certain questions – in particular, whether climate should be the governing factor in building design or if cultural or religious elements should be paramount. The resultant new buildings in KL – the Maybank, Tabung Haji, the Dayabumi and the National Library – have seen traditional elements interacting with innovative architectural expressions, often with strikingly original effect. Some architects have looked to the past and combined the archetypal sloping Malay roof and Islamic arches with the latest functionalist thinking; others consider a more fundamental principle to be the country's climate, which results in buildings which use solar panelling for heating and water concourses to regulate the internal temperature. In addition, KL's architects have started to work closely with new sculptors, integrating two- and three-dimensional artworks into their designs; see p.106 for more on this.

The architect who best demonstrates the contemporary fusing of essentially religious motifs with new design is **Hijjas Kasturi**, who was responsible for the Maybank and Tabung Haji buildings. The **Maybank Building** (p.94) is perhaps his most impressive work, where the dominance of the colour white denotes purity while the smooth, cool contours of the building's arresting height are reminiscent of a mosque's minaret. As for the **Tabung Haji**, on jalan Tun Razak at the intersection with jalan Ampang, the five columns which support the structure represent the five pillars of Islam, its single tower symbolizing unity with God. Appropriately, the building is the headquarters of the *Islamic Bank of Malaysia*.

The new **National Library** on jalan Tun Razak is a good example of a building reinterpreting traditional Malay forms. Although dominated by a gleaming roof covered in large blue ceramic tiles, architect Shamsuddin Muhammad's starting point was a typical east

The account below starts at Merdeka Square and heads south along the main jalan Sultan Hishamuddin to the national art gallery and museum, and on to the Lake Gardens and Parliament House, before returning to Jame Mosque. From there you can dive at will into the noisy, exhausting but always riveting traffic-clogged streets which comprise Chinatown, Little India, the jalan TAR area and the Golden Triangle.

The colonial district

The small **COLONIAL DISTRICT** (see over page for map), which developed around the confluence of the Gombak and Klang rivers in the 1880s, is unlike any other area of KL, its eccentric fusion of building styles at extreme odds with the rest of the city. The district is centred on the beautifully tended, two-hundred-metre long **Merdeka Square** on the west bank of the Klang. Once both English cricket field and Malay *padang* (field), it's now the most famous stretch of green in Malaysia, as it was here that Malaysian independence – simply called *merdeka* (freedom) – was proclaimed on August 31, 1957. On the eastern edge of the square you'll see the 95-metre-high flag-pole, the tallest in the world, and nearby is a large video screen which displays adver-tisements and religious messages – leading the onlookers alternatively into the ways of modern Malaysia's twin creeds, consumerism and Islam.

The **Royal Selangor Club** on the square was the British elite's favourite watering hole. Colonial wags used to refer to the low, black-and-white mock-Tudor building as "the Spotted Dog" in memory of the club mascot, a dalmatian, which a former member used to tie up at the steps. Dating from 1890, the club is now theoretically open to anyone who can afford membership, though old colonial prejudices die hard – the rule barring women from the bar is still in force and it's only possible to visit if invited by a

coast house, built on stilts and encompassing an intimate space more often than not made from a warm material like wood. Within the library he incorporated everyday cultu-ral symbols, using the shapes of traditional earthenware pots as one of the subjects for its interior sculpture, and the patterns on the *songket* headscarves worn by Malay women on the walls.

Another leading architect, **Ken Yeang**, considers Malay culture and religion as a side issue. For him the chief consideration is climate, and his **Menara Measiniaga** skyscraper – on the way to Subang Airport – is the latest in a string of tropical buildings which make maximum use of natural light and ventilation. His intention is to make it possible for the occupants to experience as much of the country's natural climate as possible: the windows are shaded to reduce heat, plants spiral up the walls in what is known as vertical landscap-ing, while energy efficiency, like solar panelling, is integral to the design.

Nik Mohammed's **Dayabumi Complex** (p.90), combines both climatic and Islamic ideas, although at heart it's much more functional than any of the later buildings, with office space more important than cosmetic flourishes. Nevertheless, as one of the earliest new buildings it set the standard by being unmistakably Malaysian, modern and differ-ent. Undoubtedly the most spectacular new building in KL wasn't designed by a Malaysian at all, though its Islamic themes are expressed more strongly than just about anywhere else. Cesar Pelli's **Petronas Towers** – office space for the state oil company – is due to be completed in 1996, when at just over 490 metres high, it will become the tall-est building in the world (until China's Chongquing Tower or Norman Foster's projected Millenium Tower for Tokyo top out). Tapered twin towers resembling minarets are joined by a bridge forty-odd floors up, forming a megalithic gateway, while the interior design is a profusion of squares and circles symbolizing harmony and strength. Here is the ultimate expression of Malaysia's intention to stand at the economic heart of modern Southeast Asia while maintaining its tradition and faith.

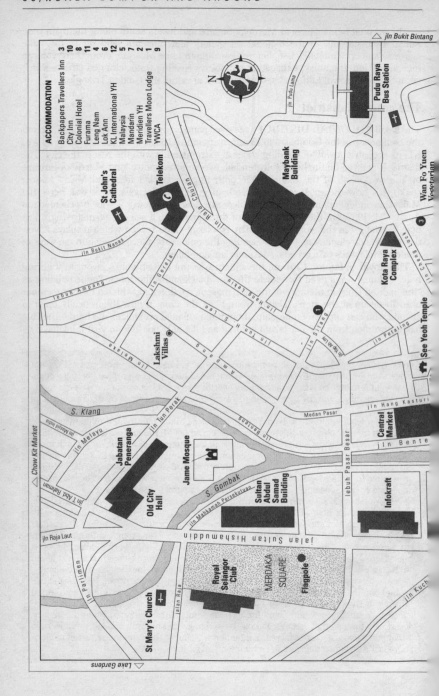

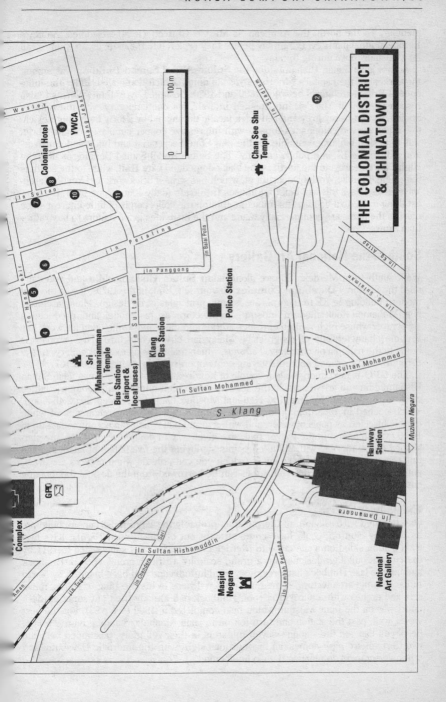

THE COLONIAL DISTRICT
& CHINATOWN

0   100 m

Wesley

YWCA   9

Colonial Hotel   8

Jln Sultan

7   10   11

Hang Lekir

6

5

4

Jln Petaling

Jln Baba Polis

Jln Panggong

Sri
Mahamariamman
Temple

Bus Station
(airport &
local buses)

Klang
Bus Station

Jln Sultan

Police Station

Jln Sultan Mohammed

Jln Sultan Mohammed

S. Klang

Chan See Shu
Temple

Jln Stadium

12

Jln S. Sulaiman

Jln Sa Atap

Railway
Station

▽ Muzium Negara

Jln Damansara

GPO

Complex

Jln Sultan Hishamuddin

Jln Chendra

Jln Sri

Jln Tugu

Jln Lembah Perdana

Masjid
Negara

National
Art Gallery

member. To the north, the Anglican **St Mary's Church** (1894) welcomed the city's European inhabitants every Sunday before they repaired to the club; if you want to call in, it's usually open during the day.

Across jalan Sultan Hishamuddin, the **Sultan Abdul Samad Building** was among the earliest of the capital's Moorish-style buildings, which dominated under the influence of British architects between 1890 and 1920. Designed by Anthony Norman (also responsible for St Mary's) and finished in 1897, it's contemporary with the Railway Station, its two-storey grey-and-red-brick facade dominated by a forty-metre-high clocktower and curved colonnades topped with impressive copper cupolas. Norman's brief was to design buildings suitable for the new State Secretariat and his grand construction still serves KL in a public capacity. The Sultan Abdul Samad Building is now the High Court; nearby, to the north is the black-domed old **City Hall**, while to the south is the original Public Works Department, which has striped brickwork and keyhole archways. These days this last building houses **Infokraft** (daily 10am–7pm; free), the closest thing in KL to a handicrafts museum, though the collection is of little interest since most of the items are commercially made and the main idea is for visitors to buy rather than browse.

South to the National Art Gallery

Walk south from Merdeka Square along **jalan Sultan Hishamuddin** and you can't miss the 35-storey **Dayabumi Complex** on your left. Built in the 1970s, it was the first modern building in KL to incorporate Islamic principles in its design. Malay architect Nik Mohamed took modern mosque architecture as his model and produced a skyscraper whose high-vaulted entrance arches and glistening white open fretwork has become charactersistic of progressive Malaysian city architecture. The complex is home to the national oil company, *Petronas*, which maintains an exellent gallery, *Galeri Petronas*, on the ground floor, displaying contemporary Malaysian art (see p.107).

The **GPO** is next door, while a couple of hundred metres further down jalan Sultan Hishamuddin you arrive outside the seventy-metre high minaret and geometric lattice work of the **Masjid Negara**, the National Mosque (9am–6pm except Fri 2.45–6pm), which opened in 1965. It's an impressive building, its sweeping rectangles of white marble bisected by pools of water, and with a grand hall which can accommodate up to 10,000 worshippers. In the prayer hall, size gives way to decorative prowess, the star-shaped dome adorned with eighteen points signifying the five pillars of Islam and the thirteen states of Malaysia. To enter (which you can only do when prayers are over), you need to be properly dressed: robes can be borrowed from the desk at the mosque entrance.

The Railway Station

One hundred metres south of the mosque, probably the city's most famous building, its **Railway Station**, could have come straight out of the Arabian Nights. KL's first train station stood on a site close to Merdeka Square, but was superseded in 1911 by the current building, designed on a grand scale by a British architect, A.B. Hubbock and built to last. Hubbock had previously lived in India and had been inspired by North Indian Islamic architecture, something reflected here in his meshing of spires, minarets and arches with a hardy iron roof; Hubbock had already tried out some of these flourishes on the Jame Mosque which he'd completed in 1909 (see p.93). For the best views, walk past the station and turn left on to jalan Kinabula. Standing on the bridge here, you can see the station's seven minarets in their full glory, positioned between two thirty-metre high domes, an incongruous sight with the futuristic Dayabumi and other skyscrapers dominating the skyline behind.

The National Art Gallery

Across from the station, next to the the Railway Administration offices, what was once the colonial *Majestic Hotel* now houses the country's **National Art Gallery** (daily 10am–6pm; free). The ground floor is given over to temporary exhibitions, usually of painting, sculpture or photography from Malaysia and other Southeast Asian countries, with the permanent collection occupying the second and third floors. If you were hoping to expand your knowledge of Malaysian artists, you'll be disappointed by the poorly referenced collection, which provides only the artists' names and dates of the works. Still, it is instructive to wander from the more contemporary canvases on the second floor – which include several colourful abstract works, some inspired by Islamic design – to the more traditional works on the top floor. Here, landscapes and portraits offer historical insights and reveal images of another, more rural Malaysia, where handicraft-making and music-playing predominate.

The Muzium Negara

Past the art gallery, ten minutes' walk along jalan Damansara leads to the **Muzium Negara**, Malaysia's National Museum (daily 9am–6pm, closed Fri noon–2.45pm; $2), built in 1963 with a sweeping roof, characteristic of Sumatran *Minangkabau* architectu- tre, and a main entrance flanked by Italian mosaics. Much of the original collection, housed in the old Selangor Museum, was destroyed by World War II bombing, which makes the extensive ethnographic and archeological exhibits on display today even more of an impressive collectors' assembly than usual.

The **ground floor** is mostly taken up with life-size dioramas depicting various aspects of traditional Malaysian life, from the prosaic activities – fishing, farming and weaving – taking place in a Malay *kampung* to the pomp and ritual of a wedding or a Malay circumcision ceremony. At the end of the room, a cross section of a Melaka *Baba* house is revealed, loaded with mahogany furniture, intricate carpets and orna- ments made from silver, brass and gold. Also on the ground floor are *wayang kulit* (shadow play) displays, which show how the wooden puppets used in this ancient artis- tic tradition differ in design and colour depending on their provenance.

On the **upper floor**, a large but uninspiring zoological section of stuffed birds and animals needn't detain you long, certainly not if you're waylaid by the much more impressive collection of weapons, including a large number of *kris* daggers, *parangs* (machetes), swords and miniature cannons. Finally, tucked away down a passage, there's a fabulous section on traditional musical instruments: the *serunai*, a reed with a multicoloured end; the *rebab*, a kind of fiddle played like a cello; numerous two-metre- long Kelantanese drums and smaller *rebana* drums; and Chinese lutes, gongs and flutes. Although Malay instruments are still in common use at festivals and ceremo- nies, traditional Chinese music in Malaysia was virtually extinct by independence, but has now been partially revived – if you're interested in hearing the music produced by these instruments, check out the venues listed on p.107.

The Lake Gardens and around

At the National Museum you're only a short walk from the southern entrance to the **Lake Gardens**, one hundred hectares of close-cropped lawns, gardens and hills originally laid out in the 1890s by the British state treasurer to Malaya, Alfred Venning, though much of the spectacular landscaping has been completed within the last twenty years. Spread around a lake (Tasek Perdana), the park incorporates a number of sights – the National Monument, Butterfly House and Bird Park, Orchid and Hibiscus Gardens – while just beyond, on the northern edge, is Malaysia's Parliament House.

From the Muzium Negara, head along jalan Damansara for about 50m, watching out for the small pathway leading into a tunnel at the junction with jalan Kebun Bunga. This takes you to the southern edge of the gardens, from where it's a good twenty-minute walk along the lake and up the hill to the garden headquarters where the bird park and flower gardens are located. The second, and much more heavily used, way in is to head due west of Merdeka Square along jalan Parlimen – all told it's a thirty-minute walk before you reach the main entrance, on the northern side of the gardens, and another ten minutes once inside to the headquarters. By bus to the main entrance, it's either the blue #30 from jalan Sultan Mohamed, or the pink #22 or #38 from lebuh Pasar Besar.

In the gardens

Opposite the main entrance, off jalan Parlimen, 50m along jalan Tamingsabi, is the **National Monument**, a great bronze sculpture designed by Felix de Weldon, better known for his work on the Iwo Jima Memorial in Washington DC. The fifteen-metre-high shiny slab was constructed in 1966 to commemorate the nation's heroes yet strangely, the seven military figures protruding from it appear to be European rather than any of the various Malaysian ethnic groups who fought in World War II and the Emergency. Reached by a path leading up from the car park, the monument stands surrounded by a moat with fountains and ornamental pewter water lilies – a tranquil spot. Back at the car park, looking down on jalan Parlimen, is a **sculpture garden**, to which neighbouring countries contributed abstract works of marble, iron, wood and bamboo.

The **Butterfly House** (daily 9am–5pm; $5) – first left from the National Monument inside the Lake Gardens – holds a diverse collection of butterflies (dead and alive), though more likely to hold your attention is the excellent **Bird Park** (daily 9am–6pm; $5), nearby; retrace your steps from the Butterfly Park to the main road and turn left uphill, following the road for 200m and it's on your left. Modelled on Singapore's Jurong BirdPark, walkways loop around streams and pools taking in the habitats of indigenous species like hornbills, the Brahminy Kite and the Hawk Eagle, as well as specimens of the largest pheasant in the world, the Argus Pheasant. You may as well nip into the **Orchid** and **Hibiscus Gardens** (daily 9am–6pm; free), opposite, where hundreds of plants are grown – and sold; the hibiscus section especially provides a wonderful assault on the senses.

The main road through the gardens then weaves down past a field of deer, to the **Memorial Tun Abdul Razak**, a house built for the second Malaysian Prime Minister – his motorboat and golf trolley are ceremonially positioned outside. Beyond is the **lake** itself, where you can rent boats and pedaloes and buy food and drink from a number of stalls. It takes nearly an hour to walk all the way round the lake, while from here you're only twenty minutes from the southern entrance (for access to the Muzium Negara).

Parliament House

If you coincide with the parliamentary sessions, you might want to tie in a visit to the gardens with one to **Parliament House**, 300m further down jalan Parlimen from the main entrance. Here, two white buildings – the House of Representatives, an ultra-modern high-rise, and the Senate, a lower building with a curved roof and protruding circular windows – emerge from a lush green hill and command an excellent view of the Lake Gardens. You need to get prior permission for your visit by calling in person at the City Hall (Mon–Thurs 9am–noon, Fri 9am–12.30pm) – and make sure you're properly dressed: women in long sleeves, trousers or long dresses, and men with a long-sleeved shirt and long trousers.

Jame Mosque to Central Market

At the southern end of Merdeka Square, lebuh Pasar Besar runs over KL's busiest bridge, connecting the colonial district with the commercial sector. Just north of here, on a promontory at the confluence of the Klang and Gombak rivers, stands KL's most attractive devotional building, the **Jame Mosque**. It's a site replete with significance, since it was here – on a section of dry land carved out from the enveloping forest – that the pioneers from Klang arrived in the 1850s on their search for tin, establishing a base that soon turned into a boomtown. The mosque itself formed part of the second great period of expansion in KL, completed in 1909 by the British architect A.B. Hubbock and incorporating features he had copied from Moghul mosques in North India – pink brick walls and arched colonnades, topped by oval cupolas and squat minarets. There's an intimacy at work here that isn't obvious at the much larger national mosque (which replaced the Jame as the centre of Muslim faith in KL), and the grounds, bordered by palms, are a pleasant place to sit and rest; the main entrance is on jalan Tun Perak.

Head south down jalan Benteng, over the junction with lebuh Pasar Besar, and you reach the Art-Deco **Central Market** (daily 9am–10pm). Backing onto the Klang river, this large pastel-coloured brick hangar was built in the 1920s as the capital's wet market, but now houses restaurants, craft shops and stalls selling anything from T-shirts to porcelain statues of Hindu and Chinese deities. The ground floor has batik textiles, hand-painted shadow-play masks, silk scarves, hats, bags, baskets and wooden *orang asli* sculptures; the first and second floors feature hawker stalls (busiest at 1–3pm and 6–8pm); while directly outside the market, on the west side, are more cafés and a **bandstand** on which are staged free cultural performances, usually during the evenings from Thursday to Sunday.

Chinatown

Spreading out from Central Market is **CHINATOWN**, KL's commercial kernel since the first traders arrived in the 1860s. Bordered by jalan Petaling to the east and jalan Tun Perak to the north, the area had adopted its current borders by the late-nineteenth century; along narrow streets like jalan Tun H.S. Lee and jalan Sultan, southern-Chinese style shophouses, coffee shops and temples sprang up in ever increasing numbers. Much is unchanged since those days, like the traditional apothecaries displaying medicines on the street corners, though behind other glass frontages you're now as likely to find stacks of computers and sound systems as tools, pots and pans, while what remains of the early architecture is dwarfed by the surrounding skyscrapers. For the moment, family businesses still predominate, but the few remaining genuinely old spots, like the **wet market** between jalan Petaling and jalan Tun H.S. Lee, may well soon be cleared for development. In the meantime, a stroll down Chinatown's narrow lanes still reveals delapidated shops and Chinese pharmacists, while large baskets of cured and dried meats alternate with the street-vendors' ranks of brightly coloured sweet drinks, soya milk and cigarette lighters.

In the early years of this century, **jalan Petaling** used to boast brothels and gambling dens. Nowadays, dozens of colourful umbrellas shield the street vendors from the fierce sun, while tourists spend their time bartering hard for mock Gucci watches, bric-a-brac and clothes: at nos. 86, 90 and 96 you can buy beads, stones, necklaces, masks, sculptures and conches. After 6pm, the street is closed to vehicles and the entire area is transformed into a *pasar malam* (nightmarket), where food stalls offer *loong kee* – rectangular slices of pork – and bananas, deep-fried in batter, and expert hagglers can pick up bags, sunglasses, clothes and crafts at tremendous prices.

See Yeoh and Chan See Shu Yuen temples

At the junction of jalan Tun H.S. Lee and lebuh Pudu is the **See Yeoh Temple**, founded by Yap Ah Loy, KL's early headman (see p.77), who promptly became the temples' chief deity when he died in 1885. It's not particularly interesting – though it comes to life on festival days – and you're better off visiting the area's largest temple, **Chan See Shu Yuen**, at the very southern end of jalan Petaling. The main deity here is Chong Wah, an Emperor in the Sung Dynasty. The inner shrine is covered in gold-painted scenes of lions, dragons and mythical creatures battling with warriors. Statues representing the temples' three deities stand behind a glass wall, above them a mural of a brilliant yellow sun. From outside, you can see the intricately carved roof, its images depicting more monumental events in Chinese history and mythology and decorating the edge of the pavilion are blue ceramic vases and small statues of peasants – the guardians of the temple – armed with poles crowned with lanterns.

Sri Mahamariamman Temple

Oddly perhaps, KL's main Hindu temple, is also located in the heart of Chinatown, on jalan Tun H.S. Lee, between the two Buddhist temples. Outside the pyramid-shaped entrance to the **Sri Mahamariamman Temple**, garland-makers sell their wares, and sweetmeats and other delicacies are often available. The earliest temple on this site was built in 1873 by Tamil immigrants and named after the Hindu deity, Mariamman, whose intercession was sought to provide protection against sickness and "unholy incidents". In the case of the Tamils, who had arrived to build the railways or to work on the plantations, they needed all the solace they could find from the appalling rigours of their working life. Significant renovation of the temple took place in the 1960s when sculptors from India were commissioned to design idols to adorn the five tiers of the gate tower – these now shine with gold embellishments, precious stones and exquisite Spanish and Italian tiles. Above the gate is a hectic profusion of Hindu gods, frozen in dozens of scenes from the *Ramayana*.

During the Hindu **Thaipusam** festival the temple's golden chariot is paraded through the streets on its route to Batu Caves, on the northern edge of the city (see p.111). For the rest of the year, the chariot is kept in a building at the side of the temple, and can be seen if you walk along jalan Hang Lekir, the first street on the left back along jalan Tun H.S. Lee from the temple. The temple is always open to the public and is free to visit, although you may want to contribute a dollar or so towards its upkeep.

Chinatown's eastern edge

Chinatown's main west–east thoroughfares, jalan Tun Perak and jalan Cheng Lock (the latter the route of the original railway track through KL) converge at the Pudu Raya roundabout, just off which stands the **Malay Banking (Maybank) Building**. Built in the late 1980s by Hijjas Kasturi, it's a structure typical of the new KL, designed with Islamic principles in mind (see p.86); unlike many of the other modern skyscrapers, there's actually a reason to venture inside, too; to visit either the excellent art gallery on the ground floor (see p.107) or the **Nurismatic Museum** (Mon–Fri 10am–5pm; free), on the first floor. This is an unusually interesting collection, arranged in chronological fashion, starting with pre-coinage artefacts once used for transactions in Southeast Asia – tin ingots, gold dust and bars of silver or, for what the caption describes as "ordinary people", cowrie shells, rice and beads. Coins were gradually introduced into the region along with the arrival of the various colonizing powers; early sixteenth-century Portuguese coins on display here are delicately engraved with miniatures of the Malay peninsula and of tiny kites billowing in the air. The first mass-produced coins were those issued by the East India Company, bearing the company's coat-of-arms, a practice seen up to the late eighteenth century when tokens were minted by timber and rubber companies to pay their expanding labour pool. The very first notes were produced by a private bank in 1694, although they were only issued officially around fifty years before the outbreak of World War II. During the Japanese invasion, the occupying administration produced its own notes which, after the Japanese surrender, the British diligently collected and stamped "not legal tender" and "specimen only".

Walk around the Pudu Raya roundabout from the Maybank and you'll see the bus station on the right, inhabiting an oblong island in the wide road. Immediately to the left is a little street, jalan Pudu Lama, 20m up which is KL's second most important Hindu shrine, the **Court Hill Ganesh Temple**, a small and often crowded place, with dozens of stalls outside selling garlands, incense, sweatmeats and charms. Sited just below the old law courts, this was a favoured stop by visitors on their way to KL's original law courts, once sited nearby, where they were able to pray to the chief deity, Lord Ganesh, who specializes in the removal of all obstacles to prosperity, peace and success.

East: jalan Ampang and the Golden Triangle

Just north of the Maybank and the *Telekom* building, **jalan Ampang** swings east out of the city, jumping back a century as it goes. Mansions started to be built along here as the early profits from the tin industry flooded in, and during the first years of this century Chinese *towkays* and British businessmen and administrators took up

residence in houses that took their architectural inspiration from various sources – Islamic to Art Deco. One is now the information office, MATIC, at no. 109 (see p.82), while a little further along on the same side of the road, another became *Le Coq D'Or* restaurant (p.103), supposedly built by one tin baron to impress another who had refused to let his daughter marry the first because he had once been too poor. Other surviving period residences along here are now foreign embassies and high commissions, although many of those further out along jalan Ampang were pulled down in the 1980s to make way for more modern developments, like the Ampang Shopping Complex, Yuan Chuan Plaza and City Square, all at the junction with jalan Tun Razak, around 3km from the centre. Blue bus #15 from the Central Market comes out this way, to the junction of jalan Ampang and jalan Tun Razak.

The Golden Triangle

The grid of roads south of jalan Ampang – with jalan Sultan Ismail and jalan Bukit Bintang at its heart – comprises what locals refer to as the **GOLDEN TRIANGLE**, the only area of the city which keeps really late hours. Here, among the hotels, shopping malls, neon signs and nightclubs, smartly dressed Kuala Lumpun youth and thousands of expats drift from bar to club to shop, taking in the arts and handicraft stalls and food centres along the way.

North: Little India to Chow Kit Market

Just to the north of Chinatown, **LITTLE INDIA** – the commercial centre for KL's Indian community – lies on the site of an original Malay *kampung* dating from the very earliest days of the settlement. Although covering a much smaller area than Chinatown, Little India is equally fascinating to the casual browser; it's the main area in the city for buying silk goods, especially *sarees*, *songkets*, scarves and skull caps, as well as handmade jewellery. Here and there, soap-box salesmen sell anything from herbal

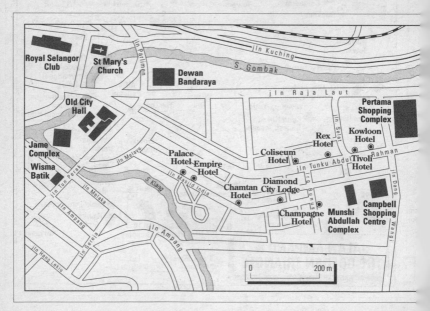

remedies to shoeshines. If you need a specific target, stroll up to **Wisma Batik** (Mon–Fri 9am–5pm, Sat 9am–1pm), on jalan Tun Perak at its junction with jalan Melaka, which has a tremendous selection of batik clothes and bags (see p.108).

Turning into **jalan Masjid India**, it's soon clear you've entered the Tamil part of the city, with *poori* and *samosa* vendors and cloth salesmen vying for positions on the crowded streets outside the cafés and hotels. Ten minutes' walk north, lorong Bunus branches off to the right and leads to a small market where you'll see **garland makers** busy at their craft. There's another nightly *pasar malam* here, too, a good place to come to eat tandoori chicken and other dishes.

Along jalan TAR

KL's largest day market, Chow Kit, is 2km north of Little India, along **jalan Tunku Abdul Rahman** (or **jalan TAR** as it's always known). The street – named after the first Prime Minister of independent Malaysia – is at its most alluring at its extremities, so having dawdled around the southern end catch a bus north. In an (unsuccessful) attempt to ease the city's chronic traffic congestion, jalan TAR only carries one-way traffic, southbound, so you have to skip over a block to the northbound jalan Raja Laut for the bus – virtually every bus or minibus heading north will take you towards Chow Kit.

On foot, a few hundred metres from Merdeka Square, jalan TAR passes the plain façade of the **Coliseum Hotel** where the British owners of the rubber plantations once met to drink tumblers of whisky and water (*stengahs*) and eat steak. It's still one of KL's most fashionable places, serving up good meals (see p.102) and ice-cold beers; the adjacent *Coliseum Cinema* puts on a strict diet of kung fu films, and Indian and Malay romances and dramas.

On Saturday nights this whole section of jalan TAR becomes a **pasar malam** (Sat 7pm–2am), where blind street musicians and Filipino rock bands entertain the mingling crowds. It's KL's longest and busiest street market, and includes items from clothes to children's toys, but is strongest on food, soft drinks and, bizarrely, kitchenware.

Another five minutes' walk up jalan TAR from the *Coliseum*, down narrow jalan Medan Tunku, **Wisma Loke** (Mon–Fri 10am–6.30pm, Sat 10am–5pm) occupies a beautiful colonial building, once the home of Loke Yew, a Chinese business baron, and now an antique and handicraft gallery, also known as the *Artequarium*. Its display pieces – sandalwood and mahogany furniture, pewter and ceramic pots and jars – are rather overpriced, but looking them over at least gives you an excuse to poke around the white two-storey building, taking in the sumptuous interior with its ornate ceiling, blue floor tiles and exotic pillars.

Chow Kit Market

At the northern end of jalan TAR, the entrance to **Chow Kit Market** (daily 9am–5pm) is announced by a gaggle of stalls crowding the pavements – the best place in KL to buy cheap secondhand clothes, like checked shirts and trousers. Inside, in the city's largest market, precarious plankways lead past stalls overladen with meat, fish, vegetables, spices, tofu and fruit. In the middle of it all vendors beseech you to buy worms squirming in baskets (you eat them, if you were wondering), while crabs and lobsters crawl around in near-empty tubs of water. It's not just food; there are clothes, shoes, cassettes and fabrics, and at the northern end of the market food stalls serve up excellent *roti canai*, *tee tarek* and high-quality *nasi campur*. This all adds up to one of the most interesting markets in the city, though more lurid accounts suggest it's also the haunt of pickpockets and drug addicts. The Malaysian government for one believes its own warnings, and the police regularly trawl the area for illegal aliens (usually Indonesians) supposedly orchestrating various nefarious activities, sweeping through the warren of narrow paths in the early morning, checking everyone's passes and throwing the unlucky ones into jail.

To reach the market from jalan Raja Laut, get out of the bus at jalan Haji Taib and walk east for ten minutes, crossing jalan TAR to the market entrance.

Kampung Bharu

Ten minutes' walk east of Chow Kit Market along jalan Raja Alang is the oldest Malay residential area in KL, **KAMPUNG BHARU**, founded in 1899 and the site of another well-known weekly *pasar malam*. On the way, you'll pass Kuala Lumpur's main Sikh temple (not open to the public), a red-and-white brick building, its facade reminiscent of the city's prewar shophouses, most of which have now been demolished. At the junction of jalan Raja Alang and jalan Abdullah – the *kampung's* main street – the district's **mosque** was built in 1924, a strong concrete structure at odds with most of the surrounding traditional Malay wooden houses.

Continuing along jalan Raja Alang leads you to the junction with jalan Raja Muda Musa, where a narrow twist of *lebuhs* houses Saturday's nightmarket, the **Pasar Minggu**, which runs from 6pm–1am. There's a thoroughly Malay atmosphere here and poking around turns up a number of jewellery, handicraft and fabric shops, alongside the usual hawker stalls. In particular, there are two excellent handicraft shops located where the main, narrow market street branches off from jalan Raja Muda Musa, as well as a number of stalls which sell batik and *songket* fabrics at knock-down prices.

Out from the centre

KL's urban sprawl is infamous. Main drags south like jalan Syed Putra and jalan Tun Sambanthan are choked solid at rushhour and, increasingly, at other times of the day as well. Most people take one look at the traffic and decide to stay put, within the confines of the city centre, until it's time to move on. It's worth venturing into the suburbs, though, for a couple of destinations, not least **Lake Titiwangsa**, a couple of kilometres north of Chow Kit, and the terrific **Thean Hou Temple**, just to the south of the city; slightly further south, the Indian area of **Brickfields** and adjacent **Bangsar** are both good places to come and eat. Further out than all of these is KL's zoo, north of the city, and the Rubber Museum, neither exactly must-see attractions but diverting enough if you have a couple of hours to kill.

Lake Titiwangsa

Set in a small park close to jalan Pahang, 2km north of Chow Kit, **Lake Titiwangsa** is an opal-shaped lake, usually swamped with locals who come here to rent boats ($5 an hour) and fool around on the water. There are concerete walkways through the landscaped park, but most people don't do anything too energetic. The best thing by far is to head for one of the numerous hawker stalls, though many eat instead at the *Lake Titiwangsa Restaurant*, at the northwestern edge of the lake (see p.103).

To get to the lake catch blue bus #174 from lebuh Ampang on the northern edge of Chinatown, or bus #169 from Pudu Raya; ask for the lake stop, and you'll be dropped off opposite jalan Titiwangsa. Walk along here for ten minutes then turn right onto jalan Kuantan – the lake is 100m up on the left.

Thean Hou Temple

KL's newest Buddhist temple, the **Thean Hou Temple** (daily 9am–6pm; free), is located on a hilltop 1.5km south of the city centre, between a sacred Bodhi tree and a one-hundred-year-old Buddhist shrine. The temple is always busy, with busloads of tourists constantly descending to take in the marvellous views north over the city and south to the satellite town of Petaling Jaya. It's also the most popular place in KL for Chinese marriages, and sports its own registry office on the first floor of the temple complex.

The main focus of excitement is the pagoda, in whose inner temple stands the shrine to Thean Hou's main deity, Kuan Yin, the Goddess of Mercy, who – legend has it – appears on earth in a variety of forms and can be identified by the precious dew flask which she always holds. The decor is as ornate as you'd expect, with a ceiling whose intricate patterns contain hundreds of green lanterns. In the centre of the line of sculpted deities sits Thean Hou, with Kuan Yin to her right, in front of whom visitors gather to burn offerings of joss sticks and paper money.

The easiest way to get here is by pink minibus #27 from Klang bus station, getting off at the jalan Kelang Lama junction on jalan Syed Putra (ask the driver for the temple). From there, the temple is five minutes' walk up a steep hill on the right.

Brickfields and Bangsar

Located on either side of jalan Tun Sambanthan and around 3km south of the city centre, **BRICKFIELDS** was first settled by Tamils employed to build the railways, and named after the brick yards which lined the railway tracks. The main street runs along the back of the original rail line and many of the turn-of-the-century buildings still remain. It's a great place to come to eat (see "Eating" below), while you might also venture this far afield for the *Temple of Fine Arts* (daily 11am–9pm; free; see also p.107), at 116 jalan Berhala, which features monthly Indian concerts and special events during Hindu festivals; music and dance lessons are offered in the early evening, and there's a café as well. To get to Brickfields, take blue bus #28 from Central Market; or take one of the more frequent Bangsar buses from Central Market and get off at jalan Travers, which is a short walk from jalan Tun Sambanthan, Brickfield's main thoroughfare.

Four kilometres further south, along jalan Bangsar, is **BANGSAR** itself. Only five years ago, this small grid of streets was a quiet, middle-class residential area with a few good cafés and a popular *pasar malam*. Nowadays, it's the trendiest area in KL to eat in the evening, with dozens of excellent restaurants, two hawkers' areas – one inside a giant hangar, the other in the adjoining street where there's also an excellent bookshop, called *MPH*.

The National Zoo

Malaysia's **National Zoo**, the *Zoo Negara* (daily 9am–6pm; $5), is 14km north of the city centre, beyond jalan Tun Razak on jalan Ulu Klang; blue bus #170 and pink mini-bus #17 run regularly from lebuh Ampang. Set in large grounds, you'll need to devote at least three hours to it if you want to see everything, unless you take advantage of the shuttle bus ($5 for three rides) which drops you off at main spots like the tiger and lion enclosures. The zoo is particularly strong on indigenous species, like the musang, civet, tiger, bearded pig and rhino, and also features an exceptional collection of **snakes**, including the Sumatran pit ulper and the Indian rock python. However, several of the cages and fenced areas are almost devoid of vegetation, and many of the animals look cramped and ill-at-ease, an exception being the little island containing two smooth-coated otters, who appear to adore the attention. An **aquarium** is located at the back of the zoo proper and although rather dark is worth venturing into to catch a glimpse of rare species and various coral reef fishes.

The Rubber Museum

The Malaysian rubber story began in 1877 with an Englishman, Henry Wickham, who collected 70,000 seeds from Brazil and took them to Kew Gardens in London, where they were germinated. Of these, twenty-two were sent to Singapore and nine to Kuala Kangsar, where they were planted in Resident Hugh Low's garden; by the 1930s, tens of thousands of hectares were under production and Malaya's rubber industry had dwarfed that of Brazil.

You can trace the development of the industry in the city's **Rubber Museum** (Mon–Fri 8am–4.15pm, Sat & Sun 10am–3pm; free), in the grounds of the Rubber Research Institute, 40km northwest of KL in a *kampung* called Sungei Buloh. Very few people make the effort to visit the museum – mainly because it's so far out – and it may be necessary to pick up the keys from the manager, who lives in the adjacent bungalow. Inside the museum, photographs, diagrams and drawings record in great detail the various changes in technology from manual distillation techniques to large-scale automation. More intriguing, perhaps, is the charting of the social life endured by tens of thousands of immigrants – mostly Tamil Indians and Teochew Chinese – who worked on the vast estates, clearing malarial swamps for plantation.

From KL, catch bus #144 or #145 from stands 21–23 at Pudu Raya bus station, which leave about every forty minutes (a 70-minute journey); ask for the Rubber Research Institute (RRI) and you'll be dropped at the gates.

Eating

KL boasts an extraordinary number of hawker stalls, coffee shops and restaurants, all of which boast a high standard of cuisine, and many of which are very inexpensive. The vast majority of places to eat serve Malay, Chinese or Indian food; KL is not noted for its international cuisine, although Japanese, Thai, Korean and fast food outlets are rapidly multiplying.

Locals make little distinction between eating at inexpensive **hawker stalls** and pricier **restaurants** – the quality of food at a stall is usually just as good and many offer regional dishes which aren't available elsewhere. There is, though, a difference between the stalls themselves: traditionally, they were open-air and many still line the traffic-choked roads in little enclaves throughout the city, but increasingly stalls are found grouped together in food courts inside buildings, where the food is usually no more expensive but the surroundings are air-conditioned. Good as the stalls can be, for real top-quality cooking you'll need to dine out at one of the big hotels, since most Malay restaurants in KL serve a rather limited range of dishes. The exception is at

Outside the city, don't forget the large choice of excellent hawker stalls, cafés and restaurants in **Petaling Jaya**, the southwestern satellite of KL – see p.115 for all the details.

festival times when the stops are pulled out and imaginative Malay cuisine is available throughout the city – watch out for hotels offering special buffets. Finding good Chinese or Tamil and North Indian food is much easier; it's served in cafés and restaurants in both Chinatown and Little India. In the latter especially, the cafés and hawkers do a manic trade at lunchtime in excellent banana leaf curries, *murtabak*, *dosai* and *roti*.

Hawker stalls

Indoor hawker stalls tend to be in shopping malls and complexes and open all day between 10am and 10pm. Outdoor stalls don't usually start business until 6pm or 7pm, but then stay open until 2am or so; exceptions are noted below.

Indoor

Ampang Shopping Complex, jalan Ampang at junction with jalan Tun Razak. The food court in this hi-tech mall is a mix of international and Asian tastes, designed to please Ampang's abundant middle class. Blue bus #15 from the Central Market.

Central Market, 1st and 2nd floors, jalan Hang Kasturi. Best are the superb Malay stalls on the top floor where plates of *nasi campur* cost just $2.

Hilton Hotel, jalan Sultan Ismail. Just behind the hotel, this opens late morning for *nasi campur*, Malay salad (*ulam*), Chinese noodles, Indian and Malay curries and fried fish amongst others; there are also fresh juice and beer vendors here, too. Closes at around 2pm.

Medan Hang Tuah, basement and 4th floor, *The Mall*, jalan Putra. Here, dozens of stalls sell everything from burgers to Chinese "steamboats" of fish, meat and vegetables. In the basement is a mix of Chinese noodle dishes and Malay *nasi* options. Closes at around 10pm.

Naan Corner, 200m from the *International School*, Ampang. A long trawl by pink minibus #32 or #34 from lebuh Ampang, but this Indian hawker centre serves sensational north Indian food and is good for parties. Probably the best-quality Indian in KL after *Annalakshmi* in Bangsar (see below).

Pudu Raya Bus Station, 1st floor, jalan Pudu. A dozen stalls serving a mix of Chinese, Malay and Indian *nasi*, *roti* and noodles. This has longer hours than many, and a few stalls are open all night.

Semua House, basement, jalan Masjid India. Very popular and crowded lunch-time spot, where you can opt for a fabulous *nasi campur*, or an equally good banana leaf curry.

Sungei Wang Plaza Hawker Centre, jalan Bukit Bintang. KL's oldest mall, with a crowded food centre selling Malay and Chinese fast food.

Jalan Telawi Tiga Food Centre, jalan Telawi Tiga, Bangsar. Recently the vibrant hawkers from the top of the street were moved into this new, unatmospheric building, but the food is great with the Indian tandoori stalls outstanding, Take any Bangsar bus from outside Central Market.

Outdoor

Bangsar Hawkers, jalan Telawi Tiga, Bangsar. Behind the *Jalan Telawi Tiga Food Centre* (see above) are a dozen or so excellent stalls including Korean, north Indian tandoori and Malay. Open after 6pm only. Take any Bangsar bus from outside Central Market.

Brickfields Hawkers, jalan Thambapillai, Brickfields. A cluster of predominantly Chinese cafés, though *Sri Vani's Corner* – just beside the *YMCA* – is renowned as the best tandoori hawker in KL. It's not always open, but it's worth a try. Stalls open after 6pm only. Bus #28 from Central Market.

Chinatown, jalan Tun H.S. Lee and jalan Petaling market. Essentially a wet fish (and meat and vegetable) market, there are some great Chinese noodle stalls in this warren of plankways reached by looking for the narrow openings halfway down either street. Open early morning til 7pm.

Chow Kit Market, jalan Sultan Suleiman. At the top end of Chow Kit Market there are some good *roti canai* hawkers, and tucked away in a building just south of jalan Sultan Suleiman some *nasi campur* stalls. Open from 8am–7pm.

Golden Triangle, jalan Alor. A wide street with lots of Chinese cafés which put tables out into the street after dark. If you like fried chicken wings, this is the best place to go in KL. Open after 7pm.
Little India, jalan Masjid India. Along the main street there are dozens of excellent food stalls, not only Indian. Although lunch time is best, there's still plenty to eat up until 11pm.

Restaurants and cafés

All the **restaurants and cafés** listed below are open daily from 11am or noon until midnight, unless otherwise stated. Most restaurants stay open throughout the year, though note that eveything will be closed during the two-day Hari Raya festival (Feb/ March), and most Malay restaurants close during Ramadan (Feb). It's difficult to be precise about **prices** at restaurants in KL, save to say that you'll always spend more than at a hawker stall. That said, even in top-class restaurants it's possible to sit down and just order a plate of noodles at lunchtime; the reviews give an idea of how much you can generally expect to pay for a decent meal.

Phone numbers are given below for restaurants where it's necessary to reserve a table in advance – or just call in earlier in the day. For those staying outside the Golden Triangle, the best way to get there is to take one of the pink minibuses from outside Central Market which run east to the centre of the district, to the junction of jalan Sultan Ismail and jalan Bukit Bintang; coming back, after midnight, you'll have to take a cab.

Central KL

Ang Patt Meng Café, 97 jalan Petaling, Chinatown. There are many cheap Chinese cafés like this, with morning noodles and, after midday, *nasi campur* with meat, fish and vegetable dishes.
Bangles, 60 jalan TAR, Little India (☎298 6770). You should book in advance for evening meals at this superb Indian restaurant, whose speciality is chicken tandoori; around $40 for two.
Bilal Restaurant, 33 jalan Ampang. At the western, city centre, end of jalan Ampang, this is one of KL's most revered north Indian restaurants, and is particularly popular for its chicken and mutton curries and naans. Prices are very reasonable, at about $20 for two.
Coliseum Café, 98 jalan TAR. Colonial hotel-restaurant famous for it's sizzling steaks, but also offering chicken, fish, salad and Chinese dishes, too. Steak meals cost around $15–20 per head.
Hameeds Café, ground floor, Central Market, jalan Hang Kasturi, Chinatown. Superb, busy, north Indian cafe serving tandoori chicken, curries and rice dishes. Open when the market's open.
Hamid Shah Café, 30 jalan Silang, Chinatown. Excellent, busy, café for Malay and North Indian curries and *roti*. Very good value at around $10–12 for two. Open 8am–6pm.
Kenanga Seafood Restaurant, 1st floor, MARA Building, jalan Raja Laut. Malay restaurant noted for its squid, crab and prawn dishes – from around $20 a head.
Lakshmi Villas, lebuh Ampang, Little India. On the edge of Chinatown, this is the best south Indian café in KL. The ground floor serves various *dosai*; the first floor specializes in banana leaf, with extra meat and vegetable curries from midday; a bargain at around $6 for two. Closes at 7pm.
Seng Kee Restaurant, 100 jalan Petaling, Chinatown. Frenetically busy restaurant with great prawn and duck dishes; well priced at around $25 for two.
Wan Fo Yuan Vegetarian Restaurant, lebuh Sultan, Chinatown. The area's best-known vegetarian restaurant serving rather bland tofu dishes; supplement your meal with fresh green vegetables.

Golden Triangle

123 Restaurant, 159 jalan Ampang (☎261 4746). One of KL's most popular spots for expats, *123* is worth the trip: the setting, under a thatched roof, is great, the seafood dominated menu excellent, and reasonably priced, at around $30 for two – though you could spend a lot more here if you tried.
Café Capri, Ground Floor, Life Centre, jalan Sultan Ismail. A pleasant, European-style café with a terrace and international food including sandwiches and pasta dishes; prices are around $15 a head.
Cal's Diner, Basement, Lot 10 Shopping Centre, jalan Bukit Bintang. The full American effect here, with hamburgers, coffee, desserts and an old jukebox stacked full of rock and roll classics. Prices are around $25–30 for two, but it's a surefire hit with KL's youth.

Eden Seafood Village, 260 jalan Raja Chulan (☎241 4027). Popular family restaurant, with dozens of types of fish cooked Cantonese-style and a Malaysian cultural show. Two will spend around $50.

Golden Phoenix, at the *Hotel Equatorial*, jalan Sultan Ismail (☎261 7777). Top-of-the-range Chinese restaurant specializing in exotic seafood dishes; expect to spend over $30 a head.

Hard Rock Café, *Concorde Hotel*, 2 jalan Sultan Ismail. The usual burgers, steaks and salad for around $15 a head (drinks extra), accompanied by loud music and related pop and rock artefacts.

Koryo-Won Restaurant, Antara Bangsa Complex, jalan Sultan Ismail. Top Korean restaurant, next to the *KL Hilton*, specializes in chilli-hot meat and fish dishes. Expensive, but makes a nice change.

Le Coq D'Or, 121 jalan Ampang (☎242 9732). Housed in a converted tin *towkay*'s mansion, you could easily spend up to $50 a head (or just come for a drink on the verandah). The French, Malay and Chinese dishes aren't bad, but it's the elegant ambience that's the real draw. Dress smart.

Rasa Utara, BB Plaza, jalan Bukit Bintang. A northern Malay menu characterizes this busy restaurant; try the *ayam percik*, a hot, sour chicken dish from the state of Kelantan. Moderately priced.

Teochew Restaurant, 272 jalan Pudu. Well-known and extremely busy Chinese restaurant, noted especially for its high-quality *dim sum* (served daytime only) at around $50 for two.

Shang Palace, *Shangri-La Hotel*, jalan Sultan Ismail (☎241 6572). One of the most popular places in KL for *dim sum*; dinner, too, is highly regarded but not cheap.

Sze Chuan Restaurant, 42 jalan Sultan Ismail (☎242 7083). Hot, spicy cooking from China's Szechuan province, at reasonable prices ($30–40 for two). This is one of the best Chinese restaurants in KL for both quality and cost, and you'd do best to book early in the day.

Yazmin Restaurant, 6 jalan Kia Peng (☎241 5655). Quite expensive, at $35 a head for tasty regional Malay dishes, but includes a cultural performance (see "The arts and entertainment", below).

North of the centre

Cili Padi Thai Restaurant, 2nd Floor, The Mall, jalan Putra. Excellent, moderately priced Thai restaurant, good on Bangkok-style cuisine, including elaborate chicken and seafood dishes.

Hoshigaoki Restaurant, The Mall, jalan Putra. Superb Japanese food at reasonable prices – *sushi* is around $6 a portion and set meals are from $12. There's a more central branch at Lot 10 Shopping Centre, jalan Bukit Bintang, in the Golden Triangle.

Lake Titiwangsa Restaurant, jalan Kuantan, off jalan Pahang, Lake Titiwangsa (☎422 8600). Built on a floating platform, this seafood-based restaurant includes Malay and Chinese dishes. Although overpriced at around $50 for two, this includes a cultural show of Malaysian singing and dancing. Blue bus #174 from lebuh Ampang in Chinatown, or #169 from Pudu Raya.

Omar Khayyam, 5 jalan Medan Tunku, off jalan TAR, close to *Wisma Loke*. A Mughal-style menu with heavy, rich meat curries; portions are large and prices reasonable at around $25 for two.

South of the centre

For bus details to Bangsar and Brickfields, see p.99.

Annalakshmi, 46 jalan Maarof, Bangsar (☎282 3799). Most people opt for the as-much-as-you-can-eat buffet, with delicious vegetable curries, dhal and pastries at this excellent south Indian vegetarian restaurant. It's a fine place and the price is very reasonable at around $20 each.

Bangsar Seafood Village, jalan Telawi Tiga, Bangsar. Over-expensive seafood specialists but attractively located in a large garden.

Beijing Inn Restaurant, 20 jalan Telawi Tiga, Bangsar. Chinese restaurant with tables overlooking the street. The menu includes chicken in chilli or cashew nuts, spare ribs, and a range of fresh green side dishes in lashings of garlic.

Hong Kong Tim Sum & Noodle House, 8 jalan Telawi Tiga, Bangsar. Sublime Chinese restaurant – try the chicken in chillies and butter prawns. Eat on the street then follow up your meal with an ice cream at *Baskin-Robbins* round the corner.

Puteri Restaurant, 146 jalan Tun Sambanthan, Brickfields. One of a number of good north Indian cafés in Brickfields with fine *roti canai* and curries.

Sri Devi Restaurant, jalan Travers, Brickfields. Brickfields' best, selling excellent banana leaf curries from midday onwards and wonderful *dosais* all day. Extremely cheap.

Sri Thai Restaurant, 14 jalan Telawi Tiga, Bangsar. The oldest Thai restaurant in KL, it has a wide variety of dishes including some from Chiang Mai in north Thailand. Good value at $30–40 for two.

Drinking and nightlife

KL has a growing number of excellent bars and fashionable clubs and discos, especially in the more monied districts along jalan Bukit Bintang and jalan Ampang. **Bars** here are often called pubs, a hangover from the British colonial presence and a draw for the British and Australian expats resident in the city. Many of the larger places feature live music, usually performed by Filipino bands, although a seemingly insatiable appetite for **karaoke** has engulfed KL recently – the specialist karaoke bars mostly appeal to visiting businessmen, although tourists are attracted by the promise of a certain laugh, usually at their own expense. Although beer is relatively expensive throughout KL – usually around $6–7 a glass – most places have "happy hours" where the price drops by a couple of dollars. Most bars are open throughout the day from noon onwards, and close after midnight; karaoke bars tend to open from 9pm to 1am or 2am, and don't have a cover charge.

The daily "Metro" section in *The Star* newspaper has **club** listings and leaflets sometimes given out in Central Market advertise new places. The most fashionable – and most interesting – events are usually unpublicized, so unless you meet an in-the-know local you're unlikely to get to hear of them. Doors usually open at around 9pm, though nothing much tends to happen before midnight, with clubs closing at 3am. Entrance charges are high, around $20, which makes them the preserve of expats and the Malaysian middle class. The music played is a diverse mix of international and Malay pop, soul and rock, although KL is increasingly opting into the international dance music circuit with Western club DJs making guest appearances at various clubs. For more on the Malaysian music scene, see *Contexts*, p.587.

Concerts featuring Malay pop stars or visiting big names from other Southeast Asian countries (and further afield) play large-scale venues like Merdeka Stadium or the Civic Centre in Petaling Jaya (for this, see p.115) outside the city. Concerts are always over early – by 11pm – to ensure that everybody can get home easily by public transport. Ticket prices start at around $20 and tickets are available either by going to the venue itself or to a ticket agency (see box opposite); the easiest one to find is the *Horizon Music Centre* on the ground floor of Central Market.

Bars and pubs

Barn Thai, 370b jalan Tun Razak. East of the centre, an atmospheric wooden bar where the live music, including jazz, rock and world music, kicks off at about 11pm and goes on until 3am.

Bull's Head, Central Market, jalan Benteng. A very busy bar, popular with expats, tourists and business people alike. Closes at midnight.

Ceejay's, ground floor, Menara SM1, 6 lorong P. Ramlee (behind the *Shangri-La Hotel*), Golden Triangle. Unexceptional bar, whose main attraction is bands playing cover versions. Open til 2am.

Centrepoint, jalan Setiapuspa, off jalan Medan Damansara. Great bar with live rock groups and a young, energetic, clientele; the best time to go is 10am–2am. It's west of the centre – take a taxi.

Club Fukiko, Menara Promet, jalan Sultan Ismail, Golden Triangle. Upmarket bar with expensive drinks and seriously trained karaoke-wannabes dominating the mike.

Coliseum Hotel, 98 jalan TAR. Always busy, the *Coliseum* bar has a rich history and relaxed atmosphere. The cartoonist, Lat (p.106), drinks here and his work is on the walls. Open 10am–midnight.

Dinty's, jalan Tun Sambanthan. Brickfields' top bar isn't worth the trip in itself, but if you're staying at the YMCA, you may want to drop in. Open 6am–midnight.

Lai-Lai Karaoke Lounge, Sungei Wang Plaza, jalan Sultan Ismail, Golden Triangle. Close to the junction with jalan Bukit Bintang, this is the best karaoke bar, especially at around 10pm, when you're likely to get a turn yourself.

London Pub, lorong Hampshire, off jalan Ampang (behind the *Ming Court Hotel*). Lively stomping ground for British expats, perfect if you want to play darts and drink draught beer.

The Pub, *Shangri-La Hotel*, jalan Sultan Ismail. Non-residents can drink in *The Pub*, which is better than most hotel bars; a good atmosphere and a chance to look round KL's most opulent hotel.

Riverbank, Central Market, jalan Benteng. Well-placed bar, opposite the river, with occasional music – a good place to sit if there's a group or a cultural performance on at the nearby bandstand.

Discos and clubs

Baze, 3rd floor, Wisma Central, opposite *Ming Court Hotel*, jalan Ampang. Happening club frequented by KL's well-heeled youth; soul, reggae and dance music are played. Open 9pm–4am.

Betelnut, corner of jalan Pinang and jalan P. Ramlee. KL's best-known club, but not so popular these days with the trendy young, attracting instead a crowd of expats and businessmen who don't mind high prices. The music tends towards 1960s' and 1970s' classics. Open 8pm–4am.

Blue Moon, *Hotel Equatorial*, jalan Sultan Ismail (opposite the MAS Building). The only place in KL where you'll hear Malaysian golden oldies from the 1950s, French shmaltz and famous singer, the golden-voiced baritone, P. Ramlee. One of the cheaper club venues. Open 7pm–midnight.

Deluxe Night Club, 2nd floor, Ampang Shopping Complex, jalan Ampang. Mainstream club with mainstream sounds catering for the Ampang middle class. Open 9pm–2am.

Fire, 6 lorong P. Ramlee, off jalan P. Ramlee (behind the *Shangri-La Hotel*). Fashionable club which plays Western dance music. High door prices and crowds of punters. Open 9pm–4am.

Hollywood East, Ampang Shopping Complex, rooftop, jalan Ampang. Supposedly one of the world's largest discos, playing Malay and Western pop to a mixed crowd. Open 8pm–3am,

Renaissance, 3rd Floor, Yuan Chuan Plaza, jalan Tun Razak. Local bands sometimes play here; otherwise listen to the taped Malay rock and pop. Free admission. Open 6pm–midnight.

Sapphire Discotheque, 3rd Floor, Yuan Chuan Plaza, jalan Tun Razak. Busy disco where rock bands often play. Open 8pm–2am.

Live music

Bantai, jalan Ampang, at the jalan Tun Razak intersection, opposite *Micasa Hotel*. Upmarket seated club with live jazz at the weekends. Open 8pm–3am; entrance will cost around $20.

Hard Rock Café, *Concorde Hotel*, 2 jalan Sultan Ismail, Golden Triangle. Rock bands from 9.30pm; otherwise open 11am–midnight. Gets absolutely packed on Friday and Saturday nights – you don't have to eat if you've come to see the band.

Merdaka Stadium, jalan Hang Jebat. Stages occasional large concerts, mostly of visiting Western rock acts, ballad singers and (a must-see) Malay heavy metal bands – look for posters around town.

Pyramid, jalan Damansara. KL's top live music venue where brilliant world music/jazz fusion band, Aslabeat, plays. It's a $6 taxi ride west of the centre. Open 8pm–3am; $30 entrance includes dinner.

The arts and entertainment

Culturally speaking, KL has a fairly provincial feel, with little happening in the performing arts. Contemparary dance is very much in its infancy, as is theatre, and the only time you can really guarantee seeing traditional theatre, dance and music is at festivals. Otherwise, you'll have to depend on the cultural shows performed in some restaurants and other venues, which combine such activities, though often to lame and inauthentic effect. There are bright spots, though, including a number of promising

---

TICKET AGENCIES

The following agencies sell tickets for music, theatre and dance events, and are open Mon–Sat 11am–6pm.

Bon Ton, jalan Kia Peng, Golden Triangle (☎241 3614).
Eastwood Music, 30 jalan Telawai Tiga, Bangsar (☎254 2655).
Galerie Wan, 4 jalan Binjai, off jalan Ampang (☎261 4071).
Horizon Music Centre, Central Market, jalan Hang Kasturi (☎274 6778).
Topaz, 1–2 jalan Taman Bukit Tunku, Taman Tunku (☎293 0397).

theatrical companies, like the *Instant Café Theatre*, which has caused a stir in recent years with its subtle satirical treatment of Malaysian life. Unfortunately, there is no national theatre in KL and companies like this have to hunt around for appropriate space whenever they want to stage something.

Cinema is popular but of limited interest to most visitors since the majority of movies are either Western ones dubbed into Malay, Cantonese or Tamil, or domestic movies made in those languages. Listings appear in *The New Straits Times*, *The Star*, *The Sun* (weekly) and *The Malay Mail*; tickets cost $10–15. There are occasional festivals of English-language films but the government's draconian censorship laws usually mean that many are cut to threads.

Where KL is strongest is in the **visual arts**, with numerous private galleries stocked with new work and visiting exhibitions, notably from Southeast Asian countries, and getting rave reviews in the press. Banks and oil companies – like the state-owned *Petronas* who run the gallery in the Dayabumi Complex – sponsor art and sculpture in KL, which in the case of the Maybank's pioneering ground-floor gallery has led to dozens of Malay (and, increasingly Indian and Chinese) artists selling work and rapidly gaining international reputations. Top talents to watch out for include colourful abstract painters like Ismael Latiff, S. Chandhiran and Tajuddin Ismail, and more naturalistic artists who home in on images from everyday life: Rahmat Ramli, Maamor Jantan and Sani Mohamad Dom. **Sculpture** in public places is also a growth area, with impressive works like Lee Kiew Sing's *Vision 2020* outside the *Public Bank*, on jalan Raja Laut, and Syed Ahmaed Jamal's iron and marble figures at the UNBC Building on jalan Kuching.

Art galleries

Anak Alam Gallery, 905 Pesiaran Tun Ismail, off jalan Parliamen. Specializes in canvases of traditional *kampung* scenes.

Artfolio, 2nd floor, City Square, 182 jalan Tun Razak. Stacks of watercolours, oil paintings and ceramics to choose from, at high prices.

LAT

Malaysia's most famous artist is **Lat**, a cartoonist who more than any fiction writer or essayist successfully holds his culture's foibles up for forensic examination. In his early forties, Lat has published four books and is seldom out of the country's most influential paper, *The New Straits Times*. In his first book, "Kampung Boy", he applied bright watercolour sketches to separate the present from the past, drawing a contrast between his traditional Malay upbringing in the *kampung* and modern life in the city suburbs. The pictures he creates are full of wit, telling, for example, how the boys in the *kampung* were so proud of their shorts, despite the fact that the inner linings of the pockets were made from flour sacks and carried the words "Best Quality".

Lat quickly became a national institution and it's a commonly held view in Malaysia that he can get away with criticizing contemporary society in his work, which the government wouldn't tolerate coming from anyone else. Banks and galleries display his work, despite the fact that in many of his drawings the holders of Malaysia's purse strings are cleverly caricatured. As with any great cartoonist, Lat draws out the prime characteristics of his subject, so most Malay women are covered by a headscarf, but some – the ambitious urban generation – wear power clothing and high heels. Likewise, Malay men are mostly drawn in relaxed, even lazy, demeanour, sitting about in their sarongs, but others are sketched as power-hungry, attention-seeking egotists.

Lat is one of the few cultural commentators who can get away with pointing the finger at excesses without it seeming like subversion. Malaysians see themselves in his cartoons – if often as grotesque generalities – and visitors wanting to get inside Malaysian society could do worse than buy his work and get an instant and accessible sociological update.

Art House, 2nd floor, Wisma Stephens, jalan Raja Chulan, Golden Triangle. Painting and ceramics.

Case Galleries, Lot T, 117B, 3rd floor, City Square, 182 jalan Tun Razak. Run by artist Raja Azhar Idris, this is both a gallery for new work and a workshop for conservation, framing and restoration.

Galeri APS, 2nd floor, City Square, 182 jalan Tun Razak. New work by young artists.

Galeri Petronas, ground floor, Dayabumi Complex, jalan Sultan Hishamuddin. Large space with excellent temporary exhibitions, often on naturalistic themes like the rainforest or the oceans.

Impression Arts, 1st floor, Wisma Stephens, jalan Raja Chulan, Golden Triangle. Another commercial outlet for KL's artistic talent.

Maybank Building, ground floor, Pudu Raya roundabout. KL's most influential art gallery, with shows that change monthly – the best place to gain an insight into contemporary Malaysian art.

National Art Gallery, jalan Sultan Hishamuddin. Ironically, fairly poor at displaying new work, but the temporary exhibitions on the ground floor are usually worth visiting.

Cinemas

Cathay, jalan Bukit Bintang, opposite the *Federal Hotel* (☎242 9942). Screens thoroughly mainstream material from Malay epics to Chinese kung fu.

Coliseum, jalan TAR, next to the *Coliseum Hotel* (☎292 5995). Shows the latest Cantonese and Taiwanese blockbusters.

Federal, jalan Raja Laut, at corner of jalan Sultan Ismail (☎442 5041). Specializes in Malay cinema, which ranges from corny romances to historical epics.

Odeon, jalan TAR, corner of jalan Dang Wangi (☎292 0084). Provides a wide spread of material, including Indian musicals.

Pavilion, jalan Pudu at the junction with jalan Bukit Bintang (no phone). Shows Malay, Chinese and Tamil films.

President, Sungei Wang Plaza, jalan Sultan Ismail (☎248 0084). Screens the odd English-language films, usually a few months behind US and European release.

Cultural shows, dance and traditional music

Eden Seafood Village, 260 jalan Raja Chulan (☎241 4027). Large Chinese restaurant which stages pan-Malaysian dances nightly.

Lake Titiwangsa Restaurant, jalan Kuantan, off jalan Pahang, Lake Titiwangsa. Atmospheric location overlooking the lake, though featuring a rather tame song-and-dance troupe.

Malaysian Tourist Information Complex (MATIC), 109 jalan Ampang (☎243 4929). Costumed shows every evening at 7.30pm, price $5; you don't need to book, but call first to check on performances. There are occasionally shows held in the gardens outside, too.

Sri Melayu, jalan Conlay, behind the *KL Hilton*. New venue with a regular and enthusiastic cast which perform Chinese, Indian and Malay dances.

Temple of Fine Arts, 116 jalan Berhala, Brickfields (☎274 3709). Arts organization which preserves Tamil Hindu culture by promoting dance, theatre, folk, classical music and craft-making.

Yazmin Restaurant, 6 jalan Kia Peng, Golden Triangle (☎241 5655). The best of KL's regular cultural evenings, held in a restaurant where the $35 cover price includes food and a 9–10.30pm show. The in-house cultural troupe plays traditional melodies on gongs, percussion and wind instruments. The show reaches its peak with the staging of a Malay wedding ceremony.

Markets and shopping

Most of KL's malls are open daily from 10am to 10pm; elsewhere, shops are usually open from Monday to Saturday 9am to 6pm. Although **handicrafts** are best picked up outside KL, there are some outlets worth perusing in the city. Pewter production is of a very high standard, and a visit to the *Royal Selangor Pewter Factory* gives an insight into the scale and sophistication of the production process, and provides an opportunity to buy items at lower prices than in the shops. Of course, if you're in the market for them, you can also pick up batik products, including textiles, bags, belts and hats, as well as carvings, artwork and sculpture – check the list of shops below for the best deals.

However, the unchallenged top shopping activity for most locals is to visit the **night-markets** – the *pasar malams* – where goods of all sorts are sold at competitive prices; bargains are easy to come by and the atmosphere is always gregarious, almost like a festival. Most markets have already been covered, but there's a round-up below.

Markets

Tun Razak, jalan Jujur, at the intersection with jalan Tun Razak. Saturday nightmarket including cut-price clothing.

Central Market, jalan Hang Kasturi, Chinatown (daily 9am–10pm). See p.93.

Chow Kit, jalan Haji Hussein, off jalan TAR (daily 9am–5pm). See p.98.

Pasar Minggu, jalan Raja Muda Musa, Kampung Bharu (Sat 6pm–1am). See p.98.

Jalan Petaling, Chinatown (daily 9am–10pm). See p.93.

Pudu Market, bordered by jalan Yew, jalan Pasar and jalan Pudu, 2km southeast of the centre (Mon–Sat 8am–4pm). A massive market selling mostly food. Bus from Central Market.

Jalan TAR (Sat 7pm–2am). See p.97.

Batiks and handicrafts

Aked Ibu Kota, jalan TAR, opposite the *Coliseum*. A shopping centre on KL's busiest main street which sells local handicrafts, including batiks.

Batik Malaysia, corner of jalan Tun Perak and jalan Ampang. Large stock of batik cloth by the metre and a wide range of men's shirts, sarongs and Malay women's dresses, *baju kurung*.

Central Market, jalan Hang Kasturi. Some of the craftsmen work here, so you can buy batik clothing and handicrafts, like bags, caps, kites and masks which you've just watched being made.

Chin Li, 13 jalan Tun Mohammad. Stocks a wide range of painting, sculptures and finely made furniture at steep prices.

Karayenaka, jalan Raja Chulan, Golden Triangle. An arts and crafts centre which has recently closed down the demonstration houses showing the architecture of Malaysia's ethnic groups. It stocks a wide variety of sculpture, pictorial art and textiles, amongst others, but the prices are high.

Kutang Kraf Batik Factory, jalan Damansara. The best place to go to purchase batiks at warehouse prices. You'll need to take a taxi; it's west of the centre.

Jalan Masjid India, Little India. Excellent for sarees and other colourful Indian fabrics, and also religious paraphernalia, metalware and handicrafts from the Middle East, Indonesia and north Asia.

Wisma Batik, jalan Tun Perak. Offers a wide selection of shirts, sarongs, blouses, trousers, bags and local drawings and paintings, with prices cheaper than in the Central Market.

Pewter

Dai-Ichi Arts and Crafts, 122 mezanine floor, *Park Royal Hotel*, jalan Sultan Ismail. An impressive collection of highly priced pewter products.

Royal Selangor Pewter Factory, 4 jalan Usahawan, Sentul, 4km northeast of the centre. It's worth visiting in working hours (Mon–Fri 9am–6pm, Sat 9am–noon) to see how pewter is made. Take bus #167 or #169 from lebuh Ampang.

Shopping malls

BB Plaza, jalan Bukit Bintang, Golden Triangle. The mall with the most frequent sales; excellent deals on cameras, electronic equipment and shoes.

City Square, jalan Tun Razak. The *Metro* department store, Malaysia's most popular chainstore, has pride of place here, with brand-name clothing at reasonable prices and in Western sizes.

Imbi Plaza, jalan Imbi, Golden Triangle. Focuses on computers, with hard- and software on sale.

Lot 10 Shopping Centre, junction of jalan Bukit Bintang and jalan Sultan Ismail, Golden Triangle. KL's latest trendy shopping venue specializes in designer clothes, sportswear and music, and includes an outlet of the Japanese department store *Isetan*.

The Mall, jalan Putra. Besides the food centres in the basement and on the fourth floor, the main attraction is the Japanese store, *Yaohan*, on the first and second floors. It incorporates the best bookshop in the city and the widest range of designer clothing in KL.

Wisma Stephens, jalan Raja Chulan, Golden Triangle. A complex which includes bars, an art gallery, music stores, clothes shops and cafés.
Yuan Chuan Plaza, jalan Tun Razak. Specializes in arts and crafts, and also has a brace of clubs.

Listings

Airlines Most airlines have offices in and around the Golden Triangle. Major airlines include: *Aeroflot*, ground floor, 1 jalan Perak (☎261 3231); *American Airlines*, Angkasa Raya Building, 123 jalan Ampang (☎248 0644); *Bangladesh Airlines*, Subang Airport (☎746 1118); *British Airways*, Wisma Merlin, jalan Sultan Ismail (☎242 6177); *Cathay Pacific*, UBN Tower, 10 jalan P. Ramlee (☎238 3377); *China Airlines*, Level 3, Amoda Building, 22 jalan Imbi (☎242 2383); *Czechoslovak Airlines*, 12th floor, Plaza Atrium, 10 lorong P. Ramlee (238 0176); *Delta Airlines*, UBN Tower, 10 jalan P. Ramlee (☎232 4700); *Garuda*, 1st floor, Angkasa Raya Building, 123 jalan Ampang (☎248 2524); *Japan Airlines*, 1st floor, Pernas International Building, Lot 1157, jalan Sultan Ismail (☎261 1733); *KLM*, Shop 7, ground floor, President House, jalan Sultan Ismail (☎242 7011); *MAS*, MAS Building, jalan Sultan Ismail (☎261 0555); *Pelangi Air*, c/o *MAS* (☎262 4448); *Quantas*, UBN Tower, 10 jalan P. Ramlee (☎238 9133); *Royal Brunei*, 1st floor, Wisma Merlin, jalan Sultan Ismail (☎242 6511); *Singapore Airlines*, Wisma SIA, 2 jalan Sang Wangi (☎298 7033); *Thai International*, Kuwasa Building, 5 jalan Raja Laut (☎293 7100); *United Airlines*, MAS Building, jalan Sultan Ismail (☎261 1433).

Banks and exchange Leading bank HQs are: *Bank Bumiputra*, jalan Melaka; *Bank of America*, 1st floor, Wisma Stephens, jalan Raja Chulan; *Chase Mahattan*, 1st floor, Pernas International Building, jalan Sultan Ismail; *Hongkong Bank*, 2 lebuh Ampang; *Maybank*, 100 jalan Tun Perak; *Standard Chartered Bank*, 2 jalan Ampang; *United Malayan Banking Corporation*, UMBC Building, jalan Sultan Sulaiman. Almost all of their branches exchange money (Mon–Fri 10am–4pm, Sat 9am–12.30pm), but you get better rates from official moneychangers, of which there are scores in the main city areas; the kiosk below the General Post Office, on jalan Sultan Hishamuddin, also gives good rates.

Bookshops For English-language books try *Berita Book Centre*, Bukit Bintang Plaza; *MPH*, jalan Telawi Lima, Bangsar and at BB Plaza, jalan Bukit Bintang; *Times Books*, Yuah Chuan Plaza, jalan Ampang; *Minerva Book Store*, 114 jalan TAR; *Yaohan Book Store*, 2nd floor, The Mall, jalan Putra.

Car rental All main companies have offices at the aiport; or contact *Avis*, 40 jalan Sultan Ismail (☎242 3500); *Budget*, 163 jalan Ampang (☎261 1122); *Hertz*, 2nd floor, Antara Bangsa Complex (☎243 3433); *Mayflower-Acme Tours*, 18 jalan Segambut Pusat (☎626 7011); *National Car Rental*, 70 jalan Ampang (☎248 0522).

Embassies and consulates *Australia*, 6 jalan Yap Kwan Seng (☎242 3122); *Brunei*, 113 jalan U Thant (☎261 2860); *Canada* 7th floor, MBF PLaza, 172 jalan Ampang (☎261 2000); *Indonesia*, 233 jalan Tun Razak (☎984 2011); *Netherlands*, 4 jalan Mesra, off jalan Damai (☎243 1141); *New Zealand*, 193 jalan Tun Razak (☎248 6422); *Thailand*, 206 jalan Ampang (☎248 8222); *UK and Ireland*, 13th floor, Wisma Damanara, jalan Semantan (☎248 7122), Passport Office at 186 jalan Ampang (☎248 7122); *US*, 376 jalan Tun Razak (☎248 9011).

Emergencies Dial ☎999 for ambulance, police or fire. For the *Tourist Police Unit* call ☎241 5522 or ☎243 5522.

Hospitals and clinics *Assunta Hospital*, Petaling Jaya (☎792 3433); *Pantai*, jalan Pantai, off jalan Bangsar, Bangsar (☎757 5077); *Pudu Specialist Centre*, jalan Pudu (☎242 9146). There are 24-hour casualty wards at all of the above.

Immigration At 3rd floor, jalan Pantai Bahru, off jalan Damansara (Mon–Fri 9am–4.30pm; ☎757 8155). This is where you come for visa extensions.

Laundry Most hotels, guest houses and lodges will do your laundry for you for a few dollars.

Left-luggage office At Pudu Raya bus station, jalan Pudu (daily 8am–10pm; $2 per item).

Police The main city police station is in Chinatown at the southern end of jalan Tun H.S. Lee (☎232 5044), where you report stolen property and claim your insurance form.

Post office The GPO is on jalan Sultan Hishamuddin, opposite Central Market (Mon–Fri 8am–5pm, Sat 8am–midday); poste restante/general delivery mail comes here.

Sports Bowling at *Federal Bowl, Federal Hotel*, jalan Bukit Bintang (daily 10am–11pm; $10); golf at *Kelab Golf Negara*, Subang, near the airport (green fees $60–100); most large hotels have swimming pools though the only public one is at *Bangsar Sports Complex*, jalan Bangsar, Bangsar (daily 8am–10pm; $8 adults, $4 children; ☎254 6065), where there's also squash, tennis and badminton courts. Finally, play tennis at *Kelanga Sports Complex*, jalan Padan Belia, Brickfields (daily 8am–10pm; $12 an hour).

Taxis To call a cab, use one of the following numbers: *Comfort Radio Taxi Service* (☎733 0507); *Koteksi* (☎781 5352); *Radio Teksi* (☎442 0848).

Telephone offices The cheapest places to make international calls are the *Telekom Malaysia* offices dotted around the city. The largest is the one in Wisma Jothi, jalan Gereja; and there's also *Kedai Telekom*, at Subang International Airport; making calls from the major hotels costs at least 50 percent more.

Tour operators The larger tour operators listed here are all able to organize tailor-made adventure trips across Malaysia: *Angel Tours*, lower ground floor, City Tower, jalan Alor (☎241 7018); *Asian Overland Services*, 35 jalan Dewan Sultan Sulaiman (☎292 5637); *Borneo Travel*, Lot 36–37, The Arcade, *Hotel Equatorial*, jalan Sultan Ismail (☎261 2130); *Fairwind Travel*, Lot T, Sungei Wang Plaza, jalan Sultan Ismail (☎248 6920); *Insight Travel*, 9th floor, Plaza MBF, jalan Ampang (☎261 2488).

Travel agencies *MSL Travel*, Asia Hotel, 69 jalan Haji Hussein, (☎298 9722); *Reliance Travel*, 3rd floor, Sungei Wang Plaza, (☎248 6022); *Semestra Travel*, 52 jalan Bulan, jalan Bukit Bintang (☎243 4802); *Tina Travel*, 1st floor, *Holiday Inn*, jalan Raja Laut (☎457 8877).

AROUND KL

The biggest attractions around KL are north of the city, where limestone peaks rise up out of the forest and the roads narrow as you pass through small *kampungs*. There's dramatic scenery as close as 13km from the city, where the Hindu shrine at **Batu Caves** attracts enough visitors to make it one of Malaysia's main tourist attractions. Further north, **Templer Park** encompasses the nearest portion of primary rainforest to the capital, while some distance beyond – 50km northeast of KL – the much-hyped **Genting Highlands** is the first, and least inspiring, of the country's hill stations.

Frankly, if you've visited the northern hills, you've seen the best of the countryside surrounding the city. Travelling southwest along Route 2 into the state of Selangor, you enter one of the most polluted and ugliest parts of Malaysia, with much of the **Klang Valley** from KL to Klang itself resembling a vast building site with half-built structures marooned in seas of gashed earth and puddles of water. Three towns spread along the valley, all effectively outsize satellites of KL. At **Petaling Jaya** (PJ), a large conurbation easily the size of central KL, the renowned restaurants and nightlife attract locals and visitors out from the capital. The National Mosque at adjacent **Shah Alam** is the biggest in Southeast Asia and you can combine a visit here with the neighbouring agricultural park, an interesting blend of environmental protection, educational displays and commercial good sense. Perhaps the most alluring single destination, though, is Selangor's first capital, **Klang**, whose old centre retains a warehouse now turned into a fascinating tin museum and one of the country's most atmospheric mosques.

Finally, northwest of the city, close to **Kuala Selangor**, itself a historic town of some repute, the coastal **Kuala Selangor Nature Park** and the spectacle of the nearby fireflies might tempt those with time to spare, although these are tricky destinations to reach by bus and you'll need either a rented car or taxi.

See the map on p.76 for the location of destinations around Kuala Lumpur.

The telephone code for KL and its environs is ☎03.

Batu Caves

Long before you reach the entrance to the **BATU CAVES**, you can see them ahead: small, black holes in the vast limestone thumbs which comprise a ridge of hills 13km north of the city centre. The caves were first discovered by the American explorer William Hornaby, and ten years later, in 1891, local Indian dignitaries convinced the British colonial authorities that the caves were ideal for worship. Soon devotees were visiting the caves in ever increasing numbers to pay homage to the shrine established here to Lord Muruga – better known as **Lord Subramaniam**. The temple complex was later expanded to include a shrine to the elephant-headed deity **Ganesh**, while today the caves and shrines are surrounded, too, by the full panoply of religious commercialism, with shops selling Hindu idols, pamplets, bracelets, postcards and cassettes. The caves are incredibly popular, and always packed with visitors, but the numbers most days are nothing compared to the hundreds of thousands of devotees who descend here during the three-day Thaipusam festival (see box over page) held at the beginning of every year.

The caves are just off the old Gombak road, which branches off from jalan Pahang beyond Lake Titiwangsa – catch **minibus** #11 from the Pertama Shopping Centre or blue **buses** #68 or #70 from lebuh Ampang in Chinatown, for the forty-minute journey. On the way, the bus passes **Pak Ali's House** (daily 9am–6pm, $3), a good example of a traditional Malay stilt house, common in Kuala Lumpur in the early years of the century. It was built in 1917, using timber hewn from the nearby jungle, its verandah, stairs and roof carved with opulent shapes and ornate designs. You'll get a fleeting view from the bus.

During Thaipusam, extra buses operate services to the caves and it's advisable to get there early – say 7am – for a good view of the proceedings. Although there are numerous cafés at the caves, you should also take plenty of water and snacks with you as the crowds are horrendous.

The caves

To the left of the 272-step brick staircase which leads up to the main Temple Cave, follow a small path to the so-called **Museum Cave**, which contains dozens of striking multicoloured statues of deities, portraying scenes from the Hindu scriptures. As well as these dioramas – including a naked goddess astride a five-headed snake, flanked by figures with goats' heads carrying tools – flamboyant murals line the damp walls of the cave: jungle settings, mythic battles and abstract designs.

After climbing to the top of the stairs there's a clear view through to the **Subramaniam Swamy Temple** (daily 6.30am–10pm), set deep in a large cave around one hundred metres high and eighty metres deep, and illuminated by shafts of light from gaps in the ceiling high above. The cave walls are lined with idols which represent the six lives of Lord Subramaniam and in the small inner temple, devoted to Lord Subramaniam and the deity Rama, a dome is densely sculpted with more scenes from the scriptures. Two figures stand guard at its entrance, their index fingers pointing upwards towards the light. In a chamber at the back of the temple, the statue of Rama, who watches over the well-being of all immigrants, is adorned with silver jewellery and a silk sarong. If you want to look closely at the inner sanctum, the temple staff will mark a small red dot on your forehead, thus giving you a spiritual right to enter.

THAIPUSAM AT BATU CAVES

The most important festival in the Malaysian Hindu calendar, **Thaipusam** honours the Hindu deity Lord Subramaniam. Originally a Tamil festival from southern India, it's a day of penance and celebration, held during full moon in the month of "Thai" (between Jan 15 and Feb15), when huge crowds arrive at Batu Caves – a site chosen a century ago as centre for the devotions probably because its spectacular geography was thought to be reminiscent of the sacred Himalayas. What was originally intended to be a day of penance for past sins has now become a major tourist attraction, with both Malaysians and foreigners flocking to the festival every year.

Thaipusam starts with the early morning passage of a golden chariot bearing a statue of Subramaniam which makes a slow procession from KL's Sri Mahamariamman Temple to the caves, with thousands of devotees following on foot. The trip takes around seven hours and, after reaching the caves, the statue is placed in a tent before being carried up to the temple cave by the devotees. As part of their penance – and in a trance-like state – the devotees carry numerous types of *kavadi* ("burdens" in Tamil), the most popular being milk jugs decorated with peacock feathers placed on top of the head, which are connected to the penitents' flesh by hooks. Others wear wooden frames with sharp spikes protruding from them which are carried on the back and hooked into the skin; trident-shaped skewers are placed through some devotees' tongues and cheeks. This rather grisly procession – which only now occurs in Malaysia, Singapore and Thailand – has its origins in India, where most of Lord Subramaniam's temples were sited on high ridges, up which devotees would walk, carrying heavy pitchers or pots to honour the deity. At Batu, climbing the 272 steps up to the main chamber signifies the fact that it is not easy to reach God without expending effort.

Once in the temple cave the devotees participate in ceremonies and rituals to Subramanian and Ganesh, finishing with a celebration for Rama, when the milk from the *kavadi* bowl can be spilt as an offering – incense and camphor is burned as the bearers unload their devotional burdens. The festival takes many hours to complete and the atmosphere becomes so highly charged that police are needed to line the stairs and protect the onlookers from the entranced *kavadi*-bearers and their instruments of self-flagellation.

Templer Park

Another 10km or so north of the Batu Caves, **TEMPLER PARK** (daily 8am–6pm; free) makes a great day out from the city, boasting a number of beautiful waterfalls, small trails and abundant bird life. Opened in the 1950s, and named after Sir Gerald Templer (the last of Malaya's British High Commissioners), it's the closest you'll get to primary rainforest if you haven't got time to visit the state parks in the interior. Coming from the city, take bus #66 from Pudu Ray bus station; the trip takes a little over an hour and costs around $1.50. Alternatively, you can combine the park with a trip to the Batu Caves, from where you catch the #11 minibus out to the main Ipoh road and then wait for the the blue Tanjung Malim bus (#66), which originates at Pudu Raya bus station.

The park is at its busiest at weekends, when trippers arrive from the capital, but you don't need to make too much of an effort to escape the crowds. The park covers 300 acres of primary forest, dominated by a belt of limestone outcrops set into a valley which cuts through the hills for five kilometres. A narrow road winds from the entrance to an artificial lake, 300m to the east, before shrinking to a narrow path, which snakes up into the forest. This trail leads back and forth across the shallow, five-metre-wide sungei Templer, reaching a dramatic waterfall after an hour's walk. From there you can follow the riverside path through primary jungle for another hour or so, but you'll have to return by the same route. An alternative is to leave the main path on a trail to the left of the waterfall, from where a one-hour trek hugs the edge of the hillside and later meets the concrete road near the park entrance. Other paths snake up into the forested hills and pass natural swimming lagoons and waterfalls. The highest point is **Bukit Takun** (740m) which rises on the western side of the river in the northern corner of the park. Few animals can now be seen in the park, as what's left of the jungle here is surrounded by development, which has frightened off much of the wildlife.

The park authorities permit **camping**, although there isn't an official campsite, or any toilets, washing or cooking facilities – as long as you're prepared to rough it, it's a rewarding experience.

The Orang Asli Museum

Like Templer Park, KL's **Orang Asli Museum** (Mon–Thurs & Sun 9am–5.30pm; free) holds a certain interest if this is as far into rural Malaysia as you're going to get. Located 24km north of the city, the museum, which is organized and run by the government-sponsored Centre for Orang Asli Affairs, provides a fine illustration of the cultural richness and demographic variety of the *orang asli* (Malay for "the first people") – Malaysia's indigenous inhabitants (see *Basics*, p.55). As you enter the unobtrusive timber building, a large map of west Malaysia shows that the separate *orang asli* groups are found, in varying numbers, in just about every part the country, which may well surprise visitors who often see little sign of them during their travels. Many of the *orang asli* maintain a virtually pre-industrial lifestyle – some still rely on blowpipes for hunting – and pursue their traditional occupations in some isolation, whether it's hunting and gathering in the fast-depleting forests, fishing along the increasingly polluted Johor coastline, or carving their extraordinary handicrafts. Partly, too, it's believed that the *orang asli* try to keep out of the way because they see their cultures are under threat, and too much exposure to modern Malaysia is likely to do them more harm than good.

Although the museum is small, an awful lot is crammed into it. There's an explanation of the incidence of the various groups of *orang asli*, while various displays vividly portray the tools of their trade – from fishing nets and traps to guns and blowpipes. More interesting, hidden in an annexe, are examples of traditional handicrafts including the **head carvings** made by the Mah Meri tribe, from the swampy region on the borders of Selangor and Negeri Sembilan, and the Jah Hut, from the slopes of Gunung Benom in central Pehang; the carvings are around half a metre high and fashioned from a particularly strong, heavy hardwood. They still have religious significance – the central image used, the animist deity Moyang, represents the spirit of the ancestors – and are prevalent in contemporary religious ceremonies, when the masks are worn during dances honouring a pantheon of gods. The *orang asli's* animist religion is influenced by early Hindu beliefs, and the carvings here show similiarities with those of some Hindu deities. At the far end of the museum's main room are photographs of *orang asli* militias commandeered by the government to fight the Communist guerillas in the 1950s (for more, see p.000), while other displays describe the changes forced on the *orang asli* over the past thirty years – some positive, like the eradication of serious disease and the development of health and school networks, others less encouraging, including the disintegration of the family system as the young men drift off to look for seasonal work.

Blue **bus** #174 leaves lebuh Ampang in Chinatown every thirty minutes, and the fifty-minute trip along the old Gombak road pases the International Islamic University and the *Mimaland Amusement Park*. The museum is the second stop after the park, where two run-down shops are located, and the entrance is 50m to the right along a narrow, steep road (ask the driver to tell you when you've arrived as it's not obvious). For the return trip, wait outside the shops for the bus.

The Genting Highlands

Of the three hill stations located on the western side of the Banjaran Titwangsa mountain range north of KL, the **GENTING HIGHLANDS** is the odd one out. Whereas visits to Fraser's Hill (p.121) or the Cameron Highlands (p.127) revolve around short treks, visits to waterfalls and a fair degree of colonial tranquillity, Genting – 50km northeast of the city – can be stress-inducing in the extreme. Although the highlands themselves are eminently attractive – something that's obvious from the journey there, as the bus zig-zags its way gingerly up the road – upon arrival you're deposited at a brain-numbingly noisy, concrete resort, perched on top of the hill, where the focus of attention is a quadrangle of high-rise hotels, with their shopping arcades and restaurants. An exclusive golf course is the only "green" recreation the hill station has to offer and you'd be hard pushed to find any trails reaching out from the hotels. Before the early 1980s, when the development began, the whole area was covered in forest, but now Malaysians flock here from the city in their thousands to frequent the only casino in the country and to spoil their families in the fast-food outlets and swimming pools.

On the way up to the top, the bus passes the *Awana Golf Club and Country Resort* on the right; to the left, a **cable car** (every 20min, Mon 12.15–8.30pm, Tues–Sun 8.30am–9.30pm; $5) offers an alternative and precipitous journey up the remaining few kilometres to the resort hotel at the top. By bus, you are deposited in the bowels of the eighteen-storey *Genting Highlands Resort Hotel* (☎211 1118; ⑥), where one-armed bandits and computer games vie for your attention. Two floors above is the **Casino** (open 24hr; minimum age 21), where the chips start at ten dollars; outside, 20m from the concrete forecourt which is usually full of exhaust-belching buses, there's a **swimming pool** and a small area set aside for picnicking. There are two other hotels beside the resort hotel, *The Pelangi* (☎211 2812; ⑤) and *The Highlands* (☎211 2812; ⑤), both of which also have overpriced restaurants. There's no budget accommodation, though rooms at *The Pelangi* sometimes drop to vaguely affordable rates during midweek.

Transport here is by the Genting **bus** from either the Pudu Raya (tickets from booth 43) or Pekeliling stations, (every 30min 6.30am–10.30pm; journey time 1hr; $5). Getting a seat on a return bus can be hard, and often involves competing for space with a crowd of young Malaysians – get to the stop at the *Genting Highlands Resort Hotel* early. You can take a share taxi for $40 per taxi from the second floor at Pudu Raya.

The Klang Valley

Three hundred years before KL was founded, the **Klang Valley** – southwest of the modern capital – was one of the most important regions in Malaysia, the sultans of Selangor based at the royal town of **Klang**. In the late nineteenth century, with the discovery of new tin deposits further inland, Klang lost its importance but the valley remained ripe for development as KL expanded rapidly. The first road linking Klang to KL wasn't built until the 1920s – previously all goods were carried along a narrow horse track, or went by river – but a decade later, the railway line between the two towns came into existence and was only abandoned in the late 1980s. These days, transport is along Route 2, which cuts from the capital to the coast, running through the modern satellite towns of **Petaling Jaya** and **Shah Alam**. If you're based in KL, you may fancy a day out in these parts, though each destination in itself isn't of huge interes. Note, though, that the ferries to Sumatra from **Port Klang**, 8km southwest of Klang, provide another reason for making the trip.

Petaling Jaya

PETALING JAYA, or PJ as it's known locally, is 12km southwest of the city centre, covering a sprawling area divided into 25 different planned sections. Originally conceived as an overspill suburb for KL, it provided low-cost, modern housing for those who flocked to the city to find work in the 1970s when the Malaysian economy began rapidly to expand. Now it's very nearly a separate city, with a manufacturing base rooted in electronics, computers and textiles, and a population of several hundred thousand, and while this is of no intrinsic interest to visitors, KL's cash-rich middle class come out here to eat in PJ's swanky restaurants and sample the booming nightlife; some of the best places are covered below.

The town is split into sections, the main ones being "State", "Damansara Utama" and the Orwellesque "Section 2" (or SS2). **State** is the closest thing PJ has to a municipal centre and boasts an enormous Civic Centre, which stages large-scale concerts and exhibitions, and a high-quality eating area along jalan Penchala, famous among locals for its excellent Chinese cuisine. **SS2** is probably the most interesting section for foreign visitors, its *pasar malam* – held on Mondays around a massive square known locally as "glutton square" – the most extensive in the whole of KL. Here, you'll find hawkers selling *satukeping*: delicious pancakes layered with brown sauce and shredded vegetables. Later at night, the focus shifts to **Damansara Utama**, a massive rectangular spread of shopfronts incorporating dozens of restaurants and nightclubs along its four sides, which stay open until 4am over the weekend.

Practicalities

From KL, **minibuses** #28, #30, #33 and #35 from Klang bus station (every 10min), run to State in about twenty minutes, where you change for buses to other sections of town. Addresses in PJ can be confusing at first glance, though once you appreciate that the city was planned on a grid system, and that streets have numbers and not names, you're halfway there.

PJ's main **eating** area is based around the hawker stalls at SS2, upon which hundreds of people descend from dusk until 2am, grazing on a mix of foods including burgers, pizza and Korean food, but also with plenty of Chinese and Malay noodle and rice dishes too. For specific restaurants, Damansara Utama is the place: *Baluchi's*, at 3 jalan SS21/60, is a high-quality north Indian restaurant, with excellent chicken tikka and masalas, and superb naans; just beside it, the huge *Mahligai's Vegetarian Chinese* caters mostly for family groups, with good food costing around $30 for two.

Most of the **nightlife** is in Damansara Utama, too. *All That Jazz*, at 14 jalan 19/36 (open 8am–3pm; $20; ☎755 3152), is a favourite watering hole for PJ sophisticates, with live jazz, while the *Longhorn Pub* (7pm–2am; free, $10 after 11pm), is KL's foremost country and western spot, where local groups perform the classics. All the really big acts which make it to Malaysia usually play at the **PJ Civic Centre**, jalan Penchala, in State (☎757 1211), a state-of-the-art venue which puts on rock and classical concerts, musicals and exhibitions.

Shah Alam and around

Further downvalley, **SHAH ALAM**, designated the state capital of Selangor in 1982, is still in the process of being completed. Much of its ultra-modern centre is generally devoid of interest, the only exception being the stunning **Sultan Salahuddin Abdul Aziz Shah Mosque** (10am–noon & 2–4pm; closed Fri). Completed in 1988 at a cost of $162 million, this is the largest mosque in Southeast Asia, a vast complex incorporating massive blue marble pillars and set in acres of shining concrete and glistening water –

the prayer hall alone can hold 16,000 people. The 92-metre-high dome was designed by computer and has a striking blue and white design, its main panels emblazoned with Koranic inscriptions. The dome itself is porous – when rain falls between the joints of the outer panels, it's collected in a special channel, from which the water then flows into a storage tank and is pumped up into one of the four minarets. Worshippers taking their ablutions before prayers trigger the flow of water from the tank by breaking a photo-electric beam.

To visit the mosque, women must wear a *tudong* (plain headscarf) and a long dress or trousers, and men long-sleeved shirts and long trousers. Take any Shah Alam bus from KL's Klang bus station, which leave every thirty minutes; you'll need to ask for the mosque, though most services will drop you right outside; it's just 1km from the centre.

The Agricultural Park

Three kilometres west of Sham Alam, the **Bukit Cahaya Sri Alam Agricultural Park** (daily 8am–6pm; free) presents traditional Malaysian agrarian activities in a beautiful natural setting. It's aimed particularly at school groups, but it doesn't make a bad day out if you can summon up any enthusiasm at all for tropical horticulture and agro-forestry. Four roads fan out from the **park headquarters** (daily 8am–6pm; ☎550 6922), where you can pick up a map and brochures describing the park activities. The road going northeast leads past a rice field, an aviary and mushroom, spice and orchid gardens, to a dam and a freshwater fish-breeding centre. North, there's a campsite and another dam, from where there is a short, well-signposted pathway leading into primary jungle. Other roads lead to food stalls, an open-air theatre, insect house, a tropical fruits plantation, and even a small *orang asli* village – whose inhabitants no longer pursue a traditional lifestyle. You can **camp** or rent **chalets** in the park (park headquarters has the details), though in truth you'd do better at almost any minor stop in the interior.

Hourly buses – either the #338 or #222 from Klang bus station (around $4) – take eighty minutes to reach the park. The bus drops you within sight of the park entrance, with the headquarters a further ten minutes' walk beyond. Coming back, either walk back outside the park to the main road and wait for the #338 or #222, or catch the (less regular) Shah Alam town bus, which leaves from next to the park HQ and runs to the PNKS Complex in Shah Alam, from where the #222 or #206 run on to KL.

Klang

The highway that runs the length of the Klang Valley comes to a final stop in **KLANG**, 30km southwest of KL. As erstwhile royal seat and historic capital of Selangor state, Klang is hundreds of years older than KL, and from the early sixteenth century onwards was at the centre of one of the most important tin-producing areas in Malaysia, its development inextricably bound up with the gradual expansion of tin production. But in this was sown the seeds of its own decline, since it was from Klang that the expedition up the Klang river to seek new tin deposits was organized, which led to the founding of Kuala Lumpur in the 1850s (see p.77). In 1880, KL superseded Klang as state capital (more than a century later it moved again to Shah Alam) and the old river port ceased to have any political or ceremonial importance.

Although still a bustling, commercial centre, with fishing its main industry these days, Klang's historic buildings – the tin museum, the mosque, the government offices and the old Istana – reflect a more dignified, graceful past, where the call to prayer dictated the pace of life. Most of these buildings are found in the **old quarter** of town – to get there, follow the main road past the bus station and cross the bridge over the Klang river. Immediately below you, on your right, is the Gedung Rajah Abdullah, an old tin warehouse built in 1856 and now housing the **National Tin Museum** (9am–4pm except Fri 9am–noon & 2.45–4pm; free) within its black sloping roof and white-washed walls. The warehouse was built by Rajah Abdullah – the Sultan of Selangor's son – both as a home and storehouse for the tin he owned; it was at Abdullah's prompting that the pioneers rafted their way up the Klang river in 1857 to look for new sources of tin. As well as an extensive photographic record detailing the history of tin and the town, the museum contains examples of currency made from tin, including tortoise-shaped ingots, and various pieces of production equipment; try and catch the hourly video show, which briefly covers the history of tin production in the region.

To reach the Istana and mosque follow jalan Besar, which runs under the bridge opposite the museum, deeper into the old part of Klang. The road passes well-maintained Chinese terraced shops and cafés, before reaching the main street, jalan Istana, which leads to the nineteenth-century **Istana**, another 200m to the north. As is usual, you can only visit the magnificent palace during the two-day Hari Raya festival, but the walk up the road past the well-tended plants, trees and flowerbeds, offers a ravishing prospect, its main golden spire gleaming in the sun. If you return the way you came and take the first right onto jalan Kota Raja, which passes the padang, ten minutes' further on is Klang's mosque, the intimate **Masjid Sultan Suleiman**. Its seven yellow domes and grey stone outer walls are marvellously atmospheric: low, arched entrances set into the walls lead into narrow passages, where the worshippers sit and read the Koran, and onwards into the inner prayer room, whose stained-glass windows provide a luminous light.

Practicalities

There are hourly **buses** – the #51, #58 or #225 – from Klang bus station in KL, which take an hour to reach Klang. If you don't want to return directly to the capital, services from Klang's bus station head north on Route 5 to Kuala Selangor and its nature park (see below) – though realistically, given the paucity of facilities in both towns, you're only going to continue in this direction if you have your own transport.

On to Indonesia

Most Klang buses continue on the 8km to **PORT KLANG**, from whose jetty comfortable air-conditioned **boats** leave two or three times a week to Belawan in Indonesia. From the bus stop it's 200 metres to the *Sea View* restaurant at the port, with the boat ticket offices just to the right and the port entrance to the left. There are money changers by the *Sea View*, though none apparent at Belawan. **Tickets** to Belawan cost around $120 one-way, $220 return and the price includes the onward bus journey at the other end to Medan. If you're stuck in Port Klang for a while, apart from the *Sea View* there's also the *Restoran Sri Thanakshmi Villas*, opposite the bus stop, which serves excellent *masala dosai*.

Kuala Selangor and around

The other main target around KL is the former strategic royal town of **KUALA SELANGOR**, 67km to the northwest, lying on the banks of sungei Selangor. Today, the town is no more than one main street of two-storey concrete buildings and is really only worth a stop if you're on your way to either of the local natural attractions (see below). All that remains of Kuala Selangor's more glorious past are the remnants of two forts overlooking the town, the largest of which, **Fort Altingberg** (daily 9am–4.30pm; free), recalls a period in Malaysian history when this part of the country changed hands, bloodily, on several occasions. Originally called Fort Melawati, Altingberg was built by local people during the reign of Sultan Ibrahim of Selangor in the eighteenth century, but was later captured by the Dutch (who renamed it) as part of an attempt to wrestle the tin trade from the sultans. Later, the fortress was partly destroyed during local skirmishes in the Selangor Civil War (1867–73). The fort is now a museum, the exhibits comprising a cannon and an execution block as well as other military bric-a-brac.

Kuala Selangor is reached on hourly bus #141 from bay 23 at Pudu Raya bus station; the ninety-minute trip costs around $4.

Kuala Selangor Nature Park

Eight kilometres southeast of from Kuala Selangor by road – although directly below the fort – is the **KUALA SELANGOR NATURE PARK** (daily 8am–7pm), opened in 1987. Among the different habitats in this reclaimed mangrove swamp are mud flats, lakes and a small patch of forest which holds around 130 species of bird, with thirty more passing along the coastline annually. This is the only site in Malaysia, for example, where the Spoonbilled Sandpiper has been sighted. Silver leaf monkeys live in the forest while along the coast the mangroves provide a home for a variety of crabs and fish.

There are several clearly marked **trails** in the park, but none are more than a few hundred metres long. **Accommodation** here ranges from sturdy A-frame tents for around $15, to small two-bed chalets for $30, either of which can be booked through the *Malayan Nature Society* (☎791 2185), although it's possible to reserve once you've arrived, if there's room; call in at the warden's house. Weekends are always busy. Buses run here up Route 5 from Klang; get off the bus 8km before Kuala Selangor on at the *Mobil* station and follow jalan Klinik 200m to the park entrance.

The fireflies

Most people make the trip to Kuala Selangor to see the **luminous fireflies** which glow spectacularly in the early evening along the banks of the Selangor river, around 8km inland of Kuala Selangor itself, at a small village called **KAMPUNG KUANTAN**. For $10 each, visitors are taken out in boats and rowed upriver for forty minutes to observe the extraordinary fireflies and glow-worms, which have developed a striking synchronized flashing pattern. They are found glowing from the riverbank foliage either singly or in groups; most leave the trees at dawn and are found in grass blades until around an hour before dusk.

There's no public transport to Kampung Kuantan, and you'll have to take a taxi which will cost around $100 from KL, or $50 from Kuala Selangor, for the return trip.

travel details

All departures given below are from Kuala Lumpur; for terminals, see p.81

Buses

North

Alor Setar (9 daily; 9hr); Butterworth (every 30min; 7hr); Cameron Highlands (hourly; 4hr 30min); Ipoh (every 30min; 4hr); Kampar (4 daily; 4hr); Kuala Kedah (6 daily; 8hr); Kuala Perlis (6 daily; 9hr); Lumut (6 daily; 4hr); Penang (every 30min; 8hr); Taiping (9 daily; 5hr).

South

Johor Bahru (5 daily; 6hr); Melaka (every 30min; 2hr); Muar (4 daily; 3hr); Seremban (8 daily; 1hr); Singapore (7 daily; 7hr); Tanjong Bidara (3 daily; 2hr).

East Coast and Interior

Genting Highlands (every 30min; 1hr); Kuala Kuba Bharu (8 daily; 2hr); Kuala Lipis (4 daily; 4hr); Kota Bharu (7 daily; 10hr); Kuala Terengganu (3 daily; 7hr); Kuantan (every 30min; 5hr); Mersing (1 daily; 8hr); Temerloh (every 30min; 3hr).

Trains

Kuala Lumpur to: Alor Setar (4 daily; 10hr); Butterworth (4 daily; 8hr); Gemas (5 daily; 4hr); Ipoh (4 daily; 3hr);Johor Bahru (4 daily; 6hr); Padang Besar (4 daily; 12hr); Seremban (4 daily; 1hr 30min); Singapore (4 daily; 6hr 30min); Tapah Road (4 daily; 2hr).

Flights

Kuala Lumpur to: Alor Setar (6 daily; 50min); Ipoh (5 daily; 35min); Johor Bahru (8 daily; 45min); Kota Bharu (6 daily; 50min); Kuala Terengganu (2 daily; 45min); Kuantan (4 daily; 40min); Langkawi (4 daily; 55min); Penang (18 daily; 45min); Singapore (18 daily; 55min).

CHAPTER TWO

THE WEST COAST

T he **west coast** of the Malaysian peninsula, from Kuala Lumpur north to the Thai border, is the most industrialized and densely populated – not to mention cosmopolitan – part of the whole country. Its considerable natural resources have long brought eager traders and entrepreneurs here, but it was the demand for the region's tin in the late nineteenth century that spearheaded Malaysia's phenomenal economic rise. Immigrant workers, most of whom settled in the region for good, bestowed a permanent legacy in the predominantly Chinese towns that punctuate the route north. **Perak** state – once boasting the richest single tin field in the world – and its capital, the old tin-boom city of Ipoh, are still littered with historical reminders of the recent industrial past. But even when the light industry surrounding Malaysia's other major commodity, rubber, took over from the dying tin trade in the 1950s, it didn't quite obliterate the essentially agricultural nature of much of the region. The state of **Kedah**, along with **Perlis**, tucked into the northern border, shares the distinction of being the historical *jelapang padi*, or "rice bowl", of Malaysia, where rich, emerald paddy fields are disturbed only by the jutting limestone outcrops that form the peninsula's most dramatic scenery.

This, too, is the area in which the **British** held most sway, attracted by the political prestige of controlling such a strategic trading region. Although they had claimed administrative authority since 1826 in the Straits Settlements (which included Singapore and Melaka as well as Penang) it was the establishment here of the Federated Malay States (of Perak, Pahang, Selangor and Negeri Sembilan), fifty years later, that gave the British the opportunity to extend their grasp over the whole peninsula.

Despite the rich heritage on show, most visitors are too intent on the beckoning delights of Thailand to bother stopping at anything other than the major destinations. Nowhere are the rural delights of the country more prominent than at the **hill stations** north of KL, originally designed as cool retreats for colonial administrators. **Fraser's Hill** is closest to the capital, though it's easily overshadowed by **Cameron Highlands**, 95km further north, Malaysia's largest hill station and one of the most significant tourist spots in the country. Both are justifiably popular mountain retreats, providing the opportunity for forest treks and indulging in the traditionally English comforts of crackling log fires and cream teas.

Due west, tiny **Pulau Pangkor**, whilst falling short of the idyll promised by the islands of the peninsula's east coast, is nevertheless an increasingly visited resort, sporting the best beaches in the area. But the fastest development is on its far northern rival, **Pulau Langkawi**, the largest island in the glittering and largely unpopulated Langkawi archipelago. Most travellers wisely give the port of **Butterworth**, the transportation hub for the whole region, a wide berth, using it merely for access to the island of **Penang**, whose vibrant capital **Georgetown** combines modern shopping malls with ancient Chinese shophouses, and whose beaches still continue to draw the crowds in spite of superior competition elsewhere.

These main sights aside, there's a whole host of intriguing and under-visited places off the beaten track, like **Ipoh**, 200km north of Kuala Lumpur, which proclaims its erstwhile prosperity with elegant colonial buildings and mansions at every turn, and its northern neighbour, the royal town of **Kuala Kangsar**, a place of quiet architectural pleasures. The route north also passes through the old mining town of **Taiping**, whose small hill station, **Maxwell Hill**, is now fading gently into insignificance. State capital of Kedah is **Alor Setar**, the last major town before the border (and the last significant stop other than Pualu Langkawi). Long a stamping ground for successive invaders, the region still reveals a Thai influence in its cuisine, although Alor Setar itself is a staunch Muslim stronghold. From here it's a short hop from any of the **border towns** – Kuala Perlis, Kangar and Arau – into Thailand itself.

Because of its economic importance, the west coast is the most well-connected part of the country. The newly completed **North–South Highway**, pristine and little used, virtually shadows the already adequate **Route 1**, running from Singapore all the way to Malaysia's northern border at Bukit Kayu Hitam. The **train line**, which runs more or less parallel to these roads, is less utilised, though its border crossing at Padang Besar at least facilitates easy connections with Hat Yai, the transportation crossroads of southern Thailand. Both roads and train line pass through all the major towns – Ipoh, Taiping, Butterworth and Alor Setar – with **express buses** providing the backbone of the services, while **local buses** maintain a link with the hills and the coast.

Fraser's Hill

The buildings and facilities strung across **FRASER'S HILL** – actually seven hills – 1500m up in the Titiwangsa mountain range, were erected to provide welcome relief for the British expatriate community from humid Kuala Lumpur, 100km to the southwest. Its origins, though, were slightly more mysterious, linked to the economic expansion engendered by the finding of KL in the 1860s. The seven hills which comprise the hill station were originally known as *Ulu Tras*, a name soon abandoned with the arrival of a solitary English pioneer, called James Fraser, in the 1890s. An accountant by profession, he had travelled to Australia at the peak of its gold rush and then on to Malaya, and although gold wasn't found in any quantity in the hills here, Fraser did find plentiful **tin** deposits. This was excavated by Chinese miners and then hauled by mules through thick jungle along a perilous hill route down to the nearest town, Raub, where Fraser set up a camp and a gambling den on one of the hills for his workers. But after 25 years Fraser mysteriously disappeared and when a search party trekked up into the area to look for him in 1917, the camp and mines were deserted. However, the excellent location recommended itself to the party, who soon convinced the British authorities that it would make a perfect hill station.

It was never as popular as the much larger Cameron Highlands to the north and even today there are less than one hundred dwellings in the region. The surrounding mountainous jungle provided perfect cover for some of the Communist guerillas' secret

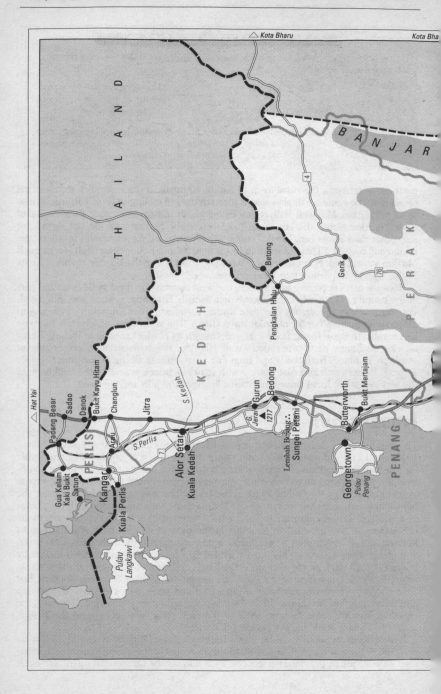

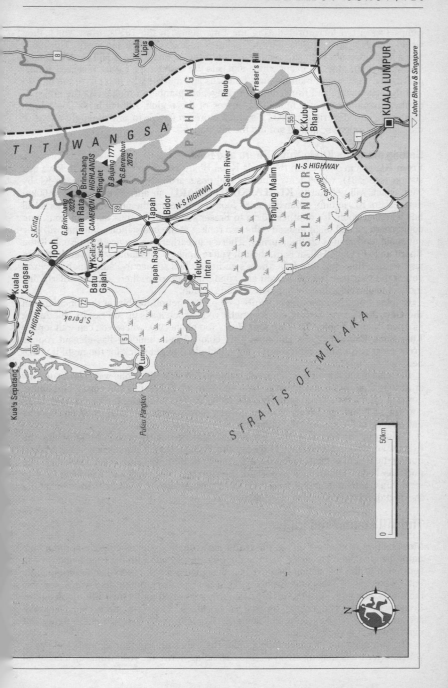

camps (see p.196 for more) during the Emergency in the 1950s, from which they would launch strikes on British-owned plantations and neighbouring towns. The 1960s saw a kind of revival with the establishment of the annual Fraser's Hill Bird Watching Festival, held in May, an event which still sets the tone for the rather reserved atmosphere here. Visitors are mainly Kuala Lumpans and tourists who don't have the time to visit the state parks, and they come in manageable numbers which eases the pressure on the environmental and human resources of the region. Although it's possible to come here on a day trip from KL, it's much more preferable to stay the night at one of the hotels or lodges scattered around the hill station.

Getting there: via Kuala Kubu Bharu and Raub

From KL, you need to catch the Kuala Kubu Bharu bus from bay 21 at Pudu Raya bus station (see p.81), which leaves hourly and costs around $3.50. Aim to leave KL by 9am, which will get you to **KUALA KUBU BHARU**, an attractive small town 60km northeast of KL, in time to have a quick look round before the up-country Fraser's Hill bus leaves at noon. It's another 40km to Fraser's Hill and the bus takes an hour; you could charter a taxi ($35) instead – the taxi rank is at the bus station – but that will only cut about ten minutes off the journey. There's an earlier bus service from Kuala Kubu Bharu up to Fraser's Hill, at 8am, though you're unlikely to want to stay overnight here just to catch this; if all else fails, there's an hourly bus service to Raub which can drop you at the Gap (see below). If you are killing time in town, there's a particularly fine Indian Muslim café, directly opposite the bus station.

Coming from the interior, via **Raub** (see p.212), get off the bus at the junction with **the Gap**, the narrow, twisting ten-kilometre road which leads up to Fraser's Hill. At the junction, there's a hotel, *The Gap Rest House* (no phone; ①), where you can wait for the Kota Kubu Bahru–Fraser's Hill bus. This colonial-style building has elegant rooms, great views and a fine dining room – not a bad place to get stuck for the night if needs be.

Because of the size of the Gap road, traffic to Fraser's Hill is one-way – up or down – at various times of the day between 6am and 8pm: up to Fraser's Hill during odd hours, down at even hours. Overnight, though, between 8pm and 6am, the road's open to all comers, so if you are driving at night go very slowly since you might well meet someone coming in the opposite direction.

Halfway up the Gap road you'll see a sign, "Emergency Historical Site", marking the exact spot where **Sir Henry Gurney**, the British High Commissioner for Malaya during the height of the Communist insurgency in 1951, was ambushed and killed. The guerillas hadn't known how important their quarry was; their aim had been only to steal guns, ammunition and food, but when Gurney strode towards them demanding they put down their weapons, they opened fire.

The hill station and trails

Most visitors want to get out on the **trails** fairly quickly, and since none of them take more than two hours to cover, you can negotiate every one within a couple of days – in fact much of the hill station territory is a designated forest reserve and consequently out of bounds to the general public. This isn't primary jungle and you'll see few mammals, although Fraser's Hill is particularly renowned for its **bird life** – look out for flycatchers and woodpeckers, as well as hornbills. There's a more comprehensive account of the region's flora and fauna in *Wildlife*, p.583, if you want to figure out exactly what it is you're seeing.

The two main routes which loop around the hills start from the central clocktower, with shorter trails snaking off on all sides. Heading north, the road winds up a beautiful

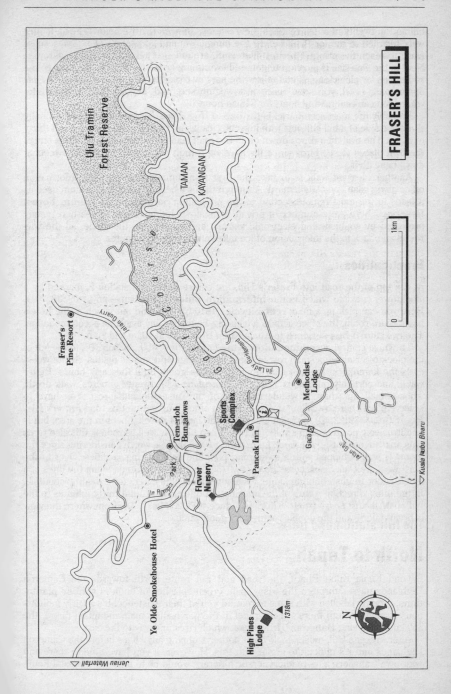

hill and in twenty minutes reaches the *Temerloh Bungalows* (see below). For a longer walk turn left at the fork just before the bungalows and go past *Ye Olde Smokehouse Hotel* to reach the tranquil **Jeriau Waterfall**, around 4km (1hr) from the clocktower. Next to the waterfall is a concrete encased swimming area – the water's freezing cold – and tables for picnicking. If you follow the narrow road opposite the turn-off to *Ye Olde Smokehouse Hotel*, you soon reach a flower nursery and, beyond that, a small **lake** where you can rent rowing boats for $15 an hour.

Probably the most scenic trail is the one to *High Pines Lodge*, which weaves initially along the side of a hill buzzing with insects, cicadas and flying beetles for around thirty minutes. The trail then drops down on to the road leading to the lodge, which is one of the best places to see birds since it's sited on a high point, with the forest sweeping down beneath it..

Another pleasant walk is to take the first right immediately past the information office along jalan Lady Guillemard. Although this is a cement road, it is seldom used as it leads to the most remote section of the hill station bordering **Ulu Tramin Forest Reserve**. There are a number of private bungalows hidden along drives here, many protected by sophisticated electronic alarms, and completing the circle, all the way round and back to the information office takes around ninety minutes.

Practicalities

At the top of the road into Fraser's Hill, the centre of the hill station is marked by a clocktower, next to which is the **information office** (daily 8am–6pm; ☎09/382201). Here you can pick up a map, **rent bicycles** ($10 hr) and find out which of the hotels has a spare room; the office acts as a clearing house for any available accommodation. The two **return bus services** to Kuala Kubu Bharu are at 10am and 2pm.

The most central **accommodation** is the *Pancak Inn* (☎09/382055; ④), to the left of the clocktower above a small row of cafés selling rice and noodle dishes. At the weekends the karaoke in the golf club opposite keeps going until the early hours. Better value, and certainly quieter, is *Temerloh Bungalows* (③), twenty minutes' walk north, whose small huts have a wonderful view of the mist-enfolded forest. You have to reserve places here by calling the information office. Further up this road *Fraser's Pine Resort* (☎09/382122; ④), on jalan Quarry, is the largest development in the area, but is unobtrusively positioned in a valley between two hills. As well as rooms, this also rents outs apartments during the week for around $200 a night – worth considering since the *Resort* is well equipped with a swimming pool and self-catering facilities. Over to the northwest, *Ye Olde Smokehouse Hotel* (☎09/382226, ⑥) is designed along the lines of a mock-Tudor English hunting lodge; it's a small place and caters for a wealthy clientele. In the other direction, south of the information office, it's around thirty minutes to the hilltop *Methodist Lodge* (☎09/282236; KL office ☎03/232 0477, ④), from where the view is breathtaking and the double rooms very good value.

North to Tapah

Beyond Kuala Kubu Bharu, the road and rail route north towards the Cameron Highlands passes through the wispy, pale green splashes of endless **rubber plantations**, proudly labelled with signs to remind you of their existence. It's a fairly monotonous stretch, though there's visual relief in the peninsula's main mountain range, the 350-kilometre-long **Banjaran Titiwangsa**, which rises up away to the east.

After Fraser's Hill, most people don't bother stopping anywhere before the Cameron Highlands and it's difficult to argue with this. However, if you have time to spare and your own transport, a more idiosyncratic itinerary would be to follow the coastal Route

5 north out of Klang, southwest of KL, which passes through Kuala Selangor – see p.116–117 for both of these destinations. You run through low-lying marshland almost all the way to **TELUK INTAN**, 157km northwest of Kuala Lumpur, where you can stop off at least long enough to survey the pagoda-like clocktower and grab a bowl of noodles before taking some fairly minor back roads to connect with Bidor, 32km further northeast. Back on the main road route, the North–South Highway and Route 1 both pass through **TANJUNG MALIM**, on the border of Selangor and Perak states, **SELIM RIVER** and **BIDOR**, dull and featureless towns all – follow your instincts and keep going to Tapah.

Tapah

The small town of **TAPAH** – virtually no more than a crossroads – is the jumping-off point for the Cameron Highlands. For the highlands, you need the **bus station** on jalan Raja, off the main street through town; for long-distance services (including those to Hat Yai in Thailand) you have to buy a ticket from one of the express bus agencies in town, like the *Kah Mee*, opposite the bus station, or *Caspian* on the main road. They'll either tell you where to catch your bus or, more than likely, will flag it down for you, since express buses only stop briefly in Tapah to allow new passengers to join. The **train station**, for routes up and down the west coast, is a few kilometres west of town (the station is called "Tapah Road"), but it's easy enough to get from the station into town by local bus (which runs at least half-hourly from 7.20am–7.20pm) or taxi, which takes fifteen minutes into Tapah itself.

You're unlikely to get stuck in Tapah, as it's only a two-hour journey from Kuala Lumpur and buses run hourly (8.15am–6.15pm) on the further two-hour trip up to Tanah Rata in the Cameron Highlands. However, if disaster srikes there are some reasonable **hotels**. The *Bunga Raya* (☎05/411436; ①), on the corner of the main street and jalan Raja, is pretty basic; the *Utara* (☎05/412299; ②), on jalan Stesen, parallel to jalan Raja, an improvement. Much better value all round is the *Timuran* (☎05/411092; ①) further along jalan Stesen, which is very clean; all the rooms here have attached bathrooms. There's also a number of cheap but nondescript Indian and Chinese **restaurants** dotted around town.

Cameron Highlands

Nestling amid the lofty peaks of Banjaran Titiwangsa, the various ouposts of the **CAMERON HIGHLANDS** (1524m) form Malaysia's most extensive hill station. It took its name from William Cameron, a government surveyor who stumbled across the plateau in 1885 during a mapping expedition. Unfortunately – doubly so for a surveyor – Cameron failed to mark his find on a map, and it wasn't until the 1920s that the location of the plateau was finally confirmed by a consensus of reports from subsequent expeditions. Sir George Maxwell, a senior civil servant, saw the same potential here when he visited in 1925 as he'd seen in Fraser's Hill, and quickly conceived the idea of developing a hill station. Others, too, were quick to see the benefits of the region and early tea planters were followed by Chinese vegetable farmers and wealthy landowners in search of a weekend retreat – a spate of development that culminated in the hotels and luxury apartments that now exist here.

Despite seventy years of tourism, the Cameron Highlands today can still be recognized in William Cameron's early, glowing descriptions which talked of the plateau's gentle slopes surrounded by dramatic peaks. There's a quintessential English character to the lush, rolling green fields, dotted with country cottages, farms and a golf course, and while weekenders flock here in their thousands, it's no great challenge to avoid the hordes. Leisure activities tend to be rather wholesome, with the emphasis on

The telephone code for the Cameron Highlands is ☎05. Note that all Malaysian telephone numbers are being changed in a rolling programme lasting several years. Some of the numbers given in this chapter, while correct at the time of going to press, are likely to have changed.

fresh air and early nights. The vast plateau and surrounding hills and forests are ideal for **walking** and even the most slothful are cajoled by the cooler climate into indulging in some moderately rigorous hiking. Other pleasures are simple – in fact, there's precious little else to do here, particularly in the evenings when **eating** provides just about the sole diversion. The Highlands' colonial past means you can round off a day on the trails with an English cream tea, followed by dinner incorporating the local speciality, the steamboat – the Malaysian equivalent of the Swiss fondue – which involves dunking raw vegetables and other titbits into a steaming broth until cooked, making for a filling (and lengthy) meal.

Orientation

The Cameron Highlands encompasses three small towns lying just within the western corner of the state of Pahang, 219km from KL. As you make your way up the winding mountain road from Tapah, you first encounter **Ringlet**, 45km to the north, a rich agricultural area and site of the famous tea plantations. Another 300m up, and 13km away, is **Tanah Rata**, the principal settlement, where the drop in temperature heralds a change in scenery to streams, waterfalls and mountains, making it an ideal walking base. About 3km further north, **Brinchang** is a newer town, also renowned for its farms, most of which are located to the north towards the *kampungs* of Tringkap and Raja.

You'll want to stay at either Tanah Rata or Brinchang, since this is where the best accommodation is situated; they're also convenient for **tours** of the farms and tea estates, since many operators will collect you from your hotel or guest house. If your time here is limited then you could do worse than take a tour of the whole region. They're organized by the Tanah Rata tourist office (3hr tour; $15) and though a bit "whistle-stop" in character, do at least cover all the main sights and destinations in one swoop. The inevitable shopping stop at the end is mercifully low-key, too.

Useful information

Since the **weather** in the Cameron Highlands is as British as the countryside, you can expect freak rainstorms even in the dry season. For this reason, it makes sense to avoid the area during the monsoon itself, and you should also steer clear at major holiday times (Christmas, Easter and Hari Raya), unless you relish sharing the trails with hundreds of rowdy picknickers and children. Temperatures drop dramatically at night – whatever the season – so you'll need socks and a jumper as well as waterproofs.

There's plenty of **accommodation**: Tanah Rata is right in the thick of things and has the greatest number of cheaper hotels and backpackers' hostels, the latter offering dormitory beds for $5–7 as well as ordinary rooms, information and, occasionally, self-catering facilities. Between Tanah Rata and Brinchang are a few upmarket hotels, all of which have good views but are a bit isolated without your own transport; while in Brinchang itself are several more inexpensive and mid-range hotels. If you're travelling in a group and plan to stay for some time, there are a few **bungalows** and **apartments** for rent dotted around the region. Because of the steady flow of visitors throughout the year, there's no great incentive for hotel owners to be especially competitive – **prices** soar at peak holiday times when you can expect to add at least $20 to the price of an ordinary room. It can also be difficult to find a space at this time, so book ahead if you can. Needless to say, it's always worth bargaining out of season. You'll want to make

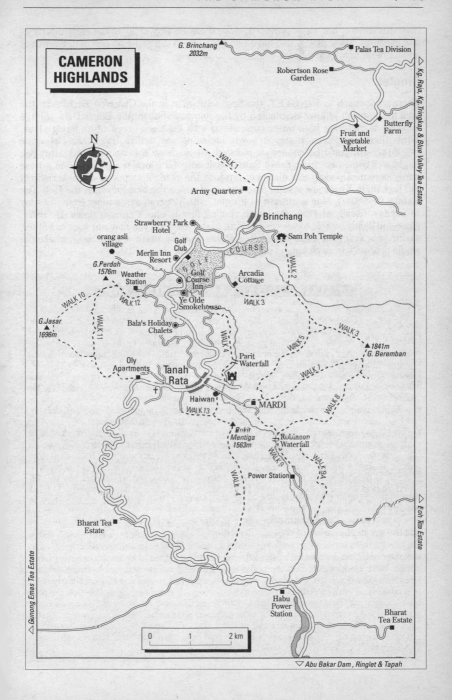

CAMERON
HIGHLANDS

N

G. Brinchang
2032m

Palas Tea Division

Robertson Rose
Garden

Butterfly
Farm

Fruit and
Vegetable
Market

WALK 1

Army Quarters

Brinchang

Strawberry Park
Hotel

Sam Poh Temple

orang asli
village

Golf
Club

G. Perdah
1576m

Merlin Inn
Resort

GOLF COURSE

Weather
Station

Golf
Course
Inn

Arcadia
Cottage

WALK 2

WALK 10

WALK 12

Ye Olde
Smokehouse

WALK 3

WALK 3

G. Jasar
1696m

WALK 11

Bala's Holiday
Chalets

WALK 4

WALK 5

1841m
G. Bereman

Oly
Apartments

Parit
Waterfall

WALK 7

Tanah
Rata

WALK 8

Haiwan

MARDI

WALK 13

Bukit
Mentiga
1563m

Robinson
Waterfall

WALK 9A

WALK 9

Power Station

WALK 4

Bharat Tea
Estate

Habu
Power
Station

Bharat
Tea
Estate

Gunong Emas Tea Estate

Kg. Raja, Kg.Tringkap & Blue Valley Tea Estate

Ifoh Tea Estate

0   1   2 km

Abu Bakar Dam , Ringlet & Tapah

sure that there is hot water provided, since it can be very chilly in the early mornings and evenings. Some places also have real fires, which can make no end of difference to an otherwise uninspiring hotel.

Ringlet

There's not much to **RINGLET**, the first settlement in the Cameron Highlands, the area to the north of town dominated by the immense Sultan Abu Bakar Dam, a huge expanse of glittering blue water contrasting with the deep green of its forest cloak. While there are places to stay in town, including one deluxe hotel, *The Lakehouse* (☎996142; ⑥), you'd be somewhat isolated if you chose this as your base. But you might well come here from Tanah Rata to visit one of the local **tea plantations**, whose hardy perennial plants, at a distance, produce the verdant carpet so characteristic of the highlands. There are several plantations, of which the best known is the **Boh Tea Estate** (☎996032), 8km northeast of Ringlet, which operates free tours from Tuesday to Sunday, usually at 11am; it's worth ringing first to check current times. However, since you'll only be able to see the packing of the tea here, you may not want to bother, saving your visit instead for the estate's **Palas** division, north of Brinchang, where the whole process – from picking to packing – takes place (see p.134).

WALKING IN THE CAMERON HIGHLANDS

The Cameron Highlands features a number of **walks**, varying in difficulty according to your level of fitness and stamina. While the landscape, more forest than jungle, can sometimes obscure the views, the trails here take in some of the most spectacular scenery in Malaysia, encompassing textured greenery and misty mountain peaks. Some of the walks are no more than casual strolls; others veer off into what seems like the wild unknown, giving a sense of isolation rarely encountered in lowland Malaysia. You're unlikely to come across much wildlife on the trails, perhaps the odd wild pig or squirrel, but the **flora** at all times of the year is prolific and most common sightings are of ferns, pitcher plants and orchids.

Unfortunately, the trails themselves are often badly signposted and maintained, though there are various sketch **maps** on sale at the Tanah Rata tourist office and at many of the hotels which – despite their apparent vagueness – do all seem to make sense on the ground. About the best is the black-and-white sketch map available for 50c, which has all the walks fairly clearly marked. There used to be more official trails than now exist but many were closed during the 1970s due to the supposed threat of Communist guerillas hanging out in the undergrowth. Even now, if you want to attempt any **unofficial routes** then a guide recommended by the tourist office is essential and you must also obtain a permit from the District Office (see "Tanah Rata: Listings", p.134), which is tricky and expensive.

However, the **official trails**, detailed below (and marked on our map) are varied enough for most tastes and energies. The timings given are estimates for one-way walks by people with an average level of fitness. You should always inform someone, preferably at your hotel, where you are going and what time you expect to be back. On longer trips, take warm clothing, water, a torch and a cigarette lighter or matches to facilitate basic survival should you get lost. If someone else doesn't return and you suspect they may be in **trouble**, inform the District Office immediately. It's not a fanciful notion that the hills and forest are dangerous. The most notable victim to date was Jim Thompson, the renowned American-born Thai silk entrepreneur, who came on holiday here at Easter 1967 and disappeared while walking in the forest. The services of *orang asli* trackers, dogs and even mystics failed to provide any clue as to what fate befell him – a warning to present-day trekkers of the hazards of jungle life.

Buses from Tapah stop on the main road in Ringlet before moving on to Tanah Rata. There are buses from Ringlet to the *Boh Tea Estate* at 6.30am, 11.30am, 3.15pm and 5.15pm, with return journeys at 7.20am, 12.20pm, 3.45pm and 6pm. It's easy enough to get to Ringlet from Tanah Rata, since there are buses every 30 minutes throughout the day, though the quickest way to get to reach the tea estate here directly is to take a taxi from Tanah Rata, which will cost around $8 one way.

Tanah Rata

The tidy town of **TANAH RATA** is the highlands' main development, a genteel, neat-looking place festooned with hotels, buildings with white balustrades, flowers and parks. It comprises little more than one street (officially called jalan Pasar, but usually just known as "Main Road"), which is where you'll find most of the hotels, all the banks and other services, as well as some of the best restaurants in the Cameron Highlands, all lined up in a half-kilometre stretch. Since the street also serves as the main thoroughfare to the rest of the region, it suffers from the constant honking of departing buses during the day, but at night it becomes the centre of Cameron Highlands' social life, a popular promenade, with many of the restaurants spilling their tables out onto the pavement.

Walk 1 (1hr): not marked on any of the maps, this is a short but tough walk up a rarely used and unmaintained track by the army quarters north of Brinchang. You must come back the same way – given which it's barely worth following.

Walk 2 (1hr 30min): begins just before the Sam Poh Temple below Brinchang. Often a hands-and-knees scramble rather than a straight footpath, you'll need to be fit (and have some spare clothes). The route undulates severely for the first part and eventually merges with Walk 3.

Walk 3 (2hr 30min): starts at *Arcadia Cottage* to the southeast of the golf course, crossing streams and climbing quite steeply to reach the peak of Gunung Berembhan (1841m). Moderately arduous.

Walk 4 (20min): to Parit Waterfall, a stroll to a disappointing waterfall and rubbish-strewn picnic spot.

Walk 5 (1hr): branches off from Walk 3 and ends up at the Malaysian Agriculture Research and Development Institute (*MARDI*). It's an easy walk through peaceful woodland and then you can cut back up the road to Tanah Rata.

Walk 6: the official numbering system falls down here: this walk doesn't exist.

Walk 7 (2hr): starts at *MARDI* and climbs steeply to Gunung Beremban (see Walk 3), an arduous hike.

Walk 8 (3hr): another route to Gunung Beremban, a tough approach from Robinson Waterfall.

Walks 9 & 9A (1hr): the descent from Robinson Waterfall to the Power Station is reasonably steep and strenuous; the station caretaker will let you through to the road to Boh. Walk 9a branches off from the main route to emerge in a vegetable farm on the Boh road and is less steep than Walk 9.

Walks 10 & 11 (2hr –2hr 30min): starts next to the road to the weather station for the fairly strenuous climb to Gunung Jasar (1696m), and emerges on the way to Tanah Rata near the *Oly Apartments*. Good views on the way. The less challenging (and slightly shorter) Walk 11 bypasses the summit.

Walk 12 (1hr): a turn-off to Gunung Perdah (1576m) from Walk 10 that's easy to miss. A moderate walk giving panoramic views over the *orang asli* village.

Walk 13 (1hr): A new trail which starts 30 minutes behind the *Cameronian Holiday Inn* and eventually merges with Walk 14.

Walk 14 (3hr): a moderate, though initially steep, route to Bukit Mentiga (1563m) with great views; it begins at Haiwan (vet centre) and continues south, joining the road 8km from Tanah Rata.

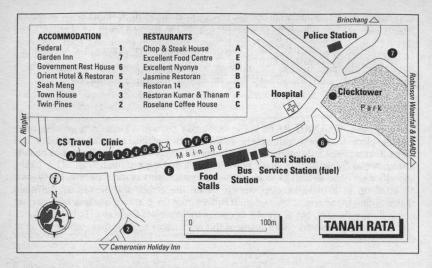

TANAH RATA

All the local and long-distance **buses** only go as far as Tanah Rata; to move onto Brinchang and other destinations you'll have to change here. Long-distance buses stop outside the helpful **tourist office** (daily 7.30am–7pm; ☎901266) at the southern end of town; local buses depart from the **bus station**, about halfway along the main road, 250 metres away from the tourist office. The **taxi station** is just a little further along. At the far end of town, past the hospital and the police station, the road bends round to the left to continue on to Brinchang.

Since many of the Cameron Highlands' **walks** start from nearby (see "Walking in the Cameron Highlands", p.130–131), Tanah Rata makes an ideal base; a couple of waterfalls, a mosque and three reasonably high mountain peaks are all within hiking distance. Several of the walks pass through, or close to, the **Malaysian Agriculture Research and Development Institute** (*MARDI*; ☎901255), a couple of kilometres east of town, which is open for tours by appointment, though it's a rather dry activity for anyone other than a specialist.

Accommodation

The places strung along the main road can be a bit noisy what with all the comings and goings – the best are picked out below. For more solitude you'll have to pay the higher prices charged at the comfortable hotels out on the Brinchang road, or rent one of the **apartments** or cottages in the locality. There are places advertised in shop windows in Tanah Rata – rates quoted are usually per day and a residential cook or caretaker are often offered for an additional cost. Try one of the following: *Golf View Villa* (six-roomed bungalow for $360; ☎901624); *Lutheran Bungalow* (sleeps 20 at $20 a head; ☎901584); *Rose Cottages* (two-roomed place for $230; ☎901173); or *Country Lodge* (6–9 people for $200–360; ☎901811). All the accommodation below is marked either on the Tanah Rata map or the main map of the highlands.

Cameronian Holiday Inn, 16 jalan Mentigi (☎901327). The self-proclaimed "Home of the Budgets", this hostel is further around the corner from *Twin Pines* in a secluded spot. The rooms are relatively luxurious, and there's also a sitting room and small library. ②.

Excellent Lodge, 27a Main Rd (☎901922). Marked "rooms for rent", this small, informal hostel (rooms and dorms) has TV, stereo and free tea and coffee. It's just up from the post office. ①.

Father's Guest House (☎902484). This long-running place retains a loyal following – just before the bridge as you enter town from Ringlet, take the road on the right which curves around the bottom of the convent hill; follow the stone steps to the top. Basic corrugated iron bunkers with shared kitchen facilities and free tea and coffee. ①.

Federal, 44 Main Rd (☎902377). Clean but spartan – there are better bargains to be had, although prices remain fairly reasonable in high season. ②.

Garden Inn (☎901911). Take the road on the right just past the clocktower. The cheaper rooms are dingy, but they have balconies and excellent bathrooms. Prices are negotiable out of season. ④.

Goverment Rest House (☎901254). Doesn't look up to much – it resembles a 1950s' municipal building – but it's nearly always full; there's an averagely priced restaurant and tennis courts. ④.

Orient, 38 Main Rd (☎901633). Very good value with thoughtfully furnished airy rooms, although prices rocket in season. ①.

Seah Meng, 39 Main Rd (☎901618). Clean, well-kept rooms; one of the best-value hotels. ②.

Town House, 41 Main Rd (☎902868). Adequate rooms in a small, well-run hotel, with a very helpful manager. It's also an authorized agency for *Nasional Ekspres* bus tickets. ②.

Twin Pines, 2 jalan Mentigi (☎902169). Set back from the main road, reached by a turn-off opposite the clinic, this small blue-roofed building is currently topping the popularity stakes. There's an attractive patio garden and books full of travellers' tips. ②.

ON THE BRINCHANG ROAD

Bala's Holiday Chalets (☎901660). About 1km or so towards Brinchang, this English country cottage has a wide variety of rooms, including small dorms, as well as a lounge and two dining rooms, a real fire and beautiful gardens. Some rooms are cheaper than this category suggests. ②.

Golf Course Inn (☎9011411). Monstrous concrete exterior but inside it's relaxed and friendly, if slightly down-at-heel, with the best views in the locality, over the golf course. ④.

Merlin Inn Resort (☎901205). More promising from the outside than inside. Standard, bland rooms, some overlooking the golf course, and a pool/snooker room. ⑤.

Strawberry Park Hotel (☎901166). High-class hotel in superb location at the top of a hill, which makes it inaccessible; you're reliant on the hotel minibus. There's also a swimming pool ⑥.

Ye Olde Smokehouse (☎941214). Twenty rooms, most with four-poster beds, just on the tasteful side of kitsch; leaded-light windows and wooden beams belie the fact that this country pub is only 55 years old. Given the high standard of decor, the bathrooms are a bit shabby. ⑤.

Eating and drinking

There are a number of places in Tanah Rata offering Western dishes, particularly pepper steak, but nothing especially imaginative. Much cheaper than the restaurants, and often more satisfying, are the Malay **food stalls** along the main road. Open in the evening, they serve satay, *tom yam* (spicy Thai soup) and the usual rice and noodle combinations, for about $2 per dish.

Chop and Steak House, 50 Main Rd. Sparklingly clean restaurant with a Western menu offering pizza, steak and cream teas. Meals for around $9.

Excellent Food Centre, on the main road opposite the post office. Lives up to its name with a large, inexpensive menu of Western and Asian dishes – great for breakfast, open during the day only. In the adjacent *Fresh Milk Corner*, you can get wonderful shakes and lassis (yoghurt drinks).

Excellent Nyonya, 40 Main Rd. Budget-priced and good for Straits Chinese cuisine.

Jasmine Restoran, 45 Main Rd. Popular with German and Dutch travellers for its *rijstafel* set meals. It has karaoke in the evenings when the beer is more expensive. Good value at other times.

Orient Restoran, 38 Main Rd. Standard Chinese food in the restaurant below the hotel. The set meals are reasonable value, as are the steamboats.

Restoran 14, 14 Main Rd. Popular with locals, serving Indian curries at bargain prices.

Restoran Kumar, Main Rd. Along with the nearby *Thanam*, the *Kumar* specializes in clay pot rice.

Roselane Coffee House, 44 Main Rd. The various set menus and low-price meat grills here make up for the nauseatingly twee decor.

Ye Olde Smokehouse (☎941214). Halfway to Brinchang, the hotel opens its restaurant to non-residents to provide very intimate surroundings for a romantic splash-out. It's hugely expensive: the traditional English menu features a choice of roast meat dinners for around $70, and other dishes start at $20. You'll need to book in advance.

Listings

Banks All situated on the main road and open standard banking hours.

Cinema In the grounds of the *Garden Inn,* showing Cantonese blockbusters as well as some recent English-language films daily at 2pm, 8pm & 10pm; tickets $3.

Clinic 48 Main Rd; open 8.30am–12.30pm, 2–5.30pm & 8–10pm. Ring doorbell after clinic hours.

District Office Main Rd (☎901066). Contact immediately if you suspect someone has got lost on a walk. Also call here to obtain permits for unofficial trails.

Garage There are service stations in both Tanah Rata and Brinchang.

Hospital Main Rd, opposite the park (☎901966).

Laundry There's a reasonably priced service at *Highlands Laundry,* Main Rd (☎901820).

Police Station Main Rd, opposite the *Garden Inn* (☎901222).

Post Office Main Rd (☎901051); pick up poste restante/general delivery mail here.

Sport *Cameron Highlands Golf Club* (☎901126) has an 18-hole course; green fees $40 ($60 weekends, equipment rental extra); there's a strict dress code. Tennis courts at the golf club ($4/hr for court, $5 for racket) and at the *Government Rest House,* bookable at District Office.

Taxi station Main Rd (☎901234).

Travel agents *CS Travel* and *Town House Hotel,* both on Main Rd, are agents for express bus tickets from Tapah to all major destinations.

Brinchang and around

After Tanah Rata, **BRINCHANG**, 3km or so further north, seems like a scruffy conurbation. Sprawling messily around a central square and the main road through town, it lacks the charm of its neighbour, although its saving grace is the lively **nightmarket** which opens up at about 4pm. In the holiday periods, you may have to resort to Brinchang as an alternative to Tanah Rata in order to find a room – not a major disaster since some of the walks are easily approached from here, too, while reaching the farms and tea estates to the north is also quicker. A more challenging option to the local trails is to hike to the summit of **Gunung Brinchang** (2032m), the highest peak in Malaysia accessible by road. This takes two to three hours from Brinchang and although the road is tarmacked, it's still an extremely steep and exhausting climb. On a clear day, though, the views back down over the broad valley are unparalled. At some point during your stay here, you might also walk to the **Sam Poh Temple,** 1km below Brinchang, a gaudy modern place with a monastery which was built in 1965.

Buses leave Tanah Rata for Brinchang and Kampung Raja, the furthest point north, every hour or so between 6.40am and 6pm. A taxi from Tanah Rata to Brinchang costs around $5. You can also head direct to the *Palas Tea Estate* (see below) from Brinchang's own **bus station**, just south of the square, at 9.30am, 11.45am and 1.45pm – if you go in the afternoon, on the 1.45pm bus, you'll have to make your own way back to the main road to pick up the more regular Brinchang-bound bus from Kampung Raja, adding another twenty-minute walk to your journey, since the last *Palas* bus returns at 2.10pm.

Palas Tea Etate

The **Palas Tea Estate** (tours Tues to Sun, usually at 11am; free; ☎996032) is probably the best tea estate to visit, as you can watch the entire process there, from picking to packing. Despite the romantic imagery used on the packaging, handpicking, although the best method for producing the highest quality tea, is now far too labour-intensive to be economical. Instead, the small, green leaves are picked every ten days or so using shears and wicker basket by the mainly Tamil workers who live on the estates. Once in the factory, the full baskets are emptied into large wire vats where the leaves are withered by blowing alternate blasts of hot and cold air underneath them for sixteen to eighteen hours; this removes around fifty percent of their moisture. The leaves are then sifted of dust and impurities and rolled by ancient, bulky machines. This breaks up the leaf and releases the moisture for the all-important process of fermentation, when the leaves begin to emit their distinctive, pungent smell. After ninety minutes of grinding in another machine, the soggy mass is fired at 90°C in what is effectively a spin-dryer, to halt the fermentation process, whereupon the tea turns black. After being sorted into grades, it matures for three to six months before being packaged and transported to market.

How much you glean of this process from your guide is dependent on the acuteness of your hearing, for parts of the factory are so deafening that all other sounds bar the roar of the driers are obliterated. Some areas of the building are also made extremely dusty by the tea impurities, so take a handkerchief to cover your mouth and nose.

The farms

All over the Cameron Highlands – but especially north of Brinchang – you'll pass small sheds or greenhouses by the roadside, selling cabbages, leeks, cauliflower, mushrooms and strawberries. These come from various fruit and vegetable **farms**, which thrive in the temperate climate, and if you aim to pass by one of the farms during a walk, you'll usually find someone willing to show you the cultivation process. Narrow plots are cut out of the sheer hillsides to increase the surface area for planting, forming giant steps all the way up the slopes. However, such ingenious terrace farming poses a problem for the transportation of the harvested crop, since the paths between the terraces are only wide enough for one nimble-footed person. This has been solved by the introduction of a **cable system**, initially operated by brute force but now powered by diesel engine, which hoists the large baskets of vegetables from the terraces to trucks waiting by the roadside high above, from where they are taken to market – over forty percent of the produce is for export to Singapore, Brunei and Hong Kong.

A couple more specific targets might entice you out into the countryside north of Brinchang. At the **Butterfly Farm** (daily 8am–6pm; $3), 5km north, scores of butterflies fly free among the flowers, with the sound of running water from an artificial pond in the background; the Kampung Raja bus from Brinchang passes outside. Better is the **Robertson Rose Garden** (daily 10am–6pm; free), 2km to the northwest, on the way to the *Palas Tea Estate*, to which a visit is rewarded by superb views of the sculpted sweep of the surrounding hills. Rose bushes aside, the shop here sells honey and cordials, as well as attractive dried flowers and arrangements.

Accommodation

The hotels here all line the east and west sides of the central square, and although the numbering system leaves a lot to be desired, you shouldn't have too much difficulty locating them.

Brinchang Hotel, 36 Main Rd (☎901755). Good-sized rooms with colour TV and phone. Some rooms have a nice view over the food stalls. ③.

East Garden Hotel (☎902380). On the northwest corner of the square; clean with well-equipped bathroom, but overpriced for what you get. ③.

Kowloon Hotel, 34–35 Main Rd (☎901366). Small, comfortable rooms; quads are good value. ③.

Parkland Hotel, 45 Main Rd (☎901299). Thirty plush rooms with great views over town. ④.

Hotel Plastro, 19 Main Rd (☎901009). This middle-of-the-range hotel has eleven bright rooms with attached bathrooms, a TV/video lounge and helpful management. ②.

Hotel Sentosa, 38 Main Rd (☎901907). Next door to the *Plastro*, this friendly hotel is basic but clean and the best you'll find for the money. The eleven rooms all have attached bathroom. ①.

Silverstar Hotel, 10 Main Rd (☎901387). Fifteen basic, fair-sized rooms with *mandi*. Rates are subject to negotiation and sometimes drop as low as $10 per person in a shared room. ②.

Wong Villa YHA (☎901145). Just past the post office, this rather run-down place is not worth the hike unless you bring your own crowd for company. ①.

Eating and drinking

As well as the Malay **food stalls** in the central square, the following cafés and restaurants are worth a try.

Carl's Jnr, Main Rd, next to the service station. Burger joint for those desperate moments when nothing else will do.

Hong Kong, Main Rd, west side of square. Looks more upmarket than it actually is, serving the usual Chinese dishes and steamboats.

Kowloon, 34–35 Main Rd. Smart, efficient restaurant with prices to match. But the dishes from the very large Chinese menu are worth the extra cost.

Restoran Sakaya, Main Rd. Near the *Hong Kong*, this is one of three good budget Chinese eating houses (as well as *You ho* and *Kuan Kee*), with buffet lunches on offer from $3 for three dishes, with rice.

Parkland, 45 Main Rd. Part of the hotel, this pleasant, airy restaurant has good views over town but is fairly pricey for the bland, international cuisine that is served.

Ipoh and around

Eighty kilometres north of Tapah in the Kinta valley is **IPOH**, the state capital of Perak and third biggest city in Malaysia. It grew rich on the tin trade, which turned it from a tiny *kampung* in a landscape dominated by dramatic limestone outcrops to a sprawling boomtown within forty years; now a metropolis of over 500,000 people, it's a far cry from the original village on this site whose name was derived from the *upas* tree which once thrived in the area and whose sap was used by the *orang asli* for arrow-head poison. Perak had been renowned for its rich tin deposits since the sixteenth century, which made it vulnerable to attempts from rival chiefs to seize the throne and thus gain control of the lucrative tin trade. However, it wasn't until the discovery of a major field in 1880 that Ipoh's fortunes turned. Before long it had become a prime destination for pioneers, merchants and fortune-seekers from all over the world, transforming it into something of a cosmopolitan city, which is still reflected in the broad mix of cultures present today. To accommodate this rapidly increasing population, the city expanded across sungei Kinta between 1905 and 1914 into a "new town" area, its economic good fortune reflected in a multitude of **colonial buildings** and Chinese **mansions**. Despite the later decline in demand for tin, when Malaysia turned to oil to resurrect its hopes of prosperity, the export of tin is still the fifth largest earner of foreign currency in the country, and Ipoh has remained a major player in Malaysia's meteoric rise to the top of Southeast Asian economic league table.

Yet despite its historical significance and present-day administrative importance, Ipoh proves to be a disappointment to many visitors – the colonial parts of Georgetown are far more interesting. In fact, the main reason people stop is to visit the outlying attractions – the Chinese cave temples of **Sam Poh Tong** and **Perak Tong**, the anachronistic ruin of **Kellie's Castle** and the unique development at the **Yook Lin Hot Springs** – though to do these justice you're likely to have to spend at least one night in the city.

The city

The layout of central Ipoh is reasonably straightforward since the roads form, more or less, a grid system. What *is* confusing is that some of the old colonial **street names** have been changed in favour of something more Islamic, though the street signs haven't always caught up; hence, jalan CM Yusuf instead of jalan Chamberlain, jalan Mustapha Al-Bakri for jalan Clare and jalan Bandar Timar for jalan Leech, although in practice, people will know either name. The muddy and lethargic **sungei Kinta** cuts

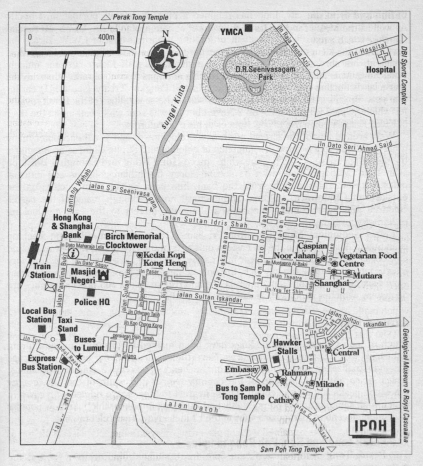

the centre of Ipoh neatly in two; most of the hotels (see below) are situated east of the river, whilst the **old town** is on the opposite side between the two major thoroughfares, jalan Sultan Idris Shah and jalan Sultan Iskander.

Although most of what might attract you to Ipoh is located on its outskirts, there are a few diversions here that are worth at least a cursory glance, starting as you get off the train. The most prominent reminder of Ipoh's economic heyday, the **train station**, was built in 1917 at the height of the tin boom, a typical example of the British conception of "East meets West", with its Moorish turrets and domes and a verandah that runs the entire two-hundred-metre-length of the building. Like other colonial train stations, in KL and Hong Kong, it sported a plush hotel (under renovation for some time now) in which the planters, traders and administrators sank cocktails in their suites.

The modernist **Masjid Negeri** on jalan Sultan Iskandar is one of the more outstanding landmarks in the centre of town, all tacky Sixties' cladding, with a minaret that rises over forty metres above its mosaic-tiled domes – evidence that despite the maelstrom of immigrants to the city, Ipoh has retained a buoyant Islamic population. Directly opposite the mosque, on the parallel jalan Dato' Sagor, stands the **Birch Memorial Clocktower**, a square white tower incorporating a portrait bust of J.W.W. Birch, the first British Resident of Perak who was murdered in 1874. When Birch was installed as Resident, his abrupt manner and lack of understanding of Malay customs quickly offended Sultan Abdullah, who resented Birch's attempts to control rather than advise, a crucial distinction that had been laid out in the Pangkor Treaty (see p.141) earlier that year. Birch's manner proved to be an insult to the sensibilities of the Perak royalty, for which he paid with his life – on 2 November he was shot while bathing in the river at Kuala Kangsar, on a trip to post notices of his own reforms.

Walk around any of the streets north of the clocktower and you'll encounter many other buildings which show the influence of colonial and Straits Chinese architecture, the most impressive of which is the white stucco **Hong Kong and Shanghai Bank** on jalan Dato' Maharaja Lela, with its second-storey Corinthian columns and unusual pillared tower. Turning right from the bank into jalan Sultan Yusuf, you're on the outskirts of **Chinatown**, of equal architectural note, although many of the pastel-coloured nineteenth-century shophouses along the streets to the east are looking rather tatty nowadays.

Ipoh's **Geological Museum** (Mon–Fri 8am–4.15pm, Sat 8am–12.45pm; free) on jalan Sultan Azlan Shah on the far eastern outskirts of the city (a taxi ride away, around $5), does its best to make tin appear interesting, but other than granting a perfunctory insight into what made the city rich, the only achievement here is comprehensiveness – over six hundred samples of minerals and an array of fossils and precious stones are on display, which is about as fascinating as it sounds.

Around Ipoh

Much of Ipoh's striking surroundings have been marred by unsightly manufacturing industries which dominate the suburbs. Nevertheless, it's not long before you escape the industrialization and find yourself in the heart of extensive rubber plantations, typical of so much of this part of the country. North and south of the city, craggy limestone peaks add a bit of colour. Those nearest to the city are riddled with caves in which Ipoh's immigrant workers established Buddhist temples, which are now popular pilgrimmage centres, particularly during the Chinese New Year celebrations.

The Perak Tong and Sam Poh Pong temples
The **Perak Tong Temple** (daily 8am–6pm; free), situated 6km north of Ipoh, is the more impressive of the two Chinese cave temples just outside the city, housed in dramatic surroundings and doubling as a centre for Chinese art. Get there by taking bus #141 (to Kuala Kangsar) from the local bus station for the twenty-minute ride. The gaudiness of its exterior – bright red and yellow pavilions flanked by feathery willows and lotus ponds – gives you no preparation for the eerie atmosphere to be found inside the temple, where darkened cavern upon cavern honeycombs up into the rock formation. The huge first chamber is dominated by a fifteen-metre-high golden statue of the Buddha, plump and smiling, while two startled-looking companions on each side dance and play instruments for his amusement. A massive bell, believed to be more than a century old, fills the chamber with its booming echoes from time to time, rung by visiting devotees to draw attention to the donation they've just offered. Walking past the bell into the next chamber, as your eyes become more accustomed to the gloom you'll notice the decorative walls, covered with complex calligraphy and delicate paintings of flowers. Towards the back of this musty hollow, a steep flight of 385 crudely fashioned steps climbs up and out of the cave, leading onto a sort of balcony,

which affords excellent views over the surrounding area, studded with large, bold limestone outcrops jutting forcefully out from the earth – views that would be fantastic were it not for the ugly factory buildings that sprawl across the valley between here and the city centre.

The **Sam Poh Tong Temple** (daily 8am–6pm; free), just to the south of the city, is also a popular place of pilgrimage for Chinese Buddhists. Built into a rock face, the huge limestone caverns open towards the rear to give more impressive views over the surrounding suburbs and hills. Unfortunately, the upkeep of the temple leaves a lot to be desired and the place is covered with litter and graffiti. There's an expensive bar nearby and a good Chinese vegetarian restaurant. A visit to the temple makes an easy half-morning's trip: catch the green "Kinta" bus #66 (to Kangar) from the local bus station, or from the roundabout near the *Embassy* hotel; it's a ten-minute journey.

Kellie's Castle

If you only have time for one trip from Ipoh then make it to **Kellie's Castle**, a mansion situated in a thousand acres of the Kinta Kelas Rubber Estate, about 12km south of the city. It stands out as a symbol of the prosperity available to many an enterprising foreigner who saw the potential of the rubber market in the early 1900s. The mansion, with its weighty rectangular tower and apricot-coloured bricks, was to have been the second home of William Kellie Smith, a Scottish entrepreneur, who settled here in order to make his fortune. Designed with splendour in mind, there were even plans for a lift to be installed, the first in Malaysia. However, during the mansion's construction in the 1920s, an epidemic of Spanish influenza broke out, killing many of the Tamil workers. In an act of appeasement, Smith had a Hindu temple built near the house and here, among the deities represented on its roof, you can see a figure dressed in a white suit and topi, presumably Smith himself. While work resumed on the "castle", Smith left on a trip to England in 1925 but never returned, as he fell ill and died in Portugal. The crumbling, warren-like remains, set in lush, hilly countryside – there's an excellent panorama from the roof – are now covered in graffiti dating back to 1941, recording the visits of tourists down the years.

Getting to the castle from Ipoh involves some determination. You need to take bus #36 or #37 from the local bus station for the half-hour journey to Batu Gajah (departures every 1hr 20min or so) and, once there, either walk the remaining 4km on road A8 (clearly marked) or catch bus #67, which passes the castle fairly frequently. It's easiest to take a taxi from Batu Gajah – around $4.

Yook Lin Hot Springs

At the **Yook Lin Hot Springs** (Tues–Sun 4–9pm; $7.50), 8km northeast of Ipoh, you can indulge in a hot, mineral-rich soak in the two thermal swimming pools, one cooler than the other, which are fed naturally by hot springs – no mean feat of engineering, as the enthusiastic owner will probably tell you. All around, steaming pools of slimy water break through the surface of the earth, and for a further $3.50 you can crawl into the corner of a nearby limestone cave for a natural sauna (not for the claustrophobic), or amuse yourself with a game of snooker or ten-pin bowling using the four-lane alley ingeniously built into the principal cave. Another of the surrounding caves was once inhabited by a Japanese monk and later by Japanese soldiers in hiding during World War II, hence the painted characters on some of the cave walls. There are rather expensive **hotel rooms** (☎05/554407; ⑤) surrounding the pools, whose bathrooms are – of course – fed by the natural hot water supply.

To reach the hot springs, take the "Rambutan" bus from the local bus station for about thirty minutes until you see the signpost for "Resort Air Panas", off to the right of the main road; the springs are a further 1km down a dirt track.

Practicalities

All the transport facilities are located in roughly the same area. The **train station** is on jalan Panglima Bukit Gantang Wahab (or just jalan Panglima), west of the old town, with the **GPO** practically next door. The **local bus station** is 500m south of the train station, at the junction of jalan Tun Abdul Razak and jalan Panglima. The **taxi stand** is opposite; **express buses** operate from behind a bank of ticket booths across the road. Buses to **Lumut** (the departure point for Pulau Pangkor; see opposite) depart from a seperate forecourt, beside a row of shops, a little further along jalan Tun Abdul Razak. You might conceivably fly into Ipoh: the Sultan Azlan Shah **airport** is 5km from the city (info on ☎05/202459).

There are two **tourist offices**: one in the State Economic Planning Unit close to the train station on jalan Dewan (Mon–Thurs 8am–12.45pm & 2–4.15pm, Fri 8am–12.15pm & 2.45–4.15pm, Sat 8am–12.45pm; ☎05/532800), another at the rather inconveniently sited *Royal Casuarina* hotel, 18 jalan Gopeng, at the eastern end of town (same hours as above; ☎05/532008 ext. 8123), though the latter is rather more helpful. The main **banks** are on jalan Sultan Idris Shah and jalan Yang Kalsom. For **car rental**, contact *Avis* (☎05/206586) or *Hertz* (☎05/207109), both with offices at the airport.

Accommodation

Most of the **places to stay** in Ipoh are found east of the river, around jalan CM Yusuf and jalan Mustapha Al-Bakri, the latter with a more seedy feel, though it's generally much quieter. The most famous place in town is the elegant *Station Hotel* (☎05/512588; ⑤), on the third floor of the train station, off jalan Panglima. Rather run-down in recent years, renovations plan to recapture the fine colonial style which made it so sought-after in its prime.

The best option at the lower end of the scale is the *Cathay*, 88–94 jalan CM Yusuf (☎05/513322; ①), a typical Chinese hotel with a very knowledgable manager. The *Shanghai*, at 85 jalan Mustapha Al-Bakri (☎05/512070; ②), is pleasant enough for the money, while the *Embassy* on jalan CM Yusuf (☎05/549496; ②) is better than most, all rooms having attached bathrooms. At the top of its range, the *Caspian*, 6–10 jalan Jubilee (☎05/542324; ②), has good rooms with air-con and hot water. Also worth a mention is the *Central*, 20–26 jalan Ali Pitchay (☎05/500142; ③), where all the rooms come with TV and balcony – excellent for the price. The *Mikado* (☎05/505855; ④), on jalan Yang Kalsom, is a wonderful slice of Japanese kitsch although the decor is oppressive in parts. Ipoh's *YMCA* (☎05/540809; ③) is too far out of the centre, at 211 jalan Raja Musa Aziz, to be useful, although the $10 dorm beds may be a draw for some.

Eating and drinking

Many of Ipoh's **restaurants** close in the evenings, so you may have to resort to the **hawker stalls** near the train station or those at the top of jalan CM Yusuf. At lunchtime, however, the choice is much more extensive. Regional specialities are *kuey teow* (a chicken-based dish in soup or fried form) and *sar hor fun*, flat rice noodles served in a chicken stock soup, to which prawns, fried shallots and bean sprouts are added – available at most Chinese restaurants in Ipoh.

On jalan Mustapha Al-Bakri are the very clean *Mutiara* and the *Vegetarian Food Centre*, a rare treat in meat-orientated Malaysia. Jalan CM Yusuf boasts the restaurant at the *Cathay* hotel, which is very popular with Chinese locals, and the *Rahman*, an extremely friendly Indian restaurant. Around jalan Bandar Timar in the old town are several Chinese restaurants, the oldest and best known of which is the *Kedai Kopi Kong Heng* (lunchtime only) where you wander round the bustling stalls and pick your dish; someone else will then offer you drinks at your table. There are also several **bakeries** in town serving lovely fresh bread and pastries; try the *Noor Jahan* on jalan Raja Ekram.

Pulau Pangkor

PULAU PANGKOR is one of the west coast's more appealing islands, with some of the best beaches to be found on this side of the Malay peninsula. It's also one of the most accessible, lying just a thirty-minute ferry ride from the port of Lumut (85km southwest of Ipoh), a short hop which has turned Pangkor into an increasingly popular weekend resort. This is naturally affecting the levels of both development and prices on the island: there's a brand new airport and two international-standard hotels, while the adjacent island of Pangkor Laut, just off the southwest coast of Pulau Pangkor, is now privately owned by a hotel which charges visitors for the use of its beaches. These facilities are disproportionate with Pangkor's small size and at odds with the quiet, almost genteel, atmosphere that still pervades much of the island. Pangkor has managed to keep its fairly relaxed atmosphere, its inhabitants' livelihood still largely based on the fishing and boat-building businesses rather than tourism. Indeed, there's a distinct split still between the two, as most of the thriving local villages lie in a string along the east coast while the tourist accommodation and the best beaches are on the west side of the island. The interior is mountainous and dense with jungle, inaccessible but for a few tiny trails and one main road that connects the two coasts, but there's plenty to occupy you around the rim, from superb stretches of sand to various historical relics.

The historical sites themselves – a seventeenth-century Dutch fort and several temples – are less significant than the role played by the island in the modern development of Malaysia; it was the site of the signing of the ground-breaking **Pangkor Treaty** of January 20, 1874. Until this time, British involvement in Malay affairs had been unofficial, but late in 1873, Raja Abdullah of Perak (in which state Pangkor lies) invited the new Governor of the Straits settlements, Andrew Clarke, to appoint a Resident (colonial officer) to Perak, in exchange for Abdullah's being recognised as the Sultan of Perak instead of his rival, the intractable Sultan Ismail. This held some appeal for the British, eager to foster stability and facilitate economic progress in the region, and the Pangkor Treaty was signed between Clarke and Abdullah, who agreed to accept the advice of the Resident "on all questions other than those touching Malay religion and custom". It is doubtful that the Malays had any idea of the long term consequences of the treaty. The original version indicated that the decision-making process would be collective, much like the Malays' own courts; more significantly, the political and religious distinction was from the start a nonsensical concept to the Malays, for whom all action was dictated by the laws of Islam. Sultan Abdullah, bent on acquiring local power and status, therefore inadvertantly provided a foot in the door for the British which eventually led to their full political intervention in the peninsula.

Getting there: Lumut

Although you can now **fly** direct to Pulau Pangkor from KL (daily 8.35am; $120 one-way) or from Penang (Mon, Thurs & Sat; $100 one-way) with *Pelangi Air*, most people still cross to Pulau Pangkor by ferry from the quiet coastal town of **LUMUT**, around 85km southwest of Ipoh. Once a relatively obscure fishing village, it has since become the main base of the Royal Malaysian Navy whose towering apartment buildings dominate the coastline from the sea. In an attempt to cash in on the success of Pulau Pangkor, Lumut too has seen its own spate of development, but this is still mercifully low-key, and the town manages to retain some of its erstwhile charm, with multicoloured fishing boats bobbing in the tiny marina, and stores specializing in shell and coral handicrafts, for which Lumut is famed locally. However, all this is a mere diversion from your main purpose, which is to jump straight on one of the numerous ferries to Pulau Pangkor.

Lumut's **bus station** is behind the public gardens opposite the jetty; there are services from Ipoh roughly every 45 minutes, which take an hour and a half. If you're coming from the Cameron Highlands or from the south, there's a twice-daily direct bus from Tapah – around $9 – though, since it originates in Kuala Lumpur, it's often full. There's a branch of *Maybank* in Pangkor Town on Pulau Pangkor but it can be difficult to change travellers' cheques, so it's best to **change money** first at one of the several money changers in Lumut.

You'd have to be very unlucky to need to spend the night in Lumut, but late arrivals might need the services of either the *Phin Lum Hooi*, 93 jalan Panjang (☎05/935938; ①), the cheapest place in town, or the *Indah*, 208 jalan Iskander Shah (☎05/935064; ②), which makes reductions for single travellers; they're both very close to the jetty. There's also a small *Government Rest House* (☎05/935938; ④) on the seafront, east of the jetty, which shows signs of faded grandeur at less faded prices. There isn't much choice when it comes to **eating** – the *Phin Lum Hooi* has a decent restaurant, or there are some hawker' stalls in the bus station.

FERRIES

The **express ferries to Pulau Pangkor** run approximately every fifteen minutes (daily 6.45am–7.30pm; $4 return); while six boats a day also run to the *Pan Pacific Resort* at the north end of the island ($4 return), and four to Pangkor Laut ($6 return). At the ferry ticket offices, next to the jetty, don't be won over by the loudest voice emanating from behind the glass, but head instead for the jetty itself to check which boat is leaving first, otherwise you could find yourself watching a number of boats pulling out as you wait for your particular company's vessel to depart. Hang onto your ticket for the return journey – and, contrary to popular opinion, note that the tickets are not transferable to other companies' ferries on the way back. The express ferry calls first at Kampung Sungei Pinang Kecil before reaching the main jetty at Pangkor Town, which is where you'll want to get off.

Around the island

Pulau Pangkor has a surfaced **road** of varying quality all the way around its circumference; because of the mountainous interior this only crosses the island at one point, from Pangkor Town, where the ferry docks, to the tourist developments at Pasir Bogak on the west coast, 2km away. **Renting** a motorbike or pushbike from one of the hotels or guest houses on the west coast – the *Pangkor Standard Camp* has a good selection – costs around $30 and $15 respectively per day. At just 3km by 9km, a trip **around the island** is easily accomplished in one day. Travelling by motorbike you could visit all the sights in about five hours, stopping en route for lunch – add another couple of hours if you're travelling by pushbike. Otherwise the only other means of transport are the **minibus taxis** ($3 to Pasir Bogak, $10 to Teluk Nipah and $24–$30 for a round-island trip), and the infrequent **local buses**, which run from Pangkor Town to Pasir Bogak. It might only be a couple of kilometres from Pangkor Town across to the west coast, but don't even think of walking it in the heat of the day – there's no shade.

Pangkor Town

The ferry from Lumut drops you at the jetty in **PANGKOR TOWN**, the island's principal settlement, whose few dusty streets feature *kedai kopis* graced with Nonya marble-topped tables and antique clocks. The best part of the town, by far, is the port to which the fishing boats return in the early morning with their catch, which is then immediately packed into boxes of crushed ice to be despatched to the mainland. The island is particularly renowned for *ikan bilis* (anchovies).

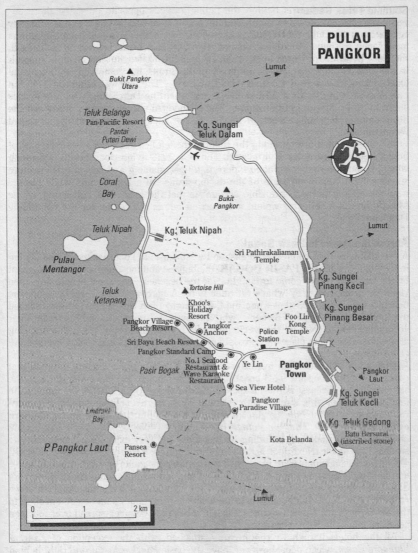

While it makes for a decent stretch of the legs once you've got off the ferry, there's very little reason to stop long; buses and taxis to the beaches on the other side of the island leave from the jetty. There are, though, a couple of reasonably attractive **places to stay**: the *Chuan Full*, 60 Main Rd (☎05/951123; ②), a characterful hotel with a rear balcony overlooking the water; and, nearer the jetty, *Hotel Min Lian* at no. 1a (☎05/951294; ②), another basic but friendly place. A number of Chinese **restaurants** keep the locals fed, but the most unusual place to eat is the *No.1 Seafood Restaurant*, next to the jetty, easy to spot since it's shaped like the bow of a ship complete with portholes.

South to Teluk Gedung

Following the coastal road south out of town, after 1.5km you'll come to pretty **KAMPUNG TELUK GEDONG**, a gathering of traditional wooden stilted houses named after the bay in which it is cradled. Here, set back from the road on the right, is the **Kota Belanda**, or Dutch Fort, originally built in 1670 for the storage of tin supplies from Perak and to keep a check on piracy in the Straits, but destroyed in 1690 by the local Malays who were discontent with Dutch rule. The fort was rebuilt in 1743 but only remained in use for a further five years, when the Dutch finally withdrew after several further attacks by the Malays. The abandoned site was left to decay and the disappointing, half-built structure that you see today is, unbelievably, a recent reconstruction.

Just a few metres further along the road on the left lies the **Batu Bersurat**, a huge boulder now almost covered in graffiti. The year 1743 is inscribed beside a drawing which, if you use your imagination, depicts a tiger mauling a child – a grisly picture supposedly in commemoration of the disappearance of a Dutch child while playing near the rock. The more plausible account is that the infant was kidnapped by the Malays, one of a series of violent acts carried out as retribution for the continuing Dutch presence.

Across the island to Pasir Bogak

A two-kilometre road connects the east and west coasts of Pulau Pangkor, terminating in the holiday village of **PASIR BOGAK**, the biggest and most upmarket development on the island. If you've come to Pangkor for the beaches – and most people do – then you'll be disappointed by what's on offer here. A narrow strip of grubby sand, the beach is virtually nonexistent when the tide is high, a fact that seems to have escaped the notice of the chalet owners, who continue to renovate and upgrade their accommodation to cater for the weekend trade. If you plan to stay, it's worth shopping around because some places are grossly overpriced, and rates can rocket everywhere at weekends.

Only a few of the **chalets** front the beach itself; most are lined along the road that continues north along the west coast, but even so, they're all reasonably close to the sea. About the cheapest is the *Pangkor Standard Camp* (☎05/951878; ②), one of the few places left on this stretch with A-frame huts; there's another similar but more run-down set-up at the *Pangkor Anchor* (☎05/951363; ②) further up. At the far northern end of the strip, the *Pangkor Village Beach Resort* (☎05/952227; ②–⑤) has a wide choice of accommodation, including budget tents and very expensive chalets, but the site has little shade. Next door is the long-running *Khoo's Holiday Resort* (☎05/951164; ③), an increasingly upmarket place with comfortable mosquito-proof chalets, hot water and fantastic views, a computer games room and indoor badminton court; rates here drop considerably over a three-night stay. Up a significant notch is the *Sea View Hotel* (☎05/951605; ⑤), with a good beachside location, or if money's no object, check in to the *Sri Bayu Beach Resort* (☎05/951929; ⑥), a beautiful complex spread over fourteen acres, popular with KL's in-crowd.

All the hotels here have **restaurants** attached, with the exception of *Pangkor Standard Camp*, which does, however, have the basic *Pangkor Restaurant* right behind it. By far the best value is *Ye Lin*, slightly away from the principal cluster, on the cross-island road, offering huge plates of excellent Chinese food, while the finest view belongs to the *Pangkor Paradise Village* up a dirt track to the south of the main strip, whose beachfront restaurant on stilts over the water is great for a beer at sunset. Otherwise, the food here – like the accommodation – is overpriced. Back in the thick of things, the *No.1 Seafood Restaurant* and adjacent *Wave Karaoke Restaurant*, both serve standard dishes for $6–7.

Teluk Nipah and the northeast coast

Much better beaches than that at Pasir Bogak are to be found about 2km further north at **TELUK KETAPANG**, a bay which has been known to harbour the increasingly rare giant leatherback turtle (Teluk Ketapang means "Turtle Bay") which swims thousands of miles to lay its eggs on Malaysia's beaches. Although the turtles normally favour the peninsula's eastern coast (see p.255 for more info), you might be lucky with a few sightings here between May and September. Otherwise, take the opportunity to stretch out on white sand beaches, backed by palm trees, which are slightly less crowded than Pasir Bogak and much wider and cleaner.

Since there's no accommodation at Teluk Ketapang, you'll have to make do with staying in Pasir Bogak or, better, continuing north a couple more kilometres to **TELUK NIPAH**, where there are a few inexpensive places to stay, but more crucially, some splendid beaches. Of these, **Coral Bay** is the best – a near-perfect cove with crystal-clear sea lapping at smooth white sand, backed by dense jungle climbing steeply away to one of the island's three summits, Bukit Pangkor. That the bay is inaccessible by road only serves to make the beach more exotic: to reach it you have to climb over the rocks at the northern end of Teluk Nipah – watch the tide or you might have to swim back – though if you haven't the energy for this, the main bay of Teluk Nipah more than suffices.

At present the atmosphere at Teluk Nipah is much more informal and friendly than elsewhere, the accommodation still mainly simple A-frames. How much longer this will continue is uncertain since the authorities are likely to rule against this type of chalet in order to appeal to a more exclusive crowd. In the meantime though, the huts are set back about 100m from the beach in the *kampung* and include *Coral Beach Camp* (☎05/951745; ①) and *Nazri Nipah Camp* (no phone; ①), both with A-frames and rooms of a much better standard; both serve meals, too. Two much pricier places – *Sukasuka Beach Resort* (☎05/952494; ④) and *Nipah Bay Villas* (☎05/952198; ⑤) – include all meals with the deal, but the additional comfort they offer is hardly worth the extra money.

The road cuts inland from Teluk Nipah and crosses to the northeastern tip of the island, where it branches off left to the high-class *Pan Pacific Resort* (☎05/951091; ⑥), situated in secluded **TELUK BELANGA**. You can get here directly by ferry from Lumut, though unless you're staying at the resort you'll be charged $30 to use the beach (collected at the entrance gate), for which price they generously include a snack. The bonus is the good sports facilities here, including a golf course, and a beach, **Pantai Puteri Dewi** (Beach of the Beautiful Princess), that holds its own with the best that Pangkor has to offer – a fine stretch of crunchy white sand.

Doubling back to the junction with the main road, continue straight past the new airport over the steep and craggy headland for 3km before descending into the first bay on the east coast.

The east coast: north of Pangkor Town

There's not much to see on the northeast side of the island until you reach **KAMPUNG SUNGEI PINANG KECIL**, which is little more than a few straggling dwellings by the roadside and the first stop for the ferry from Lumut. The **Sri Pathirakaliaman** Hindu temple just before the village, overlooking the sea, is only worth a cursory glance before continuing on to the more substantial **KAMPUNG SUNGEI PINANG BESAR**, less than a kilometre away. Here, down a small turning off to the right, you'll find the **Foo Lin Kong** temple, a cross between a place of worship and a theme park. Inside the dim, rather spooky room that houses the shrine are some authentic-looking shrunken heads designed to ward off evil spirits and a few incongruous *Guinness* bottles as offerings, while surrounding the temple itself is a miniature Great Wall of China spreading up the hillside, a small children's playground and a dismal zoo. Back on the main road, a few hundred metres more brings you back to Pangkor Town.

Other islands

There are several small islands around Pulau Pangkor to which some of the hotels arrange fishing and snorkelling **day trips** for around $30 a head. No accommodation is available except on **PULAU PANGKOR LAUT**, off the southwest coast, where the *Pansea Resort* (☎05/935495; ⑤) will charge you $30 for the privilege of setting foot on the island in the first place. This is worth it for Emerald Bay alone, whose superb sand and waters across the island from the resort match anything found elsewhere in Malaysia. There are four daily ferries to and from Lumut ($6 return), or a service every fifteen minutes from Pangkor jetty ($2 return). It is also possible to get a boat across from Pasir Bogak, but this seems to be a more ad hoc service, only taking place if there is enough demand.

PULAU SEMBILAN, an archipelago of nine islands two hours south by boat from Pulau Pangkor, is the setting for an annual **fishing safari**, a competitive event held in conjunction with the lavishly celebrated *Lumut Pesta Laut* (in Lumut), a popular festival that takes place every October or November. Only one island in the clump, Pulau Lalang, has fresh water and accessible beaches, and at present there is nowhere to stay. You can charter a boat from Lumut jetty or Pasir Bogak for around $250, or arrange a day-trip package through *Faza Holidays* (☎05/509315) in Lumut, starting at $50 per person.

Kuala Kangsar

While Ipoh is the state administrative capital, **KUALA KANGSAR** – 50km to the north-west – is its royal town, home to the Sultans of Perak since the fifteenth century and with the monuments to match. Built by a grandiose sweep of the Perak river, it's a neat, attractive town of green parks and flowers, which sees few tourists – another reason to make time for at least a couple of hours' stop-over between Ipoh and Taiping. Nineteenth-century accounts of Kuala Kangsar rhapsodized about its situation: Ambrose B. Rathborne, in his *Camping and Tramping in Malaya* (1883) thought it boasted "one of the prettiest views in the Straits. . . overlooking the Perak river, up whose beautiful valley an uninterrupted view is obtained," though since he'd just camped and tramped his way through the jungle on an elephant (the only way to reach Kuala Kangsar in the nineteenth century), he was perhaps overly enthusiastic.

With the planting of nine rubber plant seedlings here in 1877, at the beginning of Hugh Low's Residency (see feature below), Kuala Kangsar was in at the start of colonial Malaya's most important industry, but despite the town's one-time importance as an administrative centre, not much has survived from that period. However, a clutch of monuments on the outskirts of town provide a snapshot of Kuala Kangsar's indigenous royal and religious importance.

Heading east from the clocktower in the centre of town, follow jalan Istana as it curves around the fast-moving river, passing through the ornamental gateway that straddles the street. After about 2km, as you begin to notice the gentle gradient of Bukit Chandan, you'll reach the **Ubudiah Mosque**, whose large gold onion domes soar skywards – squashed out of proportion to its width, it looks like Islam's answer to Cinderella's castle. Built in 1917, its construction was interrupted several times, most notably when two elephants belonging to Sultan Idris rampaged all over the imported Italian marble floor. Non-Muslims should ask before entering the mosque.

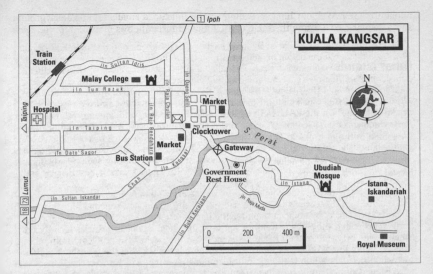

A further fifteen-minute walk up the same road brings you to the imposing, white marble **Istana Iskandariah**, the Sultan's ultra-modern, official palace. It's closed to the public, but stroll around to the left of the huge gates and you'll get a good view down the river. An early legend associated with sungei Perak explains why there is no crown in the Sultan's regalia. A former prince was caught in a severe storm while sailing down the river and, throwing his crown overboard in order to calm the waves, he saved the sinking ship but not, it seems, his headwear, which eluded the efforts of his followers to recover it. Since that day, new Sultans have been enthroned to the sound of drumming rather than by being crowned.

Close by, off to the left as you circle the palace to rejoin the road, the **Royal Museum** (*Muzium di Raja*; Mon–Wed, Sat & Sun 9.30am–5pm, Thurs 9.30am–12.45pm; free) is of greater architectural significance. This former royal residence, the erstwhile *Istana Kenangan*, is a traditional stilted wooden structure – apparently built without the use of a single nail – with intricate friezes and geometric-patterned wall panels on its exterior. Inside, the museum displays a collection of royal artefacts (medals, costumes and so on), although the photographs of past and present royalty in Perak are more stimulating.

Back in town the most evocative memory of colonial days is provided by the **Malay College**, on jalan Tun Razak, its elegant columns and porticos on view as you approach the centre from the train station. Founded in January 1905, it was conceived by British administrators as a training ground for the sons of Malay nobility, an "Eton of the East", where discipline and tradition was more English than in England – although the schoolboys were required to wear formal Malay dress. The success of many of the college's pupils in finding good jobs in the newly created Malay Administrative Service, left parents clammering for places for their offspring and started a craze for English education elsewhere in the country.

Practicalities

The **train station** is on the northwestern outskirts of town, a twenty-minute walk from the clocktower in the centre. Buses from Ipoh, Butterworth or Taiping pull up at the **bus station** at the bottom of jalan Raja Bendahara, close to the river. Although you

THE RESIDENTIAL SYSTEM

The creation of the **Residential System** formed the backbone of the Pangkor Treaty of 1874 and furthered the notion of indirect British rule. The British Resident – one for each state – was to have an advisory role in Malay affairs of state in return for a sympathetic observance of their own customs and rituals. The interpretation of the newly created post was in the hands of **Hugh Low** (1824–1905), the very first Resident, whose jurisdiction of Perak (1877–1889) was based in Kuala Kangsar. The personable Low lived modestly by British standards in the Residency building (no longer extant) and, together with his two pet chimpanzees for company, kept open house during his ten-hour working day. Together with his assistant George Maxwell – later destined for greater things – his adroit linguistic skills won him favour with the local chiefs with whom he could soon converse fluently and whose practices he quickly understood. Having spent nearly thirty years in Borneo, he had become great friends with Charles and James Brooke and sought to replicate their benign system of government.

The approval of the Malay nobility – by no means guaranteed, as the Birch incident shows (see p.138) – was vital to the success of the Residency scheme, and this was induced principally by compensation for the income they had lost from taxes and property. This suited the Sultans well, for not only did they establish financial security for themselves by virtue of their healthy stipends, but they were also protected from other rivals. As time went on, lesser figures were given positions within the bureaucracy, thus weaving the Malays into the fabric of the administration, of which the cornerstone was the **State Council.** Although the Sultan was the ceremonial head, it was the Resident who chose the constituent members and who set the political agenda, in consultation with his deputies, the **District Officers**, and with the Governor.

The increasing power of central government soon began to diminish the consultative side of the Resident's role, and by the 1890s fewer and fewer meetings of the council were being held. Religious matters were the only things exempt from British control, but even here the goal posts were often moved to suit British purposes. Furthermore, there were few Residents as talented and sympathetic as Hugh Low and so, predictably, the involvement of the British in Malay affairs became less to instruct their subjects in new forms of government and more to affirm British status.

won't necessarily want to stay in Kuala Kangsar, there are a couple of options if you do get stuck. Opposite the bus station is the *Double Lion*, at 74 jalan Kangsar (☎05/ 851010; ②), while a quieter option, on the way to the Ubudiah mosque, is the *Government Rest House* (☎05/851699; ②), whose decor and facilities do not, unfortunately, match the stately riverside location.

Taiping and Maxwell Hill

Set against the backdrop of the mist-laden Bintang hills, **TAIPING**'s origins – like so many places in Perak – lay in the discovery of tin here in the first decades of the nineteenth century. As a mining centre, overrun by enthusiastic prospectors, its early history was predictably turbulent. Originally known as Larut, the town was torn apart in 1871 by violent wars between various Chinese secret societies whose members had come to work in the mines. A truce was finally declared in 1874, after British intervention as a result of the Pangkor Treaty, and the town was somewhat hopefully renamed Taiping, meaning "everlasting peace" – which, incidentally, makes it the only sizeable town in Malaysia today with a Chinese name.

From these shaky beginnings Taiping thrived and its expanding prosperity helped fund many firsts at a time when Kuala Lumpur was barely on the map: the first railway in the country to facilitate the export of the tin, connecting Taiping with the coastal port of Fort Weld (now Kuala Sepetang); the first English-langauge school in 1878; the first museum in 1883; and the first English-language newspaper (the *Perak Pioneer*) in 1894. With the establishment of the nearby hill station of **Maxwell Hill** (now Bukit Larut) as a retreat for its administrators, Taiping was firmly at the forefront of the colonial development of the Federated Malay States. For years, tin was its life force, mined and traded by a largely Chinese population which was superstitious to the point of obstinacy. The mere presence of a European close to a tin mine was disliked and resented, while Ambrose B. Rathborne, off tramping again, noted that "No greater offence can be given to a gang of miners than by descending their mine with boots on and an umbrella opened overhead, as it is popularly supposed that such a proceeding is an insult to the presiding spirits, who, out of revenge will make the tin ore disappear." The actual reason for the eventual depletion of the tin deposits was, needless to say, rooted more in geological reality, but the diminished market for tin did later take its toll on the wealth of the town. Nowadays, bypassed by the North–South Highway and replaced in administrative importance by Ipoh, Taiping has started to decline gracefully, its tattered two-storey shop fronts symptomatic of the run-down atmosphere that pervades the town. The main reason people visit is to relax at Maxwell Hill, but allow yourself at least half a day to explore the sights of Taiping – its gardens, the Perak Museum and the fine buildings which line the wide roads.

The town

Taiping is an easily walkable size and since the central streets are laid out on a grid system there's no problem finding your way around. The four main streets which run parallel to each other are jalan Taming Sari, jalan Pasar, jalan Kota and jalan Iskander. The gardens – Taman Tasik – spread to the northeast of town, close to the foot of Maxwell Hill, with the museum a little to the northwest.

A wander around the shop-lined streets surrounding Taiping's active **central market** does little to detract from its reputation as a seedy old mining town. Wizened old *towkays* lurk at the rear of musty shophouses, while dingy *kedai kopis* now keep the town ticking in place of the erstwhile gambling dens and bottle shops. More promising are the numerous food markets which add a welcome splash of colour. On the southwestern outskirts of the town, you can pay a visit to the three **temples** representing the Hindu, Chinese and Muslim communities, before heading up jalan Pesar to the **padang** and the sparkling white **District Office**, which marks the northern limit of the Chinese district.

Then make your way northwards up jalan Taming Sari to **All Saints' Church**, whose foundation in 1887 makes it the oldest Christian church in Malaysia. It cuts a forlorn figure these days: built entirely of wood, the termites are slowly destroying the structure and there's talk of completely demolishing and rebuilding it to "preserve" the church for future generations. In some ways, the tiny churchyard is more interesting, providing a pertinent reminder of the hidden costs of building an empire, since it contains the graves of the earliest British and Australian settlers, many of whom died at an unusually early age, or who, after many years of service to the Malay states, failed to gain a pension to enable them to return home.

Another hundred metres further on, the **Perak Museum** (daily 9.30am–5pm, Fri closed 12.15–2.45pm; free), housed in a cool and spacious colonial building, boasted as many as 13,000 exhibits when it opened in 1883. Often billed as the best museum in Malaysia, it's difficult to understand the accolade and even the collection of stuffed rare snakes fails to excite much interest, although there is an extensive collections of ancient weapons and *orang asli* implements and ornaments. Opposite the museum, the **prison** was built by the Japanese during World War II: it carries out most of the executions of Malaysia's drug offenders. To the left, the **Ling Nam Temple** is one of Taiping's main Chinese centres of worship.

Backtracking down jalan Taming Sari takes you to the *padang*, from which it's a ten-minute stroll to **Taman Tasik**, the 62-acre lake gardens which are landscaped around two former tin-mining pools. At the height of the industry's success, large areas of countryside were being laid to waste, creating unsightly muddy heaps and stagnant pools. In Taiping, at least, the Resident kept a colonial sense of propriety and turned this area into a park in 1890. It's still immaculately kept, with a gazebo, freshwater fish in the lakes and a profusion of flowers. There's also a nine-hole golf course and even a small zoo (daily 10am–6pm; $1).

A short walk to the northeast of the park, past the lotus pond, takes you to the **Commonwealth War Cemetery**, a serene memorial to the casualties of World War II, split in two by the road to Maxwell Hill, leaving an all-too-neat division of Indians on one side, British and Australians on the other. There are over five hundred graves here, many of them unmarked, including Taiping's recipient of the Victoria Cross.

Maxwell Hill

MAXWELL HILL – 12km northeast of Taiping – is Malaysia's smallest (and oldest) hill station, named after the first Assistant Resident of Perak, George Maxwell. At approximately 1035m above sea level the climate is wonderfully cool and on a clear day there are spectacular views of the west coast. Unfortunately its reputed status as the wettest place in Malaysia also means that it's frequently too cloudy at the top to see much at all. Nevertheless, it's worth visiting if only for the few tame forest **walks** – they're not marked so you'll have to use your initiative if you want to depart from the surfaced road – and the climb to Cottage, the only accessible **summit**, which takes you through groves of evergreens and the largest variety of sunflowers in the country. Leeches can be a problem in the forest: wear long trousers, and socks and shoes rather than sandals.

The narrow road up to the hill station twists and turns round some terrifying bends and is only accessible by government **land rover**: private vehicles are not allowed. The service begins at the foot of the hill, ten minutes' walk from the lake gardens (hourly 8am–6pm; $2.50 one-way) and takes twenty minutes to reach the top. If you're only making a day trip, it's advisable to **book your seat** there in advance (call ☎05/827243), otherwise at busy times you could find yourself hanging around waiting for a space. Alternatively, book your return journey up at the station itself in the booth by the *Rumah Beringin* rest house.

Many people prefer to **walk** up from Taiping instead, which takes from two-and-a-half to three hours. This way you get more time to take in the views and you can still make it down again by early evening; the marked path starts at the land rover pick-up point. About midway to the summit is the *Tea Garden House*, which was once part of an extensive tea estate. It's an ideal place to stop for a cuppa: the view at this point is superb with the town of Taiping and the mirror-like waters of the gardens visible below.

Practicalities

The **train station** is just over a kilometre west of the centre of Taiping, behind the hospital, on jalan Stesyen; it's a twenty-minute walk to the nearest hotel. The **express bus station** is right in the centre of town, in a small square between jalan Kota and jalan Iskander; the **taxi station** is right next door. The **local bus station** is a very grotty affair further down jalan Iskander on the left, but you probably won't need to use this; there's another agency for KL/Singapore buses nearby.

Accommodation

For a town of its size, Taiping has a remarkable number of hotels, which is just as well because in high season it often has to cater for the overspill from Maxwell Hill. For those on a tight budget, or who prefer a bit more action, the town rather than the hill station is definitely the place to stay. One or two of the places are old-style wooden Chinese houses with shutters, which can be a bit grotty but still retain some character.

The best of the budget options in **Taiping** is the *Aun Chuan* (☎05/825322, ①), on the corner of jalan Halaman Pasar and jalan Kota, above *Kentucky Fried Chicken*, a clean and spacious place with wooden floors. The *Peking* on jalan Idris Taiping (☎05/822975; ①), close to the express bus station, has a traditional wooden exterior (though modern rooms); this, too, is good value and the management is friendly. More seedy is the *Hotel Peace*, 30–32 jalan Iskander (☎05/823379; ①), whose original tiles and stained glass make up for the distinct lack of peace and quiet. In the northeastern part of town, just south of Taman Tasik, is the *Lake View*, at 1a Circular Road (☎05/824911; ①), a modern hotel with well-appointed rooms, although the karaoke bar can make it very noisy. The *Panorama*, 61–79 jalan Kota (☎05/834111; ④), is the plushest hotel in town, but fairly reasonably priced for all that and centrally located.

At **Maxwell Hill**, the choice is between rest houses and bungalows, and since there is only room for a total of 53 people you'll need to **book in advance** (call ☎05/827241 to reserve at any of the places mentioned here). The rest houses are the cheapest choice, either *Rumah Beringin* (②), *Rumah Rehat Bukit Larut* (①) – the only place with a single room – or, the furthest up, *Rumah Rehat Gunung Hijai* (②), all situated along the road beyond the land rover drop-off point. Bungalow prices are for the whole building rather than for individual rooms, and you can choose from *Rumah Cendana* (⑤), or the VIP-class *Rumah Cempaka* (⑥) and *Rumah Tempinis* (⑥) – all sleep four to six people.

Eating and drinking

The most entertaining meals to be had in town are those at Taiping's numerous **food-markets**. One of the best is *Larut Matang* on jalan Iskander, a big bright eating hall with every kind of rice and noodle dish imaginable. For other daytime food, *Kedai Kopi Tai Chien* on jalan Pasar, one block west of the clocktower, is very good, famed for its *popiah, mee goreng* and fruit juices; it also has a surprisingly explosive ice-crunching machine. For a more upmarket meal, try the *Nagaria Steak House* on jalan Pasar, where Western meals go for around $12.

At **Maxwell Hill** meals are available at each of the rest houses, while at the bunga-lows, the caretaker can arrange for food to be prepared for you, or you can do your own cooking – buy provisions in Taiping.

Butterworth

Heading north from Taiping towards the coast, the landscape becomes increasingly flat and arid, as the road eases away from the backbone of mountains that dominates the western seaboard. There's nothing of note in the 94km before **BUTTERWORTH**, a dusty, industrial town with an anomalous status: it lies within Seberang Prai, the penin-sular province of the largely island state of Penang. Butterworth's fumes and noise do nothing to encourage a stop, but unfortunately it's the transportation hub for the whole area, and the only place on the peninsula from which to reach the island of Penang and its capital Georgetown (for which, see below). As a halfway house between Bangkok and Singapore, Butterworth is also the most common stopover point on that journey, so you could find yourself spending a short time here, whatever your eventual destination.

The **bus station, port complex, taxi stand** and **train station** are all next door to each other, lying right on the quayside, so with a little luck you should never have to venture any further. Although on a branch line from the main north–south railway, there is only one daily train that does not pass through Butterworth and that stops at the nearby main line station of Bukit Mertajam, a short bus or local train ride to the southeast.

Realistically, the only reason to spend any time at all in Butterworth is to sort out your **transport to Penang** – which can usually be done within half an hour of arrival. All the details for services to Penang are covered on the opposite page. If you get stuck, there are plenty of **places to stay**, although many of the hotels are a fair way from the port. Some of the nearer options are *G7 Lodge* (☎04/312662; ①), on jalan Pantai – turn immediately left out of the bus station. There are dorm beds here, too, and a lower charge for day use of the rooms and showers – handy if you're waiting for a connection between Bangkok and Singapore. A bit further along jalan Pantai is the *Beach Garden* (no phone; ②), which is overpriced and basic. Otherwise, the *Ambassadress* (☎04/342788; ③) is just one of many along jalan Bagan Luar, the main road running out of Butterworth; facilities are better here, but it's more than walking distance from the terminals.

Penang

PENANG, 370km from Kuala Lumpur on Malaysia's northwestern coast, is a confusing amalgam of state and island. The entire interest in Penang state is on Penang Island – **Pulau Pinang** (Betel Nut Island) in Malay – a large island of nearly 300 square kilometres upon which was sited the first British settlement on the Malay peninsula. The mainland strip of Penang state – Seberang Prai (formerly Province Wellesley) – is of little or no interest, centred on the industrial town of Butterworth (see above), to which there would be no point in going at all were it not for the ferry services across to the island. The confusion gets worse when you consider that the island's likeable capital, **Georgetown**, Malaysia's second largest city, is also often referred to as "Penang". Once there, though, things quickly fall into place. A fast-moving, go-ahead place, Georgetown has a reputation as a duty-free shopping mecca that accords with its history as a trading port; the epitome of its commercial development is the gigantic high-rise KOMTAR building, visible even from the mainland.

Nonetheless, Georgetown has sacrificed few of its traditional buildings and customs to modernity. In one of Malaysia's most vibrant Chinatowns, faded two-storey shop-houses and ornate temples predominate, legacies of the massive influx of immigrants attracted by the early establishment of a colonial port here. Hot on their heels were the Indian merchants, bringing with them spices, rich cloths and religious customs, nowhere more evident in the city than during the annual festival of Thaipusam. Also dotted here and there is some of the best British colonial architecture in the country, exemplified in the buildings that surround crumbling Fort Cornwallis, the island's oldest structure; while to the northwest of the centre, huge mansions and elegant gardens bear witness to the rewards earned by many an early entrepreneur.

While the city is likely to be your base during a stay on Penang, most visitors make day trips out, traditionally to the beaches at **Batu Ferringhi** and **Tanjung Bungah** along the north coast. No longer the hippy hangout of the 1970s, this is now five-star resort territory, and although pollution and overdevelopment have taken their inevitable toll, the beaches themselves aren't bad and the nightlife keeps most people happy. It's still all too easy, though, to run away with the idea that the beaches are the only reason to come to Penang and you'll get a much more balanced picture of the island if you make the effort to spend some time away from the coast. There's enough in the busy Georgetown streets to occupy at least a couple of days – markets, temples and historic buildings – while journeys south and west reveal a startlingly rural and mountainous interior with a population that retains many of its traditions and industries.

The island is the focus of several important **festivals** throughout the year, starting with Thaipusam in February. Perhaps the best known of the rest is the Penang Bridge Run held in May, when thousands of competitors hurtle across the bridge to Butterworth at dawn as part of a half-marathon. June is also a busy month, with the International Dragonboat Race, the Equestrian Carnival and a beach volleyball tournament on the northern coast. In July the flower festival and Grand Parade provide colour, while the Cultural Festival provides a showcase for the various ethnic groups — the Malays, Chinese and Indians – who make up Penang's population.

Getting there

The most convenient approach from the mainland is on the 24-hour passenger and car **ferry service from Butterworth** (daily: every 20min, 6am–midnight; hourly, midnight–6am; passengers 40c return, cars $7 return), which takes fifteen minutes and docks at the centrally located terminal on Pengkalan Weld in Georgetown. The **Penang Bridge**, the longest in Asia at 13km, crosses from just south of Butterworth at Perai to a point on jalan Udini, 8km south of Georgetown on the east coast; there's a

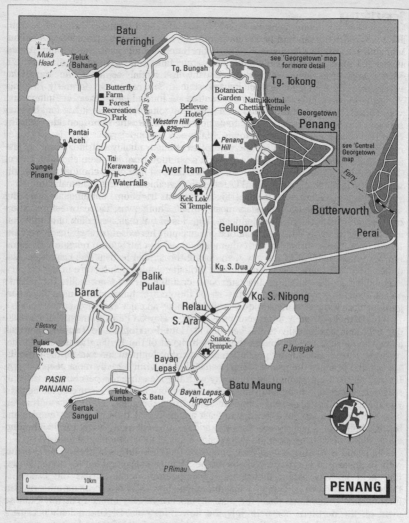

PENANG

one-way toll of $7 payable on the mainland – if you are coming over by **long-distance taxi** from any point on the peninsula, check whether or not the toll is included in the fare. The **airport,** at Bayan Lepas on the southeastern tip of the island, handles some direct international flights, though most are routed through KL. Yellow bus #66 or #83 (on the hour 6am–midnight; $1.80) takes about thirty minutes to run into Georgetown, dropping you next to the Pengkalan Weld ferry terminal; otherwise a taxi costs around $15 – buy a coupon beforehand from inside the terminal building. Finally, **ferries** from Medan (Indonesia) and Langkawi (p.180) dock in Georgetown at Swettenham Pier, a few hundred metres up the dockside from Pengkalan Weld.

For **arrival and information details in Georgetown,** see p.156.

Some history

Until the late eighteenth century, Pulau Pinang was ruled by the **Sultans of Kedah**. For many years Kedah had been harrassed by enemies, which meant that its Sultan, Mohammed J'wa Mu'Azzam Shah II, was prepared to afford trade facilities to any nation that would provide him with military protection. Enter **Francis Light** in 1771, a ship's captain of the European trading company of Jourdain, Sulivan and de Souza, who was in search of a regional trading base for both his company and the East India Company. According to contemporary accounts, Captain Light was a charming man, well trained in the art of diplomacy, and it was not long before the Sultan had housed the captain in his fort at Kuala Kedah, conferred upon him the honorary title of "Deva Raja" (God-king) and taken him into his confidence.

Light knew that the East India Company wanted to obtain a strategic port in the region to facilitate its trade with China and as a refuge from its enemies in the Bay of Bengal. In forwarding the Sultan's offer of the island of Penang to the Company, Light drew particular attention to its safe harbour and the opportunities for local commerce. In 1772 the Company sent its own agent, Edward Moncton, to negotiate with the Sultan, but the talks soon broke down and it was another twelve years before agreement was reached, spurred by the accession of a new Sultan, Abdullah, and the East India Company's mounting concern that other countries were gaining a regional foothold – the French, at war with Britain, had acquired port facilities in northern Sumatra, having already made a pact with Burma, and the Dutch were consolidating their position in the Straits of Melaka.

In accordance with an agreement arranged by Light, the Company was to pay Sultan Abdullah $30,000 a year. Unfortunately for the Sultan, the Company's new Governor-General Charles Cornwallis firmly stated that he could not be party to the Sultan's disputes with the other Malay princes or promise to protect him from the Burmese or Siamese. This rather pulled the rug from under Light's feet because it was on the basis of these promises that the Sultan had ceded the island of Penang in the first place. Undeterred, Light decided to conceal the facts from both parties and formally **established a port** at Penang on August 11, 1786 on his own initiative. For the next five years Light adopted stalling tactics with the Sultan, assuring him that the matter of protection was being referred to authorities in London. The Sultan eventually began to suspect that the Company had reneged on the agreement and attempted to drive the British out of Penang by force, but the effort failed and the subsequent settlement imposed by the British allowed the Sultan an annual payment of only $6000, and no role in the future government of the island.

So it was that Penang, then inhabited by less than a hundred indigenous fishermen, became the **first British settlement** in the Malay Peninsula. Densely forested, the island was open to settlers to claim as much land as they could clear – in somewhat debonair mood, Light encouraged the razing of the jungle by firing coins from a cannon into the undergrowth. After an initial, late eighteenth century influx, of mainly Chinese immigrants attracted by the possibilities of new commerce, Penang quickly became a major colonial administrative centre – within two years, four hundred acres were under cultivation and its population had reached ten thousand. Francis Light was made Superintendent and declared the island a free port, renaming it "Prince of Wales Island" after the British heir apparent, whose birthday fell the day after the founding of the island. Georgetown was, unsurprisingly, named after the king at that time, George III; and it retained its colonial name, even after the island reverted to the name of Penang.

For a time, all looked rosy for Penang, with Georgetown proclaimed as capital of the newly established **Straits Settlements** (incorporating Melaka and Singapore) in 1826. But the founding of Singapore in 1819 was the beginning of the end for Georgetown and as the new colony overtook its predecessor in every respect (replacing it as capital of the Straits Settlements in 1832), Penang's fortunes rapidly began to wane. In retrospect, this had one beneficial effect, since with Georgetown stuck in the economic doldrums for a century or more, there was no significant development within the city – which meant many of its colonial and early Chinese buildings survive to this day. Although occupied by the Japanese in 1942 during World War II and placed under the authority of a Japanese governor, the strategic significance of Singapore once more proved to be Penang's saving grace and there was little or no bomb damage to the island.

Georgetown

On arriving in **GEORGETOWN** in 1879, stalwart Victorian traveller Isabella Bird thought it "a brilliant place under a brilliant sky" and it's hard to improve on this simple statement – Malaysia's most fascinating city retains more of its cultural history than virtually anywhere else in the country. Fort Cornwallis, St George's Church and the many buildings on and around lebuh Pantai all survive from the earliest colonial days, while the communities of Chinatown and Little India have contributed some of the country's finest temples. Later Thai and Burmese arrivals left their own mark around the city, but its predominant character is formed by the rows of peeling two-storey Chinese shophouses, shutters painted in pastel colours, with bright red Chinese lettering covering their colonnades and cheerfully designed awnings to shield their goods from the glare of the sun. While the confusion of trishaws, buses, lorries and scooters make parts of Georgetown as frenetic and polluted as most others in the region, life in the slow lane has changed very little over the years: the rituals of worship, eating out at a roadside stall, the running of the family business, have all continued with little concern displayed for Georgetown's contemporary technological development. It may no longer be a sleepy backwater – most of the island's one-million strong population now lives here – but the city's soul is firmly rooted in the past.

Strategically sited Georgetown is no stranger to visitors, since ships from all over the world have been docking at present-day Swettenham Pier since Francis Light first established his port here in 1786. Over the years, not surprisingly, it acquired a rather dubious reputation for back street dives frequented by boisterous sailors on shore leave. Where once ships' chandlers and supply merchants ran thriving businesses, modern-day maritime trade is of an entirely different nature: neon-lit bars and dingy brothels help to boost the spirits of foreign navy crews who make regular forays around the city's streets. There's been a gradual change, though, especially since the late 1970s, when foreign tourists first descended upon Penang in significant numbers. Nowadays, parts of downtown Georgetown sparkle with the state-of-the-art hotels and air-con shopping malls familar to much of modern Malaysia. Perhaps more than any other place in the country, too, Georgetown is a magnet for budget travellers – the city is something of a hangout, a place not only to renew Thai visas, but also to settle down and observe the street life from one of the pavement cafés in between trips to the beach.

Arrival, information and getting around

Arriving at either the bus station, taxi stand or ferry terminals on **Pengkalan Weld** or at nearby **Swettenham Pier** puts you at the eastern edge of Georgetown, just a short walk from the hotels and major amenities. **Driving** into the city is not for the traffic-shy, though the major routes are well signposted. Better than trying to navigate

The **telephone code** for Geogetown and Penang is ☎04. Note that all Malaysian telephone numbers are being **changed** in a rolling programme lasting several years. Some of the numbers given in this chapter, while correct at the time of going to press, are likely to have changed.

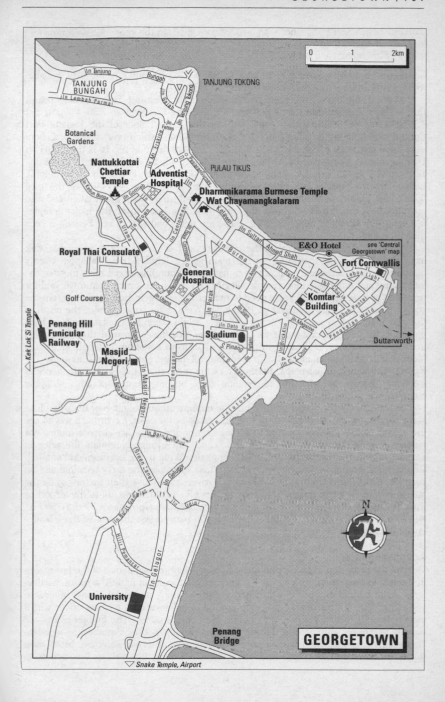

For **departure information from Penang**, see the box on p.170.

Georgetown's narrow streets is to park in the KOMTAR building on jalan Penang, which is within easy walking distance of the hotel area.

On arrival, the most convenient tourist office is the **Penang Tourist Association** (Mon–Thurs 8.30am–1pm & 2–4.30pm, Fri 8.30am–12.30pm & 2.30–4.30pm, Sat 8.30am–1pm; ☎616663), which you'll find on the ground floor of the Penang Port Commission building on jalan Tun Syed Sheh Barakbah, which produces an excellent island and city **map** which costs $1. A couple of doors down at no. 10 is the **Tourism Development Corporation** (Mon–Thurs 8am–12.45pm & 2–4.15pm, Fri 8am–12.15pm & 2.45–4.15pm, Sat 8am–12.45pm; ☎620066), which is slightly more helpful. Best of all is the **Tourist Information Centre** (daily 10am–6pm; ☎614461) on the third floor of the KOMTAR building, which is really clued up on local information and also operates half- and full-day tours of the city, including ones to all the major temples ($20) and the northern beaches ($40); these are not a bad way to see Penang if your time is limited.

The best way of **getting around the city** is on foot. It's fairly small – you could walk from Pengkalan Weld to the top of the main street, lebuh Chulia, in about twenty minutes – and in any case, unless you're pavement-pounding you'll miss most of the interesting and otherwise inaccessible alleyways. For longer journeys in town, and for travelling around the island, you'll need to master the excellent **bus service**. From the station next to the ferry terminal on Pengkalan Weld, blue buses service the north of the island, and yellow buses the south and west, while green buses also run from here on routes through the city out towards Ayer Itam. For buses **around the city** and its immediate environs, *MPPP* (red-stripe) buses run from a station on lebuh Victoria, a block north of Pengkalan Weld. In addition, all buses stop at the station by the KOMTAR building on jalan Ria. **Fares** are rarely more than a dollar and the services frequent, though by 8pm in the evening they become more sporadic, stopping completely at midnight.

The traditional way of seeing the city is by **trishaw**, though lounging back in a low-slung carriage while the driver strains on his pedals is, for most, too brutal a way to see the sights. Still, some people like to arrange tours and there are drivers touting for custom outside the major hotels and all along lebuh Chulia. Negotiate the price in advance; a ride from the ferry terminal at Pengkalen Weld to the northern end of lebuh Chulia costs around $3. Otherwise, there are **taxi** stands by the ferry terminal and on jalan Dr. Lim Chwee Long, off jalan Penang. Drivers rarely use their meters so fix the fare in advance – a trip across town runs to about $5, while a ride out to the airport or Batu Feringghi costs $15. To book a taxi in advance, call *Georgetown Taxi Service* on ☎617098. For **bike or car rental** – useful if you plan to see the rest of the island – check the list of addresses on p.171.

Accommodation

Despite the profusion of hotels and guest houses, Georgetown is one of the few places in the whole country where you might experience difficulty in finding a **room**, particularly at the budget end of the scale. Arrive early or book ahead by phone; otherwise you either face a great deal of traipsing around or reliance on a trishaw driver who'll usually be able to find you a room (though for a commission). The budget places are mostly found on and around **lebuh Chulia**, usually within ramshackle wooden-shuttered mansions, often with a portico and elegant internal staircase. Most have **dorm beds** as well as rooms and other useful services, like selling bus tickets to

Thailand, obtaining Thai visas and so on. Given the choice it barely seems worth mentioning the two official **youth hostels**, the *YMCA*, 211 jalan Macalister (☎362211; ②), and the *YWCA*, 8 jalan Mesjid Negeri (☎681855; ②), which are miles away from the city centre.

In Georgetown's mid-range places – mostly in the same noisy area – you're often just paying for air-con and more modern furniture. Top-of-the-range hotels are more or less all located on **jalan Penang** and **lebuh Farquhar**, west of the centre, at all of which 15 percent tax is added to the quoted price.

All the places to stay listed below are keyed on the map on p.162–165.

ALONG LEBUH CHULIA

Lebuh Chulia starts with number 1 at the eastern end (nearest the ferry terminal).

Eastern, no. 509 (☎614597). Tiny box-like rooms with "saloon" doors. It's next to the mosque, so expect it to be noisy. ②.

Eng Aun, no. 380 (☎04/612333). Long-running backpackers' haunt with dorms and the cheapest rooms in town (though you get what you pay for); renovations may increase prices soon. Laundry service and pleasant café, too. ①.

Hang Chow, no. 511 (☎610810). Basic – and not terribly welcoming – hotel at the upper end of the scale, with some large, but also some very small, rooms and miniscule bathrooms. ①.

Honpin, no. 273b (☎625243). Above *Hsiang Yang* restaurant, the rather average rooms don't quite live up to the promise of the grand marble lobby. ③.

Lum Thean, no. 422 (☎614117). Modern frontage but with an interesting inner courtyard and a grand staircase. The large scruffy rooms have luxurious sprung mattresses. ①.

My Palace Hostel, no. 103a (☎894663). New and somewhat cobbled together, this place only has dorm beds, some in the corridor. Room for 40 and the management are very obliging. ①.

Paradise Bed and Breakfast, no. 99 (☎628439). Clean place though rooms are rather small and internal ones have no windows. There's a helpful information board, and breakfast is included. ②.

Sky, no. 348 (☎622323). Basic, but air-con rooms are good value. A few dorm beds available, too. ②. **Swiss**, no. 431 (☎620133). Another popular hostel (no dorm) that tends to get full before noon. Set back from the road with parking and an airy café. Also has laundry, travel and visa sevices. ①.

Theeba Hostel, no. 41 (no phone). This small, shabby place is one of the closest hostels to the ferry terminal; it has overpriced rooms but decent dorms. ②.

Tye Ann, no. 282 (☎614875). Another backpackers' favourite with small but clean rooms and dorm, all with shared bathroom. There's no communal area after the café (see p.169) closes at 5pm. ①.

AROUND LEBUH CHULIA

Cathay, 15 lebuh Leith (☎626271). Stylish old colonial mansion dating from 1910. The cool greys of the interior decor, the spacious rooms and courtyard fountain make for a tranquil environment. ③.

D'Budget Hostel, 9 lebuh Gereja (☎634794). Five minutes' walk from the ferry terminal, with plenty of dorm space and small partitioned rooms, but clean, well kept and secure. Shared bathroom with hot showers and Western style toilets and the usual ticket service and notice board. ①.

Joy Planet, 26 jalan Kuala Kangsar (☎619043). Basic rooms but with a helpful information service and rooftop beer garden. Some may find its location, opposite the meat market, offputting ①.

Modern, 179c lebuh Muntri (☎635424). On the corner of lebuh Leith this standard hotel gets some good reports. Top-floor rooms have balconies. ①.

New China, 22 lebuh Leith (☎631601). Old-style hotel with rear bar and a steady flow of regular and backpacking clientele. Roomy with some dorm space. ①.

Noble, 36 lorong Pasar (☎612372). Tucked away in a small side street this lacks the atmosphere of those places on lebuh Chulia. It's very cheap but doesn't have much else going for it. ①.

Popus Inn Guest House, 34 jalan Kedah (☎280436). New guest house that welcomes families, with its self-catering facilities, TV and music room. Very reasonably priced. Dorm beds, too. ①.

Tiong Wah, 23 lorong Cinta (☎622057). Cell-like rooms in a quiet area. Air-conditioned bar adds interest. ①.

Wan Hai, 35 lorong Cinta (☎616853). A good place with dorms and lower prices for single people occupying rooms. Friendly, helpful management. ①.

ALONG JALAN PENANG AND LEBUH FARQUHAR

City Bayview, 25a lebuh Farquhar (☎633161). Modern high-rise hotel close to the sea with fantastic views over bay and town. The price includes tax. ⑥.

Continental, 5 jalan Penang (☎636388). Impersonal and squeaky-clean hotel with nightclub, karaoke lounge and a very central location. ⑤.

Eastern & Oriental, 10 lebuh Farquhar (☎630630). Legendary colonial hotel (known universally as the *E&O*) whose classy rooms, beautiful gardens and swimming pool make it a surprisingly good-value treat. ⑤.

Federal, 39 jalan Penang (☎634179). Reasonably attractive hotel, but the front rooms are noisy and the bathrooms very small. ③.

International Youth Hostel, 8 lebuh Farquhar (☎630558). Next door to the *E&O*, this has the cheapest dorm beds in town, but if you can afford more, do, as it's scruffy and unappealing. ①.

Oriental, 105 jalan Penang (☎634211). Excellent-value mid-range hotel with particularly good low-season rates Nov–Feb. ④.

Polar Café, 48a jalan Penang (☎622054). Comfortable rooms, sprung mattresses and inclusive continental breakfast make this a good choice – the only drawback is the sing-along bar at the front that keeps you awake till the small hours. ②.

Towne House, 70 jalan Penang (☎638621). Plush and well-appointed rooms that are among the cheapest in this category. ④.

White House, 72 jalan Penang (☎632385). Very clean, large rooms, although ones at the front tend to be a bit noisy. It's at the bottom end of this price category, and consequently very good value for money. ②.

The city centre

The main area of interest in Georgetown is the central square kilometre or so bordered by the sharply curving coast, the north–south jalan Penang and east–west jalan Magazine. The most prominent, if not most aesthetically pleasing, landmark is the Komplex Tun Abdul Razak (or KOMTAR), a huge high-rise of shops and offices towering over the western corner of the city centre. The whole of this area could effectively be termed **Chinatown**, since the entire centre of Georgetown is dominated by shuttered two-storey shophouses and a liberal scattering of *kongsis* (clan associations) that have stood here in various forms since the late eighteenth century. Struggling to survive this cultural domination is the tiny **Little India** between lebuh Queen and lebuh King, while the remnants of the city's **colonial** past – Fort Cornwallis, St George's Church and the building housing the Penang Museum – are all clustered relatively close together at the eastern end of town, not far from Swettenham Docks. For a reminder of Penang's past economic success, typified by millionaire's row and the *Eastern and Oriental* (*E&O*) *Hotel*, the area around **jalan Penang**, west of the central area, is worth exploring.

STREET NAMES IN GEORGETOWN

The most confusing thing about finding your way around Georgetown is understanding the **street names**. All of them used to bear names reflecting the city's colonial past, but the current political climate encourages either a Malay translation of existing names or complete renaming. Thus, Penang Road has become jalan Penang, Penang Street is lebuh Penang, Weld Quay has become Pengkalan Weld, and Beach Street is now lebuh Pantai. This would be relatively straightforward were it not for the fact that the new names have not always been popularly accepted and even on official maps, you'll sometimes see either name used. For example, lebuh Cinta is almost universally known as Love Lane, while the most awkward name is jalan Mesjid Kapitan Kling, the clumsy new title for the erstwhile Pitt Street, which more often than not is referred to simply as lebuh Pitt.

FORT CORNWALLIS AND THE WATERFRONT

The site of **Fort Cornwallis** (daily 8am–7pm; $1) on the northeastern tip of Pulau Pinang marks the spot where the British fleet, under Captain Francis Light, first disembarked on July 16, 1786. A fort was hastily thrown up, fronting the blustery north channel, to provide barracks for Light and his men, and was named after Lord Charles Cornwallis, Governor-General of India. The present structure dates from around twenty years later, but for all its significance there's little left to excite the senses except the peeling surrounding walls and the seventeenth-century **Sri Rambai cannon**, sited in the northwest corner of the citadel. Presented to the Sultan of Johor by the Dutch, this was later confiscated by the British in 1871 during their attack on Selangor, who loaded 29 guns including the cannon onto the steamer "Sri Rambai" and on reaching Penang, threw it overboard where it remained submerged for almost a decade. According to local legend, the cannon "refused" to leave the sea bed during the subsequent salvage operation and only floated to the surface when Tunku Qudin, the former Viceroy of Selangor, tied a rope to it and ordered it to rise. Since then it's been considered a living entity with mystical powers; the local belief is that barren women can conceive by laying flowers on its barrel.

Elsewhere, inside the fort, there's a craft shop, a replica of a traditional Malay house and, close to the cannon, an airless underground bunker detailing the history of Penang – unimaginatively presented, but informative if you're not claustrophobic. An open-air auditorium, which consumes much of the central area, hosts local music and dance festivals – keep an eye on the local press for the latest shows.

The large expanse of green that borders the fort, the **Padang Kota Lama**, was once the favourite promenade of the island's colonial administrators and thronged with rickshaws and carriages. On the south side, opposite the grand sweep of the Esplanade, there even used to be a bandstand where Filipino groups played to the strolling passers-by. Now used for sports and other public events, the Padang is bordered by some superb examples of Anglo-Victorian architecture: the **Dewan Undangan Negeri** (State Legislative Building) with its weighty portico and ornate gables, and the **Dewan Bendaran** (Town Hall) of equal aesthetic if not political merit, the city's affairs now being conducted from the KOMTAR tower.

Turning left past the food stalls outside the fort brings you to the Moorish-style **clocktower**, at the junction of lebuh Light and lebuh Pantai, which was presented to the town in 1897 to mark Queen Victoria's Diamond Jubilee (its sixty-foot height represented one foot for each year of her reign). A turn to the right and you're at the top of one of Georgetown's oldest streets, **lebuh Pantai**, the heart of the business district. This narrow and congested road once fronted the beach – its swaying palms providing the first sight of the island to anyone approaching from the mainland. But the scores of moneylenders squeezed cheek-by-jowl between the imposing bank and government buildings, not to mention the constant buzz of the motor scooters, are a far cry from this. Gracefully lining an otherwise ill-proportioned street are some of Georgetown's best colonial buildings, like the *Standard Chartered Bank* and the *Hong Kong and Shanghai Bank*, the heavy pillars of the former providing an elegant archway and a welcome escape from the traffic.

A left turn down any of the adjoining streets leads to the **waterfront**, but there's little of interest here except the passage of the lumbering yellow ferries to and from Butterworth. Much is made of the quaint lifestyle of the inhabitants of the stilted settlement, known as **Kampung Ayer**, close to the ferry terminal. This is also known as "Clan Piers", since each of the jetties is named after a different Chinese clan (see below); the unsanitary and semi-derelict properties here are home to the hundreds of families of harbour workers prevented from moving elsewhere because of the high cost of land.

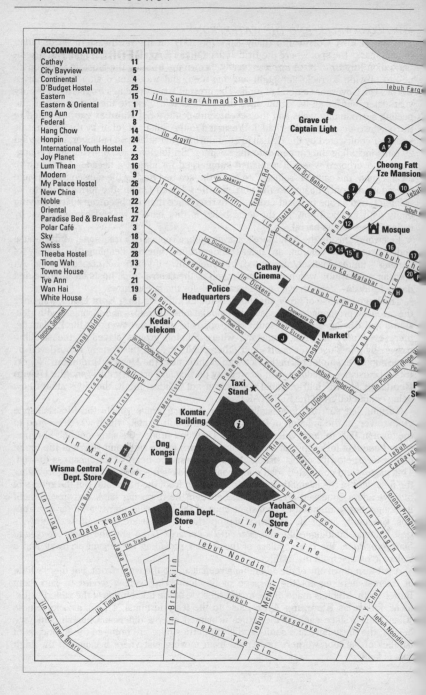

ACCOMMODATION

Cathay	11
City Bayview	5
Continental	4
D'Budget Hostel	25
Eastern	15
Eastern & Oriental	1
Eng Aun	17
Federal	8
Hang Chow	14
Honpin	24
International Youth Hostel	2
Joy Planet	23
Lum Thean	16
Modern	9
My Palace Hostel	26
New China	10
Noble	22
Oriental	12
Paradise Bed & Breakfast	27
Polar Café	3
Sky	18
Swiss	20
Theeba Hostel	28
Tiong Wah	13
Towne House	7
Tye Ann	21
Wan Hai	19
White House	6

Grave of
Captain Light

Cheong Fatt
Tze Mansion

Mosque

Cathay
Cinema

Police
Headquarters

Kedai
Telekom

Market

Taxi
Stand

Komtar
Building

Ong
Kongsi

Wisma Central
Dept. Store

Gama Dept.
Store

Yaohan
Dept.
Store

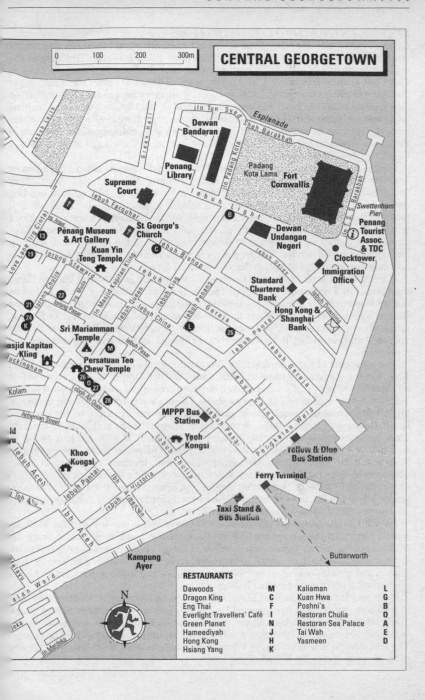

CENTRAL GEORGETOWN

0   100   200   300m

Jln Tun Syed Sheh Barakbah

Esplanade

Dewan Bandaran

Penang Library

Supreme Court

Padang Kota Lama

Fort Cornwallis

lebuh Farquhar

Penang Museum & Art Gallery

St George's Church

Kuan Yin Teng Temple

lebuh Light

lebuh Bishop

Dewan Undangan Negeri

Swettenham Pier

Penang Tourist Assoc. & TDC

Clocktower

lebuh Union

Immigration Office

Standard Chartered Bank

Hong Kong & Shanghai Bank

lebuh Downing

Sri Mariamman Temple

Masjid Kapitan Kling

Persatuan Teo Chew Temple

lebuh China

lebuh Gereja

lebuh Pantai

lebuh Gereja

Pengkalan Weld

MPPP Bus Station

Yeoh Kongsi

Yellow & Blue Bus Station

Khoo Kongsi

Ferry Terminal

lebuh Pantai

lebuh Aceh

lebuh Victoria

lebuh Chulia

Taxi Stand & Bus Station

Butterworth

Kampung Ayer

N

RESTAURANTS

Dawoods	M	Kaliaman	L
Dragon King	C	Kuan Hwa	G
Eng Thai	F	Poshni's	B
Everlight Travellers' Café	I	Restoran Chulia	O
Green Planet	N	Restoran Sea Palace	A
Hameediyah	J	Tai Wah	E
Hong Kong	H	Yasmeen	D
Hsiang Yang	K		

ST GEORGE'S CHURCH TO LEBUH CHULIA

On the western side of lebuh Pantai you're in Chinatown again, a leisurely five-minute stroll through which leads to jalan Masjid Kapitan Kling (or lebuh Pitt), one of the city's main thoroughfares. At its northern end, the Anglican **St George's Church** (Tues–Sat 8.30am–12.30pm & 1.30–4.30pm, open all day Sun) comes into view, one of the oldest buildings in Penang and as simple and unpretentious as anything built in the Greek style in Asia can be. It was constructed in 1817–1819 by the East India Company using convict labour and its cool, pastel-blue interior must have been a welcome retreat from the heat for its new congregation. In 1886, on the centenary of the founding of Penang, a memorial to Francis Light was built in front of the church in the form of a Greek temple – Victoriana at its most inappropriate.

Next to the church on lebuh Farquhar, a street which takes its name from a former Lieutenant-Governor of the settlement, is the **Penang Museum and Art Gallery** (daily 9am–5pm except Fri 9am–12.15pm & 2.45–5pm; free), housed in a building dating from 1821 that was first used as a school. It has an excellent collection of memorabilia that brings to life the various episodes in the island's history: rickshaws, press cuttings, faded black-and-white photographs of early Penang's Chinese million-aires, and a panoramic photograph of Georgetown taken in the 1870s – note just how many buildings still survive. The art gallery upstairs displays temporary exhibitions of contemporary paintings and photographs – it's a bit hit-and-miss.

A few minutes' walk south of St George's Church along jalan Masjid Kapitan Kling, the **Kuan Yin Teng** temple is dedicated to the Buddhist Goddess of Mercy and while not the finest example of a *kongsi* (temple-meeting hall) – that honour goes to the Khoo Kongsi (see below) – it can claim the title of the oldest Chinese temple in Penang. Originally constructed in 1800, it was completely ravaged during World War II; what you see today, including the massive roof dominated by two guardian dragons, is a renovation.

The area east of here, enclosed by the parallel roads of lebuh Queen and lebuh King, forms Georgetown's compact **Little India** district. Despite being surrounded on all sides by Chinatown, it's a vibrant, self-contained community whose outward face, at least to visitors, is of saree and incense shops, banana leaf curry houses and the towering **Sri Mariamman Temple** (open early morning to late evening), on the corner of lebuh Queen and lebuh Chulia. A typical example of Hindu architecture, the lofty entrance tower teems with brightly coloured sculptures of 38 gods and four swans, as well as the hundreds of pigeons that make it their home. At times, the compound becomes quite frenetic with the activities of the devotees of the main deity, Mariamman, found within the inner sanctum under a nine-metre-high dome, which alone contains statues of forty other deities and lions. Within a few metres of here, across lebuh Chulia, the **Persatuan Teo Chew Temple** features fiercesome temple guardians painted on the insides of the temple doors.

Lebuh Chulia itself – the central artery of Chinatown – was the area the southern Indian immigrants chose for establishing their earliest businesses (*chulia* being the Malay word for "South Indian merchant"), and Indian shops here still deal in textiles. But the area (like much of central Georgetown) looks predominantly Chinese, its shop-houses and arcades selling everything from antiques and bamboo furniture to books, photographic services and foreign holidays.

Back on jalan Masjid Kapitan Kling, follow the road along for 500 metres past lines of jewellery stores, each one guarded by a sleepy-looking octogenarian armed guard. You'll see the **Masjid Melayu** ahead, tucked away on lebuh Acheh, and although this is the oldest mosque in Penang, it's only unusual in having an Egyptian-style minaret. The real interest is nearby, across lebuh Aceh, where in a secluded square at the end of an alleyway stands the Khoo Kongsi.

THE KHOO KONGSI

Kongsi is the Hokkien word for "clan-house", the building in which Chinese families gather to worship their ancestors. In Penang, the *kongsis* were originally formed for the mutual help and protection of nineteenth-century immigrants, who naturally tended to band together in clans according to what district they came from. This led to rivalry and often violence between the different Chinese communities, though these days the *kongsis* have reverted to their supportive role, helping with the education of members' children, settling disputes between clan members or advancing loans. Consequently, they are an important means of solidarity, although traditionally women have been excluded from many of the functions and are rarely represented in the hierarchy.

Many of the *kongsis* in Penang are well over a hundred years old and are excellent examples of traditional Chinese architecture. The **Khoo Kongsi** (Mon–Fri 9am–5pm, Sat 9am–1pm; free) is no exception, featuring a spacious courtyard in front of the clan-house, opposite which is a stage for theatrical performances, and two halls in the main building itself, one containing the shrine of the clan deity, the other for the display of the ancestral tablets (the equivalent of gravestones). The original building was started in 1894, an ambitious and extensive project with a roof styled in the manner of a grand palace. It took eight years to complete but was immediately gutted by a mysterious fire. Suspecting sabotage, the clan members rebuilt the house on a lesser scale with the public excuse that the previous design had been too noble to house the ancestral tablets of ordinary mortals. Less extensive it may be, but the present structure was still meticulously crafted by experts from China. The saddle-shaped roof itself reputedly

---

THE PENANG RIOTS

Chinese immigrants in Penang brought their traditions with them, including the establishment of triad (secret society) branches that had evolved in China during the eighteenth century as a means of overthrowing Manchu rule. Once in Penang, the societies provided mutual aid and protection for the Chinese community, their position later bolstered by alliances with Malay religious groups which had originally been established to assist members with funerals and marriages. As the societies grew in wealth and power, gang warfare and extortion rackets became commonplace. The newly appointed Governor-General Sir Harry Ord and his inefficient police force, largely made up of those outside of the Chinese community, proved ineffective in preventing the increasing turmoil and in 1867 matters came to a head in the series of events known subsequently as the **Penang Riots**.

For nine days Georgetown was shaken by fighting between the **Tua-Peh-Kong** society, supported by the Malay **Red Flag,** and the **Ghee Hin**, allied with the Malay **White Flag**. Police intervention resulted in a temporary truce, but a major clash seemed inevitable when, on August 1, 1867, the headman of the Tua-Peh-Kong falsely charged the Ghee Hin and the White Flag societies with stealing cloth belonging to the Tua-Peh-Kong dyers. All hell broke loose and fighting raged around Armenian, Church and Chulia streets. Barricades were erected around the Khoo Kongsi, where much of the fiercest fighting took place, and you can still find bullet holes in the surrounding shops and houses. The authorities were powerless since the battery of artillery normally stationed at Fort Cornwallis had just left for Rangoon and the relief forces had not yet arrived. Countless arrests were made but the police soon had to release many from custody as there was no more room for them in the overflowing jails.

The fighting was eventually quelled by sepoys (Indian troops) brought in from Singapore by the Governor-General, but by then hundreds had been killed and scores of houses burned. As compensation for the devastation suffered by the city, a penalty of $5000 was levied on each of the secret societies, some of which was later used to build four police stations strategically placed to deal with future trouble.

weighs 25 tons, while the central hall is made dark by heavy, intricately carved beams and pillars and bulky mother-of-pearl inlaid furniture. An Art Deco grandfather clock stands somewhat incongruously in the corner. Behind this is a separate chamber, with delicate black-and-white line drawings depicting scenes of courtly life. The hall on the left is a richly decorated shrine to Tua Peh Kong, the god of prosperity; the right-hand hall contains the gilded ancestral tablets. Connecting all three halls is a balcony minutely decorated in bas-relief, whose carvings depict episodes from folk tales – even the bars on the windows have been carved into bamboo sticks. Although entrance to the *kongsi* is free, you must register in the office on your right as you enter the courtyard.

ALONG JALAN PENANG

East of St George's Church, **jalan Penang** separates the traditional commercial district from the residential quarter further to the west, an elegant part of town formerly frequented by many a colonial resident.

At the far northern end of the road, on lebuh Farquhar, stands the legendary **Eastern and Oriental Hotel**, once part of the Sarkies brothers' select chain of colonial retreats (together with the *Raffles* in Singapore; see p.503), and now the epitome of Penang's faded grandeur – keeping up appearances with its *Palm Court* lobby and *Planters' Bar*, and turning a blind eye to the peeling edges. Rudyard Kipling and Somerset Maugham both stayed here, taking tiffin on the terrace and enjoying the cooling sea breeze; stroll in for a drink at least, if not to actually stay. Continuing west along lebuh Farquhar, after about five minutes the road merges with sea-facing jalan Sultan Ahmad Shah, across which you'll find the overgrown churchyard where Francis Light is buried. Further along, the huge, stylish mansions set back from the road in acres of manicured lawn led to the road's rather predictable nickname of "millionaires' row", and though the preposterous upkeep costs have seen several fall into disrepair, what remains still provides an ostentatious reminder of the wealth that once typified Penang.

Backtracking towards jalan Penang, five more minutes' walk east brings you to lebuh Leith, on the corner of which is the stunning **Cheong Fatt Tze Mansion**, whose outer walls are painted in a striking rich blue. It's the best example of ninteenth-century Chinese architecture in Penang, built by Thio Thiaw Siat, a Cantonese businessman. Restoration work is well under way in the elaborate halls of ceremony, bedrooms and libraries, separated by cobbled courtyards, small gardens and heavy wooden doors. Sadly, much of the house's furniture and antiques disappeared long ago, but it is planned to replace these with faithful reproductions.

Back on jalan Penang, don't let the sophisticated shop fronts put you off from bargaining a little, something that's a necessity in the cramped tourist **market** opposite the police station, a little further along. This is the place to pick up leather goods – particularly bags and wallets. Further along still, you'll come to the ordered calm of the **KOMTAR** building, the nucleus of Penang's business and government administration, comprising five levels of air-conditioned shops, offices and fast-food joints, topped by a gigantic circular tower which provides a handy orientation point.

The outskirts

There are several sights on the western and northern **outskirts** of Georgetown worth exploring, most of which provide a welcome break from the frenetic city. Trips to Ayer Itam and Penang Hill especially are a cool alternative to heading for the northern beaches for the day. *MPPP* buses run to all the destinations below from the station on lebuh Victoria, though you can also pick them up at the station at the KOMTAR building on jalan Ria.

THREE TEMPLES AND THE BOTANICAL GARDENS

A fifteen-minute bus ride on *MPPP* #2 or blue buses #93, #94 or #95 (towards Batu Ferringhi) brings you to **Wat Chayamangkalaram** on lorong Burma, a Thai temple painted in yellow and blue and flanked by two statues, whose fierce grimaces and weighty swords are designed to ward off unwanted visitors. Inside, a statue of the Reclining Buddha stretches out its 33-metre length, surrounded by elaborately decorated images of the Buddha covered with gold leaf. The **Dharmmikarama Burmese Temple** across the road is less spectacular, although the white stone elephants at the entrance are attractive and the temple's two stupas are lit to good effect at night. Entrance to both temples is between sunrise and sunset, and is free.

Further west on jalan Kebun Bunga is the **Nattukkottai Chettiar Temple**, a seven-kilometre bus ride from the city centre on *MPPP* #7. This is the focus of the Hindu Thaipusam festival in February, in honour of Lord Subramanian, when thousands of devotees walk through the streets bearing *kavadis* (sacred yokes) fixed to their bodies by hooks and spikes spearing their flesh. The biggest such event in Malaysia is at Kuala Lumpur's Batu Caves (see p.111); if you can't catch that, the festivities here are a similar blend of hypnotic frenzy and celebration. At other times of the year, you're free to concentrate on the temple itself, in which an unusual wooden colonnaded walkway, containing some exquisite pictorial tiles, leads up to the inner sanctum. Here, a life-sized solid silver peacock – featured as a theme throughout the temple – crouches, bowing its head to the deity, Lord Subramanian.

Just five more minutes along jalan Kebun Bunga (Waterfall Road) from the temple, the **Botanical Gardens** (daily 7am–7pm; free) lie in a lush valley. It's a good place to escape the city and enjoy the fresh air, although the waterfall that gives the road its name has been cordoned off.

AYER ITAM AND THE KEK LOK SI TEMPLE

A thirty-minute bus ride west on *MPPP* #1, Ayer Itam is an appealing wooded hilly area (almost 250m above sea level), spread around the **Ayer Itam Dam**, built in the early 1960s. Despite its 550-million litre capacity, it's rather dwarfed by the vertiginous surroundings, through which snake several short trails. If you're looking for a stroll outside the city, you'll do better at Penang Hill (see below), although you might come on up to the dam after visiting the nearby Kek Lok Si Temple, a couple of kilometres back down the road.

The sprawling, fairy tale complex of **Kek Lok Si Temple** (open morning to late evening; free) certainly makes for an intriguing sight as you approach Ayer Itam, the tips of its colourful towers peeking cheekily through the tree tops. Supposedly the largest Buddhist temple in Malaysia, its sheer exuberance makes it hard to dislike – flags and lanterns bedecking various fantasy temples, and imaginative statues and pagodas, linked by hundreds of stupa. The entrance to the complex is approached through a tunnel of trinket stalls stretching a few hundred metres, but as well as being a major tourist spot, it's a serious place of worship. The "Million Buddhas Precious Pagoda" is the most prominent feature of the compound, with a tower of simple Chinese saddle-shaped eaves and more elaborate Thai arched windows, topped by a golden Burmese *stupa*. A donation is required to climb to the top, which affords a great view of Georgetown and the bay.

PENANG HILL

The other major trip outside Georgetown is to the small hill station of **Penang Hill** (Bukit Bendera), an 821-metre-high dome of tropical forest due west of Georgetown. This was once the retreat for the colony's wealthiest administrators but nowadays is a popular weekend excursion for the locals. The cooler climate encourages flowering trees and shrubs, and there are several gentle, well-marked walks through areas whose names (Tiger Hill, Strawberry Hill) conjure up colonial days. You can also walk from here down to the Botanical Gardens, a steep descent taking about an hour.

Take *MPPP* bus #1 to the end of the line and then #8 for the 45-minute journey which terminates at the base of Penang Hill, the final climb up which is made by **funicular railway** (daily 6.30am–9.30pm, Wed & Sat until midnight; departures every 30min; $4 return). This takes 25 minutes and deposits you at the top, where there's a post office, police station and a few food stalls, as well as a hotel, the *Bellevue* (☎699500; ④), five minutes from the station, which has a terrace with the best view of Georgetown. It's really just for hotel guests, but if you ask nicely, it's usually possible to have a drink or a meal there – perfect at sunset when the city's lights flicker on in the distance.

Eating

Georgetowns status as Malaysia's second city means thaere's no shortage of cafés and restaurants. Surprisingly, however, it's only really standard Malay, Chinese and Indian cuisine which are represented in great numbers, though a few places serve seafood, north Indian and Nonya specialities. **Hawker stalls** dish out the cheapest meals and are located either in permanent sites, in which case they're open all day and evening, or spring up by the roadside or down an alleyway at meal times. In addition, a roving **pasar malam** (nightmarket) is held every two weeks at various venues around town (near the stadium is a favourite) – any of the tourist offices will have the latest details.

Of the **cafés** (usually open 8am–11pm), the ubiquitous Chinese *kedai kopis*, sometimes hard to distinguish from stalls when their tables spill out onto the pavement, serve reliable *nasi* and *mee* standards, although many also specialize in fine Hainan chicken rice; the other local favourite is Penang *laksa*; noodles in thick fish soup, garnished with vegetables, pineapple and *belacan* (shrimp paste). The Indian *kedai kopis* around jalan Penang and Little India offer *murtabaks*, *rotis* and biriyanis as well as a bewildering array of curries, but none serve alcohol. The main travellers' hangouts are dotted on or around lebuh Chulia, often little more than hole-in-the-wall joints, serving Western breakfasts, banana pancakes and milkshakes, for less than a couple of dollars each. These tend to open from around 9am to 5pm; the exceptions are noted below. For **Western fast foods**, the KOMTAR building on jalan Penang (10am–10pm) has a *Kentucky Fried Chicken*, *McDonald's* and a *Pizza Hut*.

Jalan Penang is home to a handful of more upmarket **restaurants**, mainly specializing in seafood, while for high-class Western, Malay, Japanese or Chinese food you should head to the top hotels. Set meals here can sometimes work out quite reasonably and are a good opportunity to sample more unusual dishes, often with some sort of cultural entertainment thrown in; you only need to book in advance on Saturday night.

Note that during **Ramadan** (in Feb/March) some places only open after sunset and can be very busy coping with the burst of activity from Penang's hungry Muslims.

HAWKER STALLS

Chinatown: lebuh Kimberley and lebuh Cintra.
Food Court, ground floor of the KOMTAR building.
Jalan Tun Syed Shah Barakah, near Fort Cornwallis at the end of the esplanade.

CAFÉS

Eng Thai, lebuh Chulia. Close to the junction with lebuh Cintra, this is popular for breakfasts, great milkshakes and snacks. Only open during the day. The *Seng Hin* across the road is a similar set-up.
Everlight Travellers' Café, 42 lebuh Cintra. There's a good salad bar here, and vegetarian food available, too. More pricey than average but the set dishes are good value; otherwise expect to pay around $5 per dish. Open 8am–2pm & 5–10pm.

Green Planet, 63 lebuh Cintra. Roomy and comfortable, with tasteful rattan and bamboo decor, this café serves international veggie food (falafel, quiche, waffles, pizza), with some ingredients organically grown, and wonderful baguettes and wholemeal bread. Open 10am–midnight.

Tai Wah, lebuh Chulia. At the eastern end, near jalan Penang, this regular all-hours café has fast and efficient service and becomes a bar in the evening (see below).

Tye Ann, 282 lebuh Chulia, beneath the hostel of the same name. Light and airy with the usual travellers' food, although the service is sometimes very slow.

RESTAURANTS

Dawoods, 63 lebuh Queen. Well-known South Indian restaurant with a limited menu. The speciality, *Curry Kapitan*, spicy chicken with ginger and coconut milk, is worth a try.

Dragon King, 99 lebuh Bishop. Upmarket restaurant that specializes in Nonya cuisine – try any of the *assam* fish dishes. Expensive.

Eliza, 14th floor, *City Bayview Hotel*, 25a lebuh Farquhar. The set meal ($18 per head) in "authentic" Malay atmosphere is accompanied by live traditional music, and the food is surprisingly tasty and well presented.

Hameediyah, 164 lebuh Campbell. They'll try and haul you in from the street if you look remotely interested. Let them: it's great Indian food at reasonable prices, around $4 a head for a full meal.

Hong Kong, 29 lebuh Cintra. Although this looks like any number of *kedai kopis* in the area, the food is of much better quality than usual, something reflected in the prices. There's an extensive Chinese menu with "specials" at $4–8 per main dish, and the portions are huge.

Hsiang Yang, lebuh Chulia. More like a hawker centre with tables sprawling out on the pavement, this bustling, inexpensive place serves a great variety of Chinese as well as some Malay dishes.

Kaliaman, lebuh Penang. Very good North and South Indian food, which arrives quickly. Standard korma, jalfrezi and biriyani dishes for around $4 each.

Kashmir, basement of *Oriental Hotel*, 105 jalan Penang. Very popular high-class north Indian restaurant; you'll need to book at weekends. Expensive – $7 per dish and upwards – but chic.

Kuan Hwa, lebuh Chulia. One of the many places claiming to serve the best Hainan chicken rice in Penang; around $4 a head.

Poshni's, 3–5 lebuh Light. Neat and clean Thai restaurant with fiery dishes for around $4.

Restoran Chulia, lebuh Chulia. Spacious and clean, with Indian/Malay curry dishes laid out buffet-style. An inexpensive place to indulge yourself.

Restoran Sea Palace, 50 jalan Penang. One of the least expensive of the many seafood restaurants in this part of town, with meals averaging $15. Smart service, and with the walls surrounded by fish tanks, from which your dinner is plucked, you can at least guarantee that the food is fresh.

Sky Café, 348 lebuh Chulia. Very popular with the locals and one of the few places serving Chinese/Malay food until late (11.30pm). Fish-head *bee hoon* (a hot noodle dish) is a speciality.

Yasmeen, 177 jalan Penang. Busy and friendly neighbourhood Indian café-restaurant that does excellent *roti canai*.

Drinking, nightlife and entertainment

Most of Georgetown's **bars** are comfortable places in which to hang out – some of the best are detailed below. With the arrival of the fleet, though, a good many turn into rowdy meat markets and a place that may have been perfectly allright the night before could become unpleasant for women visitors, so choose carefully. Usual opening hours are 6pm–2am and occasional **happy hours** (usually 6–8pm) make the cost of beer more reasonable; otherwise, a night's drinking can be expensive. The only thing you can count on in Georgetown's **discos** is that there'll be no hint of the latest Western club sounds. The majority are located in the sterile environment of the city's top hotels and the evening is just as liable to turn into a not-so-impromptu karaoke session. This said, they do at least stay open until the early hours; there's usually a cover charge of around $10. Other entertainment is thin on the ground: the *Cathay* (jalan Penang) and *Rex* (jalan Burma) **cinemas** show recent releases of English-language movies; check the *New Straits Times* for details. There's no cultural centre in Penang, so it's up to the five-star hotels both in town and at Butu Ferringhi to put on shows; this is expensive as you have to pay for a meal in order to watch them.

Anchor Bar, *E&O,* 10 lebuh Farquhar. The traditional decor conjures up the era of the good old colonial times. Pricey place for a beer, though.

Cheers, 22 jalan Argyll. Not like its American counterpart, but with a happy hour 6–8.45pm.

Hong Kong Bar, 371 lebuh Chulia. Tiny, long-running serviceman's bar with none-too-recent hits on the jukebox and a stupefyingly sexist visitors' book.

Hotlips, corner of jalan Penang and jalan Sultan Ahmed Shah. A tasteless pair of giant red lips glows like a beacon outside this tacky club. Open 8pm–2am playing karaoke and disco.

No name bar, lebuh Chulia. Further up from the *Hong Kong Bar* by the bus stop, this basic place always hosts a steady stream of elbow-bending travellers.

Penny Lane, basement, *City Bayview,* 25a lebuh Farquhar. One of the better of the hotel clubs, this concentrates on hits from the Sixties.

Polar Café, 48a jalan Penang. Family-run sing-along bar with organist and music machine, bright lighting and TV. A hamburger stall operates outside at night.

Tai Wah, lebuh Chulia. Daytime café turns into a lively bar in the evening with the cheapest beer in town. The resident Tom Waits impersonator provides musical diversion until the small hours.

20 lebuh Leith. This renovated 1930s' Straits-style mansion is littered with film memorabilia; it has a large video screen and plenty of tables in the beer garden. Slightly pricey, but interesting.

LEAVING PENANG

Details of airline offices, travel agencies and the Thai consulate (for Thai visas) in Georgetown are given in "Listings", below.

Airport
Bayan Lepas International Airport (flight information on ☎834411); take yellow bus #83 or #63 (on the hour 6am–midnight) from Pengkalan Weld or the KOMTAR building. *MAS* operates a daily morning flight to Medan in Sumatra, a busy and popular route. Other direct flights are to Singapore, Bangkok, Hat Yai, Phuket and Madras.

Ferries
The 24-hr passenger and car ferry from Pengkalan Weld to Butterworth (daily: every 20min, 6am–midnight; hourly, midnight–6am) is free on the return leg. Express ferries to Medan depart in the mornings on Mon, Wed, Thurs and Sat, and to Langkawi daily at 8am, both leaving from Swettenham Pier. Tickets for either route can be purchased in advance from the office next to the Penang Tourist Association, or for Langkawi from the *Kuala–Perlis–Langkawi Ferry Service* (☎625630) at the PPC Shopping Complex; travel agencies on lebuh Chulia will also book for you.

Across the bridge: trains and buses
The nearest **train station** is in Butterworth (information on ☎347962), but there is a booking office in the Pengkalan Weld ferry terminal (☎610290) where you can reserve tickets to anywhere on the peninsula. Unless you're driving, it doesn't make much sense to use the Penang Bridge to get back to the mainland, given the existence of the ferries; taxis from Pengkalan Weld charge at least $10 to Butterworth station. Although some **buses** depart from Pengkalan Weld for destinations on the peninsula, most use the terminal at Butterworth. This isn't as awkward for onward travel as it sounds, since there are any number of travel agencies on lebuh Chulia who can book seats for you – in any case, services are so numerous throughout the day that you can just turn up without booking beforehand.

To Thailand
In addition to the train routes to Hat Yai, Surat Thami and Bangkok which can be picked up in Butterworth, **long-distance taxis** depart from several hostels (like the *New China* on lebu Leith) to Hat Yai, although unless there are four of you this doesn't work out particularly economical.

Listings

Airlines *Cathay Pacific*, 28 lorong Penang (☎620411); *Garuda*, 41 lorong Aboo Sitee (☎365257); *Malaysia Airlines*, 3rd floor, KOMTAR, jalan Penang (☎620011); *Qantas Airways*, *E&O Hotel Arcade*, lebuh Farquhar (☎634428); *Singapore Airlines* Wisma Penang Gardens, jalan Sultan Ahmed Shah (☎363201); *Thai International*, Wisma Central, jalan Macalister (☎366233).

American Express Office at 274 lebuh Victoria (9am–5pm; ☎362690). Credit card and travellers' cheque holders can use the office as a poste restante/general delivery address.

Banks and exchange Major banks (Mon–Fri 10am–3pm, Sat 9.30–11.30am) are along lebuh Pantai, including *Standard Chartered* and the *Hong Kong and Shanghai*, but since they charge a hefty commission, the licensed moneychangers on lebuh Pantai and lebuh Chulia (daily 8.30am–6pm) are more convenient – they charge no commission and the rate is often better.

Bike rental Outlets on lebuh Chulia rent out motorbikes and pushbikes: $20 a day for a motorbike (you need a valid driving licence – in practice, you'll rarely be asked to show it), $10 for a pushbike.

Bookshops *United Book Ltd*, jalan Penang, has a large selection of English-language books including travel books; the bookshop at the *E&O* hotel sells popular fiction, classics and local history; there are also lots of secondhand bookshops on lebuh Chulia.

Car rental *Avis*, *E&O Hotel Arcade*, lebuh Farquhar (☎631685) and Batu Ferringhi (☎811023); *Hertz*, 38 lebuh Farquhar (☎635914) and at the airport (☎830208); *National*, 1 Pengkalan Weld (☎629404), 17 lebuh Leith (☎629404) and at the airport (☎834205).

Consulates *Bangladesh*, 15 lebuh Bishop (☎621085); *Denmark*, 3rd floor, Hong Kong Bank Chambers, lebuh Downing (☎624886); *France*, Wisma Rajab, 82 lebuh Bishop (☎629707); *Indonesia*, 467 jalan Burma (☎374686); *Japan*, 2 jalan Biggs (☎368222); *Netherlands*, c/o *Algemene Bank Nederland*, 9 lebuh Pantai (☎622144); *Norway*, Standard Chartered Bank Chambers, lebuh Pantai (☎625333); *Sweden*, Standard Chartered Bank Chambers, lebuh Pantai (☎625333); *Thailand*, 1 jalan Tunku Abdul Rahman (☎378029); *Turkey*, 7 Pengkalan Weld (☎615933); *UK*, Standard Chartered Bank Chambers, lebuh Pantai (☎625333). There is no representation for citizens of the USA, Canada, Ireland, Australia or New Zealand – KL has the nearest offices (see p.109).

Hospitals *Adventist Hospital*, jalan Burma (☎373344) – take blue buses #93, #94 or #95 or *MPPP* #2; *General Hospital*, jalan Western (☎373333) – green bus #92, blue buses #136 or #137, or *MPPP* #1, #5 or #10.

Immigration office *Pejabat Imigresen*, lebuh Pantai, on the corner of lebuh Light (☎610678). For on-the-spot visa renewals.

Pharmacy There are several pharmacies along jalan Penang; open 10am–6pm.

Police In emergencies dial ☎999; the police headquarters is on jalan Penang.

Post office The GPO is on lebuh Downing (Mon–Sat 8am–6pm). The efficient poste restante/general delivery office is here, and parcel-wrapping is available from shops on lebuh Chulia.

Sport Play golf at *Bukit Jambul Country Club*, 2 jalan Bukit Jambul (☎842255; green fees $100, $150 weekends), or the *Penang Turf Club Golf* (☎876701; green fees $50, $80 weekends), there's racing at the *Penang Turf Club*, jalan Batu Gantung (☎362333) – see the local paper for fixtures.

Telephone offices Calls within Penang made from public telephone booths cost a flat rate of 10c and can be dialled direct. For international calls it is better to use a *Telekom* office at either the GPO, on lebuh Downing, or *Kodai Telekom*, 1st floor, jalan Burma, both open 24 hours.

Travel agents Try the *MSL Travel*, 340 lebuh Chulia (☎616154) for student and youth travel. There are a large number of other agencies along lebuh Chulia. Look for one that is *TDC* registered.

The northern beaches

The 15km or so along Penang's **north coast** have been aggressively marketed since the early days of package tourism and even more so in recent years with the growth in popularity of condominiums, particularly among the Japanese. The narrow strip of coastline, hemmed in by the densely forested interior, is punctuated by a series of bays and beaches, linked by a twisting road lined with resort hotels which advertise themselves as being part of the "Pearl of the Orient". The filthy ocean rather detracts from this image, but while the water may flunk the pollution tests, the sand is golden, crunchy and relatively clean – although it's fair to say that if you've visited the east coast of Malaysia, you'll see nothing here to touch it. More worryingly, though, once you see its already extensive capacity, is that the area is still being developed. Huge apartment buildings are springing up all over the place, the rooms within them often sold before they've even been completed. It makes you wonder how much more a short stretch of beach, reached through already congested streets, can take.

There are three main developments strung out along the northern coast: Tanjung Bungah, Batu Ferringhi and Teluk Bahang. The first two have arisen purely to serve tourism's needs, rather than by growing out of a local community, and this is particularly obvious at Tanjung Bungah, which lacks a heart and focus. Occupied for the most part by a string of deluxe resorts, Batu Ferringhi is the biggest of the three, and has gone a fair way towards establishing a community and spirit of its own; Teluk Bahang, with just one modern hotel, is the only place to maintain its fishing village roots. If you want to stay at any of the beaches, it's wise to ring the hotels and guest houses first from Georgetown to check on space, especially during Christmas, Easter and Hari Raya.

Tanjung Bungah

Although there are beaches closer to Georgetown, **TANJUNG BUNGAH**, 12km and twenty minutes' bus ride (blue buses #93, #94 or #102; every 20min) from the city outskirts, is really the first place that is pleasant enough to inspire you to linger. That said, it's a largely uncoordinated string of properties and the beach is not as good as further west. By far the best budget **accommodation** is at *The Lost Paradise*, c/o *Green Planet Restaurant* in Georgetown (☎616192; ②), about a ten-minute walk from the bus stand, opposite the *Marvista* condominiums and marked by a large number "261". Comprising renovated turn-of-the-century villas and a gazebo, it has a private cove and its own gardens with a variety of accommodation from dorm beds to air-con rooms, as well as self-catering facilities. The next best low-budget option is the *Seaview Hotel*, (☎802582; ③), further out towards Batu Ferringhi up some steps on the left-hand side of the road; it has a bearable piece of beach, but is otherwise fairly isolated.

For **eating**, you're pretty much restricted to your own hotel. The *Seaview* serves fairly inexpensive food, but *The Lost Paradise* usually only caters for its own guests. The upmarket hotels along here offer a variety of food, although all at five-star prices.

Batu Ferringhi

BATU FERRINGHI (Foreigner's Rock), a ten-minute bus ride further west on blue bus #93, earned its name from the foreigners who hung out here in the early Seventies when the island's waters really were jewel-like. Although it is almost unrecognizable since its hippy-haven heyday, for most visitors it still provides the right mix of relaxation and excitement – the beach during the day, shopping and eating in the evening, and drinking at night in the bars and discos.

Orientation is very simple: the road runs more or less straight along the coast for 3km, along which all the hotels and restaurants are lined up side by side. The "centre", such as it is, lies between two bridges a couple of kilometres apart and sports a *Telekom* office, post office and police station, opposite which is the mosque and clinic; it is here that the bus from Georgetown stops. The **beach** is remarkably clean – it's in the interests of the big resorts to keep it so – and since every major hotel has a pool, with luck you'll never have to swim in the sea. Even if you're not staying, it's worth looking around some of the hotels for sheer astonishment value: cascading foyer waterfalls, glass elevators, extravagant mock-Malay architecture, all handsomely represented. The trinket stalls, tailors' shops and street hawkers remain fairly unobtrusive during the day, but become the main focus when the sun goes down. In fact, it's at night that the real bargains are to be had, when the road becomes alive with brightly lit stalls selling batik, T-shirts and fake designer watches.

ACCOMMODATION

Towards the western end of Batu Ferringhi there is a small enclave of **budget guest houses** facing the beach – take the road by the *Guan Guan Café* – but don't expect any great bargains here; rooms are generally more expensive than in Georgetown. One of the nicest is the *Ah Beng* (☎811036; ②) which has polished wood floors, a sea-facing communal balcony and a washing machine. Another spotless and friendly place is nearby *Baba's* (no phone; ②) offering dorm beds as well as regular rooms. *Ali's* (☎811316; ②) is also very popular, with a decent open-air café.

Independent travellers don't get particularly good deals in the expensive hotels, most of whose business is with tour groups. The *Casuarina Beach* at the far western end (☎811711; ⑤) is the most tasteful – an intimate, low-rise, open-plan hotel which attracts a quieter crowd. This is definitely not the case at the *Golden Sands Resort* (☎811911; ⑥), whose active social programme, lush gardens and pool makes it one of the most lively places. Two other high-class choices are the elegant *Park Royal* (☎811133; ⑥), and the *Rasa Sayang* (☎811811; ⑦), on the eastern edge, which makes the biggest concession to traditional Malay architecture.

EATING AND DRINKING

There are virtually no budget **restaurants** in Batu Ferringhi since most places cater for the overspill from the large hotels, all of which have several restaurants of their own. But there are some fine seafood restaurants, if you can afford it, and a few interesting places to eat Malay cuisine.

The roadside **stalls** (evening only) by the *Guan Guan Café* sell inexpensive, local food, or try *Andrew's Café*, by the western bridge, for tasty banana leaf curries. The *Guan Guan Café* is one of a few similar, moderately priced establishments with a wide selection of food. At the huge *Eden Seafood Village* the boast is "Anything that swims, we cook it", but it's far from cheap, at around $20 a dish; a cultural show accompanies the meal. The bright and bustling *Ferringhi Village*, back towards the *Rasa Sayang*, serves a good range of Chinese food, seafood and steaks. For excellent North Indian cuisine, head for the *Moghul Arch*, set back from the road, where thalis and tikka masalas go for around $8. Finally, *Papa Din's Bamboo Restoran*, hidden at the end of an unlikely looking path over the western bridge, features the septuagenarian *bomoh* (medicine man), Papa Din, who subjects you to a well-rehearsed self-adulation session as you tuck into an excellent three-course set meal.

Teluk Bahang

Another 5km west, the small fishing *kampung* of **TELUK BAHANG** is the place to come to escape the development. The long and spindly pier towards the far end of the village is the focus of daily life, where the latest catch is hauled in off the multitude of fishing boats. Beyond the pier, a small path disappears into the forest for the two-hour trek westwards to the lighthouse at **Muka Head**. The beaches around this rocky headland are better than the ones at Teluk Bahang itself, but since the big hotels run boat trips out here, it's unlikely that you'll have them to yourself. Other diversions are to the south, up the road into the interior, where the Butterfly Farm and Forest Recreation Park (see below) are just 200m from the village.

Accommodation is somewhat limited. Friendly *Rama's Guest House* (☎811179; ①) is about the cheapest place, with some basic dorm beds as well as rooms; take the left turn at the roundabout and it's about 50m down the road on the right. *Madame Loh's* is another long-running option but it's a bit more expensive; ask at the *Kwong Tuck Hing* shop on the main road. At the other end of the scale is the *Penang Mutiara*, on the main road (☎812828; ⑥), beautifully decorated and with a good beach.

Tanjung Bungah's real attraction is its plethora of inexpensive **places to eat** on the little stretch of main road, including an excellent seafood restaurant called the *End of the World* just by the pier. The huge fresh prawns are a particular speciality.

The rest of the island

If you're going to see the **rest of the island**, you'll have to get round it in one day, for apart from the hotels on the north coast, there is no other accommodation on Penang. The trip *can* be done by bus which takes in most of the points of interest picked out below: heading southwest from Georgetown take yellow bus #66 to Balik Pulau, yellow bus #76 from there to Teluk Bahang, then blue bus #93 through Batu Ferringhi back to town; make sure you leave Georgetown by 8 or 9am in order to get round the island. But this route rather misses the point, which is to get away from the main road and explore the jungle, beaches and *kampungs* at leisure. It's much better to **rent a motorbike**, or even a pushbike, from one of the outlets on lebuh Chulia – it's a seventy-kilometre round trip so you have to be fairly fit to accomplish it using pedal-power, especially since some parts of the road are very steep. Once clear of the outskirts of Georgetown the roads are blissfully traffic-free.

South to Gertak Senggal

Take the road south from Pengkalan Weld in Georgetown past the university to the **Snake Temple**, 12km out of town. This is a major attraction for bus tour parties (and their video cameras) and the usual bunch of stalls clutter up the otherwise impressive entrance, guarded by two stone lions, the doors featuring brightly painted warrior gods. The figure of Chor Soo King, a monk who came from China over a hundred years ago and gained local fame as a healer, sits in the main square, a black statue clothed in red and yellow. Inside the temple, draped lazily over parts of the altar, are dozens of poisonous green snakes, which – legend has it – mysteriously appeared upon completion of the temple in 1850 and have made it their refuge ever since. They're fairly lethargic – supposedly drugged by the incense – and most have been doctored, so it's considered safe enough to have your photograph taken with the snakes curled over you.

Continuing south, the road takes you past the airport at Bayan Lepas to **BATU MAUNG**, 13km further on from the snake temple. There's not much here except pretty coastal scenes and an expensive Chinese restaurant, and you'll have to backtrack the couple of kilometres to the main road, which runs on 3km to **TELUK KUMBAR**, where the sea looks particularly uninviting and the beach, though reasonable, gets very crowded at weekends. West of here, the stretch of road along the south coast towards **GERTAK SANGGUL** is one of the most attractive spots on the island: gently winding and tree-lined, with the odd tantalising glimpse of glittering ocean. The road ends at a scenic bay where you can watch the local fishing boats at work.

North to Teluk Bahang

Backtracking almost to Teluk Kumbar, the road north winds steeply up to the village of **BARAT**, where you have the choice of heading northeast to **BALIK PULAU** or southwest to **PULAU BETONG**. Neither are particularly enthralling, though there's something attractive in the quiet pace of life hereabouts and in the friendliness of the local people, who are always keen to point you in the right direction. Balik Pulau is probably the best choice, simply because of the string of cafés along the main road – any of them is good for a refreshment stop. If you want to cut the trip short, you can head back to Georgetown via Ayer Itam. The small track northeast out of Balik Pulau (officially a dead end and only accessible by bike) takes an interesting course through the jungle past some huge boulders that look as if they had been carefully placed by Henry Moore. It climbs steeply and soon becomes increasingly impractical as a means of getting anywhere fast.

Back in the Balik Pulau, the road north continues the circuit of the island. Next stop, and a small detour off the main road to the west, are **SUNGEI PINANG** and **PANTAI ACHEH**, Chinese fishing villages built along a narrow and largely stagnant river. If you don't mind feeling conspicuous – and can stand the pervasive rotting fish smell – it's a good place to watch the fishermen, painstakingly maintaining their low-lying, wooden boats.

Back on the main road, the route once more climbs very steeply as it winds round the jungle-clad hillside, offering the occasional excellent viewpoint over the flat forested plain, which stretches towards the sea. A couple of kilometres from the junction for Sungei Pinang are the disappointing **Titi Kerawang Waterfalls**, for most of the year little more than a dismal, rubbish-strewn trickle. However, there is fresh fruit on sale at stalls by the roadside.

After only a little more climbing, the road levels and straightens out until you reach the **Forest Recreation Park** (9am–1pm & 2–5pm, except Fri 9am–12pm & 2.45–5pm; closed Mon), on the right-hand side of the road. A museum introduces visitors to the differing forest types evident on Penang; several well-marked forest trails and a children's playground offer a modicum of light relief. The **Butterfly Farm** (Mon–Fri 9am–5pm, Sat, Sun and holidays 9am–6pm; $4) and nearby **batik factory**, less than 1km from the park, provide an uninspiring end to the island circuit, the latter more a shop than a factory, with prices hiked up in expectation of the descending bus tours. Within sight, around 200m away, is the roundabout at Teluk Bahang, a right turn at which brings you onto the northern coastal road, 20km or so from Georgetown.

Sungei Petani and around

From Butterworth, train and highway shoot north, running quickly into the state of **Kedah** and through the small town of Sungei Petani, 35km away. Few people stop and those that do are drawn by the archaeological remains at Lembah Bujang (Bujang Valley), 10km northwest, and the beacon of Gunung Jerai (Kedah Peak), 20km north, rather than any delights the town itself has to offer. Even these attractions are fairly specialist in nature – particularly the archeological site – and if you're at all short on time, keep going north.

Sungei Petani

SUNGEI PETANI is the nearest point from which to reach both sites. A clocktower dominates the main road through town, jalan Ibrahim, to the right of which is a road leading to the **train station**. Long-distance buses depart from the stand marked "MKDM" by the clocktower. The local **bus station** and **taxi stand** are next door to each other on jalan Puteri, which branches off left from the main road, about 200m south of the clocktower.

If you plan to visit both Lembah Bujang and Gunung Jerai in one day, you'll need to stay overnight in Sungei Petani at one of its three **hotels**, all within easy reach of the bus station. Turn left and the first is the *Duta* (☎04/412040; ③), with reasonably priced air-con rooms; less expensive options are the optimistically named *Bright Hotel* further along on the opposite side (no phone; ①), and the nearby *Lih Pin* (no phone; ①) – the same price but very dingy. Out of town on jalan Kolam Air, and in another price league altogether, is the *Sungei Petani Inn* (☎04/413411; ⑤), incongruously flash for the area.

There's a very popular Chinese **restaurant** at the *Bright Hotel*, and a small but lively nightmarket a few blocks to the north.

Lembah Bujang

Lying between Gunung Jerai to the north and the sungei Muda to the south, **Lembah Bujang** is the site of some of Malaysia's most important archeological discoveries. Most of what's known of the country's history before 1400 AD has been somewhat sketchily pieced together from unreliable, and often contradictory, contemporary accounts – until, that is, the early nineteenth century, when, "the relics of a Hindoo colony" were discovered in the Bujang valley. This important find by Colonel James Low, a member of the Madras Army stationed at Penang and a keen amateur archaeologist, gave credence to the prevailing theories that Hinduism was the dominant ideological force in early Malaya, sustained by the fifth-century kingdom of Langkasuka and later by the mighty Srivijaya empire based in Sumatra. Unfortunately, Low's rather unscientific methods have not stood the test of time, since early twentieth-century excavations revealed fifty or so temples (known as *candis*) in the Bujang basin displaying **Buddhist influences** – a discovery which changed the thrust of subsequent historical theories and created controversy in academic circles which continues today.

At the cornerstone of the new theories is **Candi Bukit Batu Pahat**, one of the tenth-century temples now reconstructed on the Lembah Bajang site, which embodies the styles of Mahayana Buddhism as well as of the cults of Siva and Visnu. The argument runs that, because there is no direct equivalent of the structure in India – the origin of both Hindu and Buddhist religions – this signifies that outside influences actually adapted to suit the local culture, thereby creating a new modified theology.

Since excavations are still taking place, most of the site is off limits to the public, but there is an **archeological museum** (daily 9am–5pm; free) which displays photographs of some of the finds *in situ*, as well as a number of relocated stone pillars, pots and jewels. The historical information is fairly turgidly written and there are precious few contextual comments on the artefacts, but behind the museum, eight *candis* (including Candi Bukit Batu Pahat) have been reconstructed using original materials – though they appear rather bare to anyone not armed with specialist knowledge.

Since the whole project is in its infancy, it is still quite difficult to reach the museum. From Sungei Petani take a local bus to the small village of Bedong, 8km north; here you'll see a signpost giving the direction of the museum; another, rather infrequent, bus from Bedong takes you the final 15km, but it only drops you on the main road – the museum is another two-kilometre walk away. A taxi is a better bet and should only cost $8–10 one-way, to charter from Bedong.

Gunung Jerai

Gunung Jerai (1200m), a massive limestone outcrop 10km north of Lembah Bujang as the crow flies, dominates the landscape for miles around. It's the highest peak in Kedah and on clear days various vantage points offer panoramic views of the rolling rice fields stretching up to Perlis in the north, and of the coastline from Penang to Langkawi. While it is stretching things to call the settlement on the peak a "hill station" – there's no colonial tradition here – there is one hotel, which can provide a pleasant overnight stop (though it's cheaper to stay at Sungei Petani). Wherever you stay, a few hours is enough to stroll around the **Sungei Teroi Forest Recreation Park** halfway up the mountain, with its rare species of orchids, and animals like the lesser mouse-deer and the long-tailed macaque for which the conservation area is renowned.

Gunung Jerai is a mountain replete with history and legend. Tales abound of the infamous "Raja Bersiong" (the king with fangs) who once held court over the ancient kingdom of Langkasuka. Archeological digs revealed the existence of a water temple (Candi Telaga Sembilan) at the summit which many believe was the private pool of Raja Bersiong. A **Museum of Forestry** (Mon, Wed & Sat 9am–3pm; free), at the top of the path leading to the recreation park, is of limited interest.

The jumping-off point for Gunung Jerai is just north of the town of Gurun on the Butterworth–Alor Setar road. Local bus #2 from Sungei Petani (every 30min) drops you at the bottom of the mountain after a thirty-minute ride. If you don't want to walk to the summit, a gentle two-hour climb, **jeeps** make the journey every 45 minutes (daily 8.30am–5pm; $5 return). At the top, you can stay at the *Peranginan Gunung Jerai* (☎04/ 729788; ④), which has a restaurant as well as comfortable chalets – and the owners can provide tents (②) if you prefer sleeping *al fresco*.

Alor Setar

Another 58km north of Sungei Petani, **ALOR SETAR** (pronounced "Alor Star"), the tiny state capital of Kedah, is the last major stop before the Thai border. It's a city that is keen to preserve its heritage – witness the many royal buildings and museums – and since Alor Setar has useful transportation connections to the east coast as well as to Thailand, you might well spend at least a short time here.

Kedah's history is a sad catalogue of invasion and subjugation, most pervasively by the Thais, lasting more or less up until the beginning of this century. But even from the earliest days, the state was noted for its independent spirit of resistance: an eleventh-century Chola inscription mentions "Kadaram (Kedah) of fierce strength". By the thirteenth century, Kedah was already asserting its own economic power over that of the Srivijaya empire, by sending ships to India to trade jungle products for such exotic goods as Arab glass and Chinese porcelain. As a vassal state of Ayudhya – the mighty Thai kingdom – during the mid-seventeenth century, Kedah still managed to express its defiance. For decades, the Malay states had been left to get on with their own affairs, provided they sent monetary tributes from time to time. But when, in 1645, the Kedah ruler was summoned to appear at the Thai court in person – an unprecedented request – he refused point-blank, claiming that it was beneath the dignity of a Sultan to prostrate himself before another ruler. To avoid further embarrassment, the king of Ayudhya sent a statue of himself to Kedah, instructing the court to pay homage to it twice a day. At the beginning of the nineteenth century, Kedah's relationship with its Thai conquerors degenerated into a *jihad*, or "holy war", led by Sultan Ahmad. The strength of religious feeling frightened the Bangkok government which deposed Ahmad, but in 1842 the British, anxious to see peace in the region and realizing the strength of Ahmad's hold over his people, forced the Sultan's reinstatement. Even this

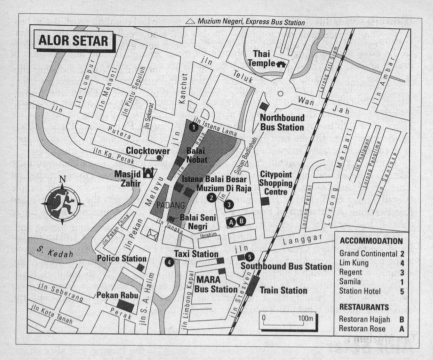

gesture had little effect on stubborn Kedah: as recently as the beginning of this century, when Kedah was transferred by the Thais to British control, it adamantly refused to become part of the Federated Malay States.

Something of Kedah's past is evident in Alor Setar today since many Thais still live here, worshipping in the Thai temple, running businesses and restaurants. For all that, Alor Setar is one of most Malay towns you'll find on the west coast, sustained in part by the predominance of Islam which, throughout the years of Kedah's external domination, played an important part in the maintenance of traditional Malay values.

The town

The Kedah river runs along the western and southern outskirts of Alor Setar. The main sights are located to the west of the town around the **Padang**, or central square, which is entirely paved and with a large modern fountain at its centre. The **Masjid Zahir** dominates the western side of the square, its typical Moorish architecture highlighted at night by thousands of tiny lights. Facing the mosque, on the opposite side of the square, the elegant **Istana Balai Besar** (Royal Audience Hall) – the principal official building during the eighteenth century – stands serene amid the roaring traffic. The present two-storey, open-colonnaded structure only dates back to 1904, however, when the original hall was rebuilt to host the marriages of the Sultan Abdul Hamid's five eldest children. So grand was the refurbishment and so lavish the ceremony, that the state was nearly bankrupted.

Just behind the Balai Besar, the old royal palace now serves as the **Muzium Di Raja** (Mon–Thurs & Sat–Sun 10am–6pm, Fri 9am–noon & 3–6pm; free), an excellent way of preserving this dainty little 1930s' building. Better laid out than most, it still has its fair share of eulogistic memorabilia – medals and fond recollections of the current Sultan's salad days – but some of the rooms have been kept exactly as they were used by the Sultan and his family.

Across the way stands a curious octagonal tower, the **Balai Nobat**, housing the sacred instruments of the royal orchestra. Played only during royal ceremonies – inaugurations, weddings and funerals – the collection consists of three ornate silver drums, a gong, a long trumpet and a double-reeded instrument similar to the oboe, which combine to produce the haunting strains of "nobat" music. Since the instruments are regarded as the most treasured part of the Sultan's regalia, so the musicians themselves are given a special title, *orang kalur*, relating to the time when they were also keepers of the royal records. The Kedah Nobat is the oldest and most famous of all the royal orchestras, chosen to be played at the installation of independent Malaysia's first constitutional monarch in 1947. Unfortunately, the tower, together with its priceless contents, remains closed to the public.

However, you are free to wander round the grandiose, white stucco **Balai Seni Negeri** (Mon–Thurs & Sat–Sun 10am–6pm, Fri 10am–noon & 2.30–6pm; free), an art gallery directly across the Padang from the tower, displaying largely uninspiring and derivative works showing the influence of traditional Malay culture on contemporary artists. Rural scenes abound, as you might expect.

A glimpse of contemporary culture can be found at the **Pekan Rabu**, or "Wednesday Market", now a daily affair, running from morning to midnight. Situated just over the river, there's a large collection of stalls selling anything from local farm produce to handicrafts – it's also a good place to sample traditional Kedah food like the "Dodol Durian", a sweetcake made from the notoriously pungent durian fruit.

The Muzium Negeri

Hop on bus #31 heading north from jalan Raja, adjacent to the Padang, and after about 1.5km you'll pass the **Muzium Negeri** (Mon–Thurs & Sat–Sun 9am–4pm, Fri 9am–12.15pm & 2.45–5pm; free), on jalan lebuhraya Darulaman. Apart from some background information on the archeological finds at Lembah Bujang (see p.176), the museum fails to ignite much interest, though standing out a mile above the other exhibits is a delicate replica silver tree, close to the entrance, called the *bunga mas dan perak*, literally "the gold and silver flowers". This refers to a practice, established in the seventeenth century, of honouring the ruling government of Thailand by a triennial presentation of two small gold and silver trees, about a metre in height, meticulously detailed even down to the birds nesting in their branches – the cost was estimated at over a thousand Spanish dollars, no mean sum for those times. While the tradition was seen by Ayudhya as a recognition of its suzerainty, the gift was considered by the Kedah rulers as a show of goodwill and friendship – a typical refusal to acknowledge their vassal status.

Practicalities

Alor Setar has a rather confusing array of bus stations, each serving different areas. The **express bus station** for services to Hat Yai and destinations within Malaysia is north of the centre, down an unsignposted left turning off jalan Pekan Melayu, past a piece of waste ground around which the ticket booths are arranged – it's a ten-minute walk from here to the Padang. **Northbound local buses** go from the station off jalan Sultan Badlishah – there are more long-distance booking booths and departure points here, too. For **southbound buses**, there is a station on jalan Langgar, right in the centre of town (also the station for bus #106 for the 30-min journey to Kuala Kedah for the ferry to Langkawi), and a smaller station for the *MARA* buses to Sungei Petani, a little further south behind the *Hankya Jaya* supermarket; the **taxi station** is in front of the *MARA* bus station. The **train station** is a five-minute walk east of the centre on jalan Stesyen. Alor Setar is a principal station on the west coast route and a place to pick up the daily express train to Hat Yai and Bangkok (3.20pm) on its way from Butterworth; strangely though, it doesn't stop here on the return leg. The domestic **airport** (*MAS* office; ☎04/711106), 11km north of town, is accessible by the hourly "Kepala Batas" bus from the northbound bus station.

The helpful **tourist office** (Mon–Fri 8am–4pm; ☎04/722088) is in the Wisma Negeri building on jalan Raja. All the major **banks** are also on jalan Raja.

Accommodation

Most **budget hotels** are close to the southbound bus station along jalan Langgar. Furthest away from the station, but by far the best value, is the *Lim Kung* (☎04/728353; ①); the dark corridors look unpromising but the rooms are the largest you'll find in town for the price and the manager is exceptionally friendly. The *Station Hotel*, right above the bus station (☎04/733786; ①), is more expensive, but once you get past the grubby entrance the rooms are large and have bathrooms. Up a significant notch in price and standard is the comfortable *Regent* (☎04/711900; ②) on jalan Sultan Badlishah. Most of the top-class hotels are inconveniently situated on the outskirts of town, though of the more central ones, the *Grand Continental* on jalan Sultan Badlishah (☎04/735917; ⑤) is a large landmark; the *Samila* (☎04/722344; ④), just north of the Padang, has more character and is at the bottom end of its category – excellent value for its plush, well-appointed rooms.

Eating

You'd do well to sample some regional Thai cuisine while in town. The *Restoran Hajjah* on jalan Tungku Ibrahim, parallel to jalan Langgar, has a wide-ranging Thai-Muslim menu including some unusual fried rice options. The printed menu has no prices so ask before you order. Otherwise, one of the best-value places is the nearby *Restoran Rose*, on jalan Sultan Badlishah, which serves excellent, filling Indian food. For a variety of dishes under one roof head for the Pekan Rabu market, while if your budget can stand it, the restaurant at the *Samila* gets good reports for its Western-orientated cuisine.

Langkawi

Situated 30km off the coast at the very northwestern tip of the peninsula is a cluster of 104 tropical islands, dotted liberally throughout the Straits of Melaka, known collectively as **LANGKAWI**. Most are little more than deserted, tiny scrub-clad atolls; only two are inhabited, including the largest of the group, **Pulau Langkawi**, once a haven for pirates and now a sought-after refuge for monied tourists. It's seen unparalled development in recent years enhanced by its duty-free status, making it Malaysia's premier island retreat. Some of the country's most luxurious hotels are here, while a new airport has been built to cope with the increasing number of visitors. Perhaps because of Langkawi's size (around 500 square kilometres), this development doesn't appear to have encroached unduly on the traditional way of life of the island's inhabitants, and its natural attractions – a mountainous interior, white sands, limestone outcrops and lush vegetation – have remained relatively unspoiled. Indeed, the longstanding lure of the Langkawi archipelago's beauty has fostered traditional stories of the "Islands of Legends" and in true Malay fashion almost every major landmark has a myth associated with it – each ruthlessly hijacked by the tourist authorities to promote the islands' charms. Chiefly, these consist of lazing around on Pulau Langkawi's beaches and enjoying the sunshine, although a day trip by bike or taxi around the island can take in the ancient **Makam Mahsuri**, various splendid waterfalls and the **Telaga Air Panas** hot springs; designated **wildlife and marine parks** on neighbouring Pulau Singa Besar and Pulau Payar provide a little extra interest. You can also explore other, **uninhabited islands** in the archipelago, though the only way to do this is by taking an expensive day trip, organized either by the tourist office or one of the hotels on Pulau Langkawi.

The principal town on Pulau Langkawi is **Kuah**, an untidy straggle of hotels and shops in the southeast of the island, where you'll find most of the duty-free bargains. The main tourist development has taken place around three bays on the western side of the island, at **Pantai Tengah**, **Pantai Cenang** and **Pantai Kok**. Of these, Cenang is by far the most commercialized, although there is still some budget accommodation available. More recent building work has taken place at two beaches on the north coast, **Pantai Datai** and **Tanjung Rhu**, where accommodation is limited to top-class resorts.

Getting there

Langkawi is most commonly reached from Kuala Perlis (see p.188), adjacent to the Thai border, from where there are nine fast boats every day ($13 one-way; 45min); ferries also operate six times daily from **KUALA KEDAH** ($13 one-way; 1hr 10min), 51km south – or just 8km from Alor Setar (see p.177). There's rarely any need to book tickets in advance – just turn up when you want to go. Both services run to the jetty on the southeastern tip of the island, about ten minutes' drive from Kuah itself. Buses supposedly run from the jetty into Kuah, but in practice it's easier to get a **taxi**, which should cost around $4 for the car.

Alternatively, there's a once-daily direct express boat **from Penang** ($36 one-way; 2hr) which docks at the jetty in Teluk Ewa on the north coast, from where it's another taxi ride (about $12) to any of the beaches and accommodation. The **airport** is 20km west of Kuah, near Pantai Cenang, receiving internal flights from KL, Penang and Ipoh, and services from Singapore and Phuket in Thailand. Again, you'll have to take a taxi – it'll cost less than $5 to any of the western beaches or $12 to Kuah.

There are also ferry services **from Thailand**: three times daily from Satun on the border ($35; 2hr), or twice weekly from Phuket ($90; 3hr); both ferries dock at Kuah.

The Langkawi **tourist office** (Sat–Wed 9am–5pm, Thurs & Fri 9am–1pm; ☎04/788209) is very helpful, but located somewhat inconveniently at the *Langkawi Island Resort* almost 1km from the Kuah jetty. The *MAS* office (☎04/916622) is here, too.

Pulau Langkawi

Having docked at Kuah, most people immediately hop in a taxi and strike out for the beaches on the west coast. There is basically one circular route around the island, with the other main road cutting the island in two, connecting north and south; various minor roads are well surfaced and signposted.

However, public transport around the island is limited. The bus service runs on only three routes out of Kuah, departing from the bus stand opposite the hospital: hourly (8am–6.15pm) to Pantai Cenang, a similar service to Padang Lalang and every two hours (8am–4.30pm) to Pantai Kok. It's easier to get around by **taxi**: most longer journeys cost $12–15, while a taxi tour of the island runs to around $50. Many of the chalets and motels offer **motorbike rental** for around $25 per day. Travelling by bike would take a full day to see everything, but there are plenty of places to stop for a drink or a bite to eat if you need a break, and fuel stops at regular intervals, too.

Kuah

Its population of nearly 11,000 easily makes **KUAH** the largest town on Langkawi. Lining a large sweep of bay in the southeastern corner of the island, there's not much more to it than a ragged stretch of modern hotels and shops along the main road,

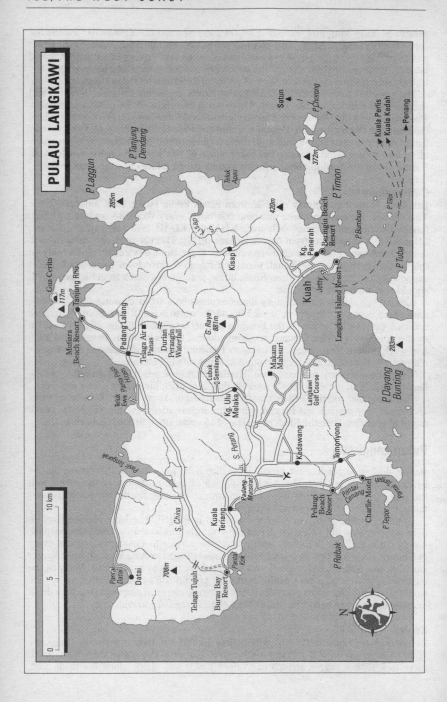

which hugs what little beach there is. The sand and water here aren't too bad, but it's more of a fishing beach than a recreational one. Kuah isn't an unattractive place – the waterfront dominated by the whitewashed **Masjid Al-Hana** – but despite the multitude of hotels, it's not somewhere you're really likely to want to stay. However, it will probably constitute your first sight of Langkawi and it is the place to sort out any business matters. As well as the numerous duty-free shops along the main road, selling everything from hooch to handbags, you'll find the **post office, police station** (☎04/916222) and **hospital** (☎04/916333) close to each other. Behind the *MAYA* shopping complex, also on the main road, are three parallel streets where you'll find all the **banks** (virtually the only places to change money on the island) together with the **Telekom** centre.

If you insist on **staying**, one of the better choices is the *Malaysia* (☎04/916298; ①), about halfway along the main road heading west, which is a bit scruffy but has a helpful information board and can arrange motorbike rental. Another clean and reasonable option is the *Langkawi*, at no. 6–8 on the main road (☎04/916248; ②); while for a real bargain in its price category, try the *Region* (☎04/917719; ④), down a turning opposite the mosque, which has very comfortable rooms.

As you make your way back towards the jetty, lying just off the main road, is the very secluded *Beringin Beach Resort* (☎04/916966; ④), a small cluster of well-appointed chalets in a tiny bay (though part of the beach has been taken over by mangroves). Closer to the jetty, but still a taxi ride from Kuah, is the flashy *Langkawi Island Resort* (☎04/788209; ⑤), whose lobby is a hotch-potch of shops and offices (including the tourist office and *MAS* outlet); the hotel also operates a good range of sports activities and day trips.

There are numerous eating houses of various standards, from the **hawker stalls** – past the post office heading towards the jetty – to the pricier seafood **restaurants** on the front, like the *Sari* and the *Orchid*. Despite the ready availability of fresh fish, these are fairly expensive, each dish setting you back at least $8 – there are better places on the island.

Towards the west coast beaches

Heading west from Kuah just past the *Langkawi Golf Club*, whose dress code for women states – alarmingly – that "skirts should not be higher than six inches from the shoulder", a signpost about 10km from town directs you to **Makam Mahsuri** (the tomb of Mahsuri), in Kampung Mawat, the site of Langkawi's most famous legend. It recalls the story of a young woman named Mahsuri, born over two hundred years ago, whose beauty inspired a vengeful accusation of adultery from a spurned suitor – or, as some versions have it, a jealous mother-in-law – while her husband was away fighting the invading Siamese. Mahsuri protested her innocence but was found guilty by the village elders who sentenced her to death. She was tied to a stake, but as the ceremonial dagger was plunged into her, she began to bleed white blood, a sign that was interpreted as proving her innocence. With her dying breath, Mahsuri muttered a curse on Langkawi's prosperity to last seven generations – though judging by the island's increasing income in recent years, this must be beginning to wear off at last. The white marble tomb stands alone in a shady garden, and the $1 entrance fee (open 10am–6pm) also gains you access to a reconstruction of a traditional Malay house.

Heading north, skirting around the airport, a right turn brings you to the **Padang Matsirat** (The Field of Burnt Rice). Shortly after Mahsuri's death, the Siamese conquered Kedah and prepared to attack Langkawi. The inhabitants of the island set fire to their staple crop and poisoned their wells in order to halt the advance of the invaders, and to this day, so the legend goes, traces of burnt rice resurface in the area after a heavy downfall of rain.

Pantai Tengah

Back on the main road, a further 8km brings you to a junction where a left turn, clearly signposted, takes you to the first of the western beaches, **PANTEI TENGAH**, 6km away. A quiet beach, the sand itself isn't at all bad, but the secluded nature of the bay means that the water isn't renewed by the tide and appears quite murky. There are also jellyfish present: take local advice before you swim.

Accommodation is limited to a couple of smart resorts and a handful of low-key chalet places, about the best of which is the popular *Charlie Motel* (☎04/911200; ②), at the top end of its price bracket, with chalets and an attractive beachfront patio restaurant. A bit further along the *Sugary Sands Motel* (☎04/911553; ②) is one of three plots uncharacteristically – and unimaginatively – bunched together on a bare piece of ground; the others are *Green Hill Beach Motel* (☎04/911935; ②) and the *Tanjung Malie* (☎04/911891; ②), both of a similar standard. Close by, and much better, is the *Sunset Beach Resort* (☎911751; ③), a pretty set-up with good rooms, gardens and a beachfront restaurant and bar. Finally, closer to the road, next door to each other, are the *Langkawi Village Resort* (☎04/911511; ⑤) and the *Langkawi Holiday Village Beach Resort* (☎04/911701; ⑥); there's very little to choose between them – both are in a secluded position at the very end of the beach.

Eating is limited to the restaurants attached to the various motels and resorts – local enterprise has yet to hit Pantai Tengah. Both *Charlie* and *Sunset* have mellow beachside restaurants, hosting the occasional **barbecue** at around $10 a head.

Pantai Cenang

Five hundred metres north of Tengah, the development at **PANTAI CENANG** is the most extensive on the island, with a whole string of cramped chalet sites slotted in side by side. By and large, though, the buildings are unobtrusive, largely because of the government's requirement that any beachfront accommodation must not exceed the height of a coconut tree. The bay forms a large sweep of wide, white beach with crisp, sugary sand, but again the water here doesn't win any prizes for cleanliness. Less dedicated sun-worshippers will find the lack of shade on the beach a problem, but its sheer length and breadth means that, despite the package-tour clientele, it never gets too crowded. Plenty of places offer **watersports** and **boat rental**, otherwise only available at the large resorts elsewhere on the island. One of the more organized centres is *Langkawi Marine Sports* (☎04/911389), where costs are negotiable depending on the season – expect to pay around $165 per boat (which can take 6 people) for a round-the-island boat tour, $110 for a day's fishing or $25 for ten minutes' waterskiing.

There are dozens of **places to stay**, although not many good options at the budget end of the scale – if money's tight, you're unlikely to be able to afford a sea view. The cheapest place is the *Suria Beach Motel* (☎04/911776; ①), about 100 metres north from the promontory which separates Cenang from Tengah, with small, ramshackle rooms. A bit further along, the *Sandy Beach Motel* (☎04/911308; ②) has a wide variety of accommodation, although you'll pay more for the beach front bungalows. Back at the promontory, the *Delta Motel* (☎04/911307; ②) has a fine location together with good-value chalets; of a similar standard are the *Samila Beach Motel* (☎04/911964; ②), which has simple corrugated-roof A-frames with bathrooms, and the friendly *AB Motel* (☎04/911300; ②), an attractive development with gardens, hammocks and a terrace restaurant. The *Semarak Langkawi* (☎04/911377; ④) is the best place in its price range and boasts spacious, wooden-floored bungalows in a large garden compound. The island's finest accommodation is at the *Pelangi Beach Resort* (☎04/911011; ⑥) – which hosted the 1989 Commonwealth Conference – a luxurious, two-storey timber development which echoes traditional Malay buildings. If you want to get away from it all, about halfway along the bay, at *Majari's Rent and Camp* (☎04/911409), $70 fixes you up with a six-person tent and all the equipment you need for a night in the wild, either on Langkawi itself or on any of the permitted islands; there are considerable reductions for further nights' rent.

Most of the "motels" also have attached **restaurants** with the emphasis on Westernized local dishes. The *Delta* is good value, but doesn't serve alcohol, and the *Semerak Langkawi* has a pleasant, if slightly expensive, terrace restaurant; the *AB Motel* is better value. Aside from the motels, there is a reasonable Italian restaurant, the *Prizzo*, about halfway along the stretch, one of the less expensive of the outfits along the main road. For a top-notch meal, head for the *Pelangi Beach Resort*, where a meal in its excellent Chinese or Japanese restaurants could set you back around $50 a head.

Pantai Kok

Continuing round the island road, another couple of kilometres uphill you pass the *Sheraton Langkawi* (☎04/911901; ⑥), perched somewhat inconveniently on a cliff top, before reaching the next place of any consequence, **PANTAI KOK**, lying on the far western stretch of Langkawi. It's the best beach on the island, a large sweep of powdery white sand with relatively clear and shallow water – quieter and more secluded than Cenang, more intimate in feel, and with little to do in the evening except swing in a hammock looking up at the stars. You're also only 2km from the splendid falls at Telaga Tujuh, just to the north (see below).

A number of attractive **chalets** are strung out along the beach. In spite of its name, the best is *The Last Resort* (☎04/911046; ②) with timber and atap rooms; the luxury detached beachfront bungalows here are in the next price category up. Least expensive rooms are at the *Pantai Kok Motel* (☎04/911048; ①), but it's very run-down. Better, but riding somewhat on its reputation, is the *Country Beach Motel* (☎04/911212; ①). Next door, the *Kok Bay* (☎04/911407; ②) faces the *Coral Beach* (☎04/911000; ②), both neat and tidy, if rather regimented, rows of huts. For something a bit out of the ordinary, the reasonably priced chalets at the *Iduman Bay Resort* (☎04/911066; ④) are arranged

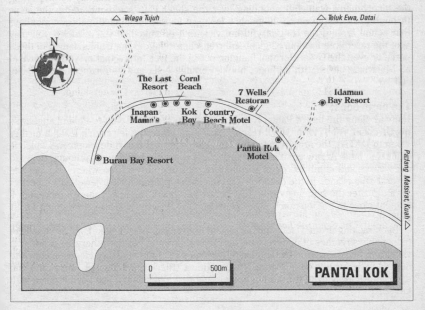

around a freshwater pool reached by wooden walkways, and come with air-con, hot water, TV and phone. The one upmarket place on this beach is the *Burau Bay Resort* (☎04/911061; ⑥) at the western end, sister to the *Pelangi* at Cenang, and frankly not on a patch on its relative.

Most of the chalets again have their own **restaurants**. The best food around also happens to be the cheapest, at the tiny *7 Wells Restoran,* on the corner of the road to Datai – it has wonderful home cooking with either chicken or fish dishes cooked to order. Another good option is at *The Last Resort*, which has an attractive, airy restaurant, though it's a little on the expensive side. At the lively *Idaman Bay*, the restaurant overlooks the pool and serves hot, Thai-influenced dishes; the bar balcony is built on stilts over the river which whirls underneath you when the tide comes in. Finally, *Inapan Mama's* has hamburgers on the menu and is a good spot for drinking late into the night.

Telaga Tuju

A dirt track on the right just before the *Burau Bay Resort* leads up to the island's most wonderful natural attraction, **Telaga Tujuh** or "Seven Pools", a cascading freshwater stream that has pounded large recesses into the rock. The mossy surface covering the rock enables you to slide rapidly from one pool to another, before the fast-flowing water disappears over the cliff to form the waterfall you can see from below – it's only the depth of the water in the last pool that prevents you from shooting off the end too. This being Langkawi, there is of course another legend suggesting it is the playground of mountain fairies; a special kind of lime and *sintuk* (a climbing plant with enormous pods) roots found around these pools are believed to have been left behind by the fairies, and the locals use them as a hair wash to rinse away bad luck.

You can only go a short way up the track to Telaga Tujuh by vehicle, but the steep two-hundred metre climb to the pools that follows is well worth it – in total, it's about a 45-minute walk from the road near the *Burau Bay Resort*. About halfway up, bypassing the ninety-metre **waterfall** pounding over the sheer cliff face, continue up the steps through the forest to reach the pools – look out for the long-tailed macaque monkeys that bound around the trail, playful but vicious if provoked. If you're lucky, you may spot the rarer cream-coloured giant squirrel scampering up the trunks, famed in these parts, or even the Great Hornbill hanging out in the tree tops – that most distinctive of all Malaysian birds, with its huge, hooked orange beak and its distinctive cackle-like call.

The north coast

Halfway along the bay at Pantai Kok is a right turn that takes you to Pulau Langkawi's **north coast**. After 10km you'll reach a new road off to the left which leads a further 12km to **DATAI**, the area targeted for Langkawi's newest resort development, which is still being built. At present it's not a particularly rewarding diversion, although the road does curve and climb to reveal a couple of secluded coves from where you can see several Thai islands in the distance. The sea at this point is a clear jewel-blue – perfect for a dip after the hot, dusty ride. Just before you reach the resort there's more development close to the top-notch *Datai Bay Golf Club*. Private villas here are going for $1 million.

Backtracking from Datai, further round the coast, past Teluk Ewa, a couple of reasonable stretches of undeveloped beach look inviting, but the otherwise panoramic view from here is marred by the unsightly factory belching out large clouds of concrete dust. A little further on is **Pantai Pasir Hitam** (Black Sand Beach), where the cliff drops down away from the road to reveal sand that looks as if it has been washed with tar.

Five kilometres further east the road intersects the main north–south route across the island at the village of **PADANG LALANG**. Turn left and a couple of kilometres through some swampy land will bring you to **Tanjung Rhu**, also known as "Casuarina Beach" because of the profusion of the trees here. There are two developments here, a large incongruous block of condominiums, *Mutiara Court*, and the *Mutiara Beach Resort* (☎04/916488; ⑤) next door. Close to the beach, past the sign that warns "Alcohol is the root of all evil", are some food and drink stalls – which don't sell beer. Although the sand here is a bit gritty, the sea – sheltered by the curve of the bay – is unusually tranquil, almost lagoon-like. The tide goes out far enough at certain times of the day for you to walk to the nearby islands of **PULAU PASIR** and **PULAU GASING**, only a few metres or so away across the sand and perfect spots for a bit of secluded sunbathing. On a promontory accessible only by boat from Tanjung Rhu (costing around $80), you'll find the isolated **Gua Cerita** (Cave of Tales), facing the Thai coastline. Avoiding the voluminous bats' droppings, if you look closely inside the cave you can make out verses of the Koran written in ancient script.

Back at the crossroads, it's another 2km east to the site of **Telaga Air Panas** (Hot Springs), reputedly formed during a quarrel between the island's two leading families over a rejected offer of marriage. Household items were flung about in the fight: the spot where gravy splashed from the pots became known as "Kuah" (gravy), and here, where the jugs of boiling water landed, hot springs spouted. There's not much to see and what there is has been subsumed within the **Air Hangat Village**, which now encompasses the hot springs and an arts pavilion, designed in traditional Malay *kampung* style. It's $4 to enter, for which you get demonstrations of folk and classical dance, *silat* and kick boxing at various times of the day. There is also an expensive restaurant that puts on a cultural show every evening, catering inevitably for tour groups.

Another 2km further on is the turn-off for **Durian Perangin**, a waterfall reached along a difficult and rocky path, and fairly disappointing unless you happen to catch it after the wet season when the water level is high. Shortly after this the road curves to the south for the remaining 10km to Kuah.

Other islands

While most of the Langkawi archipelago is uninhabited (and uninhabitable), expensive day trips are run to some of the nearer islands – fine if you're into snorkelling and fishing, but otherwise providing little incentive to leave the main island. Trips are organized at the tourist office or the *Langkawi Island Resort* in Kuah, or by various hotels at Pantai Tengah or Pantai Cenang.

Mountainous **PULAU TUBA**, 5km south of Langkawi, is the only island with accommodation and then only one option – the *Sunrise Beach Resort* (☎010/332882; ④), with its own swimming pool. There's barely enough space around the rim for the dirt track which encircles the island, although negotiating it is rewarded by deserted beaches. It's awkward to get to Tuba – a matter of hanging round the Kuah jetty until someone offers to take you across in one of the small speedboats; a one-way trip costs $8.

PULAU DAYANG BUNTING (Island of the Pregnant Maiden) is the second largest island in the archipelago, about an hour's boat ride from Pulau Langkawi. It's the exception to the rule in having at least a couple of specific points of interest, but you'll have to visit on a day trip as there's nowhere to stay. **Tasik Dayang Bunting**, a large and tranquil freshwater lake, is reputed to have magical properties whereby barren women who drink from it can become fertile. The area is overwhelmed by massive, densely forested limestone outcrops, which are at their most dramatic around the **Gua Langsir** (Cave of the Banshee), a towering 91-metre-high cave on the island's west coast, with a reputation for being haunted – probably induced by the echo of the thousands of bats which reside inside. The boat, which leaves from Kuah, Pantei Tengah and Pantei Cenang and costs around $18 a head, drops you at a jetty near the lake, before continuing on to the cave, 8km to the north.

Langkawi's most recent attempt at "green" tourism is realized on **PULAU SINGA BESAR**, a wildlife sanctuary 3km off the southern tip of Pantai Tengah. The organized day trip includes the services of a guide, since for obvious reasons you're not allowed to roam around at will. Monkeys, mouse deer, iguanas and peacocks are among the wildlife to have been freed on the island, although how many animals you actually see is, as ever, a matter of luck.

You'd have to be a really dedicated enthusiast to visit the **PULAU PAYAR MARINE PARK** – a one-way, three-hour boat charter south from Langkawi will cost in the region of $120. Schools of tropical fish abound and south of the island, 13km west of the peninsula, lies a coral garden supporting the largest number of coral species in the country. Again, no accommodation is available and to camp you must first obtain permission from the Fisheries Department at Alor Setar (☎04/725573).

North to the Thai border

The tiny state of **Perlis** – at 800 square kilometres, the smallest in Malaysia – lies at the northwestern tip of the peninsula bordering Thailand. Together with neighbouring Kedah, it's traditionally been viewed as the country's agricultural heartland, something reflected in the landscape which is dominated by lustrous, bright green paddy fields. There's no special reason to stop here; most people pass quickly through the state's dull towns on their way to Thailand – it's likely you'll want to do the same. Although both main roads and train line cut inland to the border, it's easy enough to catch local buses to the coastal villages covered below.

Kuala Perlis

Boats to and from Langkawi dock at the little town of **KUALA PERLIS**, 45km north of Alor Setar, and although it's the second-largest settlement in the state it has no more than two streets. Buses drop you at an unmarked stand adjacent to the jetty, from where a wooden footbridge connects with the older, more interesting part of town, a ramshackle collection of buildings on stilts. The *Kuala Perlis–Langkawi Ferry Service* has an office here (☎04/754494), but it's just as easy to turn up and board; there are five departures throughout the day.

There are two **banks** in the main part of town, near the jetty. While express buses to Padang Besar, Alor Setar and Butterworth are fairly frequent, there are a couple of **hotels** if things get desperate, the cheapest of which is the *Asia* (☎04/755392; ②), signposted a short five-minute walk out of town. An upmarket alternative is the antiseptic *PENS Hotel* (☎04/754122; ④), just along from the jetty on the road towards Kangar. A few *kedai kopis* provide **snacks**, but don't expect any great gastronomic delights.

You can reach Satun in **Thailand** directly from Kuala Perlis by small long-tailed boat from the jetty, which leave when full, charging $3.50 for the thirty-minute journey, making it the quickest cross-border option if you're coming from Langkawi (otherwise, you have to cross by bus or train; see below). At weekends you'll be charged an additional $1 for the immigration officers' overtime payment!

Kangar, Arau and Kaki Bukit

Buses north run on to **KANGAR**, 12km from Kuala Perlis, the state capital, another unremarkable modern town, and stop at the centrally located bus station where you have to change buses for the border. The nearest **train station** is at **ARAU**, 10km east, and the least interesting of all the Malaysia's royal towns – the Royal Palace (closed to the public) on the main road looks little more than a comfortable mansion. The town is only really handy for the daily train to Hat Yai and Bangkok (which doesn't stop here on the return journey), and there are less convenient once-daily connections to Butterworth, Alor Setar, Sungei Petani, Taiping, Ipoh, Tapah Road and Kuala Lumpur.

With your own transport, and time to kill before crossing the border, you could visit **Gua Kelam Kaki Bukit**, a 370-metre-long limestone cave that is now a working tin-mine, which runs through to a village on the other side of a hill, 14km before the border checkpoint at Padang Besar. Its name literally means "at a foothill (kaki bukit) lies a cave of darkness (gua kelam)" and the subterranean stream that runs through the mine was once used to carry away the excavated tin ore to the processing plant near the cave's entrance. Access to the tin face is by way of a suspended wooden walk-way that gives visitors a unique vantage point for observing the proceedings, athough it is also used by locals – and their motorbikes – as a means of getting to the other side of the valley. **KAKI BUKIT** itself is easily reached by bus from Kangar, but since this means carting your luggage with you through the mine and back again, you'll probably want to give it a miss and carry straight on to Padang Besar.

Crossing the border

The two land **border crossings** are at the villages of Padang Besar and, further south-east, Bukit Kayu Hitam.

The **train** comes to a halt at **PADANG BESAR**, where a very long platform connects the Malaysian service with its Thai counterpart. You have to change trains here and go through customs at the station. By **bus**, frequent services from Kangar drop you on the road at the border, which is closed from 6pm to 6am. The first train gets to Padang Besar at 7.40am, the last at 4.20pm, while buses run regularly through-out the day. The **North–South Highway** runs to the border at **BUKIT KAYU HITAM**, from where it is about a five-hundred-metre walk to Danok on the Thai side.

Once you've passed through immigration, there are regular bus connections from both places with Hat Yai, 60km away, southern Thailand's transportation hub. The train passes through here, too, on its way north to Bangkok.

travel details

Note that connections for overland transport from Penang are from Butterworth; see p.170 for details of leaving Penang.

Trains

Alor Setar to: Arau (3 daily; 30min–1hr); Bangkok (1 daily; 18hr 15min); Butterworth (1 daily; 2hr 45min); Hat Yai (1 daily; 2hr 20min); Ipoh (1 daily; 4hr 30min); Kuala Lumpur (1 daily; 8hr 50min); Padang Besar (2 daily; 1hr 15min); Sungei Petani (2 daily; 50min–1hr 10min); Taiping (1 daily; 3hr); Tapah Road (1 daily; 5hr 40min).

Butterworth to: Alor Setar (2 daily; 1hr 40min–2hr 20min); Bangkok (1 daily; 19hr 55min); Hat Yai (1 daily; 4hr); Ipoh (5 daily; 2hr 55min–4hr 22min); Kuala Kangsar (5 daily; 2–3hr); Kuala Lumpur (5 daily; 7hr 10min–10hr); Sungei Petani (2 daily; 2hr 15min); Taiping (5 daily; 1hr 30min–2hr 10min); Tapah Road (5 daily; 3hr 50min–6hr 10min).

Ipoh to: Butterworth (5 daily; 3hr 25min–5hr 10min); Kuala Kangsar (5 daily; 1hr–1hr 30min); Kuala Lumpur (6 daily; 4hr 15min–5hr); Taiping (6 daily; 1hr 40min–2hr 30min); Tapah Road (6 daily; 55min 1hr 45min).

Kuala Kangsar to: Butterworth (5 daily; 2hr 30min–3hr 40min); Ipoh (5 daily; 50min 1hr 15min); Kuala Lumpur (5 daily; 4hr 10min–7hr); Taiping (5 daily; 40min–1hr); Tapah Road (5 daily; 1hr 45min–3hr).

Padang Besar to: Alor Setar (1 daily; 3hr 25min); Bangkok (1 daily; 17hr 15min); Butterworth (1 daily; 2hr 40min); Hat Yai (1 daily; 1hr 20min); Ipoh (1 daily; 8hr); Kuala Lumpur (1 daily; 12hr 15min); Sungei Petani (2 daily; 1hr 40min–4hr 15min); Taiping (1 daily; 6hr 30min); Tapah Road (1 daily; 9hr).

Taiping to: Alor Setar (1 daily; 3hr 30min); Butterworth (5 daily; 1hr 50min–2hr 40min); Ipoh

(6 daily; 1hr 25min–2hr 10min); Kuala Kangsar (5 daily; 30min–1hr); Kuala Lumpur (6 daily; 5hr 40min); Padang Besar (1 daily; 4hr 45min); Sungei Petani (1 daily; 2hr 45min); Tapah Road (6 daily; 2hr 20min–4hr).

Tapah Road to: Alor Setar (1 daily; 7hr); Butterworth (5 daily; 4hr 20min–6hr 20min); Ipoh (6 daily; 1hr 10min); Kuala Kangsar (5 daily; 1hr 50min–2hr 45min); Kuala Lumpur (6 daily; 3hr 20min–3hr 50min); Padang Besar (1 daily; 8hr 10min); Sungei Petani (1 daily; 6hr); Taiping (6 daily; 2hr 30min–3hr 40min).

Buses

Alor Setar to: Butterworth (every 30min–1hr 30min; 2hr 30min); Hat Yai (2 daily; 3hr); Ipoh (2 daily; 6hr); Johor Bahru (2 daily; 16hr); Kota Bharu (2 daily; 8–9hr); Kuala Lumpur (2 daily; 8hr); Kuala Perlis (every 30min; 1hr 30min); Kuala Terrenganu (2 daily; 8hr); Kuantan (1 daily; 9hr 30min); Tapah (3 daily; 6hr).

Butterworth to: Alor Setar (every 30min–1hr; 2hr 30min); Bangkok (2 daily; 18hr); Hat Yai (2 daily; 5hr 30min); Ipoh (6 daily; 3hr 45min); Kota Bharu (2 daily 6hr); Kuala Lumpur (at least 15 daily; 7hr); Kuala Perlis (5 daily; 3hr 45min); Kuala Terengganu (2 daily; 8hr); Kuantan (3 daily; 12hr); Lumut (4 daily; 4hr); Melaka (11 daily; 6–10hr); Padang Besar (5 daily; 4hr); Singapore (at least 2 daily; 16hr); Seremban (4 daily; 8–9hr); Sungei Petani (10 daily; 1hr 15min); Surat Thani (2 daily; 10hr 30min); Taiping (14 daily; 2hr 15min); Tapah (3 daily; 4hr 30min).

Ipoh to: Alor Setar (2 daily; 6hr); Butterworth (6 daily; 3hr 45min); Kangar (2 daily; 6hr); Kuala Kangsar (every 45min; 1hr); Kuala Lumpur (every 30min–1hr; 4hr); Kuala Terrenganu (1 daily; 11hr); Kuantan (5 daily; 8hr); Lumut (every 30min–1hr; 1hr 30min); Penang (2 daily; 4hr 30min); Singapore (5 daily: 10–11hr); Taiping (every 30min; 1hr 30min); Tapah (hourly; 1hr 20min).

Lumut to: Butterworth (4 daily; 4hr); Ipoh (every 30min–1hr; 1hr 30min); Kuala Lumpur (6 daily; 5hr 30min); Kuantan (5 daily; 9hr 30min); Taiping (every 30min; 1hr 10min); Tapah (2 daily; 2hr).

Tapah to: Alor Setar (3 daily; 6hr); Butterworth (3 daily; 4hr 30min); Hat Yai (1 daily; 10hr); Ipoh (hourly; 1hr 20min); Kuala Lumpur (at least 10 daily; 2hr–2hr 30min); Kuala Terrenganu (1 daily; 7hr); Kuantan (2 daily; 6hr); Lumut (2 daily; 2hr); Melaka (2 daily; 3hr 30min); Singapore (2 daily; 10hr).

Ferries

Butterworth to: Penang (every 20–60min, 24hr service; 15min).

Kuala Kedah to Langkawi (6 daily; 1hr 10min).

Kuala Perlis to Langkawi (9 daily; 45min).

Langkawi to: Kuala Kedah (6 daily; 1hr 10min); Kuala Perlis (9 daily; 45min); Penang (1 daily; 2hr); Phuket (2 weekly; 3hr); Satun (3 daily; 1hr).

Penang to: Butterworth (every 20–60min, 24hr service; 15min); Langkawi (1 daily; 2hr); Medan (Indonesia; 4 weekly; 4hr).

Flights

Ipoh to: Johor Bahru (at least 4 daily; 55min); Kuala Lumpur (at least 6 daily; 35min); Langkawi (2 weekly; 45min).

Langkawi to: Ipoh (2 weekly; 45min); Johor Bahru (1 daily; 2hr 20min); Kuala Lumpur (at least 7 daily; 55min); Penang (at least 3 daily; 30min); Phuket (1 weekly; 40min); Singapore (at least 7 daily; 1hr 25min).

Penang to: Bangkok (1 daily; 1hr 40min); Johor Bahru (at least 6 daily via KL; 1hr 5min–3hr 45min); Kota Bharu (1 daily; 40min); Kuala Lumpur (at least 19 daily); Langkawi (4 daily; 30min); Medan (1 daily; 20min); Phuket (1 daily; 30min); Singapore (at least 12 daily; 1hr 10min–3hr 55min).

CHAPTER THREE

THE INTERIOR

The **interior** states of Pahang and Kelantan were the last regions of Peninsular Malaysia to excite the interest of the British colonial authorities. Until the 1880s the Bendahara (Prince) of Pahang, Wan Ahmed, ran his southern central state as a private fiefdom, unvisited by outsiders except for a hundred or so Chinese and European gold prospectors who had established contacts with a few remote Malay villages and *orang asli* settlements. When explorer and colonial administrator Sir Hugh Clifford visited he noted that the region "did not boast a mile of road and it was smothered in deep, damp forest, threaded across a network of streams and rivers. . . flecked here and there by little splashes of sunlight." What Clifford also noted – indeed the reason for his visit – was that Pahang was "wonderfully rich in minerals" and an agreement with Wan Ahmed gave the British mining and planting rights in exchange for providing military protection against the incursions of the Siamese or Kelantanese.

First to arrive were British officials, then the tin and gold prospectors, followed by investors in rubber and other plantation enterprises. The new arrivals initially used the rivers to get around, though the larger companies soon began to clear tracks into the valleys and along the mountain ridges, the forerunner of today's roads. Development was made much easier when the jungle railway opened in the 1920s (see below). Slowly, small towns like Temerloh, Raub and Kuala Lipis grew in size and importance, while new settlements like Gua Musang were established to cater for the influx of Chinese merchants and workers.

Since the 1980s, when the only highway into the interior, Route 8 (from Bentong to Kota Bharu), was finished, the whole region has been transformed. If still not entirely accessible – there are corners whose "utter remoteness from mankind" have changed little since Clifford's day – the impact of the timber, rubber and palm-oil industries cannot be underestimated. Much of the primeval landscape, hitherto the preserve of *orang asli*, a few Malays and the odd Chinese trader, has been rapidly tamed, providing economic incentives for people from both east and west coasts to move into these areas. This encroachment has had a huge effect on the indigenous tribes of the interior and since the late 1950s the greater part of the *orang asli* have opted out of their traditional lifestyle. It's probable that only a few hundred truly nomadic tribespeople remain and even those have been tainted by economic progress: *orang asli* expert, Iskandar Carey, wrote in the 1970s, "There are groups of Senoi in the deep jungle who have never seen a road, although they are familiar with helicopters, a word for which has been incorporated into their language." The *Centre of Orang Asli Affairs* coordinates a variety of policies, including health and educational drives, which, although inevitably diluting the purity of *asli* culture, has lifted their standard of living and begun a process – still in its early stages – of integrating the *orang asli* into mainstream, multi racial Malay culture.

Barisan Titiwangsa (Main Range) forms the western boundary of the interior; to its east is an H-shaped range of steep, sandstone mountains with knife-edge ridges and luxuriant valleys in which nestle small towns and *kampungs*. The rivers which flow from these mountains – sungeis Pahang, Tembeling, Lebir, Nenggiri and Galas – provide the northern interior's indigenous peoples, the Negritos and Senoi, with their main means of transport. Visitors, too, can travel by boat to perhaps the most stunning of all Peninsula Malaysia's delights, **Taman Negara**, the country's first national park

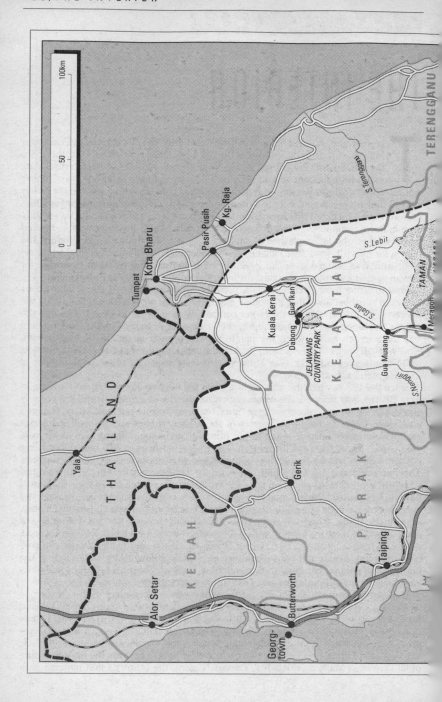

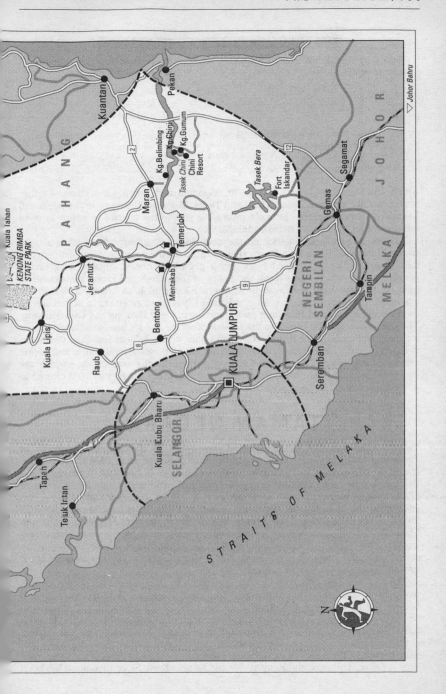

which straddles the borders of Pahang, Kelantan and Terengganu states. Further south, two lake systems, **Tasek Chini** and **Tasek Bera**, are the home to the Jakun and Semelai groups – perhaps the most promising part of the interior in which to meet *orang asli* who still live in a quasi-traditional way.

Drivers cut across the interior on the new **Route 8**, a journey that takes around twelve hours from KL to Kota Bharu (not allowing for the occasional landslide or rock fall). However, unless you're in a real hurry to get to either coast, consider a trip on the **jungle railway** which winds along the floors of the valleys and round the sandstone hills on its route from Mentakab in southern Pahang to Kota Bharu, 500km to the northeast. There are interesting stops at **Kuala Lipis** (the former capital of Pahang), at the **Kenong Rimba** and **Jelawang** parks, and the caves at **Dabong** and **Gua Musang**. The train was originally known as the *Golden Blowpipe* and it's hard to imagine a more inappropriate name, since it runs at a snail's pace and is seldom less than two hours behind schedule. Nevertheless, it's a foolproof way of meeting local people and seeing remote Malay villages, as well as the interior's spectacular landscapes – which are increasingly hard to view by car or bus, since much of the jungle has been cleared to make way for roads and new settlements.

TAMAN NEGARA

Two hundred and fifty kilometres northeast of KL is the southern boundary of Peninsular Malaysia's largest and most important protected area, **TAMAN NEGARA**, spread over large tracts of the interior of the three states of Kelantan, Terengganu and Pahang. Taman Negara means simply "the national park" and, within its 4300 square kilometres, lie dense lowland forest bisected by rivers; higher-altitude cloud forest enveloping the highest peak, **Gunung Tahan**; and numerous hills, *orang asli* settlements, hides, campsites and the *Taman Negara Resort*, the most chic jungle retreat in Malaysia. From the clear-water tributaries which snake down from the mountains feeding fierce waterfalls, to the multitudinous flora and fauna viewed from every step of the parks' trails, the Taman Negara experience – as the *Resort's* publicity material never tires of telling you – is second to none.

The area was first protected by state legislation in 1925 when 1300 square kilometres was designated as the Gunung Tahan Game Reserve; thirteen years later it became the King George V National Park, after the British monarch, and at independence it was renamed Taman Negara and extended to its current boundaries. In 1991, the Malaysian Parks and Wildlife Department decided it was best to split the running of the park into two sections. The department would continue to oversee the ecological management of the park, but the accommodation and eating facilities at the three main sites – Tahan, Trenggan and Keniam – would be privatized. Since then there has been substantial redevleopment by the Singapore-based *Pernas* hotel chain: at Kuala Tahan a massive cash injection has financed over one hundred deluxe chalets, with smaller, less obtrusive developments taking place at Kuala Trenggan and Kuala Keniam.

The park itself forms by far the largest undivided tract of rainforest in Peninsular Malaysia; indeed it contains some of the **oldest rainforest** in the world – older than the Congo or Amazon – having had a continuous history of evolution for 130 million years. Although for many the chance of seeing sizeable **mammals**, especially elephants, is one of the park's big draws, very few visitors have any success unless they are either prepared to undertake a three- or four-day trek, or journey upriver to remote Kuala Keniam and head into the forest from there. But stay overnight in the hides – tree houses positioned beside salt licks – and you'll often spot mouse deer, tapir and *seladang* (wild ox), especially during the rainy season. That said, it's quite possible to spend a week in the park and see nothing more exciting than a mound of elephant dung, armies of ants and leeches, and a colourful shape – maybe an Argus Pheasant – sprinting noisily through the undergrowth. **Bird life**, at least, is ever-present – the park has over three hundred species – and many are quite easy to spot with good binoculars and patience. For a full rundown of the park habitats and species on view, see the wildlife account in *Contexts*, p.584.

There's a map of Taman Negara park on p.206.

Every **trek** into the forest has its fascinations. For those unfamiliar with the tropical rainforest environment, just listening to the bird, insect and animal sounds, smelling the rich, intoxicating air, wondering at the sheer size of the *dipterocarp* trees and peering into the rainforest canopy is bound to be a memorable experience. Walks always reveal a myriad of entrancing sights: flowering lianas, giant bamboo stands with funghi which glow in the dark, chattering macaque monkeys rattling across the tree tops. A few dozen nomadic Batek *orang asli*, a sub-group of the Negritos, still remain in the park and on the paths which weave along the west side of sungei Tembeling and curl off north into the jungle you may pass their low, makeshift shelters built of vines and forest brush, built to stand only for a few days before the inhabitants move on again – but you'll seldom see the *asli* themselves. The Batek are mostly hunters and gatherers and the authorities turn a blind eye to them hunting game here, though some Batek also work for the park authorities at the *Resort*.

The undoubted success of the *Taman Negara Resort* – over 30,000 people a year now visit the park – brings its own problems. According to some Malaysian environmentalists, the increasing number of visitors is having an unsustainable impact on the park's ecosystem: the popular trail to Gunung Tahan is suffering accelerated **erosion** due to the large number of hikers who, moreover, leave rubbish on the trail, so despoiling a formerly pristine environment. Also of concern is the effect on the biological food chain of the gradual migration of large mammals from the noisy Kuala Tahan area around the *Resort*.

The best time to **visit** the park is between March and September, during the "dry" season, although it still rains most days even then. The park used to close in the wet season (mid-Oct to Feb), but under the new management is now staying open during this period. The main effect of the wet conditions on the visitor are some restrictions on the trails and boat trips. Those wanting a tranquil, at-one-with-nature experience may well not take to **Kuala Tahan** and would be better advised to stay upstream at **Nusa Camp**, which is smaller and more basic. Alternatively head straight for the upriver camps at **Kuala Keniam** and **Kuala Trenggan**; or even camp at one of the twelve designated campsites dotted around the park.

Getting there

Although it's possible to fly from KL to close to the park, the vast majority of visitors take a bus to Tembeling jetty, from where it's a three-hour boat trip up sungei Pahang and then the narrower sungei Tembeling to the park headquarters at Kuala Tahan. By jungle railway, there's access from one of two stops – either Jerantut, a small town 10km from the jetty, or Kuala Tembeling, a *kampung* further north, from where the jetty is only a thirty-minute walk. As there is no accommodation at Kuala Tembeling, many stay the night at Jerantut (see below for details).

THE EMERGENCY, THE ORANG ASLI AND LAND RIGHTS

During the **Emergency** years (1948–60), Chinese Communist guerillas – many of them originally members of the Malayan Communist Party – built jungle camps deep in the forested interior from which to operate against both British and Malayan forces. The effect of this on the way of life of the Sakai – the *orang asli* groups inhabiting areas north of the Kuantan Highway (Route 2) as far as Kuala Kerai in Kelantan – was dramatic. All but the most remote tribes were subject to intimidation and killings, from the guerillas on one side and the government forces on the other. In effect, the *orang asli*'s centuries-old invisibility ended, with the population of Malaysia now aware of their presence and the government of their strategic importance.

The *orang asli* had no choice but to grow food and act as porters for the guerillas, and most important of all, provide an intelligence service to warn them of the approach of the enemy. In turn, government forces built eleven jungle forts, including ones near the towns of Raub and Tanjung Malim, and in near desperation implemented a disastrous policy – soon abandoned – of removing *orang asli* from the jungle they had occupied for centuries and relocating them in new **model villages** near Raub and Gua Musang, which were no more than dressed-up prison camps. Thousands were placed behind barbed wire and hundreds died in captivity before the government dismantled the camps, but by then, not surprisingly, more of the *orang asli* actively supported the insurgents – although they switched their allegiance to the security forces when the guerillas' fortunes waned and defeat became inevitable.

At the peak of the conflict around ten thousand guerillas were hiding out in dozens of camouflaged jungle camps. For a long time they milked a support network of Chinese-dominated towns and villages in the interior, in many cases cowing the inhabitants into submission by means of public executions – although in some areas many of the poor rural workers identified with the struggle to wrest the ownership of the large rubber plantations away from the British. It was only when the government successfully started to plant informers that the security services started to get wind of guerilla operations.

As far as the *orang asli* were concerned, the attempt by the government to control their living patterns throughout the Emergency led inexorably to the imposition of a structural framework of laws, social strategies and programmes during the 1960s and 1970s. This has ranged from providing basic health and education facilities to subjecting the *orang asli* to Islamic proselytising, but in recent years *asli* activists and legal experts have begun to contest a number of these government-sponsored initiatives. The **land rights** issue is now considered by a growing number of people to be the most urgent affecting the *orang asli*. According to one commentator, Lim Heng Seng, "the *asli* find themselves virtually squatters on state land" and as long as the problem of legal entitlement to land is not resolved, there will be a steady stream of cases of outsiders encroaching on *asli* land. Indeed, land is everything to the *orang asli* – in the Semai language, land is called *nerng-rik*, which means "country". Life has changed very rapidly for most *orang asli* since the Emergency years, but it pays to remember that what is seen as progress for many other Malaysians, could all too easily be a cultural trap that is closing in on the indigenous people.

From KL
Flights from KL's Subang airport with *Pelangi Air* (Wed, Fri & Sun; around $170 return) take only 45 minutes to reach the **sungei Tiang airstrip**, from where it's a further thirty minutes north by boat to Kuala Tahan (around $10). Motorized sampans are always there to meet the plane.

The scheduled **bus route** to the park involves two stages. First, take the Temerloh/ Jerantut bus from KL's Pudu Raya station (p.81), which leaves hourly, for the three-hour trip to Jerantut (around $10). From there, take a local bus for the 16-km trip to Tembeling jetty (40min; around $3); as these only leave at 8am, 11am and 1.30pm, many visitors stay overnight in Jerantut and catch the 8am bus the next day. The 7am or 8am bus from KL gets you to Jerantut in time to catch the 11am bus to the jetty, but, as there are only two boat departures from the jetty for the park headquarters – at 9am and 2pm – this leaves you with a long wait. Note that the 1.30pm Jerantut–Tembeling bus doesn't arrive at the jetty in time for the 2pm boat.

By train KL involves travelling first to Gemas (trains leave KL at 8am and 2.45pm), where you change to the jungle train, which leaves Gemas at 2.20am, arriving in Jerantut at 5.30am. The train arrives at the tiny station at **KUALA TEMBELING** thirty minutes later at 6am (tell the guard on the train if you want to get out at Kampung Tembeling as it's an unscheduled stop), which leaves plenty of time to walk the 2km west to the jetty for the 9am boat – there are unlikely to be any taxis as this is a very remote stop. The total price for the train trip from KL is around $12.

From the east coast
Trains leave **Wakaf Bharu**, 7km from Kota Bharu (see p.239), at 8.10am on Wednesday, Friday and Sunday, reaching Kuala Tembeling at around 1pm (if the train is on time, you will be able to catch the 2pm boat departure; if not you'll have to spend the night in Jerantut). Alternatively, the 2.20pm from Wakaf Bharu arrives at Jerantut at around 9.10pm. **From Kuantan**, two daily buses (8am & noon; $12) go straight to Jerantut, or there's an hourly service to Temerloh, where you change for Jerantut (usually within the hour).

Jerantut
JERANTUT is a small, busy town with only one main street, jalan Besar, lined with concrete Chinese cafés and houses. From Jerantut's **bus station** – where the buses arrive from KL and Kuantan and leave for Tembeling jetty – it's a five-minute walk south to jalan Besar and the centre of town; the **train station** is off jalan Besar, just behind *Hotel Sri Emas*.

Jerantut is well equipped with good value accommodation and places to eat. One kilometre west of the train station on jalan Besar is the excellent *Jerantut Rest House* (☎09/264438; ①–②), which has comfortable twin-bed chalets with bathrooms. As tour groups often stay here, it may be possible to hitch a ride on their bus to the jetty. In the middle of town, at the junction of jalan Besar and the road which leads to the train station, is *Hotel Sri Emas* (☎09/264499; ②), a modern Chinese-run hotel with small, neat rooms. A third option is the *Hotel Jerantut*, 100m east on jalan Besar from the junction (☎09/265568; ①) which usually has rooms available. There's an excellent **hawker centre** (daily 5pm–1am), opposite the bus station, which sells particulary good Thai food; otherwise the Chinese cafés serve the usual dishes.

Tembeling jetty to park headquarters
With up to a dozen sleek, motorized sampans leaving daily at 9am and 2pm, **Tembeling jetty** on sungei Pahang has developed into something of a mini-bazaar, with a hundred or more visitors waiting for a connection at any one time. At the jetty

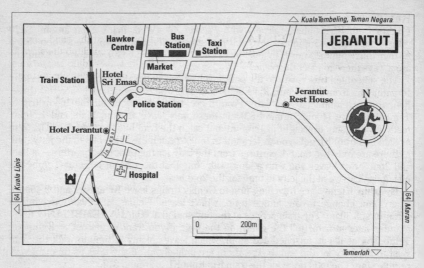

there is a handicraft shop (daily 9am–6pm), three small cafés (same hours) selling *nasi campur*, noodles and snacks and, up some nearby steps, the *Taman Negara Resort* and *Nusa Camp* **ticket offices** – boats owned by both companies leave at the same time.

The sixty-kilometre, three-hour boat trip starts on wide sungei Pahang but after three hundred metres or so the sampans leave the river's main passage for the narrower **sungei Tembeling**. At first, you'll see huts high up on the bank beside small pepper orchards and oil palm plantations, but soon the moss-draped trees reach down to the water, the forest canopy thickens and undulating hills waver on the horizon – only the occasional dab of brown leaves or the sporadic outbreak of red flowers interrupt the various shades of green. Occasionally white-horned cows and buffalo can be seen wallowing in the water, and birds skeet across the bows of the sampan, swooping into the trees.

Staying at Taman Negara

The sampans run to two separate points: *Taman Negara Resort* at Kuala Tahan – the park headquarters – and *Nusa Camp*, a private initiative, 2km further northeast on sungei Tembeling, but outside the park boundary on the east side of the river. If you are staying at *Nusa Camp*, or intend to head straight for the upriver sites at Trenggan and Keniam, you will still have to break your journey at Kuala Tahan to check in.

As with most of Malaysia's parks, facilities are heavily used at the weekends (and especially over festivals and holidays), but are far less crowded during the week. It's also worth noting that the park is, in general, a more pleasant place to explore when there are fewer people around – another good reason for avoiding peak times. For **accommodation** at most places in the park you need either to book at *MATIC* in KL (see p.82) or call the *Taman Negara Resort* direct (☎09/263500). It's best to book around two weeks in advance of your trip if possible, although if you're planning to camp it isn't necessary to reserve in advance. There are more accommodation details below in the relevant sections.

Kuala Tahan

The attractive park site at **KUALA TAHAN** nestles in the forest, at the confluence of the Tahan and Tembeling rivers. After disembarking at the jetty you climb the steps to the *Taman Negara Resort* **office**, where you acquire a Parks and Wildlife Department permit ($1), sign in and get taken to your accommodation. An excellent site and park **map** is available here for no charge – and if you are staying in a *Resort* chalet, you'll also get a glossy brochure giving details about the park and listing the on-site facilities. The information desk in the office deals with queries from all park visitors, regardless of whether you're staying here or at *Nusa Camp*. You also have to book your return boat trip at this office, although there is nearly always room on the sampans for anyone making a snap decision.

Orientation

East from the *Taman Negara Resort* office lie most of the **chalets**, while just along the path which runs through them, there's the **hostel**, a small library and annex – where slide shows about the park take place nightly at 8.30pm. The **library** (daily 8am–midnight) has a diverse selection of geographical journals and accounts of the park; the slide show gives an entertaining, if out-of-date, rundown of the park's main features. Further along the path, close to the point where the chalets end and the forest crowds in, there's the *Teresek Cafetaria*. Just west of the office is the *Tahan Restaurant*; while behind the office is the official **Parks and Wildlife Department** headquarters and two **shops**, one selling basic provisions and the other renting out **camping** gear. Following the path beside the shops leads up some steps to the **campsite**.

Accommodation

Accommodation at Kuala Tahan has to be booked in advance at *MATIC* in KL or by contacting the *Taman Negara Resort*. The two-storey, two-bedroom **bungalows** (⑥) are the height of luxury (around $400 each), with balcony, bathroom with hot showers and kitchen. Next down in price, the hundred-plus twin-bed **chalets** with bathroom (⑤–⑥) are also highly impressive with fiercer air-con than in most expensive hotels. Significantly less expensive is the hundred-bed **hostel** (①), a long brick building, with rather cramped four-berth rooms, at the back of which are washbasins and toilets but no cooking facilities. Lastly, there is the **campsite**, 300m from the *Resort* office, which looks directly onto the jungle (campers are advised not to leave any food outside their tents otherwise the monkeys will get it). You can rent tents for $5 a night from the camping shop, and there's a small site charge of $1 per tent.

Eating and drinking

There are four different **places to eat**. The *Tahan Restaurant* (daily 8am–11pm) is expensive (around $20 a head), although the buffet is good and worth the occasional splurge. Cheaper, but of significantly lower quality, is the *Teresek Cafetaria* (daily 8am–9pm) – a lovely, quiet spot at which to spend time, though you soon tire of the fried noodles and mixed rice; the free hot water is handy if you've brought your own tea or coffee. By far the best food at the site is served at the *KT Restoran* (daily 7am–11pm), which you'll find on a secure raft to the left of the jetty. It's a private enterprise and offers excellent food, both Malaysian and Western, at low prices, around $6 for a full meal. It's also the best place to order an inexpensive **packed lunch**. The last option is to cross sungei Tembeling by sampan from the jetty and eat on the shingle beach below Kampung Tahan, where there are a number of inexpensive **hawker stalls**.

Nusa Camp

The far smaller **Nusa Camp** is 2km further upstream on sungei Tembeling. *Nusa Camp* boats from Tembeling jetty will take you straight there, stopping briefly at Kuala Tahan first to get a park permit. *Nusa Camp* is far smaller than the *Resort* with just twenty huts and chalets, and one café. Although accommodation and food is cheaper, the disadvantage of staying here is that you are dependent on the sampans to ferry you over the river to the park proper, or down to Kuala Tahan, and these trips add up, as the boatmen charge around $4 each way. Note, too, that there aren't any hikes starting from the east side of the river, which is outside the park boundary.

For accommodation, you again need to book in advance at *MATIC* or call *SPKG Tours* (☎09/262369), both in KL. Most expensive accommodation is in the twin-bed **chalets** (②), which are a lot more basic than the ones at the *Resort*, but nevertheless have an attached bathroom. The tiny **teepee**-like pyramid buildings (sleep two; ①) have an external toilet and shower; while the forty-bed **hostel** costs just $7 a night. *Nusa Camp* has one small **cafeteria** which sells inexpensive food (daily 8am–10pm).

Other sites

There is also accommodation available at lodges, hides and campsites throughout the park, the sites of which are covered in more detail in the relevant accounts below. The **lodges** (③–④) upriver at Trenggan (1hr from Kuala Tahan by sampan) and Keniam (2hr) are built along the same lines as the chalets at Tahan, although they're less luxurious. They should be booked in advance if you're planning to go straight there; otherwise leave booking until you arrive in Tahan. There isn't an official campsite at either of these places, but it's possible to put up a tent if you want to. Along sungei Keniam in the remote northeast of the park is *Perkai Lodge* (①), run by the Parks and Wildlife Department. It's very basic, with just eight beds, and you don't need to book – though you will need to take your own bedding. Both Trenggan and Keniam have **cafeterias**, although stocks of food are usually low unless a group is expected, when a boatful of provisions will be brought in from Kuala Tahan. Staying at *Perkai Lodge*, you have to bring your own food which you can cook on the rudimentary barbecue at the back of the lodge.

There's no charge to stay overnight in the various **hides** (see feature on p.204) dotted around the park, but it's best to reserve a place at the *Resort* office in Kuala Tahan as each can only accommodate four to six people. Although you don't need to reserve a spot at any of the twelve **campsites**, check with the Parks and Wildlife Department office which are actually open, since they're rotated to avoid overuse. All the campsites, with the exception of the one at Kuala Tahan, have no facilities whatsoever – you'll even have to take your own bottled water.

Visiting the park

If your stay at Taman Negara is a short one, **essential places to visit** close to the *Taman Negara Resort* include the tough climb up nearby Bukit Teresek, from where there's a panoramic view north across the park; the Canopy Walkway, a swaying aluminium-and-rope bridge 30m above the ground from which you can see a crosssection of jungle life; and Gua Telinga, a deceptively large limestone cave, just one of a number in the park. With three days to spare, your itinerary could also include guided forest walk or a night in one of several hides, positioned deep in the jungle overlooking salt licks where you can spy animals arriving to drink the salty water.

Naturally, all these places and activities tend to be among the most frequented in the park because of their proximity to Kuala Tahan, and to get into the undisturbed forest you really need to stay for a week or more. A seven-day visit, for example, could start with the thirty-kilometre **Rentis Tenor trail**, a lassoo-shaped trek leading south from Kuala Tahan to Gua Telinga, before heading northwest into deep forest to the campsite at sungei Tenor, where you stay in a small clearing beside a beautiful river. Back at base, you could catch a sampan upriver to Kuala Keniam, visit *Perkai Lodge*, and walk along the wild **Keniam trail** – where elephants are sometimes sited – spending the night in a hide at Kumbang, before taking a sampan from Kuala Trenggan back to park headquarters. Unless the park is very busy you're unlikely to see more than a handful of people during the week.

The most adventurous activity of all is the nine-day, sixty-kilometre trek to **Gunung Tahan**; for this you must plan to be in the park at least eleven days, and all groups have to be accompanied by a guide from the Parks and Wildlife Department. The trail involves crossing sungei Tahan numerous times – quite a challenge if the waters have been swollen by rain – and some steep climbing towards the end. One of the chief thrills of the route is that it passes through various terrains, from lowland jungle to cloud forest, before reaching the 2187-metre-high summit, where the vista is breathtaking.

The account of the park below is divided into three sections: day trips that you can make from Kuala Tahan, longer trails – the Rentis Tenor and Gunung Tahan – which require a certain commitment, and trips made from the upriver sites at Trenggan and Keniam. For certain treks you'll require specific equipment and resources, which are detailed where appropriate. None of the trails themselves, however, require any special skills, beyond an average level of fitness, patience and endurance. There's a map showing the area around Kuala Tahan on p.202, and a map of the whole park on p.207.

Getting around

Transport around the park is by sampans, which come in varying sizes depending on the depth of the river. The smaller, lighter craft run along the shallow tributaries like sungei Tahan and sungei Tenor, with the more powerful boats used to reach Trenggan and Keniam upriver on sungei Tembeling. Sampans also **cross the river** at Kuala Tahan, a short trip that costs just $1.

To **rent a boat** either ask the staff at the *Taman Negara Resort* office, who will arrange a trip on your behalf, or – the less expensive option – approach the boatmen directly, at the jetty, and sort out a price with them. In general, you can expect to spend at least $30 a day per person on boat expenses, an amount which will get you as far as the upriver sites or to Lata Berkoh on sungei Tahan. To reach the furthest navigable spot in the park, *Perkai Lodge*, is more likely to cost $100 per person for the return trip. When renting a sampan to the upriver sites, remember to book your return trip at the same time, since the boatmen only operate out of Kuala Tahan and *Nusa Camp*.

Besides river transport the main way of getting about is, of course, on **foot**. The park is dotted with trails, which take from one hour to a few days; the longest, to Gunung Tahan, takes nine days there and back. Many visitors combine boating and trekking, leaving in the morning by sampan and returning later by trail.

Day trips

From Kuala Tahan, there are various possible day trips involving trail walking, river and waterfall excursions and hide visits. For clothing, you can get away with T-shirt and shorts and strong sports shoes, but always have a hat, mosquito repellent and water to hand. Whether you're an ornithologist or not, it's a good idea to take binoculars on

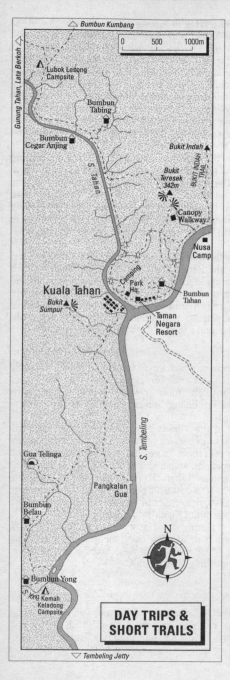

Bumbun Kumbang

0   500   1000m

Gunung Tahan, Lata Berkoh

Lubok Lesong
Campsite

Bumbun
Tabing

Bumbun
Cegar Anjing

S. Tahan

Bukit Indah

Bukit
Teresek
342m

BUKIT INDAH TRAIL

Canopy
Walkway

Nusa
Camp

Camping

Park
Hq.

Kuala Tahan

Bumbun
Tahan

Bukit
Sumpur

Taman
Negara
Resort

S. Tembeling

Gua Telinga

Pangkalan
Gua

Bumbun
Belau

N

Bumbun Yong

Yong Kemah
Keladong
Campsite

**DAY TRIPS &
SHORT TRAILS**

Tembeling Jetty

either the short, or the longer, trails, to get the best possible look at birds from the jungle floor. Also, a magnifying glass is a welcome addition, as it can open up a whole new world of insects, leaf and bark formations.

Bukit Teresek

Although undoubtedly the most heavily used trail in the park, the route to **Bukit Teresek** (which also leads on to Bukit Indah; see below) is an excellent starter, and enables you to acclimatize to the hot, humid conditions. Follow the path which weaves between the chalets east of the *Resort* office, beyond which a trail heads northeast away from the river. It's wide and easy to follow, hitting primary jungle almost immediately; for around 500m most of the tree types have been labelled along the way. After around twenty minutes the trail divides, left to Bukit Teresek and straight on for the Tabing hide (see feature below) and Bukit Indah.

The climb up **Bukit Teresek** – a 342-metre hill – is best negotiated early in the morning, before 8am. It takes one hour at an even pace to reach the top where there's a shelter set on exposed sandstone – a good spot to take in the marvellous views north over the valley to Gunung Tahan and Gunung Perlis (1279m). Along the trail you might hear gibbons or hill squirrels in the trees. The monkeys, especially, are relentless pursuers of any type of food, so keep it out of sight.

Back at the base of the hill, the canopy walkway is just 300m to the north along a clearly marked, springy path of slippery tree roots.

The canopy walkway

Only a small group of people can gain access to the **canopy walkway** (daily 8am–noon; $10) at any one time, so it's best to buy a ticket in advance from the Parks and Wildlife Department office. You may have quite a wait if you just turn up.

The walkway, a sixty-metre-long swaying bridge made from aluminium ladders bound by rope and set 30m above the ground, takes between five and fifteen minutes to negotiate depending on the tree life on view. It's reached by climbing a sturdy wooden tower – two 250-year-old *tualang* trees support the walkway at twenty-metre intervals and you return to terra firma by another wooden stairwell at the end of the third section. Once you've got used to the swaying, it's a pleasurable experience, taking in the fine views of sungei Tembeling and closely observing the insect life and tree parasites which abound at that height. Geckos, cicadas, crickets and grasshoppers hop and fly about, often landing on the walkway, if only to find their bearings before leaping back on to a branch or leaf. Other species usually in sight include the grey banded leaf monkey, with a call that sounds like a rattling tin can, and the white-eyed dusky leaf monkey, with its deep, nasal ha-haw cry, both loping about in groups of six to eight.

The Bukit Indah trail

Past the canopy the route divides, north and slightly uphill to the Tabing hide, another 1km further on, or northeast – heading marginally downhill and cutting back towards sungei Tembeling – along the lovely **Bukit Indah trail**. Intially, this follows the river-bank, and again, you are bound to see monkeys, plenty of bird life, squirrels, shrews and a multitude of insects and, if early or late in the day, perhaps tapir or *seladang*. The path to Bukit Indah itself leaves the main riverside trail (which continues to Kuala Trenggan, 6km away) and climbs at a slight gradient for 200m; the top of the hill offers a lovely view over sungei Tembeling and is an excellent spot to hear, and perhaps catch sight of, monkeys and squirrels. In all, it's a three-kilometre, ninety-minute return trip from the *Resort* office.

Gua Telinga and Kemah Keladong

Another major trail leads south alongside the river, with forks branching off to the lime-stone outcrop of Gua Telinga, to the Belau and Yong hides, and the campsite at Kemah Keladong.

From the jetty by the *KT Restoran*, take a sampan across sungei Tahan. On the other side, follow the trail through a small *kampung* (where some of the resort and Park and Wildlife Department staff live) into the trees and dense foliage. The undulating trail heads across some steep spurs and traverses magnificent lowland rainforest, before descending to the flat land of the river terrace along sungei Tembeling. The forest here has a quite different appearance from that on the hill slopes, partly the effect of flooding, notably that of 1926 which devastated extensive areas of forest around Kuala Tahan. After 3km, you follow the sign north for a futher 200m to reach **Gua Telinga**, where you will need to catch your breath after the tiring walk.

The limestone cave looks small and unassuming, but it's deceptively deep – something you only really discover when you slide through it. Although in theory it's possible to follow a guide rope through the eighty-metre-long cave, in practice only small adults or children are agile enough to tug themselves through the narrow cavities; most people will have to crawl along narrow passages in places and negotiate areas of deep, squishy guano. Thousands of tiny roundleaf and fruit bats reside in the cave, as well as giant toads, black-striped frogs and whip spiders (which aren't poisonous). The roundleaf bats are particularly interesting, so-called because of the shape of the "leaves" of skin around their nostrils, which help direct the sound signals transmitted to assist the bat in navigation.

From Gua Telinga, it's another 500m to the Belau hide through beautiful tall forest, and another kilometre to that at Yong (for both, see the feature below), where the trail divides, north to Kemah Rentis (see below) and left to the tranquil **Keladong** campsite, 500m further, on the terraced bank of sungei Yong. Given an early start, it's quite possible to reach this point, have a swim in the river, and get back to the *Resort* before dusk, but bring at least a litre of water per person and a packed lunch.

Lata Berkoh

Most people visit the "roaring rapids" of **Lata Berkoh** by boat, as it's an eight-kilometre, three-hour trip on foot. Alternatively, you could always walk the trail there, but arrange for a boat to pick you up for the return journey, that way getting the best of both worlds.

Sampans from the jetty at Kuala Tahan cost around $10 each (provided you can get a group of four together) and take roughly thirty minutes, heading upstream on sungei Tahan, the most frequented of the parks' tributaries. The jetty at the other end is just a 100m from the rudimentary *Berkoh Lodge*, a small building, set back from the river in a clearing. If you're intending to sleep here, check first on space with the Parks and Wildlife Department office in Kuala Tahan, and bring your bedding and food – mattresses and a barbecue frame with a few cooking utensils are provided. On the opposite bank is the Melantai **campsite** (see also "The Gunung Tahan trail" below); you can ford the river to reach this most of the year, but in the rainy season you'll have to get there instead on the trail which runs from the *Taman Negara Resort*.

THE HIDES

Spending a night in one of the park's six **hides** (known as *bunbuns*) doesn't guarantee sightings of large mammals, especially in the dry season when the **salt licks** – where plant-eating animals come to supplement their mineral intake – are often so waterless that there's little reason for deer, tapir, elephant, leopard or *seladang* to visit. But it'll be an experience you're unlikely to forget. Not only are the hides at the very roughest end of the accommodation scale – the mattresses are sometimes sodden and not without the odd flea, there's a simple chemical toilet and no washing or cooking facilities – but you're deep in the jungle with only a flashlight (an indispensable item) for illumination.

It's best to go in a group and take turns keeping watch, listening hard and occasionally shining the flashlight at the salt lick – if an animal is present its eyes will reflect brightly in the torch beam. Talking should be kept to a minimum since noise lessens the likelihood that timid animals will use the salt lick. Many people leave scraps of food below the hide to attract the animals, although environmentalists disapprove since this interferes with their naturally balanced diet. As well as a flashlight, take rain gear, hat and sleeping bag, and all the food and drink you will need – and bring all your rubbish back for proper disposal at the *Resort*. You should book your bunk in the hide at the *Resort* office, although during the week there's often room if you just turn up on the off chance. For a full rundown of the wildlife you're likely to see from the hides, turn to *Contexts*, p.584.

There are four hides north of the *Taman Negara Resort* and two to the south. Of the northern ones, the closest is the six-bed **bumbun Tahan** which is situated just south of the junction with the Bukit Teresek trail. However, much more promising ones are the eight-bed **bumbun Tabing**, on the east bank of sungei Tahan (see "Bukit Teresek" for directions), and the eight-bed **bumbun Cegar Anjing**, an hour further and slightly to the south on the west bank of sungei Tahan, beside the old airstrip and reached by fording the river; in the wet season this hide can only be reached by boat as the river's too powerful to wade across. The most distant hide to the north of the *Resort* is the six-bed **bumbun Kumbang**, an eleven-kilometre walk from Kuala Tahan, which, because of its remote location, is the best spot to catch sight of animals.

To the south, there's the six-bed **bumbun Belau** on the Gua Telinga trail, and beyond the cave, the eight-bed **bumbun Yong**, at either of which there's only a small chance of spotting wildlife as the hides are quite close both to the traffic on sungei Tembeling and the *Resort's* vast electricity generator – the combination of these noises has frightened most animals away.

The waterfall itself is 50m north of the lodge, its gurgling waters streaming over hundreds of large rocks. There's a deep pool in which you can swim and the rocky area overlooking the swirling water is an ideal site for a picnic. If you ask the boatman to cut his engine, you'll improve your chances of hearing the sounds of the forest, and of seeing kingfishers with their yellow-and-red wings and white beaks, large grey and green fisheagles, the multicoloured straw-headed bulbuls and, on the rocks, camouflaged monitor lizards.

The **trail** from the *Resort* to Lata Berkoh starts at the campsite and leads through dense rainforest, past the turning for the Tabing hide to the east. After around 3km you reach the campsite at **Lubok Lesong**, just to the left of which there's a broad, pebbled beach leading down to a deep pool in sungei Tahan. The route to the waterfall veers west from the main trail around thirty minutes after the campsite, crossing gullies and steep ridges, before reaching the river, which must be forded. The final part of the trail runs north along the west side of sungei Tahan before reaching the falls.

Longer trails

The two main long trails in the park are the nine-day trek to **Gunung Tahan** and back and the four-day, circular **Rentis Tenor** trail, which reaches the beautiful sungei Tenor before dipping back east. For either, you'll need loose-fitting, lightweight cotton clothing with long sleeves, long trousers to keep insects at bay, a raincoat or poncho, and a litre bottle of water plus water-purifying tablets. Also take a lightweight tent, a powerful torch and spare batteries, map, cooking equipment and compass, all of which can be rented from the camping shop at Kuala Tahan; check with your guide (see below) how much food you'll need to take. For Gunung Tahan you will also need a sleeping bag for the two nights spent at a high-altitude camp. To keep out the leeches – a serious problem after heavy rain – wear walking boots, or sports shoes, with your trousers tucked into heavy duty socks, and spray on insect repellent liberally every hour or so. The *orang asli* approach is to go barefoot and flick off the leeches as they begin to bite, but this requires an advanced-level jungle temperament.

Perhaps the most important advice on all long-distance trails is to know your limitations and not run out of time. Slipping and sliding along in the dark is no fun and can be dangerous – it's easy to fall at night and it's impossible to see snakes or other forest floor creatures which might be on the path.

The Gunung Tahan trail

The sixty-kilometre trek to Peninuslar Malaysia's highest peak, **Gunung Tahan** (2187m), is the highlight of any adventurous visitor's time in Taman Negara – but you have to allow at least eleven days to accomplish it: nine to complete the trek and one day either side to get in and out of the park. Although in peak season hundreds of people trudge along the trail every week, the sense of individual achievement after fording sungei Tahan dozens of times, hauling yourself up and down innumerable hills and camping out every night – let alone the final, arduous ascent through montane forest habitat – is supreme. Not for nothing do successful hikers proudly display their "I climbed Gunung Tahan" T-shirts.

The weather conditions can't be relied upon: the moss forest, which ranges from 4000–6000m, is often shrouded in cloud and even at the summit, cloud cover can prevent a full appreciation of the view below. But if it's clear, you can see at least fifty kilometres in all directions. To the indigenous inhabitants of the region, the Batek *orang asli*, Gunung Tahan is the **Forbidden Mountain** and in their folklore the summit is the home of a vast monkey, who stands guard over magic stones. Because of this, they venture into the foothills on hunting expeditions, to find wild pig, monkey or squirrel, but rarely head further up the mountain.

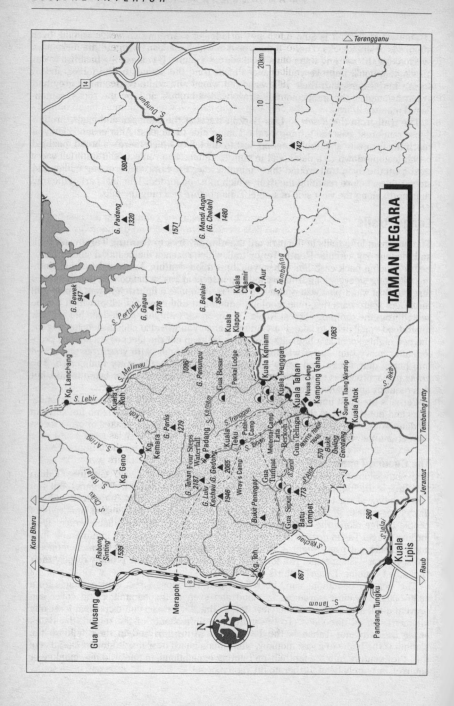

TAMAN NEGARA

To reach the summit you have to follow precarious ridges which weave around the back of the mountain, since the most obvious approach from sungei Tahan would involve scaling the almost sheer one-thousand-metre-high Teku gorge – which the first expedition, organized by the Sultan of Pahang, tried and failed to do in 1863. The summit was finally reached in 1905 by a combined British-Malay team led by the explorer Leonard Wray, who followed the Mengkuang route.

The Gunung Tahan trail is the only one in the park on which you must be accompanied by a **guide** (which costs around $500 total for the nine days), although in truth the trail is easy to follow with a compass and map. Head first for the Parks and Wildlife Department office, where you can discover if a trek has already been planned during the period you want to go – it's easy to join up with a group, hence splitting the cost. Most trekkers go in groups of between four and ten; groups of twelve or more have to take two guides, according to park regulations.

THE ROUTE

The first day involves an easy six-hour walk to **Melantai**, the campsite on the east bank of sungei Tahan, across the river from Lata Berkoh. On the second day more ground is covered, the route taking eight hours and crossing 27 hills, including a long trudge up Bukit Malang, which means "unlucky hill". This section culminates in the traverse of Gunung Rajah (576m), before descending to **sungei Puteh**, a tiny tributary of the Tahan, where you strike camp. The third day's trek to the campsite at **Kuala Teku** is spent fording the Tahan half a dozen times – if the river's high, extra time and energy is spent following paths along the edge of the river, crossing at shallower spots.

On the fourth day you climb from 168m to 1100m in seven hours of steady, unrelenting trekking which takes you up onto a ridge. Prominent among the large trees along the ridge is *seraya*, with a reddish-brown trunk, as well as oaks and conifers, but these thin out when the ridge turns to the west. Here, the character of the landscape changes dramatically, becoming montane oak forest where elephant tracks are common. Park experts believe that elephants live around this point – where the forest is more open and less dense than lower down but is still rich enough in foliage to provide food. The night is spent at the Gunung Tahan base camp, **Wray's Camp**, named after the explorer Leonard Wray.

The fifth day's trek comprises six hours of hard climbing along steep gullies, before reaching the highest campsite, the **Padang**, on the Tangga Lima Belas ridge, sited on a plateau which, in contrast to the harsher more open conditions on the other ridge, is sheltered by tall trees. The summit is now only two and a half hours away through open, hilly ground sporting exposed rocks, knee-high plants and peaty streams, which support thick shrubs and small trees. The trail follows a ridge into moss forest and soon reaches the **summit**, where if the weather's on your side, there's a stupendous view, although thick mists often envelop the plateau and reduce visibility. It's a pristine environment: pitcher plants, orchids and other rare plants grow in the crevices and gullies which punctuate the summit.

On the return trip, the sixth night is spent back at the Padang, the seventh at Wray's Camp, the eighth at Sungei Puteh, and by the end of day nine you're back at Kuala Tahan.

To Four-Steps Waterfall

The seven-day (50km) trail to **Four-Steps Waterfall**, east of Gunung Tahan, follows the same route as that described above for the first three days. At Kuala Teku, hikers take the right fork instead, which after eight hours of following the course of the Ulu Tahan reaches the foot of the falls. Although the falls are only thirty metres high, the gorgeous setting is what makes the trek worthwhile: flat stones on the path side are a good point to rest, listen to the sound of the water and look out for birds and monkeys.

You can camp below the falls at **Pasir Panjang** (Panjang pass), which can be reached in around three hours by a clear path to their right.

The Rentis Tenor trail

The other major long-distance trail is the four-day, thirty-kilometre, circular **Rentis Tenor**, which leads south to sungei Yong, then northwest to the campsite at Kemah Rentis and southeast back to Kuala Tahan. The initial route is the same as that to Gua Telinga (see above), bearing north at the Yong hide (two hours from the *Resort*), before following the course of sungei Yong and reaching the campsite at **Kemah Yong**, just under 10km from the *Resort*. Two hundred metres south of the campsite a side trail leads off to the left to **Bukit Guling Gendang** (570m), a steep, two-hour climb best undertaken in the morning, after a good night's rest – from the top, there's a lovely view north to Gunung Tahan, west to Gua Siput and beyond to the highest limestone outcrop in Peninsular Malaysia, Bukit Peningat (713m), on the western edge of the park. Towards the summit the terrain changes from lowland tropical to montane forest, where tall conifer trees allow light to penetrate to the forest floor and squirrels are the dominant animals, with the black giant and cream giant the main species. Both are as big as a domestic cat, their call varying from a grunt to a machine-gun burst of small squeaks.

On day three the main trail continues on into the upper catchment of sungei Yong, then over a low saddle into the catchment of sungei Rentis. From here the path narrows through thick forest alongside the Rentis river, crossing it several times, until it joins **sungei Tenor** three hours later, where there's a remote and beautiful clearing, **Kemah Rentis**, beside the river, where you camp. It's a fifteen-kilometre hike back to the *Resort* from here, and some trekkers go easy and spend a fourth night at **Kemah Lameh** (4km from Kemah Rentis) or the campsite at **Lubok Lesong** (8km from Rentis) on sungei Tahan.

As for the trail itself from sungei Tenor, follow the river downstream through undulating terrain to the rapids at **Lata Keitiah** (which takes around 1hr), beyond which another tributary stream, sungei Lameh, enters the Tenor. You are now in lowland open forest where walking is fairly easy and after four hours the trail leads to **bumbun Cegar Anjing** (another possible overnight stop; see the feature on "The Hides"), from where it's 3km back to the *Resort*.

Trenggan, Keniam and Perkai lodges

The **upriver lodges** are excellent sites from which to explore several far less visited parts of the park. The boat journey there, along the rapid-studded **sungei Tembeling**, is exciting, while the lodges themselves are set in tranquil surroundings, from which various hikes take in visits to caves and to spots ideal for bird-watching and fishing.

The closer lodge, at **KUALA TRENGGAN**, is 12km upstream from *Taman Negara Resort* and you can go either by boat, which takes less than an hour, or by one of two trails, which take between six and eight hours. The shorter and more direct **trail** runs alongside sungei Tembeling (9km) on a well-trodden, lowland forest path; an inland route (12km) runs north past the campsite at Lubok Lesong, bearing right into dense forest where elephant tracks are often seen, and then crosses the narrow sungei Trenggan 500m to the north, to reach the lodge. The **river trip** costs around $40 per boat; on the way, look out for water buffalo on the east bank of the river. **Trenggan Lodge** itself – a collection of wooden chalets – is partially hidden by forest on a bend in the river; in the largest chalet, an elevated building with a verandah, there's a small café where you can get refreshments and food.

A further 20km north along sungei Tembeling is **KUALA KENIAM** (2hr from the *Resort*; $60 per boat), where **Keniam Lodge** comprises several more chalets and another small café. If you plan to stay a couple of nights at Keniam, ending with the trek back to Trenggan (see below), then on your first day hike upstream along sungei Perkai (which cuts away from sungei Tembeling, 200m north of the lodge) for 3km to *Perkai Lodge*, a popular spot for fishing and bird-spotting. The two-hour **Perkai trail** runs roughly parallel to the river; in places it's possible to leave the main path and find a way down to the water. This far from Kuala Tahan the region is rich in wildlife, including banded and dusky leaf monkeys, long-tailed macaques and white-handed gibbons, all of which are relatively easy to spot, especially through binoculars. As for big mammals, elephants certainly roam in these parts and although the park staff will tell you tigers are present, too, there hasn't been a sighting for several years. Smaller animals like tapirs, civets and deer are best seen at night or early in the morning.

The trail ends at a small clearing on the river's edge, where stands **Perkai Lodge**. There are eight bunk beds here in all and the lodge doesn't have any resident staff unlike at Trenggan and Keniam, so you must bring food, drink and bedding if you intend to stay. There is at least a barbecue area and some crockery out the back. Very few people use the lodge so there isn't any need to book, unless *Keniam Lodge* is uncommonly busy whereupon some people may decamp to *Perkai Lodge*.

The Keniam–Trenggan trail

After Gunung Tahan, the thirteen-kilometre **Keniam–Trenggan trail** is the great highlight of the park, combining the possibility of seeing elephants – or at least their droppings – with visits to three caves, one of which is large enough for a small army to camp in. It's a full day's hike, although in dry conditions it can be covered in around six hours. Some people take two days instead, pitching their tent either in one of the caves or on a stretch of clear ground near a stream – there aren't any designated campsites in this remote corner of the park. The trail is a tough one, with innumerable streams to wade through, hills to circumvent, and trees blocking the path.

The trail cuts southwest from *Keniam Lodge* along a narrow, winding path through dense forest dominated by huge *meranti* trees with red-brown fissured bark. It's two hours before you enter limestone cave country, first reaching **Gua Luas** which, although impressive externally, has no large internal cavity. One hundred metres south is **Gua Daun Menari** (Cave of the Dancing Leaves), which does have a large chamber through which a gentle wind blows leaves and other jungle debris. Climb up the side of the cave and you'll see small dark holes leading into the cave chamber where, in the pitch-darkness, live thousands of roundleaf bats.

To regain the main trail, go back 50m towards Gua Luas and look for an indistinct path on the left; follow this for another 30m, at which point you should see the main trail ahead. Bear left here – the third cave, **Gua Kepayang**, is around ten minutes' walk further on. This has a very large chamber at the eastern side of the outcrop which is easy to enter and an excellent place to put up a tent. The fourth cave, **Kepayang Kecil**, is the last limestone outcrop on the trail. A line of fig plants drop a curtain of roots down the rock and behind lies a small chamber, with a slightly larger one to the right, containing half-a-metre long stalactites and stalagmites.

After passing Kecil you are about halfway along the trail but there are plenty more streams to cross – and armies of ants, flies and leeches on the move every few metres. The trail is illuminated in places by patches of sunlight highlighting tropical mushrooms on the trees and plants, though you're soon back in the gloom again. Parts of the path are wide and easy to follow, while other sections are far narrower, passing through tunnels of bamboo: be careful to avoid brushing against bushy green plants with razor sharp stems. The final two hours comprise more boggy crossings as the trail descends slightly to the Trenggan valley, arriving at *Trenggan Lodge*.

LEAVING THE PARK

Most people **leave the park** the way they came, by boat down sungei Tembeling – book your seat on the sampan at the *Resort* office, unless you're staying at *Nusa Camp*, which has its own Tembeling jetty-bound boat. There are, however, more adventurous – but appreciably more difficult – ways to leave the park. One route heads upstream on sungei Tembeling and then branches off east into the jungle through Terengganu state; the other leaves the Gunung Tahan trail at the Padang and heads west out of the park to Merapoh in Kelantan, a village which is accessible by jungle railway and Route 8.

THE TERENGGANU ROUTE

To reach **Terengganu state** you'll need to take a guide to the beginning of the trail (around $100) or at least make sure that the boatman knows where to drop you. You will need camping gear and food for two days. The sampan costs around $100 to take you the four hours upstream on sungei Tembeling to the start of the trail at Kampung Besar, on the east bank of the river. From here there is a trail through the jungle, where after around four hours' walking you make camp, and the next day continue west for another six hours until you reach a laterite road. Going east on this takes you to a small *kampung*, where you can camp overnight, and then get a bus out to the south–north Highway 14 (Kuantan to Kuala Terengganu).

THE KELANTAN ROUTE

The route to **Kelantan** is reached from the Gunung Tahan trail – you will need a guide to get you onto the trail, which runs west northwest before joining a four-wheel drive track to **Merapoh**, two day's walk from the Tahan trail's Padang camp (see "The Gunung Tahan trail" above) and lying on the bus and train route between Kuala Lipis and Gua Musang. More traffic, however, tends to go the other way and it's possible to take a land cruiser from Merapoh to the end of the track, where you camp, reaching the Padang camp in a day's walk.

KL TO THE NORTHEAST COAST

Two routes cut across the interior, from KL to the northeast coast, with travellers following either the jungle railway or Route 8. The main stopping points are the sleepy town of **Kuala Lipis**, 170km northeast of KL, erstwhile capital of Pahang in the tin-mining days of the last century; the nearby state park at **Kenong Rimba**, which attracts a fraction of the tourists Taman Negara does but has much to offer; and, further north, the caves of **Gua Musang** and the **Jelawang** park. But the chief reason for making the trip is the chance to spend time amid the green forests and sandstone hills which pepper the landscape, an environment far from the economic expansionism of the west coast and the beach-dominated muggy torpor of the east. In this lush and rugged region, Senoi *orang asli* groups still live semi-nomadic lives along inaccessible river basins.

Many **Senoi** live in the wide catchment area served by the jungle railway. The lifestyles of the two main Senoi groups, the Temiar and the Semai, revolve around a combination of shifting cultivation – where there is still enough accessible land left for this to be feasible – the trading of forest products and, where possible, fishing and animal trapping. The Temiar, in particular, are mountain dwellers, although some are based near rivers, like the Temiar of southern Kalantan who can sometimes be seen rafting timber down sungei Kelantan to **Kuala Kerai**, before selling the wood on to the Chinese middlemen. Although the Temiar are increasingly exploiting the forest for timber, their logging practices are marginal compared to those of the State Forestry Department. The **Semai**, in contrast, prefer to live in lowland jungle or open flat country, and there are several Semai communities close to Merapoh in southern Kelantan.

Rail and road routes

The five-hundred-kilometre **jungle railway** from Gemas, southeast of KL, to Tumpat on the northeast coast, has been in full operation since 1931 (the first section from Gemas to Kuala Lipis was opened in 1920), and much of its rolling stock has not been upgraded since. The line took eight years to build, the workers mostly indentured Tamils, and initially it was used exclusively for freight – first for tin and rubber, and later for oil palm, before a passenger service opened in 1938. If you want to cross the interior quickly, you should avoid the train – it takes fourteen hours to get from Gemas to Kota Bharu, five hours longer than it takes by bus. But as a way of encountering rural life it can't be beaten: for the Malays, Tamils and *orang asli* who live in these remote areas, the railway is the only alternative to walking and your fellow passengers range from cheroot-smoking old men in sarongs to fast-talking women hauling kids, poultry and rice to and from the nearest market. The ancient carriages are always packed to bursting point as the trains rumble through the isolated *kampungs* of Pahang and Kelantan, crossing wide rivers on iron bridges with craggy mountains towering on either side.

From KL, there are two **road routes** into the interior. The first leaves Route 1 at the Kuala Kubu Bharu turning (Route 55) and heads northeast past Fraser's Hill, joining Route 8 at Raub. Otherwise, take Route 2 past the Genting Highlands and turn north at Bentong, where Route 8 begins. From Taman Negara, Route 64 connects Jerantut with Route 8 north of Raub. Beond Kuala Lipis, **Route 8** heads due north, running parallel with the railway for 100km until it bears east at Gua Musang, meeting the railway again 80km further on at Kuala Kerai. The final section of Route 8,

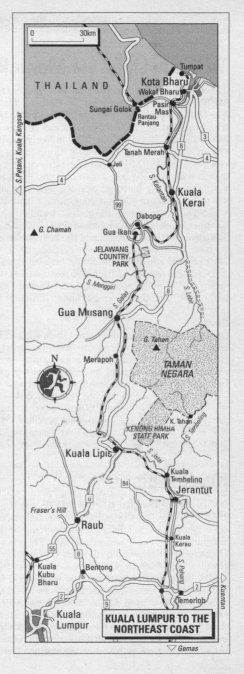

KUALA LUMPUR TO THE NORTHEAST COAST

onwards to Kota Bharu, intersects with the east–west Route 4, the eastern turning lead-ing to the Kuala Terengganu road, Route 3.

To Kuala Lipis: via Mentakab and Raub

The most common approach to the jungle railway from KL is to take a bus to **MENTAKAB**, a small town on the Kuantan Highway (Route 2), under 100km east of KL. These run twice an hour from KL's Pudu Raya terminus on the two-and-a-half-hour trip; note that the 11.35am **train** from Gemas (100km south of Mentakab) reaches Mentakab at 1.50pm. Although it's unlikely you'll want to stay if you're heading north, you might need to on the return trip, heading south, as one of the two daily trains reaches Mentakab at 10.10pm (the other arrives at around 2.20pm). To reach the train station walk from the bus station out onto the main road, jalan Tun Razak, and bear left for 100m to a big junction; turn left again on jalan Ponniah, walk another 200m and watch for a narrow road on your right, marked to the train station – a fifteen-minute walk. There are numerous budget **hotels** behind the bus station, including *Hotel Continental*, 90 jalan Haji Kassin (☎09/272622; ②); *London Café and Hotel*, 71 jalan Temerloh (☎09/271119; ①); and the best option, the friendly if very basic *Hotel Hoover*, 25 jalan Mok Hee Kiang (☎09/271622; ①). Best place to **eat** is the North Indian *Malabar Restoran* (8am–midnight), on jalan Ponniah.

Leaving Mentakab by train, the route passes through Jerantut and Kuala Tembeling (see p.197 for both), access points for Taman Negara. Note that Temerloh (p.225), just to the east, is another overnight option if Mentakab doesn't appeal.

Raub

By road to Kuala Lipis, the route leaves KL and heads northeast on Route 55 to Kuala Kubu Bharu, a two-hour trip and departure point for buses to Fraser's Hill (see p.121). Beyond Kuala Kubu Bharu, the scenery gets ever more spectacular, the road following ridges along the sides of large hills, with small plantations and forests stretching below. *Kampungs* become fewer and so do cars.

The only stop worth making by car or bus is at **RAUB**, on Route 8, a former gold-mining town which in the 1950s acquired an infamous reputation as one of the main areas sympathetic to the Communist guerillas. Overlooking the *padang* is the two-storey *Rest House* and the 1910-vintage Courthouse and District Office. The bus station is adja-cent to the town's main street, where there are several elegant Chinese shophouses.

Kuala Lipis

It's hard to believe that **KUALA LIPIS** was the state capital of Pahang from 1898 to 1955, for today it's a sleepy, inconsequential place of only five thousand people, situated on a bend of sungei Jelai (a tributary of the Pahang), dwarfed by steep hills and surrounded by forest and plantations. There's none of the tin-mining fervour which characterized the town's peak years (1910–30) – it's the sort of place where shops still close for a midday break and the bus station disappears under a hundred stalls each Friday night for the *pasar malam*, when rural Malays and Semai tribespeople arrive with their produce on the train from as far afield as Kuala Kerai.

Kuala Lipis started life as a small riverside settlement in the early nineteenth century, the population growing quickly from a few dozen to around two thousand by the 1890s. By then it was a **trading centre** for *gaharu* – a fragrant aloe wood used to make joss sticks – as well as other jungle products, collected by the Semai and traded with Chinese *towkays* based in the region. Until the first road was built from Kuala

Lumpur in the 1890s – a 170-kilometre journey by bullock cart – the river was the only means of transport; the trip from Singapore by ship and then sampan took over two weeks. Nevertheless, because of its early importance as a transit point on sungei Pahang for locally mined tin, and because of its central geographical position, the colonial government set up its state administrative quarters here. Yet the tin deposits soon evaporated and the fabled gold supposed to stud the interior never materialized. The rise of Kuantan marginalized Kuala Lipis, which slipped into genteel obscurity – today there's a disproportunately large amount of fine period buildings, scattered around a town whose main street is only 400m long. Nearby Kenong Rimba State Park (see p.215) is the main reason most travellers stop in Lipis, promising rainforest hikes without the crowds which frequent nearby Taman Negara.

The town

Heading left from the train station takes you down the narrow jalan Besar past a jumble of Chinese shophouses, which incorporate a number of busy bars, general purpose shops and the town's two hotels. Each Friday, the buses are moved from the **market** area, next to the bus station, and the whole district is transformed into a vibrant *pasar malam*, an event for which everybody in town turns out. Stalls here sell everything from pet birds to cleaning utensils, while the hawkers prepare massive trays of cooked noodles and seafood, pies and deep-fried prawn cakes, and superb cornmeal puddings.

Pahang's most famous Resident, Hugh Clifford, lived on Bukit Residen, a four-hundred-metre-high hill overlooking the town, and his house – a graceful one-storey

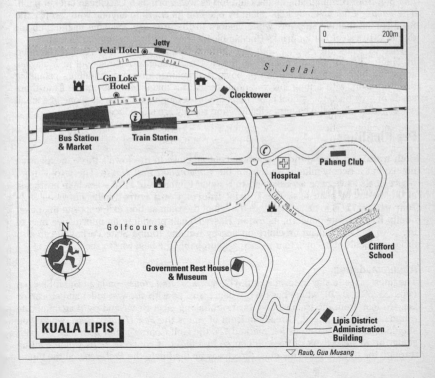

colonial building – now does duty as the *Government Rest House*, within which lies a **museum** (daily 8am–10pm) detailing the town's cultural history. The exhibits line the walls of the corridors and main drawing room, and originally belonged to colonial civil servants, both British and Malay, who had lived in this building and others like it around Kuala Lipis. It's mostly bric-a-brac – oblong brass boxes for betel leaf, coconut oil lamps and embroidered sashes – though there's more interest in the line of photographs, including one of the *Rest House* at the time of the great flood of 1926, when the level of the flood waters was recorded on the outside wall. In the drawing room to the right of the main entrance is a collection of *kris* daggers, with highly ornate handles, spears and *parangs*, ceramic vases, cups and plates; while upstairs, outside the grand bedroom with its marvellous views over the town and beyond to Kenong Rimba and Taman Negara parks, there are more photographs, this time of Pahang's royal family.

On the hill opposite stands the town's largest colonial structure, the **Lipis District Administration Building**, around ten minutes' walk from the train station. Dating from 1919, it's been beautifully maintained, and now serves as the local law courts. The other central hill, Bukit Lipis, also sports two lovely period buildings, most obviously the **Pahang Club** (1867), with its distinctive black Chinese-tiled sloping roof. Every bit the archetypal colonial club in the tropics, it was the first building constructed by the British in the town, later serving as a temporary residence for Hugh Clifford. The occasional large function is still held in the main room, with its dark mahogany floor, but most of the action these days takes place in the musty, tobacco-stained bar, through the hall to the right. Its once-tended gardens have now been almost reclaimed by the jungle, but the billiard room is still in use, housing a massive billiard table made in 1910 by *Padmore and Son* from Birmingham, its dark felt top as well worn as a Caribbean cricket pitch. The *Pahang Club* has only kept afloat by opening its doors to anyone who can pay the $100 annual membership fee, while visitors to the area are welcome in the club for dinner ($10 a steak) or for drinks (the bar closes when the last customer has left).

Directly below the *Pahang Club*, the **Clifford School** was built in 1913, part-funded by Hugh Clifford, and maintained as the first multiracial private school in Malaysia, admitting both British and Chinese boys. A grandiose group of buildings painted a deep crimson, with a long low verandah beneath a magificent roof made from thousands of grey tiles, the school is perhaps the most famous in Malaysia – one of a small select group where the country's leaders and royalty are still educated.

Practicalities

Both **train and bus stations** are very central, close to the town's three inexpensive hotels, but a twenty-minute walk from the *Government Rest House*. The **jetty** – from where boats leave once a week (Sat) to Kenong Rimba State Park – lies 50m northeast of the market on jalan Jelai. The **Tourist Information Centre** (daily 8am–noon & 2–7pm; ☎09/313277) is tucked away to the left of the train station exit, opposite the ticket booth. It's a private concern, its owner Hassan Tuah providing an informative map of the town and a colourful brochure on nearby Kenong Rimba State Park; you can also discover details of his own tour to the park, probably the best way to see it.

Accommodation

The finest place to stay in town is at the *Government Rest House*, on jalan Bukit Residen (☎09/312599; ②–③), which has twenty bedrooms, all with shower, toilet and air-con or fan. On foot, from the train station, turn right along jalan Besar and right again on the roundabout, 100m ahead. Directly in front of you is the *Pan Holiday Hotel*, where you should follow the road to its left marked "To the Golf Course"; after 50m take the path along the western flank of the golf course to a flight of concrete steps which lead up through the trees – this is the most direct way up the hill to the *Rest House* at the top.

Two inexpensive hotels in the town itself draw most of the budget travellers. The *Gin Loke Hotel*, 64 jalan Besar (☎09/311654; ①), is very friendly, with clean rooms, shared toilet and shower, a book exchange system, and a small café serving food to order all day. The owner also runs trips into Kenong Rimba park. The other budget hotel, *Jelai Hotel*, at 44 jalan Jelai (☎09/311574; ①), overlooks the river, one street north of jalan Besar. The twin-bed rooms are small, with shared toilet and shower.

Eating and drinking
Aside from a smattering of below-average Chinese **cafés** on jalan Besar, and the café at the *Gin Loke*, the only restaurant of note in Kuala Lipis is the the one at the *Rest House* (Mon–Sat 8–10am, noon–2pm & 7–11pm), which specializes in traditional Pahang dishes like river trout in durian sauce and chicken in coconut and lemon grass. There's no alcohol served here; for a beer, head for one of the noisy **bars** on jalan Besar.

Kenong Rimba State Park

KENONG RIMBA STATE PARK is fast becoming one of the best reasons to travel the jungle railway into the interior and, if coupled with a visit to Kuala Lipis, makes for a perfectly balanced three- to five-day stop-off en route from KL to Kota Bharu. Rimba's main attraction is that it offers a compact version of the Taman Negara experience – jungle trails, riverside camping, mammal-spotting and excellent bird-watching – at much reduced prices and without the brouhaha characterizing the larger park, which shares its southwestern border with Rimba. The park is one tenth of the size of Taman Negara, stretching over 128 square kilometres of the **Kenong Valley**, east of Banjaran Titiwangsa. It's dotted with limestone hills, which are riddled with caves of varying sizes, and crossed by trails which snake along the forest floor. The park is also a promising place to spot big mammals, many of which have been inadvertently driven away from Taman Negara by the increase in tourism and have ventured across into Rimba. That said, it's still unlikely you'll catch sight of a tiger or elephant, although there's certainly more of a chance here than in Taman Negara.

Getting there
The easiest way there is to travel **from Kuala Lipis** on Saturday, when a flat-rate sampan ($15) leaves the jalan Jelai jetty at 2pm (returning people to their *kampungs* from the *pasar malam*), arriving at the Tanjung Kiara jetty (see below) at around 4.30pm. On other days of the week, you can charter a sampan directly from Kuala Lipis, but this is expensive (around $150 per boat). It's cheaper to take the 6.30am local train to **BATU SEMBILAN**, (30min; $1) just three stops to the north of Kuala Lipis, where you walk left (east) along a narrow road 50m to the jetty on sungei Jelai. Here sampans take you on the thirty-minute trip downstream ($30 per person), turning left into sungei Kenong to reach the **Tanjung Kiara jetty**.

However you get here, it's then a forty-minute walk on a wide road from the jetty through the rather spread-out **KAMPUNG DUSUN**, past a small store on your right to a bridge where the park proper begins. After a further thirty minutes along a narrow path through lowland forest, you reach the **park headquarters** at **GUNUNG KESONG**, a clearing beside sungei Kesong where chalets, a café and park office are situated.

Hassan Tuah, who runs the information office at Kuala Lipis (see above), organizes three-day **tours** to the park ($150 inclusive), including obtaining the necessary permit. If you are travelling independently, you need to go to the park office on arrival and buy the **permit** (around $1).

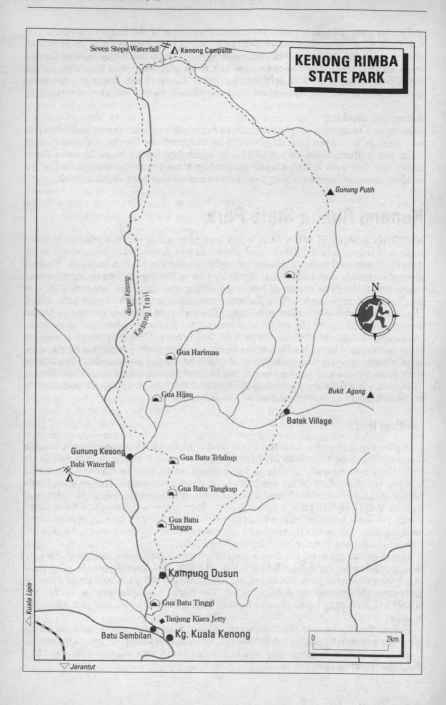

KENONG RIMBA
STATE PARK

Seven Steps Waterfall △ Kenong Campsite

▲ Gunung Putih

Sungei Kesong

Kesong Trail

Gua Harimau

Gua Hijau

Bukit Agong ▲

Batek Village

Gunung Kesong

Babi Waterfall
△

Gua Batu Telahup

Gua Batu Tangkup

Gua Batu
Tangga

△ *Kuala Lipis*

Kampung Dusun

Gua Batu Tinggi

Tanjung Kiara Jetty

Batu Sembilan **Kg. Kuala Kenong**

0   2km

▽ *Jerantut*

Staying at the park

At the park, you either stay in chalets or camp. The twelve self-contained wooden **chalets** (③–④) have two beds in each, and it's advisable to book in advance at the information office in Kuala Lipis. The **campsite** is close to the chalets, and it only costs a few dollars to put up your tent; there are toilets and showers on site but no cooking facilities. Some campers use Kesong as a base and then head further into the park to camp, often at the Kenong campsite, four hours' walk away in the north of the park (see below). **Eating** is very limited at Kesong with just one café serving basic, inexpensive meals of rice, meat, vegetables, soup and *roti canai*.

As Rimba is small, you can see most of the main sights within three days: one day to check out the caves, which are all within 2km of each other; another to get to the Kenong campsite; and the third to return to base via the Batek *orang asli* village. No special equipment is needed, besides a tent and blanket for sleeping. Be sure, however, to take lots of mosquito repellent and always carry at least one litre of water with you on the trails – at Kesong campsite it's safe to drink the water from the waterfall.

The caves

The first of the six **caves** in Rimba is outside the park proper, close to the Tanjung Kiara jetty. About ten minutes' walk from the jetty along the road watch out for a path on your left (west) which leads to **Gua Batu Tinggi**, a small cave which has a cavity just big enough to clamber into. Inside, there's a surprising variety of plant life – including orchids and fig trees – while there's a waterfall 100m further along the trail which is an excellent place for swimming.

Gua Batu Tangga (Cave of Rock Steps) can be reached direct from the camp at Gunung Kesong, though you can also get there from Tinggi by returning on the same trail and crossing the road, following the path to the left of a house set in a well-kept garden – there's a sign pointing to the cave, another twenty minutes' walk further on. Shaped like an inverted wok, the large limestone cave has a wide, deep chamber and in the northwest corner a row of rocks form ledges or steps, which give the cave its name. The cave is sometimes occupied by elephants – the trail through the cave narrows between rocks rubbed smooth over time, probably by the passage of the great creatures – but you're more likely to catch sight of mouse deer or porcupine scurrying away. Two smaller caves, **Gua Batu Tangkup** and **Gua Batu Telahup**, are just a few hundred metres beyond Tangga on the same trail.

The last two caves are close to park headquarters: **Gua Hijau** (Green Cave) is just five minutes' walk away, home to thousands of bats; while **Gua Harimau** is a little further along on the right, scarcely more than an overhang and reputedly the lair of tigers.

The trails

The main trail in the park, the Kesong trail, is to **Seven Steps Waterfall** (10km), which heads north from the headquarters. If you don't want simply to retrace your steps on the return trip, there's an alternative route which runs back to the southeast and passes close to the Batek village.

From park headquarters, the three-hour trail to the waterfall runs alongside sungei Kesong through lowland forest, through which little sunlight penetrates. Over the years, the Batek have cleared portions of forest around this trail for agricultural purposes, which could account for the jungle's impenetrability, as secondary forest tends to grow back more thickly than primary forest. The trail crosses over the river on a number of bridges and 1km before the waterfall you cross sungei Kesong for the final time to reach the Kenong **campsite**. From here, you're very close to the water-fall, the trail continuing through high forest, to a set of rapids, with jungle closing in all around. There's nowhere to rest except on the boulders, but sitting on these, close to the edge of the river, you can listen to the loud hiss of the water dropping over the nearby falls.

Returning on the southeastern loop of the trail takes longer, around five hours, so it's best tackled after staying the night at the waterfall campsite. This trail is harder going as it traverses small hills – Gunung Putih (884m) is the largest – and follows a less well-defined path. After three hours you pass close to a **Batek village**, where someone may invite you to their hut or display some wares to sell or trade. Although this isn't an official campsite, ask if you want to pitch a tent near the huts, especially if you decide to climb **Bukit Agong** (1800m), a tiring climb of around two hours each way from the village. Returning to headquarters from the village takes around another two hours on the main trail (there is no connecting path from Bukit Agong).

Gua Musang

Back on the road and train route, the jungle landscape changes near Merapoh, 80km north of Kuala Lipis, where it becomes dominated by large, round sandstone hills. From Merapoh, it's another hour to **GUA MUSANG**, the largest town in the interior of Kelantan. It's a largely unappealing place, though one which has expanded fast over the last decade as logging money has flowed in, quickened by the arrival of Route 8, which made accessible remote tracts of forest hitherto undisturbed by the timber saws. Most of the timber merchants and their employees are Chinese and there's a distinct frontier spirit here, typical of many towns in rural Malaysia. Gua Musang positively churns with Toyota land cruisers and motorbikes, cheap hotels and cafés full of people making business deals day and night. At weekends, dozens of young Chinese prome-nade up and down the two-street town, hunting down karaoke bars or flocking to the kung fu movies shown at the only cinema.

The caves

The main reason tourists stop is to visit the **caves** that riddle the massive limestone hunk hovering above town. Both caves – and the town – are named after a small crea-ture, the *musang*, which looks like a civet and used to live up in the caves; they're now almost extinct. Cross the railway track and walk through the tiny, cramped *kampung* which languishes in the shadow of the rock behind. Here you'll have to ask for a guide; it is possible to reach the caves on your own, but the trail – which is directly at the back of the huts – is difficult to negotiate after rain, when it's likely to be extremely slippery. Wear strong shoes and take a flashlight for inside the cave.

Once you've climbed almost vertically up 20m of rock face you'll see a narrow ledge; turn left and edge gingerly along until you see a long slit in the rock which leads into a cave – you'll need to be fairly thin to negotiate this. Once through, though, the cave is enormous, 60m long and 30m high in places, and well illuminated. The main cave leads through to other ones, which have rock formations jutting out from the walls and ceil-ings. The only way out is by the same route, which you'll need to take very carefully, especially the near vertical descent off the ledge and back down to the *kampung*.

Practicalities

Trains leave Kuala Lipis for Gua Musang at 6.30am and 3.30pm, arriving at 8.30am and 5.10pm respectively. The **train station** is situated directly below the limestone rock, in front of which is the town's main street, jalan Besar, where most of the **hotels** are located. Three Chinese cheapies – *Hotel Merling, Hotel Alishan* and *Hotel Mesra* (☎09/

901813; all ①) – lined along the right-hand side of the street, are owned by the same people; the slightly more upmarket *Hotel Gunung Emas* (☎09/902892; ②) is on the left. There's a small day-market where the street forks left and becomes jalan Pulai, 200m along which, past the Chinese temple, watch for a right-hand turn to *Kesadar Inn* (☎09/901229; ③–⑤). This stylish hotel actually comprises chalets set in a lovely lawn beside sungei Galas, with meals served on a patio overlooking the river. If you're planning on coming at the weekend it's a good idea to book ahead.

Gua Musang is not particularly renowned for its food, but the stalls near the station serve good *nasi campur* and the Chinese **cafés** on jalan Besar cook hearty meals.

Dabong and around

From Gua Musang the next stop – 50km north – is **DABONG**, a quintessentially Kelantanese Malay village, sited on sungei Galas and surrounded by flat-topped limestone peaks and dark green forest. Simple wooden *kampung* huts line the two narrow unpaved streets, and three café-cum-shops look out over the only concrete building, the school. It's not an uninteresting place to pass the time: timber-stilted houses peep out from between banana trees and a brightly painted, single platform train station looks like it hasn't changed in fifty years.

There is only one **place to stay** in Dabong, two rooms with bunk beds at the back of a shop on the main street (①). Ask at the train station or at one of the shops opposite the school about availability. The main reason for getting out of the train here is to visit **Gua Ikan**, a deep cave, 3km to the southwest, or – more excitingly – the **Jelawang** country park, which perches on a mountain futher south.

Gua Ikan

The caves at **Gua Ikan** – distinguished by a stream running through a wide cavity – are a little way south of Dabong. To get there on foot, cross the railway track and walk east for 3km along a wide, paved road; or ask at the train station about a van-taxi ($10). The limestone caves are clearly marked off to the right, set in a small, unmaintained park. In the main cave – forty metres long and twenty metres high – a small river runs along the bed, which you can follow provided you've brought a flashlight and water-tight boots (the rocks are too slippery to go barefoot). This leads out to the other side of the cave to a small rock-enclosed area; a lovely spot to rest awhile, listening to the birds and monkeys.

Jelawang Country Park

The **JELAWANG COUNTRY PARK** has much in common with Kenong Rimba. Its facilities are very basic – visitors should expect to rough it – but the trade-off is its easy access to beautiful hiking country and the distinct possibility of seeing large mammals and rare birds. It also boasts Peninsular Malaysia's highest waterfall, **Lata Jeri**.

To get there from Dabong, walk south through the village to the jetty (where boats arrive from Kuala Kerai; see below), take a sampan across sungei Galas and catch the van-taxi which will be waiting on the other bank; it's then a four-kilometre ride east to Kampung Jelawang ($3). Where the van drops you, walk to the left along a small road towards the vast limestone hill, **Gunung Stong** (1421m), directly ahead – you can actually see the Lata Jeri's cascading water from the road.

The hike up Gunung Stong to the park's waterfall campsite takes around ninety minutes and is fairly gruelling, involving some sheer, muddy sections, though rocks at the side of the trail allow you to rest and look back over the forest. The **campsite** is snugly sited beside the waterfall amid large trees, where two dozen **huts** (1–4 beds; ①–②) blend in with the surrounding forest and incorporate a basic kitchen and two lean-tos which pass for the park's eating area. The rates include three daily meals served by the camp staff; there are two chemical toilets close by, but no showers – instead, most visitors make good use of the waterfall's small rockpools. There's no way of booking in advance at the site, but even if you turn up and the huts are full, the staff here will erect a lean-to shelter for you (and charge you less than the usual rate).

The site is a reasonably pleasant spot at which to soak aching feet, after which you'll want to strike out on one of the local **trails**, which require a guide. The three-hour **Seven Waterfalls** hike (around $10 per person) takes you up the west side of the waterfall in a roundabout way to the top then heads down the east side. The longer trail is the **Elephant Trek** (around $40), which follows the main path up the mountain for two hours to reach the top of Gunung Stong, before winding along the ridge and crossing over onto neighbouring Gunung Ayan. Although it's possible to return to the waterfall campsite the same day on this trek, it's preferable to camp for the night at a clearing along the trail, near a small stream – you'll need some warm clothing and a sleeping bag. The Jelawang park staff say they've seen elephants here, and there's a high chance of encountering tapir, monkey and deer in the early morning or early evening.

Access from Kota Bharu

A **tour** to the country park is promoted fairly vigorously in Kota Bharu (p.230) as the "Jelawang Jungle Trail", and travel agencies or guest houses (like the *Town* or *Windmill*) there can arrange a trip – not bad value at around $100 for a four-day tour. If you're **travelling independently** from the northeast coast, you'll need to leave Kota Bharu by 9am, taking bus #5 ($4) from the local bus station for the one-and-a-half-hour journey to Kuala Kerai (see below). From there, the journey to Dabong is either by train or boat, though since there are only two trains a day, both in the afternoon, the boat is best, a two-hour journey costing $5 – see "Kuala Kerai" below for details. Heading back to Kota Bharu, you'll almost certainly need to stay overnight in Dabong unless you're prepared to take the evening train, a terribly slow (and frequently delayed) service taking three hours to Wakaf Bharu.

On to Tumpat

Moving on from Dabong, there's a choice of transport. A **boat** from the jetty (daily except Fri at 2pm; $5) runs as far as **Kuala Kerai**, which takes ninety minutes, as does the daily **train** service which heads north at 9.50am (south at 4.35pm). From Kuala Kerai, this continues to **Tumpat**, at the end of the line, though most people get off at Wakaf Bharu, the nearest station to Kota Bharu.

The train ride is splendid, chugging along valley floors where trees and plants sprout from the bank, almost enveloping the track, and then climbing steep gradients to cross long, metal bridges over a network of rivers. Along the route the train passes through seven tunnels and, when the minimal lighting malfunctions, the swaying carriages are plunged into darkness. The few stations along the way are hardly more than lean-tos; if there is anywhere left in the Malay peninsula that is truly remote it's here. Obscure little settlements, squeezed into the dense green cloak of jungle, have Senoi *orang asli* names like Renok, Kemubu and Pahi, from which the local people materialize, to board the train with their massive bundles of goods.

Kuala Kerai

The only town of any size between Gua Musang and Kota Bharu, **KUALA KERAI**, on the east bank of the two-hundred-metre wide sungei Kelantan, is a busy commercial centre serving inland Kelantan. Once, great barges laden with goods were floated from here down to the coast, though nowadays, most of the local traffic is confined to the road – Route 8 runs within 2km of the town centre – or to the jungle railway, which passes to the south of the town. But despite Kerai's regional importance, the pace of life here is slow, and there's very little going on through the baking hours of the early afternoon.

The town is formed simply around one east–west street, jalan Sultan Yahya Petra, and the north–south jalan AN Sang, where you'll find most of the hotels and services. About the only distraction is to take a walk up to the **Mini Zoo** and **Museum** (daily 9am–12.30pm & 2–5pm; $1), ten minutes out of town on a well-marked road. The zoo is eminently missable, a pathetic array of ill-kept and unkempt animals; further up the hill, in a large Malay house, the museum commands a fine view of the town. Besides the ubiquitous stuffed animals, there are photographs of town dignitaries, markets, street life and *orang asli* in traditional dress, while other exhibits include a church organ, whose chair sports intricately designed Kelantanese symbols, various musical instruments, and a large wall hanging displaying the Kelantan royal family tree.

Practicalities

The **train and bus stations** are at the northern end of jalan AN Sang, with the **jetty** just 50m to the west. For **accommodation**, there's *Hotel Kerai*, 190 jalan AN Sang (②), which, despite its elegantly fading shutters and red-tiled *kampung*-style roof, has little atmosphere and only basic facilities. Opposite, the *Joomui Hotel*, 189 jalan AN Sang (②), is a better bet, with its industrial fans, a TV and, close to the rooms, bucket-over-the-head showers. There are good Muslim **cafés** on the corner of the two streets, where tasty *nasi campur* and *roti canai* are served until about 9pm, while further along jalan AN Sang on the right, the busy Chinese hawker centre, *Jade Garden*, serves superb seafood dishes, including Kelantese specialities like river trout and perch. At the other end of town, on the approach from Route 8 along jalan Sultan Yahya Petra, just past the zoo and museum, there's a line of satay stalls.

Moving on

Trains north leave at 11.10am and 7pm for the two-hour trip to Wakaf Bharu (the stop for Kota Bharu); and at 5.40am, 1.40pm and 3.40pm for the trip south. **Buses** north to Kota Bahru leave every thirty minutes from 6.30am to 6pm (around $4), and there are also services to Gua Musang (around $3) every hour and one daily to KL at 10.30 am (around $15).

Boats to Dabong leave at 10.45am daily except Friday ($5), for the ninety-minute journey down sungei Kelantan into sungei Galas. There's no need to book, but get to the jetty at least fifteen minutes before departure – from jalan AN Sang, take the left turn at the junction with jalan Sultan Yahya Petra, and keep going until the road peters out. The jetty consists of a leaky bamboo raft connected to the riverbank by a single, bowed plank – not very practical if you're carrying any luggage.

To Tumpat

The final section of the jungle railway – the 75km from Kuala Kerai **to Tumpat** on the northeast coast – sees the geography change from mountainous, river-gashed jungle to rubber, pepper and palm oil plantations. This is also cattle country, where cows are a constant problem for the train drivers, as they tend to graze along the railway sidings, often straying onto the track. The trains usually travel slow enough to avoid hitting the cows, but occasionally there's a collision. Along the route, villages become more numerous and the train swells with Malay traders and *saree*-clad Indian women heading for Kota Bharu. The penultimate stop is Wakaf Bharu, for Kota Bharu, 7km away by bus, with the end of the line at Tumpat, another thirty minutes northwest of Wakaf Bharu – see "Kota Bharu and around" (Chapter 00) for all the details.

TASEK CHINI AND TASEK BERA

The main interest in the southern part of the interior, below the KL–Kuantan road (Route 2), lies in its two lake systems, **Tasek Chini** and **Tasek Bera**, beautiful areas where *orang asli* groups live and work. Chini is much more developed than Bera and has a small resort and a large village at its northern end, where there's inexpensive accommodation and excellent handicrafts for sale. The larger lake system at Bera is sparsely populated and has fewer facilities for visitors but if anything, it's even more stunning than Chini. Access to Tasek Bera is via **Temerloh**, the main town on Route 2, which is of slight interest, but is at least well endowed with reasonable hotels and places to eat.

The **Jakun** *orang asli* around Tasek Chini live in settled communities and occasionally work in seasonal jobs. At more remote Tasek Bera, the **Semelai** cultivate tapioca, rice, vegetables, sugar cane, sweet potatoes and peppers, and also trap fish and collect forest products for a living. There are crocodiles in the lake here, and the Semelai believe their ancestors concluded a pact with the mythic supreme crocodile of the lake, forging a relationship of mutual respect. The Semelai live on the edge of the jet-black lake in elevated houses built of wood, tree bark and *atap* leaves; their sturdy boats are made from hollowed out tree trunks, although these days they tend to buy them from the Malays, rather than make them themselves. Along the seemingly endless tunnels through the rushes on Tasek Bera a loud and eerie sound can be heard, which emanates from the *berbeling*, crude windmills made of bamboo which guide the Semelai through the swamps.

Tasek Chini

TASEK CHINI is a conglomerate of twelve connecting lakes of varying sizes spanning an area of around twenty square kilometres. The lakes have attracted a plethora of myths and legends through time, which is hardly suprising given their serene beauty – the waters here are a deep black, though from June to September, the surface is enlivened by shimmering pink-and-white lotus blossoms. The creation legend of the indigenous Jakun has it that they were planting crops one day, when an old woman with a walking stick appeared and said that the group should have sought her permission before clearing the land. But she allowed them to stay, and to legitimize their right she stabbed her stick into the centre of the clearing and told them never to pull it out. Years later, during a particularly ferocious rainstorm, a tribe member accidentally pulled out the stick, leaving a huge hole which immediately filled with water, creating the lake. Another legend tells of the existence of an ancient city which, when threatened with external attack, was flooded by its inhabitants using a system of aqueducts, with the intention of draining it later. Curious Malaysian scientists have embarked upon several research projects over the years, but nothing has ever been found. Some Jakun believe a serpent – or *naga* – guards the lakes, though sightings are as elusive as any real evidence of a lost city.

All the lakes in the system can be explored by boat, from either *Chini Resort*, in the south, or nearby Kampung Gumum. During the summer months *Chini Resort* attracts enough visitors to support a small-scale tourist industry, including a growing number of *orang asli* **carvers** who live and display their work here.

Getting there

From KL, catch an hourly (non-express) KL–Kuantan bus from either the Pekeliling or the Pudu Raya bus stations to the small town of **MARAN**, 180km (3hr; $10) east of KL on Route 2. You'll need to leave KL at around 7am or 8am to be in in good time for the noon bus from Maran to **KAMPUNG BELIMBING**, on sungei Pahang (other Maran–Kampung Belimbing buses depart at at 6am, 9am and 3pm), which takes another hour and costs around $2. From Belimbing jetty, close to the road, you can rent a boat (around $50) to take you to the lake, a trip of around forty minutes up sungei Pahang before branching south along the small sungei Chini for the final 4km to the lake. Along the way lianas cloak the giant trees leaning across the narrow river and, in the early morning or late afternoon, the boat may well pass a group of Jakun fishermen gingerly pulling up their nets to get at the catch.

From Kuantan, any non-express Kuantan–KL bus can drop you at the Chini turn-off where you wait for the Maran–Bembeling bus (aim to be at the junction around 20min after the bus leaves Maran), or in Maran itself. The other way to get to Chini from Kuantan is to take bus #121 ($10) to **KAMPUNG CHINI**, an uninteresting village set in a monotonous landscape of oil palms, 8km east of the lake. The bus leaves

Kuantan three times daily and takes two hours to reach the *kampung*, where you will have to take a motorbike-taxi (around $20) to Kampung Gumum or *Chini Resort*. From Chini, the bus back to Kuantan leaves at 8am, 11am, 2pm and 5pm.

Chini Resort

Most boats take you to the jetty below **Chini Resort** (☎011/344969), a quiet place nestling in the forest on the edge of the main lake, and the only place with a range of accommodation. It can get very busy at weekends when large groups often make block-bookings, so it's best to go in the week – during the wet season (Oct–Jan) you may have the place to yourself. The five small **dormitories** have ten beds in each (①), while the nine two-bed **chalets** (④) can also be equipped with extra mattresses for around $20 extra per person. There's a **café**, which serves meals throughout the day, a **restaurant** (noon–2pm & 7–11pm) and a **Ranger's Camp** where you can rent inexpensive tents, calor-gas stoves and sleeping bags.

There's a detailed **map** of the lake system on the wall in the café and the resort staff double as guides, available to lead day hikes around the periphery of the lakes (see below). For **boat trips**, go back to the jetty where there's a small office (daily 8am–7pm) which deals with bookings, although any local you meet will probably offer to take you on trips around the lakes. Most trips last from one to two hours and cost between $20 and $40.

Kampung Gumum

Five minutes by boat east of the *Chini Resort* is **KAMPUNG GUMUM**, a dispersed Jakun *orang asli* village of one hundred *kampung*-style huts, a small store and two places to stay. The village hasn't got a jetty, so boats just pitch up on the beach, directly in front of *Nadia's Shop*, one of the best places around to buy *orang asli* handicrafts – engraved wooden boxes, wonderful miniature wooden elephants, blowpipes of various sizes, and flutes and whistles. Nadia sometimes has spare rooms in her house in the *kampung,* just five minutes' walk behind the beach (①, including food).

Walking along the beach for a few metres to the south (right) and up a path into the forest leads to *Rajan Jones' Shop*, the only place in Gumum to get a meal. Jones, like Nadia, also has a guest house in the village, with room to sleep six people in three huts (①). Again, food is included in the price if you're staying; a well at the bottom of the garden provides the only means of washing.

Boat trips and trails

The shortest **boat trip** is to the *orang asli* **show village**, close to the *Chini Resort*, only twenty minutes away. The Jakun have built a traditional house here, made of bamboo and *atap* leaves and elevated on wooden stilts, but most of the people actually live in Gumum – there's the same range of carvings and blowpipes on sale as at *Nadia's Shop*. Better are the two-hour trips west and south to **Laut Melai**, the lake where the pink-flowering lotuses are most plentiful, and to **Laut Babi**, the biggest lake in the system. If the water is low, clumps of spiky *pentenas* grass can be seen protruding from the water, and gulls often swoop down to pluck fish from the water. In May, the few resident Chini turtles lay their eggs, and the boatmen may know where to find them.

The most used **trail** is the one leading along the side of Tasek Chini from the resort to Gumum, a two-kilometre trip. The path, however, can be hard to follow after heavy rain, and may involve wading through water. A longer, four-hour trail from the resort goes to a **campsite** at **Laut Terembau**, the path weaving in and out of mangrove, forest and oil palm plantations. The campsite is merely a clearing and doesn't have any facilities so bring food and water with you. The trail continues beyond the camp and after around 5km leads to a secondary road, east along which after 20km leads to the Segamat–Kuantan road (Route 12).

There is a further campsite on the west side of the lake system at **Palau Babi**, which can only be reached by boat, and another where sungei Chini divides off from sungei Pahang at the top of the lake complex, not far from Bembeling.

Tasek Bera

At around 27 kilometres long and five kilometres wide, **TASEK BERA** is the most extensive lake system in Malaysia. Like Chini, Bera's warren of channels lead from one lake to another through waterways where *nemkung rasau*, a sharp, high grass with a sticky yellow fruit, grows with abandon, and reeds sprout from the water. The main lake is incredibly beautiful, its peat-fringed watercourse and peat-floored bed rendering the waters jet black in places. At the edges, the centuries-old Semelai *orang asli* practice of shifting cultivation has helped create a forest of great diversity, in which large trees have been thinned and a wide variety of edible plants like pepper and root vegetables have been sown. Apart from the Semelai, the only visitors the lake has seen in recent years are staff from Pahang's Fisheries Department, who come to take samples of the water and fish to ensure the *orang asli* aren't using chemicals or poisons to boost their catch. There's not a great deal to do at the lake beyond taking boat rides around the channels and staying at the island house – the local Parks and Wildlife Department is planning a headquarters within the lake system, which will include visitor facilities, but this is still in its early stages.

Access: Temerloh

You may have no choice but to spend the night at **TEMERLOH** on your way to Tasek Bera. The best day to arrive is Tuesday, when a *pasar malam* is set up on the Kuantan road, but also there's a market on Saturday afternoon, close to the bus station.

Accommodation is easy to find and generally inexpensive, with the hotels located behind the bus station on jalan Tengku Bakar. There's little to choose between the *Hotel Hung* (☎09/2929097; ①) at no. 1, *Hotel Isis* (☎09/293136; ①) at no. 12, and *New Ban Hin Hotel* (☎09/292031; ①) at no. 40, as all have communal showers and toilets, and are equipped with fans. For **eating** after dark the only option is the Malay hawker centre next to the bus station, although there are some good Indian **cafés** open during the day on jalan Tengku Bakar.

To reach the lake, take any **bus** from the terminus south to Teriang (hourly service 7am–5pm, except 11am & noon; $3) and get off at Kereyong, a thirty-minute ride. From here, either take a taxi all the way (28km; $30) or catch the infrequent local bus ($2) to a point 20km east where the route to Bera leaves the road – the track through oil palm plantations sees quite a lot of traffic, including plantation staff vans and motorbikes belonging to the Semelai (which charge around $10 to take you to the lakeside).

Staying at the lake

A Semelai hut belonging to Sham Sudin marks the only point on Bera where **boats** can be rented; Sudin charges around $50 for a two- to three-hour trip around the lake and as he speaks some English, can answer basic questions on the local flora and fauna. He has also built a **pilau kuram** (island house), a simple hut on stilts, overlooking the lake (①), which is the only place to stay in this wild, undisturbed marshland. If you intend to stop the night here, bring some supplies, although Sudin's family will cook you rice and fish to take to the *kuram*. Once there, you can walk around the side of the lake, watch the birds from the verandah, fish and even swim – though only in designated places, since crocodiles may put in an appearance.

From Tasek Bera to Kuantan

The only way of reaching the southern sections of Tasek Bera is by car. Pass through Teriang and 30km further on turn east just before Bahau on Route 11, which leads to the southernmost point on the lake, a small *kampung* called **FORT ISKANDER**. This far south in the interior, the land is flat and most areas have been deforested, making way for agricultural plantations. There are a number of Semelai villages along the riverbanks here and it may be possible to find a house in which to spend the night, although taking a tent is more sensible. Travelling on east from Iskander, Route 11 joins Route 12 where, 50km north, is the left turn to Kampung Chini. On Route 12, buses from Segamat to Kuantan pass hourly, and, once the 12 meets the Kuantan Highway, they become very frequent.

travel details

Trains

Gemas to: Gua Musang (1 daily; 11hr); Jerantut (1 daily; 3hr); Kuala Lipis (2 daily; 8hr); Mentakab (1 daily; 4hr); Tumpat (1 daily; 13hr 20min); Wakaf Bharu (2 daily; 14hr 30min).

Kuala Lumpur to: Gemas (5 daily; 3hr).

Wakaf Bharu to: Dabong (2 daily; 3hr); Gemas (2 daily; 13hr); Gua Musang (2 daily; 6hr); Jerantut (2 daily; 10hr 30min); Kuala Kerai (3 daily; 2hr); Kuala Lipis (2 daily; 9hr); Kuala Tembeling (2 daily 10hr); Mentakab (2 daily; 12hr 30min).

Buses

Gua Musang to: Kuala Kerai (hourly; 3hr).

Jerantut to: Kuala Lipis (hourly; 1hr 30min); Tembeling jetty (3 daily; 40min).

Kuala Kerai to: Kota Bharu (every 30min; 2hr 30min); Kuala Lumpur (1 daily; 8hr).

Kuala Lipis to: Gua Musang (hourly; 3hr).

Kuala Lumpur to: Gua Musang (4 daily; 6hr); Kota Bharu (6 daily; 10hr); Kuala Kerai (4 daily; 8hr); Kuala Lipis (6 daily; 3hr); Mentakab (hourly; 1hr 15min); Raub (10 daily; 90min); Temerloh (every 30min; 1hr 30min).

Temerloh to: Jerantut (every 30min; 1hr).

Ferries

Dabong to: Kuala Kerai (1 daily; 2hr).

Kuala Lipis to: Kenong Rimba (at 2pm Sat; 3hr).

Tembeling jetty to: Taman Negara (daily departures at 9am & 2pm; 3hr).

Flights

Kuala Lumpur to: Sungei Tiang for Taman Negara (3 weekly; 45min).

CHAPTER FOUR

THE EAST COAST

The 400km from the northeastern corner of the peninsula to Kuantan, roughly halfway down the **east coast**, display a quite different cultural legacy to the more populous, industrialized western seaboard. For hundreds of years, the Malay rulers of the northern states of **Kelantan** and **Terengganu** were vassals of the Thai kingdom of Ayutthaya, suffering the indignity of repeated invasions as well as the unruly squabbles of their own princes. Nevertheless, the relationship forged with the Thais allowed the Malays a great deal of autonomy which, together with the rigorous adoption of Islam in the seventeenth century, helped the region foster a strong sense of identity and independence; a state of affairs perpetuated by the influence of Persatuan Islam Sa-Tanah Melayu (*PAS*), the Pan-Malayan Islamic Party that has dominated local politics in Kelantan since the 1950s. It's still the most "Malay" region in Malaysia, offering a chance to see **cultural traditions** that have long since died out elsewhere.

Remaining free from British control until 1909, the region's history is also one of isolation from the economic and social changes that rocked the western Malay peninsula during the nineteenth century. Cut off by the mountainous, jungle-clad interior from the technological advances taking place in the the the Federated Malay States, the states of Kelantan, Terengganu and Pahang retained their largely rural character: while immigrants poured into the tin and rubber towns of the west, the east remained underdeveloped and, as a result, today lacks the ethnic diversity of the rest of the country. The recent discovery of oil off the shores of Terengganu has dramatically increased the standard of living for some east coast residents, whose per capita income was previously well below the national average. But for the most part, the economy – one of the poorest in the federation – is still based on small-scale sea and river fishing and rice farming.

For the visitor at least, this manifests itself in a settled pace of life that provides a welcome contrast to the entrepreneurial west coast. The casuarina-fringed beaches and coral reefs on three of the most beautiful islands in the South China Sea, **Pulau Perhentian**, **Pulau Redang** and **Pulau Kapas**, are perhaps the greatest attraction, but the two main cities also have a certain traditional appeal: **Kota Bharu**, the last major town before the Thai border, whose inhabitants still practise ancient Malay crafts such as kite-making and top-spinning; and **Kuala Terengganu**, 160km to the south, an up-and-coming oil-rich town which retains an old Chinese quarter and a traditional boat-building industry. Both are infinitely preferable to the urban disaster that is **Kuantan**, though you'll find it hard to avoid passing through, since its equidistance from Kota Bharu, Kuala Lumpur and Johor Bahru makes it the transportation hub for the whole east coast. In particular, it's connected to the nation's capital by the congested and perilous Route 2, which slices the peninsula in two (and, incidentally, boasts the highest accident rate in the whole country).

Much of the east coast – from Kota Bharu to Kuantan – is virtually out of bounds between November and February because of the annual **monsoon**, and the heavy rains and sea swell are too great to allow boats to reach any of the islands. Since there are no rail links, travel throughout the region is limited to the relatively traffic-free Route 3, hugging the coast, and Route 14 which runs virtually parallel a little way inland, linking Kuala Terengganu with Kuantan. It's the coastal road that's the most interesting,

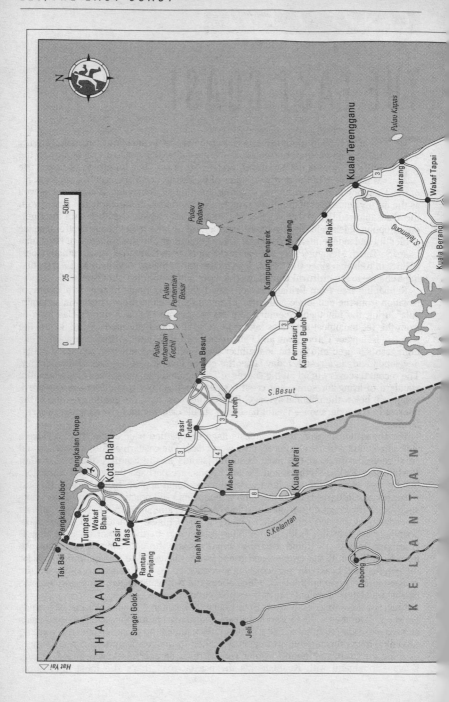

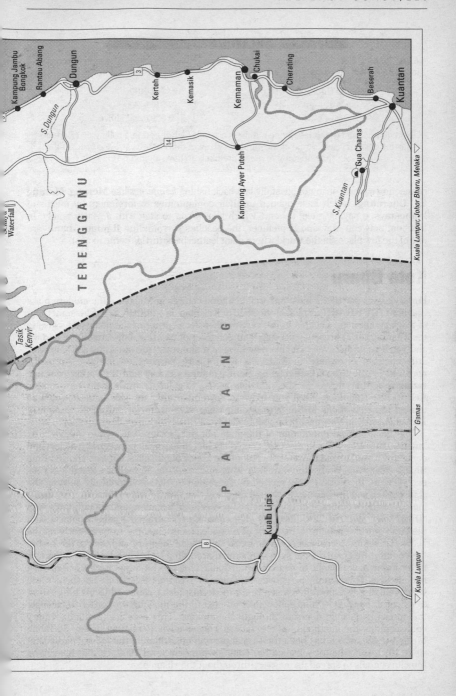

connecting a whole string of blissfully laid-back fishing *kampungs* like **Merang**, **Marang** and **Cherating**, which have opened up their communities to foreigners by means of **homestays**, a paying guest scheme which allows you to stay with a Malay family. In addition, between May and September, the beaches surrounding **Rantau Abang** are one of the few places in the world where giant leatherback turtles come to nest.

Kota Bharu

For saying it's one of the most important cultural centres in Malaysia, the modern mass that is **KOTA BHARU**, capital of the state of Kelantan, is – initially at least – something of a disappointment. Located in the very northeastern corner of the peninsula, close to the Thai border, it presents a scruffy and nondescript exterior, but scratch the surface and you'll soon discover that this new town is a showcase for old skills and customs, little-practised elsewhere in Malaysia. Kota Bharu parades its traditions proudly, nurtured by the town's **Gelanggang Seni** (Cultural Centre) and the various **cottage industries** that thrive in the outlying areas. Regular festivals help to promote Kelantanese traditions and if you arrive in September after the rice harvest, you'll be treated to celebrations in the surrounding villages; conversely, during the month of Ramadan, early in the year, strongly Muslim Kota Bharu virtually shuts up shop.

The geographical quarantine of the state not only fostered a unique culture – so much so that a traveller in the 1820s noted distinct differences between the dialect and dances of Kelantan and those of the rest of the Malay peninsula – but also allowed Kota Bharu greater political autonomy than other state capitals. In fact, it existed in a relative vacuum: the railway only arrived in the region in 1931, symbolically skirting the state capital, and the journey to Kuala Lumpur at that time involved thirteen ferry crossings. Kelantan's embrace of **Islam** helped preserve its isolation, and though links with other Malay states were limited, its long coastline encouraged trading contacts with the Arab world, enabling a free-flow of new ideas and customs from as early as the 1600s. Travel to Mecca was common by the nineteenth century and, unlike the rest of the country, Kelantan's legal system operated according to Islamic law – an important factor in the maintenance of national pride under Thai overlordship. Kota Bharu's most famous son, **To' Kenali**, a renowned *ulama,* or religious teacher, who spent some years studying in Cairo, then a centre for modernist ideas, returned to his home town to establish *pondoks* – "hut" schools set up next to the mosque – in order to facilitate the spread of Islamic doctrine throughout the state. This sees its twentieth-century equivalent in the methods of the radical conservative Persatuan Islam Sa-Tanah Melayu (*PAS*), which has been the largest party in opposition in the federal parliament since 1959, and which controlled the state government until 1990, relying heavily on Muslim schools to spread its message throughout the villages.

Kota Bharu's population is still predominantly Malay, it being one of only three towns in Malaysia (together with Kuala Terangganu and Dungun) to have a Malay majority. This is evident the minute you enter town – women are dressed much more circumspectly than elsewhere, and attending the mosque is a prominent feature of the day. Foreign women sometimes complain about feeling uncomfortable in Kota Bharu, but while it's hardly the place to sport beach wear, there's a relaxed air about the town which belies its political conservatism and mitigates its male-dominated outlook.

While you might well be drawn away from the centre by the opportunity to witness the various trades at first hand – kite and top construction, batik-printing and weaving – this shouldn't distract you from Kota Bharu's **historical buildings**, sited around Padang Merdeka, or its fine markets. Using the town as your base, you can also head out to the local **beaches** and into the surrounding agricultural countryside, hard on the border with Thailand and sporting its share of temples and distractions.

Arrival, information and getting around

Long-distance **buses** arrive at one of the two bus stations, inconveniently situated on the southern outskirts of town: the state bus company, *SKMK,* operates from the

ACCOMMODATION

Family Garden	8	Nora	11	Tokyo Baru	3
Ideal Travellers' House	1	Perdana	9	Town Guest House	5
Indah	2	Rainbow Inn	7	Windmill	6
Meriah	4	Sentosa	10		

RESTAURANTS

Golden City Restoran	A
Meena	B
Qing Lang	C

Langgar bus station on jalan Pasir Puteh, as does the *MARA* company, which runs buses to KL and Singapore; other companies use the larger bus station on jalan Hamzah to the west, which also has a left-luggage facility. If you arrive in the dead of night, you're at the mercy of the unofficial taxis that tout for custom at the stations, which ask for up to $15 for the two-kilometre drive to the centre, compared to the daytime charge of around $4 – unfortunately there's no alternative. The **local bus station** is on jalan Padong Garong, although, confusingly, *SKMK* also operates some services from here and has an information counter (8am–9pm except Fri 8am–12.45pm & 2–9pm). The **long-distance taxi** stand is behind the bus station on jalan Pendek.

The nearest **train station** to Kota Bharu is 7km to the west at Wakaf Bharu, the penultimate stop on the "Jungle Railway" through the interior from Gemas. From here into town, it's a twenty-minute ride on bus #19 or #27, both of which run to and from the local bus station. There's a local **airport**, too, 9km northeast of the centre – a share-taxi into town should cost around $3 per person.

For details of **leaving Kota Bharu**, see the relevant entries in "Listings", p.236–237; if you're heading **into Thailand**, see the feature below.

Information

The **Tourist Information Centre** (8.30am–6pm, Thurs 8.30am–1.15pm; ☎09/7441511) on jalan Sultan Ibrahim, close to the clocktower, is very helpful, offering informative handouts on the town, as well as their own **tours**: a half-day city tour includes visits to various craft workshops and costs $35.

City transport

Although most of the sights in Kota Bharu are within easy walking distance of each other, you may want to opt for a **trishaw**, particularly if you are staying at one of the more distant guest houses. Trishaws can be found along the roads around the bus station and nightmarket, and the normal fare for a ten-minute journey is $3 – make sure you agree the price beforehand. For longer journeys, a **taxi** is more convenient; they operate from a stand behind the local bus station on jalan Pendek, and for sightseeing the rate is roughly $10–15 per hour per taxi (not per person).

CROSSING THE BORDER INTO THAILAND

From Kota Bharu, you can cross the Thai border by sea or by land. In either case, you'll first need a **visa**, easily obtainable from the town's consulate (see "Listings", p.237), unless you can provide an air ticket to prove that you'll be leaving Thailand within fifteen days. Both **border posts** are open daily between 6am and 6pm – remember that Thai time is one hour behind Malaysian time.

The coastal access point is at **Pengkalan Kubor**, 20km northwest of Kota Bharu, which connects with the small town of Tak Bai on the Thai side. Take bus #27 or #43 from the local bus station for the half-hour journey ($1.20), followed by a 50 *sen* car ferry.

More convenient for onward travel in Thailand is the land crossing at **Rantau Panjang**, 30km southwest of Kota Bharu. Bus #29 departs from the local bus station in Kota Bharu every thirty minutes (6.45am–6.30pm) for the 45-minute trip ($2) or you can take a share-taxi from Kota Bharu for $6; from Rantau Panjang, it's a short walk across the border to Sungei Golok on the Thai side. Trains depart from there at 7.55am and 3pm for the eighteen-hour trip to Bangkok via Hat Yai and Surat Thani, or there are buses which leave at 8am and 12.30pm; buses to Hat Yai take four hours, leaving at 7am and 3pm. Train information can be checked with the State Railway of Thailand in Sungei Golok on ☎073/611162, although they're unlikely to accept a seat reservation over the telephone. There's no longer a Malaysian train service from Wakaf Bharu to Rantau Panjang.

Accommodation

Competition between the many **guest houses** in Kota Bharu ensures some of the lowest-priced (if sometimes a little basic) accommodation to be found in Malaysia, the rates often including breakfast. Some places allow you to do your own cooking, although given the cost of eating out this hardly seems worthwhile. All guest houses provide dorms as well as ordinary rooms, unless otherwise stated; common rooms, TV and laundry facilities are standard, while a few places offer batik workshops, bicycle rental and cultural tours. An alternative option is the **homestay programme** run by the Tourist Information Centre, which offers the chance to stay with a family, often expert in a particular craft, which costs $280 per person for two nights/three days, including all meals – expensive, but at the time of writing a new, cheaper scheme was being considered at around $20 per day. Given the other choices available, the budget hotels are poor value, and are often dirty, noisy and located in seedy areas close to the local bus station. However, you'll find quite a few mid-range bargains, and while top-class options are very limited, the choice is wider if you stay out of town at one of the beach resorts (see "Around Kota Bharu", p.237). All the places listed below are keyed on the map on p.231.

Family Garden, 4945-D lorong Islah Lama (no phone). Near the Thai consulate, this homely place offers free breakfast and transport to the out of town bus stations. ①.

Ideal Travellers' House, 3954-F jalan Kebun Sultan (☎09/742246). Down a quiet lane off the main road to the northeast of town, this popular place is often full. Good atmosphere, with a garden. ①.

Hotel Indah, 236-B jalan Tengku Besar (☎09/785081). Reasonably priced but old-fashioned rooms with excellent views over the river and Padang in this centrally located hotel. No dorm. ④.

Meriah, 1183J-M jalan Ismail (☎09/781340). Spacious, but tatty, rooms, though since they come with hot water, this is good value. ①–②.

Nora, 5229-H jalan Sultan Ibrahim (☎09/748455). By far the best of the bunch in the price range, with spotless carpeted rooms and dorms, although it's quite a distance from the town centre. ②.

Hotel Perdana, jalan Mahmood (☎09/7385000). A monstrosity of a building houses all the features you'd expect for the price, including a swimming pool and a good sports centre. ⑤.

Rainbow Inn, 4423-A jalan Pengkalan Chepa (no phone). Interesting paintings and laid-back atmosphere make up for basic rooms. There's a garden, batik workshop and bikes for rent. ①.

Sentosa, 3180-A jalan Sultan Ibrahim (☎09/743200). Close to the Cultural Centre, this friendly hotel has fresh, comfortable rooms, though no other facilities (and no dorm either). ④.

Tokyo Baru, 3945 jalan Tok Hakim (☎09/744611). Welcoming lobby, but impersonal rooms, though they do have great balconies overlooking the town centre. ③.

Town Guest House, 4959-B jalan Pengkalan Chepa (☎09/785192). Conscientious management and a warm welcome make this the nicest guest house in town. Clean and comfortable, with a delightful rooftop café and a batik workshop. Will make train reservations to Thailand for guests. ①.

Windmill, 286 jalan Pengkalan Chepa (☎09/773113). A notch above most in this category, with classy timber decor and a coffee shop. Bike rental available, as well as organised cultural trips ①

The town

The centre of Kota Bharu, hugging the eastern bank of sungei Kelantan, is based on a grid pattern, with a busy roundabout sporting a curious pink rocket-like clocktower marking the junction of the town's three major roads: jalan Hospital, jalan Sultan Ibrahim and jalan Temenggong. The area surrounding the clocktower is where you'll find most of the shops, banks and offices, while around jalan Padang Garong, a few blocks to the north, are Kota Bharu's **markets**. Further north still, close to the river, the quiet oasis of **Padang Merdeka** marks Kota Bharu's historical centre, a compact square of fascinating buildings. With so much to see on the streets themselves, it's easy to overlook the **State Museum** and the **Gelanggang Seni** (Cultural Centre), south of the clocktower, which give a rather more ordered visual documentation of Kota Bharu's cultural inheritance. Most of these sights are within easy walking distance of each other and, at a stretch, you could complete a tour in a day, perhaps taking in a show in the evening.

Around Padang Merdeka

While the clocktower is the nucleus of the town's commercial sector, the small **Padang Merdeka** to the north is its historical heart. Despite its grand title – "Independence Square" – it's not much more than a grassy patch of land, on which the British displayed the body of the defeated Tok Janggut ("Father Long Beard"), a peasant spiritual leader who spearheaded a revolt against the colonial system of land taxes and tenancy regulations in 1915, one of the few specifically anti-colonial incidents to occur on the east coast.

The Padang is bordered on its northern side by the white **Masjid Negeri**, known as *Serambi Mekah* – or "Verandah of Mecca" – because of its prominent role in the spread of Islam throughout Kelantan. Dominating the eastern end of the square, the immense **Sultan Ismail Petra Arch** is a recent timber construction commemorating the declaration of Kota Bharu as a cultural city; beyond is a pedestrianized area around which are grouped the royal palaces. Half-hidden behind high walls and entrance gates, the single-storey **Istana Balai Besar** was built in 1844 and contains the Throne Room and State Legislative Assembly, but is now used primarily for ceremonial functions and is closed to the public. To the right of the palace gates, the former Kelantan **State Treasury Bank** is easily missed, a stone bunker no more than two metres high, which remained in use until well into this century and which gives the square its unofficial name of "Padang Bank" – somehow it's hard to imagine the Sultan's employees queueing up outside what looks like a coal shed to receive their wages.

Adjacent to the former treasury building, the **Istana Jahar** (daily except Fri 10am–5.45pm; $2) houses the Royal Customs Museum. Although not the oldest structure in the square – it was originally constructed in 1887 – it is certainly the most traditional in style, with a timber portico and highly polished decorative panels adorning the exterior. The building takes its name from the *jahar* tree, the burnt-orange "flame of the forest", a specimen of which was planted outside in the courtyard by Sultan Mohammed IV. The Sultan ordered extensive renovations to the palace in 1911, adding an Italian marble floor, which lends a crisp coolness to the interior, and a wrought-iron spiral staircase that's still in use today. The ground floor of the palace is given over to a display of exquisite textiles – intricate henna-coloured *ikat* weaving and lustrous *songkets* – together with samples of the ornate gold jewellery belonging to the Royal Family. Upstairs you'll see lifesize reconstructions of various traditional royal ceremonies, from weddings to circumcisions – in the childbirth ritual, the mother is made to sit over a hot stove, supposedly to encourage the delivery of the afterbirth.

As you leave the museum, turn the corner to your left and after a few metres you'll spot the sky-blue **Istana Batu** (daily 10.30am–5.45pm; $2), an incongruous 1930s' villa, built as the Sultan's residence. One of the first concrete constructions in the state (its name means "stone palace"), it's now the Kelantan Royal Museum, with the rooms left in their original state. Pictures of the ruler and his family glare down from the walls, surveying the vast amounts of English crockery and glassware which crowd the handsome dining-room table – kitsch and clutter beyond belief. Still, it's worth a half-hour wander through, from reception rooms to scullery, if only for comparison with the relatively humble standards of previous rulers.

Directly opposite, another large pedestrianized square is the site of the **Kampung Kraftangan** (10am–5pm; closed Friday), or "Handicraft Village", still in its infancy, designed to give demonstrations to tourists of traditional various arts and crafts, with a chance to participate in weaving and batik work. The Handicraft Museum (entrance fee

$2) occupies one of several authentic timber houses in the compound, though it displays a disappointingly limited range of crafts.

The markets

To the south, away from Padang Merdeka, are two of the most vibrant markets you're likely to experience in Malaysia. The **Central Market** (daily 9am–5pm) contained within an unsightly octagonal warehouse, is the focal point of the town, abuzz with stalls selling products of all kinds, from meat and fresh vegetables on the ground floor, to cooking pots and batik sarongs on the second and third. Virtually all the stall-holders are female, the coloured headscarves of their traditional Muslim dress augmenting the vivid display. The scene is best viewed from the third floor, where the vegetables, neatly coordinated in piles around each vendor, take on an almost geometric aspect, the yellow perspex roof casting a soft, jaundiced light over the sprawling mass below. Look out, too, for the local fish speciality, *keropok batang*, greyish brown and sausage-like in its raw state, but distinctly more appetizing once fried and dipped in chilli sauce.

One block to the south, hundreds of brightly lit food stalls set up each evening in a car park, forming a **nightmarket** of epic proportions. As well as offering a gastronomic experience (see "Eating", below), this performs a social function, too, as it's the place to catch up on all the local gossip, making competition for tables fierce.

The State Museum and the Gelanggang Seni

Situated on the corner of jalan Hospital and jalan Sultan Ibrahim, the **State Museum** (daily except Fri 10.30am–5.45pm; $2) houses an odd collection of paintings depicting romanticized rural Malay scenes juxtaposed with lots of earthenware pots. Better is the collection of musical instruments on the first floor, among which is the *kertok*, a large coconut with its top sliced off and a piece of wood fastened across the opening to form a sounding board. Decorated with colourful pennants and hit with a cloth beater, it's one of the percussion instruments peculiar to Kelantan. To see these in action, visit the **Gelanggang Seni**, Kota Bharu's Cultural Centre, on jalan Mahmood, one block behind the museum, reached via either jalan Sultan Ibrahim or jalan Hospital. Free performances here, held every Monday, Wednesday and Saturday from February to October except during Ramadan (check with the Tourist Information Centre for details), feature many of the traditional pastimes of Kelantan – using *gasing* (spinning tops) and *rebana* (giant drums; see next page) – as well as Wednesday evening *wayung kulit* (shadow play) performances. The *Mak Yong* dance dramas, mounted on Saturday nights, are unique to Kelantan, derived from nineteenth-century court entertainments heavily influenced by Thai tradition and providing a fine balance between singing, dancing, romance and comedy – colourful enough for outsiders, though hardly fast-moving. Despite a growing tendency towards commercialism, with souvenir stalls and performers wearing logo T-shirts, a visit to the centre is still the easiest way to see many of the arts that are dying out elsewhere in Malaysia, and the standard is consistently high.

Eating

Easily the most exciting place to eat is Kota Bharu's **nightmarket** (daily 6.30pm–midnight), whose stalls sell an amazing variety of food – although vegetarians could find themselves limited to vegetable *murtabak*s. If you ask, you'll get a spoon and fork; otherwise use the jug of water and roll of tissue on each table to clean your hands before and after – and eat with your right hand only. Try the local speciality *ayam percik* (barbecued chicken with a creamy coconut sauce) or the delicious *nasi kerabu* (purple, green or blue rice with a dash of vegetables, seaweed and grated coconut), finish off with a filling *pisang murtabak* (banana pancake), and you won't have parted with much more than $5. The town's **restaurants** come as bit of a letdown after the

TRADITIONAL PASTIMES IN KELANTAN

Gasing Uri or **top-spinning** is one of the most vigorous of the sports played in the state and, with none of the childish connotations it has in the West, is taken very seriously, requiring a great deal of strength and dexterity. There are two types of competition: the straightforward spin, in which the winner is simply the one whose top spins the longest – the record time in Kelantan is 1 hour 47 minutes – and the striking match whereby one top has to knock out the other. The launching process is the same, however: a long length of rope is tightly wound around the top, the loose end of which is fastened to a tree trunk, and the top is flung from shoulder-height rather like a shot put – no mean feat when you consider that it weighs about 5kg. The spinner then has to rely on the nimble fingers of his partner, the "scooper", to whip up the top from its landing place and transfer it to the arena where its progress is judged. Competition is fierce, particularly in the knockout game, which takes place in an atmosphere almost like a boxing match; try to see it in a local village context if you can – the Tourist Information Centre can tell you when a competition is being held (September is the usual month).

Kite-flying (*wau ubi*) is a hugely popular activity, so much so that the emblem for the national airline, *MAS*, features the *wau bulan*, or "moon kite", the most common of all the designs. Originally regarded as a means of contacting the gods, the kites are highly decorated in order to find favour among the deities. The contest in which a kite-flyer had to cut the string of an opponent's kite was banned some time ago since it caused so many heated disputes – quite apart from the fact that the string, which contained ground glass to make it sharp, was also highly dangerous. Nowadays, competitions are a much more muted affair, with participants being judged purely on their handling skills and the height achieved.

The playing of *rebana* – **giant drums** – might not seem like a sport, but once you witness the energy required to produce the thunderous roll on these massive instruments, you'll begin to understand why it's classified as such. The brightly coloured drums have a diameter of over one metre, weigh 100kg each and are decorated with bamboo sticks that fan out from the rim like bicycle spokes. A festival every July incorporates a competition to determine the most skillful group of players. Each team comprises six players who play different-sized drums nonstop for around thirty minutes, maintaining fast and complex rhythms using a combination of hands and sticks – the winner is the group deemed to have displayed the most consistent and harmonious technique. Again, the spectacle is best seen outdoors, conducted in the traditional costume of tunic, *songket* and headdress.

nightmarket, many closing in the evenings in the face of such stiff competition. Note that the only places which serve alcohol are the Chinese *kedai kopis*.

Golden City Restoran, jalan Padang Garong. Lively and brightly lit *kedai kopi* serving standard Chinese food. Try the *wan tan mee* or *curry mee* – spicy noodle dishes for around $3.

Golden Jade Seafood Restoran, *Hotel Perdana*, jalan Mahmood. A pricey outlet lacking in atmosphere, although the Cantonese and Shanghainese dishes are recommended. Around $15 per dish.

Meena, jalan Gajah Mati. Excellent, inexpensive banana-leaf curries; much frequented by locals.

Pata Seafood Restoran, *Hotel Indah*, 236-B jalan Tengku Besar. Wide-ranging menu including crab and prawns from $2.50–$4 per dish.

Qing Lang, jalan Zainal Abidin. A totally meat-free menu with prices a touch above average (around $3 per dish); closed in the evenings.

Listings

Airlines *MAS*, Komplek Yakin, jalan Gajah Mati (☎09/747000).

Airport Sultan Ismail Petra Airport is 9km northeast of town, operating a domestic service only. Flight info on ☎09/737000.

Banks and exchange *Bank Bumiputra*, jalan Doktor; *Hong Kong and Shanghai*, jalan Mahmood; *Standard Chartered*, jalan Padang Garong.

Bookshops *Johan Bookshop* on jalan Padang Garong has a small selection of English-language books; *Central Bookstore* on jalan Temenggong by the clocktower has a larger choice.

Buses The *SKMK* information counter (8am–9pm except Fri 8am–12.45pm & 2–9pm; ☎09/740114) at the local bus station gives the rundown on local and long-distance services. *SKMK* services and *MARA* routes to KL and Singapore depart from the Langgar bus station on jalan Pasir Puteh; for other companies and destinations, head for the station on jalan Hamzah.

Car rental *Avis*, office in the *Hotel Perdana* lobby (☎09/7385000)

Hospital The *General Hospital* is on jalan Hospital (☎09/785533).

Immigration On-the-spot visa renewals at the Immigration Department at 2nd Floor, Wisma Persekutuan, jalan Sultan Zainab (8.30am–5.30pm except Fri; 8.30am–1.15pm; closed Fri; ☎09/782120). **Left luggage** At the bus station on jalan Hamzah (daily 8am–10pm).

Police Headquarters is on jalan Sultan Ibrahim (☎09/785522).

Post office The GPO is on jalan Sultan Ibrahim (Mon–Thurs & Sun 8am–4.30pm; ☎09/784033). Efficient poste restante/general delivery at counter 20.

Shopping Kota Bharu offers a vast range of home-produced items in several modern multistorey shopping complexes. The *Bazaar Bulu Kubu* on jalan Hulu, south of Padang Merdeka, houses a cinema, as well as souvenirs and handicrafts. *Syarikat Kraftangan* on jalan Sultan has higher prices compared to other markets, but better-quality kites, weaving and puppets. The shops along jalan Sultanah Zainab are a good bet for antiques and silverware.

Taxis The long-distance taxi stand is behind the local bus station on jalan Pendek (☎09/747104); fares (per person) are around $12 to Kuala Terengganu, $25 to Kuantan and $35 to KL.

Telephones The *Telekom* centre is on jalan Doktor (daily 8am–5pm).

Thai visas From the *Royal Thai Consulate*, 4426 jalan Pengkalan Chepa (☎91/782545; Mon–Thurs & Sun 9am–noon & 1.30–3.30pm). Visas are issued within 24 hours and cost $32.

Trains From the station at Wakaf Bharu (departure info on ☎09/796986), services run south on the "Jungle Railway" to Kuala Lipis and the interior. For the route into Thailand by train, see "Crossing the Border into Thailand" on p232.

Around Kota Bharu

While there's plenty in Kota Bharu itself to keep you occupied for at least a couple of days, the outlying areas soak up many visitors, who either aim for a spot of relaxation at the **beaches** to the north and south of town, or want to see at first hand the **cottage industries** responsible for the local crafts. The area north of town towards the border is unsurprisingly Thai in character, boasting a few **temples** dotted among the emerald green rice paddies.

It's also worth noting that some travel agencies and a number of guest houses in Kota Bharu arrange trips south into Kelantan's obscure interior, on the Jelawang Jungle trail – all the details are given on p.220–221.

The beaches and the border region

The **beaches** each side of town are popular with the locals, often becoming crowded at weekends, although the conservative attitudes within the state are not, on the whole, conducive to relaxed sunbathing. Compared to what's on offer further south, the sands are nothing special and, in many cases, their wistfully romantic names are better than the beaches themselves.

Pantai Cinta Berahi

The best-known and most-visited beach is **PANTAI CINTA BERAHI** (commonly shortened to PCB), 11km north of Kota Bharu, a thirty-minute ride on bus #10 from outside the central market. As every guidebook tells you, it's optimistically nicknamed

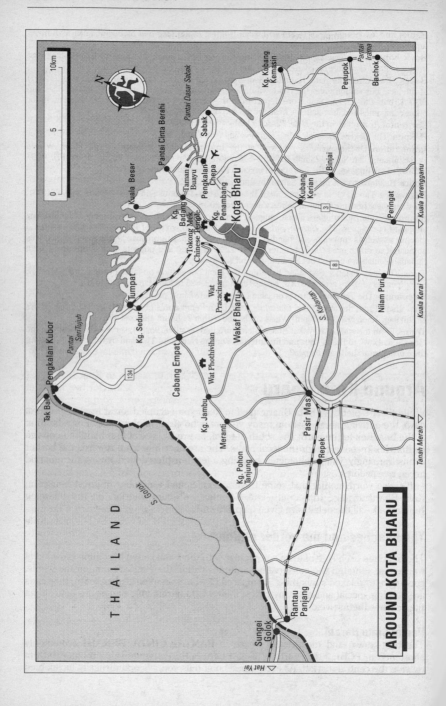

AROUND KOTA BHARU

the "Beach of Passionate Love", which is about its best feature; the sand is for the most part clean and golden, but the murky, choppy sea doesn't do it any favours. About 100m back from the beach, off the main road, the entrance fee to the signposted **Taman Buayu** (crocodile farm; $2) treats you to a recreational complex, including a "House of Mirrors", as well as a small zoo, snake farm and, of course, the crocodiles, who loll around in the sun snapping at passers-by.

On the way to PCB, you could stop off at the **Tokong Mek Chinese Temple**, about 6km outside Kota Bharu, singposted off to the left of the main road, where you'll find a peaceful little temple, with some unusually dramatic three-dimensional wall sculptures featuring tigers and dragons. Bus #10 passes right by the turn-off.

There are several **places to stay** at Pantai Cinta Berahi, although there's not much action here during the week. The best place is the *KB Resort* (☎09/734993; ②–④), a secluded spot about 300m down a path past the *Perdana Resort*, with a wide range of A-frames and chalets, together with a beachfront restaurant. It's a friendly place, and they have cheap dorm beds, too. A marginally more comfortable option is the *Longhouse Beach* (☎09/731090; ②), right next to the final bus stop, also with its own restaurant. For complete luxury, stay at the *PCB Resort* (☎09/732307; ④), a very pleasant, if slightly old-fashioned, complex, with well-appointed chalets, pool and a restaurant.

Pantai Seri Tujuh, Wakaf Bahru and the Tumpat region

Buses #19 or #43 depart regularly from the local bus station in Kota Bharu for the trip to **PANTAI SERI TUJUH**, a two-kilometre stretch of coastline that looks far more idyllic on the map than it actually is – its lagoons have now turned into muddy puddles.

The buses pass several Thai temples en route, in various states of disrepair. One of the most glamorous is **Wat Pracacinaram**, easily spotted just outside Wakaf Bharu, on the road to Cabang Empat; it's a brand new building, with a triple-layered roof elaborately decorated in gold, sapphire and red.

WAKAF BAHRU itself is the site of the nearest train station to Kota Bharu, but otherwise a nondescript little town. The end of the line is 12km further north at **TUMPAT**, a small town at the edge of a lush agricultural area. Tumbledown Thai temples punctuate field upon field of jewel-green rice paddies, visions of rural tranquility that are only interrupted by the occasional blue flash of a kingfisher. At the **Wat Phothivihan**, 15km west of Kota Bharu, a forty-metre-long Reclining Buddha is said to be the second largest in the world (although this is not a unique claim in these parts). The colossal, if rather insipid, plaster statue contains ashes of the deceased, laid to rest here according to custom – although there's a popular rumour that it has an alternative function as a secret cache for the temple's funds. Other pavilions within the complex, somewhat dwarfed by the central structure, are of little interest, except for a small shrine to the left which honours a rather wasted-looking hermit – perhaps a warning against the excesses of asceticism. You can reach Wat Phothivihan by bus from Kota Bharu – #19 or #27 from the local bus station brings you to Cabang Empat, from where it's a 3.5-kilometre walk, or a short taxi ride ($4 per car).

Pantai Dasar Sabak and Pantai Irama

Back on the coast, 13km northeast of Kota Bharu, **PANTAI DASAR SABAK** is of interest only because of its historical significance as the first landing place of the Japanese in 1941, before they began their invasion of the peninsula. It's a desolate place, a rough, windswept stretch of coast, punctuated by the boom and crash of the waves hitting a crumbling World War II bunker.

PANTAI IRAMA, a further 12km south, strikes a less solemn note as the "Beach of Melody", and it would indeed be relatively harmonious were it not for the tidemark of rubbish along the water's edge. That said, it *is* the nicest beach within easy reach of

Kota Bharu, a quiet, tree-fringed stretch of white sand, freshened by the sea breeze; but you should bear in mind that this is a conservative Muslim village, so stripping off is likely to attract attention. To get here, take the #2a or #2b bus to Bachok from Kota Bharu's local bus station (the buses leave every 30 minutes and the journey takes 45 minutes); the beach is about 500m north of the bus station at Bachok.

Local cottage industries

The **workshops** that line the road from Kota Bharu to Pantai Cinta Berahi offer an excellent opportunity to observe the skills of master craftsmen in the various industries for which Kelantan is renowned. **KAMPUNG PENAMBANG** is particularly good for weaving and batik, while **KAMPUNG KIJANG** specializes in kite-making; needless to say, there's always an opportunity to buy at the end of each demonstration; most workshops are open daily from 9am to 5pm. Both villages are barely beyond the town suburbs on the #10 or #28 bus routes, which leave from the local bus station in Kota Bharu.

The making of the *gasing* (spinning top) – resembling a discus except for a short steel spike inserted in one side – entails as much an art as does its use. The process of carefully selecting the wood which must be delicately planed and shaped, together with the precise balancing of the metal spike, can take anything up to three weeks. An intricate *wau* (kite), typically about 1.5 metres long by two metres across, takes around two weeks to complete, the decorations being unique to each craftsman, although tradition dictates leaf patterns and a pair of birds as the principal elements in the design. The most unusual aspect of the kite's structure is the long projection above its head, supporting a large bow that hums when the kite is flying, the musical quality of which can be judged in competition. Finally, batik-printing and weaving are the commonest crafts in Malaysia, and most of the workshops here will allow you to experiment with the techniques and create your own designs.

Pulau Perhentian

PULAU PERHENTIAN, just over 20km off the northeastern coast, remained a very well-kept secret until the late 1980s. Actually two islands rather than one – Perhentian Kecil (Small Island) and Perhentian Besar (Big Island) – both are textbook tropical paradises, neither more than four kilometres in length, whose idyllic nature is enhanced by the almost total lack of electricity, modern plumbing or telephones (bar a few mobiles). There's no doubt, however, that the Perhentians' cover has now been well and truly blown: they are fast becoming a popular getaway for KL and Singaporean weekenders, and now also see a regular stream of backpackers. Nevertheless, the low-budget chalet accommodation has still to be forced out by upmarket resorts – as has happened on some of Malaysia's other islands – the big money so far put off by the lack of any kind of infrastructure. Furthermore, government projects afoot on nearby Pulau Redang (see p.252), a larger island a few kilometres to the south, feature a major resort and golf course – an investment that is bound to keep the perils of mass-market tourism away from the Perhentians for at least a little while longer.

In the meantime, although the islanders say that the place has changed beyond belief in recent years, life on Pulau Perhentian remains delightful, with only the passing flying foxes, monkeys and lizards for company as you draw up the well water for your daily shower. Neither island boasts a raging nightlife – in fact, with no electricity or alcohol in most places, you'll probably be tucked up in bed by 10pm. However, the local people, though Muslims, seem to have no objection to you bringing your own

booze over from the mainland. The harsh east coast **monsoon** means that the islands, reached by slow and unsophisticated fishing boats from Kuala Besut, are accessible only between March and October. Conversely, during the middle of the dry season, from June to August, some places can suffer from a shortage of fresh water.

Getting there: Kuala Besut

The ragged little town of **KUALA BESUT**, 45km south of Kota Bharu on the coastal Route 3 (and just over the border in Terengganu state), is the departure point for Pulau Perhentian. It's easily reached by bus #3, which leaves Kota Bahru's local bus station every fifteen minutes throughout the day for the hour's ride to Pasir Puteh, then the #96 (every 30min) for the remaining half-hour journey to Kuala Besut itself.

There are no banks in Kuala Besut, or on the islands, so **change money** before you go. If you're desperate, the *Sawagan* travel agency will exchange cash only, but the rate is lousy. There's always a chance that unfavourable weather conditions may force you to spend the night in town and though there's not much choice, one of the better **places to stay** is *D'Rizan Resort* (no phone; ①), a beachside place with basic A-frames, first on the left over the bridge on the main road, about 1km from the centre. If you're feeling flush, try the *Primula Beach Resort* (☎09/976311; ⑤), a white concrete complex a couple of kilometres or so further south; you'll have to take a taxi.

Boat services

In season, **boats** depart from two points on the Kuala Besut quayside, just behind the bus station. Services operate every two hours or so between 9am and 5pm, the journey taking about an hour and a half – morning departures are preferable, since the weather tends to be more reliable then. Tickets cost $15 one-way though it's better to buy a return ticket ($30), since the boat is then obliged to bring you back on request, even if you're the only passenger. Five travel agents in town sell boat tickets and advise on accommodation on the islands: *Bonaza Express* (☎09/970290), *Perhentian Island Information Centre* (☎09/970189), *Perhentian Pleasure Holidays* (☎09/970313), *Sawagan* (☎09/970090) and *Sea Breeze* (☎09/979818) – all within walking distance of the quay. If you don't have a firm accommodation choice in mind (see below), they often try and pressurize you into staying where they have "connections", but the agencies can be useful for checking which chalets have space.

The islands

It's better to have some idea of which island you want to stay on, and where, before you leave Kuala Besut. Only Perhentian Besar's western beach and Long Beach on Perhentian Kecil have a variety of **chalet** operations from which to choose; elsewhere, you're pretty much confined to the bay in which you're dropped, though on Perhentian Besar you can simply walk along the beach, occasionally scrambling over the rocks. The interiors of both islands consist of largely inaccessible, tree-covered rocky hills, although a few well-trodden paths offer some unchallenging **walks** through the jungle.

The **boats** will drop you at the bay of your choice, although those without a jetty entail a bit of wading to reach the shore. To get around once there, most chalet operations have small speedboats and they don't usually bother charging. Facilities are fairly basic, though almost all the places to stay have their own **restaurant** – you don't have to be staying there to eat at them. Be warned, though, that the food, infinite variations on the *nasi* and *mee* themes, with fish thrown in as a highlight, can be a little monotonous. On balance, there's a more lively scene at the beach cafés on Besar; Kecil is much more isolated. It's worth noting that new chalets are springing up all the time, so the coverage below is only a guide to what's currently available.

Perhentian Kecil

On the southeastern corner of **PERHENTIAN KECIL** lies its sole village, **Kampung Pasir Hantu**, together with the island's only jetty, its police station, school and clinic – but the village's littered beach and scruffy houses mean you won't want to stay here.

The west-facing coves have the advantage of the sunsets, a major event in the Perhentian day. **Coral Bay**, about halfway along the island, has two chalet developments, *Coral Bay* itself (①), with secluded, beach-facing chalets, and *Rajawali* (②), a more luxurious establishment, high up on the rocky headland. About 1km south on the same side, a tiny bay houses the popular *Mira's Place* (☎011/976603; ①), a small cluster of chalets with a communal TV and radio – not the place if you really want to get away from it all. The south-facing *Petani* (③), just around the headland (accessible by a small overgrown track), has more upmarket chalets, but like its neighbour *Mira's*, it can have problems with fresh water in the height of the dry season.

East-facing **Long Beach** has been the target of most development on Kecil, not surprising since it boasts a wide stretch of uncluttered, glistening white beach, with deep, soft sand. However, it's more exposed to the elements, forcing the chalet owners to close up from September to April, since boats are unable to approach safely. Throughout the rest of the season, the water's pretty tame and shallow at low tide, giving easy access to the coral-like rocks at either end of the bay, perfect for snorkelling. The best accommodation is at *Mata Hari* (①), thirteen simple but well-designed chalets, complete with mosquito nets and hammocks, and a good restaurant with a wide-ranging menu. It's set back from the beach, though, so views may be obscured by any future developments. Not so at nearby *Cempaka* (①), where A-frames have been built on tall stilts against the hillside to ensure an uninterrupted panorama. Your first sight in the morning, however, as you open your door at *Cottage Hut* (①) next door, is likely to be of the A-frames tightly packed in front of you. This, too, has its own restaurant, but it's not as good as that at *Mata Hari*.

The only other place to stay on Kecil is at the very northeast tip of the island, where *D'Lagoon* (①), set in a tiny, very isolated cove, offers tents, rooms and chalets. From here, you can clamber across the narrow neck of the island to the turtle-spotting beach on the other side (though the best place to see turtles is on Besar – see below).

Perhentian Besar

All the accommodation on **PERHENTIAN BESAR** is on the western half of the island – there's a lot to choose from so it shouldn't be too difficult to find somewhere suitable if your first option is full. South of *Mama's Place*, however, the boats drop you right at the southern end of the bay, entailing quite a walk.

The *Perhentian Island Resort* (☎011/345562; ③–⑤) has by far the best beach of the whole island group – a majestic sweep of sugar-like sand, fringed by jungle, and offset by glassy, turquoise water. The basic A-frames clinging to the hillside are overpriced though, as is the chaotic restaurant, but the family chalets are comfortable enough, and the dive centre is well patronized (see below). A flat trail leads from behind the *Perhentian Island Resort* to the large bay in the south (see below), taking 45 minutes.

Just around the corner, over the rocks, are the rather regimented chalets belonging to *Coral View* (☎011/970943; ③). The restaurant, overlooking two bays, is worth the outlay, offering tasty chicken and beef dishes. *Mama's Place* (①), a little further down, has very basic, pastel-coloured chalets and a well shower. The beach here is liberally scattered with coral, making a dip in the sea a bit hazardous.

An impassable rocky headland separates this from the shingle beach to the south, home to *Cozy Chalets* (☎011/326822; ②), whose modern huts with fans herald the start of a crowded string of developments. There's little to choose between them, but two of the better ones are *Ibi's* (②) and *Abdul's* (①) at the southern end of the stretch, with beach-facing chalets and an excellent strip of sand.

Continuing south, a set of wooden steps traverses the rocky outcrop to two tiny restaurants, *Isabella Café* and *Coral Cave Seafood*, both serving Western breakfasts, snacks and set meals (around $4–6). The trail across to the bay on the southern side of the island begins just past the second jetty, behind some disused private villas. A steep 45-minute climb brings you to the first of the developments on the island's south side. *Pelangi Chalets* (②) is good value, if slightly unimaginative in layout; its neighbour, *Flora Bay* (☎011/977266; ③), appeals to a more upmarket crowd, while *D'Lagoona* (①) is the only truly budget accommodation on this windswept expanse of smooth, powdery sand, a pleasant little encampment of ramshackle A-frames.

The best place on the islands for **turtle watching** is undoubtedly Three Coves Bay on the north coast of Besar. A stunning conglomeration of three beaches, separated from the main area of accommodation by rocky outcrops and reached only by speedboat, it provides a secluded haven between May and September for Green and Hawksbill turtles to come ashore and lay their eggs (see also "Rantau Abang", p.255).

Snorkelling, diving and fishing

You'll also get a chance to spot turtles if you go **snorkelling** – equipment can be rented from most chalets, and boat trips around either island to undeveloped coves cost around $10 per person – just ask at the place you're staying. The conditions are superb:

tranquil currents and visibility of up to twenty metres, although the seasonal sea lice can be a problem, inflicting an unpleasant but harmless sting not unlike that of a jelly fish. A foray around the rocks at the ends of most bays turns up a teeming array of brightly coloured fish and live coral – don't break any off, since it's razor-sharp and you'll also be damaging the subaqua ecosystem.

For the more adventurous still, the small centre at the *Perhentian Island Resort* on Besar runs **dive courses**, or most chalets offer a single dive for qualified divers for a pricey $120. If all this sounds too energetic for your liking, you can take a **fishing trip** with the local fishermen for $30, a chance to see the way of life that sustains most islanders – though the swell of the water, combined with the smell of the landed fish, can make you queasy.

Merang

There's absolutely nothing to do in **MERANG** (not to be confused with Marang, 57km further down the coast) – and that's the attraction. A tiny coastal *kampung* 120km south of Kota Bharu, Merang began to attract foreign travellers in the 1970s, drawn by the peaceful surroundings. The only places to stay were in the homes of the villagers and soon this became the very reason people wanted to come here – to break away from the bland and impersonal atmosphere of tourist hotels. Only relatively recently have a few enterprising locals turned this into a more formal arrangement, with the introduction of **homestays**. Surprisingly perhaps, Merang is still beautifully tranquil, the simple fishing community remaining virtually unchanged by its guests.

All this may soon be lost with the development of Pulau Redang (see p.252) as a major resort, since there is talk of building a jetty in Merang, which will shorten the present three-hour boat journey from Kuala Terengganu by two hours. Although you *can* currently sail to Redang from Merang ($30 one-way), it's an ad hoc arrangement and involves the Kuala Terengganu boat making a brief stop in Merang, on request, before continuing its journey. You must also book accommodation on Redang in advance from one of the agencies in Kuala Terengganu (see p.253 for all the details).

The village

The *kampung* at Merang is clustered around a small T-junction close to the beach, with rough yellow sand sloping steeply towards the sea. It gets more littered the closer you get to the village, but it's reasonable enough for swimming. The best spot is in front of the "resort", a small, downmarket motel to the north of the main village, while dominating this sweep of bay, a large mound serves as an ideal lookout across the blustery coastline – Pulau Perhentian and Pulau Redang are clearly visible from here. Just before the start of Ramadan in February, the beach becomes the focus of a local festival; visitors are invited to join in with traditional games and music. For the rest of the year, fishing forms the mainstay of village life – if you get up early enough (around 6am), you'll see the fishermen returning with the day's catch.

Practicalities

Coming from the north, take any bus bound for Kuala Terengganu as far as Permaisuri, just before Kampung Buloh on the main route through the coastal flatlands. From here, taxis ($15 per car) or a regular minibus service (known as an *econovan*; $6) run to Merang, a further 33km. From the south, a local bus takes you as far as Batu Rakit, one of a string of pretty coastal *kampungs*, from where *econovans* ply the remaining 16km ($3) to Merang.

Merang's **homestays** are the only worthwhile accommodation options, costing $10–$15 per person, including all meals. The best of the bunch is *Naughty Dragon's Green*

Planet, run by a young German/Malay couple, signposted right at the main T-junction, then a further fifty metres or so on the left. It has four rooms in a shady palm grove close to the beach, free tea and coffee, and – surprisingly – an international phone/fax facility for guests; room-only rates are available. *Razak's Kampung House* is run along similar lines to its neighbour *Naughty Dragon*, with a dorm as well as ordinary rooms, although no meals are provided. The long-running *Man's* has always been a popular place, just two rooms in a friendly family house, about a kilometre back from the junction on the Penarik road; you're made to feel very welcome and the food is good. Otherwise motel-style rooms or beachfront A-frames are available at the *Merang Beach Resort* (☎011/970853; ③) on the beach.

Since most of the homestays provide food, there's little in the way of separate **restaurants**, but there are two basic *kedai kopis* at the junction, and two or three provision stores for other snacks.

Kuala Terengganu and around

As you approach **KUALA TERENGGANU**, 160km south of Kota Bharu, a huge hillside sign in Malay and Arabic greets you: "God Save Terengganu" – or as locals wryly remark, "'God Save the Oil', more like". The discovery of oil in the South China Sea, just off the coast here, has undoubtedly been the main factor in Terengganu state's recent prosperity, and evidence of the new wealth is immediately apparent as you enter Kuala Terengganu, the state capital, where high-rise office buildings and banks jostle for position in the busy commercial sector.

As recently as the early 1970s, though, Kuala Terengganu was virtually little more than an oversized fishing village that just happened to be the seat of the Sultan, whose descendants established themselves here in the early eighteenth century. There was a certain amount of trade from the town, with neighbouring states and countries particularly interested in Kuala Terengganu's local crafts – boat-building, weaving and brassware. But economic development was slow, and what wealth there was accrued only to the rulers: a short-lived **peasants' revolt** in 1928 (see feature on next page) was the direct result of the imposition of new taxes and regulations on an already overburdened populace, though its true significance was as the only rebellion in the peninsula to be led by religious leaders, taking on the character of a *jihad* (holy war) against infidels and one of the few involving the normally passive peasantry.

Even in these nouveau riche times for Kuala Terengganu, the outward trappings of modernity have not changed the essence of this tiny Muslim metropolis, sited in what is still a fairly conservative, strongly Islamic state. For the casual visitor, there's plenty of immediate appeal, from the *Istana* and the Chinatown streets, to the lively market and waterfront. For those who are prepared to delve deeper, the handicraft skills that thrive in the surrounding areas, such as offshore Pulau Dayong, reveal a continuation of tradition that stretches back centuries. Using the city as a base, you can also venture inland to **Tasik Kenyir** and the **Sekayu Waterfall** to experience something of the outdoor life for which the state's interior is renowned, or out to sea as far as the marine park of **Pulau Redang**, bathed by the crystal waters of the South China Sea.

Arrival, information and accommodation

At present, the **local bus station** is on the corner of jalan Masjid Abidin and jalan Sultan Ismail, with the **express bus station** across town on jalan Sultan Zainal Abidin. At some point in the near future, the two stations are due to merge and relocate to a new site halfway down jalan Masjid Abidin. The **taxi stand** is at the far western end of jalan Sultan Abidin Ismail, close to the Pulau Dayong jetty. The **airport** is

THE TERENGGANU PEASANTS' REVOLT

In the first three decades of the twentieth century, major changes were being wrought on the Terengganu peasantry. The introduction by the Malay rulers of the system of *cap kurnia*, or royal gifts of land, created a new class of absentee landlords, and reduced farmers who had previously been able to sell or mortgage their land to the status of mere tenant cultivators. Furthermore, the installation of the British Advisory system in 1910 sought to consolidate colonial power by imposing new land taxes, a costly registration of births, deaths and marriages, and permits for everyday things like collecting wood to repair houses.

These ploys were greatly resented by the peasantry, whose response was expressed primarily in religious terms – the deterioration of their living conditions signalled to the faithful the imminent coming of the *Imam Mahdi* who would restore tradition and true faith. Consequently, their actions were directed against all *kafir* (unbelievers) including the Malay rulers, who were seen to be in collusion with the colonists.

The campaign of resistance began in 1922 with a series of anti-tax protests, organized by the village *imams* and spearheaded by two charismatic *ulamas* (Islamic scholars), **Sayyid Sagap** and **Haji Drahman**. As the peasants' courage and militancy increased, so relations with the government deteriorated, until one incident in April 1928 triggered a **full-scale revolt**. A group of around five hundred armed men angrily confronted three officials who were investigating an illegal felling near Tergat, deep in the Terengganu interior, in an attempt to provoke the British into defending their interests. Instead, Sultan Sulaiman himself travelled upstream to hear the crowd's grievances, which he duly promised to consider. The resulting legislation was a compromise that failed to satisfy the peasantry, who decided on a major assault on Kuala Terengganu. Moving upriver, they first captured the District Office at Kuala Berang and then proceeded to Kuala Telemong where they were to join forces with a local band. But the rendezvous never happened. Impatient to capitalize on previous successes, the gang at Kuala Telemong, a motley crew by comparison with the well-armed band at Kuala Berang, decided to attack the government installation alone, walking straight into the line of fire. Many of their leaders, who had previously been considered invulnerable, were killed, taking the wind out of the sails of the deeply disillusioned peasants.

However, it was the behaviour of the two *ulamas* that dealt the most powerful blow to the rebellion. Sayyid Sagap denied that he had ever been involved, claiming to be a loyal subject of the Sultan; luckily for him, he had remained too far in the background for him to be successfully implicated. On hearing about the Kuala Telemong shooting, Haji Drahman fled to Patani, although he eventually returned voluntarily to face trial. Malay and British officials alike not only feared him personally but realized that he was too influential a figure to imprison, and so persuaded him to call off the hostilities in return for comfortable exile to Mecca and a healthy stipend from the government to keep him there. The peasants, having had their collective will broken, were not only deserted by their leaders but then subject to the unfettered and strangling effects of British bureaucracy.

13km northeast of the town centre, a $12–15 taxi ride away; the local bus marked "Kem Seberang Takir" picks up from the road directly outside and runs to the local bus station.

The **Tourist Development Corporation** (Sat–Wed 8.30am–6pm, Thurs 8.30am–1.15pm; closed Fri; ☎09/621433) is inconveniently situated at the eastern end of jalan Sultan Zainal Abidin, on the ground floor of the Wisma MCIS building. Much handier is the helpful **Tourist Information Centre** (same hours as the TDC; no phone) on the same road, but more centrally located near the GPO. The town is easy to get around on foot, though for some of the far-flung places, you might want to take a bus or taxi (details in relevant sections below).

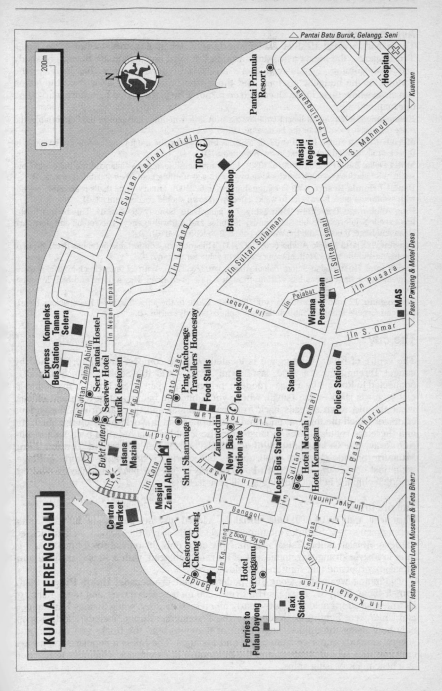

KUALA TERENGGANU

△ Pantai Batu Buruk, Gelangg. Seni

Pantai Primula Resort

Hospital

▷ Kuantan

Jln S. Mahmud

Jln Persinggahan

Masjid Negeri

Jln Sultan Zainal Abidin

TDC

Brass workshop

Jln Ladang

Jln Sultan Sulaiman

Jln Sultan Ismail

Jln Pusara

Jln Pejabat

Pejabat

Jln Pelabat

Wisma Persekutuan

Jln S. Omar

MAS

▷ Pasir Panjang & Motel Desa

Express Bus Station

Kompleks Taman Selera

Jln Nesan Empat

Seri Pantai Hostel

Seaview Hotel

Taufik Restoran

Jln Kg. Dalam

Ping Anchorage Travellers' Homestay

Jln Dato Isaac

Food Stalls

Telekom

Stadium

Police Station

Jln Sultan Zainal Abidin

Bukit Puteri

Istana Maziah

Jln Zainal Abidin

Shri Shanmuga

Zainuddin

New Bus Station site

Jln Masjid

Jln Tok Lam

Local Bus Station

Hotel Meriah

Hotel Kenangan

Jln Sultan Ismail

Jln Batas Baru

Jln Kota

Jln Masjid

Central Market

Masjid Zainal Abidin

Restoran Cheng Cheng

Jln Banggol

Banggol

Jln Ka Tiong 2

Jln Kg. Tiong 2

Jln Engkusa

Engkusa

Hotel Terengganu

Jln Bandar

Jln Ayer Jarneh

▷ Istana Tengku Long Museum & Feta Bharu

Jln Kuala Hiliran

Ferries to Pulau Dayong

Taxi Station

N

200m

0

Accommodation

There isn't a great deal of choice, or quality, when it comes to **hotels** in Kuala Terengganu – the inexpensive ones around the local bus station are downright seedy and unwelcoming. Fortunately, there are several good **hostels** that increase the options for the budget-conscious, and those who prefer to stay away from the action can always hole up at Pulau Dayong (see p.250). The places listed below are marked on our map.

Kenangan, 65 jalan Sultan Ismail (☎09/622688). A little run-down and musty, but comfortable; the more expensive rooms offer the best value. ③.

Meriah, 67 jalan Sultan Ismail (☎09/622652). A bit basic for the money, but rooms are spacious in this centrally located hotel, next to the *Kenangan*. ②.

Motel Desa, Bukit Pak Api (☎09/623033). Fairly inaccessible, quite a distance from the centre, but set in quiet gardens on a hill overlooking town with a swimming pool. Well-appointed rooms. ⑤.

Pantai Primula Resort, jalan Persinggahan (☎09/622100). Luxury hotel that's reasonably priced; with swimming pool. It's too far to walk; a taxi from town should cost around $3. ⑤.

Ping Anchorage Travellers' Homestay, 77a jalan Dato' Isaac (☎09/620851). This budget hostel has excellent information boards, laundry facilities and a travel agency. The rooms and dorm are clean and large, if noisy, and the rooftop café is a welcome retreat. ①.

Seaview, 18a jalan Masjid Abidin (☎09/621911). This modern, comfortable hotel has great views of the Istana and the waterfront, offering excellent value for money. ②.

Seri Pantai Hostel jalan Sultan Zainal Abidin (☎09/632141). With 24-hour check-in, this place is convenient for the express bus station, though a little overpriced. Has a dorm and bicycle rental. ①.

Terengganu, 12 jalan Paya Bunga (☎09/622900). Close to the jetty, this hotel has spacious rooms with comfortable fittings, although the atmosphere is fairly sterile. ②.

The city

The centre of Kuala Terengganu is located within a compact promontory formed by sungei Terengganu – a wide, fast-flowing river – and the South China Sea, and is connected to Route 3 by a large, modern bridge. The main artery through the commercial sector is jalan Sultan Ismail, where you'll find the banks and government offices, while the **old town** spreads back from jalan Bandar and the waterfront. The various crafts for which the town is renowned are all practised in **workshops** on the outskirts, and there are regular buses to most from the local bus station. Also each a short bus ride away, the **Gelanggang Seni** (cultural centre) and the **Istana Tengku Long Museum** provide excellent opportunities to experience the state's cultural heritage, while just across the estuary, **Pulau Duyong** is the last place in Malaysia where a unique technique in boat building is still practised.

The old town

The neat and precise **Istana Maziah** (closed to the public) is one of Kuala Terengganu's few historic monuments, set back from the sea in well-manicured gardens on jalan Sultan Zainal Abidin. Now used only for official royal functions, it is built in a style strangely reminiscent of a French chateau, with a steeply inclined gunmetal-grey roof and tall, shuttered windows.

Continuing westwards along the pedestrianized promenade, **Bukit Puteri** (daily 9am–5.45pm; 50c), or "Princess Hill", rises 200 metres above river and town. Relics of its time as a stronghold during the early nineteenth century, when Sultans Muhammed and Umar were fighting each other for the Terengganu throne, include a fort, supposedly built using the unlikely ingredient of honey to bind the bricks and mortar, and several cannons imported from Spain and Portugal. The hill is a popular spot, always crawling with school children, and the lighthouse at its pinnacle continues to function as a beacon for passing ships.

Turn to your left after you've descended the steps from Bukit Puteri to walk along **jalan Bandar**, the continuation of jalan Sultan Zainal Abidin. The dusty, narrow street forms the centre of **Chinatown**, its decaying shophouses providing a sharp contrast to the high-rises of the modern town: the whiff of lost opportunity hangs in the air, while every so often, a contemporary structure juts out rudely from between the older buildings. No greater contrast to this can be found in Kuala Terengganu's **Central Market** (daily 8am–9pm), a little further down on the right, close to the junction with jalan Kota. Housed in a modern multistorey building which backs onto the river, it oozes vitality and prosperity. Upstairs, above the crowded and claustrophobic wet market, is the best place to search out batik, *songkets* and brassware.

After leaving the market, either continue southwards along jalan Bandar through the remainder of Chinatown, or head east along jalan Kota, at the far end of which you'll pass the **Masjid Zainal Abidin**, an unremarkable modern structure built in 1972 on the site of the original nineteenth-century wooden mosque.

Gelanggang Seni and the craft centres

At the far southeastern end of town, about 2km from the centre, is the **Gelanggang Seni**, a modern cultural complex facing the town's beach, Pantai Batu Buruk. Showtime is every Friday between 5pm and 6.30pm, and Saturday between 8.30pm and 11pm (except during Ramadan) when traditional dances and *silat* are performed for free by amateur groups – check with the tourist office for current details.

Of perhaps greater interest – certainly if you're looking to buy souvenirs – are the various arts and crafts centres scattered around town. Terengganu artisans have long been known for their **brassware** in particular, working in a metal alloy called "white brass" unique to the state, a secret combination of yellow brass, nickel and zinc. The small **workshop** (8.30am–6pm) on jalan Ladang, close to the TDC office, uses the traditional "lost-wax" technique, whereby a wax replica of the article is covered with clay inside and out, placed in a kiln to fire the clay and melt the wax, leaving a clay mold in which to pour the molten metal. When the metal hardens, the clay is chipped off, leaving the metal surface to be polished and decorated. White brass, formerly the luxury of the Sultans, is now used to make decorative articles such as candlesticks and large gourd-shaped vases.

The wide, rougher *mengkuang* style of **weaving** reaches its pinnacle in Terengganu: using the long thin leaves of pandanus trees, similar to bulrushes, women fashion delicate but functional items like bags, floor mats and fans. *Ky Enterprises*, about 3km due

---

THE KRIS

The **kris** occupies a treasured position in Malay culture, a symbol of manhood and honour believed to harbour protective spirits. All young men crossing the barrier of puberty will receive one, which remains with them for the rest of their lives, tucked into the folds of a sarong; for an enemy to relieve someone of a *kris* is tantamount to stripping him of his virility. The weapon itself is intended to deliver a horizontal thrust rather than the more usual downward stab; when a sultan executed a treacherous subject, he did so by sliding a long *kris* through his windpipe, just above the collar bone, thereby inflicting a bloody – though swift– death.

In accordance with their symbolic function, the daggers can be highly decorative. While the iron blade is often embellished with fingerprint patterns or the body of a snake, it is the hilt, shaped like the butt of a gun to facilitate a sure grip, which is the distinguishing feature of the dagger. Materials used for the hilt vary from ivory to wood and metal, but designs are usually based on the theme of a bird's head. The hilt can also be used in combat if the owner has not had time to unsheath the weapon, inflicting a damaging blow to the eye or head.

south of the centre on jalan Panji Alam, is a good place to watch the process; take the "Gong Pak Maseh" or "Gong" bus for the fifteen-minute ride from the local bus station.

There are several other craft workshops in neighbouring Pasir Panjang, about half a kilometre west of jalan Panji Alam. Perhaps the most famous is that belonging to Abu Bakar bin Mohammed Amin on lorong Saga (9am–5.30pm), a **kris** maker (see feature above). Here you can watch the two-edged dagger and its wooden sheath being decorated with fine artwork, a process which, together with the forging, can take several weeks to complete. Take a "Pasir Panjang" bus from the local bus station and get off at the sign marked "Sekolah Kebangsaan Psr. Panjang".

Pulau Duyong

Accessible by a five-minute ferry ride (50c) from the jetty at the end of jalan Sultan Ismail, **PULAU DUYONG** is the largest of the islets dotting the Terengganu estuary. This dank and muddy area, the condition of which has worsened since the construction of the Kenyir Dam further upstream, is famous for its **boat building**, a skill that has developed from a traditional art form into a burgeoning commercial enterprise. In the island's dry docks, old-fashioned deep sea fishing boats line up alongside state-of-the-art luxury yachts – but whatever the price tag, the construction method is the same. The craftsmen work entirely from memory rather than from set plans, building the hull using strong hardwood pegs to fasten the planks, then applying special sealant derived from swampland trees, which confers a degree of resistance to rot. Unusually, the frame is then fitted afterwards, giving the whole structure strength and flexibility.

There's not much else to do on Pulau Duyong other than stroll up and down the seafront, passing from workshop to workshop, but the village here is pleasant enough, with a myriad of brightly painted wooden houses. *Awi's Yellow House* (①) is a delightful timber complex of huts and walkways, replete with pot plants, built on stilts over the water. Relatively hard to find – turn left when you get off the boat and follow the river as closely as possible – it's nevertheless known by all the locals, and offers a variety of **accommodation** from basic huts to a spacious dorm, complete with mosquito nets. With transport connections to the city so unreliable – buses across the bridge are infrequent, and the ferries stop running early at around 7pm – *Awi's* is not an ideal base, but with its own cooking facilities, it's perfect for self-catering and beautifully peaceful.

The Istana Tengku Long Museum

The new **Istana Tengku Long Museum**, 3km west of the town centre in an idyllic riverside site, is destined to be among Malaysia's most exciting cultural complexes once it's fully operational. Among other things it will house the contents of the now-defunct State Museum in an outsized modern interpretation of the triple-roofed houses common in this area. For the present, set in a landscaped area next to the wide sungei Terengganu, are two examples of the sailing boats for which Kuala Terengganu is famed (see above), as well as numerous ancient timber palaces. The supreme example of these is the **Istana Tunku Nik**, originally built in 1888 entirely without nails (which to a Malay signify death because of their use in coffins). Like the majority of east coast houses dating from before this century, the hardwood rectangular building has a high pointed roof and a pair of slightly curved wooden gables at either end. Each gable is fitted with twenty gilded screens, intricately carved with verses from the Koran and designed to admit air but also provide protection from driving rain.

The museum is easily reached by a twenty-minute journey on the "Losong" minibus which departs regularly from the local bus station, passing through some attractive *kampungs* – on the way look out for the traditional high-gabled stilted houses.

MALAY DOMESTIC ARCHITECTURE

The **traditional Malay house** is now found only in rural areas – hence the generic term **kampung architecture** – with the best examples being in the states of Kelantan and Terengganu. Since the house is basically a timber structure, you won't see any over a hundred years old, due to both weathering and termites taking their toll over the years. Raised on stilts to afford protection from floods and wild animals, the wooden walls have many windows to let in the maximum amount of light and air, and are often embellished with elaborate carvings displaying skills and artistry garnered over centuries. Inside, a large, rectangular room acts as the principal family area and as a reception room for guests, with bedrooms and storerooms behind, while the kitchen is connected to the main part of the house by an open courtyard. The roof is covered by *atap* (palm thatch), though these days tiles or corrugated iron are just as common. Regional variations in these village houses are most pronounced in the state of Negeri Sembilan, between KL and Melaka, whose *Minangkabau* settlers from Sumatra brought with them their distinctive saddle-shaped roofs – sweeping, curved structures often termed "buffalo horns". The states of Kelantan and Terengganu show the influence of their Thai neighbours to the north in their gables and tiled roofs, with fewer windows and more headroom, while those in Melaka are characterized by a decorative, tiled stairway leading up to an open-sided verandah. The simple, airy *kampung* architectural style, with its emphasis on timber, is being adopted by many new hotels and public buildings to evoke a more informal atmosphere and to emphasize Malay traditions, often to award-winning success.

Eating

There are excellent **food stalls** on jalan Tok Lam and on the first floor of Kompleks Taman Selera, serving the usual Malay dishes (11.30am–midnight). By comparison other restaurants are poor value, although there are one or two notable exceptions.

Restoran Cheng Cheng, jalan Bandar. The excellent buffet in this authentic, but tourist-oriented, Chinese *kedai kopi* price-codes your plate with coloured pegs – lunch costs around $5.

Shri Shanmuga, jalan Tok Lam, by junction with jalan Dato' Isaac. Great banana leaf curries.

Taufik Restoran, jalan Masjid Abidin. A popular Indian place serving *murtabak*s and curry dishes starting from $2. Closed in the evening.

Zainuddin, jalan Tok Lam. A smart, air-con restaurant offering a broad Thai-influenced menu that's surprisingly inexpensive at around $3 per dish, and very popular with locals.

Listings

Airlines The *MAS* office is at 13 jalan Sultan Omar (☎09/621415).

Airport Sultan Mahmmud Airport is 13km northeast of town, flight info on ☎00/664500.

Banks and exchange *Standard Chartered, UMBC* and *Malayan Banking*; all on jalan Sultan Ismail.

Buses Kuala Terengganu has regular buses to all points on the Peninsula. Local buses go every 30min to Marang (7am–6pm; $1) and to Dungun and Rantau Abang (7.30am–6pm; $2).

Hospital The state hospital is off jalan Sultan Mahmud on jalan Peranginan (☎09/633333), 1km or so southeast of the centre.

Immigration The *Wisma Persekutuan* office on jalan Pejabat. (Sat–Wed 8.30am–6pm, Thurs 8.30am–1pm; closed Fri) issues on-the-spot-visa renewals.

Police Main police station is on jalan Sultan Ismail (☎09/622222).

Post office The GPO (for poste restante/general delivery) is on jalan Sultan Zainal Ibrahim.

Telephones There's a *Telekom* office on jalan Tok Lam (8.30am–4.15pm).

Tours and travel agents The Tourist Information Centre on jalan Sultan Zainal Abidin near the GPO arranges tours to most local places including Tasik Kenyir and Sekayu Waterfall (from $60), and can also recommend other agencies. *Ping Anchorage Travel and Tours*, 77a jalan Dato' Isaac (☎09/620851), is very informative and efficient.

Around Kuala Terengganu

There are three main excursions that can be made from Kuala Terengganu: to **Tasik Kenyir**, a huge artificial lake 55km southwest of the city; to the **Sekayu Waterfall**, 56km south; and to **Pulau Redang**, a stunning marine park 45km off the Terengganu coast. With the exception of Sekayu, all visits must be arranged through a travel agent (see "Listings", above), since recent government regulations for protected areas prevent independent travel to these parts. This makes exploring not only expensive but also rather regimented. Nevertheless, if you want to strike out a little off the beaten east coast track, this is your chance.

Tasik Kenyir

Malaysia's largest hydroelectric dam may not seem a promising start for a "back-to-nature" experience, but on the other side of the immense concrete wall is **Tasik Kenyir**, a lake of some 360 square kilometres, enveloping 340 islands, created when the valley was flooded. Currently being developed as an alternative gateway to Taman Negara, it was once an area of lush jungle, as indicated by the partially submerged trees that jut out of the waters. The stark stumps lend a rather desolate air to the scene – perhaps heightened by the knowledge that the rotting trunks have contributed to the reduction in oxygen levels in the water, causing fish to hunt for food in more congenial surroundings. Otherwise, however, the water is clear, and tours visit the many waterfalls whose plunge pools allow swimming, as well as the limestone Bewah Caves, deep in the hills that surround the lake, filled with stalactities and bat droppings.

There are two types of **accommodation** available at Tasik Kenyir: upmarket floating chalets, with full facilities, or more basic houseboats. The latter are not only cheaper but, surprisingly, provide better access to the lake. Typical packages for a one-night stay cost from $100 per person in a houseboat and $140 in a floating chalet, including bus transfer from Kuala Terengganu, meals and a guided tour – not a bargain by anyone's standards, particularly when the second day's schedule concludes at lunchtime.

Sekayu Waterfall

If you can't face parting with the money for the Tasik Kenyir experience, then a trip to **Sekayu Waterfall** is a good compromise, not least because you can include a visit to the dam on the way. Part of a government park complex, known as **Hutan Lipur Sekayu** (daily 9am–6pm; $1), the park is a busy weekend picnic spot, even if the environment has been somewhat tamed, with rustic shelters, a bird park, mini zoo and an "all-you-can-eat" fruit farm.

Take a local bus for the forty-five-minute journey to Kuala Berang ($2.20), and after taking a peek at the dam, hop in a taxi for the further fifteen minutes to the park ($10 one-way for the car); don't forget to arrange a pick-up time with your driver as there is no taxi stand at the park.

However, if you want to stay at the park, there are a number of **chalets** and a **rest house** (both ②) which must be booked in advance at the District Office in Kuala Berang (☎09/811259). Most travel agents in Kuala Terengganu can arrange a day trip costing $35.

Pulau Redang

Forty-five kilometres northwest of Kuala Terengganu, the unspoilt island of **PULAU REDANG** forms the latest of Malaysia's government-designated marine parks, designed to minimize the damage caused to the spectacular coral reefs found in the waters here. About two hundred families live on the island (a mere 5km by 8km), in an attractive stilted village on the estuary of sungei Redang, an ancient fishing community about to be relocated further upstream to make way for a rather less ecologically sound luxury resort and golf course. Camping grounds, hiking tracks and boardwalks through the mangrove forest are all part of a determined effort to protect the environment, while at the same time promoting public awareness – an honourable motive that may be undermined by the effects of the impending leisure complex. Already, the dwindling importance of fishing has forced some of the inhabitants to raid the caves on the northeastern side of the island for valuable edible birds' nests, thereby threatening some rare species of birds.

The delicate balancing act between tourism and conservation has been carried off more successfully when it comes to protecting the underwater treasures of Pulau Redang. The island boasts abundant **marine life** sustained by the coral reef which thrives in the mangrove-sheltered waters of the estuary. The reef had barely recovered from the havoc wreaked by a large-scale attack of "crown of thorns" starfish in the mid-1970s (then suffering a second attack in the early 1990s), when agricultural development and the building of a road to the upper reaches of the river in the late 1980s deposited silt and caused more massive damage to the coral. Happily, coral reefs have a remarkable ability for self-renewal, and through the elimination or regulation of certain harmful activities, such as spearfishing, trawling and watersports, it is hoped to create a more conducive environment for survival.

Your movements around the island and in the sea are restricted. The best legal snorkelling is off the southern coast around the islets of Pulau Pinang and Pulau Ekor Tibu, while scuba diving is recommended around Redang's northeastern region. Among the most common fish are batfish, angel fish, box fish and butterfly fish, luminous multi-coloured creatures which feed off the many anemone, sponges and bivalves to be found around the rocks. Towards the north of the island itself, an area sandwiched between the two rocky hills that run the length of Redang has been set aside for recreational purposes, allowing for some easy walks through the forest.

At present, there are three **places to stay** on Pulau Redang: the *Redang Beach Resort* (☎09/638188), *Redang Bay* (☎09/636048) and *Redang Pelangi* (no phone), although at each you must book an all-inclusive package in Kuala Terengganu, costing from $180 for one night in a tent to $220 for a luxury chalet; this includes all meals and activities. Prices are likely to come down as Redang becomes more popular (already Singaporeans come in large numbers), and hopefully the greater demand will eventually produce a wider choice than the "team games and karaoke" packages currently on offer. The boat leaves from the jetty on Sultan Zainal Abidan in Kuala Terengganu.

Marang and Pulau Kapas

Times are changing in **MARANG**, a tiny coastal village 17km south of Kuala Terengganu. Its conservative residents have long been used to the steady trickle of foreign visitors, drawn to the place by the promise of "old Malaysia", as well as the delights of nearby Pulau Kapas, 6km offshore. But the village, home to a handful of guest houses and batik shops as well as local traders and nicknamed "Cowboy Town" because of its dusty one-horse feel, is about to get a face-lift. At the time this book went to press, the dingy, ramshackle wooden shops and houses that lined the road were due to be razed to the ground and replaced by a block of uniform concrete units. While visitors might bemoan Marang's loss of character, you won't hear many of the locals complaining, since they welcome the improved safety and sanitation that the new buildings bring. Shades of the old Marang linger in the sleepy backwater to the north of the main street, a community living under the shade of coconut trees beside a lovely lagoon, in whose glassy waters colourful fishing boats loll languidly. The beach here, and 2km further to the south at **RHU MUDA**, seems imperfect given the paradigm of Pulau Kapas, though the empty stretches at both are hard to beat for solitude.

Practicalities

Any Dungun- or Rhu Muda-bound **bus**, leaving at half-hourly intervals from Kuala Terengganu, will drop you on the main road at Marang, from where a five-minute walk down one of the roads off to the left will bring you into the centre. Marang-bound buses drive right down the main street, terminating at the bus stand about halfway along; the **taxi stand** is next door. Although the northern end of Rhu Muda is easy enough to walk to, you can also pick up a bus on the main road.

There are no banks in Marang, though there is a police station and a post office just before the bridge at the south end of the village. The **ferry companies** running boats over to Pulau Kapas have their offices on the main road, all offering the same deal of $15 for a return trip, but arrangements can just as easily be made through most of the guest houses. The **jetty** is just off the main street; sailings are dependent on the whim of the tide, since the harbour is incredibly shallow – mid-morning is the most usual departure time. During the monsoon months of November to February, Pulau Kapas is completely inaccessible.

Accommodation and eating

Even with development afoot, it's likely you'll want to **stay** a night or so in Marang. One of the best places is the *Ping Anchorage II* (☎09/682132; ①) – sister of the one in Kuala Terengganu at the south end of town – with dorms and single rooms. The little enclave at the far northern end of town, past the lagoon, is fast becoming popular. The long-running *Kamal's* (☎09/682181; ①) is the cheapest here, with some reasonable chalets, a shabby dorm and communal showers, kitchen and seating area. Much better is the *Marang Guest House* (☎09/681976; ①) up on the hill behind *Kamal's*, with fresh, comfortable rooms and A-frames, and an excellent vantage point over the lagoon and sea. The *Island View Resort* (☎09/682006; ①) next to *Kamal's*, is a messy mishmash of different styled chalets, but the new, pricier rooms are very good value. Most guest houses have their own **restaurants**, serving Westernized food, while the food stalls near the market are worth checking out for local dishes.

Rhu Muda

Unless you have your own transport, staying at Rhu Muda puts you out on a limb, for although there are a whole string of beach resorts, there's not the same sense of community that there is in Marang itself. About the best of the **accommodation** is the *Angullia Beach House Resort* (☎09/681322; ②), 2km south of Marang, a spacious grassy compound with variously priced chalets, all with their own verandahs. The *D'Costa Hut* (☎09/681589; ①), about another 2km further on, is promising, with a large beach-facing restaurant but very dark, windowless rooms and dormitory.

Pulau Kapas

A thirty-minute ride by fishing boat from Marang takes you to **PULAU KAPAS**, a tiny island less than 2km in length. It's a fine spot, the beach coves on the western side of the island accessible only by sea or by clambering over rocks – you'll be rewarded by excellent sand and aquamarine water, though the latter can be too littered with dead coral for comfort. Access to the remote eastern side is via a track that leads back from the jetty, taking around 45 minutes, but the sheer cliffs which plummet to the water's edge make the approach unwelcoming. Like many of its neighbours, Kapas is a designated marine park, the best snorkelling being around the rocky islet, Pulau Raja, just off its northwestern shore, while the northernmost cove is ideal for turtle-spotting.

At present, the only **accommodation** is at the two western coves that directly face the mainland. The best value is *Zaki Beach Chalet* (☎010/933435; ②), a laid-back place set in a shady grove, with comfortable A-frames, though its cheaper rooms near the generator are very noisy. Its restaurant is definitely the place to be in the evenings. Close by, the welcoming *Pulau Kapas Garden Resort* (☎011/971306; ②) is worth checking out, with well-equipped A-frames and more luxurious rooms; it's the only place on this bay to have a beachside restaurant and a resident diving instructor – courses start from $750. Skip the cramped *Mak Cik Gemuk Beach Resort* between these two developments – its generator is turned off at 1am, leaving you to swelter throughout the night without fans. A wooden walkway over the rocks leads to the jetty in the next bay, and to the *Primula Village Resort* (☎09/622100; ⑤), an exclusive set of Malay-style chalets, with a swimming pool and extensive watersports facilities. At the far end of the bay, the *Sri Kapas Lodge* (no phone; ③) is an attractively designed longhouse of dark, polished timber, with some budget dorm beds – though with only a well shower and no electricity, it's a touch overpriced.

Rantau Abang

Coastal Route 3 marches southwards, passing through numerous fishing *kampungs* before reaching **RANTAU ABANG**, 43km from Marang. Although the village is no more than a collection of guest houses strung out at regular intervals along a couple of kilometres of dusty road, it has made its name as one of a handful of places in the world where the increasingly rare **giant leatherback turtle** comes to lay its eggs, returning year after year between May and September to the same beaches. While other species, including the hawksbill, the Olive Ridley and green turtles, are also to be found in these parts, it is the sight of the huge, ponderous leatherbacks, with their unusual coat of black, rubbery skin, lumbering up the beach, that is the real attraction.

Measuring a metre and a half in length, and weighing on average of about four hundred kilos, only the female ever comes ashore, heaving herself out of the water at night with her enormous front flippers until she reaches dry sand. The turtle's back flippers make digging movements to create a narrow hole fifty to eighty centimetres deep in which she deposits up to a hundred eggs. The turtle then covers the hole with her rear flippers, while disguising the whole nest site by churning up more sand with the front ones. It is this action which causes the turtle to wheeze and shed tears in order to remove the kicked-up sand from her eyes and nose – although a more romantic explanation has it that the creature is grieving for her lost eggs.

Although a single turtle never lays eggs for two consecutive seasons, it can nest three or four times within the same season at two-weekly intervals. The eggs incubate for fifty or sixty days, the temperature of the sand influencing the sex of the hatchlings – warm sand produces more females, cooler sand favours males. The hatchlings – no more than a hand-span length – then crawl to the surface of the sand, leaving their broken shells at the bottom of the pit. The first few hours of a hatchling's life are particularly hazardous, for if it hasn't been destroyed by larvae or funghi in the sand, then it can be picked off by crabs, birds and other predators before even reaching the sea. Usually emerging under the cover of night, they propel themselves rapidly towards the water's edge using their outsize flippers, the element of the turtle's behaviour that most baffles scientists. While it was once thought that they headed towards the lightest area in their vision (other sources of light such as torches were known to disturb their progress), other studies showed that the hatchlings were also moving away from the land's higher horizon. In so doing, it is thought that the turtles somehow memorize the beach on their speedy scuttle towards the water, which could account for their ability to re-locate Rantau Abang in later life. This theory is supported by the observation that, once in the water, turtles swim in the direction from which the waves are coming, as if guided by a sense of magnetic direction. But at the end of the day, nobody knows why a mature fifty-year-old turtle, swimming in waters as far away as South America, can find its way back to nest on the coast of Terengganu.

Turtle watching

Shamefully, turtle-watching was once something of a sport, with tourists riding the sensitive and harmless creatures for the sake of a good photograph – behaviour that, not surprisingly, was scaring the turtles away. Moreover, the freshly laid eggs are considered a delicacy among Malays, a fact which wasn't helping to maintain turtle numbers. The coastline 10km either side of Rantau Abang has now been set aside as a **sanctuary** for nesting turtles by the State Government with the support of the World Wildlife Fund, and specific nesting areas have been established on the beach, fenced off from the curious human beings. Also off limits are the **hatcheries** set up to protect the eggs from theft or damage; the eggs are dug up immediately after the turtle has laid them and reburied in a safe site surrounded by a wire pen tagged with a date marker. When the hatchlings have broken out of their shells, they are released at the top of the beach, and their scurry to the sea is supervised to ensure their safe progress.

The **Turtle Information Centre** (May–Aug Mon–Thurs & Sat 9am–1pm, 2–6pm & 8–11pm, Fri 9am–noon & 3–11pm; Sept–April Mon–Wed & Sat 8am–12.45pm & 2–4pm, Thurs 8am–12.45pm; free), to the north of the central two-kilometre strip, has a map showing the extent of the restricted areas, as well as an interesting video and other displays relating to the turtles found in the locality.

Although there are specific places where the public are allowed to watch the nesting turtles, you are asked to keep at least five metres away and refrain from using torches, camera flashes and fires as well as making a noise. Better still, you can get a volunteer to come and wake you at your guest house for a fee of $2 if a turtle is sighted, guaranteeing you a better night's sleep, as well as minimizing the disturbance for the turtles.

THE MARINE TURTLE – AN ENDANGERED SPECIES

While the striking leatherback turtle is an emotive cause for concern, the population of all marine turtles – green, black, Olive Ridley, Kemp's Ridley, hawksbill, loggerhead – is at risk. Although the authorities have gone some way towards controlling the on-shore conditions for visiting turtles at Rantau Abang, the real damage to the population is inflicted elsewhere. Harmful fishing methods, such as the use of trawl nets, are responsible for the deaths of more than 100,000 marine turtles each year – a figure that explains the dramatic reduction in turtles nesting on the Terengganu coast from 2,000 in the 1950s to a mere 200 in 1989. With a survival rate of only 50 percent among hatchlings, this is bound to have drastic consequences for the survival of the species: current estimates reckon on a figure of between 70,000 and 75,000 females left in the world.

But in Southeast Asia in particular, the turtles have a far more menacing predator – human beings. While its meat is forbidden by religious law in Malaysia, neighbouring nations such as Indonesia and the Philippines have traditionally relied on the turtle as an important source of nutrition. More worrying, however, was the deliberate slaughter of turtles for their shells – each worth around US$375 – which were fashioned into ornaments, like bowls and earrings, primarily for the Japanese market. Until 1992, when a ban was enforced, Japan imported 20 tons of hawksbill shells annually for this purpose, which involved killing over 30,000 turtles.

Practicalities

Local buses from Kuala Terengganu and Marang run every thirty minutes (7.30am–6pm) for the hour's journey to Rantau Abang. If you're coming by express bus from the south, you have to change at Dungun, 13km to the south (see below), from where you can easily get a local bus for the remainder of the journey. Buses drop you on the main road, just a short walk from all the accommodation and the *Turtle Information Centre*.

There are surprisingly few **accommodation** options, all of them close to the beach. Prices double when the turtles are in town, from May to September; the price codes refer to the high season rate. The best place is the upmarket *Rantau Abang Visitor Centre* (☎09/841801; ⑤), about a kilometre north of the *Turtle Information Centre*, with ten timber chalets complete with fridge and TV arranged around a peaceful lagoon. Of the budget options, *Dahimah's Guest House* (☎010/934500; ②), at the far southern end of the strip, rates highly, with very comfortable rooms and chalets surrounding a central courtyard; many of the rooms are a good deal cheaper than this category suggests, making them excellent value. Costing still less, and with much more of a backpackers' feel, is the long-running and central *Awang's* (☎09/843500; ①), a little run-down but friendly, with a variety of simple rooms as well as some overpriced air-con chalets. *Ismail's* (☎09/841054; ①), next door, is very basic and not as good. Both places are handily located, near the *Turtle Information Centre*.

All guest houses have their own **restaurants**, serving the usual traveller-orientated food. In addition, there are **food stalls** near *Awang's*, and the excellent *Kedai Makan Rantau Abang*, 750m further south, a cheerful local eating house offering substantial rice and noodle dishes. For **midnight snacks** while turtle-watching, the modern *R&R Plaza* (open 24hr), on the main road opposite the *Turtle Information Centre*, is the place to head, with a wide-ranging menu featuring Western and Malay dishes.

South to Cherating

The **route south** from Rantau Abang is a further indictment of the rampant development that has accompanied Terengganu's economic success: ugly oil refineries and huge residential complexes for their employees, built with little or no regard for the local environment. This rapid industrialization hasn't deterred the growth of tourism however, as illustrated by the success of the award-winning *Tanjung Jara Beach Hotel* (☎09/841801; ⑥), a luxury Malay-style resort, 8km south of Rantau Abang. There are, in fact, several resorts along this stretch, though the sight of the offshore rigs in these parts may be offputting for sun-seekers. It's only when you reach the secluded bay of Cherating that the scenery takes a distinct upturn.

Dungun to Chukai

The backwater town of **KUALA DUNGUN**, a further 5km south, is predominantly Chinese, with a handful of shophouses and a weekly nightmarket each Thursday. Aside from sorting out transport connections, there's no reason to spend much time here: the local bus station (for services to Rantau Abang) is in the town, on the west side of the *padang*, while express buses (to KL and Singapore) depart from outside the hospital on route 3 itself – tickets can be purchased from either the *A.A.* or *Aziz* restaurants on the main road. With local buses leaving every thirty minutes to Rantau Abang (25min) en route to KL (2hr) and every thirty minutes to Kemaman (2hr), you probably won't need to spend the night; if you do, the *Kasanya* at 223–227 jalan Tumbun (☎09/841704; ②), the town's main street, is about the best option.

Continuing south, the highway swerves suddenly inland to avoid a small promontory before rejoining the coast at **PAKA**, a small fishing village now dwarfed by the immense power plant just to the south. This marks the beginning of a dreary string of developments including Kerteh and Kemasik that are best passed through swiftly. **KEMAMAN**, an untidy, sprawling town halfway between Dungun and Kuantan – and barely distinguishable from its neighbour, **CHUKAI** – is significant only in that it's here that you'll have to change buses to reach any of the small *kampungs* along the road to Kuantan, including Cherating.

Cherating

About 40km north of Kuantan, the fast-expanding travellers' hangout of **CHERATING** hugs the northern end of a windswept bay, protected from the incessant breeze by the shelter of a rocky cliff. Although most of the locals have long since moved to a small village further south, the settlement still tries to reflect *kampung* life by offering simple chalets and homestays at a modest charge to visitors. Ramshackle stilted huts with unashamedly hippy-dippy names nestle engagingly in palm groves, while a handful of beach bars lead the gentle carousing well into the night. The sum total of Cherating's billing as a "cultural village" seems to be the opportunity to learn batik-printing at one of the many outlets around – though even this seems to be a thinly disguised front for marketing off-the-peg clothes at inflated prices. Cynicism aside, nothing really detracts from the laid-back pace of life here, making Cherating an ideal place in which to unwind, with a nightlife that comes as close as the east coast gets to raging.

Any express or local bus between Kuala Terengganu and Kuantan will drop you off at Cherating, which lies within easy walking distance of Route 3. Two rough tracks lead from the road down into the main part of the village, about five minutes' away, although the one nearest the bridge is the most direct. Chalets shaded by tall, gently swaying palm trees are dotted either side of the path, increasing in density when you reach the main drag, a tiny surfaced road that runs roughly parallel to the beach. This is where you'll find most of the restaurants and bars, as well as the provisions stores; a rental outlet, *Checkpoint Cherating*, offering everything from a mountain bike ($20 a day) to a boat; and a small travel agency, *Mimi's Service and Tours* (☎011/952820), at which you can book tours to Gua Charas (see p.265), as well as local river and snorkelling trips ($15 including equipment).

With a reliable sea breeze, Cherating is ideal for **windsurfing**, and some of the beach bars and chalets rent out equipment, from $15 an hour. If that's a bit too active for your liking, try a brisk walk westwards along the **beach** to where the rippling tide makes fascinating patterns on the sand. The revoltingly brown and polluted sungei Cherating that runs into the bay here is really only passable at low tide, effectively cutting off the route further west. Clambering over the rocks at the eastern end of the bay brings you to a tiny secluded cove, though the beach isn't as good as that belonging to the exclusive *Club Med* over the next outcrop. Low tide is less of a problem here than in the main part of the bay, where you'll have to walk out at least two hundred metres to reach the sea, and still further to get deep enough to swim.

Accommodation

True to form for somewhere that has doubled in size in the last five years, Cherating has no shortage of **places to stay** and new places are springing up all the time. Most aren't yet on the phone; the best are reviewed below and marked on the map above.

Greenleaves Inn. There's a real "jungle getaway" feel to this place, with basic chalets hidden away in the groves by a river. A relaxed atmosphere with breakfast included in the price. ①.

Mak Long Teh's (☎09/439290). Set back from the main road, this is one of the original "homestays", offering rooms without fans, and excellent all-you-can-eat meals in a warm family environment. ②, but cheaper without food.

Matahari. Spacious, sturdy chalets each with its own refrigerator and large verandah, as well as a separate communal area with a TV room and cooking facilities. ①.

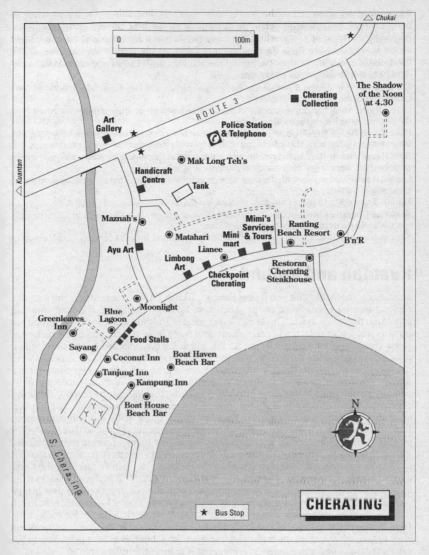

Map labels:
△ Chukai
0 — 100m
ROUTE 3
△ Kuantan
Art Gallery
Cherating Collection
Police Station & Telephone
The Shadow of the Noon at 4.30
Handicraft Centre
Mak Long Teh's
Tank
Maznah's
Mimi's Services & Tours
Ranting Beach Resort
Matahari
Mini mart
B'n'R
Ayu Art
Lianee
Limbong Art
Checkpoint Cherating
Restoran Cherating Steakhouse
Moonlight
Greenleaves Inn
Blue Lagoon
Sayang
Food Stalls
Coconut Inn
Boat Haven Beach Bar
Tanjung Inn
Kampung Inn
Boat House Beach Bar
N
S Cherating
★ Bus Stop
CHERATING

Maznah's. Wacky decor and a lively atmosphere make up for the dilapidated A-frames, most without attached bathrooms. All-day breakfast and tasty evening meals included in the price. ②.

Ranting Beach Resort. Well-appointed and centrally located chalets surrounding an airy restaurant . ③.

Tanjung Inn. The garden compound that stretches down to the beach houses well-spaced, comfortable huts run by a friendly family. ②.

The Shadow of the Moon at Half-Past Four. Five chalets with attached bathroom, tucked away in a beautiful wooded area. *The Deadly Nightshade* bar and lounge are the real attraction. ②.

Eating and drinking

It's no surprise that **eating** is the main focus of nightlife in Cherating, though more unusually for Muslim Malaysia, many lively **bars** offer a convincing alternative. Most chalet operations have their own restaurants – with monotonously similar menus. The **food stalls** operating in the evening on the road through the village offer Malay standards like *nasi lemak, rojak ayam* and *cendol*.

B'n'R. Attractively designed restaurant, though the chicken and fish dinners for around $6 don't quite live up to the promise of the decor.

Blue Lagoon. Busy bar and restaurant whose Chinese-based menu attracts the expat crowd from the local oil refineries; averages $6 per dish.

Boat Haven Beach Bar. An imaginatively constructed bow of a ship forms this beachfront bar, with tables and logs in the sand. Has interesting sculptures, volleyball competitions and camp fires.

Boat House Beach Bar. Archetypal beach bar that's one of the few places selling wine and spirits, as well as beer: an excellent spot to view the sunset.

Lianee. A long-running joint with the most wide-ranging menu: Malay, Thai and seafood dishes averaging $2.50–$4 a plate.

Moonlight. A mostly Chinese (and pricey) menu, but the all-day breakfasts are good value.

Restoran Cherating Steakhouse. Overpriced German cuisine, including grills at $20. The daily specials for $9 are worth trying though. Closed Mon.

Sayang. Nice surroundings and great North Indian tandoori food, but at $6 per dish, it's not cheap.

Kuantan and around

It's virtually inevitable that you'll pass through **KUANTAN** at some stage, since it's the region's transport hub, lying at the junction of Routes 3, 14 and 2, the latter running across the peninsula to KL. The brash state capital of **Pahang**, confidently sprawling out from its thriving commercial centre, Kuantan's roots lie in the administrative failure of Kuala Lipis, the old state capital (see p.212), and in the disappointed hopes surrounding the gold and tin mines located deep in the state interior. These valuable minerals were discovered as far back as the fifteenth century, giving rise to Pahang's legendary reputation as "the richest and most favoured state in the peninsula". Although accounts of its potential wealth quickly dug deep into Malay folklore, the deposits were too widespread ever to be mined effectively and communications to Kuala Lipis too slow and cumbersome for expectations to be realized. Kuantan, more conveniently located on the coast, took up the economic slack, though ironically the geographical location that boosted its prosperity in the nineteenth century can be blamed for many of its current problems. Although handy for shipping, its situation on a promontory means that traffic up the east coast faces a significant diversion inland up the Kuantan river before reaching the town, a factor which many consider has played its part in the failure to capture business from Singapore. All this is about to change, however, with the construction of a new bridge connecting the centre of Kuantan directly to the southern Route 3 – though how much this will alleviate the chaotic congestion in the town's streets is a matter for conjecture. Land prices in the vicinity of the bridge have soared, however, fuelled by developers keen to take advantage of the improved transport links, but this in turn is leading to the eviction of traditional communities no longer able to meet the inflated rents.

While there's little to capture your imagination in the dull, concrete buildings of the town centre – aside from the magnificent Masjid Negeri – the fishing communities to the south of town make an interesting diversion. The beach satellites of **Teluk Chempedak** or **Beserah** just to the north are more pleasant places to stay than the centre itself, and those with more time to spare should not miss out on **Gua Charas**, a limestone cave temple within easy reach of the town. The trip here is worth it for the stunning setting alone, dramatic outcrops jutting rudely out from otherwise undisturbed and virtually deserted plantation country.

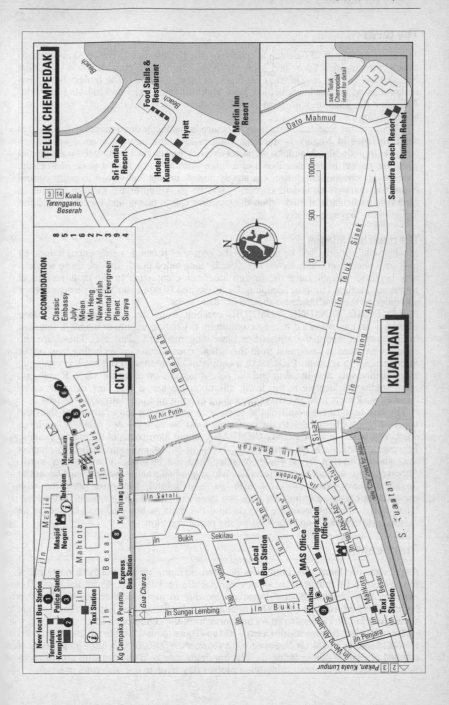

TELUK CHEMPEDAK

Beach

Food Stalls & Restaurant

Beach

Sri Pantai Resort

Hotel Kuantan

Hyatt

Merlin Inn Resort

Dato Mahmud

see 'Teluk Chempedak' inset for detail

Samudra Beach Resort

Rumah Rehat

Jln Teluk Sisek

Jln Teluk Ali

3 14 Kuala Terengganu, Beserah

ACCOMMODATION
Classic 8
Embassy 5
July 1
Meian 6
Min Heng 2
New Meriah 7
Oriental Evergreen 3
Planet 9
Suraya 4

N

0   500   1000m

KUANTAN

Jln Tanjung Ali

S. Kuantan

see City inset for detail

CITY

Jln Beserah

Jln Air Putih

Jln Setali

Jln Mesiid

Masjid Negeri

Telekom

Makan Kuantan

Tksi

Jln Teluk Lumpur

Ke Tanjung Lumpur 8

Jln Bukit

Sekilau

Jln Merdeka

Jln Beserah

Sisek

Jln Mahkota

New local Bus Station

Terentum Kompleks

Police Station

Taxi Station

Express Bus Station

jln Besar

Kg Cempaka & Peramu

Gua Charas

jln Sungai Lembing

Jln Bukit

Jln Junid

Jln Haji

Jln Tun Ismail

Jln Gambut

Local Bus Station

MAS Office

Immigration Office

Jln Haji Abdul Azir

Khalsa

Ubi 9

Mahkota

Taxi Station

jln Penjara

Jln Wong Ah Jang

The town

The commercial part of Kuantan is relatively small, conveniently clustered around two parallel streets, jalan Besar and jalan Makhota. The former, running close by sungei Kuantan and leading into jalan Telok Sisek, is home to most of the budget hotels and restaurants, while, one block behind, jalan Makhota (which changes to jalan Haji Abdul Aziz after the junction with jalan Bank) is where you'll find the GPO, *Telekom* and police station.

While most of Kuantan's urban architecture is distinctly unmemorable, its one real sight, the **Masjid Negeri**, is stunning. Built in 1991, the mosque bears down imperiously on frenetic jalan Makhota, its pastel exterior (green for Islam, blue for peace and white for purity) more reminiscent of a huge birthday cake than a place of worship. Despite its conventional design – a sturdy square prayer hall with a looming central dome and minarets at all four corners – it's the most impressive modern mosque in Malaysia, particularly at dusk when the plaintive call to prayer and the stunning lighting combine to magical effect.

The riverside villages

Most people's priority will be to escape the centre of Kuantan, easily enough done by making a short hop south across the river by long-tailed boat – though these services may begin to dwindle once the bridge has been completed. In the communities of Kampung Tanjung Lumpur, Kampung Cempaka and Peramu you'll find plenty of peace and quiet, as the inhabitants go about their daily tasks.

KAMPUNG TANJUNG LUMPUR, reached from the jetty behind the *Hotel Classic*, is an impoverished fishing community consisting mainly of illegal Indonesian immigrants, to whom the authorities have long turned a blind eye. These are the people who stand to lose most from the bridge construction, as rocketing land prices force families to relocate. **PERAMU**, a couple of kilometres up the road, is changing more visibly, with new housing and the recent installation of mains water. Recalling a more traditional lifestyle is the lively afternoon market, a long line of stalls a few minutes' walk away from the riverside, selling everything from clothes to vegetables.

The coastline to the south of the town is in many ways more appealing than the beach at Teluk Chempedek to the north, not least because it is still relatively undeveloped. The beach at **KAMPUNG CEMPAKA**, about 3km south of Kampung Tanjung Lumpur, is particularly pleasant: a wide sweeping expanse of sand bathed by shallow sea, whose currents are a whole lot safer than the buffeting waves further north. Although close enough to town for a day trip, a good alternative would be to stay at the *Sanubari Beach Resort* (☎011/952518; ⑤), a delightful, family-run operation with comfortable chalets, a swimming pool and excellent cuisine. To get here, take a long-tailed boat to Peramu from the jetty behind the express bus station, followed by an exhilarating motorbike-taxi ride ($5) for the remaining 7km.

Practicalities

At present, the **local bus station** is on jalan Stadium, on the northern outskirts of town, soon to be relocated to a more central site on jalan Haji Abdul Rahman. The **express bus station** on jalan Besar is also due to move, further out to jalan Tun Ismail. The **taxi station** (☎504478) is between jalan Besar and jalan Makhota, while the **airport** is 13km east of town – a taxi there from the centre costs $10.

The **Tourist Information Centre** (Mon–Thurs 8am–12.45pm & 2–4.15pm, Fri 8am–12.45pm & 2.45–4.15pm, Sat 8am–12.45pm; ☎09/503026), in a large glass booth at the end of jalan Makhota facing the playing fields, can help you out with accommodation in and around Kuantan, and also organizes **day trips** to the surrounding area.

Accommodation

Kuantan has no shortage of **hotels**, though at the bottom end of the market the basic Chinese-run boarding houses are poor value. If you can stretch to a few extra dollars, those in the middle range are a good deal more agreeable. Top-class hotels are almost all located in Teluk Chempedek rather than in town itself, though there are one or two less costly alternatives; likewise, Beserah's hostels provide good-value, fume-free respites for the budget-conscious – see over for details of both these places.

Classic, jalan Besar (☎09/554599). The best hotel in town, with large bright rooms, huge bathrooms and great views of the river. ④.

Embassy, 60 jalan Telok Sisek (☎09/527486). One of the more upmarket Chinese hotel; all rooms have attached bathrooms. ②.

July, 73 Lorong Rusa 1, off jalan Bukit Ubi (☎09/500760). This spotless hotel near the new bus station offers small but comfortable rooms, though the decor is a little twee. ②.

Meian, 78 jalan Teluk Sisek (☎09/520949). Basic, neat and clean, though a little overpriced. ①.

Min Heng, jalan Makhota (☎09/504885). Characterful old hotel, with a central location near the taxi station and the cheapest rooms in town. ①.

New Meriah, 142 jalan Telok Sisek (☎09/525433). Large, carpeted, though slightly dingy rooms and bathrooms with hot water make this a very good option. ②.

Oriental Evergreen, 157 jalan Haji Abdul Rahman (☎09/500168). Tucked down a side street off the main road, this is surprisingly plush, with well-appointed rooms and good facilities. ④.

Planet, 77 jalan Bukit Ubi (no phone). Budget hostel with 24-hour check-in, flexible check-out and free hot drinks. The basic rooms are attractively decorated, and the manager is eager to please. ①.

Suraya, 55 jalan Haji Abdul Aziz (☎09/554266). Not quite international standard, but this place still rates highly, with tasteful, subtly lit rooms and a health club. ④.

Eating

Kuantan's **restaurants** win no gastronomic awards; even the **food stalls** near the mosque on jalan Makhota and those by the river behind the bus station do little to tickle the tastebuds. More of a handicap is that many restaurants close in the evenings – a fact which does more to curtail your nightlife than disappoint your palate.

Khalsa, jalan Bukit Ubi. One of several on this road serving Malay/Indian food. Busy and cheerful.

Kum Leng, jalan Bukit Ubi. Popular upmarket air-con Chinese restaurant, with mid-price menu.

Makanan Kuantan, jalan Haji Abdul Aziz. Bright, bustling and specializing in seafood (average dish price $8) with unusual Chinese dishes, such as "Holland Bean and Prawns Rice", though with little choice for vegetarians. Try the "sizzlers" or some tiger prawns from the tank. Open until 2am.

Min Heng Steakhouse, jalan Makhota. A reasonably priced menu makes up for the Alpine-lodge decor in this air-con restaurant. Grills cost around $9–12.

Tiki's, jalan Makhota. Good-value Western breakfasts; relax with a paper over eggs, tea and toast.

Listings

Airlines *MAS*, 7 Ground floor, Wisma Bolasepak Pahang, jalan Gambut (☎09/622457).

Airport The Sultan Ahmad Shah airport is 13km west of town; flight info on ☎09/581291.

Banks *OCBC*, *UMBC*, *Standard Charter Bank* and *Hong Kong Bank* are all situated around the intersection of jalan Besar and jalan Bank.

Buses Express services run from the station on jalan Besar to most points on the Peninsula, including services hourly (8am–5pm) to Temerloh (for Tasik Chini and Tasik Bera) and twice daily to Kuala Lipis (for Taman Negara).

Car rental *Avis*, 102 jalan Telok Sisek (☎09/523666); *Hertz*, c/o Samudra River View Hotel, jalan Besar (☎09/528041); *National*, 49, jalan Telok Sisek (☎09/527303).

Immigration The immigration office is on the first floor, Wisma Persekutuan, jalan Gambut (☎09/521373) for on-the-spot visa renewals (Mon–Fri 9am–4.15pm).

Post and Communications The GPO, with poste restante, is on jalan Haji Abdul Aziz; the *Telekom* office is on jalan Makhota (9am–4.15pm).

Taxis The long-distance taxi stand is on jalan Makhota (☎09/504478); fares per person are $15 to Kuala Terengganu, $20 to KL, $15 to Mersing and $35 to JB.

Teluk Chempedak

TELUK CHEMPEDAK, around 5km east of Kuantan, is a leafy suburb of wide roads and grand houses – in effect, the exclusive beachfront neighbourhood of the town. Sitting on the tip of the peninsula, the beaches have spawned a small collection of resort hotels and pricey trinket shops, all eager to capitalize on the urban disaster that is Kuantan, and edging out all but the most tenacious of the budget hostels. The narrow, sloping beach on the eastern side is reasonable, even if the sea, churned up by the constant wind into a grey broth, is less than inviting, but the western shallows that overlook Kuantan itself are terribly murky. Nevertheless, the clean air and tree-lined avenues are a welcome break from the polluted convolutions of the town centre.

Bus #39 runs regularly to Teluk Chempedak – catch it at the stop on jalan Telok Sisek, just past jalan Merdeka. The bus stops at the beach on the eastern side of the peninsula and most of the **hotels** are off to the right, while a number of restaurants and snack bars face the sea itself to the left. If you can afford its rates, the nicest place to stay is the *Hyatt* (☎09/501234; ⑥), whose open walkways and restaurants are pleasantly freshened by the sea breeze. Its near neighbour, the *Merlin Inn Resort* (☎511388; ⑥), comes a very poor second, an ugly white structure, long overdue for renovation. The quaint *Hotel Kuantan* (☎09/554980; ③), opposite the *Hyatt*, is somewhat chaotic but oozing with charm, while the cheapest rooms to be had are at the *Sri Pantai Resort* (☎09/525250; ②), rather grandly named for the facilities on offer, though with a wide variety of rooms ranging from grotty to reasonable. The western side of the promontory has fewer options: the government-run *Rumah Rehat* (☎011/976946; ④) isn't bad, but it's often full, while the *Samudra Beach Resort* (☎09/505933; ④), with twenty motel rooms, is much better value.

The **places to eat** in Teluk Chempedak are considerably more inspiring than those in Kuantan, although they are limited to the busier eastern side. The *Hyatt* has several restaurants, including a pizzeria, but you won't get away with less than $20 a dish. Facing the beach at the far end of the row of shops are some basic **food stalls**, while a few doors up, the *Massafalah* and *Pattaya* restaurants serve good seafood and steamboats for $6–12.

Beserah

Ten kilometres north of Kuantan on the road to Kuala Terengganu, the small village of **BESERAH** is famous for its salted fish and *keropok* (fish crackers). Fishermen still haul the day's catch to the processing areas by buffalo cart – a mode of transport that is becoming increasingly rare in techno-conscious Malaysia. Although it functions as yet another "cultural village" for Kuantan's tourists, supplied with a few handicraft workshops looking remarkably like souvenir outlets, Beserah is on the whole an unassuming place, whose ways have remained virtually unchanged for decades.

A few guest houses have popped up in Beserah, making it a convenient and altogether more pleasant place to stay than Kuantan, particularly since buses #27, #28 and #30 from the local bus station ply the route regularly from 7am to midnight. Get off at the "Pantai Beserah" sign on the right and follow the road past the sign round to the left for about 25m, where you'll find the friendly *Belia Perkasa* (☎09/588178; ②), affiliated to the *IYHF*, with cheap dorms. The *Beserah Guest House* (☎09/587492; ②) is about 100m further on, past the post office, an old-fashioned wooden boarding house facing a grey sand beach, with strict house rules and shabby rooms. If you turn right instead of left at the "Pantai Beserah" sign and walk for 1km, you'll come to *La Chaumiere* (☎09/587662; ②), the last house on the beach and considerably more laid back. The price includes breakfast and they'll collect you from Kuantan for $6. Further up the main road, a sign on the left points you to *Jaafar's Guest House* (no phone; ②), about 500m down a well-marked trail. This tranquil woodland is the setting for the longest-running homestay in the area, a relaxed family home where the price includes all meals and free tea. Places **to eat** are rather thin on the ground, but all of the guest houses offer evening meals.

Gua Charas

If you have any time to spare in Kuantan, you should visit **GUA CHARAS**, a cave temple 25km northeast of Kuantan, built into one of the soaring limestone outcrops surrounding the town. It can be seen as a leisurely day trip: bus #48 from the local bus station departs regularly for the half-hour journey to the villlage of Panching; look out about halfway along for the well-kept Chinese cemetery clinging to the hillside on the right. At Panching, a sign to the caves points you down a four-kilometre track through overgrown rubber plantations and rows upon rows of palm oil trees – agricultural legacies responsible for the large numbers of Tamils living in the area, descendants of the indentured workers brought from southern India in the nineteenth century. It's a long, hot walk – take plenty of water with you.

Once you've reached the outcrop and paid your $1 entry fee, you're faced with a steep climb up almost vertical steps to reach the Thai Buddhist **cave temple** itself. About halfway up, a rudimentary path strikes off to the right, leading to the entrance to the main cave. Descending into the eerie darkness is not for the faint-hearted, even though the damp mud path is dimly lit by florescent tubes. Inside the vast, echoing cavern with its algae-stained vaulted roof and squeaking bats, illuminated shrines gleam out from gloomy corners, guiding you to the main shrine deep in the far reaches of the cave. Here, an eight-metre sleeping Buddha seems almost dwarfed by its giant surroundings. Retracing your steps back through the cave, steps lead to another, lighter hollow. It's nothing special, but if you go as far as you can to the back, the wall opens out to give a superb view of the surrounding countryside, a patchwork of stubby palm oil trees marching in regimented rows towards the horizon.

travel details

Trains
Kota Bharu to: Gemas (2 daily; 9hr 30min–12hr 50min); Kuala Lipis (2 daily; 4hr 15min–5hr 20min); Singapore (3 weekly; 11hr 55min). For trains into Thailand see the feature on p.000.

Buses
Kota Bharu to: Alor Setar (2 daily; 8hr); Butterworth (2 daily; 6hr); Johor Bahru (2 daily; 12hr); Kuala Lumpur (2 daily; 7hr); Kuala Terengganu (6 daily; 3hr); Kuantan (5 daily; 6hr 30min); Melaka (1 daily; 12 hr).
Kuala Terengganu to: Alor Setar (2 daily; 9hr 30min); Butterworth (2 daily; 8hr); Ipoh (1 daily; 11hr); Johor Bahru (2 daily; 10hr); Kota Bharu (6 daily; 3hr); Kuala Lumpur (2 daily; 8–9hr); Kuantan (8 daily; 3hr 30min); Marang (every

30min; 30min); Melaka (3 daily; 7hr); Mersing (2 daily; 6hr); Rantau Abang (every 30 min; 1hr).
Kuantan to: Alor Setar (3 daily; 13hr 30min); Butterworth (3 daily; 12hr 30min); Ipoh (5 daily; 8hr); Johor Bahru (6 daily; 6hr); Kota Bahru (5 daily, 7hr), Kuala Lipis (2 daily; 6hr); Kuala Lumpur (at least 6 daily; 5hr); Kuala Terengganu (6 daily; 3hr 30min); Melaka (2 daily; 5hr); Mersing (6 daily; 3hr 30min); Singapore (6 daily; 7hr); Temerloh (hourly; 2hr).

Flights
Kota Bharu to: Alor Setar (1 daily; 35min); Kuala Lumpur (6 daily; 50min); Penang (2 daily; 40min).
Kuala Terengganu to: Kuala Lumpur (at least 2 daily; 45min).
Kuantan to: Kuala Lumpur (at least 5 daily; 40min); Singapore (4 weekly; 50min).

CHAPTER FIVE

THE SOUTH

The **south** of the Malaysian peninsula, below Kuala Lumpur and Kuantan, features some of the most historically and culturally significant towns in the country. The foundation of the small city of **Melaka**, on the west coast, in the fifteenth century led to a Malay "Golden Age" under the Muslim Melaka Sultanate, during which were planted the social and cultural roots of *Melayu*, or "Malayness", which still pervade much of modern Malaysia. For all its influence, though, the Sultanate was surprisingly short-lived and its fall in the early sixteenth century to the Portuguese marked the start of centuries of colonial interference in Malaysia – all the more galling given the glory of the Melaka Sultanate. The Dutch and British followed the Portuguese in Melaka, the British soon to worm their way inextricably into the eighteenth- and nineteenth-century development of the country. The resulting juxtaposition of colonial influences and architectural styles is one of the main reasons people come to Melaka; other attractions include the unique cultural blend offered by the *Peranakan*, or Baba-Nonya, the society that arose here following the intermarriage of early Chinese traders and Malay women.

A different historical strand is presented by **Johor Bahru** (or JB), at the peninsula's tip, although its chaotic, snarling streets are a far cry from its erstwhile lustre. Although JB's modern history dates back only to 1855, and to the establishment of a settlement (originally called Tanjung Puteri) across the Johor Straits from Singapore, the city slots into a chain of events spanning several centuries, set in motion by the fall of Melaka to the Portuguese in 1511. Elsewhere, while other foreigners came and went, the intrepid **Minangkabau** tribes from Sumatra settled in what is now the state of Negeri Sembilan, between KL and Melaka, making their mark in the spectacular architecture of **Seremban** and **Sri Menanti**, just over an hour south of the capital.

Melaka – in the centre of a small state of the same name and just two hours by bus from KL – makes a logical starting point for exploring the south. While its sights are liable to keep you absorbed for several days, other local destinations make good day trips: the easy going towns of **Muar** and **Segamat**, the offshore **Pulau Besar**, and the coastal villages of **Tanjung Bidara and Tanjung Kling**. Most people then head for the active little seaport of **Mersing** in order to reach **Pulau Tioman** and the other sparkling islands in the **Seribuat archipelago** – a draw for divers and snorkellers as well as those who simply like the idea of soft sandy beaches and transparent waters.

Other than these destinations, visitors tend to steam up and down either east or west coasts, between KL, Kuantan and JB, avoiding the mountainous core, and there is little encouragement from the poor interior road network to do otherwise. The west coast North–South Highway (and the train line) connects KL with Singapore, while its counterpart on the east coast, the narrow and undulating Route 3, is similarly light in load and a good deal more varied as it wends its way for 300km through palm oil country and past luxuriant beaches. However, those who relish the idea of time travel should get off the main routes and attempt an exploration of the primeval **Endau Rompin National Park**, the southernmost tropical rainforest in the peninsula. Just beginning to open up to the possibilities of tourism, it's a worthy alternative to the much-visited Taman Negara, further north.

ACCOMMODATION PRICE CODES

All the places to stay listed in this book have been given one of the following price codes; for more details, see p.40

① Under $20   ④ $61–100
② $21–40   ⑤ $101–200
③ $41–60   ⑥ $201 and above

Note that all Malaysian telephone numbers are being **changed** in a rolling programme lasting several years. Some of the numbers given in this chapter, while correct at the time of going to press, are likely to have changed.

Negeri Sembilan: Seremban and Sri Menanti

Nowhere did the Minangkabau tribes from Sumatra establish themselves more thoroughly than in the Malay state of **Negeri Sembilan**, whose modern-day capital is the town of **Seremban**, 67km south of Kuala Lumpur, but whose cultural nucleus is the royal town of **Sri Menanti**, 30km further east. Centres of Minangkabau civilization (see the feature on p.272) since the early years of the Melaka Sultanate, both towns boast attractive buildings which either retain or adapt traditional Minangkabau architecture – typified by distinctive, sweeping buffalo-horn peaked roofs, a style now echoed in buildings across the peninsula.

The moden state of Negeri Sembilan is based on an old confederacy of nine districts (hence its name – *sembilan* means nine in Malay) whose early origins are uncertain. What is clear is that by the middle of the nineteeth century, British control over the area and its thriving **tin trade** was virtually complete, with the colonial authority administered from the British base at Sungei Ujong (today's Seremban). Wars between rival Malay and Minangkabau groups for control over the mining and transportation of tin were commonplace, most notably between the Dato Kelana, the chief of Sungei Ujung, and the Dato Bandar, who controlled the middle part of sungei Linggi, further to the south. The heavy influx of Chinese immigrants at this time – who numbered about half the total population of Negeri Sembilan by the time of the first official census in 1891 – only had the effect of prolonging the feuds, since their various secret societies, or triads, attempted to manipulate the situation in order to gain local influence.

The most significant figure to emerge from this period was **Yap Ah Loy**, a charismatic leader who helped orchestrate clan rivalry in a series of violent skirmishes, one of which resulted in the sacking of Sri Menanti. He later moved to the newly established tin-mining town of Kuala Lumpur, where he quickly became an equally influential figure (see p.77). In an attempt to control a situation that was rapidly sliding out of control, the British Governor Jervois installed Abu Bakar of Johor as overlord, a man not only respected by the Malays but who also appeared sympathetic to the colonists' aims. However, two prominent British officials, Frank Swettenham (later Resident at the time of KL's early meteoric expansion) and Frederick Weld, were less than convinced about Abu Bakar's loyalty and bypassed his authority with the use of local British officials. Learning from the mistakes in Perak, where the hurried appointment of a British advisor had caused local uproar, their approach this time was cautious, although eventually a treaty was signed in 1895, which served to narrow the divide between the British government and the Minangkabaus that had been the cause of so much previous strife.

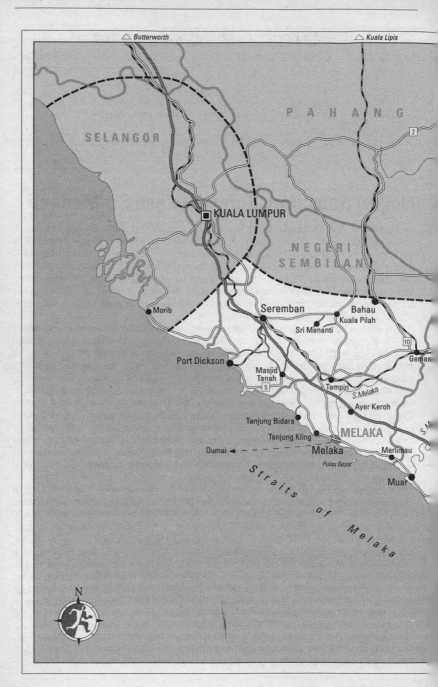

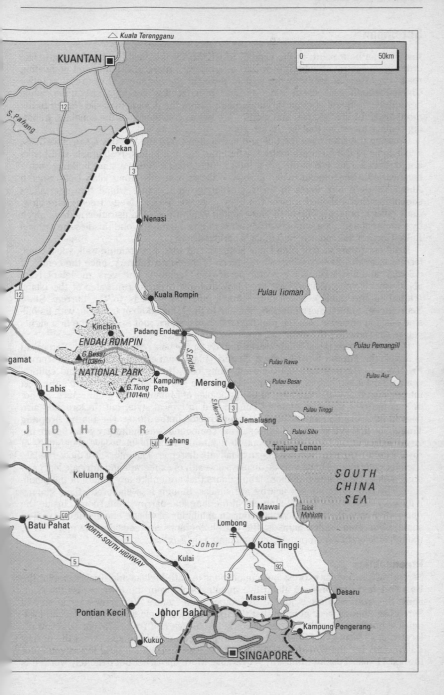

Seremban

Just over an hour south of the capital, **SEREMBAN** is a bustling town, the grid-like order of its central streets thrown into disarray by a maze of twisting and undulating roads over the parklands to the east of town. In the commercial centre, decorative Chinese shophouses nestle side by side with faceless concrete structures, while Seremban's frequent attempts at modernism – from the designer Masjid Negeri to the more tasteful Minangkabau imitations – are not as convincing as the solid and imposing colonial mansions that line its streets.

Crossing the river from the bus and taxi stations, past the **Wesley Church** of 1920, you'll come to the business district, where most of the hotels, restaurants and banks are located. Facing you is the great hulk of the *Oriental Bank*, a stout building with a half-hearted Minangkabau-inspired roof. Walking past this along jalan Dato' Sheikh Ahmad, a right turn leads to the recreation ground, across which the nine pillars supporting the scalloped roof of the grey concrete **Masjid Negeri** come into view. Each pillar represents one of the nine states local of the administration and is topped by a crescent and star, symbols of Muslim enlightenment. Beyond this lies the artifical **Lake Garden**, the focus of Seremban's parkland area.

Head northwards along jalan Dato' Hamzah and after a ten-minute walk you'll come face to face with the sparkling white stucco of the **State Library**, once the centre of colonial administration, its graceful portico and columns the very model of Neo-classicism. If you continue past the black and gilt wrought-iron gates of the Istana (closed to the public), a left turn shortly afterwards leads to the current **State Secretariat**, a much more effective homage to the Minangkabau tradition, with its hillside position ensuring that the multilayered, buffalo-horn roof is one of the first sights you see as you enter the town.

However, all this is just window-dressing. By far the best reason to come to Seremban is to visit the **Taman Seni Budaya Negeri** (10am–6pm except Thurs 8.15am–1pm & Fri 10am–12.15pm & 2.45–6pm; closed Mon; free), the state's museum and cultural centre, 3km northwest of the centre, close to the North–South Highway. It's the best introduction that you could have to the principles of Minangkabau architecture, for not only is the new museum building constructed in typical style, but the grounds also contain three original timber houses, reconstructed in the 1950s. The **Istana Ampang Tinggi**, the first you see as you approach the compound, was built forty years before the larger palace at Sri Menanti (see opposite), passing through successive generations of royalty until 1930, after which it began to fall into disrepair. The interior of the verandah, used for entertaining male guests, displays a wealth of exuberant and intricate leaf carvings, with a pair of heavy timber sliding doors that are unlike any others in the peninsula. The two other houses nearby are similar, though less elaborate, their gloomy interiors relieved only by the shutters in the long and narrow front rooms. Inside the museum proper, the lower floor contains an exhibition of village handicrafts, as well as some moth-eaten stuffed animals; the old photographs are considerably more lively, though little of the accompanying commentary is in English.

Practicalities

Seremban has regular express bus connections to both Melaka and Kuala Lumpur; the **bus and taxi stations** are about five minutes' walk from the town across the river, while the **train station** is just to the south of the centre. You may want to stay in Seremban, though bear in mind that the town has a chronic shortage of decent, inexpensive **hotels**. One of the better places is the *Golden Hill* (☎06/735760; ①), centrally located at 42 jalan Dato' Sheikh Ahmad, with air-con double rooms. Avoid the nearby *Continental*, but the *Oriental* (☎06/730119; ②), easily visible on your left as you enter town at 11 jalan Tuanku Munawir, is bearable. More upmarket but definitely worth it is

ACCOMMODATION

Golden Hill	3
Nam Keow	1
Oriental	2
Tasik	4

0   200m

▽ Port Dickson

the spotless *Nam Keow* (☎06/735578; ①), at 61–62 Jalan Dato' Bandar Tunggal – it's at the very bottom of this price range. If you're after more luxury, there's the *Tasik* (☎06/730994; ⑤), in a great location on jalan Tetamu on the far side of the Lake Gardens, a Minangkabau-style hotel with a swimming pool.

There's no shortage of cafés in town, and although none particularly recommend themselves, the *Bilal* at 100 jalan Dato' Bandar Tunggal serves reliable Indian dishes. There are **food stalls** along jalan Tuanku Munawir and close to the train station.

Sri Menanti

For a town of its size, **SRI MENANTI**, 30km east of Seremban, enjoys a disproportionate importance as the royal capital of Negeri Sembilan, flaunting its palaces – ancient and modern – in a lush, mountainous landscape. Minangkabau architectural tradition reached its apogee in the town's **Istana Lama**, a timber palace set in geometric

THE MINANGKABAUS

The **Minangkabaus** are a racial group whose cultural heartland is in mountainous western central Sumatra (Indonesia) and who established a community in Malaysia in the early fifteenth century. Their **origins** are somewhat sketchy and since they had no written skills until the arrival of Islam, accurate recorded history is negligible. Their own oral accounts trace their ancestry to Alexander the Great, while the *Sejarah Melayu* (Malay Annals) talk of the equally fanciful story of a mysterious leader, Nila Pahlawan, who was pronounced king of the Palembang natives by the spittle of an ox, which had magically turned into a man. Oxen feature prominently, too, in the legend surrounding the origins of the name of the group. Their original home in Sumatra had been under attack from the Javanese, causing the native people to agree to a contest whereby the outcome of a battle fought between a tiger (representing the Javanese) and a buffalo (representing the natives) would determine who controlled the land. Against all the odds, the buffalo killed the tiger, and henceforth the inhabitants called themselves *Minangkabau*, meaning "the victorious buffalo".

In early times the Minangkabaus were ruled in Sumatra by their own overlords or rajas, though political centralization never really rivalled the role of the strongly autonomous *nagari* (Sumatran for "village"). Each *nagari* consisted of numerous **matrilineal clans** (*suku*) who took the name of the mother and lived together in the *adat* house, the ancestral home. The *adat* house was also the corporate body in control of ancestral property which was passed down the maternal line. The *sumando* (husband) stayed in his wife's house at night but was a constituent member of his mother's house, where most of his day was spent. But although the idea that the house and clan name belonged to the woman remained uppermost, it was the *mamak* (mother's brother) who was the administrative figurehead, the authority for the proper distribution of ancestral property, and who took responsibility for the continued prosperity of the lineage. Political and ceremonial power was therefore in the hands of men, while the women were once more relegated to the domestic sphere.

While population growth and land shortage encouraged **migration**, it was the lack of ties to his wife's family and his traditional role as a commercial entrepreneur that facilitated the *sumando*'s wanderlust. Culturally, this was represented as a man's desire to further his fame, fortune and knowledge which, when Islam became more established, saw its realization in religious studies under famous teachers or visits to Mecca. When and why the Minangkabaus initially emigrated to what is now **Negeri Sembilan** in Malaysia is uncertain, but – frequently called upon to supplement the armies of ambitious Malay princes and sultans – their history is closely bound up with that of Melaka and Johor.

Correspondingly little is known of their interaction with the native population, although evidence of intermarriage with the region's predominant tribal group, the Sakai, indicates an acceptance by the Malays of the matrilineal system. What *is* certain is that the Minangkabaus were a political force to be reckoned with. Their dominance in domestic affairs was aided by their reputation for supernatural powers, rumours of which were so widespread that the early eighteenth-century trader Alexander Hamilton noted, "Malays consider the Minangkabau to have the character of great sorcerers, who by their spells can tame wild tigers and make them carry them whither they order on their backs."

Although migration remained standard practice, after the mid-nineteeth century the drift was towards urban centres, and communal living in the *adat* house became relatively rare. This century, two important adaptations to the matrilineal system have been documented: the tendency for families from the various clans to migrate rather than just the husband; and a change in the hereditary customs, whereby individually earned property can be given to a son, becoming ancestral property only in the next generation. However, although certain matrilineal ties have weakened, most aspects of Minangkabau society have remained virtually unchanged – as a Minangkabau proverb says:

The old adat, *ancient heritage,*
Neither rots in the rain,
Nor cracks in the sun.

gardens, which was the seat of the Minangkabau rulers, whose migration to the Malay peninsula began during the fifteenth century, during the early years of the Melaka Sultanate. The sacking of Sri Menanti during the Sungei Ujong tin wars destroyed the original palace – this four-storey version was designed and built in 1902 by two Malay master craftsmen, who used no nails or screws in its construction. The palace was used as a royal residence until 1931, with the first floor functioning as a reception area, the second as family quarters, and the third floor providing the Sultan's private apartments. The tower, used as the treasury and royal archives, can only be reached by ladder from the Sultan's private rooms, thus ensuring a measure of security.

What is special about the structure is the forked projection at the apex of the central tower, known as "open scissors", now seen very rarely, but reproduced in the roof of the Muzium Negara in Kuala Lumpur (see p.91). The whole rectangular building is raised nearly two metres off the ground by 99 pillars, 26 of which have been carved in low-relief with complex foliated designs. The main doors and windows are plain, but a long external verandah is covered with a design of leaves and branches known as *awan larat*, or "driving clouds"; the most elaborate part is above the front porch, where a pair of fantastic creatures with lions' heads, horses' legs and long feathery tails suggest that the craftsmen probably weren't Malay, but Chinese from Melaka.

Unlike Seremban's Istana Ampang Tinggi, the best carving at the Istana Lama is on the outside, the inside being of little or no decorative interest. The palace now houses the lacklustre **Muzium Di Raja** (10am–12.45pm & 2–6pm except Thurs 8am–12.45pm & Fri 10am–12.15pm & 2.45–6pm; closed Mon; free), in which the reconstructions of the state rooms lack atmosphere, although some of the fabric hangings are reminiscent of north Indian patchwork and mirrorwork. Bedecked in yellow, the royal colour, the rooms contain the usual old costumes, ceremonial *krises*, golfing memorabilia and photographs of past Sultans and British administrators, all of which fail to excite.

Reaching Sri Menanti is relatively straightforward, if a little long-winded without your own transport. From Seremban, take a *United* **bus** for the 45-minute journey to Kuala Pilah; then, either wait for an infrequent local bus to Sri Menanti, or take a share taxi, a ten-minute ride costing no more than $1.50 per person. You'll be dropped at a delapidated row of shops, not far from a small mosque, and walking past this you'll spot the Istana Lama. Don't be misled by the sign for the Istana Besar, the rather imposing current royal palace, topped by a startling blue roof.

The coastal route to Melaka

The somewhat dismal coast stretching south of the capital to Melaka is nevertheless a major draw for KL weekenders, who are attracted by the populous resort of **Port Dickson** and who turn a blind eye to its horribly polluted sea. Things improve marginally the further south you go, in the smaller beach satellites of **Tanjung Bidara** and **Tanjung Kling**, though it's unlikely that you'll be detained here too long given the lure of nearby Melaka. Regular bus connections with KL ensure ease of access to all points en route, though the coastal road gets a little tortuous in places – but it's a more varied journey than that offered by the monotonous highway.

Port Dickson

It's hard to see why **PORT DICKSON**, 34km southwest of Seremban, is so popular. The port town-cum-beach resort itself is not much more than a few shops and banks, while Port Dickson's beach, stretching as far as the Cape Richardo lighthouse 16km to the south, is marred by the sight of passing oil tankers, sludgy brown sand, dishwater-grey sea and the enormous sewage pipe spilling out its contents to the north of the bay. Yet it attracts a growing number of regular weekenders, to whom the town is affectionately known as PD, though in truth their patronage probably has more to do with Port Dickson's convenience – halfway between KL and Melaka, and just a couple of hours from either – than for its dubious charms. Whatever the reason, Port Dickson's hoteliers are rubbing their hands with glee and to cope with the increasing demand, new hotels and condominiums are constantly springing up along the length of the coastline – though most developers are sensible enough to have built swimming pools.

Practicalities

It's worth deciding on where you want to stay in advance, since the best places are strung out along the coastal route, jalan Pantai, for several kilometres to the south of Port Dickson, their location marked out in milestones. Buses from KL stop at the bus station in the commercial part of town, but it's easy enough to hop on any Melaka-bound bus until you reach the hotel of your choice; buses from Melaka trawl down the coastal road before reaching the bus station, so you can get off at any time.

The cheapest **accommodation** is at *Asrama Belia* (☎06/472188; ①), affiliated to the *IYHF*, behind a row of shops and restaurants at the six-mile marker, with clean, newly renovated chalets and dorms offering a rather wholesome environment. Close by, the *Regency* (☎06/474090; ⑥) is Port Dickson's most upmarket hotel, built in striking Minangkabau style and featuring watersports and tennis. *Moon Chalets* (☎06/406944; ④) at the seven-mile marker has small but plush chalets, though the area is somewhat shadeless. A little further south, the *Ming Court* (☎06/405244; ⑤) is one of the longest-running resorts, though it doesn't match up to the *Regency*; while another kilometre or so down the coast, the *Kong Ming* (☎06/405683; ②) is about the least expensive in this stretch, basic but bearable.

Most chalets and hotels have their own **restaurants** but there are many others lining the road, of which the nicest is the Muslim *Pantai Ria*, near the seven-mile marker, specializing in seafood. Several **food stalls** offer everything from burgers to freshly caught fish.

Tanjung Bidara

The road south of Port Dickson follows the coast closely for about 20km before heading inland to a junction at the town of Masjid Tanah. The small beachside village of **TANJUNG BIDARA** is a short detour through lush paddy fields off the Port Dickson–Melaka road (Route 5) – take bus #47 from Masjid Tanah – but the beach is much better than that either at Port Dickson or Tanjung Kling (see below). There are two fine **places to stay**: the *Tanjung Bidara Beach Resort* (☎06/542990; ⑤), with pleasant rooms, family chalets and a pool, or the budget-rated *Bidara Beach Lodge* (☎06/543340; ②), a delightful little guest house a little further along.

Tanjung Kling

Rejoining Route 5 and heading south, the road becomes increasingly narrow and winding, though there's plenty to catch your eye in the small towns and *kampungs* en route. Around 18km from the turn-off to Tanjung Bidara, you'll reach the village and beach resort of **TANJUNG KLING** –"kling" now being a derogatory term for the Tamil immigrants who first populated this village. New developments are popping up all around this area, despite the fact that the permanently grey-looking beach and sea are less than inviting, and the community lacks facilities and a focus.

A right turn at the mosque, following the signpost to the *Malacca Club*, brings you to **Makam Hang Tuah**, the grave of the famous fifteenth-century warrior (see feature, p.283). It was formerly known locally only as *Makam Tua* or "Old Grave" in order to conceal its presence from the Portuguese who went about destroying all buildings connected with the Melaka Sultanate on their takeover in 1511. The fact that the newer part of the tomb is built from old Dutch bricks suggests that their colonial successors were more lenient.

Back on the main road, a string of small resorts begins, of which the most appealing is *Shah's Beach Resort* (☎06/511120; ④), whose Art Deco frontage shields intriguingly designed chalets incorporating elements of Portuguese architecture and boasting genuine antique furniture. Good facilities include an open-air *atap*-roofed restaurant, as well as tennis courts and a pool.

Moving on, Route 5 heads southeast through Melaka's suburbs of stylish Peranakan mansions, passing the **Masjid Tranquerah** on the left about 2km out of town, another of the pagoda-like Melakan mosques dating from the eighteenth century, where Sultan Hussein, who ceded Singapore to Stamford Raffles in 1819, is buried.

Melaka and around

Happy is a nation that has no history.
Anon.

It is often said that when Penang was known only for its oysters and Singapore was just a fishing village, **MELAKA** (formerly "Malacca") had already achieved world-wide fame. Under the auspices of the Melaka Sultanate, founded in the early fifteenth century, political and cultural life flourished, helping to shape a definition of what it was to be Malay. Yet beginning in 1511, there followed a series of successive takeovers and botched administrations by the Portuguese, Dutch and British, causing the humiliating subjugation of the Malay people. These turbulent events can be traced throughout the town by the survival of some of the country's oldest buildings – though these have to be viewed against the relative paucity of structures over a hundred years old in the rest of the peninsula. Perhaps because of the perceived value of its cultural legacy, there's something about Melaka that smacks of over-preservation, all too easily apparent in the brick-red paint wash that covers everything in the so-called "historical centre". At its core, the **Dutch Square** sports a fake windmill and nineteenth-century fountain, bordering dangerously on pastiche.

For a more authentic encounter with the past, it's far better to strike out into **Chinatown**, where the rich Baba-Nonya heritage is displayed far less stiflingly in a set of opulent merchants' houses and elegant restaurants that line the narrow thoroughfares. Poignant reminders of the human costs of empire building also remain in the shape of the many Christian churches and their graveyards scattered around the town, where tombstones tell of whole families struck down by fever and of young men killed in battle. The **Portuguese Settlement** to the east of the centre symbolizes something of the decaying colonial heritage that typifies Melaka, while the land reclamation in the new town area, **Taman Melaka Raya**, southeast of the centre, points to the urban regeneration that the city badly requires. Out of the centre, a couple of places of interest take up any extra time you may have: the green-belt area of **Ayer Keroh**, 14km north of the city, and the offshore beach resort of Pulau Besar.

A little history

The foundation of Melaka had its roots in the struggles between Java and the Thai kingdom of Ayutthaya for control of the Malay peninsula in the fourteenth century. The *Sejarah Melayu* (Malay Annals) record that when the Sumatran prince Paramesvara from Palembang, in the Srivijaya empire, could no longer tolerate subservience to Java, he fled to the island of Temasek (later Singapore), where he set himself up as ruler.

The intervention of the Javanese subsequently forced him to flee north to Bertam where he was welcomed by the local community. While his son, Iskandar Shah, was out hunting near modern-day Melaka Hill, a mouse deer turned on the pursuing hunting dogs, driving them into the sea. Taking this courageous act to be a good omen, Shah asked his father to build a new settlement there and in searching for a name for it, he remembered the *melaka* tree, under which he had been sitting.

Melaka rapidly became a cosmopolitan marketplace, boasting reliable storage facilities for goods, mainly spices from the Moluccas in the eastern Indonesian archipelago and textiles from Gujurat in northwest India. Exacting a levy on all imported goods soon helped to make it one of the wealthiest kingdoms in the world. Melaka's meteoric rise was initially assisted by its powerful neighbours, Ayutthaya and Java, who found its trading facilities a boon. But they soon had a serious rival, since Melaka sought to satisfy its own growing needs by **territorial expansion** which, by the reign of its last ruler Sultan Mahmud Shah (1488–1530), included the west coast of the peninsula as far as Perak, the whole of Pahang, Singapore, and most of east coast Sumatra. By the beginning of the sixteenth century, Melaka's population had increased to 100,000, and it would not have been unusual to count as many as 2000 ships in its port. Culturally, too, Melaka was held to be supreme – its sophisticated language, dances and literature were all benchmarks in the Malay world. Equally significant was the establishment of a court structure (see feature on p.285), which defined the nature of the Melaka state and the role of the individuals within it, a philosophy which remained virtually unchanged until the nineteenth century. The linchpin of the state was the ruler, the Sultan, who by virtue of his ancestry which could be traced back to the mighty empire of Srivijaya, embodied the mystique which set Melaka apart from its rivals. With the adoption of **Islam** in the early fifteenth century Melaka consolidated its influence, for it was said that to become a Muslim was to enter the society of Melaka Malays.

But a sea change was occurring in Europe which was to end Melaka's supremacy. The **Portuguese**, in their "Age of Discovery", sought to establish their own links in Asia by dominating key ports in the region and in 1511 Afonso de Albuquerque led the **conquest of Melaka**. Eight hundred officers were left to administer the new colony and although subject to constant attack, the Portuguese – or "white Bengalis" as they were known by the Malays – maintained their hold on Melaka for the next 130 years, introducing Catholicism to the region through the efforts of **St Francis Xavier**, the "Apostle of the East". Little tangible evidence of the Portuguese remains in Melaka today – bar the Eurasian community to the east of town – a reflection of the fairly tenuous nature of their rule, which relied on the internal squabbles of local leaders to dissolve any threats to their position.

The formation of the *Vereenigde Oostindische Compagnie* (VOC), or **Dutch East India Company**, in 1602, spelled the end of the Portuguese. Having already founded Batavia (modern-day Jakarta), the VOC set its sights on Melaka, for the saying was at the time, "Whoever controls Melaka has his hands on the throat of Venice". The ascendancy of Johor (see p.296), an enemy of the Portuguese, gave the Dutch a natural ally, but although they made several attempts on Melaka from 1606 onwards, it wasn't until January 14,1641, after a five-month siege, that they finally captured the city. Where the Portuguese had tried to impose rule on the Malays, the Dutch sought to integrate them in society, finding them useful in matters of etiquette when negotiating with other Malay rulers. Chinese immigrants were drawn to the city in large numbers, often becoming more successful in business than their European rulers; many of the Chinese married Malay women, creating a new racial mix known as **Peranakan** or Baba-Nonya (see p.287). The Protestant Dutch made half-hearted attempts at religious conversion, including translating the Bible into Malay, but on the whole the attitude to the Catholic Melakans was tolerant. However, the settlement never really expanded in the way the VOC had hoped. High taxes drove merchants away to more profitable

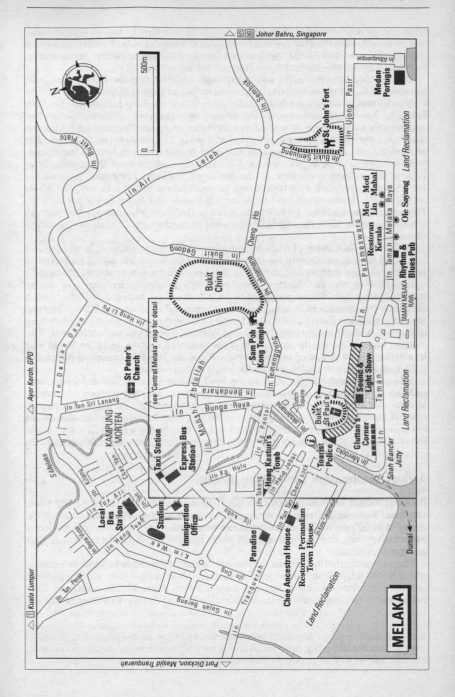

△ 5 50 Johor Bahru, Singapore

Jln Albuquerque

Medan Portugis

Jln Ujong Pasir

St John's Fort

Jln Sembok

Jln Bukit Senuang

Jln Bukit Piatu

Leleh

Jln Air

Cheng Ho

Jln Bukit Gedong

Moti Mahal

Mei Lin

Restoran Kerala

Jln Parameswara

Ole Sayang

Jln Taman Melaka Raya

Rhythm & Blues Pub

TAMAN MELAKA RAYA

Land Reclamation

Bukit China

Jln Laksamana

Jln Hang Li Po

St Peter's Church

Jln Durian Daun

see Central Melaka map for detail

Sam Poh Kong Temple

Jln Temenggong

Jln Munshi Abdullah

Jln Bendahara

Dutch Square

Bukit St Paul's

Sound & Light Show

Jln Taman

Land Reclamation

△ Ayar Keroh, GPO

Jln Tun Sri Lanang

KAMPUNG MORTEN

Jln Bunga Raya

Jln Kg Pantai

Glutton's Corner

Taxi Station

Express Bus Station

Jln Kg Hulu

Hang Kasturi's Tomb

Jln Hang Jebat

Jln Kubu

Tourist Police

Jln Merdeka

Shah Bandar Jetty

△ ☐ Kuala Lumpur

S Melaka

Jln Kilang

Jln Bunga Vista

Jln Hang Tuah

Local Bus Station

Stadium

Immigration Office

Jln Tokong

Jln Hang Tuah

Cheng Lock

Paradise

Chee Ancestral House

Restoran Peranakan Town House

K Jln Wee

Jln Ong

Jln Tranquerah

Jln Galah Berang

Jln Tun Perak

Jln Kota Laksamana

Land Reclamation

Dumai →

MELAKA

▽ Port Dickson, Masjid Tranquerah

500m

0

ports like the newly founded Penang, and the Dutch relied ever more on force to maintain their position in the Straits – which lost them the respect of their Malay subjects. A ditty put about by their British rivals at that time had it that: "In matters of commerce, the fault of the Dutch/ Is offering too little and asking too much".

The superior maritime skills and commercial adroitness of the British East India Company (EIC) provided serious competition for the control of Melaka. Weakened by French threats on their posts in the Indies, the Dutch were not prepared to put up a fight and handed Melaka over to the British on August 15, 1795, initially on the understanding that the EIC was to act as a caretaker administration until such a time as the Dutch were able to resume control. For a while Melaka flew two flags and little seemed to have changed: the language, the legal system and even some of the officials remained the same as before. But the EIC were determined upon the supremacy of Penang and against the advice of the Resident, **William Farquhar**, ordered the destruction of Melaka's magnificent fort to deter future settlers. In fact, the whole population of Melaka would have been forcibly moved to Penang had it not been for Thomas Stamford Raffles, convalescing there at the time, who managed to impress upon the London office the impracticality – not to mention the harshness – of such a measure.

Despite the liberalizing of trade by Farquhar, the colony continued to decline and looked set to disintegrate with the establishment of the free-trade port of Singapore in 1819. British administrators – just thirty in number, rising slowly to around 330 by 1931 – attempted to revitalize Melaka, introducing progressive agricultural and mining concerns; while the Chinese continued to flock to the town, taking over former Dutch mansions. But investment in new hospitals, schools and a railway did little to improve Melaka's spiralling deficit, and it wasn't until a Chinese entrepreneur, Tan Chey Yan, landed on **rubber** as a potential crop that Melaka's problems were alleviated. The industry boomed during the early years of the twentieth century, but after World War I, even that commodity faced mixed fortunes. When the Japanese **occupied Melaka** in 1942, they found a town exhausted by the interwar depression.

Modern-day developments, such as the **land reclamation** in Taman Melaka Raya and the reorganization of the chaotic road network, are still working to reverse Melaka's long-term decline. Yet whatever damage was wrought during its centuries of colonial mismanagement, nothing can take away the enduring influence of Melaka's creation of a Malay language, court system and royal lineage – a powerful legacy established in a mere hundred years that was to change forever the path of development in the peninsula.

Arrival, information and getting around

Both bus stations are located on the northern outskirts of the city, off jalan Hang Tuah. The **local bus station** operates services to most destinations within the conurbation, as well as to Singapore. The chaotic **express bus station** is beyond the **taxi station**, a block to the south, in a tiny square by the river. From either, it's just a ten-minute walk into the town centre.

Many people arrive by **ferry** on the three-hour daily service from Dumai in Sumatra, which docks at the Shah Bandar jetty on jalan Merdeka, within easy walking distance of both the historical centre and the budget hostel area. Melaka's **airport**, Batu Berendam, is 9km north of the city and handles *Pelangi Air* services from Singapore,

The telephone code for Melaka is ☎06. Note that all Malaysian telephone numbers are being **changed** in a rolling programme lasting several years. Some of the numbers given in this chapter, while correct at the time of going to press, are likely to have changed.

Ipoh and Pekan Baru in Sumatra. Buses from the airport into the centre are irregular, so it's best to take a taxi, which costs around $10. There's no **train station** in Melaka itself, the nearest being at Tampin, 38km away; buses from Tampin drop you at the local bus station.

The **Tourist Information Centre** is on jalan Kota (8.45am–5pm except Fri 8.45am–12.15pm & 2.45–5pm & Sun 9am–5pm; ☎236538), 400m from the Shah Bandar jetty, and is reasonably helpful; the information board outside displays the times of the river trips to Kampung Morten (see p.288).

City transport

Most of the places of interest are located within the square kilometre that forms the town's nucleus, the historical centre, and are best visited **on foot**. The area around Padang Pahlawan is the only concession to pedestrianization, however, and even this is partially blocked by the entrance to the Istana and its gardens.

For longer journeys, **taxis or trishaws** are the best bet, both costing roughly the same (though trishaw drivers are more difficult to negotiate with) – from the bus station to the centre costs around $4. A sightseeing tour by trishaw, covering all the major sights including Medan Portugis, costs from $15 per hour for two people – though you'll have to have nerves of steel to stand weaving between the snarling traffic; you should find a trishaw around the Dutch Square. Taxis are quite hard to find on the street, but you can always get one from the taxi station.

The **town bus service** has several useful routes for visitors: #17 or #25 runs to Taman Melaka Raya and Medan Portugis, and #19 out to Ayer Keroh; fares run from 50 *sen* to $1.20 per journey and buses depart from the local bus station in the first instance. **Drivers** should park their cars at the first possible opportunity and get around the city by bus, trishaw or taxi: the streets are hair-raisingly tight and the one-way system is liable to lead you away from the very sights you want to reach. **Car rental** outlets are given in "Listings" on p.291.

LEAVING MELAKA

Airport
Batu Berendam Airport is 9km from the city centre, and caters only for small aircraft. *Pelangi Air* runs a service to both Singapore ($110) and Ipoh ($100) on Monday, Wednesday and Saturday, and there's a Friday flight to Pekan Baru in Sumatra ($145). For flight information call ☎222648, and for tickets contact *MAS*, on the first floor of the *City Bayview Hotel*, jalan Bendahara (☎235722).

Buses
Melaka is well serviced by buses to all points on the peninsula. There are frequent departures from the express bus station to KL, Ipoh, Butterworth and Alor Setar, while most express services to Singapore leave from the local bus station. There's rarely any need to book in advance; just turn up before departure and buy a ticket from one of the booths in the bus station.

Ferries
Two companies combine to offer a daily service to Dumai in Sumatra (3hr; $80): *Madai Shipping* at 321a jalan Tun Ali (☎240671), near the bus station, and *Tunas Rupat* at 17a jalan Merdeka (☎232506).

Trains
The nearest train station is in Tampin (☎411034), 38km north of the city, although Melaka itself has a ticket-booking office on Taman Pringgit Jaya (☎223091). There are regular buses to Tampin from the local bus station.

Accommodation

Melaka has a huge selection of **hotels**, although prices are a little higher than in other Malaysian towns. Most in the lower price bracket are, needless to say, located in the noisiest areas, around the bus stations or main shopping streets. In the Taman Melaka Raya area there's a rapidly growing number of budget **hostels**, all offering broadly the same facilities; touts often wait at the local bus station to show you photographs of their place, which can save you time wandering around places that are already full. Town bus #17 from the local bus station takes you there, or a taxi or rickshaw costs around $5. All the hotels and hostels below are marked on the central Melaka map.

Central, 31–41 jalan Bendahara (☎222984). One of the cheapest in town, this typical run-down Chinese hotel is nevertheless clean and friendly, and well soundproofed. ①.

Chong Hoe, 26 jalan Tokong Emas. One of the few hotels in Chinatown offering standard and air-con rooms, but in a noisy location opposite the mosque. Arranges tours to outlying districts. ①.

Grand Continental, 20 jalan Tun Sri Lanang (☎240048). Standard hotel that is very reasonably priced, its facilities including a pool and coffee house. ⑤.

Majestic, 188 jalan Bunga Raya (☎222367). A colonial hotel that is fading away, with musty air-con rooms, antediluvian bathrooms and Raj-like service in the bar and breakfast-restaurant. ③.

Malacca, 27a jalan Munshi Abdullah (☎222252). A noisy, basic hotel close to the bus station, which benefits from being housed in an elegant old building. ②.

Malacca Renaissance, jalan Bendahara (☎248888). The town's top residence, with an imposing lobby complete with huge chandeliers, matched by elegant, well-furnished rooms. ⑥.

May Chiang, 59 jalan Munshi Abdullah (☎222101). Modest hotel with small but very clean rooms that are a delight; the double glazing helps, too. Well worth the money. ③.

Paradise, 4 jalan Tengkera (☎230821). Just west of Chinatown, this has large rooms, some air-con, and dorms. Facilities including an air-con TV lounge, games room, kitchen and an aquarium. ①.

Robin's Nest, 246b Taman Melaka Raya (☎229142). Friendly, family-run hostel, with small rooms but two pleasant lounges: video, hot showers and communal meals. ①.

SD Rest House, 258b Taman Melaka Raya (☎247080). This comfortable, upmarket guest house has well-furnished, mostly air-con rooms and hot water. The family room can double as a dorm. ②.

Shirah's Guest House, 229b Taman Melaka Raya (no phone). Ten rooms, the front ones with a balcony; it has 24-hour check-in, hot showers, video and dartboard and a mini batik workshop. ①.

Sunny's Inn, 253b Taman Melaka Raya (☎237990). A clean and homely place with hot showers, offering car as well as bicycle and motorbike rental. ①.

Traveller's Lodge, 214 Taman Melaka Raya (no phone). Small and well-kept hostel, with a floor-cushioned lounge and breezy roof garden. ①.

The city

The centre of Melaka is deftly split in two by the murky brown **sungei Melaka**, the western bank of which is occupied by **Chinatown** and, 700m to the north, **Kampung Morten**, a small collection of stilted houses. On the eastern side of the river lies what could be termed the colonial core – the main area of interest – with **Bukit St Paul** at its centre, encircled by jalan Kota. Southeast of here is a section of reclaimed land known as **Taman Melaka Raya**, a new town that is home to most of the budget hotels, restaurants and bars.

There are a few sights further east of the centre, and an exploration of **Medan Portugis** (Portuguese Square), **St John's Fort** and **Bukit China**, the Chinese community's ancestral burial ground, neatly encompasses two of the most important ethnic communities, together with some important elements of Melaka's history in the process. They're all a little too far flung to be comfortably covered on foot – Medan Portugis is 3km from the centre – but town buses #17 or #25 run regularly to Medan Portugis, from which St John's Fort is only about a kilometre's walk. Take a taxi or trishaw from there to Bukit China (around $6), and you'll have spent the best part of half a day.

It's a pity that the authorities felt the need to drown Melaka's central buildings in a uniform brick-red paint, proudly baptizing each afflicted monument "historical". Intended to symbolize the red laterite from which many of Melaka's original structures were built, this actually destroys part of the individual character of each landmark by smoothing out its careworn edges under a false veneer. That said, it has at least meant that the buildings have been maintained and a tour of them is essential for anyone bent on discovering more about the development of Malay culture. At a push you could get

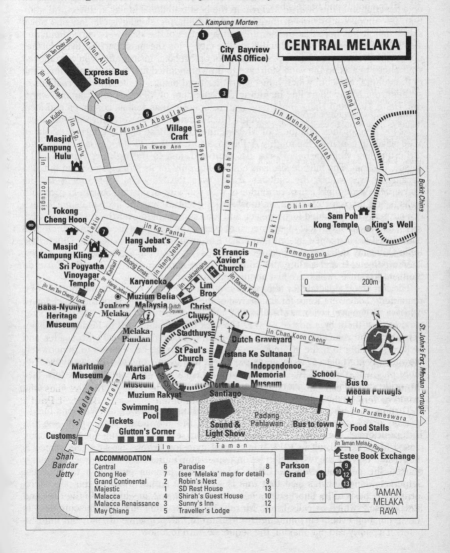

CENTRAL MELAKA

ACCOMMODATION			
Central	6	Paradise	8
Chong Hoe	7	(see 'Melaka' map for detail)	
Grand Continental	2	Robin's Nest	9
Majestic	1	SD Rest House	13
Malacca	4	Shirah's Guest House	10
Malacca Renaissance	3	Sunny's Inn	12
May Chiang	5	Traveller's Lodge	11

around the colonial core in a day; to take things at a more leisurely pace, and see Chinatown and the outskirts, it's probably better to spend the best part of three days in Melaka. Many visitors find that it's a city that grows on them the longer they stay.

The Istana and around

The **Istana ke Sultanan** (daily 9am–6pm, closed Fri 12.15pm–2.45; $1.50) on jalan Kota is not only in the geographical centre of town but stands at the very centre of Malaysian history. This dark timber royal palace, set imposingly in neatly manicured gardens, is a contemporary reconstruction of the original fifteenth-century *istana* based on a description in the *Sejarah Melayu*. In the best traditional Malay architectural tradition, its complex structure of multilayered and sharply sloping roofs contains not a single nail. It was here that the administrative duties of the state were carried out, and also where the Sultan resided when in the city – for the most part he lived further upriver at Bertam, safe from possible attacks on Melaka. Inside, after you've removed your shoes to ascend the wide staircase to the verandahed first floor, spend some time in the cultural museum which houses a rather tired display of life-sized re-creations of scenes from Malay court life, including the epic duel of Melaka's most famous warriors, Hang Tuah and Hang Jebat (see feature opposite), as well as costumes and local crafts. When all is said and done, though, the building alone is worth the entrance fee.

At the time of their conquest of Melaka, the Portuguese used the forced labour of 1500 slaves to construct the mighty **A Famosa** fort; all that is left today is a single gate, the crumbling whitewashed **Porta de Santiago**, just to the right as you leave the palace museum. The hillside site was chosen not only for its strategic position but also because it was where the Sultan's *istana* was located – its replacement by the Portuguese stronghold a firm reminder of who was now in charge. Square in plan with walls nearly three metres thick, its most striking feature was the keep in its northwestern corner, which loomed forty metres and four storeys high over the rest of the garrison. This was no mean feat of engineering, even if the design of the fort as a whole was considered old-fashioned by contemporary European observers. When the Dutch East India Company defeated the Portuguese in 1641, it used the fort as its headquarters, later modifying it and adding the company crest and the date 1670 to the Porta de Santiago – features which are just about distinguishable today.

The fort stood steadfast for 296 years and no doubt there would be much more of it remaining today were it not for the arrival of the British in 1795. With their decision to relocate to Penang, orders were given in 1807 to destroy the fort in case it was later used against them by a hostile power. The task of demolition fell to Resident William Farquhar, who reluctantly set about with gangs of labourers armed with spades and pickaxes. Failing to make an impression on its solid bulk, he resorted to gunpowder, blowing sky-high pieces "as large as elephants and even some as large as houses". A more poignant epitaph is that of Sultan Munshi Abdullah who noted that the fort "was the pride of Melaka and after its destruction the place lost its glory, like a woman bereaved of her husband, the lustre gone from her face".

Turning your back on the gate, and facing **Padang Pahlawan**, or "Warrior's Field", a large open green that forms the centre of the downtown area, you'll see the **Independence Memorial Museum** (9am–6pm except Fri 9am–noon & 3–6pm; closed Mon; free). Built in 1912, this elegant mansion, whose classic white stucco is moderated only by the two golden onion domes atop either side of its portico, formerly housed the colonial **Malacca Club**, whose most famous guest was the novelist Somerset Maugham. It's said that this is where the author was told the tale which formed the basis of his short story *Footprints in the Jungle*, in which both the *Club* and Melaka itself (which he calls Tanah Merah) feature prominently. The museum depicts the fascinating events surrounding the lead up to independence in 1957, but unfortunately it's poorly laid out, making the sequence hard to follow.

A CLASSIC CONFRONTATION

If any ruler puts a single one of his subjects to shame, that shall be a sign that his kingdom will be destroyed by Almighty God. Similarly it has been granted by Almighty God to Malay subjects that they shall never be disloyal or treacherous to their rulers, even if their rulers behave evilly or inflict injustice on them.

From the *Sejarah Melayu*

The tale of the duel between **Hang Tuah** and **Hang Jebat**, recounted in the *Hikayat Hang Tuah*, a seventeenth-century epic, stands as a symbol of the conflict between absolute loyalty to the sovereign and the love of a friend. These two characters, together with Hang Kasturi, Hang Lekir and Hang Lekiu, formed a band known as "The Five Companions", because of their close relationship since birth, and were highly trained in the martial arts. When they happened to save the life of the Bendahara Paduka Raja, the highest official in the Malay court, Sultan Mansur Shah was so impressed by their skill that he appointed them as court attendants. Hang Tuah rapidly became the Sultan's favourite and was duly honoured with a beautiful *kris*, **Taming Sari**, which was said to have supernatural powers. This overt favouritism rankled with other long-serving officials who, in the absence from court of the rest of the companions, conspired to cast a slur on Hang Tuah's reputation by spreading the rumour that he had seduced one of the Sultan's consorts. On hearing the accusation, the Sultan was so enraged that he ordered the immediate execution of Hang Tuah. But the Bendahara, knowing the charge to be false, took it upon himself to hide Hang Tuah as a chance to repay his debt to him, reporting back to the Sultan that the deed had been carried out.

When Hang Jebat returned to the palace, he was shocked to discover Hang Tuah's supposed death and rampaged through Melaka, killing everyone in sight as retribution for the life of his treasured friend. The Sultan, in fear of his own life, soon began to regret his decision, at which point the Bendahara revealed the truth and Hang Tuah was brought back to protect the Sultan from Hang Jebat's fury and to exact justice for the murders committed. Hang Tuah wrestled hard with his conscience before deciding that the Sultan had the absolute right to dispose of his subjects how he wished. So, with a heavy heart, Hang Tuah drew his *kris* against Hang Jebat and, after a protracted fight, killed him – a much-recounted episode whose moral was considered to set the seal on the Malay system of government.

Bukit St Paul

Walking back through the Porta de Santiago, either climb the steps behind, past the trinket and painting sellers, up to **Bukit St Paul**, or skirt round the base of the hill to the left along jalan Kota, where Melaka's newest museums are situated. The **Muzium Rakyat**, or People's Museum (daily 9am–6pm, closed Fri 12.15pm–2.45; $1) is the first, showing the development and successes of Melaka during the last decade – fine if you're into housing policy and the structure of local government – while the **Islamic and Martial Arts Museum**, housed in a superbly renovated Dutch house, is still in the throes of establishment. In between these two, a steep set of steps is the alternative route up to St Paul's Church on the summit of Bukit St Paul.

The ghostly shell of **St Paul's Church** – roofless, desolate and smothered in ferns – has been a ruin for almost as long as it was a functioning church. Constructed in 1521 by the Portuguese, who named it "Our Lady of the Mount", the church was visited by the Jesuit missionary **St Francis Xavier** between 1545 and 1552, and on his death in 1553 his body was brought here for burial – a brass plaque on the south wall of the chancel marks the spot where he was laid. A grisly story surrounds the exhumation of the saint's body in 1554 – allegedly showing very few signs of decay after nine months of burial – for its transferral to its final resting place in Goa in India. In response to a request for canonization, the Vatican demanded the right arm from the body which, when severed, appeared to drip blood. Even more macabre is the tale of the marble statue of St Francis that has stood in front of the church since 1952. On the morning following its consecration ceremony in 1953, a large casuarina tree was found to have fallen on the statue, severing the right arm.

The Dutch Calvinists changed the denomination of the church when they took over in 1641, renaming it St Paul's Church, and it remained in use for a further 112 years until the construction of Christ Church at the foot of the hill (see below). The British found St Paul's far more useful for military than religious purposes, storing their gunpowder here during successive wars, and also finding occasion to build the light-house that still guards the church's entrance. The tombstones that lie against the interior walls, together with those further down the hill in the **graveyard** itself, are an interesting catalogue of the times. As the only major port in the Straits, many visitors were buried here, including Bishop Peter of Japan, who was a missionary in Melaka in 1598; as well as large numbers of Portuguese, Dutch and British notables, whose epitaphs have long been obscured by lichen. Note the tomb of the Velge family, in the graveyard on the slopes below, five members of which died within twenty days of each other during the diphtheria epidemic of 1756.

The Dutch Square and around

A winding path beside St Paul's Church brings you down into the so-called **Dutch Square**, one of the oldest surviving parts of Melaka, although two of its main features date from much later times. The central fountain is an ornate Victorian marble addition, erected in 1904 to commemorate Queen Victoria's Diamond Jubilee, while the baldly unimaginative clock tower was constructed in 1886 in honour of Tan Beng Swee, a rich Chinese merchant.

Presiding over the entire south side of the square is the sturdy **Stadthuys**, now housing the **Museum of Ethnography** (daily 9am–6pm, closed Fri 12.15pm–2.45; $2). The simple, robust structure – more accurately a collection of buildings built between 1660 and 1700 – was used as a town hall throughout the whole period of Dutch and British administration. Although the long wing of warehouses projecting to the east is the oldest of the buildings here, recent renovations revealed remains of a Portuguese well and drainage system, suggesting that this was not the first development on this site. The wide, monumental, interior staircases, together with the high windows that run the length of the Stadthuys, are typical of seventeenth-century Dutch municipal buildings, though are rather less suited to the tropical climate than they are to European winters. Look out of the back windows onto the whitewashed, mould-encrusted houses that line the courtyard and you could be viewing a scene from any of Vermeer or De Hooch's masterpieces. The museum itself displays an array of Malay and Chinese ceramics and weaponry; the reconstruction of a seventeenth-century Dutch dining room is an exception. The rooms upstairs are filled with endless paintings giving a blow-by-blow account of Melakan history, although it becomes more absorbing in the later part of the exhibition, when old photographs of the town show just how little it has changed over the last hundred years.

Turn to the right as you leave the Stadthuys and you can't miss **Christ Church** (daily except Wed 9am–5pm; free), also facing the fountain. Built in 1753 to commemorate the centenary of the Dutch occupation of Melaka, its simple design, with neither aisles nor chancel, is again typically Dutch; the porch and vestry were nineteenth-century afterthoughts. A cool, whitewashed interior is relieved only by decorative fanlights high up on the walls, while the most significant features are the heavy timber ceiling beams, each cut from a single tree, and the elaborate, two-hundred-year-old hand-carved pews. The plaques on the walls tell a sorry tale of early deaths by epidemics – the Westerhouts feature prominently here – while more contemporary losses are recorded on a wooden plaque to the rear of the western wall of the church, including local planters who were drafted in World War II. A small detour down the lane on the left of the church, forking right at the old Courthouse to skirt round the foot of Bukit St Paul, leads to the overgrown remains of the **Dutch Graveyard**. This was first used in the late-seventeenth century, when the VOC was still in control, hence the name, though British graves easily outnumber those of their predecessors. The tall column towards the centre of the tiny cemetery is a memorial to two of the many officers killed in the Naning War in 1831, a rather costly attempt to include the region as part of Melaka's territory under the new Straits Settlements.

North to St Peter's Church

Back at Christ Church, moving quickly past the **Muzium Belia Malaysia** (daily 9am–6pm, closed Fri 12.30pm–2.45; free) – replete with pictures of smiling, wholesome youths shaking hands with Dr Mahathir – head north along jalan Laksamana towards **St Francis Xavier's Church**, a twin-towered nineteenth-century neo-Gothic structure. Further up from here, skirting the busy junction with jalan Temenggong and taking

MALAY COURT STRUCTURE

One of the most outstanding achievements of the Melaka Sultanate was to create a **court structure** setting a pattern of government that was to last for the next five hundred years, and whose prominent figures are still reflected in the street names of most towns in the country.

At the top of the tree was the **Sultan**, who – at least in legend – could trace his ancestry back to the revered leaders of Srivijaya. Far from being an autocratic tyrant, a form of social contract evolved whereby the ruler could expect undying loyalty from his subjects in return for a fair and wise dispensation of justice – the crux of the confrontation between Hang Juah and Hang Tebat (see feature on p.283). Sultans were not remote ceremonial figures: many supervised the planting of new crops, for instance, or wandered freely in the streets among the people, a style that may explain the relative humility of the palaces they occupied.

Below the ruler was a clutch of **ministers**, administrators with well-defined tasks who undertook the day-to-day matters of government. The most important of these was the **Bendahara**, who dealt with disputes both among traders and the Malays themselves. In effect, he was the public face of the regime, wielding a great deal of power, backed by his closest subordinate, the **Penghulu Bendahari**, who supervised the *Syahbandars* (harbourmasters) and the Sultan's domestic staff. Training for a potential Bendahara could be gained in the office of **Temenggung**, who was responsible for law and order, working in close partnership with the **Laksamana**, the military commander whose strongest arm was the navy.

Wide-ranging consultation regarding new measures took place in a **council of nobles**, who had earned their titles either through land ownership or from blood ties with royalty. However, given the consensual nature of politics between men of rank and power, it became necessary to emphasize the position of the ruler by indications of their separateness. The colour yellow was only allowed to be used by royalty and no one but the ruler could wear gold – unless it was a royal gift. In addition, commoners could not have pillars or enclosed verandahs in their houses or windows and reception rooms in their boats. Nevertheless, despite these methods of distinction, threats to the throne were commonplace – particularly from the Bendahara. Although little is known of the **common people** of Melaka, it is certain that they had no part in the decision-making process; though the *Sejarah Melayu* nevertheless speaks of them in glowing terms: "Subjects are like roots and the ruler is like the tree; without roots the tree cannot stand upright."

jalan Bendahara directly ahead, you're in the centre of Melaka's tumbledown **Little India**, a rather desultory line of incense and *saree* shops, interspersed with a few eating houses. After about five minutes' walk, you'll come to a sizeable crossroads with jalan Munshi Abdullah, beyond which is **St Peter's Church** set back from the road on the right. The oldest Roman Catholic church in Malaysia, it was built in 1710 by a Dutch convert as a gift to the Portuguese Catholics, and although ostensibly Romanesque in appearance, the interior of the church, with its barrel-vaulted ceiling and Gothic side walls, is very unusual – indicating a considerable amount of restructuring over the years. The church really comes into its own at Easter as the centre of the Catholic community's celebrations.

The river and docks

If you feel like a rest from pavement pounding, take a **boat trip** up sungei Melaka, leaving from the small jetty behind the Tourist Information Centre (hourly until 2pm; $6) – buy your tickets at the office, or on the boat itself. The 45-minute trip takes you past "Little Amsterdam", the old Dutch quarter of red-roofed *godowns*, which back directly onto the water. Look out for the slothful monitor lizards that hang out on either side of the bank, soaking up the sun, and the local fisherman who line the route, mending boats and nets. The boat turns round without stopping at Kampung Morten (see p.288), opposite which, on the right bank, you can just make out a few columns and a crumbling aisle poking out from beneath the undergrowth, all that remains of the late-sixteenth-century Portuguese church of St Lawrence.

On the return journey, you're taken beyond the jetty to the **docks**, crowded with low-slung Sumatran boats, heavy wooden craft that are still sailed without the aid of a compass or charts, bringing in charcoal and timber which they trade for rice. From here, you can also see the new **Maritime Museum**, on the quayside off jalan Merdeka, incomplete at the time of writing, housed in a towering replica of the Portuguese cargo ship, *The Barinel*, which sank in Melaka's harbour in the sixteenth century. The best time to catch the activity at the docks is around 4.30pm, when the multicoloured fishing boats leave for the night's work.

Chinatown

Melaka owed a great deal of its nineteenth-century economic recovery to its Chinese community: Tan Chey Yan first planted rubber here, and one Tan Kim Seng established an early steamer company, which later became the basis of the great *Straits Steam Ship Company*, providing regular communication between different parts of the colony. Most of these early entrepreneurs settled in what became known as **Chinatown**, across sungei Melaka from the colonial district, where they spent lavishly. Turn left after the bridge by the Tourist Information Centre, then first right to follow the one-way system and you'll see plenty of evidence for this in **jalan Tun Tan Cheng Lock**, fondly known as "Millionaires Row". Strictly speaking, the elegant townhouses that line the narrow road are the ancestral homes of the **Baba-Nonya** community (see feature on next page), descendants of the original Chinese pioneers who married local Malay women – it is said that Chinese women of high class were reluctant to emigrate. The wealthiest and most successful built long, narrow-fronted houses, a ploy to minimize the "window tax" by the incorporation of several internal courtyards, also designed for ventilation and the collection of rainwater.

At no. 48–50, the **Baba-Nyonya Heritage Museum** (daily 10am–12.30pm & 2-4.30pm; $7), actually an amalgam of three adjacent houses, is an excellent example of the Chinese Palladian style, and the informative 45-minute tour is a good introduction to the genre. Typically connected by a common covered footway, decorated with hand-painted tiles, each front entrance has an outer swing door of elaborately carved teak,

THE BABA-NONYAS

Tales of Melaka's burgeoning success brought vast numbers of merchants and entrepreneurs to its shores, eager to benefit from the city's status and wealth. The Chinese, in particular, came to the Malay peninsula in droves, anxious to escape Manchu rule – a trend that began in the sixteenth century, but continued well into the nineteenth – and many intermarried with local Malay women; descendents of these marriages were known as **Peranakan** or "Straits-born Chinese". While their European counterparts were content to while away their time until retirement, when they had the option of returning home, the expatriate Chinese merchants had no such option and so became the prinicpal wealth-generators of the thriving city. The **Babas** (male Sino-Malays) were unashamed of flaunting their new-found prosperity in the lavish townhouses which they appropriated from the Dutch and transformed into veritable palaces. They filled their houses with Italian marble, mother-of-pearl inlay blackwood furniture displaying strong Victorian and Dutch influences, hand-painted tiles and Victorian lamps. The women, known as **Nonyas** (commonly spelt Nyonya), held sway in the domestic realm and were responsible for Peranakan society's most memorable legacy – the **cuisine**. Taking the best of both Malay and Chinese traditions, dishes rely heavily on sour sauces and coconut milk; the social etiquette of eating, however, is Malay – using fingers, not chopsticks.

while a heavier internal door provides extra security at night. Two red lanterns, one bearing the household name, the other messages of good luck, hang either side of the doorway, framed by heavy Greco-Roman columns. But it is the upper level of the building that is the most eye-catching: a short canopy of Chinese tiles over the porch frames the shuttered windows, almost Venetian in character, whose glass is protected by intricate wrought-iron grilles, while the eaves and fascias are covered with painted, floral designs. Inside, the homes are filled with gold-leaf fittings, blackwood furniture inlaid with mother-of-pearl, delicately carved lacquer screens and Victorian chandeliers.

Further up the road, at no. 107, the **Restoran Peranakan Town House** is another former mansion that is now a restaurant specializing in Nonya cuisine (see "Eating", p.290). Beyond, at no. 117, you can't fail to notice the **Chee Ancestral House**, an imperious Dutch building of white stucco topped by a silver dome, and home to one of Melaka's wealthiest families, who made their fortune from tapioca and rubber.

The parallel **jalan Hang Jebat** – formerly named "Jonkers Street" or "Junk Street" – is Melaka's **antiques** centre (see "Shopping", p.301) and it's worth a wander even if you don't intend to buy. Shortly on the left after you enter the street, crammed in between the Chinese temples and the shophouses, is the small, whitewashed tomb of **Hang Kasturi**, one of the "Five Companions" (see feature on p.283). Turning into jalan Hang Lekiu (still signposted as Fourth Cross Street), and then into jalan Tokong Emas, puts you outside the **Masjid Kampung Kling**, dating back to 1748, and displaying an unusual combination of styles. The minaret is more of a pagoda; English and Portuguese glazed tiles adorn the building; while a Victorian chandelier in the prayer hall hangs down over Corinthian columns and a pulpit carved with both Hindu and Chinese designs. The Hindu **Sri Pogyatha Vinoyagar Temple** next door is comparatively disappointing; its run-down and gloomy inner sanctum contains the elephant-headed deity, Ganesh, and its exterior is a faded and peeling Brahmin blue.

The nearby **Tokong Cheng Hoon**, the "Merciful Cloud Temple", back over the junction with jalan Hang Lekiu, is reputed to be the oldest Chinese temple in the country – though there are several others that would dispute the title. Dedicated to the Goddess of Mercy, the main prayer hall's heavy saddled roof and oppressive dark timber beams are reminiscent of its counterpart in Georgetown. The temple authorities act as the trustees for Bukit China, the ancestral burial ground to the northeast of town, still the centre of an ongoing controversy (see "Bukit China" below) – newspaper clippings detailing the story are displayed prominently in the temple. Smaller chambers devoted to ancestor worship are filled with small tablets bearing a photograph of the deceased, strewn amongst which are wads of fake money and papier-mâché models of luxury items, symbolizing creature comforts for the dead.

From the temple, a right turn into jalan Portugis and then taking the second right brings you to **Masjid Kampung Hulu**, thought to be the oldest mosque in Malaysia. Constructed around 1728 in typical Melakan style, it's a solid-looking structure, surmounted by a bell-shaped roof, covered with green Chinese tiles and, again, with more than a hint of pagoda in its minaret. Such architecture has its origins in Sumatra, perhaps brought over by the Minangkabaus (see p.272) who settled in nearby Negeri Sembilan.

An alternative route back to the centre of town is to walk to the end of the road containing the mosque, turning right into jalan Kampung Hulu as it follows the river and merges into jalan Kampung Pantai. At the junction with jalan Hang Kasturi, a couple of minutes further on, you can pause for a moment at **Hang Jebat's Tomb**, another tiny mausoleum to one of the great warriors of the Golden Age.

Kampung Morten

The village of **KAMPUNG MORTEN**, named after the British District Officer who donated $10,000 to buy the land, is a surprising find in the heart of the city. It's easiest to explore this community on foot: take the footbridge down a small path off jalan Bunga Raya, one of the principal roads leading north out of town. The wooden stilted houses here are distinctively Melakan in style, with their long, rectangular living rooms and kitchens, and narrow verandahs approached by ornamental steps. On the left as you cross the footbridge the **Villa Sentosa** (daily 9am–5pm; voluntary donations), with its *kampung* doll's house and mini lighthouse, acts as a beacon for disorientated visitors. The warm and welcoming family will gladly show you artefacts and heirlooms handed down by the old patriarch, Tuan Haji Hashim Hadi Abdul Ghani, who died recently at the age of 98 – much to the relief of the Civil Service, who were still paying his pension.

Medan Portugis and St John's Fort

The road east of Taman Melaka Raya leads, after about 3km, to Melaka's Portuguese Settlement; turn right into jalan Albuquerque, clearly signposted off the main road, and you enter its heart. The government was prompted by the depletion of the community's numbers – barely any higher than the two thousand recorded in the first census in 1871 – and increasing levels of poverty, to establish this village in 1933 on the historic site of their original community. Today you're likely to recognize the descendants of the original Portuguese settlers only by hearing their *patois*, a unique blend of Malay and old Portuguese, or seeing their surnames – Fernandez, Rodriguez and Dominguez all feature as street names.

Although there's no longer anything in the domestic architecture to indicate the heritage of the inhabitants, the **Medan Portugis** (Portuguese Square), at the end of the road, is European to the hilt, and you could be forgiven for thinking that its white-washed edifice, gently eroded by the salty winds, was a remnant from Alberquerque's time. Progressing through the archway, the souvenir shop and tourist-oriented restaurants surrounding the central courtyard soon make it clear that this is a purpose-built "relic", dating only from 1985. Having said that, the square is a good place for a quiet beer at sunset, cooled by the sea breeze, and on Saturday nights the place is transformed into a Portuguese fiesta, with tables covering every inch of the open-air arena (see "Nightlife and entertainment"; 290). To get here, pick up bus #17 or #25 from jalan Parameswara, just outside Taman Melaka Raya.

Heading back into town, make a brief detour to **St John's Fort** by turning left at the traffic lights about 500m after the settlement. Just before the next roundabout, a right turn, followed by another up an easily missable track, brings you to the base of the hill, a popular jogging spot for Melaka's fitness fanatics. The fort itself, a relic of the Dutch occupation and somewhat dwarfed by the adjacent water tower, isn't terribly exciting, but it offers panoramic views over the Straits and the town.

Bukit China

Bukit China, the ancestral burial ground of the town's Chinese community, is the oldest and largest outside China itself. Although Chinese contacts with the Malay peninsula probably began in the first century BC, it wasn't until the Ming Emperor Yung-Lo sent his envoy Admiral Cheng Ho in 1409 that commercial relations with Melaka were formally established, according the burgeoning settlement with vassal status. The **temple** at the foot of the hill is dedicated to Cheng Ho, upon whom was conferred the title of "Sam Poh" or "Three Jewels" in 1431. Contemporary accounts are vague about the arrival of the first Chinese settlers, though the *Sejarah Melayu* recounts that in the marriage of Sultan Mansur Shah (1446–59) to the daughter of the Emperor, Princess Hang Liu, the five hundred nobles accompanying her stayed to set up home on Bukit China. It was supposedly these early pioneers who dug the well behind the temple; also known as the **King's Well**, it has been of such importance to the local inhabitants as a source of fresh water that successive invading armies all sought to poison the well, leading the Dutch to enclose it with a protecting wall, the ruins of which still remain.

Climb the steep incline to the top of Bukit China, across which horseshoe-shaped graves stretch as far as the eye can see. On the way up, you'll pass the oldest grave in the cemetery, belonging to Tin Kap – the first Chinese *kapitan*, a mediatory position created by the VOC which made it possible for them to rule the various ethnic communities. He was succeeded by Captain Li, whose grave on the other side of the cemetery is the subject of local myth. A fortune teller, asked to advise on the location and construction of the grave, prophesied that if it were to be dug three feet deep, Li's son would benefit, but any deeper and all profit would go to his son-in-law. Whether by accident or design, the grave was made three and a half feet deep, and the son-in-law, Chan Lak Koa, went on to found the elaborate Cheng Hoon Teng temple as an expression of gratitude for his prosperity.

The burial ground has been the subject of a bitter legal battle between the cemetery's trustees and the civil authorities since 1984. Competing plans to develop the area into a cultural and sports centre provoked a claim by the government for a $2 million bill for rent arrears, stating that the exemption over the previous centuries had been a "clerical error". This outraged the Chinese community who flatly refused to pay and the controversy has still not been settled.

Eating

Surprisingly, there are very few quality restaurants in the centre of town – in fact, aside from a few places in Chinatown, it's hard to find much open at night. Instead, **Taman Melaka Raya** is fast becoming the favoured food centre, featuring Chinese, Nonya, Malay, Indian and seafood restaurants. Budget meals are hard to find – even the city's principal **food stalls** on jalan Taman Melaka Raya, known as "Gluttons' Corner", are overrated and expensive: seafood is unpriced on the menu but calculated according to weight, so make sure you don't get less than you've been charged for. Far better to try the stalls just off jalan Parameswara, though these are only open during the day. It goes without saying that sampling **Nonya cuisine** is a must at some stage in your stay, though it is generally more expensive than other types of food; "house" specialities are mentioned below, but the emphasis is on spicy dishes, using sour herbs like tamarind, tempered by sweeter, creamy coconut milk. By contrast, the city's few remaining **Portuguese** restaurants are generally disappointing, expensive and tourist-oriented.

Usual restaurant **opening hours** are 9am–11pm, unless otherwise stated; **phone numbers** are given where it's necessary to book (usually only on Saturday nights).

Gluttons' Corner, jalan Taman. More a collection of permanent restaurants rather than food stalls, the city's highest profile eating area also has high prices and aggressive service. One of the better restaurants is *Bunga Raya*, which is popular with the locals. A full meal is at least $10 a head.

Jonkers Melaka, 17 jalan Hang Jebat. In a beautiful *Peranakan* house, this café is also a gift shop and art gallery. Good for vegetarians – try the spinach and feta samosas with coriander relish; *Nonya* meals ($16), including Assam fish and bitter-gourd curries, are also great. Open 10am–5pm.

Long Feng Chinese Restaurant, *Malacca Renaissance Hotel*, jalan Bendahara. Excellent Cantonese and Szechuan dishes in a classy setting. It's not cheap, however – around $20 per dish.

Mei Lin, 542 jalan Taman Melaka Raya. The menu of this friendly vegetarian restaurant lists items like Lemon Chicken and Sizzling Pork Ribs – but they're all made of soya. Most dishes cost $3–5.

Melaka Pandan, jalan Kota. Behind the tourist office and with a shady garden, this is the only open-air café in Melaka. A wide-ranging menu features Western and local cuisine; snacks average about $4, and there's a set breakfast at $7. Open 9am–10pm.

Moti Mahal, 543 jalan Taman Melaka Raya (☎237823). Upmarket North Indian restaurant serving all the usual favourites. Around $6 per dish.

Ole Sayang, 198–199 jalan Taman Melaka Raya (☎234384). A moderately priced *Nonya* restaurant with re-created *Peranakan* decor. Try the beef *goreng lada*, in a rich soy-based sauce, or the *ayam lemak pulut*, a spicy, creamy chicken dish; both cost around $7. Open 11.30am–2.30pm & 6–9.30pm.

Restoran Kerala, 194 jalan Taman Melaka Raya. Cheap and cheerful South Indian food in a sparklingly clean establishment. Excellent banana-leaf curries as well as *idli* and *dosa* for about $3.

Restoran D'Nolasco, Medan Portugis. A Mediterranean atmosphere with Oriental food – eg crabs in tomato and chilli sauce with soy. Saturdays include a cultural show: price is around $15 a head.

Restoran Peranakan Town House, 107 jalan Tun Tan Cheng Lock (☎245001). Marble tables with white-lace tablecloths, and a reasonably priced Nonya menu. Try spicy *rendang* dishes ($7) or *clay pot ayam* ($8). There are cultural shows nightly except Saturdays, so you may have to reserve.

Nightlife and entertainment

While the centre of town is comatose at night – bar the discos in the top hotels – **Taman Melaka Raya** comes alive. If karaoke bars (8pm–2am) are your definition of entertainment, then there's no shortage of options here, though both these and the discos are somewhat lacking in character. In some ways, you'd be better off eschewing the Western-style bars in favour of one of the grotty Chinese bottle shops in the centre of town. Melaka is also an ideal place to take in a **cultural show**, not much because of the quality of the entertainment, but because you don't have to pay five-star hotel prices to watch; the *Restoran Peranakan Town House* (see above) is just one venue.

Black Widow Disco, *Plaza Inn*, jalan Munshi Abdullah, near the river. An impressive laser system and lukewarm sounds hardly compensate for the hefty $15 cover charge.

Medan Portugis. The best place to be on Saturday night. Amateur dance groups and a band reflecting both Portuguese and Malay cultural traditions perform from about 8.30pm (entrance $2), making for a thoroughly Mediterranean evening. Get there early to ensure a good spot in the square; you can eat here (see above) or just come for a drink. Bus #17 or #25 from jalan Parameswara, just outside Taman Melaka Raya.

Rhythm and Blues Pub, 176a Taman Melaka Raya. Gloomy lighting in this small bar tries to induce the moody atmosphere that the live music does its best to destroy.

Sound and Light Show, Padang Pahlawan. A must for fans of high drama ("Something is rotten in the state of Melaka"); the buildings are well lit and the sound system is used imaginatively – take lots of mosquito repellent. Shows are nightly at 9.30pm in English (except during Ramadan when they begin at 8.30pm) and last an hour – tickets ($5) from the booths at each end of the Padang.

Shopping

Melaka is famed for its **antiques**, and along jalan Hang Jebat and jalan Tun Tan Cheng Lock are many specialist outlets. Prices are usually fixed, although it doesn't hurt to bargain, and you can find anything from Nonya tableware to HMV gramophones in the musty shop interiors. If it's a genuine antique – and many shops fill their windows with colourful but inauthentic clutter – then check that it can be exported legally and fill in an official clearance form; the dealer should provide you with this. Jalan Bunga Raya and jalan Munshi Abdullah form the modern shopping centre, where you'll find a variety of Western and local goods.

Abdu Co., 79 jalan Hang Jabat. A good place for china and glass.

Dragon House, 65 jalan Hang Jebat. The best value for old coins and banknotes, with helpful staff.

Karyaneka, jalan Laksamana. Opposite the post office, this is the place to go for fixed-price crafts such as brassware, lacquerware and rattan articles.

Koo Fatt Hong, 92 jalan Tun Tan Cheng Lock. Specialists in "Asia Spiritual and Buddha images".

Orang Utan, 59 lorong Hang Jebat. Here, a local artist sells his paintings and original T-shirts.

Parkson Grand, Taman Melaka Raya. A huge air-con supermarket whose upper floors contain clothing and shoe departments; food in the basement.

Ringo, 12 jalan Hang Jebat. British bikes and old biker artifacts, as well as unusual toys; pricey.

Village Craft, 124 jalan Munshi Abdullah. Pricey but good quality clothes, etc, from Southeast Asia.

Wah Aik, 92 jalan Hang Jebat. Renowned for making silk shoes for bound feet, a practice that happily no longer exists – they're now lined up in the window as souvenirs, at a mere $75 per pair.

Listings

Banks and exchange *Bank Bumiputra*, jalan Kota; *Hongkong and Shanghai*, 1a jalan Kota; *Overseas Chinese Banking Corporation*, jalan Hang Jebat. Moneychangers are often more convenient and offer as good rates as the banks: *Malaccan Souvenir House and Trading*, 22 jalan Tokong; *Sultan Enterprise*, 31 jalan Laksamana.

Bookshops *Estee Book Exchange*, Taman Melaka Raya, offers a good selection of English-language classics and other fiction; *Lim Bros*, 20 jalan Laksamana, has books on the Malaysian economy and politics, as well as colonial memoirs and expensive travel guides.

Car rental *Avis*, 27 jalan Laksamana (☎235626); *Thrifty*, G5 Pasar Pelancong, jalan Tun Sri Lanang (☎249471).

Cinema The *Cathay* and the *Rex* on jalan Bunga Raya both show English-language films. Check in English-language papers for what's on where and when.

Hospital *The Straits Hospital* is at 37 jalan Parameswara (☎235336).

Immigration The immigration office is on the 2nd floor, Bangunan Persekutuan, jalan Hang Tuah (☎224958) for on-the-spot visa renewals.

Police The Tourist Police office (☎222222) is on jalan Kota and is open 24 hours.

Post office The GPO is inconveniently situated on the way to Ayer Keroh on jalan Bukit Baru – take town bus #19. A minor branch on jalan Laksamana sells stamps and aerograms.

Sport The *Merlin Melaka* sports centre on jalan Munshi Abdullah offers ten-pin bowling, snooker, squash, and roller skating.

Swimming There's a public swimming pool on jalan Kota which costs $2.

Telephones The *Telekom* building is on jalan Chan Koon Cheng (daily 8am–5pm).

Travel agents Try *Atlas Travel* at 5 jalan Hang Jebat (☎220777) for plane tickets.

Around Melaka

While there's more than enough to keep you occupied in Melaka itself, you may well fancy a break from sightseeing in favour of more relaxed pleasures, while still using the city as a base. Heading north to the more rural area of **Ayer Keroh** or to Melaka's nearest resort island of **Pulau Besar** guarantees leisurely traffic-free pursuits.

Ayer Keroh

Fourteen kilometres north of the centre, **AYER KEROH** – despite its position adjacent to the North–South Highway – is a leafy recreational area that provides a pleasant alternative to staying in the city itself. Town bus #19 runs every thirty minutes from the local bus station and once there, the major attractions are all within a few hundred metres or so of one another, but heavy traffic on the main road can make walking a bit of a liability.

Apart from the **Hutan Rekreasi** (daily 7am–6pm; free), an area of woodland area set aside for walking and picnicking, all the attractions are somewhat contrived: the **Taman Buaya**, or Crocodile Farm (Mon–Fri 9am–6pm, Sat–Sun 9.30am–7pm; $3); the **Melaka Zoo** (Mon–Fri 9am–6pm, Sat & Sun 9.30am–6.30pm; $3), purportedly the second largest in the country; and the **Taman Rama Rama** (Butterfly Farm; daily 8.30am–5.30pm; $4), with its walk-through aviary and small marine centre. The only display that demands more than fleeting attention is the **Taman Mini Malaysia** (Mon-Fri 10am–6pm, Sat & Sun 9.30am–6.30pm; $3), a large park fifteen minutes' walk north of the Crocodile Farm, filled with full-sized reconstructions of typical houses from all thirteen Malay states. The specially constructed timber buildings are frequently used as sets for Malaysian films and soap operas, while cultural shows featuring local music and dance are staged at the park's open-air arena – ask at the ticket office for details.

The area around the lake, just off the main road, is where you'll find most of the **places to stay**, limited exclusively to up-market resort accommodation. The best of the bunch is the *Malacca Village Park Plaza Resort* (☎06/323600; ⑥), an unpretentious place using traditional timber and rattan decor, with comfortable rooms around the swimming pool. Next door, *D'Village Resort* (☎06/328000; ⑤), is the least attractive option, with hot, blue-roofed chalets cramped together, though it does have the cheapest rooms. **Places to eat** are more or less limited to those in the resorts, save for a few tourist-oriented food stalls at the main attractions. In addition, the *Malacca Village Park Plaza Resort* has an area devoted to hawker stalls, offering standard Malay favourites.

Pulau Besar

Long before it was turned into an exclusive beach resort, **PULAU BESAR**, about 5km off the coast of Melaka, was known as the burial ground of passing Muslim traders and missionaries, tales of whom live on in distorted local legends even today. Although its historic sites have been vigourously promoted by the tourist authorities, they consist of little more than a few ancient graves, several wells and remnants of the Japanese occupation, such as a bunker and dynamite store. However, the island's beaches and hilly scenery are pleasant enough, and its compact size makes it easy to stroll around in a day – the name, "Big Island", is misleading, since Pulau Besar is only about 16km square.

Pulau Besar is easily reached by air-con **ferry** ($8 return), currently departing four times a day (at 8am, noon, 3pm & 11pm) from the Shah Bandar jetty in town. You can also get there by simpler fishing boat from the **Pengkalan Pernu jetty** in Umbai (on request; $8 return), 10km southeast of Melaka, a half-hour journey from the city on bus #91. The various departure times allow you to spend a full day on the island, though you might want to stay overnight in the luxury *Tapa-Nyai Island Resort* (☎06/242088; ⑥), the only available **accommodation**; it's a well-organized set-up, with superior rooms and facilities, though the resort is also developing a range of simpler chalets (③). You have slightly more freedom when it comes to **eating**, since aside from the pricey in-house restaurant at the resort, a couple of local *kedai kopis* serve *nasi* and *mee* dishes.

Inland: Gunung Ledang and Segamat

Heading **inland** from Melaka into the state of Johor, a maze of minor roads covers the sparsely populated lowland, whose horizon is disturbed only by the soaring conical protuberance of **Gunung Ledang**. Further inland still, you'll meet up with the sweep of Route 1, connecting a string of lifeless towns, of which the least dull is **Segamat**.

Gemas, 25km northwest of Segamat, is a grubby little place, whose merit is only as the transportation hub of the train network; it's here that you'll have to change if you want to venture into the interior on the so-called Jungle Railway (see *The Interior* for all the details). Otherwise, transport connections throughout inland Johor are uncomplicated, with a good network of buses serving all destinations.

Gunung Ledang

Formerly called Mount Ophir by the British, **Gunung Ledang** (1276m) is the highest mountain in the state of Johor and, like many other mountains, is believed by the animist *orang asli* to be endowed with spirits. The best-known legend associated with Gunung Ledang is that concerning the betrothal of Sultan Mansur Shah to the mountain's beautiful fairy princess. A lengthy list of requirements was presented to the Sultan, on fulfilment of which the princess would consent to marry him, and while the Sultan was not daunted by such items as trays of mosquito hearts and a vat of tears, he drew the line at a cup of his son's blood, and swiftly withdrew his proposal.

Today, Gunung Ledang offers rather more worldly pastimes in the form of its dramatic **waterfall** and challenging **treks**, though the latter are restricted to experienced climbers with their own camping equipment. Once you're past the clutter of trinket stalls at the approach to the waterfall, the surroundings become gradually more leafy and refreshing, leading to the start of the trail to the summit. A series of rapids, which the main path follows closely, form natural pools, ideal for a cooling dip, though the water is a bit murky in places. To reach the waterfall's source requires stamina and in any case is disappointing in the dry season, so you can be excused for sticking to the lower reaches. All this rural frolicking may change, however, when threatened plans for a resort, including a large hotel, chalets and a golf course, get underway.

The mountain is easily reached by a Segamat-bound express bus from Melaka – ask to be dropped at **SAGIL**, 11km north of Tangkak on Route 23. Here, the waterfall is clearly signposted ("Air Terjun") off the main road, from where it is a 1500 metre walk to the beginning of the rapids.

Segamat

While there's no real reason to continue on to **SEGAMAT**, 52km northeast of Tangkak, it's not an unpleasant town and if you're driving through on Route 1, then stop for a drink and a wander around the grassy *padang*. This is bordered by some elegant old colonial buildings, such as the **Sekolah Tinggi**, formerly the English High School, as well as the District Office and an ill-proportioned Catholic church. The more modern, anonymous commercial centre is more than 1km to the south.

Central Segamat offers plenty of **accommodation**, including the comfortable *Pine Classic Inn* at 30 jalan Genuang (☎07/923009; ③), on the main thoroughfare; the basic *Tai Ah* (☎07/911709; ①), over the road at no. 42–25; and the mid-bracket *Segemat Inn* (☎07/911401; ②), in the UMNO building next to the GPO on jalan Awang.

South to JB

It's 206km southeast from Melaka to Johor Bahru (see p.296) and the first 45km, to the Malay town of **Muar**, is through verdant countryside dotted with neatly kept timber stilted houses with double roofs. These houses – in some of the prettiest *kampungs* in Malaysia – are especially numerous along Route 5 and, with time to spare en route between Melaka and Maur, you could stop to visit one of them, **Penghulu's House**. Further south, the towns of **Batu Pahat** and **Pontian Kecil** are of scant interest; Batu Pahat, slightly inland, has even managed to acquire a reputation as a red-light resort for day- (and night-) tripping Singaporeans. If you do want to stop anywhere else before JB and Singapore, aim for **Kukup**, right at the southern end of the west coast, a terrific place to eat seafood.

Penghulu's House

Just off the main road on the right, a little more than 2km south of the village of **MERLIMAU**, the striking **Penghulu's House**, a chieftain's house, was built in 1894, with elaborate wood carvings adorning the verandah and eaves, and the front steps covered in colourful Art Nouveau hand-painted tiles. It is still inhabited by the chieftain's descendents, who will show you around inside; a donation towards the upkeep of the house is always appreciated.

Muar

The old port town of **MUAR** – also known as Bandar Maharani – exudes an elegance, affluence and calm that attracts surprisingly few tourists. Legend has it that Paremesvara, the fifteenth-century founder of Melaka, fled here first from Singapore, seeking to establish his own kingdom on the southern bank of sungei Muar, before finally being persuaded to choose Melaka as his site. Although rejected by the Sumatran prince, Muar later became an important port in the Johor empire (see p.567), as well as a centre for *ghazal* music (see p.588), which originated in Africa – and the place whose dialect is considered the purest *Bahasa Malaysia* in the peninsula.

Today, Muar's commercial centre looks like any other, with Chinese shophouses and *kedai kopi*s cluttering its parallel streets, jalan Maharani, jalan Abdullah and jalan Meriam. But turn right out of the bus station on jalan Maharani, following the river as the road turns into jalan Petri, and you'll see an altogether different side to town. Gently declining under the shade of huge rain trees, the neo-Classical, colonial buildings that form the administrative core, the **Custom House** and **Government Offices** (Bangunan Sultan Abu Bakar) on the right, and the **District Police Office** and **Courthouse** on the left, still reek of confident prosperity from their days as an administrative centre for the British regime. The graceful **Masjid Jamek**, a further 100m or so on the right, though a little peeling in places, is the most impressive of them all.

Practicalities

Bus #2 runs frequently from Melaka's local bus station, arriving in Muar at the station on jalan Maharani. It's less than an hour and a half away, but if you prefer to stay, there are plenty of reasonable **hotels**, the best value the initially unpromising *Park View* (☎06/916655; ②), which has the best views over town and the river, even if the rooms are a touch dog-eared. Also good, but costing less, is the *Kingdom* (☎06/921921; ②) at 158 jalan Meriam, two blocks back from the bus station, with small, modern rooms. Finally, the *Rest House* (☎06/927744; ③), signposted "Rumah Persinggahan" on jalan Sultanah, reached by a left turn at the far end of jalan Petri, offers the quietest, most upmarket accommodation, with huge rooms complete with TV and telephone, a children's play area, as well as some family chalets.

Aside from **eating** houses in the commercial centre of town, none of which can be particularly recommended, the *Medan Selera* near the bridge on jalan Maharani serves Malay snacks, while the *Park View* has a bearable restaurant with a wide-ranging menu averaging $5 per dish.

Batu Pahat and Pontian Kecil

Heading south, Route 5 hugs the palm-fringed coast as far as **BATU PAHAT**, which has garnered something of a reputation as a venue for "dirty weekends". A slightly more noteworthy association is with a couple of important political events. UMNO, a coalition of organizations opposed to the British-inspired Malayan Union, had its origins here in 1946. Years later, during the Constitutional Crisis of 1983, Prime Minister Dr Mahathir held a mass rally in the town to protest against the position taken by the hereditary rulers, urging the people to assert their constitutional rights and elect him. The choice of Batu Pahat as the venue for this conscience-stirring symbolized Dr Mahathir's desire to remind the rulers of UMNO's role in reversing their original acquiescence to the Malayan Union may years before. There's not much that brightens up today's town bar the Art Deco **Masjid Jamek** and Straits Chinese **Chamber of Commerce**. Keep on going.

Further south, you head into plantation country – in this case pineapples, piled high on roadside stalls in season filling the air with their sweet fragrance. The next place of any consequence is the unassuming town of **PONTIAN KECIL**, 70km southeast of Batu Pahat, where you can stop off for a cup of tea at the cutesy, old-world *Rest House*, just up from the bus station (regular services to JB) on the seafront.

Kukup

Two giant king prawns flank the roadside at **KUKUP**, waving their tentacles in eager expectation at the money you're about to part with. This small fishing community, just 19km from Pontian Kecil, has opened its doors to the Singapore package-tour trade, whose clients come to ogle the ancient, stilted houses built over the murky river – and to sample Kukup's real attraction: the seafood.

As you enter its single tumbledown street packed with restaurants, you might as well dive straight into one for lunch, although most tours usually include an appetite-inducing trip to the offshore **kelong**. This huge fish trap has rickety wooden platforms, from where the nets are cast, which float on their moorings, rather than being anchored to the sea bed. The agency right by the jetty or any one of the restaurants can sell you a ticket for the 45-minute tour ($5).

There's a dearth of transport from Pontian Kecil to Kukup, so you're better off catching a **taxi** for around $3 per person. There are at least half a dozen places to **eat**, from the enormous *Makanan Laut*, closest to the jetty, where you can see the food being prepared in a vast array of woks, to the more modest *Restoran Zaiton Hussin* immediately opposite, where the emphasis is on Malay rather than Chinese-style seafood. Expect to pay $13 for fish, $12 for prawns and $6 for mussels.

To and from Indonesia

Kukup is a little-known exit point from Malaysia to **Tanjung Balai in Indonesia**, a 45-minute ferry ride leaving from the jetty at 10am every Monday, Wednesday and Friday ($45 one-way); you'll need a visa beforehand as it's not a recognized departure point. The problem with **arriving** in Kukup from Indonesia is that onward travel connections are sketchy – and there's nowhere to stay in Kukup.

Johor Bahru

The southernmost Malaysian city of any size, **JOHOR BAHRU** – or simply **JB** – is the gateway into Singapore, linked to the city-state by a 1056-metre causeway carrying a road, a railway, and the pipes through which Singapore imports its fresh water. Around 50,000 people a day travel across the causeway and the ensuing traffic, noise and smog affects most of unsightly downtown Johor Bahru. The town has long had to tolerate unflattering comparisons with squeaky-clean Singapore, for which it has served as a red-light haunt for many years, but things do at last seem to be changing. The past two decades have seen the state of Johor – of which JB is the capital – become one of the three sides of an economic "Growth Triangle", together with Singapore and Batam island in the Indonesian Riau archipelago. Confronted by mounting production costs in their own country, Singaporean investors have flooded across the causeway to take advantage of low labour costs, and JB has prospered accordingly. Today, the air of decay which hangs over much of downtown JB is slowly being dispelled, as Johor's manufacturing boom finances new international hotels and ever more dazzling shopping malls. Development is particularly evident among the arcades of **Taman Century Estate**, a couple of kilometres north of the city centre along the Tebrau Highway.

Despite these improvements, JB remains ill-equipped to win the hearts of visitors. By day, it's a hectic city whose only real attraction is the royal **Istana Besar**; by night, its main streets are lit by the neon lights of its hostess bars and night clubs. If you've arrived from Singapore, there's little to detain you from the quick getaway provided by the North–South Highway to the considerable attractions of Melaka and Kuala Lumpur.

Historically, though, JB stands with Melaka as one of the most important sites in the country. Chased out of its seat of power by the Portuguese in 1511, the Melakan court decamped to the Riau archipelago, south of modern-day Singapore, before upping sticks again in the 1530s and shifting to the upper reaches of the Johor river. A century of uncertainty followed for the infant kingdom of Johor, with persistent offensives by both the Portuguese and the Acehnese of northern Sumatra, forcing the court to shift its capital regularly. Stability was finally achieved by courting the friendship of the Dutch in the 1640s; the rest of the seventeenth century saw the kingdom of Johor blossom into a **thriving trading entrepôt**. By the end of the century, though, the questionable rule of the wayward and tyrannical Sultan Mahmud had halted Johor's pre-eminence among the Malay kingdoms, and piracy was causing a decline in trade. In 1699, Sultan Mahmud was killed by his own nobles and with the Melaka-Johor dynasty finally ended, successive power struggles crippled the kingdom, as Buginese immigrants, escaping the civil wars in their native Sulawesi, eclipsed the power of the Sultans. Though the Buginese were finally chased out by the Dutch in 1784, the kingdom was now a shadow of its former self.

The Johor-Riau empire – and the Malay world – was split in two once and for all, with the Melaka Straits forming the dividing line following the Anglo-Dutch treaty of 1824. As links with the court in Riau faded, Sultan Ibrahim assumed power, amassing a fortune based upon hefty profits culled from plantations in Johor. The process was continued by his son Abu Bakar, who in 1885 was named Sultan of Johor, and is widely regarded as the "Father" of modern Johor. Abu Bakar it was who in 1866 named the new port across the Johor Straits *Johor Bahru*, or "New Johor".

The city

Today, redeeming features are few and far between in scruffy **downtown JB**. A stroll through the claustrophobic ways of the city's sprawling **market**, below the Komtar Building on jalan Wong Ah Fook, reveals products as diverse as "one-thousand-year-

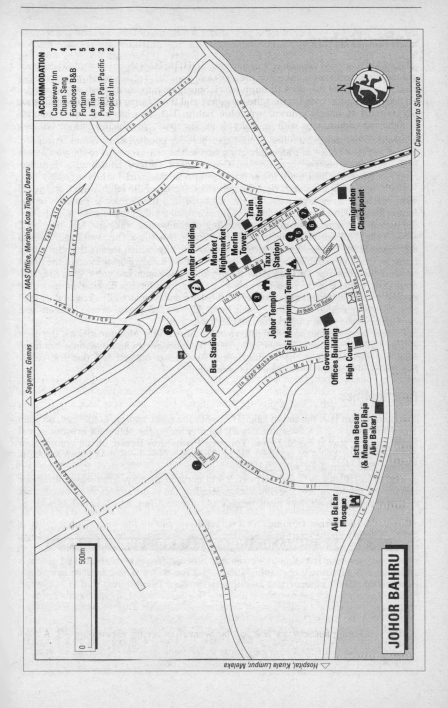

JOHOR BAHRU

ACCOMMODATION
Causeway Inn 7
Chuan Seng 4
Footloose B&B 1
Fortuna 5
Le Tian 6
Puteri Pan Pacific 3
Tropical Inn 2

Causeway to Singapore

MAS Office, Mersing, Kota Tinggi, Desaru

Segamat, Gemas

Hospital, Kuala Lumpur, Melaka

Komtar Building
Market/Nightmarket
Merlin Tower
Train Station
Taxi Station
Immigration Checkpoint
Johor Temple
Sri Mariamman Temple
Government Offices Building
High Court
Bus Station
Istana Besar (& Museum Di Raja Abu Bakar)
Abu Bakar Mosque

500m

old eggs" (actually preserved for a year under a mixture of lime, ash and tea leaves), machetes and silk; while a little way south, the **Sri Mariamman Temple** lends a welcome splash of primary colour to the cityscape. Underneath its *gopuram*, and beyond the two gatekeepers on horseback who guard the temple, is the usual collection of vividly depicted figures from the Hindu pantheon. There's another temple, just west of the Sri Mariamman, on jalan Trus, the **Johor Temple** which – dating back over a hundred years – is JB's oldest, its murals of traditional Chinese life darkened by years of incense smoke.

After the cramped streets of the city centre, the spaciousness of the western **seafront** comes as a great relief. From here, there are good views of distant Singapore, and of the slow snake of traffic labouring across the causeway. En route, you'll pass jalan Timbalan's austere, grey-bricked **Government Offices Building**, a 64-metre-high construction whose stark tower provides a useful landmark for new arrivals.

Walk west along the water, past the garlanded facade of the **High Court**, and you'll soon reach the grey arch marking the entrance into the expansive gardens of the **Istana Besar** – the former residence of Johor's royal family. Ornate golden lamps line the path to the Istana, a magnificent building of chalk-white walls and low, blue roof, set on a slight hillock, overlooking the Johor Straits. Nowadays, the royal family lives in the Istana Bukit Serene, a little further west of the city, which means that the Istana Besar is open to the public: bearing to the right of the building brings you to the ticket booth of the **Museum Di Raja Abu Bakar** (daily 9am–5pm, last entry 4pm; $18, children $8). The bulk of the pieces on show are gifts from foreign dignitaries, including exquisite ceramics from Japan, crystal from France and furniture from England, as well as more recognizably Southeast Asian items like stuffed tigers, ornate daggers and even an umbrella stand crafted from an elephant's foot.

Further west, the four rounded towers of the **Abu Bakar Mosque** make it the most elegant building in town. Completed in 1900, the mosque can accommodate two thousand worshippers; as at the Istana, Sultan Abu Bakar himself laid the first stone, though he died before the mosque was completed.

Practicalities

The **bus station** is at the top of jalan Trus, with the **train station** to the east, off jalan Tun Abdul Razak. It's a five-minute walk from either to the abundant brochures and knowledgeable staff at the **Malaysia Tourism Promotion Board**, on the ground floor of Komplex Tun Abdul Razad, jalan Wong Ah Fook (Mon–Fri 8am–4.15pm, Sat 8am–12.45pm, Sun 10am–4pm; ☎07/223590).

Flights to JB land at **Senai airport**, 25km north of the city, from where a regular bus service ($1.40) runs to the bus station. Heading out to the airport, *MAS* passengers can take the $4 shuttle bus from outside the *Tropical Inn*, which connects with all

---

TRAVEL BETWEEN SINGAPORE AND JOHOR BAHRU

Two **bus services** run throughout the day between Singapore and JB. The air-con *Singapore-JB Express* (every 10min, 6.30am–11.30pm; $1.80) is the most comfortable, though the #170 is cheaper ($1) and runs every fifteen minutes from 6am to 12.30am. There's also an *MAS* bus service ($10) from JB's Senai airport to Singapore's *Novotel Orchid* – buses connect with all major departures and arrivals. **Taxis** between Singapore and JB cost $6–7 per person, and leave only when they are full.

The buses drop passengers outside the immigration points at each end of the causeway and **immigration** procedures take around ten minutes. If you want to avoid this hassle, you can make the journey by **train**, as the formalities are carried out on board, though at $8 for a second-class seat, this is more expensive.

major flights. Alternatively, you can get a taxi to the airport for about $20 from the taxi stand, between the Sri Mariamman temple and jalan Wong Ah Fook. The *MAS* office is at Level 1, Menara Pelangi, jalan Kuning Taman Pelangi (☎07/341001).

If you want to explore Malaysia out of Singapore, it's far cheaper to **rent a car** in JB. Contact either *Avis*, at the *Tropical Inn* (☎07/237971); *Budget Car Rental*, Suite 216, 2nd Floor, Orchid Plaza, jalan Wong Ah Fook (☎07/243951); *Hertz*, 1 jalan Trus (☎07/237520); or *National*, 50-B Bangunan Felda, jalan Segget (☎07/230503). There are **moneychangers** in the main shopping centres, or track down *Malayan Bank*, 11 jalan Selat Tebrau; *Bank Bumiputra*, 51 jalan Segget; *Hong Kong & Shanghai Bank*, 1 jalan Bukit Timbalan; or *OCBC*, jalan Ibrahim.

Accommodation

JB's manufacturing boom means the city attracts more businessmen than tourists, so **hotel** prices tend to be a little higher than elsewhere in mainland Malaysia. Moreover, since the city's nightlife continues to appeal to Singaporeans looking for a night out, some or its budget hotels post hourly rates. The majority of JB's lower-priced hotels are on or around jalan Meldrum, bang in the centre of town.

Causeway Inn, 6A-F jalan Meldrum (☎07/248811). Amiable hotel near the waterfront, whose sizeable rooms come with air-con, TV and private toilet. ④.

Chuan Seng Hotel, 35 jalan Meldrum (no phone). Grotty Chinese hotel, complete with hideous partitioned rooms, but the lowest-priced beds in JB if *Footloose* is full (see below). ②.

Footloose B&B, 4H jalan Ismail (☎07/242881). Run by a friendly Scottish woman, this is basic but tidy with one double room and one small dorm; evening meals are good value at $4 a head. ②.

Fortuna Hotel, 29A jalan Meldrum, (☎07/228666). Central hotel whose position above a karaoke bar makes it noisy; the rooms and toilets have seen better days, but at least the linen is clean. ②.

Hotel Le Tian, 2A-D, jalan Sui Nam (☎07/248151). Unremarkable hotel with air-con and toilets in all its cramped rooms. ③ .

Puteri Pan Pacific Hotel, The Kotaraya, jalan Trus (☎07/233333). JB's most opulent address, with 500 sumptuous rooms and a wide choice of restaurants. ⑥.

Tropical Inn, 15 jalan Gereja (☎07/247888). A JB landmark; comfortable, with good rooms and decent restaurants. ⑤.

Eating

Scores of **restaurants** operate in JB, serving anything from Pakistani to Japanese dishes. If it's a quick and modest snack you're after, there's a large **nightmarket** across the footbridge from the train station, and a smaller one on the waterfront in front of the General Hospital on jalan Skudai.

Granee's Restaurant, 27 jalan Seggat. Unbeatable for good, economical banana leaf curries ($3.50) and Indian breads. Daily 8am–9.30pm.

High Street Café, 60 jalan Ibrahim. Fresh and pleasing café serving Chinese and Malay meals and snacks. Daily 8am–10pm.

Jaws 5 Restaurant, *Straits View Hotel*, 1D jalan Skudai. Open-air restaurant with backdrop of traditional Malay houses; its inexpensive menu has fish and shark's fin dishes. Daily 11.30am–midnight.

Restoran Hua Mui, 131 jalan Trus. Western and Chinese dishes rub shoulders on the menu in this two-floored restaurant. Daily 7am–9.30pm.

Sedap Corner, 11 jalan Abdul Samad. Choose from a picture-menu of inexpensive Malay dishes. Daily 8am–9pm.

Selasih Restaurant, *Puteri Pan Pacific*, The Kotaraya, jalan Trus. Serves tasty dishes from all 13 states in Malaysia; the set lunches are good value at $40 a head. Daily 11.30am–3pm & 6.30–11pm.

Shalimar, 43/44 jalan Ibrahim. Large portions of North Indian and Pakistani dishes, served by charming staff – highly recommended. Daily 11.30am–3pm & 6.30–10pm.

Snow White Restaurant, 9A & 11A jalan Siaw Nam. Affordable, open-sided restaurant up above the thrum of JB's traffic; specializes in Cantonese seafood and steamboats. Daily 11am–2am.

Tong Ah Restaurant, 14 jalan Ibrahim. No-frills *nasi padang* restaurant, lined by aged cigarette posters. Daily 7am–8pm.

Warong Saga, 5 jalan Mahmudiah. This amiable restaurant serves cheap Chinese staples; its decor is a mixture of portraits of Malay royalty, seven-inch singles and coolie hats. Daily 7am–7pm.

Across to the east coast

Without the patronage of neighbouring Singapore, the area **around Johor Bahru** would have quietly nodded off into a peaceful slumber. Not that it's exactly a thrilling region even now: the likes of Kukup on the western seaboard (see p.295) and the desultory seaside resort of **Desaru** on the eastern coast have flourished, one suspects, more for their geographical rather than aesthetic merits. Most people heading **east** beat a hasty path along Route 3 to Mersing, neglecting to stop even at **Kota Tinggi**, whose waterfall constitutes the region's most enduring sight.

Kota Tinggi and around

The undistinguished town of **KOTA TINGGI**, 40km northeast of JB, clings to the wide and fast-flowing sungei Johor, and although it's not worth a visit in its own right, you may want to stop at the **waterfall** (daily 8am–8pm; $1) at **LEMBONG**, 15km north out of the town centre. Despite the unattractive concrete buildings housing restaurant and toilet facilities, the area cannot be robbed of its stunning setting, with wild jungle creepers trailing down to the tumultuous, steaming water. Of the two falls here, the pool at the bottom of the farthest one is the biggest and the best for swimming, deep and unobstructed by boulders. If you remain on dry land, you'll still be soaked by the fine spray given off by the pounding water. Another minor diversion is to take the road off to the east, about 15km northeast of Kota Tinggi, which leads past the forgotten royal mausoleums of past Johor sultans at **MAWAI** to the uninspiring resort bay of **TELOK MAHKOTA**, amid bleak and desolate marshland.

Practicalities

Buses from JB run every thirty minutes on the 45-minute trip to Kota Tinggi, stopping at the centrally situated bus station, which caters for both express and local services. Bus #43 leaves hourly from Kota Tinggi (7am–7pm; $1), winding up through rubber-plantation country to the entrance to the waterfall. The chalets (☎07/831146; ③) **at Lembong** make a good alternative to staying in Kota Tinggi itself, though some of the older ones are very shabby; there's a campsite ($10) for die-hards. The Chinese *Restoran Air Terjun* just by the entrance has a sound menu.

The hotels **in Kota Tinggi** are located around the bus station, best value of which is the modern and spotless *Sin May Chun* at 26 jalan Tambatan (☎07/833573; ①); the *Bunga Raya* further along at 12 jalan Jaafar (☎07/833023; ①) is also well kept. The *Nasha* at 40 jalan Tambatan (☎07/838000; ③) is the most upmarket option, but its rooms are small and musty. Seafood is a speciality in the town, with a number of flashy **restaurants** close to the river, including the popular *Restoran Kota*, the *Sin Mei Lee* and the *Mui Tou* – prices are surprisingly reasonable at around $6–8 per dish, so this is the place to try out crab, lobster and prawns.

Desaru

DESARU is the first major beach resort outside Singapore and as beaches go, it's not that bad, with its sheltered, casuarina-fringed bay. But there's better to be found further up the coast and the wide, well-kept but rather soulless streets don't inspire any lengthy stays. It's nearly 100km by road from JB, so most visitors from Singapore come by sea from Changi Point (see "Leaving Singapore", p.480–481). The transportation system is geared towards this, with shuttle buses running the 45 minutes from the Malaysian port of Kampung Pengerang to Desaru itself. In addition, the *PGB* company runs bus #5 from JB, and there are also local connections with Kota Tinggi.

The three **places to stay** in Desaru are all under the auspices of the *Desaru Garden Beach Resort* (☎07/821101), with a full range of accommodation from a fairly poor campsite ($5 per person) and dorms ($12 per person), home-from-home chalets (at the bottom end of ④), through to two hotels, the *Desaru View* (⑤), and the newer and more pleasant *Desaru Hotel* (⑤), both with pools. Be warned that rates rise dramatically at weekends. All the places have **restaurants**, predominantly Chinese and Japanese, and a very average meal costs a minimum of $15 a head.

Mersing

Large white letters spelling the name of the town welcome you Hollywood-style to the fishing port of **MERSING**, 130km north of Johor Bahru, sitting astride the languid sungei Mersing. A bustling and industrious little town, it's the gateway to Pulau Tioman and the other smaller islands in the Seribuat archipelago, so is unlikely to delay you longer than one night. Services have sprung up to cater for the seasonal floods of tourists – hotels, restaurants and travel agencies – and it pays to work out exactly what you want to do before arriving in Mersing, or else be prepared to be bamboozled into a decision by the ever-eager entrepreneurs that hang around the jetty.

Mersing itself is grouped around two main streets, jalan Abu Bakar and jalan Ismail, fanning out from a roundabout on Route 3. Mersing's Chinese and Indian temples, just south of the roundabout, are unremarkable, and the only real sight in town is the square **Masjid Jamek**, on a nearby hilltop, its cool, pastel-green tiled dome and minaret lit to spectacular effect at night, when it appears to hang in mid-air, high in the sky. In the centre of town, by a mini-roundabout on jalan Abu Bakar, is a historic Chinese **shophouse**, built by Poh Keh, a Mersing pioneer, its prominent verandah and flowery wall motifs a little too prettily renovated.

Practicalities

Express buses from Singapore, JB or Kuantan drop you off just before the roundabout, while the **local bus station** for services to Kota Tinggi, Endau and elsewhere is on jalan Sulaiman, close to the riverfront. If you're thinking about heading out to one of the islands the same day, then head straight to the **jetty**, which is about ten minutes' walk from the roundabout along jalan Abu Bakar. For details of getting to the islands, see "Leaving for the islands" below. One problem with **leaving Mersing** is that few buses originate here, so there can be a fight for seats in the peak season. Express tickets can be bought in advance from *Restoran Malaysia*, which is where you catch buses to destinations in the peninsula, though Singapore-bound services depart from the *R&R Plaza* near the jetty.

Accommodation

If you've missed the day's sailings, you'll have to spend the night in Mersing. There's no shortage of low-budget **hotels** and if you're staying at either of the two places to the north of town, a local bus runs this route every thirty minutes, or a taxi costs $3.

Country, jalan Abu Bakar (☎07/791799). Near the bus station, this hotel is more upmarket than its price suggests; each carpeted room has comfortable furniture, a bathroom and balcony. ②.

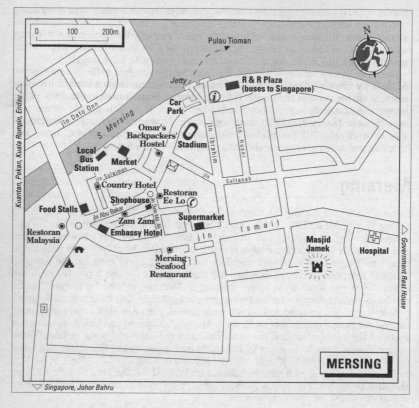

Embassy, 2 jalan Ismail (☎07/793545). Clean and comfortable, this relatively quiet and well-run place has dorms, with only two or three beds to a room, in addition to ordinary doubles. ①.

Government Rest House, jalan Ismail (☎07/792102). A good-value place with large, slightly run-down rooms, some facing the sea; at the eastern end of jalan Ismail, fifteen minutes' walk from town. ②.

Kali's Guest House (☎07/793613). A charming place by the sea, 1km north of town, with a peaceful garden and a choice of A-frames, chalets or dearer cottages. Phone for collection from town. ①.

Merlin (☎07/791312) The best hotel in town is 1km north of the roundabout, and has a pool and elegant restaurant, though rather musty rooms. ⑤.

Omar's Backpackers' Hostel, jalan Abu Bakar (☎07/793125). Opposite the GPO, this is one of the cheapest places in Mersing, with dorm beds and excellent value double rooms. ①.

Eating

Mersing is a great place for **eating**, with seafood topping the menu. The **food stalls** near the roundabout are particularly good – try the great satay and banana fritters.

Golden Dragon, *Embassy Hotel*, 2 jalan Ismail. The widest-ranging Chinese and seafood menu in town, though a touch more expensive than some. Averages $8 per dish.

Kali's Pizzeria, attached to *Kali's Guest House* (see above). Near-to-genuine pizzas and spaghetti go for around $8, served in a rustic bistro atmosphere.

Mersing Seafood Restaurant, jalan Ismail. One of the best seafood (and air-con) restaurants in town, with a good selection of crab, prawn and mussel dishes at around $8 each.

Restoran Ee Lo, jalan Dato Md. Ali, on the jalan Abu Bakar mini-roundabout. A variety of Chinese-based dishes, as well as a limited range of seafood.

Zam Zam, jalan Abu Bakar. Always busy, this serves tasty Indian food including great *roti canai*.

Leaving for the islands

At the jetty there's a cluster of agency booths representing various islands, boats and resorts, known collectively as the **Tourist Information Centre** – but don't expect impartial information.

If you're heading to **Pulau Tioman** itself, rather than any of the smaller islands, you may as well take your chances with accommodation once there and just buy a boat ticket – even in the busiest season (May–Oct) you're unlikely to have difficulty finding a place to stay. Inside the nearby *R&R Plaza* – a collection of restaurants, moneychangers and more resort offices – you'll find a large signboard indicating which company's boats sail at what time that day – the latest departure will normally be no later than about 2pm, depending on the tide. You can then buy your ticket from the agency booth whose timings suit you best. For the **other islands**, it's better to head for the particular island office itself, each of which are based around the jetty, or to one of the many **travel agencies** in town – mostly along jalan Abu Baker – to book in advance, since boat services are less regular and accommodation more at a premium.

Whatever you decide, make sure that you **change money** before you leave as rates on the islands are lousy; there are branches of *Malayan Banking* and *Bank Bumiputra* on jalan Ismail. If you have your own transport, there's a secure **car park** by the jetty which charges $5 per day.

Pulau Tioman

Shaped like a giant apostrophe floating away in the South China Sea, **PULAU TIOMAN**, 30km east of Mersing, has long been one of Malaysia's most popular holiday islands. Thirty-eight kilometres in length and nineteen kilometres at its widest point make it the largest of the 64 volcanic islands that form the Seribuat archipelago, and it is the sheer size and inaccessibility of its mountainous spine that has preserved its most valuable asset – the dense, variegated **jungle**. As you approach, Tioman looms with smouldering intensity, clouds forever shrouding its hump back: the two peculiar granite pinnacles of Bukit Nenek Semukut on its southern tip stick up like donkeys' ears – though they are known as *chula naga* (dragon's horns). According to legend, the origins of Pulau Tioman lie in the flight of a dragon princess on her way to China, who fell in love with the surrounding waters and decided to settle here permanently by transforming her body into an island. First mention of the island in official records dates back to 1403, when a Chinese trading expedition to Southeast Asia and Mecca found Tioman, with its abundant supplies of fresh water, a handy stopping place. Shipping charts called it Zhumaskan, though local inhabitants believe the island to be named after the *tiong* (Hill Mynah bird) that is commonly found here.

Ever since the 1970s, when it was voted one of the ten most beautiful islands in the world by *Time* magazine, crowds have been flocking to its palm-fringed shores, in search of the mythical Bali H'ai for which it was the chosen film location in the Hollywood musical, *South Pacific*. But twenty-odd years is a long time in tourism. Where slow fishing vessels used to ply the seas for the arduous five-hour journey to Tioman, noisy express boats now complete the trip in less than two hours and these, combined with the several daily flights from Singapore and other parts of the peninsula, have helped destroy the sense of romantic isolation that once made the island so popular. Those in search of unspoilt beaches will also be disappointed: for the most part, the rocky shoreline collects unsightly debris which is revealed at low tide – though there are some superb exceptions. But although years of tramping hordes have taken their toll, most notably in the damage inflicted on the surrounding coral and marine life, the island displays a remarkable resilience, and to fail to visit Tioman is to miss out on somewhere very special – the greater part of the island has still not lost its intimate, village atmosphere.

Tioman presents an array of **activities**, particularly diving (see feature on p.307) and watersports, though you can also go **wildlife**-spotting on its few easy hikes. The mouse deer and flying lemur are the biggest creatures to be found here, though the long-tailed macaques and monitor lizards that hang out in the forest can grow to quite a size. Look out for the clusters of greater frigate birds that gather on the surrounding islands and rocks; occasionally you'll see Christmas Island frigate birds, breeding only on the island after which they are named, more than 2000km south of Tioman. Like the rest of the peninsula's east coast, Tioman is affected by the **monsoon**, making the island virtually unreachable by sea between November and February, while July and August are the busiest months, when prices increase and accommodation can be tough to find. Even in the dry season, it rains almost daily, since clouds seem to hang permanently around the island's mountainous ridge, frustrating sun-worshippers but causing great swathes of mist to arise from the jungle, to the delight of photographers.

Accommodation possibilities range from the island's one international-standard resort, through to chalet developments and simple beachfront A-frames – the latter being gradually edged out by identical, tin-roofed box chalets. Most of the habitation on Tioman is along the west coast, with the popular budget places being in the main village of **Tekek** and the bay of **Air Batang**; while the east coast's sole settlement, **Juara**, is less developed – you'll easily find a place to stay in the latter two villages for under $20. **Genting** and **Salang** are noisy, more upmarket resorts, while **Paya** and **Nipah**, together with **Mukut** on the island's southern coast are just opening up to tourism. Long gone are the days when you had to resort to a hurricane lamp at night – everywhere has electricity, albeit from a local generator. Nightlife has still to take off, however, though beer is freely available everywhere on the island except at Juara.

Getting there

Four companies operate **express boats from Mersing** (see p.303): *Cheang Fong*, *Seagull*, *Open Sea* and *Damai*, each service taking roughly one and a half to two hours, depending on the tide; tickets are uniformly priced at $25 for the one-way trip, though travel agents in Mersing may offer discounts if you buy an open-return ticket (see "Leaving Tioman" below). Slower and less comfortable **bumboats** take anything up to five hours, and are a little cheaper at $15–20 one-way – though these are fast dying out in the face of stiff competition from the express boats. Whichever service you use, it's important to decide in advance which bay or village you want to stay in, since the boats generally make drops only at the major resorts of Genting, Tekek, Air Batang and Salang (in that order); there's one boat a day from Mersing to Juara on the east coast.

SANDFLIES

Sandflies can be a real problem on all of the Seribuat islands, though reputedly Juara, on the east coast of Tioman, is the worst place, depending on the season. These little pests look like tiny fruit flies, with black bodies and white wings and, though harmless, can suck blood and cause an extremely itchy lump, which can sometimes become a nasty blister, especially if scratched. Short of dousing yourself all over with insect repellent or hiding out in the sea all day long, there's virtually nothing you can do, although using suntan oil rather than lotion or cream is supposed to confound their attempts to bite.

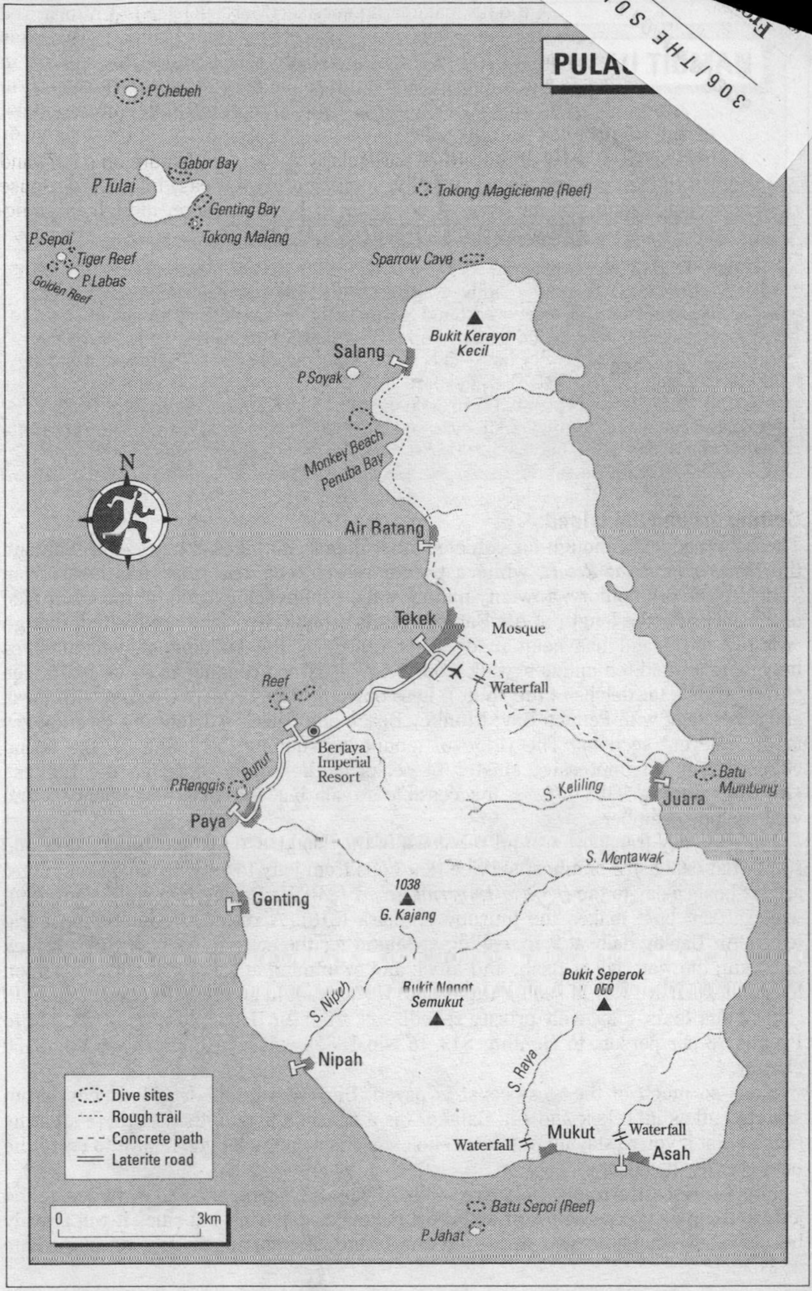

P.Chebeh

Gabor Bay

P.Tulai

Genting Bay

Tokong Malang

P.Sepoi

Tiger Reef

P.Labas

Golden Reef

Tokong Magicienne (Reef)

Sparrow Cave

Bukit Kerayon Kecil

Salang

P.Soyak

Monkey Beach

Penuba Bay

N

Air Ratang

Tekek

Mosque

Reef

Waterfall

Berjaya Imperial Resort

P.Renggis

Burut

S. Keliling

Batu Mumbang

Juara

Paya

S. Montawak

Genting

1038

G. Kajang

Bukit Seperok

060

Bukit Nonot

Semukut

S. Nipeh

S. Raya

Nipah

Waterfall

Mukut

Waterfall

Asah

Batu Sepoi (Reef)

P.Jahat

Dive sites
..... Rough trail
- - - Concrete path
=== Laterite road

0   3km

Singapore, there's a daily catamaran service (March–Oct; $143 return; see Leaving Singapore", p.480–481 for details), which takes four and a half hours and runs directly to the *Berjaya Imperial Resort*. Arriving **by air**, you'll land at the airstrip in Tekek, from where there's a half-hourly shuttle bus to the *Berjaya Imperial Resort*, 2km to the south, along the only proper road on the island. Otherwise, you'll have to make your own way from the airport to the other beaches, involving a trip on the sea bus or sea taxi (see below) from the nearby Tekek jetty.

LEAVING TIOMAN

Although many of the travel agencies in Mersing may try to sell you an open-return boat ticket to Tioman, tickets are readily available from outlets at any of the bays on the island. **Express boats** all leave at around 8–9am daily, making their pick-ups from each jetty, so it matters little which company you go for. Slower bumboats usually leave before midday, picking up from every bay – check with your chalet-owner. There are also daily **flights** to Kuala Lumpur ($141), Singapore ($167) and Kuantan ($72) with *Berjaya Air* (☎03/244 1718), *Pelangi Air* (☎03/746 3000 or ☎02/336 6777) and *Tradewinds* (☎02/225 4488). You can make reservations for *Berjaya Air* and *Pelangi* Air at the *Berjaya Imperial Resort* (☎09/445445).

Getting around the island

The only road wide enough for vehicles other than motorbikes is between Tekek and the *Berjaya Imperial Resort*, while a two-metre-wide concrete path runs north from Tekek to the promontory, a twenty-minute walk, commencing again on the other side of the rocks for the length of Air Batang. **Trails** around the island are limited, though crossing the island has been made a lot easier by the building of cement steps beginning around ten minutes' walk from Tekek jetty and running as far as Juara (see "Juara", p.311, for details of the route). Less obvious trails connect Genting with Paya, and Air Batang with Penuba Bay, Monkey Beach and Salang – details are given below in the relevant sections. The ridge of mountains running the length of the island culminates in an impressive cluster of peaks in the south, of which the highest, **Gunung Kajang** (1038m), is inaccessible to all but the most experienced and well-equipped climbers.

For everyday transport around the coast of the island, use the **sea bus**, a slow and somewhat expensive bumboat service that hops from jetty to jetty. From Tekek, there are six boats a day to the *Berjaya Imperial Resort* ($3), Air Batang ($3) and Salang ($9), while a 9am boat makes the journey to Juara ($18). A **round-the-island** boat trip leaves Air Batang daily at 9am, calling at Mukut for the splendid view of Bukit Nenek Semukut, the waterfall at Asah, and lunch and swimming at Juara – at $30 per person it's an inexpensive way of seeing the island. If you want to go elsewhere, you'll have to rely on **sea taxis**, effectively private speedboats: from Air Batang to Monkey Bay or to Paya is $8 per person, to Genting $13, to Nipah $53, while to Juara is a costly $150 charter.

Since so much of the west coast is paved, **bicycle rental** – at $4 an hour from several outlets in Tekek and Air Batang – is a sensible option, though there's hardly much point if you're staying outside Tekek since at some point you'll have to carry the bike over the headlands.

The **Tourist Information Centre** (daily 7.30am–11.30am), situated right beside the jetty at Air Batang, can help you with boat tickets or day trips, but since it will already be closed by the time you arrive on the island, it's not much use for immediate assistance.

Tekek

The sprawling village of **TEKEK** is the main settlement on the island – and these days is completely overrun with tourist services. You'll find moneychangers in the new Terminal Complex next to the airstrip and, a ten-minute walk south of the main jetty, the police station and a post office. The shabby central beach is finally getting a facelift, while the beach south of the jetty is pretty decent, with good budget accommodation; but the incessant stream of chugging ferries, the daily roar of aeroplanes and the churning of concrete mixers all combine to make Tekek one of the least inspiring parts of Tioman.

For a break from the beach, pop into the **Tioman Island Museum** (daily 9.30am–5pm; free) in the Terminal Complex. Displaying some twelfth- to fourteenth-century Chinese ceramics, which were lost overboard from early trading vessels, it also outlines the facts and myths concerning the island. North of the main jetty, at the very end of the bay, it's hard to miss the government-sponsored **Marine Centre** with its hefty concrete jetty and dazzlingly blue-roofed buildings. Set up to protect the coral and marine life around the island, and to patrol the fishing taking place in its waters, it also contains an aquarium and samples of coral (daily 9.30am–5pm; free).

SNORKELLING AND DIVING

With such abundant **marine life** in its surrounding waters, it's unlikely that you'll want to spend the whole time island-bound. Many of the nearby islets provide excellent opportunities for **snorkelling**, and most of the chalet operations offer **day trips**, costing around $20 (not including equipment). Many **dive centres** on Tioman offer the range of PADI certificates, from an intensive five-day "Open Water" course which includes three days of theory and between seven and nine dives (around $650), through to the ten-day "Dive Master" ($790) – though you should check that qualified English-speaking instructors are employed, and that the cost includes all the necessary equipment.

Most of the best dive sites are around **Pulau Tulai**, a large island about 6km off the northwestern coast of Tioman, though spots close to the *Berjaya Imperial Resort* and off the southern coast are also good; the calm, deep waters of **Monkey Bay** are ideal for beginners. Some of the most rewarding dive sites include:

Golden Reef (depth: 10–20m). Fifteen minutes off the northwestern coast, cliff-like rocks provide a breeding ground for marine life, as well as producing many soft corals.

Pulau Cheheh (depth: 15–25m). In the northwestern waters, this is a massive volcanic labyrinth of caves and channels. Napoleon fish, trigger fish and turtles are present in abundance.

Pulau Labas (depth: 5–15m). South of Pulau Tulai, tunnels and caves provide a home for puffer fish, moray eels and corals such as fan and sweetlip nudibranch.

Pulau Renggis (depth: 5–13m). Directly opposite the resort, a sheltered spot suitable for training and night dives. Good for spotting barracuda, stingray, angel fish

and buffalo fish, as well as two resident, harmless black-tip sharks.

Tiger Reef (depth: 10–25m). Southwest of Pulau Tulai, and deservedly the most popular site, with yellow tail snappers, trevally and tuna, spectacular soft coral and gorgonian fans.

Tokong Magicienne (depth: 3–25m). Due north of Pulau Tioman, this colourful, sponge-layered coral pinnacle is a feeding station for larger fish – silver snappers, golden-striped trevally, jacks and groupers.

Tokong Malang (depth: 5–15m). Just off the southeastern tip of Pulau Tulai, this shallow reef traversed by sand channels is full of sponges. Watch out for barracuda, large cuttlefish, yellow-spotted stingray and leopard shark.

Accommodation

There are lots of **places to stay** in Tekek, though choices are significantly better south of the jetty. Tioman's only true resort is the *Berjaya Imperial Resort* (☎09/445445; ⑥), 2km south of the village, with excellent facilities, including a pool, tennis courts, horse riding, watersports and a golf course – though, surprisingly, the rooms aren't up to much. *Samudra Swiss Cottage* (☎07/242829; ③), the first place north of the resort, lies in a shady jungle setting, with a dive shop and small restaurant; but by far the best atmosphere and value is at *Sri Tioman Chalet* (☎011/711256; ②), further north, where hill-facing or sea-facing chalets sit in a secluded, leafy compound with its own small restaurant. North of the jetty, along the path, are a whole string of down-at-heel A-frames, one of the better places *Ramli's House* (①) with chalets close to the beach in a little garden. If you can face the twenty-minute walk, the best place is friendly *Manggo Grove* (☎011/952932; ①), in the shadow of the rocky headland – chalets overlooking the sea here are the cheapest in Tekek, and there's a batik shop and restaurant.

Eating and drinking

One of Tekek's nicest **restaurants**, *Liza*, is at the far southern end of the bay, with a wide-ranging menu specializing in seafood and Western snacks – dishes average around $6. Most of the other places are attached to the chalet groups; the best are those with beachside settings, such as *Manggo Grove* and *Tioman Sinar*. A rickety bridge crosses a small, stagnant lagoon just past the airstrip, over which you'll find *Norhidayah Café*, serving snacks, fried rice and noodles; it's also good for sunset drinks.

Air Batang

Despite its ever-increasing popularity, **AIR BATANG**, 2km north of Tekek from jetty to jetty, is still one of the best areas on Tioman, competing with Juara for the budget market. Although there's plenty of accommodation, it has a more spacious feel than Tekek or its northern neighbour Salang, and what development there is tends to be relatively tasteful and low-key. The cement path that runs its length is interrupted by little wooden bridges over streams, overhung with greenery. A jetty divides the bay roughly in half; the beach is better at the southern end of the bay, close to the promontory, though the shallow northern end is safer for children. A fifteen-minute **trail** leads over the headland to the north which, after an initial scramble, flattens out into an easy walk, ending up at **PENUBA BAY**. This secluded cove is littered with dead coral right up to the sea's edge, which makes it impossible to swim comfortably, though many people still prefer its peace and quiet to the beach at Air Batang. From here, it's an hour's walk to Monkey Beach, beyond which is Salang; see below for both.

Accommodation

As you get off the boat, a signpost helpfully lists the direction of all the numerous places to stay in the bay; the best are listed below. Not all have fans – the gentle sea breeze is usually adequate – or their own bathrooms, though mosquito nets are usually provided. All these places are marked on the map opposite.

ABC (☎011/349868). At the far northern end of the bay, this long-running operation is still the best in Air Batang: basic but pretty chalets in a well-tended garden with its own freshwater stream. More expensive chalets, up on the rocks, have a great view over the bay. ①–②.

CT's Cottage (no phone). Smart, *atap*-roofed chalets which are a departure from the usual design, surrounded by a garden. ②.

Johan's (no phone). A good choice with well-spaced chalets and new, larger ones up the hill. ①.

Mokhtar Place (no phone). South of the jetty, this place is more upmarket, though all the chalets are a touch cramped together and face inwards, rather than out to sea. ③.

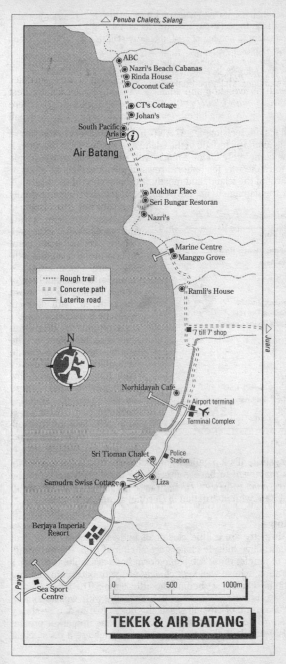

TEKEK & AIR BATANG

Nazri's (☎011/349534). At the southern end of the bay, this rides rather on its long-standing reputation, with shabby, overpriced rooms; however, it has the best bit of beach on the strip. ③.

Nazri's Beach Cabanas (☎07/793244). A truly spectacular outfit (afiliated to *Nazri's*), with large, air-con cottages set in spacious grounds, and some ordinary, cheaper chalets at the back. ②–④.

Penuba Chalets (no phone). The only place to stay in Penuba Bay, and you're committed to eating here every night, too, unless you fancy a scramble over the headland in the dark. Its stilted chalets cling perilously high up on the rocks and have fantastic views out to sea. ①.

Rinda House (no phone). A good spot in a neat and shaded setting, perfect for watching the sun go down from one of their hammocks. ①.

South Pacific (no phone). Close to the jetty, it's a little run-down these days, though all the chalets have bathrooms, and some are right on the beach. ①.

Eating, drinking and nightlife

Though hardly swinging, Air Batang has the best **nightlife** scene on the island. Most of the chalets have their own **restaurants**, though you don't have to be staying there to eat at them. Menus tend to reflect Western tastes and fish is a staple feature.

ABC (see above). Good-quality, inexpensive food – chicken and fish dishes average $4 – and fresh fruit juices. A late bar (*Ten-on*) and good sound system mean this friendly joint is always rocking.

Aris. Overlooking the jetty and overhanging the beach on stilts, the food here is a cut above average, although the service is on the slow side. Expect to pay around $7 for a meal.

Coconut Café. Though the restaurant is nothing special, the satay stall that sometimes sets up outside in the evenings makes this a lively spot.

Nazri's Beach Cabanas. The food is more expensive than elsewhere, and runs to things like chicken-in-a-basket and burgers, averaging $8; its balcony makes a great place for a sunset beer.

Seri Bungur Restoran. Serves traditional Malay food and you won't part with more than about $4.

Salang

No longer the secluded idyll it's often claimed, **SALANG** has been subject to the sort of merciless development that is uncharacteristic of the island as a whole. Since the stretch along the beachfront is now completely chock-a-block with new buildings, the jungle behind is being torn down to make way for uniform rows of identical chalets, all over-priced compared to other parts of the island, and mostly without a view of the sea at all. This is a shame, not only for the damage to the environment, but also as Salang actually

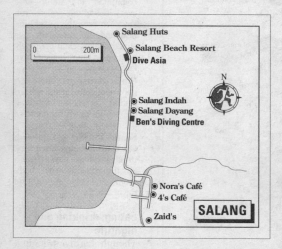

has one of the loveliest beaches on Tioman (its northern half excepted, where rocks and coral debris prohibit all sunbathing and swimming) – though the constant hum of people milling up and down the concrete path detracts from the beautiful setting.

A rough trail takes you over the headland to the south for the 45-minute scramble to **Monkey Beach**. There are few monkeys around these days; the silent rainforest backing the beach is strangely free of the tell-tale rustle in its tree tops; but the well-hidden cove is more than adequate compensation. It's a popular spot for trainee divers because of its clear, calm waters, and you may want to base yourself here to take advantage of the two good **dive schools**, *Dive Asia* and *Ben's Diving Centre*, both running courses at least every four days ($625–1200), with instruction in German as well as English.

Accommodation and eating

On the right as you leave the jetty are a little cluster of budget **places**, the best of which is *Zaid's* (②), whose attractive hillside chalets are sheltered from the surrounding maelstrom by the cover of jungle; there are some dorm beds available, too. *Nora's Café* is a friendly family operation, whose well-kept chalets (①) with bathroom, fan and mosquito nets make them the best value, set behind the little lagoon. The largest outfit, towards the centre of the bay, is *Salang Indah* (☎011/730230), with well-appointed chalets to suit every budget, from run-of-the-mill sea-facing boxes (①) to double-storey family chalets (④). The *Salang Beach Resort* (☎07/792337; ③) has upmarket pretensions, with comfortable, hillside chalets, though the sea-facing ones are a bit steep at double the normal price. At the far end of the bay, the standard chalets at *Salang Huts* (②) are considerably quieter than others along the stretch, though they overlook unattractive piles of rocks and there's no beach to speak of.

There's a polarized choice when it comes to **eating**, from the expensive restaurants at *Salang Dayang* and *Salang Beach Resort*, where the emphasis is on Malay cuisine and seafood at around $8 per dish, to the more informal *Nora's Café*, serving excellent Western and Malay dishes for no more than $2–3. For **nightlife**, the *4's Café* is about your only choice, a candle-lit beer bar.

Juara

As Tioman's west coast becomes more and more developed, many people are making their way to **JUARA**, the only settlement on the east coast. Life is simpler here, the locals speak less English and are much more conservative than elsewhere on the island: alcohol isn't served, and it's even forbidden to drink your own in private. There's only one sea bus and one fast ferry a day, so at any other time the journey to this isolated bay must be made **on foot** through the jungle, a moderate trek that takes under two hours from Tekek. The start of the trail (a 5-min walk from the airstrip) is easy enough to identify since it's the only concrete path that heads off in that direction, passing the local mosque before hitting virgin jungle in about fifteen minutes. There's no danger of losing your way: cement steps climb steeply through the greenery, tapering off into a smooth, downhill path once you're over the ridge. Gentle light filtering through the leaves pinpoints some unusual blue ferns, and some of the rarer trees are labelled. After 45 minutes, a **waterfall** provides a refreshing break, though it's now forbidden to bathe in it, since it supplies Tekek with water. From here, it's another hour or so to Juara village.

Although Juara's seclusion may have saved it so far from the excesses all too apparent on the west coast, everywhere has electricity and new chalets are already springing up. For the time being, however, Juara is refreshingly free from the buzz of speedboats and motorbikes, while its wide sweep of beach is far cleaner and less crowded than anywhere on the other side. A constant sea breeze means that fans aren't necessary, though the downside to this is that the water is always choppy, and the bay, facing out to the open sea, is the most susceptible on the island to bad weather.

Juara in fact consists of two bays, the northern one possessing the jetty, opposite which the cross-island path emerges. Most of the accommodation and all the restaurants are here, too, within a five-minute walk of the jetty. Although the southern bay does have a few chalets, you'll face a long scramble over the rocks or a dark walk along the concrete path that runs behind all the developments to get to the nearest restaurants; everything listed below is in the main (northern) bay.

Accommodation and eating
Starting at the northern end, the best options are *Paradise Point* (①), which has the cheapest A-frames, and chalets a little apart from the rest of the clutch. *Atan's* (①–②), past the cross-island path, boasts an interesting, two-storey guest house, rather like a Swiss chalet; while *Mutiara* (①–②) is the biggest operation, with a wide variety of room types and prices – these are also the people to see if you want to arrange a boat trip for fishing or snorkelling. A little further south, *Basir* has good sea-facing chalets (②), with some cheaper huts as well, while at the very end of the strip, *Sunrise* and *Rainbow* have characterful, painted A-frames right on the beach (both ①).

While there's less choice for **eating**, portions tend, on the whole, to be larger and the menus more imaginative than on the west coast. *Paradise Point* does good *rotis* and unusual dishes, such as fish with peanut sauce and fried rice with coconut, averaging around $5. Two simple places nestle side by side at the jetty, *Ali Putra* and *Beach Café*, both with a huge range of local and Western dishes. To the south, *Happy Café* is always busy, serving ice cream among other things accompanied by good music, while *Sunrise* is open for breakfast and lunch with muesli, home-baked bread and cakes.

Asah and Mukut

South of Juara are the deserted remains of the village at **ASAH**; the round-the-island boat trip (see "Getting around the island", on p.306) calls here, or take a sea taxi from Genting ($60 per person), the nearest point of access. These days, the only signs of life are the trails of litter left by day-trippers dropping by to visit the famous **waterfall**, the setting for the "Happy Talk" sequence in *South Pacific*. A fifteen-minute walk from the ramshackle jetty, the twenty-metre-high cascade is barely recognizable even to avid cineastes, though the tinkling rivulets are certainly photogenic enough. While the deep-plunge pool at the foot of the waterfall provides a refreshing dip, there's not much else to detain you in Asah apart from the stunning view of the dramatic, insurmountable twin peaks of **Bukit Nenek Semukut**.

Mukut

Far better to spend time at nearby **MUKUT**, a tiny fishing village just five minutes from Asah by sea taxi, in the shadow of the towering granite outcrops, which are just beginning to open up to tourism – though more commonly for group bookings than to individuals. Shrouded by dense forest, and connected to the outside world by a solitary card phone, it's a wonderfully peaceful and friendly spot to unwind, though be warned that this is still a conservative place, unused to Western sunbathing habits.

Having paid handsomely to get here, you'll probably want to make it worth your while by staying for some time. The nicest position is occupied by *Chalets Park* (③), with secluded chalets shaded by trees. Those at *Sri Tanjung Chalets* (②), at the far western end of the cove, overlook a patch of beach from their hillside spot – ask at the house in the village where the name is painted on a tyre. The places to **eat** serve only very basic food. The *Sri Sentosa* is a bit on the dingy side, though popular with the locals, while the views from *Mukut Coral Resort* and the *7-eleven* café just by the jetty make up for their lack of variety.

Nipah

For almost total isolation head to **NIPAH** on Tioman's southwestern face. Comprising a clean, empty beach of coarse, yellow sand and a landlocked lagoon, there's no village to speak of, so you'll have to rely on the *Dive Centre* and canoeing to keep you amused. If you're persuasive, you might be lucky enough to get the ferries from the mainland to drop you here since there is an adequate jetty, but it's more likely that you'll have to come by sea taxi from Genting, costing around $30 per person.

There's only one **place to stay**: the *Nipah Village Beach Resort* (☎011/328134; ③), offering basic chalets and more expensive A-frames, as well as a nicely designed restaurant; the food can get a little monotonous. The air-con longhouse, *Nipah Paradise*, at the far end, caters only for prebooked packages from Singapore.

Genting

Usually the first stop from the mainland, **GENTING**, at the western extremity of the island, is hardly a heartening welcome, an ugly blot on the landscape that will probably make you feel more like turning back. The cramped developments cater largely for Singaporean tour groups and the settlement is awash with discos and karaoke bars.

Except on weekends and holidays when prices rise dramatically, it has a rather gloomy out-of-season feel.

The southern end of the beach is the best, which is also where most of the low-budget **accommodation** is situated. There's little to choose between *Genting Jaya* (☎011/731005; ②) and the many more similar, unnamed places nearby. At the far northern end of the concrete path, the *Sea Star Beach Resort* (☎011/718334; ②) is not bad for the price, though *Sun Beach* (☎011/713866; ③), the largest enterprise just north of the jetty, has the widest variety of rooms and a large balcony restaurant. Places to eat are generally limited to large, open-plan **restaurants** attached to the resorts, whose emphasis is on catering to large numbers rather than providing interesting, quality meals. Prices are predictably inflated, though the *Yonghwa Restaurant* in front of the jetty has more moderately priced dishes on its Chinese-based menu.

Paya

By contrast to its noisy neighbour, the understated developments at **PAYA**, further up the west coast (and just 5km from Tekek), seem relatively peaceful, helped by the fact that the mainland ferries rarely stop here. Once again, package tours are the norm, and as a consequence, individual travellers turning up at this narrow stretch of pristine beach will find their options somewhat limited. **Jungle walks** are worth exploring here, as the greenery is at its most lush, despite the minor inroads made by the resorts. You can even walk to Genting from Paya, a tough, overgrown and at times steep trek taking about an hour from jetty to jetty. The easier thirty-minute walk north to Bunut provides greater rewards in the shape of the fantastic, deserted talcum-powder beach at the end of the trail – though rumours are that the Pahang royal family, who own it, are planning a new resort here. From here it's a hot 45 minute walk through the golf course to the *Berjaya Imperial Resort* and a further half hour to Tekek.

The only budget **accommodation** in Paya is at the *Paya Holiday* (☎011/716196; ②), right in the centre of the small bay. A little further to the north, the *Paya Beach Resort* (☎07/791432; ④) has reasonable facilities, including sea sports and snooker, though its chalets are shoddily built. By far the best operation is the *Paya Tioman Resort* (☎011/324121; ④), set back in the woodland, with open-air restaurant and barbeque facilities.

The other Seribuat islands

Though Pulau Tioman is the best-known and most visited of the 64 volcanic islands which form the **SERIBUAT ARCHIPELAGO**, there are a handful of other accessible islands whose beaches and opportunities for seclusion outstrip those of their larger rival. For archetypal azure waters and table-salt sand, four in particular stand out: **Pulau Besar**, **Pulau Tinggi**, **Pulau Sibu** and **Pulau Rawa** – though none of them are particularly geared to a tight budget. All the islands are designated **marine parks** and, like Tioman, belong to the state of Pahang, unlike their port of access, Mersing, which lies in Johor.

Pulau Besar

The long and narrow landmass of **PULAU BESAR**, four kilometres by one kilometre, is also known as Pulau Babi Besar, or "Big Pig Island". Just over an hour's ferry ride from Mersing (departs daily around midday; $24 return), it's one of the most developed islands, with a variety of resorts and chalets, but despite this, outside the main holiday periods, you're still likely to have the place to yourself. The island claims to be

sheltered from the worst of the monsoon, but there's a strong undertow and constant sea breeze even in the dry season. Topped by two peaks, Bukit Atap Zink (225m) and Bukit Berot (275m), the island has three relatively easy **trails** crossing it: a short ten-minute stroll from behind the *Hillside Chalet Island Resort* at the northern end of the island brings you to the Beach of Passionate Love; while an hour's walk starting either from behind the central jetty or from just beyond the *Perfect Life Resort* leads to secluded bays. However, neither beach is as good as the west-facing one where all the accommodation is situated.

Accommodation and eating

The **resorts** on Besar are all well spaced out facing the mainland. The *Radin Island Resort* (☎07/791413; ⑤), more or less in the middle of the bay, is the best place on the island, with superbly designed chalets. The only budget-orientated place is a set of four A-frames (②) right by the sea, not far from the *Radin Island* – ask at the small shop by the phone and post box. The *Perfect Life Resort* (☎07/793948; ⑤), at the far southern end of the bay, has its own jetty and the best bit of beach on the island; its clapboard buildings look a bit motley at first sight, but they're quite comfortable inside. Next door is *Sundancer II* (☎011/716029; ②), with simple but homely chalets set far apart from each other in a well-tended flower garden. Right at the far northern end of the island, the exclusive *Hillside Chalet Island Resort* (☎07/236603; ⑤) has an isolated setting, a good half-hour walk from the rest of the developments. Its beach isn't that special, but the chalets are comfortable and arranged in flourishing green gardens.

All the places to stay have their own **restaurants**; that at the *Hillside* is the most expensive at around $20 per head, although the room rates include breakfast. The *Radin* has an elegant open-air restaurant designed to catch the sea breezes, while *Sundancer II* serves reasonable meals, such as *nasi goreng* for around $4.

Pulau Tinggi

One of the largest of the island group, **PULAU TINGGI** is also the most distinctive, with its towering volcanic peak sticking up like a giant upturned funnel (*tinggi* actually means "tall" or "high"). You can climb the mountain, an arduous four-hour trip, though you will need a local guide to help you as the route can be quite dangerous. A gentler excursion is to the **waterfall**, pretty disappointing outside the rainy season, about half an hour over the headland along a well-worn path – but with such a splendid beach, you'll probably never want to move away from it.

The island is a two-hour boat ride from Mersing ($30 return). **Accommodation** is currently limited to two resorts, *Smailing Island Resort* (☎011/716559; ⑤), badly in need of refurbishment, but with a good swimming pool, and the friendly *Tinggi Island Resort* (☎011/762217; ⑤) with relatively basic chalets but good watersports facilities. You can **eat** at both of the resorts, for about $10 for a meal, or try the local food stalls by the jetty, where *nasi goreng* is served.

Pulau Sibu

PULAU SIBU lies closest to the mainland, the most popular – if the least scenically interesting – of the islands after Tioman, though the huge monitor lizards and the butterflies here make up for the lack of mountains and jungle. Like the rest of the islands, Sibu boasts fine beaches, though the sand is yellower and the current more turbulent than some. Shaped like a bone, the island's narrow waist can be crossed in only a few minutes, revealing a double bay know as Twin Beach; while most of the coves offer good offshore coral.

Most of the resorts on Sibu operate their own boats **from Tanjung Leman**, a tiny village about 30km down the coast from Mersing and an hour's boat ride from the island. It's not an established route, however, so you must notify your resort in advance which will arrange to pick you up. The exception to this is *O&H*'s boat, the distinctive "Black Sausage", which runs the two-and-a-half-hour journey to and from Mersing daily. Tanjung Leman is awkward to get to without your own transport, though it's clearly marked off Route 3. A taxi from Johor Bahru or Mersing costs around $60, but since there is no stand at Tanjung Leman, you must arrange a pick-up in advance. Secure parking is available for $5 per day.

Accommodation and eating

Halfway along the eastern coast, *O&H Kampung Huts* (☎07/793125; ①–③) is the best place to stay on the island if you're on a budget, a friendly and relaxed set-up of A-frames and some dearer but still fairly basic chalets. Also on the eastern side, the *Sea Gypsy Village Resort* (☎011/717109; ⑥) is much more exclusive, aiming for the diving market, with all-inclusive packages costing around US$100 per night for two people. It's a tasteful place, with simple chalets and an attractive lounge and dining area. For something more unusual, try *Rimba Resort* (☎011/231493; ⑥), on the north coast, whose simply furnished cottages have an African theme and whose communal areas are scattered with floor cushions. They offer a package including boat transfer and all food. *Sibu Island Cabanas* (☎07/317216; ③) is one of the lower-priced options – its chalets are shabby, but it has a good stretch of beach. Head back from the *Cabanas*, over the small ridge in the centre of the island, to get to *Twin Beach Resort* (☎03/2415562; ③), the only place with sunrise- *and* sunset-viewing; its A-frames and pricier chalets are run-down, but you can also camp here.

Eating on Pulau Sibu is a pleasure. *O&H* has excellent fish and chicken curries with rice, vegetables and salad, as well as Western options, at around $15 for a full meal. *Sea Gypsy* also offers great cuisine, but for resort guests only. The restaurant at *Twin Beach* specializes in (reasonably priced) Chinese food.

Pulau Rawa

Nobody has a bad word to say about **PULAU RAWA**, an hour and fifteen minutes' boat ride ($20 return) from Mersing; its sugary sands and transparent waters get uniformly rave reviews. There's only one **place to stay**, the deluxe *Rawa Island Resort* (☎07/791204), where there are comfortable, well-equipped chalets (⑤), or cheaper *atap*-roofed A-frames (③), and every facility for watersports. Try to book a couple of days in advance, especially at weekends. Rawa is close enough to visit as a day trip – though you'll be subject to a $4 cover charge, and you're not allowed to bring your own food and drink onto the island.

Endau Rompin National Park

One of the few remaining areas of lowland tropical rainforest left in Peninsular Malaysia, the **ENDAU ROMPIN NATIONAL PARK** covers approximately 870 square kilometres – about one and a half times the area of Singapore. Surrounding the headwaters of the lengthy sungei Endau and sitting astride the Johor-Pahang state border, the region took shape during violent volcanic eruptions more than 150 million years ago. The force of the explosions sent up huge clouds of ash, creating the quartz crystal ignimbrite that's still very much in evidence along the park's trails and rivers, its glassy shards glinting in the light. Endau Rompin's steeply sloped mountains level out into odd, sandstone plateaux, spawning their own particular vegetation, but it is for the richness of **species** of both flora and fauna that it is valued by conservationists. Although the park is known as the habitat of the increasingly rare **Sumatran rhinoceros** – who hide out in the far western area of the park, which is off limits to visitors – the dense, lush habitat has also nurtured several species new to science, including at least three trees, eight herbs and two mosses, documented by the Malaysian Nature Society during its 1985–86 expedition, which in part helped to establish the need for a properly controlled park. The restrictions imposed as a result of Endau Rompin's establishment as a National Park in 1989 at last ensure its protection from the damaging logging that took place here in the 1970s. For the less specialized nature-lover, there's plenty on offer, from gentle **trekking** to more strenuous mountain-climbing and **rafting**. Although gradually becoming accustomed to the exploits of tourists, Endau Rompin still has a long way to go before it suffers the over-use that afflicts Taman Negara, and for the time being at least, its trails remain refreshingly untrampled.

The aboriginal people of the Endau Rompin area are commonly referred to by the generic term **orang ulu**, meaning "upriver people". Traditionally collectors of forest products such as resins, rattan and camphor wood, much of their lives revolves around the rivers – you can still see dug-outs made from a single tree trunk and canoes made of lengths of bark sewn together with twine. In recent years, these nomadic peoples have become more settled, living in permanent villages such as Kampung Peta, accessible only by an old logging track two hours' drive from the nearest tarmac road.

Visiting the park requires a certain degree of determination, however, in the acquisition of permits (see "Practicalities" on the next page), and once there, conditions are fairly primitive: sleeping under canvas is the only comfort you can expect. Administrative complications and a series of charges mean that there is a strong case for booking a tour (see box on p.318). During the monsoon, the park is completely inaccessible, since many of its waterways are swollen and the trails too boggy to use.

The park

The park is watered by three **river systems** based around the main tributaries of sungei Marong, sungei Jasin and sungei Endau, reaching out to the south and east like gnarled and bony fingers. At the confluence of the latter two, at the eastern end of the park, lies Endau Rompin's base camp at **KUALA JASIN**, at whose Visitors' Control Centre you must register on arrival; they will arm you with a map. Although the park's boundaries lie some distance beyond the rivers, it is only in these valleys that you can roam freely. **Rafting** down the peaty sungei Endau is a possibility, too, with short stretches of stony bed and relatively sluggish flow interspersed by white-water rapids and huge boulders. After the river merges with sungei Kinchin, the flow becomes slower and the scenery generally less exciting. Ask at the Visitors' Control Centre for advice on arranging a rafting trip.

The Janing Barat plateau
The accessible area includes the **Janing Barat plateau** (710m), to which a relatively easy four-hour trail leads southeast of the base camp. Topped by a giant sandstone slab, the outcrop marks an abrupt change from the lush growth of wild ginger, characterized by its bright crimson flowers, and the ever-present betel-nut palm, in favour of tough fan palms. On the ridge of the mountain, at around 450m, is a boggy, water-logged area, producing a small patch of heath forest, though it is past this, in the taller forest, that most of the wild animals can be found – look out for the occasional group of pigs, or a solitary tapir chewing at the bark of the trees.

The waterfalls
Each river boasts a major waterfall, the best of which are along sungei Jasin, southwest of base camp. Two routes lead from the base camp to the head of the river, where the spectacular **Buaya Sangkut** cascades in a forty-metre torrent over three levels, splaying out almost as wide as it is high. A track along the northern bank leads directly to the falls, a six-hour hike crossing the multiple ridges of Bukit Segongong (765m). An *orang ulu* legend tells of an old crocodile who lived in the pools above the waterfall, and one day got stuck between some rocks, its body transforming itself into the white-water rapids – the translation of the waterfall's name in fact means "trapped crocodile". A longer, less-defined trail branches off south, about ten minutes out of base camp, crossing sungei Jasin to reach the estuary, Kuala Marong, about 45 minutes later. From here, you can head off eastwards along sungei Marong as far as Kuala Bunuh Sawa (2hr), or continue along sungei Jasin to the **Upeh Guling** waterfall, just ten minutes further on. Although initially less impressive than Buayu Sangkut, one striking feature is the collection of deep potholes near the top of the falls, whose steep sides have been eroded by the water into smooth, natural bath tubs – a good place to soothe aching feet. Following the river closely for a further two hours will bring you to **Batu Hampar** waterfall, where you can either pitch a tent, or continue the additional three hours to Buaya Sangkut.

Flora and fauna in the park
At the upper levels of the jungle, epiphytes are common: non-parasitic plants which take advantage of their position on tree branches to get the light they need for photo-

synthesis. Here, too, massive palms are common, but it's mostly orchids and ferns that flourish. Lower down in the forest shade, where straight, unbranched trunks stand like massive pillars, moths and spiders camouflage themselves among the greyish brown lichen that covers the bark; squirrels and lizards can also be seen scurrying up and down. Much closer to eye level, where most of the light is cut out by the virtually impenetrable canopy, are live **birds** like babblers and woodpeckers; as well as tree frogs, whose expanded disc-like toes and finger tips, sticky with mucus, help them cling to leaves and branches. The forest floor is mostly covered by **ferns and mosses**, as well as tree seedlings struggling to find a chink in the canopy.

It's all too easy to look at your feet while trudging along the trails, or to have your eyes trained on the middle distance for the sight of wild pigs, but most of the animals you're likely to see hang out in the upper levels of the forest. There are at least seven species of **hornbill** (see feature on p.393 for more details) in the park, hard to miss – particularly in flight, when their oversized, white-tipped wings counterbalance their enormous curved orange bill. Early in the morning, the cautious hooting of the male **gibbon** joins the dawn chorus of insects, cuckoos and babblers. This is the time of day when the wildlife is most active; by noon all activity has ceased. The late afternoon cool heralds a second burst of action, and is a particularly good time for bird-watching, while at night, owls, frogs, rats and pythons can all be heard. If you're on a tour with a guide (see below), then you've a better chance of spotting tiger or elephant **footprints**, though wild pigs, mouse deer and colourful toads are far more usual sightings.

Practicalities

At present, there are two ways of entering Endau Rompin National Park, both requiring your own transport to get you as far as the main access points.

From Mersing, take Route 3 as far as Jemaluang, then the smaller and windier Route 50 west for a further 42km. Take a right turn just after a bridge, signposted to the Kahang palm oil mill, 5km before Kahang itself. Continue north for 48km along logging tracks until you reach the *orang asli* settlement of Kampung Peta; from here, it's another 15km to the base camp at Kuala Jasin, taking close to three hours on foot, though by boat it's just 45 minutes (departures on request; $10 per person). If this isn't adventurous enough for you, then you can take a trip upriver **from Endau**, 33km north of Mersing – a six-hour trip on a motorboat as far as Kampung Peta, costing around $200.

Admission and accommodation

To enter the park, you need a **permit**, which costs $20 and is available on the spot from Johor State Economic Unit, Level 2, Bangunan Sultan Ibrahim, Johor Bahru (Mon–

ENDAU ROMPIN TOUR OPERATORS

The following agencies have been recommended by the Malaysian Tourist Development Corporation, but always check exactly what is included in the price before paying.
Giamso Safari, 27 jalan Abu Bakar, Mersing (☎07/792263).
Malaysian Nature Society, 485 jalan 5/53, 46000 Petaling Jaya (☎03/791 2185).
Memories Holiday Resort, 29a jalan Barat (off jalan Imbi), 55100 Kuala Lumpur (☎03/245 0746).
Mohammed Travel and Adventure, 7 lorong Teratai, Kampung Melayu, 86000 Kluang (☎07/733290).
Wilderness Experience, 6b jalan SS 21/29, Damansara Utama, 47400 Petaling Jaya (☎03/717 8221).

Thurs 8am–1pm & 2–4.15pm, Fri 8am–12.45pm & 2.15–4.1a5pm; ☎07/237344). Charges don't stop there, however; once inside the park, it costs $30 per person per day to visit the Upeh Guling waterfalls, Kuala Marong or the Janing Barat plateau, and $50 for the Buayu Sangkut waterfalls; you'll also be charged an extra $10 to use your camera.

Both the Johor and Pahang authorities (both of whose territories include the park) and the Malaysian Nature Society advise you to book an **organized tour** through a travel agency (see the box on the previous page), which can spare you the hassle of arranging permits and travel. A typical four-day/three-night package costs around $250, including guides but not camping equipment. Take loose-fitting, lightweight cotton clothing that will help to protect you from scratches and bites and is quick to dry – even in the dry season you're bound to get wet from crossing rivers. Waterproofs will come in handy, and you'll need tons of insect repellent – and maybe a lighter to burn off leeches.

Although new chalets are planned, for now the only facilities available are at the designated **camping grounds** at the Upeh Guling, Batu Hampar and Buaya Sangkut waterfalls, which cost $10 per person per night. If you're on a tour, your guide cooks simple **food** for you, but take energy-giving snacks as well. If you're not on a tour, you'll have to fend for yourself – remember that carrying cooking pots in addition to the rest of your gear can get very wearing in dense jungle.

Pekan

Nearly 200km up the east coast from Mersing and just 44km from the state capital of Kuantan (see p.260), lies the unassuming royal town of **PEKAN** – its name meaning "small town". Although the state capital of Pahang until 1898, Pekan's sleepy complacency gives the impression that nothing much has happened here for a very long time. Its neat and sober streets are lined with multifarious palaces, some modest, some vulgar – all products of the state's rapid turnover of Sultans – which, together with a handful of colonial buildings in varying states of decay, document Pekan's history.

The town

From the bus station in the northeast of town, at the edge of the tiny commercial sector, turn into jalan Tengku Ahmad facing the languid riverfront and walk past a row of turn-of-the-century shophouses shaded by huge rain trees, until you reach the **Muzium Sultan Abu Bakar** (9.30am–5pm except Fri 9.30am–12.15pm & 2.45–5pm; closed Mon; free). The mustard and cream exterior enhances the elegant columns and cool shutters of a well-proportioned Straits colonial building that has been used for various purposes down the years – from the Sultan's *istana*, and the centre of British administration, to the headquarters of the Japanese army during the occupation. Today it houses the State Museum of Pahang, and its hotch-potch collection – including splendid Chinese ceramics recently salvaged from the wreck of a junk in the South China Sea and an impressive display of royal regalia in the new east wing – is well worth an hour or two. Don't leave without picking up the free guide to the museum; it contains a useful town map, marking all the historical sights as well as a few "interesting trees".

Continuing from the museum along jalan Tengku Ahmad, within a few metres you'll see the unusual **Masjid Abdullah** which was built during the reign of Sultan Abdullah (1917–32). No longer used for active worship, this Art Deco-type structure, whose blue dumpling domes look more Turkish than Southeast Asian, is now home to the Pusat

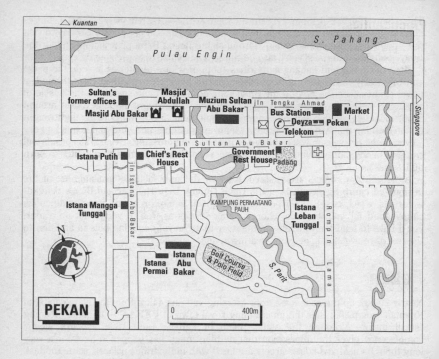

Dakwah Islamiah, the state centre for the administration of religious affairs. Next door, the current mosque, **Masjid Abu Bakar**, has a familiar style, with gold, bulbous domes.

Turn the corner at the end of the road, past the unremarkable former offices of the Sultan, and you'll shortly come to a crossroads. An archway built to resemble elephants' tusks marks your way ahead to the royal quarter of the town, past the fresh, white **Istana Putih** on the corner, which is currently under restoration. Opposite, the **Chief's Rest House** of 1929 seems bereft of a role today, its wooden terraces being left to decay gently. Turn left shortly after the unpretentious, sky-blue **Istana Mangga Tunggal**, and the **Istana Permai** (closed to the public) comes into view, a tiny blue-roofed subsidiary palace that is home to the Regent of Pahang. Dominating the vista is the rectangular facade of the **Istana Abu Bakar**, the palace currently occupied by the royal family. Topped by garish yellow inverted umbrella-type objects, it is an example of misplaced opulence that's generally untypical of the buildings to be found in Pekan; its expansive grounds are now a royal golf course and polo ground.

With the Istana Abu Bakar behind you, take a sharp left immediately before the sports field and a narrow winding lane brings you into **Kampung Permatang Pauh**, the quiet and secluded village area of Pekan, whose simple wooden stilted houses possess an old-world dignity. After about ten minutes' walk, take a right turn, shortly crossing sungei Parit, and continue to the end of the narrow street. Turn left, then immediately right, and facing you is the most impressive of Pekan's royal buildings, the **Istana Leban Tunggal** – a refined wooden structure, fronted by a pillared portico, with an unusual hexagonal tower on each side to complete the symmetry.

Practicalities

Transport connections to Pekan are patchy and slow. If you're coming from the south, it's easier to travel via Kuantan, from where it's a 45-minute journey on bus #31, departing every thirty minutes from the express bus station. Likewise, if you want to continue south, it's better to backtrack to Kuantan to pick up one of the many express buses than wait around for the infrequent local services.

Places to stay in town are limited, and with regular connections to Kuantan, you shouldn't need to stop. The best place is the *Government Rest House* (☎09/421240; ②), in the corner of the Padang, where the rooms and bathrooms are vast, if a little crusty, and the service very attentive. Close to the bus station at 102a jalan Tengku Arrif Bendahara is the *Deyza* (☎09/423690; ①), which is basic but clean – the *Pekan* next door is not as good. The choice of **restaurants** is grim, the best being the couple of Indian places along jalan Tengku Arrif Bendahara. The food stalls near the bus station are very uninspiring.

travel details

Trains

Johor Bahru to Gemas (7 daily; 3–5hr); Kuala Lipis (3 weekly; 7hr); Kuala Lumpur (5 daily; 6hr 20min–7hr 10min); Seremban (5 daily; 4hr 20min–7hr 20min); Singapore (8 daily; 25min); Tumpat (3 weekly; 12hr).

Kuala Lumpur to: Gemas (5 daily; 3hr 40min–4hr 15min); Johor Bahru (5 daily; 6hr 45min–9hr); Segamat (5 daily; 3hr 35min–5hr 10min); Seremban (5 daily; 1hr 50min–2hr 10min).

Seremban to: Gemas (5 daily; 1hr 45min–2hr 20min); Johor Bahru (5 daily; 5–7hr); Singapore (5 daily; 6hr); Kuala Lumpur (5 daily; 2hr–2hr 45min).

Buses

Johor Bahru to: Alor Setar (2 daily; 16hr); Butterworth (at least 2 daily; 14hr); Ipoh (4 daily; 9hr); Kota Bharu (2 daily; 12hr); Kuala Lumpur (every 30min; 7hr); Kuala Terengganu (2 daily; 10hr); Kuantan (8 daily; 6hr); Melaka (5 daily; 4hr); Mersing (at least 2 daily; 2hr 30min); Singapore (every 30min; 1hr).

Melaka to: Alor Setar (11 daily; 8hr); Butterworth (11 daily; 6hr); Ipoh (11 daily; 4hr); Johor Bahru (5 daily; 4hr); Kota Bharu (1 daily; 11hr); Kuala Lumpur (14 daily; 2hr); Kuala Terengganu (1 daily; 8hr); Kuantan (1 daily; 6hr); Mersing (2 daily; 5hr); Singapore (9 daily; 5hr).

Mersing to: Johor Bahru (at least 2 daily; 2hr 30min); Kluang (every 45min; 2hr); Kuala Lumpur (2 daily; 7hr); Kuantan (3 daily; 3hr 30min); Melaka (2 daily; 5hr); Singapore (4 daily; 3hr 30min).

Seremban to: Butterworth (4 daily; 9hr); Ipoh (2 daily; 5hr); Johor Bahru (3 daily; 5hr 30min); Kota Bharu (4 daily; 10hr); Kuala Lumpur (every 10min; 1hr); Mersing (2 daily; 5hr).

Ferries

Melaka to: Dumai (1 daily; 2hr 30min);

Mersing to: Pulau Besar (1 daily; 1hr 10min); Pulau Rawa (1 daily; 1hr 15min); Pulau Sibu (1 daily; 2hr 30min); Pulau Tinggi (1 daily; 2hr), Pulau Tioman (at least 4 daily; 1hr 30min–5hr).

Pulau Tioman to: Singapore (6 weekly; 4hr 30min).

Flights

Johor Bahru to: Ipoh (1 daily; 2hr 10min); Kota Kinabulu (1 daily; 2hr 20min); Kuala Lumpur (at least 7 daily; 45min); Kuching (at least 1 daily; 1hr 25min); Langkawi (1 daily; 2hr 20min); Penang (1 daily; 1hr).

Melaka to: Ipoh (5 weekly; 50min); Singapore (5 weekly; 55min).

Pulau Tioman to: Kuala Lumpur (up to 8 daily; 45min); Kuantan (1 daily; 20min); Singapore (3 daily; 30min).

CHAPTER SIX

SARAWAK

S ix hundred kilometres from the mainland, across the South China Sea, the two East Malaysian states of Sarawak and Sabah occupy the northern flank of the island of Borneo (the rest of which, save the enclave of Brunei, is Indonesian Kalimantan). **Sarawak** is the larger of the two states and a more different place than Peninsular Malaysia it's hard to imagine. Clear rivers spill down the jungle-covered mountains to become wide, muddy arteries nearer the sea, while the surviving rainforest, highland plateaux and river communities combine to form one of the most complex and diverse ecosystems on earth. Monkeys, deer and lizards abound, although both deforestation caused by the logging industry and overuse by indigenous agriculturalists have had a serious effect on mammals like the orang-utan, proboscis monkey and rhino, which are now all **endangered species**. Ironically, even Sarawak's official state emblem, the large, squawking hornbill (see feature on p.393), is at risk – the bird's ivory beak has been used for centuries by indigenous tribespeople to carve images from the natural and supernatural worlds.

Indeed, perhaps the most convincing reason for hopping across the sea is the possibility of contact with the **indigenous peoples** of Sarawak, who make up around half the state's population. They fall into groups known historically either as Land Dyaks, Sea Dyaks or *orang ulu* (people of the interior) who for centuries have lived in massive longhouses, a visit to which is the highlight of most trips to Sarawak. With journeys through the sprawling interior often taking days, rather than hours, travellers have traditionally been dependent on the goodwill of longhouse residents for food, accommodation and safe passage. More formally, tour operators based in Kuching and Miri now pay certain longhouses an annual stipend in exchange for bringing in foreign travellers, sums which pay for structural renovations, and travel and education costs for the longhouse children. However, the increasing contact with the outside world has undoubtedly had a detrimental effect on several of the communities. Visits to the semi-nomadic Penan, especially, who number no more than two thousand in total, have forced the modern age upon them with alarming rapidity. It's argued that contact with tourists can leave groups like this expecting, if not dependent on, food and consumer items from outside.

Other factors also are endangering the survival of the indigenous peoples. The Malaysian government is keen to see the semi-nomadic Penan, and others like them, move into permanent settlements, despite their showing strong signs of wanting to remain forest-dwelling hunter-gatherers. However, the main reason for encouraging tribes to "reap the dividends of development" in this way is to take the sting out of the **anti-forestry campaigns** currently being waged in Sarawak. Timber barons and politicians are afraid that an increase in the number of successful court cases, proving the indigenous groups' customary ownership of the forest, could prevent the lucrative trade in exporting hardwood to the developed world. Although the timber cartels have been successful in buying off some local communities with money and extravagant promises, all across Sarawak, and especially along the Baram river in the north, native tribes backed by environmental groups are resisting the loggers. There's more on the politics of logging and the environment in *Contexts* on p.579.

Most people start their exploration of Sarawak in the capital **Kuching**, in the south-west. This is also the starting point for visiting Iban longhouse communities in the

Batang Ai river system and the Bidayuh dwellings near the Indonesian border, south of the city; and provides a base for seeing nearby **Bako National Park**. Although Sarawak is not noted for its beaches, there's a fine one at **Sematan**, the most westerly point in the state, four hours' ride from the capital by bus. Northeast of Kuching and another four-hour ride away, this time by boat, **Sibu** marks the start of the popular route along **batang Rajang**, Sarawak's longest river. Most people stop at **Kapit** and from there visit longhouses along the Katibas and Baleh tributaries, though you can continue as far along the river as **Belaga**, a remote interior settlement where the Penan occasionally appear to trade.

The route north from Sibu is by bus, along Sarawak's only main road – and even this is not paved in places. You pass through the town of **Bintulu** before reaching **Niah National Park**, whose vast cave system is overwhelming; there's inexpensive accommodation at the park headquarters and accessible hikes in the forest. The road then heads north to **Miri**, a busy town built on oil money, on its way to the Brunei border. East of here, along the **Baram** river, thousands of kilos of hardwood logs – the fruit of the state's aggressive policy of deforestation – are floated down from the forests upstream. Express boats go as far upriver as **Marudi**, from where smaller boats or planes head further east to **Gunung Mulu National Park**, Sarawak's chief natural attraction, featuring the astonishing limestone **Pinnacles** and numerous extraordinary caves and undiscovered passageways under the park's three mountains. Also from Miri or Marudi, flights connect with **Bario** in the northeastern **Kelabit Highlands**, a forested plateau from where it's possible to visit Kelabit longhouses and perhaps even experience the odd encounter with the Penan, who roam these parts.

A little history

Sarawak's first inhabitants were cave-dwelling **hunter-gatherers**, distant ancestors of the Penan, who lived here as long as 40,000 years ago; evidence of their lives was discovered in 1958 at Niah Caves by a team from the Sarawak Museum headed by its curator, Tom Harrisson. The various tribes lived fairly isolated lives and there was little contact with the wider world until the first trading boats from Sumatra and Java arrived in the sixth century AD, exchanging cloth and pottery for jungle produce. These merchants were mainly Hindus, some of whom subsequently settled in Sarawak, while a larger group of Muslim Malays from Java and Sumatra founded the city of Vijayapura in northern Borneo, close to Brunei, in the eleventh century. But isolated settlements like this, on the northernmost fringes of the Sumatran Srivijaya empire, were always vulnerable to attack from pirates and Muslim rivals.

As the Srivijaya empire collapsed at the end of the thirteenth century, so regional trading patterns changed and **Chinese merchants** became dominant, bartering beads and porcelain with the coastal Melanau people for bezoar stones – from the gall bladders of monkeys, and birds' nests, both considered aphrodisiacs by the Chinese. In time, the traders were forced to deal with the rising power of the Malay sultanates, which by the fifteenth century had widened their net of control to include the northwest of Borneo. Paramount was the **Sultan of Brunei**, at the height of whose power even the indigenous peoples of Sarawak, based on the coast and in the headwaters of the large rivers in the southwest, were being taxed heavily; clashes were frequent and bloody. Meanwhile, Sarawak was attracting interest in Europe. Pigafetta, the chronicler of Magellan's voyage in the sixteenth century, described meeting Sea Dyak groups near Brunei Bay, while in the seventeenth century the **Dutch** and **English** established short-lived trading posts near Kuching in order to extract pepper and other spices.

With the eventual decline in power of the Brunei sultanate, the region became impossible to administrate – at the beginning of the eighteenth century civil war had erupted due to feuding between various local sultans, while piracy threatened to

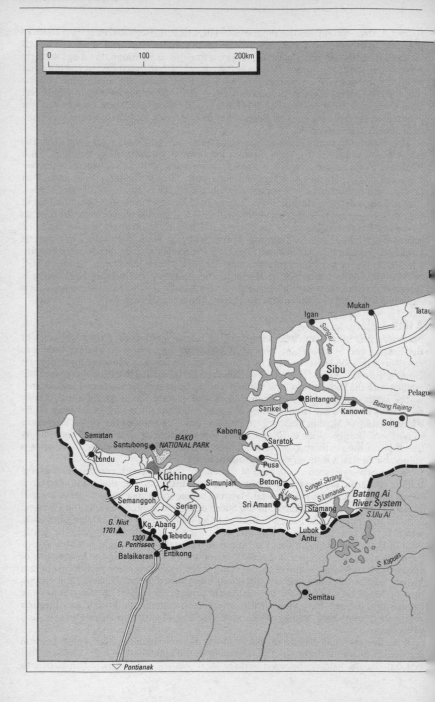

SARAWAK PRACTICALITIES

It matters little what time of year you travel to Sarawak. The riverine **climate** and humid rainforests aren't seriously affected by the monsoon, though you can depend upon it raining steadily most days, with the odd persistent outburst, more often at night than during the day. What will affect your travel plans is the **budget factor**. The flights alone from Peninsular Malaysia to Sarawak can dig deep into the pocket and the basics – accommodation and internal travel – cost more than on the mainland. However, food and soft drinks are always a bargain, and ethnic artefacts bought in longhouses are usually good value too.

Getting there

MAS flights to **Kuching** are the most straightforward approach. The most regular service is from **Kuala Lumpur** (9 daily; $240 one-way); otherwise, there are *MAS* flights from **Kuantan** (4 daily) costing a shade less, and from **Johor Bahru** (4 daily; around $170). There are *MAS* flights from **Singapore**, too (3 daily; around $230), but you'd do better skipping over the causeway to JB and flying from there. The other main service is from **Kota Kinabalu** (5 daily; around $230). From elsehere in the region, *MAS* flies from the Kalimantan city of **Pontianak** on Mondays and Thursdays ($170 plus) and the Indonesian carrier *Merpati* has a Friday flight for around $150; while *Royal Brunei* flies from **Bandar Seri Begawan** on Monday, Tuesday and Friday ($250).

Reaching **Miri**, in the north, usually involves taking an *MAS* internal flight from Kuching (around $230 one-way), though there are a few direct flights daily from KL (around $400). There are also flights to Miri from Kota Kinabalu (4 daily; around $100).

BY BOAT AND OVERLAND

There are daily boat services **from Brunei** to both Lawas (p.384) and Limbang (p.383), the two far northern divisions of Sarawak – see "Leaving Bandar Seri Begawan", p.459.

The main **overland** route into Sarawak is by bus or taxi **from Kuala Belait** in Brunei to Miri, a very straightforward crossing involving a ferry across the Belait river; see p.469 for all the details. The other main crossing is via **Sipitang** in Sabah (see p.426) to Lawas, either by local bus or taxi or by the daily *Lawas Express* which originates in Sabah's capital Kota Kinabulu (see p.408).

From Indonesian Kalimantan, there are remote border crossings to villages in the northeastern Kelabit Highlands (see p.394), though you're unlikely to be approaching from this direction. More straightforward is the overland route into southwest Sarawak, crossing **from Entikong** to Tebedu, around 100km south of Kuching. On this route, the express bus leaves Pontianak in Kalimantan at 6am, arriving in Kuching at 5pm.

destroy what was left of the trade in spices, animals and minerals. In addition, the indigenous groups' predilection for **head-hunting** had led to a number of deaths among the traders and the sultan's officials, while violent confrontations between the more powerful ethnic groups over territory were increasing.

Matters were at their most explosive when Englishman **James Brooke** took an interest in the area. Born in India, Brooke had joined the Indian army and had been wounded in the First Anglo-Burmese War, before being sent to his family home in Devon to convalesce. Returning to the East, he arrived in Singapore in the 1830s, where he learned of the troubles the Sultan of Brunei was having in Sarawak. The Sultan's uncle, Hashim, had recruited Dyak workers to mine high-grade antimony ore in the Sarawak valley near present-day Kuching, but conditions were intolerable and the Dyaks, with the support of local Malays, had rebelled. Brooke – having chartered a schooner in Singapore and gathered together a small but well-armed force – quelled the rebellion and, as a reward, demanded sovereignty over the area around Kuching. The Sultan had little choice but to relinquish control of the difficult territory and in

Getting around

Boats – the main mode of transport – come in three sizes and nearly always run to a relia-ble timetable. Sea-bound **launches** ply the busy stretch from Kuching to Sarikei, at the mouth of batang Rajang; long, thin, turbo-charged *ekspres* **boats** shoot up and down the main rivers; while smaller, diesel-powered **longboats** provide transport along the tributaries.

Occasionally it may be necessary to **rent a longboat**, particularly for travel along the more remote tributaries, though it can be prohibitively expensive if you aren't travelling as part of a group: it's common to pay in excess of $100 a day to visit the more distant longhouses. In addition, although the distances travelled from one longhouse to another are often not that great – around 30km on average – travel upstream against the current, in shallow waters and through rapids is hard going; sometimes you even have to get out of the boat and help pull it over the rocks.

In some areas, you'll need a **permit** before you can visit, though it's usually a straight-forward matter to obtain one; all the details are given where necessary.

Accommodation

Most towns in Sarawak have mid-range hotels, lodging houses and cut-price *rumah tumpangan* (guest houses); the only places with top-class **hotels** are Kuching, Miri and Bintulu.

Budget travellers often head as quickly as possible to the **longhouses**, where gifts or a small cash donation (around $10 a night) take the place of a room rate. The more remote the longhouse, the more basic the gifts can be and local foodstuffs will usually do, though if you plan to stay at a longhouse for a few days then more exotic gifts from Kuching or from your home country are the order of the day. Although it's possible, in theory, to stay for a while at a longhouse, most visitors only remain for a day or two, and you certainly shouldn't plan a budget which includes staying for next to nothing at a long-house every night.

Don't expect to save funds by **camping**: either. There are no campsites: locals seldom, if ever, sleep out in the open, and to do so would at the very least invite much curiosity, and at worst, increase the chances of contracting an unpleasant disease or tangling with unfriendly wildlife.

All the places to stay listed in this book have been given one of the following **price codes**; for more details, see p.40

① Under $20	③ $41–60	⑤ $101–200
② $21–40	④ $61–100	⑥ $201 and above

1841 Brooke was installed as the first **"White Rajah"** of Sarawak, launching a dynastic rule which lasted for a century.

Brooke signed treaties with the Sultan and tolerated the business dealings of the Chinese, though his initial concern was to stamp out piracy and pacify the warring tribal groups. Displaying an early environmental awareness, Brooke also opposed calls from British and Singapore-based businessmen to exploit the region commercially which, he believed, would have been to the detriment of the ethnic groups, whom he found fascinating. In the 1840s he wrote: "Sarawak belongs to all her peoples and not to us. It is for them we labour, not for ourselves." Laudable words, which didn't, however, prevent him from building a network of **forts** to strengthen his rule, or from sending officials into the malarial swamps and mountainous interior to contact the inaccessible *orang ulu* tribes.

Brooke's administration was not without its troubles. In one incident his men killed dozens of Dyaks, who were part of a pirate fleet, while in 1857 Chinese **Hakka gold-miners**, based in the settlement of Bau on the Sarawak river, opposed Brooke's attempts to eliminate their trade in opium and suppress their secret societies. They attacked Kuching and killed a number of officials; Brooke got away by the skin of his teeth. His nephew, **Charles Brooke**, assembled a massive force of warrior Dyaks and followed the miners – in the battle that ensued over a thousand Chinese were killed.

The acquisition of territory from the Sultan of Brunei continued throughout Charles Brooke's reign, which started in 1863. River valleys, known as divisions, were bought for a few thousand pounds, the Dyaks living there either persuaded to enter into deals or crushed if they resisted. Elsewhere, Brooke set the warrior Iban against the Kayan, whose stronghold was in the central and northern interior, and by 1905 his fiefdom encompassed almost all of the land traditionally occupied by the coastal Malays, as well as that of the Sea Dyaks along the rivers and of the Land Dyaks in the mountains. Brunei itself had shrunk so much it was now surrounded on all three sides by Brooke's Sarawak.

During the 1890s Charles Brooke encouraged Chinese **immigration** into the area around Sibu and along the Rajang river, where pepper, then later rubber, farms were established. Bazaars were set up and traders travelled the rivers bartering with the ethnic groups. Brooke thought that these few intrepid Chinese traders – mostly poor men forever in debt to the *towkays* (merchants) in the towns who had advanced them goods on credit – might undermine the indigenous way of life, so he banned them from staying in longhouses and insisted they report regularly to his officials.

The third and last Rajah, **Vyner Brooke**, consolidated the gains of his father, Charles, but was less concerned with indigenous matters. Although the new constitution, which he proposed in 1941, would have accelerated the process of bringing the sub-colonial backwater of Sarawak into the twentieth century, it was the **Japanese invasion** which effectively put an end to his absolute control. Brooke escaped but most of his officials were interned, and some subsequently executed. With the Japanese surrender in 1945, Australian forces temporarily ran the state; Vyner returned the next year and ceded Sarawak to the British government. Many Malays opposed this, believing that **British rule** was a backward step and their protest reached its peak in 1949 when the colonial British Governor was murdered. With Malaysian independence in 1957, attempts were made to include Sarawak, Sabah and Brunei in the **Malaysian Federation**, inaugurated in 1963, with Brunei exiting at the last minute. Sarawak's inclusion in the Federation was opposed by Indonesia and skirmishes broke out along the Sarawak-Kalimantan border, with Indonesia arming communist guerillas inside Sarawak, who opposed both British and Malay rule. The insurgency, known as the **Konfrontasi**, continued for three years, but was eventually put down by Malaysian troops aided by the British.

Throughout the 1960s and 1970s reconstruction programmes strengthened regional communities and provided housing, resources and jobs. These days, Sarawak is a predominantly peaceful, multiracial state, though in recent years social tensions have been triggered by the government's economic strategy, chiefly the promotion of the **timber industry** over the indigenous groups' traditional claims to the land. Despite progress on the question of land rights, communities usually lose the battle for the forests, often forfeiting their former economic autonomy and ending up worse off as wage earners in seasonal employment. Although the rate of deforestation is slowing down, and the state government is now processing more timber in the state rather than exporting whole trunks, hopes for sustainable management of the remaining fifty percent of Sarawak's rainforest cover seem unrealistic – largely because the powerful timber lobby and the state's politicians go hand in glove, unwilling to relinquish control of the highly lucrative logging industry.

SOUTHWEST SARAWAK

Southwest Sarawak is the most densely populated part of the state, supporting around one and a half million inhabitants. It's also the only part of the state to be well served by road, a reflection of its long-standing trading importance: Malays from Sumatra and Java first arrived 1300 years ago; Chinese traders have been visiting the region since the eighth century; while Iban tribes migrated here from the Kapuas river basin in present-day Kalimantan around three hundred years ago, supplanting the original Bidayuh population. A second wave of Chinese immigrants settled here in the eighteenth century, initially to mine gold and antimony, a mineral used in medicines and dyes and which was in great demand in Europe. Later, when the bottom dropped out of the antimony market, the Chinese switched their endeavours to growing pepper and rubber.

A visit to **Kuching** – set upriver from the swamp-ridden coastline – is likely to be a starting point for the more adventurous travelling found beyond Sibu, four hours away by boat. But the city and surroundings contain enough to occupy a couple of weeks' systematic sightseeing if you were so inclined. Kuching's **Sarawak Museum** holds the state's best collection of ethnic artefacts, antique ceramics, brassware and natural history exhibits, while easy day trips include visits to the **Semanggoh Wildlife Rehabilitation Centre** and **Jong's Crocodile Farm**, both to the south, and the **Sarawak Cultural Village**, on the Santubong Peninsula to the north. You'll need more time for **Bako National Park** – at least a couple of days – as you will to see either the **Bidayuh longhouses** near the remote Kalimantan border or the languid coastal village of **Sematan** to the west. The Iban longhouses on the **batang Ai river system**, east of the capital, are a more long-winded proposition altogether, but it's a trip that's rewarded by the warm reception most visitors receive from their hosts.

Kuching

Despite obvious signs of modernity, **KUCHING** – capital of Sarawak – remains a highly attractive place, the city's elegant colonial buildings crumbling under the fierce equatorial sun and lashing rains. The restored courthouse and Istana still serve their original purpose, while the commercial district – in the heart of the old town – is a warren of crowded lanes in which Kuching's Chinese community run cafés, hotels, general stores and laundries. Main Bazaar, the city's oldest street, sports the remains of its original *godowns*, now converted into shops but still overlooking sungei Sarawak, Kuching's main supply route since the city's earliest days. In 1841 James Brooke came up the river, arriving at a village known as "Sarawak", which lay on a small stream called sungei Mata Kuching (cat's eye), adjoining the main river. It seems likely that the stream's name was shortened by Brooke and came to refer to the fast-expanding settlement, though a much repeated tale has the first Rajah pointing to the village and asking its name. The locals, thinking Brooke was pointing to a cat, replied – reasonably enough – "kuching" (a cat). Either way, it wasn't until 1872 that the Charles Brooke officially changed the name from Sarawak to Kuching.

Until the 1920s, the capital was largely confined to the south bank of sungei Sarawak, stretching only from the Chinese heartland around jalan Temple, east of today's centre, to the Malay *kampung* around the mosque to the west. On the north bank, activity revolved around a few dozen houses reserved for British officials and the fort. It was the pre-war **rubber boom** which financed the town's expansion: jalan Padungan, an elegant tree-lined avenue, 1km east of the centre, became the smart place in which to live and work, while the *kampung* areas increased in size, too, as the population was swollen by the arrival of a new bureaucracy of Malay civil servants, as well as by Dyaks from the interior and immigrants from Hokkien province in mainland China looking for work. The city escaped serious destruction during **World War II**, since Japanese bombing raids were mainly intent on destroying the oil wells in the north of Sarawak – the few bombs that were dropped on Kuching missed the military base at Fort Margherita and set fire to a fuel store. Since independence, business has boomed and though many of the impressive nineteenth-century buildings were restored others have been destroyed to make way for new roads and office developments. However, the planners cast a sympathetic eye over perhaps the most important part of Kuching. Following a large-scale, and painfully slow, renovation of the river esplanade – which hindered access along Main Bazaar for years – a spacious riverwalk once again integrates the city with the river to which it owes its growth. Yet despite the inevitable structural changes, the city still feels like a colonial outpost, albeit one tattered at the edges and lazily acquiescing to a benign takeover bid by a cosmopolitan alliance of Chinese businesses, urbanized Dyaks and curious tourists.

On the whole, Kuching is underrated by visitors. Most stop only for a day or two to organize trips to Bako National Park, or to the longhouses and the interior. But there's a fair amount to keep you occupied, pottering around the centre's historic buildings and resting in the landscaped gardens. The city's 250,000 inhabitants are divided between Chinese, Malays, Indians and the various indigenous groups (mostly Iban, Bidayuh and Melanau) with the **Chinese** forming the largest group. Indeed, Chinese enterprise has been pivotal to Kuching's economic success, while Chinese clan houses play a central part in the cultural life of the city; at the main temple, there are musical events, theatrical performances and religious rituals most weekends (and nonstop at Chinese New Year). Despite the Iban accounting for around thirty percent of the state population, the various indigenous groups have little impact in Kuching, although they come out in force on Saturday (market day) and at the annual festivals.

Arrival and information

Kuching **airport** is 10km south of the city, from where you either take a taxi into the centre (around $15) or the #12A bus, from directly outside the terminal (every 40min, daily 7am–8pm; $3); it's a thirty-minute ride into the city. Long-distance buses from Pontianak (in Kalimantan) or from Sarikei bring you into the city along the esplanade road, Main Bazaar, terminating at the **bus station** on lebuh Jawa, west of the centre, a good fifteen-minute walk from the main hotels and lodging houses. Buses from the airport also end their run at this station; on their way, they swing by lebuh Temple, in the old part of town, close to jalan Green Hill, the most popular accommodation area – ask the driver to drop you off here, before you reach the terminal.

The **boats** from Sibu and Sarikei dock at the Express Association Wharf, 5km west of the city centre in the suburb of Pending. Walk down to the main road, 100m away, and catch bus #17 or #19 into the centre (every 30min, daily 6am–7pm; $1), a thirty-minute trip. These buses also run via lebuh Temple before reaching the bus station at lebuh Jawa.

Information

There is a small **Sarawak Tourist Association** (STA) desk in the airport (daily 8am–9pm; ☎240620), but the main office is in a beautifully restored *godown* on Main Bazaar, at the junction with jalan Tun Haji Openg (Mon–Thurs 8am–12.45pm & 2–4.15pm, Fri 8–11.30am & 2.30–4.45pm, Sat 8am–12.45pm; ☎248088). This has plenty of maps, bus

The telephone code for Kuching is ☎082.

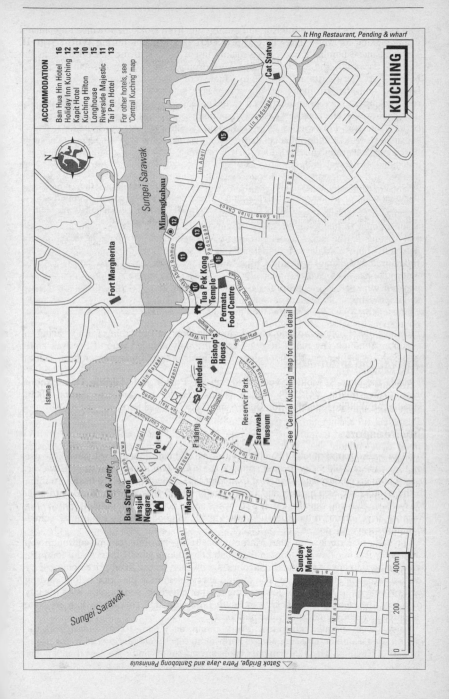

KUCHING

△ It Hng Restaurant, Pending & wharf

ACCOMMODATION

Ban Hua Hin Hotel	16
Holiday Inn Kuching	12
Kapit Hotel	14
Kuching Hilton	10
Longhouse	15
Riverside Majestic	11
Tai Pan Hotel	13

For other hotels, see
'Central Kuching' map

Cat Statve

Sungei Sarawak

Minangkabau

Fort Margherita

Jln Abdul Rahman

Jln Abell

Jln Padungan

Jln Ban Hock

Jln Song Thian Cheok

Jln Bukit Mata Kuching

Tua Pek Kong
Temple

Permata
Food Centre

Istana

Bishop's
House

Main Bazaar

Jln Carpenter

Cathedral

Jln Wayang

Jln Ban Huat

Jln Tun Openg

Jln Courthouse

Jln McDougall

Reservoir Park

Sarawak
Museum

Jln Tun Haji Openg

Padang

Police

Jln Mosque

Jln India

Jln Jawa

See 'Central Kuching' map for more detail

Pier & Jetty

Bus Station

Masjid
Negara

Market

Jln Gambier

Jln Satok

Jln Haji Taha

Jln Palm

Jln Nanas

Jln Reservoir

Sunday
Market

Jln Palm

Jln Abbah Abol

Sungei Sarawak

0   200   400m

LEAVING KUCHING

For details of airline offices, the national parks office and Indonesian consulate in Kuching, see "Listings", p.341. For tour operators see box on p.342.

Airport
Take a taxi, or the #12A bus from the station on lebuh Jawa out to the airport (flight enquiries on ☎454242). There are services to Bandar (3 weekly; $360), Bintulu (9 daily; $120), Johor Bahru (4 daily; $240), Kota Kinabalu (5 daily; $325), KL (9 daily; from $230), Kuantan (1 weekly; $335), Miri (13 daily; $325), Sibu (11 daily; $75), Singapore (3 daily; $300) and Pontianak (3 weekly).

Boats
Boats to Sarikei ($20) and Sibu ($29) leave from the Express Association Wharf at Pending (daily at 8.30am and 1pm); the much slower cargo boat departures (around $15) are on Wednesday and Saturday at 6pm. Take buses #17 or #19 from lebuh Jawa, Main Bazaar or jalan Tunku Abdul Rahman to the wharf; buy your ticket on the boat. You don't need to book in advance.

Buses
The main bus terminal is at lebuh Jawa. Among companies operating out of here are *Chin Lian Long* (☎327666), which runs the city buses, and *Sarawak Transport Company* (☎242967) for Semanggoh every 2hr, daily 8am–6pm; $1.50) and Sarikei (daily at 6.15am & 1.15pm; $18).

---

timetables, hotel listings and dozens of glossy leaflets on everything from weaving to tattooing. Although city maps here are free, the only detailed map of Sarawak state costs $50 – available from the bookshop in the foyer of the *Holiday Inn* on jalan Tunku Abdul Rahman.

Inside the main STA office, you'll also find the **Parks and Wildlife Department** office (same hours; ☎442180), which issues permits for and information about Semanggoh Wildlife Rehabilitation Centre and Bako National Park.

City transport

You can **walk** around much of Kuching with ease and consequently will have little use for the white-and-blue **city buses**, run by the *Chin Lian Long* company. However, some of the green *Sarawak Transport Company* (*STC*) **local buses** are useful, running to the boat wharf, Semanggoh and the coast. The **STC bus station** is close to jalan Market – though you can also catch *STC* buses at the post office or outside *Holiday Inn Kuching*. Buy tickets on the bus and always arrive in good time, as sometimes scheduled buses leave as soon as they're full.

The main **taxi rank** is on jalan Market, close to the two bus stations, although you can usually flag one down in front of the plush hotels along jalan Tunku Abdul Rahman; avoid going into any of the hotel concourses, however, as the fixed prices charged by the taxis are a lot steeper there. You should always negotiate the price before starting the trip – often the "fixed rate" lowers after a bit of haggling, and to get across the city from, say, the *Holiday Inn Kuching* to lebuh Jawa shouldn't cost more than $8. Note that fares increase significantly after midnight.

Noisy, diesel-operated **sampans** (every 15min, daily 6am–10pm) depart from the jetty on jalan Gambier, crossing sungei Sarawak to reach Fort Margherita in the northern part of Kuching. The boat trip only takes a few minutes and costs less than a dollar each way.

Accommodation

Finding inexpensive **accommodation** in Kuching is not easy – be prepared to pay around $30 for a double room if the budget places are full. Moving up a grade, the mid-range lodging houses are reliable enough; there are at least a dozen in the jalan Green Hill area, the best of which are reviewed below. At the top end of the scale, most of the expensive hotels have great views over the river, as well as swimming pools and 24-hour service. If you want to stay on the coast, head for the *Holiday Inn Damai Beach* on the Santubong Peninsula (see p.344). All the hotels below are marked either on the map of greater Kuching above or central Kuching below.

Ah Chew Hotel, 3 jalan Jawa (☎286302). Noisy, as it overlooks the bus station. Used by a mostly young Chinese clientele, the rooms have communal bathrooms and paper-thin walls. ①

Anglican Rest House, jalan McDougall (☎240188). Kuching's best deal is set in the gardens of the Anglican Cathedral. It's often full (particularly in August), so call to book ahead. The main two-storey, wooden colonial building has comfortable, twin-bed rooms with high ceilings and shared bathrooms. There are also two self-contained apartments with bedroom, verandah and bathroom. ①–②

Arif Hotel, jalan Haji Taha (☎241211). Snug and friendly place, handily positioned for the night market. A variety of rooms are available, with fan, air-con or bath. ②

Aurora Hotel, jalan McDougall (☎240281). The oldest and once the most prestigious hotel in Kuching has recently been modernized. Comfortable air-con rooms with shower. ④

Ban Hua Hin Hotel, 36 jalan Padungan (☎242351). Aimed at Chinese workers rather than tourists; basic and friendly. ①

Borneo Hotel, 30 jalan Tabuan (☎244122). Top-class hotel whose lovely rooms have polished wooden floors, air-con, bath or shower, and TV. ⑤

Fata Hotel, junction of jalan Temple and jalan MacDougall (☎248111). Excellent location a few metres from Reservoir Park. The small rooms are equipped with air-con, shower and TV. ③

Holiday Inn Kuching, jalan Tunku Abdul Rahman (☎426169). Overlooking the river with some of the rooms looking directly out onto the fort on the opposite bank; has a pool, restaurant and bookshop. ⑥

Kapit Hotel, 59 jalan Padungan (☎244179). Away from the centre and popular with a Malaysian business clientele. Rooms have air-con, shower and TV. ②

Kuching Hilton, jalan Tunku Abdul Rahman (☎248200). Another top-class hotel, whose front rooms have a great view of the river. There's a pool and revolving bar. ⑥

Kuching Hotel, 6 jalan Temple (☎413985). About the best budget option if the *Rest House* is full. That said, it's very basic, spartan and a bit dirty, with one shower and toilet on each floor, although each room has a fan and sink. ①

Hotel Longhouse, jalan Abell (☎419333). East of the centre, and frequented mainly by visiting business people. Rooms have air-con, shower and TV. ③

Mandarin, 6 jalan Green Hill (☎418269). One of the most promising places in Green Hill. Full facilities – air-con, shower, toilet and TV – but most rooms are rather small ②

Orchid Inn, 2 jalan Green Hill (☎411417). Like the *Mandarin,* this is fairly comfortable and is close to some excellent cafés; particularly friendly staff, too. ②

Riverside Majestic, jalan Tunku Abdul Rahman (☎247777). Large parts of Chinatown were flattened to make way for Sarawak's priciest hotel, a ten-floor marble and glass extravaganza. ⑥

Tai Pan Hotel, 93 jalan Padungan (☎082/417363). Cosy, family-run place, situated on a lane just off the main street. The small rooms have air-con, shower and TV. ②

The city

The central area, sandwiched between jalan Courthouse to the west, jalan Temple to the east and Reservoir Park to the south, is usually referred to as **colonial Kuching**. The Courthouse, the Post Office and the Sarawak Museum are the most impressive buildings here, with the museum itself the city's most absorbing attraction. Set within this small area is **Chinatown**, which incorporates the main shopping streets – Main

Bazaar, jalan Carpenter and jalan India. To the east of jalan Temple lie jalan Green Hill and jalan Tunku Abdul Rahman, the principal accommodation districts. Further south from the old town's narrow, busy streets – yet only fifteen minutes' walk from the river – is **Reservoir Park**; while bordering the colonial area, on the western edge of the centre, is the state **mosque** and main Malay residential area, dominated by detached *kampung*-style dwellings with their sloping roofs, intricate carvings around the windows and elevated verandahs. Southwest, Satok bridge leads to Kuching new town and the timber museum, while north, across the river, is **Fort Margherita** – now the Police Museum – and the **Istana**, still the residence of Sarawak's head of state.

Colonial Kuching

If you exclude the Sarawak Museum, Kuching's colonial buildings will occupy only an hour or two of your time. The most obvious place to start is at the square white **Courthouse**, overlooking the river on the south bank at the junction of Main Bazaar and jalan Tun Haji Openg. Built in 1874, and sporting impressive Romanesque columns and a balcony, this is where the rebellious Chinese miners, who nearly ended James Brooke's tenuous rule in the 1850s, were sentenced to death. Today the four-room court has less dramatic sessions – to which the public are admitted (Mon–Thurs 10am–noon) – and it's worth going inside the main court chamber in any case to see the **murals** on the ceiling and walls. The traditional motifs were painted by artists from various tribal groups, the vividly coloured paintings representing scenes from long-house life: a woman weaving *pua kumba* cloth on her loom (see p.352), men hunting with blowpipes, and celebrations after the rice harvest.

Straight across jalan Tun Haji Openg, the **Round Tower** was originally built as a dispensary in the 1880s, its austere dimensions explained by the fact that it was designed to double as a fort in an emergency. Nearby, the **Charles Brooke Memorial**, a twenty-foot-high granite obelisk built in 1924, has a bronze panel sunk into each corner on which stone figures representing the four most numerous races in Sarawak are set in relief: the Chinese, Dayaks, Malays and *orang ulu*. There's also a marble relief of Charles Brooke and an inscription giving details of his life.

Walking away from the river, it's one block south to the absurdly grand **Post Office**, whose massive ornamental columns, semicircular arches and decorative friezes were outmoded almost as soon as they were completed in 1931. Continue on up jalan Tun Haji Openg, turn left onto jalan McDougall and you'll see the modern Anglican **Cathedral**, a walk through whose grounds leads to the oldest surviving building in Kuching, the large, two-storey wooden **Bishop's House**, built in 1849 – nowadays, privately owned and not open to the public.

The Sarawak Museum

Further up jalan Tun Haji Obeng, overlooking the spacious Padang, is Kuching's prime tourist attraction, the **Sarawak Museum** (daily 9am–6pm; free), whose main building (the largest colonial structure in Kuching) was built in the 1890s and is set back from the road in lovely gardens. A new wing, opened in 1983, lies on the other side of jalan Tun Haji Openg – you can get from one to the other by using the bridge over the road. Charles Brooke first conceived the idea of a museum in Kuching, prompted by the nineteenth-century naturalist Alfred Russell Wallace, who spent two years in Sarawak in the 1850s; Wallace's natural history exhibits now form the basis of the collection on show in the main building. The museum's best known curator was **Tom Harrisson,** whose discovery of a 39,000-year-old skull in the caves at Niah in 1957 prompted a radical reappraisal of the origins of early man in Southeast Asia. Under the museum's auspices, Harrisson frequently visited remote *orang ulu* tribes, bringing back ceremonial artefacts from their longhouses which comprise some of the museum's greatest assets, on display in the new wing.

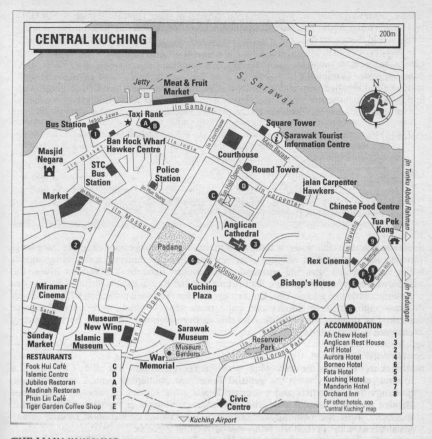

CENTRAL KUCHING

0   200m

S. Sarawak

N

Jetty   Meat & Fruit Market

Jln Gambier

Taxi Rank

Bus Station   Lebuh Jawa

Ban Hock Wharf Hawker Centre

Jln India

Square Tower

Sarawak Tourist Information Centre

Main Bazaar

Jln Market

Masjid Negara

STC Bus Station

Police Station

Courthouse

Round Tower

jalan Carpenter Hawkers

Jln Carpenter

Jln Khoo Han

Jln Hun Yeang

Market

Jln Mosque

Chinese Food Centre

Tua Pek Kong

Padang

Anglican Cathedral

Jln Wayang

Rex Cinema

Jln McDougall

Jln Temple

Bishop's House

Jln Green Hill

Miramar Cinema

Jln Satok

Kuching Plaza

Museum New Wing

Sunday Market

Islamic Museum

RESTAURANTS
Fook Hui Café   C
Islamic Centre   D
Jubilee Restoran   A
Madinah Restoran   B
Phon Lin Café   F
Tiger Garden Coffee Shop   E

Sarawak Museum

War Memorial

Museum Gardens

Jln Hall Open

Reservoir Park

Jln Reservoir Park

Jln Lorong Park

Civic Centre

Jln Tunku Abdul Rahman

Jln Padungan

ACCOMMODATION
Ah Chew Hotel   1
Anglican Rest House   3
Arif Hotel   2
Aurora Hotel   4
Borneo Hotel   6
Fata Hotel   5
Kuching Hotel   9
Mandarin Hotel   7
Orchard Inn   8
For other hotels, see
'Central Kuching' map

Kuching Airport

THE MAIN BUILDING

There's an information desk at the main entrance, beyond which is the **natural science** section whose varied exhibits include a massive hairball from a crocodile's stomach and fairly pedestrian displays highlighting the diverse range of plant, animal and bird species in Borneo. The **ethnographic** section on the upper floor is of an altogether different standard, despite the occasionally vague descriptive labelling. Here you can walk into an authentic wooden Iban longhouse and climb up into the rafters of the *sadau* (loft), which is used to store bamboo fish baskets, ironwork and sleeping mats; you're also free to finger the intricately glazed, sturdy Chinese ceramic jars and fine woven *pua kumbu* cloth. The Penan hut here is a much simpler affair, constructed of bamboo and rattan creeper, within which are blowpipes and *parangs* (machetes), animal hides, coconut husks used as drinking vessels, and hardy back-baskets, made from the *pandanus* palm and the *bemban* reed. At the other end of the floor, there's a collection of fearsome Iban war totems, and woodcarvings from the Kayan and Kenyah ethnic groups who live in the headwaters of the Rajang, Baram and Balau rivers. One carving – a ten-metre-high ceremonial pole made of hardwood – sports a pattern of grimacing heads and kneeling bodies stretching up in supplication. Towering above all

LONGHOUSE LIFE

In the last century observers described Sarawak's **longhouses** as being up to one kilometre long, but these days few have more than one hundred doors – representing the number of families living there. Traditionally, longhouses were erected by rivers (the main means of transport for Sea Dyaks – the Iban and Melanau – and *orang ulu* groups like the Kenyah, Kayan and Kelabit), though the predominant Land Dyak group, the Bidayuh, built their dwellings away from rivers, in the hills. Most longhouses are made from timber laced with bamboo and rattan cord. A communal verandah runs parallel to the private section where the families eat, sleep and keep their artefacts, some of which (like the ceramic jars) can be centuries old. On the verandah the inhabitants socialize, dry rice, weave baskets and textiles, and greet visitors. A near vertical ladder is often the only way up, while underneath the longhouse pigs and chickens rummage around, eating the various bits of debris thrown from above. Outlying huts, set away from the main house, are used to store grain. In the more hierarchical ethnic groups, like the Kayan, natives not born in the longhouse but who desire entry live for several years in nearby huts, awaiting the higher status which would allow them access to the big house, which only comes about when the *tuai* (headman) decides.

of this, on one of the walls, is a massive mural, whose images are excerpts from longhouse life: sowing and reaping rice, hunting, fishing, dancing and playing music. Elsewhere, you'll also find **musical instruments** used by the various tribes: the Bidayuh's heavy copper gongs, Iban drums and the Kayan *sape,* a stringed instrument looking a little like a lute. Also, keep an eye out for the small collection of Iban *palangs* – two-centimetre-long rhinocerous bone penis pins – which were once a popular method of re-energizing a wilting lovelife in the longhouse; inserted horizontally, in case you were wondering.

THE NEW WING

Across the road, in the new wing, a recent reorganization has shifted the exhibits around considerably, with the **ground floor** now containing a book and gift shop, paintings by local artists and a section detailing the history of Sarawak from James Brooke until the present day. The real interest, though, is upstairs, with separate, extensive sections containing the museum's unparalleled collection of antique ceramics and brassware, prehistoric relics and early trading goods.

Heading round anticlockwise, initial displays are of **prehistoric artefacts**, including ceramic fragments found at Tom Harisson's Niah and Santubong excavation sites – in particular remnants of plain, globular Neolithic vessels used in funerary rites. Early **Chinese ceramics** are well represented, too. Typical of the Song Dynasty is the dish decorated with carved lotus petals, and there's also a vase in the shape of two fishes with their stomachs joined and sharing a common mouth. The Tang and Yuan Dynasty wares represent a qualitative step forward – look for the beautiful blue-white glazed teapot decorated with a pair of dragons whose heads protrude from the body forming the spout, the tails the handle and the legs the feet. Later fifteenth-century wares – the products of larger, more complex kilns – are more elaborate still and the museum contains some wonderful examples of work adorned with sprig moulding (embroidering with representations of twigs and other images): one dish is decorated with a four-clawed dragon pursuing a flaming pearl.

From the tenth century onwards, Borneo's tribal groups traded rhinocerous horns, ivory and spices for Chinese ceramics, most notably colourful **storage jars**, which became closely linked to tribal customs and beliefs. The status and wealth of a person depended on how many jars they possessed, with the most valuable ones only used for funereal purposes or for ceremonies like the *gawai kenyalang* (the rite of passage for a mature, prosperous man). Others would be used for storage or to brew rice wine, as a dowry in marriages, or as fines for adultery and as settlements in divorces. Among the Berawan in northern Sarawak, when a person died, the corpse was packed into a jar in a squatting position; as decomposition took place, the liquid from the body was drained away through a bamboo pipe. Jars – it is said – can also possess the power of foretelling future events and can summon spirits through the sounds they emit when struck.

Many of the hundreds of jars here are magnificent objects, in brown, black and vivid green glazes, with dragon-emblazoned motifs. One spectacular giant is almost a metre high, coloured blue and white, and adorned with scenes of real and mythic Chinese life, incorporating the intricate detail of plant petals, houses and epic landscapes. Another is decorated with the outlines of a fighter holding a stick. Contemporary ceramics take their influence from these early jars, with skilled Chinese potters – mainly immigrants from Kwantung Province – adopting the traditional decorative patterns of the ethnic groups, often deploying animist images of birds, plants and fish.

The other major section is devoted to the exquisite **brassware** collection. Many of these superbly wrought cannons and kettles were crafted in Brunei and, again, many found their way into interior longhouses through exchange with traders and merchants, where they were traditonally used as a means to store wealth and as a unit of currency. Both kettles and cannons are strikingly ornate, adorned with miniature animals – which, in the case of the dragons on the cannons, make up the very body of the instrument itself.

From the Sarawak Museum to Reservoir Park

Behind the new wing of the museum, the **Islamic Museum** (daily 9am–6am; free) is housed in a one-storey building, painted in brilliant white and with a cool interior with tiled floors. Each of the four main rooms is devoted to a different aspect of Islamic culture: architecture, history, music and prayer.

Back across the road at the Sarawak Museum's main building, a path through the sloping garden leads to the war memorial – less than five minutes' walk away. You'll pass the **Kuching Aquarium** (daily 9am–6pm; free) on the way, which contains a small collection of marine life, including turtles from Sipidan in Sabah. Following the path past the memorial takes you to the corner of the museum gardens and out onto narrow Jalan Reservoir, across which lies **Reservoir Park**, a beautiful, if artificial, tropical environment with many resident bird species and wildlife. It's not a very large place you can walk its circumference in less than thirty minutes – but there's a café (daily 8am–4.30pm), a drinks kiosk, boats for rent, a playground and stretching frames for work out enthusiasts. Quiet during the day, it perks up in late afternoon when joggers take to the paths and couples to the benches. The other road bordering the park, Jalan Lorong Park, leads up to the **Civic Centre** on Jalan Budaya, an ultra modern building which includes a planetarium and has space for temporary exhibitions. The Sarawak Tourist Association office has information on current events here, though most visitors come for the restaurant on the top floor which has fine views over the city.

Chinatown and further east

The grid of streets running eastwards from Jalan Tun Haji Openg to the main Chinese temple, Tua Pek Kong, constitutes Kuching's **Chinatown**. On busy Main Bazaar and, one block south, Jalan Carpenter, numerous cafés, restaurants, laundries and stores go about their business, many operating out of renovated two-storey *godowns*, originally built by Hokkien and Teochew immigrants who arrived in the 1890s. The *godowns* were originally divided into three sections: the front room was where the merchant conducted business and stored his goods, from salt and flour to jungle products collected by the ethnic groups and salted fish caught and prepared by Malay fishermen; the back room was the family quarters; while the loft was where the business partners would sleep. Previously, many of these warehouses stood at the water's edge, though there's now a concrete esplanade between the river and the warehouses.

Overlooking the river on jalan Temple stands the oldest Taoist temple in Sarawak, **Tua Pek Kong**, built in 1876, its position – in accordance with Chinese tradition – carefully divined through geomancy. Plenty of people drop by during the day to pay their respects to the temple deity, Loh Hong Pek, who looks after the people of the surrounding area; and to burn paper money and joss sticks; and to pray for good fortune. The temple maintains an immensely busy cultural life and during Chinese New Year especially, there are theatrical and musical performances, readings and rituals.

Jalan Tunku Abdul Rahman heads east from the temple, past several of the swankier hotels, changing its name to **jalan Padungan**, which runs to a roundabout on the eastern edge of the city, separating Kuching proper from its outskirts. The one-kilometre walk along the tree-lined avenue takes you past some splendidly ornate houses, and you can't fail to spot the avenue's **great cat of Kuching**, a five-metre-high white plaster effigy, her paw raised in welcome. Created by local artist Yong Kee Yet as a nod to the supposed derivation of the city's name, it's a popular spot for family photos.

West of Chinatown: market, kampung and mosque

Heading west along the riverfront from Main Bazaar puts you on jalan Gambier, fronting which is the **cargo port** – less important than it once was, but still a fascinating place around which to wander. In the late afternoon you'll see cargo boats come from West Kalimantan unloading tons of tropical fruits to be sold in the nearby **markets**. One block back from jalan Market a series of open-air food stalls are very much the focal point for Kuching's traders and buyers, who tuck in throughout the day to noodle soups and stir fries, *roti canai* and *daal.* East of here a handsome arch leads into **jalan India**, the busiest pedestrian thoroughfare in Kuching, and the best place to buy shoes and cheap clothing. The street is named after the Indian coolies who arrived in the early part of this century to work at the docks; at 37 jalan India, a dim passageway leads to the oldest of the Indian community's mosques.

Follow the curve of the river southwest for 300m or so and you reach the **Malay kampung**, which retains many well-preserved family houses, built at the turn of the century by well-to-do government officials. Even the smaller buildings here share the same attractive features, like the floor-level windows fronted by curved railings.

On the steep hill above stands the **Masjid Negara**, whose golden yellow roof glints in the dying sun at evening prayers. There's been a mosque on this site for around two hundred years, though this one only dates from the 1960s, festooned with gold cupolas. If you want to go inside (9am–3pm; closed Fri), men must wear long trousers and women skirts and headdress; the women's clothing is provided by the mosque at the entrance.

The Malay enclave's southern boundary is the wide, traffic-clogged **jalan Satok**. At its junction with jalan Palm, opposite the *Miramar Cinema*, lies the site of Kuching's **Sunday market**, which actually kicks off on Saturday afternoon; it continues until about 2am on Sunday morning, picks up again at 6am and finally ends around midday. Buses #4A and #4B get you there from the lebuh Jawa bus station, or from outside the post office, in five minutes. This is the place for picking up supplies of everything from rabbits to knives; other stalls sell satay, curry pie, sweets and *lycheesank,* a soft drink made with beans, rice pellets, sugar and lychees. Amid the congested confusion, look out for the alley where Dyaks sell fruit, vegetables and handicrafts – a good place to pick up inexpensive baskets and textiles. Note that the market is the one place in Kuching where you should watch your bag and keep your money in a secure place.

Across sungei Sarawak

A Malay *kampung* had grown up on the north side of the river before the arrival of James Brooke, and within forty years – during the reign of Charles Brooke – two of Kuching's most important buildings had come to dominate the district. A boat crosses from the jetty on jalan Gambier, on the south side (every 15min, daily 6am–10pm), and once across the river, you can follow a marked path towards the **Istana**, built by Charles Brooke in 1869 and still the official home of Sarawak's governor. It is an elegant, stately building with a distinctive shingle roof, set amid a long, sloping garden with an excellent view of the Courthouse on the opposite bank. Various pieces of Brooke memorabilia and other relics are kept in one of the rooms, but unfortunately you can only visit the Istana on two days of the year, over the Hari Raya holiday at the end of Ramadan.

Along the river bank, 1km to the east, is **Fort Margherita**; if you retrace your steps back to the jetty, there's a marked path leading to it. The first fort built on this site was James Brooke's most important defensive installation and commanded a breathtaking view along sungei Sarawak – a location deliberately chosen to overlook the long straight stretch of river approaching Kuching. However, the fort was burned to the ground in 1857 by rebel Chinese gold-miners and wasn't rebuilt until 1879, by Charles Brooke, who named this building after his wife. It remains the finest example of the Brooke's system of fortifications; around twenty other forts, most of humbler construction, lie on prime riverine positions throughout Sarawak, strategically placed to repel pirates, or Dyak or Kayan war parties. Looking for all the world like a defensive English castle, Fort Margherita is the only one of the forts open to the public, and renovations have ensured that it looks much as it did last century, with the grounds and interior now housing a **Police Museum** (Tues–Sun 10am–6pm; free; take your passport). Outside the central keep stand old cannons and other pieces of artillery, while inside there is a solid collection of swords, guns and uniforms. There's even a reconstructed opium den, and exhibits on illegal games and drugs, while photographs recall the Communist insurgency and *Konfrontasi*, which required the small Sarawak army to call upon British military aid to help defend the bazaar towns in the interior.

Petra Jaya, the Timber Museum and Cat Museum

Across Satok bridge, southwest of the centre, the road careers round to the northern part of Kuching and the new town, known as **Petra Jaya**. This is an ugly area, devoid of any real interest and, compared to the older parts of Kuching, apparently devoid of life, too. Still, it's where you'll find most of the government offices, including the national headquarters of the Parks and Wildlife Department, as well as two wildly contrasting museums.

The appropriately log-shaped **Timber Museum** (Mon–Fri 8am–4pm, Sat 8am–12.30pm; free) is next to the stadium on jalan Wisma Sumbar Alam, which is the main thoroughfare in Petra Jaya; buses run here from outside the post office. Built in 1985 for the express purpose of putting across the timber industry's point of view in the increasingly acrimonious debate on tropical deforestation, the museum does its job well, featuring informative displays and exhibits, and presenting plenty of facts and figures about tree types and the economic case for logging. Hardly surprisingly, the other side of the argument – the devastation of land which has been farmed for generations by the tribal groups – isn't addressed at all here. The rationale that economic development must come before all other considerations fails to address the simple fact that most of the timber-related wealth either goes into the pockets of big business tycoons, or is syphoned off in state taxes to the national goverment. The displays even suggest that the Dyaks, who have lost much of their customary land through deforestation, have ultimately gained as they now live in less remote areas with health and education facilities nearby. But many ethnic groups, which have recently set up representative committees, would say the forests are their livelihood – remove the forests and tribal culture eventually withers and dies.

There's light relief – though not much – in the recently relocated **Cat Museum** (Tues–Sun 10am–6pm; free) in the new town's DBKU Building, visible from just about all over Kuching. Claiming to be the only such museum in the world, the exhibits take as their starting point the supposed derivation of the city's name from the Malay word for "cat" – which means displays of cats from around the world, *Garfield* comic strips and feline folklore. Take bus #2B from jalan Khoo Hun, by the market.

Eating

Many of the **cafés** and **hawker stalls**, especially those along jalan Carpenter, close at around 7pm and even the top restaurants close early, with last orders at around 10pm, so don't leave eating out too late. This aside, Kuching is a great city for food – but you've got to know what to ask for. The local speciality is *kuey teow* (thick rice noodles, with meat and vegetables in gravy), while Kuching also has its own version of *laksa*, a mixed soup where rice vermicelli is combined with shredded chicken and prawns, bean sprouts, chilli and vegetables. Seafood is also splendid here, especially lobsters, local oysters, prawns, crab and *sotong* (squid); while Kuching "steamboats" – meat and vegetables, cooked fondue-style – are among the best in Malaysia.

Food centres and hawker stalls

Ban Hock Wharf Hawker Centre, jalan Market. Massive hawker centre that's very cheap and popular with locals for basic rice, noodle and curry dishes.

Chinese Food Centre, jalan Carpenter. Opposite the Chinese temple, and good for fresh vegetable dishes and simple meat ones.

Geran Anjekarasa Hawker Centre, jalan Satok, under the bridge. Famous for its barbecued chicken and steaks. It's a bit of a trek but a whole chicken plus rice and vegetables only costs around $10 for two. Take any jalan Satok bus, but check it goes as far as the bridge.

Jalan Carpenter Hawkers, jalan Carpenter. Compact centre with a range of dishes including excellent laksa. Popular with Kuching's young Chinese.

Permata Food Centre, junction of jalan Padungan and jalan Song Thian Cheock. A large selection of stalls, a few of which serve pizza, and steak and chips. Best though is the Chinese *Nafya* stall, right at the back, for excellent buttered prawns, ginger chicken, and fern tips in garlic. Meals cost around $20 for two, while the *Food Centre* itself stays open late (daily 11am–11pm).

Rex Cinema Hawker Stalls, jalan Temple. Popular for its satay and noodles, but, irritatingly, only open until 5pm.

Restaurants and cafés

Fook Hui Café, jalan Tun Haji Openg. Opposite the post office, this is Kuching's best-known coffee shop. Try the coconut tarts, or choose from a wide range of very cheap and tasty Chinese rice and noodle dishes.

Islamic Centre, jalan Carpenter. Serves halal food, curries and unleavened bread from mid-morning until around 9pm. Very popular with visitors and inexpensive – around $3–4 a head.

It Hng, MBKS Swimming Pool Building, jalan Pending. Kuching's best – a highly popular Teochew restaurant with spectacular, regional cuisine, including an excellent *yam basket*. Meals here are quite expensive, around $30 for two.

Jubilee Restoran, jalan India. Set amid busy textile stores, this is the best and most stylish North Indian restaurant in town. The *kacang goreng* (peanuts in fish paste), *sayur* (green beans in chilli and lemon) and *tahu* (fried bean curd) are particularly tasty house specials. Full meals from $8 for two. The adjacent *Madinah* is a good second choice.

Meisan Restoran, ground floor, *Holiday Inn Kuching*, jalan Tunku Abdul Rahman. Spicy Szechuanese food. Although lunchtime *dim sum* is reasonably priced, evening meals are expensive, at $50 for two including beer, but worth splashing out for.

Minangkabau, jalan Chan Chin Ann. Excellent Indonesian restaurant with a range of dishes which you can't find anywhere else in Kuching. It specializes in chilli-hot fish curries and beef *rendang*, all for the very reasonable cost of around $10–15 for two.

Phon Lin Café, jalan Green Hill. Taxi drivers' haven and local café for those who stay in the nearby inns. No real food served until 11am, when delicious chillied beans, sweet and sours, and stir fries appear for around $3 a portion. Run by a very friendly family.

Singapore Chicken Rice, various outlets throughout town. Fast food Southeast Asian style, which tastes a lot better than the tacky decor suggests.

Tiger Garden Coffee Shop, jalan Temple, Green Hill. The best Chinese dumplings in town and great for other Chinese staples, too – $3 a head, including coffee or tea.

Shopping

Kuching is the best place in Sarawak to buy just about anything, although it would be unwise to stock up on tribal textiles and handicrafts here if you are visiting Sibu, Kapit or the longhouses in the interior. Still, if you need to fill in the gaps in your purchases, there are a dozen shops catering for the ethnic artefacts market. Most of the **handicraft** and **antique** shops are along Main Bazaar, jalan Temple and jalan Wayang. There are some **ceramics** stalls on the road to the airport, but it's better to visit the **potteries** (open daily 8am–noon & 2–6pm) themselves, clustered together at Kilang Pasa, 8km from town – take the #12A bus from the post office. You can walk around and watch the potters in action on the wheel and at the firing kilns, and each pottery also has a shop on site, though the work isn't particularly innovative.

Arts of Asia, 68 Main Bazaar. Some of the most comprehensive artwork in town, including naturalistic painting and sculpture, but an expensive store.

Eeze Trading, just past the *Holiday Inn Kuching* on jalan Tunku Abdul Rahman. Souvenirs for the person who has everything – the only shop in the city selling dried insects.

Sarakraf, in the STA building, Main Bazaar. Small stock of baskets, textiles and ironwork.

Sarawak Batik Art Shop, 1 jalan Temple. A fine collection of Iban *pua kumbu* textiles (see feature on the Iban on p.352–353).

Sarawak House, 67 Main Bazaar. Flashy and expensive but usually worth a look.

Sarawak Plaza, jalan Tunku Abdul Rahman, close to the *Holiday Inn Kuching*. This mall is the major focus for Western products – fashion accessories, shirts and shoes, and dance music cassettes. The handicraft store has a good range of bags, T-shirts and ethnic jewellery; though perhaps the most useful stop is the pharmacy on the first floor.

Sing Ching Loon, 57 Main Bazaar. Pricey handicrafts and antiques, but good for a browse

Tan Brothers, jalan Padungan, close to junction with jalan Mathies. Baskets, carvings and bags.

Yeo Hing Chuan, 46 Main Bazaar. Interesting carvings and other handicrafts; a quality hardwood carved figure 30cm tall costs about $400.

Listings

Airlines *MAS*, jalan Song Thian Cheok (☎246622); *Merpati*, c/o *Sin Hwa Travel Service*, 8 lebuh Temple (☎246688); *Royal Brunei Airlines*, at the *Kuching Hilton*, jalan Tunku Abdul Rahman (☎248200); *Singapore Airlines*, at the *Riverside Majestic*, jalan Tunku Abdul Rahman (☎247777).

Banks and exchange *Hong Kong* and *Shanghai Bank*, 2 jalan Tun Haji Openg; *Overseas Union Bank*, junction of Main Bazaar and jalan Tun Haji Openg; *Standard Chartered*, Sarawak Plaza, jalan Tunku Abdul Rahman, and at 20 jalan Pandungan. There are moneychangers at the airport (daily 8am–8pm) and in all the main shopping complexes.

Bookshops The one inside the *Holiday Inn* foyer is the best in Sarawak and the only place to get a large-scale map of the state; it also sells the English-language *Borneo Post*, which features international news and a small section on events in the state. *Sky Book Store*, 57 jalan Padungan, and *Star Books*, Main Bazaar, are also good for geographical, cultural and anthropological material.

Car rental *Mahang Rent A Car*, 18G, Level 1 (☎411370) and *Petra Jaya Car Rental*, Level 1, Lot 788 (☎416755), both in the Taman Sri Sarawak Mau Building, jalan Borneo.

TOUR OPERATORS IN KUCHING

The standard of the tours on and around sungei Lupar and sungei Skrang, 300km east of Kuching, is high. Most of the Iban longhouses here aren't over-commercialized, though it's best to go in small groups – no more than eight, so always check how many are going on your tour. Most companies charge the same, around $100 a day per person – quite steep but the tour is packed with activity, and especially good if you're short on time.

Asian Overland, 286-A 1st floor, Westwood Park, jalan Tubuan (☎251163). The best for longhouse trips in the Kuching vicinity and the batang Ai river system (see p.350–354 for details). Also arranges trips further afield to Mulu National Park and on the "headhunters trail" from Mulu to Lawas.

CPH Travel Agencies, 70 jalan Padungan (☎243708). Sarawak's oldest operator, with good contacts in the native communities.

Ibanika Expedition, 411a, 4th floor, jalan Wisma Saberkas (☎424022). Operates longhouse tours and supplies guides who can speak French, German and Japanese.

Tour Exotica, 1st floor, 1–3 Jalan Temple (☎254607). Run by Winston Marshall, whose best deal is the one-day tour to a Bidayuh longhouse. No other company visits the gunung Braang region near the Kalimantan border, south of Kuching, or offers a day package (around $140 for two) to a traditional Bidayuh community.

Hospitals *Kuching General*, jalan Ong Kie Hui (☎257555); *Normah Medical Centre* (private hospital), 937 jalan Tun Datuk Patinggi, Petra Jaya (☎440055). There is no emergency or ambulance number – call *Kuching General*.

Immigration 1st floor, Bangunan Sultan Iskander, jalan Simpang Tiga, Petra Jaya (Mon–Fri 8am–noon & 2–4.30pm; ☎240301), for visa extensions.

Indonesian Consulate At 5a jalan Pisang (Mon–Thurs 8.30am–noon & 2–4pm; ☎241734) – take bus #5A or #6 from the state mosque. Visas cost $10, and allow at least two working days – though you may no longer need one to cross at Entikong.

Laundry *All Clean Services*, 175G jalan Chan Chin Ann (☎243524).

National Parks and Wildlife Office Wisma Sumbar Alam, Petra Jaya (☎442180). For leaflets and info on national parks in Sarawak. Permits for Bako National park are issued in the Parks and Wildlife Office, inside the tourist office on Main Bazaar.

Pharmacy *Apex Pharmacy*, Electra House, lebuh Power (☎246011), and 2nd floor, Sarawak Plaza, jalan Tunku Abdul Rahman.

Police Main HQ is at jalan Badruddin (☎245522). Come here to report stolen and lost property.

Post office The main post office is on jalan Tun Haji Openg (Mon–Fri 8am–6pm, Sat 8am–noon); poste restante/general delivery can be collected here – take your passport.

Swimming There's a pool at MBKS Building, jalan Pending (Mon–Fri 2.30–9pm, Sat 6.45–8.45pm, Sun 9.30am–9pm; ☎426915); $2 adults, $1 children. Closed on public holidays.

Telephones The *Telekom* office, jalan Batu Lintang (Mon–Fri 8am–6am, Sat 8am–noon), is the only place, other than hotels, from where you can make international calls.

Day trips from Kuching

The area **around Kuching** is well served by road, unlike other parts of Sarawak, and two days' worth of interesting excursions can be made by bus and boat, without going to the trouble of hiring guides and porters. Within an hour's bus ride of the capital you can visit a crocodile farm, a wildlife rehabilitation centre deep in the forest, and the riverside villages of the Santubong peninsula. Some people stay out at the peninsula, at the *Holiday Inn*, next to which is the Sarawak Cultural Village, a showpiece community where model longhouses are staffed by guides from each of the ethnic groups.

Jong's Crocodile Farm

To reach **Jong's Crocodile Farm** (daily 9am–5pm; $5), 18km south of Kuching on the Serian Highway, take the #6 *STC* bus from lebuh Jawa; currently, it runs at 8.20am, 10.30am, noon and 1.30pm, returning to Kuching at 10am, noon, 2pm and 4pm. The journey takes twenty five minutes. Crocodiles are an endangered species in Sarawak and various species are bred on the premises – though some of those are killed at a tender age and their skins sold. The farm is hardly an essential trip since apart from at feeding times (daily at 9am and 3pm) there isn't a great deal to see, but it's worth a look in, especially if you haven't got time to head along the rivers into Sarawak's interior, where you might have a more authentic, heart-stopping meeting with a crocodile. Just to keep you on your toes, the farm features some grisly photographic reminders that people are frequently attacked by crocodiles; one photo shows a dead croc's stomach which has been cut open, revealing an assortment of masticated animals.

Semanggoh Wildlife Rehabilitation Centre

It's another 15km further south along the Serian Highway, through hillier terrain, which gives way to rubber plantations and patches of secondary jungle, to the **Semanggoh Wildlife Rehabilitation Centre** (daily 8am–4.15pm; free). This was established in 1976 to rehabilitate wild animals and birds – mostly endangered species which had either been confiscated from apprehended poachers, or found injured in the forest. The official line is that you need a permit from the Parks and Wildlife Office on Main Bazaar in Kuching to visit the centre, but in practice, you can just turn up. It's a twenty-minute walk from the entrance to the centre's headquarters (closed 12.30–2pm), where you can pick up a free, detailed information pack, and buy snacks and drinks. If you didn't apply for a permit in Kuching, all you have to do here is to sign your name in a book.

At the centre, the animals are first put into cages and later released into the **forest reserve**, after which they can be returned to the wild proper – usually the area where they were first found. Because of this system, it's best to time your visit with the animals' feeding times at 9am and 2.30pm, when the "advanced stage" animals, who are out in the reserve, sometimes return to their cages to get their share of the papaya, bananas and melons.

Along an elevated wooden walkway, a minute from the headquarters, the number of animals and birds undergoing the first stage of rehabilitation varies. In the dozen cages there are usually proboscis monkeys, orang-utans (a protected species in Sarawak), gibbons, hornbills, porcupines, honey bears and eagles. It doesn't take long to stop by all the cages, including that of Bullet, a fully grown orang-utan who has been at the centre since it opened. Shot by a hunter (hence her name), Bullet has long recovered from her wounds, but over the years has become too institutionalized to be returned to her natural habitat. After seeing the animals, you can return to the road by one of the **trails** which cut into the forest from the track leading to the headquarters, where staff have labelled tree and plant species, highlighting *dipterocarp* tree types, including *meranti* and *engkabang* species, and wild fruit trees, among them *cempedak* and *durian*.

Coming from Jong's Crocodile Farm, take the #6 bus from the main road, straight to the wildlife centre's main gate. Buses return to Kuching from here every two hours, from 10am to 4pm, although you can get a bus after 4pm by walking along the track opposite the gates which leads to the main road; from here, buses regularly travel back to the city until 7pm.

The Santubong Peninsula

Santubong Peninsula, 30km north of Kuching, is dominated by the 2500-metre Gunung Santubong which looms over the peninsula above the point where sungei Sarawak meets the sea. Once the site of an early trading settlement, the peninsula is a region full of strangely shaped rocks within patches of secondary forest and is accessible enough to mean that stretches of the river and coastline are being rapidly developed as a tourist area, with the *Holiday Inn Damai Beach* setting the pace. Other than *Holiday Inn* punters, most people come out to the peninsula to stay in one of the guest houses in the small riverside villages of Buntal and Santubong, or to visit the much-hyped Sarawak Cultural Village, next to the *Holiday Inn*.

Buntal, Santubong and the Holiday Inn

From Kuching's lebuh Jawa depot, the #2B bus (every 40min, daily 5.30am–5pm) makes the forty-minute trip through occasional housing developments and small rubber and pepper plantations, before leaving the main road and running along the edge of the river to **BUNTAL**. This quiet riverside *kampung* is bordered by forest and has one good place to eat, the *Seafood Centre,* and several inexpensive guest houses (①). There's a small beach, too, while locals offer short boat trips along sungei Sarawak.

From Buntal, the bus returns to the main road and weaves up the lower reaches of Gunung Santubong, before turning east down a narrow road for 2km to the village of **SANTUBONG**, a very pretty place, set on an inlet with fishing boats hauled up onto the beach. Two Chinese cafés, *Son Hong* and the *Santubong,* whip up tasty stir-fry and rice dishes and one of the houses opposite the *Santubong* takes lodgers (①). There's not much else to do but you might take time to search out some interesting **rock graffiti** near Santubong. Head back along the Kuching road for 200m and turn left just before the six-kilometre sign. Thirty metres down the track you'll see a path running between two rocks leading to some curiously carved boulders, one featuring a prone human figure, though the other forms are hard to decipher. An exact dating hasn't been made, although archaeologists think the rock images could be around a thousand years old.

The bus continues from Santubong for another 5km and, after winding further up the densely forested mountain road, dips down to the **Holiday Inn Damai Beach** (☎082/411777; ⑤) nestling in a natural hollow at the end of the road. "Sarawak's best-kept secret" is in fact a mini-resort, with pool and tennis courts alongside a private, yellow sand, palm-fringed beach. There's also a fleet of vans available to take you anywhere – at a price – though the #2B bus stops right outside the hotel gates.

Sarawak Cultural Village

Beside the entrance to the hotel is the **Sarawak Cultural Village** (daily 9am–5.30pm, stage shows at 11.30am & 4.30pm; $40), a kind of theme park for the state's ethnic communities, where six authentically built longhouses stand in a dramatic setting: the sea to one side, a lake in the middle of the site and Gunung Santubong looming behind. The longhouses are functioning daytime communities, demonstrating weaving, cooking and instrument-playing, although the tribespeople working here live in Kuching. The stage shows – the village's big draw – are actually fairly poor, and involve a quite astounding trivialization of ancient forest skills. In one, a slim Penan boy moves in slow motion, mimicking the practice of hunting with a blowpipe and aiming it at the audience, before turning his sharpshooting to balloons dangling from the roof of the auditorium. Each show ends with the "cast" singing an anodyne anthem to peace and prosperity, all of which may be highly entertaining, but as an insight into traditional longhouse life, it's fairly meaningless. Indeed, Penan tribal representatives want nothing to do with the project as they feel it misrepresents the true predicament in which their people find themselves.

Bako National Park

BAKO NATIONAL PARK, a two-hour bus and boat journey northeast of Kuching, is Sarawak's oldest national park, occupying the northern section of the Muara Tebas peninsula at the mouth of sungei Bako. The area was once part of a forest reserve – a region set aside for timber growing and extraction – but in 1957 it was gazetted as a national park and fully protected from exploitation. Although relatively small, Bako is spectacular in its own way: its steep rocky cliffs, punctuated by deep bays and lovely sandy beaches, are thrillingly different from the rest of the predominantly flat and muddy Sarawak coastline. The peninsula is composed of sandstone which, over the years, has been worn down to produce delicate pink iron patterns on cliff faces, honey-comb weathering and contorted rock arches rising from the sea. Access to some of the beaches is difficult, requiring tricky descents down nearly vertical paths; above, the forest contains various species of wildlife, and rivers and waterfalls for bathing. The hike to the highest point, **Bukit Gondol** (1500m), is among the most popular of the trails which criss-cross the park, its peak offering a wide view over the park to the South China Sea.

Getting there

First stop for the trip to Bako is the Parks and Wildlife Department desk at the *STA* office in Kuching (see p.332), where you need to get a **permit** and reserve your accommodation (see below). This is done over the counter and only takes a few minutes. Once at the park, it's generally a straightforward business to extend your stay if you want to.

To **get to the park**, take the #6 bus ($2) from jalan Market or use one of the share **vans**, also from jalan Market ($5 per person), both of which run hourly to the jetty at **KAMPUNG BAKO**, where you have to rent a **longboat** for the thirty-minute cruise to the park headquarters ($25 per boat). By car from Kuching, the 37-kilometre journey takes around forty minutes and there's a car park at Kampung Bako, where you can leave your vehicle safely. There's rarely a delay in catching a longboat at the *kampung*, unless a large tour group is being relayed out to the park. In any case, you wouldn't want to hang around since it's extraordinarily dirty, with garbage spreading from the line of shops to the river.

Staying at the park

Once at the **park headquarters** you need to sign in. The ranger will then give you a detailed and informative **map** of the park and take you to your accommodation. You may want to give yourself an hour to look around the excellent displays and exhibits at the headquarters; these identify the flora and fauna in the park as well as describe in detail its history and unique characteristics.

Accommodation and eating

At park headquarters, various types of **accommodation** have been built along the side of the forest, divided from the beach 50m away by a row of coconut trees. Although seldom full during the week, Bako tends to get very busy at weekends and bank holidays. For budget travellers the **hostel** is good value (①) and the shared kitchen is fully equipped. Going up the scale, there's also a semi-detached **lodge** (①–②), a standard **rest house** (②) and a new rest house (③), all of which provide bed linen, fridge and cooking facilities. Some hikers prefer to **camp** on the trails – tents can be rented from the headquarters for $4, although it's not much more to stay at the hostel.

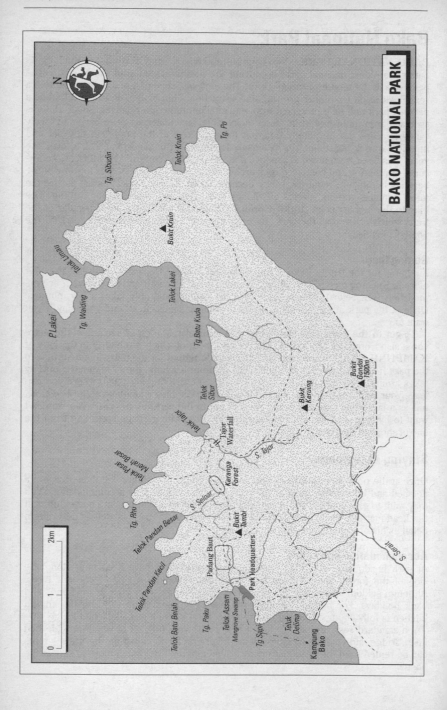

The **café** at park HQ is very basic, with a daily menu of rice with vegetables, meat or fish and egg dishes, all at budget prices. The park **shop** has a limited range of goods but can keep you supplied with tins, rice, fruit and a few vegetables, so there's not much point in lugging provisions out from Kuching unless you can't survive without a few luxuries.

Around the park

Given the easy access to and inexpensive accomodation within the park, many people stay a few days longer than planned at Bako, taking picnics to one of the seven **beaches**, relaxing at the park headquarters itself, or going slow on the trails to observe the flora and fauna. In all, you'll come across seven different **vegetation** types, including peat bog, scrub and mangrove; most of the sixteen trails themselves run through a highly enjoyable mixture of primary *dipterocarp* forest and *keranga*, a sparser type of forest characterized by much thinner tree cover, stubbier plants and more open pathways. On top of the low hill on the Lintang trail, the strange landscape of Padang Baut is covered in rock plates, where, among the shrubs, you'll find **pitcher plants**, whose deep, mouth-shaped lids open to trap water and insects which are then digested in the soupy liquid. Elsewhere, on the cliffs, delicate plants cling to vertical rock faces or manage to eke out an existence in little pockets of soil, while closer to park HQ the coastline is thick with mangrove trees.

You're more likely to catch sight of the **wildlife** while lazing at the chalets than out on the trails. Monkeys on the lookout for food are always lurking around, so it's important to keep the kitchen and dormitory doors locked. Even the rare flying lemur has been sighted swinging from the trees around the park headquarters. The best time to see wildlife on the trails is at night or in the early morning and, if you're lucky, you might catch sight of proboscis, macaque and silver leaf monkeys, snakes, wild boar, giant monitor lizards, squirrels, mouse deer, and possibly even the very rare honey bear which is dangerous if cornered. The park headquarters and the open paths in the *keranga* are the best places for **bird-watching**: 150 species have been recorded in Bako, including two rare species of hornbills (for more on which, see p.393).

Along the trails

It's best to get an early start on the **trails**, taking much-needed rests at the strategically positioned viewpoint huts along the way. The sixteen trails are all colour-coded: every twenty metres, paint splashes denoting the trail are clearly marked on trees and rocks. You'll need to carry a litre of water per person (you can refill your bottle from the streams), a light rainproof jacket, mosquito repellent and sunscreen. Wear comfortable shoes with a good grip (there's no need for heavy-duty walking boots), light clothing like T-shirt and shorts, and take a sunhat. Don't forget your swimming gear either, as cool streams cut across the trails, and beaches and waterfalls are never far away. The park map clearly shows the trails, which all start from park HQ.

Probably the most popular trail is the three-and-a-half kilometre hike to **Tajor Waterfall**, a hike estimated at two and a half hours, though it can easily be done in ninety minutes if you don't linger too long for rests or plant study. The initial half an hour's climb from the jetty, along a steep and circuitous, root-bound path up the forested cliff is the hardest section. At the top you move swiftly through scrubland into *keranga* – a section without much shade, along which you'll encounter a profusion of pitcher plants. The path leads to a simple wooden hut with a fine prospect of the peninsula. Moving on, you return to sun-shielded forest, where the dry, sandy path gives way to a muddy trail through peat bog, which leads eventually to the waterfall itself, a lovely spot for swimming and eating your picnic.

Alternatively, if you leave the main trail at the wooden hut and viewpoint and turn west, a path descends to two beautiful **beaches**, Telok Pandan Kecil and Telok Pandan Besar, each around a thirty-minute hike from the viewpoint. During the week you'll probably be the only person at either, with Kecil in particular involving a steep, rugged descent down sandstone rocks to reach the refreshingly clean water. The other two beaches at Bako – Sibur and Limau – are much harder to reach, but just as enjoyable once you've got there. To find **Telok Sibur** beach, continue past Tajor Waterfall, following the main trail for around forty minutes, before turning west on the black-and-red trail. The demanding descent to the beach takes anything from twenty minutes to an hour to accomplish. You have to drop down with the help of creepers and roots which cling to the cliff face and your troubles aren't over when you reach the bottom either, since you're then in a mangrove swamp and must tread carefully lest you lose your footing among the stones. After wading across a river, you reach the beach – the longest on the peninsula and, not surprisingly, seldom visited.

The hike to **Telok Limau**, estimated at seven hours, can be done in five at a push. The terrain alternates from swampland and scrub to primary and secondary forest, and incorporates gradients which grant fabulous views around the whole peninsula. The beach itself marks the most northerly point in the park and, as such, it's not really on to get there and back in a day. Either bring a tent and food and camp on the beach, as perfect a spot to lay your weary head as you will ever find, or arrange with park HQ for a boat to pick you up for the return trip, which costs around $200. Once out at Limau you could detour on the way back along the marked trail to **Kruin**, at the eastern end of the park – an area where you're most likely to spot wildlife. There is a secluded freshwater pond on the way and further on, from the top of the nearby hill, a grand view of the park's eastern edges.

The route to Sematan

The most westerly inhabited point in Sarawak is the pretty seaside village of **Sematan**, 100km from Kuching. There's no coastal road from the city and the only way to reach Sematan is by heading southwest by bus to **Bau**, and then northwest to **Lundu**; there you change onto a bus which runs past newly established **Gunung Gading National Park** to the coast. The Lundu–Sematan bus isn't that frequent, and you won't get to Sematan and back in one day, which is actually a bonus – Sematan is just the place to kick your heels in the sand for a while, and go swimming, hiking and fishing.

Bau, Lundu and Gunung Gading National Park

The #2B bus from Kuching's lebuh Jawah depot to Lundu departs four times daily (at 8am, 11.30am, 2.15pm & 4pm; $10). The bus stops briefly in nondescript **BAU** after which the road deteriorates, the bus clattering through a landscape which gradually changes from plantation to forest, with jungle-wrapped hills close by. At **LUNDU** you change buses for Sematan and during the one-hour wait there's time to walk around the small market, where you can buy fresh fruit, or go to one of the cafés bordering the town's only square; the *Jouee* serves excellent noodles.

The bone-shaking bus ride to Sematan from Lundu takes another hour, passing **GUNUNG GADING NATIONAL PARK** on the way, which encompases an area selected for conservation because *rafflesia*, the world's largest plant, grows here. Discovered by – and named after – Sir Stamford Raffles, its flowers grow up to 45 centimetres across, smell of rotting meat, and are pollinated by carrion flies; perhaps because of which there are, as yet, no visitor facilities at the park. However, it is possible to follow some of the trails which start from a group of wooden buildings that do duty as the park's temporary headquarters. The main trail is well marked, running northwards from the buildings, an hour along which – following an incline which winds along the side of Gunung Gading, the route accompanied by the cacophonous sounds of the jungle – you'll reach some attractive waterfalls deep in the rainforest.

Sematan

Thirty minutes beyond the national park, the village of **SEMATAN** is quietly located at the end of the road. The mostly deserted long beach – its yellow sand clean but for driftwood – is wonderful, partially hidden from the narrow road by coconut palms. If you tire of the laid-back beach atmosphere, Sematan also has several local **trails**, starting from the wood just a couple of minutes across the bay, 200m away. Ask one of the men hanging around the small jetty to take you over – it should only cost a few dollars. At the other end, the boatman can point out the start of a circular trail which runs through plantations and a tiny *kampung*, before winding around to join the road on which the bus came in on; all in all, it's a two-hour trip.

Another walk – this time in open countryside – follows the coastline westwards from the village, past the bungalows, reaching rugged **Cape Belinsah** after an hour where there's little to do except clamber around on the rocks. From here it may be possible to visit the island of **Talang Talang**, clearly visible a few kilometres north of the cape, where there is a small turtle sanctuary, but you'll need to obtain permission from the local district officer – ask at the Parks and Wildlife office in Kuching if you're interested.

For **accommodation** in Sematan, the *Sematan Hotel* (☎088/711162, ②), on Sematan Bazaar, is a friendly place with small, clean rooms, or you can stay at the *Lai Sematan Bungalows* (☎082/711133, ②), beautifully positioned among coconut palms on the beach. The detached chalets are fairly basic but can sleep four; it's necessary to reserve in advance, since the janitor needs to make a special journey to Sematan to give you the keys. Two or three Chinese **cafés** in the village serve hot meals; the local crabs are particularly tasty.

The Kalimantan border: Bidayuh longhouses and Gunung Penrissen

One hundred kilometres south of Kuching, up in the mountains straddling the border with Kalimantan, are several authentic **Bidayuh longhouses**, which offer a fascinating insight into the culture of the only remaining Land Dyaks in Sarawak. Unlike other ethnic groups, the Bidayuh built their multi-levelled, elevated longhouses at the base of hills rather than on rivers and, as a consequence, endured violent attacks during the last century from other more aggressive groups, especially the Iban, who were migrating across the mountains from the Kapuas river region in West Kalimantan. Bidayuh longhouses were frequently raided, the men's heads severed and shrunk, the children taken as slaves, and the woman offered a choice between becoming the victors' wives or losing their heads, too. The Bidayuh, for their part, weren't exactly passive victims: they are the only ethnic group which traditionally erected a separate structure in each community called a **head-house**, where the heads of their enemies were kept and which served as a focus for male activities and rituals. Given the constant attacks, it's not surprising that the Bidayuh are among the more introverted of Sarawak's ethnic groups, yet they welcome sensitive visitors just as much as the more demonstrative Iban or Kelabit. Many Bidayuh traditions are thriving; they make the best **carpets** of all the indigenous groups and also excellent mats. But only a small percentage of the remaining Bidayuh population in Sarawak, which totals around 50,000, still live in the longhouses. Most of the young men prefer seasonal employment in logging, or work on the rubber and pepper plantations, while many of the children go on to further education before taking jobs in the burgeoning clerical and service industries.

Visiting the longhouses

To visit the longhouses you need to set off early for the first leg of the trip to **SERIAN**, 100km southeast of Kuching. Buses leave the lebuh Jawa depot every thirty minutes; the best departures are at 6.40am or 7am. At Serian depot ask for the Penrissen road bus, which makes a slow two-hour ride along a terrible road to the **BENUK** longhouse. Another service, the Padawan bus, runs through a small village, Kampung Abang, and on to the largest Bidayuh settlement in the area, **ANNA RAIS**, a similar distance from Serian. There's a small charge to visit both communities in return for which you'll be shown round, offered food and drink and invited to watch and participate in craft demonstrations. The best time to go is at the weekend when the children are back from school and the wage-earners back from their logging and city jobs. Most visitors stay a couple of hours, returning to Kuching the same day, but you can stay the night, though if you want to do this, remember to bring some gifts. Alternatively, you can sleep in the community hall at **KAMPUNG ABANG**, a useful overnight stop if you want to trek up nearby Gunung Penrissen the next day.

Gunung Penrissen

The most accessible of the one-thousand-metre-plus mountains bordering Kalimantan is the spectacular 1300-metre **Gunung Penrissen**, the hike up which involves tough walking along narrow paths and crossing fast-flowing streams which descend from the source of sungei Sarawak; vertical ladders help you on the last section. This and other nearby peaks are criss-crossed by narrow paths, known only to locals and a few trained trackers, so it's inadvisable to venture on to them without a **guide**: William Nub (☎082/410858) will arrange one, starting from either of the longhouses detailed above or from Kampung Abang. Although the ascent and descent of Penrissen can be done in one hard day, you may prefer to set up camp at the foot of the summit; if so bring a lightweight tent and food supplies.

Gunung Penrissen was strategically important in the 1950s' border skirmishes between the Malaysian and Indonesian armies and there's still a Malaysian **military post** close to the summit, from where exhausted walkers gaze over the rainforest into Kalimantan to the south and east, and to the South China Sea over the forests to the north.

The border crossing

A few kilometres southeast of Gunung Penrissen is the **border crossing** at **TEBEDU**, 120km from Kuching. There are buses from Serian to Tebedu and again, you'll need to set off first thing, as local buses, from Tebedu across the border the few kilometres south to the Indonesian town of **ENTIKONG** and on to Pontianak, stop running in the early afternoon. Tebedu is tiny, little more than an administrative centre, with a couple of dispirited hotels. The border crossing at Entikong is open from 6am to 5pm and you need a valid Indonesian visa, available in Kuching (though this may soon no longer be necessary).

The batang Ai river system

Although Sibu – and batang Rajang – is only four hours by boat from Kuching, the most popular destination for **longhouse visits** from the capital remains the **batang Ai river system**, 200km east of the city, a distance which takes as least six hours to cover. Many of the tour operators in Kuching have established good relations with the friendly Iban communities here; indeed many of the operators' staff are Iban from the longhouses themselves. It's quite possible, however, to try your luck without travelling under the protective – and expensive – wing of a tour group, and find a longhouse which hasn't yet been greatly disturbed by the patter of tour group feet. Access is via the town of **Sri Aman**, 150km southeast of Kuching, reached by buses from the lebuh Jawa depot at 8am, 12.30pm and 3pm, taking three hours to Sri Aman.

Sri Aman

SRI AMAN is the second biggest town in southwest Sarawak and is the administrative capital of this part of the state. It sits upriver on sungei Lupar, whose lower reaches are over 1500 metres wide, though the river narrows dramatically as it meanders through the flat alluvial plain. Just before Sri Aman, a small island in the river obstructs the flow of the incoming tide, producing the town's renowned "tidal bore". At regular intervals, when enough water has accumulated, a billowing wave rushes by with some force: longboats are hauled up onto the muddy bank and large vessels head for mid-stream in an attempt to ride the bore as evenly as possible. At its most impressive, the bore rolls up like a mini tidal wave, rocking boats and splashing the new Chinese temple which is set back from the pier. Somerset Maughan was caught by the wave in 1929 and nearly drowned, a tale he recounted in "Yellow Streak" in his *Borneo Tales*.

The busy town itself has a central defensive fort, **Fort Alice**, built by Charles Brooke in 1864 and thus predating Fort Margherita in Kuching. More compact than the one in the capital, the fort (now a government office and not open to the public) has pronounced turrets, a courtyard and, oddly, a drawbridge. Charles Brooke based himself in this region for many years, heading a small force which repelled the down-river advances of pirates and the upriver internecine scraps between warring Iban factions.

There are three **hotels** in town: the *Champion Inn*, 1248 Main Bazaar (☎085/320140; ②) is the most central; *Hoover Hotel*, 139 jalan Club (☎085/322578; ②) the best value; while the smartest is the *Alishan Hotel*, 120 jalan Council (☎085/322578; ③).

Visiting the longhouses

The **sungei Lupar** and **batang Ai region**, around 40km southeast of Sri Aman, is Iban territory and although there was a major demographic displacement in the 1960s, caused by the building of the batang Ai reservoir, most Iban here still maintain their traditional lifestyles. It is common to meet young men and women who have done a stint in a logging camp or at a hawker stall in Sri Aman or Kuching, and yet have returned to the longhouse life. Nevertheless, many people have moved away permanently and the onus on keeping the essentially agricultural way of life going is being increasingly placed on the women and adolescents.

The numerous **Iban longhouses** on the Lupar's four main tributaries – the Engkari, Lemanak, Ulu Ai and the Skrang – are fairly accessible from Sri Aman. All the Kuching-based tour operators (see p.342) offer two- to five-day trips and most have adopted a longhouse. For travellers on a short stay, tours like this are ideal, but check that the size of the group doesn't exceed six to eight people or else things can get a bit congested. If you want to make your own way to a longhouse, in the first instance you need to head for the small town of **Lubok Antu**, 50km southeast of Sri Aman.

Stamang

One particularly good tour is that run by *Asian Overland* (see p.342 for address and details) to the **Stamang** longhouse on the Engkari river, 30km east of Sri Aman, on the

THE IBAN

The **Iban** – one of the ethnic groups categorized as Sea Dyaks – comprise nearly one-third of the population of Sarawak, making them easily the most numerous of Sarawak's indigenous peoples. They originated in the Kapuas river basin of West Kalimantan, on the other side of the mountains which separate Kalimantan and Sarawak, but having outgrown their lands they migrated to the Lupar river in southwest Sarawak in the early sixteenth century, looking for **new land** to cultivate. Once in Sarawak, the Iban soon clashed with the coastal Melanau, and by the eighteenth century they had moved up the Rajang into the interior, into areas that were traditionally Kayan lands. Inevitably, great battles were waged between these two powerful groups, with one contemporary source recording seeing "a mass of boats drifting along the stream, while the Dyaks were spearing and stabbing each other; decapitated trunks and heads without bodies, scattered about in ghastly profusion."

Head-hunting become established during the Iban migrations, a practice generally sponsored by the need to top up the spiritual reserve in a new longhouse, though revenge too played a part. It didn't matter how the head was taken or to whom it belonged. An account which appeared in the *Sarawak Gazette* in 1909, just when Charles Brooke hoped his policy of stopping head-hunting was at last becoming effective, reported that: "Justly are the Dyaks called head-hunters, for during the whole of their life, from early youth till their death, all their thoughts are fixed on the hunting of heads. The women, in their cruelty and blood-thirstiness, are the cause. At every festival the old trophies are taken from the fireplace and carried through the house by the women who sing a monotonous song in honour of the hero who cut off the head, and in derision of the poor victims whose skulls are carried around. Everywhere, the infernal chorus, 'Bring us more of them', is heard." Although conflicts between the various ethnic groups stopped with the slowing down of the migrations, heads were still being taken as recently as the 1960s during the *Konfrontasi* skirmishes, when Indonesian army units came up against Iban fighters in the Malaysian army.

After the Melanau, the Iban are the most "modernized" of Sarawak's ethnic groups. Around ten percent live in towns – mostly Kuching, Sri Aman and Sibu – and work in a variety of trades, from handicrafts to manufacturing. Even the bulk of the rural Iban, the vast majority of whom still live in longhouses, undertake seasonal work in the rubber and oil industries, and it is not a small irony that **logging** – the business which most devastates their own customary lands – provides plentiful and lucrative work.

Unlike most of the other groups, the Iban are a very egalitarian people – the longhouse *tuai* (headman) is more of a figurehead than someone who wields hierarchical power. Nevertheless, women in the community have different duties to men: they never go hunting or work in logging, but are considered to be great weavers. In this context, they're most renowned for their beautiful **pua kumbu** (blanket or coverlet) work, a cloth of intricate design and colour. The *pua kumbu* once played an integral part in Iban rituals, when they were hung prominently during harvest festivals and weddings, or used to cover structures containing charms and offerings to the gods. And, when head-hunting

road to Lubok Antu (see below). Ten kilometres from Lubok Antu you reach the jetty at the batang Ai reservoir, from where the longhouse is an hour away by longboat, across the reservoir and along shallow sungei Engkari. On either side steep hillsides leading up to the forest-topped peaks have been cleared for rice growing and other cultivation. When the river is very low, everybody gets out of the longboat and pushes.

The thirty-door Stamang longhouse has not yet been swamped by tourists and consequently the traditional Iban lifestyle hasn't been unduly affected. A three-day trip gives you two nights and a complete day at the longhouse, with time to visit the agricultural plots, go fishing and watch daily life unfold in this industrious community. There is little time to yourself on the first evening, as you are introduced to all the inhabitants, was still a much-valued tradition, the women would wear the *pua kumbu* to receive the "prize" brought home by their menfolk. The cloth is generally made by using the *ikat* technique, which involves binding, tieing and dyeing the material so as to build up complex patterns.

The Iban are extremely gregarious and love an opportunity to throw a **party**, drinking *tuak*, eating piles of meat and fish and cracking jokes (the Iban lexicon is rich with double entendres). The games any visitor finds themselves playing when visiting the Iban are often designed to get as many laughs at their expense as possible. It's best to play along and work out a way of getting your own back. The best time to visit is during June when the **gawai** (harvest) **festival** gets into swing – the months after the rice harvest (May and June) are customarily a time for relaxing, hunting, craft-making and merrymaking.

Of all the customs maintained by the Iban, perhaps the most singular is their style of **tattooing**, which is not just a form of ornamentation, but also an indication of personal wealth and other achievements. Many designs are used, from a simple circular outline for the shoulder, chest or outer side of the wrists, to a more elaborate design, such as a dog, scorpion or dragon for the inner and outer surfaces of the thigh. The two most important places of the anatomy are considered to be the hand and the throat. A tattoo on the hand indicates that you have "taken a head" – some elders still have these – while one on the throat means that you are a fully mature man, with wealth, possessions, land and family. For women, the more elaborate the tattoo the higher their social status in the community. The actual process is usually carried out by an experienced artist, either a longhouse resident or a travelling tattooist who arrives just prior to the *gawai* season. A carved design on a block of wood is smeared with ink and pressed to the skin, the resulting outline then punctured with needles dipped in dark ink, made from a mixture of sugar juice, water and soot. For the actual tattooing a hammer-like instrument is used that has two or three needles protruding from its head. These are dipped in ink, the hammer placed against the skin and hit repeatedly with a wooden block, after which rice is smeared over the inflamed area to prevent infection.

Each longhouse hosts at least one open weekend during *gawai* when visitors are welcome as long as they bring **gifts**. Anything will do, from basic food supplies like meat, salt and sugar to Western clothes and cassettes – gifts for children are guaranteed to endear you to the kids. But as you are supposed to socialize with the chief's family first – unless you've met anyone else en route – the gifts should be given to the chief to distribute accordingly. Other **house rules** include never walking straight into a longhouse unless you are following your guide – wait to be invited. Shake hands with everybody who wants to shake yours but don't touch the locals anywhere else, ie, don't tousle the heads of the children. Eat as much as possible and don't worry if it looks like you are eating the family's entire supply of food – it is the custom to stuff visitors, whether foreigners or next door neighbours, and there is usually more in reserve. You should also accept the offer to swim in the river – everybody goes, usually in small groups, for a wash at the start of the day and at dusk – but be careful not to reveal your anatomy; wear a sarong or shorts.

offered yam and tea, taken to the river for a bathe, fed again on chicken, jungle ferns and rice, and later subjected to traditional *Ngayat* dancing, music and Iban games. It takes nearly a day to get there from Kuching, and you can expect to pay around $400 per person for the three-day trip.

Lubok Antu and other longhouses

It's perfectly possible to make your own way to other longhouses on the Engkari – Stamang is just one of twelve on the river – as well as to the score or so of others on the muddier, but still picturesque, sungei Ulu Ai and sungei Skrang, reached by longboats from the jetty at the Ai reservoir.

Take the bus from Sri Aman southeast to **LUBOK ANTU**, a small town 50km away which has a predominantly Iban population. Here, you'll need to ask for the bus to the **batang Ai reservoir jetty**, about 10km to the northeast; this is not a regular service, so arrive as early as you can in the morning. Once at the jetty, get talking to some of the Iban who go back and forth along the rivers to the longhouses and when they realize why you've come, they'll soon invite you over to their longhouse. If you get to Lubok Antu late and can't reach the jetty, you'll have need of the grandly named, but extremely basic, *LA Hilton* (①), above a shophouse on the main street.

For the pretty, but muddier sungei Lemanak, get off the Sri Aman–Lubok Antu bus at the modern roadside longhouse of **Rumah Bareng** in Sebeliau, just after the bridge (30km from Sri Aman). Again, talk to the guys messing around on the boats here and you'll soon be offered a look round a local Iban longhouse.

SIBU AND THE RAJANG BASIN

The 560-kilometre long **Rajang** river, known as *batang* (big river) rather than *sungei*, because of its great width and length, lies at the very heart of Sarawak. In many ways, it's changed little since the nineteenth century, when Chinese and Malay adventurers took boats from Sibu wharf to the bazaar town of **Kapit**, before heading up the Rajang to the frontier settlement of **Belaga**, to trade with the nomadic Penan. This is the world of head-hunting Iban and of isolated colonial forts, of longboat trips along clear tributaries brimming with fish to stately longhouses, where massive woodcarvings guard the entrance and where, on the verandah above, the community's *tuai* (headman) beckons you up the log stairs into his home. Once the little town of **Song** on the Rajang has been reached, **Iban longhouses** along the Katibas and Baleh tributaries become easily accessible; while guides in Kapit and Belaga can lead you on jungle treks to **Kayan longhouses** or visits to **Penan** communities.

Approaching along the coast from Kuching, initial impressions of the Rajang are of a wide, dirty channel, used to transport logs from the interior of the state to the outside world. From the small town of Sarakei, near the mouth of the Rajang, to beyond Kapit, over 200km to the east, hundreds of log-laden barges chug downstream with their immense loads past dozens of processing factories and storage depots. Despite the state government's commitment to slowing down the pace of deforestation, there are few signs of this along the lower reaches of the Rajang. Around ninety minutes upriver from the coast, the major port of **Sibu** is the headquarters of the timber cartels – indeed, now that the accessible forests of the north have been thoroughly logged, Sibu has overtaken Miri and Marudi as the focal point of Sarawak's timber industry.

A little history

For centuries, the Rajang was rife with tribal conflict. In the fifteenth century – the height of power of the Malay Sultanates – Malays living in the estuaries of southern Sarawak pushed the immigrant Iban up the rivers towards present-day Sibu. This antagonized the indigenous people of those regions, especially the Baleh and upper Rajang Kayan, and throughout the seventeenth and eighteenth centuries they skirmished among themselves for territory and heads. Occasionally, when they felt threatened, the Malays and the Ibans would form an uneasy alliance to attack inland Kayan tribes and carry out piratical raids on passing Indonesian and Chinese ships.

With the arrival of the British, it was clear that no serious opening out of the interior could go ahead until the region was made relatively safe – which meant controlling the land and subjugating, or displacing, many of the indigenous inhabitants. James Brooke bought a section of the Rajang river, from its mouth to beyond Kapit, from the Sultan of

Brunei in 1853, while his successor, Charles, asserted his authority over the Iban and Kayan tribes, and encouraged **Chinese pioneers** to move into the interior. Some of the more intrepid Chinese pioneers started to trade upriver with the Iban and, with support from the Malay business community and Brooke officials, built settlements at Kanowit and Sibu in the late nineteenth century, hacking out farms in the jungle, on which, with varying degrees of success, they grew rice, vegetables, pepper and rubber. Indeed, Sibu's early growth was largely financed by the proceeds of rubber cultivation. But the pioneers faced numerous disputes with the Iban, who, historically angry with the Malays for pushing them away from the estuaries, now resented the Chinese for clearing and growing crops on land the Iban believed belonged to them.

The life of the upriver pioneers was a dangerous one: most lived on their *atap*-roofed boats, never leaving them, even while trading with the Iban. Some, however, learned the tribal languages and customs and, although banned from doing so by Brooke, would spent nights in the longhouses; a few even took Dyak wives. The pioneers would spend a month or more plying the tributaries, leaving cloth, salt and shotgun cartridges on credit with the Dyaks and then returning to pick up **jungle produce** in exchange, like birds' nests, camphor, beeswax, honey and bezoar stones. But it was a risky life, especially when faced with an Iban tribesman who had decided that the only way out of a credit impasse was to do away with the trader to whom he owed the goods.

Sibu

SIBU, 60km from the coast up batang Rajang, is Sarawak's second largest city and the state's biggest port. It veritably seethes with activity, most of the action taking place along the half-kilometre length of jetties, with their separate bays for passenger boats, commercial craft and logging barges. Most of the local population are Foochow Chinese (the town is known locally as the New Foochow) and its remarkable modern growth is largely attributed to these industrious and enterprising immigrants. Sibu, unlike Kuching or Miri, never retained a large contingent of Brooke officials which means its Chinese character has never really been diluted. Following the success of the early rubber plantations, manufacturing industries (largely textiles and consumer items) were established here, while later, after independence, Chinese businessmen moved into the lucrative trade in **timber**. But it wasn't all untrammelled expansion. In 1928 the Chinese *godowns* along the wharf and many of the cramped lodging houses and cafés were destroyed by fire. The town was devastated again in World War II by advancing Japanese forces, and was occupied for three years, during which time much of the Chinese population was forced into slave labour.

There is still a wild edge to Sibu: the traders are louder and more persuasive; the locals more assertively friendly; while everywhere are the signs of the timber cartels' wealth – a staggered skyline of multistorey commercial buildings on the outskirts, brand new Toyota pick-ups on the streets, and gangs of Chinese middlemen in the cafés, surrounded by beer and whisky bottles, slapping down dozens of twenty-dollar notes during a session of mahjong. The town's most striking landmark is the towering, seven-storey pagoda, next to the temple, while behind it is the old Chinatown, with its warren of narrow streets, along which are most of the cheap hotels, the hawker stalls and the cramped fish, meat and vegetable markets. Beyond simply soaking up the town's vibrant atmosphere, there's little else for visitors to get to grips with in Sibu, though you'll want to check out the bustling night market and the small museum on the edge of town, which focuses on the Chinese migration and the displaced ethnic communities. However, in the end, most people are here because it's the first stage of an expedition upriver – though don't be surprised if you end up feeling sorry to leave.

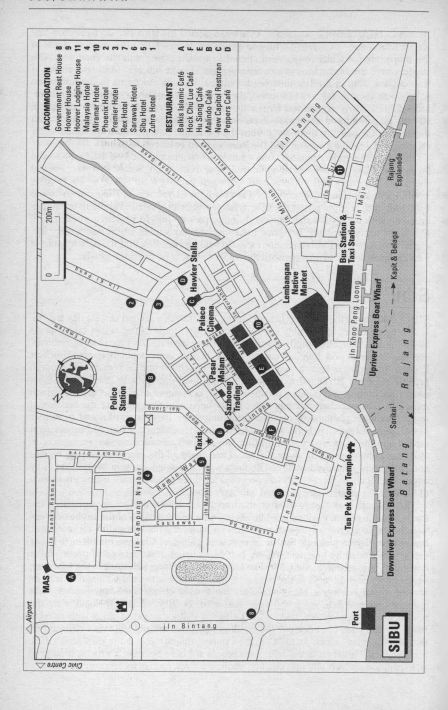

SIBU

ACCOMMODATION
Government Rest House 8
Hoover House 9
Hoover Lodging House 11
Malaysia Hotel 4
Miramar Hotel 10
Phoenix Hotel 2
Premier Hotel 3
Rex Hotel 7
Sarawak Hotel 6
Sibu Hotel 5
Zuhra Hotel 1

RESTAURANTS
Balkis Islamic Café A
Hock Chu Lue Café F
Hu Siong Café E
Malindo Café B
New Capitol Restoran C
Peppers Café D

Arriving and information

The **airport** for arrivals from Kuching, Bintulu and Miri, is 6km south of the centre. The taxi drivers at the airport tend to be a fairly assertive breed and will tell you not to bother with the bus, but they'll charge you $12 for the journey into the centre. Otherwise, make your way out of the tiny terminal and on to the main road where there is a bus stop for the #1 into town (every 40min, daily 7am–6pm). This takes you to the **bus and taxi station** on jalan Khoo Peng Loong, 200m west of Chinatown, where all the budget hotels are located; this is also where the long-distance bus from Bintulu arrives.

Travelling by boat from Sarikei, you dock at the **upriver boat wharf**, 100m east of the bus terminal. This is where you come to catch the *ekspres* boat on to Kapit and Belaga, while for **downriver boats** – the ones *from* Kapit and *to* Sarikei – there's another jetty, 100m further east, just beside the Chinese temple. Walking directly behind the pagoda leads to jalan Tukang Besi and on to jalan Central, another main street with accommodation and restaurants. For more **departure details**, see the relevant sections in "Listings", below.

Although there's no tourist office in Sibu, you can get leaflets and an accommodation list, together with **information** on town and longhouse tours, from Frankie Ting's office, *Sazhoong Trading*, at 4 jalan Central (Mon–Sat 8am–4.40pm).

Accommodation

It is fairly easy to find **accommodation** in Sibu although many of the hotels are in the old town, where the day-market, hawker stalls and cafés – open from before dawn – make sleeping in an impossibility. The nightmarket makes going to bed early difficult too, though things quieten down around 11pm. Prices are cheaper than in Kuching, though the standard of the rooms is not as high.

Government Rest House, jalan Pulau (☎084/330406). Fifteen minutes' walk from the wharf in a large colonial building at the far end of jalan Pulau. The double rooms are pricey, but comfortable, and some overlook a tranquil garden at the back. Visiting officials take priority, so you are more likely to get a room here at the weekends. ③

Hoover House, jalan Pulau (☎084/332491). Quiet situation, basic double rooms with communal bathrooms and a friendly caretaker. Book in advance. ①

Hoover Lodging House, 34 jalan Tan Sri (☎084/334490). Unobtrusively positioned in a cramped side street close to the bus station. The rooms are small with fan, shared toilet and shower. ①

Malaysia Hotel, jalan Kampung Nyabor (☎084/332298). A popular, but fairly shabby place, located on a busy main road, with small rooms, shared toilet and shower, however it's family-run and very friendly. ②

Miramar Hotel, 47 jalan Channel (☎084/332433). Right on top of the market: grubby, not very friendly, but centrally located – looking directly down on the nightmarket. ②

Phoenix Hotel, jalan Ki Peng, off jalan Kampung Nyabor (☎084/313877). Smart and friendly; one of the best upmarket hotels, with spacious modern rooms, some with baths, and TV. ④

Premier Hotel, jalan Kampung Nyabor (☎084/323222). Top-class hotel; you can tell by the chilly air-con when you approach the doorway. ⑤

Rex Hotel, 32 jalan Lintang (☎084/330625). Cheap, functional rooms with fan and shared facilities. Air-con rooms are more expensive. ①–②

Sarawak Hotel, 34 jalan Lintang (☎084/333455). Recently had a facelift and now with an elevator to the tastefully decorated rooms on four floors. Predictably, more expensive than in the old days; the large rooms now equipped with TV, air-con and shower. ③

Sibu Hotel, jalan Marshidi Sidek (☎084/330784). Small rooms, some with air-con, others just with fan; all with shared shower and toilet. ①

Zuhra Hotel, jalan Kampung Nyabor (☎084/310711). Quality hotel with smallish, modern rooms with air-con, TV and shower. ③.

The town

For a century or more the Rajang has been the town's commercial and industrial life-line. Along the **wharf**, on jalan Khoo Peng Loong, plankways lead to several points where the boats dock, while stalls line the road selling basic provisions for journeys up and down the Rajang. At the western edge of the harbour is the **Rajang Esplanade**, a small park built in 1987 on reclaimed land. It's a popular place to sit and enjoy the evening breeze, and there are occasional cultural events held here, too, like ethnic dancing and Chinese firework displays.

Head back past the boat wharf and jalan Khoo Peng Loong merges with jalan Pulau close to the **Tua Pek Kong Temple**. There was a small, wooden temple on this site as early as 1870, though soon afterwards it was rebuilt on a much grander scale, with tiled roof, stone block floor and decorative fixtures imported from China. Two large concrete lions guard the entrance, while the fifteen-metre-wide main chamber is always busy with people paying respects to the deity, Tua Pek Kong, a prominent Confucian scholar. The statue of Tua Pek Kong, to the left of the front entrance, is the most important image in the temple and survived both the fire of 1928 and Japanese bombardment. Elsewhere, the roof and columns are decorated with traditional dragon and holy bird statues, while emblazoned on the temple wall to the left of the entrance are murals depicting the animals which symbolize the signs of the Chinese zodiac. For a small donation, the caretaker, Tan Teck Chiang, will tell you the story of the temple and give you a brief rundown on the significance of these and other images. In 1987 the rear section of the temple was replaced by the $1.5-million, seven-storey **pagoda**, from the top of which there's a splendid view of the Rajang snaking away below.

Across the way, in the network of streets between jalan Market, jalan Channel and jalan Central, is **Chinatown** with its plethora of hardware shops, newspaper stalls, rowdy cafés, textile wholesalers, cassette sellers, food and fruit juice vendors and hotels. The central artery, **jalan Market**, runs from jalan Pulau beside the temple, and forms the hub of possibly the most vibrant *pasar malam* (nightmarket) in Sarawak. At dusk, hundreds of stalls are set up, offering a wide variety of foods, many of which are specific Sibu delicacies like stuffed dumplings, grilled fish and chicken wings, or – not for the faint-hearted – pig or duck's head and a range of offal.

On the southwestern edge of the old town, in between jalan Mission and jalan Channel, the daily **Lembangan Market** opens before dawn and closes around 5pm. There are hundreds of stalls here, many of the hawkers Iban from nearby longhouses selling anything from edible delicacies like flying fox, squirrel, snake, turtle, snail, jungle ferns and exotic fruits, to rattan baskets, beadwork, charm bracelets and leather belts and thongs.

The Civic Centre

On the outskirts, the one place worth visiting is the modern **Civic Centre**, 2km south-east of the centre, which contains a small but high-quality collection of exhibits in its museum (Tues–Sat 3–8pm, Sun 9am–noon & 2–8pm) on the ground floor. Take the jalan Tun Abang Haji Openg bus from the bus terminal and ask for the Civic Centre. The displays detail the development of Sibu and the other settlements on the Rajang, best seen in a set of photographs, dating from 1880 onwards, which record their growth. The Chinese migration is well covered, too, especially the history of the numerous cultural associations which were the immigrants' first port of call when they arrived. In exchange for voluntary labour, the associations would find the new arrivals paid work and lodgings and induct them into the business and cultural life of the city. Rather more perfunctory is the coverage of the ethnic tribes the Chinese often displaced, although imitation longhouse rooms contain textiles, kitchen utensils and other paraphernalia belonging originally to the Iban and *orang ulu*.

Eating

Throughout town there are Chinese cafés selling Sibu's most famous dish, Foochow noodles – steamed and then served in a soy and oyster sauce with spring onions and dried fish. Other local favourites include *million* (a type of wild fern), *kung muan bee* (a fat noodle) and *kong bian* (baked biscuit). Prawns and crabs are of a high quality and, in season, tropical fruit like star fruit, rambutan and guava are easily available from market stalls. Although Sibu has some fine air-con **restaurants**, most people prefer to be outside when the weather's good; and even the most conspicuously wealthy opt to eat at **hawker stalls**: busiest in the morning are those at the Lembangan Market; in the evening everyone congregates at the *pasar malam* in the town centre, though you can't sit down and eat here – if you buy snacks from the nightmarket, you'll have to wander down to the Esplanade to eat.

Most cafés are **open** throughout the day, from around 7am to 8pm, with the Chinese coffee houses staying open until around midnight. Restaurants open from around 11am until 11pm.

Balkis Islamic Café, 69 jalan Osman. Very good North Indian staples like *roti canai, murtabak* and curries. It's near the *MAS* office and post office and costs around $3 a head. Open 7am–8pm.

Hock Chu Leu Restoran, 28 jalan Blacksmith. Well-known Foochow restaurant with great baked fish and fresh vegetables. The cost is around $25 for two, including beer.

Hu Siong Café, jalan Market. Busy place popular with locals, near the market and jetty. Great for drinking beer or tea and watching frenetic Sibu bustle by.

Malindo Café, 20 jalan Kampung Nyabor. Tasty, spicy Indonesian food – the stuffed crab is particularly good and extremely inexpensive at around $4–5 a head.

New Capitol Restoran, jalan Workshop. Expensive Chinese restaurant though worth the splurge at around $25–30 a head, including drinks. The nearby hawker stalls are popular, too, specializing in Malay food – crisp green bean and chilli, and curried chicken and beef dishes – with plenty of tables protected from the elements.

Peppers Café, *Tanahmas Hotel*, jalan Kampung Nyabor. A wide menu including some Western dishes as well as Malay fish curries. The international flavour is very popular with Sibu businesspeople, but it's not cheap at around $40 for two.

Listings

Airport For flight info call ☎084/334351; *MAS* is at 61 jalan Tuanku Abdul Rahman (☎084/26166). There are services to Bintulu (6 daily); Kuching (11 daily) and Miri (7 daily).

Banks *Bumiputra*, Lot 6 & 7, jalan Kampung Nyabor; *Public Bank,* 2–6 jalan Tuanku Osman.

Boats Departures to Kapit from the upriver wharf (hourly 6am–2.45pm, $16), to Belaga from the upriver wharf at 6am and 9am; to Sarikei from the downriver wharf (hourly 7am–3pm; $8); to Kuching via Sarikei from the downriver wharf (daily at 7am & 11.30am; Mon and Fri at 11pm). For more on upriver departures, see the section following.

Buses Departures to Bintulu are daily at 6.15am, 9.15am, 12.15pm and 2.15pm.

Handicrafts *Chai Chiang Store,* 5 jalan Central, for woodcarvings, beadwork, bamboo and rattan baskets, and mats. Prices are cheaper than in Kuching. There are also stalls selling basketware where jalan Channel hits the wharf. There are three ceramic factories close to Sibu: two on jalan Ulu Oya, one on jalan Upper Lanag; buses every hour from the bus station.

Hospital *Lau King Hoe,* jalan Pulau, next to the *RPA* building (☎084/313333).

Laundry *Dobi Sibu,* 5G jalan Bindang.

Police On jalan Kampung Nyabor (☎084/322222).

Post office The main office is on jalan Kampung Nyabar (Mon–Fri 8am–6pm, Sat 8am–noon).

Tour operator *Ibrahim Tourist Guide,* 1 Lane One, Jalan Bengkel (☎084/318987). As Sibu is usually first stop on a trip further up the Rajang, few people organize tours from here. But if you're not going any further, *Ibrahim's* overnight tour to an Iban longhouse close to Sibu is good value at around $200 for two.

Up the Rajang: Kanowit, Song and the Katibas

From Sibu the *ekspres* heads up the Rajang, stopping first at **Kanowit** and then **Song**, from where explorations of **sungei Katibas** are possible, before heading onwards to Kapit (see below). The distance between each wood-processing yard steadily lengthens until Song is reached; they rarely disturb the thick jungle thereafter. Along the way, small Iban boats can be seen, hugging the sides of the river to get as far away as possible from the swell that the fast boats create.

The *ekspres* **boat** for Kapit leaves Sibu daily on the hour from 6am; the last one is at 2.45pm. The trip takes four hours and costs $20. The 6am and 9am boats go further than Kapit, right the way to the upper reaches of the Rajang to Belaga (see p.367). You can't book in advance – seats are on a strictly first-come, first-served basis – so always arrive at least fifteen minutes early to bag your seat, and then nip off to buy any provisions you require for the journey.

> There's a map of the Rajang river system on p.365.

Kanowit

An hour from Sibu, the boat reaches the small settlement of **KANOWIT** and although there's a hotel on the waterfront, the *Kanowit Air Con,* and a few cafés, the only real reason to get out here is to see **Fort Emma**, one of the first defensive structures built by James Brooke. It's just a couple of hundred metres to the left of the jetty. Built in 1859 of timber and bamboo, the fort took its name from James' beloved sister, its presence intended to inhibit the numerous raids by the local Iban on the remaining Rajang Melanau tribes. However, soon after it was built it was overrun and future attacks were only repulsed by stationing a platoon here, mostly comprising Iban and Malays in the pay of Brooke's officials. Up until the Japanese occupation, Fort Emma was the nerve centre of the entire district but with the passing of colonial rule the building fell into disuse: there were no more pirates to repulse, head-hunters to pursue, or rebellious Chinese miners to suppress. Nonetheless, despite years of neglect, the fort is still impressive, perched on high ground, its turrets surveying its surroundings. Like others, though, it's now a government office and it's not possible to get inside.

Song and sungei Katibas

The next stop is at **SONG**, another ninety minutes upstream, which lies at the head of one of the Rajang's major tributaries, sungei Katibas, which winds and narrows southward towards the mountainous border region with Kalimantan. There's not much to the place, which is little more than a jetty, a playground, a small Chinese temple, and one hotel, the *Capital* (②), on the waterfront street New Bazaar, which has clean rooms. Elsewhere along here the usual Chinese **cafés** and stores occupy the *godowns*, built in the 1920s. Song does have a helpful **guide**, Richard Kho, who can arrange visits to Iban longhouses on the Katibas (for more on which, see below) – ask at the hotel for him or try calling ☎084/777228.

Exploring sungei Katibas

To explore **sungei Katibas**, you need to catch the passenger longboat which leaves Song twice each morning; departure times change so ask at the jetty. On the Katibas are several Iban longhouses worth visiting, including the large community at the junction of the Katibas and one of its own small tributaries, sungei Bangkit. It takes between two and three hours to reach **BANGKIT**, which comprises a massive, one-hundred door longhouse and a dozen smaller dwellings on the opposite bank. This is the boat's final port of call, so most of your fellow passengers will get off here: one is bound to extend an invitation to you to visit. The longhouse women are excellent weavers, and you can buy a wall hanging or thin rug here for around $300. There are another twelve Iban longhouses in all along the banks of the river, each maintaining their own rice fields, clinging to the inclines. To travel further down sungei Bangkit or the Katibas may mean **renting a boat**, though if you're lucky you'll be able to tag along with a smaller longboat heading your way. Negotiate the fare before you start the trip – you shouldn't have to pay more than $50 for a half-day's travel.

Despite their proximity to big-town Sibu, the river communities still hold their customs dear. Along the banks of the Katibas and the Bangkit you'll catch sight of small **burial houses** set back on the banks. For a good 300m either side of the burial spots, the jungle is left undisturbed; these areas are strictly out of bounds to locals from neighbouring longhouses and other visitors. The surrounding areas also remain uncultivated: the ancestors would be displeased if the living showed disrespect to the dead by harvesting close to their last resting place.

Kapit and around

KAPIT – four hours east of Sibu – is a fast-growing town with a frontier atmosphere; a riverside settlement in the middle of thick jungle being made more accessible by the day. It started life as a remote bazaar for a small community of British officials and Chinese *towkays* trading with the region's indigenous population; but these days, the signs of rapid expansion are everywhere: heavy boxes of rifle cartridges, machine parts and provisions are unloaded from the tops of the *ekspres* boats, and local landowners drive around in Toyotas, picking up workers to clear land or build houses. There remains a strong native presence; fruit sellers are much more forthright here than in Sibu or Kuching because – for the time being at least – this is still their territory. The timber trade employs native workers from distant longhouses on short-term contracts and the bright lights of Kapit is where they come to spend their wages – karaoke lounges, snooker halls and brothels are all much in evidence.

Although most travellers stay just one night, waiting for boats either way along the Rajang or for connecting longboats along sungei Baleh (see p.366), it's easy to get to like Kapit. The place itself is tiny – little more than a few streets cleared out of the luxuriant forest which threatens to engulf it. However, there are lots of good cafés in which to while away time, a decent museum collection, and – out of town – the chance to visit Sebabai Park, 10km away along a dusty track. Kapit is also a good place to organize trips to nearby Pelagus Rapids and to local Iban communities, with one of a number of legitimate **tour operators** based in town (see "Around Kapit" on p.364 for details).

The town

Close to the the jetty lies Kapit's main landmark, **Fort Sylvia**, built in 1880 (and renamed in 1925 after Vyner Brooke's wife) in an attempt to prevent the warring Iban attacking less numerous and more pacific groups like the upriver Ukit and Bukitan. The fort also served to limit Iban migration along the nearby sungei Baleh and confine them to the section of the Rajang below Kapit. Its most famous administrator was **Domingo de Rozario**, the son of James Brookes' Portuguese chef. Born in the Istana kitchen in Kuching, de Rozario's memoirs record that life in Kapit was pleasant and that he got on well with the natives, but he found it most troublesome when dealing

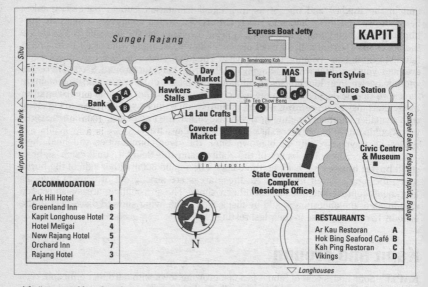

Along the map:

KAPIT

Sungei Rajang

Express Boat Jetty

◁ Sibu

jln Temenggong Koh

Day Market ❶

Kapit Square

MAS

Fort Sylvia

Police Station

Hawkers Stalls

❷ ❸ Ⓐ Ⓑ

Bank

Ⓓ ❹ ❺

◁ Airport Sebabai Park

⊠ La Lau Crafts

jln Teo Chow Beng Ⓒ

Covered Market

❻

Sungei Baleh, Pelagus Rapids, Belaga ▷

❼

jln Airport

jln Selirik

Civic Centre & Museum

State Government Complex (Residents Office)

N

ACCOMMODATION	
Ark Hill Hotel	1
Greenland Inn	6
Kapit Longhouse Hotel	2
Hotel Meligai	4
New Rajang Hotel	5
Orchard Inn	7
Rajang Hotel	3

RESTAURANTS	
Ar Kau Restoran	A
Hok Bing Seafood Café	B
Kah Ping Restoran	C
Vikings	D

▽ Longhouses

with "cases of heads taken on raids." These days the fort houses administrative offices and there's little of period interest inside Sylvia, though if you're curious, the officials will let you take a look.

Along Kapit's oldest riverside street, **jalan Temenggong Koh**, the rows of simple shophouses which once nestled between patches of jungle have now given way to stores and cafés housed in concrete buildings, which can withstand the fires and deluges which regularly occur. The **jetty** is always a hive of activity, too, with dozens of longboats bobbing up and down at their moorings and scores of people making their way back and forth between the *ekspres* boats and smaller craft with bulky bundles of goods. Merchants, timber employers and visitors watch the goings-on from the wood- and marble-topped tables in the *Chuong Hin Café,* opposite the jetty.

Kapit's main square, simply called **Kapit Square**, lies to the east of the jetty around 50m along jalan Temenggong Koh, surrounded by shops selling everything from post-cards to rope. The walk along the northern edge of the square, on jalan Teo Chow Beng, leads to the **day-market** where tribespeople rail at you until you buy a cluster of tropical fruit, and more measured traders point out boxes of eels and shrimps which are still wriggling. On Fridays and Saturdays live animals are sold, including frogs, turtles, birds and monkeys. There's a wet fish section too, and textile and shoe stalls upstairs in the main building; while the stalls in front of the market sell great Sarawakan fast food – prawn cakes, *pau,* curry pies and sweet pastries. Opposite the market there's an excellent **handicraft** store, *Putena Jaya,* with a small but very well-priced selection of antique and new handicrafts. The only other place in town to buy ethnic artefacts is *La Lau Crafts,* just off jalan Airport, which has an excellent collection of rugs, sarongs, baskets, *pua kumbu* textiles, woodcarvings, beads and ceramics.

Back from the jetty, near the pond, is the **Civic Museum** (Mon–Fri 2–4.30pm; free), which has a collection of interesting exhibits on the tribes in the Rajang basin, includ-ing a well-constructed longhouse and a mural painted by local Ibans. Artist Timothy Chua's sketches and watercolours of Kapit, Belaga and Song are descriptive accounts of a life which is slowly disappearing, while the museum also covers the lives of the Hokkien traders who were the early pioneers in the region.

Practicalities

The **airport** is 4km south of town, from where you should be able to jump in a Toyota van for the ride to central Kapit Square ($2). If not, a taxi into the centre charges $10. The *ekspres* **boats** dock at the town jetty, from where it is a few minutes' walk to anywhere in town. The only **information** available is from Tan Teck Chuan, whose office is at 11 jalan Sit Leong; he has a few tour brochures and accommodation details.

You need a **permit** to travel upriver to Belaga and beyond, or along any of the tributaries off the Rajang, available from the **Resident's Office** (Mon–Fri 8am–12.30pm & 2.15–4.15pm), on the first floor of the State Government Complex, 100m north of the jetty on jalan Selinik. Take your passport with you; the process is a formality and there's no charge.

Accommodation

Ark Hill Hotel, 10 jalan Airport (☎084/796168). On the edge of the centre with small, clean rooms, including air-con and shower. ②–③

Greenland Inn, jalan Teo Chow Beng (☎084/796388). Recently opened, the *Greenland* is cashing in on Kapit's growth. The rooms are small and clean, some with good views over the Rajang. Facilities include air-con and bathroom. ②–③

Kapit Longhouse Hotel, 21 jalan Berjaya (☎084/796415). The cheapest hotel in town with a lovely position at the river's edge. Although grubby, only the *Rajang* is more popular with travellers. The rooms, with fans, are basic; bathrooms are shared. ①

Hotel Meligai, jalan Airport (☎084/796817). The only upmarket hotel in town – and full of brash businessmen. The large rooms have full facilities, and it has a good restaurant attached. The receptionist, Sia Majau, organizes trips to nearby longhouses. ③

New Rajang, 104 jalan Teo Chow Beng (☎084/796600). Small rooms which are all fully equipped with air-con, shower and TV. ②–③

Orchard Inn, 64 jalan Airport (☎084/796325). Rooms with air-con, shower and TV. ②–③

Rajang Hotel, 28 jalan Temenggoh, New Bazaar (☎084/796709). One of Sarawak's best known travellers' hotels, where the guys at reception strum guitars and have sing-songs during siesta. The large rooms, many overlooking the river, have efficient fans and good bathrooms. ①–②.

Sing Soon Hing Hotel, 26 jalan New Bazaar (☎084/461257,①). Chinese cheapie with small, dusty rooms communal bathroom. ①

Eating

Kapit is a great place to **eat** on the hoof – which is ironic as it's one town where you may spend a lot of time just sitting around. The food from **hawker** stalls and **markets** is great and, as a rule, better than many of the few sit-down **restaurants**.

Ar Kau Restoran, jalan Berjaya, beside *Kapit Longhouse Hotel*. Specializes in local recipes: wild boar, steamed fish, jungle vegetables, and as much rice as you can eat, for around $25 for two with beer.

Covered Market, jalan Airport. A dozen separate stalls serving Chinese, Malay and Dyak dishes. *Gerai Islam* sells *roti canai* and various noodle dishes with local vegetables, seafood and meat. The optimum time to eat here is between noon and 3pm, though it's open until 9pm.

Day Market Stalls, jalan Teo Chow Beng. Sarawak fast food like curry puffs, prawn cakes, cornmeal cake and *tofu* buns. Open 7am-5pm.

Hock Bing Seafood Cafe, 8 jalan Temenggoh. Tables along the pavement at this bustling café, which serves the best prawn dishes in Kapit. Friendly, atmospheric and excellent value at around $20 for two including beer.

Kah Ping Restoran, Kapit Square, jalan Teo Chow Beng. Good spot to watch Kapit life go by; the best dishes on the menu are the Chinese noodle and rice dishes.

Ming Hock Restoran, 1st floor, Day Market building, jalan Teo Chow Beng. Situated above the day-market, this large but often empty restaurant has an excellent view but a limited menu.

Vikings Restaurant, corner of jalan Wharf and jalan Teo Chow Beng. It had to come to Kapit: Western fast food including fried chicken, french fries and hamburgers, all at local prices.

Around Kapit

Although the roads around Kapit don't go very far in any direction, worthwhile trips can be made to Sebabai Park, and to the few **longhouses** accessible by road (although these don't compare with visiting the traditional Iban communities along sungei Baleh; see next section). You might also consider a trip to the spectacular **Pelagus Rapids**, an hour upstream.

You'll need a **guide**, or be part of a small **tour group**, to go to Pelagus and the more inaccessible longhouses. When approached – as you will be early on in your stay – ask whether the person is registered with the Sarawak Tourist Association (STA); some unregistered guides are unreliable and since many charge over $100 a day just to take you to their longhouses you want to be sure you're getting a good deal. It's always best to haggle a little, as well as checking exactly what the price includes: there shouldn't be any extra costs, like contributions for food, once the trip has started. The best person in Kapit to consult is the STA-approved **Tan Teck Chuan** (11 jalan Sit Leong, Kapit Square; ☎084/796655), a *towkay* and explorer who knows sungei Baleh and its tributaries very well. He organizes one- and two-night tours to longhouses and has good contacts with Iban *tuais,* and also runs inexpensive (around $80 for the day) trips to the Pelagus Rapids. A Kapit Iban with good contacts is **Donald Ding** (☎084/ 797639); he is often in the *Ar Kau* restaurant and will take you on an overnight trip to his family's longhouse on sungei Mujong, a tributary of the Rajang about two hours away by longboat. This is not a particularly traditional community but the people there are friendly, and Ding's family serves up a hearty meal. At the *Hotel Meligai,* the receptionist **Sia Majau** (also STA-approved) co-ordinates the following: a one-day trip to the Pelagus Rapids (about $350 for a boat which can seat six); much more expensive four-day trips to a Kayan longhouse, Long Singgit, far up sungei Baleh; or three-day trips along the Baleh's Gaat and Mujong tributaries to visit **Iban communities** which still perform the *mering* ceremony, the procedure for welcoming strangers. The *tuai* sings a song before touching eggs, tobacco and rice cakes; visitors in turn copy his actions, after which everyone can sit down and informal conversation, tea-drinking and eating can commence.

Sebabai Park

To reach **SEBABAI PARK**, take the irregular Toyota van to Sebabai longhouse, a ten-kilometre trip east which costs $5; the Toyota stop is in front of the day-market on jalan Teo Chow Beng. Although the park is a popular picnic spot for locals at weekends, few people come in the week, when you will have the place to yourself. The bus weaves up and down the hilly road through the forest, passing houses and occasionally stopping for locals carrying wood or bringing sacks of rice from the market. At the end of the road by the longhouse, a sign points up a hill to the park. The path leads down into dense primary forest, crosses streams and, after about fifteen minutes, ends at a small **waterfall**, where insects, birds and monkeys chatter alongside the mesmeric trickle of running water – perfect for swimming. There aren't any facilities here so bring water and some food if you're going to stay a while. Returning, note that no vans run between noon and 2pm – the drivers are taking a break in the longhouse.

Pelagus Rapids

Another easy trip is to take one of the local *ekspres* boats to the **Pelagus Rapids**, a stretch of deceptively shallow river an hour upstream on the way to Belaga, where large, submerged stones make any passage through treacherous. On either side of the river, dense rainforest hugs the steep banks; there's a twenty-door Iban longhouse a ten-minute walk away, in the forest. A resort, called the *Park Cresent,* which will include chalets, is planned for the area immediately above the rapids on the west bank.

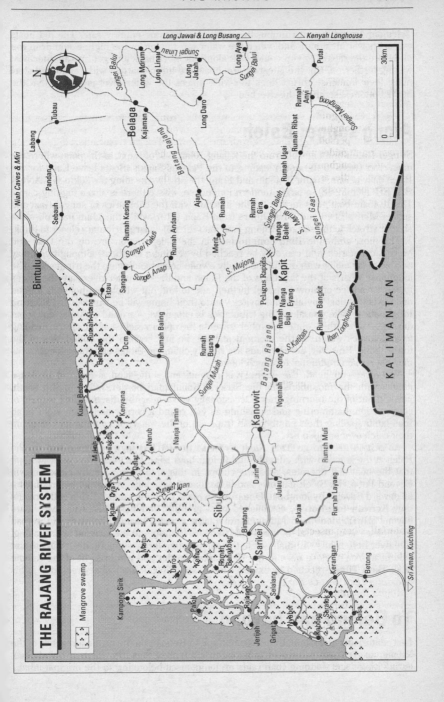

THE RAJANG RIVER SYSTEM

Mangrove swamp

It's only recently that running the rapids has become entirely safe. The old boats weren't powerful enough and, when the water was too low or too high, would drop you off before the rapids so you could walk along the river bank and get into another boat waiting further on. But the latest *ekspres* boats are turbo-charged with reinforced steel hulls; their immense thrust does the trick unless the water level is so low that the boat's bottom is scraping the riverbed.

Along sungei Baleh

Sungei Baleh branches off from the Rajang 10km east of Kapit, at the point where the main river twists to the north leading to the Pelagus Rapids. Boats leave Kapit for the Baleh daily at 7am, 10am, 10.45am and 11am, the first two heading the 20km to **NANGA BALEH** (90min; $8), a large, modern longhouse, where there is also a logging camp. The 10.45am boat goes further, to the junction with the tributaries of sungei Gaat and sungei Merirai, two and a half hours from Kapit ($10); while the 11am boat plies the shorter stretch to the sungei Mujong junction (1hr; $6) – a large tributary closer to Kapit.

The most authentic **Iban longhouses** in the Baleh region are on the Gaat and Merirai tributaries, and can only be reached by renting a longboat, although you may be able to tag along with one of the locally owned boats heading up the tributaries. The longhouse wharfs at the junctions of the Baleh and these smaller rivers are the places to ask for advice on how to travel further, and to find out which longhouse is a good one to visit; almost anyone who invites you to their home will be trustworthy. **Renting longboats** to take you along the tributaries is expensive – around $100 per day – but during good weather, quite a number traverse the upper reaches of the rivers, heading to longhouses which, at the moment at least, lie just beyond the boundaries of the timber zone. However, access roads are rapidly changing things and these longhouses may not remain traditional for much longer.

Wherever you head, the **scenery** is magnificent – the land is covered in dense jungle, with the mountains on the Sarawak-Kalimantan border, 50km to the south, peeping out of the morning mist. Occasionally you'll hear the disembodied sounds of conversation, hammering and splashing as you round a corner and catch sight of an Iban family pulling their bamboo fish traps out of the water, or cooking and smoking their catch over an open fire.

An *ekspres* used to go from Kapit as far as the **PUTAI** logging camp, way up the Baleh at the junction with sungei Putai (a four-hour trip). You'll have to check in Kapit that the boat still operates, as some camps in this area have recently closed down. Beyond Putai, the Baleh narrows and is no longer navigable by regular *ekspres* boat – all onward travel is by longboat. One place to make for on the upper Baleh is the river's only **Kenyah longhouse**, established by a group of Indonesian Kenyah, two hours beyond Putai by longboat. Although not a large wooden beauty like many of the Iban longhouses along the Baleh, the people here are friendly and the location breathtaking. The river here brims with fish, while the surrounding forest supports deer, buffalo and wild boar. You're close here to the Kalimantan border and within sight of the remote peak, **Batu Tiban**, reached by explorer Redmond O' Hanlon, a journey recorded in his book *Into The Heart Of Borneo*.

To Belaga and beyond

Last century the 150-kilometre trip from Kapit to **Belaga**, on the furthest reaches of the Rajang, used to take two weeks in a longboat, a treacherous trip which involved negotiating rapids and dodging Iban raids on longhouses belonging to the original inhabitants of the upper Rajang, the **Kayan.** After Charles Brooke bought the region from the Sultan of Brunei in 1853, a small bazaar was built in Belaga and Chinese pioneers arrived to trade with both the Kayan and the nomadic **Penan** who roamed over a wide swathe of the forest. The British presence in this region was tiny – officials would occasionally brave the trip from Kapit but no fort was built this far up the river.

These days the trip takes up to six hours, depending on the river level. Occasionally the boat companies cancel departures: if the water level's very low, Pelagus Rapids (see "Around Kapit" above) can be particularly hazardous; if it's high, the Rajang becomes a raging torrent and anyone who can avoid moving on the river does so. However, if the conditions are right, it's an excellent trip. Logging camps are scarcer in this stretch of the river and as you near the centre of Sarawak, wispy clouds cloak the hills; while the screech of rainforest monkeys and birds can be heard when the boat cuts its engine.

Longhouses are dotted along the river bank. As far as **LONG PILA**, ninety minutes from Kapit, the people are all Iban, though between here and Belaga there are many tribes, including the Bukitan, Tanjong and Sekapan. Before the 1860s the Kayan were numerous here, too, but when they protected the killers of two government officials, Charles Brooke led a punitive expedition against them, driving them back to the Belaga river, upstream of Belaga itself.

Belaga

BELAGA, which lies at the confluence of the Rajang and sungei Balui, is as remote as you can get in the Sarawak interior but it's not uncharted territory by any means. As early as 1900, Chinese *towkays* had opened up Belaga to trade and were supplying the tribespeople with kerosene, cooking oil and cartridges, in exchange for beadwork and mats, beeswax, ebony and tree gums. In more recent years it's been possible to cut northwest to the coast, via Tubau, from this isolated spot by getting rides in loggers' vehicles from a camp just to the north on the Belaga river, but timber production is slowing down in the area and consequently there are fewer four-wheel drives going to and forth between the camps. This means that the only real reason for coming to Belaga these days is to travel along **sungei Balui**, which weaves and curls eastwards over 200km until it reaches its headwaters in the mountains which divide Sarawak from Kalimantan. This requires a certain amout of planning, though, and a great deal of money since fuel prices are inflated this far away from the urban centres: diesel is three times more expensive here than on the coast and renting a longboat is really only feasible if you're in a group, preferably of between four and six people. There is a guide in Belaga (see "Practicalities" below) while solo travellers wanting to visit the Kayan communities (see feature on p.368) on the Balui may be able to join a larger group, paying just a single share of the tour price.

There's nothing particular to do in Belaga itself except watch the comings and goings. Sometimes the Penan arrive to sell things – their uniqely carved knives can be picked up for a third of the price you would pay in Sibu. A seasonal appearance is also made by the **wild honey collectors** from Kalimantan, who arrive in March and again in September to trade their jungle produce for supplies. Other faces on Belaga's small network of streets show the diversity of upriver life: Kayan and Kenyah, with their fantastic tattoos and elongated ear lobes wander through the bazaar; longhouse chiefs on a visit eat wild boar and fried ferns in the Chinese cafés; and the small group of uniformed Malay officials laugh and smoke, making the most of their remote posting.

From the jetty, everything is fairly close by: market, shops selling provisions, a few nondescript houses and, beyond, a small track snaking towards the formidably dense forest, a few hundred metres away. Twenty minutes' walk along a small path which runs south and adjacent to the river, there's a pretty *kampung* where the Kejaman (a small ethnic group, now almost extinct, related to the Kayan) burial pole on display outside the Sarawak Museum in Kuching was found in the early years of this century. The path weaves through pepper gardens and past wooden, stilted houses, to a school where curious children stop their games to stare at strangers. Looking over the river, just before the playing field beyond the *kampung*, you can see a Kayan *salong* or **burial tomb** on the opposite bank – a small wooden construction with a multicoloured wooden sculpture sporting the image of a face. It's taboo for anyone other than the dead person's family to go within a hundred metres of the tomb. As the Kayan prefer to build their longhouses on tributaries, yet position *salongs* on the main rivers, they are often all you see for many kilometres when you travel along sungei Balui.

Practicalities

Belaga's three **hotels** all offer similar rooms, which are of quite a high standard considering how isolated the town is. *Hotel Belaga,* 14 Main Bazaar (☎086/461244; ②), is the favourite – the rooms have bathroom and fan. Owner Andrew Tong and his family run a café downstairs which is the best place to eat in town. The *Bee Lian Inn,* 11 Main Bazaar (☎086/461416; ①), and *Hotel Sing Soon Huat,* 27 New Bazaar (☎086/461257; ②), are the alternatives, both with small, basic rooms.

Officially, you need a **permit** to travel onwards on the Balui, or to attempt the overland route to Tubau, for either of which see below. The government office (Mon–Fri 8am–noon & 2–4.15pm) is the first building on your right along the path from the jetty.

If Belaga's only **guide**, Eddie John Balarik, is in Belaga, he'll soon find you, though you can leave a message for him at the *Bee Lian Inn.* Eddie's the acknowledged local expert, with excellent contacts with the Penan. He organizes a three-day expedition to Long Jakah, a Kayan settlement a day's travel northeast of Belaga on sungei Linau; as well as a jungle trek, which follows an ancient trade path, staying overnight with the Penan, and with an option to go hunting and fishing. These trips cost around $100 a

---

THE KAYAN AND KENYAH

The **Kayan** and the **Kenyah** are the most numerous and powerful of the *orang ulu* groups who live in the upper Rajang, and along sungei Balui and its tributaries. The Kayan are the more numerous, numbering around 40,000 people, while the Kenyah population stands at around 10,000 (though there are substantially more over the mountains in Kalimantan). Both groups migrated from East Kalimantan into Sarawak around 600 years ago, although during the nineteenth century, when Iban migration led to clashes between the groups, they were pushed back to the lands they occupy today. The Kayan and the Kenyah have a lot in common: they are class-conscious, with a well-defined social hierarchy (unlike the Iban or Penan), and they have a completely different language from the other groups, with Malay-Polynesian roots. Traditionally, the **social order** was topped by the *penghulu* (chief) of the longhouse, followed by a group of lesser aristocrats (usually three or four in each community), lay families and slaves – although slavery no longer exists today. Both groups take great pride in the construction of their **longhouses** which are very impressive: Tom Harrisson, of the Sarawak Museum, learned of a longhouse on the upper Balui which was nearly one kilometre long, and in the Kenyah town of Long Nawang across the border in Kalimantan, a longhouse as high as a three-storey building and hundreds of metres long can be visited. Artistic expression plays an important role in longhouse culture, the Kayan especially maintaining a wide range of **musical traditions** including the lute-like *sape*, which is used to accompany long voice epics. **Textiles** are woven by traditional techniques in the upriver longhouses, and Kaytan and Kenyah **woodcarvings**, which are among the most spectacular in Southeast Asia, are produced both for sale and for ceremonial uses. Potent **rice wine** is still drunk by some Kayan, although many communities have now converted to Christianity, the missionaries successfully banning alcohol in many areas.

day all in. He will go as far as Long Busang, too (see "River Expeditions from Belaga", below), but this kind of trip requires lightweight camping gear, medicines, food and gifts for the locals. To get to Long Busang and back takes a week, and costs $3000–4,000 per group for longboat hire and Eddie's fee.

River expeditions from Belaga

Visiting longhouses and trekking into the forest are the only reasons why visitors come this far into the interior, but even if you're not up for a full expedition, you can see some nearby places without a guide. The *ekspres* to the north along sungei Balui leaves in the late morning, with the first main stop at **LONG MURUM**, a large Kayan longhouse where the chief is the *penghulu* for the region. There is a charge (around $10) for spending the night here, so you don't need to take gifts. The second stop is at the mouth of **sungei Linau**, at the small Kayan settlement of **LONG LINAU**, three hours from Belaga, though if you want to explore any further along the Linau, it's best to ask about longboats in Belaga as Long Linau hasn't got much traffic feeding through it.

If you're lucky, there may well be a longboat at Long Murum heading southeast along the winding Balui to the large, traditional Lahanan longhouse, **LONG LAHANAN**, beyond the mouth of the Linau, two hours from Long Murum. Another very rewarding place to try and reach is **LONG DARO**, a Kayan community a full day's outboard motoring from Lahanan. Dano's architecture is spectacular, the whole of the communal verandah one huge mural depicting Kayan designs. Four hours further east along the Balui lies **LONG AYA**, the only Ukit longhouse in Sarawak. There aren't many Ukits left now, and some of those left are still nomadic, living off hunting and the gathering of jungle plants.

The last but one settlement eastwards on the Balui, **LONG JAWAI**, lies in the foothills leading to the Kalimantan border. From here, British troops led operations against the Indonesians during the *Konfrontasi* in 1963, and most of the debris from the fighting is still around and used in ingenious ways: ammunition boxes for trunks and bridge strips as floorboards. Although most of the five-hundred-plus population are Kayan, other *orang ulu* people live here and there's occasional trade with the Penan, Ukit and the timber personnel: a new track has been hacked out of the jungle to facilitate logging in this previously pristine region of primary rainforest. The last village on the Balui, **LONG BUSANG**, takes a full two days to reach from Belaga.

Onwards to Kalimantan

It's possible to reach Indonesian Kalimantan from Belaga, although it's a predictably expensive trip due to the cost of chartering longboats. You'll also need to get your passport stamped at the Resident's office in Kapit (see p.363), as there's no immigration department in Belaga. The guide, Eddie John, will know if any boats are heading in the right direction, via Long Busang (see above), two days' southeast of Belaga, and then leaving the Balui at the junction with sungei Aput, which flows to the border. You'll need to a guide to show you where the trail leaves the river, leading over the unmarked border to **LONG NAWANG**, a large Kenyah settlement, where there's an Indonesian immigration post. It's a fascinating area in which to trek, but few organized tours are available from the Kalimantan side, so travellers have to rely on local guides, initiative and luck.

Onwards to Tubau and Bintulu

It's now much harder to reach the coastal port of Bintulu (see over page) from sungei Belaga, a route which entails taking logging vehicles northwest through a deforested area to **TUBAU** and then boats west down sungei Kemena to Bintulu. After five years of sustained timber harvesting in this area, demand has lessened and fewer four-wheel drives make the rough, overland trip. It's best to ask Eddie John Balarik in Belaga or Tan Teck Chuan in Kapit before setting out or else you might waste a day at a logging camp before having to retrace your steps to Belaga. **Coming from Bintulu** you could take the *ekspres* to Tubau (see p.374, "Listings" for details), which is a pleasant enough trip, and ask around there if trucks are going to Kastima camp and beyond to sungei Belaga. This route aside, the only other way out of Belaga is to get the 6am *ekspres* to Sibu which connects with the 2pm bus to Bintulu, another four hours ($18) away.

THE COAST FROM SIBU TO LAWAS

Most of the coast from the Santubong peninsula, north of Kuching, to Bintulu, 400km northeast, comprises impassable mangrove swamp; there are no roads and very few communities. Even the 150km of inland road from Sibu to Bintulu is only partly paved, and much of the four-hour bus journey is along a potholed track; but the route along the western flank of Sarawak towards Brunei is one of the most travelled in the state, and for visitors offers diversions into some of Sarawak's – indeed Malaysia's – best national parks. The state's newest, **Similajau National Park**, 20km northeast of the industrial town of **Bintulu**, is a long thin strip of beach and forest with, as yet, few visitor facilities; **Lambir Hills National Park**, further up the main highway, 30km south of Miri, is more established, and scientific reports have suggested that its vegetation types and tree species are more numerous than anywhere else so far studied. However, either of these are just preparation for Sarawak's most famous park, **Niah National Park**, halfway between Bintulu and Miri. Noted for its formidable limestone caves – the mouth of the main cave is the largest in the world – the park was put on the map in the mid 1950s when the curator of the Sarawak Museum, Tom Harrisson, discovered human remains and rock graffiti inside the caves; subsequent dating has suggested that Southeast Asia's earliest inhabitants were living in Sarawak as long as 40,000 years ago.

After Niah it's another two hours to **Miri**, which, like Sibu, is a predominantly Chinese town and an important administrative centre – though there the similarities end. The region developed commercially much later than southwestern Sarawak, with Miri's rapid expansion stimulated by the discovery of massive oil reserves. Since World War II, Bintulu has grown to rival Miri, specializing in the tapping of abundant pockets of natural gas on its doorstep. Both towns have a smaller percentage of indigenous inhabitants than Sarawak's other main settlements and although Iban and Melanau live in the area, there are very few longhouses to visit. However, you will need to pass through Miri en route to batang Baram for river trips to Marudi and Gunung Mulu park, or to catch a flight to the Kelabit Highlands (for all of which see "The Northern Interior", p.385). It's also the starting point for the onward trip to Brunei: from Miri the road runs along the coast to Kuala Baram (the mouth of the Baram river) and on to Kuala Belait and the **Brunei border**. East of here, tucked into the folds of Brunei are two peculiar "divisions" of Sarawak: finger-shaped **Limbang**, with **Lawas** beyond, the most northerly strip of Sarawak, stretching north to meet Sabah.

Bintulu and around

BINTULU is at the centre of Sarawak's fastest growing industrial area. Up until twenty years ago, the settlement was little more than a convenient resting point on the route from Sibu to Miri, but when large **natural gas** reserves were discovered off-shore in the 1960s, speedy expansion began. Since then Bintulu has followed in Miri's footsteps as a primary resources boomtown, with a population which has tripled in a decade to 60,000 and an industrial output that incorporates over six million tonnes of liquified natural gas a year, and around 1000 tonnes of ammonia and 1500 tonnes of urea for fertilizers per day. All this is a long way from the town's origins. Before Bintulu was bought by Charles Brooke from the Sultan of Brunei in 1853, Melanau pirates preyed on the local coast and would lay waste any ships which dared to pass by, decapitating the crew in the process. The name Bintulu is derived from the Malay *Menta Ulau* – "the place for gathering heads".

Modern Bintulu is very ordinary, a flat, compact rectangle of streets bordered by the airfield to the east and sungei Kemena to the west, with nothing much of interest in between. But inexpensive accommodation is easy to find, the restaurants are excellent and the markets sell local delicacies like fresh fish grilled with *blanchan* (shrimp paste). Although most people just stay overnight to await a bus connection to Niah National Park, longer stays can take in **Bintulu Wildlife Park** (see p.373), just north of the centre, and nearby **Simulajau National Park** (covered on p.374).

Arriving, information and accommodation

The **airport**, incredibly, is right in the town centre, within 100m of most of the hotels and restaurants. The long-distance **bus station** is over the road on jalan Somerville, with the local bus station ten minutes' walk northwest along the parallel jalan Keppel. Boats for trips up sungei Kemena to Tubau dock at the **jetty**, four blocks across town from the long-distance bus station. The town's main **taxi rank** is directly in front of the Chinese temple, 100m or so northwest of the jetty. There is no tourist office, although some leaflets, including an accommodation list, can be picked up from the foyer of the *Plaza Hotel,* on jalan Abang Galau, close to the esplanade. You can get also a map of the Bintulu Wildlife Park (see below) and other leaflets on the town from the **Bintulu Development Authority**, on jalan Somerville (☎086/331552).

Accommodation

There's quite a wide range of **accommodation** in Bintulu, though the only real budget choices are the *rumah tumpangano* down by the river, basic lodging houses with dormitory-style rooms catering for timber camp workers and oil company employees. They're often full and in any case, there have been complaints from solo women travellers about conditions and behaviour in several of them; the places listed below are all a grade up and much nicer.

Capital Hotel, jalan Keppel (☎086/31167). This is a popular travellers' hotel: cheap, basic and noisy. The shared bathrooms have bucket-over-the-head showers. ②

City Inn, 149 jalan Masjid (☎086/337711). The rooms here are small but do come with air-con, TV and shower. ③

Hoover Hotel, jalan Abang Galau (☎086/337166). Smart but overpriced rooms equipped with air-con and shower. ④

Kemena Lodging House, 78 jalan Keppel (☎086/331533). This is a popular place, with decent rooms, run by a friendly family. A good first choice. ③

King's Hotel, jalan Masjid (☎086/337337). Modern, clean and cool rooms with all the usual facilities. ③

National Inn, jalan Abang Galau (☎086/337222). Small rooms with ferociously cold air-con. ③

Plaza Hotel, jalan Abag Galau (☎086/35111). The top end of the hotel spectrum, with a swimming pool, and large modern rooms with full facilities. ⑤

Royal Hotel, 10 Jalan Padada (☎086/332166). Popular with well-heeled locals. ④

Hotel Salehah, New Commercial Centre, jalan Abang Galau (☎086/332122). This mid-range hotel has large rooms with the usual facilities, but it's not as clean as the inns. ③

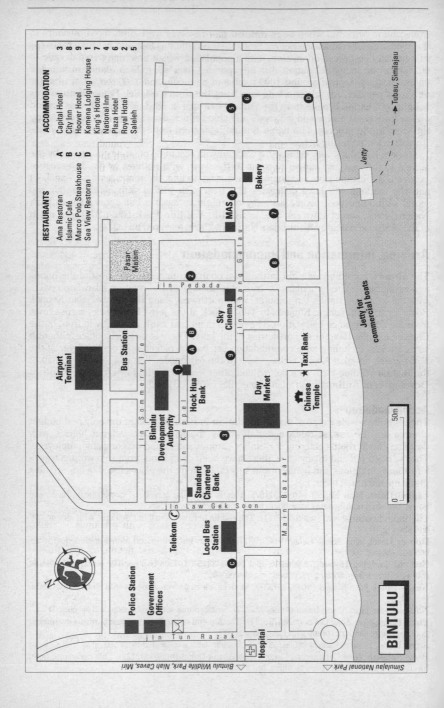

RESTAURANTS

A Ama Restoran
B Islamic Café
C Marco Polo Steakhouse
D Sea View Restoran

ACCOMMODATION

Capital Hotel   3
City Inn   8
Hoover Hotel   9
Kemena Lodging House   1
King's Hotel   7
National Inn   4
Plaza Hotel   6
Royal Hotel   2
Saleleh   5

Airport Terminal

Bus Station

Bintulu Development Authority

Standard Chartered Bank

Hock Hua Bank

Pasar Malam

Jln Pedada

Sky Cinema

Jln Sommerville

Jln Keppel

Jln Law Gek Soon

Telekom

Local Bus Station

Police Station

Government Offices

Jln Tun Razak

Hospital

Day Market

Taxi Rank

Chinese Temple

Main Bazaar

MAS

Bakery

Jln Abang Galau

Jetty

Jetty for commercial boats

→ Tubau, Similajau

0   50m

BINTULU

Bintulu Wildlife Park, Niah Caves, Miri

Similajau National Park

The town

Bintulu's main commercial street, **jalan Keppel**, named after an early British official who did a long stint here, is lined with cafés spilling over with a boisterous beer-drinking clietele, while the stores are overflowing with shoes, clothes and electrical equipment. A couple of blocks to the west, Main Bazaar passes the **Chinese temple**, less impressive than those in Kuching or Sibu, but a rallying point for the town's Hokkien-descended population in the evening. Fifty metres north of here on Main Bazaar is the **day-market** – two large, open-sided circular buildings with blue roofs overlooking the river; seafood and vegetables are sold on the ground floor, while a variety of Malay and Chinese cafés can be found upstairs. Although the market stalls stay open until 5pm, the cafés close at 2pm. Adjacent is the site of the old market, where locals still bring in small quantities of goods and lay them on rough tables to sell. Across town, the **pasar malam** starts up at around 6pm in the car park on jalan Somerville and gets very crowded by 9pm. It's a great place to browse, eating grilled fish, meat pastries and sweets, and almost impossible to avoid talking to locals wanting to practise their English.

Within view of the boat jetty, across the wide sungei Kemena, lies **KAMPUNG JEPAK**, the traditional home of the local Malay and Melanau-descended population. It's well worth the hour's trip, if only to escape the hustle and bustle of the town centre for a short while, since the *kampung* has a completely different atmosphere to Bintulu itself, with few cars, lots of children and old people, and a much slower pace of life. Small diesel-powered *sampans* (every 20min; $1) make the crossing from the jetty. Jepak is famous for its pungent shrimp paste, *blanchan*, which you will find on sale all over Sarawak and Peninsular Malaysia; and although most blanchan is produced in factories, cottage industries still proliferate here – the production season is December to January. Another major *kampung* activity used to be sago-processing, stemming from the days when sago, together with fish, was the staple food, though most of the production these days takes place in factories at Kidurong Industrial Estate, 20km north of town.

Bintulu Wildlife Park

Two kilometres north of town is **BINTULU WILDLIFE PARK**, a 250-acre tropical recreation area, with a sizeable collection of animals and birds. Get any bus from the local bus station, heading along jalan Tanjung Batu, and ask for the stop closest to the park – it's a pleasant five-minute walk north from the main road.

Extending across a hill with lovely views over the sea, the park is criss-crossed with walkways and wooden steps and is home to a small wood, bougainvillea plants, fruit trees and a fernery, all accessed from paths which dip under small avenues of creepers and run alongside streams. Mynah birds tackle passers-by with greetings – "hello, goodbye and how-are-you" – while other diversions include an orang-utan on a little island, two tigers, and a variety of Southeast Asian birds, flamingos and ducks. Unfortunately the **beach** opposite the entrance to the park is dirty and no effort is made to maintain it.

Eating

Although no culinary capital, Bintulu has a number of fine Chinese and north Indian **restaurants**. There are **hawker stalls** at both the day-market and the pasar malam, the latter in particular serving great steamed seafood and stir-fried noodles, though as in Sibu, there aren't any tables – the locals take theirs home to eat.

Ama Restoran, jalan Keppel. Excellent curries, and particularly busy at lunchtime.

Islamic Café, jalan Keppel. Tuck in to superb *roti canai*, delicious curries and pineapple and cucumber salad at this very friendly spot and expect to pay $12 for a full meal for two, including *teh tarek*.

Marco Polo Steakhouse, jalan Abang Galau. This upmarket steakhouse (100m north of the day-market) has an in-house band which makes talking impossible, though at least it's better than the karaoke which picks up later in the evening.

Sea View Restoran, 254 Esplanade. An atmospheric Chinese café, pleasantly positioned overlooking sungei Kemena and away from the traffic. The food is of a high standard and meals go for around $15 a head, including beer.

Listings

Airport Flights to Kuching (10 daily; $120), Sibu (7 daily; $70) and Miri (4 daily; $70). Also, two planes fly daily to Sabah's capital, Kota Kinabalu. Call ☎086/331073 for flight information. *MAS* is on jalan Abang Galau (☎086/31554).

Banks *Standard Chartered*, 89 jalan Keppel; *Hock Hua Bank*, jalan Keppel.

Boats *Ekspres* boats to Tubau, 60km east, leave dialy at 7am, 9am, 10.30am, noon and 1.30pm (2hr 30min; around $16). From here it's possible to cut through the forest to Belaga; see p.369 for more details. Boats return from Tubau at 6am, 7.30am, 9am, 10.30am and noon.

Buses *Suria Bas Company* (☎086/34914) and *Syarikat Bas Express* (☎086/31522) are both at the long-distance bus station, running daily air-con services north to Miri via Batu Niah (for Niah National Park, see below) daily at 7.20am, 10.30am, noon and 1.30pm (5hr; $20) and south to Sarikei and Sibu at 6am and noon respectively (both 5hr 30min; $24). There's an extra Batu Niah bus at 3pm ($9) and one to Miri at 6pm which will drop you at the Batu Niah junction but charge you the full fare to Miri.

Government offices on jalan Tun Razak: Parks and Wildlife Department (☎086/36101); Immigration Department (☎086/31441); Resident's Office (Mon–Fri 8.30am–noon & 2–4.15am; ☎086/335575).

Hospital On jalan Abang Galau (☎086/331455).

Laundry *Teo Soon*, 48 Main Bazaar; same-day service costs around $5.

Police Main HQ on jalan Tun Razak (☎086/332044).

Post office Main office on jalan Tun Razak (☎086/332375).

Telephone *Telekom* office, jalan Keppel (Mon–Sat 8.30am–4.30pm).

Similajau National Park

The recent opening of **SIMILAJAU NATIONAL PARK**, 20km north along the coast from Bintulu, might well persuade you to stop in the region a bit longer. The park has a lot in common with Bako, near Kuching, with its long, unspoiled sandy beaches broken only by rocky headlands and freshwater streams. Beach walks and short hikes are possible, either along the 30km of coastline or following the trails which run alongside small rivers winding into the forest, their source in the undulating hills which rise only a few hundred metres from the beach. Shrubs grow on the cliff faces, pitcher plants can be found in the ridges and orchids hang from the trees and rocks. Twenty-four species of mammal have been recorded in the park, including gibbons and long-tailed macaques, mouse deer, wild boar, porcupines, civets and squirrels. The monkeys are quite friendly but sightings of anything else are quite rare unless you're very patient. Salt-water crocodiles are found occasionally wallowing in some of the rivers, especially after rain – one good reason for not swimming in the river close to the park centre – and there have even been sightings of dolphins and porpoises out in the waves.

    Speedboats rented from Bintulu jetty cost $300 per day, an almost prohibitive sum unless there are at least six people sharing the cost. Boats arrive at the jetty at the headquarters, from where starts the short trail heading north to the beach. You can also get to Simulujau by **road** by leaving the trunk road to Batu Niah (see over page) after 15km and bearing left along a newly paved road to a small *kampung*, Kuala Likau, at the entrance to the park. Buses don't yet come out this way, though the Parks and Wildlife Department in Bintulu (see "Listings" above) will have the latest transport details; a taxi from town shouldn't cost more than $40.

Accommodation at the park ranges from chalets with rooms (②) to the hostel (beds ①, rooms ②) and the **campsite**, where rented tents cost only a few dollars. As well as the chalets, the park HQ comprises a canteen and an **information centre** (daily 8am–5pm), with a small display on the local flora and fauna. You can book accommodation in Bintulu at the Bintulu Development Authority (see above for details).

The trails

At just 30km by 1.5km, the park hasn't any particulary arduous trails but it's as well to wear light boots, long-sleeved shirts and long trousers on the trails, as well as headgear as the sun is very fierce in this part of Sarawak. A water bottle is useful although the river water is quite drinkable.

By far the greatest attractions are the beaches, on which turtles occasionally nest in April and May. The two-hour walk north to **Turtle Beach** starts from the park headquarters, the first stage involving crossing sungei Likau in a motorized longboat. The trail ascends into the forest and soon reaches a viewpoint which looks out over the South China Sea. The path then follows the coastline to Turtle Beach, an hour beyond which is **Golden Beach**, noted for its fine sand. Ten minutes' walk north along Golden Beach and you reach the trail which runs inland along the side of sungei Sebubong. Although the park offers a boat trip from the headquarters to this point, it's much more enjoyable to walk – the route into the forest is especially gratifying after the lack of shade and heat of the open beach. After fifteen minutes the trail reaches **Kolam Sebubong**, a freshwater pool, whose waters are stained with harmless tannin acid from the nearby peat swamp, which turns it a remarkable ruby red.

The other worthwhile trail leads to the **Selansur Rapids**. Follow the Turtle Beach trail for one hour and look for a marked trail which heads into the forest parallel to a small river, sungei Kabalak. It passes through sparse *keranga* forest before climbing the sides of hills where you'll hear monkeys high up in the trees and the omnipresent chainsaw-like call of the cicadas. After around ninety minutes you reach the rapids, a pleasant place to rest and take a dip.

Niah National Park

Visiting **NIAH NATIONAL PARK**, 130km north of Bintulu, is a highly rewarding experience – in less than a day you can see one of the largest caves in the world, as well as prehistoric rock graffiti in the remarkable Painted Cave, and hike along primary forest trails. The park consists of 31 square kilometres of lowland forest and limestone massifs, the highest of these **Gunung Subis**, rising to nearly 400m and riddled with caves. Although the region wasn't designated a National Park until 1975, it has been a National Historic Monument since 1958, when Tom Harrisson discovered evidence that early man had been using Niah as a cemetery. In the outer area of the present park, deep excavations revealed **human remains**, including skulls which dated back 40,000 years and artefacts like flake stone tools, sandstone pounders, mortars, bone points and shell ornaments – the first evidence that people had lived in Southeast Asia that long ago.

> Some of the caves at Niah are frequented year-round by bird's nest harvesters (after swiflet nests for soup), a state of affairs that has worried the park authorities who are concerned about the effect on the bird population. Officially, the nests should only be collected during two specific seasons, before the swifts lay their eggs and after the departure of the young, when the nests are no longer needed. Consequently, Niah National Park has been **closed** for several months at a time on recent occasions in an attempt to stop the collectors' activities – check to see if Niah is still open for visitors before going.

Getting there: Batu Niah

The park is roughly halfway between Bintulu and Miri, 10km off the main road close to the small town of **BATU NIAH**, which you can reach by regular local bus from either Bintulu or Miri. There are a few average Chinese cafés here, and the *Niah Cave Aircon Hotel* (②) is the best **accommodation** option, with rooms overlooking the river. The caves are 2km south of Batu Niah, which you reach either by a pleasant walk along the forest path – which takes thirty minutes – or by **longboat** (daily 8am–4pm; $10) or taxi ($10).

Staying at the park

The path from Batu Niah leads straight to the **park headquarters**, located in a beautiful position on the southern banks of sungei Niah, and well shaded by coconut trees, with the forest deep and thick on the other side of the river. The **hostel** here is excellent, providing bunk beds in one of three twelve-bed dorms (①); you get a sheet, blanket and cooking utensils as well. From the hostel verandah, there's a fine view of the river. Across the river from park HQ, reached by *sampan* (on request during the hours of daylight; $1), there's a more expensive hostel which has cosier rooms (③) with four beds, and four two-bed **chalets** (①). You'll only need to book accommodation in advance (at the Parks and Wildlife Department offices in Bintulu or Miri) if you intend to visit at weekends, when the park is at its busiest. The hostels have cooking facilities and there's a **shop** (daily 7am–10pm) where you can buy basic foodstuffs. The **canteen** (daily 7.30am–10pm) has a limited range of dishes, including stir-fries, noodles and omelettes, at very reasonable prices.

The caves

From the park headquarters it's a thirty-minute walk to the **caves**, heading north on the only trail into the park. After crossing the narrow sungei Niah by *sampan*, the trail follows a wooden walkway through dense rainforest where monkeys, hornbills, birdwing butterflies, tree squirrels and flying lizards compete to be heard. A clearly marked path leaves the walkway on the left after forty minutes, running to an Iban longhouse, **RUMAH CHANG**, where you can buy soft drinks and snacks.

Further along the main walkway a rock-and-creeper-encrusted jungle wall looms up ahead and the path takes you up through the **Trader's Cave** to the west mouth of the Great Cave. Crude steps have been dug out of the rock for the final ascent. From within the immense, draughty darkness disembodied voices can be heard above the squeal of a million bats. The voices come from the **bird's nest collectors** who, despite official scrutiny, are close to exhausting the fragile stocks of swiftlet nests, used to make the famous bird's-nest soup (see feature above); three species of swiftlet breed here, co-existing in the cave's voluminous rafters with the bats. Thin beanstalk poles snake up from the cave floor and the collectors can just be made out on top of them.

Once inside, the walkway continues on to the Painted Cave, via Burnt Cave and Moon Cave, and the smell of guano intensifies as the path leads around extraordinary rock formations, where the sound of everything – your voice, dripping water, bat-chatter and the nest collectors' scrapes – is magnified considerably. As the walkway veers to the right, the light through the cave mouth ebbs and artificial lighting takes over. As the planks are often slippery with guano, it's best to wear shoes with a grip and take a flashlight.

After thirty minutes' careful walking you reach the **Painted Cave** itself, in which early Sarawak communitites buried their dead in **boat-shaped coffins**, arranged around the cave walls. When Harrisson first entered, the cave had partially collapsed, and the contents were spilled all around, although subsequent dating pinpointed the finds at around 1000AD, as bartered Chinese stoneware was discovered in the remains. These finds were much more recent than Harrisson's other discoveries in the region, but proved that the caves had been used as a cemetery for many thousands of years.

One of these wooden coffins is still perched on an incline, as though beached after a monumental journey, its contents long since removed to the Sarawak Museum for safe-keeping. Despite the light streaming from an opening at the far end of the cave, it's hard to distinguish the **wall paintings** that give the cave its name, but they stretch from the dark right-hand corner behind the coffin – a thirty-metre long picture depicting boats on a journey, the figures apparently either jumping on and off, or dancing. This image fits various Borneo mythologies where the dead undergo water-bound challenges on their way to the afterlife. The markings, although crude, can be made out, but the brown paint strokes are now extremely faded.

The only way back to the entrance is by the same route – try to be there at dusk when the swiftlets return and the bats swarm out for a night's worth of fruit-seed disposal, an airborne change of shift worth catching. Even if you miss this, there's plenty to keep you occupied on the march back, including fireflies and luminous funghi visible from the walkway – switch off your flashlight and let your eyes accustom themselves to the dark.

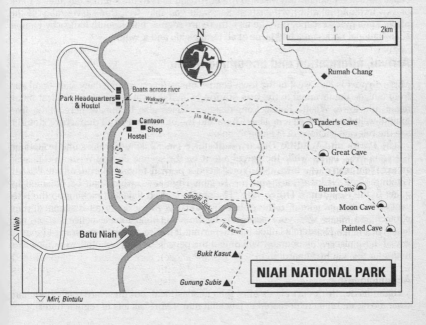

The trails

There are two **trails** in the park which, after the claustrophobic darkness of the caves, offer a much-needed breath of fresh air. The first, **jalan Madu**, splits off to the right from the plank walkway around 800m from the park headquarters and cuts first east, then south, across a peat swamp forest, where you see wild orchids, mushrooms and pandanus. The trail runs west along the banks of sungei Subis and it takes about an hour in all to reach sungei Niah, from where a river path leads you back towards the headquarters, another thirty-minute walk. The other, and more spectacular trail, is that to **Bukit Kasut**, its starting point a small wharf at the confluence of sungei Niah and sungei Subis. After crossing the river, the clearly marked trail winds through *keranga* forest, round the foothills of Bukit Kasut and up to the summit – a hard one-hour slog, at the end of which there's a view both of the impenetrable forest canopy and Batu Niah.

Miri and around

These days **MIRI**, rather than Kuching, is the largest town in Sarawak (with a population of around 400,000) and, despite historic links with Western businesses – specifically the oil producer *Shell* – and a significant expatriate community, it retains a strong Chinese character. Some of the town's earliest inhabitants were pioneering Chinese merchants who set up shops to trade with the Kayan who lived in longhouses to the northeast along batang Baram. But Miri remained a tiny, unimportant settlement up until the time oil was discovered in 1882, though it wasn't until 1910 that the black gold was drilled in any quantity. Since then, over six hundred wells have been drilled in the Miri area, on and off shore, and the main refineries are just 5km up the coast at Lutong. On first appearances Miri appears to be a traffic-congested place, bursting out of the constraints of its topography – sea to the north and hills to the south – but after a week or two trekking in wild northeastern Sarawak, you may well think favourably of the place. For a quick escape from the city, there are regular buses south to nearby Lambir Hills National Park, not a bad place at all for a picnic and a swim.

Arrival, information and accommodation

Miri's **airport** is 8km west of the town centre: buses (every 40min, daily 7am–6pm) run from outside the terminal to the **bus station**, which is located next to the tallest building in the town, Wisma Pelita. Long-distance buses also terminate here. It's a five-minute walk from here east to jalan China and the old town. For all **departure details**, see the relevant sections of "Listings", below.

The **Parks and Wildlife Department** office (see "Listings") has some leaflets on Niah and Mulu parks, while the **travel agent** on the second floor of Wisma Pelita sells an excellent map of the town ($2). You'll need a **permit** to visit Marudi on the Baram, Gunung Mulu National Park and the Kelabit Highlands, which can be obtained by going to the **Resident's Office** (see "Listings") on jalan Raja and picking up the relevant form: fill it in, take it to the **police** headquarters next door, get it stamped, then photocopied (along with your passport) in the shop opposite the police station, and head back to the Resident's Office for the permit. If you're going on an arranged tour to any of these places, the operator will obtain the permit for you, but otherwise allow two hours for the whole rigmarole.

Accommodation

Lodging houses with dorm beds offer the cheapest deal, but these are really basic and none too clean. If you're prepared to pay a bit more, Miri has lots of regular hotels.

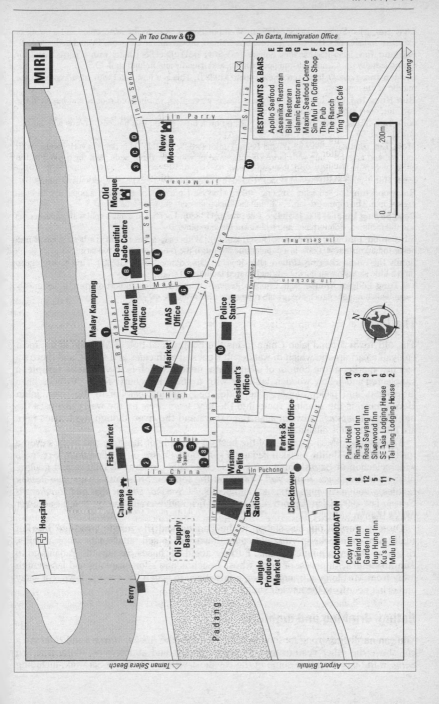

MIRI

△ jln Teo Chew & 12   △ jln Garta, Immigration Office

▷ Lutong

jln Yu Seng

jln Parry

jln Sylvia

RESTAURANTS & BARS

Apollo Seafood	E
Aseanika Restoran	H
Bilal Restoran	B
Islamic Restoran	G
Maxim Seafood Centre	I
Sin Mui Pin Coffee Shop	F
The Pub	C
The Ranch	D
Ying Yuan Café	A

New Mosque

jln Merbau

Old Mosque

Beautiful Jade Centre

jln Yu Seng

jln Madu

Tropical Adventure Office

MAS Office

jln Bendahara

Malay Kampung

jln Brooks

Police Station

jln Setia Raja

jln Kwangtung

jln Hockein

N

Market

jln High

jln Raja

Resident's Office

Fish Market

jln Raja Square

jln China

Wisma Pelita

Parks & Wildlife Office

jln Pujut

Chinese Temple

ACCOMMODATION

Cosy Inn	4	Park Hotel	10
Fairland Inn	8	Ringwood Inn	3
Garden Inn	12	Rosa Sayang Inn	9
Hup Hung Inn	5	Silverwood Inn	1
Ku's Inn	11	SE Asia Lodging House	6
Mulu Inn	7	Tai Tung Lodging House	2

jln Puchong

Bus Station

Clocktower

Hospital

Oil Supply Base

jln Malay

jln Padang

Ferry

Jungle Produce Market

Padang

0   200m

△ Airport, Bintulu   △ Taman Selera Beach

Cosy Inn, jalan Yu Seng (☎085/415522). Well positioned close to the *MAS* office and a string of excellent Indian cafés. However, the rooms are small, though all have air-con, TV and bathroom. ③

Fairland Inn, jalan Raja, at Raja Square (☎085/413981). Excellent hotel with a perfect roof for drying laundry on. Clean, well-equipped rooms, and friendly and helpful staff. ②

Garden Inn, Lot 290, jalan Teo Chew (☎085/419822). This is a new hotel with small rooms in the middle of the new town. ③

Hup Hung Inn, jalan Raja, at Raja Square. Inexpensive place with shared rooms, and bunks in the corridor; don't stay if you want any privacy. ①

Ku's Inn, 3 jalan Sylvia (☎085/37333). Located on a busy street, this has cosy rooms with air-con and shower. ③

Mulu Inn, jalan Raja, opposite Wisma Pelita Tunku (☎085/410611). This place is very popular with tourists and is good value with large rooms, some of which fit three beds. Ask for a room at the back, away from the busy road. Recommended. ②

Park Hotel, jalan Raja (☎085/414555). Top-of-the-range hotel with expensive, extensive rooms. ⑤

Ringwood Inn, Lot 826, jalan Yu Seng (☎085/415888). Upmarket place which is popular with businesspeople. The rooms are large with full facilities – air-con, showers and TV. ④

Rosa Sayang Inn, Lot 566, Jalan Lee Tak (☎085/413880). Located in a quiet spot with small rooms and full facilities. Comfortable, and a pleasant place to stay. ③

Silverwood Inn, jalan Bendahara (☎085/420577). With easy access to Miri's best seafood and north Indian restaurants, this is a popular one although the rooms are none too large. ②

South East Asia Lodging House, jalan Raja, at Raja Square (☎085/416921). This is very cheap (and a little sleazy), with dorm beds and shared facilities. ①

Tai Tung Lodging House, jalan China (jetty end). Situated in the old part of town, it has mostly dorm beds but more expensive private rooms are also available. ①–②

The town

The **old town** around jalan China forms the commercial hub of Miri and is the most enjoyable part around which to wander. It's packed with cafés and shops, and there's a wet fish market at the bottom of jalan China, next to which is the **Chinese temple**, a simple red-and-yellow wooden building with a small forecourt where devotees burn joss sticks and paper money. The wide road running parallel to the river, **jalan Bendahara**, is the simplest route into the new town area; on the way you'll pass the old Malay *kampung,* between jalan Bendahara and the river, though the houses here are now extremely dilapidated.

The **shops** in Miri are some of the best on this side of the state and there's even a mall, at **Wisma Pelita**, on jalan Padang. *Pelita Book Centre*, on the first floor here has a wide selection of English-language books, especially on Sarawak culture and geography; while *Longhouse Handicraft Centre*, on the top floor, has rattan bags, *pua kumbu* textiles, wooden carvings, jars, hats and beads. At *Syarikat Unique Arts and Handicrafts Centre*, Lot 2994, jalan Airport, 4km out of Miri, native crafts can be bought at lower prices than in town.

Directly west of the bus station is the Padang and the **jungle produce market** (daily 6am–2pm) where *orang ulu* come downriver to sell rattan mats, tropical fruits, rice wine and even jungle animals. Further afield, all buses passing the Padang go to **Taman Selera**, 4km west of town, whose beach is one kilometre long and far enough away from Miri to be a tranquil spot, a fine place to watch the sun go down, eat satay and drink beer from the hawker stalls.

Eating, drinking and nightlife

You can hardly go wrong for food in Miri, although the *Apollo, Maxim's* and *Bilal* are a cut above the other **restaurants** for value, quality and atmosphere. Along jalan Yu Seng in the new town are some of the rowdiest watering holes in Sarawak, including

The Ranch and *The Pub* – rock-music-playing, hard-drinking **bars** where expat oil personnel and other Europeans meet. The best time to go is when a Filipino band is playing live.

Apollo Seafood Centre, 4 jalan Yu Seng. Very popular with expats and visitors alike. The grilled stingray and pineapple rice is exquisite, although eating here is not cheap at around $40 for two including beer.

Aseanika Restoran, jalan China. Malay café serving excellent *rotis* and curries. Closed during Ramadan.

Bilal Restoran, Lot 250, Beautiful Jade Centre. Superb North Indian food: *rotis*, naan, *murtabak*, and outstanding tandoori chicken at around $6 for each giant-sized portion.

China Street Food Stalls, near the temple. Known for their delicious *laksa* noodles and *congee* (Chinese rice porridge).

Islamic Restoran, 233 jalan Maju. Around the corner from the *Bilal*, this is another excellent place whose speciality is spiced Malay dishes.

Maxim Seafood Centre, Lot 342, jalan Miri-Pujut. Although a bit of a trek (take a taxi), *Maxim's* is still Miri's most popular restaurant. Serves a superb array of grilled fish with *blanchan;* and delicious vegetable dishes with chilli, herbs and garlic. Around $40 for two including beer.

Sin Mui Pin Coffee Shop, 5 jalan Yu Seng. A third high-quality fish restaurant, with an even more vibrant atmosphere than the others. Again, the stingray is excellent – order your rice and vegetables from the people at the rear. Unless you want a long wait, get here before 8pm.

Tanjong Seaview, Taman Selera beach. This food centre is very popular with young Miri couples and families, and offers superb satay at low prices.

Ying Yuan Café, Lot 55, jalan Bendahar. Busy Chinese café noted for its mixed rice which includes prawns, chicken, baby sweetcorn and okra: cheap, filling and delicious.

Listings

Airport Daily flights to Kota Kinabalu (7 daily; $95), Kuala Lumpur (3 daily; $425), Kuching (13 daily; $325), Sibu (5 daily; $115), Marudi (2 daily; $40), Gunung Mulu (3 daily; $70), Bario (1 daily; $80), Bintulu (4 daily; $70), Limbang (4 daily; $50), Lawas (2 daily; $60), Long Lelland (2 weekly; $80) and Pontianak (2 weekly; $300). For flight enquiries call ☎085/414242. *MAS* is on jalan Yu Seng (☎085/414144).

Banks and exchange *Standard Chartered,* jalan Raja *Bank Bumiputra*, jalan Bendahara (11am–3pm only). There are moneychangers off jalan China.

Buses All buses leave from the bus station. *Bus Suria* (☎085/412173), for Bintulu and other locations south; *Miri Transport* (☎085/418655) for Lambir Hills; *Miri Belait Transport* (☎085/31046) for Kuala Belait and Brunei (5 daily; $15; note last departure from Belait to BSB in Brunei is around 3.30pm, so set off early).

Car rental *A&Z Motor,* Lot 108, jalan Bendahara (☎085/412692); *Mewah Bunga*, 81 jalan Permaisuri (☎085/655639).

Hospital *General Hospital,* jalan Peninsula, north side of sungei Miri (☎085/32222). The ferry runs across every 15min (6.30am–8pm).

Immigration office At jalan Garta (Room 3; Mon–Fri 8am–noon & 2–4.15pm). You can extend your Sarawak visa here, but only by a few days. The officials insist that you have to leave the state and then return if you want to spend more time in Sarawak.

Laundry *Miri Laundry and Cleaning Service*, jalan Krokop.

Parks and Wildlife Department The office is on jalan Pujut (Mon–Fri 8.15am–noon & 2–4.15pm; ☎085/36637).

Police Headquarters on jalan King (☎085/33777).

Resident's office On jalan Raja (Mon–Fri 8.15am–noon & 2–4.15pm; ☎085/33203).

Telephones *Telekom* office on jalan Garta (daily 7.30am–10pm).

Tour operators *Tropical Adventure,* Lot 228, 1st floor, jalan Maju (☎085/419337), is Miri's oldest and most reliable tour operator specializing in treks to the Baram, Gunung Mulu Park and the Kelabit Highlands. Expect to pay $750 for two for a five- or six- day trek. *Borneo Overland,* Raghavan Building, 37 jalan Brooke (☎085/30255), has similar tours, at roughly the same prices.

Lambir Hills National Park

Situated 30km south of Miri, **LAMBIR HILLS NATIONAL PARK** is perfect for a day
trip and is particularly popular with Miri locals at the weekends. Its history goes back
sixty million years, when a vast area of sedimentary rock was laid down, stretching from
present-day western Sarawak to Sabah, bequeathing the region quite a geological cocktail: limestone and clay at lower levels, and sandstone and shale closer to the surface.
Subsequent upheavals created the hills and the rich soil substrata, and gave rise to the
local rainforest, where various distinctive vegetation types predominate. Mixed *dipterocarp* forest makes up over half the area with the vast hardwood trees – *meranti, kapur*
and *keruing* – creating deep shadows on the forest floor; the *keranga* forest, with its
peaty soils, low-lying vegetation and smaller trees, is lighter and drier.

Arrival and accommodation

Buses leave Miri's bus station every thirty minutes (daily 6.30am–4.30pm) for the
forty-minute trip. Approaching from Niah National Park, you can take the Batu Niah–
Miri bus which takes ninety minutes; ask for the Lambir Hills stop.

Accommodation at the park is limited, so it's best to book in advance at Miri's
Parks and Wildlife Department office (see "Listings" above). The two options are the
hostel which has very cheap dorm beds (①), and the rest house, whose rooms have
two beds (②). Both places are close to the road, next to the **park headquarters** (daily
9am–5pm), which issues permits and park maps, and the **canteen** (daily 8am–7pm). If
you intend to go on the longer trails, bring hiking boots, water bottle, torch, sun hat
and insect repellent.

The trails

Twelve well-marked **trails** criss-cross the south part of the park; most can be walked in
a day, but as there are also seven **waterfalls** of varying sizes, you will only be able to
get to one or two if you're just here on a day trip.

The longest trail – the four-hour trek to the summit of **Bukit Lambir** – is tough but
rewarding, the view from the top, looking across the park, a lovely sight. An unbroken
deep green canopy of tree tops obscures the many hills and waterfalls, with the sounds
of insects and birds echoing below. The trail cuts across deceptively steep hills, where
gnarled roots are often the only helping hand up an almost vertical incline – you may
well catch sight of monkeys, lizards, or snakes on the trail.

To reach the three **Latak waterfalls**, 1km from park HQ, follow the trail marked
"Latak" which branches off east from the Bukit Lambir trail. The falls aren't particularly
impressive, but they're easily accessible and good for swimming. There are more spectacular falls further afield; it takes two and a half hours to reach the **Pantu** and **Pancur**
waterfalls – watch for the narrow paths which lead down to the rivers from the main
Bukit Lambir trail. These are fine places to stop and eat, and take in a deliciously cool
swim. The most remote waterfall, **Tengkorong**, is a further thirty minutes' walk from
Pancur.

North of Miri: the border region

The trip by road and water from Sarawak **to Brunei** is fiddly and, if you head on to
Sabah, can take up to two days – many people prefer to fly straight from Miri to Kota
Kinabalu. The advantage of the land and sea route is that you can visit the territorial
divisions of **Limbang** and **Lawas,** which contrast greatly with the land around Miri as
they are sparsely populated by an ethnic mix of Iban, Murut, Berawan and Kelabits.
This is a hard area to get around, though, as there are few boats and no roads.

Travelling to Brunei

Heading straight for Brunei from Miri, the trunk road north runs a few kilometres in from the coast alongside rubber plantations to **KUALA BARAM**, 30km away, a small town situated at the mouth of batang Baram. Here, all vehicles and pedestrians have to cross the river by ferry (every 20min, daily 6am–8pm) and then make their way on towards the **border** at the Bruneian town of Kuala Belait (see p.469), another 6km further.

At Kuala Belait, you hop on board a Bruneian bus which runs to Seria, for connections to the capital, Bandar Seri Begawan. The last bus from Kuala Belait to get you to the Bruneian capital the same day leaves at around 3.30pm; from Seria, the first bus to the capital leaves at 7am, after which the service is very regular.

Limbang and around

Just to the south of Bandar is **Limbang**, a strip of Sarawak roughly 30km wide and 50km deep, sandwiched between the two parts of Brunei. It's a seldom visited, inaccessible district, yet travel is possible along sungei Limbang, which snakes into the interior from the mangrove-cloaked coast, and provides access to Gunung Mulu National Park by an adventurous three-day river trip along sungei Medalam (see "Limbang Town" below and p.391). For centuries, Limbang was a trading centre run by Malays, who bartered the jungle produce collected by the Berawan, Kelabit and Murut peoples, with fellow Chinese and Malay merchants. Although the White Rajahs never actually bought Limbang from the Sultan of Brunei, as they did the areas to the south, Charles Brooke occupied the region in 1890, following demonstrations by the ethnic groups against the increasingly decadent rule of the Sultan. Brooke's main reason, however, for interceding was to acquire as large a slice of what was left of Brunei as possible, before his Sabah-based rivals in the *British North Borneo Chartered Company* overran it.

Limbang town

The only building of note in the only settlement, **LIMBANG TOWN**, is the **fort**, the most northerly of Charles Brooke's defensive structures, sited on the river bank 50m west of the jetty. Constructed in 1897, it was renovated in 1966 when much of the woodwork was replaced by more durable materials like concrete and belian. It was originally designed to serve as an administrative centre, but was instead used to monitor native insurgency in the early years of this century; now it's a centre for Islamic instruction and education. The rest of the small town is composed of a few streets set back from the river; the main street, jalan Bunagsiol, leads to the **market**, which is at its busiest on Friday when fruit, animals and vegetables are brought in from the forest to be sold.

The **airport** is 2km south of the town and you'll need to get a **taxi** (around $6) into the centre; there are daily flights to and from Miri and Lawas, which cost around $25. The **jetty** is just east of the fort: two boats leave each morning for Brunei, a thirty-minute ride away ($10), and one daily ($20) on the longer journey across to the other Sarawak division of Lawas (see below). Several daily boats also travel the 50km upstream on sungei Limbang to Naga Medamit – the junction with sungei Medalam, a couple of hours away – from where an irregular longboat heads along the Medalam. Thirty minutes along this river is an Iban longhouse – the most northerly Iban community in Sarawak – where you can stay, after which it's possible to travel onto Gunung Mulu. There are buses to Naga Medamit, too, from jalan Buangsiol, every two hours from 9am until 3pm, the trip taking around three hours, twice as long as the boat.

The new *Government Rest House* (①) on the river, 1km west of the centre, offers the only budget **accommodation**, though there are a number of inexpensive hotels, including the *Borneo Hotel*, Main Bazaar (②), and three more upmarket ones along jalan Buangsiol. The stalls at the river's edge above the market offer a limited range of Chinese **food** and perhaps the best place to eat is *Maggie's Cafe*, jalan Buangsiol, which has a good view of the river.

Lawas

Boxed between Sabah and Brunei's sparsely inhabited Temburong District is Sarawak's most northwesterly division, **Lawas**, a little larger than Limbang and with appreciably more coastline. It was bought by Charles Brooke from the Sultan of Brunei in 1905, and from its origins as a remote bazaar and trading centre for Berawan, Kelabit and Chinese pioneers, **LAWAS TOWN** – the only settlement of any size in the area – has grown into a bustling centre on the Lawas river, becoming prosperous from its timber industry. Above the river is the town's main focal point, the posh new market, with stalls selling tropical fruits and vegetables, and several food stalls upstairs. Saturdays are busiest, when traders from Sabah sometimes arrive to sell clothes and textiles. Otherwise, the only diversion in town is the Chinese temple five minutes north of the market, on jalan Bunga Teratai, remarkable only for the unusual fact that a large portion of it is open to the elements.

North of town, jalan Punang leads, after around 10km, to **PUNANG** itself, the site of a reasonable attractive beach – minibuses ($2) leave from the bus station on jalan Pengiran.

Practicalities

Lawas **airport** is around 3km south of town – a bus usually meets the daily flights from Kota Kinabalu, Limbang, Bario and Ba Kelalan in the Kelabit Highlands. The *MAS* agent is *Eng Huat Travel Agency*, at 2 jalan Lian Siew (☎085/5570), next door to the *Gaya Inn* on jalan Punang. **Boats** arrive and depart from the jetty beside the town market: the *Utama Lawas* leaves for Brunei (daily at 7.15am; $18) and there are also boats to Sabah's Pulau Labuan (daily at 7.30am; $20) and to Limbang (daily at 9am; $20). Tickets are sold at the jetty just before departure, or go to the ticket office below the *Do Re Mi Cinema* in the centre of town.

Overland to and from Brunei's Temburong District, the journey is by (expensive) taxi; while minibuses and taxis run to the **border with Sabah**, where you can pick up another bus or taxi to Sipitang (see p.426), an hour's journey all told. There's also a daily through-bus to Kota Kinabalu, the *Lawas Express*, which leaves at 7.30am ($20), and also passes through Sipitang. The only other way out of Lawas is by **land cruiser** (daily; around $35) to the lowland Kelabit settlement of Ba Kelalan (see p.399), 90km south; most of the trip is on a rough unpaved road and takes five hours – go to the area below the *Mee Yan Hotel* for details.

The best low-price **accommodation** in Lawas is the *Hup Guan Lodging House* (②) above a snooker hall and below the park in the town centre. The *Mee Yan Hotel* (①), at the bottom of the town, is less expensive, but also darker and appreciably more sleazy. More upmarket is the *Federal Hotel* (③) on jalan Punang, and the top-of-the-range *Shangsan Hotel* (⑤) on jalan Trusan.

For inexpensive **food**, head for the upper floor of the market or for the stalls beside it. There's no menu at the tidy *Soon Seng* restaurant below the hotel of the same name, but the Chinese food there is good. For *dim sum*, try the *Bee Hiong* Restaurant, in the block above the *Mee Yan Hotel*; Malay staples are served at *Restoran Hj Narudin Bin Matusop*, opposite the market.

THE NORTHERN INTERIOR

The **northern interior**, loosely defined as the watershed of **batang Baram** – the wide river to the northeast of Miri – incorporates both the wildest, most untouched areas of Sarawak, and the most environmentally degraded. At the northernmost point of the White Rajahs' reach – and almost completely ignored by the Sultan of Brunei – the Baram featured a number of Brooke fortifications, but the tribal groups living along the river's reaches were largely left to their own devices. More recently, though, Baram was the first part of Sarawak to be heavily logged and timber yards now line the river for 50km from **Kuala Baram** to **Marudi**, the largest town in the region, and for a score more to the east. The scale of the industry can be judged by the number of timber rafts which float down the wide, silt-clogged river. Although the state government is cutting back production in the north, the forests are still being harvested at the rate of over 300,000 hectares a year and some estimates suggest that over fifty percent of Sarawak's inland forests have already gone. The very obvious environmental problems apart, there's great concern at the impact that **logging** has had on the region's indigenous inhabitants, mostly Kayan, Kenyah, Kelabit and Penan. Soil erosion as a result of the deforestation has damaged their lands, water catchments are murky and often unfit for drinking, and the food supply – either game in the forest or from agricultural land – is diminishing. Disease is rife, too, spread principally by contact with timber personnel and water-born parasites. The Penan are the worse affected because, as hunters and gatherers, they rely solely on the forest for survival. However, resistance to logging has been vigorous, with various groups constructing barricades in disputed territories. Some local communities have applied to set up **Communal Reserves**, both to protect the remaining areas of primary rainforest and to maintain the secondary areas where they practise shifting cultivation, harvest fruit trees and plants, and hunt. The state government has refused most of these applications, and the communities have reacted by taking their cases to the courts.

Despite the despoilation, the northern interior holds many of Sarawak's most renowned natural delights. One of batang Baram's tributaries, **sungei Tutoh**, branches off east when the Baram dips south, and runs to **Gunung Mulu National Park**, which contains the famous Pinnacles and many impressive cave systems. Further east still, straddling the border with Kalimantan and only accessible by plane, lies the magnificent **Kelabit Highlands**, a lush, sparsely populated mountain plateau, which, because of its pleasing climate and low humidity, is the best place in the state for long treks in the rainforest.

Travel in the region is very efficient, due to the excellent rural air service and the reliable river boats. In a ten-day trip you could cover visits to Gunung Mulu, the Kelabit Highlands, the bazaar town of Marudi and a Kenyah longhouse on the Tutoh.

Marudi and around

MARUDI, 80km southeast of Miri on batang Baram, is the only bazaar in the whole Baram watershed, supplying the interior with consumer items, from outboard engines to plastic buckets. Marudi's **jetty**, where dozens of *ekspres* boats and larger vessels crowd the water, is the centre of the community; stalls and cafés here do a brisk trade as the boats disgorge those who come to visit or barter. Conspicuous wealth is not hard to detect: timber magnates in jeans and dark glasses drive by in brand new Toyota vans – even the mobile phone has reached here – while groups of young men wait for temporary labour in the timber camps, processing yards and nearby rubber estates. Charles Brooke bought Marudi from the Sultan of Brunei in 1882 and called it

Claudetown, after the first official James Brooke had sent to administer the area. Brooke encouraged Iban tribespeople from the middle Rajang to migrate here, to act as a bulwark against Kayan war parties who, at their peak in the mid-nineteenth century, amassed up to three thousand warriors on expeditions downriver in search of human trophies.

The town is dominated by two features, the jetty and the hilltop fort, **Fort Hose**, which is reached by walking past the main Bazaar Square, west of the jetty, and following jalan Fort to the top of the hill. The fort was named after the most well known of the Residents to have occupied the position here, the naturalist Charles Hose. Built in 1901, its ironwood tiles are still in perfect condition, as are the ceremonial brass cannons at the front. The fort is now a government office, but part of it houses a **Penan handicraft centre** (Mon–Fri 9pm–2am), where baskets, metalwork and textiles are for sale. Five minutes' further along the hilltop road is the old Resident's house, which, though sturdy and quite habitable, is currently vacant and beginning to erode in the tropical climate.

Practicalities

It only takes a few minutes to walk from Marudi's **airport** into town, although **taxis** usually meet the morning flights from Gunung Mulu, Bario and Miri. The boat **jetty** (see "River trips from Marudi" below for more) is north of the centre and only five minutes' walk from the main hotel, the *Grand* (☎085/55712; ①), which is just off the airport road, jalan Cinema, and provides far and away the best **accommodation** in town. The hotel is massive with clean and quiet rooms, and at the reception you'll find details of Gunung Mulu tours and visits to longhouses. The *Alisan,* on jalan Queen, off jalan Cinema (☎085/55601; ②), is a very good deal, too. Other options include the *Hotel Zola,* a stone's throw from the jetty on jalan Cinema (☎085/755311; ②); *Jaya Hotel,* Lot 950, jalan Newshop (☎085/756425; ③), which has small clean air-con rooms; and the most expensive place in town, the *Victoria Hotel,* Lot 961, in Bazaar Square (☎085/756067; ③), which has good views over the river.

There are two excellent **restaurants**: the Indian *Restoran Koperselara,* just past the *Alisan* hotel on jalan Cinema, sells *roti canai,* curries and refreshing *teh tarek* (a full meal costs around $4); while *Boon Kee Restoran,* set behind the main street in jalan Newshop, is a great place for dinner, with outdoor tables. A favourite meal here is sweet and sour prawns, greens in garlic and rice, plus beer – something that will cost around $15 a head. Otherwise, a couple of cafés beside the jetty and on the square do adequate rice and noodle dishes.

River trips from Marudi

The upriver Baram *ekspres* (daily at 8.30am, 10am & 2.30pm) goes to the settlement of **LONG LAMA**, 80km southeast (around $15), with return boats leaving for Marudi at 6.45am and 10am. The longhouse at Long Lama has sleeping facilities and it's possible to arrange trips further down the Baram to **LONG AKAH**, another 60km east, although renting a longboat for this journey is expensive.

Another daily departure from Marudi is the Tinjar *ekspres* (8am), which takes two hours to reach the Kayan longhouse at **LONG TERU**, where there's a logging track leading to a timber camp, at which most of the inhabitants work. The only boat along the Tutoh river to **LONG TERRAWAN** (where there's a connection for Gunung Mulu National Park) leaves at noon. Although most people travel this route specifically to go to the park, you pass many traditional Kayan longhouses on the way which are worth visiting. An hour from Marudi along the Tutoh, you reach the periphery of the loggers' activities; from here on, the river is clear, the jungle closing in around the river banks.

Finally, the boat (hourly 7am–3pm; $12) west from Marudi to Kuala Baram (see p.383), takes three hours, with numerous buses waiting at the other end for onwards travel for Miri or Brunei.

Gunung Mulu National Park

GUNUNG MULU NATIONAL PARK is Sarawak's premier national park and largest conservation area, located deep in the rainforest. Until 1992, when commercial flights started, it was accessible only from Marudi by a full day trip along the Baram, Tutoh and Melanau rivers, but the region has been a magnet for explorers and scientists since the 1930s, who continue to make new discoveries here: at the last count, Mulu featured 20,000 animal species and 3500 plant species. Quite apart from Mulu's primary rainforest, which is the size of southern England and characterized by clear rivers and high-altitude vegetation, the park has three mountains dominated by dramatically eroded features, including fifty-metre-high razor-sharp limestone spikes known as the **Pinnacles**; there's also the largest limestone **cave system** in the world, much of which is still being explored. The two major hikes, to the Pinnacles on Gunung Api and to the summit of **Gunung Mulu**, are daunting, but you're rewarded with stupendous views of the rainforest, stretching as far as Brunei.

Most of the world's limestone landscapes have been modified by glaciation within the last two million years and although Mulu is far older (the region formed over twenty million years ago) and has been weathered by a combination of rainfall, rivers and high temperatures, it's never been moulded by ice. The caves, which penetrate deep into the mountains, were created by running water and are very ancient: the oldest formed around five million years ago, the youngest during the last 50,000 years. The surface water driving down the slopes of Mulu has eroded vast amounts of material, shaping the landscape outside, as well as carving cave passages within, dividing the great chunks of limestone into separate mountains.

Modern **explorers** have been coming for well over a century, starting in the 1850s with Spenser St John, who – although he didn't reach the summit of Gunung Mulu – wrote inspiringly about the region in his book *Life in the Forests of the Far East*. A more successful bid was launched in 1932 when the South Pole explorer Lord Shackleton got to the top during a research trip organized by Tom Harrisson, who would later become the curator of the Sarawak Museum. After his successful ascent Shackleton recorded that "Although it was steep, the going during the first day or two was comparatively good, for the forest still consisted of big timber rising to a height of over one hundred feet. But it grew colder and soon we entered at around four thousand feet that extraordinary phenomenon, the moss forest. Sometimes we found ourselves plunging deeper and deeper, not knowing whether we were walking on the top of the wood or on the forest floor and occasionally having to cut tunnels through the squelching moss."

More recently, a Royal Geographical Society trip in 1976, led by Robin Hanbury-Tenison, put forward a quite overwhelming case for designating the region a national park, based on studies of the flora, fauna, caves, rivers and overall tourist potential. Over 250km of caves have now been explored, yet experts believe this is only around thirty percent of the total. By 1985 the park was open for tourists, and it now attracts 20,000 visitors a year. There are still no roads into the area, but Mulu is under threat from **developers**. A large hotel, financed by the Japanese, has just been built and there are plans to cut down acres of forest to build a golf course and an international airstrip.

Planning a trip

Although you can arrive unannounced and book into the park hostel, most visitors come to Mulu as part of a **tour group** (see "Kuching", p.342; "Miri", p.381, and "Kuala

Lumpur", p.110; for addresses). That way, all the incidental costs, including the guides which are mandatory for the treks and cave visits, are taken care of. But prices are high – around $600 per person, for example, for a three-night, four-day trip to climb the Pinnacles and see the caves. Going independently, preferably in a group of two to four people, you should be able to undercut these costs, but allow yourself an extra day at the beginning of the visit to discuss options and prices with one of the guides, based at the park headquarters (and try to avoid arriving at the weekend or on a public holiday when the park is at its busiest).

The **minimum individual costs** for a guide and the various activities are: the **Pinnacles** (two nights/three days; around $90); **Mulu summit** (three nights/four days; around $120); **adventure caving** (around $60 per day); adventure caving in **Sarawak Chamber** (two days; $90); and the **show caves** – ie the ones open to the public ($20 per cave). If you need a **porter** the charge is another $25 for one day and night. You've also got to shell out for **boat travel** (around $10 for short trips, $30–50 for long ones), but once there it's possible to hitch rides along sungei Melanau, the main thoroughfare through the park, connecting the airport with the headquarters, the caves and the main trails.

You'll need three **permits** to visit Mulu: one from the National Parks office, one from the Resident's office and a Police clearance permit. If you're on a tour, the operator will obtain them on your behalf. Independent travellers should wait until they arrive at park HQ to get them, since the offices in Miri (see p.378) may ask to see evidence that you are travelling with a tour operator before granting the permits.

Among **equipment** you'll need is a large plastic water bottle, comfortable walking shoes with a good tread, sun hat and swimming gear, a poncho/rain sheet, flashlight, mosquito repellent, headache pills, salt solution, ointment for bites, and a basic first aid kit. On the trails it's best to wear light clothing – shorts and T-shirts – rather than fully cover the body; this way, if the conditions are wet, it'll be easier to see any leeches that might be clinging to you. For the Pinnacles, Mulu and Head-hunter trails, bring long trousers and long-sleeved shirts for the dusk insect assault, and for the occasional cool nights. And a thin mat is useful on the trails.

Getting there

To **fly** to Mulu from Miri (daily at 8.40am, 10.10am, 11.50am & 3pm; around $70) or Marudi (daily at 9.20am; around $40), book ahead as the tiny Twin-Otters carry only 19 passengers each. The **airport** is 2km east of park HQ, just outside the park boundary, and longboats meet the planes to take you to the headquarters or wherever you have arranged accommodation (see below).

Reaching Mulu **by boat** from Miri involves four separate stages and takes all day. The first step is to take an early bus ($3) or taxi ($20) to Kuala Baram, at the mouth of batang Baram, which takes thirty minutes. From there, take the *ekspres* boat upriver to Marudi, which leaves hourly ($12) – you'll need to catch the 7am or 8am to be in time to catch your connection which is the noon *ekspres* to Long Terrawan (around $20). When the river's low, this boat may only go as far as Long Panai-Kuala Apoh ($12), though you can then take a longboat ($10) from there to Long Terrawan.

LEAVING THE PARK

Return **flights** to Miri and Marudi leave the park daily at 11am, 2.10pm and 3.50pm. For the return trip **by boat** you have to arrange with the park office for the longboat to pick you up at 6am. This connects with the *ekspres* or longboat at Long Terrawan at 7.15am, which gets you to Marudi between 10.30am and 11am, in time to get the noon boat to Kuala Baram.

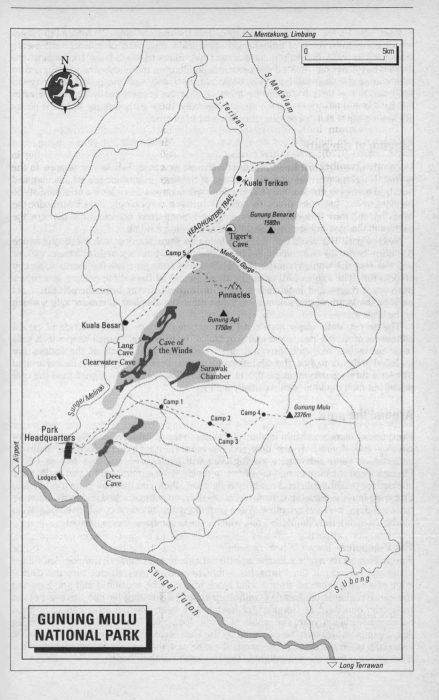

△ Mentakung, Limbang

0   5km

N

S. Medalam

S. Terikan

Kuala Terikan ●

HEADHUNTERS TRAIL

Gunung Benarat
1580m ▲

Tiger's
Cave ○

Camp 5 ●

Melinau Gorge

Pinnacles

Gunung Api
1750m ▲

Kuala Besar ●

Lang
Cave
Cave of
the Winds

Clearwater Cave

Sarawak
Chamber

Sungei Melinau

Camp 1 ●

Camp 2 ●

Camp 3 ●

Camp 4 ●   Gunung Mulu
2376m ▲

Park
Headquarters ■

△ Airport

Lodges ■

Deer
Cave

Sungei Tutoh

S. Ubong

GUNUNG MULU
NATIONAL PARK

▽ Long Terrawan

Soon after leaving Marudi the boat turns into the narrow sungei Tutoh and the scenery changes from lines of timber yards to thick forest, with occasional settlements stretching down to the bank. It takes about three hours to reach Long Terrawan where there'll be a longboat ($25–50 per person depending on the number of passengers) to take you on the final two-hour trip, down sungei Tutoh and into its tributary, sungei Melanau, to the park. It's along the Melanau that the scenery really becomes breathtaking: the multiple greens of the forest deepening in the early evening light, the peaks of Gunung Mulu and Api peeping through a whirl of mist.

Staying at the park

Upon arrival at the **park headquarters** you must sign in and show – or acquire – your permit. If you have arranged to sleep at one of the tour groups' lodges, which are a few hundred metres upstream, then the longboat will take you there after a brief stop at the headquarters. The parks office (no phone) has got surprisingly little information on Mulu but the **tour lodges** are better equipped. Some have books on the caves, while each of the lodges' guest diaries makes for fascinating reading.

Next to park HQ you'll find various **places to stay**, starting with the hostel which has dorm beds (①) and cooking facilities. The chalets have six beds to a room (①), or you can rent the whole room for $60; while top of the range are the four-bed, air-con chalets (③). The lodges further up the river, owned by the tour operators, sometimes have spare rooms and independent travellers can often stay here cheaply (①) – get back on the longboat and ask to be dropped off at the *Tropical Adventure* lodge, which is the largest.

The air-con **café** (daily 8am–8pm) at the headquarters serves a range of meals, consisting of mostly rice, meat and vegetables. Next door is a small shop which sells basic provisions like rice, tins and dried meat and fish. Meals at the **lodges** are included in the tour price, though independent travellers can pay a fixed rate of around $12 for a three-course main meal, and around $6 for breakfast – higher than the café prices but then the food is substantially better.

Around the park

Everyone's itinerary at Mulu includes trekking to the **Pinnacles** and visiting the show **caves** – and, if you have the time and the money, either scaling **Gunung Mulu** or undertaking some **adventure caving**. You will need three full days to trek to the Pinnacles and the caves, and four or five to reach Mulu summit; and if you really are a stickler for punishment (and unaffected by cost), then you can end your trip to Mulu by caving into the Sarawak Chamber – altogether, an action-packed and fairly unforgettable ten days' worth of activities. When planning your itinerary, consider leaving Mulu by the three-day Head-hunter's Trail, which runs to Limbang (see opposite).

The Pinnacles

Five million years ago a constant splatter of raindrops dissolved Gunung Api's limestone and carved out the **Pinnacles** – fifty-metre-high grey shapes with the cutting edge of a samurai sword, from a solid block of rock. The erosion is still going on and the entire region is pockmarked with deep shafts penetrating far into the heart of the mountain: one third of Gunung Api has already been washed away and in perhaps another ten million years the whole of it will disappear. From 1200m up on Gunung Api, it's impossible not to be overawed by the sheer size and grandeur of the Pinnacles, especially when the setting sun causes them to cast shadows far across the top of the trees growing from the soil caught in the crevices near their base.

From the lodges park HQ the first part of the trip is by longboat upstream along sungei Melanau; you may have to help pull the boat through the rapids if the water level is very low. After landing at Kuala Berar, there's a two-and-a-half-hour trek through lowland forest to reach **Camp 5**, close to the Melanau gorge with nearby **Gunung Api** (1750m) and Gunung Benarat (1580m) casting long shadows across it in the fading afternoon light. Most Pinnacle climbers spend two nights at Camp 5, where there's a large hut for sleeping and cooking facilities partially protected by a rocky overhang. A hazardous rope bridge straddles the river and on the other side a path disappears into the jungle; this is the first stage of the Head-hunter's Trail (see below).

The demanding **ascent** up the south face of Gunung Api to get a good view of the Pinnacles is a six-to-seven-hour-plus return trip. The trail is honeycombed with holes and passages through which rainwater immediately disappears, and it's vital to bring water – a litre per person at the very least – as there's none on the trail. Carry little else with you – wear light clothing and a hat, and bring a snack – or you'll be too weighed down. Indeed tour operators are being economical with the truth when they describe the climb as "moderate" – to the less than perfectly fit, climbing to the Pinnacles can be extraordinarily taxing. Only a few metres from Camp 5 the track quickly leads to the face of the mountain where it disappears among tree roots and slippery limestone debris. After two hours' climb, including rests, a striking vista opens up: the rainforest stretches below as far as the eye can see and wispy clouds drift along your line of vision. The climb gets tougher as you scramble between the rocks and the high trees give way to **moss forest**, where pitcher plants feed on insects, and ants and squirrels dart in and out of the roots of trees.

The last thirty minutes of the climb is almost a sheer vertical manoeuvre. Ladders, thick pegs and ropes help you on this final ascent and just when your limbs are finally giving way, you arrive at the top of the **ridge** which overlooks the Pinnacles. The ridge is itself a pinnacle, although sited across a ravine from the main cluster, and if you tap the rocks around you, they will reverberate because of the large holes in the limestone underneath. The vegetation is sparse, but includes the *balsam* plant with pale pink flowers, and pitcher plants full of nutrient-rich liquid. After taking in the stunning sight of the dozen or more fifty-metre-high grey limestone shapes, jutting out from their perch in an unreachable hollow on the side of the mountain, it's time for the return slog, which takes three to four hours, or longer if the route is particularly slippery.

Walks from Camp 5

Once back at the camp, most people rest, swim, eat and sleep, preferring to start the return trip to park HQ the following day. But there are a few interesting alternatives if you want to stay longer and explore the area. A path from the camp follows the river further upstream and ends below the **Melanau gorge**, where a vertical wall of rock rises 100m above the river, which vanishes into a crevice on the way back to its underground source. This is a beautiful spot although there is nowhere other than slippery rocks to rest before returning to Camp 5, a return trip of around two hours. Another short trail from Camp 5 begins on the other side of the rope bridge, where you take the path to the right to the base of **Gunung Benarat** and to the lower shaft of **Tiger's Cave**, a trip of around three hours there and back.

A third, much longer option from Camp 5 is to follow the so-called **Head-hunter's Trail**, a route supposedly traced by tribal war parties in days gone by. Once across the bridge you turn left and walk along a wide trail passing a large rock, Batu Rikan (around 4km), from where the trail is clearly marked to **KUALA TERIKAN**, four hours (11km) away, a small Berawan settlement on the banks of sungei Terikan where you'll find basic hut accommodation. Next day, the trail continues for two hours and reaches sungei Medalam, down which you can take a longboat to the 23-door Iban longhouse at **MENTAKUNG**. It's best to stay here and then continue next day down sungei Medalam in a longboat into sungei Limbang and on up to Limbang Town (see p.383), a trip that takes all day. This is a particularly good route for those wanting to get to Brunei from Mulu, as boats run frequently from Limbang to Bandar.

Gunung Mulu

The route to the summit of **Gunung Mulu** (2376m), was first discovered in the 1920s by Tama Nilong, a rhinoceros-hunter. Earlier explorers hadn't been able to find a way around the huge surrounding cliffs, but Nilong discovered the southwest ridge trail by following rhinoceros tracks, enabling Lord Shackleton in 1932 to became the first mountaineer to reach the summit. It's a more strightforward climb these days, though much of the route is very steep, but any reasonably fit person can complete it.

The first stage is from park HQ to **Camp 3**, an easy three-hour walk on a flat trail which crosses from the park's prevalent limestone to the sandstone terrain of Gunung Mulu en route. **Hornbills** (see feature opposite) fly low over the jungle canopy and if you watch the trail carefully, you may see the tracks of wild boar and mouse deer. The first night is at the open hut at Camp 3, which has cooking facilities. Day two comprises a hard, ten-hour, uphill slog; there are two resting places on the way where you have time to wash your tired limbs in small rock pools. From here onwards you're in a moss forest in which great clumps of dripping vegetation cover the trees and rocks, and small openings on the trail reveal lovely views of the park. The next part of the trail is Nilong's **southwest ridge**, a series of small hills negotiated by a narrow, twisting path. When the rain has been heavy, there are lots of little swamps to negotiate, with one known as "Rhino's Lake" – so-called because it was around here that the last rhinoceros in the area was shot in the 1950s. For some decades the rhino was believed to be extinct in Sarawak although what appear to be rhino tracks have been recently discovered on the slopes of Mulu, so there's hope that the rhino may be seen again in the near future. The hut at **Camp 4** is at 1800m. It can be cool here – you'll need a sleeping bag.

Most climbers set off well before dawn for the ninety-minute hard trek to the **summit**, if possible timing their arrival to coincide with sunrise. After an hour's climbing – just before dawn – you pass an overgrown helicopter pad. Now the forest is waking up, the insect and bird chorus reverberating in the thin, high-altitude air. On this final stretch there are big clumps of pitcher plants, though it's easy to miss them as by this point you are hauling yourself up by ropes onto the cold, windswept, craggy peak. From here, the view is exhilarating, as you look down on Gunung Api and, on a clear day, far across the forest to Brunei Bay. Below are the various levels of forest and sungei Melanau can just be made out, a pencil-thin wavy light-brown line, bisecting the deep-green density of the lush forest carpet.

It's just possible to do the whole **return trip** from the summit to park HQ in one day. This takes around twelve hours and cuts out the last night at Camp 4. The red-and-white marks on the trees marking the trail are easy to see, so you won't lose your way in fading light.

The caves

Only four of the 25 caves so far explored in Mulu are open to visitors – Deer Cave, Clearwater Cave, Lang's Cave and the Cave of the Winds – and as these are Mulu's most popular attraction, there's the occasional log jam along the plankways leading to the caves. Guided tours to Sarawak Chamber and connecting passages in the Clearwater Cave system can also be arranged; caving equipment is included in the cost.

The most immediately impressive cave in the park is **Deer Cave**, the nearest to the headquarters, which is believed to contain the largest cave passage in the world. Once inhabited by deer, which used to shelter in its cavernous reaches, Deer Cave would have been known to the Berawan and Penan but was never used for burial purposes,

HORNBILLS

Hornbills are bizarre, almost prehistoric-looking, inhabitants of tropical forests, whose presence (or absence) is an important ecological indicator of the health of the forest. The novice observer should have little difficulty in recognizing one: they are large, black-and-white birds with disproportionately huge (often decurved) bills, topped with an ornamental casque a piece of generally hollow horn attached to the upper mandible of the bill. The function of the casque is unknown, but it may play a role in attracting a mate and in courtship ceremonies. In addition to this, the birds have a long tail and broad wings which produce a highly audible "whooshing" sound as they glide and flap across the forest canopy.

Hornbills are heavily dependent upon large forest trees for nesting, using natural tree cavities as nest sites. The female seals herself into the cavity by plastering up the entrance to the nest hole with a combination of mud, tree bark and wood dust. This prevents snakes, civets, squirrels and other potential predators from raiding the nest. She spends up to three months here, totally dependent on the male bird to provide herself and the offspring with a diet of fruit (mainly figs), insects and small forest animals. A narrow slit is left in the plaster wall, through which the male passes food to his mate, and through which the female and the youngsters defecate. When the young bird is old enough to fly, the female breaks open the mud wall to emerge back into the forest. Given their nesting habits, it is essential that large, undisturbed, good-quality tracts of forest are retained in order to secure a future for hornbills. Sadly, hornbill populations in many parts of Asia have declined or been driven to the point of extinction by human encroachment, overhunting and deforestation.

Ten of the world's 46 species of hornbill are found in Malaysia and as many of these species are endangered, or only present in small, isolated populations: visiting Malaysia's larger forested areas offers the only real opportunity of seeing one. Two of the most commonly seen species are the pied hornbill and the black hornbill. The **pied hornbill** can be identified by its white abdomen and tail, and white wing tips in flight. It's the smallest hornbill you're likely to encounter, reaching 75cm in length. It appears more tolerant to forest degradation than other species and during the non-breeding season gathers in noisy flocks which are generally heard well before they are seen. The **black hornbill** is another small species, slightly larger than the pied hornbill, and all black save for the white tips to the outer tail feathers. Some individuals also show a white patch behind the eye. Two of the larger species of hornbill found in Malaysia are the **helmeted hornbill** and the **rhinoceros hornbill**. Both of these are over 120cm in length, the helmeted having central tail feather plumes of up to 50cm. Both species are mainly black in colour, with white tails and bellies. The rhinoceros has a bright orange rhino horn shaped casque (hence the name), whereas the helmeted has a bright red head, neck and helmet-shaped casque. The call of the helmeted is a remarkable series of "took" call notes which start off slowly and then accelerate to reach a ringing crescendo of cackling laughter.

Other than Gunung Mulu National Park, where there eight species of hornbill are present, good places to spot hornbills elsewhere in Malaysia are Taman Negara (several species present), Fraser's Hill (several species including rhinoceros and helmeted hornbills), Langkawi (three species), Sabah's Danum Valley (seven species), and Mount Kinabalu National Park (several species).

unlike the smaller caves dotted around the park. From the headquarters, there's a well-marked, three-kilometre plankway which runs through a peat swamp forest and passes an ancient Penan burial cave in which were found fragmented skulls, now in the Sarawak Museum. Once in Deer Cave itself, the statistics become unfathomable: the cave passage is over 2km long and 200m high, while up above, hundreds of thousands of horseshoe bats live in the cave's nooks and crannies. You follow the path through the cave for an hour to an area where a large hole in the cave roof allows light to penetrate. Here, in the so-called **Garden of Eden**, scientists of the 1976 RGS expedition discovered luxuriant vegetation undisturbed for centuries; Robin Hanbury-Tenison noted that "even the fish were tame and gathered in shoals around a hand dipped in the water". It's an incredible spot: plants battle for the light, birds and insects celebrate the warm, bright air, giant ferns cluster around pebbles and small families of grey-leaf monkeys scuttle about unafraid. The best – and the busiest – time to visit Deer Cave is in the late afternoon: wait around the cave entrance at dusk and you'll see vast swarms of bats streaming out of the cave into the darkening skies, off on a search for food.

Clearwater Cave is best visited on your way to or from the Pinnacles, the main entrance (an hour downstream from Kuala Berar) reached by a one-kilometre boat journey along sungei Melanau from park HQ. The longboats moor at a small jungle pool, after which the cave is named, at the base of the one-hundred-step climb to the cave mouth. Discovered in 1988, the cave tunnels here weave deep into the mountain and stretch for over 60km, although ordinary visitors can only explore the small section close to the entrance, where lighting has been installed along a walkway leading 300m to **Young Lady's Cave**, which ends abruptly in a fifty-metre-deep pothole. Deep inside the main body of Clearwater is an underground river which flows through a five-kilometre passage averaging ninety metres high and wide. One of the caving tours takes you some distance down it in special lightweight canoes, although much of it remains unnavigable.

The entrance to the **Cave of the Winds** is ten minutes further west along sungei Melanau, past the backwater which leads to Clearwater Cave – subterranean passageways actually join the two caves. Reached by steps leading up from the river, the cave is fairly small in comparison with the others, but contains a great variety of golden, contorted rock shapes, stalactites and stalagmites, all revealed by subtle lighting. Further along the path from the river, past the Cave of the Winds, is **Lang's Cave**, similar in shape but even smaller, and worth a look, if only to gaze at its distinctive smooth-shaped formations, especially the curtain stalactites and coral-like growths – helictites – which grip the curved walls.

The Kelabit Highlands

One hundred kilometres east of Mulu and accessible only by air, the long, high plateau of the **KELABIT HIGHLANDS** runs along the border with Kalimantan. Home to the Kelabit people for hundreds of years, Western explorers had no idea of the existence of this self-sufficient mountain community until the turn of this century, when Brooke officials made a few brief visits. But the Highlands were literally not put on the map until World War II, when British and Australian commandos, led by Major Tom Harrisson, used a number of Kelabit settlements as bases for waging a guerrilla war against the occupying Japanese forces. After parachuting into the forest, Harrisson and his team were taken to the largest longhouse in the area, in the village of **Bario**, to meet the *penghulu*. With his help Harrisson set out to contact the region's other ethnic groups and within twelve months was in a position to convince Allied Command in Manila that the tribes were thirsty for retaliation.

Before Harrisson's men built the airstrip at Bario, trekking over the inhospitable terrain was the only way to get there – it took two weeks from Marudi to the west, which, according to early accounts, required hacking through moss forests and circumnavigating sharp limestone hills and savage gorges; and it was another seven days through similar conditions to the furthest navigable point on batang Baram, **Lio Matoh**, just off the edge of the plateau. After the war, missionaries arrived and converted the animist Kelabit into the alien ways of Christianity with the consequence that many of their traditions, like burial rituals and the promiscuous parties called *iraus* – where

Chinese jars full of rice wine were consumed – disappeared. What's more, the Kelabits' magnificent **megaliths** – associated with these traditions – were soon swallowed by the jungle: dolmens, urns, rock carvings of human faces and ossuaries containing bones and skulls used in funereal processes, were all lost to the elements. Carvings of human faces also celebrated feats of valour, like a successful head-hunting expedition, and birds were also popular images – a motif that still survives in their beadwork and also in the craftwork of neighbouring ethnic groups. Now the three most populous Kelabit settlements – Bario, Long Lellang to the southwest and Ba Kelalan to the north – have a daily air service in tiny 21-seater Twin-Otter planes, giving the highland people the chance of daily contact with the world beyond, and curious tourists the opportunity to visit them with relative ease.

For all the recent contact, the highlands remains one of the most unspoiled regions on earth, displaying dazzlingly vivid flora, abundant game and a cool refreshing climate. Not surprisingly, these factors have made the highlands a popular place for walkers, attracted by jungle **treks** and meetings with friendly local people, many of whom live in sturdy **longhouses** surrounded by their livestock, fruit trees and wet paddy fields. Visiting the longhouses is an unmissable part of any trip to the highlands and as Kelabits aren't as concerned as the Iban or Kayan with formality, there's less etiquette to observe. Once you've attracted the attention of an adult longhouse dweller, you'll inevitably be invited in, soon after which the *penghulu* will arrive and take charge, urging you to eat with his family and, probably, insisting that you stay in his rooms. But if you've already made friends with another family, no harm's done by turning the chief down and staying with them. Your arrival will usually

be an excuse for a mini-party, with much laughing, joking and cross-cultural leg-pulling. Swimming in the river below the longhouse is a delight and if a hunter offers to take you on a night trek, go.

A number of excellent inclusive **tours** – which include trekking and visits to long-houses – are available from companies based in Miri. *Tropical Adventure* (see p.381 for address and details) in particular has four-day tours to Bario, which include short walks to Pa Umor and Pa Berang; and more strenuous five-day visits to longhouses around Ramudu, Pa Dalih and Long Dano. There's also an adventurous trip which follows Penan forest trails through Long Ugong, Long Semadoh and Long Uping. All these tours work out at around $170 per night for two people.

Bario

The central settlement of **BARIO** is approximately 10km west of the border with Indonesian Kalimantan, and a few days' hard hike from the other local villages Long Lellang to the south, and Ba Kelalan to the north. It's a small but widely dispersed settlement, set among the plateau's rolling hills and surrounded by rice fields. Next to the turf landing strip, a small cluster of buildings constitute the centre, with a lodging house, two stores, and around twenty dwellings. Two kilometres west is Bario Asal, where a large longhouse is situated. There are no telephones or cars, and the pace of life could hardly be slower, with only the planes' arrival disturbing the tranquillity.

Practicalities

The daily **flights** from Miri and Marudi bring in pieces of machinery, food and house-hold and agricultural utensils as well as visitors. The planes don't land when the weather's bad so, once in Bario, you may well get stuck – bring along enough funds, as there are no banks. Trying to get on the flight from Miri in the first place can be hard as Bario people tend to book ahead and the flights fill up quickly: ask to be put on the reserve list and call back the day before you want to fly. It's best to avoid Friday and Saturday, as Kelabits in Miri go back for the weekend.

Bario **airport** *is* the centre of town; the hut next to which the planes stop doubles as the *MAS* office (daily 10am–noon). One hundred metres north of the airfield on Bario's only street is *Tarawe's*, a relaxed **lodging house** (①) run by John Tarawe and Englishwoman Karen Hedderman. It has four rooms with three beds in each, and mats for occasions when large groups arrive. Inexpensive, hearty meals are available here, including wild boar, ferns in garlic, rice and other seasonal dishes (around $8 per person), with a breakfast of noodles and eggs at around $5.

Other than this, there are two **cafés** next to the *MAS* building which sell soft drinks, noodles, cakes and rice dishes in the daytime. The only other place to stay, *Bario Lodging House*, is no longer open to the general public, as the owners don't need to look any further than their own extended family to fill the two spare rooms.

Day trips from Bario

A good way to acclimatize to the high-altitude conditions is to embark on short treks from Bario – the walk to the longhouse at Pa Umor is especially rewarding. Follow the track past *Tarawe's* for thirty minutes, then turn down a narrow path to the right, and after about an hour you'll reach **PA UMOR**, a modern longhouse, where someone's bound to invite you in. From Pa Umor the path leads past the fork to the Kalimantan frontier post at Lembudud (six hours away) and over a precarious bridge, past remnants of an earlier longhouse, into a lovely copse, from where there are fine views of the lush highlands. Watch out for a right fork along a buffalo track, which leads into a thick, aromatic forest. At the end of this path is one of only two functioning **salt licks** on the highlands. Extracting fine grey salt from the muddy water at the bottom of the small well is a traditional Kelabit industry which goes back centuries. The salt is then cooked and dried, and heaved back on the narrow trail to the longhouses.

Two other longhouses, **PA UKAT** and **PA LUNGAN**, lie further along the main track. Ignore the right turn to Pa Umor and keep walking; it takes around forty minutes to get to Pa Ukat, and Pa Lungan is three hours further along the winding road. Both are pleasant, easy walks but get in an early start if you're heading to the latter as there's little shade.

Another short walk from Bario is the twenty-minute stroll west from the village, along the road adjacent to the airstrip, to the largest longhouse in the area, **ULUNG PALLANG**, which replaced the traditional longhouse from where Tom Harrisson planned his rebellion.

South to Lio Matoh

To get to the older, more traditional, but thriving Kelabit longhouses of **Long Dano** and **Pa Dalih** requires hiking into primary forest. The longhouses, at which you can stay, are the first stage on a gruelling six-to-eight-day trip south, on the **Harrisson trail** to the Baram river settlement of **Lio Matoh**.

Bario to Long Dano

It's best to take a guide on the six-hour trek from Bario to Long Dano, so ask at *Tarawe's* if any locals are heading that way. The initial route is across the airfield and along the path to the new longhouse at **KAMPUNG BARU**, 1km past which you follow a path to the left over a wobbly steel-and-bamboo bridge, which leads onto a narrow, undulating buffalo path. If it's been raining, mud will have collected in troughs along the route. The path weaves up and down the sides of the hills and occasionally drops into mud pools, bathing holes for the buffaloes, the Kelabits' most valuable livestock. There are several resting places en route and you're likely to pass, overtake or be overtaken by Kelabit families taking produce back and forth to Bario, including hefty gadgets like generators and rolls of wire – all that's necessary to bring electricity to the most isolated of longhouses.

After around seven hours you cross over a small river on a swinging rattan bridge to reach the thirty-door longhouse of **LONG DANO**, which nestles in fields beside a small brook, with the forest crowding in around. Visitors spend most of their time on the communal bamboo verandah, from where can be glimpsed tiny apartments, one for each family. Below the verandah are storerooms for the stocks of rice, other grains and fried fish. A Christian community, Long Dano incorporates a Methodist church and even a tiny shop, and is surrounded by tended fields; the river nearby is full of fish and abundant hunting is close at hand. Jobs like rice harvesting, mat-making and textile-weaving are dictated by the time of year – the rice cycle starts in August with the clearing and planting of the fields, and the crop is cultivated in February. After the hard labour required in processing the rice, the Kelabit women turn their attention to crafts and the men to hunting or fishing, going on trips to other longhouses or to big towns like Miri and Marudi.

Some Dano Kelabits leave to work in Miri or in the logging industry, but most return for the **iraus**, which centre around massive feasts of wild boar, crackers, rice and traditional games. The conversion to Christianity since the war has meant that rice wine has been banned – there are copious jugs of lemonade and *milo* instead.

Long Dano to Lio Matoh

It's another two hours east from Long Dano on the circuitous trail through the rainforest to the larger longhouse at **PA DALIH**. The chief's son speaks English and is well travelled, and will receive you in the customary Kelabit way – which usually means a feast and games which go on deep into the night. From Pa Dalih, it's a seven-hour hike to three spectacular **waterfalls**, which are very close to the Kalimantan border; however, you'll need a guide (around $40 each day) to take you from Pa Dalih, as the trail is not marked clearly enough to follow. Night is spent under a typical Kelabit lean-to, made with the branches and leaves of large trees.

From Pa Dalih the settlement at **REMADU** is three hours further south, where you can stay the night in a longhouse. The people of Remadu are famed for their skilfully weaved rattan back baskets and they may have a surplus of stock which you can bargain for. The trail beyond Remadu is a hard physical slog: you must carry enough water and food for each day; if it's wet, leeches will be out in force. The trail follows the watershed of sungei Kelapung, taking a full day to reach the jungle shelter at **LONG OKAN**, which hasn't any facilities, so you'll need a light blanket for sleeping. The next day it's four more hours along a hard, hilly trail to **LONG BERUANG**, a large Penan settlement, whose inhabitants are semi-nomadic, preferring sago-collecting and hunting to the settled rice-growing of the Kelabits. Have a few little gifts, like food or tobacco, at hand.

A day on from Long Beruang gets you to the longhouse at **LONG BANGA**, from where it's a two-hour walk downhill off the plateau to the timber camp and longhouse at **LIO MATOH**, the most easterly settlement on batang Baram. For the Kelabits especially this seems like a thriving, busy community in contrast with the jungle longhouses up the track. From Lio Matoh, small longboats travel downriver daily – it's a question of asking around and negotiating a price. You should pay no more than $120 to Marudi if you are sharing a boat, but if you can't avoid renting the whole thing, it will cost about $800 for the three-day journey. If there's no alternative, rent a boat to the next busy point, Long Palai, less than a day away, and try to join a boat there.

Bario to Pa Tik

Another challenging trek from Bario is that to the Penan community at Pa Tik, which takes two days. You've got to have a guide for this route; ask at *Tarawe's*. You'll also need enough food for the outward journey, and the Penan at Pa Tik will give you provisions for the return leg. The first part of the five-day return trip follows the airport road past the turning to Ulung Pallang, and twenty minutes later you're in **BARIO ASAL**, the start of the trail to Pa Tik. The first day's trek up slippery jungle-covered mountains takes eight hours, reaching the jungle shelter of **LONG MANAU**, an elevated shed with a fireplace and dry wood available. (Wood should be replaced for the next passers-by.) A walking stick is advisable as the route is very taxing on the knees, especially if you avoid crossing the rivers on the slippery log bridges, preferring instead to wade through at knee-depth. The second day contains more of the same, and with an early start you can reach Pa Tik by 3pm.

Pa Tik village and around

The kind of gifts you should take for the Penan at **PA TIK** include coffee, tea, sugar and salt, while shotgun cartridges guarantee a good meal. Although the language spoken here is Penan, some people know a little Malay, so a phrase book comes in useful. The settlement has around fifty permanent residents and twice that number of dogs. The head of the village will fix you up with **accommodation**, which will be a mat on the floor. Strict vegetarians will run into problems, as all meals consist of rice and wild boar, or sometimes mouse deer; *tapioca,* fried in wild boar oil, tastes just like french fries.

For trips around Pa Tik, Penan guides can be hired for $25 per day. The trek to the remote Penan village of **LONG SEMADO** takes one and a half days (a return trip for guides must be paid for, too). If you're lucky, your guide may be able to lead you to the nearest Penan nomads for a demonstration of the their legendary tracking skills.

North to Ba Kelalan

The last of the main trails from Bario are the two which lead to the large Kelabit village of **Ba Kelalan**, to the north, which has an airstrip, from where it's possible to travel overland to Lawas (see p.384). An easier trek (including some stages by motorcycle) goes northeast from Bario through **Indonesian villages** in Kalimantan. The tougher, more interesting, option is the two-to-four-day trail due north through the villages of **Pa Lungan** and **Pa Rupai**. On the second trail, it's possible to make side trips to climb **Gunung Lawi** (2039m), or **Gunung Murud** (2438m), the twin peaks of the former making it the most impressive mountain in the area. The Kelabits traditionally believed Gunung Lawi had an evil spirit and so never went near it, and although animist beliefs don't play much part in Kelabit life these days, climbers will still have difficulty finding a local Kelabit prepared to act as a guide to Lawi. The lower peak can be climbed without equipment, but the other sheer-sided peak requires proper gear – it was only scaled for the first time in 1986. Gunung Murud is the highest mountain in Sarawak, an extremely hard climb and only accessible to highly experienced mountaineers.

Bario to Ba Kelalan via Pa Lungan

The time required for this trek depends on fitness and finances. Although a Kelabit could pull it off in ten hours, it's best to allow three days – this is some of the richest, thickest forest in Borneo and after this trail, almost any other walk will seem easy.

The route from Bario heads past the longhouse at Pa Ukat (see "Day trips from Bario", p.396); watch out for the **trailside boulder** a few kilometres along the trail, on which are carved some human faces, the only known example of funerary art remaining in the highlands. After about eight hours you reach **PA LUNGAN**, which consists of detached family units around a large rectangular field for pigs and buffalo. Visitors stay in the longhouse, usually in the chief's quarters.

On the second day, it takes around four hours to get to the abandoned village of **LONG RAPUNG**. On the way, before the forest closes in around you, look out for Gunung Murud on your left, if it's not shrouded in mist. A small shelter still exists at Long Rapung, which is nothing more than just an intersection of paths and a place to rest – you could spend the night here, allowing for a less strenuous third day. Otherwise, press on to **PA RUPAI**, four to five hours away, on a hard narrow trail, infamous for its leeches. A long downward slope passes through irrigated rice fields to the village – you're now in Kalimantan, although there are no signs to prove it.

It takes two more hours before the village of **LONG MEDANG** comes into sight, where you can rent a motorcycle to the town of Long Nawang in Kalimantan and fly onto Tarakan (provided you have a visa). The last stage of the trail to Ba Kelalan curves out of Long Medang and climbs a short, steep hill – this point marks the frontier with Kalimantan. You then walk alongside rice fields to the army outpost outside Ba Kelalan where you need to show your passport.

BA KELALAN is smaller and more compact than Bario, comprised of single dwellings, a large longhouse and a few shops selling basic provisions. As in Bario the airport is right in the centre of the town, with the main street running parallel. There's a small **hotel**, the *Green Valley Inn* (①) and two coffee shops. **Flights** leave mid-morning to Lawas or else you can trek north to Buduk Aru for two hours where a land rover travels the logging road, taking four dusty – or mud-splattering – hours to reach Lawas. Along much of the road the signs of deforestation are only too apparent: wide gashes in the forest open out the scenery and piles of timber await collection.

Bario to Ba Kelalan via Long Bawang

This trail is easier to follow and can be done without a guide. An early start from Bario is recommended as the first day's walk is eight hours: the hike doesn't involve much of a climb and the track is well-trodden, if often muddy. Take the path from Bario to Pa Umor (see "Day trips from Bario", p.396) and look out for the sign on your left that says "Indonesia". Ten minutes down this track through secondary forest there are some rice paddies: this is the only confusing part of the walk, as the trail vanishes for about 100m, but if you cut across the open area in a straight line you should find the next bit of the path. After three hours you arrive at the border with Kalimantan, after which the trail becomes a road which you follow to **LEMBUDUD**. Report first to the army post and then find the village headman, who will probably offer you floor space in his house for the night.

Lembubud to **LONG BAWANG** is an easy three-hour walk north along a hot open road, but a motorcycle can be chartered for around $50 for this section. At Long Bawang, it's best to report to the police, where a form is filled in and a fee of $10 levied. The small town has a **lodging house** where you can rent rooms (①).

The trail on to Ba Kelalan takes another five hours and goes through three Indonesian villages including **LONG API**. Again, much of this is along a track good enough for motorcycle traffic. You'll pass the Indonesian checkpoint and soon reach the Malaysian army outpost, where you will need to show evidence of a valid Sarawak state visa stamp, before reaching Ba Kelalan.

travel details

Buses

Batu Niah to: Bintulu (4 daily; 2–3hr); Miri (4 daily; 2–3hr).

Bintulu to: Batu Niah (5 daily; 2–3hr); Sarikei (3 daily; 4hr); Sibu (4 daily; 4hr).

Kuching to: Bako (12 daily; 1hr); Damai beach (every 40min; 1hr); Lundu (4 daily; 2hr); Sarikei (3 daily; 5–6hr); Serian (4 daily; 1hr); Semanggoh (4 daily; 1hr); Sri Aman (3 daily; 3hr); Tebedu (1 daily; 10hr).

Miri to: Batu Niah (4 daily; 2–3hr); Bintulu (4 daily; 4hr); Kuala Baram (every 15min; 45min); Kuala Belait (6 daily; 3hr); Lambir Hills (every 30min; 40min).

Sarikei to: Bintulu (4 daily; 4hr); Kuching (3 daily; 5–6hr).

Sibu to: Bintulu (4 daily; 4hr).

Boats

Belaga to: Kapit (2 daily, at same time; 4hr).

Bintulu to: Tubau (5 daily; 2–3hr).

Kapit to: Belaga (2 daily; 4–5hr); sungei Gaat (1 daily; 2hr); Mujong (1 daily; 2hr); Nanga Baleh (2 daily; 4hr).

Kuala Baram to: Marudi (7 daily; 3hr)

Kuching to: Sarikei (2 daily; 2–3hr); Sibu (2 weekly; 14hr).

Long Lama to: Marudi (3 daily; 3hr).

Marudi to: Kuala Baram (7 daily; 2–3hr); Lapok (1 daily; 2hr); Long Lama (3 daily; 3hr).

Sarikei to: Kuching (2 daily; 2–3hr); Sibu (2 daily; 1–2hr); Sibu (8 daily; 1–2hr).

Sibu to: Kapit (9 daily; 3–4hr); Kuching (2 weekly; 14hr).

Tubau to: Bintulu (5 daily; 2—hr).

Flights

Bandar Seri Begawan (Brunei) to: Kuching (3 weekly; 1hr 10min).

Bario to: Marudi (1 daily; 50min); to Miri (1 daily; 1hr 15min).

Bintulu to: Kuching (9 daily; 1hr); Miri (4 daily; 35min); Sibu (7 daily; 1hr).

Johor Bahru to: Kuching (4 daily; 1hr 20min).

Kapit to: Sibu (2 weekly; 40min).

Kota Kinabalu to: Kuching (5 daily; 2hr 20min); Miri (5 daily; 40min).

Kuala Lumpur to: Kuching (9 daily; 1hr 40min).

Kuantan to: Kuching (1 weekly; 1hr 20min).

Kuching to: Bandar (3 weekly; 1hr 10min); Bintulu (9 daily; 1hr); Johor Bahru (4 daily; 1hr 20min); Kota Kinabalu (5 daily; 2hr 20min); Kuala Lumpur (9 daily; 1hr 40min); Kuantan (1 weekly;

1hr 20min); Miri (13 daily; 1hr); Pontianak (3 weekly; 1hr); Sibu (11 daily; 40min) Singapore (3 daily; 1hr 20min).

Marudi to: Bario (1 daily; 50min); Miri (4 daily; 20min).

Miri to: Bario (1 daily; 1hr 15min); Bintulu (4 daily; 35min); Kapit (2 weekly; 40min); Kota Kinabalu (5 daily; 40min); Kuching (8 daily; 1hr); Lawas (4 daily; 45min); Limbang (7 daily; 45min); Marudi (4 daily; 20min); Sibu (7 daily; 1hr).

Pontianak to: Kuching (3 weekly; 1hr).

Sibu to: Bintulu (6 daily; 35min); Kuching (11 daily; 40min); Miri (7 daily; 1hr).

Singapore to: Kuching (3 daily; 1hr 20min).

CHAPTER SEVEN

SABAH

Sabah, bordering Sarawak on the northwestern flank of Borneo, boasts an ethnic and geographical make-up every bit as idiosyncratic as its neighbour's. Until European powers began to gain footholds here last century, the northern tip of this remote landmass was inhabited by tribal peoples who had only minimal contact with the outside world, with the result that costumes, traditions and languages have developed that are quite unique to the region. However, although any mention of Borneo typically evokes images of head-hunters and impenetrable jungle, it would be wrong to over-romanticize the state of Sabah, part of the Malaysian Federation since its foundation in 1963. The **logging** industry, which reached its destructive peak in the 1970s and 1980s, has raped vast portions of the natural forest cover; World War II bombs and hurried urban redevelopment have conspired to produce a capital city and a chain of towns almost devoid of architectural worth; while a lack of funding from Kuala Lumpur has left the state's infrastructure and economy in a state of disrepair.

It's a bleak picture, but one which neglects the natural riches on parade in a fertile region, whose name – according to some sources – means "the land below the wind", its 72,500 square kilometres falling just below the typhoon belt. Sabah encompasses various **terrains** from swampy, mangrove-tangled coastal areas, through the dazzling greens of paddy fields and rainforests to the dizzy heights of the Crocker Mountain Range – home to the loftiest mountain peak between the Himalayas and New Guinea. These surroundings maintain an astounding range of indigenous **wildlife**, from the forest-dwelling proboscis monkeys, orang-utans, bearded pigs and hornbills to the turtles who swim ashore to lay their eggs on Sabah's east coast.

Among Sabah's **ethnic** groups, more than eighty dialects are spoken, by over thirty races, though with traditional costumes increasingly losing out to T-shirts and shorts, it would take a trained anthropologist to distinguish one tribe from another. The peoples of the Kadazan/Dusun tribes constitute the largest indigenous racial group, with the Murut of the southwest and Sabah's so-called "sea gypsies", the Bajau, also populous; while more recently, Sabah has seen a huge influx of Filipino and Indonesian immigrants, particularly on the east coast. The best time to witness the music, dance, food and handicrafts of tribal Sabah is during the *Sabah Fest* every May, a week-long celebration that's the climax of *Pesta Kaamatan*, the Kadazan/Dusun harvest festival. Otherwise, try to visit one of the **tamus**, or market fairs, held (usually weekly) in towns and villages across the state. The *tamu* has long been an important social focal point of tribal life in Sabah, and each draws crowds of people from the surrounding region, who come to catch up with local goings-on as much as to buy and sell produce.

Its relative inaccessibility and expense make Sabah a place to visit with a specific purpose in mind, the classic reason being to climb 4101-metre-high Mount Kinabalu in the northwest. Most trips start in the friendly capital **Kota Kinabalu**, from where Sabah's main road heads south to **Beaufort**, beyond which the state's only railway takes advantage of the swathe cut through the Crocker Mountain Range by the broad Padas river to head into the rural **interior**. Here, southeast of the towns of **Tenom** and **Keningau** is Murut territory, isolated enough to allow a taste of the adventures that travelling in Sabah once entailed; while a short way north, Kadazan/Dusuns tend the patchwork of paddy fields that quilts **Tambunan Plain**.

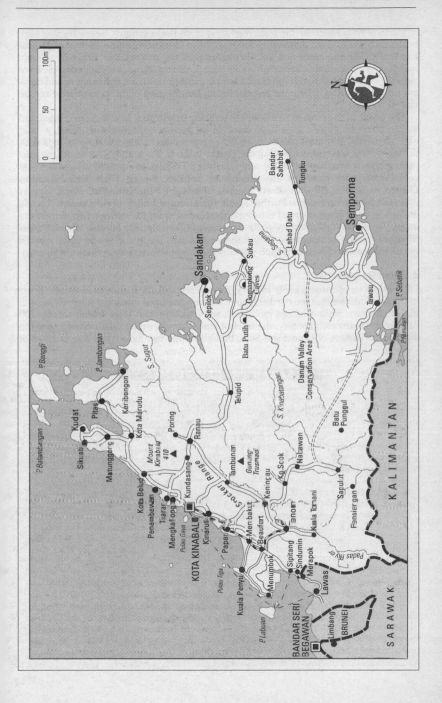

North of Kota Kinabalu, the main road strays into Bajau country, before turning east-wards through lowland *dipterocarp* forest and the awesome granite shelves of **Mount Kinabalu**. The mountain is a joy, its challenging but manageable slopes seemingly tailor-made for amateur climbers; from its jagged summit there are staggering views of Sabah's west coast, through the clouds below. Further north are the beaches and coco-nut groves of **Kudat**, where the few remaining **longhouses** of the Rungus tribe can be visited.

The towns of the eastern seaboard are unlikely to win your heart: impoverished and still troubled by pirates, they have come to be known, collectively, as Sabah's "wild east". Nevertheless, most people go as far as **Sandakan**, a busy community built with timber money, and base for visiting the **Turtle Islands Park**. Indeed, if wildlife is your main reason for coming to Sabah, you'll doubtless be keen to continue around the east coast since more close-ups are possible at **Sepilok Orang Utan Rehabilitation Centre**, as well as along the lower reaches of **sungei Kinabatangan**, which support clans of proboscis monkeys. Further south, the **Danum Valley Conservation Area** is embarking on a programme of eco-tourism intended to let the surrounding virgin rain-forest pay its way. Of more specialized interest is Sabah's only oceanic island, **Pulau Sipadan**, just off Semporna on the southeastern coast. It's touted as one of the world's top diving havens, though sky-high prices make it a destination for serious divers only.

A little history

Little is known of Sabah's **early history**, though archeological finds in limestone caves in the east indicate that the northern tip of Borneo has been inhabited for well over ten thousand years, while Chinese merchants were trading with local settlements by 700 AD. By the fourteenth century, the tract of land now known as Sabah came under the sway of the sultans of Brunei and Sulu, though of this fact its isolated communities of

---

SABAH PRACTICALITIES

Sabah is just north of the equator which means its **climate** is hot and humid. Temperatures can reach 33°C, but an average of 27–28°C throughout the year is more typical. The **wet season** lasts from November until February, but you'll experience rain at most times of the year – especially if you're in the rainforest or up Mount Kinabalu. Perhaps a more important consideration is what you can afford to do when you get there. Sabah is 600km and a pricey air ticket away from the mainland, while several of its high-lights will cut large chunks out of your **budget**, so it's worth doing some sums before committing yourself.

Getting there

Kota Kinabalu (KK) is almost certain to be your first port of call in Sabah. *MAS* flies from **Kuala Lumpur** (7 daily; from $310) and from **Johor Bahru** (4 daily; $350) – though only one flight a day out of JB is direct. There are also departures out of **Kuching** (4 daily; $228), though only the Wednesday and Saturday flights are direct. From the Bruneian capital **Bandar Seri Begawan**, services are with *Royal Brunei* (3 weekly; $117). From **Manila**, *Philippine Airlines* (3 weekly) tickets to KK are undercut by *MAS* (5 weekly; $500), while the *Cathay Pacific* subsidiary, *Dragon Air*, makes the trip from **Hong Kong** to KK (3 weekly; $940). Finally, from Tarakan in **Kalimantan**, there are *Bouraq* (3 weekly; $185) and *MAS* (2 weekly; $210) flights to Tawau.

Daily **boats** from **Brunei** (p.459), and from **Lawas** (p.384) and **Limbang** (p.383), in northern Sarawak, run to Pulau Labuan (p.424), from where there are regular connec-tions with KK. Also, there's a ferry from northeastern **Kalimantan** to Tawau (see p.449) once or twice a week. The only **overland route** into Sabah is from Lawas from where several buses daily make the short run to the border at Merapok; see p.384 for more.

hunter-gatherers would have been generally unaware. In 1521, Europe's superpowers first arrived, when the ships of the Portuguese navigator Ferdinand Magellan stopped off at Brunei and later sailed northwards. But it was to be almost 250 years before any significant development occurred, when – in 1763 – one Captain Cowley established a short-lived trading post on Pulau Balambangan, north of Kudat, on behalf of the British East India Company. Further British involvement came in 1846, when Pulau Labuan (at the mouth of Brunei Bay) was ceded to them by the Sultan of Brunei and in 1878 the Austrian, **Baron von Overbeck** – with the financial backing of British businessman Alfred Dent – agreed to pay the Sultan an annuity of $15,000 to cede northern Borneo to him. Shortly afterwards a further annual payment of $5,000 was negotiated with the Sultan of Sulu, who also laid claim to the region. Von Overbeck hastened to England to finalize matters and in 1881 the **British North Borneo Chartered Company** was registered, with full sovereignty over northern Borneo. Shortly afterwards, von Overbeck sold his shares to Dent.

With the company up and running, the first steps were taken towards making it pay its way: rubber, tobacco and, after 1885, timber, were commercially harvested, and an early map of the territory details a telegraph line all the way from the Klias Peninsula (opposite British-held Labuan) to the new capital, Sandakan. By 1905 a **railway** linked Jesselton on the coast (later called Kota Kinabalu) with the resource-rich interior. When the Company introduced taxes the locals were understandably ill-pleased and native resistance followed – most notably that of **Mat Salleh**, the son of a Bajau chief, whose followers sacked the company's settlement on Pulau Gaya in 1897. Another uprising, in **Rundum** in 1915, resulted in the slaughter of hundreds of Murut tribes people by British forces.

No other major disturbances troubled the *Chartered Company* until New Year's Day, 1942, when the Japanese Imperial forces invaded Pulau Labuan. Less than three weeks

Getting around

Unless you rent your own transport in KK (see p.416), you'll rely almost exclusively upon **buses, minibuses** and **landcruisers** for getting around. The state's roads have been much improved in recent years and a sealed U-shaped road now stretches from Beaufort around to Tawau, from where logging roads complete the loop. Whether a decent road will ever be laid along this last stretch is anyone's guess – a proposed extension was under consideration at the turn of the century, when it showed up on an early map of the state. Minibuses are by far the most common form of public transport, following both local and long-distance routes, always at breakneck speed. Roomier, though much slower, are full-sized buses, which operate locally in Kota Kinabalu, Sandakan and Tawau, as well as making scheduled, early morning trips across the state. Outsize jeeps, called land cruisers, are fastest of all, though these are correspondingly more expensive. Sabah is also criss-crossed by a good **plane** network, with daily flights between Kota Kinabalu, Sandakan and Tawau. There's no equivalent in Sabah to Sarawak's *express boats*, and you'll have to rent your own **boat** if you're intent on a river trip – usually a substantial outlay.

Accommodation

Accommodation in Sabah generally means locally run Chinese hotels, ranging from seedy lodging houses that double as brothels to charming mid-range establishments. **Hostels** catering specifically for budget travellers are few and far between – only in Kota Kinabalu, Sandakan and Mount Kinabalu Park are dormitory beds available. There's less of a **longhouse** scene in Sabah than there is in Sarawak, though it's quite feasible to stay overnight in one of the longhouses around Sapulut, or the Kudat Peninsula. If you do, the etiquette is the same as in Sarawak – see p.353 for all the details.

later Sandakan fell and over two years of occupation followed, before the Japanese surrendered on September 9, 1945. The years of **World War II** were devastating ones for Sabah: occupied by the Japanese, it soon found itself bombed by Allied forces eager to neutralize its harbours. By the time of the Japanese surrender, next to nothing of Jesselton and Sandakan remained standing. Even worse were the hardships that the captured Allied troops and civilians endured – culminating in the Death March of September 1944, when 2400 POWs made a forced march from Sandakan to Ranau. Only six men, all Australians, survived.

Unable to finance the rebuilding of North Borneo, the *Chartered Company* sold the territory in 1946 to the British Crown and Jesselton was declared the new capital of the **Crown Colony of North Borneo**. However, within fifteen years, plans had been laid for a federation consisting of Malaya, Singapore, Sarawak, North Borneo and Brunei. Although Brunei pulled out at the last minute, the **Federation** was still declared and at midnight on September 15, 1963, colonial rule ended in North Borneo – which was quickly renamed Sabah. Objecting to the inclusion of Sarawak and Sabah in the Federation, Indonesia's president Sukarno initiated his anti-Malaysian *konfrontasi* policy and sporadic skirmishes broke out along the Sabah-Kalimantan border for the next three years.

In 1967, Jesselton was renamed Kota Kinabalu; the decade that followed saw Sabah's **timber industry** reach its destructive peak. More recently, there have been moves to establish a secondary industry in timber processing, a move that gained in urgency when the Federal Government limited the state's exporting of logs in 1991. Indeed, relations with Kuala Lumpur have been strained since the mid-1980s. Sabah towed the *UNMO* party line until 1985, but then the *Parti Bersatu Sabah* (*PBS*), led by the Christian **Joseph Pairin Kitingan**, was returned to office – the first time a non-Muslim had attained power in Malaysia. Subsequently, Sabahans have complained of minimal funding of their state's infrastructure – resulting, they say, in a corresponding loss of foreign investment – and of blatant pro-Muslim propaganda, which has run as far as offering Christians cash incentives to convert to Islam. Anti-federal feelings are worsened by the fact that 95 percent of the profits from Sabah's flourishing crude petroleum exporting industry are syphoned into KL. More recently, Pairin himself was charged with corruption, accused of awarding a lucrative contract to a relative, with many Sabahans interpreting the charge as an attempt to discredit his Christian government. Whatever the truth, early 1994's **state elections** saw Pairin and the *PBS* retain power, only to yield it to the *Barisan Nasional* just weeks later, when first three, and then many more of his assemblymen defected to the opposition – a defection that left many in KK suspicious of corruption, though so far without proof. Sabah's new chief minister is Tan Sri Sakaran Dandai; Pairin's case remains unconcluded.

Kota Kinabalu and around

Since 1946, Sabah's seat of government has been based at **KOTA KINABALU**, halfway up the state's western seaboard. KK (as it's universally known) certainly isn't one of the world's magical cities – World War II bombing all but robbed it of charismatic buildings, and first impressions are of a grim concrete sprawl – but the friendliness of its citizens and its proximity to a clutch of idyllic islands still conspire to charm visitors; which is lucky, since you'll be hard-pressed to avoid KK on a trip to Sabah.

The telephone code for KK is ☎088.

Modern-day Kota Kinabalu can trace its history back to 1882, the year the *British North Borneo Chartered Company* first established an outpost on nearby **Pulau Gaya**. This was burned down by followers of the Bajau rebel, Mat Salleh, in 1897. The mainland site chosen by the Company for a new town was known to locals as *Api Api*, or "Fire, Fire": one explanation is that the name referred to the firing of the original settlement; another, that it reflected the abundance of fireflies inhabiting its swamps. Renamed **Jesselton**, after Sir Charles Jessel, the vice-chairman of the *Chartered Company*, the town prospered and by 1905, the Trans-Borneo Railway (see p.423) reached from Jesselton to Beaufort, meaning that for the first time rubber could be shuttled efficiently from the interior to the coast.

The Japanese invasion of North Borneo in 1942 marked the start of three and a half years of **military occupation**: of old Jesselton, only the Atkinson Clock Tower and the post office (today's tourist office) survived the resulting Allied bombing. However, progress since the war has been startling and today, with a population approaching 200,000, Kota Kinabalu (the name, meaning simply Kinabalu City, was coined after Malaysian *merdeka* in 1963) is a thriving seaport once more.

Most of downtown KK has been reclaimed from the sea during the past century – so ruthlessly in some places that pockets of stilt houses have been left stranded in land-bound lakes. On the resulting new patches of land, large complexes of interconnecting concrete buildings – the Sinsuran and Segama complexes are two – have been constructed, their ground floors taken up by shops, restaurants and businesses, the upper floors turned into apartments. The city has a limited number of sights, best of which are its **markets** and the **State Museum**, while south of the centre a series of *kampungs* provide a glimpse into the region's relatively recent tribal past. But KK's highlight is, without doubt, offshore **Tunku Abdul Rahman Park**, whose five unspoilt islands (including Pulau Gaya, site of the first British settlement) are just ten minutes by speedboat from the city centre.

Arrival, information and getting around

KK's **airport** is 6km and fifteen minutes south of the centre. Six yellow-and-red buses a day travel from the airport into town (first bus 6.30am, last bus 5.30pm; 65 *sen*), stopping opposite the GPO on jalan Tun Razak. Otherwise, walk out to the main road and catch a minibus ($1.50) into town; or take a taxi, for which you buy a $10 coupon in the arrival hall and present it to the next car in line outside.

Trains from Tenom and Beaufort pull in close to the airport at **Tanjung Aru Station**, which is beside jalan Kepayan, the main road to points south of KK, so you'll have no trouble catching a bus heading into town. **Long-distance buses** from Sandakan and elsewhere congregate on the open land east of jalan Padang, from where it's no more than a five-minute walk to any of KK's central hotels. **Ferries** to and from Labuan dock in front of the *Hyatt Hotel*, on jalan Tun Fuad Stephens. For all **departure information**, see "Leaving KK" below.

Information

At the **Sabah Tourism Promotion Corporation** (*STPC*; Mon–Fri 8am–4.15pm, Sat 8am–12.45pm; ☎218620), in the old GPO at 51 jalan Gaya, the staff are friendly and will inform you of any forthcoming events. While you're here, pick up a free **map** of the city – the best one available. **Tourism Malaysia** (Mon-Fri 8am–12.45pm & 2–4.15pm, Sat 8am–12.45pm; ☎211732), across jalan Gaya in the Wing On Life Building, can answer questions about Peninsular Malaysia or Sarawak.

If you're travelling to Mount Kinabalu and Poring (see p.429), you need to go to the **Sabah Parks** office (Mon–Fri 8.30am–4pm, Sat 8.30am–noon; ☎211881), in Block K of

LEAVING KK

See "Listings", p.415, for details of airline offices, tour operators and the Indonesian consulate in KK.

Airport
From KK's **airport** there are regular connections with the mainland, Singapore, Manila, Brunei and Hong Kong. Six buses a day run from oposite the GPO (first bus 6.30am; 65 *sen*); otherwise take a Putatan- or Petagas-bound minibus from the terminal on jalan Tun Fuad Stephens and tell the driver your destination – he might charge an extra $1 for the detour.

Buses
Long-distance buses for points north, south and east of KK leave from the open land east of jalan Padang. Apart from a number of very early morning buses to Sandakan and one to Kudat, buses leave when full; turn up by 7am to ensure a seat. This terminus is also the departure point for the daily *Lawas Express* (1.30pm) to Lawas in Sarawak.

Trains
Although there is a rail link from KK to Beaufort, the bus gets you there in half the time. The stretch of line between Beaufort and Tenom (see p.422) is the best part of the Sabahan train system. Call ☎52536 for up-to-date timetable information.

Ferries
There are three services to Pulau Labuan (see p.424). The *Labuan Express II* departs from KK at 8am, returning at 1pm; while the *Duta Muhibbah II* makes the same journey at 1.30pm returning at 8.30am, – one-way tickets cost $28 second-class and $33 first-class. The *Express Kinabulu* ($15) leaves for Labuan at 10am, returning at 3pm. All tickets are sold at the jetty and it's worth booking ahead if you plan to travel at the weekend or over a holiday.

---

the Sinsuran Complex, jalan Tun Fuad Stephens, to book your accommodation; this is also the place to come to arrange accommodation in Tunku Abdul Rahman (see below) and Pulau Tiga (p.424) parks. For reservations at the Danum Valley Conservation Area (p.446), drop by the offices of the **Innoprise Corporation**, 1km southwest of the centre in Block D, Sadong Jaya Complex (Mon–Fri 8am–12.45pm & 2–4.15pm, Sat 8am–12.45pm; ☎243245), where reservations can be made. Finally, enquiries for the *Batu Punggul Resort* (see p.420) can be made at *Korporasi Pembangunan Desa*, 9 Tuaran Road (☎428910 ext. 234).

What's on information is in short supply in KK, though you'll find details of cultural events in any of Sabah's English-language newspapers – the *Borneo Mail*, *Sabah Times* and *Daily Express*. Otherwise, the **notice boards** at the *Travellers' Rest Hostel* and *Jack's B&B* (see below) are valuable sources of information.

City transport
The city centre is compact enough to traverse **on foot** in fifteen minutes; even the museum is only a further twenty minutes' hike southwest of town, though you'll probably want to take a bus or taxi. **Taxis** crop up all over the city and are inexpensive provided you agree a price before setting off. It'll cost no more than $4 to travel right across the city centre; you'll find taxi ranks outside the *Hyatt Hotel* on jalan Datuk Salleh Sulong, at the GPO on jalan Tun Razak, and at Centrepoint shopping centre on lebuh Raya Pantai Baru. See "Listings" for taxi booking numbers.

Taking a **bus** is more complicated, since until the planned terminal materializes, there's no central station in KK, just one patch of land for minibuses and another for

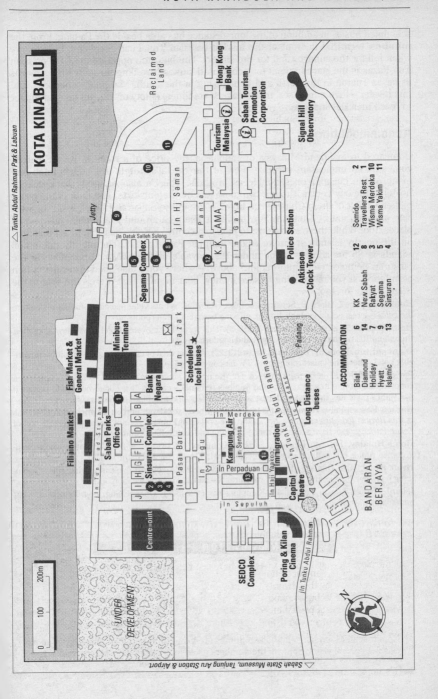

△ Tunku Abdul Rahman Park & Labuan

KOTA KINABALU

Reclaimed Land

Hong Kong Bank

Sabah Tourism Promotion Corporation

Tourism Malaysia ⓘ

ⓘ

Signal Hill Observatory

Jetty

jln Datuk Salleh Sulong

Segama Complex

jln Hj Saman

jln Pantai

K.K.

jln Gaya

Police Station

Atkinson Clock Tower

Filipino Market

Fish Market & General Market

Minibus Terminal

Scheduled local buses

jln Tun Razak

jln Tun Fad Stephens

Sabah Parks Office

Sinsuran Complex

Bank Negara

jln Pasar Baru

jln Merdeka

Kampung Air

jln Sentosa

jln Tegu

Immigration

jln Perpaduan

jln Haji Yaakob

jln Sepuluh

Capitol Theatre

jln Tunku Abdul Rahman

jln Pasar

Padang

Long Distance buses

BANDARAN BERJAYA

Centre-oint

UNDER DEVELOPMENT

SEDCO Complex

Poring & Kilan Cinema

jln Tunku Abdul Rahman

0   100   200m

N

△ Sabah State Museum, Tanjung Aru Station & Airport

ACCOMMODATION

Bilal	6	KK	2
Diamond	14	New Sabah	1
Holiday	7	Rakyat	10
Hyatt	9	Segama	11
Islamic	13	Sinsuran	
		Somido	
		Travellers Rest	12
		Wisma Merdeka	8
		Wisma Yakim	3
			5
			4

scheduled buses, in addition to the long-distance bus area beside the Padang. From the **minibus terminal** in front of the market on jalan Tun Fuad Stephens, buses leave when full for the suburbs and for the airport. The bus stop opposite the GPO on jalan Tun Razak is the starting point for **scheduled buses** travelling through KK's suburbs as far as Tuaran in the north and Penampang in the south. Marginally cheaper – and much safer – than minibuses, these leave at set times, empty or full, but take far longer to reach their destinations.

Accommodation

Compared to mainland Malaysia or Indonesia, the price of a room in Kota Kinabalu comes as an unpleasant surprise. Few of the capital's **hotels** are budget-rated and many of the cheaper ones double as brothels. There's also only one backpackers' hostel in the city centre, though two more just on the outskirts. The bulk of the possibilities – most of them Chinese-run hotels – are in the Sinsuran Complex, on the west side of town, and in Kampung Air, beside it; the area around jalan Pantai has several places, too. While there's nowhere to **camp** in central KK, it's possible to set up a tent on the nearby islands in Tunku Abdul Rahman Park (p.412). The nightly rate on all islands is $5 for adults, $2 for under-18s, payable at the *Sabah Parks* office in the Sinsuran Complex (see "Information" above) – where you'll also need to secure written permission. If you're camping to save money, bear in mind that there's the boat to the island to pay for, too.

Hotel Bilal, Lot 1, Block B, Segama Complex (☎56709). Set above an excellent Indian restaurant, the *Bilal* is a respectable establishment, offering basic but clean rooms. ②.

Hotel Capital, 23 jalan Haji Saman (☎231999). This recently renovated hotel boasts few amenities, though its 102 rooms are spacious, light and comfortable. ⑤.

Diamond Inn, Block 37, Kampung Air (☎213222). A great deal of effort has gone into this comfortable hotel, where the smart rooms have TV, air-con and fridge. ④.

Farida's B&B, 413 jalan Saga, Mile 4 1/2, Kampung Likas (☎428733). A delightful family-run concern, fifteen minutes away from the minibus terminal – catch a "Kg Likas" bus – and perfect if you want a quiet life. Rooms and dorms are wonderfully airy, and fitted out in varnished wood. ②.

Gayana Resort, Pulau Gaya (☎223034). Dormitory beds at $40 per person, or pricey double rooms at this *Borneo Expeditions*-run resort, in the one corner of Pulau Gaya not under the jurisdiction of *Sabah Parks*; guests have access to canoes, fishing and snorkelling equipment. ⑤.

Hotel Holiday, Lot 1/2, Block F, Segama Complex (☎213116). A friendly hotel, whose well-groomed rooms err on the pricey side, despite their TV, air-con and bathroom. ④.

Hyatt Hotel, jalan Datuk Salleh Sulong (☎221234). All the comforts you might imagine – swimming pool, business centre, choice of restaurants – and at a central location. ⑥.

Islamic Hotel, 8 jalan Perpaduan, Kampung Air (☎254325). Unappealing, no-frills option – but undeniably inexpensive. ②.

ACCOMMODATION PRICE CODES

All the places to stay listed in this book have been given one of the following price codes; for more details, see p.40

① Under $20	④ $61–100
② $21–40	⑤ $101–200
③ $41–60	⑥ $201 and above

Note that all Malaysian telephone numbers are being **changed** in a rolling programme lasting several years. Some of the numbers given in this chapter, while correct at the time of going to press, are likely to have changed.

Jack's B&B, no. 17, Block B, jalan Karamunsing (☎232367). One kilometre southwest of the mini-bus terminus, *Jack's* is as spotless and as friendly a place as you could want, its dorms fitted with air-con and fan; recommended. ②.

KK Hotel, 46 jalan Pantai (☎213888). The most affordable of several hotels on and around jalan Pantai with spick-and-span tiled rooms; shared bathrooms are kept scrupulously clean. ②.

Hotel New Sabah, Lot 3/4, Block A, Segama Complex (☎224590). Ordinary hotel, slightly tattier than the *Holiday*, whose tiled rooms (all with attached bathroom) are functional but soulless. ③.

Pulau Mamutik Rest House, Pulau Mamutik (arrange through *Sabah Parks* office; see "Information" above). This beachside rest house, sleeping eight people, costs 33 percent more at the weekend; no restaurant, but there are cooking facilities ⑤–⑥.

Pulau Manukan Chalets, Pulau Manukan (also through *Sabah Parks*). Twenty attractive chalets – each has two double rooms and is let as a unit – are located on or overlooking an idyllic beach, and have use of a restaurant and swimming pool; prices increase by a third at the weekend. ④.

Hotel Rakyat, Lot 3, Block I, Sinsuran Complex (☎211100). The nine pleasant rooms offer a modi-cum of comfort; a few extra dollars secure you a private bathroom. ③.

Hotel Segama, Lot 1, Block D, Segama Complex (☎221327). Tolerable at the price, though its rooms are dark, box-like and tawdry – a last resort. ②.

Shangri-La Tanjung Aru Resort, Tanjung Aru Beach (☎088/225800). Superior hotel with two pools, several restaurants, a fine beachside setting – and prices to match. ⑥.

Sinsuran Inn, Lot 1, Block I, Sinsuran Complex (☎088/211158; ③). Though undecorated, the rooms are capacious and clean, and have TV, bathroom and air-con.

Hotel Somido, Lot 8, Block I, Sinsuran Complex (☎211946). Not a very distinguished place, though another budget choice, and clean enough. ②.

Travellers' Rest Hostel, Lot 5/6, Block L, Sinsuran Complex (☎240625). KK's original guest house, and still the city's best budget choice: dorms and rooms are simple but very clean (prices include breakfast), the owners are friendly and helpful, and there's an informative notice board, which includes details of the hostel's own tours. Recommended. ②.

The city

Downtown KK was almost totally obliterated by World War II bombs and only in the northeastern corner of the city centre – an area known as **KK Lama**, or old KK – are there even the faintest remains of its colonial past. KK Lama is bordered by **jalan Pantai** (Beach Road), formerly the waterfront, and **jalan Gaya**, where the attractive old General Post Office building houses the *STPC*. A lively **street market** is held along jalan Gaya every Sunday morning, with stalls selling herbal teas, handicrafts, orchids and rabbits, and streetside coffee shops doing a roaring trade in *dim sum* and noodles.

A block east, under the shadow of Bukit Bendera (Signal Hill), stands the now-incongruous **Atkinson Clock Tower**, a quaint wooden landmark built in 1905 in memory of a district officer in the *Chartered Company*. From here, you may as well take the fifteen-minute walk up to breezy **Signal Hill Observatory**, which provides a good overview of KK's matrix of dreary buildings and of the infinitely more attractive bay. Early photographs of the city show colonial officers playing cricket on the **Padang**, which you'll pass on your way to the observatory.

It's a five-minute stroll from the Padang across town to KK's waterfront markets, the most diverting of which is the **Filipino Market**, opposite blocks K and M of the Sinsuran Complex. Its numerous stalls are run by Filipino immigrants, who stock Sabahan ethnic wares beside their Filipino baskets, shells and trinkets. Next door is the dark and labyrinthine **general market** and, behind that, the manic waterfront **fish market** – worth investigating if you can stomach the vile stench.

To the Sabah State Museum
Head southwest along jalan Tunku Abdul Rahman, past the pyramidal Catholic **Sacred Heart Cathedral** and – slightly further on – the **Sabah State Mosque**, whose eye-catching dome sits, like a Fabergé egg, on top of the main body of the complex.

After twenty minutes you reach the **Sabah State Museum** (Mon–Thurs 10am–6pm, Sat & Sun 9am–6pm; free), KK's most rewarding diversion, its buildings styled on Murut and Rungus longhouses and set in exotic grounds that are home to several splendid steam engines. Its highlight is its ethnographic collection which features a *bangkaran*, or cluster of human skulls, dating from Sabah's head-hunting days; and a *sininggazanak*, a totemic wooden figurine which would have been placed in the field of a Kadazan man who had died leaving no heirs. Photographs in the history gallery trace the development of Kota Kinabalu and include fascinating old snaps of *Chartered Company* elders and Sabahan natives, while beyond, in the Merdeka Gallery, contemporary newspaper cuttings trace the story of Malaysia's path to independence. Of rather less interest is the tired collection of stuffed animals in the natural history section, while only a fine old wooden coffin from Batu Putih (see p.444) stands out among the clay shards of the archaeology gallery. If you can't face the walk from the centre, take a bus from opposite the GPO.

The **Science Centre** (same hours; free), next door to the museum, houses a less than gripping exhibition on oil-drilling, so head upstairs to the **Art Gallery** (Mon–Thur 10am–4.30pm, Sat–Sun 9.30am–5pm; free) instead. Many of the works on display are unadventurous, postcard images of Sabah, though there are exceptions – most notably the impressionistic paintings of Suzie Majikol and a dreamlike work in oil, by Nazric Said, of four women dancing.

Fronting the museum is an **Ethnobotanic Garden** (daily 6am–6pm), whose huge range of tropical plants is best experienced on one of the free guided tours (9am & 2pm except Fri). Exquisitely crafted, traditional houses representing all Sabah's major tribes border the garden; while back in the museum is a souvenir shop with a great selection of literature.

Tanjung Aru

Past the museum, jalan Tunku Abdul Rahman continues on for another 2.5 km (becoming jalan Mat Salleh), to the beach at **Tanjung Aru**, site of the swanky *Shangri-La Resort*. The beach itself is reasonable – long and fairly narrow, and serviced by several food and drink stalls – but with so many beautiful islands just off the coast, there's no great incentive to visit. To reach Tanjung Aru direct from the centre, take a bus from opposite the GPO.

Tunku Abdul Rahman Park

Named after Malaysia's first Prime Minister, and situated just a stone's throw from central Kota Kinabalu, the five islands of **TUNKU ABDUL RAHMAN PARK** were gazetted as a national park in 1974, since when their forests, beaches and coral reefs have been the salvation of tourists stuck in the capital. All five islands lie within an eight-kilometre radius of downtown KK, with park territory just 3km off the mainland at its closest point, but unless you've got your own boat, or you're prepared to charter one for the whole day, you'll have to opt for just one island at a time.

The islands

Largest of the park's islands – and the site of the British *North Borneo Chartered Company*'s first outpost in the region – is **PULAU GAYA**, whose name is derived from *goyoh*, the Bajau word for "big". Today, a large stilt village housing thousands of KK's Filipino immigrants squats off its east coast. Although a native chief granted the island's timber rights to a certain Mr White in 1879, they were never fully exploited and lowland rainforest still blankets Gaya, best viewed by following the twenty-kilometre system of trails that snakes across it. Most of these trails start on the southern side of the island at **Camp Bay**, which is adjacent to a mangrove forest whose crabs and mudskippers can be viewed from the boardwalk that intersects it. While Camp Bay offers pleasant enough swimming, a more secluded and alluring alternative is **Police Beach**, on the north coast. Boatmen demand extra money for circling round to this side of Gaya, but it's money well spent: the bay is idyllic, its dazzling white sand running gently down to the water, lined by trees. Wildlife on Gaya includes hornbills, wild pigs, lizards, snakes and macaques – which have been known to swim over to nearby **PULAU SAPI** (Cow Island), a 25-acre islet off the northwestern coast of Gaya that's popular with swimmers, snorkellers and picnickers. Though far smaller than Gaya, Sapi too is ringed by trails and home to macaques and hornbills. Parts of the island have recently been in a filthy state – if you see any litter, you should report it to the *Sabah Parks* office.

The part's three other islands cluster together 2.5km west of Gaya. The park headquarters is situated on crescent-shaped **PULAU MANUKAN** – site of a former stone quarry and now the most developed of all the park's islands – though you'll have no cause to visit it, since all the literature available can be picked up at KK's *Sabah Parks* office. Manukan's fine beaches and coral have led to the construction of chalets, a restaurant, swimming pool, tennis and squash courts, which draw large numbers of locals at times. Across a narrow channel from Manukan is tiny **PULAU MAMUTIK**, which can be crossed on foot in fifteen minutes and has excellent sands either side of its jetty. **PULAU SULUG** is the most remote of the islands and consequently the quietest. Its good coral makes it popular with divers and on its eastern side is a long sand spit that ends in a sharp drop-off.

Practicalities

The assembly of **speedboats** that gathers daily behind KK's *Hyatt Hotel* on Jalan Tun Fuad Stephens makes getting to the islands easy, though the boatmen like to try their luck, so be prepared for some intensive haggling. Boats won't leave for less than $30–40, but if you're in a group, you shouldn't pay more than $10–12 per person for a return journey. Once you've arrived at your chosen island, don't forget to arrange a pick-up time; it's also wise to pay only when you're safely back in KK – there have been reports of tourists being left on islands overnight. Otherwise, *Coral Island Cruises* (☎223490) runs a **ferry service** to the islands (Mon–Fri at 10am, returning 3pm; Sat & Sun at 9am, 10am & 11am, returning 2pm & 4pm; $16 return, except Police Beach $24), departing from behind the *Hyatt*. If you don't have **snorkelling gear** with you, the boatmen will rent you some ($5 a day), but try it out before they speed back to KK.

The $2 **entry fee** presently charged on landing at Sapi, Manukan and Mamutik will in time apply to all the islands. All **accommodation** in the park – island camping, the *Manukan Chalets* or the *Mamutik Rest House* – must be booked through the *Sabah Parks* office (see KK's "Accommodation" and "Information" sections above, for details), except the *Gayana Resort*, on the northeastern side of Gaya, which lies in the one patch of the island outside the park perimeters. There's a **restaurant** serving the chalets on Manukan, but otherwise nowhere to eat, so take a picnic.

South of the city

Regular minibuses from Jalan Tun Fuad Stephens leave the city for the suburb of Donggongon, around 10km to the south. From the bus station here, it's only a ten-minute local bus ride past rice fields and winding streams to **KAMPUNG MONSOPIAD**, where 39 of the 42 skulls cleaved by legendary Kadazan warrior, Monsopiad, hang from a rafter in his ancestral house – tell the bus driver you want the "skull house". The present owners will happily let you into their living room to see the grisly display and recount the legends that have been passed down about Monsopiad. Among the skulls, displayed in a row like a coconut shy, and decked with *hisad* (palm) leaves signifying the victims' hair, a lone thigh bone testifies to one such story. Visiting a neighbouring village for a large feast, Monsopiad ended up in a dancing competition with a relative of his, called Gantang. When this ended unresolved, they had a drinking competition, before finally beginning to fight. His head fuzzy from the rice wine, Monsopiad forgot himself and resorted unfairly to using a bamboo spear, instead of his sword, to kill Gantang, whose thigh bone – rather than his head – was awarded to Monsopiad to remind him of his moment of dishonour. Monsopiad eventually grew too fond of harvesting heads and constituted a public menace; killed by a group of friends, he was buried beneath a stone that still stands near the house, with his own head left intact out of respect. Once a year (usually in May), a Kadazan priestess is called in to communicate with the skulls' spirits, whose job it is to watch over Monsopiad's descendants.

Once you're out in Donggongon, you might as well take the opportunity to see Sabah's oldest church, **St Michael's Catholic Church**, only a twenty-minute walk (or short bus ride) beyond the bus terminus and along the main road. Built in 1897, the sturdy granite building stands on a hillock above peaceful Kampung Dabak, its red roof topped by a simple stone cross; inside, the church is undecorated, save a mural depicting the Last Supper and framed paintings of the Stations of the Cross.

Further south: Kinarut to Papar

Further down the main road south, KK's suburbs yield to a carpet of paddy fields that stretches away to the foothills of the Crocker Mountain Range. From the minibus terminal, there are frequent departures on to the village of **KINARUT**, 21km away, the starting point for an enjoyable half-hour stroll along a quiet road to **KAMPUNG TAMPASAK**, where there's a replica of the *sininggazanak* in the State Museum (see above). From the two faded old shophouses that form the centre of Kinarut, walk across the rail track, cross the bridge to your left and turn right – the turning to the *kampung* is signposted by an overgrown tyre. On your way, you'll see two or three mysterious *menhirs*, or upright stones, thought to have been erected centuries ago either as status symbols or boundary stones, or to mark the burial places of shamans.

Two or three kilometres away at **KINARUT LAUT** (take a Papar minibus from KK), the *Seaside Travellers' Inn* (☎088/750313; ②–③) is a popular retreat for KK weekenders, its dorms and rooms a little overpriced but otherwise hard to fault; a balcony off the dining room looks out to the nearby islands of Dinawan and Muntukat, and over the inn's own unspectacular stretch of beach. The *Kinarut Riding School*, 1km back towards KK, offers **horseback** trips through the surrounding countryside (90min for $50) – call Dale Sinidol on ☎088/225525.

The one town of any size between KK and Beaufort (see p.422), **PAPAR**, is another 20km or so further south; buses run here all through the day from KK's minibus terminal. Unless you're here on Sunday for the decent weekly *tamu*, the only reason to break your journey is to visit the nearby beach – **Pantai Manis** – reached by minibus ($1) from the centre of Papar's old shophouses.

Eating, drinking and nightlife

Finding somewhere to eat in KK causes no headaches, with Malay, Chinese and Indian **restaurants** catering for all pockets in abundant supply; and a good selection of central **hawker stalls**. Problems arise, though, if you want to sample Sabahan cuisine: while the indigenous peoples all have their own dishes, their total absence from the menus of KK is a big disappointment. Note that quite a few restaurants are closed by mid evening, so be prepared for an early dinner; specific opening hours (daily unless otherwise stated) are given below. Opening hours for Hawker stalls listed below are usually daily 6–11pm; the exception is the central market, whose stalls operate daily from 9am–6pm.

KK only has a handful of **bars** and **clubs**, and they're not up to much. Best of the bunch is *Rocky Fun Pub & Café*, Lot 52, jalan Gaya (open until 2am), a good-time bar favoured by expats, and featuring a karaoke area, dance floor, and café. Otherwise, try the glitzy *Tiffiny Discotheatre*, Block A, jalan Karamunsing (open until 2am, Sat until 3am), where live bands appear nightly, and a Happy Hour runs from 8.30 to 9.30pm; there's a cover charge of $12–15 depending on the night.

Hawker stalls

Central Market, jalan Tun Fuad Stephens. The handful of *nasi campur* stalls on the upper floor provide filling, good-value meals.

Night Market, behind the Filipino Market, jalan Tun Fuad Stephens. Fried chicken and barbeque fish are the specialities here.

SEDCO Square, Kampung Air. Restaurant-lined square, whose scores of outdoor tables are a fine place for barbecued meat and fish.

Tanjung Aru Beach. Busiest and best at the weekend, when large numbers of locals come for satay and barbecued seafood.

Cafés and restaurants

Restoran Bilal, Block B, Segama Complex. A classic North Indian Muslim eating house, with a buffet-style range of tasty and inexpensive curries. Open 6am–9pm.

Restoran Haj Anuar, Block H, Sinsuran Complex. Cosy, open-fronted place opposite the *Sinsuran Inn*, with a Malay menu including *soto*, *nasi lemak* and *nasi campur*. Open 7am–7pm.

Houng Kee Seafood Restaurant, 5 Mosque Valley, jalan Padang. The garden fronting this charming restaurant makes it an appealing place to relax over a meal. House speciality is steamed fish; two people can feast for $40. Open 7am–10.30pm.

Nan Xing Restaurant, 33–35 jalan Haji Saman. A decent Cantonese menu that includes a range of *dim sum* as well as steaks and chops. Open noon–2.30pm & 6–9pm.

New Fortune Eating House, Block 36, jalan Laiman Diki, Kampung Air. A busy place housing several stalls, the best of which serves superb *dim sum* at breakfast and later. Open 6am–7pm.

Phoenix Court Restaurant, *Hyatt Hotel*, jalan Datuk Salleh Sulong (☎221234). Superior Cantonese and Szechuan food, and elegant surroundings. Expect to pay $30–40 a head, and reserve in advance. Open 11am–2pm & 7–11pm.

Port View Restaurant, jalan Haji Saman. Lively at night, when the roadside tables fill up with locals choosing from a wide range of (live) seafood. Open 6pm–2am, Sat until 3am.

Restoran Sri Rahmat, Lot 7, Block D Segama Complex. A basic Malay restaurant – though with an air-con room – that's worth frequenting for the delicious *laksa* alone. Open Mon–Sat 7am–9pm, Sun 7am–5pm.

Shiraz Restaurant, Lot 5, Block B, SEDCO Complex. Sabah's finest Indian restaurant, serving huge portions of Mughlai food. The chicken biyriani is especially good; around $12 a head. Open 11am–2.30pm & 5.30–10pm.

Sri Melaka, 9 jalan Laiman Diki, Kampung Air. A popular establishment that's great for Malay and Nonya food; try the excellent *assam fishhead* (the $8 portion feeds two). Open 8.30am–9.30pm.

Sri Pama Vilas Restoran, jalan 4 no. 33, Bandaran Berjaya. The banana-leaf meal in this no-frills, south Indian restaurant, is a mountainous, all-you-can-eat feast ($3.50 for vegetarian, $6 for meat), served by really friendly staff. Open 6.30am–2am.

Listings

Airlines *Dragon Air*, ground floor, Block C, Kompleks Kuwasa, jalan Karamunsing (☎54733); *MAS*, Kompleks Karamunsing, jalan Tuaran (☎213555); *Philippine Air*, Kompleks Karamunsing, jalan Tuaran (☎239600); *Royal Brunei*, ground floor, Kompleks Kuwasa, jalan Karamunsing (☎242193); *Singapore Airlines*, ground floor, Block C, Kompleks Kuwasa, jalan Karamunsing (☎55444); *Thai Airways*, ground floor, Block C, Kompleks Kuwasa, jalan Karamunsing (☎232896).

American Express Lot 3.50 & 3.51, 3rd floor, Kompleks Karamunsing (Mon–Fri 8.30am–5.30pm; ☎241200).

Banks and exchange *Hong Kong & Shanghai Bank*, 56 jalan Gaya; *Sabah Bank*, Block K, Sinsuran Complex; *Standard Chartered Bank*, 20 jalan Hj Saman. Moneychangers (Mon–Sat 10am–7pm) in Wisma Merdeka include *Ban Loong Money Changer* and *Travellers' Money Changer*, both on the ground floor; there's also an office in the *Taiping Goldsmith*, Block A, Sinsuran Complex.

Bookshops *Arena Book Centre* (Block L, Sinsuran Complex), *Iwase Bookshop* (Wisma Merdeka), and the *Yaohan* book store (2nd floor, Centre Point), all have a few shelves of English-language novels. For an unparalleled array of books on Southeast Asia, head for *Borneo Crafts* (Wisma Merdeka), or to their branch at the Sabah State Museum; the *Hyatt*'s *Rahmat* bookshop stocks a modest range of international newspapers and magazines.

Car rental *Ais Rent-A-Car*, Lot 1, Block A, Sinsuran Complex (☎238954); *Kinabalu Rent-A-Car*, Lot 3.60, 3rd floor, Kompleks Karamunsing (☎232602), and at the *Hyatt Hotel*; *Sabah Holiday Rent-A-Car*, Lot 20, Wisma Sabah, jalan Tun Razak (☎245106). Rates start from around $150 per day, though four-wheel drives (from $250) are advisable if you plan to get off the beaten track.

Cinemas The *Poring and Kilan Cinema*, and the *Capitol Theatre*, below the SEDCO Centre at the western edge of downtown KK, both have regular screenings of English-language movies. Proramme listings are in the *Borneo Mail* or *Sabah Times*.

Consulates The nearest consular representation for most nationalities is in KL; see p.109.

Danum Valley Reservations for the Danum Valley Conservation Area (see p.446) can be made at the *Innoprise Corporation*, Block D, Kompleks Sadong Jaya (☎243245).

Hospital *Queen Elizabeth Hospital* is beyond the Sabah State Museum, on jalan Penampang (☎218166). In an emergency, dial ☎999.

Immigration Office 4th floor, Wisma Dang Bandang, jalan Hj Yaakob (Mon–Fri 8am–12.30pm & 2–4.15pm, Sat 8am–12.45pm; ☎216711). Visa extensions up to a month are available and cost $2.

Indonesian Immigration The *Konsulat Jenderal Indonesia*, jalan Kemajuan (☎218600), issues one-month visas for Kalimantan.

Laundry *Bright Laundry*, Wisma Merdeka; *Daily Clean Laundry*, Block B, Sinsuran Complex.

TOUR OPERATORS IN KK

A large number of **tour operators** are based in KK, and though prices are often high, many of the adventure tours on offer are only possible through an agency; some of the best are listed below. Expect to pay around $40 for a half-day KK city tour; $100 for day trips to Tunku Abdul Rahman Park, the Rafflesia Centre or Kinabulu National Park; $180 for a day's white-water rafting; and $600 upwards for extended tours into the forested interior, depending on the size of the group.

Api Tours, ground floor, Wisma Sabah (☎221233). For rafting, besides more demanding trips like the Mount Trusmadi Trek.

Borneo Expeditions, 3rd floor, Wisma Sabah (☎245168). A white-water rafting specialist, but organizes inland tours, too.

Borneo Divers, ground floor, Wisma Sabah (☎222226). The most prestigious outfit for diving trips and scuba courses; three days (two nights) on Sipidan with them costs US$660.

Borneo Sea Adventures, 1st floor, 8A Karamunsing Warehouse (☎553900). One-day trips to Sipadan out of Semporna ($200) for groups of four or more.

Borneo Wildlife Adventure, Block L, Sinsuran Complex. For tailor-made adventure tours along the Sarawak and Kalimantan borders.

Discovery Tours, Shopping Arcade, *Shangri-La Tanjung Aru Resort* (☎216426). Half- and full-day tours in the KK area.

Journey World Travel, 3rd floor, Nosmal Court, 62 jalan Gaya (☎221586). Imaginative operator devising tailor-made adventure tours along the Sarawak and Kalimantan borders.

Sipadan Dive Centre, 10th floor, Wisma Merdeka (☎240584). A newish organization, which has chalets for rent on Sipadan.

Travellers' Rest Hostel, Block L, Sinsuran Complex (☎240625). Provides the most competitive rates for trips out of Sandakan.

Pharmacies *Centre Point Pharmacy*, Centre Point; *Farmasi Gaya*, 122 jalan Gaya; *Metropharm*, Block A, Sinsuran Complex.

Police The main police station, *Balai Polis KK* (☎58191 or ☎58111), is below Atkinson Clock Tower on jalan Padang.

Post office The GPO (Mon–Sat 8am–5pm, Sun 10am–1pm) lies between the Sinsuran and Segama complexes, on jalan Tun Razak; poste restante/general delivery is just inside the front doors.

Sabah Parks Block K, Sinsuran Complex (Mon–Fri 8.30am–4pm, Sat 8.30am–noon; ☎211881).

Shopping *Borneo Handicraft* (1st floor, Wisma Merdeka) has a good choice of woodwork, basketry and gongs; *Borneo Handicraft & Ceramic Shop* (ground floor, Centre Point) stocks ceramics, antiques and primitive sculptures; also good are the souvenir shops at the Sabah State Museum and the *STPC*; while the Filipino Market's scores of stalls sell both local and Filipino wares.

Telephones There are IDD facilities at *Kedai Telekom* (daily 8am–10pm), in Kompleks Sadong Jaya. Phone cards, available at the GPO and any shops displaying the *Uniphone Kad* sign, can be used for international calls in orange, but not yellow, public phone booths – there are some in Centre Point.

Taxis Book a taxi on either ☎ 52113 or ☎51863.

Southwestern Sabah and the interior

Sabah's **southwestern** reaches are dominated by the ridge of the **Crocker Mountain Range**, which divides the state's west coast and swampy Klias Peninsula from the area christened the **interior** in the days of the *Chartered Company*. At one time, this sparsely populated region was effectively isolated from the west coast by the mountains. This changed at the turn of the century, when a railway was built between Jesselton (modern-day KK) and the interior in order to transport the raw materials being produced by the region's thriving rubber industry. Today, logging has taken precedence, though the Kadazan/Dusun and Murut peoples still look to the interior's fertile soils for their living, cultivating rice, maize and cocoa there.

Travelling by bus and train, it's possible to circumnavigate the region from KK, starting with a drive southeast over the mountains to the Kadazan/Dusun town of **Tambunan**, which nestles on a plain chequered with paddy fields. From Tambunan, the road continues further south to **Keningau**, the centre of the interior's timber industry. Following the circular route to KK entails travelling on to **Tenom**, but Keningau is also the launch pad for more adventurous detours deeper into the heart of the interior. Both Tenom and Keningau mark the start of Murut territory, which stretches down to the Kalimantan border. The traditional ways of the Murut are fast dying out, but those prepared to venture into the less accessible areas south of Keningau and Tenom – using remote **Sapulut** as a base – will come across isolated tribes to whom home is still a longhouse, albeit a modernized one.

Tenom itself sits on the bank of the Padas river, whose turbulent waters you'll have to negotiate if you sign up for a white-water rafting tour. The train line connects Tenom with **Beaufort**, from where you can head one of three ways: northwards, back to KK; south to Sipitang, the terminus for buses and taxis into Sarawak; or west into the Klias Peninsula, an infertile shoulder of former swamp forest that forms the northeastern reach of Brunei Bay. From Kuala Penyu, in the northern corner of the peninsula, boats travel to **Pulau Tiga Park**; while ferries and speedboats connect Menumbok, on its southern side, with the duty-free island of **Pulau Labuan**.

The Crocker Mountain Range

Unless you take a Tenom-bound train from Beaufort (see p.422), the only way to reach the interior of Sabah is to follow the eighty kilometres of road from KK, southeast to Tambunan (see below); buses leave regularly from beside the Padang in KK. Ten kilometres out of the city, paddy fields give way to the rolling foothills of the **CROCKER MOUNTAIN RANGE** and buses start the long, twisting haul up to the 1649-metre-high Sinsuron Pass. As you go, you'll be treated to peerless views of the surrounding countryside and even, weather permitting, of mighty Mount Kinabalu; the occasional lean-to shack balances by the side of the road, piled with pineapples, bananas and vegetables for sale – often there's no one attending them, as some locals believe that anyone pilfering risks death by black magic.

A few kilometres beyond the Sinsuron Pass, the **Rafflesia Complex** (Mon–Fri 8am-12.45pm & 2–5pm, Sat & Sun 8am–5pm; free) houses examples of the Rafflesia flower, a parasitic plant whose rubbery, liver-spotted blooms can reach up to one metre in diameter – making it the world's largest flower. Its full name, *Rafflesia Arnoldii*, recalls its discovery, in Sumatra in 1818, by Sir Stamford Raffles and his physician, the naturalist Dr Joseph Arnold. "The petals", Raffles recorded, "are of a brick-red with numerous pustular spots of a lighter colour. The whole substance of the flower is not less than half an inch thick, and of a firm fleshy consistence." There's no need to hire one of the guides ($20) advertised at the complex's informative Visitors' Centre, as the park's paths are simple to follow and you're not going to miss a plant that size; someone at the centre should be able to direct you to one in bloom, though it's a good idea to phone the Visitors' Centre's hotline (☎011/861499) before leaving KK, to avoid a wasted journey – each flower only lasts a few days before dying.

Tambunan Plain

Seventeen kilometres short of Tambunan, a kink in the road reveals the gleaming emerald paddy fields of **Tambunan Plain** below. Flanked by groves of bamboos – the result of a colonial regulation that for every pole cut, twenty more be planted – and threaded by the Pegalam river, the plain is thought to have been named after two warriors, Tamadons and Gombunan, whose peoples joined forces centuries ago to expel invading tribes. **Gunung Trusmadi**, Sabah's second highest mountain (2642m), towers above the plain's eastern flank.

If you want to visit the forest-framed, fifteen-metre-high **Mawah Waterfall**, you'll have to get off the bus when you hit the main Ranau–Tambunan road, and catch another bus ($2) going northeast (to Ranau). After 7km, you reach the wide gravel trail leading to the waterfall from **KAMPUNG PATAU**, from where it's another two-hour hike through an idyllic bowl of hills stepped with groves of fern and bamboo.

Tambunan

After such a wonderful approach, the small Kadazan settlement of **TAMBUNAN**, centred around an ugly square of modern shophouses, is bound to disappoint. The most generous thing that can be said about Tambunan, administrative centre of Tambunan District, is that it's a quiet and spacious town, the site, every Thursday, of a lively *tamu*, for which a smart new market building has been erected.

Buses to and from KK, Ranau and Keningau stop in the main square, around which are several unspectacular eating houses. There are also two **places to stay** in town: the *Government Rest House* (☎774339; ④), a five-minute walk through town from the main road, set on a small hill, and with memorable views of Tambunan Plain; or the *Tambunan Village Resort Centre* (*TVRC*; ☎087/774076; ④), 1km north of town, the fruit of a 1987 Operation Raleigh venture, whose bamboo chalets sleep up to twelve people. As well as a restaurant, the centre boasts a cottage industry producing *lihing* – the rice wine for which Tambunan is locally renowned.

Although now a sleepy agricultural district, Tambunan featured in one of the more turbulent periods in Sabah's history, when it witnessed the demise of folk hero and rebel, **Mat Salleh**, who in 1897 burned down the British settlement on Pulau Gaya, in protest at taxes being levied by the *Chartered Company*. Branded an outlaw with a price on his head, Salleh finally negotiated a deal with William Clarke Cowie of the *Chartered Company* that allowed him and his men to settle in Tambunan. Such a humiliating outcome outraged other members of the company and Salleh hurriedly withdrew to Tambunan Plain, where he erected a fort of bamboo and stone. Sure enough, government forces descended into the plain at the beginning of 1900 and besieged Salleh's fort; by the end of January, Salleh was dead, killed by a stray bullet. At **KAMPUNG TIBABAR**, a few kilometres north of Tambunan, a stone memorial marks the site of his fort.

Keningau

A fifty-kilometre jaunt down the road from Tambunan brings you to the rapidly expanding town of **KENINGAU**, the interior's forestry capital. It's a hectic, noisy place, its streets bulging with tooting buses and taxis, its pavements inhabited by women hawking cigarettes and children offering "shoeshine, boss" from morning to night. At the weekend, the town attracts crowds of labourers from the sawmills and logging camps that have scarred the hills around it – a phenomenon in part responsible for a burgeoning prostitution trade which puts several of the town's hotels off limits.

Keningau's single attraction is its **Chinese temple**, situated right beside the bus terminus. The brightly painted murals that cover its walls and ceilings are more reminiscent of those in a Hindu temple, while in the forecourt is a statue of a fat, smiling Buddha, resplendent in red and yellow gown. If you're in town on **market** day (Thursday), check out Keningau's *tamu*, a short walk up the main Keningau–Tambunan road. The only other distraction is the minibus ride twenty minutes northeast of town, through paddy fields and small *kampungs*, to **Taman Bandukan**. This pleasant riverside park is packed with picnicking locals on Sundays, but at other times grazing cows and scores of butterflies are your only company; the river is clean and swimmable, while from above its far banks – reached by a wobbly suspension bridge – there's a good view of the surrounding hills. Take a minibus from the central square to Bingkor, telling the driver where you're headed.

Rather than heading on, either to Tenom or Tambunan, a more exciting alternative is to head for Sapulut (see below) to explore Sabah's Murut heartland; this remote region is effectively a dead end and accessible only from Keningau, to which you'll have to backtrack afterwards. It's also possible to take a land cruiser and strike east along the logging roads which connect the interior with Tawau, the largest town in southern Sabah (p.448), though this is a really tough route, for the committed only.

Practicalities

Unless you're arriving by **land cruiser** from Tawau (in which case you'll be dropped at the southwest side of town), **buses** and **taxis** terminate in and around the town's central square. It isn't possible to book a seat on a land cruiser to Tawau ($80) and drivers only set off with a full load, so turn up as early as you possibly can.

A couple of adequate **hotels** – *Hotel Hiap Soon* (☎087/331541; ②) and the pricier *Hotel Tai Wah* (☎087/332092; ②) – are nearby, though the majority are found in the new part of town, five minutes' walk behind the Chinese temple, up jalan Masuk Spur. It's here that you'll find Keningau's friendliest budget choice, *Wah Hin* (☎087/332506; ②); others nearby are brothels.

Locals swear by the boiled duck at the *Yung On* coffee shop, a five-minute walk to the right of the Chinese temple's neighbour, the *Yuk Yin* School, at the northeastern edge of town. Nearby are *Restoran Shahrizal*, which serves fine *rotis* and curries behind its bamboo facade; and Keningau's best **restaurant**, the *Mandarin*, where one of the specialities is freshwater fish. Across town, near the *Hotel Wah Hin*, the *People*

Restaurant dishes up *dim sum* and noodles. For a more economical meal, try the cluster of **food stalls** beside the bus stop, bearing in mind that most are closed by dusk.

Into the interior: Sapulut and beyond

One or two buses ($20) a day make the 116-kilometre journey from Keningau southeast to Sapulut, deep in the heart of Murut country, and the departure point for some exhilarating river expeditions. The time-honoured customs of Sabah's indigenous peoples are dying out at an alarming rate, but along the rivers around Sapulut you can still witness traditional longhouse community life, little changed over the centuries. Moreover, the experience of sitting at the prow of a boat that's inching up a churning Bornean river under a dense canopy of forestation, is one that's hard to beat. If you do make the trip, bear in mind that you'll need a few days spare and that afterwards you'll have to retrace your steps to Keningau, as the road runs out at Sapulut.

The trip starts inauspiciously: the terrain towards Sapulut has been so scarred by logging that, for much of the journey, you'll wonder why you bothered coming. Moreover, you'll be lucky if you make it to Sapulut without the bus suffering a buckled suspension or a puncture: the scraps of tyre and inner tube littering the length of the unsealed road testify to its treacherousness. To make matters worse, endless logging trucks loom terrifyingly out of the dust cloud that hangs permanently over the route.

Around an hour out of Keningau is tiny **KAMPUNG SOOK**, barely more than a wide stretch of the road, with a few stalls and split bamboo houses and a huge district office. Beyond Sook, keep your eyes peeled for roadside shelters, erected by the Murut over their buried dead and draped with painted cloths. While crosses decorate several of these cloths, others feature more imaginative designs, even including representations of soccer players.

Sapulut

It takes four hours to reach **SAPULUT**, situated at the convergence of the Sapulut and Talankai rivers, and hemmed in by densely forested hills. It remains an appealing *kampung* in spite of its ugly tapioca mill, and though the main reason for coming here is to continue up- or downriver, there's enough of interest to warrant a day in the village itself. Across the pedestrian suspension bridge that spans sungei Talankai is Sapulut's former schoolhouse (dating back to Japanese occupation, but now overgrown) and its **Mahkamah**, or native court building. The hollowed sandstone rock you can see outside the court is the *batu Kelasan*, or spirit stone, by which men found guilty were entitled to test their innocence, the theory being that if they touched it and took an oath of honesty (a "sumpah"), and didn't subsequently die, they were telling the truth. A two-hour climb through the secondary forest above the mill leads to a panoramic view of the surrounding *kampungs* and countryside.

The one **place to stay** in Sapulut is at the home of Lantir Bakayas (②), the boatman who arranges trips to Batu Punggul (see below). Lantir's wife serves up simple but filling **meals** ($5) throughout the day, and Lantir himself will happily show you around the village. Minibus drivers will drop you at Lantir's house, which is on the left-hand side of the road, beyond the mill.

Beyond Sapulut

The best trip out of Sapulut is up the Sapulut river to **Batu Punggul**, a 250-metre-high limestone cliff that rears out of the virgin jungle around it. The climb to the summit is rewarded by outstanding views of the forest, while another few minutes' walking brings you to the impressive **Tinahas Caves**, whose walls are lined with swifts' nests and roosting bats. The *Korperasi Pembangunan Desa* (*KPD*), which controls Sapulut's tapioca mill, operates the *Batu Punggul Resort*, twenty minutes' walk from the cliff; as well as its rest house, guests can stay in a traditional Murut longhouse, and there's a canteen, too. For an extra charge, villagers from a nearby longhouse will lay on a Murut cultural evening, complete with jars of lethal *tapai* (rice wine). A six-berth **boat** to Batu Punggul costs $250; the trip takes around two and a half hours (though it could be two or three times as long, depending on the weather), and passes isolated river-bank *kampungs* and longhouses on the way. Both the boat and accommodation should be booked ahead with a tour operator in KK (see feature on p.416), but arrangements can be made directly with Lantir, subject to there being space at the resort.

The going gets tougher – and pricier – if you travel downriver from Sapulut to visit one of the *kampungs* towards the Kalimantan border. The first settlement of any size, forty minutes south of Sapulut, is **KAMPUNG PAGALONGAN**, a surprisingly large community, where local villagers pick up supplies. It's another ten minutes to the bend in the river commanded by **KAMPUNG SILUNGAI**'s huge 120-metre longhouse. Despite its jarring zinc roof, the longhouse is an appealing construction of green and white wooden slats, centring around a ceremonial hall, and home to around six hundred extremely friendly villagers. More traditional longhouses can be seen at nearby **PENSIANGAN**, but their future is uncertain since the logging industry is moving unerringly towards this settlement – already there's reputed to be a track from Sapulut, though minibuses don't run this far. Finally, provided you have an Indonesian visa, it's possible to follow the Sapulut river **into Kalimantan**, though renting a boat for such a journey is prohibitively expensive.

The person to contact if you want to explore the territory south of Sapulut is Lantir, who arranges **tailor-made trips** to these parts, though at a price: chartering a boat for a day's river meandering – say to Pensiangan and back – weighs in at $400 for up to six people. Very occasionally, much cheaper **passenger launches** ply this stretch of the river – ask Lantir to check with the *KPD* office, in Salong, 5km south of Sapulut, before you charter a boat, though bear in mind that you could get stuck in a *kampung* for a long time awaiting a lift out.

Tenom and around

After Keningau, the small town of **TENOM**, 42km to the southwest, comes as a great relief. The heady days when Tenom was the bustling HQ of the Interior District of British North Borneo are now long gone, and today it's a peaceful, friendly backwater. It has its fair share of dreary concrete buildings, but is given a certain grace by its mantle of lushly forested hills, while the centre boasts a selection of charismatic wooden shophouses and mansions, and a blue-domed mosque. The surroundings are extremely fertile, supporting maize, cocoa and soya beans – predominantly cultivated by the indigenous Murut people.

The **Tenom Agricultural Research Station** (Mon–Thurs 7am–3pm, Fri 7am–noon, Sat 7am–12.30pm), a 35-minute bus ride from below the *padang*, is where the state's Agricultural Department carries out feasibility studies on a wide range of crops. The research station is renowned for its **Orchid Centre** where a profusion of orchids cascade from trees and tree trunks, lending the site a look of studied disarray. Less tempting, but actually much better than it sounds, is the nearby **Crop Museum** (free), where you can easily spend an hour strolling through the groves of exotic fruit trees and tropical plants, like durian, rambutan, jackfruit, coffee and okra – all tended by women in wide-brimmed hats. Views from the Research Station's own *Rest House* (☎087/735661; ③) are beautiful, though it's a fair walk from the station HQ.

Murut villages

A string of tiny **Murut villages** runs along the road south of Tenom, most accessible by catching a bus bound for Kuala Tomani, 37km from Tenom. The Murut are

Christians – the result of some fairly vigorous missionary work early this century – which accounts for the area's several powder-blue churches, made of wood and sporting names like True Jesus Church. Traditional longhouses have disappeared from the region, but a few **ceremonial halls** are still standing, inside which you'll find *lansaran*: Murut trampolines, made of planks and pliant logs, and used for dancing jigs on special occasions. To see one, ask your bus driver to stop at **KAMPUNG MAMAI TOM** (around 28km from Tenom) or, better still, at **KAMPUNG KAPARUNGAN**, close to Kuala Tomani, where the bamboo benches in the ceremonial hall have gaps in them to take *tapai* jars. Sadly, the Murut rarely don their traditional costumes these days, unless tourists pay them to do so. The proposed **Murut cultural village**, to be built between Tenom and Melalap, may or may not materialize – contact the *STPC* in KK, or ask around in Tenom, if you're interested.

Practicalities

Buses north to Keningau ($5) – from where you can continue on to KK – and south to Kuala Tomani ($4), circle around Tenom all day long, looking for takers; you can always pick one up on the main street, at the western edge of the *padang*. **Share-taxis** to Keningau also cost $5 and leave from the main street whenever they've assembled four passengers. Moving on to Beaufort to the northwest is by **train** – Tenom marks the end of Sabah's only stretch of railway and the track skirts the southeast edge of town. Tenom Station is on the southern edge of the *padang* – call for reservations to be sure of a railcar seat (see "Beaufort" below for timetable and details).

If friendly *Hotel Kim San* (☎087/735485; ②) at the southwestern end of town is full, all is not lost: **rooms** at the *Hotel Sri Jaya* (☎087/735077; ②), on Tenom's main street, are spick and span, or there's the simpler and less expensive *Hotel Sabah* (☎087/735534; ②), off a side road by the market. **Places to eat** are plentiful, with a clutch of coffee shops and restaurants in the area around the *Hotel Kim San*. For a tasty *mee* soup, try the *Restoran Double Happiness*, below the *padang*; or, for something a bit more lavish, head 2km south of town to the cavernous *YNL Restaurant* (daily 6pm–1am), where the speciality is fresh fish caught in the nearby Padas river.

Beaufort

Named after the elaborately monikered Leicester P. Beaufort, one of the early governors of British North Borneo, **BEAUFORT** is a well-to-do, though uneventful town, normally only strayed into by tourists taking a train to Tenom, or on their way to the white-water rafting on nearby sungei Padas. Beaufort's commercial importance has declined markedly since the laying of a sealed road from KK into the interior lessened the importance of its rail link with Tenom. The town's position on the banks of the sungei Padas leaves it prone to flooding, which explains why its shophouses are raised on steps – early photographs show Beaufort looking like a sort of Southeast Asian Venice. But once you've poked around in the town market, inspected angular St Paul's Church at the top of town and taken a walk past the stilt houses on the river bank, you've exhausted its sights.

Practicalities

The **train** station is next to the Padas river at the southern side of town, from where it's a minute or so on foot into the centre – walk up the road opposite the station forecourt. **Buses** stop in the centre itself, beside the market.

Beaufort's only two **hotels** are the *Beaufort* (☎087/211911; ②), east of the market, and the *Mandarin Inn* (☎087/212798; ②), five minutes' walk across the river – they're practically identical, though rooms at the *Mandarin* just have the edge in terms of freshness. When it comes to **eating**, you could do a lot worse than *Christopher's Corner*

Parking, across from the train station, whose friendly owner will rustle you up a really good Western breakfast. *Restoran Kim Wah*, a sizeable establishment below the *Hotel Beaufort*, serves simple Chinese food, while across the river at *Restoran Merdeka*, Malay food and banana leaf curries are the order of the day. There are also hawker stalls upstairs in the town market and more next to the bridge.

Taking the train

> *Over the metals all rusted brown,*
> *Thunders the "Mail" to Jesselton Town;*
> *Tearing on madly, reck'ning not fate,*
> *Making up time – she's two days late*
> *See how the sparks from her smokestack shower,*
> *Swaying on wildly at three miles an hour.*

As this 1922 rhyme illustrates, Sabah's only railway line is more a curio than a practical mode of transport. Although the line runs all the way from KK to Tenom, travelling between Beaufort and the capital is far quicker by **bus**, and it's only the two-and-a-quarter-hour journey from Beaufort to Tenom – a boneshaking ride tracing the twists and turns of the Padas river – that's really worth making. The train passes tiny stations and winds through dramatic jungle that at times arches right over the track. Three types of train – diesel, cargo and railcar – ply the route daily; the fastest, most comfortable, and therefore most expensive option is the compact railcar, whose front windows afford an unimpeded view of the oncoming countryside; but it only holds a handful of passengers, so phone or call in at the station to book ahead. See the box below for all the details.

TRAIN TIMETABLE

Beaufort–Tenom
Mon–Sat: 8.25am (railcar); 10.50am (diesel); noon (cargo); 1.55pm (diesel); 3.50pm (railcar).
Sun: 6.45am (diesel); 10.50am (diesel); 2.30pm (diesel); 4.05pm (railcar).

Tenom–Beaufort
Mon–Sat: 6.40am (railcar); 7.30am (diesel); 8am (cargo); 1.40pm (diesel); 4pm (railcar).
Sun: 7.20am (railcar); 7.55am (diesel); 12.10pm (diesel); 3.05pm (diesel).

Railcar: $8.35 one-way.
Diesel & Cargo: $2.75 one-way.

Information on ☎087/221518 (Beaufort) or ☎087/4735514 (Tenom).

West of Beaufort: the Klias Peninsula and Pulau Tiga Park

Immediately west of Beaufort and served by regular minibuses from the centre of town is the **Klias Peninsula**, from whose most westerly settlement, tiny **MENUMBOK**, several ferries depart daily for Pulau Labuan (see below). Meanwhile, it's a jarring, hour-long bus ride from Beaufort northwest to **KUALA PENYU**, at the northern point of the peninsula, the departure point for Pulau Tiga Park and not a place to visit for its own sake. If you get stuck here, your only hope is a room at the *Government Rest House* (☎087/884231; ③), five minutes beyond the *Shell* garage on the waterfront. **Moving on**, if there are no buses leaving Penyu for major destinations, take a local bus to nearby Kampung Kayul and wave down a bus coming from Menumbok heading either for KK or Beaufort.

Pulau Tiga Park

Originally, the **PULAU TIGA PARK** – north of Kuala Penyu in the South China Sea – comprised three islands, but wave erosion has reduced one of them, Pulau Kalampunian Besar, to a sand bar; the remaining two, Tiga and Kalampunian Damit, offer good snorkelling, plus the chance to see some unusual wildlife.

PULAU TIGA itself was formed by erupting mud volcanoes and you can still see smaller versions, occasionally squirting strings of mud into the air, at the top of the island. Circled by fine sand beaches and good coral, and criss-crossed by lengthy trails, Tiga's forested interior harbours wild pigs and monitor lizards; if you're down on the sands, look out for Tiga's most famous inhabitants, its megapodes, or rotund incubator birds – so-called because they lay their eggs in mounds of sand and leaves.

PULAU KALAMPUNIAN DAMIT, 1km northeast of Pulau Tiga, is known locally as Pulau Ular, or "Snake Island", as it attracts a species of sea snake called the yellow-lipped sea krait in huge numbers – on an average day, at least a hundred of these metallic grey and black creatures come ashore to rest, mate and lay their eggs. Though dozy in the heat of the day, the sea kraits are poisonous, so you're best off accompanied by a ranger if you want to see them.

To **get to the park**, call the owner of the local Kuala Penyu boat, the *Stompock* (☎087/884772), or speak to the *Sabah Parks* office in KK (see p.407). The return journey typically costs a minimum of $200 for one to ten people, and $20 for each extra passenger – though there's no harm in bargaining. From Tiga, bank on $30 more for a boat to visit Kalampunian Damit. The only **accommodation** is on Tiga itself, where a night in one of the *Rest House*'s three double rooms costs $30 a head; if that's too pricey, there's space for camping. Bookings are handled by *Sabah Parks* in KK.

Pulau Labuan

PULAU LABUAN, around 10km west of the Klias Peninsula, is a small, arrowhead-shaped island that boasts a history disproportionate to its size. The terms of treaty with the Sultan of Brunei yielded the island to the British Crown long before neighbouring Sabah was procured by the *Chartered Company* and on Christmas Eve 1846, Captain G.R. Mundy took possession of it in the name of Queen Victoria. In addition to Labuan's fine anchorage and consequent potential as a trading post, it was its **coal deposits** – the northern tip of the island is still called *Tanjung Kubong*, or Coal Point – which attracted the British, keen to establish a coaling station for passing steamships. With trade in mind, the island was made a free port in 1848; by 1889, it had been incorporated into British North Borneo, a state of affairs that lasted until it joined the Straits Settlements a few years into the new century.

World War II brought the focus of the world upon Labuan. Less than a month after the bombing of Pearl Harbour, the island was occupied by the invading Japanese army, on New Year's Day, 1942, and it was through Labuan that the Japanese forces penetrated British North Borneo. The island spent its war years known as **Maida Island**, in memory of General Maida, Commander-in-Chief of the Japanese forces in British Borneo, who was killed in a plane crash on his way to declare its airport open. In June 1945, the men of the Ninth Australian Infantry Division landed on Labuan and three and a half years of occupation came to an end; having witnessed the arrival of Japanese forces, it was only fitting that Labuan should also witness their surrender, which took place on September 9, 1945. Labuan, along with Sabah, reverted to the British Crown in July 1946, though it was a further seventeen years before it actually became part of Sabah. Then, in 1984, the island was declared part of Malaysian Federal Territory, governed directly by Kuala Lumpur. Today, Labuan – with a population fast approaching 50,000 – is a still a duty-free port, though its present status as both a sordid getaway for Bruneians and Sabahans after prostitutes and cheap beer, and a base for Filipino smugglers, is at odds with its pretensions to becoming an offshore banking centre. Still, with ferries from KK and Brunei interconnecting here, you may well end up spending at least some time here.

The island

The centre of Labuan, previously known as Victoria but now referred to simply as **LABUAN TOWN**, lies on the southeastern side of the island, its central streets thronging with Malaysian businessmen and Russian sailors, Bruneian shoppers and Filipino traders. The *gerai*, or permanent **market**, at the far western end of town, is rather downbeat, though its upper level affords good views of the modest **water village** northwest of town, its surrounding waters bristling with rotting foundations. Below the market is a gathering of tin shacks, where Filipinos sell seashell models, stuffed turtles, leather bags, brassware, cloths and silks.

Just 500m north of town, the dome of the **Masjid Negeri** resembles a concrete shuttlecock, but from there you'll have to travel further afield to amuse yourself. *Layang Layangan* minibuses from the bus area (see below) will drop you at Labuan's **war memorial**, next to a sleepy *kampung* 4km north of town. Occupying a peaceful seaside site, the memorial – a concave concrete bridge covered in grass – remembers all those who died in Borneo in World War II; just below, an enclosure marks the site of the Japanese surrender of 1945. Locals swim on the thin **beach** beside the memorial, strewn with driftwood and coconut husks, though the better stretch is around 1km further north. There's another decent beach across the island, below the **chimney**, that's all that remains of Labuan's coal industry; while on the way out to the airport is a large **Allied war cemetery**.

Practicalities

Jalan Merdeka, running along the seafront below the town centre, forms the spine of Labuan Town; along it, you'll find the GPO and a branch of the *Hong Kong Bank*. Running northwards from the middle of jalan Merdeka, and effectively splitting the town in two, is jalan Tun Mustapha. **Ferries** from Kota Kinabalu, Menumbok, Limbang and Lawas in Sarawak, and Bandar Seri Begawan (in Brunei) dock at the ferry terminal, below jalan Merdeka; see below for all departure details. Labuan's **airport** is 3km north of town and connected to it by regular, inexpensive minibuses from the **minibus area** on jalan Bunga Raya; there's a *MAS* office in Wisma Kee Chia, on jalan Bunga Kesuma (☎087/412263).

There are plenty of **places to stay** in Labuan, though unless you're prepared to brave one of the places over on the east end of town which double as brothels, none are in the budget price range. Best deal in town is a room with a fan in the Indian-run *Pantai View Hotel* (☎087/411339; ②) – turn left out of the ferry terminal and then right up jalan Bunga Tanjung. Right opposite the terminal in jalan Perpaduan is friendly but spartan *Hai Thien Lodging* (☎007/411261; ③) and, beyond it, *Melati Inn* (☎087/416307; ③), where double rooms come with TV, air-con and bathroom. From there, prices climb steadily: of the cluster of decent hotels east of Jalan Tun Mustapha, best is *Hotel Labuan* (☎087/412502; ⑤), boasting its own swimming pool.

Along jalan Merdeka and jalan OKK Awang Besar you'll find a number of no-frills, Chinese and Indian **restaurants** – the latter featuring American wrestling videos day and night. Particularly good for *rotis*, *murtabaks* and curries is *Restoran Farizah*, next to the *Pantai View* (see above); while two blocks north, facing each other on jalan Bunga Mawar, there's the Muslim *Madina Restaurant* and the *Restaurant Pulau Labuan*, an air-con restaurant with a wide Chinese menu. For great *dim sum* and Chinese tea, try *Restoran Ramai Ramai* above the taxi stand at the intersection of jalan Merdeka and jalan Tun Mustapha. At night, make a beeline for the stalls behind the *Hong Kong Bank* on jalan Merdeka, where you'll find delicious barbecued chicken wings. Altogether more upmarket is the *Hotel Labuan*'s *Nagalang Chinese & Japanese Restaurant*, while below it is the 24-hour *Kiamsam Terrace* coffee shop.

Ferries from Labuan

Tickets are sold sporadically at the arrival points at the ferry terminal area, though if the booth is closed, there are two outlets nearby: *Duta Muhibbah Agency* (daily 8am–4pm; ☎087/413827) and *Sin Matu Agency* (Mon–Sat 8am–5pm, Sun 8am–noon; ☎087/412261), at 52 and 55 jalan Merdeka respectively.

Although schedules are susceptible to change, there are presently three departures a day to **Kota Kinabalu**, at 8.30am and 1pm ($28 second-class, $33 first-class), and at 3pm ($15); and three also to **Brunei** at 8am, 12.15pm and 2pm ($22). For **Limbang**, a ferry leaves daily at 12.30pm; while a **Lawas** ferry departs at 1pm – both cost $20. Finally, there are plenty of speedboats to **Menumbok**, from where it's a two-hour bus ride to Kota Kinabalu.

To Sarawak: Sipitang

Forty-seven kilometres or so on the bumpy gravel road southwest of Beaufort, **SIPITANG** is a sleepy seafront town worth bearing in mind if you need a place to stay en route to Sarawak. Aproaching from the north, a bridge marks the start of town – look out for the pretty stilt houses to your left as you cross. Just over the bridge, there's a jetty from which a **boat** leaves daily (7am; $20) to Labuan; 250m beyond that, you're in the town centre. Buses for Beaufort, KK and Lawas (see below) congregate in the centre of town; right next to the bus terminus is the taxi stand. Except for a trip to **Taman Negara** – a beachside picnic spot a few kilometres south of town, and favoured by locals at the weekend, when there'll probably be a minibus service – there's nothing to do in Sipitang. On the bright side, a couple of **restaurants** have used the town's location on the shore of Brunei Bay to their advantage. Best is the *Kelong Restaurant*, 100m south of town and built on stilts, which serves up reliable Chinese, Malay and Western food. Back in town, *Restoran Anda* is a charming establishment with tables overlooking the sea. Of the **hotels** along the main road, the *Hotel Asanol* (☎087/821484; ②) is the friendliest and most affordable; failing that, neighbouring *Hotel Lian Hin* (☎087/821008; ②) is all right, though a bit pricier.

Crossing to Sarawak

The easiest way to travel from Sipitang **to Lawas in Sarawak** is to take a minibus or taxi (both $10) from the centre of town, which take one hour. It's cheaper to wait for the *Lawas Express* ($6), which leaves KK daily at 1.30pm, passing through Sipitang around 4pm and getting to Lawas some time after 5pm; or catch a $2 minibus to Sindumin, on the Sabah side of the border, and then connect with a Sarawak bus. Whichever you choose, the driver will wait while you pass through the passport controls flanking the border – one in Sindumin, the other a couple of hundred metres away at Merapok in Sarawak.

North of Kota Kinabalu

North of Kota Kinabalu, Sabah's trans-state road hurries through the capital's drab suburbs and past the timber yards of **Tepilok**, en route to the more pastoral environs of **Tuaran**. From here, the *atap* houses of the Bajau water villages, **Mengkabong** and **Penambawang**, are both a stone's throw away. Although the main road veers eastwards to Ranau (see p.435) just outside Tuaran, a lesser fork shoots north, dragging its heels over the foothills of Mount Kinabalu before reaching **Kota Belud**, the site of a weekly *tamu* that attracts tribespeople from all over the region. The landscape really hots up north of Kota Belud: jewel-bright paddy fields abut the road for much of the way up to the **Kudat Peninsula**, and behind them looms Mount Kinabalu. Journey's end is signalled by the coconut groves and beaches of **Kudat**, formerly capital of the British North Borneo, but now a focal point for the Rungus people who dwell in modernized longhouses in the surrounding countryside.

Buses for Tuaran and Kota Belud leave KK throughout the day, and both destinations make for decent day trips out of the capital. However, it's worth thinking twice before committing yourself to the longer trip to the Kudat Peninsula: the region's inaccessible beaches and modern longhouses have left many visitors disappointed.

Mengkabong and Penambawang

It takes just under an hour to travel 34km from Kota Kinabalu to **TUARAN**, from where it's possible to visit two water villages. On the way, you'll pass the **Yayasan Sabah Building** – a vast glass cylinder in Likas Bay, which houses the Sabah Foundation, an organization that channels profits from its huge timber concession into schools, hospitals and a flying doctor service.

Of the two villages, **MENGKABONG**, ten minutes out of Tuaran on a local bus, is the most accessible – with the result that it's a favourite destination with KK's tour agencies. The sight of a village built out over the sea on stilts is usually a compelling one, but Mengkabong is a noisy, charmless example, and you'd do well to make the extra effort to reach **PENAMBAWANG**. Minibuses to Kampung Surusup – the tiny settlement from where you can catch a boat to Penambawang – leave from the road west of Tuaran's brown clock tower: it's a twenty-minute drive (on a nightmarish road) through idyllic paddy fields. Once in Surusup, you'll need to ask around for a boat – Penambawang is fifteen minutes northeast, across a wide bay skirted with mangroves, and the return ride shouldn't cost more than $10 or $15. Except for a handful of zinc roofs, it's a timeless village, with houses of *atap*, bamboo and wood interconnected by labyrinthine boardwalks – called jambatan – along which fish are laid out to dry. The village's welcoming inhabitants are Muslim Bajau.

Kota Belud

For six days of the week, **KOTA BELUD**, 75km northeast of KK on the road to Kudat, is a drab little town, its main street occupied by listless teenagers and packs of scraggy dogs. Each Sunday, though, it springs to life, as hordes of villagers from the surrounding countryside congregate at its weekly *tamu*, ten minutes' walk out of town, and said to be the biggest in Sabah. The *tamu* fulfills a social, as much as a commercial, role, and tribes represented include the Rungus and Kadazan/Dusun, as well as the Bajau, who occasionally ride in on horseback and in traditional apparel.

Kota Belud's popularity among KK's tour operators means it's always laced with tourists; even so, you're far more likely to see dried fish, chains of yeast beads (used to make rice wine), buffaloes and betel nut for sale, than souvenirs. At Kota Belud's annual *tamu besar*, or "big market", in addition to the more typical stalls, there are cultural performances, traditional horseback games and handicraft demonstrations. The *tamu besar* usually takes place in November; for more details, call in at the *STPC* in KK.

To catch the weekly *tamu* at its best, plan to leave KK at 7am. Buses ($5) leave from the far side of the *Shell* garage near the GPO; or catch a Kudat-bound bus ($5) from the long-distance station; it's a scenic ninety-minute trip.

Practicalities

Buses stop in the main square, and with onward connections so good, there's really no need to spend the night here: a far better idea is to book a bed at the Kinabalu National Park (see p.429), which can be reached via Tamparuli, or to carry on to Kudat. If you insist on **staying**, there's only the *Hotel Kota Belud* (☎087/976576; ②) on jalan Francis, whose nine clean rooms all have air-con, but shared bathrooms. There's not much in the way of **restaurants**, either; for Malay food, try *Restoran Rahmat* next to the bus terminus, or one of the lean-to stalls beyond the far side of the bus terminus. Otherwise, *Kedai Makan Sin Hing*, behind the hotel, serves up basic Chinese meals.

Kota Marudu and around

The 26km from Kota Belud north to Kampung Timbang take in some of Sabah's most dramatic scenery, with the grand peaks of Mount Kinabalu reflected – rice harvest allowing – in the still waters of the paddy fields to the east. At the base of Marudu Bay, the road forks, the right turn leading to **KOTA MARUDU** – a town with two hotels and several restaurants, but with nothing to entice you to stop and try them out. East of Kota Marudu, a potholed road passes seaside *kampungs* and huge sawmills before reaching Pitas, from where it's possible to catch a bus to Kenibongon, the departure point for boats to Pulau Jambongon, though the activities of pirates in its waters currently make the island unsafe to visit.

Kudat and its peninsula

Coconut groves and paddy fields line the upper portion of the badly surfaced road that runs northwest of Marudu Bay. Many of the coconuts end up at the dessicated coconut plant 9km out of **KUDAT**, right on Borneo's northern tip – from the bus, you'll see piles of discarded husks, resembling bleached skulls.

Kudat nestles on the western shore of Marudu Bay and its good natural harbour resulted in its being declared the administrative capital of British North Borneo in 1881, though control was switched to Sandakan two years later. Although it's lively and indisputably friendly, there's not much to bring you here, save for a stroll around the busy **waterfront** – where wiry old men carry sacks to and from the *godowns* which back Jalan Lo Thien Chock's shophouses – and a visit to the adjacent **stilt village** at the southern end of town.

The **Kudat peninsula** is home to the Rungus people and until recently their longhouse dwellings, or *binatang*, were the region's main attraction. They still exist, and their size still impresses, but today they're often made with sheets of corrugated zinc, the durability of which is preferred to traditional materials like timbers, tree bark, *rattan* and *nipah* leaves. **KAMPUNG TINANGGOL**, set back from the KK road, 37km south of Kudat, boasts three 25-family longhouses and a quaint white church. The *STPC* is constructing an authentic *binatang* in the village which, when finished, will allow visitors to spend a night with local families in a traditional environment. Further south, at **KAMPUNG MATTUNGONG**, a footpath leads eastwards over a wire suspension bridge, through bamboo groves, to **KAMPUNG MOMPILIS**, which has two dilapidated longhouses; though it's really the walk that makes the trip worthwhile.

The beaches

Kudat's most famous beach is **Bak Bak**, 12km north of town, though **Tajau**, a few kilometres north of it, is favoured by some locals. Across on the west coast, there's **Bangau Beach**, near the town of **SIKUATI** – any bus headed for KK can drop you at the turning, but then it's a six-kilometre hike to the beach. Sikuati itself is only a small coastal settlement, though it hosts a good-sized Sunday *tamu*.

Quite a few locals visit Bak Bak on a Sunday; otherwise local buses to *kampungs* near Kudat's beaches are so erratic as to be totally impractical. Taking a taxi is the only practical solution, but prices start at around $16 for the return journey.

It's also possible to take a ferry to **PULAU BANGGI**, off Sabah's north coast, though only if you've got a few days to spare, as departures are unpredictable, and the only way to get around the island once you're there is to hitch on local boats. The island boasts forest and beaches, and there's a small government *Rest House* (☎088/612511; ③) at Kampung Kalaki, the main settlement – contact the *Urusetia* in Kudat (see below) for details.

Practicalities

Downtown Kudat centres around the intersection of jalan Ibrahim Arshad and jalan Lo Thien Chock – the latter Kudat's main street, with most of its shops, as well as a *Standard Chartered Bank*. **Minibuses** congregate a few yards east of the intersection, as do the town's **taxis**, though the two main KK-bound **buses** (daily at 7.30am & noon) stop west of jalan Lo Thien Chock, along lorong Empat. For **ferries** to Pulau Banggi, head for the jetty at the southern end of jalan Lo Thien Chock.

Accommodation starts with the *Hotel Oriental* (☎088/61677; ②), at the portside end of jalan Lo Thien Chock, whose bright and clean rooms are only marred by an insalubrious hallway and shared toilets. Otherwise, there's the similarly priced *Hotel Islamik*, (☎088/613063; ②) which is above a Muslim restaurant north of the town centre, on jalan OKK Abdul Ghani. For a bit more comfort, best bet is the *Hotel Greenland* (☎088/62211; ②), five minutes' east of the town centre, in Block E of the SEDCO Shophouse development. *Hotel Sunrise* (☎088/611517; ②), in the middle of jalan Lo Thien Chock there is another decent establishment; here, an extra $16 or so gets you your own bathroom and TV. Finally, enquiries about Pulau Banggi's *Rest House* can be made at Kudat's *Urusetia*, or District Office (☎088/611511), beyond the golf course.

Restoran Sri Pelangi, at the northern end of jalan Lo Thien Chock, is the friendliest **restaurant** in town, serving Malay and Indonesian food; while the *Silver Inn*, along the road and below the *Sunrise Hotel*, dishes up a ham-and-eggs breakfast as well as a range of good Chinese dishes. At the *Keng Nam Tong Coffee Shop*, opposite the *Silver Inn*, you can have coffee and cake on a marble-topped table; and there's good fried chicken and fresh fruit at the stalls beyond the *Hotel Islamik*.

Kinabalu National Park

There's no more astounding sight in Borneo than the cloud-encased summit of **Mount Kinabalu** – at 4101 metres, half the height of Everest – shooting skywards from the 750 square kilometres of **KINABALU NATIONAL PARK**. Eighty-five kilometres northeast of KK and plainly visible from Sabah's west coast, Kinabalu's jagged peaks appear impossibly daunting at first sight, but in reality, the mountain is relatively easily climbed, by means of a well-defined, eight-and-a-half-kilometre path which weaves up its southern side to the bare granite of the summit, passing on its way a vast range of flora and fauna. Limbs that are weary from the climb up the mountain will welcome the warm, sulphurous waters of the **Poring Hot Springs**, around 40km away, on the park's southeastern flank, while between these two sites is the small town of **Ranau**, an accommodation option if you arrive too late to reach the springs.

A *TUT* bus leaves KK's long-distance terminal for the park at 7.30am daily, after which minibuses depart when they're full; don't forget to arrange your accommodation at the *Sabah Parks* office before you board (see "Practicialities", p.433, for all the details).

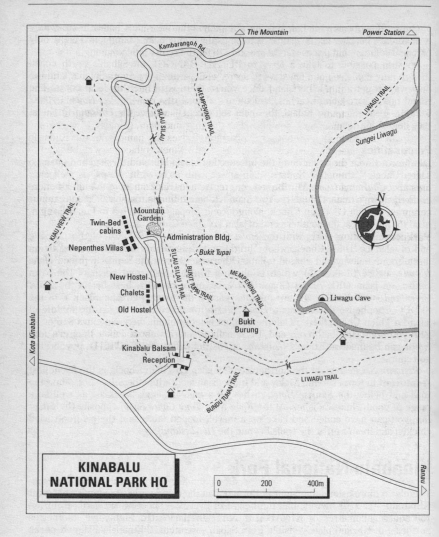

KINABALU
NATIONAL PARK HQ

0   200   400m

Mount Kinabalu

Conquering **MOUNT KINABALU** today is far easier than it was in 1858, when Spenser St John, British Consul-General to the native states of Borneo, found his progress blocked by Kadazans "shaking their spears and giving us other hostile signs". Hugh Low, at the time British colonial secretary on Pulau Labuan, had made the first recorded ascent of the mountain seven years earlier, though he baulked at climbing its highest peak, considering it "inaccessible to any but winged animals". The peak – subsequently named after Low, as was the mile-deep gully that cleaves the mountain-top – was finally conquered in 1888 by John Whitehead. **Low's Gully*** splits the summit into a U-shape, which led early explorers to conclude that Kinabalu was volcanic; in fact, the mountain is a granite pluton – an enormous ball of molten rock which has solidified and forced its way through the Crocker Mountain Range over millions of years. This process continues today, with the mountain gaining a few millimetres annually.

The origin of the mountain's name is uncertain; one legend tells how a Chinese prince travelled to Borneo to seek out a huge pearl, guarded by a dragon at the summit of the mountain. Having slain the dragon and claimed the pearl, the prince married a Kadazan girl, only to desert her and return to China. His wife was left to mourn him on the slopes of the mountain – hence *Kina* (China) and *balu* (widow) – where she eventually turned to stone. Another explanation derives the name from the Kadazan words *Aki Nabalu* – "the revered place of the dead". Nineteenth-century climbs had to take into account the superstitions of local porters, who believed the mountain to be a sacred ancestral home. When Low climbed it, his guides brought along charms, quartz crystals and human teeth to protect the party, and Kadazan porters still offer up chickens, eggs, cigars, betel nut and rice to the mountain's spirits at an annual ceremony.

Park Headquarters and around

Most climbers spend their first night at the mountain around the **park headquarters** and set off early the next morning. Exploring the 20km of **trails** that loop the montane forest around the headquarters is as good an introduction as any to the park – you can join the free guided tour that leaves daily from the administration office at 11.15am. Less dramatic, but still interesting, are the labelled plants of the **Mountain Garden** (Mon–Fri 8am–4.30pm, Sat 8am–5pm, Sun 9am–4pm), below the administration office. The **Multivision Show** (daily at 1.30pm; $1), screened in the office itself, and the **Slide Show** (Mon & Fri–Sat at 7.30pm; $1) are less informative – instead, head upstairs for the photos, visuals and mounted exhibits of the **Exhibit Centre**, where you should look out, in particular, for the monster stick insect.

Up the mountain

Aim to be at the park reception by 7am, where, besides your $10 climbing **permit**, you'll be asked to pay for an obligatory **guide** – an outlay that can be minimized by tagging along with other climbers: guides cost $25 a day for one to three persons, but only $30 for seven or eight persons. Porters are also available ($25 a day for carrying of loads up to 24lb), though the **lockers and saferoom** at reception make this an unnecessary expense. Useful things to take with you include a torch, headache tablets (for altitude sickness), suntan lotion and strong shoes or hiking boots. To combat the cold – which is bitter before dawn on the summit – bring any warm clothes you can muster. Adequate raincoats are sold at the park's souvenir shop. It's over an hour's walk from the reception to the power station that marks the start of the mountain trail proper, so you might like instead to take the **shuttle bus** ($2) that's laid on.

Climbing to your first night's accommodation, at around 3350 metres, takes between three and six hours, depending on your fitness. The **trail** uses the roots and stones it passes as steps, and features wooden "ladders" laid up its muddier stretches. The air

---

* Mount Kinabalu grabbed the world's headlines in March 1993, when two British army officers and three Hong Kong soldiers went missing on a training exercise down Low's Gully – described by Spenser St John as "a deep chasm, surrounded on three sides by precipices, so deep that the eye could not reach the bottom. . . There was no descending here". Defeated by impassable waterfalls and boulders, the men set up camp in a mountain cave and left out an SOS marked out with white pebbles. Treacherous weather conditions and inhospitable terrain repeatedly thwarted rescue attempts, but they were finally found, on day thirty of what should have been a ten-day mission – by which time they were surviving on a diet of *Polo* mints.

gets progressively cooler as you climb, but the walk is still a hard and sweaty one, and you'll be glad of the regular water tanks and **sheltered rest points** en route.

Two or three hours into the climb, incredible views of the hills, sea and clouds below you start to unfold (if the weather is kind); higher up, at just above 3000 metres, a detour to the left brings you to **Paka Cave** – no more than a large overhanging rock, and the site of overnight camps on early expeditions. The end of your first day's climbing is heralded by the appearance of the mighty, granitic slopes of the **Panar Laban** rock face, veined by trickling waterfalls. From the rest houses (see below) at the foot of Panar Laban – the name is a corruption of a Dusun word meaning "place of sacrifice" – views of the sun setting over the South China Sea are exquisite, and it's here that you'll spend your night on the mountain.

Plan to get up at 2.30am the next morning to join the pseudo-religious candle-lit procession to the top. Although ropes have been strung up much of this segment of the trail, none of the climbing is really hairy. That said, the air this high up is quite thin, so

---

FLORA AND FAUNA IN THE PARK

If you dash headlong up and down Mount Kinabalu and then depart, as some visitors do, you'll miss out on many of the region's natural riches. The national park's diverse terrains have spawned an incredible assemblage of plants and wildlife, and you are far more likely to glimpse some of them by walking its trails at a leisurely pace.

Flora
Around a third of the park's area is covered by **lowland dipterocarp forest**, characterizedby massive, buttressed trees allowing only sparse growth at ground level. The world's largest flower, the parasitic – and very elusive – *Rafflesia* (see p.418), occasionally blooms in the lowland forest around Poring Hot Springs. Between 900 and 1800m, you'll come across the oaks, chestnuts, ferns and mosses (including the *Dawsonia* – the world's largest moss, which can reach a height of one metre) in the **montane forest**.

The higher altitude of the **cloud forest** (1800–2600 metres) supports a huge range of flowering plants – around a thousand orchids and 26 varieties of rhododendron are known to grow in the forest, including Low's Rhododendron, whose yellow flowers can attain a width of 30 centimetres. The hanging lichen that drapes across branches of stunted trees lends a magical feel to the landscape at this height. It's at this level, too, that you're most likely to see the park's most famous plants – its nine species of cup-shaped **pitcher plants**, which secrete a nectar that first attracts insects and then drowns them, as they are unable to escape the slippery sides of the pitcher. Early climber Spenser St John is alleged to have seen one such plant even digesting a rat.

Higher still, above 2600 metres, only the most tenacious plantlife can survive – like the agonizingly gnarled *Sayat-Sayat* tree, and the Heath Rhododendron, found only on Mount Kinabalu – while beyond 3300 metres, soil gives way to granite. Here, grasses, sedges and the elegant blooms of Low's Buttercup are all that survive.

Fauna
While **mammals** that dwell in the park include orang-utans, Bornean gibbons, tarsiers and clouded leopards, you're unlikely to see anything more exotic than squirrels, rats and tree shrews. You might just catch sight of a mouse deer or a bearded pig, if you're lucky. The higher reaches of Mount Kinabalu boast two types of **birds** seen nowhere else in the world – the Kinabalu Friendly Warbler and Kinabalu Mountain Blackbird. Lower down, look out for hornbills and eagles, as well as the Malaysian Tree Pie, identifiable by its foot-long tail. You're bound to see plenty of **insects**: butterflies and moths flit through the trees, while down on the forest floor roam creatures like the Trilobite Beetle, whose orange-and-black armour plating lend it a fearsome aspect. You'll spend a lot of time looking at your feet as you scale the mountain, so tell your guide what you want pointed out *en route*.

headaches, nausea and certainly breathlessness are a possibility. The spectacle of sunrise will rob you of any remaining breath, and then it's back down to Panar Laban for a hearty breakfast before the two-hour amble down to park headquarters. And, when you finally arrive back at HQ, it's worth reflecting on the fact that Nepalese runner, Kusang Gurung, the winner of the 1991 **Kinabalu Climbathon**, ran up and down the mountain in a staggering two hours, 42 minutes and 33 seconds.

Practicalities

It's a good idea to book a **place to stay** in the park as soon as possible – especially if you're planning to go at the weekend, when it's at its busiest. If you're really organized, you can book by post or phone: postal bookings should be addressed to the Park Warden, Sabah Parks Office, Lot 1-3, Block K, Sinsuran Shopping Complex, PO Box 10626, Kota Kinabalu (☎088/211585). Otherwise, drop in at the office, where the friendly staff will help you plan your ascent. You'll need at least two days to climb Mount Kinabalu – three if you want to carry on by bus to Poring – though you'll be glad of a spare day or two, in case cloud cover spoils the view from the summit. Only accommodation is paid for in KK – permits and guide fees are levied at the park itself (see "Up the mountain" above).

Upon **arrival**, buses stop at the extended cluster of lodgings, restaurants and offices known as Park Headquarters, depositing you outside the **park reception** office (daily 7am–7.30pm), where you go to check into your accommodation. Staff here will provide you with useful maps and information sheets, while at the neighbouring souvenir shop there's a wide range of T-shirts, postcards and Borneo-related books. The staff at the park reception can also arrange charter buses ($60) to Poring.

A cluster of **hotels** has sprung up along the main road outside the park, but there's a perfectly adequate range of choices in the park itself. For those on tight budgets, the *Old* or *New Fellowship* **hostels** are basic but salubrious dormitory set-ups ($10 a head) with cooking facilities. From there, prices take a hike, with a variety of cabins all working out at roughly $40 a head. The twin-bed **cabins** (③ weekdays, ④ weekends) command magnificent views and are convenient for the park's administration office, while both the four-person **annexe rooms** (③ weekdays, ④ weekends), and the two-person **basement rooms** (③ weekdays, ④ weekends) are in the office itself. Top of the range are the *Nepenthes Villas* (⑤ weekdays, ⑥ weekends) – tasteful wooden chalets, each sleeping four people – and the swish *Kinabalu Lodge* (⑥).

Huts **up the mountain** couldn't be more basic – with the exception of *Laban Rata Rest House* (dormitory bed $25) which has its own restaurant, as well as central heating and hot-water showers. Otherwise, *Gunting Lagadan*, *Panar Laban* and *Waras* huts all have $10 dormitory beds, electricity and cooking facilities. *Sayat-Sayat Hut* ($10 a bed) is an hour further up the mountain, and lacks even an electricity supply.

The park's best **restaurant** is the *Kinabalu Balsam* (daily 6am–10pm, Sat until 11pm), whose balcony has fine views of the mountaintop; inside the entrance is a shop which sells chocolate, corned beef and biscuits for the climb. Alternatively, make for the administration office and the *Liwagu Restaurant* (daily 6am–10pm, Sat until 11pm), which, despite boasting all the ambience of a school canteen, serves well-cooked dishes, both Western and Asian. Higher up, unless you're catering for yourself, the only option is the restaurant in the *Laban Rata Rest House* (daily 7am–8pm & 2am–3.30am), where the food is fortifying, if on the pricey side.

Poring Hot Springs

Sited 43km from park HQ, on the southeastern side of Kinabalu National Park, are the **PORING HOT SPRINGS** ($2, free for overnight guests). The complex was developed by the Japanese during World War II, though the wooden tubs they installed have

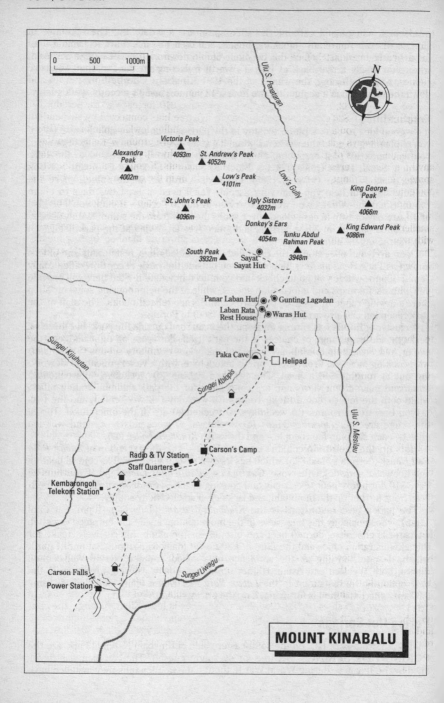

0   500   1000m

Victoria Peak
4093m
St Andrew's Peak
4052m
Alexandra Peak
4002m
Low's Peak
4101m
King George Peak
4066m
St John's Peak
4096m
Ugly Sisters
4032m
Donkey's Ears
4054m
King Edward Peak
4086m
Tunku Abdul Rahman Peak
3948m
South Peak
3932m
Sayat Sayat Hut

Ulu S. Penataran

Low's Gully

N

Sungei Kijuhutan

Panar Laban Hut
Gunting Lagadan
Laban Rata Rest House
Waras Hut

Paka Cave
Helipad

Ulu S. Mesilau

Sungei Kolopis

Radio & TV Station
Carson's Camp
Staff Quarters

Kembarongoh Telekom Station

Carson Falls
Sungei Liwagu
Power Station

MOUNT KINABALU

been replaced by functional rows of tiled baths. After a few days' hiking up the mountain, a soak in its hot (120–140°F) sulphurous waters is just the ticket – if a little like sitting in a sheep dip. The baths are a couple of minutes from the main gates, across a suspension bridge that spans the Mamut river; there's a plunge pool adjacent and two enclosed baths with jacuzzi.

A fifteen-minute walk beyond the baths brings you to Poring's **canopy walk** (daily: 10.30am–3.30pm, $2; 6pm–6am, $30 for 1–3 persons, $10 for each extra person; 6–10.30am, $60 1–3, $20 extra; camera $5), where five tree huts connected by suspended walkways afford you a monkey's-eye view of the surrounding lowland rainforest. Views from the walkways – at their highest point, 60 metres above ground – are tremendous, though the shouts of giddy tourists negotiating them thwart your chances of seeing anything more interesting than birds, butterflies and ants. If you're set on witnessing some wildlife, arrange a more expensive trip at night or in the early morning, when it's cooler and quieter.

A more conventional trail strikes off to the right of the baths, reaching 150-metre-high **Langanan Waterfall** about an hour and a half later. On its way, the trail passes smaller **Kepungit Waterfall** – whose icy pool is ideal for swimming – and a cave lined with squealing, fluttering bats, as well as groves of towering bamboo (*poring* means "bamboo" in Kadazan). Be warned: if it's been raining, there'll be leeches on the trail. A strong flick with the finger sometimes despatches them, though all too often you'll only end up transferring the leech onto your hand; a more foolproof method is to burn them off with a cigarette.

Practicalities

If you're in a group, it's best to charter a **minibus** to take you from Kinabalu Park HQ to Poring – the alternative is to wave down a passing Ranau-bound minibus (see below), and change there. The journey takes around half an hour. Minibuses drop you beside Poring's **reception** hut, inside the complex gates, where you can arrange an onward minibus when you leave. A proposed restaurant at the springs still hasn't materialized, though there are two unspectacular **places to eat** just outside the gates: the *Poring Restoran* (daily 8am–8pm), which serves uninspiring Chinese food, and the *Kedai Makanan Melayu* (daily 8am–6pm), three doors along, whose simple Malay dishes take an age to reach your table.

No permit is needed to visit Poring, though you'll have to book your accommodation at the *Sabah Parks* office in KK. Unless you're camping ($5 per person) on the grounds beyond the reception, the most affordable **place to stay** is at one of the two dorm units comprising the *Poring Hostel* ($10 a head), both of which have good cooking facilities. Two more upmarket **cabins** are also available: the *New Cabin* (③ weekdays, ④ weekends), which can accommodate four, and *Old Cabin* (④ weekdays, ⑤ weekends), sleeping up to six.

Ranau

Set in a pleasant bowl of hills, the small town of **RANAU** huddles around a square on the south side of the main KK–Sandakan road, 20km from Kinabalu National Park. There's nothing to do here, but it's a handy stopping point if it's too late to travel the extra 19km to Poring. Like KK, Ranau is based around a grid of ugly, lettered blocks; street names are in short supply, though one exception is Jalan Kibarambang – the first turning on the right if you're coming from KK, and home both to a rickety old market and a new Chinese temple, its gleaming white walls striped by red pillars. The first day of every month sees a lively *tamu*, around 1km out of town, towards Sandakan.

Incidentally, between Kinabalu Park HQ and Ranau is **KUNDASANG**, where a war memorial 150m off the main road commemorates the victims of the "Death March" of

September 1944, when Japanese troops marched 2400 POWs from Sandakan to Ranau (see p.442).

Practicalities

Minibuses stop at the eastern edge of town, on a patch of land beside Block A. At present, **long-distance buses** from KK to Sandakan stop briefly across town, on jalan Kibarambang – also the site of Ranau's **share taxi** stand – though there is talk of incorporating them both at the minibus terminus.

Ranau has three **hotels**, the best of which is the quiet, six-room *View Motel* (☎088/876445; ②) in Block L. The *Hotel Ranau* (☎088/875661; ③), next to the *Bank Bumiputra* at the top of the square, has a range of rooms from box-like singles to more spacious aircon doubles with bathrooms; while the *Kinabalu Hotel* (☎088/876028; ②), below the square in Block A, is a smartly painted place with cosy rooms and shared bathrooms. Enquiries about the *Government Rest House* (☎088/875337; ② or ④, depending on the whim of the manager), 500m east of town, should be made at the District Office opposite the Chinese temple – but be prepared to pay double the local rate.

Jalan Kibarambang has several **restaurants and coffee shops**, including the excellent *Restoran Muslim* (daily 6.30am–10pm), where you can eat great fried chicken to the strains of the Indian pop hits on the jukebox. Interesting Chinese food is in short supply in Ranau, though the *Sin Mui Mui Restoran* (closed Fri afternoon) at the south of the square has one of the town's wider choices. Also good is the *Mien Mien Restoran*, opposite. For Malay food, make for the *Restoran Sri Tanjung* (daily 7am–10pm), below the *View Motel*.

Sandakan and around

Sandwiched between sea and cliffs, and lacking Kota Kinabalu's sense of space, **SANDAKAN** isn't an immediately appealing city. Like the capital, Sandakan was all but destroyed during World War II, and its postwar reconstruction was worked around an unimaginative – and, in Sabah, all too familiar – grid system of indistinguishable concrete blocks. That said, the town is the springboard to several of Sabah's most fascinating destinations, including the Turtle Islands Park (p.442), Sepilok Orang Utan Rehabilitation Centre (p.441), and even the town centre itself is not without its redeeming features.

Although eighteenth-century accounts exist of a trading outpost called Sandakan within the Sultanate of Sulu (whose epicentre was in what is now the Philippines), the town's modern history began in the early 1870s, with the arrival of a group of European adventurers. Except for one, William Clarke Cowie, a moustached Scot who ran guns for the Sultan of Sulu, nothing is known about these men, but Kampung German, the name of the settlement they established on Pulau Timbang, points to their predominant nationality. The area of northeast Borneo between Brunei Bay and sungei Kinabatangan had been leased by the Sultan of Brunei to the *American Trading Company* in 1865. The company's attempt to establish a settlement here failed after a year and in 1877 the Anglo-Austrian partnership of Baron Von Overbeck and Alfred Dent took up the lease, naming Englishman William Pryer as the first Resident of the East Coast. After Kampung German burned down a year later, nearby Buli Sim-Sim was chosen by Pryer as the site of his new town, which he named *Elopura*, or "Beautiful City", although locals persisted in referring to it as Sandakan (in Sulu, "to be pawned"). By 1885, Sandakan was the capital of British North Borneo, its natural harbour and its proximity to sources of timber, beeswax, rattan and edible birds' nests transforming it into a thriving commercial centre. Sabahan timber was used to build

Peking's Temple of Heaven and much of Sandakan's early trade was with Hong Kong; today, there's still a strong Cantonese influence in town.

In January 1942, the Japanese army took control, establishing a POW camp from where the infamous Death March to Ranau commenced. What little of the town was left standing by intensive Allied bombing was burned down by the Japanese, and the end of the war saw the administration of Sabah shift to KK. Nevertheless, by the 1950s a rebuilt Sandakan had become the economic engine of the state, while the timber boom of the 1960s and 1970s generated such wealth that for a while the town was reputed to boast the world's greatest concentration of millionaires. When the region's good timber ran out in the 1980s, Sandakan looked to oil palm and cocoa, crops which now dominate the surrounding landscape.

Arrival, information and getting around

The **long-distance bus station** is below jalan Leila, ten minutes' walk west of the town centre; long-distance taxis and land cruisers also work out of this area. The **airport** is 11km north of town, and connected to it by taxis (around $12) and minibuses ($1.50) – the latter shuttling to and from the southern end of jalan Pelabuhan throughout the day. Downtown Sandakan's **addresses** take a little getting used to, reliant on numbers, not names; indeed, less central addresses are pinpointed according to their distances out of the downtown area, hence "Mile 1 $1/_2$", "Mile 3", and so on (given below). There's no tourist office as such, though the *Sabah Parks* office (see "Listings" below for address) – which you may need to visit anyway, if you want to go to the Turtle Islands Park – hands out **free maps** for tourists.

City transport
Sandakan's two local bus stations are within a couple of minutes' walk of each other, in the centre of town. The scheduled services of the *Labuk Road Bus Company* leave from the waterfront **Labuk Road Station** – blue-and-white buses travel up Labuk Road itself, while those sporting red, yellow and green stripes are bound for points west, along jalan Leila. A short walk west along jalan Pryer brings you to the **minibus area**. The two stations have many destinations in common, so it's worth checking each in turn to find the earliest bus to your destination.

Taxis speed around town throughout the day, but if you can't spot one, make for the southern end of Fourth Street, where they gather in numbers.

Accommodation

Only two establishments in or around town cater specifically for budget travellers. The majority of hotels are in the blocks forming the town centre, though several others cluster in the suburb of Bandar Ramai-Ramai, reached in five minutes on any west-bound bus.

Hotel City View, Block 23, Third Avenue (☎089/271122). Central hotel with spacious rooms. ⑤.

Hung Wing Hotel, Block 13, Third Avenue (☎089/272217). The absence of a lift means rooms get less expensive as they get higher: top-floor rooms, smallish but tidy, are a bargain. ②.

Hotel London, Block 10, jalan Buli Sim-Sim (☎089/216366). The bare but presentable rooms in this friendly hotel next to Wisma Khoo have air-con and private bathroom. ③.

Mayfair Hotel, 24 jalan Pryer (☎089/219855). Clean but spartan rooms, situated over the *Malaysian Textile Centre*. ③.

Hotel Paris, Third Avenue (☎089/218488). Tatty Chinese hotel with budget-rated fan rooms; air-con rooms are 50 percent more expensive. ②.

Ramada Renaissance Hotel, jalan Utara (☎089/213299). Sandakan's five-star finest, with swish restaurants, business centre, swimming pool and sports facilities. ⑥.

Hotel Ramai, Mile 1 ¹/₂ jalan Leila (☎089/273222). Real effort has been made in this excellent mid-range hotel, whose 44 spacious rooms complete with bathroom, TV and air-con, are within striking distance of downtown Sandakan; recommended. ④.

Resort Lodge Hotel, Mile 1 ¹/₂ jalan Leila (☎089/45211). Like the *Hung Wing*, more affordable as you climb higher; not a budget choice, but competitive if you want a modicum of comfort. ③.

Sanbay Hotel, Mile 1 ¹/₂ jalan Leila (☎089/275000). Smart new hotel west of the town centre. ⑤.

Travellers' Rest Hostel, 2nd Floor, Apartment 2, Block E, Bandar Ramai-Ramai (☎089/43454). Sister hostel to the well-established KK namesake, offering clean, bargain-priced dorms ($10) and rooms with breakfast included. Owner Chris Perez can arrange trips to his jungle camp ($85 return, then $13 a day) and elsewhere (see p.442). ②.

Uncle Tan's, Mile 17 ¹/₂ Labuk Road (☎089/531639). Perennially popular guest house, where the $20 charge for a bed in a basic wooden hut includes three meals. Uncle Tan himself arranges tours of the surrounding area (see p.442), including trips to his jungle camp ($130 return, then $15 a day). Coming from KK by bus, ask to be dropped at *Tan's*, which is around 28km west of Sandakan. ②–③.

The town

Sandakan town stands on the northern lip of Sandakan Bay – much of it on land reclaimed from the sea early this century. Stretching west of the dense maze of numbered streets and avenues that makes up the downtown area is jalan Leila, while to the east, running up round the bay, is jalan Buli Sim-Sim. The heart of the town centre is its **padang** – one of the few surviving reminders of Sandakan's colonial heritage.

First stop should be the uproarious **waterfront markets** (daily 7am–6pm) along jalan Pryer, down whose dark aisles you'll find exquisite conches and turtle eggs illegally imported from the Philippines. A row of weather-beaten old fishing boats moors behind the fish market, Sabah's largest. Despite the strong police presence along this stretch of jalan Pryer, pickpocketing is still rife, so be vigilant.

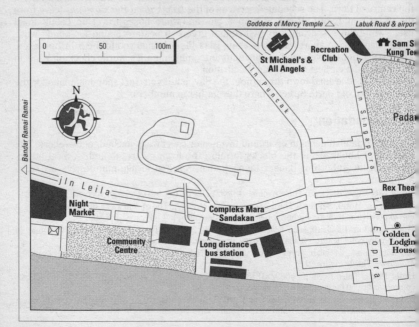

Speedboats from below jalan Pryer run across to **Pulau Berhala** 4km offshore, below whose vertical sandstone cliffs is a decent beach; with a lot of bargaining, the return journey should come to $20. Berhala once housed a leper colony, and in World War II was used as a POW camp by the Japanese, housing American author Agnes Keith (see "Books", p.599) and her son George, amongst others.

A fifteen-minute walk east, along Jalan Buli Sim-Sim, deposits you in front of Sandakan's modern, minimalist **mosque** which stands on a promontory and commands fine views of the bay. Flanking its eastern side is **Kampung Buli Sim-Sim**, the water village around which Sandakan expanded last century, whose countless photogenic shacks spread like lilies out into the bay, criss-crossed by walkways. There's a marked contrast between the delapidation of the water village and the well-tended surroundings of Sandakan's colonial remnants, especially the quintessentially English **St Michael's and All Angels' Church**, northwest of the *padang*, a five-minute walk up Jalan Puncak. Here, varnished pews, memorial plaques and faded photographs evoke a sense of antiquity rarely felt in Sabah. Steps lead down from the far side of the church grounds to jalan Singapore across which, on jalan Tokong, **Sam Sing Kung Temple** rears up above the *padang*. Inside, its smoke-stained walls are lined with wooden boards etched with Chinese characters written in gold; while above the entrance hangs a wonderful woodcarving of a boatful of people coursing through an ocean teeming with prawns, crabs and fish. Sandakan's oldest temple is the **Goddess of Mercy Temple**, five minutes further up jalan Singapore, in a grove of magnificent palms; although modernization has robbed it of any character.

A ten-minute walk up Jalan Utara, across on the eastern side of the *padang*, brings you to the foot of jalan Istana, from whose **Observation Point** are good views of the town, boats and islands below. Turn right down the road beyond it, and bear left after

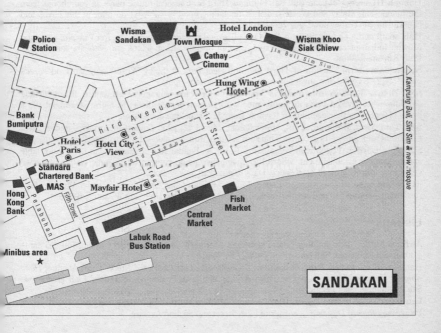

SANDAKAN

Sandakan's half-Tudor, half-*kampung*-style **Istana**, and you're in the huge town **cemetery**, its thousands of green and sky-blue, semicircular graves banked impressively up a hillside. Once this far, you may as well continue along the path to the **Japanese cemetery** where, besides the graves of Japanese soldiers killed in action in World War II, are those of Japanese girls sold into prostitution in the late nineteenth and early twentieth centuries.

There's another pleasing view of Sandakan Bay from the **Puu Jih Shih Temple**, a new complex high up on the cliffs, 4km west of town. Inside, three tall statues of Buddha, carved from imported teak and embellished with gold foil, stand on the altar, ringed by 32 dragon-entwined pillars – also of teak. Come early in the morning and your visit will be accompanied by the songs of scores of birds that swoop around the temple's rafters. Sibuga buses from the Labuk Road Station drop you off nearby.

Eating and drinking

Sandakan may not be able to match KK's variety of good **restaurants**, but there's still enough choice here to suit most people, with Malay, Chinese, Indian and Western food all well represented. Most places are in the town centre or along jalan Leila, though several renowned seafood restaurants open every evening on Trig Hill, high up above the town, with fine views of Sandakan Bay. For **hawker stalls**, the market on jalan Pryer is unbeatable, or there's the grandstand on jalan Singapore, under which a makeshift cluster of satay stalls sets up every evening. There's nothing in the way of nightlife in Sandakan, though beer is widely available in Chinese restaurants and coffee shops.

Kedai Kopi Subur, Compleks Mara Sandakan, jalan Leila. No-frills coffee shop specializing in *coto makassar* – a tasty, meaty broth with chunks of rice cake. Daily 8am–9pm.

Kim Fah, behind the long-distance bus station, off jalan Leila. Rough and ready Chinese seafood restaurant, rescued by the views of the bay from its verandah. Daily 11am–2pm & 5pm–3am.

Habeeb III, corner of jalan Buli Sim-Sim and Third St. Classical music plays as you choose from the Indonesian, Malay and Western dishes (including good breakfasts) on offer in this cheap and cheerful air-con restaurant. Daily 7am–11pm.

Haji, south of the *padang*, Second Ave. One of several restaurants below the *Rex Cinema*, a popular Muslim Indian place with an air-con dining room upstairs; fresh juices and *rotis* are memorable. Daily 8.30am–9.30pm.

Selera Samudera, junction of Third Ave and jalan Puncak. Spicy West Malaysian food served buffet-style – $3 buys rice, meat and vegetables. Daily 8am–9pm.

SRC Deluxe Restaurant, *Sandakan Recreation Club*, jalan Singapore. Cantonese dishes include delicious whole baked duck in plum sauce ($35), which serves three; at night, steamboat ($9 a head) is served on the second-floor terrace. Daily 11.30am–2pm & 5–10pm.

Srie Tom Yam Makanan Laut, Hotel Ramai, Mile 1 $1/_2$ jalan Leila. Comfortable, understated, restaurant seek out for its excellent Thai soups. Open Mon–Sat 8am–11.30pm, Sun 10am–10pm.

Supreme Garden Vegetarian restaurant, Block 30, Bandar Ramai-Ramai, jalan Leila. Affordable and welcoming establishment, where the imaginative menu runs to mock meat dishes like fried vegetarian frog with black bean sauce. Daily 10am–2pm & 5.30–9pm.

XO Steakhouse, Hsiang Garden Estate, Mile 1 $1/_2$ jalan Leila. Sandakan's premier Western food restaurant, serving fish and seafood as well as Australian steaks. Daily 11am–2pm & 6–10pm.

Listings

Airlines *MAS*, Sabah Building, jalan Pelabuhan – formerly jalan Edinburgh – open Mon–Fri 8am–4.30pm, Sat 8am–3pm, Sun 8am–noon (☎089/273966).

Banks and exchange *Bank Bumiputra*, opposite *Standard Chartered Bank*, Third Avenue; *Hong Kong & Shanghai Bank*, corner of Third Avenue and jalan Pelabuhan; *Standard Chartered Bank*, Sabah Building, jalan Pelabuhan.

Laundry *Sandakan Laundry*, on Third Avenue, between Third and Fourth streets.

Pharmacy *Borneo Dispensary*, corner of Fifth Street and Second Avenue.

Police The main police station is on jalan Sim Sim (☎089/211222).

Post Sandakan's GPO is five minutes' walk west of town, on jalan Leila; Mon–Fri 8am–5pm, Sat 10am–1pm.

Sabah Parks 9th floor, Wisma Khoo (Mon–Fri 8am–12.45pm & 2–4.15pm, Sat 8am–12.45pm; ☎089/273453)

Telephones At the *Telekom* office, 6th floor, Wisma Khoo (daily 8.30am–4.45pm); IDD calls can presently only be made on card phones.

Tour operators *SI Tours*, 3rd floor, Yeng Yo Hong Building, arranges tours of the sights around Sandakan, as does *Wildlife Expeditions*, 903, 9th floor, Wisma Khoo Siak Chiew (☎089/219616). For budget trips to the Turtle Islands Park, Gomantong and the Kinabatangan, contact the *Travellers' Rest Hostel*, or *Uncle Tan's*.

Wildlife Department 6th floor, Urusetia Building, Mile 7, Labuk Road (☎089/666550), for permits for the Gomantong Caves.

Sepilok Orang Utan Rehabilitation Centre

One of only three orang-utan sanctuaries in the world, the **SEPILOK ORANG UTAN REHABILITATION CENTRE** (daily 9am–noon & 2–4pm; feeding times station A 10am & 2.30pm and station B 10.30am; $10), 25km west of Sandakan, occupies a 43-square-kilometre patch of lowland rainforest. The centre was established in 1964 as a retraining centre for orangs liberated by a law prohibiting the catching and keeping of them as pets – though the timber boom has meant that Sepilok's more recent arrivals come from regions where logging has robbed them of their homes. At the centre, young and domesticated orang-utans (the name means "man of the forest" in Malay), whose survival instincts are undeveloped, are trained to fend for themselves. Although not always successful, this process has so far seen around a hundred orangs reintroduced to their natural habitat. To aid the integration process, bananas and milk are made available to those still finding their forest feet at two **feeding stations**; the diet is never varied, as a way of encouraging orangs to forage for other foodstuffs in the trees.

Orang-utans – tailless, red haired apes – can reach a height of around 1.65m, and can live to be as old as thirty. Solitary, but not aggressively territorial animals, they live a largely arboreal existence, eating fruit, leaves, bark and the occasional insect. At the **visitors' centre** that fronts the Sepilok sanctuary, a blackboard outlines the day's events, while inside there's an exhibition on forest preservation. Close to feeding time a warden leads you for ten minutes along a wooden boardwalk to **station A**, passing the **nursery**, where baby orang-utans are taught elementary climbing skills on ropes and branches. Nothing prepares you for the thrill of seeing young orangs swinging, shimmying and strolling – and some carried by their mothers – towards their breakfast, jealously watched by gangs of macaques that loiter around for scraps. Once replete, wilier orangs take away enough bananas for a picnic lunch in the trees. Most visitors see only station A, though up to fifteen people a day are allowed to take the thirty-minute hike to station B, where there's a better chance of seeing semi-mature and more independent orangs; ask at reception when you arrive, if you're interested. Sepilok is also a halfway house for honey bears, elephants and other wild animals that are either sick or en route for other reserves in Sabah. You can't see any of these though – nor the four extremely rare Sumatran Rhinos kept for breeding at the centre.

Buses leave for the centre daily at 9.20am, 11.30am, 1.30pm and 3pm from Sandakan's Labuk Road Station, but if you want an earlier start, head for the minibus area and take a "Batu 14" bus.

Taman Buaya and the War Memorial Park

On your way back into Sandakan, you might consider a couple of minor diversions – neither of them thrilling – along Labuk Road. At **Taman Buaya** (daily 7am–5pm; $2), Sabah's only crocodile farm, a raised boardwalk lets you view over a thousand croco-

diles languishing in dreary concrete moats. If this wasn't bad enough, the stuffed crocodiles, eggs and foetuses on sale in the souvenir shop are a study in tastelessness.

A mile further in towards Sandakan, and along jalan Rimba, the **War Memorial
Park** marks the site of the World War II POW camp where the Death March of 1944
originated. In 1942, 2750 British and Australian soldiers were transported from
Singapore to Sandakan and set to work building an airstrip. By early in 1945, many had
died, but the surviving 1800 Australians and 600 British troops were force-marched to
Ranau, where they were to start work on a new project. Just six Australian soldiers
survived the 240-kilometre march through mud and jungle. Dominating the park is a
simple white block dedicated to the Allied soldiers who fought in North Borneo, to the
locals who helped POWs, and to those involved in the Sandakan underground
movement. Remnants of the camp are scattered around the sadly neglected grounds of
the park.

Turtle Islands Park

Peeping out of the Sulu Sea some 40km north of Sandakan, three tiny islands comprise
Sabah's **TURTLE ISLANDS PARK**, the favoured egg-laying sites of the Green and
Hawksbill **turtles**, varying numbers of which haul themselves laboriously above the
high-tide mark to bury their clutches of eggs. To protect them, a turtle closed season
was introduced as early as 1927 by the *British North Borneo Chartered Company*. In
1966, Malaysia's first turtle **hatchery** was established here and today all three of the
park's islands (Pulau Selingaan, Pulau Bakkungan Kechil and Pulau Gulisaan) have a
hatchery – though only Selingaan has amenities for tourists. As at Malaysia's other
protected turtle-watching site – Rantau Abang (see p.255), on the peninsula's east coast
– you're guaranteed an extraordinary sight, especially as the newly hatched turtles are
liberated on the beach, to waddle, Chaplin-like, into the sea.

On your way to Turtle Islands Park, you'll pass scores of *bagang*, or fish traps. At
night, the light of the kerosene lamps hung from their bamboo frames attracts shoals
of anchovies, which are then caught in raisable nets – though on certain days of the
month the moon is too full and bright for the process to work. The *bagang* are washed
away by the annual storms of the November monsoon and rebuilt early the next year.

Turtle watching

Turtles begin to come ashore around 7.30pm – **rangers** scout the island after dark and
they'll alert you once a sighting has been made. While turtles visit the park every day
of the year, the peak nesting time falls between July and October. Typically, it takes
half an hour for sea turtles to lurch up the sand, dig a nesting pit and lay their slimy,
ping-pong-ball eggs – an average clutch will contain upwards of a hundred eggs. All the
egg-laying turtles are tagged, to aid research into the distribution and size of Southeast
Asia's turtle population; their eggs, meanwhile, are taken for reburial to the hatchery,
where they are safeguarded from hungry rats. With hatchings a nightly event, you're
almost guaranteed the stirring sight of scores of determined little turtles wriggling up
through the sand. In the meantime, Selingaan's quiet **beaches** are good for swimming
and sunbathing, or you can go snorkelling off nearby Bakkungan Kechil ($15 a person,
minimum four people; details from park headquarters).

Practicalities

You can only visit the park as part of a tour. The best deals are offered by *Uncle Tan's*
and the *Travellers' Rest Hostel* (see "Accommodation" above): Tan charges $110 (mini-
mum six people) for the boat transfer plus a night's accommodation (meals extra);
Chris Perez at the *Traveller's Rest* charges the same, but will depart with half as many

people. Otherwise, go to the *Sabah Parks* office in Wisma Khoo in Sandakan where, subject to availability, you'll be able to arrange a lift with the next group out, and pay for your accommodation, all for around $130. If you book through an agency you'll be looking at around $250 for the same package. *Sabah Parks* allows no more than twenty visitors a night onto Selingaan, all of whom are put up in the island's four comfortable **chalets** and eat at *Roses' Cafe*, inside the visitors' centre; set breakfasts, lunches and dinners are available, but sticking to the menu ensures better value.

Gomantong Caves

Further afield, the **GOMANTONG CAVES**, south of Sandakan Bay, are inspiring enough to warrant a visit at any time of the year, though you'll get most out of the trip when the edible nests of their resident swiftlets are being harvested. The caves are administered by Sabah's Wildlife Department, which permits just two harvests a year – one between February and April, allowing the birds time to rebuild before the egg-laying season, the other between July and September, when the young have hatched and left. Bird's-nest soup has long been a Chinese culinary speciality and Chinese merchants have been coming to Borneo to trade for birds' nests for at least twelve centuries.

Of the two major caves, **Simud Hitam** is the more accessible. Reaching a height of ninety metres in places, it supports a colony of black-nest swiftlets, whose nests – a mixture of saliva and feathers – sell for US$40 a kilogram. Above Simud Hitam is larger but less accessible **Simud Putih**, home to the white-nest swiftlet, whose nests are of pure, dried saliva and can fetch prices of over US$500 a kilogram. Harvesting is a dangerous business: workers scale impossibly precarious rattan ladders and ropes – some up to sixty metres high – to collect the nests; there are occasional fatalities. Outside the caves, there's a picnic site and an **information centre** that will fill you in on the caves' ecosystem, while ringing the whole area is a patch of virgin jungle supporting wildlife as dramatic as orang-utans and elephants – neither of which you're likely to see.

It's easiest to go with a tour agency (anywhere from $60–300 per person), but under your own steam, one minibus a day (6am) leaves Sandakan's long-distance bus station for **SUKAU**, a riverside town beyond Gomantong. This drops you on the main road, from where it's 5km down a former logging road to the caves. Permission is presently required from the Wildlife Department (see "Listings" above) to explore the caves – which can also tell you whether **chalets** planned for the site have materialized.

The Kinabatangan river

East of the entrance to Sandakan Bay, Sabah's longest river, the 560-kilometre **Kinabatangan**, ends its northeasterly path from the interior to the Sulu Sea. The dual threats of piracy and flooding have kept its lower reaches largely free of development, and the area consequently boasts a wealth of Bornean wildlife. Elephants, orang-utans, macaques and crocodiles all dwell in the forest flanking the river, and the resident **bird life** is equally impressive: with luck, you may glimpse hornbills, egrets, exquisite blue-banded kingfishers or oriental darters, which dive underwater to find food. The Kinabatangan's greatest natural assets, however, are its **proboscis monkeys** (see feature below), found beside the water's edge each afternoon: instantly recognizable, looking not unlike Batman's arch-foe, the Penguin.

Again, the only way to see the Kinabatangan is through a tour operator, who can arrange afternoon boat and monkey-spotting trips out of Sandakan, though to appreciate the full beauty of the river, it's best to stay in one of the several **jungle lodges** on its banks. Those run by *Uncle Tan's* and the *Travellers' Rest Hostel* (see

> ### PROBOSCIS MONKEYS
>
> For many naturalists, a trip to Borneo would not be complete without having encountered a **proboscis monkey**, a shy animal confined to riverine forests and mangrove swamps of the Bornean coast and found nowhere else in the world. It derives its name from the enlarged, drooping, red nose of the adult male monkey; females and young animals are snub-nosed. The role of the drooping nose, which seems to straighten out when the animal is issuing its curious honking call note, is largely unclear, although it is likely to help in attracting a mate. The monkeys are reddish-brown in colour, with a dark red cap; in addition, the adult males have a cream-white collar (or neck ruff). All of them have long, thick, white tails and white rumps, and the adult males in particular have large bellies, giving them a rather portly, "old gentleman" appearance. Males are significantly heavier than females, weighing up to 23kg, compared with a maximum female weight of 10kg. All in all, this combination of features has earned male proboscis monkeys the (not entirely complimentary) name of *orang belanda* or "Dutchman" in parts of Borneo.
>
> The monkeys live in loose groups, spending their days in trees close to water, feeding on young leaves, shoots and fruit. They are most active at dawn and dusk, when moving to and from feeding sites. Although they are mostly arboreal (tree-living), they will walk across open areas when necessary, and are proficient swimmers, aided by having partly-webbed feet. They are quite choosey feeders, preferring the leaves of the Sonneraita mangrove tree, a rather specialist diet which means that large areas of forest need to be protected to provide groups of monkeys with sufficient food. This fact, coupled with the restricted range of the proboscis monkey, makes the species vulnerable to habitat loss and hunting pressure.
>
> Visitors can hope to see proboscis monkeys in several of the national parks in Sabah and Sarawak, apart from the admittedly remote Kinabatangan area: in Sarawak in particular, the animals can be seen in Bako National Park (p.345) and in the Mangroves Forest Reserve near Kampung Salak.

"Accommodation", p.438) boast the most competitive prices: *Uncle Tan's* charges $130 for the return journey, then $15 a night expenses, while with the *Travellers' Rest Hostel*, expect to pay around $90 for transport and $15 a night.

Batu Putih

Within the limestone outcrop of **BATU PUTIH** (known locally as Batu Tulug), 1km north of the Kinabatangan Bridge on the road between Sandakan and Lahad Datu, small caves contain wooden coffins well over a hundred years old. When the former curate of the Sarawak Museum, Tom Harrisson, explored the caves in the 1950s, he found many hardwood coffin troughs and lids, as well as a wooden upright, grooved with notches that were thought to represent a genealogical record. It was from here that the two-hundred-year-old coffin lid with a buffalo's head carved into its handle, displayed at the Sabah State Museum, was taken; other coffins are still in their original spots, though unless archeology is your passion, think twice about making the detour to see them. All buses to Lahad Datu pass by the caves.

South of Sandakan

Below Sandakan Bay, the horseshoe of Sabah's main road continues southwards over the Kinabatangan Bridge to the towns of **Lahad Datu** and **Tawau**. This far east, the state's central mountain ranges taper away, to be replaced by lowland – and sometimes swampy – coastal regions lapped by the **Sulu** and **Celebes** seas, and dominated by oil palm plantations. Archeological findings around **Madai**, off the road between Lahad

Datu and Tawau, prove this area of Borneo has been inhabited for well over ten thousand years. Nowadays, this is Sabah's "wild east", where streets teem with Filipino and Indonesian immigrants trying to scratch a living and where pirates working out of islands in the nearby Filipino waters pose a real threat to fishermen. You'll sense a profound change of mood if you arrive direct from KK. Filipinos and Indonesians have been migrating into Sabah since the 1950s, when they were drawn in search of work on Sabah's plantations, but the influx of Filipinos rose sharply in the 1970s, as a result of the civil unrest in Mindanao.

The lowland rain forest runs riot at the **Danum Valley Conservation Area**, which can be reached via Lahad Datu. Closer to Kalimantan, and around the southern lip of wide **Darvel Bay**, the oceanic island of **Sipadan** is acclaimed as one of the world's top diving spots, its flawless coral ablaze with exotic fishes and sea creatures. More prosaically, you'll find yourself this far around the state if you're **heading to Indonesia**: a boat from Tawau is the cheapest way to reach northeastern Kalimantan.

If you're heading back to KK, there is an alternative to retracing your steps around the crown of the state. From Tawau, land cruisers depart daily for Keningau (p.419), travelling on logging roads that complete a **ring road** of sorts around Sabah.

Lahad Datu

A discomfiting sense of lawlessness prevails in **LAHAD DATU**, 175km south of Sandakan, on shallow Darvel Bay. In recent years, this unattractive boomtown has been flooded by immigrants – many of whom you'll see eking out a living by hawking cigarettes and nuts – while pirates are known to work the adjacent coastline. In 1986, a mob of heavily armed pirates stormed the *Standard Chartered Bank* and *MAS* office on Jalan Teratai, Lahad Datu's main street, making off with almost $100,000.

As Lahad Datu is the jumping-off point for trips to the Danum Valley Conservation Area (see below), your first port of call will probably be the *Innoprise* office (☎089/81092), in Block 3 of the Fajar Centre, north of the town centre. Here you can book trips to the valley, if you haven't already done so in KK, or pick up the bus (Mon, Wed & Fri at 3pm; $30) if you have. The only tourist sight in town is **Kampong Panji**, a run-down water village on the western edge of town.

Practicalities

Buses stop at the terminus on jalan Bunga Raya, a couple of minutes southeast of the town centre – look inland and you'll see the tall, chocolate- and beige-coloured building that marks the eastern end of jalan Teratai, on which you'll find Lahad Datu's *MAS* office (☎089/81707). The **airport** is a short taxi ride north of town.

Budget **accommodation** centres around the eastern (bus terminus) end of Jalan Teratai; the *Ocean Hotel* (☎089/81700; ③) has adequate if dingy rooms, but for rock bottom prices, head up the side street 20m west of it, to seedy *Rumah Tumpangan Malaysia* (☎089/83358; ②), where the absence of a lift means rooms get cheaper as they get higher. Opposite, the *Malaysia Venus Hotel II* (no phone; ②) is the best deal in town, with clean but spartan rooms with attached bathroom; or try the well-furnished *Hotel Jago Kota* (☎089/82000; ③) on jalan Kampong Panji, or jalan Teratai's slightly shoddier *Hotel Mido* (☎089/81800; ④).

A handful of decent **restaurants** make a forced stay in Lahad Datu more bearable. There's the cave-like Chinese *Restoran Melawar*, a block west of the *Hotel Mido*; while the *Restoran Auliah* (closes at 7pm), next door, does a fine biyriani. Otherwise, go for the good-value *Lahad Datu Seafood Restaurant* (open until midnight), housed in waterfront buildings and serving Chinese and Malay seafood dishes; adjacent is the town's swish new **market**, whose upstairs stalls command pleasant views out to sea.

To Sahabat

Although good stretches of beach do exist along the coastline east of Lahad Datu, the threat of piracy puts them off limits. The only exception is the beach at **TUNGKU**, a seaside village that has its own police station – though 70km is a long way to go for a dip in the sea; look for a Tungku minibus at Lahad Datu's terminus.

A wiser plan is to continue east into **SAHABAT**, a vast area of land which Sabah's Federal Land Development Agency (*FELDA*), has blanketed with oil palms. Here, the plantation settlement of **BANDAR SAHABAT** provides the unlikely backdrop to a tasteful seafront hotel, the *Sahabat Beach Resort* (⑤), a quiet place at which to tread water for a time. While the hotel's palm-fringed beach can't be called idyllic – abutting it is a jetty at which boats are loaded with palm oil – it's breezy and clean enough. Plans afoot include a water sports complex and tours of local plantations. Those on a tighter budget should stay instead at the adjacent *Sahabat Resort Annexe* (③), whose rooms are perfectly cheery – though bear in mind that prices here may increase as the resort's amenities improve. Bookings at both places can be made on ☎089/776533.

Madai Caves

If you didn't get to Gomantong Caves (see p.443), it's worth breaking your journey to Tawau for a trip to the **MADAI CAVES**, 13km west of the unremarkable coastal town of Kunak. Although humans have dwelt in them for over ten thousand years, the caves of the Madai limestone massif are most remarkable for the bird life they support; here, as at Gomantong, the nests of swiftlets are harvested for bird's-nest soup. The entrance to the cave system is marked by a motley gathering of fragile stilt huts – home, in season, to Idahan nest-harvesters. Once beyond the front aperture, you'll discover a succession of vast chambers in which swiftlets dive, bats squeak and guano lies ankle-deep. In season, harvesters will offer to show you the remnants of old Idahan coffins that the caves hold – but at a price. The caves are pitch-black, so a flashlight is essential.

Tawau-bound minibuses will drop you in the Madai area for $5, though with the caves 3km off the main road, it's worth paying an extra $2 to be driven all the way.

Danum Valley Conservation Area

Sabah's **DANUM VALLEY CONSERVATION AREA** (DVCA) spans 438 square kilometres of primary lowland rainforest west of Lahad Datu. Established in 1981 for the purpose of rainforest-related research and education, the DVCA supports a wealth of wildlife from bearded pigs to orang-utans, Sumatran rhinos to Asian elephants, and hornbills to pheasants. Tourism at the DVCA is in a state of flux: until recently, the hub of all activity was the **Danum Valley Field Centre**, 85km west of Lahad Datu, on the DVCA's eastern edge, established to provide facilities for visiting scientists. In addition to its laboratory, library and computer room, it has three observation platforms and 50km of tracks, which provide tourists with a unique opportunity to explore the rainforest. Now, though, the centre is being partially phased out, to be superseded by the **Borneo Rainforest Lodge**, a major new initiative aiming to show that eco-tourism can positively aid the protection of the rainforests. Sited on a bend in the Danum River, the lodge specializes in "natural history tourism": wildlife treks and marked nature trails weave through the surrounding forest, while a canopy walkway, and video and slide shows, illustrate how the rainforest functions. Other activities include trips to the field centre and night safaris by jeep; or you can see the recently unearthed coffins and jars of a Dusun burial site at a two-hundred-metre escarpment near the lodge.

Practicalities

Buses to the *Field Centre* and *Borneo Rainforest Lodge* depart from the *Innoprise* office in Lahad Datu (Mon, Wed and Fri at 3pm; $60 return); otherwise you'll have to charter your own transport for $260. Though it's sometimes possible to arrange a visit to the DVCA once you reach Lahad Datu, it's wiser to do so in Kota Kinabalu (see p.416). Upon arrival at either site, there's a $25 entrance fee; at the field centre it's also obligatory to hire a guide ($20 for a half-day) for your first foray into the forest.

Whether **accommodation** will be available at the *Field Centre* in future is unclear; presently, it's much the cheapest option in the DVCA, with a tidy rest house whose seven twin rooms have attached bathrooms (④), and a hostel ($36 per person) where bathrooms are shared. Camping costs $15 per person, and you'll need your own tent. Check ahead (☎088/243245) to find the current state of play.

As for the *Borneo Rainforest Lodge* (⑤), it plans a total of 24 twin rooms in comfortable chalets built around a central lodge. Aimed squarely at the upper end of the tourist market, the place is far from a bargain, though prices do include meals and all activities. Again, call ☎088/243245 for details.

Semporna

Like Lahad Datu, **SEMPORNA** is worth visiting only as a springboard to better things – in this case, Pulau Sipadan (see below), for where boats depart most days. Sited 108km to the east of Tawau, the whole of this Bajau fishing town seems in danger of spilling into the sea: stilt houses are clustered either side of the town, and its one concession to tourism, the *Semporna Ocean Tourism Centre* (*SOTC*), balances on a causeway jutting out into the sea – even its chaotic market, where buses stop, is built half on land and half on stilts.

The rectangular sails of Bajau boats drift across the bay east of Semporna, which is studded by many small **islands**; some possess good beaches, though none to compare with Pulau Sipadan. Still, Pulau Gaya, Pulau Sibuan and Pulau Mabul are all recommended locally for snorkelling and swimming – staff at the *Dragon Inn Hotel* (see below) can arrange boats for the day for around $200–250, though you may pay less by haggling with a fisherman at the water's edge beyond the market.

Practicalities

The chances are that the company taking you to Sipadan will have booked you in at its *Dragon Inn Hotel* (☎089/781088; ④); if not, one economical option, the adequate *Hotel Semporna* (☎089/781378; ④), sits right in the centre of town. Three **tour operators** – *Borneo Divers*, *Sipadan Dive Centre* and *Borneo Sea Adventures* – have offices at the *SOTC*, as does *Today Travel Service*, Semporna's *MAS* agent.

Barring the uninspiring restaurants downtown, Semporna's only **eating** options are both on the same causeway as the *SOTC*: the classy *Pearl City Restaurant*, which has views out to sea, and the nearby, more decrepit, *Floating Restaurant*.

Pulau Sipadan

In the past few years, a trip to tiny **PULAU SIPADAN** – 30km south of Semporna in the Celebes Sea – has become *de rigueur* for the hardcore scuba diving fraternity. Acclaimed by marine biologist Jacques Cousteau, Sipadan is a cornucopia of marine life, its waters teeming with turtles, moray eels, sharks, barracuda, vast schools of gaily coloured tropical fish, and a diversity of coral that's been compared to that at Australia's Great Barrier Reef.

Pulau Sipadan represents the crown of a limestone spire that rises six hundred metres from the sea bed, widening at the top to form a coral shelf shaped like an artist's palate. The diving highlights include a network of marine caves – the most eerie being **Turtle Cavern**, a watery grave to the skeletal remains of turtles which have strayed in and become lost. **Whitetip Avenue** is frequented by basking White-tip sharks, while the **Hanging Gardens** is an extraordinarily elegant profusion of soft coral hanging from the underside of the reef ledge.

The island itself is carpeted by lush forest, and fringed by flawless white sand **beaches**, up which Green turtles drag themselves to lay their eggs. Recently, Malaysia's ownership of the area has been disputed by the Indonesian government; the outcome could alter the face of marine tourism on Sipadan.

Practicalities

With limited **accommodation** on the island, the only way to stay on Pulau Sipadan is by booking through a tour operator – all but one of the companies selling diving trips operate out of Kota Kinabalu (see p.416 for details), the exception being *Pulau Sipadan Resort*, which is based in Tawau (see below). It is possible to make independent day trips to the island: locals with boats (and snorkelling equipment) for rent are plentiful on the *SOTC* causeway in Semporna, though you're looking at around $350–450 for the day for the boat and a few dollars more for the snorkelling equipment.

Tawau

Beyond the Madai Caves, 150km southwest of Lahad Datu, is **TAWAU**, Sabah's south-ernmost town of any size. Tawau was originally a small Bajau settlement, until the *British North Borneo Chartered Company*, attracted by its fine harbour and the rich volcanic soil, transformed it into the thriving commercial port it is today. As in so many regions of Sabah, while the town's prosperity relied at first upon the cultivation of cocoa, nowadays oil palm plantations and timber logging are in the ascendency, attract-ing many Filipino and Indonesian immigrants. Tawau is also a major departure point for Kalimantan – the Indonesian portion of Borneo (see feature on next page).

Central Tawau is an orderly blend of quaint rows of wooden shophouses and concrete buildings. There's little to see or do here, though the **market** beside *Hotel Soon Yee* is worthy of a browse. That apart, you might stroll along Tawau's backbone, jalan Dunlop; its *Teo Chew Association* building is crowned by a Chinese temple, while the sprawling provisions market on the square of reclaimed land opposite is mildly diverting.

An hour's drive north of town is the **TAWAU HILLS STATE PARK**, a patch of lowland rainforest with trails, hot springs and a waterfall, though reaching it is trickier than it's worth, with public buses only making the trip on a Sunday.

Practicalities

Long-distance **buses** terminate below the eastern end of Tawau's main street, jalan Dunlop, with land cruisers to Keningau (see below) leaving from the same site; the **local bus** terminus is on jalan Stephen Tan, in the centre of town, while **share taxis** park at the foot of jalan Domenic. The **airport** is only a little over 1km northwest of town – take one of the hotel courtesy buses waiting there, or hail a taxi ($3). The sole Sipadan operator not based in KK is *Pulau Sipadan Resort*, Block P, Bandar Sabindo (☎089/765200). **Ferries** to Indonesia depart from Customs Wharf, 150m south of jalan Dunlop's *Shell* station.

As well as several **banks**, the commercial estate known as the Fajar Centre, east of jalan Dunlop, houses both the *Telekom* building in Block 35, and the *MAS* office in *Wisma Sasco*; you'll find the **post office** across the other side of jalan Dunlop.

Tawau is the main stepping stone for onward **travel to Kalimantan**. The only ferry plying the route is the *Sasaran Muhibbah*, for which tickets can be bought from *Sasaran Tinggi*, at 120 jalan Chester (☎089/772455), on the west side of the local bus terminus – though there are reports that this office is to move location in the near future. The ferry has no set schedule, departing instead to connect with the Indonesian ferry *Tidar*, Nunukan ($25) is an hour from Tawau, after which it's a further three hours to Tarakan ($65).

The only **airlines** making the half-hour flight to Tarakan are *MAS* (Mon & Sat; $210) and the Indonesian *Bouraq* (Tues, Thurs & Sat; $185), whose agent in Tawau is *Merdeka Travel*, south of jalan Dunlop in Block M, Bandar Sabindo (☎089/772531).

Since Indonesian **visas** aren't issued in Nunukan or Tarakan, you'll need to arrange one in advance. This can either be done in KK (see p.416), or by taking a bus from Tawau's local station to the **Indonesian Consulate**, at Mile 1 ¹/₂, jalan Apas. The Malaysian immigration office is on the first floor of the Persekutuan Tawau (Tawau Federal Building), 200m southeast of the long-distance bus station.

Most of Tawau's budget **hotels** are along jalan Stephen Tan or jalan Chester, the best of which is *Hotel Soon Yee* (☎089/772447; ①), a very friendly Chinese hotel on jalan Stephen Tan. Near-neighbour *Hotel Murah* (②) is pricier, though its rooms have air-con, TV and bathroom; while *Peningpan Kinabalu* (①), a block south on jalan Chester, has bare, seedy – but extremely low-priced – lodgings over a Muslim Indian restaurant. Jalan Dunlop has a couple of mid-range establishments, like the *North Borneo Hotel* (☎089/763060; ③), west of jalan Masjid. The classiest address in town is the swish *Marco Polo* (☎089/777988; ⑤), at the top of jalan Masjid.

Two blocks below jalan Dunlop's eastern end, a two-hundred-metre stretch of **open-air restaurants** and **stalls** sets up daily; best-value are the Malay stalls, and bargain seafood is sold at night. You'll find several good Indian Muslim restaurants in this corner of town too, but the Fajar Centre, to the east, has a virtual monopoly on more stylish venues. Pick of the bunch is the *Mint* (closed Mon), in Block 38, a tastefully decorated Nonya restaurant serving mouthwatering desserts like red bean soup. The open-fronted *Restaurant Teo Chew* (daily 7am–2am), in Block 41, couldn't be more basic, but is still reliable. Otherwise, you might try the *Hut* in Block 29, which has generous Western set meals, or *Restoran Asnur,* in Block 38, if you want to go Thai or Malay. Finally, the *Marco Polo Hotel*'s elegant *Kublai Restaurant* has a *dim sum* breakfast on Sunday morning.

Tawau has only two **bars** – one is the *Marco Polo*'s pleasant lobby bar, the other the *Lighthouse*, just west of *Hotel Oriental*, and occasionally lively at night.

Circling Sabah: west of Tawau

A network of **logging roads** spanning the southern portion of Sabah makes it possible to travel back to KK overland, without having to retrace your steps. While not cheap, the journey by **land cruiser** (vehicles leave only when full; $80) from Tawau's long-distance bus terminus to Keningau, along a track that parallels the Kalimantan border, is worth taking for its excitement value alone.

The journey feels comfortable enough as you leave Tawau, as passengers are taken in two vehicles past the police road block outside town that checks on overcrowding – but then you're all transferred into one land cruiser. At **MEROTAI**, some 20km out of Tawau, the sealed road ends and the jolting ride begins, taking you past cocoa and palm plantations, lush forest and, less romantically, vast timber mills. Two thirds of the way to Keningau, a quarry marks the left turn for Sapulut (see p.420), though if it's dark, you're better off going on to Keningau, as vehicles are few and far between. Closer to **KAMPUNG SOOK**, look out for Murut graves by the roadside. Assuming your land cruiser doesn't experience difficulties – and the assumption is an optimistic one – you should reach Keningau in the early evening.

travel details

Trains

Beaufort to: KK (2 daily; 4hr); Tenom (5 daily; 2hr 30min).

KK to Beaufort (2 daily; 4hr); Tenom (2 daily; 7hr).

Tenom to: Beaufort (5 daily; 2hr 30min); KK (2 daily; 7hr).

Buses

Sabah's long-distance buses run to schedules, normally departing early in the morning. Minibuses and land cruisers leave as soon as they can muster a full quota of passengers. The list below is of the approximate number of buses travelling daily between the major towns, but schedules and services change constantly.

Beaufort to: KK (15 daily; 2hr); Kuala Penyu (8 daily; 1hr); Menumbok (8 daily; 1hr 30min); Sipitang (9 daily; 50min).

Keningau to: KK (15 daily; 2hr 30min); Sapulut (2 daily; 4hr); Tambunan (10 daily; 1hr); Tawau (2 daily; 6–8hr); Tenom (20 daily; 50min).

KK to: Beaufort (15 daily; 2hr); Keningau (15 daily; 2hr 30min); Kinabalu National Park (8 daily; 1hr 45mins); Kota Belud (16 daily; 2hr 10min); Kudat (10 daily; 4hr); Lawas, Sarawak (1 daily; 4hr); Menumbok (6 daily; 2hr 30min); Papar (20 daily; 40min); Ranau (10 daily; 2hr); Sandakan (12 daily; 5hr 30min); Tambunan (11 daily; 1hr 30min); Tawau (2 daily; 9hr); Tuaran (10 daily; 50min).

Sandakan to: KK (12 daily; 5hr 45min); Lahad Datu (6 daily; 2hr 30min); Ranau (8 daily; 3hr 30min); Tawau (6 daily; 4hr 30min).

Tawau to: Keningau (1–2 daily; 6–8hr); KK (2 daily; 9hr); Lahad Datu (8 daily; 2hr); Sandakan (6 daily; 4hr 30min); Semporna (14 daily; 1hr 30min).

Tenom to: Beaufort (20 daily; 50min).

Ferries

KK to: Labuan (3 daily; 2hr).

Labuan to: Brunei (3 daily; 1hr 30min); KK (3 daily; 2hr); Menumbok (10 daily; 25min); Sipitang (1 daily; 1hr 10min).

Tawau to: Nunukan (2–3 weekly; 1hr); Tarakan (2–3 weekly; 4hr).

Flights

KK to: Kudat (2 weekly; 40min); Labuan (5 daily; 30min); Lahad Datu (2 daily; 50min); Sandakan (7 daily; 50min); Tawau (5 daily; 45min).

Sandakan to: KK (7 daily; 50 min): Kudat (6 weekly; 45min); Lahad Datu (1 weekly; 1hr 5min); Tawau (3 weekly; 1hr 40min).

Tawau to: Tarakan (4 weekly; 30min).

CHAPTER EIGHT

BRUNEI

The tiny Islamic **Sultanate of Brunei** perches on the northwestern coast of Borneo, surrounded, and at one point even split in two, by the meandering border of Sarawak. At its peak in the sixteenth century, Brunei was the seat of the proudest empire in Borneo, its sultans receiving tribute from as far away as Manila. But by the end of the nineteenth century, its glory days were long since forgotten and Brunei was a country in fear for its life. European adventurers methodically chipped away at its territory, absorbing it into their new colonies, eventually leaving the Sultanate confined within 5765 square kilometres, a fraction of its erstwhile size.

Today, however, the Sultanate of Brunei is thriving. Its 260,000 inhabitants (Malays account for 70 percent of these; the rest are Chinese, Indians, indigenous tribes and ex-patriates) enjoy a quality of life almost unparalleled in Southeast Asia: education and healthcare are free; houses, cars, even pilgrimages to Mecca are subsidized; income tax is unheard of; and the average per capita income is around US$19,000 per annum. The explanation for this dramatic turn round is simple: **oil**, first discovered in 1903, at the site of what is now the town of Seria. Although it took until 1931 for the reserves to yield solid financial returns, the Sultanate's natural resources (oil was later joined by natural gas) have produced a national wealth that's the envy of surrounding states.

Despite the presence of such lucrative resources, much of Brunei has remained unchanged for centuries. It lies on a slim coastal plain, threaded by several substantial rivers; most of the country lies below 150 metres on an alluvial coastal plain, its lowland rainforest, peat swamp and heath forest running down to sandy beaches and mangrove swamps. The country is divided into four districts: **Brunei Muara**, which contains the capital, Bandar Seri Begawan; agricultural **Tutong**; oil-rich **Belait**; and **Temburong**, a sparsely populated backwater, severed from the rest of Brunei by the Limbang district of Sarawak. Because of the oil, Brunei has never needed to exploit its forestry to any great degree, with the result that primary and secondary tropical forest still cover around 75 percent of the total land area.

Oil has made Bruneians rich, but none more so than Brunei's 29th **Sultan, Hassanal Bolkiah** (his full title is 31 words long). The *Guinness Book of Records* and *Fortune Magazine* have both credited the present Sultan as the richest man in the world, claiming his assets to be around US$27 billion. The Sultan himself disputes such claims, asserting that he doesn't have unlimited access to state funds. Nevertheless, he has managed to acquire hotels in Singapore, London and Beverly Hills; a collection of three hundred cars, housed at his residence, the US$350-million Istana Nurul Iman; a private fleet of aircraft at his personal disposal; and over two hundred fine polo horses, kept at his personal country club.

The quality of life has engendered in Bruneians an acquiescence towards their royal family's showy extravagance that extends to their country's **political climate**. Sleepy Brunei certainly doesn't seem like a place under a state of emergency, but it has been since 1962, when the last recorded democratic elections resulted in an attempted coup; provisions still exist for the detention, without trial, of citizens. Furthermore, popular involvement in government decision-making remains minimal: the Sultan fulfills the dual roles of Prime Minister and Defence Minister, while the posts of Minister of Foreign Affairs and Minister of Finance are held by his brothers, Prince Mohamed and

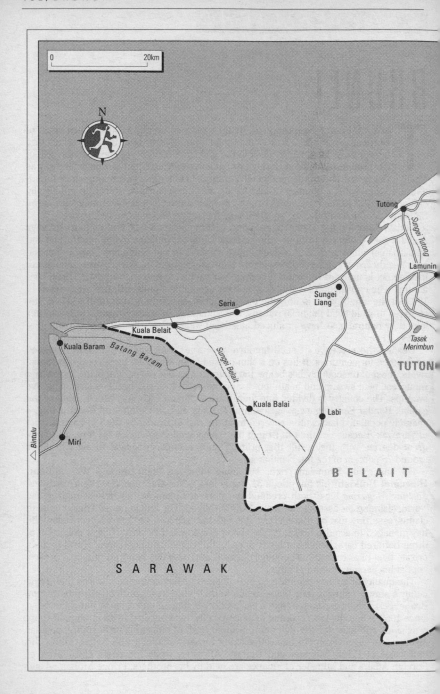

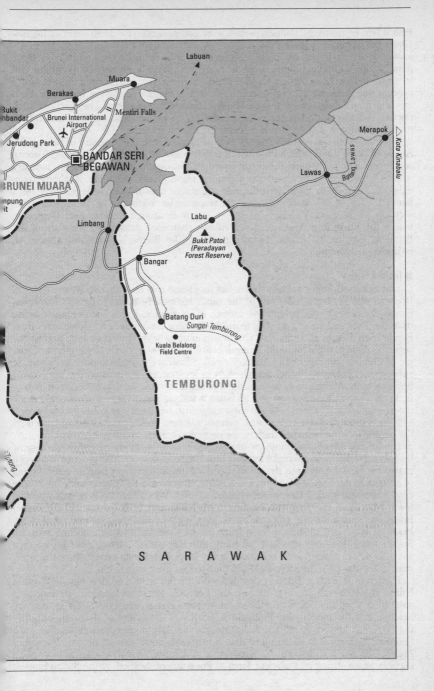

Prince Jefri respectively. Political parties were countenanced for three years in the mid-1980s, but outlawed again in 1988.

Worse still is the government's attitude towards Brunei's most populous ethnic minority, the **Chinese**. Chinese Bruneians are not automatically classed as citizens and to enjoy the perks accorded to all Bruneians, their citizenship must be proven, a process that demands not only a lengthy history of familial residence, but also a rigorous and humiliating written test in Malay language and customs. The discrimination doesn't end there: foreign businesses operating in Brunei tend to show favouritism towards Malays over Chinese when recruiting their workforce.

The sultanate's full name is *Negara Brunei Darussalam*, the "Country of Brunei, the Abode of Peace", and peaceful is a fair, if rather polite, description of the state. There's really very little to do here, the result of a disinclination to develop a tourism industry which the state's natural resources render unnecessary. Nightlife is almost non-existent, and indeed, since 1991, the sale and public consumption of liquor have been banned. Even so, it's worth extending a stopover for a glimpse of the capital alone. Virtually all the country's places of interest are in or around **Bandar Seri Begawan**, where the **Kampung Ayer**, or water village, that once constituted the core of the Bruneian Empire still exists, dwarfed nowadays by Bandar's formidable **Omar Ali Saifuddien Mosque**.

A little history

Contemporary Brunei's modest size belies its pivotal role in the formative centuries of Bornean history. Little is known of the Sultanate's **early history**, though trade was always the powerhouse behind the growth of its empire. Coins and ceramics dating from the Tang and Sung dynasties found in the Kota Batu area, a few kilometres from Bandar Seri Begawan, verify that China was trading with Brunei as long ago as the seventh century, while allusions in ninth-century Chinese records to payments of tribute to China by the ruler of an Asian city called *Puni* are thought to refer to Brunei. In subsequent centuries, Brunei benefited from its strategic position on the trade route between India, Melaka and China, and exercised a lucrative control over merchant traffic in the South China Sea. As well as being a staging post, where traders could stock up on supplies and offload some of their cargo, Brunei itself was commercially active, with local produce such as beeswax, camphor, rattan and brasswork being traded by the *nakhoda*, or Bruneian sea traders, for ceramics, spices, woods and fabrics.

By the mid-fifteenth century, as the Sultanate courted foreign Muslim merchants' business, **Islam** began to make inroads into Bruneian society. The process was accelerated by the decamping to Brunei of wealthy Muslim merchant families after the fall of Melaka to the Portugese in 1511. Certainly, Brunei was an Islamic sultanate by the time it received its first **European visitors** in 1521. When Antonio Pigafetta, who had travelled to Southeast Asia with Ferdinand Magellan, arrived at the head of the Brunei River, he found a thriving city ruled over by a splendid and sophisticated royal court. Pigafetta and his companions were taken on elephant-back to an audience with the Sultan, whom they met in a hall "all hung with silk stuffs" – though not before they were taught "to make three obeisances to the king, with hands joined above the head, raising first one then the other foot, and then to kiss the hands to him".

Pigafetta's sojourn in Brunei coincided with the Sultanate's **golden age**. In the first half of the sixteenth century, Brunei was Borneo's foremost kingdom, its influence stretching along the island's northern and western coasts, and even as far as territory belonging to the modern-day Philippines. Such was the extent of Bruneian authority that Western visitors found the Sultanate and the island interchangeable: the word "Borneo" is thought to be no more than a European corruption of Brunei. The fall of Melaka did much to bolster the importance of Brunei, though the foundation of its success was a strong and efficient form of government, headed by the Sultan himself

BRUNEI PRACTICALITIES

Brunei's **climate**, like that of neighbouring Sabah and Sarawak, is hot and humid, with average temperatures in the high twenties throughout the year. Lying 440km north of the Equator, Brunei has a tropical weather system, so even if you visit outside the official **wet season** (usually November to February) there's every chance that you'll see some rain. Brunei is most commonly visited as a stepping stone to either Sabah or Sarawak, but if you are having to watch your **budget** carefully, you may find an internal *MAS* flight between the two Malaysian states a less expensive alternative. For **general information** on visiting Brunei, see the relevant sections of *Basics*.

Getting there
Air services are either with *Royal Brunei* or *MAS*. From Kuala Lumpur, there are six *Royal Brunei* flights a week to Bandar (M$600), though their prices are substantially undercut by *MAS* (also 6 weekly; M$441). *MAS* flights also compare well from from Kota Kinabalu (6 weekly; M$83) and Kuching (3 weekly; $M250); the equivalent Royal Brunei flights cost around M$120 and M$360 respectively. The once-daily *Singapore Airlines* flights from Singapore's Changi Airport cost S$377. *Royal Brunei* also has flights from Hong Kong (3 weekly) and Jakarta (4 weekly); while there are also services from Manila with *Philippine Airlines* (3 weekly) and Bangkok with *Thai Airways*.

Boats to Brunei depart daily from Lawas (see p.384) and Limbang (see p.383) in northern Sarawak, and from Pulau Labuan (see p.426), itself connected by boat to Kota Kinabalu in Sabah. From Miri (see p.378) in Sarawak, several **buses** travel daily to Kuala Belait, in the far western corner of Brunei; while the overland route from Sabah to Brunei necessitates taking a bus to Lawas, and then a taxi into Temburong District, from where it's only a short boat trip (see p.466) to Bandar.

Getting around
If you intend to explore Brunei, you've got little option but to **rent a car**. South of the main coastal roads, **bus** services are nonexistent, while **taxis** are expensive if you want to cover much ground outside the capital. Apart from short hops across the Brunei River in Bandar's river taxis, the only time you're likely to use a **boat** is to get to Temburong District (see p.466), which is isolated from the rest of Brunei by the Limbang area of Sarawak.

Accommodation
The country's natural resources mean it has no need to court tourists and with one exception, **hotels** in Bandar are all up in the mid- to upper-range price brackets. While **longhouses** do exist in the interior, their inacessibility means you aren't likely to stay at them.

The following **price codes** have been applied to all accommodation listings, and refer to the cheapest available room for two people. For more information, see p.40.

① Under $25	④ $60–100	⑥ $200–400
② $25–40	⑤ $100–200	⑦ $401 and over
③ $40–60		

and represented in the outer regions of Bruneian territories by his *pengiran*, or noblemen. But by the close of the sixteenth century, things were beginning to turn sour for the Sultanate. Trouble with Catholic Spain led to a sea battle off the coast at Muara in 1578; the battle was won by Spain, whose forces took Brunei City, only to be chased out days later by a cholera epidemic. The threat of piracy caused more problems, scaring off passing trade. Worse still, at home the sultans began to lose control of the *pengiran*, as factional struggles ruptured the court.

Western entrepreneurs arrived in this self-destructive climate, keen to take advantage of gaps in the trade market left by Brunei's decline. One such fortune-seeker was **James Brooke**, whose arrival off the coast of Kuching in August 1839 was to change the face of Borneo for ever. For helping the Sultan to quell a Dyak uprising (see p.326), Brooke was offered the governorship of Sarawak; Brunei's contraction had begun. Over subsequent decades, the state was to shrink steadily, as Brooke and his successors used the suppression of piracy as the excuse they needed to siphon off more and more of its territory into the familial fiefdom. This trend culminated in the cession of the Limbang region in 1890 – a move which literally split Brunei in two.

Elsewhere, more Bruneian land was being lost to other powers. In January 1846, a court faction unsympathetic to foreign land-grabbing took power in Brunei and the chief minister was murdered. British gunboats quelled the coup and Pulau Labuan (see p.424) was ceded to the British crown. A **treaty** signed the following year, forbidding the Sultanate from ceding any of its territories without the British Crown's consent, underlined the decline of Brunei's power. Shortly afterwards, in 1865, American consul Charles Lee Moses negotiated a treaty granting a ten-year lease to the *American Trading Company* of the portion of northeast Borneo that was later to become Sabah. By 1888, the British had declared Brunei a **Protected State**, which meant the responsibility for its foreign affairs lay with London.

The turn of the twentieth century was marked by the **discovery of oil**: given what little remained of Bruneian territory, it could hardly have been altruism that spurred the British to set up a Residency here in 1906. Initially, though, profits from the fledgling oil industry were slow to come and the early decades of the century saw rubber estates springing up at Berakas, Gadong and Temburong. However, by 1931, the Seria Oilfield was on stream and by 1938 oil exports, engineered by the *British Malayan Petroleum Company*, had topped M\$5 million. Despite the hefty slice of profits appropriated by the British, the Sultanate was still able to pay off debts from the lean years of the late nineteenth century.

The **Japanese invasion** of December 1941 temporarily halted Brunei's path to recovery. As in Sabah, Allied bombing over the three and a half years of occupation that followed left much rebuilding to be done. While Sabah, Sarawak and Pulau Labuan became Crown Colonies in the early postwar years, Brunei remained a **British Protectorate** and retained its British Resident. Only in 1959 was the Residency finally withdrawn and a new constitution established, with provisions for a democratically elected legislative council. At the same time, Sultan Omar Ali Saifuddien (the present Sultan's father) was careful to retain British involvement in matters of defence and foreign affairs – a move whose sagacity was made apparent when, in 1962, an armed coup led by Sheik Azahari's pro-democratic Brunei People's Party was crushed by Gurkhas of the British Army. Since the coup, itself the result of Sultan Omar's refusal to convene the first sitting of the legislative council, Brunei has been ruled by the decree of the Sultan, in his role as nonelected Prime Minister.

Despite showing interest in joining the planned **Malaysian Federation** in 1963, Brunei suffered a last minute attack of cold feet, choosing to opt out rather than risk losing its new-found oil wealth and compromising the pre-eminence of its monarchy. Brunei remained a British Protectorate until January 1, 1984, when it attained full **independence**. Meanwhile, **oil reserves** have fulfilled all expectations: in 1956, onshore oil fields yielded 114,000 barrels a day and by the end of the decade offshore fields were yielding further profits. But it was only in the 1970s that the money really began to roll in, by which time the state's **natural gas** reserves were also being fully exploited. Nevertheless, Brunei's hydrocarbon resources are finite and as the government casts around for alternative sources of income for the future, it may well start to invest in tourism. Until then, Brunei remains of only limited interest to tourists.

Bandar Seri Begawan

BANDAR SERI BEGAWAN, or Bandar as it's known locally, is the capital of Brunei and the Sultanate's only settlement of any real size. Until 1970, Bandar was known simply as Brunei Town; the present name means "Town of the Seri Begawan" – the title Sultan Omar Ali Saifuddien took after abdicating in favour of his son Hassanal Bolkiah in 1967. Straddling the northern bank of a twist in the Brunei River, the city is characterized by its unlikely juxtaposition of striking modern buildings and traditional stilt houses. Brunei's original seat of power was **Kampung Ayer**, the water village which still houses around half of the city's population, with the Sultan's palace the only building constructed on dry land. With the arrival of the British Residency in 1906 came an attempt to coax the *kampung* people onto dry land, but although the streets which form downtown Bandar were laid out, the *kampung* dwellers stayed put, preferring to retain their traditional way of life. More recently, the Bruneian government has tried to entice its water villagers onshore by means of modern housing projects, though Kampung Ayer still accounted for fifty percent of Bandar's population in 1986.

As recently as the middle of this century, Brunei's capital was a sleepy water village. That contemporary Bandar has become the attractive, clean and modern waterfront city it is today is due, inevitably, to oil. With the new-found wealth of the 1970s came large-scale urbanization north of the Brunei River, resulting in housing schemes, shopping centres and, more obviously, the magnificent **Omar Ali Saifuddien Mosque**, which dominates the skyline of Bandar. First-time visitors are pleasantly surprised by a sense of space unusual for a Southeast Asian city. Unfortunately, the contrasts with neighbouring capitals don't end there: lacking the frenetic vitality of other cities, Bandar is not a place which normally engenders much affection. Nor is it a cheap place to visit: with car ownership high, public transport remains woefully undeveloped, while the fact that most visitors to Brunei are businesspeople has set room prices at a prohibitively high level. Nevertheless, the sights of Bandar are interesting enough to warrant a day or two's stopover.

Arrival, information and getting around

Flying into Bandar, you'll arrive at plush **Brunei International Airport**. If you need to book a room upon arrival, there are free public phones to your right beyond passport control; while to the left, as you walk out of the arrivals concourse and into the car park, is a **tourist information booth**, where information is sadly scarce. The easiest way to cover the 11km into Bandar is to take a taxi, though at $15–20, this is expensive. Unless you're able to sweet-talk yourself onto a hotel shuttle bus, the alternative is to take the short walk up to the main road and hail one of the public buses that pass by every twenty to thirty minutes. **Boats** from Pulau Labuan, Lawas and Limbang all dock centrally, at the foot of jalan Roberto; while bus arrivals from Sarawak and the west of Brunei terminate at the **bus station** below jalan Cator.

Once in Bandar, the only official source of information is the **Tourism Section** of the Economic Development Board, Ministry of Finance, Jalan James Pearce (Mon–Thurs & Sat 7.45am–12.15pm & 1.30–4.30pm; ☎240243); don't expect too much.

City transport

With as much as half of Bandar's population living in the various villages that make up Kampung Ayer, it makes sense that the highest-subscribed form of **public transport**

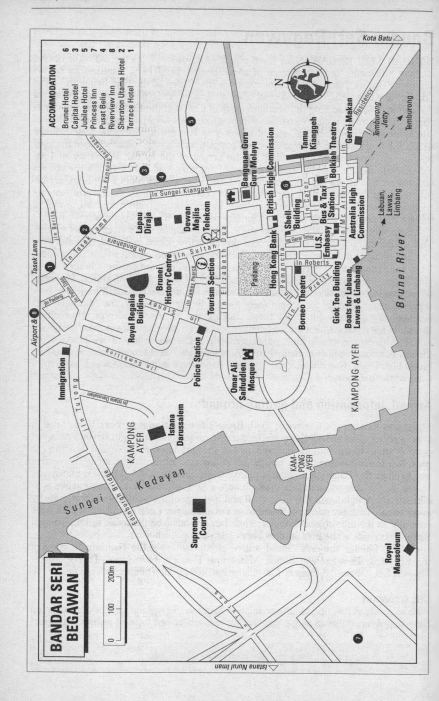

BANDAR SERI BEGAWAN

Kota Batu △

N

ACCOMMODATION

Brunei Hotel	6
Capital Hostel	3
Jubilee Hotel	5
Princess Inn	7
Pusat Belia	4
Riverview Inn	8
Sheraton Utama Hotel	2
Terrace Hotel	1

Residency

Tamburong Jetty

Temburong

Bangunan Guru Guru Melayu

Tamu Kianggeh

British High Commission

Bolkiah Theatre

Gerai Makan

Jln Sungei Kiangngeh

Lapau Diraja

Dewan Majlis

Telekom

Jln Kampong Berangan

Shell Building

Jln Cator

Bus & Taxi Station

Australia High Commission

Labuan, Lawas, Limbang

Jln Bendahara

Jln Tasek Lama

U.S. Embassy

Irg Gerai Timor

Jln Sultan

Jln Elizabeth Dua

Hong Kong Bank

Jln Mc Arthur

Brunei History Centre

Jln Pemancha

Tourism Section

Jln Jawa Piatos

Royal Regalia Building

Jln Stoney

Padang

Jln Roberts

Borneo Theatre

Giok Tee Building

Boats for Labuan, Lawas & Limbang

Jln Pretty

Brunei River

△ Tasek Lama

△ Airport & 8

Jln Berita

Jln Padang

Jln Elizabeth

Jln Sumbiling

Police Station

Omar Ali Saifuddien Mosque

KAMPONG AYER

Immigration

Jln Tutong

Jln Istana Darussalam

Istana Darussalem

KAMPONG AYER

Kedayan

KAM-PONG AYER

Sungei

Edinburgh Bridge

Supreme Court

KAMPONG AYER

Royal Mausoleum

△ Istana Nurul Iman

0	100	200m

in the city should be its **water taxis**. A veritable armada of these skinny speedboats plies the Brunei River night and day, costing only $1–2 for a short hop – pay your fare on board. If you want a longer tour of the water villages, or want to see the Sultan's palace from the river, a half-hour round trip will cost around $15–20 per person – but prices are negotiable. It's obviously cheaper the more of you there are intent upon making the trip. The jetty below the intersection of jalan Roberts and jalan MacArthur is the best place to catch a water taxi, though it's also possible to hail one from jalan Residency.

Buses to points north, east and west of Bandar leave infrequently from the bus station, underneath the multistorey car park below jalan Cator; most stop running in the early afternoon. There's no published timetable, but it's always worth checking the boards on the windscreens of the buses parked there just in case, before exploring other modes of transport. Relevant bus details to destinations outside the capital are given where appropriate throughout the rest of the chapter.

Taking a **taxi** to and from Bandar's points of interest is far easier, though obviously more expensive than taking a bus. Taxis congregate beside the bus station and a short journey – say, from the city centre to the Brunei Museum – should only cost around $6–8. Make sure you agree a price before setting off on longer trips. For the addresses of **car rental** agencies, see "Listings", p.464.

LEAVING BANDAR SERI BEGAWAN

For addresses and details of airlines, travel agents and consulates in Bandar, see "Listings", p.464.

Airport
There is no shuttle bus between Bandar and the airport, though buses from the station below jalan Cator bound for Berakas (every 20min, 7am–5pm; 50 *sen*) will drop you at the airport upon request. Taxis ($15–20), congregate at the bus station. For **flight information** call ☎331747. Don't forget the **airport tax:** $5 for flights to Malaysia and Singapore, $12 for all other destinations.

By boat
Boats for Labuan, Lawas and Limbang leave from beside the Customs and Immigration Station at the junction of jalan Roberts and jalan MacArthur. Tickets for **Labuan** (daily at 8am, 1pm & 3pm; $20/25) and **Lawas** (daily at 11.30am, $25) are sold by *Kutu Sumudra*, #03-201 Giok Tee Building, jalan MacArthur (☎243057), and *Halim Tours*, lorong Gerai Timor, off jalan MacArthur (☎226688); for **Limbang** (several departures 7am–5.30pm according to demand; $10), tickets are sold at the open stalls opposite lorong Gerai Timor, on jalan MacArthur. From Labuan, there are daily connections on to Kota Kinabalu and Menumbok in Sabah, though to ensure you catch one, it's wise to leave Bandar early in the day. Note that tickets to Labuan should be booked as early as possible – especially if you want to travel over a weekend or a holiday. Also be aware that schedules change, so double-check departure times to all destinations.

Boats to Bangar in **Temburong** (every 45min, 6.30am–4.30pm; $7) depart from jalan Residency; tickets are sold beside the jetty. From Temburong's largest settlement, Bangar, it's possible to travel overland to both Lawas and Limbang (see below).

By road
The most obvious means of exiting Bandar overland is to take a bus to Seria, change there for Kuala Belait and catch another bus or taxi from there to Miri, in Sarawak (see p.468–469 for all the details). Alternatively, from Bangar (p.466) you can take a taxi to Lawas, from where buses depart daily for Sabah; or there are buses from the Brunei/ Sarawak border in Temburong District, to Limbang (see p.466).

Accommodation

Brunei is almost bereft of budget **accommodation**, with the *Pusat Belia* (youth hostel) the only real option. Some visitors have resorted to taking a bus to the coast and sleeping on the beach, though this is hardly advisable. If you've got money in your pocket, there's a fair selection of comfortable hotels from which to choose, though most establishments are firmly mid- to upper-range in price, with double rooms starting at $80.

Brunei Hotel, 95 jalan Pemancha (☎242372). Comfortable and well appointed (at the bottom of its price category) – Bandar's most central commercial hotel. ⑥.

Capital Hostel, jalan Kampung Berangan, behind *Pusat Belia* (☎223561). A budget option by Bruneian standards, and a useful stand-by if you can't get into the neighbouring *Pusat Belia*. ④.

Jubilee Hotel, Jubilee Plaza, jalan Kampung Kianggeh (☎228070). East of Kianggeh Canal, a well-groomed, mid-range hotel set opposite a patch of traditional *kampung* houses. ⑤.

Princess Inn, jalan Tutong (☎241128). Away over Edinburgh Bridge, though offering guests regular shuttles to and from the centre. ⑤.

Pusat Belia, jalan Sungai Kianggeh (☎222900). Brunei's youth hostel, and by far the least expensive option in town, providing you can get in – you'll need an *ISIC* or *IYHF* card. Rooms ($10 for three nights) are shared with three others, and there's a pool ($1) downstairs. ①.

Riverview Inn, Km 1, jalan Gadong (☎238238). Just as good as the *Brunei*, but an annoying distance from the centre. ⑥.

Sheraton Utama Hotel, jalan Tasek Lama (☎244272). Brunei's first international-standard hotel, with 156 swanky rooms and suites, plus a well-equipped business centre. ⑥.

Terrace Hotel, jalan Tasek Lama (☎243554). Reasonable hotel, where prices reflect the slightly worn, dated appearance of its rooms; outside is a quiet pool. ⑤.

The city

Downtown Bandar is hemmed in by water: to the east is sungei Kianggeh; to the south, the wide Brunei River; and, to the west, sungei Kedayan, which runs up to the **Edinburgh Bridge**. The **Omar Ali Saifuddien Mosque**, overlooking the compact knot of central streets, is Bandar's most obvious point of reference. The mosque sits in a cradle formed by **Kampung Ayer** (water village), which spreads like water lilies over a pond across large expanses of the river. Over Edinburgh Bridge, **jalan Tutong** runs westwards and past the Mile 1 area (a grid of shopping complexes and hotels), reaching Istana Nurul Iman 3km later; in the other direction, **jalan Residency** hugs the river bank on its way to the **Brunei Museum** and its neighbouring attractions.

The Omar Ali Saifuddien Mosque

At the very heart of both the city and the Sultanate's Muslim faith is the magnificent **Omar Ali Saifuddien Mosque** (Mon–Wed 8am–noon, 1–3.30pm & 4.30–5.30pm, Thurs closed to non-Muslims, Fri 4.30–5pm, Sat & Sun 8am–noon, 1–3.30pm & 4.30–5.30pm). Built in classical Islamic style, and mirrored in the circular lagoon that abuts it, it's a breathtaking sight, whether viewed in the dazzling sunlight or seen illuminated a lurid green at night. The mosque was commissioned by and named after the father of the present Sultan, and completed in 1958 at a cost of US$5 million, making splendid use of opulent yet tasteful fittings – Italian marble, Shanghainese granite, Arabian and Belgian carpets, and chandeliers and stained glass from England. Topping the cream-coloured building is a 52-metre-high golden dome whose curved surface is adorned with over three million pieces of Venetian glass mosaic. It is sometimes possible to obtain permission to ride the elevator up the adjacent, 44-metre-high minaret, and look out over the water village below. A replica of a sixteenth century royal barge, or *mahligai*, stands in the lagoon, and is used on special religious occasions. The usual dress codes – modest attire, and shoes to be left at the entrance – apply when entering the mosque.

Kampung Ayer

From the mosque, it's no distance to Bandar's **Kampong Ayer**, or water village, whose sheer scale makes it one of the great sights of Southeast Asia. Stilt villages have occupied this stretch of the Brunei River for hundreds of years: Antonio Pigafetta, visiting Borneo in 1521, described a city "entirely built on foundations in the salt water . . . it contains twenty-five thousand fires or families. The houses are all of wood, placed on great piles to raise them high up". Today, an estimated 30,000 people live in the scores of sprawling villages that compose Kampung Ayer, their dwellings interconnected by a maze of wooden boardwalks. These villages now feature their own clinics, mosques, schools, fire brigade, even a police station, while homes boast piped water, electricity and TV. Despite all these amenities, Kampung Ayer's charm lessens as you get closer, its waters distinctly unsanitary, its houses prone to fire. Even so, a strong sense of community has meant that attempts to move the inhabitants onto dry land and into housing more in keeping with a state that can claim the highest per capita income in the world, have met with little success.

The meandering ways of Kampung Ayer make it an intriguing place to explore on foot. For a real impression of its dimensions, though, it's best to charter one of the water taxis that zip around the river (see "City transport" above). A handful of traditional **cottage industries** continue to turn out copperware and brassware (at Kampung Ujong Bukit), and exquisite sarongs and boats (Kampung Saba Darat), and the boatmen should know of the whereabouts of some of them.

Along jalan Sultan

Just to the east of the Omar Ali Saifuddien Mosque, Bandar's main drag, broad **Jalan Sultan**, runs north past several of the city's lesser sights. First up is the **Brunei History Centre** (Mon–Thurs & Sat 8am–noon & 1–4.30pm; free), a research institution whose dull displays (maps showing Brunei's changing shape, and tables outlining the genealogy of past sultans) will have you hurrying on to the **Royal Regalia Building** (Mon–Thurs 8.30am–5pm, Fri 9–11.30am & 2.30–5pm, Sat & Sun 8.30am–5pm; free) next door, and opened in 1992 as part of the Sultan's Silver Jubilee celebrations. The exhibition, which is housed in a magnificent, semicircular building fitted out with lavish carpets and marble, uses photographs and exhibits to chart the life of the present Sultan. The sycophantic labelling apart ("Since childhood His Majesty has a very cheerful, generous and benign personality"; of schooldays: "He picked up his lessons very fast within a short time"; of Sandhurst: "popular with fellow cadets as well as higher officers") there's some quite interesting stuff here – including a surprisingly happy, smiling shot of the Sultan taken during his circumcision ceremony, as well as a golden hand and forearm used to support his chin during the coronation, and a beautifully ornate crown. The **Constitutional Gallery** in the same building is inevitably drier, but its documents and treaties are worth a scan. Fronting the whole collection is the coronation carriage, or *Usungan*, ringed by regalia from the coronation ceremony – which took place right across jalan Sultan in the **Lapau Diraja** (Royal Ceremonial Hall), on August 1, 1968. The hall's slightly tacky exterior belies the grandeur of its huge inner chamber, whose western side is approached by a mini escalator. Beyond this, rows of red, black, pink and white pillars, run up to the golden *patarana*, or royal throne. Although the hall is not officially open to the public, it's usually possible to take a peak at its lavish interior. Next door is the Parliament building, the **Dewan Majlis**, which used to house the Legislative Assembly.

East of the Lapau Diraja and parallel to jalan Sultan is jalan Sungai Kianggeh, which runs past the daily market, **Tamu Kianggeh**, and Bandar's most central Chinese temple, before arriving at jalan Tasek, the turning to tranquil **Tasek Lama Park**, five minutes' walk from the main road. Bear left and pass through the pretty gardens to a small waterfall, in whose rather muddy waters locals have been known to swim; bear right along the sealed road and right again at the fork and you'll end up at a bottle-green reservoir.

East to the Brunei Museum

Jalan Residency runs eastwards from sungei Kianggeh, bordered to the right by the Brunei River and to the left by a hillside Muslim cemetery whose scores of decrepit stones are shaded by an orchard of gnarled frangipani trees. After a little less than 1km, the road reaches the **Brunei Arts and Handicrafts Training Centre** (Mon–Thurs & Sat 7.45am–12.15pm & 1.30–4.30pm, Fri & Sun 8am–noon & 2–4pm; free), an organization dedicated to perpetuating the Sultanate's cultural heritage. Here, young Bruneians are taught traditional skills, such as basketry, brass casting and the crafting of the *kris*. Apart from the occasional weaving demonstration, though, the training process is off limits unless you've applied in advance for written permission, so you'll probably have to make do with browsing through the **craft shop**'s decent selection of reasonably priced basketry, silverware and spinning tops.

From here it's 4km to the Brunei Museum (eastbound buses run, occasionally, from the bus stop opposite the centre), shortly before which is **Sultan Bolkiah's tomb**. Bolkiah (1473–1521) was Brunei's fifth sultan, holding sway at the very peak of the state's power before dying on his way back from Java. It's worth setting aside an hour or two for the **Brunei Museum** (Tues–Thurs 9.30am–5pm, Fri 9–11.30am & 2.30–5pm, Sat & Sun 9.30am–5pm; free), which has several outstanding galleries. In the inevitable *Oil and Gas Gallery*, set up by *Brunei Shell Petroleum*, exhibits, graphics and captions recount the story of Brunei's oil reserves, from the drilling of the first well in 1928, to current extraction and refining techniques. Also interesting, though tantalizingly sketchy, is the *Muslim Life Gallery*, whose dioramas allow glimpses of social traditions, such as the sweetening of a new-born baby's mouth with honey or dates, and the disposal of its placenta in a *bayung*, a palm leaf basket which is either hung on a tree or floated downriver. At the back of the gallery, a small collection of early photographs shows riverine hawkers trading off their boats in Kampung Ayer. The museum's undoubted highlight, though, is its superb *Islamic Art Gallery* where, among the riches on display, are a number of beautifully illuminated, antique Korans from India, Iran, Egypt and Turkey, and some exquisite prayer mats, as well as quirkier items like a pair of ungainly wooden slippers.

Steps around the back of the museum drop down to the riverside **Malay Technology Museum** (9.30am–5pm except Fri 9–11.30am & 2.30–5pm; closed Tues), whose three galleries provide a mildly engaging insight into traditional Malay life. Of greatest interest is *Gallery Three*, whose exhibits include the *pelarik gasing*, a machine which evenly cuts spinning tops, the *lamin keleput*, used for boring blowpipes, and other devices worked by Brunei's indigenous people from the forest materials at hand. In the same gallery are authentic examples of Kedayan, Murut and Dusun dwellings, while elsewhere in the building, you'll see dioramas highlighting stilt-house and *atap* roof construction, boat-making and fishing methods.

The Istana Nurul Iman

Bandar's complement of noteworthy buildings is wrapped up by the **Istana Nurul Iman**, the official residence of the Sultan, sited at a superb riverside spot 4km west of the capital, from where it is partially visible. Bigger than either Buckingham Palace or the Vatican, the Istana stands as a lasting monument to self-indulgence. Its design, by Filipino architect, Leandro Locsin, is a sinuous blend of traditional and modern, with Islamic motifs such as arches and domes, and sloping roofs fashioned on traditional longhouse designs, combined with all the mod cons you'd expect of a house whose owner earns an estimated US$5 million *a day*.

James Bartholomew's book, *The Richest Man in the World*, lists some of the mind-boggling figures at play in the palace. Over half a kilometre long, it contains a grand total of 1778 rooms, including 257 toilets. Illuminating these rooms requires 51,000 light bulbs, many of which are consumed by the palace's 564 chandeliers; while simply getting around them all has led to the installation of 18 lifts and 44 staircases. The throne room is said to be particularly sumptuous: twelve one-ton chandeliers hang from its ceiling, while its four grand thrones stand against the backdrop of a sixty-foot arch, tiled in 22-carat gold. In addition to the throne room, there's a royal banquet hall that seats 4000 diners, a prayer hall where 1500 people can worship at any one time, an underground car park for the Sultan's hundreds of vehicles, a state of the art sports complex, and a helipad. Inevitably, the palace is rarely open to the general public, though the Sultan does declare open house every year during Hari Raya. Otherwise, nearby **Taman Persiaran Damuan**, a kilometre-long park sandwiched between jalan Tutong and the Brunei River, offers the best view; or you can fork out for a boat trip and see the palace lit up impressively at night from the water. Opposite the park is **Pulau Ranggu**, where proboscis monkeys congregate on the shore towards dusk.

All westbound buses travel along jalan Tutong, over the Edinburgh Bridge and past the Istana, though walking isn't out of the question. En route you'll pass the city's **Mile 1** area, in whose southwestern corner the **Royal Mausoleum and Graveyard** are tucked away. Sultans have been buried here since 1786, though only the last four were laid to rest in the mausoleum.

Eating and drinking

Fortunately, Bandar's **restaurants** are more reasonably priced than its hotels and there's a modest range of decent establishments, reflecting the multicultural make-up of the city's population. Several of Bandar's better eateries are situated in the newly developed area west of Edinburgh Bridge, a short taxi ride – or an interesting walk beyond the Omar Ali Saifuddien Mosque and through Kampung Ayer – from downtown. If you're on a tight budget, head for the night **stalls** behind the Chinese temple on jalan sungei Kianggeh, where the bursting flames and billowing smoke of chicken being barbequed over charcoal fires lend proceedings a hellishly dramatic aspect. Malay favourites are laid out buffet-style here, but the lack of tables and chairs makes life difficult. Alternatively, there's a cluster of stalls behind the Temburong jetty on jalan Residency, whose lack of panache is somewhat redeemed by good and cheap *soto ayam*, *nasi campur* and other Malay staples.

One thing you won't find downtown is a bar. Drinking **alcohol** in public has been outlawed in Brunei since New Year's Day, 1991, though if you're gasping for a beer, an expat haunt, the *Brunei International Club*, a ten-minute taxi ride from the city at Simpang 197, jalan Berakas, seems to be tolerated by the authorities.

Café Melati, *Sheraton Utama Hotel*, jalan Sungei Kianggeh. The generous buffet lunch ($25) in this bright and breezy establishment fills you up for the day; buffet dinner ($30) features a different international culinary theme every night. Open Mon–Sat noon–2pm & 7–10pm, Sun 7–10pm.

Hua Hua Restaurant, 48 Jalan Sultan. Steamed chicken with sausage is one of the highlights in this hole-in-the-wall Chinese establishment, where $15 feeds two people. Open daily 7am–9pm.

Mei Kong Coffee Shop, 108 jalan Pemancha. Coffee shop, fronted by a chicken rice bar, serving noodles, *rotis* and *panggang* (rice and prawns cooked in banana leaves). Open daily 5am–8pm.

Phongmun Restaurant, 2nd floor, Teck Guan Plaza, Jalan Sultan. Classy and centrally located Chinese restaurant, lined with wall panels depicting roses and dragons, and serving *dim sum* until late afternoon. Open daily 6.30am–11pm; *dim sum* served 6.30am–4.40pm.

Popular Restaurant, Shop 5, Block 1, Putri Anak Norain Complex, Batu 1, jalan Tutong. Bare but clean Indian restaurant, serving peerless *dosai*, tandoori breads and curries. Open Mon 4pm–10pm, Tues–Sun 8am–10pm.

Rang Mahel, Ist floor, 3A Bangunan Mas Panchawarna, Batu 1, jalan Tutong. Cosy and well-respected North Indian place; below is the *Regent's Den*, where cheaper Indian snacks are available, daily 7.30am–10.30pm.

Rasa Sayang Restaurant, top floor, Bangunan Guru Guru Melayu, jalan Sungei Kianggeh. Chinese/Nonya restaurant that verges on the chintzy, but boasts friendly staff and a *dim sum* menu; around $10 a head. Open daily 6.30am–11.30pm; *dim sum* 6.30am–5pm & 8–11.30pm.

Restoran Intan Seri Taman Selera, 1–2 Bangunan Mas Panchawarna, Batu 1, jalan Tutong. Popular, buffet-style Malay restaurant with a satay stall outside at night. Open daily 7am–9.30pm.

Snoopy Restaurant, 108 Bangunan Guru Guru Melayu, jalan Sungei Kianggeh. Small and simple Indian joint, producing good curries and a delicious chicken biryani. Open Mon–Sat 6am–8.30pm, Sun 6am–1.30pm.

Sri Indah, 66 jalan MacArthur. Sweaty, cramped place churning out *murtabaks* and *rotis* that hit the spot. Open daily 7am–9pm.

Listings

Airlines *MAS*, 144 jalan Pemancha (☎224141); *Philippines Airlines*, 1st floor, Wisma Haji Fatimah, jalan Sultan (☎222970); *Royal Brunei Airlines*, RBA Plaza, jalan Sultan (☎242222); *Singapore Airlines*, 49–50, jalan Sultan (☎227253); *Thai Airways*, 4th floor, Komplek Jalan Sultan, 51–55 jalan Sultan (☎242991).

American Express Unit 401–3, 4th floor Shell Building, jalan Sultan (Mon–Fri 8.30am–5pm; Sat 8.30am–1pm; ☎228314).

Banks and exchange *Hong Kong & Shanghai Bank*, jalan Sultan; *International Bank of Brunei*, jalan Roberts; *Overseas Union Bank*, RBA Plaza, jalan Sultan; *Standard Chartered Bank*, jalan Sultan. Banking hours are Mon–Fri 9am–3pm & Sat 9–11am.

Bookshops *Best Eastern Books* (Mon–Sat 9am–6.30pm), G4 Teck Guan Plaza, jalan Sultan stocks a modest range of English-language books and magazines.

Car rental *Avis*, *Sheraton Hotel*, jalan Sungai Kianggeh (☎227100); *National*, 1st floor, jalan Gadong (☎224921); *Roseraya Car Rental*, Britannia House, jalan Sungei Kianggeh (☎241442).

Cinemas *Borneo Theatre*, on jalan Roberts, and *Bolkiah Theatre*, on jalan Sungai Kianggeh, both screen English-language movies; prices around $5.

Embassies and consulates *Australia*, 4th floor, Teck Guan Plaza, jalan Sultan (☎229435); *Indonesia*, Simpang 528, Lot 4498, Sungei Hanching Baru, jalan Muara (☎330180); *Malaysia*, 437 Kampung Pelambayan, jalan Kota Batu (☎228410); *Philippines*, 4th & 5th floor, Badi'ah Building, jalan Tutong (☎241465); *Singapore*, 5th floor, RBA Plaza, jalan Sultan (☎227583); *Thailand*, 13, Simpang 29, Kampung Kiarong (☎229653); *UK*, 3rd floor, Hong Kong Bank Chambers, jalan Sultan (☎222231); *USA*, 3rd floor, Teck Guan Plaza, jalan Sultan (☎229670).

Hospital The *Raja Isteri Pengiran Anak Saleha Hospital* is across Edinburgh Bridge on jalan Putera Al-Muhtadee Billah (☎02/222366). For an ambulance, call ☎223366.

Immigration The Immigration Office (Mon–Thurs & Sat 7.45am–12.15pm & 1.45–4.30pm) is opposite jalan Sumbiling, on jalan Tutong.

Laundry *Superkleen*, opposite *Brunei Hotel*, jalan Pemancha.

Pharmacies *Khong Lin Dispensary*, G3A, Wisma Jaya, jalan Pemancha; *Sentosa Dispensary*, 42 jalan Sultan.

Police Central Police Station, jalan Stoney (☎222333).

Post office The GPO (Mon–Thurs & Sat 8am–4.30pm) is at the intersection of jalan Elizabeth Dua and jalan Sultan. Poste restante/general delivery is at the Money Order counter.

Telephones *Telekom* (daily 8am–midnight) is next to the GPO on jalan Sultan; international calls can be made from here, or else buy a phone card ($10, $20, $50 and $100 are available) and use a public telephone.

Travel agents A number of travel agents around the city offer tours around the state; *Zura Travel Service*, Room 101, Bangunan Guru Guru Melayu, jalan Kianggeh (☎225812); and *Freme Travel Services*, 4th floor, Hong Kong Bank Chambers, jalan Sultan (☎228845), are central. Both offer three-hour city ($40) and countryside ($50) tours.

Brunei Muara

Once you've exhausted all that Bandar has to offer, you may consider ranging further afield in **BRUNEI MUARA** – the district of Brunei containing the capital. It's worth making the point that none of Brunei Muara's destinations are unmissable and few are served by direct buses: unless you are willing to pay through the nose for taxis, or rent a car, think twice before making for these destinations. Principal among the attractions that ring the capital are **Kampung Parit** and **Bukit Shahbandar Forest Recreation Park**, the former an evocation of how Bruneians lived in the days before oil and concrete, the latter a sizeable nature reserve; both make pleasant day trips. For a glimpse of Brunei's countryside, with a little determination it's possible to head for the cultivated land that flanks jalan Mulaut; or you may prefer simply to head for one of the area's several **beaches**.

Along jalan Mulaut

Some 15km west of Bandar along the road to Tutong, a mosque marks the turning southwards onto **jalan Mulaut**. From here, it's a further 10km to **KAMPUNG PARIT** (daily 8am–6pm; free), where a number of old-style Bornean dwellings have been erected to shed light on traditional Bruneian village life. Amongst the exhibits, which were built by artesans from local villages using only forest materials, is a replica of Kampung Ayer, pre-timber and zinc. The park's children's playground, picnic site and cluster of food stalls make it popular with Bruneian weekenders. Even so, access is not easy: unless you take a taxi, the only public transport access is by bus to Tutong; you have to get off after 15km, at the turning, and make your own way from there.

South of the park, jalan Mulaut continues across some fine countryside, on its way to the Sarawak border. Rice cultivation dominates this region of Brunei, much of which belongs to the **Wasan Rice Project**, a rice farm established in the late 1970s to promote rice self-sufficiency through cultivation and research. Around 6km beyond the farm, jalan Mulaut reaches an immigration checkpoint, from where it's possible to push on into Sarawak.

Muara and around

Northeast of the city, beyond the Brunei Museum, jalan Kota Batu stretches all the way up to **MUARA**, an oil town and Brunei's main port. The town was originally established to serve the now-defunct Brooketon Coal Mine, which was situated a few kilometres to the west. While there's nothing to bring you to Muara itself, nearby **Muara Beach** boasts a good stretch of sand, as well as food stalls and changing rooms. Buses ($2) to Muara from the capital pass along jalan Kota Batu, skirting the Brunei River's north bank. En route is **PULAU CHERMIN**, a tiny island whose unremarkable royal tombs are all that remain of the royal fortress which stood here three centuries ago. The island has been a protected archeological site since broken pieces of Ming and Tang Dynasty pottery were found on it, and is off limits unless you have permission to visit from the state museum. Pulau Chermin is opposite Kampung Sungei Besar, around 10km out of Bandar. Five kilometres further up the road to Muara, the chain of pools at **Mentiri Falls** offers good swimming amid lush forest. The path to the falls starts at the side of a river on the left hand side of the road, beyond Simpang 378.

The coast: Crocodile Beach and Bukit Shahbandar

From Muara, a highway more or less follows the northern coast for 18km to Tutong. A few kilometres out of town, the highway passes the turning to Pantai Meragang, known locally as **Crocodile Beach**, and considered by many to be the best in the area. The beach is slightly more than 1km west of the intersection of jalan Muara and the Muara–Tutong Highway.

Around 20km west of Muara is the **BUKIT SHAHBANDAR FOREST RECREATION PARK** (daily 8am–6pm; free), its seventy hectares of acacia, pine and heath forest scored by unchallenging trails and dotted with shelters and look-out points affording views over Bandar and the South China Sea. Marking the entrance into the park is an information centre with displays on the surrounding terrain. **Camping** is allowed, provided you have permission from the Director of Forestry's office on jalan Roberts. Unfortunately, Bukit Shahbandar is tricky to reach: unless you're prepared to pay for a taxi, you'll have to take a bus to Berakas and try to hitch from there.

Temburong District

Hilly **TEMBURONG DISTRICT** has been isolated from the rest of Brunei since 1884, when the strip of land to the west of it was ceded to Sarawak. Sparsely populated by Malay, Iban and Murut groups, the region is swathed in rainforest that can be explored in the forest reserves at Peradayan and Batu Apoi. Temburong is an important source of gravel for Brunei, and timber, too, is culled from its land, though not, so far, on a large scale. The district is accessible only by a hair-raising **speedboat journey** from Bandar (see p.459). The boats, whose shape has earned them the name "flying coffins" scream through a network of narrow mangrove estuaries that are home to crocodiles and proboscis monkeys, swooping around corners and narrowly missing vessels travelling the opposite way, before shooting off down sungei Temburong. Boatmen don't mind if you sit on top of the cabin, but think twice before deciding to do so.

All boats terminate at Bangar, the crossroads for the district's two main roads. Temburong has over 60km of good roads, providing links into Sarawak, with Limbang (p.383) to the west, and Lawas (p.384) to the east.

Bangar: crossing to Sarawak

Temburong's one settlement of any size, **BANGAR** stands beside the bridge which takes the district's main road across sungei Temburong. After the thrilling boat trip from the capital, the town is a disappointment, its main street, which runs west from the jetty to the ugly town mosque, lined only by a handful of nondescript **coffee shops** and provision stores. Across the bridge is Bangar's grandest building, its new District Office, whose waterfront café is the town's most salubrious **place to eat**. Enquiries can be made here about the *Government Rest House* at the turning to Batang Duri, five minutes' walk west of town.

If you're planning to cross **into Sarawak** – either to Limbang or to Lawas – you'll first have to make for the **immigration post** beside the turning for Kampung Puni, 5km west of Bangar. Limbang is easiest and cheapest to reach: take a ferry ($1) across the river which marks the border with Malaysia, and then catch one of the connecting buses ($2) which run into Limbang until 5pm. Lawas is accessible by road, via Labu (see below), but only by a very expensive taxi ride from Bangar.

Around Bangar

On its way to Lawas, the road east of Bangar trundles past a few small settlements and the occasional saw mill, reaching the **PERADAYAN FOREST RESERVE** after 15km. From the road, it's a ninety-minute walk through the reserve's *dipterocarp* rainforest, to the top of 310-metre **Bukit Patoi**, whose plateau affords excellent views of the surrounding terrain, and of Lawas in Sarawak. Camping on Bukit Patoi is not unheard of, though there are no facilities. A few kilometres beyond the reserve, the road reaches **LABU**, a mysterious place whose existence amounts only to a sign reading "Labu 0km"'. From here, it's only a few kilometres to the border with Sarawak – but bear in mind that the immigration outpost is way back beyond Bangar (see above).

The end of the 17km of road running south of Bangar is marked by **BATANG DURI**, whose smart Iban longhouse is lived in by around two hundred people. A short walk beyond the longhouse leads to a small waterfall whose cool waters make for a refreshing swim. There's more river swimming a couple of kilometres back up the road, at **TAMAN BATANG DURI**, a well-manicured park that's blighted by its very sad mini zoo. With permission from Bangar's District Office, it's possible to camp at the park.

Much of the area south of Batang Duri now makes up the **BATU APOI FOREST RESERVE**, which spans around five hundred square kilometres and incorporates the **Kuala Belalong Field Centre**, built as a joint venue between the *Universiti Brunei Darussalem* and *Brunei Shell* to facilitate research into the surrounding rainforest. Several trails lead into the reserve and visitors can stay at one of the *Field Centre*'s chalets, provided there's not a full house of researchers. Bookings should be made through the Department of Biology, at the *Universiti*; bear in mind, though, that the five-kilometre boat trip up sungei Temburong from Batang Duri to reach the field centre is an expensive one.

Taxis are available in Bangar to all of these places, with return fares starting from $15.

Tutong District

West of Muara District is wedge-shaped **TUTONG DISTRICT**, whose main settlement **Tutong** is a little over 40km west of Bandar. Though a coastal highway now connects Tutong with Muara District, buses ($3) from the capital still make the one-hour journey via inland jalan Tutong, which is skirted by scrublands and grasslands. The wide plug of mountains that runs down through Borneo from Sabah misses all but the Temburong District of Brunei; accordingly, the terrain of Tutong District never manages more than a gentle roll, making it ideal for the heightened agriculturalism the government is presently trying to develop in the area.

Tutong

Bruneian settlements don't come any sleepier than **TUTONG**. The town has witnessed none of the development that the discovery of oil has caused further west, but though Tutong makes no real demands upon tourists' time, it's an amiable enough place to break the trip between Sarawak and Bandar. Tutong's one street of any size, jalan Enche Awang, is flanked by rows of shophouses on one side, and on the other by broad sungei Tutong, its far bank teeming with palm trees.

You won't find anywhere to stay in Tutong, but there are several **restaurants**: try the *Haji K-K-Koya* at no. 14 for Muslim staples, or the Chinese *Ho Yuen* at no. 12. If you're in town on a Friday morning, you should visit the animated **Tamu Tutong**, which draws fruit and vegetable vendors from the interior of Brunei. The market takes place on a patch of land 1km from central Tutong, and can be reached by walking out of town along jalan Enche Awang and taking a left turn at the fork in the road.

Ignoring this fork and continuing on across the coastal highway brings you, after fifteen minutes, to the best stretch of beach in the area, the peninsular **Pantai Seri Kenangan**. Its name translates as "Unforgettable Beach" and though this may be rather stretching the point, it's pleasant enough, its yellow sands dividing Sungei Tutong from the South China Sea.

Tasek Merimbun

Tutong District's most impressive geographical feature is **Tasek Merimbun**, an S-shaped lake, the largest in Brunei. It would be a charming place to visit, if only it wasn't so awkward to reach: wooden boardwalks from the attractively landscaped shore run across to Pulau Jelandung, a tiny wooded island, and around the lake itself are pathways and picnic spots. However, unless you've rented a car, you aren't likely to get here: the lake is around 25km inland from Tutong and not served by buses; a return taxi fare costs well over $50. If you're driving, follow jalan Tutong out of Bandar and take the left turn to Lamunin, after around 30km. From there, signposts lead you to Tasek Merimbun, along negotiable roads that bisect glistening paddy fields.

Belait District

BELAIT DISTRICT, west of Tutong and over sungei Tutong, is oil and gas country, and has been the economic heart of the Sultanate ever since the Seria Oilfield first came on stream in 1931. The oil boom led directly to the rise of the region's two main coastal towns, **Seria** and **Kuala Belait**. Inland, though, it's a different story: down fifty-kilometre-long **Labi Road**, Iban **longhouses** and tiny *kampungs* survive in the face of the tremendous changes brought about by the Sultanate's sudden wealth and the substantial population shift to the coast.

Labi Road

Flat scrublands line the road westwards from Tutong to Seria. The sands along this stretch of Brunei's coast are as brilliant white as any you'll see, due to their high silicon content; in time, as the Bruneian authorities look to moneymaking alternatives to their finite oil reserves, these sands could well spawn a glass industry. A few kilometres over sungei Tutong, a turning south marks the start of **Labi Road**, which offers the chance to explore the state's interior.

First stop, 500m up the road, is the **SUNGEI LIANG FOREST RESERVE**, whose 14 hectares of thick lowland forest can be explored by following one of the well-kept walking trails emanating from the lakes, information centre and picnic shelters clustered around the entrance. With your own car, it's possible to push on down Labi Road from the reserve. Some 25km further on is **LABI** itself, a small agricultural settlement whose surrounding hills have refused to yield up their known oil riches, despite much speculative drilling. In the meantime, Labi relies upon its harvests of durian and rambutan for its livelihood. It was Labi's oil potential which led to the construction of Labi Road; shortly after Labi, it peters out, though a passable track pushes on towards the border with Sarawak, passing several modern Iban longhouses, the biggest of which, **RUMAH PANJANG MENDARAM BESAR**, houses around a hundred people. Just beyond the longhouse, a footpath to the left leads, after twenty minutes, to **Wasai Mendaram**, a low waterfall whose pool offers refreshing swimming. Another longhouse, **RUMAH PANJANG TERAJA**, marks the end of Labi Road, with only swamp forest beyond.

Seria

At the very epicentre of Brunei's oil and gas wealth is **SERIA**, 65km west of Bandar. Until oil was first discovered here at the turn of the century, the area where the town now stands was nothing more than a malarial swamp, known locally as Padang Berawa, or "Wild Pigeon's Field": an oil prospector researching in the area in 1926 reported that "walking here means really climbing and jumping over naked roots, and struggling and cutting through air roots of mangroves of more than man's height". It took until 1931 for S1, the Sultanate's first well, to deliver commercially, after which Seria expanded rapidly, followed in more recent times by offshore drilling, the construction of a gas processing plant in 1955 and the opening of an oil refinery in 1983.

As you approach from Tutong, you'll see numbers of small oil wells called "nodding donkeys" because of their rocking motion, though they actually bear a closer resemblance to praying mantises. Around the town are green-roofed housing units and bungalows, constructed by *Brunei Shell* for their employees; while on the waterfront is the **Billionth Barrel Monument**, whose interlocking arches celebrate the huge productivity of of the first well. Seria town centre is a hectic place, dominated by the Plaza Seria shopping mall, across from the bus station. Budget **restaurants** and coffee shops abound, though for a more upmarket meal try the *New China Restaurant*, in Plaza Seria. The rooms in the *Seria Hotel*, Lot 173 jalan Sharif Ali (☎03/222804; ③), are a useful last resort if you've missed the last bus to Bandar or to Sarawak; walk through the taxi rank in front of the bus station, and bear right.

Kuala Belait and on into Sarawak

It's a little under 20km from Seria to the neighbouring oil town of **KUALA BELAIT**, the attendant scenery an incongruous blend of oil pipes and palm trees. There's nothing very enticing about Kuala Belait, but with all buses to and from Miri in Sarawak stopping here, it's a place you may have to visit. The town is ringed by a band of suburban development that caters for its expat community, while central Kuala Belait is characterized by the many workshops and businesses that the local oil industry has spawned. If Kuala Belait seems dozy today, pity the poor expats consigned to its drilling stations in the early part of the century. A contemporary rhyme encapsulated the torpor and isolation they felt:

> *Work of course gets sometimes weary*
> *Up in Belait*
> *And the evenings long and dreary*
> *Up in Belait*
> *But when again New Year draws nigh*
> *Let's go to Miri, they all cry.*

Buses stop at the intersection of jalan Bunga Raya and jalan McKerron, across which is the town's **taxi** stand. Jalan McKerron houses several good **restaurants** – the best of which are the tastefully decorated *Buccaneer Steakhouse* at no. 94, whose mid-priced international food is aimed squarely at the expat market; and the *Akhbar Restaurant*, at no. 99A, boasting a Malay and North Indian menu which includes excellent *dosai*. Next door to the *Buccaneer*, at no. 93, is one of Kualal Belait's two **hotels**, *Hotel Sentosa* (☎03/234341; ⑤), its rooms capacious, well appointed and welcoming. The alternative is the slightly more expensive *Sea View Hotel* (☎03/332651; ⑤), about 2km back along the coastal road towards Seria. You can **change money** in town at the *Hongkong Bank* (Mon–Fri 9am–3pm, Sat 9–11am); the *Sei Kai* bookshop opposite the bus station will change Malaysian currency only.

Buses to Sarawak leave Kuala Belait's bus station at 7.30am, 9.30am, 11am, 1.30pm and 3.30pm; the price ($9.50) includes the ferry across sungei Belait and the connecting Sarawakian bus over the border. **Taxi** drivers charge around $100 for a full car to Miri, though you should be able to haggle them down substantially.

Upriver: Kuala Balai

Kuala Belait squats on the eastern bank of calm **sungei Belait**, and motorboatmen whose craft are moored at the back of the central market on jalan McKerron will take you upriver – it'll cost at least $100 for the return trip. Unless it's the boat trip itself you're interested in, there's very little reason to make the trip. After around forty minutes, **KUALA BALAI** comes into sight. Once a thriving centre for sago-processing,

Kuala Balai has seen its population dwindle from hundreds to just a handful, as inhabitants have left in search of work on the oil fields; it's now little more than a ghost town. As you approach Balai, look out for the wooden cage of human skulls on stilts over the river – a grim remnant of Borneo's head-hunting days.

travel details

Buses

Brunei has a generous ratio of cars to citizens, so its bus network is skimpy. If you want to make a day trip out of Bandar, you'll have to start early in the morning as bus services stop by mid-afternoon.

Bandar Seri Begawan to: Muara (every 30min until 4.30pm; 30min); Seria (every 45min until 2pm; 1hr 45min); Tutong (every 45min until 2pm; 1hr).

Kuala Belait to: Miri (every 2hr, 7.30am–3.30pm; 1hr 30min); Seria (hourly until 6.30pm; 45min).

Seria to: Bandar Seri Begawan (every 45min until 2pm; 1hr 45min); Kuala Belait (hourly; 45min).

Boats

Bandar Seri Begawan to: Bangar (every 45min; 50min), Lawas (1 daily; 2hr); Limbang (several daily; 30min); Pulau Labuan (3 daily; 1hr 30min).

CHAPTER NINE

SINGAPORE

Singapore is certainly the handiest city I ever saw, as well planned and carefully executed as though built entirely by one man. It is like a big desk, full of drawers and pigeon-holes, where everything has its place, and can always be found in it.

W. Hornaday, 1885.

Despite the immense changes the past century has wrought upon the tiny island of **Singapore**, natural historian William Hornaday's succinct appraisal is as valid today as it was in 1885. Since gaining full independence from Malaysia in 1965, this absorbing city-state – which measures just 580 square kilometres and is linked by a kilometre-long causeway to the southern tip of Malaysia – has been transformed from a sleepy colonial backwater to a pristine, futuristic shrine to consumerism. It's one of Southeast Asia's most accessible destinations, its downtown areas dense with towering skyscrapers and gleaming shopping malls, while sprawling new towns with their own separate communities and well-planned facilities ring the centre. Yet visitors prepared to peer beneath the state's squeaky-clean surface will discover a profusion of age-old buildings, values and traditions that have survived in the face of profound social and geographical change. Nor has this change turned the island into a drab, urban slum – even as you make your way in from the airport, you'll be struck immediately by Singapore's abundance of parks, nature reserves, and lush, tropical greenery. Inevitably, given its geographical position, the state is seen by most people as a mere stopover and, because of its size, you can gain at least an impression of the place in just a few hours. However, justifying a lengthier stay is easily done. Quite apart from the cultural highlights, you'll find several days spent in Singapore invaluable for arranging financial transfers, seeing to medical problems and generally gathering strength before continuing on to the region's less affluent – and often more demanding – areas.

Singapore's progress over the past three decades has been remarkable. Lacking any noteworthy natural resources, its early prosperity was based on a vigorous free trade policy, in place since 1819 when Sir Stamford Raffles first set up a British trading post here; later, mass industrialization bolstered the economy, and today the state boasts the world's second busiest port after Rotterdam, minimal unemployment, and a super efficient infrastructure. Almost the entire population has been moved from unsanitary *kampungs* into swish new apartments, and the average per capita income is over US$12,000. Yet none of this was achieved without considerable compromise – indeed, the state's detractors claim it has sold its soul in return for prosperity.

Put simply, at the core of the Singapore success story is an unwritten bargain between its government and population, which stipulates the loss of a certain amount of personal freedom, in return for levels of affluence and comfort that would have seemed unimaginable thirty years ago. "When you are hungry, when you lack basic services . . ." former Prime Minister, and now Senior Minister, Lee Kuan Yew has gone on record as saying, "When you are hungry, when you lack basic services, freedom, human rights and democracy do not add up to much". Outsiders often bridle at these sentiments, and it's true that some of the regulations in force here can seem extreme: neglecting to flush a public toilet, jaywalking, or chewing gum and eating on the subway all carry sizeable fines, while the case of American teenager, Michael Fay, caught the world's headlines in early 1994, when he was given four strokes of the *rotan*

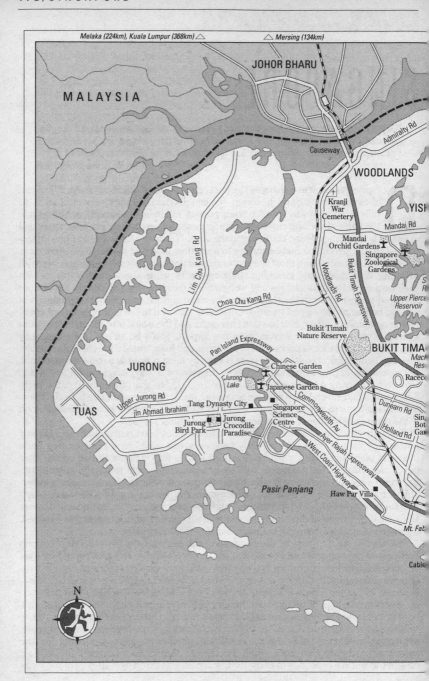

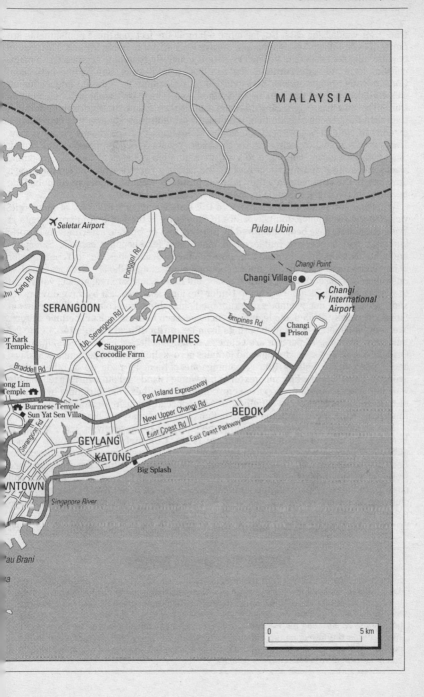

MALAYSIA

Seletar Airport

Pulau Ubin

Ponggol Rd

Changi Point

Changi Village ●

Changi
International
Airport

Chu Kang Rd

SERANGOON

Up. Serangoon Rd

TAMPINES

Tampines Rd

Changi
Prison ■

or Kark
Temple

■ Singapore
Crocodile Farm

Braddell Rd

ong Lim
Temple

Pan Island Expressway

BEDOK

♦ Burmese Temple

New Upper Changi Rd

♦ Sun Yat Sen Villa

Serangoon Rd

East Coast Rd

East Coast Parkway

GEYLANG

KATONG

Big Splash

NTOWN

Singapore River

au Brani

a

0   5 km

(cane) for vandalizing cars. But far more telling is the fact that these punishments are rarely, if ever, inflicted, as Singaporeans have learned not to break the law. The population, trusting the wisdom of its leaders, seems generally content to acquiesce to a paternalistic form of **government** that critics describe as soft authoritarianism. Consequently, Singaporeans have earned a reputation for cowed, unquestioning subservience, a view that can be overstated, but which isn't without an element of truth. The past has taught Singaporeans that, if they follow their government's lead, they reap the benefits. In addition, they take a pride in their country that occasionally extends to smugness – witness the huge celebrations that accompany National Day, Sinagapore's annual collective pat on the back. Yet there is good reason to be proud: Singapore is a clean, safe place to visit, its amenities are second to none, its public places smoke-free and hygienic. And as the nation's youth – who don't remember a time before the improvements they take for granted – begin to find a voice, public life becomes increasingly, if gradually, more liberal and democratic.

Whatever the political ramifications of the state's economic success, of more relevance to the five million annual visitors to Singapore is the fact that improvements in living conditions have been shadowed by a steady loss of the state's **heritage** as historic buildings and streets are bulldozed to make way for shopping centres. Singapore undoubtedly lacks the personality of some Southeast Asian cities, but its reputation for being sterile and sanitized is unfair. Shopping on state-of-the-art Orchard Road is undoubtedly a major draw for many tourists, but to do Singapore real justice, you've got to venture beneath its affluent sheen. Under the long shadows cast by the giddy towers and spires are the dusty temples, fragrant medicinal shops, and colonial buildings of old Singapore, neatly divided into historical enclaves, each home to a distinct ethnic culture. Much of Singapore's fascination springs from its **multicultural population**: of the 2.7 million inhabitants, 78 percent are Chinese, a figure reflected in the predominance of Oriental faces, shops, restaurants and temples across the island; 14 percent are Malays; and 7 percent are Indians (the remaining one percent is made up of other ethnic groups). This diverse ethnic mix textures the whole island, and often turns a ten-minute walk into what seems like a hop from one country to another. One intriguing by-product of this ethnic melting pot is **Singlish**, or Singaporean English, a patois which blends English with the speech patterns, exclamations and vocabulary of Chinese and Malay.

The entire state is compact enough to be explored exhaustively in just a few days. Forming the core of downtown Singapore is the **Colonial District**, around whose public buildings and lofty cathedral the island's British residents used to promenade. Each surrounding enclave has its own distinct flavour, ranging from the aromatic spice stores of **Little India**, to the tumbledown backstreets of **Chinatown**, where it's still possible to happen upon calligraphers and fortune tellers, or the **Arab Quarter**, whose cluttered stores sell fine cloths and silks. **North** of the city, you'll find the country's two nature reserves – Bukit Timah Nature Reserve and the Central Catchment Area – and the splendid **Singapore Zoological Gardens**. In the **west** of the island, the East

---

WHEN TO GO

Singapore is just 136km north of the equator, which means that you should be prepared for a hot and sticky time whenever you go. **Temperatures** are uniformly high throughout the year, but it's the region's humidity levels which make the heat really uncomfortable. Be prepared for **rain** during your stay, too – November, December and January are usually the coolest, and the wettest, months, but rain can fall all year round. On average, July records the lowest annual rainfall. Otherwise, the only other consideration is the possibility of coinciding with one of the many **festivals** (see *Basics*), of which the liveliest and most extensive is Chinese New Year.

meets Disneyworld at **Tang Dynasty City** and **Haw Par Villas**; while the **east coast** features good seafood restaurants, set behind long stretches of sandy beach. In addition, over fifty islands and islets lie within Singaporean waters, all of which can be reached with varying degrees of ease. The best day trips, however, are to **Sentosa**, the island amusement arcade which is linked to the south coast by a short causeway (and cable car), and to **Pulau Ubin**, off the east coast, whose inhabitants continue to live a *kampung* life long since eradicated from the mainland.

A little history

What little is known of Singapore's ancient history relies heavily upon legend and supposition. Third-century Chinese sailors could have been referring to Singapore in their account of a place called Pu-Luo-Chung, or "island at the end of a peninsula". In the late thirteenth century, Marco Polo reported seeing a place called Chiamassie, which could also have been Singapore: by then the island was known locally as Temasek – "sea town" – and was a minor trading outpost of the Sumatran Srivijaya empire. The island's present name – from the Sanskrit *Singapura*, meaning "Lion City" – was first recorded in the sixteenth century, when a legend narrated in the Malay annals, the *Sejarah Melayu*, told how a Sumatran prince saw a lion while sheltering on the island from a storm; however, the name had been in common use since the end of the fourteenth century.

Throughout the fourteenth century, Singapura felt the squeeze as the Ayutthaya and Majapahit empires of Thailand and Java struggled for control of the Malay peninsula. Around 1390, a Sumatran prince called Paramesvara threw off his allegiance to the Javanese Majapahit Empire and fled from Palembang to present-day Singapore. There, he murdered his host and ruled the island until a Javanese offensive forced him to flee north, up the peninsula, where he and his son, Iskandar Shah, subsequently founded the Melaka Sultanate. A grave on Fort Canning Hill (see p.505) is said to be that of Iskandar Shah, though its authenticity is doubtful. With the rise of the Melaka Sultanate, Singapore devolved into an inconsequential fishing settlement; a century or so later, the arrival of the Portuguese in Melaka forced Malay leaders to flee southwards to modern-day Johor Bahru for sanctuary, and a Portuguese account, in 1613, of razing an unnamed Malay outpost at the mouth of sungei Johor to the ground, marked the beginning of two centuries of historical limbo for Singapore.

By the late eighteenth century, with China opening up for trade with the West, the British East India Company felt the need to establish outposts along the Straits of Melaka to protect its interests. Penang was secured in 1786, but with the Dutch expanding their rule in the East Indies (Indonesia), a port was needed further south. Enter **Thomas Stamford Raffles**. In 1818, the Governor-General of India authorized Raffles, then Lieutenant-Governor of Bencoolen (in Sumatra), to establish a British colony at the southern tip of the Malay Peninsula; early the next year, he stepped ashore on the northern bank of the Singapore River.

At the time, inhospitable swampland and tiger-infested jungle covered Singapore, and its population is generally thought to have numbered around 150, although some historians suggest it could have been as high as a thousand. Raffles recognized the island's potential for providing a deep-water harbour, and immediately struck a treaty with **Abdul Rahman**, *Temenggong* (chieftain) of Singapore, establishing a British trading station there. The Dutch were furious at this British incursion into what they considered was their territory, but Raffles – who still needed the approval of the Sultan of Johor for his outpost as Abdul Rahman was only an underling – disregarded Dutch sensibilities. He approached the Sultan's brother, Hussein, recognized him as the true Sultan, and concluded a second treaty with both the Temenggong and **"His Highness the Sultan Hussein Mohammed Shah"**. The Union Jack was raised, and Singapore's future as a free trading post was set.

Strategically positioned at the foot of the Straits of Melaka, and with no customs duties levied on imported or exported goods, Singapore's expansion was meteoric. The population had reached 10,000 by the time of the first census in 1824, with Malays, Chinese, Indians and Europeans arriving in search of work as coolies and merchants. In 1822, Raffles set about drawing up the demarcation lines that divide present-day Singapore. The area south of the Singapore River was earmarked for the Chinese; a swamp at the mouth of the river was filled and the commercial district established there; while Muslims were settled around the Sultan's Palace in today's Arab Quarter. The Singapore of these times was a far cry from the late twentieth century's spotless version. "There were thousands of rats all over the district" wrote Abdullah bin Kadir, scribe to Stamford Raffles, "some almost as large as cats. They were so big that they used to attack us if we went out walking at night and many people were knocked over."

In 1823, Singapore was ceded outright to the British; in 1826, the fledgling state united with Penang and Melaka (now under British rule) to form the **Straits Settlements**, which later became a British crown colony. For forty years the island's economy boomed, though life was chaotic and disease rife. More and more immigrants poured onto the island and by 1860 the population had reached 80,000, with each arriving ethnic community bringing its attendant cuisines, languages and architecture. The British, for their part, erected impressive Neoclassical theatres, courts and assembly halls; in 1887 Singapore's most quintessentially British establishment, the *Raffles Hotel*, opened for business.

By the end of the nineteenth century, the opening of the Suez Canal and the advent of the steamship had consolidated Singapore's position at the hub of international trade in the region, with the port becoming a major staging post on the Europe–East Asia route. In 1877, Henry Ridley began his one-man crusade to introduce the **rubber plant** into Southeast Asia, a move which further bolstered Singapore's importance as the island soon became the world centre of rubber exporting; between 1873 and 1913 trade increased eightfold, a trend which continued well into the twentieth century.

Then, in 1942, the bubble burst. In December 1941, the Japanese had bombed Pearl Harbour and invaded the Malay Peninsula. Less than two months later they were at the top of the causeway, safe from the the guns of "Fortress Singapore", which pointed south from what is now Sentosa island. The inhabitants of Singapore had not been prepared for an attack from this direction and on February 15, 1942, the **fall of Singapore** (which the Japanese then renamed Syonan, or "Light of the South") was complete. Winston Churchill called the British surrender "the worst disaster and the largest capitulation in British history"; cruelly, it later transpired that the Japanese forces had been outnumbered and their supplies hopelessly stretched immediately prior to the surrender.

Three and a half years of brutal Japanese rule ensued, during which thousands of civilians were executed in vicious anti-Chinese purges and Europeans were either herded into **Changi Prison**, or marched up the peninsula to work on Thailand's infamous "Death Railway". Following the atomic destruction of Hiroshima and Nagasaki in 1945, Singapore was passed back into British hands, but things were never to be the same. Singaporeans now wanted a say in the government of the island and in 1957 the British government agreed to the establishment of an elected, 51-member legislative assembly. Full internal **self-government** was achieved in May 1959, when the People's Action Party (PAP), led by Cambridge law graduate **Lee Kuan Yew**, won 43 of the 51 seats. Lee became Singapore's first Prime Minister, and quickly looked for the security of a merger with neighbouring Malaya. For its part – and despite reservations about aligning with Singapore's predominantly Chinese population – anti-Communist Malaya feared that extremists within the PAP would turn Singapore into a Communist base, and accordingly preferred to have the state under its wing.

In 1963, Singapore combined with Malaya, Sarawak and British North Borneo (modern-day Sabah), to form the **Federation of Malaysia**. The alliance, though, was an uneasy one and within two years Singapore was asked to leave the federation, in the face of outrage in Kuala Lumpur at the PAP's attempts to break into federal politics in 1964. Hours after announcing Singapore's **full independence**, on August 9, 1965, a tearful Lee Kuan Yew described the event, on national TV, as "a moment of anguish". One hundred and forty-six years after Sir Stamford Raffles had set Singapore on the world map, the tiny island, with no natural resources of its own, faced the prospect of being consigned to history's bottom drawer of crumbling colonial ports.

Instead, Lee's personal vision and drive transformed it into an Asian economic heavyweight – a position achieved at a price. Heavy-handed censorship of the media was introduced, and littering offenders submitted to the public humiliation of forced litter duty, though most disturbing of all was the Government's attitude towards political opposition. The archaic **Internal Security Act** still grants the power to detain without trial anyone the government deems a threat to the nation, which has kept political prisoner Chia Thye Poh under lock and key since 1966 for allegedly advocating violence. Population policies, too, have brought criticism from abroad. These began in the early 1970s, with a **birth control campaign** which proved so successful that it had to be reversed: the 1980s saw the introduction of the "Go For Three" project, which offered tax incentives for those having more than two children in an attempt to boost the national – and some say, more specifically the Chinese Singaporean – birth rate. Lee Kuan Yew also made clear his conviction that Singapore's educated elite should intermarry, thereby breeding the sort of babies that would serve the country well in the future.

At other times, Singapore tries so hard to reshape itself that it falls into self-parody. "We have to pursue this subject of fun very seriously if we want to stay competitive in the 21st century" was the reaction of former Minister of State for Finance and Foreign Affairs, George Yeo, when challenged on the fact that some foreigners found Singapore dull. Whether Singaporeans will continue to suffer their government's foibles remains to be seen. Adults beyond a certain age remember how things were before independence and, more importantly, before the existence of the Mass Rapid Transit (MRT) system, housing projects and saving schemes. Their children and grandchildren have no such perspective, however, and telltale signs – presently nothing more extreme than feet up on MRT seats, or jaywalking – suggest that the government can expect more dissent in future years. Already a substantial brain drain is afflicting the country, as Singaporeans with skills to offer choose to move abroad in the pursuit of heightened civil liberties.

Orientation

The squidged diamond-shaped island of Singapore is 42km from east to west at its widest points, and 23km from north to south. The downtown city areas huddle at the southern tip of the diamond, radiating out from the mouth of the **Singapore River**. Two northeast–southwest roads form a dual spine to the central area, both of them traversing the river. One starts out as **North Bridge Road**, crosses the river and, fittingly, becomes **South Bridge Road**; the other begins as **Victoria Street** (at whose western end is found most of Singapore's budget accommodation), which becomes Hill Street and skirts Chinatown as **New Bridge Road**.

At the very heart of the city, on the north bank, the **Colonial District** is home to a cluster of buildings that recall the days of early British rule – Parliament House, Cathedral, Supreme Court, Cricket Club and, most famously, the *Raffles Hotel*. Moving west, the fringes of **Fort Canning Park** house several attractions, including Singapore's National Museum and Art Gallery; from here, it's just a five-minute stroll to the eastern end of **Orchard Road**, the main shopping area in the city. Go north instead from Fort Canning Park and you're rapidly into **Little India**, whose main road – Serangoon Road – is around fifteen minutes' walk from *Raffles Hotel*. Ten minutes' southeast, Singapore's traditional **Arab Quarter** squats at the intersection of North Bridge Road and Arab Street.

South, across the river, the monolithic towers of the **Financial District** cast long shadows over **Chinatown**, which stretches for around 1km as far as Cantonment Road. Singapore's **World Trade Centre** is a fifteen-minute hike southwest of the outskirts of Chinatown, from where cable cars run across to **Sentosa**.

Out of the centre, the various sights and attractions fall neatly into distinct geographical areas: north, east and west. The island is developing a system of expressways, of which the main ones are the east–west **Pan Island Expressway** and the **East Coast Parkway/Ayer Rajah Expressway**, both of which run from Changi to Jurong; and the **Bukit Timah Expressway**, which branches off north from the Pan Island Expressway at Bukit Timah new town and runs north to Woodlands. At Woodlands, the road (shadowed by the train from the Railway Station near Chinatown) crosses the **causeway** linking Singapore with Malaysia.

Arrival and information

Most people's first glimpse of Singapore is of Changi Airport, and a telling glimpse it is. Its two terminals, connected by the *Skytrain* monorail, are modern, efficient and air-conditioned – in other words, Singapore in a microcosm. Other arrivals are from over the causeway from the Malaysian city of Johor Bahru (p.296), or by boat from the Indonesian archipelago. Wherever you arrive, the well-oiled infrastructure means that you'll have no problem getting into the centre. For **departure information**, see the box over the page.

Changi Airport

Changi Airport is at the far eastern end of Singapore, 16km from the city centre. As well as duty-free shops, moneychanging and left-luggage facilities, the airport boasts a 24-hour post office and telephone service, hotel reservations counters, day rooms, saunas, and a business centre. There's also a *MacDonald's* and a *Swenson's* ice cream parlour; below *MacDonald's*, in Terminal One's basement, is a food centre – the cheapest and most authentically Singaporean option. That said, the likelihood is that you'll barely get the chance to take in the place at all – baggage comes through so quickly at Changi that you can be on a bus or in a taxi within fifteen minutes of arrival. Be sure to pick up one of the free maps the Singapore Tourist Promotion Board (STPB) leaves at the airport.

Since Singapore's underground train system doesn't extend as far as the airport (yet), you'll have to take either a taxi or a public bus into the centre. The **bus** departure points in the basements of both terminals are well signposted; take the #16 or #16E – departures are every ten minutes (daily 6am–midnight; $1 or $1.20 air-con) – and note that Singapore bus drivers don't give change. The bus heads west to Stamford Road (ask the driver to give you a shout at the YMCA stop, and cross over Bras Basah Park to reach Bencoolen Street) before skirting the southern side of Orchard Road. **Taxis** from the airport charge a $3 surcharge on top of the fare. Again, the pick-up points are well signposted, and a trip into downtown Singapore costs around $15 and takes twenty minutes or so. There are also **car rental agencies** at the airport (see "Listings", p.557), though you'd be advised not to travel around Singapore by car (see "City transport", p.480, for better ways of getting around).

Across the causeway

Singapore is linked to Johor Bahru by a 1056-metre-long **causeway** which runs across the Strait of Johor to Woodlands town, in the far north of the island. All buses and trains **into Singapore from Malaysia** currently pass over the causeway, though there is talk of a second connection being constructed further east.

By bus

Buses stop at one of two terminals in Singapore. Local buses **from Johor Bahru** (JB) arrive at **Ban San Terminal** at the junction of Queen and Arab streets, from where a two-minute walk along Queen Street, followed by a left along Rochor Road takes you to Bugis MRT station. Buses **from elsewhere in Malaysia** and **from Thailand** terminate at **Lavender Street Terminal**, at the corner of Lavender Street and Kallang Bahru, around five minutes' walk from Lavender MRT. Alternatively, walk a short way in the other direction to the end of jalan Besar and hop on bus #122 or #139, either of which travel along Bencoolen Street. In addition, bus #145 passes the Lavender Street Terminal on its way down North Bridge and South Bridge Roads.

By train

Trains from Malaysia end their journey at the **Singapore Railway Station** on Keppel Road, southwest of Chinatown. Oddly, you haven't officially arrived in Singapore until you step out of the station – which is owned by Malaysia – and into the street, as a sign above the main station entrance ("Welcome to Malaysia") testifies. The grounds of Singapore's railway system were sold lock, stock and barrel to the Federal Malay States in 1918, though recently the Singapore government has been buying back piecemeal segments of it. From Keppel Road, bus #97 travels past Tanjong Pagar MRT and on to Selegie and Serangoon roads.

By sea

Boats from the Indonesian archipelago of Riau (through which travellers from Sumatra will approach Singapore) dock at the World Trade Centre, off Telok Blangah Road, roughly 5km east of the centre. From Telok Blangah Road, bus #97 runs to Tanjong Pagar MRT; the #65 goes to Selegie and Serangoon roads, via Orchard Road; for Chinatown, take bus #166. It's also possible to reach Singapore by bumboat from Kampung Pengerang on the southeastern coast of Johor in Malaysia (see p.301 for details). These moor at Changi Village, beyond the airport, from where bus #2 travels into the centre, via Geylang, North Bridge and South Bridge roads.

Information and maps

The Singapore Tourist Promotion Board (STPB) maintains two **Tourist Information Centres**, both of which have toll-free information lines. One is at #02-34 *Raffles Hotel* Shopping Arcade, 1 Beach Road (daily 8.30am–8pm; ☎1-800/3341335 or 3341336); the other just off Orchard Road at #02-03 Scotts Shopping Centre, 6 Scotts Road (daily 9.30am-9.30pm; ☎1-800/7383778 or 7383779). Don't underestimate the utility of the phone lines – the staff on hand are experts at guiding confused tourists from A to B. It's also worth dropping in at one of these offices to pick up their free hand-outs, the biggest of which – the *Singapore Official Guide* – is very informative and features some handy maps. Other **maps** worth having include that published by the *Asian Business Press* and endorsed by the STPB, and the *Singapore Street Directory* – a snip at $6 and invaluable if you're going to rent a car.

LEAVING SINGAPORE

For Changi airport flight enquiries, and the addresses and telephone numbers of airlines, travel agencies and the Malay, Indonesian and Thai consulates in Singapore, see "Listings", p.557.

Airport
There are good deals on plane tickets from Singapore to Australia, Bali, Bangkok and Hong Kong. However, if you're planning to head for either Malaysia or Indonesia by air, it might be worth going to JB (p.296), across the causeway, or Batam, the nearest Indonesian island (see "Boats" below), and buying a flight from there.

Bus #390 (daily 6am–midnight; $1.20) to **Changi Airport** runs frequently down Orchard Rd and Bras Basah Rd; flagging down a taxi on the street will cost around $12–15. For **Seletar Airport**, from where *Tradewinds* and *Pelangi Air* fly to Tioman island in Malaysia ($125 one-way), take bus #103 from New Bridge Rd, Hill St or Serangoon Rd, or a taxi ($10). Note that there's a **departure tax** of $5 levied on all flights to Malaysia and Brunei, and $12 on flights to all other destinations.

Buses and taxis
To Malaysia: easiest way across the causeway is to get the #170 JB-bound bus from the Ban San Terminal (every 15min, 6am–12.30am; around $1) or the plusher air-con *Singapore–JB Express* (every 10min, 6.30am–11.30pm; $1.80), both of which take around an hour (including border formalities); both stop at JB bus terminal. From the taxi stand next to the terminal, a car to JB (seats 4) costs $30. The *Singapore–KL Express* leaves from the Ban San Terminal daily at 9am, 1pm and 10pm (8hr; $17.30); the afternoon departure doesn't leave much time to find a room on arrival. Buy your KL ticket from the booth in the terminal, a couple of days in advance at holiday times.

For other destinations, go to the Lavender Street Terminal, where buses to Butterworth ($29), Penang ($30), Kota Bharu ($30) and Ipoh ($27) tend to leave in the late afternnon; those to Melaka ($11), Mersing ($11) and Kuantan ($17) depart in the early morning and afternoon. For KL ($17) there are both morning and night departures from this terminal. Book as far in advance as possible – operators at the terminal include

---

A number of publications offer **what's on** listings and recommendations. Two – the *Singapore Visitor* and *This Week Singapore* – are available free at hotels all over the island, but are really nothing more than advertising vehicles for Singapore's swankier shops. The "Life!" section of the *Singapore Straits Times* has a decent listings section, though best of all is *8 Days* magazine, which is published weekly and costs $1.20. Finally, scanning **notice boards** in guest houses can unearth helpful pointers to life in the city.

City transport

All parts of the island are accessible by bus or MRT – the underground rail network – and fares are reasonable; consequently, there's little to be gained by renting a car. However you travel, it's best to avoid rush hour (roughly 8–9.30am and 5–7pm) if at all possible; otherwise, the roads are jam-free. A *Transitlink Guide* ($1), available from bus interchanges, MRT stations and major bookshops, outlines every bus and MRT route on the island in exhaustive detail – there's even a five-step explanation of how to board a train. You needn't be afraid that jumping in a **taxi** will break the bank either; Singapore has thousands of easily available and affordable cabs.

Getting around **on foot** is the best way to do justice to the central areas. Bear in mind, though, that you are in the tropics: apply sun screen and stay out of the midday

Pan Malaysia Express (☎2947034), *Hasry Ekoba Express* (☎2926243), *Malacca–Singapore Express* (☎2925915) and *Masmara Travel* (☎2947034). It's slightly cheaper to travel to JB and then catch an onward bus from the bus terminal there – though it still pays to make an early start from Singapore.

To Thailand: buses leave early morning from Beach Road Golden Mile Complex. You can buy a ticket all the way to Bangkok (though it might well be cheaper just to buy one as far as Hat Yai and pay for the rest of the journey in Thai currency once there). Fares to Hat Yai (16hr) start at around $30, while Bangkok will set you back around $70. Try *Phya Travel* Service (☎2945415) or *Sunny Holidays* (☎2927927), and don't forget to allow two working days for securing a Thai visa (needed for stays of over 15 days).

Trains

You can make free seat reservations up to one month in advance of departure at the information kiosk (daily 8.30am–2.30pm & 3.05–7pm; ☎2225165) in the Railway Station. The 11pm *Express Senandung Malam* gets into KL early the next morning; or the 7.30am *Express Rakyat* arrives there at 2.25pm – this continues to Butterworth, arriving at 10.10pm.

Boats

To Malaysia: from Changi Point (bus #2 to Changi Village) bumboats run to Kampung Pengerang, on the southeastern tip of Johor (for access to the beach resort of Desaru; p.300) boats leave when they're full (daily 7am–4pm; $5 one-way) and the trip takes 45 minutes. Between March and October there's a catamaran service from the World Trade Centre to Tioman island, daily at 7.50am ($143 return), a four-and-a-half-hour trip; information and tickets from *Resort Cruises* (☎2784677).

To Indonesia: Boats to Batam in the Riau archipelago depart throughout the day from the World Trade Centre (7.45am–7pm; $16 one-way), docking at Sekupang, from where you take a taxi to Hangnadim airport for internal Indonesian flights. There are also four boats a day ($51 one-way; info and tickets from *Dino Shipping*, ☎2700311, or *Auto Batam*, ☎2714866) from the WTC to Tanjung Pinang on Pulau Bintan, from where cargo boats leave three times a week for Pekanbaru in Sumatra; there are also boat services from Kijang Port, south of Tanjung Pinang, to Jakarta.

sun. Orchard Road shopping centres are air-conditioned, and here you'll be whizzing up and down escalators as often as not. Elsewhere, strolling through the remaining pockets of old Singapore entails running the gauntlet of uneven five-foot ways (the covered pavements that front Singapore's old shophouses) and yawning storm drains.

The MRT (Mass Rapid Transit) System

Singapore's **MRT** system was officially opened on March 12, 1988, and now boasts 67 kilometres of track passing through 42 stations. In terms of cleanliness, efficiency and value for money the system is second to none – compared to London's tubes or New York's subways, a trip on the MRT is a joy. Nor is there any possibility of delays owing to a passenger falling on the line – the automatic doors dividing the platform from the track open only when a train arrives and is stationary. The system has two main lines: the *north-south* line, which runs down the island from Yishun to Marina Bay, and the *east-west* line, connecting Boon Lay to Pasir Ris; see the MRT map below for more details. Trains run every four to five minutes on average, daily from 6am until midnight. For **information**, pick up the free *MRT Handy Guide* from any station, or call the **MRT Information Centre** (toll-free, ☎3368900).

A **no-smoking** rule applies on all trains, and eating and drinking is also outlawed. Another policy is alluded to by signs in the ticket concourse that appear to ban hedgehogs from underground travel. In fact, the sign means "no durians" – not an

---

---

unreasonable request if you've ever spent any time in a confined space with one of these pungent fruits. Bear in mind also that there are no toilets on MRT platforms.

Tickets cost between 60c and $1.50 for a one-way journey. If you don't have any coins for the ticket machines (inside the main hall at each station), change machines will provide you with some; larger notes can be broken at the information counter. Feed your change into the machine and you'll get a plastic card; to get to the platforms, feed this card into the turnstile, walk through, and pick it up at the other side.

Most Singaporeans avoid the rigmarole of buying a ticket every day by purchasing a **Transitlink Farecard** – a stored-value card that's valid on all MRT and bus journeys in Singapore, and is sold at MRT stations and bus interchanges for $12 or $22 (including a $2 deposit). The cost of each journey you make is automatically deducted from the card when you pass it through the turnstile; any credit on the card when you leave Singapore will be reimbursed if you take it to a *Farecard* outlet.

An **MRT Tourist Souvenir Ticket** is also available for $6, sold at leading hotels and central MRT stations. Note, though, that it only has a stored value of $5.50.

Buses

Singapore's **bus** network is slightly cheaper to use than the MRT system, and far more comprehensive – you'll probably spend more time on buses than on trains and there are several routes which are particularly useful for sightseeing (see box on next page). Two bus companies operate on the roads of Singapore: the **Singapore Bus Service** (*SBS*) and **Trans-Island Bus Services** (*TIBS*). Most of their buses charge distance-related fares ranging from 50–90c (60c–$1.20 for air-con buses). Others are flat-fare buses, whose price is displayed on the destination plates on the front of the bus. Unless you are on a route rarely frequented by tourists, the driver is likely to know of anywhere you could possibly be heading for; signs posted at bus stops alert you when you are near an attraction. For bus route **infomation**, call ☎2872727 (*SBS*) or ☎4823888 (*TIBS*).

Tell the driver where you want to go, and he'll tell you how much money to drop into the metal chute. Change isn't given, so make sure you have coins. If you are in town for a while, buy a **Transitlink Farecard** (see above), which you insert into the validator as you get on; press the button to select your fare, which is then deducted from the stored value. Another ticket option is the **Bus Explorer Ticket** ($5 one-day, $12 three-day), though frankly, you'd have to do an awful lot of travelling to make these tickets pay. The same is true of using the **Singapore Trolley**, a mock-antique bus that loops between the Botanic Gardens and Chinatown throughout the day. One day's unlimited travel is $9, while a "point to point" fare is $3 – hardly any cheaper than a taxi.

Taxis

More than ten thousand **taxis** prowl the streets of Singapore, trying to rake in their next fare. With that much competition, you'll hardly ever have any trouble hailing a cab, day or night. Taxis are all metered, the fare starting at $2.20 for the first 1500m:

THE MRT SYSTEM

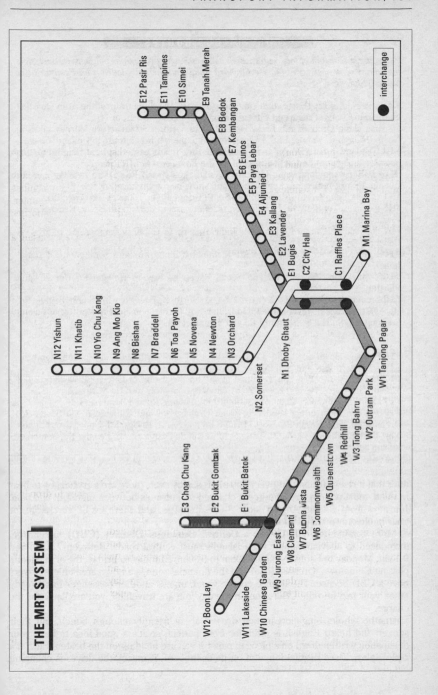

Below are a selection of bus routes which connect Singapore's major points of interest; note that many of the services from the Orchard Road area actually leave from Penang Rd or Somerset Rd.

#2 passes along Eu Tong Sen St (in Chinatown) and Victoria St (past the Arab Quarter) en route to Changi Prison and Changi Village.

#7 runs along Orchard Rd, Bras Basah Rd and Victoria St; its return journey takes in North Bridge Rd, Stamford Rd, Penang Rd and Somerset Rd en route to Holland Village.

#14 takes in Orchard Rd and Bras Basah Rd, then heads east – alight at Haig Rd for *Big Splash*; stay on until Bedok South Ave 1 for the *East Coast Sailing Centre*.

#16/16E passes down from Orchard Rd and Bras Basah Rd, before heading east for Changi Airport; returns via Stamford Rd and skirts below Orchard Rd.

#51 travels along North Bridge Rd and South Bridge Rd en route to Haw Par Villa.

#65 terminates at the World Trade Centre, after passing down jalan Besar, Bencoolen St, Penang Rd and Somerset Rd.

#97 runs along Stamford Rd to Little India, then on to Upper Serangoon Rd; returns via Collyer Quay and the GPO, and Bencoolen St.

#103 runs between New Bridge Rd Terminal (Chinatown) and Serangoon Rd (Little India).

#105 runs along Stevens Rd and Scotts Rd on its way to Holland Rd (for Holland Village).

#124 connects Scotts Rd, Orchard Rd and North Bridge Rd with South Bridge Rd, Upper Cross St and New Bridge Rd in Chinatown; in the opposite direction, travels along Eu Tong Sen St, Hill St, Stamford Rd and Somerset Rd.

#139 heads past Tai Gin Rd, via Dhoby Ghaut, Selegie Rd, Serangoon Rd and Balestier Rd.

#167 passes down Scotts Rd, Orchard Rd and Bras Basah Rd, Collyer Quay (and the GPO), Shenton Way and Neil Rd (for Chinatown).

#170 starts at the Ban San Terminal at the northern end of Queen St, passing Bukit Timah Nature Reserve and Kranji War Cemetery on its way to JB in Malaysia.

#171 runs to Singapore Zoo from Stamford Rd, Penang Rd and Somerset Rd.

#190 is the most direct service between Orchard Rd and Chinatown, via Scotts Rd, Orchard Rd, Bras Basah Rd, North Bridge Rd and South Bridge Rd, Upper Cross St and New Bridge Rd; returns via Eu Tong Sen St, Hill St, Stamford Rd, Penang Rd, Somerset Rd and Scotts Rd.

after that it rises 10 cents for every 250 metres. However, there are **surcharges** to bear in mind, most notably the 50 percent charged on journeys between midnight and 6am. Journeys from Changi Airport incur a $3 surcharge, and there's a $2 surcharge for taxis booked over the phone.

More confusingly still, there's a **Central Business District (CBD) surcharge**, introduced to alleviate jams on the island's most central roads. Between 7.30am and 9.15am Monday to Saturday, and 4.30pm to 6.30pm Monday to Friday, the area encompassing Chinatown, Orchard Road and the financial zone is a no-go area unless drivers have a CBD license. The license costs $3 and, unless another passenger has already taken your taxi into the CBD zone on the day you are travelling, you are liable for the charge.

On the whole, Singaporean taxi drivers are a friendly enough bunch, but their spoken and heard English is often far from perfect, so it's a good idea to have your destination written down on a piece of paper if you are heading off the beaten track. If a taxi displays a red destination sign on its dashboard, it means the driver is changing shift and will accept customers only if they are going in his direction. Finally, tourists confined to **wheelchairs** should note that the *TIBS Radiophone* company has ten wheelchair-accessible cabs for rent; call ☎4811211.

Vehicle and bike rental

The Singapore Government has introduced huge disincentives to driving in order to combat traffic congestion. If you want to drive into the CBD (see above) you'll have to buy a license, available at post offices and license booths at entrances to the district. Parking, too, is expensive and requires that you purchase coupons from a license booth, post office or shop. In fact, the only real reason for **renting a car** in Singapore is to travel up into Malaysia – and even then it's far cheaper to rent from a company based over the causeway (in JB), as Singaporean firms levy a $25 Malaysia surcharge. If you still insist on driving in Singapore itself, you'll find rental companies listed on p.558. For details of prices, documentation and road rules, see *Basics*, p.37.

Bike rental is possible along the East Coast Parkway, where the cycle track that skirts the seashore is always full of Singaporeans zooming around in full cycling gear. Expect to pay around $3 an hour for a mountain bike, and bring some form of ID to leave at the office. The dirt tracks that criss-cross Pulau Ubin, off Changi Point at the eastern tip of the island, are ideal for biking – a day's rental at one of the cluster of shops near the jetty costs $4–8, though the price doubles if Singapore's schoolkids are on holiday. Finally, there's a range of bikes – including tandems – available for rent next to the ferry terminal on Sentosa Island ($2–5 an hour), providing by far the best way to see the island.

Trishaws

Trishaws – three-wheeled bicycles with a carriage on the back – were once a practical transport option in Singapore, though they're a bit of an anachronism these days. You'll still see a few trishaws providing a genuine service around Little India and Chinatown, but most drivers now congregate along Waterloo Street between Bras Basah and Stamford roads waiting for the arrival of the next bus load of tourists, who'll happily pay around $40 for a 45-minute sightseeing ride.

Organized tours

If you're pushed for time, there are several reputable operators in Singapore offering **sightseeing tours**. The main ones are listed on p.559, or ask at your hotel or the tourist office. Tours vary according to the operator, but four-hour city tours typically take in Orchard Road, Chinatown and Little India, and cost around $25. For a "Round the Island Tour" (8hr) – visiting places of interest on all of Singapore's coasts, and including a trip to a modern housing project – expect to pay $60. **Specialist tours** are also available – tracing the footsteps of Raffles, horse racing, around Singapore by night, World War II sights – and prices run from $32–70 per person. For more details, contact the STPB. For **nature and bird-watching tours**, contact R. Subharaj at 8 Jalan Buloh Perindu (☎4429774), whose tours range from three-hour birding trips ($20) to personalized nature tours spanning Singapore and Malaysia, for around $600 a day for a group of one to five persons.

Members of the *Registered Tourist Guides Association* (☎7383265) charge $50 an hour for a minimum of four hours for a **personalized tour**. Finally, **free sightseeing tours** of Singapore, arranged by the STPB, are available to transit passengers at Changi Airport – call in at the tour desk in the transit lounge if you're interested.

SINGAPORE RIVER, HARBOUR AND ISLAND CRUISES

Fleets of **cruise boats** ply Singapore's southern waters every day and night. The best of these, the *Singapore River Experience*, casts off from North Boat Quay (hourly departures 9am–7pm) for a $6 cruise on a traditional bumboat, passing the old *godowns* upriver where traders once stored their merchandise. Several cruise companies also operate out of Clifford Pier and the World Trade Centre, offering a whole host of seaborne possibilities, from luxury catamaran trips around Singapore's southern isles to dinner on a *tongkang* (Chinese sailing boat). On average, a straightforward cruise will set you back around $20, and a dinner special about $60. The companies below are all recommended by the STPB. It is quite possible to **charter** your own boat – a few companies are listed below – but you can bank on forking out up to $1000 a day for the privilege. If you don't relish the idea of an organized cruise, you can haggle with a bumboat man on Clifford Pier: if you're lucky, he might take a group of you around the southern isles for $25 an hour.

Cruise companies
Eastwind Organisation (☎5333432).
J&N Cruises (☎2707100).
Resort Cruises (☎2784677).
Singapore River Experience (☎2279678).
Waterfront Cruises (☎5324497).
Watertours (☎5339811).

Charter companies
Amaril Cruises (☎2216969).
Beachcomber (☎3361690).
Fantasy Cruises (☎2840424).
Orient Charters (☎2789397).

Accommodation

Room rates take a noticeable leap when you cross the causeway from Malaysia into Singapore, but good deals still abound as long as your expectations aren't too lofty or – the budget end of the scale – if you don't mind sharing with other visitors. Singapore's status as one of the main gateways to Southeast Asia means that occupancy rates at all levels of accommodation are permanently high. Even so, you shouldn't encounter too many difficulties in finding a room, and advance booking isn't really necessary unless your visit coincides with Chinese New Year (usually Jan/Feb) or Hari Raya (usually March/April).

The **Singapore Hotel Association** has booking counters at Changi Airport (daily 8am–11.30pm; ☎5426955 or ☎5459789) which will find you a room in the city free of charge. Don't expect them to start scrabbling around at the bottom end of the market for you – the association only represents Singapore's official hotels, all of which, incidentally, are listed in a free STPB booklet. Touts at the airport also hand out flyers advertising rooms, but things can get a bit embarrassing if, once you're there, you don't like the place they represent.

The cheapest beds are in the communal **dormitories** of many of Singapore's guest houses, where you'll pay $10 or less a night. Most of the **guest houses** are situated along Bencoolen Street and Beach Road, with a few in nearby Little India and some also south of the river, in Chinatown. Singapore's classic guest house address is *Peony Mansions* on Bencoolen Street, where a cluster of establishments are shoehorned into several floors of a decrepit apartment building. Walk around here with a backpack on, and sooner or later you'll be approached by someone offering you "cheap room! cheap room". Guest houses aren't nearly as cosy as their name suggests: at the $20–30 mark, rooms are tiny, bare, and divided by paper-thin partitions; toilets are shared, and showers are cold. However, paying another $10–20 secures a bigger, air-con room, and you often get TV, laundry and cooking facilities, lockers and breakfast included. Always check that the room is clean and secure, and that the shower and air-con work before you hand over any money. It's always worth asking for a discount, too, though you stand the best chance of a reduction if you are staying a few days. Finally, since guest houses aren't subject to the same safety checks as official hotels, without sounding alarmist, it's a good idea to check for a fire escape.

The appeal of Singapore's **Chinese-owned hotels**, similar in price to guest houses, is their air of faded grandeur – some haven't changed in forty years. Sadly, faded grandeur is something the government frowns upon, with the result that there are not too many left. In more modern, mid-range hotels, a room for two with air-con, private bathroom and TV will set you back around $60–80 a night. From there, prices rise steadily and at the top end of the scale, Singapore boasts some extraordinarily opulent hotels, ranging from the colonial splendour of *Raffles* to the awesome spectacle of the *Westin Stamford* – currently the world's tallest hotel. The biggest selection of upmarket hotels is found around Orchard Road.

Camping is not really a practical option in Singapore: few sites exist, and those which do are not in convenient locations. The *Universal Adventure* shop (☎7206639) on Pulau Ubin, off the east coast (see p.531), rents out two- and four-person tents ($20/30), which can be pitched on open land on the island. The only other alternative is to go to Sentosa island (see p.536), where a four-person tent costs $16 (including the island entrance fee), pitched on a site with toilets and barbecue pits (details on ☎2707888).

Bencoolen Street and around.

Bencoolen Street has long been the mainstay of Singapore's backpacker industry – so long, in fact, that its buildings are beginning to show their age, while others have already fallen under the demolition ball. Still, the location is handy for all parts of central Singapore, and the proliferation of guest houses makes it a great place for meeting people. All the places listed here are keyed on the map on p.488.

Bayview Inn, 30 Bencoolen St (☎3372882, fax 3382880). Bencoolen Street's poshest hotel, with very comfortable rooms, a compact rooftop swimming pool and a friendly, modern café. ⑤.

Bencoolen House Traveller's Centre, 7th Floor, 27-F Bencoolen St (☎3381206). Bearable at the price, though the dorms are grottier than most. Guests have use of the kitchen. ②.

Goh's Homestay, 4th Floor, 169-D Bencoolen St (☎3396561, fax 3398606). The smartest guest house in town (at the top of its price category), with fresh and inviting (if slightly cell-like) rooms, pricier dorm beds than usual, laundry service, a bright, comfortable lounge/canteen area and a pet python. Recommended. ②.

Hawaii Hostel, 2nd Floor, 171-B Bencoolen St (☎3384187). Small, tidy, air-con rooms with breakfast included. ②.

Latin House Home Stay, #03-46 Peony Mansion, 46-53 Bencoolen St (☎3306308). The budget priced dorms are adequate, but the rooms a little run-down. ②.

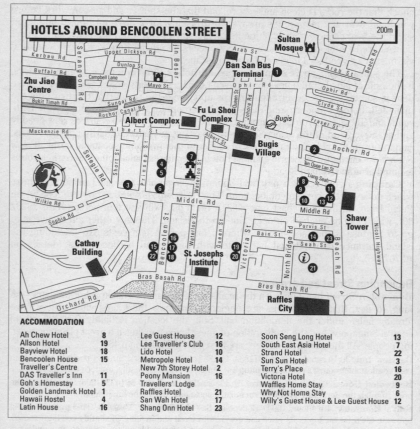

HOTELS AROUND BENCOOLEN STREET

ACCOMMODATION

Ah Chew Hotel	8	Lee Guest House	12	Soon Seng Long Hotel		13
Allson Hotel	19	Lee Traveller's Club	16	South East Asia Hotel		7
Bayview Hotel	18	Lido Hotel	10	Strand Hotel		22
Bencoolen House	15	Metropole Hotel	14	Sun Sun Hotel		3
Traveller's Centre		New 7th Storey Hotel	2	Terry's Place		16
DAS Traveller's Inn	11	Peony Mansion	16	Victoria Hotel		20
Goh's Homestay	5	Travellers' Lodge		Waffles Home Stay		9
Golden Landmark Hotel	1	Raffles Hotel	21	Why Not Home Stay		6
Hawaii Hostel	4	San Wah Hotel	17	Willy's Guest House & Lee Guest House		12
Latin House	16	Shang Onn Hotel	23			

Lee Traveller's Club, #07-52 Peony Mansion, 46–52 Bencoolen St (☎3383149). The brightest place in Peony Mansion: clean, simple dorms (a dollar more for air-con) and rooms, a pleasant breakfast area and laundry facilities. There's another *Lee*'s on Beach Rd (see below). ②.

Peony Mansion Travellers' Lodge, #04-46 Peony Mansion, 46–52 Bencoolen St (☎3385638). Moneychanging facilities, a notice board and a travel consultant's desk make this a handy place to stay. The dorms are cramped, while rooms start out cheap (between $25-40) and graduate to more expensive doubles with TV, fridge, air-con and toilet. ②.

San Wah Hotel, 36 Bencoolen St (☎3362428). Shabby but rather charming old Chinese hotel which benefits from being set back slightly from the road. A $5 surcharge buys air-con facilities. ③.

South East Asia Hotel, 190 Waterloo St (☎3382394). Spotless doubles with air-con, TV and phone for those yearning for a few creature comforts. Downstairs is a vegetarian restaurant serving Western breakfasts, and right next door is Singapore's liveliest Buddhist temple. ③.

Strand Hotel, 25 Bencoolen St (☎3381866, fax 3363149). Excellent-value hotel with clean, welcoming rooms (right at the top of this category) and a variety of services. ④.

Sun Sun Hotel, 260A&B–262A&B Middle Rd (☎3384911). Housed in a splendid 1928 building, the *Sun Sun* isn't overpriced for its high standard – decent rooms and plenty of communal bathrooms. Air-con rooms are also available, while downstairs is the wonderful *L.E. Cafe & Confectionery*. ③.

Terry's Place, #06-50 Peony Mansion, 46–52 Bencoolen St (☎3385638). Though in the heart of Singapore's "dormitory land", a relatively smart place with only (varying) singles and doubles. ②.
Why Not Homestay, 127 Bencoolen St (☎3388838). Long a popular traveller's haunt, *Why Not* is showing signs of age, and its rooms are all right but unspectacular; a café downstairs serves beers and snacks through the night. ②.

Beach Road to Victoria Street

A few blocks east of Bencoolen Street, **Beach Road** boasts a mixture of charismatic old Chinese hotels and smart new guest houses. What's more, you can brag about having stayed down the road from *Raffles Hotel* (or even in it) when you get home. These hotels are keyed on the map opposite.

Ah Chew Hotel, 496 North Bridge Rd (☎3375285). Simple but charismatic rooms with "Wild West" swing doors and crammed with period furniture, and run by a gang of T-shirted old men lounging on antique opium couches. Despite its address, it's just around the corner from North Bridge Rd, on Liang Seah St. ②.
Allson Hotel, 101 Victoria St (☎3362526, fax 3340631). Reasonable 412-room hotel with shopping arcade, health and business centres and three restaurants. Some effort has been made to cater for the disabled: there are low counters and phones and adapted toilets, but you'll need to book well ahead for the hotel's one specifically designed bedroom. ⑥.
DAS Traveller's Inn, #04-02 Chye Sing Building, 87 Beach Rd (☎3387460). Smartly tiled and cheery place, though there have been complaints about its cleanliness recently; still, it's got the cheapest double room in town, and pleasant dorms. ①.
Golden Landmark Hotel, 390 Victoria St (☎2972828, fax 2982038). More of a mustardy yellow really, though very pleasant once you get past the dated shopping centre downstairs, and handy for Bugis MRT Station and Arab St. ⑥.
Lee Guest House, #06-02 Fu Yuen Building, 75 Beach Rd (3395490). Like its Bencoolen Street counterpart, clean and friendly, with bright dormitories and spick and span communal toilets. ②.
Lido Hotel, 54/56 Middle Rd (☎3371872). A grand old Chinese hotel whose airy double rooms with fan are great value. There's a tempting cake shop next door. ②.
Metropole Hotel, 41 Seah St (☎3363611). Friendly, great-value establishment (at the bottom of its price category), just across the road from *Raffles Hotel*, whose roomy lodgings are served by the intriguing *Imperial Herbal Restaurant* (see "Eating", p.544). ⑤.
New 7th Storey Hotel, 229 Rochor Rd (☎3370251, fax 3343550). Despite its rather old-fashioned exterior, this is a clean hotel with perfectly respectable rooms, all with TV. Rooms with en-suite bathrooms are available, though the communal ones are fine. ④.
Raffles Hotel, 1 Beach Rd (☎3371886, fax 3397650). The flagship of Singapore's tourism industry, *Raffles* takes shameless advantage of its reputation: $21 buys you a Singapore Sling and a glass to take home, while the souvenir shop stocks *Raffles* golf balls, socks and cuddly tigers. Still, it's a beautiful place, dotted with frangipani trees and palms, and the suites (there are no rooms) are as tasteful as you would expect at these prices. See p.503 for more details. ⑦.

DORM BEDS

The places listed below offer the cheapest beds in Singapore. For full details, see the relevant reviews.

Bencoolen House: p.487.	*Peony Mansions Travellers' Lodge*: p.488.
Canton Guest House: p.492.	*Sandy's Place*: p.491.
Cavenagh Gardens: p.490.	*Waffles Homestay*: p.490.
Chinatown Guest House: p.492.	*Why Not Homestay*: this page.
DAS Traveller's Inn: this page.	*Willy's Guest House*: p.490.
Goh's Homestay: p.487.	*YMCA International House*: p.491.
Latin House: p.487.	*YWCA Hostel*: p.490.
Lee Traveller's Club: p.488.	

Shang Onn Hotel, 37 Beach Rd (☎3384153). Set in a quaint old building sporting attractive green shutters, the *Shang Onn* has reasonable rooms and a useful notice board. ②.

Soon Seng Long Hotel, 26 Middle Rd (☎3376318). One of a glut of old Chinese hotels in this area, the *Soon Seng Long* offers respectable, spacious rooms. ②.

Victoria Hotel, 87 Victoria St (☎3382381, fax 3344853). Unremarkable budget rooms, some with bathrooms, all with air-con and TV. Only $10 extra for a third bed in a double room. A great new food centre has recently opened next door. ③.

Waffles Home Stay, 3rd Floor, 490 North Bridge Rd (☎3341608). Not too terrible for the price (which includes breakfast and a free flow of hot drinks), though recommended only for the tightest budgets. Entrance is around the back, off Liang Seah St. ①.

Willy's Guest House, #04-02 Fu Yuen Building, 75 Beach Rd (☎3370916). Box-like but tidy rooms at competitive prices that include breakfast and hot drinks. The cheapest dorm doubles as a TV room, so it's worth paying $2 more for the air-con dorm; and there are few bathrooms, so expect queues. Willy has more rooms at quieter 101 Beach Rd, but enquire here first. Recommended. ①.

The Colonial District

A handful of expensive hotels squat at the edges of the Padang, just north of the Singapore River. Three of them – the *Marina Mandarin*, *Oriental* and *Pan Pacific* hotels – stand on the land reclamation project which robbed Beach Road of its beach. See the map on p.494 for the layout of this area.

Marina Mandarin Hotel, 6 Raffles Blvd (☎3383388, fax 3394977). Top-flight hotel, architecturally interesting and affording great harbour views; the atrium is particularly impressive. ⑦.

Oriental Singapore, 5 Raffles Ave (☎3380066, fax 3399537). Like the *Marina Mandarin*, housed in what's claimed to be South East Asia's largest shopping and hotel complex, Marina Square. It's also one of Singapore's priciest hotels. ⑦.

Pan Pacific Hotel, Marina Square, 7 Raffles Blvd (☎3368111, fax 3391861). The place to go if you prefer your pool to have an underwater sound system; several facilities available for the disabled. ⑦.

Westin Plaza, 2 Stamford Rd (☎3388585, fax 3382862). Top-of-the-range hotel whose amenities are shared with the *Westin Stamford*. Located right above City Hall MRT. ⑦.

Westin Stamford, 2 Stamford Rd (☎3388585, fax 3371554). Upper floor rooms aren't for those with vertigo, though the views are as splendid as you'd expect from the tallest hotel in the world. There are 1253 classy rooms here, 16 restaurants and an MRT Station downstairs. ⑦.

YWCA Hostel, Fort Canning Centre, 6/8 Fort Canning Rd (☎3363150). Clean rooms (some with views of Fort Canning Park) for women, couples and families. Paying $10 more gets air-con and private shower, and there's a dorm at $15. Breakfast and cheap set meals are available too. ③.

Orchard Road and around

Sumptuous hotels abound in and around **Orchard Road** and unless you opt for a dorm bed at the YMCA, you have to be prepared to spend a bare minimum of $80 double. You can multiply that figure by four or five, though, if you decide to treat yourself. See the map on p.522 for the location of the hotels in this district.

Cavenagh Garden, #03-376, Block 73 Cavenagh Rd (☎7374600). A homestay in the literal sense of the word: two dorm beds ($10) are available on a balcony off the family living room, and various rooms are dotted around the house. A steep $20 extra is demanded for a private shower. At the end of Cuppage Rd, cross the Expressway bridge and walk to the left for 300m. ③.

Cockpit Hotel, 6/7 Oxley Rise (☎7379111, fax 7373105). Renamed in 1960 due to the frequent patronage of airline crews, the Georgian facade of this 176-room hotel harks back to its beginnings in 1941 as the *London Hotel* on Beach Road. Inside its pastel-shaded rooms are serviced by several decent restaurants and bars. ⑥.

Dynasty Hotel, 320 Orchard Rd (☎7349900, fax 7335251). A superior hotel and a Singapore landmark, housed in a 33-storey pagoda-style building next door to *C.K. Tangs Department Store*. ⑥.

Goodwood Park Hotel, 22 Scotts Rd (☎7377411, fax 7328558). Don't be surprised if this opulent hotel reminds you of *Raffles* – both were designed by the same architect. The building has a long history (see p.523), but it's still a study in elegance, its arching facades fronting exquisitely appointed rooms. ⑦.

Holiday Inn Park View, 11 Cavenagh Rd (☎7338333, fax 7344593). Guests of this smart hotel with all the trimmings are next-door neighbours of Singapore's President for the duration of their stay – the Istana is just across the road. ⑥.

Hyatt Regency, 10–12 Scotts Rd (☎7331188, fax 7321696). Classy hotel, with access facilities for the disabled, and a good option if you like your nightlife: within the hotel are the trendy *Brannigan's* bar and *Chinoserie* discotheque. ⑦.

Lloyd's Inn, 2 Lloyd Rd (☎7377309). Motel-style building boasting attractive rooms and a fine location, just five minutes from Orchard Road. ④.

Mandarin Hotel, 333 Orchard Rd (☎7374411, fax 7322361). Every luxury you could hope for; even if you don't stay, take a trip up to the top floors for the magnificent view of central Singapore. ⑥.

Metropolitan YMCA, 60 Stevens Rd (☎7377755, fax 2355528). Not as central as the Y on Orchard Road, but perfectly adequate, and suitable for travellers in wheelchairs. ④.

Mitre Hotel, 145 Killiney Rd (☎7373811). Reasonable old Chinese hotel, set amid overgrown grounds, and with an endearingly shabby air about it; downstairs is a great lobby bar. ②.

Sandy's Place, 3C Sarkies Rd (☎7341431). Rooms are a touch overpriced in this friendly, laid-back place, set across a field from Newton MRT, but the dorms are tidy, and include a fruit breakfast. It's best to phone ahead. ②.

Sheraton Towers, 39 Scotts Rd (☎7376888, fax 7371072). Faultless hotel voted one of the top ten in the world by *Business Traveller* magazine; the lobby area is dazzling and there's even a waterfall out the back. ⑦.

Sloane Court Hotel, 17 Balmoral Rd (☎2353311, fax 7339041). As close to a Tudor house as you get in Singapore, the *Sloane Court* is tucked away in a prime residential area, near Newton MRT. ⑤.

Hotel Supreme, 15 Kramat Rd (☎7378333, fax 7337404). A budget hotel, well placed at the eastern end of Orchard Road, which levies a hefty $200 deposit at check in. ⑤.

Hotel VIP, Balmoral Crescent (☎2354277, fax 2352824). Within walking distance of Orchard Road, a quiet, affordable hotel with swimming pool. ⑤.

YMCA International House, 1 Orchard Rd (☎3373444, fax 3373140). Plush rooms, excellent sports facilities (including rooftop pool) and free room service from the *MacDonald's* downstairs. Dorm beds are the most expensive in town, though, and there's a first-day charge of $5 for non-members. Bus #390 from the airport stops right outside. ④.

Little India

Buses along Jalan Besar connect **Little India** with the rest of central Singapore. Little India's hotels and guest houses tend not to attract many Western visitors, though there are several noteworthy places, all marked on the map on p.516.

Boon Wah Boarding House, 43A Jalan Besar (☎2991466, fax 2942176). This decent Chinese hotel offers clean, if slightly cramped, rooms with TV, air-con and shower. The entrance is around the corner, on Upper Dickson Rd. ④.

Broadway Hotel, 195 Serangoon Rd (☎2924661, fax 2916414). Ugly-looking hotel, boasting pleasant enough rooms with air-con, bathroom and TV in the heart of Little India. ④.

Friendly Resthouse, 357A Serangoon Rd (☎2944058). Definitely friendly, though also a bit pokey. Still, the basic partitioned rooms here are extremely inexpensive. ①.

Little India Guest House, 3 Veerasamy Rd (☎2942866, fax 2984866). A fairly new guest house with excellent, fresh-looking rooms and spotless toilets. ③.

Mount Emily Hotel, 10A Upper Wilkie Rd, Mount Emily Park (☎3389151, fax 3396008). Rooms here are pricey and just starting to show their age, but the hotel's location beside a lovely park above the city makes it a quiet, relaxing option. ⑤.

Palace Hotel, 407A Jalan Besar (☎2983108). Friendly hotel with spacious rooms, some of which have little balconies. Recommended. ①.

Chinatown and around

Despite being such a big tourist draw, **Chinatown** isn't very well furnished with budget accommodation. On the other hand, the area does contain a mass of upmarket hotels which benefit from their proximity to the business district. The following places are all keyed on the map on p.508.

Canton Guest House, 42 Smith St (☎3231275). A bed in one of the series of cheery, carpeted, air-con dorms in this pre-war shophouse bases you in the bustling heart of Chinatown. ②.

Chinatown Guest House, 5th Floor, 325-D New Bridge Rd (☎2200671). Friendly, no-frills place and a popular choice, offering varied rooms, free breakfast and luggage storage. However, the cheapest rooms are tiny, the dorms pretty cramped and there are just three common bathrooms. ②.

Chinese YMCA, 70 Palmer Rd (☎2224666). There are fewer amenities here than in Singapore's other Ys, but the rates are less expensive and it's handy for the train station. ③.

Dragon Cityview Hotel, 18 Mosque St (☎2239228). Sizeable, comfortable rooms in the middle of Chinatown, all with air-con, TV, fridge and bathroom, and set in attractive shophouses. ⑤ .

The Duxton, 83 Duxton Rd (☎2277678, fax 2271232). Elegant rooms in the renovated shophouses that make up this hotel don't come cheap; it's in the Tanjong Pagar redevelopment zone. ⑥.

Inn of the Sixth Happiness, 9–37 Erskine Rd (☎2233266, fax 2237951). Delightful "boutique hotel" renovated from 14 shophouses and named after a 1958 film starring Ingrid Bergman. Rosewood furniture, porcelain lamps and silk robes evoke an air of Chinese nostalgia, and the VIP suites boast antique opium beds. Its a shame the rooms aren't more spacious. Recommended. ⑤.

Kwong Thye Hin Lodging House, 89 Amoy St (☎2225566). Rambling old Chinese hotel, unchanged in decades, where *mandis* (tubs from which you scoop water over yourself) are still preferred over showers. The rooms – tiny, open-topped boxes on two floors above the massive reception area – are basic and noisy but great value for two people. ①.

Majestic Hotel, 31–37 Bukit Pasoh Rd (☎2223377). Unspectacular but scrupulously clean, old-style hotel. All rooms have air-con, while those at the front boast little balconies; for a private bathroom add on $10, and for a TV, another $5. ③.

Geylang and Katong

Geylang and Katong, along Singapore's southeastern coast, have traditionally both been Malay-dominated areas. If you can't face the noise and the bustle of central Singapore, this region might appeal – certainly its cool sea breezes and Malay markets are an advantage. MRT and buses connect you quickly with downtown Singapore.

Amber Hotel, 42 Amber Rd (☎3445255). Comfortable rooms with TV, air-con and bathroom just a short walk from the east coast. ④.

Ghim Peng Hotel, 424 Geylang Rd (☎7447777). The most modern-looking place along Geylang Road, the *Ghim Peng* is tiled throughout and has rooms with air-con, TV and private bathroom. One or two people pay the same price. ④.

Hotel Malacca, 97 & 99 Still Rd (☎3457411). Good value if you want a few luxuries: every (smart) room has air-con, phone, TV and bathroom. ④.

Sing Hoe Hotel, 759 Mountbatten Rd (☎4400602). Beautifully kept colonial house, with attractive reliefs on its external walls, but overpriced for its unmemorable, air-con rooms. Look out for the amazing "gingerbread house" next door. ③.

Soon Teck Hotel, 57A Koon Seng Rd (☎3440240). A peaceful Chinese hotel with just five air-con rooms. Communal facilities are clean, and downstairs is a sleepy coffee shop. Recommended. ②.

Sentosa Island

Two luxury hotels on the island of Sentosa allow you to bypass the bustle of downtown Singapore. If you aren't too keen to negotiate any of the more long-winded means of transport to the island (for details and an island report, see p.536), it's possible to get a taxi direct from the airport to Sentosa (though note that from 7am–10pm a $6 surcharge is levied).

The Beaufort (☎2750331). A swanky hotel, elegantly appointed and fitted out in varnished wood, which is bounded by two 18-hole golf courses and a beach. A $40 price increase applies on Fri and Sat. ⑥.

Rasa Sentosa Beach Resort (☎3381201). Opened in 1993, the *Rasa Sentosa* is the first hotel in Singapore to have its own beach front, and its situation on Sentosa Island makes it a good option if you've got kids to amuse. As at the *Beaufort*, a $40 price rise applies on Fri and Sat; sea view rooms are an extra $40, too. ⑥.

Downtown Singapore

Ever since Sir Stamford Raffles first landed on its northern bank, in 1819, the area around the Singapore River, which strikes westwards into the heart of the island from the island's south coast, has formed the hub of Singapore. Etching a radius of three kilometres around the mouth of the river with a pair of compasses would produce a circle containing all of Singapore's central districts – which makes **Downtown Singapore** an extremely convenient place to tour. Although buses do run between these districts (see bus routes information on p.484), you might find that you prefer to explore the whole central region on foot. You'll need at least two days to do full justice to the main areas: the **Financial** and **Colonial** districts, **Chinatown, Little India** and the **Arab Quarter;** while Singapore's commercial mecca, **Orchard Road**, can occupy a single morning, or several days, depending on how much you enjoy shopping.

The Financial District and Singapore River

As the colony's trade grew in the last century, the **SINGAPORE RIVER** became its main artery, clogged with bumboats – traditional cargo boats – which featured eyes painted onto the front of them, enabling them to see where they were going. The boat pilots ferried coffee, sugar and rice to the riverbank warehouses (*godowns*), where coolies loaded and unloaded sacks. Indeed, in the 1880s the river itself was so busy it was practically possible to walk from one side to the other without getting your feet wet. A recent campaign to clean up the waters of the river also managed to have the bumboats relocated to the west coast, though a handful still remain and offer trips downriver and around Marina Bay (see "Organized Tours" on p.485). These days, with the bumboats gone, the river is quieter, cleaner and, inevitably, less charismatic, though parts of both banks are undergoing something of a commercial revitalization as new restaurants and bars move into formerly abandoned buildings.

Until an early exercise in land reclamation in the mid-1820s rendered the zone fit for building, the patch of land south of the river, where Raffles Place now stands, was a swampland. However, within just a few years Commercial Square (later renamed Raffles Place) was the colony's busiest business address, boasting the banks, ship's chandlers and warehouses of a burgeoning trading port. The square now forms the nucleus of the **FINANCIAL DISTRICT** – the commercial heart of the state, home to many of its numerous banks (around 140) and financial institutions. Cutting through the district runs **Battery Road**, whose name recalls the days when Fort Fullerton (named after Robert Fullerton, first Governor of the Straits Settlements) and its attendant battery of guns used to stand on the site of the present GPO.

Raffles Place

Raffles Place was Singapore's central shopping area until Orchard Road superceded it in the late 1960s. Two department stores, *Robinsons* and *John Little*, dominated the area until then, but subsequent development turned Raffles Place into Singapore's financial epicentre, ringed by buildings so tall that pedestrians crossing the square feel like ants in a canyon. The most striking way to experience the giddy heights of the Financial District is by surfacing from Raffles Place MRT – follow the signs for Cecil Street out of the station – and looking up to the sky, to be confronted by a tapestry of gleaming towers, blue sky and racing clouds. To your left is the soaring metallic triangle of the **OUB** (*Overseas Union Bank*) Centre, and, right of that, the heftier **UOB** (*United Overseas Bank*) Building; in front of you are the rich brown walls of the **Standard Chartered Bank**, and to your right rise sturdy **Shell Tower** and the (as yet incomplete) **Savu Tower**. A smallish statue, entitled "Progress and Advancement", stands at

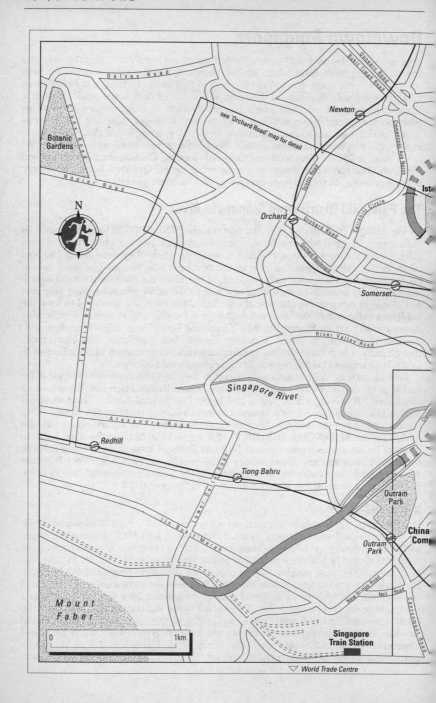

Botanic
Gardens

Dalvey Road

Cluny Road

Napier Road

Tanglin Road

see 'Orchard Road' map for detail

Newton

Bukit Timah Road

Dunearn Road

Clemenceau Ave North

Scotts Road

Ista

Orchard   Orchard Road

Cairnhill Circle

Orchard Boulevard

Somerset

N

River Valley Road

Singapore River

Alexandra Road

Redhill

Tiong Bahru

Lower Delta Road

Jln Bukit Merah

Mount
Faber

0   1km

Outram
Park

China
Com

Outram
Park

New Bridge Road

Neil Road

Cantonment Road

Singapore
Train Station

▽ *World Trade Centre*

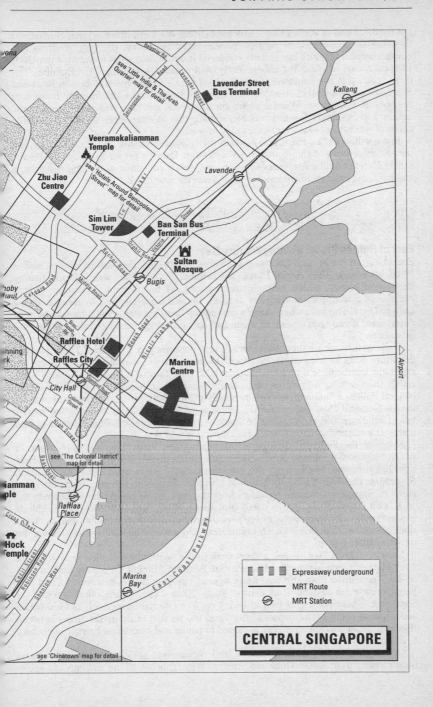

CENTRAL SINGAPORE

Lavender Street Bus Terminal

Kallang

Veeramakaliamman Temple

see 'Little India & The Arab Quarter map for detail

Lavender

Zhu Jiao Centre

see 'Hotels Around Bencoolen Street' map for detail

Sim Lim Tower

Ban San Bus Terminal

Sultan Mosque

Bugis

Raffles Hotel

Raffles City

City Hall

Marina Centre

Coleman Street

see 'The Colonial District' map for detail

amman ple

Raffles Place

Cross Street

Hock Temple

Marina Bay

East Coast Parkway

Airport

see 'Chinatown' map for detail

	Expressway underground
	MRT Route
	MRT Station

the northern end of Raffles Place. Erected in 1988, it's a miniature version of what was then the skyline of central Singapore. Somewhat inevitably, the very progress and advancement it honours has already rendered it out of date – not featured is the **UOB Plaza**, a rocket of a building only recently built beside the existing UOB Building. The three roads that run southwest from Raffles Place – Cecil Street, Robinson Road and Shenton Way – are all choc-a-bloc with more high-rise banks and financial houses; to the west is Chinatown. Wander along these streets and here and there you'll come across a refreshingly low-tech cobbler's stall; the passing high heels and sensible shoes of the business set ensure they stay in work.

Just north of Raffles Place, and beneath the "elephant's trunk" curve of the river, the pedestrianized row of shophouses known as **Boat Quay** is presently enjoying a renaissance. Derelict until a few years ago, it now sports a collection of thriving restaurants and bars, and is an excellent spot for an *al fresco* meal or drink.

> See the map on p508 for the river and Financial District.

East of Raffles Place: skirting Marina Bay

Branching off the second floor of the Clifford Centre, on the eastern side of Raffles Place, is **Change Alley Aerial Plaza**. The original Change Alley was a cheap, bustling street-level bazaar, which redevelopment wiped off the face of Singapore; all that remains is a sanitized, modern-day version, housed on a covered footbridge across Collyer Quay. The tailors here have a persuasive line in patter – you'll have to be very determined if you aren't going to waste half an hour being convinced that you need a new suit.

Walking through Change Alley Aerial Plaza deposits you at **Clifford Pier**, long the departure point for trips on the Singapore River and to the southern islands. There are still a few bumboats tied up here, though these days they're rented out as cruise boats rather than earning a living as cargo boats. Visible from the pier to the north is the elegant Fullerton Building, fronted by sturdy pillars. Built in 1928 as the headquarters for the **General Post Office (GPO)**, this was once – remarkably – one of Singapore's tallest buildings. Old photographs of Singapore depict Japanese soldiers marching past it after the surrender of the Allied forces during World War II.

Opposite the Fullerton Building is **Merlion Park** (daily 6am–midnight; free), in which Singapore's national symbol, the statue of the mythical **Merlion**, presides. Half-lion, half-fish, and wholly ugly, the creature reflects Singapore's name (in Sanskrit, *Singapura,* meaning "Lion City") and its historical links with the sea. There are good views of Singapore's colonial buildings from the park, while beside the entrance to the park is the tiny (and presently closed) **Singapore River Museum**. Best of its exhibits is a collection of photographs of barbers, hawkers, coolies and other "people of the river", but other than this it's fairly uninspiring and it would be no great loss should the museum fail to reopen.

Back at Clifford Pier it's just a short walk to the south along Raffles Quay to Telok Ayer Market, recently renamed **Lau Pa Sat Festival Market**. Originally built in 1894 on land reclaimed from the sea, its octagonal cast-iron frame has been turned into Singapore's most tasteful food centre (daily 10am–3am), which offers a range of Southeast Asian cuisines, as well as laying on free entertainment such as local bands and Chinese opera performances. After 7pm, the portion of Boon Tat Street between Robinson Road and Shenton Way is closed to traffic and traditional hawker stalls take to the street.

One of Singapore's most ambitious land reclamation projects, **Marina South**, is plainly visible from Raffles Quay and Shenton Way. This has all the makings of a splendid folly – the entertainment and recreation park which was built on it during the 1980s has already gone bankrupt and the large patch of land now seems to serve no other purpose than to carry the East Coast Parkway on its journey west – making it surely the world's biggest bridge support. Marina South is a ghost town, its only real asset an imaginative children's playground within a pleasant park; access is by MRT from Raffles Place, or bus #400 from Tanjong Pagar MRT. Below Marina South, Singapore's **port** begins its well-hidden sprawl westwards. Singapore is the world's busiest container port (the second busiest port overall after Rotterdam), and hundreds of ships are docked south of the island at any one time waiting for permission from the Port of Singapore Authority to enter one of the state's seven terminals.

The Colonial District

North of the river, take a walk down to where Coleman Street abuts Saint Andrew's Road, and look across the Padang towards the city: laid out before you is a panorama that defines Singapore's past and present. In the foreground is the Singapore Cricket Club – the epitome of Colonial Man's stubborn refusal to adapt to his surroundings. Behind that, the Singapore River snakes westwards and inland, passing the last few surviving *godowns* from Singapore's original trade boom. And, towering high above all this, are the spires of the modern business district.

The Padang ("field" in Malay, and still a grassy, open space today) is the very nexus of the **COLONIAL DISTRICT**, flanked by dignified reminders of British rule. To the south are Empress Place Building and Parliament House, to the north, the grand old *Raffles Hotel*, beyond which a string of nineteenth- and twentieth-century churches leads to Singapore's most famous entertainment centre, Bugis Street. Heading west, you pass City Hall and the Supreme Court before climbing the slopes of Fort Canning Hill, ten minutes' walk from the Padang, and one of the few hills in Singapore not yet lost to land reclamation. The late twentieth century seems strangely absent amid all these echoes of the past, though the district's most notable modern building doesn't do things by half – the *Westin Stamford*, on Stamford Road, is the world's tallest hotel.

Along the north riverbank

From Raffles Place MRT it's just a couple of minutes' walk, past the GPO, to the elegant suspension struts of **Cavenagh Bridge** – as fine a place as any to start a tour of Singapore's colonial centre. Named after Major General Orfeur Cavenagh, Governor of the Straits Settlements from 1859–1867, the bridge was constructed in 1869 by Indian convict labourers using imported Glasgow steel. Times change, but not necessarily on the bridge where a police sign still maintains: "The use of this bridge is prohibited to any vehicle of which the laden weight exceeds 3cwt and to all cattle and horses."

Stopping off the bridge, you're confronted by **Empress Place Building**, a robust Neoclassical structure named for Queen Victoria and completed in 1865. It served for ten years as a courthouse before the Registry of Births and Deaths and the Immigration Department moved in, though following a recent multi-million dollar face-lift, the building's upper chambers now house regularly changing cultural **exhibitions** (daily 9am–7.30pm; $6) with a strongly Chinese bias. Downstairs is a display room of local artwork, an antiques gallery, a restaurant and two souvenir shops – none of which need detain you very much. You're more likely to puzzle over the significance of the pyramid-shaped time capsule in the grounds in front of the building, which was sealed in 1990 as part of Singapore's silver jubilee celebrations and is due to be opened in 2015. It contains "significant items" from Singapore's first 25 independent years: the clever money says that when opened it'll yield a Lee Kuan Yew speech or two.

Next door to Empress Place Building, two fine, off-white examples of colonial architecture, the **Victoria Concert Hall** and adjoining **Victoria Theatre**, between them

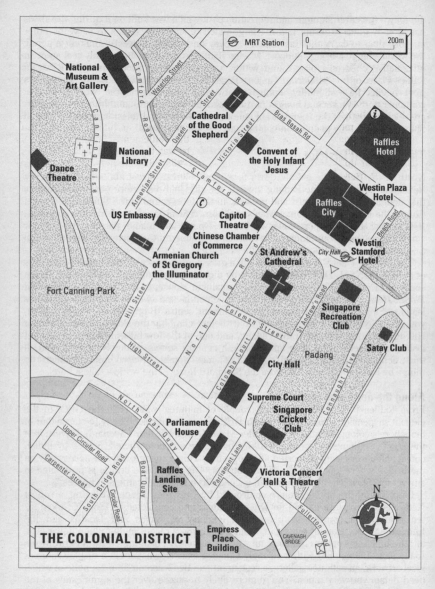

⊖ MRT Station

0   200m

National Museum & Art Gallery

Stamford Road

Waterloo Street

Queen Street

Cathedral of the Good Shepherd

Bras Basah Rd

ℹ

Raffles Hotel

Victoria Street

Convent of the Holy Infant Jesus

National Library

Canning Rise

Armenian Street

Stamford Rd

Westin Plaza Hotel

Dance Theatre

Beach Road

Raffles City

ⓒ

US Embassy

Capitol Theatre

Chinese Chamber of Commerce

City Hall

Westin Stamford Hotel

Armenian Church of St Gregory the Illuminator

St Andrew's Cathedral

Fort Canning Park

Hill Street

North Bridge Road

Coleman Street

Singapore Recreation Club

St Andrew's Road

High Street

Colombo Court

Padang

Satay Club

North Boat Quay

City Hall

Connaught Drive

Supreme Court

Singapore Cricket Club

Upper Circular Road

Parliament House

Carpenter Street

South Bridge Road

Boat Quay

Circular Road

Raffles Landing Site

Parliament Lane

Victoria Concert Hall & Theatre

Fullerton Road

N

THE COLONIAL DISTRICT

Empress Place Building

CAVENAGH BRIDGE

present some of Singapore's most prestigious cultural events. The theatre was originally completed in 1862 as Singapore's town hall while the Concert Hall was added in 1905 as a tribute to the monarch's reign. During the Japanese occupation, the clock tower here was altered to Tokyo time, while the statue of Raffles that once stood in front of the tower narrowly escaped being melted down. As luck would have it, the newly installed Japanese curator of the National Museum – where the statue was sent – valued it sufficiently to hide it and report it destroyed.

Further inland, along North Bank Quay, a copy of the statue marks the generally accepted **landing site** where, in January 1819, the great man took his first steps on Singaporean soil. Sir Stamford now stares contemplatively across the river towards the business district. The *Singapore River Experience* boats (see p.486) depart from a tiny jetty a few steps along from Raffles' statue.

Walking north from the statue up Parliament Lane, the dignified white Victorian building on the left ringed by fencing is **Parliament House**, first built as a private dwelling for a rich merchant by Singapore's pre-eminent colonial architect, the Irishman George Drumgould Coleman, who was named the settlement's Superintendent of Public Works in 1833. It is sometimes possible to watch Singapore's parliament in session from up in the Strangers' Gallery – call ☎3368811 for details. The bronze elephant in front of Parliament House was a gift to Singapore from King Rama V of Thailand (whose father was the King upon whom "The King and I" was based) after his trip to the island in 1871 – the first foreign visit ever made by a Thai monarch.

The Padang

It's the **Padang** that's the very essence of colonial Singapore. Earmarked by Raffles as a recreation ground shortly after his arrival, such is its symbolic significance that its borders have never been encroached upon by speculators and it remains much as it was in 1907, when G.M. Reith wrote in his *Handbook to Singapore*: "Cricket, tennis, hockey, football and bowls are played on the plain... beyond the carriage drive on the other side, is a strip of green along the sea-wall, with a foot-path, which affords a cool and pleasant walk in the early morning and afternoon." Once the last over of the day had been bowled, the Padang would have assumed a more social role: the image of Singapore's European community hastening to the corner once known as Scandal Point to catch up on the latest gossip is pure Somerset Maugham. Today the Padang is kept as pristine as ever by a bevy of gardeners mounted on state-of-the-art lawnmowers.

The brown-tiled roof, whitewashed walls and dark green blinds of the **Singapore Cricket Club**, at the southwestern end, manage to evoke an air of nostalgic charm. Founded in the 1850s, the club was the hub of colonial British society and still operates a "members only" rule, though there's nothing to stop you watching the action from outside on the Padang. The Singapore Rugby Sevens are played here, as well as a plethora of other big sporting events and parades; a timetable of forthcoming events is

---

SINGAPORE'S PARLIAMENTARY SYSTEM

The Republic of Singapore is governed by a unicameral parliament, led by a Prime Minister and cabinet. Its head of state is the President; former deputy Prime Minister, Ong Teng Cheong, is the present incumbent, and the first to have been installed by popular vote rather than parliamentary decision. Parliament has a life of five years, though normally a general election is held after four years, with voting compulsory for over 21-year olds. Presently there are 81 elected Members of Parliament as well as six nominated members (NMPs) invited by the President. During sittings – for which there are no scheduled dates – members can speak in Mandarin, Malay, Tamil or English, with simultaneous translation piped through to the chamber. Around twenty political parties currently operate in Singapore, but one, the People's Action Party (PAP), has held the mandate continuously since internal self-government was acheived in 1959. The only other parties of any consequence are the Workers' Party and the Singapore Democratic Party.

SIR STAMFORD RAFFLES

*"Let it still be the boast of Britain
to write her name in characters of light;
let her not be remembered as the tempest
whose course was desolation,
but as the gale of spring reviving
the slumbering seeds of mind and
calling them to life
from the winter of ignorance and oppression.
If the time shall come
when her empire shall have passed away,
these monuments will endure when her triumphs
shall have become an empty name."*

This verse, written by **Sir Stamford Raffles** himself, speaks volumes about the man whom history remembers as the founder of modern Singapore. Despite living and working in a period of imperial arrogance and self-motivated land-grabbing, Raffles maintained an unfailing concern for the welfare of the people under his governorship, and a conviction that British colonial expansion was for the general good – that his country was, as Jan Morris says in her introduction to Maurice Collis' *Raffles*, "the chief agent of human progress. . . the example of fair Government."

Fittingly for a man who was to spend his life roaming the globe, Thomas Stamford Raffles was born at sea on July 6, 1781 on the *Ann*, whose master was his father Captain Benjamin Raffles. By his fourteenth birthday, the young Raffles was working as a clerk for the East India Company in London, his schooling curtailed due to his father's debts. Even at this early age, Raffles' ambition and self-motivation was evident as, faced with a lifetime as a clerk, he resolved to educate himself, staying up through the night to study and developing a hunger for knowledge which would later spur him to learn Malay, amass a vast treasure trove of natural history artefacts and write his two-volume *History of Java*.

Abdullah bin Kadir, Raffles' clerk while in Southeast Asia, describes him in his autobiography, the *Hikayat Abdullah*: "He was broad of brow, a sign of his care and thoroughness; round-headed with a projecting forehead, showing his intelligence. He had light brown hair, indicative of bravery; large ears, the mark of a ready listener. . . He was solicitous of the feelings of others, and open-handed with the poor. He spoke in smiles. He took the most active interest in historical research. Whatever he found to do he adopted no half-measures, but saw it through to the finish."

Raffles' diligence and hard work showed through in 1805, when he was chosen to join a team going out to Penang, then being developed as a British entrepôt; overnight, his

available at the club's reception. Eurasians who were formerly ineligible for membership of the Cricket Club founded their own establishment instead in 1883, the **Singapore Recreation Club**, which lies across on the north side of the Padang.

Just to the west of the Cricket Club, Singapore's Neoclassical **Supreme Court** (formerly the site of the exclusive *Hotel de L'Europe,* whose drawing rooms allegedly provided Somerset Maugham with inspiration) was built between 1937 and 1939, and sports a domed roof of green lead and a splendid, wood-panelled entrance hall – which is as far as you'll get unless you're appearing in front of the judges, as it's not open to the public. Next door is older **City Hall**, whose uniform rows of grandiose Corinthian columns lend it the asutere air of a mausoleum and reflect its role in recent Singaporean history. Wartime photographs show Lord Louis Mountbatten (then Supreme Allied Commander in Southeast Asia) on the steps announcing Japan's surrender to the British in 1945. Fourteen years later, Lee Kuan Yew chose the same annual salary leapt from £70 to £1500. Once in Southeast Asia, Raffles' rise was meteoric: by 1807 he was named Chief secretary to the Governor in Penang and soon Lord Minto, the Governor-General of the East India Company in India, was alerted to his Oriental expertise. Meeting Minto on a trip to Calcutta in 1810, Raffles was appointed Secretary to the Governor-General in Malaya, a promotion quickly followed by the Governorship of Java in 1811. Raffles' rule of Java was wise, libertarian and compassionate, his economic, judicial and social reforms transforming an island bowed by Dutch rule.

Post-Waterloo European rebuilding saw the East Indies returned to the Dutch in 1816 – to the chagrin of Raffles, who foresaw problems for British trade should the Dutch regain their hold on the area. From Java, Raffles transferred to the Governorship of Bencoolen, on the southern coast of Sumatra, but not before he had returned home for a break, stopping at St Helena en route to meet Napoleon ("a monster"). While in England he met his second wife, Sophia Hull (his first, Olivia, had died in 1814), and was knighted.

Raffles and Sophia sailed to Bencoolen in early 1818, Sophia reporting that her husband spent the four-month journey deep in study. Once in Sumatra, Raffles found the time to study the region's flora and fauna as tirelessly as ever, discovering the *Rafflesia Arnoldii* – "perhaps the largest and most magnificent flower in the world" — on a jungle field trip. By now, Raffles felt strongly that England should establish a base in the Straits of Melaka; meeting Hastings (Minto's successor) in late 1818, he was given leave to pursue this possibility and in 1819 duly sailed to the southern tip of the Malay Peninsula, where his securing of Singapore early that year was a daring masterstroke of diplomacy.

For a man whose name is inextricably linked with Singapore, Raffles spent a remarkably short time on the island. His first stay was for one week, and the second, three weeks, during which time he helped delineate the new settlement (see p.476). Subsequent sojourns in Bencoolen ended tragically with the loss of four of his five children to tropical illnesses, while his own health also began to deteriorate. Raffles visited Singapore one last time in late 1822; his final public duty there was to lay the foundation stone of the Singapore Institution (later the *Raffles Institution*; see p.502), an establishment created to educate local Malays, albeit upper class ones.

By August 1824, he was back in England. Awaiting news of a possible pension award from the East India Company, Raffles spent his free time founding the London Zoo and setting up a farm in Hendon. But the new life he had planned for Sophia and himself never materialized. Days after hearing that a Calcutta bank holding £16,000 of his capital had folded, his pension application was refused; worse still, the Company was demanding £22,000 for overpayment. Three months later, the brain tumour that had caused him headaches for several years took his life on July 4, 1826. Buried at Hendon, he was honoured by no memorial tablet over his grave – the vicar had investments in slave plantations in the West Indies and was unimpressed by Raffles' friendship with William Wilberforce. Only in 1832 was his life rewarded with a statue in Westminster Abbey.

spot from which to address his electorate at a victory rally celebrating self-government for Singapore. Nowadays, rather less dramatic photographs are taken on the steps as newly-weds line up to have their big day captured in front of one of Singapore's most imposing buildings.

The final building on the west side of the Padang, **St Andrew's Cathedral**, on Coleman Street, gleams even brighter than the rest. The third church to be built on this site, the cathedral was constructed in high-vaulted, neo-Gothic style, using Indian convict labour, and was consecrated by Bishop Cotton of Calcutta on January 25, 1862. Its exterior walls were plastered using Madras *Chunam* – an unlikely composite of eggs, lime, sugar and shredded coconut husks which shines brightly when smoothed – while the small cross behind the pulpit was crafted from two fourteenth-century nails salvaged from the ruins of England's Coventry Cathedral, which was razed to the ground during World War II. Closed-circuit TVs have been installed, which allow the

THE SEPOY MUTINY

Plaques on the west wall of St Andrew's Cathedral commemorate the victims of one of Singapore's bloodiest episodes, the **Sepoy Mutiny** of 1915. The mutiny began when a German warship, *Emden*, was sunk by an Australian ship off the Cocos Islands: its survivors were brought to Singapore and imprisoned at Tanglin Barracks, at the western end of Orchard Road. With almost all of Singapore's troop contingent away in Europe fighting the Kaiser, soldiers of the Fifth Light Infantry, called *sepoys* – whose members were all Muslim Punjabis – were sent to guard the prisoners. Unfortunately, these men's allegiance to the British had recently been strained by the news that Muslim Turkey had come out against the Allies in Europe. A rumour that they were soon to be sent to Turkey to fight fellow Muslims upset them still further, and the German prisoners were able to incite the sepoys to mutiny. In the ensuing rampage through the city on February 15, 1915, the sepoys killed forty other soldiers and civilians before they were finally rounded up by some remaining European sailors and a band of men led by the Sultan of Johor. All were court-martialled and the resultant executions saw 36 sepoys shot before huge crowds. As for the Germans, they took the opportunity to effect an escape. Nine of them finally got back to Germany via Jakarta and one, Julius Lauterbach, received an Iron Cross in recognition of his daring and rather convoluted flight home through China and North America.

whole congregation to view proceedings up at the altar – a reflection of the Chinese fascination with all things hi-tech, since the cathedral's size barely demands such luxuries.

On the waterfront

Land reclamation has widened the Padang to the east, and left space for a new strip of parkland known as **Esplanade Park**, which merges, further east, into Queen Elizabeth Walk. A quick stroll north along the water's edge here brings you to a **sculpture** called "Joyous Rivers", which resembles an enormous heap of metal shavings. It's a perfect example of Singapore's tendency towards self-congratulation: according to its accompanying plaque, it represents "dancing waves", which "surge forward at a 60 degree angle in one direction, symbolizing Singaporeans striving with one common purpose towards a better future."

Singapore's **cenotaph** lies a few seconds' walk beyond the sculpture and, in turn, beyond that you'll find the **Satay Club** – an outdoor food centre and a marvellous place to while away a balmy Singapore evening, munching satay and quaffing *Tiger* beer. The open ground to the east is regularly the venue for funfairs while, once a year, thousands of spectators gather here to view Singapore's annual **Dragon Boat racing festival** (see "Festivals", p.63, for more details).

Raffles City and Raffles Hotel

Immediately north of St Andrew's Cathedral, across Stamford Road, is **Raffles City**, a huge development comprising two enormous hotels – one of which is the 73-storey *Westin Stamford* – a multi-level shopping centre and floor upon floor of offices. Completed in 1985, the complex was designed by Chinese-American architect I.M. Pei – the man behind the glass pyramid which fronts the Louvre in Paris – and required the highly contentious demolition of the venerable *Raffles Institution*, originally established by Raffles himself and built in 1835 by George Drumgould Coleman. The **Westin Stamford** holds an annual vertical marathon, in which hardy athletes attempt to run up to the top floor in as short a time as possible: the current record stands at under seven minutes. Elevators transport lesser mortals to admire the view from the *Compass Rose* bar and restaurant on the top floor.

If the *Westin Stamford* is the tallest hotel in the world, across the way is perhaps the most famous. The lofty halls, restaurants, bars, and peaceful gardens of the legendary **Raffles Hotel**, almost a byword for colonialism, prompted Somerset Maugham to remark that it "stood for all the fables of the exotic East". Oddly, though, this most inherently British of hotels started life as a modest seafront bungalow belonging to an Arab trader, Mohamed Alsagoff. After a spell as a tiffin house run by an Englishman called Captain Dare, the property was bought in 1886 by the enterprising Armenian Sarkie brothers, who eventually controlled a triumvirate of quintessentially colonial lodgings: the *Raffles*, the (still extant) *Eastern and Oriental* in Penang, and the *Strand* in Rangoon.

Raffles Hotel opened for business on December 1, 1887 and quickly began to attract some impressive guests. It is thought that Joseph Conrad stayed in the late 1880s; certainly Rudyard Kipling visited soon after this, though at that stage the hotel couldn't, it seems, boast such sumptuous rooms as in later years. "Let the traveller take note," wrote Kipling; "feed at *Raffles* and stay at the *Hotel de l'Europe*". The hotel enjoyed its heyday during the first three decades of the new century, decades which saw it firmly establish its reputation for luxury and elegance – it was the first building in Singapore to boast electric lights and fans. In 1902, a little piece of Singaporean history was (reportedly) made at the hotel when the last tiger to be killed on the island was shot inside the building. Thirteen years later another *Raffles* legend, the *Singapore Sling* cocktail, was created by bartender Ngiam Tong Boon. The rich, famous and influential have always patronized the hotel, but despite a guest list heavy with politicians and film stars, it is its literary connections of which the hotel is proudest. Herman Hesse, Somerset Maugham, Noel Coward and Günter Grass all stayed at *Raffles* at some time – Maugham is said to have written many of his Asian tales under a frangipani tree in the garden.

During World War II, British expatriates who had gathered in *Raffles* as the Japanese swept through the island in 1942 quickly found themselves to be POWs, and the hotel became a Japanese officers' quarters. After the Japanese surrender in 1945, *Raffles* became a transit camp for liberated Allied prisoners. Post-war deterioration earned it the affectionate but melancholy soubriquet, "grand old lady of the East" and the hotel was little more than a shabby tourist diversion when the government finally declared it a national monument in 1987. A $160-million facelift followed and the hotel reopened on September 16, 1991.

The new-look *Raffles* gets a very mixed reception. Though it retains much of its colonial grace, the shopping arcade that now curves around the back of the hotel lacks finesse, selling *Raffles*-related souvenirs, exclusive garments, leatherware and perfume. Still, if you're in Singapore, there's no missing *Raffles* and, assuming you can't afford to stay here, there are plenty of other ways to soak up the atmosphere. A free **museum** (daily 10am–7pm) located upstairs, at the back of the hotel complex, is crammed with memorabilia, much of which was recovered in a nationwide heritage search which encouraged Singaporeans to turn in souvenirs that had found their way up sleeves and into handbags over the years. In the Jubilee Hall, you can catch the 25-minute film, *Raffles Revisited* (daily at 11am, 1pm & 2pm; $5). Otherwise, a *Singapore Sling* in one of the hotel's several bars (see p.551) will cost you around $15.

Waterloo Street to Bugis Village

Bras Basah Road cuts west from Raffles, crossing Victoria and Queen streets. At the junction with the latter and at Waterloo Street, another block west, elderly trishaw drivers in regulation-yellow T-shirts tout for custom from each newly arriving bus load of tourists.

Sunday sees **Waterloo Street** at its best, springing to life as worshippers throng to its temples, churches and synagogue. The modern **Kuan Yim Temple**, named after the Buddhist Goddess of Mercy, may not boast the cluttered altars, dusty old rafters and elaborate roofs of Chinatown's temples, but is still extremely popular; all along the pavement outside, old ladies in floppy, wide-brimmed hats sell fresh flowers from baskets. **Religious artefact shops** on the ground floor of the apartment building opposite are well placed to catch worshippers on their way out – one shop specializes in small shrines for the house: the deluxe model boasts flashing lights and an extractor fan to expel unwanted incense smoke. **Fortune tellers** and street traders operate along this stretch of the road, too, and look out for the cage containing turtles and a sleepy old snake: make a donation, touch one of the creatures inside, and good luck is believed to come your way.

One block east of Waterloo Street's shops and temples, at the junction of Rochor Road and Victoria Street sits **Bugis Village** – a rather tame manifestation of infamous Bugis Street. Until it was demolished to make way for an MRT station, Bugis Street embodied old Singapore: after dark it was a chaotic place, crawling with rowdy sailors, preening transvestites and prostitutes – and as such was anathema to a Singapore government keen to clean up its country's reputation. However, Singaporean public opinion demanded a replacement, though when Bugis Village opened in 1991 it was revealed as a shadow of its former self. Beer gardens, seafood restaurants, pubs and street stalls line its cross of roads, and while local reaction has been largely negative, nonetheless a steady stream of tourists passes through nightly. The transvestites are noticeable only by their absence, the sole reminder of their heritage a weak cabaret show in the *Boom Boom Room* nightclub.

Along Hill Street to the National Museum

From Stamford Road, **Hill Street** heads south to the river, flanking the eastern side of Fort Canning Park. **The Singapore Chinese Chamber of Commerce** (at 47 Hill Street), a brash, Chinese-style building from 1964 featuring a striking pagoda roof, lies thirty metres down on the left. Along its facade are two large panels, each depicting nine intricately crafted porcelain dragons flying from the sea up to the sky. By way of contrast, the tiny **Armenian Church of Saint Gregory the Illuminator**, across the road and next to the American Embassy, was designed by George Drumgould Coleman in 1835 (which makes it one of the oldest buildings in Singapore). The place is in need of a paint job now, and the cracks in its spire are wide enough to allow vegetation to grow; inside is a single, circular chamber, fronted by a marble altar and a painting of the Last Supper. Among the white gravestones and statues in the church's grounds is the tombstone of Agnes Joaquim, after whom Singapore's national flower, the delicate, purple Vanda Miss Joaquim Orchid is named.

Around the corner at 45 Armenian Street, the **Substation**, a disused power station, has been converted into a multi-media arts centre. Even if you don't have the time to check out its classes, discussions and performances (see p.556 for more details), the coffee shop is a pleasant place to hang out for a while. A market takes place in the courtyard every Sunday afternoon, with stalls selling anything from local crafts to secondhand Russian watches.

The National Museum and Art Gallery

An eye-catching dome of stained glass tops the entrance to Singapore's **National Museum** (Tues–Sun 9am–5.30pm; $1), on Stamford Road. The museum's forerunner, the Raffles Museum and Library, was opened in 1887 and soon acquired a reputation for the excellence of its natural history collection. In 1969, the place was renamed the National Museum in recognition of Singapore's independence, and subsequently altered its bias towards local history and culture: it's a fairly low-key collection, although you might derive an hour or two's enjoyment from the three permanent exhibitions. Downstairs, the *Straits Chinese Gallery* boasts an attractive collection of opium pipes and couches, silks, exquisite pearl-inlaid furniture, enamel tiffin carriers and other everyday articles from the nineteenth century, while the *History of Singapore Gallery* features twenty dioramas depicting formative events in the State's history – from the arrival of Raffles in 1819 up to the first session of Parliament in 1965. Much duller is the *Jade Gallery*, upstairs, in which the collection of jade amassed by the Haw Par brothers can be viewed. Other exhibitions come and go; check with the local press for details. Free **guided tours** start downstairs at the ticket counter (Tues–Fri at 11am), and the free slide show, *Singapore: The Nation*, is worth catching, too (Tues–Sun at 10.15am, 12.15pm, 2.45pm & 3.45pm); a range of other local interest slide shows are also screened (Tues–Sun at 9.45am & 1.30pm).

Adjoining the National Museum is the **National Art Gallery** (Tues–Sun 9am–5.30pm; free), which suffers from not having any permanent displays; again, check the local press for details of current exhibitions by local artists.

Fort Canning Park and around

When Raffles first caught sight of Singapore, **Fort Canning Park** was known locally as Bukit Larangan (Forbidden Hill). Malay annals tell of the five ancient kings of Singapura, said to have ruled the island from this point six hundred years ago – and archeological digs have unearthed artefacts which prove it was inhabited as early as the fourteenth century. The last of the kings, Sultan Iskandar Shah, reputedly lies here, and a *keramat*, or auspicious place, on the eastern slope of the hill marks the supposed site of his grave. It was out of respect (and fear) for his spirit that the Malays decreed the hill forbidden, and these days the *keramat* still attracts a trickle of Singaporean Muslims, as well as childless couples who offer prayers here for fertility.

However, when the British arrived, Singapore's first British Resident William Farquhar displayed typical colonial tact by promptly having the hill cleared and building a bungalow on the summit; named Government House, it stood on what was then called Government Hill. The bungalow was subsequently replaced in 1859 by a fort named after Viscount George Canning, Governor-General of India, but of this only a gateway, guardhouse and adjoining wall remain today. An early European **cemetery** survives, however, upon whose stones are engraved intriguing epitaphs for nineteenth-century sailors, traders and residents, among them pioneering colonial architect, George Coleman.

History apart, Fort Canning Park is spacious and breezy, and offers respite from, as well as fine views of, Singapore's crowded streets. There's a "back entrance" to the park which involves climbing the exhausting flight of steps that runs between the Hill Street Building and Food Centre, on Hill Street. Once you reach the top, there's a brilliant view along High Street towards the Merlion. Plans are afoot to develop the hill into a major tourist attraction. Already, it houses two theatres and soon two walks will lead visitors through the fourteenth- and nineteenth-century history of the park. The **underground bunkers**, from which the Allied war effort in Singapore was masterminded, are also due to be opened to the public.

Meanwhile, **River Valley Road**, skirting the southwestern slope of Fort Canning Park, boasts a handful of B-list attractions. Next to the **River Valley Swimming Complex** (daily 8am–9.30pm; $1; bus #122 from Bencoolen Street or #104 from Scotts Road) is the **Fort Canning Aquarium** (daily 9am–10.30pm; adults $4, children $2), whose appeal palls considerably in comparison with Sentosa Island's new Underwater World attraction (see p.536); then again, it's more central and much cheaper. The aquarium holds over five hundred species of fish and other marine creatures; feeding time is daily at noon. Evidence of the recent Singapore River development drive which initiated the beautification of Boat Quay can be seen across the road, where **Clarke Quay**, a chain of nineteenth-century *godowns*, has been renovated into an attractive shopping and eating complex.

The **Chettiar Hindu Temple** (daily 8am–noon & 5.30–8.30pm), a minute's walk further west from the aquarium, at the intersection of River Valley and Tank roads, is the goal of every participant in Singapore's annual Thaipusam Festival (see p.112 for more details of Thaipusam festivities). This large temple, dwarfed by the pink *Imperial Hotel*, is dedicated to Lord Subramaniam and boasts a wonderful *gopuram* or bank of sculpted gods and goddesses. Built in 1984, it replaced a nineteenth-century temple built by Indian Chettiars (moneylenders); inside, 48 glass panels etched with Hindu deities line the roof.

Chinatown

The two square kilometres of **CHINATOWN**, bounded by New Bridge Road to the west, Neil and Maxwell roads to the south, Cecil Street to the east and the Singapore River to the north, once constituted the focal point of Chinese life and culture in Singapore. Nowadays, scarred by the wounds of demolition and dwarfed by skyscrapers, the area is on its last traditional legs. Even so, a wander through the surviving nineteenth-century streets unearths ageing craft shops, restaurants unchanged in forty years and provision stores crammed with bird's nests, dried cuttlefish, ginger, chillies, mushrooms and salted fish.

The area was first earmarked for settlement by the Chinese community by Sir Stamford Raffles himself, who decided on his second visit to the island in June 1819 that the communities should live separately. As increasing numbers of immigrants poured into Singapore, Chinatown became just that – a Chinese town, where new arrivals from the mainland, mostly from Kwangtung (Canton) and the Fukien provinces, would have been pleased to find temples, shops and, most importantly, clan associations (*kongsi*), which helped them to find food and lodgings and work, mainly as small traders and coolies. The prevalent architectural form was the **shophouse**, a shuttered building whose moulded facade fronted living rooms upstairs and a shop on the ground floor. By the mid-twentieth century, the area southwest of the Singapore River was rich with the imported cultural heritage of China, but with independence came ambition. The government regarded the tumbledown slums of Chinatown as an

---

SONGBIRDS

One of the most enduringly popular of Singaporean hobbies is the keeping and training of **songbirds** and, every Sunday morning, scores of enthusiasts – and their birds – congregate at an unnamed nondescript coffee shop on the corner of Tiong Bahru and Seng Poh roads, just west of Chinatown. Songbird competitions are commonplace in Singapore, but this gathering is an informal affair with bird owners coming to show off their pets and admire those of fellow collectors. The exquisite cages that house the birds are hung on a metal frame that fronts the coffee shop. Birds are grouped according to their breed, lest they pick up the distinctive songs of other breeds. The various breeds of bird you'll see include the delicate green *Mata Puteh*, or "white eye bird"; the *Jambul*, with its showy blackcrest and red eye patches; and the *Sharma*, with beautiful long tail feathers. You can have toast and coffee at the café while watching and listening to the proceedings, which start around 6am – a good early morning start to a tour around nearby Chinatown. Take the MRT to Tiong Bahru station and walk left along Tiong Bahru Road for five minutes. Alternatively, buses #33, #62 and #851 from North Bridge Road all pass along Tiong Bahru Road. From the coffee shop it's just fifteen minutes' walk to New Bridge Road, or take bus #33 to Eu Tong Sen Street.

The other central Sunday songbird venue is Sturdee Road, off Petain Road, which lies between Serangoon Road and jalan Besar in Little India; for details of how to get there see "Little India", (see p.515).

eyesore and embarked upon a catastrophic redevelopment campaign that saw whole roads bulldozed to make way for new shopping centres, and street traders relocated into organized complexes. Only recently did public opinion finally convince the Singaporean authorities to restore, and not redevelop, Chinatown. Renovated buildings remain faithful to the original designs, though there's a tendency to render once characterful shophouses as improbably perfect. The latest problem to threaten the fabric of Chinatown is spiralling rent, which in time will drive out the last few remaining families and traditional businesses, leaving the area open for full exploitation. All of which means that Chinatown is best visited soon. And go early in the morning, too, when the sun isn't yet hot enough to make walking around unpleasant.

Along Telok Ayer Street

Follow the signs for Maxwell Road out of Tanjong Pagar MRT and you'll surface on the southern edge of Chinatown. Take the left hand path in front of the station and cross Maxwell Road; after about fifty metres you'll hit **Telok Ayer Street**, whose Malay name – Watery Bay – recalls a time when the street would have run along the shoreline of the Straits of Singapore. Nowadays it's no closer to a beach than is Beach Road, but alongside the shops and stores there are still a number of temples and mosques that have survived from the time when immigrants and sailors stepping ashore wanted to thank the gods for their safe passage.

Facing you as you approach Telok Ayer Street is the square **Chinese Methodist Church**, established in 1889, whose design – portholes and windows adorned with white crosses and capped by a Chinese-style pagoda-style roof – testifies to its multicultural nature. Further up, shortly beyond McCallum Street, the enormous **Thian Hock Keng Temple**, the Temple of Heavenly Happiness, is a hugely impressive Hokkien building. Built on the site of a small joss house where immigrants made offerings to Ma Chu Por (or Tian Hou), the Queen of Heaven, work on the temple started in 1839 using materials imported from China. By the time the temple was finished in 1842 a statue of the goddess had been shipped in from southern China, and this still stands in the centre of the temple's main hall, flanked by the God of War on the right and the Protector of Life on the left. From the street, the temple looks spectacular: serpentine dragons stalk its broad roofs, while the entrance to the temple compound bristles with ceramic flowers, foliage and figures. Two stone lions stand guard at the entrance, and door gods, painted on the front doors, prevent evil spirits from entering. Look out, too, for the huge ovens, always lit, in which offerings to either gods or ancestors are burnt.

A block west of Telok Ayer Street is **Amoy Street**, which – together with China and Telok Ayer streets – was also designated as a Hokkien enclave in the colony's early days. The hexagonal sign that hangs outside no. 89 advertising the *K.T.H. Native Passenger Lodging Hse* is a typical testament to the street's historical connections with the newly arrived Chinese pioneers. Long terraces of shophouses flank the street, all featuring characteristic "five foot ways", or covered verandahs so-called simply because they jut five feet out from the house. Some of the shophouses are in a ramshackle state; others have been marvellously renovated, only to be bought by companies in need of some fancy office space. It's worth walking down to the **Sian Chai Kang Temple**, at 66 Amoy Street, painted a shade of red as fiery as the dragons on its roof – it's a musty, open-fronted place dominated by huge urns, full to the brim of ash from untold numbers of burned incense sticks.

Meanwhile, Telok Ayer Street continues north over Cross Street to another former waterfront temple, the well-hidden **Fuk Tak Ch'i Temple**, at no. 76. A dark, claustrophobic place, its two shrines are jam-packed with tiny, smoke-ringed effigies of Chinese deities. As you walk inside, on your left is the God of Wealth with his horse. Two doors along, the *Seong Moh Trading Company* sells prayer books and incense sticks of various sizes – all for burning as offerings.

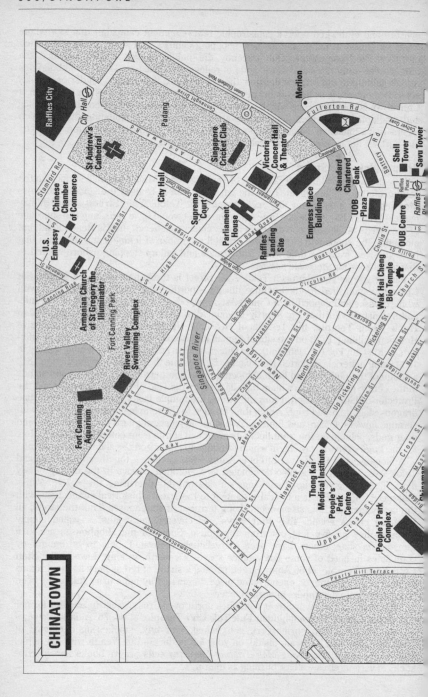

CHINATOWN

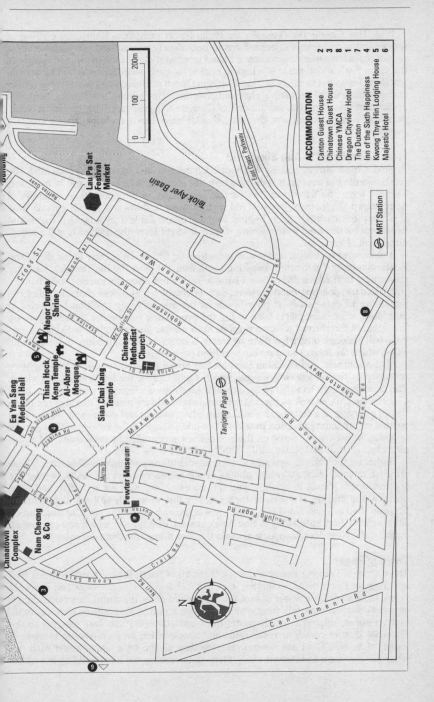

Lau Pa Sat
Festival
Market

Telok Ayer Basin

East Coast Parkway

MRT Station

Raffles Quay

Cross St

Boon Tat St

Shenton Way

Stanley St

Robinson Rd

Nagor Durgha
Shrine

McCallum St

Cecil St

Chinese
Methodist
Church

Thian Hock
Keng Temple

Amoy St

Telok Ayer St

Al-Abrar
Mosque

Maxwell Rd

Ee Yan Sang
Medical Hall

Sian Chai Kang
Temple

Ann Siang Hill

Erskine Rd

Maxwell Rd

Tanjong Pagar

Shenton Way

Palmer Rd

Wallich Rd

Peck Seah St

Pewter Museum

Murray St

Neil Rd

Duxton Rd

Tanjong Pagar Rd

Chinatown
Complex

Club St

Nam Cheong
& Co

Gemmill Rd

Craig Rd

Keong Saik Rd

Neil Rd

Cantonment Rd

N

0   100   200m

Wak Hai Cheng Bio Temple on Philip Street completes Chinatown's string of former waterfront temples, fronted by an ugly concrete courtyard criss-crossed by a web of ropes supporting numerous spiralled incense sticks. Its name means "Temple of the Calm Sea", which made it a logical choice for early worshippers who had arrived safely in Singapore; an effigy of Tian Hou, the Queen of Heaven and protector of seafarers, is housed in the temple's right-hand chamber. This temple, too, has an incredibly ornate roof, crammed with tiny models of Chinese village scenes. The temple cat meanders across here sometimes, dwarfing the tableaux like a creature from a Godzilla movie.

From China Street to Ann Siang Hill

Around **China Street** and its offshoots, Chinatown becomes more residential, the roads affording at least an insight into how the area might have appeared in its prime. The old ways still survive in this part of Singapore: in the upper floor windows of tumbledown shophouses, wizened old men in white T-shirts and striped pyjama trousers stare out rheumily from behind wooden gates, flanked by songbird cages and laundry poles threaded with washing. Down at street level, the trishaw is still a recognized form of transport.

A number of traditional trades and industries on China Street cater to the dwindling local community. On the right (walking south from the Wak Hai Bio Temple), just after the turning to Hokkien Street, is a **Chinese medicine shop**, its interior walls banked with old, dark, polished wood drawers, each engraved with Chinese characters describing its herbal contents. Next door is one of the few surviving traditional bakeries in Singapore, where charcoal is used to fire the oven. Look out, too, for the last house on the right of China Street, where a **popiah skin maker** goes about his work. By smearing a ball of dough onto a hot plate he leaves a sufficient film of mixture to harden into skins, which are then used to make deep-fried pancake rolls.

At the southern end of China Street, Club Street rises up steeply, a thoroughfare noted for its **temple-carving shops**, which you'll find on the left, a short way along. The craftsmen here hand-carve the six-inch sandalwood effigies of gods you see in all Chinese temples, as well as making temple doors and face masks. Offerings are made before a carving of a deity begins and again when its eyes and other facial features are painted on. An impromptu **flea market** often takes shape on the far side of the car park opposite, where traders squat on their haunches surrounded by catalogues, old coins, sleeveless records and phone cards, hoping to make a few cents.

Higher up Club Street, several old **clan associations** and guilds still survive. These are easy to spot: black-and-white photos of old members cover the walls; behind the screens which almost invariably span the doorway, old men sit and chat; and from upstairs, the crackle of mahjong tiles reaches the street. There's another uniquely Chinese shop at 3 Ann Siang Hill, which lies at the end, and to the right, of Club Street. The *Lee Kun Store* specializes in lion dance masks, examples of which you can see up on the walls. Next door, stop for a drink in the *Ann Siang Hill Chinese Teahouse*.

Tanjong Pagar

The district of **Tanjong Pagar** at the southern tip of South Bridge Road, between Neil and Tanjong Pagar roads, is another area that's changed beyond recognition in recent years. Once a veritable sewer of brothels and opium dens, the authorities earmarked it as a conservation area, following which over two hundred shophouses were painstakingly restored, painted in sickly pastel hues and converted into bars catering to the Financial District crowd, or restaurants and shops which prey on passing tourists. A bazaar at 51 Neil Road has several shops selling all the tat a tourist could wish for, while the **Heritage Exhibition** (daily 11am–6pm; free) in the same building is a rather grand name for what is essentially just a small room of old photographs. Another store masquerading as something more cultural is at 49a Duxton Road, where you'll find that the **Pewter Museum** (daily 9am–5.30pm; free) is little more than a showroom for the pewterware shop below.

The highlight of a trip around Tanjong Pagar is a stop at one of the traditional **teahouses** along Neil Road. At *Tea Chapter*, 9A–11A Neil Road (daily 11am–11pm), you can have tea in the very chair in which Queen Elizabeth sat when she visited in 1989 – understandably, the shop is plastered with photographs of the occasion. The Chinese take tea drinking very seriously – buy a bag of tea here and one of the staff will teach you all the attached rituals (and see the feature below); 100g bags go for $5 to over $65 and tea sets are also on sale, though they don't come cheap.

Along South Bridge Road

During the Japanese occupation, roadblocks were set up at the point where **South Bridge Road** meets Cross Street and Singaporeans were vetted at an interrogation post for signs of anti-Japanese feeling. Those whose answers failed to satisfy the guards either ended up as POWs or were never seen again. Nowadays – in stark contrast to the Tanjong Pagar conservation area – South Bridge Road is lined with numerous dingy shops that look as if they've seen no custom since the war.

Turn right out of Ann Siang Hill and you'll see **Eu Yan Sang Medical Hall** (Mon–Sat 8.30am–6pm) at 267–271 South Bridge Road, first opened in 1910 and geared up, to an extent, for the tourist trade – some of the staff speak good English. The shop has been beautifully renovated: the smell is the first thing you'll notice (a little like a compost heap on a hot day), the second, the wierd assortment of ingredients on the shelves, which to the unititiated look more likely to kill than cure. Besides the usual herbs and roots favoured by the Chinese are various dubious remedies derived from

---

TAKING CHINESE TEA

If you're in need of a quick, thirst-quenching drink, avoid **Chinese teahouses**: the art of tea-making is heavily bound up in ritual and the unhurried preparation time is crucial to the production of a pleasing brew. What's more, when you do get a cup, it's barely more than a mouthful and then the whole propcess kicks off again.

Tea drinking in China traces its origins back thousands of years. Legend has it that the first cuppa was drunk by Emperor Shen Nong, who was pleasantly surprised by the aroma produced by some dried tea leaves falling into the water he was boiling. He was even more pleased when he tasted the brew. By the eighth century, the artform was so complex that Chinese scholar Lu Yu produced a three-volume tome on the processes involved.

Tea shops normally have conventional tables and chairs but the authentic experience involves kneeling at a much lower traditional table. The basic procedure is as follows: the server places a towel in front of himself and his guest, with the folded edge facing the guest, and stuffs leaves into the pot with a bamboo scoop. Water, boiled over a flame, has to reach an optimum temperature, depending on which type of tea is being made; experts can tell its heat by the size of the bubbles rising, which are described variously, and rather confusingly, as "sand-eyes", "prawns' eyes", "fishes' eyes", etc. Once the pot has been warmed inside and out, the first pot of tea is made, transferred into the pouring jar and then, frustratingly, poured back *over* the pot – the thinking being that over a period of time, the porous clay of the pot becomes infused with the fragrance of the tea. Once a second pot is ready, a draught is poured into the (taller) sniffing cup, from which the aroma of the brew is savoured. Only now is it time to actually drink the tea and if you want a second cup, the complete procedure starts again.

exotic and endangered species. Blood circulation problems and external injuries are eased with centipedes and insects, crushed into a "rubbing licquor"; the ground-up gall bladders of snakes or bears apparently work wonders on pimples; monkey's gallstones aid asthmatics; while deer penis is supposed to provide a lift to any sexual problem. Antlers, sea horses, scorpions and turtle shells also feature regularly in Chinese prescriptions, though the greatest cure-all of Oriental medecine is said to be **ginseng**, a clever little root that will combat anything from weakness of the heart to acne and jet lag. If you need a pick-me-up, or are just curious, the shop administers free tumblers of ginseng tea.

Across the road from the front doors of *Eu Yan Sang*, the compound of the **Sri Mariamman Hindu Temple** bursts with primary coloured, wild-looking statues of deities and animals, and there's always some ritual or other being attended to by one of the temple's rugged priests, drafted in from the subcontinent, and dressed in simple loin clothes. A wood-and-atap hut was first erected here in 1827, on land belonging to Naraina Pillay – a government clerk who arrived on the same ship as Stamford Raffles, when Raffles first came ashore at Singapore. The present temple was completed in around 1843 and boasts a superb *gopuram* over the front entrance. Once inside the temple, look up at the roof and you'll see splendidly vivid friezes depicting a host of Hindu deities, including the three manifestations of the Supreme Being: Brahma the Creator (with three of his four heads showing), Vishnu the Preserver, and Shiva the Destroyer (holding one of his sons). The main sanctum, facing you as you walk inside, is devoted to Goddess Mariamman, who's worshipped for her powers of curing diseases. Smaller sanctums dotted about the open walkway circumnavigating the temple honour a host of other deities. In that dedicated to Goddess Periachi Amman, a sculpture portrays her with a queen lying on her lap, whose evil child she has ripped from her womb. Odd, then, that the Periachi Amman should be the Protector of Children, to whom babies are brought when one month old. Sri Aravan, with his bushy moustache and big ears, is far less intimidating. His sanctum is at the back on the right hand side of the complex.

To the left of the main sanctum there's an unassuming patch of sand which, once a year during the festival of **Timithi** (see p.64), is covered in red-hot coals, across which run male Hindus wishing to prove the strength of their faith. The participants, who line up all the way along South Bridge Road waiting for their turn, are supposedly protected from the heat of the coals by the power of prayer, though the presence of an ambulance parked round the back of the temple suggests that some of them aren't praying quite hard enough.

West: Chinatown Complex and beyond

After crumbling Telok Ayer and China streets, much of the section of Chinatown **west of South Bridge Road** seems far less authentic. This is tour bus Chinatown, heaving with gangs of holidaymakers plundering souvenir shops. However, until as recently as the 1950s, **Sago Street**, across South Bridge Road from Ann Siang Hill, was home to several death houses, where skeletal citizens saw out their final hours on rattan camp beds. These houses were finally deemed indecent and have all now gone, replaced by lifeless restaurants and shops stacked to the rafters with cheap Chinese vases, teapots, cups and saucers. Sago, Smith, Temple and Pagoda streets only really recapture their youth around the time of Chinese New Year. Then, they're crammed to bursting with stalls selling festive branches of blossom, oranges, sausages and waxed chickens – which look as if they have melted to reveal a handful of bones inside.

At other times of the year, give yourself an hour or so to dig out the few things worth seeing. The hideous concrete exterior of the **Chinatown Complex**, at the end of Sago Street, belies the charm of the teeming market it houses. Walk up the front steps, past the garlic, fruit and nut hawkers, and once inside, the market's many twists and turns reveal stalls selling silk, kimonos, rattan, leather and clothes. There are no fixed prices, so it's best to put your haggling head on. Deep in the market's belly is *Kan Meng* (shop 01-K6) – a calligraphers' stall, where you can have an oriental ink sign quickly drawn for you – while the *Capitol Plastics* stall (01-16) specializes in mahjong sets. There's a food centre on the second floor, while the wet market within the complex gets pretty packed early in the morning, when locals come to buy fresh fish or meat. Here, abacuses are still used to tally bills and sugar canes lean like spears against the wall.

Where Sago Street skirts to the right of the Chinatown Complex, it changes its name to **Trengganu Street**. Despite the hoards of tourists, and the shops selling *Singapore Airlines* uniforms, presentation chopstick sets and silk hats with false pony tails, there are occasional glimpses of Chinatown's old trades and industries amid the kitsch. At 30 Smith Street, soya sauce is still dispensed from huge bins, while the *Fook Weng* store at no. 34 offers shirts, watches, mobile phones, money and passports – all made out of paper – which the Chinese burn to ensure their ancestors don't want for creature comforts in the next life. *Nam Cheong and Co.*, off nearby Kreta Ayer Street, takes this industry to its logical conclusion, producing huge houses and near life-size safes, servants and Mercedes for the self-respecting ghost about town; the shop is at 01-04 Block, 334 Keong Saik Road, between Chinatown Complex and New Bridge Road.

Most of the area around Trengganu Street is best appreciated by wandering aimlessly; there is, however, one permanent museum, which warrants a special trip. The **Chinaman Scholar Gallery**, at 14B Trengganu Street (Mon–Fri 9am–4pm; $4), is

---

SHOPPING IN CHINATOWN

As well as the markets and stores covered in the text, look out for the following, all either on or near to New Bridge Road and Eu Tong Sen Street.

Chinatown Point, 133 New Bridge Road.
One of its two buildings houses bright, fashionable, Orchard Road-style shop units; the other is a handicraft centre, with scores of tourist-orientated businesses.

Hong Lim Complex, 531–531A Upper Cross Street.
Several Chinese provisions stores, fronted by sackfuls of dried mushrooms, cuttlefish, chillis, garlic cloves, onions, fritters and crackers. Other shops sell products ranging from acupuncture accessories to birds' nests.

Lucky Chinatown Complex, 11 New Bridge Road.
Fairly upmarket place with lots of jewellery shops, even an Oriental-style *MacDonalds*.

New Bridge Centre, 336 Smith Street.
The *Da You Department Store* (2nd floor) sells Chinese religious artefacts, tea sets and crockery.

Pearl's Centre, 100 Eu Tong Sen Street.
A centre for Chinese medicine. The *Chinese Patent Medicines and Medicated Liquors Centre* at #03-19 (daily 10am–9.30pm) and *TCM Chinese Medicines* at #02-21 (daily 10am–9pm) both have a Chinese clinic, where a consultation will cost you $5.

People's Park Centre, 101 Upper Cross Street.
Stall-like shop units selling cheap shoes, tapes, electronics and gold. Look into *Nison Department Store* (daily 9.30am–10pm), on the first and second floors, which has some beautiful statues and rosewood screens.

People's Park Complex, 1 Park Road.
The *Overseas Emporium* is at #02-70 (daily 10am–9.30pm) and warrants a browse through its shelves of Chinese instruments, calligraphy pens, lacquerwork and jade. Also interesting is *Tashing Emporium* (daily 10am–10pm), a Taiwanese shop at #01-79A, selling food, clothes and Oriental trinkets. Cobblers set up stall in the courtyard beside the complex, behind which is a market and food centre.

more junk shop than museum, housed in a single room within a 120-year-old shop-house. Most of its artefacts date from the early twentieth century, and the owner Vincent Tan talks his guests around them with great pride, pointing out pedestrian pieces like vases and furniture, as well as the more fascinating exhibits, like the tiny pairs of shoes worn by young girls to stop their feet growing and thus render them more beautiful.

Trengganu's cross streets – Smith, Temple and Pagoda – run west to Chinatown's main shopping drag, comprising southbound **New Bridge Road** and northbound **Eu Tong Sen Street**, along which are lined a handful of large malls (see box above). Try to pop into one of the barbecue pork vendors around the intersection of Smith, Temple and Pagoda streets with New Bridge Road – the squares of red, fatty, delicious meat that they cook on wire meshes over fires produce an odour that is pure Chinatown.

The **Thong Chai Medical Institute** has been sited at the top of Eu Tong Sen Street since 1892, when it first opened its doors with the avowed intention of dispensing free medical help regardless of race, colour or creed. Listed as a national monument, it has recently been taken over by the *Seiawan Company*, whose intentions are less charita-ble – when renovations are completed the beautiful southern Chinese-style building is to become a flashy souvenir shop, which seems a waste of its wonderful serpentile gables and wooden inscribed pillars. Northwest of the *Thong Chai* institute is a Teochew Chinese enclave based around Ellenborough and Tew Chew streets. **Ellenborough Market** incorporates a third-floor food centre serving Teochew speciali-ties, as well as a wet market where fish-mincing machines are in constant action – a sight to be avoided if you are planning to eat fishball soup again on your trip.

Telok Blangah, the World Trade Centre and Mount Faber.

A twenty-minute walk west of Chinatown comes to the area known as **Telok Blangah** in which stands Singapore's **World Trade Centre**, itself a splendid shopping centre-cum-marine terminal, from which boats depart Singapore for Indonesia's Riau Archipelago. Lots of buses come this way: #97, #125 and #166 travel down Bencoolen Street, while #65 continues on from Bencoolen Street, to Orchard Boulevard; from Scotts and Orchard roads, take bus #143. You'll know when to get off, because you'll see cable cars rocking across the skyline in front of you, on their way to and from Mount Faber.

Apart from catching one of these cable cars, either to Sentosa (see p.536), or up Mount Faber (see below), the only other thing to do here is to take a walk around the **Guinness World of Records Exhibition** at #02-70 World Trade Centre, 1 Maritime Square, (daily 9.30am–7.30pm; $5, children $3; ☎2718344), a familiar trawl through the world's tallest, shortest, hungriest and oldest people.

Once called Telok Blangah, **Mount Faber** – 600m north of the WTC – was renamed in 1845 after Government Engineer Captain Charles Edward Faber; the top of the "mount" (hillock would be a better word) commands fine views of Keppel Harbour and, to the northeast, central Singapore – views which are even more impressive at night, when the city is lit up. As you'd expect, there's a correspondingly strong souvenir shop presence, though you can escape this by moving away from the area immediately around the cable car station and up into the park. It's a long, steep walk from Telok Blangah Road up Mount Faber – better to take the **cable car** from the World Trade Centre complex (daily 8.30am–9pm; $5 return). An accident in 1983, when a ship's mast clipped the cables on which the cars are suspended, cost seven passengers their lives, but today laser eyes ensure history doesn't repeat itself. In the early days of colo-nial rule, Temenggong Abdul Rahman played Prime Minister to Sultan Hussein Shah's President, and his signature graced the treaty authorizing the East India Company to operate out of Singapore. All that's left of his settlement on the southern slopes of

Mount Faber is its pillared mosque – the **State of Johor Mosque** – and, behind that, a small Malay cemetery and a portion of the brickwork that once housed the Temenggong's baths. The mosque lies five minutes' walk east of the World Trade Centre, and is passed by all WTC-bound buses.

Little India

A tour around **LITTLE INDIA** amounts to nothing less than an all-out assault on the senses. Indian pop music blares out from gargantuan speakers outside tape shops; the air is heavily perfumed with sweet incense, curry powder and jasmine garlands; Hindu women promenade in bright sarees; and a wealth of "hole-in-the-wall" restaurants serve up superior curries.

Indians did not always dominate this convenient central niche of Singapore, just fifteen minutes from the colonial district. Its original occupants were Europeans and Eurasians who established country houses here, and for whom a race course was built (on the site of modern day Farrer Park) in the 1840s. Only when Indian-run brick kilns began to operate here did a pronouncedly Indian community start to evolve. The enclave grew when a number of cattle and buffalo yards opened in the area in the latter half of the nineteenth century, and more Hindus were drawn in search of work. Street names hark back to this trade: side by side off the western reach of Serangoon Road are Buffalo Road and Kerbau (confusingly, "buffalo" in Malay) Road. Singapore's largest maternity hospital, nearby on Bukit Timah Road, is called Kandang Kerbau (Buffalo Pen) Hospital. Indians featured prominently in the development of Singapore, though not always out of choice: from 1825 onwards, convicts were transported from the subcontinent and by the 1840s there were over a thousand Indian prisoners labouring on buildings like St Andrew's Cathedral and the Istana.

The district's backbone is the north–south **Serangoon Road**, whose southern end is alive with shops, restaurants and fortune tellers. To the east is a tight knot of roads, stretching as far as jalan Besar, that's ripe for exploration, while parallel to Serangoon Road, **Race Course Road** boasts a clutch of fine restaurants (see section on Indian and Burmese restaurants on p.546) and some temples. Little India is only a ten-to-fifteen-minute walk from Bencoolen Street and Beach Road. From Orchard Road, take bus #65, #92 or #111 and ask for Serangoon Road. Alternatively, take the MRT to Dhoby Ghaut, hop on bus #64, #65, #92 or #111 and, again, get off at Serangoon Road.

Along Serangoon Road

Serangoon Road is a kaleidoscopic whirl of Indian life, its shops selling everything from nostril studs and ankle bracelets to incense sticks and *kum kum* powder (used to make the red dot Hindus wear on their foreheads). Little stalls, set up in doorways and under "five foot ways", thread and sell garlands, gaudy posters of Hindu gods and gurus, movie soundtracks and newspapers like *The Hindu* and *India Today*. Look out for parrot-wielding fortune tellers – you tell the man your name, he passes your name on to his feathered partner, and the bird then picks out a card with your fortune on it.

At the southeastern end of Serangoon Road, the **Zhu Jiao Centre** combines many of Little India's ventures under one roof. Beyond its ground floor food centre is a wet market that's not for the faint-hearted – traders push around trolleys piled high with goats' heads, while the halal butchers go to work in full view of the customers. Elsewhere, live crabs shuffle busily in buckets, their claws tied together, and there's a mouthwatering range of fruits on sale, including mangoes and whole branches of bananas. Upstairs, on the second floor, you'll find Indian fabrics, leatherware, footware, watches, and cheap electronic bits and bobs. On Sunday, the forecourt of the centre becomes an ad hoc social club for immigrant labourers working in Singapore, most of

△ Hajjah Fatimah Mosque

**LITTLE INDIA &
THE ARAB QUARTER**

ACCOMMODATION

Boon Wah Boarding House	5
Broadway Hotel	3
Friendly Resthouse	2
Little India Guest House	4
Mount Emily Hotel	6
Palace Hotel	1

0   100   200m

Crawford St

Lavender

Lavender St
Brs Terminal

Lavender St

Horne Rd

King George's Avenue

Jln Sultan

Aliwal St

Kandahar St

Istana
Kampong
Glam

Sultan
Mosque

North Bridge Rd

Victoria St

Malabar
Mosque

Jln Kubor

ARAB ST

Rochor Canal Rd

Arab St

Weld Rd

Syed Alwi Rd

Jln Berseh

Kelantan Rd

Pitt St

Ban San

Jln Besar

Jln Besar

Upper Weld Rd

Upper Dickson Rd

5

Petain Rd

Verdun Rd

Kitchener Rd

Syed Alwi Rd

Desker Rd

Rowell Rd

Veerasamy Rd

Norris Rd

Cuff Rd

1

Leong San Temple

Sakaya Muni
Buddha Gaya
Temple

Sri Srinivasa
Perumal Temple

Perumal Rd

2

Race Course Rd

Burmah Rd

Roberts L

Serangoon Rd

Birch Rd

Kinta Rd

Race Course L

3

LITTLE INDIA

Veeramakaliamman
Temple

Serangoon

4

Race Course Rd

Kerbau Rd

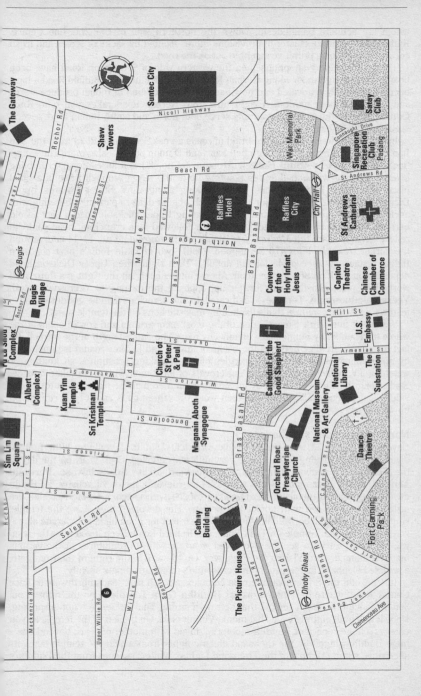

whom are actually Bangledeshi. Down the northern side of the Zhu Jiao Centre, Buffalo Road sports a cluster of provisions' stores fronted by sacks of spices and fresh coconut ground on a primitive machine out on the road.

The few remaining shophouses on the western side of Serangoon Road have been boarded up, though those along Kerbau Road – one block north of Buffalo Road – have been meticulously renovated and now harbour a proliferation of Indian produce stores and a pleasant beer garden. A right turn from Kerbau Road takes you onto **Race Course Road**, whose fine restaurants serve both north and south Indian food; several specialize in fish head curry.

In the other direction, the little braid of roads across Serangoon Road from the Zhu Jiao Centre – Hastings Road, Campbell Lane and Dunlop Street – also merits investigation. Dunlop Street's **Abdul Gaffoor Mosque** (at no. 41) is a little-known, crumbling beauty, bristling with small spires pointing up at the sky. Campbell Lane is a good place for buying Indian sandals, while walking along Clive Street towards Upper Dickson Road, you'll find on your right a batch of junk dealers patiently tinkering with ancient cookers, air-con units and TVs. Left along Upper Dickson Road – past an old barber's shop where a short back and sides is followed by a crunching head yank "to relieve tension" – are the *Madras New Woodlands Restaurant*, at no. 12–14 and, around the corner, *Komala Vilas* (76 Serangoon Road), two of Little India's best southern Indian restaurants (see p.546 for full details). Turn right when Upper Dickson Road deposits you back on Serangoon Road. Almost immediately on the right is a **flour mill** worked by pale, ghostly men; further up, opposite the turning to Veerasamy Road, **Veeramakaliamman Temple** – dedicated to the ferocious Hindu goddess, Kali – features a fanciful *gopuram* that's flanked by majestic lions on the temple walls.

You won't find **Pink Street** – one of the most incongruous and sordid spots in the whole of clean, shiny Singapore – on any city map. The entire length of the "street" (in fact it's merely an alley between the backs of Rowell and Desker roads) is punctuated by open doorways, inside which gaggles of bored-looking prostitutes sit knitting or watching TV, oblivious to the gawping crowds of local men who accumulate outside. Stalls along the alley sell distinctly un-Singaporean merchandise such as sex toys, blue videos and potency pills, while con-men work the "three cups and a ball" routine on unwary passers-by.

North: temples and shophouses

Beyond Desker Road, a five-minute walk north takes you to the edge of Little India, a diversion worth making to see three very different temples. Each year, on the day of the Thaipausam festival (Jan/Feb), the courtyard of the **Sri Srinivasa Perumal Temple**, at 397 Serangoon Road, witnesses a gruesome melee of activity, as Hindu devotees don huge metal frames (*kavadis*) topped with peacock feathers, which are fastened to their flesh with hooks and prongs. The devotees then leave the temple, stopping only while a coconut is smashed at their feet for good luck, and parade all the way to the Chettiar Temple on Tank Road, off Orchard Road. Even if you miss the festival, it's worth a trip to see the five-tiered *gopuram* with its sculptures of the various manifestations of Lord Vishnu the Preserver. On the wall to the right of the front gate, a sculpted elephant, its leg caught in a crocodile's mouth, trumpets silently.

Just beyond the Sri Srinivasa temple complex, a small path leads northwest to Race Course Road, where the **Sakaya Muni Buddha Gaya Temple** is on the right at no. 366. It's a slightly kitsch temple that betrays a strong Thai influence – not surprising, since it was built entirely by a Thai monk, Vutthisasala. On the left of the temple as you enter is a huge replica of Buddha's footprint, inlaid with mother-of-pearl; beyond sits a huge Buddha ringed by the thousand electric lights from which the temple takes its alternative name (Temple of the Thousand Lights); while 25 scenes from the Buddha's life decorate the pedestal on which he sits. It is possible to walk inside the Buddha, through a door in his back: inside is a smaller representation of the Buddha, this time reclining. The left wall of the temple features a sort of wheel of fortune – spin it (for 30c) and take the numbered sheet of paper that corresponds to the number at which the wheel stops, to discover your fortune. Further along the left wall, a small donation entitles you to a shake of a tin full of numbered sticks, after which, again, you get a corresponding sheet of forecasts.

Double back onto Serangoon Road and a five-minute walk southeast along Petain Road leads to jalan Besar, a route which takes in some immaculate examples of **Peranakan** (Straits Chinese) -**style shophouses**, their facades covered with elegant ceramic tiles reminiscent of Portuguese *azulejos*. There's more *Peranakan* architecture on display on jalan Besar itself (turn right at the end of Petain Road), while further south a daily **flea market** takes place around Pitt Street, Weld Road, Kelantan Lane and Pasar Lane – secondhand tools, odd shoes and foreign currency are all laid out for sale on plastic sheets at the side of the road.

The Arab Quarter

Before the arrival of Raffles, the area of Singapore west of the Rochor River housed a Malay village known as Kampong Glam, after the *Gelam* tribe of sea gypsies who lived there. After signing a dubious treaty with the newly installed "Sultan" Hussein Mohammed Shah (see p.475), Raffles allotted the area to the Sultan and designated the land around it as a Muslim settlement, and soon the zone was attracting Arab traders, as the road names in today's **ARAB QUARTER** – Baghdad Street, Muscat Street and Haji Lane – suggest. Even now, descendents of Sultan Hussein live in the grounds of the Istana Kampong Glam, a palace right in the centre of the district, bounded by Arab Street, Beach Road, jalan Sultan and Rochor Canal Road. Just outside the quarter, Beach Road still maintains shops which betray its former proximity to the sea – ships' chandlers and fishing tackle specialists – and you should also take the time to walk southwest from Arab Street to see the two logic-defying office buildings that together comprise **The Gateway.** Designed by I.M. Pei, they rise magnificently into the air like vast razor blades and appear two-dimensional when viewed from certain angles.

The Arab Quarter is no more than a ten-minute walk from Bencoolen Street. To get there from Orchard Road, take bus #7 to Victoria Street and get off when you spot the *Golden Landmark Hotel* on your right, alternatively, head for Bugis MRT. For a **map** of the Arab Quarter, see p.516.

Arab Street and North Bridge Road

While Little India is memorable for its fragrances, it's the vibrant colours of the shops of **Arab Street** and its environs that stick in the memory. The street boasts the highest concentration of shops in the Arab Quarter; its pavements are an obstacle course of carpets, cloths, baskets and bags. Most of the shops have been renovated, though one or two (like *Shivlal & Sons* at no. 77, and *Uttamram & Co.* at no. 73) still retain their original dark wood and glass cabinets, and wide wooden benches upon which the shopkeepers sit. Textile stores are most prominent, their walls, ceilings and doorways draped with cloths and batiks. Elsewhere you'll see leather, basketware, gold, gemstones and jewellery for sale, while the most impressive range of basketware and rattan work– fans, hats and walking sticks – is found at the intersection with Beach Road, in the *Rahmath Trading Corporation*, at no. 22–26. It's easy to spend a couple of hours weaving in and out of the stores, but don't expect a quiet window-shopping session – the traders here are masters of the forced sale, and will have you loaded with sarongs, baskets and leather bags before you know it.

The quarter's most evocative patch is the stretch of **North Bridge Road** between Arab Street and jalan Sultan. Here, the men sport long sarongs and Abe Lincoln beards, the women fantastically colourful shawls and robes, while the shops and restaurants are geared more towards locals than tourists: *Kazura Co.*, at 755 North Bridge Road, for instance, sells alcohol-free perfumes. Across the road, a cluster of shops stock rosaries, prayer mats and the *songkok* hats worn by Muslim males in mosques. In these shops you'll also find *miswak* sticks – twigs the width of a finger used by some locals to clean their teeth.

Several roads run off the western side of North Bridge Road, including jalan Pisang (Banana Street), on which a street barber works under a tarpaulin. A walk up jalan Kubor (Grave Street) and across Victoria Street takes you to an unkempt Muslim **cemetery** where, it is said, Malay royalty are buried. On Sundays, Victoria Street throngs with children in full Muslim garb on their way to study scripture at the Arabic school, **Madrasah Al Junied Al-Islamiah**.

From Istana Kampong Glam to the Golden Mile Complex

Squatting between Kandahar and Aliwal streets, the **Istana Kampong Glam** was built as the royal palace of Sultan Ali Iskandar Shah, son of Sultan Hussein who negotiated with Raffles to hand over Singapore to the British; the Sultan's descendants live here to this day, and continue to share an annual government allowance. Despite its royal provenance, the Istana is a modest, colonial-style building, run-down and dingy, its grounds dotted with huts. Back out of the Istana, there's a **stone mason's** shop on the corner of Baghdad Street and Sultan Gate, which chips out the lions that stand outside Chinese temples. Another stone mason's, nearby at 24 Baghdad Street, specializes in Muslim graves – uniformly shaped stones that look remarkably like chess pawns.

A few steps further on, Baghdad Street crosses pedestrianized Bussorah Street, from where you get the best initial views of the golden domes of the **Sultan Mosque**, or Masjid Sultan (daily 9am–1pm), the beating heart of the Muslim faith in Singapore. An early mosque stood on this site, finished in 1825 and constructed with the help of a $3000 donation from the East India Company. The present building was completed a century later, according to a design by colonial architects Swan and MacLaren, and if you look carefully at the glistening necks of the domes, you can see that the effect is created by the bases of thousands of ordinary glass bottles, an incongruity which sets the tone for the rest of the building. Steps at the top of Bussorah Street lead into a wide lobby, where a digital display lists current prayer times. Beyond, though out of bounds to non-Muslims, is the main prayer hall, a large, bare chamber that's fronted by two more digital clocks enabling the faithful to time their prayers to the exact second. An exhaustive set of rules applies to visitors wishing to enter the lobby: shoes must be taken off and shoulders and legs covered; no video cameras are allowed inside the mosque, and entry is not permitted during the Friday mass congregation (11.30am–2.30pm). The best time to come is during the Muslim fasting month of Ramadan – when the faithful can only eat after dusk. Then, Muskat Street and Kandahar Street are awash with stalls selling biyriani, barbecued chicken and cakes.

It's only a five-minute walk on to the **Hajjah Fatimah Mosque** on Beach Road, where a collection of photographs in the entrance porch show the mosque through the years following its construction in 1846 – first surrounded by shophouses, then by open land, and finally by huge housing projects. Across from the mosque, the **Golden Mile Complex** at 5001 Beach Road attracts so many Thai nationals that locals refer to it as "Thai Village". Numerous bus firms selling tickets to Thailand operate out of here, while inside, the shops sell Thai foodstuffs, cafés sell *Singha* beer and *Mekong* whisky, and authentic restaurants serve up old favourites. On a Sunday, Thais come down here in hordes to meet up with their compatriots, listen to Thai pop music, and have a few drinks.

Orchard Road

It would be hard to conjure an image more diametrically opposed to the reality of modern-day **ORCHARD ROAD** than C.M. Turnbull's description of it during early colonial times as "a country lane lined with bamboo hedges and shrubbery, with trees meeting overhead for its whole length." One hundred years ago, a stroll down Orchard Road would have passed row upon row of nutmeg trees and would have been enjoyed in the company of strolling merchants taking their daily constitutionals, followed at a discreet distance by their trusty manservants. Today, Orchard Road is synonymous with shopping. Huge malls, selling anything you could imagine, line the road, though don't expect the search to be easy or relaxing: traffic lights that are painfully slow to change, and hordes of dawdling tourists from the numerous hotels along the road, make browsing a potentially traumatic experience. The road runs northwest from Fort Canning Park and is served by three MRT stations – Dhoby Ghaut, Somerset and Orchard; of these Orchard MRT is the most central for shopping expeditions.

Orchard Road does have one or two other diversions if you get tired of staring at CDs, watches and clothes. Near its eastern extent, the President of Singapore's abode – the Istana Negara Singapura – is open to the public a few times a year, while rows of houses that hark back to old Singapore flank Cuppage Road and Emerald Hill Road. The latter road also contains a museum depicting life in a turn-of-the-century *Peranakan* house. And, way up beyond the most westerly point of the road, the Singapore Botanic Gardens make for a relaxing stroll in beautiful surroundings. On the whole, though, you really only come to Orchard Road in the daytime to shop and at night for a whole host of clubs and bars (see p.551–553 for details).

The eastern end

In the **DHOBY GHAUT** area (at the eastern tip of Orchard Road), Indian *dhobies*, or laundrymen, used to wash clothes in the Stamford Canal, which once ran along Orchard and Stamford roads. Three minutes' walk west along Orchard Road from Dhoby Ghaut MRT takes you past *Plaza Singapura*, beyond which stern-looking soldiers guard the gate of the **Istana Negara Singapura.** Built in 1869, the Istana, with its ornate cornices, elegant louvred shutters and huge mansard roof, was

ORCHARD ROAD SHOPPING CENTRES

The main Orchard Road shopping centres are detailed below; they're all marked on the map over the page.

Centrepoint. Dependable all-round complex, whose seven floors of shops include *Mark's and Spencer's* and *Robinson's* – Singapore's oldest department store.

Lucky Plaza. Crammed with tailors and electronics, this is Orchard Road's classic venue for haggling.

Ngee Ann City. A brooding twin-towered complex – Singapore meets Gotham City – with a wealth of good clothes shops.

Orchard Plaza. Tailors, leather jackets and silks galore, as well as a glut of audio, video and camera stores where haggling is par for the course.

Palais Renaissance. One of Singapore's classiest complexes, featuring *Ralph Lauren, Gucci, Karl Lagerfeld, Christian Dior* and other heavyweights.

Tanglin Shopping Centre. Unsurpassed for art, antiques and curios.

Tudor Court. Fashion shops, including Asian designers like *Dick Lee, Esther Tay* and *Arthur Yen.*

Wisma Atria. Like *Centrepoint*, a safe bet, whatever it is you're after.

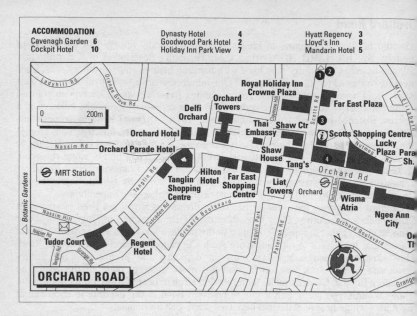

originally the official residence of Singapore's British governors, though on independence it became the residence of the President of Singapore – currently Ong Teng Cheong, whose portrait you'll see in banks, post offices and shops across the state. The shuttered Istana is only open to visitors on public holidays and is probably worth a visit if your trip coincides with one – the President goes walkabout at some point during every open day as thousands of excited Singaporeans flock to picnic on the well-landscaped sweeps and dips of its lawns, and local brass bands belt out jaunty tunes. If not, you might at least catch the **changing of the guard ceremony**, which takes place at 5.45pm every first Sunday of the month.

The **Tan Yeok Nee Mansion**, across the road at 207 Clemenceau Avenue, is currently closed and its future is unclear, though at least its survival of recent work on the Central Expressway augurs well. Built in traditional south Chinese style for a wealthy Teochew pepper and gambier (a resin used in tanning) merchant, and featuring ornate roofs and massive granite pillars, the mid-1880s mansion served as headquarters to the Singapore Salvation Army from 1940 until 1991.

Further along Orchard Road, two thirds of **Cuppage Road** have been pedestrianized, making it a great place to sit out and have a beer or a meal. **Cuppage Terrace** itself, halfway along on the left, is an unusually (for Orchard Road) old row of shophouses, containing tailors and souvenir shops, as well as several antique shops upstairs. A number of even more architecturally notable houses have also survived the developers' bulldozers in Emerald Hill Road, parallel to Cuppage Road. Emerald Hill was granted to Englishman William Cuppage in 1845 and for some years afterwards was the site of a large nutmeg plantation. After Cuppage's death in 1872, the land was subdivided and sold off, much of it bought by members of the *Peranakan* community, which evolved in Malaya as a result of the intermarriage between early Chinese settlers and Malay women. A walk up Emerald Hill Road takes you past a number of exquisitely crafted houses dating from this period, built in a decorative architectural

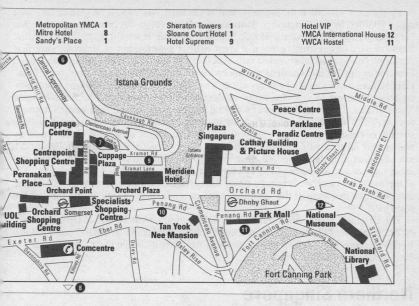

style known as Chinese Baroque, typified by highly coloured ceramic tiles, carved swing doors, shuttered windows and pastel-shaded walls with fine plaster mouldings.

Through the swing doors of 2 Emerald Hill Road, the **Show House Museum**, (Mon–Sat 10.30am–2.30pm; $4 includes guided tour), gives you a brief insight into *Peranakan* culture, with furniture and fittings in each of the house's four rooms high-lighting the lifestyle and traditions of the Straits Chinese. The museum's dining room boasts a fine collection of seventeenth-century Ching dynasty porcelain, but no chop-sticks – *Peranakans* ate with their hands at home. Look out, too, for the birdcage-like food container which could be hoisted up to the ceiling to keep the food away from rats. Meals were in three sittings: the first for the men, who were served by their daughters-in-law; the second for the elder women and daughters, again served by the daughters-in-law; only when all the others had eaten did the daughters-in-law dine with the servants – no wonder parents presented their daughters with black veils, symboliz-ing mourning, when they married into another family.

Further west

West of Emerald Hill Road, the **shopping centres** of Orchard Road begin to come thick and fast. A number of noteworthy shops are detailed above; if you want any further advice, there's a branch of the *Singapore Tourist Promotion Board* just off Orchard Road, at 6 Scotts Road (see p.479). A couple of minutes' further along Scott's Road, the impressive **Goodwood Hotel** started life in 1900 as the *Teutonia Club* for German expats. With the start of war across Europe in 1914, the club was comman-deered by the British Custodian of Enemy Property and it didn't open again until 1918, after which it served for several years as a function hall. In 1929 it became a hotel, though by 1942 the *Goodwood* – like *Raffles* – was lodging Japanese officers. Fitting, then, that the hotel was chosen, after the war, as one of the venues for a war crimes court.

By the time you reach the western end of Orchard Road, you'll be glad of the open space afforded by the **Singapore Botanic Gardens** (Mon–Fri 5am–11pm, Sat & Sun 5am–midnight; free) on Cluny Road. Founded in 1859, it was here, in 1877, that the Brazilian seeds from which grew the great **rubber plantations** of Malaysia were first nurtured. No one had taken much notice of them by the time Henry Ridley was named Director of the Botanic Gardens the following year, but Ridley recognized their financial potential and spent the next twenty years of his life persuading Malayan plantation-owners to convert to this new crop, an occupation which earned him the nickname "Mad" Ridley. The fifty-odd hectares of land feature a mini-jungle rose garden, topiary, fernery, palm valley and lakes that are home to turtles and swans. There's also an **orchid enclosure** (daily 7am–6.30pm) with 12,000 plants; orchid jewellery, made by plating real flowers with gold, is on sale here – pieces cost around $100, though prices are also quoted in Japanese yen, proving who the best customers are. At dawn and dusk, joggers and students of *Tai Chi* haunt the lawns and paths of the gardens, while at the weekend, newlyweds bundle down from church for their photos to be taken. You can pick up a free **map** of the grounds at the ranger's office, a little to the right of the main gate.

The Botanic Gardens are a ten-minute walk from the western end of Orchard Road, or catch bus #7, #14, #106 or #174 from Orchard Boulevard. The #106 passes down Bencoolen Street before heading on towards the gardens, while the #174 originates in New Bridge Road in Chinatown.

Northern Singapore

While land reclamation has radically altered the east coast and industrialization the west, the **northern** expanses of the island up to the Straits of Johor still retain pockets of the **rain forest** and mangrove swamp which blanketed Singapore on Raffles' arrival in 1819. These are interspersed today with sprawling **new towns** like Toa Payoh, maze-like Bishan and Ang Mo Kio, built in the 1970s – the latter's name (red-haired devil's bridge) refers to the nineteenth-century British surveyor, John Turnbull Thomson, under whose supervision the transport network of Singapore made inroads into the interior of the island. Man-eating tigers roamed these spaces well into this century, and it was here that Allied forces confronted the invading Japanese army in 1942, a period of Singaporean history movingly recalled by the **Kranji War Memorial** on Woodlands Road. What remains of Singapore's agricultural past still clings tenaciously to the far northern sweep of the island: you'll see prawn and poultry farms, orchards and vegetable gardens when travelling in these parts.

Dominating the central northern region are two nature reserves, divided by the Bukit Timah Expressway, which is the main road route to Malaysia. West of the expressway is **Bukit Timah Nature Reserve**, an accessible slice of primary rainforest, while to the east, the four reservoirs of the Central Catchment Area are one of Singapore's main sources of water. North of here, the zone's principal tourist attraction is the excellent **Singapore Zoological Gardens,** huddled on a finger of land pointing into the Seletar Reservoir; while to the east are two of Singapore's most eye-catching Buddhist temples – **Siong Lim Temple** and the **Kong Meng San Phor Kark See** temple complex – as well as tiny Tai Gin Road, which houses both the occasional residence of Chinese nationalist leader Dr Sun Yat Sen and Singapore's Burmese temple.

Exploring the north is a matter of pinpointing the particular sight you want to see and heading straight for it; the bus trip to the zoo, for instance, takes around 45 minutes. Travel *between* all these places is decidedly tricky unless you are driving, or in a cab, so don't expect to take in everything in a day. However, Siong Lim Temple, Sun

Yat Sen Villa and the Burmese Temple all nestle aroun
new town and could be incorporated into a single expedit
Orchid Gardens and the Kranji cemetery and memorial
Kark See temple complex really requires a separate journe

Bukit Timah

Bukit Timah Road shoots northwestwards from the juncti
roads, arriving 8km later at the faceless town of BUI
Singapore's only race course, at **Bukit Timah Turf Clu**
Singapore outside the course is restricted to the random ......, the annual
racing calendar here is understandably popular, typically featuring eight meetings,
spaced throughout the year, each spread over four days, and held over consecutive
weekends. Call ☎4693611 for race-meeting details – the most prestigious events
include the *Singapore Gold Cup* in September, the *Lion City Cup* in January, and the
Singapore Derby in October. When there's no racing in Singapore, a giant video screen
links Bukit Timah to various courses across the causeway in Malaysia. There's a fairly
strict dress code – sandals, jeans, shorts and T-shirts are out – and foreign visitors have
to take their passports with them; the day's fixtures begin after lunch, and tickets cost
$5 or $10. **Tours** comprising an afternoon's racing viewed from the members' enclosure can be booked in advance (see p.485) but you'd do far better to just turn up, eat at
the course's decent food centre and soak up the atmosphere in the stands. The bus
details are the same as for the Bukit Timah Nature Reserve – see below.

Bukit Timah Nature Reserve

Bukit Timah Road continues west past Singapore's last remaining pocket of primary
rain forest, which now comprises **Bukit Timah Nature Reserve** (daily 7am–7pm;
free). Visiting this area of Singapore in the mid-eighteenth century, natural historian
Alfred Russel Wallace reported seeing "tiger pits, carefully covered with sticks and
leaves and so well concealed, that in several cases I had a narrow escape from falling
into them. . . . Formerly a sharp stake was stuck erect in the bottom," he continued,
"but after an unfortunate traveller had been killed by falling into one, its use was forbidden." Today the 81-hectare reserve, first established in 1883 by Nathanial Cantley,
Superintendent of the Botanic Gardens, yields no such hazards and provides a refuge
for the dwindling numbers of species still extant in Singapore – only 25 mammal types,
for example, now inhabit the island. Creatures you're most likely to see in Bukit Timah
are long-tailed macaques, butterflies, insects and birds like the Dark-necked Tailorbird,
which builds its nest by sewing together leaves; but scorpions, snakes and pangolins
still roam here, too.

Recent alterations have vastly improved the reserve, which now has an informative
visitor centre (daily 8.30am–6pm) full of displays, specimens and photos relating to
the wildlife beyond. Four main paths from the centre twist and turn through the forest
around and to the top of **Bukit Timah Hill**, which – at a paltry 162.5m – is actually
Singapore's largest hill. The paths are all well signposted, colour-coded and dotted by
rest- and shelter points, and they're clearly mapped on the free leaflet handed out to all
visitors. You'd do best to visit in the early morning (when it's cooler) and in midweek
(when there are fewer visitors).

Dramatic **Hindhede Quarry** (five minutes' walk up the slope to the left of the visitors' centre) is a fine place to head for once you've explored the forest – its deep green
waters are ideal for a cooling swim. Across Bukit Timah Road from the reserve,
another forested hill, **Bukit Batok**, was where British and Australian POWs were
forced to erect a fifteen-metre-high wooden shrine, the *Syonan Tyureito*, for their

, though only the steps at its base now remain. Legend has it that the as destroyed by termites which the prisoners secretly introduced to the one, too, is the wooden cross erected by the POWs to honour their dead.

#171 and #182 both pass down Somerset and Scotts roads en route to Bukit Reserve, while the #181 can be picked up on North Bridge Road, South Bridge d or New Bridge Road; alternatively take the #170 from the Ban San Terminal on ueen Street. For Bukit Batok, the same buses apply, but stay on until you see Old Jurong Road on your left. The hill is located at the end of lorong Sesuai – the next turning left, the road itself laid by the same prisoners who constructed the shrine.

The Sun Yat Sen Villa and Burmese Temple

Between Jalan Toa Payoh to the north, and Balestier Road to the south is the **Sun Yat Sen Villa** (Mon–Fri 9am–5pm, Sat 9am–3pm; free), on tiny Tai Gin Road. Originally built to house the mistress of a wealthy Chinese businessman, this attractive bungalow changed hands in 1905, when one Teo Eng Hock bought it for his mother. Chinese nationalist leader Dr Sun Yat Sen paid his first of eight visits to Singapore the following year, and was invited by Teo to stay at Tai Gin Road, where he quickly established a Singapore branch of the *Tong Meng Hui* – a society dedicated to replacing the Manchu dynasty in China with a modern republic. After serving as a communications camp for the Japanese during World War II, the villa fell into disrepair until 1966, when it was opened to the public. Sadly, the collection of photographs inside is fairly dull unless you are familiar with the manoeuvres of that period of Chinese history; of more interest is the second-floor gallery of photos of Singapore during World War II, and an accompanying collection of combs, keys, pipes, glasses and other personal effects of victims of the Japanese occupation.

Next door is the **Sasanaramsi Burmese Buddhist Temple** (daily 6am–10pm), constructed in just two years after being forced to move from its previous site at Kinta Road, off Serangoon Road because of redevelopment. Decorated by craftsmen from Burma, the temple's ground floor is dominated by a large, white marble statue of the Buddha brought over from Burma in 1932; upstairs is another Buddha statue, this time standing, and ringed by blue skies painted on the wall behind. Tiny Buddha images are presently being "bought" by worshippers at $1000 a throw; when they're all sold they'll be mounted on the sky.

Bus #139 from Selegie Road comes out this way. You'll see a *BP* service station on the right of Balestier Road after about ten minutes – get off at the next stop, where Tai Gin Road is across the road and down a short footpath.

The Siong Lim and Phor Kark See temples

Two of Singapore's largest Chinese temples are situated in the island's central region, east of the Central Catchment Area. Both are rather isolated, but have plenty to interest temple enthusiasts and hum with activity at festival times.

The name of the popular **Siong Lim Temple**, at 184E jalan Toa Payoh (bus #8 from outside Toa Payoh MRT), means "Twin Groves of the Lotus Mountain" – a reference to the Buddha's birth in a grove of trees and his death under a Bodhi tree. Chinese Abbot, Sek Hean Wei, established the temple at the turn of the century when, passing through Singapore on his way home after a pilgrimage to Sri Lanka, he was waylaid by wealthy Hokkien merchant and philanthropist, Low Kim Pong, who supplied both land and finances for the venture. Several renovations have failed to rob the temple of its grandeur, though the urban development of Toa Payoh's outskirts around it hardly enhances its appearance. Set behind a rock garden that combines a water cascade, ponds, streams and bridges, the temple is guarded by statues of the **Four Kings of**

Heaven, each posted to keep evils out of the temple, such as the demons on which they are treading.The highly regarded collection of carved and sculpted gods inside the temple's several halls includes a **Laughing Buddha**, believed to grant good luck if you rub his stomach; a shrine to Kuan Yin, Goddess of Mercy (in the rear hall); and a number of Thai-style Buddha figures.

The largest temple complex in Singapore – and one of the largest in Southeast Asia – lies north of MacRitchie Reservoir, right in the middle of the island. **Phor Kark See Temple** (known in full as the Kong Meng San Phor Kark See Temple Complex), at 88 Bright Hill Drive, spreads over nineteen acres and combines temples, pagodas, pavilions, a Buddhist library and a vast crematorium to such impressive effect that it has been used several times as a backdrop to Chinese kung fu movies. More modern than Siong Lim, Phor Kark See boasts none of the faded charm of Singapore's older temples, but relies instead on its sheer magnitude and exuberant decor for effect. Multi-tiered roofs bristle with ceramic dragons, phoenixes, birds and human figures, while around the complex stand statues of various deities, including a nine-metre-high marble statue of Kuan Yin, Goddess of Mercy. A soaring pagoda, currently in the making, will when finished render the complex even more striking – the pagoda is to be capped by a golden *chedi* (a reliquary tower). Even the **crematorium** – conveniently placed for the nearby *Bright Hill Evergreen Home* for the elderly – doesn't do things by half. Housed below a Thai-style facade of elaborately carved, gilt wood, it's huge and can cope with five ceremonies at one time.

Below the crematorium is a pair of ponds, where thousands of turtles spend their days sunbathing precariously on wooden planks that slant into the waters. A nearby sign prohibits worshippers from letting new turtles into the ponds, a practice supposed to bring good luck. Old ladies beside the viewing gallery sell bunches of vegetables for "one dolla, one dolla", which purchasers then throw to the lucky turtles.

Take bus #130 up Victoria Street to reach the complex, alighting at the far end of Sin Ming Drive.

Along Upper Serangoon Road

Serangoon Road heads out of Little India and continues way up to the northeast coast of the island, passing several places you could fit into half a day's exploring. First stop 10 8km out of the city, at the **Singapore Crocodile Farm** (daily 8.30am–5.30pm; free), at 790 Upper Serangoon Road, where the several hundred crocs (feeding times Tues–Sun at 11am & 3pm) are joined by alligators, snakes and lizards, too. As a "farm" it's rather questionable: this is a rather tasteless commercial venture which works on the dubious premise that people who see how a crocodile is killed and skinned, and its hide treated, will then want to spend their money on the crocodile-skin products sold in the adjoining shop. Buses #97 and #106, from Selegie Road, pass by the farm, though if you want to see crocodiles still wearing their skins, make for the zoo instead (see below).

Both buses continue along Upper Serangoon Road, reaching **Bidadari Cemetery** in around another ten minutes. It's a Christian graveyard and the majority of its aged gravestones are in typical, Western style, but there are Chinese graves here, too, their semicircular design affording a natural kneeling place at which to pray for the well-being of one's ancestor. Buried somewhere in the area is A.P. Williams, a British sailor upon whose life Joseph Conrad based his novel, *Lord Jim*. In his recent travelogue *In Search of Conrad*, writer Gavin Young describes how he tracked down Williams' burial plot in the depths of Singapores' public records offices – but seeking out the number he quotes (2559) yields no sign of the grave. In the long grass of the grounds live many species of birds, and ornithologists find time spent here quite rewarding – indeed, the *Nature Society of Singapore* periodically visits the cemetery. A word of warning, though:

don't go wading into tall grass unless you are wearing ankle-high boots, as snakes also inhabit the cemetery.

Bus drivers are not particularly *au fait* with the location of Bidadari, so tell them you want the more famous Youngberg Hospital, which is just across the road from the cemetery. It takes around fifteen minutes to travel from Selegie Road to Bidadari.

Singapore Zoological Gardens

The **Singapore Zoological Gardens** (daily 8.30am–6pm; adults $7, children under 16 $3), on Mandai Lake Road, are spread over a promontory jutting into peaceful Seletar Reservoir. They attract over one million visitors a year – a fact perhaps explained by their status as one of the world's few open zoos, where moats are preferred to cages. Spacious exhibits manage to approximate the natural habitats of the animals they hold, and though leopards, pumas and jaguars still have to be kept behind bars, this is a thoughtful, humane zoo, described as "one of the really beautiful zoos" by conservationist Sir Peter Scott, who should know what he's talking about.

Over two thousand animals, representing more than 240 species, populate the zoo, so it's best to allow a whole day for your visit. A **tram** (adults $2, kids $1) circles the grounds on a one-way circuit, but as it won't always be going your way be prepared for a lot of footwork. Highlights include the komodo dragons, the polar bears, which you view underwater from a gallery, and the primate kingdom; also worth checking out is the **special loan enclosure**, which has recently played host to a giant panda, an Indian white tiger and a golden monkey. Two **animal shows** are featured daily – a primate and reptile show (10.30am & 2.30pm) and an elephant and sea lion show, the sea lions skidding, swimming and jumping to the theme from *Hawaii 5 'O'*. Children tend to get most out of these shows, and the **Children's World** area offers them the chance to ride a camel, hold young chicks and watch a milking demonstration; at 9am and 4pm daily they can even share a **meal with an orang utan** (see p.539).

Buy the $1 *Guide to S'pore Zoo* on arrival: besides riding and feeding times and a helpful map, the booklet offers suggested itineraries taking in all the major shows and attractions. At the other end of your trip, drop by the gift shop next to the exit, which stocks cuddly toys and rather less tempting bags of "zoo poo" compost. Several food and drink kiosks are dotted around the zoo, or you can head for the reasonable *Ma Kan Terrace*, bang in the centre of the grounds, where there are one or two hawker stalls.

To get to the zoo, take bus #171 from either Stamford Road or Orchard Boulevard, or take the MRT to Yishun and connect with the #171. The **Zoo Express** (☎2353111 for details) collects from all major hotels on Orchard Road and the $20 fare ($14 for children under 12) includes admission and a flying visit to nearby Mandai Orchid Gardens.

Mandai Orchid Gardens

It's only a ten-minute walk from the zoo down Mandai Lake Road to the **Mandai Orchid Gardens** (daily 8.30am–5.30pm; adults $2, children 50c), or you can take the #171 bus from the zoo, which stops right outside. Orchids are big business in Singapore: in 1991 alone, over $20 million of cut orchid flowers were exported from 56 orchid farms across the state. Here, four hectares of flowers are cultivated on a gentle slope, tended by old ladies in wide-brimmed hats. Unless you are a keen horticulturalist, the place will be of only limited interest since little effort has been taken to make it instructive. Still, if you've been to the zoo, the gardens make a colourful detour on the way home, and the price of a gift box of orchids (under $70) compares favourably with more central flower shops.

Woodlands and the Kranji War Cemetery

Five kilometres north of the zoo is the bustling town of **WOODLANDS**, from where the **causeway** spanning the Strait of Johor links Singapore to Johor Bahru in Malaysia. At peak hours (6.30–9.30am and 5.30–7.30pm) and weekends, the roads leading to the causeway seethe with cars and trucks – all full of petrol, after a recent law banned Singaporeans from driving out of the country on an empty tank. Previously, people crossed into Malaysia, filled up with cut-price fuel and then headed home; now, signs line the roads approaching the causeway requesting that "Singapore cars please top up to 3/4 tank" – or risk a $500 fine.

Bus #170 from Ban San Terminal on Queen Street heads towards Wooodlands on its way to JB, passing the **Kranji War Cemetery and Memorial**, where only the sound of birds and insects breaks the silence in the immaculate grounds. This is the resting place of the Allied troops who died in the defence of Singapore; as you enter, row upon row of graves slope up the landscaped hill in front of you, some identified only as "known unto God". The graves are bare: placing flowers is banned, as still water encourages mosquitoes to breed. A simple stone cross stands over the cemetery and, above that, the **memorial**, around which are recorded the names of more than 20,000 soldiers (from Britain, Canada, Ceylon, India, Malaysia, the Netherlands, New Zealand and Singapore) who died in this region during World War II. Two unassuming **tombs** stand on the wide lawns below the cemetery, belonging to Yusof Bin Ishak and Dr Benjamin Henry Sheares, independent Singapore's first two presidents.

As well as the #170, bus #181 from New Bridge Road and #182 from Stamford Road or Orchard Boulevard all pass the cemetery; the journey takes at least 45 minutes. It's also possible to reach Kranji from the zoo: take bus #171 (make sure the number is printed on a green plate, or you'll end up in Yishun) as far as Bukit Timah Road, cross over and hop on either the #170, #181 or #182.

Eastern Singapore

Thirty years ago, **eastern Singapore** was largely rural, dotted with Malay *kampung* villages which perched on stilts over the shoreline, harbouring the odd weekend retreat owned by Europeans or monied locals. Massive **land reclamation** and development programmes have altered the region beyond recognition, wiping out all traces of the *kampungs* and throwing up huge housing projects in their place. Today, former seafront suburbs, like Bedok, are separated from the Straits of Singapore by a broad crescent of man-made land, much of which constitutes the **East Coast Park**, whose five kilometres incorporate leisure and watersports facilities, imported sand beaches and seafood restaurants. Yet despite the massive upheavals that have ruptured the communities of the east coast, parts of it, including the suburbs of **Geylang** and **Katong**, have managed to retain a strong Malay identity.

Dominating the eastern tip of the island is Changi Airport and, beyond that, **Changi Village**, in whose prison the Japanese interned Allied troops and civilians during World War II. From Changi Point, it's possible to take a boat to **Pulau Ubin**, a small island with echoes of Singapore before the developers set to work. If your schedule allows for only one trip out of downtown Singapore, Changi and its environs should definitely be on your short list.

Geylang and Katong

Malay culture has held sway in and around the adjoining suburbs of **GEYLANG** and **KATONG** since the mid-nineteenth century, when Malays and Indonesians first arrived to work in the local *copra* factory and later on its *serai*, or lemon grass, farms. Many of its shophouses, restaurants and food centres are Malay-influenced, less so the thriving trade in prostitution that carries on here, unchecked by the local authorites. **Geylang Road** itself runs east from the Kallang River and off its main stem shoot 42 lorongs, or lanes, down which are clusters of brothrels, recognisable by their exterior fairy lights. At its far eastern end, Geylang Road meets **Joo Chiat Road**, which – after the strictures of downtown Singapore – has a refreshingly laid-back and shambolic air about it. In the **Joo Chiat Complex**, at the northern end of the road, textile merchants drape their wares on any available floor and wall space, transforming the drab interior; more market than shopping centre, it's a prime destination for anyone interested in buying cheap silk, batik, rugs or muslim.

Before striking off down Joo Chiat Road, cross Changi Road, to the north, where – on **Geylang Serai** – a hawker centre and wet market provide more Malay atmosphere, from the smell of clove cigarettes that hangs in the air to the line of sarong sellers beyond the food stalls. The contrast between this authentic slice of life and the **Malay Cultural Village**, on the other side of Geylang Serai, is huge. When the village officially opened in 1990, it was meant to be a celebration of the cuisine, music, dance, arts and crafts of the Malay people, but it's died a death, having failed both to woo tourists and to rent out its replica wooden *kampung*-style shops to locals.

As you walk south down Joo Chiat Road you'll have to negotiate piles of merchandise that spill out of shophouses and onto the pavement. In particular, there's cane and wood furniture in the *Moh Huat* shop at no. 172, while *Bor Ku Tang*, at no. 437A, specializes in antique stamps, coins and banknotes. Of the buildings, none are as magnificent as the immaculate **Peranakan shophouses** on Koon Seng Road (on your left about halfway down Joo Chiat Road), where painstaking work has restored their multicoloured facades, eaves and mouldings.

To get to Joo Chiat Road, take the MRT to Paya Lebar, from where a short walk left out of the station and left again onto Geylang Road brings you to the northern end of the road and the Joo Chiat Complex. Alternatively, bus #16 from Orchard and Bras Basah roads deposits you right in the middle of Joo Chiat Road.

Changi

Bus #2 from outside the *Victoria Hotel* on Victoria Street takes about fifty minutes to reach **Changi Prison**, the infamous site of a World War II POW camp in which Allied prisoners were subjected to the harshest of treatment by their Japanese gaolers. The prison itself is still in use (drug offenders are periodically executed here), but on its north side, through the outer gates, is the hugely moving **Changi Prison Museum** (Mon–Sat 9.30am–12.30pm & 2–4.30pm; Sun 3.30–5.30pm, followed by a religious service; free), where sketches and photographs plot the Japanese invasion of Singapore and the fate of the soldiers and civilians subsequently incarcerated here and in nearby camps. Predominant are the photos by George Aspinall, which record the appalling living conditions and illnesses suffered by POWs in Malaya and Thailand during the occupation. Aspinall, then a young Australian trooper, took his photographs using a folding *Kodak 2* camera, later developing them with a stock of processing materials which he found while working on a labour gang in Singapore's docks. Novelist James Clavell was a young British artillery officer in Singapore at the time of the Japanese invasion; later he drew on his own experience of the "obscene forbidding prison" at Changi, when he wrote *King Rat*, never forgetting that in the cells of the prison camp "... the stench was nauseating. Stench from rotting bodies. Stench from a generation of confined human bodies." Elsewhere in the museum, sketches drawn by W.R.M. Haxworth of prisoners playing bridge amongst other things betray a dry sense of humour and some stiff upper lips in the face of adversity.

Beyond the museum is a replica of a simple wooden chapel, typical of those erected in Singapore's wartime prisons; its brass cross was crafted from spent ammunition casings, while the north wall carries poignant messages, penned by visiting former POWs and relatives.

On a lighter note, among the war-related books stocked in the souvenir shop is *The Happiness Box*, the first copy of which was written, illustrated and bound by POWs in Changi in 1942 as a Christmas present for children in the prison. The Japanese became suspicious of the POWs' motives when they noticed one of the book's central characters was called Winston, but it was buried in the prison grounds before the Japanese could confiscate it.

Changi Village

Journey's end for bus #2 is at the terminal at **CHANGI VILLAGE,** ten minutes further on from the prison. There's little to bring you out here, save to catch a boat from **Changi Point**, behind the bus terminal, for Pulau Ubin (see below), or to the coast of Johor in Malaysia (see "Leaving Singapore" on p.480): the left-hand jetty is for Ubin, the right-hand one for Johor.

A stroll over the footbridge to the right of the two jetties takes you to **Changi Beach**, the execution site of many thousands of Singaporean civilians by Japanese soldiers in World War II. As a beach it wins few prizes and its most pleasant aspect is its view: to your left, as you look out to sea, is Pulau Ubin; slightly to the right is the island of Tekong (a military zone), behind which you can see a hill on mainland Malaysia; while in the water in front of you are *kelongs* (large fish traps), and boats galore, from bumboats to supertankers. Changi Village Road, the village's main drag, has a smattering of good restaurants; or try the hawker centre near the bus terminal.

Pulau Ubin

PULAU UBIN, 2km offshore, gives visitors a pretty good idea of what Singapore would have been like fifty years ago. A lazy backwater tucked into the Straits of Johor, it's a great place to head for when you get tired of shops, high rises and traffic, and it's almost worth coming for the boat trip alone, made in an old oil-stained bumboat which chugs noisily across Serangoon Harbour, belching fumes all the way. Boats depart from Changi Point throughout the day from 6am onwards, leaving whenever a boat is full. The last boat back to Changi leaves no late as 10pm, if there's a demand, but plan to be at the jetty by 8.30pm at the latest, just in case. The trip takes ten minutes and costs $1 each way.

Around the island

The boats dock at a rickety old pier in **UBIN VILLAGE**, where Malay stilt houses teeter over the sludgy, mangrove beach; the main road is lined with scores of battered old mopeds, locals sit around, watching the day take its course, while chickens run free in the dirt.

The best, and most enjoyable, way to explore the dirt tracks of Ubin is by **mountain bike**: at *Universal Adventure*, on the left hand side of the road leading west from the jetty, you'll pay $5–15 for a day's rental, depending on the bike and the season (it's most expensive during school holidays). You'll be given a baffling map of the island's labyrinthine network of tracks, though it's more fun to strike off and see where you end up – Ubin is only a small island (just 7km by 2km) so you aren't going to get lost.

Ride through the village until you come to a basketball court, where a right turn takes you past raised *kampung* houses and rubber trees to the eastern side of the island. Turning left instead takes you to the centre of the island. After about five minutes you'll come to a deep, impressive quarry, from which granite was taken to build the causeway linking Singapore to Malaysia. Further north along this track is a rather incongruous **Thai Buddhist Temple**, complete with portraits of the King and Queen of Thailand and a bookcase full of Thai books. Pictures telling the story of the life of Buddha ring the inner walls of the temple, along with ones depicting various Buddhist hells – most disturbing of which is that of demons pouring molten liquid down the mouths of "those who always drink liquor". If you follow the left track out of Ubin Village for about twenty to thirty minutes, you'll come to a steep slope: a right turn at the top takes you straight to the temple, just beyond which is another quarry, where you can take a swim and cool off.

Ignoring the right turn to the temple at the top of the steep slope and continuing straight ahead leads you towards the island's best restaurant, the *Ubin Restaurant* (see p.542), though as it's a bit tricky to find you'll have to look out for a taxi taking Singaporean diners there, to discover which track to turn down.

Western Singapore

Since the government' s industrialization programme began in the late 1960s, far **western Singapore** has developed into the manufacturing heart of the state and today thousands of companies occupy units within the towns of Jurong and Tuas. Manufacturing has proven the backbone of Singapore's economic success – for example, the state presently produces more than half the world's hard disk drives. Despite this saturation, much of the western region – crafted from former swampland and wasteland – remains remarkably verdant, and perhaps surprisingly, given the industrial surroundings, several major tourist attractions are located here, including **Haw Par Villa**, as garish a theme park as you'll ever set eyes on. But the pick of the bunch is fascinating **Jurong BirdPark**, closely followed by the **Tang Dynasty City**, where huge investment has resulted in a faithful reproduction of a traditional Chinese city. Slightly further east, the **Singapore Science Centre** is packed with imaginative and informative exhibitions, and not to be missed if you've got kids to entertain.

All of these places are easily reached from the city centre, using either buses or the MRT; specific details are given where appropriate.

Haw Par Villa

As an entertaining exercise in bad taste, **Haw Par Villa** has few equals. Located 7km from downtown, at 262 Pasir Panjang Road (daily 9am–6pm; $16), it describes itself as an "aesthetically arresting . . . park which promises you the unfolding of Chinese legends and mythologies", for which read a gaudy parade of rides, shows and over a thousand grotesque statues. Previously known as Tiger Balm Gardens, the park now takes its name from its original owners, the Aw brothers, Boon Haw and Boon Par, who made a fortune early this century selling *Tiger Balm* – a cure-all unction created by their father. When the British government introduced licensing requirements for the possession of large animals, the private zoo which the brothers maintained on their estate here was closed down and replaced by statues.

The admission price is slightly on the steep side, but you could easily spend the best part of a day here if you were determined to enjoy yourself. The park features a couple of **rides**: the rather tame *Wrath of the Water Gods Flume Ride*, and the better *Tales of China* boat ride through a dragon's belly, in which a series of splendidly gory statues show you what happens to errant humans ending up in one of the ten courts of hell. But it's the hundreds of similar **statues** crammed into the park's grounds for which the park is famous. When you get tired of these, there are various theatre and film shows to take in, retelling classic Chinese tales. Of these, the *Four Seasons Theatre* is the most fun, though if you attend a show here, be prepared to have to play a role yourself. For up-to-the-minute details of showtimes, ask at the ticket counter upon arrival. Meals and snacks can be found at the *Artisan's Eating House* or the more upmarket *Watergarden's Restaurant*.

To get to Haw Par Villa, take the MRT to Buona Vista and change on to a #200 bus to Pasir Panjang Road. Bus #51 trundles down North Bridge Road on its way to the park, while the #143 can be picked up on Scotts Road.

Holland Village

A couple of kilometres north of Haw Par Villa, **Holland Village** was previously home to some of the British soldiers based in Singapore and has now developed into an expat stronghold, with a whole row of Western restaurants and shops. The **Holland Road Shopping Centre** (211 Holland Avenue) is the place to head for if you want to buy Asian art, crafts or textiles: there are shops on two levels where you can buy anything from an Indian pram to a Chinese opium pipe, while outside, cobblers, key-cutters and newsagents set up stall. The small road alongside the shopping centre is called lorong Liput, and off it shoots lorong Mambong, home to two excellent **craft shops** – *Sin Seng Huat* at no. 16 and *Sin Huat Hing* at no. 6 – both specializing in ceramic elephants, dragon pots, porcelain ware, rattan and bamboo products. **Pasar Holland**, opposite the shops, is a small, tumbledown market that stocks fruit, flowers, fish and meat, as well as housing a handful of hawker stalls.

From Buona Vista MRT, walk up Commonwealth Avenue and then turn left onto Holland Avenue. Alternatively, buses #7 and #105 from Orchard Boulevard both pass the top of Holland Avenue – ring the bell when you see the *Esso* garage.

Around Jurong Lake and beyond

Several tourist destinations are dotted around the environs of tranquil **Jurong Lake**, about 4km northwest of the new town of Clementi. You're far more likely to want to come out this way if you've got children in tow. Of all the area's attractions, only the *Tang Dynasty City* is of universal appeal.

Singapore Science Centre

At the **Singapore Science Centre** (Tues–Sun 10am–6pm, adults $2, childen under 16 50c), seven exhibition galleries hold over six hundred hands-on exhibits designed to inject interest into even the most impenetrable scientific principles. The majority of the centre's visitors are local school children, who sweep around the galleries in vast, deafening waves, frantically trying out each interactive exhibit; the exhibits include ones which allow you to experience sight through an insect's eyes, to write in Braille and to see a thermal heat reflection of yourself, amongst others. The **Omni-Theatre** (permanent *Planetarium* show $6, children $3; movie $9, children $4; ☎5603316), within the centre's grounds, has entertaining features about science, space and history shown on a huge, engulfing dome screen above the audience.

It takes ten minutes at most to reach the Science Centre on foot from Jurong East MRT: walk left out of the station, across the road, through a housing estate, and you'll see the centre opposite you.

Chinese and Japanese Gardens

The **Chinese and Japanese Gardens** (daily 9am–7pm; adults $4, children $2), situated in the middle of Jurong Lake, defy categorization – too expensive and too far out to visit for just a sit down in the park and too dull to be a fully-fledged tourist attraction.

In the **Chinese Garden** (or Yu Hwa Yuan), pagodas, pavilions, bridges and arches attempt to capture the style of Beijing's Summer Palace – and fail. If you visit at the weekend, be prepared to be confronted by hordes of newlyweds scouring the garden for a decent photo opportunity. The Chinese Garden is best explored on the day of the annual Mooncake Festival (see p.64), when children parade with their lanterns after dark.

Walking across the impressive, 65-metre *Bridge of Double Beauty* takes you to the **Japanese Garden** (or *Seiwaen*, "Garden of Tranquillity"), whose wooden bridges, carp ponds, pebble footpaths and stone lanterns do much to help you forget the awful formica chairs and tables in the central pavilion. From Chinese Garden MRT Station, northeast of Jurong Lake, follow signs to the Chinese Garden's back entrance, three or four minutes down a footpath.

A short walk left along Yuan Ching Road, from the main exit out of the Japanese Garden, takes you to the Tang Dynasty City (see below). On the way you'll pass the **CN West Leisure Park** (Tues–Fri noon–6pm, Sat & Sun 9.30am–6pm; adults $4, children $2), Singapore's largest water fun park – which can also be reached direct from the centre on bus #154 from Boon Lay MRT.

Tang Dynasty City

You needn't worry about missing the entrance to the **Tang Dynasty City** (daily 10am–10pm; adults $15, children under 12 $10) on the corner of Yuan Ching Road and jalan Ahmad Ibrahim: enclosing this $90-million complex is a ten-metre-high re-creation of the Great Wall of China, built from bricks imported from China. Indeed, practically everything inside this cultural and historical theme park is authentic, having been made by 85 Chinese craftsmen. Alongside scheduled shows involving such events as a traditional Chinese wedding ceremony or a duel between swordsmen, is everything you'd find in an eighth-century Chinese city: a bank (where the abacus is preferred to the computer), teahouse, medicine shop stacked with herbs and potions, winery, the intriguingly named *Chamber of A Thousand Pleasures* and the courthouse, with its punishment pole for administering beatings. Pictures and artefacts at the rather lame **House of Li** give an insight into Tang fashion, music and dance, while other attractions include the **Shui Lian Cave**, birthplace of the Monkey God, complete with waterfall and monkey colony; and the **Underground Palace**, in whose vaults a 1100-strong legion of stern-looking terracotta warriors silently awaits their emperor's call to battle. Based upon the famous warriors of Xian, they're a little shorter than their Chinese counterparts due to copyright laws.

It comes as no surprise that the city doubles as a **movie lot**, boasting three studios which specialize in period and kung-fu films: hopes are high that after 1997 Singapore might take over Hong Kong's mantle as the home of Oriental cinema. There's a buffet-style **café** on site but, if you can afford them, the set meals in the *Tai He Lou Theatre Restaurant* are great fun, as you are entertained by troupes of Chinese gymnasts as you eat (see p.547).

To get to the Tang Dynasty City, take bus #154 from Lakeside MRT Station.

Jurong BirdPark and Crocodile Paradise

The twenty hectares of land which comprise the **Jurong BirdPark** (daily 9am–6pm; $6, children under 12 $2.50), on jalan Ahmad Ibrahim, contain more than 5000 birds from over 450 species ranging from Antarctic penguins to New Zealand kiwis, making it one of the world's largest bird collections. To do justice to the park, which is moulded around a string of lakes, requires a lot of walking and although paths are clearly labelled, a ride on the **Panorail** (adults $2, children $1) is a good way to get your bearings. On its way around the park, the bullet-shaped monorail skims over, past or through all the main exhibits, with its running commentary pointing out the attractions.

Be sure at least to catch the **Waterfall Walk-in Aviary**, the park's newest attraction, which allows visitors to walk amongst 1200 free-flying birds in a specially created tropical rain forest, dominated by a thirty-metre-high waterfall. Other exhibits to seek out are the colourful **Southeast Asian Birds** (a tropical thunderstorm is simulated daily, at noon with the aid of sprinklers and amplifiers); the **Penguin Parade** (feeding times 10.30am and 3.30pm); and the **World of Darkness**, a fascinating exhibit which swaps day for night with the aid of a system of reversed lighting, in order that its cute collection of nocturnal residents don't snooze throughout the park's opening hours. The best of the **bird shows** is undoubtedly the *Kings of the skies* show (4pm) – a *tour de force* of speed-flying by a band of trained eagles, hawks and falcons; entrance to this, and to the similar *World of Hawks* show (10am) and *All Star BirdShow* (11am & 3pm), is free. To get to the BirdPark, take either bus #251, #253 or #255 from the bus interchange outside Boon Lay MRT station, a ten-minute ride.

Across the car park in front of the Birdpark, **Jurong Crocodile Paradise** (daily 9am–6pm; $4.50, children under 12 $2.50) houses the biggest gathering of crocodiles in Singapore. It's no paradise for the poor beasts forced to feature in the *Crocodile Wrestling and Snake Handling Show* (11.45am & 2pm), which has them pushed, pulled and sat on in the name of entertainment. Worse still is the *Dundee Show* (10.45am & 3pm) – meant to showcase "the safe handling of crocodiles" – during which a character swathed in crocodile hide and dripping with crocodile teeth proceeds to tie up a croc's mouth, legs and tail, using rope and a stick. It comes as no surprise to find that the *Seafood Paradise Restaurant*, in the main entrance building, serves the crocs up on plates.

The Tiger Brewery

Tiger Beer, now the flagship brew of the **Asia Pacific Breweries Limited**, has been brewed in Singapore since 1931, though way back then its home was the *Malayan Breweries* on Alexandra Road, where it was developed with help from *Heineken*. A few years later, the establishment of *Archipelago Brewery* by German giants *Beck's*, seemed to set the scene for a Singaporean beer war, especially when *Tiger*'s new rival, *Anchor Beer*, was priced slightly lower (a state of affairs that still exists). But in 1941 *Archipelago* was bought out by *Malayan Breweries*, since when the organization has gone from strength to strength, moving in May 1990 into new seven-hectare holdings in Tuas, and changing its name to reflect "the new international role the company has assumed", although it's still known as the Tiger Brewery in common parlance.

Today, the tiger beneath a palm tree that adorns the label on every bottle of *Tiger Beer* is advertised across the state. The original slogan for the beer was used by Anthony Burgess as the title for his debut novel, *Time for a Tiger* – in it, as the embattled, debt-ridden police-lieutenant, Nabby Adams, gulps down another beer, "...fresh blood flowed through his arteries, the electric light seemed brighter, what were a few bills anyway?".

A **tour** of the Tiger Brewery (call ☎8606483 for details) is made up of three component parts, arranged in rising order of appeal: first comes a film show which fills visitors in on the history of the setup; next, a walk through the space-age brewing, bottling and canning halls; and finally an hour or two's free drinking in the company's own bar – Nabby Adams would have approved. You need at least ten people in the party, though all is not lost if you are travelling alone – phone up and, if there's a tour already arranged, ask to tag along. To get to Tuas, take bus #192 from Boon Lay MRT Station.

Sentosa and the southern isles

Many small **isles** – hardly islands, given their size – stud the waters immediately south of Singapore. Some, like Pulau Bukom, are owned by petrochemical companies and are offlimits to tourists. Three others – **Sentosa, St John's and Kusu** – are served by ferries and can be visited without difficulty, though their accessibility has geared them very much to tourism. If you crave a more secluded spot, you'll have to charter a bumboat to one of the more remote islands from the World Trade Centre or Clifford Pier (see p.486 for details) or head for Pulau Ubin, off Singapore's east coast (p.531).

Sentosa

Given the rampant development that over the past two decades has transformed **SENTOSA** into the most developed of Singapore's southern islands, it's ironic that its name means tranquility in Malay. Sentosa has come a long way since World War II, when it was a British military base known as Pulau Blakang Mati, or the "Island of Death Behind". Today, promoted for its beaches, sports facilities, hotels and attractions, and accessed by a speeding monorail, it's a contrived, but enjoyable, experience. The island is linked to the mainland by a brand-new five-hundred-metre causeway and a necklace of cable cars.

Sentosa is big business: the financial year of 1991–92, for instance, saw 3.32 million visitors – half of whom were locals – descend upon this tiny island, which measures just 3km by 1km. Nevertheless you'll hear mixed reports of the place around Singapore. Ultimately, it's as enjoyable as you make it; there's certainly plenty to do (though few of the attractions would make the grade at Disneyland), so much so that it's a good idea to arrive early, with a clear plan of action. Taking a round trip on the trans-island monorail upon arrival helps you get your bearings. **Admission** to several attractions is included in the Sentosa entry ticket (see "Practicalities" below), though for the more popular set-piece attractions, a further charge is levied. It's wise to avoid coming at the weekend, while public holidays should be avoided at all costs.

The attractions

Two attractions outshine all others on Sentosa. At the **Underwater World** (daily 9am–9pm; $10), near monorail station 7, a moving walkway carries you the length of a hundred-metre acrylic tunnel that snakes through two large tanks: sharks lurk menacingly on all sides, huge stingrays drape themselves languidly above you, and immense shoals of gaily coloured fish dart to and fro. If this doesn't sound all that exciting, don't be fooled: the sensation of being engulfed by sea life of all descriptions is a breathtaking one and the nearest you'll get to being on the ocean floor without donning a wet suit. A **touchpool** beside the entrance allows you to pick up star fish and sea cucumbers – the latter rather like socks filled with wet sand – while beyond that is the **Marine Theatre**, screening educational films throughout the day.

The other major-league attraction is the **Pioneers of Singapore and Surrender Chambers Exhibition** (daily 9am–9pm; $3), near monorail station 5. Here, life-sized dioramas present the history and heritage of Singapore from the fourteenth century through to the surrender of the Japanese in 1945. Though some of the wax dummies look like they've been pinched from clothes shop windows, the effect is fascinating and a couple of hours will easily pass before you know it. Highlight of the exhibition is the *Surrender Chambers*, where audiovisuals, videos, dioramas and artefacts combine to recount the events of World War II in Singapore.

A trip up to **Fort Siloso** (monorail station 6), on the far western tip of the island, ties in nicely with a visit to the *Surrender Chambers*. The fort – actually a cluster of buildings and gun emplacements above a series of tunnels bored into the island – guarded Singapore's western approaches from the 1880s until 1956, but was rendered obsolete in 1942, when the Japanese moved down into Singapore from Malaysia. Today you can explore the complex's hefty gun emplacements and tunnels and during the *Sounds of Siloso* show, booming audio effects re-create the sensation of being in the tunnels during wartime.

The rest of Sentosa is crammed with less interesting options. The **Asian Village** (daily 10am–9pm; $4), next to the ferry terminal, showcases Asian life by way of restaurants, craft shops and street performances – little more than a vehicle for shifting overpriced arts, crafts and food. A planned **village theatre**, which will present Asian dances, ceremonies and rituals, may improve things. If you end up at the **Rare Stone Museum** (daily 9am–7pm; $2), you're really scraping the bottom of the barrel – you'd do better strolling in the elegant gardens of the **Orchid Fantasy**, near monorail station 1, while for something slightly more exciting head for the **Butterfly Park and Insect Kingdom Museum** (Mon–Fri 9.30am–5.30pm, Sat & Sun 9.30am–6.30pm; $4), near monorail station 5, which is stuffed with all sorts of creepy crawlies. Also worth considering is the **Coralarium and Nature Ramble** (daily 9am–7pm; $1.50), situated way out at the eastern end of the route of bus #1: a stroll here will bring you face to face with macaws, giant land crabs, peacocks and a band of long-tailed macaques who romp mischieviously around their own playground. Head for the turtle pond at 11am or 3pm, and you could help hand-feed the green and hawksbill turtles some of the twenty kilograms of cuttlefish they consume daily.

Probably the best option, though, after a trip on the monorail and a visit to one or two attractions, is to head for the three **beaches** (monorail station 4, or take buses #A or #B) on Sentosa's southwestern coast. Created with thousands of cubic metres of imported white sand and scores of coconut palms, they offer canoes, surf boards and aqua bikes for rent – as well as plain old deckchairs. The water here is great for swimming and Singapore does not demand the same modesty on its beaches as Malaysia, although topless and nude bathing are out.

By 7pm, many of Sentosa's attractions are closed, but not so the **Musical Fountain** (shows at 7.30pm, 8pm, 8.30pm & 9pm), which is either cute, twee or appalling, depending on your age or viewpoint. The fountain dances along to such classics as the *1812 Overture*, with colourful lights and lasers adding to the effect.

Practicalities

Basic **admission** to Sentosa costs $4 (children under 12 $2.50), though this doesn't include the cost of actually reaching the island.

From the **World Trade Centre** (1 Maritime Square; buses #65, #97, #125, #143 and #166), **ferries** depart every fifteen minutes from 7.30am until 10.45pm (returning 7.45am 11pm); tickets cost $5.20, including the admission fee. However, the most spectacular way there is by one of the **cable cars** (daily 8.30am–9pm) which travel on a loop between mainland Mount Faber (see p.514) and Sentosa. A one-station trip (from the WTC to Sentosa, for instance) costs $4, two stations costs $5, and for a round trip – from the WTC up to Mount Faber, across to Sentosa and back to the WTC – you pay $6.50 (children half-price); these prices do not include the admission fee.

Crossing the bridge to Sentosa costs nothing if you walk, though you still have to pay the admission fee. Two **buses** – #A and #B – run across the bridge every ten to fifteen minutes (7am–11pm; last bus back to the mainland at 11.30pm; $5, children $3, inclusive of entrance fee): service #A originates and terminates at the WTC bus terminal, while #B picks up passengers at Tiong Bahru MRT. Ask for a **Sentosa Saver** ticket ($9.50; children $5) and, as well as the return bus trip to/from the WTC, you'll get free admission to the Pioneers of Singapore and Surrender Chambers, Fort Siloso and the Coralarium and Nature Ramble. In addition, the new **Singapore Escapade**

bus service leaves from Orchard Road's *K.T. Tangs* department store every ten to fifteen minutes: the $6 ticket gets you onto the island, pays for your basic admission and the bus back to the WTC or Tiong Bahru MRT.

Sentosa's basic admission fee gives unlimited rides on Sentosa's **monorail and bus systems** – buses #1 and #2 circle the island between 9am and 7pm, while the monorail runs from 9am until 10pm. But the best way to get about is to **rent a bike** for the day ($2–5 an hour depending on the machine) from the kiosk beside the ferry terminal; tandems are fun if you're travelling in a couple.

The *Rasa Sentosa Food Centre*, beside the ferry terminal is the cheapest **eating** option; otherwise, try the nearby *Sentosa Riverboat*, on board which is the *Canton Sea Palace Restaurant,* a pizza restaurant and a burger bar. There's a *Burger King* at the ferry terminal.

Sentosa has two international-class **hotels** and limited camping possibilities (see p.492 for more details).

Kusu, St John's and other islands

Well kept and clean as they are, Sentosa's beaches do tend to get overcrowded and you may do better to head for either **ST JOHN'S** or **KUSU** islands, which are 6km south of Singapore and connected to the mainland by a **ferry** from the WTC. This reaches Kusu in thirty minutes and then continues on to St John's, arriving shortly afterwards. On weekdays and Saturdays there are only two departures **from the WTC**, at 10am and 1.30pm; departures are **from St John's** at 11.15 am and 2.45pm, and **from Kusu** at 11.45am and 3.15pm. On Sundays and public holidays, services are more frequent.

Both islands have decent sand beaches, though the most interesting of the two is Kusu, also known as Turtle Island. Singaporean legend tells of a Chinese and a Malay sailor who were once saved from drowning by a turtle which transformed itself into an island; a pool of turtles is still kept on the island. Another legend describes how an epidemic afflicting a ship moored off Kusu was banished by the God Tua Pek Kong. Whatever the truth in these tales, once a year, around October or November, tens of thousands of Singaporean pilgrims descend upon the **Chinese temple** and **Malay shrine** a few minutes' walk from the jetty on Kusu, to pray for prosperity. The island is impossibly crowded during this time, but for the rest of the year, it offers a tranquil escape from the mainland. There is a modest cafeteria on St John's, but if you're going to Kusu it's wise to take a picnic.

Other southern islands

Since no regular ferries run to any of Singapore's **other southern islands**, you'll have to **charter a bumboat** from Jardine Steps (beside the World Trade Centre) or from Clifford Pier. Boats take up to twelve passengers, and cost at least $25 to $30 an hour. Unless you rent a boat for the whole day, don't forget to arrange to be picked up at the end of the day.

LAZARUS ISLAND and attractive **SISTER'S ISLANDS**, which lie in the same cluster of isles as St John's and Kusu, are both popular snorkelling and fishing haunts, as is **PULAU HANTU** (in Malay, Ghost Island), 12km further west and under the shadow of *Shell*-owned Pulau Bukum. Most interesting of all, though, is **PULAU SEKING**, three or four kilometres east of Hantu, where a handful of Malays continue to live in traditional stilt houses that teeter over the sea, their lifestyle almost untouched by the progress that has transformed the mainland. These islands are all very basic, so take a picnic and a day's supply of bottled water with you.

Eating

Along with shopping, **eating** ranks as the Singaporean national pastime and an enormous number of food outlets cater for this obsession. However, eating out is not afforded the same reverence that it receives in the West: as often as not, you'll find yourself eating off plastic plates in bare, unpretentious restaurants that ring to the sound of agitated conversation (invariably about food); it's the food, and not the surroundings, that's important. Singapore offers new arrivals in Asia the chance to sample the whole spectrum of the region's dishes. What's more, strict government regulations ensure that food outlets are consistently hygienic – you don't need to worry about eating food cooked at a street stall.

The mass of establishments serving **Chinese** cuisine reflects the fact that Chinese residents account for around 78 percent of the population. Singapore's development into a thriving seaport in the nineteenth century attracted labourers from many different regions of China and the cuisines they brought with them still dominate the restaurant scene – you're most likely to come across Cantonese, Beijing and Szechuan restaurants, though there's not a region of China whose specialities you can't sample. **North and South Indian** cuisines give a good account of themselves too, as do restaurants serving **Malay, Indonesian, Korean, Japanese** and **Vietnamese** food. One thing you won't find, however, is a Singaporean restaurant: the closest Singapore comes to an indigenous cuisine is **Nonya**, a hybrid of Chinese and Malay food that developed following the intermarrying of nineteenth-century Chinese immigrants with Malay women (see p.54 for more details). Several specialist Chinese restaurants and a number of Indian restaurants serve **vegetarian food**, but otherwise, tread very carefully: chicken and seafood will appear in a whole host of dishes unless you make it perfectly clear that you don't want them. **Halal food** is predictably easy to find, given the number of Muslims in Singapore; and there's a **kosher** food store at the synagogue opposite the Church of Saints Peter and Paul, on Waterloo Street. Of course, if you insist, you can even eat **Western food** in Singapore – venture beyond the ubiquitous burger chains and pizza parlours, and you'll find a host of excellent restaurants cooking anything from haggis to jambalaya.

By far the cheapest and most fun place to dine in Singapore is in a **hawker centre**, where scores of stalls let you mix and match good Asian dishes at really low prices. For a few extra dollars you graduate into the realm of proper **restaurants**, ranging from no-frills, open-fronted eating houses and coffee shops to sumptuously decorated establishments – often, though not always, located in swanky hotels.

Breakfast, brunch and snacks

Guest houses sometimes include coffee or tea and toast in the price of the room but chances are you'll want to head off elsewhere for **breakfast**. Western breakfasts are available, at a price, at all bigger hotels, most famously at the *Hilton* or *Raffles*; otherwise, there are a number of cafés serving continental breakfasts, while *MacDonald's*, *Kentucky Fried Chicken* and *Burger King* all rustle up breakfasts before reverting to chicken and burgers after 11am. For a really cheap fry-up you can't beat a Western food stall in a hawker centre: here, $8 will buy you enough steak, chops and sausage to challenge even the most starving carnivore. **Local breakfasts** available in Singapore include *congee* (Chinese porridge), *dim sum* (see "Chinese: Cantonese" below), or even curry and bread.

Breakfast With An Orang Utan, Singapore Zoo, 80 Mandai Lake Rd (☎3608509). A bumper American-style spread with seasonal tropical fruits, shared with whichever orang is on duty, costs $13 (children $11). Daily 9–10am.

Breakfast With The Birds, Jurong Bird Park, jalan Ahmad Ibrahim (☎2650022). A buffet of local and Western breakfast favourites, eaten to the accompaniment of the caged songbirds hanging above you; $12 (children $10). Daily 9am–11am.

Champagne Brunch At The Hilton, *Hilton Hotel,* 581 Orchard Rd (☎7372233). Around $50 buys a superb free flow of delicacies – oysters, salmon, curry and cakes – washed down with litres of champagne and orange juice. Reservations are essential. Sun 11.30am–2.30pm only.

Delifrance, #01-23/5 Shaw Leisure Gallery, 100 Beach Rd. This stylish café is one of a chain of French delis specializing in filled croissants and pastries. Daily 8am–9pm.

Ed's Diner, #03-12 Raffles City Shopping Centre, 252 North Bridge Rd. American-style coffee shop where toast, scrambled eggs and bacon, with coffee or tea, costs around $4.

Empire Cafe, *Raffles Hotel,* 1 Beach Rd (☎3371886). The surroundings recall the erstwhile colonial coffee shops; at breakfast, songbirds in bamboo cages are placed around the cafe. Daily 7–11am.

Famous Amos, #01-05 Specialists' Shopping Centre, 277 Orchard Rd. Sublime, hand-made cookies to take away.

Mirana Cake House. Spick and span cake and gateaux chain with branches at Chinatown Point, 133 New Bridge Road and at OUB Centre, 1 Raffles Place.

Movenpick, B1-01 Scotts Shopping Centre, 6 Scotts Rd (☎2358700). Continental ($11), three eggs with bacon ($9) and *birchermuesli* (a Swiss muesli concoction; $7) – pricey but filling. Sat & Sun 7–11am.

Mr Cucumber, #02-02 Clifford Centre, 24 Raffles Place (☎5340363). Sandwich bar with a wide variety of fillings, catering for the business district crowd. Sandwiches from $3 upwards. Mon–Fri 10am–6pm, Sat 11am–3pm.

New Nam Thong, 8-10A Smith Street. *Congee* served 4–9am, as well as *dim sum.*

Red Lantern Beer Garden, Basement, 60A Change Alley Aerial Plaza, Collyer Quay. The continental set breakfast in this enclosed beer garden is great value, at under $5. Daily 7–10.30am.

Sahib Restaurant, 129 Bencoolen St (next door to *Why Not Homestay*). Does a roaring trade in *roti prata* (fried bread) and curry sauce each morning.

Selera Restaurant, 15 Mackenzie Rd (☎3385687). The best curry puffs – curried meat and boiled egg folded into pastry – in Singapore. Two will fill a gap for around a dollar. Noon –11.30pm.

Suzuki Coffee House, #01-63/4 Centrepoint, 176 Orchard Rd (☎2355218). One of a chain of coffee houses serving good-value breakfast specials, fine coffees and cakes. Daily 9–11.30am.

Tenco Food Centre, Sim Lim Square, 1 Rochor Canal Rd. A short stroll from Bencoolen Street's guest houses is rewarded by a filling mixed grill (under $10), available at the Western stall on the left hand side of the food centre.

Tiffin Room, *Raffles Hotel,* 1 Beach Rd (☎3371886). Have your buffet breakfast here and you won't eat again until dinner; $25 per person. Daily 7.30–10am.

Hawker centres and food courts

Avoid the peak lunching (12.30–1.30pm) and dining (6–7pm) periods, when hungry Singaporeans funnel into their nearest hawker centre, and you should have no problems in finding a seat. Although **hawker centres** are kept scrupulously clean, they are often housed in functional buildings which tend to get extremely hot and, if you are seated next to a stall cooking fried rice or noodles, extremely smokey. As a consequence, a new breed of smaller, air-conditioned **food courts** has developed, where eating is a slightly more civilized affair. All are much smarter and brighter than traditional hawker centres, but are slighty less atmospheric. Hawker centres and food courts are open from lunchtime through to dinner time and sometimes beyond, though individual stalls may open and shut as they please.

Chinatown Complex, Smith St, at end of New Bridge Rd, Chinatown. A huge range of dishes with a predictably Chinese bias.

Cuppage Centre, 55 Cuppage Rd. The best hawker centre in the Orchard Road area; look out for stall 363, where *la mien* (pulled noodles) are made by hand.

Empress Place Centre, north bank, Singapore River. Spacious and central outdoor hawker centre.

NOODLE KNOWHOW

The business of buying noodles in a hawker centre is fraught with obstacles. "You wan' wet one? Dry one?" roughly translates from the Singlish as "do you want your noodles in a soup, or do you want them dry, with the soup in a separate bowl?" To this, you reply either "wet one" or "dry one", but before you reach this advanced stage, there's the problem of which noodles to plump for.

Bee hoon: extremely thin noodles, like vermicelli; *mee fun* is similar.

Kway teow: flat noodles akin to Italian tagliatelle; *hor fun* is similar.

La mien: "pulled noodles", made by spinning dough skipping-rope-style in the air.

Mee: round yellow noodles that look like spaghetti, and are made from wheat flour.

Mee suah: noodles served dry and crispy.

Festival Market, 18 Raffles Quay, Financial District. The smartest hawker stalls in Singapore. At lunch time the place is extremely busy, but it stays open deep into the night.

Geylang Serai food centre, Geylang Serai. In the heart of Singapore's Malay quarter, with a corresponding range of stalls. Turn left out of Paya Lebar MRT and left again onto Sims Avenue; the centre is five minutes' walk along, on your right.

Hill Street Centre, 64 Hill St, Colonial District. A number of fine Chinese and Indian stalls on two floors. On the far right hand side as you enter is a stall serving excellent *popiah* (spring rolls stuffed with bamboo shoots, beansprouts, prawns, and hot chilli paste).

Newton Circus Hawker Centre, north end of Scotts Rd, a short walk from Newton MRT, Orchard Road district. Prices are a little higher than other centres because it's on the mainstream tourist trail, but it has the advantage of staying open until late. Noted for its seafood stalls.

Orchard Emerald Food Court, Basement, Orchard Emerald, 218 Orchard Road. Smart food court, bang in the centre of Orchard Road, where the Indonesian buffet is great value.

People's Park Complex Hawker Centre, Eu Tong Sen St, Chinatown. Lots of good stalls selling tasty Chinese specialities.

Queen Street Hawker Centre, Block 270, Queen St, across the road from Bugis Village, Colonial District. A rough and ready centre with many Indian stalls.

Satay Club, Esplanade Park, Colonial District. A Singapore institution not to be missed, serving inexpensive chicken and mutton satay. Open evenings only, from around 7pm.

Taman Serasi, junction of Napier Rd and Cluny Rd, Orchard Road district. Opposite the main entrance to the Botanical Gardens, the speciality here is *roti john*.

Tenco Food Centre, 1 Rochor Canal Rd, Colonial District. Convenient if you are staying on Bencoolen Street, it's under the Sim Lim Square building.

Tropic Makan Place, Beach Centre, 15 Beach Road, Colonial District. Modest food court, that's handy for guest house land.

Zhujiao Hawker Centre, corner of Bukit Timah Rd and Serangoon Rd, Little India. The bulk of its stalls, naturally enough, serve Indian food.

Restaurants and cafés

Below is a representative selection of the thousands of **restaurants and cafés** that span Singapore, with the **cuisines** listed alphabetically; note that the direction "off Orchard Road" means you'll find the restaurant in the area of Orchard Road (not necessarily just off the road). **Meal prices**, where quoted, are fairly arbitrary – even in the most extravagant restaurant in Singapore it's possible to snack on fried rice and a soft drink. Equally, a delicacy such as shark's fin or bird's nest soup will send a bill soaring, no matter how unpretentious the restaurant. Individual **opening hours** are given below, daily unless otherwise specified. If possible, try to book ahead at more upmarket restaurants, particularly on Saturday nights and Sunday lunch times, when they are at their busiest; moreover, bear in mind that many restaurants close over Chinese New Year, and those that don't are often bursting at the seams. There aren't too many establishments that enforce a dress code, though it's always best to dress up a little if you're heading for a hotel restaurant.

Chinese

The majority of the Chinese restaurants in Singapore are Cantonese, ie from the province of Canton in southern China, though you'll also come across northern Beijing (or Peking) and western Szechuan cuisines, as well as the Hokkien specialities of the southeastern province of Fukien; and Teochew dishes from the area east of Canton. Whatever the region, it's undoubtedly the real thing – Chinese food as eaten by the Chinese – which means it won't always sound particularly appealing to foreigners: the Chinese eat all parts of an animal, from its lips to its undercarriage, and it's important to retain a sense of adventure when exploring menus. The other thing to note is that in many Cantonese restaurants (and in other regional restaurants, too), lunch consists of **dim sum** – steamed and fried dumplings served in little bamboo baskets.

CANTONESE

Bugis Village. Touts at the several seafood restaurants here hassle you incessantly to take a seat and a menu. The furious competition ensures prices are reasonable, despite the high proportion of tourists; all restaurants work from similar, mainstream menus. Open 5pm–3am.

Choon Seng Restaurant, 892 Ponggol Rd, Northern Singapore (☎2883472). Well regarded, particularly for its superb chilli crab and the prawn pancakes; $40 feeds two. Open noon–11pm.

Ever Happy Seafood Restaurant, 2 Lorong 25, Geylang Rd, Eastern Singapore (☎7421493). The outdoor terrace makes this a popular local spot. Seafood is recommended, as is the extensive claypot menu; *dim sum* is available day and night. Open 11am–3am.

Fatty's Wing Seong Restaurant, #01-33 Albert Complex, Albert St, Colonial District (☎3381087). A Singapore institution, where every dish on the wide Cantonese menu is well cooked and speedily delivered. Around $20 a head. Open noon–11pm.

Hai Tien Lo, 37th Floor, *Pan Pacific Hotel*, 7 Raffles Blvd, Marina Sq, Colonial District (☎3368111). If you have money enough for just one blowout, come here for exquisitely presented food and stunning views of downtown Singapore. Extravagant set meals are available, while Sunday lunchtimes are set aside for *dim sum* (10.30am–2.30pm). Open noon–2.30pm & 6.30–10.30pm.

Hillman Restaurant, #01-159, Block 1 Cantonment Rd, Chinatown (☎2215073). Extremely popular, thanks to its rich-tasting earthen pot dishes of flavoursome stews featuring various meats and seafood in a rich sauce; small pots (around $10) fill two. Open 11.30am–2.30pm & 5.30–10.30pm.

Mitzi's, 24–26 Murray Terrace, Chinatown (☎2220929). The cracking Cantonese food in this simple place, situated in a row of restaurants known as "Food Alley", draws crowds, so be prepared to wait in line. Two can eat for $30, drinks extra. Open 11am–3pm & 6–10pm.

Mouth Restaurant, #02-01 Chinatown Point, 133 New Bridge Rd, Chinatown (☎5344233). Beside a popular *dim sum* menu, this jam-packed restaurant offers classy Hong Kong new-wave Cantonese food, at under $20 a head. Open 11am–4am (*dim sum* 11.30am–5pm).

New Nam Thong, 8–10A Smith St, Chinatown (☎2232817). Characterful teahouse in the heart of Chinatown serving early morning *dim sum* delights (all under $3) before reverting to a lunchtime menu. Open 4–9am for *dim sum*, 9am–2.30pm for lunch.

Ponggol Restaurant, 896 Ponggol Rd, Northern Singapore (☎2825516). Superior seafood in a seaside setting. $22 feeds two; try the chilli, pepper or steamed crab. Open 11.30am–midnight.

Tai Tong Hoi Kee, 2–3 Mosque St, Chinatown (☎2233484). Classic teahouse where slow-moving old waiters serve 20 varieties of *dim sum*. Open 4–9am.

Tekong Seafood, #01-2100 Block 6, Changi Village, Chinatown (☎5457044). No longer on Tekong, but still cooking outstanding seafood. Open 11am–1am.

Tung Lok Shark's Fin Restaurant, #04-07/9 Liang Court, 177 River Valley Rd, Colonial District (☎3366022). The 12 types of shark's fin dishes (from $20 per person) inevitably constitute the highlight of this lavish restaurant. Meals up to $50 a head. Open 11.30am–3pm & 6.30–11pm.

Ubin Seafood, 2161 Pulau Ubin (☎5458202). One of the finest seafood restaurants in Singapore – and with a great view of Johor. Take bus #2 from Victoria St to Changi Village, and hop on a bumboat to Pulau Ubin. Then catch a taxi or rent a bike (see p.531). Open 11.30am–9pm.

Union Farm Eating House, 435A Clementi Rd, Western Singapore (☎4662776). Until 30 years ago, this used to be a poultry farm, and palms and bamboos still surround the restaurant. The house special, *Chee Pow Kai* (marinated chicken wrapped in greaseproof paper and deep fried – $14 buys enough for two), is messy and wonderful. From Clementi MRT take bus #154 and get off when you see *Maju* army camp. Open 11.30am–8.30pm.

BEIJING

Pine Court Restaurant, 35th floor, *Mandarin Hotel*, 333 Orchard Rd (☎7374411). Three elegant pine trees dominate this beautiful restaurant, where the speciality is whole Peking duck ($70) – enough for three hungry people. Cheaper set meals are available, too. You'll need to reserve in advance. Open noon–2.30pm & 7–10.30pm.

Prima Orchard Restaurant, #B1-00 *Holiday Inn Park View*, 11 Cavenagh Rd, Orchard Road district (☎7362133). Beijing food of a dependably high quality for $25 a head, before drinks; *fish afire in hot pond* (steamed fish in vinegar and pepper soup) and *white cloud over teeming sea* (shredded scallops with fish and egg white) are two of the more exotically named dishes on the menu. Open 11.30am–3pm & 6.30–11pm.

Prima Tower Revolving Restaurant, 201 Keppel Rd, Chinatown (☎2728822). Fine duck dishes and a great view are the two highlights here. Take bus #97 from Bencoolen Street or Tanjong Pagar MRT. Open 11am–3pm & 6.30–11pm.

HAINANESE

5 Star Hainanese Chicken Rice Restaurant, 224 East Coast Rd, Katong (☎4402901). Chicken rice is one of the more appealing options on a menu featuring Hainanese favourites like boneless chicken's feet and pig's intestines. Meals come in at under $10 a head. Open 5pm–1am.

Swee Kee, 51–53 Middle Rd, Colonial District (☎3385551). Venerable coffee-shop-style restaurant where the succulent Hainanese chicken rice ($3.50) is the best in Singapore. Open 10am–9.30pm.

Yet Con Chicken Rice Restaurant, 25 Purvis St, Colonial District (☎3376819). Cheap and cheerful, old-time restaurant: try "crunchy, crispy" roast pork with pickled cabbage and radish, or $10 buys chicken rice, washed down with barley water, for two people. Open 10.30am–9.30pm.

HOKKIEN

Beng Hiang Restaurant, 20 Murray St, Chinatown (☎2216695). The Hokkien chef relies heavily upon robust soups and sauces, though his most popular dish is a superbly cooked fried *mee*; the lack of a menu makes ordering distinctly tricky, but persistence is rewarded by well-cooked food at good-value prices – you can eat for under $15. Open 11.30am–2pm & 6–9pm.

Beng Thin Hoon Kee Restaurant, #05-02 OCBC Centre, 65 Chulia St, Financial District (☎5332818). Hidden inside the *OCBC* carpark, this minty green restaurant is very popular at lunchtime with city slickers from the nearby business district. Big portions make it a good and filling introduction to Hokkien cuisine. Open 11.30am–3pm & 6–10pm.

Prince Room Restaurant, #03-285 Selegie Complex, 257 Selegie Rd (☎3377141). Big, ugly restaurant improved by lanterns and a dividing screen. The steamboat set meal ($9 lunch, $11 dinner) offers vast scope for overeating; note, though, that if you take too much, you're charged $10 for every 100 grams you leave! Open 11am–2.30pm & 6–10pm.

SZECHUAN AND HUNANESE

Cherry Garden Restaurant, *The Oriental*, 5 Raffles Ave, Marina Sq, Colonial District (☎3380066 ext 3538). Elegant restaurant, designed to resemble a Chinese courtyard, and serving tasty Szechuan and Hunanese dishes. Hunanese honey glazed ham is delectable, as is the Szechuan house speciality, camphor-smoked duck and bean curd crust (both under $30); the set lunch costs $44 a head. Open noon–2.30pm & 6.30–10.30pm.

Long Jiang Restaurant, *Crown Prince Hotel*, 270 Orchard Rd (☎7321111 ext 1700). The daily buffet lunch here is an excellent initiation to Szechuan cuisine ($22 a head, weekends $26). Open 11.30am–2.30pm & 6.30–10.30pm.

Min Jiang Restaurant, *Goodwood Park Hotel*, 22 Scotts Rd, off Orchard Rd (☎7375337). This restaurant's reputation for fine Szechuan classics – like camphor and tea-smoked duck – makes reservations a good idea. A meal for two costs around $60. Open noon–2.30pm & 6.30–10.30pm.

Spice Garden Restaurant, #03-100 *Hotel Meridien* Shopping Centre, 100 Orchard Rd (☎7324122). The classic Hunanese dish, steamed minced pigeon in bamboo tube, is a highlight of the menu here; reasonable set lunches and dinners are also available. Open 11.30am–3pm & 6.30–11pm.

Taikan-En Chinese Restaurant, *Hotel New Otani*, 177A River Valley Rd (☎3383333 ext 8690). A tiny replica of a Chinese teahouse is the centrepiece of the dining room; most dishes cost under $15. Open 11.30am–2.30pm & 6.30–10.30pm.

TEOCHEW

Ban Seng Restaurant, 79 New Bridge Rd, Chinatown (☎5331471). Dishes served here are still cooked using traditional charcoal ovens: try the steamed crayfish, braised goose or stuffed sea cucumber; mid-priced. Open 12–2.30pm & 6–10pm.

Chin Wah Lin Restaurant, 49 Mosque St, Chinatown. No-frills, open-fronted restaurant where you point to what you want from the display of inexpensive Teochew dishes. The squares of red, jellyish substance you can see in trays are solidified pig's blood, long favoured by old men for its invigorating qualities. Open 7am–9pm.

Liang Kee Restaurant, #02-406, Block 2, Tew Chew St, Chinatown (☎5341029). Unpretentious, popular local restaurant that thwarts tourists with its lack of any written clues as to the food on offer. Good quality, though. Open noon–2.30pm & 6–9.30pm; closed Wed.

OTHER SPECIALITY RESTAURANTS

Imperial Herbal Restaurant, 3rd floor, *Metropole Hotel*, 41 Seah St, Colonial District (☎3370491 ext 212). The place to go if you are concerned about your Yin and Yang balance: after checking your pulse and tongue, a resident Chinese physician recommends either a cooling or a "heaty" dish from the menu. For migraine sufferers the drunken scorpions are, by all accounts, a must; rheumatics should opt for crispy black ants. Open 11.30am–2.30pm & 6.30–10.30pm.

Moi Kong Hakka Restaurant, 22 Murray St, Chinatown (☎2217758). Hakka food relies heavily on salted and preserved ingredients and dishes here, in the best Hakka food outlet in Singapore, encompass abacus yam starch beads ($6) and stewed pork belly with preserved vegetables. Open 10.30am–2.30pm & 6–10pm.

Mosque Street Taiwanese Style Steamboat House, 44 Mosque St, Chinatown (☎2229560). Take a seat at the food bar, on which 60 individual woks are set on built-in heaters, purchase your steamboat ingredients ($6 per person) – noodles, egg, prawns, pork, fish – and get cooking. Great late-night fun. Open 6pm–5am.

Siong Lee Turtle Soup, 47 Craig Rd, Chinatown (☎2278735). Turtle meat can apparently cure "bone steaming, hectic fever and debility", while the shell combats hepatitis and prolapse of the rectum – you can hardly afford to miss out. Dishes $7–30. Open Mon–Sat 11am–3pm & 6–10pm.

Snackworld, #01-12/13 Cuppage Plaza, 5 Koek Rd, off Orchard Rd. Hectic terrace restaurant where the Chinese menu is enlivened by hotplate crocodile meat ($25). Open 11am–midnight.

Top Flight Mongolian BBQ, #04-01 Park Mall, 9 Penang Rd, off Orchard Rd (☎3344888). Create your own combination from an array of meats, vegetables and sauces, hand it in at the open kitchen, where it's cooked for you on a hot griddle. Unlimited visits to the food bar cost under $20 (lunchtime) and $25 (dinner), and include starters, and desserts. Open 11.30am–2.30pm & 6–11pm.

VEGETARIAN CHINESE

Fut Sai Kai Restaurant, 147 Kitchener Rd, Little India (☎2980336). Old-fashioned Cantonese restaurant with a strongly Oriental atmosphere and fiery red decor; $20 is sufficient for two. Bean curd forms the backbone of Chinese vegetarian cooking, though, oddly, it reaches your table shaped to resemble meat or fish. Open Tues–Sun 10am–9pm.

Happy Realm Vegetarian Food Centre, #03-16 Pearls Centre, 100 Eu Tong Sen St, Chinatown (☎2226141). "The way to good health and a sound mind", boasts the restaurant's card; tasty and reasonably priced vegetarian dishes. Open 11am–8.30pm.

Hong Kong Bodhi Vegetarian Restaurant, #03-140 Marina Sq, 6 Raffles Blvd, Colonial District (☎3370703). Singapore branch of a famous Hong Kong chain, and a safe bet for reliable vegetarian Cantonese food at around $10 a dish. Open 11.30am–10pm.

Lingzhi Restaurant, #B1-17/18 Orchard Towers, 400 Orchard Rd (☎7343788). A real treat, where skewers of vegetables served with satay sauce are the highlight of an imaginative menu; there's also a takeaway counter. Open 11.30am–10pm.

European

Compass Rose Restaurant, 69th Floor, *Westin Stamford Hotel*, 2 Stamford Rd, Colonial Disdtrict (☎3388585). An expensive place, but one that boasts a panoramic view of central Singapore. Buffet lunch ($45) is the cheapest way to experience the international cuisine. Open noon–2.30pm & 7–10.30pm.

Duxton Deli and Wine Bar, 21 Duxton Hill, Chinatown (☎2277716). Pleasant wine bar on fashionable Duxton Hill where a sandwich or snack outside on the terrace will cost you less than $10. Open Mon–Sat 10am–midnight.

Fiesta Wine Bar, 18 lorong Mambong, Holland Village (☎4624510). Airy, Spanish-influenced place stocking wines at up to $200 a bottle, and serving *tapas*; Happy Hour 3–7pm. Open noon–midnight.

The Good Life, 36 Boat Quay (☎5330534). Singapore's only macrobiotic restaurant, and the only joint in town with a house magazine; choose from pastas, soups and salads, or opt for the set menus – good value at $15. Open Mon–Sat noon–3.30pm & 6–11pm.

Gordon Grill, *Goodwood Park Hotel*, 22 Scotts Rd, off Orchard Rd (☎2358637). Upmarket restaurant lent a Scottish feel by the tartan decor and the haggis with tatties: excellent food – but at a price. Set lunch ($37) is your best bet; the set dinner is a mighty $85. Open noon–3pm & 7–11pm.

Maxim's de Paris, The *Regent Hotel*, 1 Cuscaden Rd, off Orchard Rd (☎7338888). Stunning cuisine in a classic French dining room – one for a celebration. Open Mon–Fri 12.30–2.30pm & daily 6.30–10.30pm.

Movenpick, B1-01 Scotts Shopping Centre, 6 Scotts Rd, off Orchard Rd (☎2358700). Swiss specialities and good value set meals. The prime roast set lunch ($20) is a real filler. Open 11am–midnight.

Opera Cafe, 40 Boat Quay, Singapore River (☎5381870). Lunch (11am–3pm; around $15) eaten to the strains of opera, overlooking the river. Otherwise open daily 11am–1am for coffee and cakes.

HIGH TEA AND TIFFIN

Many of Singapore's swisher hotels advertise that most colonial of traditions, **high tea** in the local press; below are a few of the more permanent choices. Typically, a Singapore high tea comprises local and Western snacks, both sweet and savoury. If you really want to play the part of a Victorian settler, Singapore's most splendid food outlet at the *Raffles* still serves **Tiffin** – the colonial term for a light curry meal (derived from the Hindi word for luncheon).

Café Vienna, *Royal Holiday Inn Crowne Plaza*, 25 Scotts Rd (☎7377966). Tremendously popular among Singaporeans, so get here early and wait in line to avoid disappointment. Open Mon–Fri 3–5.30pm, Sat & Sun 3–6pm.

Fosters, #02-38 Specialists' Shopping Centre, 277 Orchard Rd (☎7378939). Devonshire teas ($10) served from 3–6pm.

Hilton Lounge, *Hilton Hotel*, 581 Orchard Rd (☎7372233). Afternoon tea at the *Hilton* is taken to the accompaniment of live musicians. The price ($15.50) increases by a couple of dollars at the weekend. Open 3–6pm.

Minton, #02-42 The Paragon, 290 Orchard Rd (☎7383368). Your $15 buys high tea in a room with a view onto frenetic Orchard Road. Daily 2.30–5.30pm.

Tiffin Room, *Raffles Hotel*, 1 Beach Rd (☎3371886). Tiffin lunch (noon–2pm) and dinner (7–10pm) both cost over $30 per person, though the spread of edibles, and the charming colonial surroundings make them worth considering. Between tiffin sittings, high tea ($21) is served, from 3.30–5pm.

Upstairs Cafe, Tudor Court, 131 Tanglin Rd (☎7336586). High tea is good value at $9, though the music from the clothes shops down the corridor is intrusive. Open 11am–7pm.

Pasta Fresca, 30 Boat Quay, Singapore River (☎5326283). Match up fresh pasta and a sauce from the menu, and sit out on the riverside terrace. Around $20 a head, drinks extra. Open 11am–10pm.

Pronto, 5th Floor, *Oriental Hotel*, 5 Raffles Ave, Colonial District (☎3380066). Affordable open-air restaurant beside the *Oriental*'s fifth-floor pool; pastas and pizzas cost around $15, meat dishes slightly more, and leave room for the delicious *tiramisu*. Open noon–10pm.

Ristorante Bologna, 4th Floor, *Marina Mandarin Hotel*, 6 Raffles Blvd, Colonial District (☎3383388). Award-winning restaurant with da Vinci prints on the walls and musicians to serenade you. Meals are fairly steeply priced – dishes average out at $40 – but the buffet lunch (noon–2.30pm; closed Sat) will fill you up for $36. Open noon–2.30pm & 7pm–midnight.

Rosette Restaurant, SHATEC, 24 Nassim Hill, off Orchard Rd (☎2359533). The *Singapore Hotel Association Training & Educational Centre* runs this place, the deal being that customers get good, fair priced Continental food in return for being part of the training procedure. Set lunches start from $13, and on Friday nights a five-course meal with wine costs $47. Open noon–3pm & 7–10pm.

Victorian Cafe, Victoria Memorial Hall, Empress Place, Colonial District (☎3397231). The marble tables and dark wood fittings in this tasteful café are offset by bare white walls. Pasta, pizzas, soup and sandwiches, all available at less than $8. Open Mon–Sat 11.30am-6.30pm.

Indian and Burmese

Annalakshmi Restaurant, *Excelsior Hotel* & Shopping Centre, 5 Coleman St, Colonial District (☎3399993). Terrific North and South Indian vegetarian food in sumptuous surroundings, with all profits going to *Kala Mandhir*, an Indian cultural association next door. Many of the staff are volunteers from the Hindu community, so your waiter might just be a doctor or a lawyer. Meals from $10 a dish. Open 11.30am–3pm & 6–9.30pm.

Burmese Cuisine, Block 3, #01-16, New Bugis St (☎3347251). House speciality, *Mo Hin Ga* (*kway teow* with fish and banana skin) is said to be good for stomach cancer. The set dinner with five dishes ($6) is good value; the pickle tea salad is intriguing. Open Tues–Sun noon–10pm.

Islamic Restaurant, 791–797 North Bridge Rd, Arab Quarter (☎2987563). Aged Muslim restaurant boasting the best chicken biriyani in Singapore, and manned by a gang of old men who plod solemnly up and down between the tables; $10 for two. Open 10.30am–9pm; closed Fri.

Kalai Restaurant, 34–36 Race Course Rd, Little India (☎2948576). Far more basic than its neighbours on Race Course Road, this hole-in-the-wall joint offers superb value for money: $3 buys a meat curry on a replenishable mountain of rice and vegetables. Open 6am–10pm.

Kinara, Boat Quay, Singapore River (☎5330412). Exquisite restaurant boasting antique fittings imported from the subcontinent; a marvellous view of the river from upstairs, and elegantly presented Punjabi dishes. Around $50 for two. Open noon–2.30pm & 6.30–10.30pm.

Komala Vilas, 76–78 Serangoon Rd, Little India (☎2936980). A cramped, popular vegetarian establishment specializing in 15 varieties of *dosai*. The "South Indian Meal", served upstairs on a banana leaf, is great value at $4.50. Open 7am–10pm.

Madras New Woodlands Restaurant, 12–14 Upper Dickson Rd, Little India (☎2971594). Functional, canteen-style place serving up decent vegetarian food at bargain prices. House specialities are the Thali set meal ($4) and the VIP Thali ($6); samosas, bahjis and other snacks are available after 3pm, and there's a big selection of sweets, too. Recommended. Open 8am–11pm.

Maharani, #05-36 Far East Plaza, Scotts Rd, Orchard Road district (☎2358840). Orchard Road's pioneering North Indian restaurant grades each dish's "heatiness" from 1- to 3-star. Around $25 a head, with beer. Open noon–10.30pm

Moti Mahal Restaurant, 18 Murray St, Chinatown (☎2214338). Not cheap, but one of Singapore's very best, serving tasty tandoori dishes in pleasant surroundings. The special is *murg massalam*, a whole chicken stuffed with rice ($50 – order in advance). Open 11am–3pm & 6.30–10.30pm.

Muthu's Curry Restaurant, 76/78 Race Course Rd, Little India (☎2932389). Rough and ready South Indian restaurant with no menu, but famous for its fish head curry. Open 10am–10pm.

Nur Jehan Restaurant, 66 Race Course Rd, Little India (☎2928033). Prize-winning cook Gurdayal Singh used to work at the legendary Singaporean restaurant *Omar Khayyam*, so expect fine food in this rather bare, but extremely friendly North Indian restaurant. Open 11am–11.30pm.

Orchard Maharajah, 25 Cuppage Terrace, Cuppage Rd, Orchard Road district (☎7326331). Set in a wonderful old *Peranakan* house, this splendid North Indian restaurant has a large terrace and a tempting menu that includes the sublime fish *mumtaz* – fillet of fish stuffed with minced mutton, almonds, eggs, cashews and raisins – worth the extra few dollars. The set lunch is good value at $16. Open 11.30am–3pm & 6.30–11pm.

Zam Zam Restaurant, 699 North Bridge Rd, Arab Quarter (☎2987011). A simple curry house, though worth a visit to see the award-winning *murtabak* maker in action. Open 7am–11pm.

Indonesian

Alkaff Mansion, 10 Telok Blangah Green (☎2786979). Built in the 1920s as a weekend retreat for the Alkaff family, the splendidly restored mansion offers a superb *rijstaffel* ($60), ten dishes served by a line of ten women in traditional *kebayas*. Or just have a beer in the bar, worth the exorbitant price for an hour or two of colonial grandeur. Bus #145 from Redhill MRT. Open 11am–midnight.

House of Sundanese Food, 218 East Coast Rd (☎3455020); and 55 Boat Quay (☎5343775). Spicy salads and barbecued seafood characterize the cuisine of Sunda (West Java), served here in simple yet tasteful surroundings. Try the tasty *ikan Sunda* (grilled Javanese fish) – an $18 fish serves two to three people. Open Tues–Sun 11am–2.30pm & 5–10pm.

Ikobana Nasi Padang Restaurant, #01-2021 Block 5, Changi Village Rd (☎5453579). This unpretentious place serves the best *padang* – highly-spiced Sumatran cuisine – food in Singapore, at around $8 for two. Take bus #2 from outside the *Victoria Hotel* and stay on until the end of the line. Open Mon–Sat 7am–4pm.

Rumah Makan Minang, 67/68 Bussorah St, Arab Quarter (☎2944805). This restaurant's full name translates as "wait and be patient day and night", which doesn't bode well for hungry customers. Service, though, is fast and friendly: $4 ensures a good feed, while $3 buys the popular barbecued fish. Open noon–2.30pm & 6–10.30pm.

Sanur Restaurant, #04-17/18 Centrepoint, 176 Orchard Rd (☎7342192). Hearty, reasonably priced food served by waitresses in traditional batik dress; the beef rendang is terrific. It's best to book ahead. Open 11.30am–2.45pm & 5.45–10pm.

Sukmaindra Restaurant, *Royal Holiday Inn Crowne Plaza,* 25 Scotts Rd, off Orchard Road (☎7317988). Singapore's only Bruneian restaurant, with an inevitably strong Indonesian influence. Well-cooked food, and no alcohol, which keeps the price down. Open 11.30am–3pm & 6.30–11pm.

Tambuah Mas Indonesian Restaurant, #04-10, Tanglin Shopping Centre, 19 Tanglin Rd, off Orchard Road (☎7333333). Friendly restaurant, approached through a *Minangkabau*-style entrance, and offering *padang* food and a smattering of Chinese dishes. Open 11.30am–2.30pm & 6–10.30pm.

Japanese

Akasaka Sushi Restaurant, #01-04 Plaza By The Park, 51 Bras Basah Rd, Colonial District (☎3383866). Unusually bright restaurant, close to Bencoolen Street, serving relatively inexpensive Japanese food; dishes on the menu start at $11, but the set lunches are better value (Mon–Fri noon–2.30pm) and include *sushi* ($20) and *sukiyaki* ($14) sets. Open 11.30am–2.30pm & 6–11pm.

RESTAURANT ENTERTAINMENT

Hilton-British Airways Playhouse, *Hilton Hotel,* 581 Orchard Rd (☎7372233). London West End plays by playwrights in the Alan Ayckbourn mould are presented periodically; tickets are expensive (over $120 per person) but include a four-course dinner.

Mandarin Hotel, 333 Orchard Rd (☎7374411). The price – around $50 – buys you an international buffet and a viewing of the *Asean Night* cultural show, music, songs and dance from all the southeast Asian countries. Dinner at 7pm; show starts at 8pm. Book ahead.

Merlion Ballroom, *Cockpit Hotel,* 6–7 Oxley Rise, off Orchard Rd (☎7379111). The nightly *Instant Asia* show is preceded by a buffet; the package costs $38, and dinner is at 7pm. Book in advance.

Singa Inn Seafood Restaurant, 920 East Coast Parkway (☎3451111). Dinner at this well-established seafood restaurant entitles you to watch the *Asian Cultural Show,* which kicks off at 8pm, Monday to Friday. Reservations recommended.

Tai He Lou Theatre, *Tang Dynasty City,* 2 Yuan Ching Rd, Jurong Lake (☎2611116). Chinese dancers and gymnasts perform as you enjoy buffet lunch (1.15pm) or dinner (7.30pm). Prices below $30, though exclusive of the Tang Dynasty City entrance fee.

Inagiku, 3rd Floor, W*estin Plaza Hotel*, 2 Stamford Rd, Colonial District (☎3388585). More of a maze than a restaurant, with four sections serving expensive, quality *tempura, teppanyaki, sushi*, and an a la carte menu – the latter the cheapest alternative. Open Mon–Sat noon–2.30pm & 6.30–10.30pm.

Sushi Kaiseki Nogawa, 4th Floor, *Crown Prince Hotel*, 270 Orchard Rd (☎7323053). Tiny *sushi* bar down a spooky corridor, where food is served by demure waitresses in kimonos; a meal for two starts from around $60. Open noon–3pm & 5–12pm.

Sushi Koharu, #02-23 Far East Plaza, Scotts Rd, off Orchard Road (☎2357172). Typical Japanese *sushi* bar where the *sashimi* mixed set ($23 per person) and *sushi* special mix ($28) offer best value. Book ahead since this place only has a handful of seats. Open noon–3pm & 6–11pm.

Korean

Hando Korean Restaurant, #05-01 Orchard Shopping Centre, 321 Orchard Rd (☎2358451). Classic dishes taken in a cushioned, traditional Korean chamber. At least $45 for two, more if you sink a few *OB* beers. Open 11am–11pm.

Hanil Korean Restaurant, 26 Tanjong Pagar Rd, Chinatown (☎2219692). Reputable barbecue restaurant in one of Singapore's biggest boom areas; *bulgogi* (Korean barbecue) will set you back $17, while the delicious ginseng chicken soup feeds two. Open 11.30am–3pm & 5.30–10pm.

Korean Restaurant Pte Ltd, #05-35 Specialists' Centre, 277 Orchard Rd (☎2350018). Singapore's first Korean restaurant, beautifully furnished and serving up a wide range of dependably good dishes at around $16–20 per dish. Open 11am–11pm.

Seoul Garden Korean Restaurant, #03-119 Marina Sq, 6 Raffles Blvd, Colonial District (☎3391339). Entertaining, busy restaurant with set lunches from $5.50 (Mon–Fri); best value is the "all you can eat" Korean barbecue – a buffet of 20 seasoned meats, seafoods and vegetables cooked by customers at their tables. Open Mon–Fri 11am–3pm & 5.30–10.30pm, Sat & Sun 11am–10.30pm.

Malay and Nonya

Aziza's, 36 Emerald Hill Rd, off Orchard Rd (☎2351130). Stylish, intimate little place serving premier Malay food; set meals are available ($34/$68), or try the house speciality, *ayam panggang kasturi* – chicken charcoal-grilled with black shallot sauce on a banana leaf. You'll need to book ahead. Open 11.30am–3pm & 6.30–11.30pm; closed Sun 11.30am–3pm.

Bengawan Solo. Excellent cake shop, specializing in Malay *kueh* (cakes) and with branches at Centrepoint, 176 Orchard Road, and at Clifford Centre, 24 Raffles Place. Open 10am–8pm.

Bintang Timur Restaurant, #02-08/13 Far East Plaza, 14 Scotts Rd, off Orchard Road (☎2354539). A periennial favourite, thanks to its reliable cooking; sticks of satay here are bigger than usual, so don't over-order. Around $12 a head without beer. Open 11am–9.45pm.

Guan Hoe Soon, 214 Joo Chiat Rd, Katong (☎3442761). Fifty years old, and still turning out fine Nonya cuisine; try the *Chen Dool* (coconut milk, red beans, sugar, green jelly and ice), a refreshing end to a meal. Around $35 for two, with beer. Open 11am–3pm & 6–9.30pm; closed Tues.

Nonya & Baba Restaurant, 262 River Valley Rd, Colonial District (☎7341382). Greatly respected Nonya restaurant lent character by its marble tables and tasteful decor; the *Otak Otak* (fish, mashed with coconut milk and chilli paste, wrapped in banana leaf) and the *Ayam Buah Keluak* (chicken with black nuts) are both terrific; other dishes cost around $7 a head. Open 11.30am–10pm.

Oleh Sayang Restaurant, 25B Lorong Liput, Holland Village (☎4689859). Diners choose from the cheap Nonya dishes and *kueh* at a counter; mounted on the walls are interesting articles describing *Peranakan* culture and foods. Open Tues–Sun 11am–3pm & 6–10pm.

Peranakan Inn, 210 East Coast Rd (☎4406195). As much effort goes into the food as went into the renovation of this immaculate, sky-blue shophouse restaurant, which offers authentic Nonya favourites at reasonable prices; around $8 a dish. Open 11am–3pm & 6–11pm.

Spring Blossoms Cafe, *Bayview Inn*, 30 Bencoolen St, Colonial District (☎3372882 ext 281). This faceless hotel café's buffet lunch is a great introduction to Nonya cuisine, and very reasonable at around $16. Open Wed, Sat & Sun noon–2.30pm.

North and South American

Cha Cha Cha, 32 Lorong Mambong, Holland Village (☎46216509). Classic Mexican dishes in this vibrantly coloured restaurant range from $10–22; outside are a few open-air patio tables, ideal for posing with a bottle of *Dos Equis* beer, but book ahead for these. Open 11.30am–10pm.

Chico's N Charlie's, #05-01 Liat Towers, 541 Orchard Rd (☎7341753). Faithfully re-created Mexican decor and food ($11–38), as well as a good value set lunch ($15 for main course, soup, garlic bread, dessert and coffee or tea). Open 11am–11pm.

Dan Ryan's Chicago Grill, #B1-01 Tanglin Mall, 91 Tanglin Rd, off Orchard Road (☎7383800). Chug back a *Budweiser* and get stuck into "American portions" of ribs, burgers and chicken in a dining room that's crammed with Americana; main courses cost around $15. Open 11am–midnight.

Hard Rock Cafe, 50 Cuscaden Rd, off Orchard Road (☎2355232). Big-boy portions of ribs, burgers and steaks served to the ear-bending accompaniment of Guns 'n' Roses, Deep Purple et al. The delicately named pig sandwich ($14) is irresistible, or there's a three-course set lunch (Mon–Fri 11am–2pm). Open 11am–10.30pm; closed Sun.

New Orleans, 2nd Floor, *Holiday Inn Park View*, 11 Cavenagh Rd, off Orchard Road (☎7338333). Jambalaya, gumbo and fried chicken are some of the highlights of this tastefully decorated creole restaurant, where you'll eat for around $35 a head. Open Mon–Sat 7–11pm; Sun 11am–2.30pm.

Ponderosa, #02-13-19 Plaza Singapura, 68 Orchard Rd (☎3360139). The perfect cure for vitamin deficiency – chicken, steak and fish set lunches (Mon–Fri 11am–4pm) come with baked potato, sundae, and as much salad as you can eat, at a bargain $11. Open 11am–10pm.

Scoops Cafe, #01-02 HPL House, 50 Cuscaden Rd, off Orchard Rd (☎7381434). Salads, hot dogs, sandwiches and *Haagen Dazs* ice cream dominate the menu in this busy café, where cartoons are screened on the TV monitors around the room. Daily 11am–11pm.

Seah Street Deli, *Raffles Hotel*, 1 Beach Rd, Colonial District (☎3371886). New York-style deli boasting the most mountainous sandwiches in Asia, at around $10 each. Huge crayons, bagels and

BUYING YOUR OWN FOOD: MARKETS AND SUPERMARKETS

Although some guest houses do have cooking facilities, you're most likely to go to a **wet market** – so-called due to the pools of water perpetually covering the floor – for the express purpose of buying a bag of fresh fruit. If you don't know a mango from a mangosteen, vendors are usually very helpful – and see p.48. Singapore also has plenty of **supermarkets**, most of which have a delicatessen counter and bakery – some offer familiar beers from back home, too.

Markets

Along **Orchard Road**, the best place to head for is *Cuppage Market*, 2nd floor, Cuppage Centre, 55 Cuppage Rd; **Little India** is served by the large wet market in the *Zhujiao Centre* (p.515), at the southern end of Serangoon Rd; both the *Chinatown Complex* (p.512) and *Ellenborough Street* (p.514) markets in **Chinatown** reward a visit, too; and you'll find other wet markets out of the city centre, in Singapore's new towns.

Supermarkets

Cold Storage, branches at Centrepoint, Orchard Rd; 293 Holland Rd; 31 Amber Rd, Katong. Local chain which stocks a wide range of Western products.

Diamaru, Liang Court Shopping Complex, 177 River Valley Rd. Japanese department store with a large food hall featuring takeaway counters.

Good Gifts Emporium, Golden Mile Complex, 5001 Beach Rd. A smallish supermarket with a leaning towards Thai produce.

NTUC Fairprice, Rochor Centre, 1 Rochor Rd. Basic supermarket that's handy for Bencoolen Street.

Sogo, Raffles City Shopping Centre, 252 North Bridge Rd. Japanese department store where you can either buy groceries or takeaway snacks.

Tashing Emporium, People's Park Complex, 1 Park Rd. Taiwanese emporium whose food hall sells some interesting Chinese produce.

Yaohan, Plaza Singapura, 68 Orchard Rd. Japanese department store and supermarket similar to *Diamaru* and *Sogo*.

wristwatches on the walls make this the most un-colonial establishment in *Raffles Hotel*. Open 11am–10pm except Fri & Sat 11am–11pm.

Thai and Vietnamese

Cairnhill Thai Seafood Restaurant, #07-03 Cairnhill Place, 15 Cairnhill Rd, Orchard Road district (☎7380703). Classic Thai dishes cooked to a dependably high standard. Open 11.30am–11pm.

Chao Phaya, #04-01 Holland Shopping Centre, 211 Holland Ave, Holland Village (☎4668068). Besides a huge menu, this excellent restaurant with roof garden has a supermarket-style seafood display: choose a fish, then decide in which of 32 ways you want it cooked. Mid-priced. Open 11.30am–2.30pm & 6.30–10.30pm.

Cuppage Thai Food Restaurant, 49 Cuppage Terrace, off Orchard Road (☎7341116). Nondescript inside, but boasting a great outdoor terrace, this cheap and cheerful restaurant offers quality Thai dishes at around the $8 mark. Open 11am–3pm & 6–11pm.

Pare'Gu Vietnamese Seafood Restaurant, #01-24/34 Orchard Plaza, 150 Orchard Rd (☎7334211). Authentic Vietnamese food; try the hot and sour soup or, if you're in a group, a fondue ($33–90). The daily lunch buffet gets you 30 dishes for $12. Open noon–3pm & 6.30pm–3.30am.

Pornping Thai Seafood Restaurant, #01-96/98 Golden Mile Complex, 5001 Beach Rd, Arab Quarter (☎2985016). Set in a complex known locally as "Thai Village" and always full of Thais waiting to catch buses home. All the standard dishes at cheap prices – $25 buys a meal for two, washed down with *Singha* beer. Open 10am–10pm.

Sai-gon Restaurant, #04-03 Cairnhill Place, 15 Cairnhill Rd, off Orchard Road (☎2350626). A posh yet affordable place which doesn't overdo the traditional Vietnamese decor. The baked fish with meat filling is reason enough to come; a set lunch is $14 (minimum 2 persons). Open 11.45am–2.45pm & 6–10.30pm.

Shingthai Palace, 13 Purvis St, Colonial District (☎3371161). Elegant little restaurant off Beach Road serving reasonably priced Thai dishes; try the *peek kai sord sai* (chicken wings with asparagus, prawns, mushrooms and meat). Around $15–20 a head. Open 11am–3pm & 6–10.30pm.

Drinking and nightlife

Singapore has much more to offer in the way of **nightlife** than it's often given credit for. The island's burgeoning **bar and pub** scene means there is now a wide range of drinking holes to choose from, with the colonial district, Tanjong Pagar and Orchard Road areas offering particularly good pub crawl potential. With competition hotting up, more and more bars are turning to **live music** to woo punters, usually cover versions by local bands. That said, big-name groups do occasionally make forays into Southeast Asia, playing Bangkok, Kuala Lumpur and Jakarta as well as Singapore. **Clubs** also do brisk business; glitzy yet unpretentious, they feature the latest imported pop, rock and dance music, though don't expect anything like a rave scene – ecstasy isn't in the Singaporean dictionary.

Bars and pubs

With the **bars and pubs** of Singapore ranging from slick cocktail joints, through elegant colonial chambers to boozy dives, you're bound to find a place that suits you. Establishments open either in the late morning (to catch the lunchtime dining trade), or in the early evening, and usually close around midnight. On Friday and Saturday, opening hours almost invariably extend by an hour or two. Many serve snacks throughout the day, and a few offer more substantial dishes. It's possible to buy a small glass of beer in most places for around $3.50, but **prices** can be double or treble that amount, especially in the Orchard Road district. A glass of wine usually costs much the same as a beer, and spirits a dollar or two more. One way of cutting costs is to arrive in time for **Happy Hour**, when bars offer local beers and house wine either at half price, or "one for one", ie you'll get two of whatever you order, but one is held back for later.

Singaporeans adore "adult-orientated" rock **music**, and a plethora of bars pander to this, presenting nightly performances by local or Filipino covers bands. Also hugely popular is **karaoke**, which almost reaches an art form in some Singapore bars.

The Colonial District and Boat Quay

Bar and Billiards Room, *Raffles Hotel*, 1 Beach Rd. A Singapore Sling ($15), in the colonial elegance of the hotel where Ngiam Tong Boon invented it in 1915, is required drinking on a visit to Singapore. Snacks are available through the afternoon, and playing billiards costs another $15 an hour. Open 11am–1am.

Compass Rose Bar, 70th Floor, *Westin Stamford Hotel*, 2 Stamford Rd. Tasteful bar from whose floor-to-ceiling windows you can see as far as southern Malaysia. Happy Hour 5.30–8.30pm; minimum charge $15 per person after 8.30pm. Open 11am–12.30am.

Harry's Quayside, 28 Boat Quay. There's live jazz Wed–Sat in this upmarket place, and a blues jam every Sun evening. Light lunches are served and prices are lower in the early evening. Open 11am–midnight.

Somerset's Bar, Level Three, *Westin Plaza Hotel*, 2 Stamford Rd. Sterile, open-plan bar improved by top-notch live jazz. Happy Hour Mon–Fri 5–8.30pm; open 5pm–2am.

The Third Man Public House, #01-02 Capitol Building, 1 Stamford Rd. "You are now entering the British zone", claims the advert; pub games, ploughman's lunches and draught *Bass* beer confirm this. Happy Hour 5–8pm and all day Sun; open 11am–midnight.

Little India and around

Khong Lock Bar, 106 jalan Besar. Set behind saloon-style swing doors, this tiny drinking den is peopled by bleary-eyed boozers; faded old beer ads and shelves lined with dusty bottles of brutal Chinese liquers line the walls, while crushed peanut shells litter the floor. Open 10am–10pm.

Leisure Pub, #B1-01 Selegie Centre, 189 Selegie Rd. Tame but endearing, darts-orientated establishment that's ideal for a quiet chat. Happy Hour 3–8pm; open 5pm–12.30am.

Rigger's Tavern, #01-01 Parklane Shopping Mall, 35 Selegie Rd. Eagles tapes play endlessly in this inexpensive pub, named after the guys who erect the bamboo poles that constitute scaffolding in the East; a café down the corridor delivers snacks. Recommended. Open 3pm–midnight.

Taj Music Lounge, 186 Syed Alwi Rd. Swinging Indian pub, with live Hindi and Tamil bands 8pm–midnight, Happy Hour 3–8pm and pricey drinks at all other times. Open 3pm–midnight.

Orchard Road

Anywhere, #04-08/09 Tanglin Shopping Centre, 19 Tanglin Rd. *Tania*, Singapore's most famous covers band, plays nightly to a boozy roomfull of expats that's at its rowdiest on Friday nights. Happy Hour Mon–Fri 6–8pm; open Mon–Sat 6pm–2am.

Brannigan's, *Hyatt Regency Hotel*, 10-12 Scotts Rd. Popular expat haunt where cocktails smooth the way during Happy Hour (5–8pm), and house bands are usually good. Open 5pm–1am.

Downunder, #01-101 Meridien Shopping Centre, 100 Orchard Rd. Aussie beers, Aussie rum, Aussie music and, occasionally, Aussie sailors. The generous Happy Hour runs 11am – 8pm; otherwise open until midnight and not expensive.

Excalibur Pub, #B1-06 Tanglin Shopping Centre, 19 Tanglin Rd. Wonderfully cluttered and cramped British-style pub that's full of weatherbeaten expats. Open 11am–10.30pm.

Fabrice's World Music Bar, Basement, *Dynasty Hotel*, 320 Orchard Rd. Hip music and decor from around the world make this Singapore's current hotspot; expect pricey cover charges after 10pm and prohibitively expensive drinks. Happy Hour 5–8pm; open 5pm–3am.

The Ginivy, #02-11 Rear Block, Orchard Towers, 1 Claymore Drive. Good-time Country & Western bar with a decent house band. Open 8pm–3am.

Lincoln's Pub, #03-22/23 Orchard Plaza, 150 Orchard Rd. Fine, serious-drinking, Indian-run pub that lets you choose your favourite music from the large tape selection. Happy Hour (4–8pm) offers two-for-one drinks. Open 4pm–midnight except Fri & Sat 4pm–2am.

Observation Lounge, 38th Floor, *Mandarin Hotel*, 333 Orchard Rd. Swanky cocktail bar offering awesome views over downtown Singapore. Open 11am–1am except Fri & Sat 11am–2am.

Saxophone, 23 Cuppage Rd. The coolest address in town, and a magnet for the beautiful people, who relax on the terrace to the sounds of the house jazz band. Classy French food is served, but it (and the drinks) isn't cheap – start elsewhere, or catch Happy Hour (6–8pm). Open 6pm–2am.

Vincent's Lounge, #06-05 Lucky Plaza, 304 Orchard Rd. Singapore's only gay bar is a very understated little place; Vincent is happy to pass on information regarding the local gay scene. Happy Hour 5–8pm; open 5pm–midnight.

Vintage Rock Cafe, #03-18 Cuppage Plaza, 5 Koek Rd. Friendly staff and locals, great R&B music on the speakers and cheapish beer: recommended. Happy Hour 5–8pm; open 5pm–midnight.

The Wall, #06-02 Far East Plaza, 14 Scotts Rd. Formerly *Woodstock*, and a mecca for heavy metal kids who come for the house band's loud cover versions of Led Zep and Sabbath classics. Happy Hour 5–9pm; open 5pm–3am.

Why? Pub, #04-06 Far East Plaza, 14 Scotts Rd. The budget prices in this tiny, lively pub attract big drinkers. Open 2pm–midnight.

River Valley Road

Front Page Pub, 9 Mohamed Sultan Rd. Stylish pub in a beautifully decorated *Peranakan*-style building, and popular with local journalists and white-collar workers. Open 3pm–1am.

The Mitre Hotel, 145 Killiney Rd. Marvellously shabby old hotel bar, with TV and dartboard.

The Yard, 294 River Valley Rd. Busy English pub with bar snacks available and where Happy Hour is 3–8pm. Open 3pm–midnight.

Tanjong Pagar

Duxton's Chicago Bar and Grill, 6–9 Duxton Hill. Good live jazz and blues, Americana on the walls and a decent adjoining restaurant; Happy Hour (noon–8.30pm) prices last all day Sunday. Open noon–1am.

Elvis' Place, 1A Duxton Hill. Elvis-devoted pub where videos of the King are screened regularly. Open Mon–Sat 3pm–midnight.

Flag and Whistle Public House, 10 Duxton Hill. Predictable British pub, complete with *Bass* beer, bar snacks and a large union jack. Open 11am–midnight.

J.J. Mahoney Pub, 58 Duxton Rd. A popular haunt for karaoke-hungry local yuppies; the bar serves *Bass* beer and snacks throughout the night; happy hour is 11am–8pm, but doesn't include *Bass*. Open 11am–1am.

Clubs

Unlike their London and New York counterparts, Singaporean **clubs** are refreshingly naive, their customers more intent on enjoying themselves than on posing. European and American dance music dominates (though some play Cantonese pop songs, too), and many feature live bands playing cover versions of current hits and pop classics.

Clubs tend to open around 9pm, though some start earlier in the evening with a Happy Hour; a few include self-contained bars or restaurants that get going at lunch time. Most have a **cover charge**, at least on busy Friday and Saturday nights, which fluctuates between $10 and $30, depending on what day it is and what sex you are, and almost invariably entitles you to a drink or two. It's worth checking the local press to see which venues are currently in favour; a scan through *8 Days* magazine will bring you up to date. Singapore also has a plethora of extremely seedy hostess clubs, in which aged Chinese hostesses working on commission try to hassle you into buying them a drink. Extortionately expensive, these joints are to be avoided, not least because they attract a decidedly unsavoury clientele. Fortunately, they are easy to spot: even if you get beyond the heavy wooden front door flanked by brandy adverts, the pitch darkness inside gives the game away.

Boom Boom Room, #02-04, 3 New Bugis St (☎3398187). The comedy and dance on show every night is tame by old Bugis St standards, though still well attended and enjoyed by locals and tourists. Cover charge Fri and Sat only; open 8pm–1am.

KARAOKE

It's hard to avoid karaoke these days in Singapore – bars, discos, restaurant, even shopping centres are infested with *KTV* (karaoke television). Request a song from the KJ (karaoke DJ), pick up the mike, look up at the TV screen in front of you and you're away. Lounges devoted to karaoke – there are several in Cuppage Plaza and Lucky Plaza, both on Orchard Road – are prohibitively expensive, so your best bet is to scour the "Bars and Pubs" listings above for an appropriate establishment. For the true devotee, *Java Jive*, 17D Lorong Liput, Holland Village, was Singapore's pioneering karaoke bar (and thus has a lot to answer for), but it's still a good-time place which absolutely heaves at the weekend (Happy Hour 6–8pm; open 6pm–1am). Another possibility is *Singsation*, in the *Plaza Hotel*, on Beach Road, Singapore's new karaoke capital, boasting a number of theme rooms that allow you to croon 'Sailing' in outer space, or 'Everything I Do' in a log cabin.

Chinoiserie, *Hyatt Regency Hotel*, 10-12 Scotts Rd (☎7331188). Big, sleek club favoured by *Singapore Airline* girls and the beautiful people; dress casual smart. Open 9pm–3am.

D'Cockpit, *Cockpit Hotel*, 6–7 Oxley Rise (☎7373068). Stars glitter on the ceiling and prisms project rainbows onto the walls in this tacky club where cha-cha-cha and samba take precedence. Open 5pm–1am.

Fire Disco, #04-19 Orchard Plaza, 150 Orchard Rd (☎2350155). A mixed bag: downstairs is teenybopper paradise; upstairs, cult Singapore covers band Energy plays nightly. Open 8pm–3am.

Rascals, *Pan Pacific Hotel*, Marina Sq, 6 Raffles Blvd (☎3388050). Generous Happy Hours (all day Mon–Fri) apply; Sunday draws a predominantly gay crowd. Open 6pm–3am.

Subway, Basement, *Plaza Hotel*, Beach Rd (☎2980011). Claustrophobic disco based on a New York-style subway station – complete with graffiti and just as crowded; a live band plays nightly. Open Mon–Sat 6pm–2am.

Top Ten, #05-18A Orchard Towers, 400 Orchard Rd (☎7323077). This glitzy, multi-tiered disco attracts expats galore, and isn't cheap. Acts like Los Lobos and Robert Palmer have played here in the past. Open 5pm–3am.

Tornado Disco, *Hotel Phoenix*, 277 Orchard Rd (☎7378666). Sprawling venue combining disco, pub and café-bar to reasonable effect. Happy Hour is 5–8pm, there's live music every evening and a rock video juke box in the bar. Open noon–3am.

Warehouse Disco, *River View Hotel*, 382 Havelock Road (☎7329922). Low cover charges and prices draw teenybopper hordes; Happy Hour 5–8pm. Open 5pm–2am.

Zouk, 17–21 Jiak Kim Street (☎7382988). Singapore's trendiest club, fitted out to create something akin to a Mediterranean feel. Famous DJs guest occasionally. Happy Hour 8–9pm; open Mon–Sat 5pm–3am.

Live music

Singapore is too far off the European and North American tour trail to attract many big-name performers, but there are occasional visits to rally the troops. Rivalling Western music in terms of popularity in Singapore is **Canto-pop**, a bland hybrid of Cantonese lyrics and Western disco beats; Hong Kong Canto-pop superstars visit periodically, and the rapturous welcomes they receive make their shows quite an experience. No matter who else is in town, you can always catch a set of cover versions at one of Singapore's bars and clubs; main venues are picked out below.

Anywhere, #04-08/09 Tanglin Shopping Centre, 19 Tanglin Rd (☎7348233). Good-time rock music by local favourites Tania.

Brannigan's, *Hyatt Regency Hotel*, 10–12 Scotts Rd (☎7331188). Contemporary sounds by Southeast Asian bands.

Duxton's Chicago Bar & Grill, 6–9 Duxton Hill (☎2224096). Reputable jazz and blues club. It's a bar next door to the grill.

Fabrice's World Music Bar, Basement, *Dynasty Hotel*, 320 Orchard Rd (☎7388887). Resident bands – from all around the world – which change every two months.

Fire Disco, #04-19 Orchard Plaza, 150 Orchard Rd (☎2350155). Accomplished covers band Energy plays two sets nightly.

The Ginivy, #02-11 Rear Block, Orchard Towers, 1 Claymore Drive (☎7375702). Country and western sounds and a lively dance floor.

Harry's Quayside, 28 Boat Quay (☎5383029). Live jazz Wed–Sat, and a blues jam on Sun evening.

Saxophone, 23 Cuppage Rd (☎2358385). Slick jazz played on a cramped stage behind the bar.

Singapore Indoor Stadium, Stadium Rd. The usual venue for big-name bands in town; tickets are available through *Sistic* (see below).

Taj Music Lounge, 186 Syed Alwi Rd (☎2953528). Hindi and Tamil bands perform 8pm–midnight.

The Wall, #06-02 Far East Plaza, 14 Scotts Rd (☎7340982). Live heavy metal nightly.

World Trade Centre, 1 Maritime Sq (☎3212717). Hosts international acts from time to time, as well as presenting free local gigs in its amphitheatre (check press for details).

The arts and culture

Of all the performing arts, **drama** gives the best showing of all, the island's theatres staging productions that range from West End farces to contemporary productions by local writers. **Dance** – Western or Asian – is more of a rarity, and events crop up only periodically. **Asian culture** is showcased in Singapore's major venues from time to time, but tends to appear more often on the street than in the auditorium, particularly around the time of the bigger festivals. Outstripping all other forms of entertainment in terms of popularity is **film**, with up-to-the-minute Asian and Western movies all drawing big crowds every day across the island.

For **information**, pick up a copy of either the *Singapore Straits Times* (whose daily *Life!* supplement has a good "what's on" section) or *8 Days* magazine. Alternatively, phone the venue's box office – all the relevant numbers are given below. Tickets for music shows, theatre and dance are sold either at the venue itself, at *C.K. Tangs* department store or *Centrepoint* shopping centre, both on Orchard Road, or through **Sistic** (☎3485555), Singapore's central ticketing agency: there are *Sistic* outlets at Forum The Shopping Mall, 583 Orchard Road; Liang Court, 177 River Valley Road; Scotts Shopping Centre, 6 Scotts Road; Festival Market, Raffles Quay; Specialists' Shopping Centre, 277 Orchard Road; Raffles City, 252 North Bridge Road; Cold Storage World Trade Centre, 1 Maritime Square; and Singapore Indoor Stadium, Stadium Road. The cost of a ticket to a cultural performance in Singapore usually starts at around $10–15, though international acts command substantially higher prices.

Classical music

At the epicentre of the Western classical music scene in Singapore is the **Singapore Symphony Orchestra**. Performances by this 85-member, multinational orchestra take place at the Victoria Concert Hall and often feature guest soloists, conductors and choirs from around the world; occasional Chinese classical music shows are included in the programme. From time to time, ensembles from the orchestra also give **lunchtime concerts**. In addition, the Singapore Symphony Orchestra gives occasional free performances in Singapore's parks, while Sentosa Island also plays host to regular Sunday concerts – the shows themselves are free, but the usual Sentosa entry fee applies.

Singapore Broadcasting Corporation's Chinese Orchestra (☎2560401, ext 2732 for info). Performances of traditional Chinese music played on traditional instruments.

Singapore Symphony Orchestra, Victoria Concert Hall, Empress Place (☎3381230). Performances on Fri and Sat evenings throughout the year.

Cultural performances

If you walk around Singapore's streets for long enough, you're likely to come across some sort of streetside **cultural event**, most usually a *Wayang*, or Chinese opera, played out on tumbledown outdoor stages that spring up overnight next to temples and markets, or just at the side of the road. *Wayangs* are highly dramatic and stylized affairs, in which garishly made-up and costumed characters enact popular Chinese legends to the accompaniment of the crashes of cymbals and gongs. *Wayangs* take place throughout the year, but the best time to catch one is during the Festival of the Hungry Ghosts, when they are held to entertain passing spooks, or during the Festival of the Nine Emperor Gods (see p.64). The STPB may also be able to help you track down a *Wayang*, and as usual the local press is worth checking. Another fascinating traditional performance, **lion dancing**, takes to the streets during Chinese New Year, and puppet theatres appear around then, as well.

The *Kala Mandhir* cultural association, based at the *Excelsior Hotel* on Coleman Street, is dedicated to perpetuating traditional **Indian** art, music and dance. Less spontaneous displays of Asian culture can be seen at **theme parks** such as *Asian Village* on Sentosa Island (p.536), *Tang Dynasty City* (p.534) and, on certain festivals, at the *Malay Cultural Village* (p.530). Finally, there are several restaurants which offer a free **cultural dinner show** to guests (see p.547).

Film

With over fifty **cinemas** spanning the island, you should have no trouble finding a movie that appeals to you, and at a price ($4–7 per ticket) that compares favourably with Europe and America. As well as Hollywood's latest blockbusters, there's a wide range of **Chinese, Malay and Indian movies**, all with English subtitles, from which to choose. Chinese productions tend to be a raucous blend of slapstick and martial arts, while Malay and Indian movies are characterized by exuberant song and dance routines. Cinema-going is a popular pastime, so if you plan to catch a newly released film, turn up early – and take along a jumper, as air-con units seem perpetually to be on full blast. Be prepared, also, for a lot of noise during shows: Singaporeans are great ones for talking all the way through the subtitled movies. The most central cinemas are listed below, but check the local press for a full rundown of any special events or one-offs that might be taking place. The *Alliance Francaise* (4 Draycott Park; ☎7378422) screens free French movies every Tuesday (7.15pm) and Wednesday (9.15pm) and there are also regular presentations at the *British Council* (see "Listings" on p.558 for address) and *Goethe Institute* (#06-01/05 Singapore Shopping Centre, 190 Clemenceau Ave; ☎3375111). Depending on when you visit, you might coincide with the **Singapore International Film Festival**. Now an annual event, it screens over 150 films and shorts – mostly by Asian directors – over two weeks. Smaller festivals are occasionally mounted by the *Singapore Film Society*.

Capitol Theatre, 1 Stamford Rd (☎3379759). Statues of maidens on winged horses flank the screen in this marvellous old Art Deco cinema screening Western blockbusters.

Cathay Cinema, 11 Dhoby Ghaut (☎3383400). Singapore's oldest cinema, and now a multi-screen affair.

Jade Classics, 4th Floor, Shaw Leisure Gallery, 100 Beach Rd (☎2942568). Like the *Picture House*, this screens slightly more cerebral movies than most.

Kreta Ayer People's Theatre, 30A Kreta Ayer Rd (☎2223972). Expect a leaning towards Oriental films, due to its location in the heart of Chinatown.

Orchard Theatre, 8 Grange Rd (☎7376588). All the latest releases, right in the heart of Orchard Road.

The Picture House, Cathay Building, 11 Dhoby Ghaut (☎3383400). A new cinema, pricier than most, screening interesting new releases.

Theatre and the performing arts

Singapore has a modest but thriving **drama** scene, with most local productions debuting at either the *Black Box*, *Substation* or *Drama Centre*, and graduating to the *Victoria Theatre* if they are successful. Foreign companies occasionally visit and usually perform at the *Victoria* or *Kallang* theatres. Performances of **dance** crop up from time to time – most notably by the *Singapore Dance Theatre*, which performs periodically at various venues.

Singapore's two-yearly **Festival of the Arts** attracts class acts from all over the world. The next festival will be held in 1996; a schedule of events is published a month before the festival begins so, unless you are in Singapore for quite a while, you'll probably have trouble getting tickets for the more popular events. Still, an accompanying **fringe festival** takes place concurrently, and its programme always includes free, street and park performances.

The Black Box, Fort Canning Centre, Cox Terrace, Fort Canning Park (☎3384077). Local productions by the *Theatreworks Company*.

Boom Boom Room, #02-04, 3 New Bugis St (☎3398187). Stand-up comedy hasn't really taken off in Singapore, though the *Boom Boom Room*'s vaguely saucy revue, featuring a camp Malay comedian whose jokes are delivered in broad Singlish (Singaporean English), is worth checking out.

Drama Centre, Canning Rise (☎3360005). Drama by local companies.

Hilton-British Airways Playhouse, Hilton Hotel, 581 Orchard Rd (☎7372233). Light comedy from London's West End.

Kallang Theatre, Stadium Walk (☎4403970). Hosts visiting companies such as the Bolshoi Ballet.

The Substation, 45 Armenian St (☎3377800). Self-styled "home for the arts" with multipurpose hall that presents drama and dance, as well as art, sculpture and photography exhibitions in its gallery.

Victoria Theatre, 9 Empress Place (☎3377490). Visiting performers and successful local performances.

Shopping

For many stopover visitors, Singapore is synonymous with **shopping**, though contrary to popular belief prices are not rock bottom across the board due to the consistently strong Singaporean dollar and a rising cost of living. Good deals can be found on watches, cameras, electrical and computer equipment, and antiques, but many other articles offer no substantial saving. The STPB's excellent *Singapore Shopping* booklet details exhaustively what you can buy and where; tucked inside, is a full list of the shops which qualify for the STPB's "Good Retailers Scheme", chosen for their courteousness and reliability, these shops all display a red-and-white merlion symbol in their windows. If you have any problems, contact *CASE* (Consumer Association of Singapore) on ☎2705433; alternatively you can go to Singapore's **Small Claims Tribunal** on Upper Cross Street (☎5352692), which has a fast-track system for dealing with tourists' complaints; having a case heard costs $10.

For clothes (either by Western or local designers – latter are far more reasonably priced), tailor-made suits, sports equipement, electronic goods or antiques, the shopping malls of **Orchard Road** will have all you could possibly want; some of the quirkier shopping centres are listed on p.521. At **Arab Street** (p.519), you'll find exquisite textiles and batiks, robust basketware and some good deals on jewellery, as well as more unusual muslim items. From here, make a beeline for **Little India** (p.515), where the silk stores and goldsmiths spoil you for choice; en route you'll pass the intersection of **Bencoolen Street and Rochor Road**, where a gaggle of shopping centres stocks electrical goods galore. As well as its souvenir shops, **Chinatown** boasts some more traditional outlets stocking Chinese foodstuffs, medicines, instruments and porcelain – Chinatown's shopping highlights are listed on p.513. For souvenirs, head for the

Singapore Handicraft Centre in New Bridge Road (see below) or for the recently reno-vated Tanjong Pagar zone (p.510) whose restored shophouses feature Oriental goods a cut above the normal tourist tat. As well as the various shops and outlets picked out in the text, check out any of the following as you travel around Singapore. Usual **shopping hours** are daily 10am–7pm, though shopping centres, especially along Orchard Road, stay open until 10pm. The only exception to this is the Christian-owned *C. K. Tang's*, which closes on Sunday

Antiques: *Antiques of the Orient*, #02-40 Tanglin Shopping Centre, 19 Tanglin Rd (☎7349351), specialists in antiquarian books, maps and prints; *Babazar*, 31A–35A Cuppage Terrace (☎2357866); *Bor Ku Tang*, 437A Joo Chiat Rd (☎3451751), for old coins, notes and stamps; *E & E Antique Co*, #03-02 Holland Rd Shopping Centre, 211 Holland Ave (☎4682621).

Buddhist-related goods: *Nanyang Buddhist Culture Service*, #01-13 Blk 333, Kret Ayer Rd (☎2237190) sells effigies, trinkets, necklaces and books.

Camping equipment: *Campers' Corner*, #01-13 Paradiz Centre, 1 Selegie Rd.

Computers and software: *Funan Centre*, 109 North Bridge Rd.

Electronic equipment: *Sim Lim Tower*, 10 Jalan Besar.

Fabrics and silk: *China Silk House*, #02-11/13 Tanglin Shopping Centre, 19 Tanglin Rd (☎2355020); *Malaya Silk Store*, #01-01/02 Orchard Shopping Centre, 321 Orchard Rd (☎2352467); *Jim Thompson Silk Shop*, #01–01 Orchard Parade Hotel, 1 Tanglin Rd (☎2354379).

Jewellery: the entire first floor of the Pidemco Centre, 95 South Bridge Rd, is a jewellery mart.

Music: *Fuli Music*, Block 335A Chinatown Complex, Smith St, boasts the cheapest tapes in Singapore; *Supreme Record Centre*, #03-28 Centrepoint, 175 Orchard Rd (☎7343598).

Porcelain: *New Ming Village*, 32 Pandan Road (Clementi MRT and then bus #78; ☎2657711), where all the work on Ming and Qing Dynasty reproductions is done by hand, according to tradi-tional methods – most fascinating is the painstaking work of the painters. This is not a place to come to unless you are dead set on buying some porcelain.

Rubber stamp makers: stamps from *Singapore Rubber Stamp Maker*, #01-115 Blk 5, New Bridge Rd (☎5354879), make inexpensive gifts.

Souvenirs: *Singapore Handicraft Centre*, Chinatown Point, 133 New Bridge Rd, gathers around 50 souvenir shops under one roof; *Chinese Cloisonne-ware Centre*, #01-37 Raffles City Shopping Centre, 250 North Bridge Rd (☎3396643); *Zhen Lacquer Gallery*, 17 Duxton Rd (☎2253801).

Listings

Airlines *Aeroflot*, #01-03/#03-00 Tan Chong Tower, 15 Queen St (☎3361767); *Air Canada*, #02-43/46 Meridien Shopping Centre, 100 Orchard Rd (☎7328555); *Air India*, #17-01 UIC Building, 5 Shenton Way (☎2259411); *Air Lanka*, #02-00B PIL Building, 140 Cecil St (☎2236026); *Air New Zealand*, #24-08 Ocean Building, 10 Collyer Quay (☎5358266); *American Airlines*, #11-02 Natwest Centre, 15 MacCallum St (☎2216988); *British Airways*, #01-56 United Square, 101 Thomson Rd (☎2538444); *Cathay Pacific*, #16-01 Ocean Building, 10 Collyer Quay (☎5331333); *Garuda*, #01-68 United Square, 101 Thomson Rd (☎2502888); *KLM*, #01-02 Mandarin Hotel Arcade, 333 Orchard Rd (☎7377622); *Lufthansa*, #05-07 Palais Renaissance, 390 Orchard Rd (☎7379222); *MAS*, #02-09 Singapore Shopping Centre, 190 Clemenceau Ave (☎3366777); *Pelangi Air*, #02-09 Singapore Shopping Centre, 190 Clemenceau Ave (☎3366777); *Philippine Airlines*, #01-10 Parklane Shopping Mall, 35 Selegie Rd (☎3361611); *Qantas*, #04-02 The Promenade, 300 Orchard Rd (☎7373744); *Royal Brunei*, #01-4A/4B/5 Royal Holiday Inn Crowne Plaza, 25 Scotts Rd (☎2354672); *Royal Nepal Airlines*, #09-00 SIA Building, 77 Robinson Rd (☎2257575); *Singapore Airlines*, 77 Robinson Rd (☎2238888), and also at *Mandarin Hotel*, 333 Orchard Rd (☎2297293) and Raffles City Shopping Centre, 252 North Bridge Rd (☎2297274); *Thai Airways*, #08-01 Keck Seng Towers, 13 Cecil St (☎2249977); *Tradewinds*, same addresses as *Singapore Airlines* (☎2212221); *United Airlines*, #01-03 Hong Leong Building, 16 Raffles Quay (☎2200711).

Airport The toll-free Changi Airport flight information number is ☎5421234.

American Express Travel services at #01-06 Lucky Plaza, 304 Orchard Rd (Mon–Fri 9am–5pm, Sat 9am–1pm; ☎2355789) and #01-04/05 Winsland House, 3 Killiney Rd (☎2355788).

Banks and exchange All Singapore's banks change travellers' cheques, with the *UOB* and *Posbank* charging the lowest commission; normal banking hours are Mon–Fri 10am–3pm & Sat 11am–1pm. Licensed money changers also abound – particularly in Arab St and the Orchard Rd shopping centres – and offer more favourable rates.

Bookshops *Times* bookshops stock a wide choice of titles, and crop up all over town: branches at #04-08/15 Centrepoint, 175 Orchard Rd and #02-24/25 Raffles City Shopping Centre, 252 North Bridge Rd. *MPH* shops are also well stocked, especially the flagship store on Stamford Rd. For secondhand books, head for *Books Paradise*, #01-15 Paradiz Centre, 1 Selegie Rd. *Select Books*, #03-15 Tanglin Shopping Centre, 19 Tanglin Rd (☎7321515), has a huge array of specialist books on Southeast Asia, while *Packir Mohamed & Sons*, #01-20/21 Orchard Plaza, 150 Orchard Rd, boasts a huge selection of magazines.

British Council At Napier Road, west of Orchard Rd (☎4731111).

Car rental *Avis, Boulevard Hotel*, 200 Orchard Blvd (☎7371668), airport Terminal 1 (☎5432331) and Terminal 2 (☎5428855); *Hertz*, #01-20 Tanglin Shopping Centre, 19 Tanglin Rd (☎7344646) – to pick up at airport, phone the downtown branch; *Sintat*, Terminals 1 & 2, Changi Airport (☎5459086 or ☎5427288).

Credit card helplines *American Express* (☎2358133); *Diners Card* (☎2944222); *Mastercard* (☎5332888); *Visa* (☎2249033).

Dentists Listed in the *Singapore Buying Guide* (equivalent to the Yellow Pages) under "Dental Surgeons", and "Dentist Emergency Service".

Disabled travellers *Access Singapore*, an informative booklet published by the *Singapore Council of Social Service*, details hotels, banks, shopping centres and hospitals with facilities for the disabled. For a copy of the booklet write to the *Council* at 11 Penang Lane.

Diving equipment *Great Blue Dive Shop*, #03-05 Holland Rd Shopping Centre, 211 Holland Ave (☎4670767), arranges local and overseas diving trips, as well as renting and selling equipment.

Embassies and consulates *Australia*, 25 Napier Rd (☎7379311); *Brunei*, 7A Tanglin Hill (☎4743393); *Canada*, #14-00 IBM Towers, 80 Anson Rd (☎2256363); *France*, 5 Gallop Rd (☎4664866); *Germany*, #14-00 Far East Shopping Centre, 545 Orchard Rd (☎7371355); *India*, 31 Grange Rd (☎7376777); *Indonesia*, 7 Chatsworth Rd (☎7377422); *Ireland*, #08-02 Liat Towers, 541 Orchard Rd (☎7323430); *Malaysia*, 301 Jervois Rd (☎2350111); *New Zealand*, 13 Nassim Rd (☎2359966); *Philippines*, 20 Nassim Rd (☎7373977); *Sri Lanka*, #13-07/13 Goldhill Plaza, 51 Newton Rd (☎2544595); *Thailand*, 370 Orchard Rd (☎7372644); *UK*, Tanglin Rd (☎4739333); *USA*, 30 Hill St (☎3380251).

Emergencies Police ☎999; Ambulance and Fire Brigade ☎995 (all toll-free); larger hotels have doctors on call at all times.

Hospitals *Singapore General*, Outram Rd (☎2223322); *Alexandra Hospital*, Alexandra Rd (☎4735222); and *National University Hospital*, Kent Ridge (☎7795555), are all state hospitals and all have casualty departments.

Immigration Department For visa extension enquiries, contact the Immigration Department, #08-26 Pidemco Centre, 95 South Bridge Rd (Mon–Fri 9am–5pm; ☎5322877).

Laundry *Washington Dry Cleaning*, 02-22 Cuppage Plaza, 5 Koek Rd (Mon–Sat 9am–7.45pm); *Washy Washy*, #01-18 Cuppage Plaza, 5 Koek Rd (Mon–Sat 10am–7pm).

Pharmacies *Guardian* pharmacy has over 40 outlets, including ones at Centrepoint, 176 Orchard Rd; Raffles City Shopping Centre, 252 North Bridge Rd; and Clifford Centre, 24 Raffles Place. Usual hours are 9am–6pm, but some stay open until 10pm.

Police Tanglin Police Station, 17 Napier Rd, off Orchard Rd (☎7330000); come here to report stolen property. In an emergency, dial ☎999.

Post offices The GPO is in Fullerton Building, Fullerton Square (Mon–Fri 8am–6pm, Sat 8am–2pm); poste restante/general delivery is here (take your passport); the front porch is open 24 hours for stamps, parcel post, phone calls and telegrams. Branches include those at Raffles City and Changi Airport.

Sports Bowling: *Orchard Bowl*, 8 Grange Rd; ice skating: *Fuji Ice Palace*, 2 Mackenzie Rd (☎3362988); sailing: *East Coast Sailing Centre*, 1210 East Coast Parkway; snooker: *Academy of Snooker*, Albert Complex, Albert St (☎3395030); tennis: *Singapore Tennis Centre*, 1020 East Coast Parkway (☎4425966); watersports: *Jasmine Ski & Recreation*, No. 8 Track 24, Punggol Point (☎2857775) and *William Watersports*, Punggol Point (☎2826879).

Swimming Most central public pool is on River Valley Rd, though *Katong Swimming Complex*, on Wilkinson Rd, and *Buona Vista Swimming Complex*, on Holland Drive, are better. For something more adventurous, try the *Big Splash* swimming complex, at 902 East Coast Parkway (Mon–Fri noon–5.45pm, Sat & Sun 9am–5.45pm; $3), whose water slides are said to be the longest in Southeast Asia; there's also a wave pool and kiddies' paddling pool.

Telephones There are 24-hour IDD, fax and telex services at the *Comcentre*, 31 Exeter Rd, and in the entrance lobby of the *GPO*; otherwise, IDD calls can be made from any public callphone – cards are sold at post offices and newsagents.

Thai visas You need a Thai visa for stays of over 15 days, which are available in person from the Thai consulate (see above for address); allow at least two working days and take along three passport photos.

Tour operators *Franco Asian Travel* (☎2938282), *Gray Line of Singapore* (☎3318244), *Holiday Tours* (☎7382622), *Malaysia and Singapore Travel Centre* (☎7378877), *RMG Tours* (☎7387776), *Singapore Sightseeing* (☎4736900), and *Tour East* (☎2355703) can all arrange sightseeing tours of Singapore (see p.485 for details).

Travel agents All the following are good for discounted air fares and buying bus tickets to Malaysia and Thailand: *Airmaster Travel Centre*, 46 Bencoolen St (☎3383942); *Airpower Travel*, B1-07 Selegie Centre, 189 Selegie Rd (☎3371392); *Harharah Travel*, 171A Bencoolen St (☎3372633); *STA Travel*, #02-17 *Orchard Parade Hotel*, 1 Tanglin Rd (☎7345681).

Vaccinations Vaccinations can be arranged through the Government Vaccination Centre, Institute of Health, 226 Outram Rd (☎2227711).

Women's Singapore *AWARE* is a women's helpline (☎2931011).

PART THREE

THE

CONTEXTS

THE HISTORICAL FRAMEWORK

The modern-day nations of Malaysia, Singapore and Brunei only came into existence as late as 1965. Before that, their history was inextricably linked with events in the larger Malay archipelago, from Sumatra, across Borneo to the Philippines. The problem for any historian is the lack of reliable source material for the region: there's little hard archeological evidence pertaining to the prehistoric period, while the events prior to the foundation of Melaka are known only from unreliable written accounts by Chinese and Arab traders.

However, there are two vital sources for an understanding of events in the formative fourteenth and fifteenth centuries: the **Suma Oriental** (Treatise of the Orient), by Tomé Pires, a Portuguese emissary who came to Melaka in 1512 and wrote a history of the Orient based upon his own observations, and the **Sejarah Melayu**, the seventeenth century "Malay Annals", which recorded oral historical tales recounted in a poetic, rather than strictly chronological, style. Although differing in many respects, not least in time scale, both volumes describe similar events.

The arrival of Portuguese and Dutch **colonists** in the sixteenth and seventeenth centuries led to an increase in written records, though these tended to concern commercial rather than political or social matters. And the wealth of information from British colonial times, from the early nineteenth century onwards – although giving detailed insights into Malay affairs – is imprinted with an imperialistic bias. It is only in the twentieth century, when Malay sources come into play, that a complete picture can be presented.

BEGINNINGS

The oldest remains of *homo sapiens* were discovered in the Niah Caves in Sarawak in 1958 (see p.375), and are thought to be those of hunter-gatherers, between 35,000 and 40,000 years old; other finds in the peninsular state of Kedah are only 10,000 years old. The variety of **ethnic groups** found in both East and West Malaysia – from small, dark-skinned Negritos through to paler Austronesian Malays – has led to the theory of a slow filtration of peoples through the Malay archipelago from southern Indo-China – a theory backed by an almost universal belief in animism, celebration of fertility and ancestor worship among the various peoples.

The development of the Malay archipelago owed much to the importance of the **shipping trade**, which flourished as early as the first century AD. This was engendered by the region's strategic geographical position, linking the two major markets of the early world – India and China – and by the richness of its own resources. From the dense jungle of the peninsula and from northern Borneo came aromatic woods, timber and *nipah* palm thatch, traded by the forest-dwelling *orang asli* with the coastal Malays, who then bartered or sold it on to Arab and Chinese merchants. The region was also rumoured to be rich in **gold**, leading to its description by Greek explorers as "The Golden Chersonese (peninsula)", a phrase that was used by later travellers, bowled over by the spectacular scenery and culture. Although gold was never found in the quantities supposed to exist, ornaments made of the precious metal helped to develop decorative traditions among craftsmen and still survive today. More significant, however, were the **tin fields** of the Malay peninsula, mined in early times to provide an alloy used for temple sculptures. Chinese traders were also attracted by the medicinal properties of various sea products, such as sea slugs, collected by the *orang laut* (sea people), as well as the aesthetic value of pearls and tortoise shells.

In return, the indigenous peoples acquired cloth, pottery and glass from foreign traders, and came into contact with new ideas, religions and cultural practices. From as early as 200 AD, **Indian traders** brought with them their Hindu and Buddhist practices, and archeological evidence from later periods, such as the tenth-century temples at Lembah Bujang (p.176), suggests that the indigenes not only tolerated these new belief systems, but adapted them to suit their own experiences. Perhaps the most striking contemporary example of such cultural interchange is the traditional entertainment of *wayang kulit* (shadow plays), still commonly performed in the eastern peninsular states, whose stories are drawn from the Hindu *Ramayana*.

Contact with **China**, the other significant trading source, was initially much less pronounced due to the pre-eminence of the overland silk route, further to the north. It wasn't until much later, in the eighth and ninth centuries, that Chinese ships ventured into the archipelago.

There's little evidence to reveal the **structure of society** in these early times. All that is certain is that by the time Srivijaya appeared on the scene (see below), there were already a number of states – particularly in the Kelantan and Terengganu area of the peninsula – that were sending envoys to China. This suggests a well-developed social system, complete with chiefs and diplomats, who were perhaps the forebears of the later Malay nobility.

SRIVJAYA

The calm channel of the Melaka Straits provided a safe refuge for ships which were forced to wait several months for a change in the monsoon winds. The inhabitants of the western peninsula and eastern Sumatra were quick to realize their geographical advantage, and from the fifth century onwards a succession of **entrepôts** (storage ports) was created to cater for the needs of passing vessels. Gradually these evolved into kingdoms, such as that of **Langkasuka** in the Patani region of what is now Thailand, and **Vijayapura** in west Borneo, with well-developed courtly practices and traditions of government.

One entrepôt stood head and shoulders above the rest to become the mighty empire of **Srivijaya**, eminent from the beginning of the seventh century until the end of the thirteenth, and encompassing all the shores and islands surrounding the Straits of Melaka. Since records are fragmentary, the exact location of Srivijaya is still a matter for debate, although most sources point to **Palembang** in southern Sumatra. The empire's early success was owed primarily to its favourable relationship with China, which it plied with tributes to ensure profitable trade. The entrepôt's stable administration attracted commerce when insurrection elsewhere frightened traders away, while its wealth was boosted by extracting tolls and taxes from passing ships. With such valuable cargoes bound for the port, **piracy** in the surrounding oceans was rife, but was kept in check in Srivijayan waters by the fearsome *orang laut* who formed the linchpin of the navy. Indeed, they might otherwise have turned to piracy themselves had not the prestige of association with the empire been so great.

During the period of Srivijayan rule there developed significant political concepts which were to form the basis of Malay government in future centuries. Unquestioning **loyalty** among subjects was underpinned by the notion of *daulat*, the divine force of the ruler (who was called the Maharaja, further evidence of Indian influence in the region), which would strike down anyone guilty of *derhaka* (treason) – a powerful means of control over what was essentially a deeply superstitious people. Srivijaya also became known as an important centre for **Mahayana Buddhism and learning**. Supported by a bouyant economy, centres for study sprang up all over the empire, and monks and scholars were attracted from afar by Srivijaya's academic reputation. When the respected Chinese monk, I Ching, arrived in 671 AD, he found more than a thousand monks studying the Buddhist scriptures.

The decision made between 1079 and 1082 to shift the capital (for reasons unknown) from Palembang to **Melayu**, in the sungei Jambi area to the north, seems to have marked the start of Srivijaya's decline. Piracy became almost uncontrollable, with even the loyal *orang laut* turning against their rulers, and soon both local and foreign traders began to seek safer ports, with the area that is now Kedah becoming one of the main beneficiaries. Other regions were soon able to replicate the peaceable conditions and efficient administration conducive to commercial success. One such was **Puni** in northwest Borneo, thought to be the predecessor of Brunei, which had been trading with China since the ninth century. Over the next three hundred years Puni continued to prosper until its capital numbered more than 10,000 people, drawn by the hospitable reception given to visiting merchants and by the entrepôt's considerable wealth.

Srivijaya's fate was sealed when it attracted the eye of envious foreign rivals, among them the Majapahit empire of Java, the Cholas of India and, latterly, the Thai kingdom of Ligor. In 1275, the Majapahits invaded Melayu and made inroads into many of Srivijaya's peninsular territories; the Cholas raided Sumatra and Kedah; while Ligor enforced its territorial claims by the instigation of a **tribute system**, whereby local Malay chiefs sent gifts of gold to their Thai overlords as recognition of their vassal status, a practice which continued until the nineteenth century (see "Alor Setar", p.177). Moreover, trading restrictions in China were relaxed from the late twelfth century onwards, which made it more lucrative for traders to go directly to the source of their desired products, bypassing the once mighty entrepôt. Around the early fourteenth century Srivijaya's name disappears from the record books.

THE MELAKA SULTANATE

With the collapse of Srivijaya came the beginning of the Malay peninsula's most significant historical period, the establishment of the **Melaka Sultanate**. Both the *Sejarah Melayu* (Malay Annals) and the Portuguese *Suma Oriental* document the story of a Sumatran prince from Palembang named **Paramesvara**, who fled the collapsing empire of Srivijaya to set up his own kingdom, finally settling on the site of present-day Melaka (see p.275 for more).

As well placed as its Sumatran predecessor, with a deep, sheltered harbour and good riverine access to its own lucrative jungle produce, Melaka set about establishing itself as an international marketplace. The securement of a special agreement in 1405 with the new Chinese Emperor, Yung-lo, guaranteed trade to

Melaka and protected it from its main warring rivals: the kingdom of Samudra-Pasai in northeast Sumatra, and that of Aru further to the south. To further ensure its prosperity, Melaka's second ruler, Paramesvara's son **Iskandar Shah** (1414–1424), took the precaution of acknowledging the neighbouring kingdoms of Ayutthaya and Majapahit as overlords. In return, Melaka received vital supplies and much-needed immigrants which bolstered the expansion of the settlement.

New laws empowered an **effective administration** to meet the needs of passing traders, guaranteeing their safety in pirate-infested waters and offering ample space in which to store their cargo and refit their vessels. Port taxes and market regulations were managed by four **Shahbandars** (harbour masters). Each was in charge of a group of nations: one for the northwest Indian state of Gujurat alone; another for southern India, Bengal, Samudra-Pasai and Burma; the third for local neighbours such as Java, Palembang and Borneo; and the fourth for the eastern nations, including China and Japan. Intimately concerned with the physical and commercial requirements of his group, the Shahbandar also supervised the giving of gifts to the ruler and his ministers, an important method of boosting the kingdom's wealth.

Melaka began to amplify its reputation by territorial expansion which, by the reign of its last ruler **Sultan Mahmud Shah** (1488–1530), included the west coast of the peninsula as far as Perak, Pahang, Singapore, and most of east coast Sumatra. But although this made it strong enough to reject the patronage of Java and Ayutthaya, it never really controlled the far north or east of the peninsula, nor did it make inroads into its competitors' territories in northern Sumatra.

Hand in hand with the trade in commodities went the exchange of ideas. By the thirteenth century, Arab merchants had begun to frequent Melaka's shores, bringing with them their religion, **Islam**, which their Muslim Indian counterparts helped to propagate among the Malays. The Sultanate's **conversion** helped to increase its prestige by placing it within a worldwide community which worked to maintain profitable trade links. But even those outside Melaka's jurisdiction embraced the doctrine with enthusiasm: the fourteenth-century **Terengganu Stone**, with its inscription espousing Islam's tenets, is deemed to be the oldest Malay text written in Arabic script.

The legacy of **Melaka's Golden Age** reaches far beyond memories of its material wealth. One of the most significant developments was the establishment of a **court structure** (see p.285), which was to lay the foundations for a system of government which lasted until the nineteenth century. The **Sultan**, as head of state, traced his ancestry back through Paramesvara to the Maharajas of ancient Srivijaya, his claimed divinity strengthened by the Sultanate's conversion to Islam, which held Muslim rulers to be Allah's representative on Earth. To further ensure his power, always under threat from the overzealous nobility, the Sultan embarked on a series of measures to emphasize his "otherness": no one but he could wear gold unless it was a royal gift; while yellow became a colour forbidden for use among the general population.

The Melaka Sultanate also allowed the **arts** to flourish. Courtly dances and music developed whose principal features can still be distinguished in traditional entertainments held today. Much more significant, however, was its refinement of **language**, adapting the primitive Malay – itself of Austronesian roots – that had been used in the kingdom of Srivijaya, into a language of the elite. Such was Melaka's prestige that all who passed through the entrepôt sought to imitate it, and by the sixteenth century, Malay was the most widely used language in the archipelago. Tellingly, the word *bahasa*, although literally meaning "language", came to signify Malay culture in general.

THE PORTUGUESE CONQUEST OF MELAKA

With a fortune as tempting as Melaka's, it wasn't long before Europe set its sights on the acquisition of the empire. At the beginning of the sixteenth century, the **Portuguese** began to take issue with Venetian control of the Eastern market. They planned instead to establish direct contacts with the commodity brokers of the East by gaining control of crucial regional ports.

The key player in the subsequent **conquest of Melaka** was Portuguese viceroy **Afonso de Albuquerque**, who led the assault on the entrepôt in 1511, forcing its surrender after less than a month's siege. Sultan Mahmud Shah fled to the island of Bentan in the Riau archipelago (see below), and Albuquerque himself departed a year later, leaving behind eight hundred officers to administer the new colony. There are few physical reminders of their time in Melaka, apart from the gateway to their fort, A Famosa (see p.282), and the small **Eurasian** community, descendants of intermarriage between the Portuguese and local Malay women. The colonizers had more success with religion, however, converting large numbers of locals to the **Catholic faith**, whose churches continue to dominate the city today. Aloof and somewhat effete in their high-necked ruffs and stockings, the Portuguese were not well liked by the Malays, perhaps because of their inability to command respect, Portuguese rule tended to be high-handed rather than sympathetic. Yet despite this, and the almost constant attacks from upriver Malays, the Portuguese controlled Melaka for the next 130 years.

CONTEMPORARY RIVALS OF MELAKA

During the period of Melaka's meteoric rise, **Brunei** had been busily establishing itself as a trading port of some renown. Ideally poised on the sea route to China, it had for a long time benefited from its vassal status to successive Ming emperors, and now with its arch rival's capture it set about filling its place. The Brunei Sultanate's **conversion to Islam**, no doubt precipitated by the arrival of wealthy Muslim merchants fleeing from the Portuguese in Melaka, also helped to increase its international prestige. When geographer Antonio Pigafetta, travelling with Ferdinand Magellan's expedition of 1521, visited Brunei, he found the court brimming with visitors from all over the world. This, indeed, was Brunei's "Golden Age", with its borders embracing land as far south as present-day Kuching, in Sarawak, and as far north as the lower islands of the modern-day Philippines. Brunei's efforts, however, were soon curtailed by Spanish colonization in 1578 which, although lasting only a matter of

For a more detailed account of Brunei's early history and its Golden Age, see p.454.

weeks, enabled the Philippine kingdom of Sulu to gain a hold in the area — a fact which put paid to Brunei's early expansionist aims.

The ambitious Thai kingdom of **Ayutthaya** had been initially willing to strike bargains with Melaka, but by 1455 had tired of its competitor's unhindered progress and launched a full-scale attack. Sources are vague as to the outcome, though it can reasonably be assumed that Ayutthaya was emphatically defeated, since the Thai kingdom made no further attempts on the entrepôt for the next forty years. It was only when Melaka's last ruler, Sultan Mahmud Shah, sought to include the Thai vassal state of Kelantan in his own territories that he provoked Ayutthaya to retaliate with another unsuccessful foray into the peninsula in the year 1500, though it was to be another 35 years — well after the fall of Melaka to the Portuguese — before they tried again.

THE KINGDOM OF JOHOR

Johor's rise to pre-eminence in the Malay world began as a direct consequence of the fall of Melaka to the Portuguese. Fleeing Melaka, Sultan Mahmud Shah made for Pulau Bentan in the Riau archipelago, south of Singapore, where he established the first **court of Johor**. When, in 1526, the Portuguese attacked and razed the settlement, Mahmud fled once again, this time to Sumatra, where he died in 1528. It was left to his son, Alauddin Riayat Shah, to found a new court on the upper reaches of the Johor river, though the capital of the kingdom then shifted repeatedly, during a century of assaults on Johor territory by Portugal and the Sumatran Sultanate of Aceh.

The **arrival of the Dutch** in Southeast Asia towards the end of the sixteenth century marked a distinct upturn in Johor's fortunes. Hoping for protection from its local enemies, the court aligned itself firmly with the new European arrivals, and was instrumental in the successful seige of Portuguese Melaka by the Dutch in 1641 (see below). Such loyalty was rewarded by trading priviledges and by help in securing a treaty with Aceh, the main aggressive force in Sumatra at that time, which at last gave Johor the breathing space to develop. Soon it had grown into a thriving kingdom, its sway extending some way throughout the peninsula.

Johor was the supreme Malay kingdom for much of the seventeenth century, but by the 1690s its empire was fraying under the irrational and despotic rule of another Sultan Mahmud. Lacking strong leadership, Johor's *orang laut* turned to piracy, scaring off the trade upon which the kingdom relied, while wars with the Sumatran kingdom of Jambi, one of which resulted in the total destruction of Johor's capital, weakened it still further. No longer able to tolerate Sultan Mahmud's cruel regime, his nobles stabbed him to death in 1699. Not only did this change the nature of power in Malay government — previously, law deemed that the Sultan was punishable only by Allah — but it marked the end of the Melaka dynasty.

THE DUTCH IN MELAKA

Already the masters of Indonesia's valuable spice trade, the *Vereenigde Oostindische Compagnie* (*VOC*), or **Dutch East India Company**, began a bid to gain control of its most potent rival, Melaka. After a five-month siege, the Dutch flag was hoisted over Melaka in 1641. Instead of ruling from above as their predecessors had tried to do, the Dutch cleverly wove their subjects into the fabric of government: each racial group was represented by a *Kapitan*, a respected figure from the community who mediated between his own people and the new administrators — often becoming a very wealthy and powerful person in his own right. The Dutch were also reponsible for the rebuilding of Melaka, much of which had been turned to rubble during the protracted takeover of the city. Many of these structures, in their distinctive northern European style, still survive today: narrow houses and *godowns* backing on to the network of canals are strangely reminiscent of Amsterdam; while the headquarters of the administration, the Stadthuys, is one of Melaka's main tourist attractions.

By the mid-eighteenth century, the conditions for trade with **China** were at their peak: the relaxation of maritime restrictions in China itself had opened up the Straits for their merchants, while Europeans were eager to satisfy the growing demand for tea. Since the Chinese had no interest in the native goods that Europe could supply in exchange, and the Dutch themselves had no knowledge of indigenous products, European traders found themselves more and more reliant on Indian items, such as cloth and opium, as bartering tools. The Chinese came to Melaka in droves and soon established themselves as the city's foremost entrepreneurs. Chinese intermarriage with local Malay women created a new cultural blend, known as **Peranakan** (literally, "Straits-born") or Baba-Nonya – the legacy of which is the opulent mansions and unique cuisine of Melaka (see feature on p.287 for more).

But a number of factors prevented Dutch Melaka from fulfilling its potential. Since the *VOC* salary was hardly bountiful, Dutch administrators found it more lucrative to trade on the black market, taking backhanders from grateful merchants, a situation which severely damaged Melaka's commercial standing. High taxes forced traders to more economical locations such as the newly established British port of **Penang**, whose foundation in 1786 heralded the awakening of British interest in the Straits (see p.155). A more significant sign of Dutch loss of control was their reliance on military rather than governmental means to sustain their supremacy, which ultimately made them vulnerable to anyone of greater strength. In the end, given the *VOC*'s overall strategy in the archipelago, Melaka never stood a chance: Batavia (modern-day Jakarta) was the *VOC* capital, and Johor's penchant for commerce suited Dutch purposes too much for it to put serious effort into maintaining Melaka's fortunes.

THE BUGIS AND THE MINANGKABAUS

Through the second half of the seventeenth century, a new ethnic group, the **Bugis** – renowned for their martial and commercial skills – had been trickling into the peninsula, seeking refuge from the civil wars which wracked their homeland of Sulawesi (in the mid-eastern Indonesian archipelago). By the beginning of the eighteenth century, there were enough of them to constitute a powerful court lobby and in 1721 they took advantage of factional struggles to capture the kingdom of Johor – now based in Riau. Installing a Malay puppet Sultan, Sulaiman, the Bugis ruled for over sixty years, making Riau an essential port of call on the eastern trade route; they even almost succeeded in capturing Melaka in 1756. Although their ousting had long been desired

by discontented Malay vassals, it was the Dutch who put paid to the Bugis supremacy in the Straits. When Riau-Johor made another bid for Melaka in 1784, the Dutch held on with renewed vigour and finally forced a treaty placing all Bugis territory in Dutch hands.

In spiritual terms, the **Minangkabaus** (see feature on p.272) had what the Bugis lacked: hailing from western Sumatra, this matrilineal society could claim cultural affinity with the ancient kingdom of Srivijaya. Although this migrant group had been present in the Negeri Sembilan region since the fifteenth century, the second half of the seventeenth century brought them to the Malay peninsula in larger numbers. Despite professing allegiance to their Sumatran ruler, the Minangkabaus were prepared to accept Malay overlordship, which in practice gave them a great deal of autonomy. Accredited with supernatural powers, the warrior Minangkabaus were not natural allies of the Bugis or the Malays, although they did occasionally join forces in order to defeat a common enemy. In fact, over time the distinction between various migrant groups became less obvious, as intermarriage blurred clan demarcations, and Malay influence, such as the adoption of Malay titles, became more pronounced.

THE END OF AN ERA

At the end of the eighteenth century, Dutch control in Southeast Asia was more widespread than ever, and the *VOC* empire should have been at its height. Instead, its coffers were bare and it faced the superior trading and maritime skills of the British. The disastrous defeat of the Dutch in the fourth Anglo-Dutch war (1781–83) lowered their morale still further and when the British, in the form of the **East India Company** (EIC), moved in on Melaka and the rest of the Dutch Asian domain in 1795, the *VOC* barely demurred.

Initially, the British agreed to a caretaker administration, whereby they would assume sovereignty over the entrepôt to prevent it falling under French control, now that Napoleon had conquered Holland. The end of the Napoleonic wars in Europe put the Dutch in a position to retake Melaka between 1818 and 1825, but in the meantime, the EIC had established the stable port of **Penang** and – under the supervision of **Sir Thomas Stamford**

Raffles (see p.500) – founded the new settlement of **Singapore** (see p.475) as their own regional entrepôt, signing a formal agreement with the Sultanate of Riau-Johor in 1819.

The strategic position and free-trade policy of Singapore – backed by the impressive industrial developments of the British at home – instantly threatened the viability of both Melaka and Penang, forcing the Dutch to relinquish finally their hold on the former to the British, and leaving the latter to dwindle to a backwater. In the face of such stiff competition, smaller Malay rivals inevitably linked their fortunes to the British.

THE CONSOLIDATION OF BRITISH POWER

To a degree, the British presence in Malay lands was only the most recent episode in a history of foreign interference that stretched back centuries. What differed this time, however, was the rapidity and extent of the takeover – aided by technological developments in the West that improved communications.

The British assumption of power was sealed by the **Anglo-Dutch Treaty of 1824**, which divided territories between the two countries using the Straits of Melaka as the dividing line, thereby splitting the Riau-Johor kingdom as well as ending centuries of cultural interchange with Sumatra. This was followed in 1826 by the unification of Melaka, Penang (together with its mainland counterpart Province Wellesley) and Singapore into one administration, known as the **Straits Settlements**, with Singapore replacing Penang as its capital in 1832. Even with this more cohesive powerbase, the official British line was minimum interference for maximum trading opportunity, a policy that was brought into sharp conflict with the desires of local empire builders by the **Naning Wars of 1831**. These erupted when the Governor of the Straits Settlements, Robert Fullerton, tried to impose Melaka's tax laws on a somewhat uppity local chief, Abdul Said. A year-long battle ensued, and though the British were finally able to cede Naning to Melaka's territories, their pyrrhic victory brought home the costs of too close an involvement in complex Malay politics.

The Anglo-Dutch Treaty did not include **Borneo**, however, and though the EIC discouraged official expansion, preferring to concentrate on expanding their trading contacts rather than geographical control, its benefits did not elude the sights of one British explorer, **James Brooke** (1803–1868). Finding lawlessness throughout the territories, Brooke persuaded the Sultan of Brunei to award him his own area – **Sarawak** – in 1841 (see p.326), becoming the first of a line of "**White Rajahs**" that ruled the state until the start of World War II. By involving formerly rebellious Malay chiefs in government, he quickly managed to assert his authority, although the less congenial Iban tribes in the interior proved more of a problem. Despite the informal association of the British with Rajah Brooke (Sarawak was not granted the status of a protectorate), trade between Singapore and Sarawak flourished – though Brooke was careful not to encourage European contacts that might challenge his hold on the state. By the mid-nineteenth century, however, the British attitude had mellowed considerably, choosing Brooke as their agent in Brunei, and also finding him a useful deterrent against French and Dutch aspirations towards the valuable trade routes.

Raffles had at first hoped that **Singapore** would act as a market to sell British goods to traders from all over Southeast Asia, but it soon became clear that **Chinese** merchants, the linchpin of Singapore's trade, were interested only in Malay products such as birds' nests, seaweed and camphor. But passing traders were not the only Chinese to come to the Straits. Although settlers had trickled into the peninsula since the early days of Melaka, new pepper and gambier (an astringent product used in tanning and dyeing) **plantations**, and the rapidly expanding **tin mines**, attracted floods of willing workers eager to escape a life of poverty in China. By 1845, the Chinese formed over half of Singapore's population, while principal towns along the peninsula's west coast – site of the world's largest tin field – as well as Sarawak's capital, Kuching, became predominantly Chinese.

Allowed a large degree of commercial independence by both the British and the Malay chiefs, the Chinese carried their traditions into the social and political arena with the formation of *kongsis*, or clan houses (see p.165), and secret societies (triads). Struggles between clan groups were rife, sometimes resulting in large-scale riots, such as those in Penang in 1867 (see p.165), where the triads allied themselves with Malay groups in a bloody street battle lasting several days.

REGIONAL CONFLICT

Malays, too, were hardly immune from factional conflicts, which frequently became intertwined with Chinese squabbles, causing a string of **civil wars**.

In **Negeri Sembilan** (1824–1869), conflict was largely brought about by contending Minangkabau heirs, although most worrying to British administrators were arguments over the control of the tin trade (see p.267). **Pahang's** skirmishes (1858–63) also involved rival political claims, by two brothers Mutahir and Ahmad, although this time the British were much more directly involved. On hearing that the Thais had backed Ahmad, the Straits Governor Cavenagh hastily aligned himself with Mutahir by attacking Kuala Terengganu (a Thai vassal town), in order to ward off further foreign involvement in the peninsula. But the British government was outraged by this decision and forbade any other action to prevent Ahmad's succession.

Perak (1861–1873) was riven with the disputes of rival Chinese clans in the central region of Larut and once again, tin was a major contributing factor. In **Selangor** (1867–1873), tax claims between Malay chiefs were the basis of the wars. The British again intervened, this time to support Tengku Kudin, the person they thought most likely to assure a peaceful resolution to the conflict. However, he was a weak figure, little respected by his own people, and the effect was to underline to the Malays that British help could even be secured for a lacklustre regime such as Kudin's.

Lawlessness like this was detrimental to commerce, giving the British an excuse to increase their involvement in local affairs. A meeting was arranged by the new Straits Governor, Andrew Clarke, on Pulau Pangkor, just off the west coast of the peninsula, between the chiefs of the Perak Malays. In the meantime, Rajah Abdullah, the man most likely to succeed to the Perak throne, had written to Clarke asking for the appointment of a British **Resident** (or advisor), in return for his own guaranteed position as Sultan. On January 20, 1874, the **Pangkor Treaty** (p.141) was signed between the British and Abdullah, formalizing British intervention in the political affairs of the Malay people.

BRITISH MALAYA

By 1888 the name **British Malaya** had been brought into use by Governor Clarke – a term which reflected the intention to extend British control over the whole peninsula. Over subsequent decades, the Malay Sultans' economic and administrative powers were to be gradually eroded, while the introduction of rubber estates during the first half of the twentieth century made British Malaya one of the most productive colonies in the world.

Each state soon saw the arrival of a **Resident** (see p.148), a senior British civil servant whose main function was as advisor to the local Sultan, but who also oversaw the collecting of local taxes. The system worked reasonably well, although relations deteriorated with J.W.W. Birch's posting as Resident of Perak. Unlike the first Resident, the respected Hugh Low, Birch was not sympathetic to the ways of the Malays, and was soon out of favour. Perak's Sultan Abdullah in particular opposed Birch's centralizing tendencies and senior British officials, fearful of a Malay rebellion, announced that judicial decisions would from now on be in the hands of the British, which was against the letter of the Pangkor Treaty. Furious Malays soon found a vent for their frustration: on November 2, 1875, Birch was killed on an upriver visit. The British brought in troops from India and Hong Kong to quell the trouble, although the attack on Birch was not followed by further assaults on colonial staff.

Agreements along the lines of the Pangkor Treaty were drawn up with Selangor, Negeri Sembilan and Pahang states in the 1880s, and in 1896 these three became bracketed together under the title of the **Federated Malay States**, with the increasingly important town of Kuala Lumpur made the regional capital.

The gradual extension of British power brought further unrest, particularly in the east coast states, where the Malays proved just as resentful of British control as in Perak. In Pahang a set of skirmishes known as the **Pahang War** took place in 1891, when Malay chiefs protested about the reduction of their former privileges. One powerful chief, Dato' Bahaman, was stripped of his title by Pahang's

For an account of the **founding of Kuala Lumpur**, see p.77.

Resident, Hugh Clifford, as a result of which the Dato' led a small rebellion which – though never a serious military threat to the British – soon became the stuff of legends. One fighter, **Mat Kilau**, gained a place in folklore as a heroic figure who stood up to the British in the name of Malay nationalism. From this time onwards, Malays would interpret the uprisings as a valiant attempt to safeguard Malay traditions and preserve Malay automomy. However, the only real impact the Pahang War had on the hitherto smooth extension of British power was to slow down briefly the pace of colonial administration. It also further underlined the contrasts between various regions of the peninsula: the economies of the northern states of Pahang, Kelantan and Terengganu developed less quickly than those of the western states, which were under more effective British control.

By 1909, the northern Malay states of Kedah, Perlis, Kelantan and Terengganu – previously under Thai control – were brought into the colonial fold: along with Johor (which joined in 1914) they were grouped together as the **Unfederated Malay States** and by the outbreak of World War I, British political control was more or less complete. The peninsula was subdivided into groups of states and regions with the seat of power split between Singapore and Kuala Lumpur. Borneo, too, had been brought under British control: the three states of Sarawak, Sabah and Brunei had been transformed into **protectorates** in 1888, a status which handed over the responsibility for their foreign policy to the British in exchange for military protection.

THE EXPANSION OF BRITISH INTERESTS IN BORNEO

The legacy of the first "White Rajah" of **Sarawak**, James Brooke, was furthered by his nephew Charles in the closing years of the nineteenth century. New regions – the Baram and Trusan valleys and Limbang – were bought, or rather wrested, from the Sultan of Brunei, while the *British North Borneo Chartered Company* handed over to Brooke the Lawas Valley in 1905. The *Chartered Company*

had assumed control over Northern Borneo (later renamed Sabah) in 1878 when an Austrian, Baron von Overbeck, with the backing of British businessmen, paid the Sultans of Brunei and Sulu an annuity to administer and develop the region; see p.405 for more on this.

Like his uncle before him, **Charles Brooke** ruled Sarawak in a paternalistic fashion, recruiting soldiers, lowly officials and boatmen from the ranks of the ethnic groups and leaving the Chinese to get on with running commercial enterprises and opening out the interior. Although the British government in London and the colonial administrators in Singapore were concerned about Brooke's territorial expansions, they accepted that the indigenous peoples were not being oppressed and that Brooke's rule was not despotic.

The rule of the last White Rajah, **Vyner Brooke**, Charles' eldest son (1916–41), saw no new territorial acquisitions, but there was a steady development in rubber, pepper and palm oil production. The ethnic peoples mostly continued living a traditional lifestyle in longhouses along the river systems and, with the end of groups' practice of head-hunting, there was some degree of integration among the country's varied racial groups.

By way of contrast, the **British North Borneo Chartered Company**'s writ in what became Sabah encountered some early obstacles. Its plans for economic expansion involved clearing the rainforest and **planting rubber and tobacco** over large areas, and levying taxes on the ethnic groups. Resistance followed, with the most vigorous action in 1897 led by a Bajau chief, **Mat Salleh**, whose men rampaged through the company's out-station on Pulau Gaya (see p.405 for more details). Another rebellion by the Murut tribespeople in 1915 resulted in a heavy-handed response from British forces who killed hundreds.

By the turn of the twentieth century, the majority of the lands of the erstwhile powerful **Sultanate of Brunei** had been dismembered – the Sultanate was now surrounded by Sarawak. But the Sultan's fortunes had not completely disappeared and with the discovery of **oil** in 1929, the British thought it prudent to appoint a Resident. Exploitation of the small state's oil beds picked up pace in the 1930s following investment from British companies; see p.456 for more details.

ECONOMIC DEVELOPMENT AND ETHNIC RIVALRIES

In the first quarter of the twentieth century hundreds of thousands of **immigrants** from China and India were encouraged by the British to emigrate to sites across Peninsular Malaysia, Sarawak, North Borneo and Singapore. They came to work as tin miners or plantation labourers, and Malaya's population in this period doubled to four million.

The main impact of what was effectively a recruitment drive by the British was to fuel resentment among the Malays who believed that they were being denied the economic opportunities advanced to others. The situation was made worse under the British **education system**, since schooling was offered at a very basic level to only small numbers of Malays, Chinese and Indians. The British barely noticed the deepening differences between the ethnic groups – a factor which contributed to resentment and racial violence in later years.

A further deterioration in Malay-Chinese relations followed the success of the mainland Chinese revolutionary groups in Malaya. The educated Chinese, who joined the **Malayan Communist Party** (MCP) from 1930 onwards, formed the backbone of the politicized Chinese movements after World War II, which demanded an end to British rule and to what they perceived as special privileges extended to the Malays. For their part, the Malays – specifically those influenced by radical Islamic movements – saw better education as the key to their future. The establishment of the **Singapore Malay Union** in 1926 gradually gained support in Straits Settlement areas where Malays were outnumbered by Chinese. It held its first conference in 1939 and advocated a Malay supremacist line.

Despite the argument put forward by the British in the 1930s that a Union for Malaya, (incorporating the Unfederated Malay States) would decentralize power and integrate the regional state groupings, little progress had been made on the burning issue of independence by the time Malaya was **invaded by the Japanese** in late 1941.

JAPANESE OCCUPATION

By February 1942, the whole of Malaya and Singapore was in Japanese hands and most of the British were POWs. The **surrender of the British forces in Singapore** (see p.476 for details) ushered in a Japanese regime which proceeded to brutalize the Chinese, largely because of Japan's history of conflict with China: up to 50,000 people were tortured and killed in the two weeks immediately after the surrender of the island by the British military command. Allied POWs were rounded up into prison camps; many of the troops subsequently were sent to build the infamous "Death Railway" in Burma.

In **Malaya**, towns and buildings were destroyed as the Allies attempted to bomb strategic targets. But with the Japanese firmly in control, the occupiers ingratiated themselves with some of the Malay elite by suggesting that after the war the country would be given independence. Predictably, it was the Chinese activists in the MCP, more than the Malays, who organized **resistance** during wartime; in the chaotic period directly after the war it was the MCP's armed wing, the **Malayan People's Anti-Japanese Army** (MPAJA), who maintained order in many areas.

The Japanese invasion of **Sarawak** in late 1941 began with the capture of the Miri oilfield and spread south, encountering little resistance. Although the Japanese invaders never penetrated the interior, they quickly established complete control over the populated towns along the coast. The Chinese in Miri, Sibu and Kuching were the main targets: the Japanese put down rebellions against their rule brutally, and there was no organized guerrilla activity until late in the occupation. What resistance there was was prompted by the presence of Major **Tom Harrison** and his team of British and Australian commandos, who parachuted into the remote Kelabit Highlands to gauge the feeling of the indigenous tribespeople; they later managed to recruit Kayan, Kenyah and Kelabit warriors in an uprising.

In **North Borneo**, the Japanese invaded Pulau Labuan on New Year's Day, 1942 (see p.424). Over the next three years the main suburban areas were bombed by the Allies, and by the time of the Japanese surrender in September 1945, most of Jesselton (modern-day KK) and Sandakan had been destroyed. Captured troops and civilians suffered enormously – the worst single outrage being the Death March in September 1944 when 2400

POWs were forced to walk from Sandakan to Ranau. Only six survived.

The Allies had been preparing to retake Singapore but just prior to the invasion the **Japanese surrendered** on September 9, 1945, on Pulau Labuan, following the dropping of atom bombs on Nagasaki and Hiroshima.

The surrender led to a power vacuum in the region, with the British initially left with no choice but to work with the MPAJA to exert political control. Violence occurred between the MPAJA and Malays, with those who were accused of collaborating with the Japanese during the occupation specifically targeted.

THE FEDERATION OF MALAYA

Immediately after the war, the British updated the idea of a Malayan **union** – a position halfway towards full independence – which would make the Chinese and Indian inhabitants full citizens and give them equal rights with the Malays.

This quickly aroused opposition among the Malays, with Malayan nationalists forming the **United Malays National Organization** (UMNO) in 1946. Its main tenet was that Malays should retain their special privileges, largely because they were the region's first inhabitants. UMNO also pushed the customary Malay line that the uniqely powerful position of the sultans should not be tampered with – indeed, they still exerted immense power despite the administrative changes wrought by the British

UMNO supporters displayed widespread resistance to the British plan and the idea of union was subsequently replaced by the **Federation of Malaya**. Established in 1948, this upheld the power and privileges of the sultans and brought all the regional groupings together under one government, with the exception of Chinese-dominated Singapore, whose inclusion would have led to the Malays being in a minority. Protests erupted in Singapore at its exclusion, with the **Malayan Democratic Union** (MDU) calling for integration with Malaya – a position that commanded little support among the Chinese population.

In **Borneo**, after the Japanese surrender, the Colonial Office in London stepped into the breach and with Vyner Brooke offering no objection, made Sarawak and North Borneo

Crown Colonies. Britain also signed a Treaty of Protection with the Sultan of Brunei, making Sarawak's High Commissioner the Governor of Brunei – a purely decorative position, as the Sultan remained the chief power in the state.

Although Sarawak's ruling body, the Council Negeri (composed of Malays, Chinese, Iban and British) had voted to transfer power to Britain, some Malays and prominent Ibans in Kuching opposed their country's new status. Protests reached a peak with the assassination in Sibu in 1949 of the top official in the new administration, Governor Duncan Stewart. But on the whole, resentment at the passing of the Brooke era was short-lived, and as the population gradually got used to the new political alignments, the economy expanded. The infrastructure of both Sarawak and North Borneo steadily improved, with new roads and a limited air service helping to open out the country to commercial development.

Brunei's most lucrative resource – its oilfields – sustained considerable damage during the Japanese invasion, and much of the postwar period was spent in rebuilding the installations. The British Governor was withdrawn in 1959 leaving the Sultan in sole charge of the region, although Britain was still responsible for defence matters and foreign relations.

THE EMERGENCY

In Peninsular Malaya many Chinese were angered by the change of the status of the country from a colony to a federation, in which they effectively became second class citizens. According to the new laws, non-Malays could only qualify as citizens if they had lived in the country for fifteen out of the last twenty-five years, and they also had to prove they spoke Malay or English.

More Chinese began to identify with the MCP, which, under its new leader, **Chin Peng**, declared its intention of setting up a Malayan republic. Peng fused the MCP with the remains of the wartime resistance movement, the MPAJA, and using the arms supplies which the latter had dumped in the forests, he recruited a secret central committee, set up **guerrilla cells** deep in the jungle and, from June 1948, launched sporadic attacks on rubber estates, killing planters and employees as well as spreading fear among rural communities.

The period of unrest, which lasted for twelve years (1948–60), was referred to as **the Emergency**, rather than a civil war, which it undoubtedly was. This was mainly for insurance purposes – planters would have had their premiums cancelled if war had been officially declared. Although the Emergency was never fully felt in the main urban areas – life went on as normal in Kuala Lumpur – the British rubber estate owners would arrive for steaks and *stengahs* at the *Coliseum Hotel* in central KL with harrowing stories of how the guerrillas (dubbed Communist Terrorists) had hacked off the arms of rural Chinese workers who had refused to support the cause, and of armed attacks on plantations.

The British were slow to respond to the threat but once Lt. Gen. Sir Harold Briggs was put in command of police and army forces, Malaya was on a war footing. The most controversial policy Briggs enacted was the **resettlement** of 400,000 rural Chinese – mostly squatters who had moved to areas bordering the jungle to escape victimization by the Japanese during the war – as well as thousands of *orang asli* seen as potential MCP sympathizers in four hundred "New Villages", scattered across the country. Although these forced migrations were successful in breaking down many of the guerrillas' supply networks, they had the effect of making both Chinese and *orang asli* more sympathetic to the idea of a Communist republic replacing British rule.

The violence peaked in 1950 with ambushes and attacks on plantations near Ipoh, Kuala Kangasr, Kuala Lipis and Raub. The most notorious incident occurred in 1951 on the road to Fraser's Hill when the British High Commissioner to Malaya, **Sir Henry Gurney**, was assassinated (see p.124). Under the new Commissioner, Sir Gerald Templer, a new policy was introduced to win hearts and minds. "White Areas" were established – regions perceived as free of guerrilla activity. Communities in these areas had food restrictions and curfews lifted, a policy which began to dissipate guerrilla activity over the next three years. At the same time, the British army – bolstered by conscripted British National Servicemen and assisted by Gurkha contingents and the Malay police force – successfully hunted down most of the Chinese leaders, although not Chin Peng. The leaders were offered an amnesty in 1956, which was refused, and Peng and most of the remaining cell members fled over the border to Thailand where they recieved sanctuary; some still live there and only formally admitted defeat in 1989.

TOWARDS INDEPENDENCE

The Emergency had the effect of speeding up the political processes prior to independence. Although UMNO stuck to its "Malays first" policy – its founder Dato' Onn bin Jaafar resigned because his call to include non-Malays was rejected – in 1955 the new leader, **Tunku Abdul Rahman** (a royal Malay whose brother was the Sultan of Kedah), forged a united position between UMNO, the moderate Malayan Chinese Association (MCA) and the Malayan Indian Association. This merger was called the **Alliance**, and it was to sweep into power under the rallying cry of *Merdeka* (Freedom). The hope was that ethnic divisions would no longer be a major factor if **Malayan independence** was granted, though the very real differences between the various ethnic groups' positions still hadn't been eradicated.

With British backing, **Merdeka** was promulgated on August 15, 1957 in a ceremony in Kuala Lumpur's Padang – promptly renamed Merdeka Square. The British High Commissioner signed a treaty which decreed that under British and Malay law the Federation of Malaya was now independent of the Crown. The first Prime Minister was Tunku Abdul Rahman. The new **constitution** allowed for the nine Malay sultans to alternate as king, and established a two-tier **parliament** – a house of elected representatives and a Senate with delegates from each of the states. Although the system was, in theory, a democracy, the Malay-dominated UMNO remained by far the most influential element in the political equation.

Under Rahman, the country was fully committed to economic expansion and full employment; foreign investment was actively encouraged. Arguments between the two dominant Alliance parties, UMNO and the MCA, were mostly over the allocation of seats in parliament and in the area of education, but Rahman refused to compromise the pre-eminent position of the Malays, and the MCA remained far less powerful than UMNO.

Despite the Alliance's aim of creating a new citizen, whose loyalties would be to the country and not to their particular ethnic group, age-old communal divisions had still not been obliterated,

Similarly, in **Singapore** the process of gaining independence gained momentum throughout the 1950s. In 1957 the British gave the go-ahead for the setting up of an elected 51-member assembly, and full **self-government** was attained in 1959, when the People's Action Party (PAP) under **Lee Kuan Yew** won most of the seats. Lee immediately entered into talks with Tunku Abdul Rahman over the notion that Singapore and Malaya should be joined administratively – Rahman initially agreed, although he feared the influence of pro-Communist extremists in the PAP.

In 1961 Tunku Abdul Rahman announced that the two Crown Colonies of Sarawak and North Borneo should join Malaya and Singapore in a revised federation. Many in Borneo would have preferred the idea of a separate Borneo Federation, but the advent of the *Konfrontasi*, an armed struggle launched by newly independent Indonesia to wrest control of the two colonies from Malaya (see below) played into Rahman's hands – those against his proposals could see how vulnerable the states were to attack from Indonesia.

Behind Rahman's proposal was the concern that demographic trends would in time lead to Malaya having a greater Chinese population than Malay. Consequently he campaigned hard for the inclusion of the two Malay-dominated Borneo colonies into the proposed federation, to act as a demographic balance to the Chinese in Singapore.

FEDERATION AND THE KONFRONTASI

In September 1963 North Borneo (quickly renamed Sabah), Sarawak and Singapore joined Malaya in the **Federation of Malaysia** – "Malaysia" being a term first coined by the British in the 1950s when the notion of a Greater Malaya had been propounded. Both Indonesia, which laid claim to Sarawak (the border of Indonesian Kalimantan ran alongside the state), and the Phillipines, which argued it had jurisdiction over Sabah as it had originally been part of the Sulu sultanate, reacted angrily to the new federation. Although the Phillipines backed down, Indonesia didn't and border skir-

mishes known as the **Konfrontasi** ensued. The conflict intensified as Indonesian soldiers crossed the border, and a wider war was only just averted when Indonesian President Sukarno backed away from costly confrontations with British and Gurkha troops brought in to boost Sarawak's small armed forces.

Differences soon developed between Lee Kuan Yew and the Malay-dominated Alliance party over the lack of egalitarian policies – although the PAP had dominated recent elections, many Chinese were concerned that UMNO's overall influence in the Federation was too great. Tensions rose on the island and ugly racial incidents developed into full-scale **riots** in 1964, in which several people were killed.

These developments were viewed with great concern by Tunku Abdul Rahman and he decided it would be best if Singapore left the Federation. This was emphatically not in Singapore's best interests, since it was an island without any obvious natural resources; Lee is reported to have cried when the expulsion was announced. Singapore thus acquired full **independence** on August 9, 1965 (see p.477 for details), and the severing of the bond between Malaysia and Singapore soured relations between the countries for some years.

BRUNEI

In **Brunei**, the Sultan's autocratic rule was tested in 1962 when, in the state's first ever general election, the left-wing **Brunei People's Party** (BPP) came to power. Sultan Omar, however, viewed democracy suspiciously and refused to let the BPP form a government. A rebellion followed, when the BPP – backed by the Communist North Kalimantan Army – gained control of parts of Seria, Kuala Belait, Tutong and Bandar, but the revolt was crushed within four days by British and Gurkha forces. Sultan Omar's powers remained unchanged and the autocratic royal rule of Brunei continues to this day. Although Abdul Rahman had wanted Brunei to join the Malaysian Federation, too, along with neighbouring Sarawak and Sabah, Omar refused when he realized Rahman's price – a substantial proportion of Brunei's oil and gas revenues. Brunei remained under nominal British jurisdiction until **independence** was declared on December 31, 1983.

ETHNIC CONFLICT

The exclusion of Singapore from the Malaysian Federation was not enough to quell the ethnic conflicts. Resentment built among the Chinese over the principle that Malay be the main language taught in schools and over the privileged employment opportunities offered to Malays. In 1969 the UMNO (Malay)-dominated Alliance lost regional power in parliamentary elections, and Malays in major cities reacted angrily to a perceived increase in power of the Chinese, who had commemorated their breakthrough with festivities in the streets. These triggered counter-demonstrations by Malays and hundreds of people, mostly Chinese, were killed and injured in the **riots** which followed, with Kuala Lumpur in particular becoming a war zone where large crowds of youths went on the rampage. Rahman kept the country under a state of emergency for nearly two years, during which the draconian **Internal Security Act** (ISA) was used to arrest and imprison activists, as well as many writers and artists.

THE NEW ECONOMIC POLICY

Rahman never recovered full political command after the riots and resigned in 1971, handing over to the new Prime Minister, **Tun Abdul Razak**, also from UMNO, who took a less authoritarian stance – although still implementing the ISA. He brought the parties in Sarawak and Sabah into the political process and initiated a broad set of directives, called the **New Economic Policy** (NEP). This set out to restructure the management of the economy so that it would be less reliant on the Chinese who previously dominated its most lucrative sectors. Ethnic Malays were to be classed as **Bumiputras** (sons of the soil) and given favoured positions in business, commerce and other professions (see p.53 for details). All schools were also required to teach Malay as a first language, rather than English, Cantonese or Tamil.

DEVELOPMENTS IN SINGAPORE

Lee Kuan Yew continued to rule **Singapore** in a similarly draconian style, also using Internal Seurity legislation to detain anyone thought to be a threat to the nation. Yet despite earlier

For a full **history of Singapore** and contemporary developments, turn to p.475.

doubts, Lee's transformation of the island's **economy** was amazing. Political alignments were made to maximize business opportunities – the government was non-Communist, ethnically mixed and (in theory at least) democratic, although like Malaysia's UMNO, no other party seriously rivalled the PAP.

The economy grew fast: per capita income increased an astonishing fourfold between 1965 and 1977, with huge profits being made in financial services, hi-tech manufacture, information technology and the petroleum industry. The high taxes these boom areas produced were used to bolster the island's infrastructure and housing, and by 1980 the impossible had been achieved: Singapore stood on the verge of becoming a **Newly Industialized Economy** (NIE), along with Hong Kong, Taiwan and South Korea. Lee had converted a tiny, highly populated country with no inherent assets into a dynamic crossroads between East and West.

But these developments came at a price. Through the 1970s and 1980s the image of Singapore as a humourless, dull place where everyone worked within the confines of a Big Brother civic apparatus started to take shape, and political intolerance became a fact of life. The **Opposition Worker's Party** won a by-election in 1984 and yet the candidate, J.B. Jeyaretnam, was unable to take his seat as he found himself charged under five offences. Although cleared, further investigations sullied his chances of developing his political career – clearly even one voice proffering criticism of Lee's policies could not be tolerated.

CONTEMPORARY MALAYSIA

For the last two decades Malaysian politics has been dominated by the present Prime Minister, **Dr. Mahathir Mohammed**, who, like all previous PMs leads the UMNO party; he has triumphed at every election since winning his party's nomination in 1981. UMNO is the dominat party in a coalition, the **Barisan National** which includes representatives from the other mainstream Chinese and Indian parties.

Over these years, UNMO's prime concern has been to extend the concept of the New

Economic Policy, which officially ended in 1990. Initially, this policy was underwritten by oil and timber revenues, while Malaysia looked away from the West, preferring to rely on other Southeast Asian countries, especially Singapore, as economic partners. But as the costs of the NEP started to bite, Mahathir galvanized Western investment, offering juicy financial incentives like low-tax rates and cheap labour. The UK soon became the main foreign investor in Malaysia.

Through tax, educational and financial breaks many Malays have got richer through the NEP's blatantly racist system of opportunities, but their share of the economy still stands at just 20 percent – way below the projected 30 percent declared when the NEP began. Although the policy was understandably popular with Malays, it was deeply resented by the Chinese and Indians, although outspoken critics of the government are few.

In 1991 the **New Development Policy** succeeded the NEP. Critics say the favoured position of the Malays is just being continued under a new name, but Mahathir has been careful to remove some of the most ill-regarded elements, such as the use of quotas to push Malays into powerful positions. Despite the lighter touch, *bumiputras* are still protected, and the Chinese and Indians have to work substantially harder for a commensurate reward in most spheres of Malaysian economic and educational life.

The structure of Malaysia's expanding **economy** has changed over the last twenty years. Manufacturing output overtook agriculture as the biggest earner in the late 1980s, while the shift to export-dominated areas, notably hi-tech industries and the services sector, has changed the landscape of regions like the Klang Valley, Petaling Jaya and Johor where industrial zones have mushroomed. The development patterns which took shape last century still hold true today: the most productive areas, with the highest per capita income, remain the west coast, particularly the urban areas of Kuala Lumpur, Ipoh, Penang, Melaka and Johor, with the east coast and interior lagging far behind, although revenue from **tourism** is changing the picture slightly.

During the 1990s Doctor Mahathir's position has been unassailable, his control over his country's political destiny aided and abetted by the impressive economic performance. National revenues have continued to increase substantially as a result either of profits from timber, mostly cut from the forests in Sarawak; the expansion of palm oil plantations often in logged areas, or cleared mangrove forests; and a further widening of the manufacturing base, especially in assembly line goods like electrical products and clothes.

EAST MALAYSIA; POLITICS AND LOGGING

The two Eastern Malaysian states have contrasting political complexions. Whereas in Sarawak the dominant Muslim party, the **Sarawak Alliance**, stands foursquare with the policies of UMNO on the mainland, in Sabah the **Parti Bersatu Sabah** (PBS) has opposed Mahathir on many issues. Led by a Christian, Joseph Pairin Kitingan, for many years – the only non-Muslim to hold political power in Malaysia – the PBS is critical of central goverment's bleeding of 95 percent of the profits of the state's crude petroleum exporting industry, and of its blatant pro-Muslim propaganda – Christians have even been offered cash incentives to convert to Islam. Pairin however lost power in the 1994 elections: a Muslim, Tan Sri Sakaran Dandai, is now the state's Chief Minister.

Although Sarawak's politics are dominated by Muslims in the Sarawak Alliance, which is part of the wider Barisan National, over the last twelve years the indigenous groups have had a small say in the political process. The **Parti Bansa Dayak Sarawak** (PBDS) was formed by defecting Iban representatives from the Sarawak Alliance, which has provided the indigenous population of the state (which makes up roughly 50 percent of the population) with an important voice.

Although Mahathir hasn't met with any substantial internal opposition, some of Malaysia's economic policies have been condemned internationally, while the issues surrounding **logging and development projects in particular** have brought severe criticism. Environmental groups in and outside the country have fought to highlight the irretrievable loss of biodiversity caused by the systematic felling of the Sarawak forests, but the angle which has most embarrassed the Sarawak state government – though less so Mahathir – is the impact of logging on the

For more on the **politics and economics of logging**, see the following feature, "Cutting Down the Rainforest".

lifestyles of the indigenous groups. Although laws exist to prevent the logging of customary land – areas which the ethnic inhabitants can prove have been lived on or used for agriculture for no less than fifty years – they are nearly impossible to enforce. Timber concessionaries frequently overstep the legal boundaries with impunity. International criticism has been met by defensive statements and at the 1992 Earth Summit in Rio de Janeiro, Mahathir suggested that Western nations had no right to tell the developing countries what they could and couldn't do with their natural resources. Currently, logging is actually on the decrease with government targets set to reduce timber harvesting by 10 percent each year. Critics counter by saying this isn't enough to save the forests, which within 30 years will cover less than 20 percent of the surface of the country, instead of the current 60 percent.

CONTROVERSY AND DEVELOPMENT

Deforestation is not the only hot topic on the environmental agenda in Malaysia; massive **dam constructions** are another. One example in Sarawak is a M$30-billion project, the **Bakun** dam in the Belaga district, which was recently approved by Kuala Lumpur. Environmentalists opposing the scheme say it flies in the face of an avalanche of scientific evidence indicating that the flooding of an area the size of Singapore will have numerous adverse effects, including the uprooting of five thousand ethnic people and the eradication of the region's unique biodiversity.

Yet the convoluted economic processes at work in modern Malaysia were highlighted again in early 1994 when it became clear that £1.3 billion's worth of defence contracts awarded to British companies had been linked to £234 million of British aid money for the building of a hydroelectric dam at **Pergau** in northern Kelantan. British civil servants declared the dam "a bad buy", but the British government went ahead, it was suggested, because the Malaysians had made the arms purchases conditional on the massive injection of funds to underwrite the dam. A Parliamentary Committee in Britain launched an inquiry, but the issue was firmly swept under the carpet in Malaysia where the press stood right behind Mahathir. Indeed, the British press coverage incensed the Malaysian government, which threatened to withhold contracts from British companies as a result.

Although the Pergau controversy harmed relations between the two countries, the thinking which underpins **Malaysian foreign policy** – essentially an open-arms approach, with slight favouritism showed to fellow-Islamic states – is unlikely to lead to any nation being viewed as a long-term enemy. Mahathir's chief goal throughout the last few years of his tenancy – Deputy Prime Minister Anwar is expected to succeed him before the end of the century – has been to raise Malaysia's profile to that of a **fully developed country** by the year 2020; to all intents and purposes, Malaysia is already a Newly Industrialized Economy. But many observers wonder how Malaysia can continue to expand its economy *and* maintain full employment, and suspect that certain skeletons in the closet, particularly the ethnic distrust which has characterized the country's recent past, will return to haunt it when recession starts to bite.

CUTTING DOWN THE RAINFOREST

Although much of the sting has gone out of the global environment debate since the Earth Summit in Rio de Janeiro in 1992, rainforest depletion continues to be a highly contentious subject in Malaysia. In recent years vociferous pressure groups have raised the profile of rainforest and wetland degradation among the general public, while the impact deforestation has had on Sarawak's ethnic groups has kept the environment debate on the boil.

However, the government in Kuala Lumpur is quick to defend itself. It insists that modern forest management programmes are increasingly sustainable, and that factors other than timber cultivation are responsible for the ecological erosion and the loss of traditional lifestyles.

Nonetheless, the main reason why deforestation remains an issue is simply because logging is so lucrative – **timber revenues** account for 13 percent of Malaysia's GNP and earn the nation nearly US$3 billion in export income per year. This makes Malaysia the planet's largest producer of tropical hardwood timber and the harvesting looks set to continue, albeit at a slower pace than in the rampant days of the 1970s and 1980s.

The government has promulgated environmental laws, most notably the obligation for timber concessionaires to conduct approved **Environmental Impact Assessments** (EIAs) before cultivation can commence. Environmental groups have had some success in limiting specific concessions by using this legislation, but the forest clearance continues apace – many Malaysian forestry professionals admit, off the record, that the laws won't work properly until more staff are employed and a greater commitment is made to tackle corruption and the over-harvesting of concession zones. The environmentalists themselves are fully stretched; the main group, *Sahabat Alam Malaysia*, has only a handful of full-time employees in the whole of Sarawak, and is consequently very limited in its sphere of operations.

THE HISTORICAL BACKGROUND

Malaysia's vast timber industry has important historical antecedents. The **sustainable exploitation** of forest products by the indigenous population has always played a vital part in the domestic and export economy of the region. For almost two thousand years, the ethnic tribes have bartered products like rattan, wild rubber and forest plants with foreign traders; first with Indian merchants, followed by Chinese, Malay, and more recently, British traders.

Commercial logging started in Sabah (then North Borneo) in the late nineteenth century. The *British Borneo Trading and Planting Company* began to extract large trees from the area around Sandakan to satisfy the demand for timber sleepers for the expanding railway system in China. By 1930 the larger **British Borneo Timber Company** (BBTC) was primarily responsible for the extraction of 178,000 cubic metres of timber, rising to nearly five million cubic metres by the outbreak of World War II, and Sandakan became one of the world's main timber ports. Most areas were logged indiscriminately and the indigenous tribal groups who lived there were brought into the economic system to work on North Borneo's rubber, tobacco and, later, oil palm plantations. The process intensified as the main players in Sabah tapped the lucrative Japanese market, where postwar reconstruction costing billions of dollars was underway. By the early 1960s, timber had accelerated past rubber as the region's chief export and by 1970 nearly 30 percent of Sabah had been extensively logged, with palm oil and other plantation crops replacing around a quarter of the degraded forest. Timber exports had accounted for less than 10 percent of all exports from Sabah in 1950; by the 1970s, this had rocketed to over 70 percent.

In **Sarawak** the development of large foreign-run plantations was hindered initially by the White Rajahs, James and Charles Brooke, who largely kept foreign investment out of their paternalistically run fiefdom. However, small indigenous timber concerns run by Chinese and Malay merchants were allowed to trade. But once the BBTC was given rights to start logging in northern Sarawak in the 1930s, timber extraction grew rapidly, especially since the third White Rajah, Vyner Brooke, was less stringent in his opposition to the economic development of the state. Timber was viewed as a vital commercial resource to be utilized in the massive reconstruction of the state, following the devastating Japanese occupation. During its short postwar period as a Crown Colony and, then after 1963, as a Malaysian state, logging in Sarawak has grown to become one of its chief revenue earners, alongside oil extraction. The state government encouraged foreign investment and issued timber concessions to rich individuals, who were encouraged to carve up ever more remote areas. Most of the Baram basin has been logged – the river is now a soupy, brown sludge due to the run off of earth and silt caused by the extraction process – and attention has switched to the remote Balui river system in the east of the state.

Peninsular Malaysia's pre-independence economy was not as reliant on timber revenues as those of Sabah and Sarawak. Although one sixth of the region's 120,000 square kilometres of forest, predominantly in Johor, Perak and Negeri Sembilan states, had been cut down by 1957, most of the logging had been done gradually and on a small, localized scale. As in Sabah, it was the demand for rail sleepers for the expansion of the Malayan train network in the 1920s which had first attracted the commercial logging companies, but wide-scale clearing and conversion to rubber and palm oil plantations in the more remote areas of Pahang, Perlis, Kedah and Terengganu didn't intensify until the 1960s. By the end of the 1970s more efficient extraction methods, coupled with a massive increase in foreign investement in the logging industry, had led to over 40 percent of the peninsula's remaining forests being either cleared for plantation purposes or partially logged.

THE CONTEMPORARY PICTURE

During the 1980s logging slowed down as a result of new legislation being enacted. Under the **National Forestry Policy** (NFP), deforestation was reduced to 900 square kilometres a year, almost a third slower than the previous rate. The government also designated 47,000 sq. km of land as **Permanent Forest Estates** in which a variety of valuable tree species are cultivated. But critics argue that these forest estates may not be able to recover from the

original depletion they suffered in the 1970s, and point out that the 1988 log output was over two million cubic metres higher than the 1986 figure – ie, far more than is considered sustainable and in apparent disregard of the NFP.

The largest share of contemporary logging takes place in **Sarawak:** – 80 percent of the total Malaysian output in the 1990s, or 2700 square kilometres a year. In principle, **customary land tenure**, which was enshrined in law throughout the White Rajah period, protects the land claimed by the state's indigenous tribal groups and formed the basis of the 1958 **Sarawak Land Code**. However, according to the groups and their supporters, much commercial logging ignores this. Not only are locations of special importance – burial places, access routes and sections of rivers used for fishing – disregarded by loggers, but even areas in which the indigenous people can prove they have lived and farmed for generations have been abused. Forests around Bintulu, Belaga and Limbang have suffered in this way, with the semi-nomadic Penan at the forefront of opposition to the encroachment onto their customary lands.

THE THREAT TO TRADITIONAL LIFESTYLES

Unlike many of the ethnic groups who can base their customary land claims on a settled history of farming, the nomadic lifestyle of the **Penan**, and the particular ways in which they utilize the land, makes it hard for their land rights to be defined and recognized. An added factor has been that since the mid-1980s the Sarawak state government's avowed policy has been to bring the Penan into what it views as the development process, by urging them to move to permanent longhouses, work in the cash economy and send their children to school.

The Penan have proved resilient to these attempts to assimilate them into the wider Malaysian social system, largely because the government diktats seem to go suspiciously hand-in-hand with an expansion of logging in their customary land areas. Very often, there's been no warning that Penan land has been earmarked for logging until the extraction actually begins – examples in remote areas of the Belaga district have been well documented by the environmental group **Sahabat Alam Malaysia**. Subsequently, the Penan have had to watch the destruction of their traditional living areas: trees are cut down; wildlife disappears along with its habitat; and the rivers become polluted by soil erosion, topsoil run off and siltation.

In retaliation, some Penan tribespeople have applied for **communal forest areas** (so-called "Penan zones") to be designated, so that some of their land would receive protection, but until now, all such applications have been refused. As a result the Penan, especially in the Baram watershed and Belaga, have resorted to **direct action**, with local people confronting logging companies, building barricades, removing and even destroying machinery. To stop the protests spreading, the state government amended the Foresty Act in 1987 to outlaw these actions, even when they took place on land proven to be owned by the locals. However, the blockades have continued, recieving worldwide publicity, which forced the state government to announce that they would set aside large areas as reserves where logging would not be allowed. This appears to be a step in the right direction, but the destruction of tribal areas still continues.

The current picture in **Sabah** is very similar, where recent aerial photographic surveys have shown that 44,000 square kilometres (over 60 percent) of the state's 74,000 square kilometres have been exploited for timber. However, there hasn't been the same level of tribal protest, simply because fewer of Sabah's indigenous people live in the deep interior where most of the logging takes place.

H3 PALM OIL CULTIVATION

Another hot issue in Sarawak in recent years has been **palm oil cultivation**. Increasingly, logged areas are being replanted with palm oil trees, now one of Sarawak's leading exports. The State Environment Department includes these monoculture plantations in its figure for the total amount of the state still under forest, but environment groups say that oil palm plantations sustain only a tiny proportion of the flora and fauna that a *dipterocarp* forest does, which they have invariably replaced. Accurate figures, however, are notoriously hard to come by. The eco-activists say less than half of Sarawak's 124,000 square kilometres remains as forest; whilst the state claims the figure is more like three-quarters – though it includes oil palm and other plantations zones in its calculations.

The **Malaysian government** is naturally keen to deflect attention away from the accusation that the timber concessions it grants are solely responsible for unsustainable timber production. In response, the government suggests that the **slash-and-burn** agricultural practices of the indigenous groups in Sarawak, and to a lesser degree, in Sabah and the interior of Peninsular Malaysia, are what cause substantial deforestation. But researchers have found that the bulk of this agricultural activity occurs in secondary rather than primary (untouched) forest. Indeed, environment groups believe that only around one hundred square kilometres of primary forest – a tiny proportion compared to the haul by commercial timber companies – is cleared by the indigenous groups annually.

Whatever the truth behind the figures for East Malaysia, there is far less of an argument about rainforest degradation in **Peninsular Malaysia**, largely because timber production there has been cut by around fifty percent in the last decade. Even so, the logged output is still estimated to stand at around five million cubic metres a year throughout the 1990s, which leaves around 50,000 square kilometres of forest out of a total surface area of 131,700 square kilometers – the remainder vanishing at the rate of nearly 1000 square kilometres each year.

However, **reforestation schemes** within the Permanent Forest Estates – government-run tracts of land given over to tree cultivation – are on the increase. An organization like the **Forest Resource Institute of Malaysia** (FRIM), which sustains an area of secondary forest on the edge of Kuala Lumpur, proves how a rainforest habitat can be renewed. Its ecological management plan ensures that a comprehensive range of flora, including tree species and a wide spectrum of plants, are planted and monitored over a long period. It must be stressed, however, that FRIM is the exception rather than the rule, and most environmentalists within Malaysia don't believe that renewable forestry can offset the damage caused by current timber extraction techniques, which seldom aid regrowth. As a rule, logging devastates over seventy percent of all the flora, topsoil and root structures in a given area.

THE FUTURE

As Malaysia – its spiralling GNP based on a solid manufacturing base – gets richer, it's likely that the revenue derived from cutting down the rainforests will decrease. As a consequence, the government hopes that the controversies surrounding logging – which have pitted "Third World" leaders like Prime Minister Dr. Mahathir against richer countries who argue that Malaysia should stop exploiting its dwindling forests for the future safety of the planet – will die down. In the meantime, however, timber remains the highest export earner.

Malaysia is slowly becoming more environmentally friendly, largely as a result of well-organized and scientifically persuasive organizations within the country, but the **pace of change** is slow. There is still a lack of effective reforestation schemes, though the Malaysian government does at least claim it will not follow the example of Thailand, where only 10 percent of the country remains forested, and it condemns the horrendous situation in lawless Burma and Cambodia where Thai and Japanese companies are clearing the remaining stocks of the world's teak forests at devastating speed. However, the complex system of logging **regulations** in force in Malaysia has, in recent years, lacked bite: if the logging is to be stopped, then the government has to apply teeth to what have hitherto been purely symbolic enforcement measures.

Perhaps more importantly, if Malaysia wants to continue talking about the country's cultural diversity in its tourist promotion brochures, then the land rights of the indigenous groups, particularly in Sarawak, have to be respected. The legislation, especially the EIA system, currently little more than a sham, must be made to work quickly.

WILDLIFE

There's an extraordinary tropical biodiversity on the Malay peninsula and in Borneo, incorporating over six hundred species of birds; more than two hundred mammal species, including the tiger, Asian elephant, orang-utan and tapir; many thousands of flowering plant species, among them the insectivorous pitcher plant and scores of others of known medicinal value; and over one hundred species of brightly coloured butterflies. This enormous variety of bird, plant and animal life makes any visit to a tropical rainforest a memorable experience.

Downtown Singapore, on the other hand, is not the sort of place you would expect to find much animal or plant life. The rapid urbanization of Singapore has had a major impact on its indigenous wildlife, and the state has consequently lost many of its original forest plant species, all its large mammals and many of its ecologically sensitive bird species such as hornbills. However, two remnant patches of tropical forest still survive amid the rampant development – at Bukit Timah Nature Reserve and the Botanic Gardens.

Although Malaysia is divided into two distinct parts – Peninsular and East Malaysia (the states of Sabah and Sarawak on the island of Borneo) – the wildlife and plant communities of both areas are very similar, since Borneo was joined to the mainland by a land bridge during the ice age. Nonetheless, there are some specific differences. The forests of the peninsula support populations of several large mammal species, such as tiger, tapir and gaur (a forest-dwelling wild cattle), which are absent from Borneo. Other large mammals, like the Asian elephant, and birds like the hornbill, occur both on Borneo and on the peninsula; while Borneo features the orang-utan (the "man of the forest") and the proboscis monkey. Indeed, this latter species is endemic to the island of Borneo.

WILDLIFE SITES

Two of the most exciting – and accessible – areas in which to **view wildlife** are featured below. The round-ups of bird, plant and animal life at **Taman Negara** and **Fraser's Hill** should be read in conjunction with the general accounts of both places in the guide. In addition, there are shorter wildlife accounts and special features throughout the guide: check the page references given below. It's worth noting that Sarawak, in particular, has endless opportunities for observing wildlife in its national parks and river systems: all the practical details for visiting the region are contained in Chapter 6.

Wherever you plan to go, it's important to remember that observing wildlife in tropical

---

A WILDLIFE CHECKLIST

Sites

Danum Valley Conservation Area: Sabah (p.446).

Fraser's Hill: Peninsula (p.121).

Kinabalu National Park: Sabah (p.429).

Pulau Tioman: Peninsula (p.303).

Rantau Abang: Peninsula (p.255).

Semanggoh Wildlife Rehabilitation Centre: Sarawak (p.343).

Sepilok Orang Utan Rehabilitation Centre: Sabah (p.441).

Singapore: Botanic Gardens (p.524) and Bukit Timah (p.525).

Taman Negara: Peninsula (p.194).

Turtle Islands Park: Sabah (p.442).

Wildlife

Hornbills (p.393).

Marine turtle (p.256).

Proboscis monkeys (p.444).

forests requires much patience, and on any one visit it is unlikely that you will encounter more than a fraction of the wildlife living in the forest. Many of the mammals are shy and nocturnal.

REFERENCE BOOKS

The following **books** are useful sources of reference and most are available on the ground in Malaysia and Singapore: the Sabah Society's *Pocket Guide to the Birds of Borneo* (Sabah Society, Malaysia); M. Strange & A. Jeyarajasingam's *Photographic Guide to the Birds of Peninsular Malaysia and Singapore* (Sun Tree Publishing, Singapore); J. Payne, C. Francis & K. Phillipp's *Field Guide to the Mammals of Borneo* (Sabah Society, Malaysia); M. Tweedie's *Mammals of Malaysia* (Longman, Malaysia); and Lord Medway's *Wild Mammals of Malaya & Singapore* (Oxford University Press).

TAMAN NEGARA

The vast expanse (4343 sq. km) of **Taman Negara** contains one of the world's oldest tropical rainforests and is generally regarded as one of Asia's finest national parks. It has an **equatorial climate**, with rainfall throughout the year and no distinct dry season. Temperatures can reach 35°C during the day, with the air often feeling very muggy. Most rain falls as heavy convectional showers in the afternoon, following a hot and sunny morning – from November to February, heavy rains may cause flooding in low-lying areas.

FOREST TREES

The natural richness of the habitat is reflected in the range of forest types found within the park. Only a small proportion of Taman Negara is true **lowland forest**, though it's here that most of the trails and hides are located. The lowlands support **dipterocarp** (meaning "two-winged fruit") evergreen forest, featuring tall tropical hardwood species and thick stemmed lianas. There are more than four hundred *dipterocarp* species in Malaysia and it's not uncommon to find up to forty in just one small area of forest. Among those present at Taman Negara are the majestic fifty-metre tall *tualang*, Southeast Asia's tallest tree; many others have broad, snaking buttress roots and

leaves the size of dinner plates. Several species of **fruit trees**, such as durian, mango, jambu and rambutan also grow wild here.

On slightly higher ground, **montane forest** predominates, mainly oak and native conifers, with a shrub layer of rattan and dwarf palm. Higher still (above 1500m on Gunung Tahan) is **cloud forest**, where trees are often cloaked by swirling mist, and the damp boughs bear thick growths of mosses and ferns. At elevations of over 1700m, miniature montane forest of rhododendron and fan palms is found, but it will be the hardy explorer who reaches such heights.

MAMMALS

The best method of trying to see some of the larger herbivorous (grazing) **mammals** is to spend the night in a **hide** overlooking a saltlick – the animals visit these natural and artificial "salt sites" to consume salt. There are six hides in the park, and to maximize your chances of spotting mammals you will need to stay overnight at one.

Animals commonly encountered include the Malayan **tapir**, a species related to horses and rhinos, though pig-like in appearance with a short, fat body, a long snout and black-and-white colouring. The **gaur** (wild cattle) is dark in colour apart from its white leg patches, looking like ankle socks; and there are also several species of **deer** you might come across: the larger *sambar;* the *kijang;* or barking deer, this the size of a roe deer; and the lesser and greater mousedeer, these the last two largely nocturnal, and not much bigger than a rabbit.

Primates (monkeys and gibbons) are found throughout the park, although they are quite shy since they have traditionally been hunted for food by the park's indigenous groups. The dawn chorus of a white-handed **gibbon** troupe – making a plaintive whooping noise – is not a sound which will be quickly forgotten. Other primates include the long-tailed and pig-tailed **macaques**, which come to the ground to feed, the latter identified by its shorter tail, brown fur and pinkish brown face. There are dusky (or spectacled – due to the white "spectacles" around the eyes and a white patch over the mouth) and banded **leaf monkeys**, too, which can be recognized by their long, drooping tails (gibbons have no tails) and their habit of keeping their bodies hidden amongst the foliage –

whereas macaques feed on the ground, both leaf monkeys and gibbons keep to the trees.

Several **squirrel** species, including the black and common giant squirrels, are present in the park, and towards dusk there's a chance of seeing the nocturnal red flying squirrel shuffling along the highest branches of a tree before launching itself to glide across the forest canopy to an adjacent tree. This squirrel can make continuous glides of up to one 100m at a time.

Other mammals you might encounter by – admittedly fairly remote – chance are the Asian **elephant**, with smaller ears and a more humped back than the African; **tigers,** of which a reasonably healthy population exists due to an abundance of prey and the relatively large size of the protected area; and **sun bears**. The latter are an interesting species: standing about 70cm high on all fours, and around 1.5m in length, they are dark brown or black, with muzzle and breast marked dirty white to dull orange. They live on fruit, honey and termites and their behaviour towards humans can be unpredictable, particularly if there are cubs nearby.

Clouded leopards are also present, a beautifully marked cat species with a pattern of cloud-like markings on the sides of the body. They live mostly in the trees, crossing from bough to bough in their search for food, eating monkeys, squirrels and birds, which they swat with their claws; they're most active at twilight. Smaller predators include the **leopard cat** (around the size of a large domestic cat) and several species of nocturnal **civet**, some of which have been known to enter the hides at night in search of tourists' food. Smooth **otters** may also sometimes be seen, in small family groups along sungei Tembeling.

BIRDS

Over 250 species of bird – including some of the most spectacular forest-dwelling birds in the world – have been recorded in Taman Negara, though many species are shy or only present in small numbers. Birds are at their most active from early to mid-morning, and again in the late afternoon and evening periods; the areas around Kuala Keniam, and the Kumbang and Tabing hides are particularly worth visiting.

Resident forest birds include several species of **green pigeon**, which feed on the fruiting trees, along with species such as **bulbuls** (vocal, fruit-eating birds which often flock to feed). **Wintering birds** from elsewhere in Asia, such as warblers and thrushes, join resident **minivets** (slender, colourful birds with long, graduated tails, white, yellow or red bands in the wings and outer tail feathers of the same colour) and **babblers** (a short-tailed, round-winged, ground-dwelling species) from September to March, and it is during this period that the visitor can hope to encounter the greatest diversity of birds. Up to seventy species alone can be seen near the park headquarters, particularly if the trees are in fruit.

Brilliantly coloured **pittas** in hues of red, yellow, blue and black are ground-dwelling birds, which generally occur singly or in pairs, though they are notoriously shy and difficult to approach. The resident species are the Giant, Garnet and Banded Pittas with Blue-winged and Hooded Pittas being winter visitors.

In addition, several species of pheasant may be seen along the trails, including the **Malaysian Peacock Pheasant**, a shy bird with a blue-green crest and a patch of bare, orange facial skin. The feathers of the back and tail have green *ocelli* (eye-spots). The Crested and Crestless **Fireback** are similar species of pheasant, differing in the Crested Fireback's black crest, white tail plumes, blue sheen upper parts and orange (rather than grey) belly. The **Great Argus** is the largest pheasant species present in the area, with the male birds reaching a maximum of 1.7 metres in length including the long tail feathers, their penetrating "kwow wow" series of call notes audible most days in the park. Finally, the **Mountain Peacock Pheasant** – very similar in plumage to the Malaysian Peacock Pheasant – is found high on Gunung Tahan and is endemic to Malaysia.

You'll also see birds of prey, with two of the most common species, the **Crested Serpent Eagle** and the **Changeable Hawk Eagle**, often spotted soaring over gaps in the forest canopy. The Crested Serpent Eagle (with a 75cm wingspan; about the size of a buzzard) can be identified by the black and white bands on the trailing edge of the wings and on the tail.

Other species confined to tropical forests are **trogons** (brightly coloured, mid-storey birds), of which five species are present at Taman Negara, and several species of **hornbill** – large, broad-winged, long-tailed forest birds with huge, almost outlandish bills (see p.393 for more on these).

REPTILES AND AMPHIBIANS

Reptiles and amphibians are well represented in the area. **Monitor lizards** (which can grow to lengths of over 2m) can be found close to the park headquarters as can **skinks** (a type of lizard which slithers along the ground a bit like a snake, not using its legs).

Several species of snake are present, too, including the reticulated **python** (which feeds on small mammals and birds and can grow to a staggering 9m in length), and the king and common **cobras**; king cobras, the largest venomous snake in the world, grow up to five metres long. These are all pretty rare in Taman Negara, though, and you're more likely to come across **whip snakes** (which eat insects and lizards) and – most common of all – harmless green **tree snakes** (which, not surprisingly, live in the trees, and eat lizards).

FRASER'S HILL

At **Fraser's Hill** visitors can escape the stultifying tropical heat of the lowlands and venture into the cool breezes and fogs of the mountain forests, where ferns and pitcher plants cling to damp, moss-covered branches. It's a noted area for bird watching, with the hill itself harbouring several montane species of bird, while mammals represented in the area include those normally restricted to more mountainous regions, in addition to some lowland species.

Much of the **forest** at Fraser's Hill is in pristine condition and the route there takes you from lowland forest through sub-montane to montane forest. Higher up on the hill, there are more evergreen tree species present, while the very nature of the vegetation changes: the trees are more gnarled and stunted, and the boughs heavily laden with dripping mosses and colourful epiphytic orchids (ie, orchids which grow on other plants and trees).

MAMMALS

The more strictly montane mammal species at Fraser's Hill include the **siamang gibbon**, a large, all-black gibbon, lacking any pale facial markings, that spends its time exclusively in trees. There are also several species of **bat**, including the montane form of the Malayan fruit bat and the grey fruit bat, and several **squirrel** species such as the Mountain Red-bellied Squirrel and the tiny Himalayan Striped Squirrel. The latter species has a pattern of black-and-yellow stripes running along the length of its back. Lowland mammal species which may be encountered are the tiger, clouded leopard, sun bear and leaf monkeys, for descriptions of which see "Taman Negara" above. However, most of these are scarce here, and you can only realistically expect to encounter monkeys, squirrels and, possibly, siamangs.

BIRDS

A feature of montane forest bird flocks is the **mixed feeding flock**, which may contain many different species. These pass rapidly through an area of forest searching for and gleaning insects as they go, and it's quite likely that different observers will see entirely different species in one flock. Species which commonly occur within these flocks are the **lesser racket-tailed drongo**, a black crow-like bird with long tail streamers; the **speckled piculet**, a small spotted woodpecker; and the **blue nuthatch**, a small species – blue-black in colour with a white throat and pale eye ring – which runs up and down tree trunks. Several species of brightly coloured **laughing thrushes**, small thrush-sized birds which spend time foraging on the ground, also occur in these flocks. One sound to listen out for is the distinctive cackling "took" call of the **helmeted hornbill** – see p.393 for more on these birds.

Fraser's Hill itself peaks at 1310 metres at the High Pines, where there is a ridge trail. Here, there's the possibility of encountering species unlikely to be seen at lower altitudes, including the brown bullfinch and the **cutia** – this, a striking bird, with blue cap, black eyeline and tail, white underparts barred black and a chestnut-coloured back.

Tony Stones

MALAYSIAN MUSIC

Like many places in the region, Malaysia is rapidly becoming Westernized at the expense of its own traditions, and lacks the dynamic indigenous music scene of its neighbour Indonesia. The creation of the modern Malaysian Federation in 1963 had the effect of pushing the traditional royal court musical styles and folk music into the background and such music now tends to be heard only at festivals or in the Islamic heartland of Kelantan state, in the northeast corner of Peninsular Malaysia. In their place are the pan-Asian pop styles that have more in common with Western pop music than Malaysian traditions.

Nevertheless, when you do track down Malaysian traditional music, there's a surprising richness to it, deriving from the peculiar blend of **ethnic influences** brought by the Arab and Chinese traders, the Indian workers and colonizers from Portugal, Holland and Britain.

The Malays adopted Arabic **instruments** such as the *gendang* (double-headed drum) and *rebana* (frame drum), the harmonium from India, and the *tawak* gong from China, to make their own folk styles. The most prominent melodic instrument is the *rebab*, the spiked fiddle of Middle Eastern origin, found also in Thailand and Indonesia. A lot of contemporary musicians use the Western violin, brought originally by the Portuguese, which they play in *rebab* style, in the lap.

The **pantum** style of Malaysian singing survives, too – centuries old and still very popular. This consists of vocal duets – sometimes with drums, but more often a cappella – which are nearly always improvised. *Pantums* developed from Islamic devotional song, where sections of the Koran would be sung. Nowadays even adverts can be sung in *pantum* and can often be witty or slapstick in character. *Pantum* has become quite an informal style with its loose metre offering opportunities for the singers to be topical and satirical, and still, occasionally, devotional.

KELANTAN: SILAT AND ZIKIR BARAT

Kelantan is the heart of the country's folk culture and the place to start a musical tour of Malaysia. Malay music and dance is performed at the cultural centre (see p.235) in Kota Bharu every week, and performances usually incorporate a wide range of different styles. A small ensemble of *aderams* (long drums), *serunai* (a cross between a clarinet and an oboe) and *tawaks* generates a loose set of cross rhythms, while two Malay gents in baggy costumes perform **silat** – an ancient dance of self-defence – in a sandpit. As the music intensifies, their flowing Tai Chi like movements change and they grip each other. The first to throw the other onto the ground is the winner. The music rises to a crescendo as the wrestling intensifies, the *serunai* screeching atonally while the drums and gongs quicken the loose rhythm.

Alongside the *silat* band are twelve men sitting in another sandpit with small, brightly coloured, wooden xylophones in front of them. The rhythm they hammer out in unison is fast and jolly, the idea being for all the players to end each piece at precisely the same time. Although a recreational activity more than an art form, this is an interesting style of communal music, known as **kertok**, which originated with the *orang asli*.

Later in the day there is usually a **wayang kulit** (shadow puppet) performance, a tradition which occurs across Southeast Asia and presents tales from the Hindu epic, the *Ramayana*. In Malaysia, however, the sound is very different to the *gamelan* (court music) that accompanies Indonesian *wayang kulit*. Here, a larger version of the *silat* band, including a xylophone, hammers out the fanfare. The puppeteer sits beside the musicians onstage behind a screen, and while he chants the epic he illustrates the story with dozens of wooden shadow puppets.

A different side of Malaysian music emerges at night in Kota Bharu, as people meet after evening prayers for supper at the market's outdoor stalls. Here, you can hear the distinct refrains of **zikir birat**. Singers chant rhythmically in *Bahasa Malaysia*, over a dense bed of percussion. Each player takes turns to chant a verse, which can be elaborated upon, allowing the performance to go on for many hours.

The form is basically a version of Islamic ritual and particularly of Sufic singing (known as *zikir*). In its most traditional form, two singers perform on the street outside mosques or in markets, alternating verses in praise of Allah to the rhythm of a single tambourine. As it took on a more secular slant, however, teams of men would chant newly composed texts about anything of topical interest. *Zikir birat* now has its pop stars, like Draman, Dollah and Mat Yeh, and is beginning to be recorded by Indian and Chinese singers, too.

KUALA LUMPUR: GHAZAL AND DONDANG

In **Kuala Lumpur**, traditional music doesn't seem to play the same integral part in everyday life. Most of the music you hear in the city, pounding from the cassette bars, is homegrown pop and rock. However, wandering the streets you do hear snatches of Islamic love songs – not unlike *ghazals* – performed by blind buskers, who accompany themselves on tinny keyboards.

More professional (and more strictly) **ghazal** artists are to be heard on cassette or in concert. The great star of this genre was the lamented **Kamariah Noor**, who died recently. She had a voice both intense and languid, bending and holding notes to inject maximum emotion into a song. Kamariah often sang with her husband, **Hamzah Dolmat**, Malaysia's greatest *rebab* player, whose slow, rather mournful style is characterized by a wonderful melodic creativity.

Other recent Malay stars include the **Kumpulum Sri Maharani** ensemble, which plays **dondang sayang**, a slow, intense,

majestic music led by sharp percussive drum rolls, which trigger a shift in melody or a change in the pace of the rhythm. This is a quintessentially Malaysian style, bringing together Indian, Arabic, Chinese and Portuguese instruments to create a mood of gentle intensity. *Tabla* and harmonium from India and the double-headed drum (the *gendang*) and tambourine from Arabia mark out the rhythms, while the violin and the *oud* provide the melodies.

Dondang traditionally accompanies classical singing – usually duets whose lyrics, like in *ghazal*, are often romantic epics. Maharani's band integrates electric keyboard and snippets of guitar into the traditional framework. Songs these days are short, starting with fast, expressive drumming. When the singers begin, the rhythm slows down, only to accelerate for dramatic emphasis towards the finale.

MELAKA: RONGGENG

Melaka makes a good musical stop, to hear the old fiddle music of the *rebab*, adapted here to the European instrument. It's a peculiarly Malaysian style of playing that is the basis of the main folk dance music across the country, **ronggeng**. Other instruments in the *ronggeng* unit include two *rebana* (frame drums) and a brass gong to mark the time.

Ronggeng fiddlers play a wide range of melodies, which, perhaps due to the music's Portuguese heritage, sound a trifle Romany or Moorish. Performances revolve around dozens of tunes that locals know instinctively. When the singers join in, the rhythm slows and the violinist switches from ebullient fiddler to plaintive accompanist.

One of the most popular dances is the **joget**. Other percussive instruments are added to the basic *ronggeng* format and most *joget* tunes end with a "chinchang passage" – the point where the drums and violin quicken and the dancers hop from one leg to another like dancing cockerels.

And then there is **zapin**, yet another musical style led by the accordion. Like in so much Malaysian folk music, Arab, European and Indian elements come together here to form something new. The *zapin* tempos start out slow but will often quicken abruptly as the accordion provides the cue for the dancers to improvise around their set steps.

COURT AND CEREMONIAL MUSIC

Nobat is almost impossible to see these days as it's the classical music of the Sultan's courts and is, by definition, played to a private audience. This music is functional rather than performed as entertainment, and is an inherent part of religious (Islamic) rituals and court ceremonies like the crowning of a ruler, weddings and funerals. *Nobat* came from the Middle East and became enmeshed with the pomp of the Sultanates soon after the region embraced Islam in the fourteenth and fifteenth centuries. The main instruments – the *nehara* (large drum), *serunai* (oboe) and *nafiri* (silver trumpet) – are fairly similar to those used in Thailand's small *piphat* classical ensembles.

At East Coast festivals watch out for **Main Puteri**, a music-cum-dance style used for healing by shamens. Its trance-like beat is played on the *rebab*, *gengang* drums and *tetawak* (gongs). The music posseses the shamen, who is then able to extract evil spirits from, and consequently purify, his client.

Among the **ethnic groups** in Sarawak, music plays an important part in dance dramas and provides an aural backdrop for ceremonies like the rite-of-passage *Gawai Kenyaalang* festival. The main instruments are a variety of gongs, a *sape* (lute) and small drums. Long epic dramas are often sung at auspicious occasions, although among most groups, especially the Kelabits of northern Sarawak, this tradition is fast disappearing.

CROONERS: POP AND ROCK

Malaysian pop music was born in the 1950s when a young singer called **P. Ramlee** rose to fame. Very much the Harry Belafonte of Malaysian music, Ramlee set romantic lyrics to Malay melodies, bringing the *dondang sayang* style up to date in duets with his wife **Saloma**. Musically, he expanded the folk instrument repeortoire, often recording with an orchestra, and reflecting the influence of Cuban mambos and cha-cha-chas in the postwar period. His singing style is a European version of classical *dondang* – an Arabic-inflected purring baritone, romantically lush but vulnerable. His great duets with Salome are Malaysian pop music's finest hour. To hear Ramlee's work, head for the *Blue Moon* in KL's *Hotel Equatorial* (see p.105).

Ramlee launched a new movement in modernizing classical singing, shortening the songs and using Western instruments. Singers like **Zaleha Hamid** continue the tradition, singing in a more upbeat but still orthodox style, backed by kit drums, keyboards, bass and flute. Along with other stars like **Sharifah Aini** and **Herman Tino**, Hamid's material is the most popular of the older-style Malaysian music.

However, the younger generation have firmly turned their back on this kind of Malay music. In the 1960s and 1970s they looked to Indonesian pop, which was adapting Western rock ideas. These days, **Malay rock and pop** cassettes outnumber *dondang*, *ronggang* and *zikir* twenty to one in the stores, but there is little to be said in its favour since it is so completely derivative – the **heavy metal** music industry is second only to Brazil's among developing countries. The only Malaysian element is the lyrics which, due to legislation, have to be sung in *Bahasa Malaysia* rather than English.

The brightest light at the soft-rock end of the spectrum is **Sheila Majid**. She has become Malaysia's first international pop star, filling halls in Indonesia and Japan. Her singing style is a kind of mellow Asian soul, with a synthesized backdrop and George Benson-style guitar rhythms. Her producer and husband Roslan Aziz is keen to introduce more traditional instrumental sounds but the market at present wants things Western. Nonetheless, Majid has provided a link between the traditional and the modern in her album "Legenda", where she covers songs by P. Ramlee.

A new development is the birth of a home-grown **rap** style, which although rhythmically taking its call from the United States, is performed in Malay with lyrics geared towards particularly Malaysian experiences. One group, **4U2C**, has had some of its material banned because of the controversial nature of the lyrics.

NEW DIRECTIONS

Although Western-style pop and rock dominate the Malaysian charts and media, over the past few years a few musicians have started looking back to their roots and to traditional melodies, while still working within a Western context. It's perhaps not enough to talk of as a movement, though it does have a name — **musica nusantara** (music of the archipelago).

The two main artists involved are **Shequal** and **Zainal Abidin**, both of whom use acoustic instruments like accordions, tabla, sitar and flute. They write their songs and melodies themselves, rather than updating classics, and they both come from rock backgrounds. Abidin used to sing with soft-rock band Headwind before leaving to search for a more indigenous direction.

He found this in what he called *kampung* (village) music, and began to write lyrics concerned with the erosion of the old ways of life. His song "Baba" warns of the threat to the Baba culture, the Malay-speaking Chinese community in Melaka. More recently, however, he has started playing what he calls "World Music", mixing rock and traditional styles with those of the African musicians, Youssou N'Dour and Papa Wemba, whom he met at a WOMAD festival in Japan.

Shequal is well worth checking out, too. His best-known song, "Balada Nusantara", is a beautiful melody led by a lovely accordion line. The mood is upbeat but relaxed, evoking the atmosphere of the coast with its slow pace of life and traditions.

Another interesting direction is evident in the releases by a fusion group called **Asiabeat**, who are causing a stir around KL with an intriguing blend of East and West, fusing traditional Eastern instruments like the *shakuhachi* (Japanese bamboo flute), played by an American, John Kaiser Neptune, with saxophones and guitars. Asiabeat often plays in KL (see p.105 for music venues).

Other musicians pursuing individual destinies include **Kit Leee**, who records way-out electronic pieces, most recently with a talented Brazilian singer, Marilia, and his friend and some-time collaborator **Rafique**, who produces KL's only music with a political edge. He gets away with criticizing the government, he says, because he is the only person doing it. His songs include "Shut Up", about the mid-1980s Internal Security Act, and "Khalwat", about the Muslim law that forbids courting couples from getting too close before marriage.

Taken (and abridged) from the Rough Guide to World Music. Thanks to Jak Kilby for additional research.

SINGAPORE IN LITERATURE

Since its foundation in 1819, Singapore has provided rich pickings for travel writers, novelists and historians. However, due to the paucity of local education in the last century, we have to rely almost exclusively on writings by foreign visitors for early depictions of the island.

The one notable exception is the historian **Abdullah bin Kadir**, born in Melaka in 1797 of Malay and Tamil stock, and later employed as a scribe by Sir Stamford Raffles. The first excerpt below comes from his autobiography, the *Hikayat Abdullah*, published in Malay in 1849, it remains a fascinating social and historic document, despite its factual inaccuracies. It is interesting to contrast Abdullah's squalid portrayal of early Singapore with the altogether more civilized picture painted by spunky English traveller **Isabella Bird**, thirty years later. By the time of her five-week tour of Singapore and the Malay states in 1879 (recorded in *The Golden Chersonese*), Bird had already seen America, Canada, Japan, Hawaii, Australia and New Zealand. Subsequent travels took her to Armenia, Persia, Kurdistan, Kashmir and Tibet, and saw her honoured as the first woman fellow of the Royal Geographical Society in 1892.

Singapore's contemporary writers are represented first by **Lee Tzu Pheng**, a lecturer at the National University of Singapore, whose poem "My Country and My People" reflects the cultural disorientation inherent in the establishment of a new nationhood. Finally, **R. Rajaram**'s short story "Hurry" is played out against a Singapore completely remoulded since the days of Abdullah, though the nineteenth-century scribe would surely have recognized the hustle and bustle that Rajaram evokes in his story.

HIKAYAT ABDULLAH

It was Colonel Farquhar's habit to go for a walk every morning looking round the district. It was all covered with thick scrub. Only in the middle of the open space already mentioned were there no thick bushes, but only myrtle, rhododendron and eugenia trees. On the side nearest the shore were many kinds of trees, *ambong-ambong*, *melpari*, *bulangan* and scattered tree trunks. On the opposite side of the river there was nothing to be seen except mangrove trees, *bakau*, *api-api*, *buta-buta*, *jeruju* and strewn branches. There was no good piece of ground even as much as sixty yards wide, the whole place being covered in deep mud, except only on the hills where the soil was clay. There was a large rise, of moderate elevation, near the point of the headland at the estuary of Singapore River.

In the Singapore River estuary there were many large rocks, with little rivulets running between the fissures, moving like a snake that has been struck. Among these many rocks there was a sharp-pointed one shaped like the snout of a swordfish. The Sea Gypsies used to call it the Swordfish's Head and believed it to be the abode of spirits. To this rock they all made propitiatory offerings in their fear of it, placing bunting on it and treating it with reverence. "If we do not pay our respects to it" they said "When we go in and out of the shallows it will send us to destruction send us to destruction." Every day they brought offerings and placed them on the rock.' All along the shore there were hundreds of human skulls rolling about on the sand; some old, some new, some with hair still sticking to them, some with the teeth filed and others without. News of these skulls was brought to Colonel Farquhar and when he had seen them he ordered them to be gathered up and cast into the sea. So the people collected them in sacks and threw them into the sea. The Sea Gypsies were asked "Whose are all these skulls?" and they replied "These are the skulls of men who were robbed at sea. They were slaughtered here. Wherever a fleet of boats or a ship is plundered it is brought to this place for a division of the spoils. Sometimes there is wholesale slaughter among the crews when the cargo is grabbed. Sometimes the pirates tie people up and try out their weapons here along the sea shore." Here too was the place where they went in for cock-fighting and gambling.

One day Colonel Farquhar wanted to ascend the Forbidden Hill, as it was called by the Temenggong. The Temenggong's men said "None of us have the courage to go up the hill because there are many ghosts on it. Every day one can hear on it sounds as of hundreds of men. Sometimes one hears the sound of heavy drums and of people shouting." Colonel Farquhar laughed and said, "I should like to see your ghosts" and turning to his Malacca men "Draw this gun to the top of the hill." Among them there were several who were frightened, but having no option they pulled the gun up. All who went up were Malacca men, none of the Singapore men daring to approach the hill. On the hill there was not much forest and not many large trees, only a few shrubs here and there. Although the men were frightened they were shamed by the presence of Colonel Farquhar and went up whether they wanted to or not. When they reached the top Colonel Farquhar ordered the gun to be loaded and then he himself fired twelve rounds in succession over the top of the hill in front of them. Then he ordered a pole to be erected on which he hoisted the English flag. He said "Cut down all these bushes." He also ordered them to make a path for people to go up and down the hill. Everyday there was this work being done, the undergrowth being slashed down and a pathway cleared.

At that time there were few animals, wild or tame on the Island of Singapore, except rats. There were thousands of rats all over the district, some almost as large as cats. They were so big that they used to attack us if we went out walking at night and many people were knocked over. In the house where I was living we used to keep a cat. One night at about midnight we heard the cat mewing, and my friend went out carrying a light to see why the cat was making such a noise. He saw six or seven rats crowding round and biting the cat; some bit its ears, some its paws, some its nose so that it could no longer move but only utter cry after cry. When my companion saw what was happening he shouted to me and I ran out at the back to have a look. Six or seven men came pressing round to watch but did nothing to release the cat, which only cried the louder at the sight of so many men, like a person beseeching help. Then someone fetched a stick and struck at the rats, killing the two which were biting the cat's ears. Its ears freed, the cat then pounced on another rat and killed it. Another was hit by the man with a stick and the rest ran away. The cat's face and nose were lacerated and covered with blood. This was the state of affairs in all the houses, which were full of rats. They could hardly be kept under control, and the time had come when they took notice of people. Colonel Farquhar's place was also in the same stateand he made an order saying "To anyone who kills a rat I will give one *wang.*" When people heard of this they devised all manner of instruments for killing rats. Some made spring-traps, some pincer traps, some cage-traps, some traps with running nooses, some traps with closing doors, others laid poison or put down lime. I had never in my life before seen rats caught by liming; only now for the first time. Some searched for rat-holes, some speared the rats or killed them in various other ways. Every day crowds of people brought the dead bodies to Colonel Farquhar's place, some having fifty or sixty others only six or seven At first the rats brought in every morning were counted almost in thousands, and Colonel Farquhar paid out according to his promise. After six or seven days a multitude of rats were still to be seen, and he promised five duit for each rat caught. They were still brought in in thousands and Colonel Farquhar ordered a very deep trench to be dug and the dead bodies to be buried. So the numbers began to dwindle, until people were bringing in only some ten or twenty a day. Finally the uproar and the campaign against the rats in Singapore came to an end, the infestation having completely subsided.

Some time later a great many centipedes appeared, people being bitten by them all over the place. In every dwelling, if one sat for any length of time, two or three centipedes would drop from the attap roof. Rising in the morning from a night's sleep one would be sure to find two or three very large centipedes under one's mat, and they caused people much annoyance. When the news reached Colonel Farquhar he made an order saying that to anyone who killed a centi-pede he would give one *wang.* Hearing this people searched high and low for centipedes, and every day they brought in hundreds which they had caught by methods of their own devising. So the numbers dwindled until once in two or three days some twenty of thirty centipedes were brought in. Finally the campaign and furore caused by the centipedes came to an end, and people no longer cried out because of the pain when they got bitten.

The above extract is taken from the Hikayat Abdullah, by Abdullah bin Kadir, translated by A.H. Hill.

THE GOLDEN CHERSONESE

Singapore, January 19, 1879.

It is hot – so hot! – but not stifling, and all the rich-flavoured, coloured fruits of the tropics are here – fruits whose generous juices are drawn from the moist and heated earth, and whose flavours are the imprisoned rays of the fierce sun of the tropics. Such cartloads and piles of bananas and pine-apples, such heaps of gold and green giving off fragrance! Here, too, are treasures of the heated crystal seas – things that one has dreamed of after reading Jules Verne's romances. Big canoes, manned by dark-skinned men in white turbans and loin-cloths, floated round our ship, or lay poised on the clear depths of aquamarine water, with fairy freights - forests of coral white as snow, or red, pink, violet, in massive branches or fern-like sprays, fresh from their warm homes beneath the clear warm waves, where fish as bright-tinted as themselves flash through them "living light." There were displays of wonderful shells, too, of pale rose-pink, and others with rainbow tints which, like rainbows, came and went - nothing scanty, feeble, or pale!

It is a drive of two miles from the pier to Singapore, and to eyes which have only seen the yellow skins and non-vividness of the Far East, a world of wonders opens at every step. It is intensely tropical; there are mangrove swamps, and fringes of coco palms, and banana groves, date, sago and travellers' palms, tree-ferns, india-rubber, mango, custard-apple, jack-fruit, durian, lime, pome-granate, pine-apples, and orchids, and all kinds of strangling and parrot-blossomed trailers. Vegetation rich, profuse, endless, rapid, smoth-ering, in all shades of vivid green, from the pea-green of spring and the dark velvety green of endless summer to the yellow-green of the plumage of the palm, riots in a heavy shower every night and the heat of a perennial sunblaze every day, while monkeys of various kinds and bright-winged birds skip and flit through the jungle shades. There is a perpetual battle between man and the jungle, and the latter, in fact, is only brought to bay within a short distance of Singapore.

I had scarcely finished breakfast at the hotel, a shady, straggling building, much infested by ants, when Mr. Cecil Smith, the Colonial Secretary, and his wife called, full of kind thoughts and plans of furtherance; and a little later a resident, to whom I had not even a letter of introduction, took me and my luggage to his bungalow. All the European houses seem to have very deep verandahs, large, lofty rooms, punkahs everywhere, windows without glass, brick floors, and jalousies and "tatties" (blinds made of grass or finely-split bamboo) to keep out the light and the flies. This equatorial heat is neither as exhausting or depressing as the damp summer heat of Japan, though one does long "to take off one's flesh and sit in one's bones.". . .

It is all fascinating. Here is none of the indo-lence and apathy which one associates with Oriental life, and which I have seen in Polynesia. These yellow, brown, tawny, swarthy, olive-tinted men are all intent on gain; busy, industrious, frugal, striving, and, no matter what their creed is, all paying homage to *Daikoku*. In spite of the activity, rapidity, and earnestness, the movements of all but the Chines are graceful, gliding, stealthy, the swarthy faces have no expression that I can read, and the dark, liquid eyes are no more intelligible to me than the eyes of oxen. It is the "Asian mystery" all over.

It is only the European part of Singapore which is dull and sleepy looking. No life and movement congregate round the shops. The merchants, hidden away behind jalousies in their offices, or dashing down the streets in covered buggies, make but a poor show. Their houses are mostly pale, roomy, detached bungalows, almost altogether hidden by the bountiful vegetation of the climate. In these their wives, growing paler every week, lead half-expiring lives, kept alive by the efforts of ubiquitous "punkah-wallahs;" writing for the mail, the one active occupation. At a given hour they emerge, and drive in given directions, specially round the esplanade, where for two hours at a time a double row of handsome and showy equipages moves continuously in oppo-site directions. The number of carriages and the style of dress of their occupants are surpris-ing, and yet people say that large fortunes are not made now-a-days in Singapore! Besides the daily drive, the ladies, the officers, and any men who may be described as of "no occupa-tion," divert themselves with kettle-drums, dances, lawn tennis, and various other devices for killing time, and this with the mercury at 80°! Just now the Maharajah of Johore, sovereign of a small state on the nearest part of the mainland, a man much petted and decorated by the British Government for unswerving fidelity to British interests, has a house here, and his receptions and dinner parties vary the monotonous round of gaieties.

The native streets monopolise the picturesqueness of Singapore with their bizarre crowds, but more interesting still are the bazaars or continuous rows of open shops which create for themselves a perpetual twilight by hanging tatties or other screens outside the side walks, forming long shady alleys, in which crowds of buyers and sellers chaffer over their goods, the Chines shopkeepers asking a little more than they mean to take, and the Klings always asking double. The bustle and noise of this quarter are considerable, and the vociferation mingles with the ringing of bells and the rapid beating of drums and tom-toms, an intensely heathenish sound. And heathenish this great city is. Chinese josshouses, Hindu temples, and Mohammedan mosques almost jostle each other, and the indescribable clamour of the temples and the din of the joss-houses are faintly pierced by the shrill cry from the minarets calling the faithful to prayer, and proclaiming the divine unity and the mission of Mahomet in one breath.

How I wish I could convey an idea, however faint, of this huge, mingled, coloured, busy, Oriental population; of the old Kling and Chinese bazaars; of the itinerant sellers of seaweed jelly, water, vegetables, soup, fruit, and cooked fish, whose unintelligible street cries are heard above the din of the crowds of coolies, boatmen and gharriemen waiting for hire; of the far-stretching suburbs of Malay and Chinese cottages; of the sheet of water, by no means clean, round which hundreds of Bengalis are to be seen at all hours of daylight unmercifully beating on great stones the delicate laces, gauzy silks, and elaborate flouncings of the European ladies; of the ceaseless rush and hum of industry, and of the resistless, overpowering, astonishing Chinese element, which is gradually turning Singapore into a Chinese city! I must conclude abruptly, or lose the mail.

I.L.B.

Letter VII (Beauties of the Tropics), extracted from The Golden Chersonese, by Isabella Bird.

MY COUNTRY AND MY PEOPLE

My country and my people
are neither here nor there, nor
in the comfort of my preferences,
if I could even choose.
At any rate, to fancy is to cheat;
and worse than being alien, or
subversive without cause,
is being a patriot
of the will.

I came in the boom of babies, not guns,
a 'daughter of a better age';
I held a pencil in a school
while the 'age' was quelling riots
in the street, or cutting down
those foreign 'devils',
(whose books I was being taught to read).
Thus privileged I entered early
the Lion City's jaws.
But they sent me back as fast
to my shy, forbearing family.

So I stayed in my parents' house,
and had only household cares.
The city remained a distant way,
but I had no land to till;
only a duck that would not lay,
and a runt of a papaya tree,
(which also turned out to be male).

Then I learnt to drive instead
and praise the highways till
I saw them chop the great trees down,
and plant the little ones;
impound the hungry buffalo
(the big ones and the little ones)
because the cars could not be curbed.
Nor could the population.
They built milli-mini-flats
for a multi-mini-society.
The chiselled profile in the sky
took on a lofty attitude,
but modestly, at any rate
it made the tourist feel 'at home'.

My country and my people
I never understood.
I grew up in China's mighty shadow,
with my gentle, brown-skinned neighbours;
but I keep diaries in English.
I sought to grow

in humanity's rich soil,
and started digging on the banks, then saw
life carrying my friends downstream.

Yet, careful tending of the human heart
may make a hundred flowers bloom;
and perhaps, fence-sitting neighbour,
I claim citizenship in your recognition
of our kind,
My people, and my country,
are you, and you my home.

"My Country and My People" by Lee Tzu
Pheng, reprinted by permission of Heinemann
Asia.

HURRY

I was running. In the centre of the road. True, I
wasn't running like the wind, but my speed
was fast enough for beads of perspiration to
run down my body and my breath to come in
short gasps.

Cars and lorries flashed past me either way.
Still I kept running. Somehow it seemed appropriate that I should be running on the white
centre line separating the dual carriageway.

Where were the vehicles heading to? I didn't
know. Did the drivers in them know where I was
running to? No, but there was a possibility that
they would think I was a lunatic. So I should not
continue to run in this manner.

I would have to cross the road, walk or run
the short distance to the MRT station to board
a train to Orchard Road. Then I would have to
disembark and cross the road to Dynasty Hotel
to meet my friend Kamal staying there.

The train would arrive at the station in two
minutes' time and I must be in it. I was running
in this wild manner all for this. I had crossed
half the road. Now running along the white
line, I tried desperately to find a way through
the thick of the moving traffic to find an opening to make my dash across. Suddenly I spied
an opening and lashed across, leaving behind
two drivers screeching to a halt as they tried to
avoid the collision. One driver even made an
obscene gesture with his hands.

I felt a sense of regret. Not at his gesture,
but that I had cut his speed of travel. Anyway,
there was no time to apologise to him. I had to
catch that train or I would really be late.

I must buy a car, I thought to myself. It
would be so convenient considering the

amount of travelling I have to do. The convenience was more than that. A motorist dares to
use foul language and rude gestures because
he knows he is safe from the poor pedestrian
out on the road. Yes, a car is definitely a
convenience in more ways than one.

Miraculously I arrived at the Jurong Station
with thirty seconds to spare. From the third
level of the station, I could see the sun had half
disappeared in the horizon. When I had left my
home in the morning, he had also been half-
hidden, but that was the dawn.

Passengers on the platform suddenly moved
forward with some standing in the yellow
safety line. I could see the train in the distance.
This wasn't a bus. There would be ample time
for all to board the train before it pulled out.
Then why the rush? To ensure that they could
get seats? But even if one pushed his way
through not everyone could get a seat. I wasn't
going to be left out however. I too rushed with
the crowd and pushed my way to the front.

As the train ground to a halt and the doors
slid open we rushed in. I was lucky enough to
grab the only seat in my compartment and sank
down gladly.

My eyes scanned the passengers. Young,
old, middle-aged, they all seemed lost in some
thoughts. What were they thinking about, or
were they just staring blankly, I wondered.

As the train pulled up at the next station,
another human wave entered the train. I
noticed my friend Ravi among them in the next
compartment. Ravi is a very close friend. Well
at least during our school days. But I still
considered him as one. Unfortunately, we had
not had many opportunities to meet as often as
we used to. As he was staying in the Jurong
area, occasionally we met like this in the train.

He had not noticed me. "Hello, Ravi!" I
shouted across. He turned, saw me and waved.
My voice, however, had shattered the silence
in the train and several dozen pairs of eyes
bored into me. I turned pink with
embarrassment.

Ravi could not come any nearer, the crowd
was that thick. No one appeared willing to
allow Ravi to walk through to me.

"How is father?" I gestured with my hands.
His father has been ill for sometime. Ravi
answered in a similar manner, giving me the
thumbs down sign. His normally cheerful face
was tinged with sadness.

As the train sped on, I wondered what I could do. I attempted to convey how I felt with expressions. He was about to say something but changed his mind, pulled out a paper from his pocket and started to scribble something.

The train reached Raffles Place Interchange. Most of us, including me had to change trains here. In no time, three quarters of the train had emptied. Ravi made his way through the crowd and as I was about to disembark, thrust the paper into my hands. As he didn't need to change trains, I didn't have the time to even exchange a few words.

As the train pulled away my train pulled into the opposite tunnel. Running with the others, I crossed over the platform and boarded it.

Eagerly I opened his note. "We have finalised marriage plans for Chitra. Father insists that he wants to see the marriage before he dies. I'll phone you later."

Chitra marrying. I sat stunned. How could she marry someone when she was my girlfriend...?

Why not? No one, not even Chitra new of my love. That's a joke isn't it!

I had wanted to tell Ravi of my love. But the opportunity had never risen, and being the coward I am I had kept postponing the discussion. Now it was too late. Who could I blame but myself? Anyway where did I have the time for courtship when I never returned from work till eleven in the night everyday.

I crumbled the note and threw it on the floor and looked up. The passenger opposite looked meaningfully at me and the note on the floor. I had littered. Sheepishly I picked up the note and shoved it into my shirt pocket.

I rritated, I reached for a cigarette. My eyes fell on the warning note directly opposite. " No smoking! $500 fine". My hand dropped to the side. I, more than anyone else, knew that every mistake had its penalty.

The train sped on through the tunnels. It was pitch dark outside. I wasn't aware where we were. This is the drawback in travelling by train. A minute's inattention, and one loses track completely of one's whereabouts. The speed with which one was travelling was the only consolation.

Some light pierced the darkness. Instantly the passengers came to life. Orchard Station. I would have to get out here. I glanced at my watch - 7.26 pm. I was pleased. Had I come by bus I would not have made it in this short time to keep my 7.30 appointment with Kamal at Dynasty Hotel's lobby.

I crossed glittering Orchard Road and walked briskly into the hotel. But Kamal was not there. Maybe he was still up in the room. Reception should be able to help.

"Can you give me Kamal's room number'"

"Mr Kamal just vacated his room. His flight was brought forward and he's left tor the airport."

If he had just left, he must be waiting for a cab outside the hotel. In my hurry, I must have missed him outside. Maybe, just maybe, I could catch him before he caught a cab, I thought as I dashed out.

"Hurry", by R. Rajaram, translated by K Sulosana, reprinted by permission of Unipress, Singapore.

BOOKS

There's no shortage of books written about Malaysia, Singapore and Brunei, though as the selction below demonstrates, the majority have tended to be penned by Western visitors to the region, rather than by local writers. Only in the latter part of the twentieth century has writing about Malaysia and Singapore, by Malaysians and Singaporeans themselves begun to gather momentum.

The best selection of local writing is available in the countries themselves, though *Skoob Books Publishing* of London are doing much to introduce Southeast Asian literature to the West.

In the reviews below, publishers are listed in the format, UK/US publisher – unless the title is available in one country only, in which case we've specified the country. Many books are published by local publishers – you may be able to order them from bookshops in your own country, and most are available in Malaysia, Singapore or Brunei; o/p signifies out of print.

TRAVEL, IMPRESSIONS, EXPLORATION & ADVENTURE

James Barclay *A Stroll Through Borneo* (Hodder & Stoughton in UK; o/p). A seminal tour of Sarawak and Indonesian Kalimantan by the doyen of travel writers; particularly perceptive on the Kayan ethnic group.

Isabella Bird *The Golden Chersonese* (OUP/Century; o/p). Delightful epistolary romp through old Southeast Asia, penned by the intrepid Bird, whose adventures in the Malay states in 1879 ranged from strolls through Singapore's streets to elephant-back rides and encounters with alligators.

Margaret Brooke *My Life in Sarawak* (OUP in UK). Engaging account by White Rajah Charles Brooke's wife of nineteenth-century Sarawak which reveals a sympathetic attitude to her subjects (which extended to rubbing eau de cologne into a Dyak warrior's forehead). Her eye for detail conveys the wonder of an unprejudiced colonial embracing an alien culture.

Spencer Chapman *The Jungle is Neutral* (Mayflower/Time-Life; both o/p). This riveting first-hand account of being lost, and surviving, in the Malay jungle during World War II reads like a breathless novel.

Oscar Cook *Borneo, the Stealer of Hearts* (Borneo Publishing Company). Written by a young district officer in the North Borneo Civil Service this is a piece of Imperial literature that's insufferably plummy, but enlightening.

G.M. Gullick *They Came To Malaya* (OUP in UK and US). A cornucopia of accounts and of people, places and events, written by the governors, planters and explorers who tamed Malaya.

Eric Hansen *Stranger In The Forest* (Abacus/Penguin). A gripping book, the result of a seven-month tramp through the forests of Sarawak and Kalimantan in 1982, that almost saw the author killed by a poison dart.

Victor T. King *The Best of Borneo Travel* (OUP in UK and US). Compendium of extracts from Bornean travel writing since the sixteenth century; an interesting travelling companion.

Andro Linklater *Wild People* (Abacus/Grove-Atlantic). As telling and as entertaining a glimpse into the lifestyle of the Iban as you could pack, depicting their age-old traditions surviving amidst the T-shirts, baseball caps and rock posters of Western influence.

Redmond O'Hanlon *Into The Heart of Borneo* (Penguin/Vintage). A hugely entertaining yarn recounting O'Hanlon's refreshingly amateurish romp through the jungle to a remote summit on the Sarawak/Kalimantan border, partnered by the English poet James Fenton.

Ambrose B. Rathborne *Camping and Tramping in Malaya* (OUP in UK; o/p). Lively nineteenth-century account with insights into the colonial personalities and working conditions of the leading figures of the day; many of Rathborne's impressions of the country still ring true today.

The Rev G.M. Reith *1907 Handbook to Singapore* (OUP in UK; o/p). Intriguing period piece which illuminates colonial attitudes in turn-of-the-century Singapore: drill hall, gaol and docks are detailed in favour of Chinatown, while the list of useful Malay phrases includes such essentials as "harness the horse" and "off with you".

Spenser St John *Life in the Forests of the Far East* (OUP in UK). A description of an early ascent of Mount Kinabalu is a highlight of this animated nineteenth-century adventure, written by the personal secretary to Rajah Brooke.

Gavin Young *In Search of Conrad* (Penguin in UK). In which Young plays detective and historian, tracing Joseph Conrad's footsteps around Southeast Asia in search of the stories and locations that inpired him. Young's time in Singapore takes him from the National Library to Bidadari cemetery in search of A.P. Williams – Conrad's Lord Jim.

HISTORY AND POLITICS

Abdullah bin Kadir *The Hikayat Abdullah* (OUP in UK). Raffles' one-time clerk, Melakan-born Abdullah later turned diarist of some of the most formative years of Southeast Asian history; his first-hand account is crammed with illuminating vignettes and character portraits.

S. Robert Aiken *Imperial Beldeveres* (OUP in UK). Sketches, photographs and contemporary accounts enliven this compact examination of the development, landscapes and attractions of the hill stations of Malaya.

Barbara Watson Andaya and Leonard Andaya *The History of Malaysia* (Macmillan St Martin's Press o/p in UK). Unlike more paternalistic histories, penned by former colonists, this standard text on the region takes a more even-handed view of Malaysia, and finds time for cultural coverage, too.

Noel Barber *War of the Running Dogs* (Arrow/Bantam; o/p). Illuminates the Malayan Emergency with a novelist's eye for mood.

James Bartholomew *The Richest Man in the World* (Penguin in UK). Despite an obvious (and admitted) lack of sources, Bartholomew's study of the Sultan of Brunei makes fairly engaging reading – particularly the mind-bending facts and figures used to illustrate the Sultan's wealth.

David Brazil *Street Smart Singapore* (Times Editions Singapore). An Aladdin's cave of Singaporean history and trivia that remains fascinating throughout.

Maurice Collis *Raffles* (Century in UK and US; o/p). The most accessible and enjoyable biography of Sir Stamford Raffles on the market – very readable.

Images of Asia series: Maya Jayapal's *Old Singapore*; Sarnia Hayes Hoyt's *Old Malacca* and *Old Penang* (all OUP in UK and US). Concise volumes which chart the growth of three of the region's most important outposts, drawing on contemporary maps, sketches and photographs to engrossing effect.

Robert Jackson *The Malayan Emergency* (Routledge in UK and US). Thorough account of the conflict between the Chinese Communist guerillas and the security forces in postwar Malaya.

James Minchin *No Man Is An Island* (Allen & Unwin in UK and US). A well-researched, and at times critical study of Lee Kuan Yew, which refuses to kowtow to Singapore's ex-PM and is hence unavailable in Singapore itself, but gleefully sold in shops throughout Malaysia.

Anthony Oei *What If There Had Been No Lee Kuan Yew* (Mandarin Paperbacks; Singapore). Ignore its overly sycophantic tone, and this is a readable enough overview of the life and works of Singapore's pre-eminent statesman; for a more opinionated account, see Minchin above.

Steven Runciman *The White Rajahs* (Cambridge University Press/Macmillan; o/p). A ponderous, blow-by-blow chronicle of the Brookes' private fiefdom, whose attention to detail compensates for its lack of colour.

C. Mary Turnbull *A Short History of Malaysia, Singapore & Brunei* (Graham Brash, Singapore). Decent, informed introduction to the region, touching on the major issues that have shaped it. Its big brother, Turnbull's *History of Singapore 1819-1988* (OUP in UK) is in contrast, as scholarly an approach to Singapore as you could wish to read.

C.E. Wurtzburg *Raffles of the Eastern Isles* (OUP in UK and US). A weighty and learned tome that's the definitive study of the man who founded modern Singapore; not for the marginally interested, who should opt for Collis's more accessible volume (above).

WWII AND THE JAPANESE OCCUPATION

Noel Barber *Sinister Twilight* (Arrow in UK). Documents the fall of Singapore to the Japanese, by re-imagining the crucial events of the period.

Russell Braddon *The Naked Island* (Penguin/ Atheneum; o/p). Southeast Asia under the Japanese: Braddon's disturbing yet moving first-hand account of the POW camps of Malaya, Singapore and Siam displays courage in the face of appalling conditions and treatment; worth scouring secondhand stores for.

Chin Kee Onn *Malaya Upside Down*. A coherent analysis of the impact of the Japanese occupation on Malaysian society; difficult to find in the UK and US, but available in Malaysian bookshops.

Agnes Keith *Three Came Home* (Eland/Little, Brown; o/p). Pieced together from scraps of paper secreted in latrines and teddy bears, this is a remarkable story of survival in the face of Japanese attempts to eradicate the "proudery and arrogance" of the West in the World War II prison camps of Borneo.

CULTURE AND SOCIETY

Iskandar Carey *The Orang Asli* (OUP in UK and US; o/p in US). The only detailed anthropological work on the indigenes of Peninsular Malaysia.

Culture Shock! Malaysia/Culture Shock! Singapore (both Kuperard/Graphic Arts Center Publishing). Cultural dos and don'ts for the leisure and business traveller to the region, spanning subjects as diverse as handing over business cards and belching after a fine meal.

Tom Harrisson *A World Within* (OUP in UK and US). The only in-depth description of the Kelabit peoples of Sarawak, and a cracking good World War II tale courtesy of Harrisson, who parachuted into the Kelabit Highlands to organize resistance against the Japanese.

William Krohn *In Borneo Jungles* (OUP in UK). An interwar years description of the infamous head-hunters of Sarawak

Leslie Layton *Songbirds in Singapore* (OUP in UK and US). A delightful examination of songbird-keeping in Singapore, detailing all facets of the pastime, from its growth in the nineteenth century to its most popular birds.

Rahman Rashid *A Malaysian Journey*. Excellent autobiographical account by a journalist returning to Malaysia in the 1990s after self-imposed exile; look it up in KL's bookshops.

Owen Rutter *The Pagans of North Borneo* (OUP in UK and US; o/p). Dry, scholarly examination of the lifestyles and traditions of

Sabah's non-Muslim peoples, which suffers from a tendency towards cultural chauvinism.

Sabah Women Action Resource Group *Women in Sabah* (SAWO in Malaysia). Occasionally interesting profile of the status and contribution of women in Sabahan society; available in KK shops.

Tan Kok Seng *Son Of Singapore* (Heinemann in US). Tan Kok Seng's candid and sobering autobiography unearths the underside of the Singaporean success story, by telling of hard times spent as a coolie.

NATURAL HISTORY AND ECOLOGY

For specific field guides to the birds and mammals of Malaysia, Singapore, Sabah and Sarawak, see p.584.

Odoardo Beccari *Wanderings in the Great Forests of Borneo* (OUP in UK and US). Vivid turn-of-the-century account of the natural and human environment of Sarawak.

John Briggs *Parks of Malaysia* (Longman Malaysia). Top tips and maps for the serious naturalist or hiker in Malaysia.

Mark Cleary & Peter Eaton *Borneo Change and Development* (OUP in UK and US). A very readable composite of Bornean history, economy and society, that's rounded off by a section dealing with issues such as logging, conservation and the future of the Penan.

Robin Hanbury-Tenison *Mulu: The Rain Forest* (Arrow/Weidenfeld & Nicolson; o/p). Hanbury-Tenison's overview of the flora, fauna and ecology of the rainforest, the result of a 1977 Royal Geographical Society field trip into Sarawak's Gunung Mulu National Park; makes enlightening reading.

Jeffrey McNeely *Soul of the Tiger* (OUP/ Doubleday). Synoptic, multi-disciplinary overview of the importance of the various facets of nature and the environment to the peoples of the region.

Alfred Russel Wallace *The Malay Archipelago* (OUP in UK and US). Wallace's peerless account of the flora and fauna of Borneo, based on travels made between 1854 and 1862 – during which time he collected over 100,000 specimens. Still required reading for nature lovers.

World Rainforest Movement *The Battle For Sarawak's Forests*. A worthy collection of writings on the acrimonious, and sometimes violent, confrontations between the State Government-sponsored loggers and tribespeople in east Malaysia.

ART AND ARCHITECTURE

Jacques Dumarcay *The House in Southeast Asia* (OUP in UK); *Palaces of Southeast Asia* (OUP in UK and US). The former is a pocket-sized overview of regional domestic architecture, covering the rituals and techniques of house construction; the latter is more specialist, but has only ten pages on Malaysia.

Norman Edwards *Singapore House and Residential Life* (OUP in UK and US). The development of the Singapore detached house, traced from early plantation villas, through colonial bungalows to Chinese landowners' mansions; beguiling photographs.

Roxana Waterson *The Living House* (OUP in UK and US). More authoritative than Dumarcay's slender introduction to Southeast Asian dwellings, and required reading for anyone with an interest in the subject.

LITERATURE

Charles Allen *Tales from the South China Seas* (Abacus in UK). Memoirs of the last generation of British colonists, in which predicatable Raj attitudes prevail, though some of the drama of everyday lives, often in inhospitable conditions, is evinced with considerable pathos.

Noel Barber *Tanamera* (Coronet/Macmillan). Romantic saga based in mid-twentieth century Singapore.

Anthony Burgess *The Long Day Wanes* (Penguin/Norton). Burgess's Malayan trilogy – *Time for a Tiger*, *The Enemy in the Blanket* and *Beds in the East* – published in one volume, provides a witty and acutely observed vision of 1950s' Malaya, underscoring the racial prejudices of the period. *Time for a Tiger*, the first novel, is worth reading for the Falstaffian Nabby Adams alone.

Chin Kee Onn *The Grand Illusion* A novel with a difference, exploring the Emergency from the perspective of a Communist guerilla cell; also good is *Twilight of the Nyonyas*, a historical novel about the life and culture of a Nynya family. Both are widely available in Malaysia.

James Clavell *King Rat* (Coronet/Dell). Set in Japanese-occupied Singapore, a gripping tale of survival in the notorious Changi Prison.

Joseph Conrad *Lord Jim* (Penguin in UK and US). Southeast Asia provides the backdrop to the story of Jim's desertion of an apparently sinking ship and subsequent efforts to redeem himself; modelled upon the sailor, A.P. Williams, Jim's character also yields echoes of Rajah Brooke of Sarawak.

J.G. Farrell *The Singapore Grip* (Phoenix in UK). Lengthy novel – Farrell's last – of World War II Singapore in which real and fictitious characters flit from tennis to dinner party as the countdown to the Japanese occupation begins.

Henri Fauconnier *The Soul of Malaya* (OUP in UK). Fauconnier's semi-autobiographical novel is a lyrical, sensory tour of the plantations, jungle and beaches of early twentieth-century Malaya, and pierces deeply into the underside of the country.

Lloyd Fernando *Scorpion Orchid* (Heinemann Educational in UK and US; o/p); *Green is the Colour* (Landmark Books in Singapore). Social politics form the basis of Fernando's works: in *Scorpion Orchid* he concerns himself with the difficulties of adjusting to the move towards Merdeka and new nationhood; while *Green is the Colour* is a remarkable novel, exploring the deep-seated racial tensions brought to light by the Kuala Lumpur demonstrations of May 1969.

K.S. Maniam *The Return* (Skoob/Heinemann; o/p); *In A Far Country* (Skoob in UK). The purgative writings of this Tamil-descended Malayian author are strong, highly descriptive and humorous; essential reading.

W Somerset Maugham *Short Stories Volume 4* (Mandarin/Penguin). Peopled by hoary sailors, bored plantation-dwellers and colonials wearing mutton chop whiskers and topees, Maugham's short stories resuscitate turn-of-the-century Malaya; quintessential colonial literature graced by an easy style and a steady eye for a story.

Southeast Asia Writes Back! Anthology (Skoob in UK). A thorough compendium of writings from the Pacific Rim that provides a useful introduction to the contemporary literature of Singapore and Malaysia.

Paul Theroux *Saint Jack* (Penguin/Pocket Books); *The Consul's File* (Penguin/Pocket Books). *Saint Jack* tells the compulsively bawdy tale of Jack Flowers, an ageing American who supplements his earnings at a Singapore ship's chandlers by pimping for Westerners; Jack's jaundiced eye and

Theroux's rich prose open windows on Singapore's past. In *The Consul's File*, a series of short stories are recounted by the ficticious American consul to interior Malaya.

Leslie Thomas *The Virgin Soldiers* (Penguin/ Little Brown; o/p). The bawdy exploits of teen-age British Army conscripts snatching all the enjoyment they can, before being sent to fight in troubled 1950s' Malaya.

Wong Phui Nam *Ways of Exile* (Skoob in UK). Chinese Malaysian poet's first collection published outside Malaysia; evocative works rooted in the interaction of cultures and ethnicity.

LANGUAGE

The national language of Malaysia, Singapore and Brunei is *Bahasa Malaysia*, which means, simply, "Malay language". It's an old language, with early roots in the central and south Pacific, and one which was refined by its use in the ancient kingdom of Srivijaya and during the fifteenth-century Melaka Sultanate into a language of the élite. Indeed, the very word *bahasa* (language) came to signify Malay culture in general.

The situation is slightly complicated by the presence of several other racial groups and languages in all three countries: in Singapore, for example, Mandarin, Tamil and English all have the status of official languages, as well as Malay; while in Malaysia itself, Cantonese, Mandarin, other Chinese languages like Hokkien and Hakka, and Tamil all form significant minority languages. In practice, however, you'll be able to get by with **English** in all but the most remote areas, since this is the common means of communication between the different races, as well as the language of business.

Nevertheless, it always helps to pick up a few words, especially since basic *Bahasa* is simple enough to learn. Understanding the quick fire, staccato speech is a different matter altogether, particularly since the spoken word is often corrupted. For example, Malays will often use *-lah* at the end of a word or sentence – hence *Minumlah Coca-cola* – a meaningless, though pervasive, suffix.

GRAMMAR

Nouns have no genders and don't require an article, while the **plural** form is constructed just by saying the word twice; thus "child" is *anak*, while "children" is *anak anak* – occasionally you'll see this written as if to the power of two, as in *anak²*. Doubling a word can also indicate "doing"; for example, *jalan jalan* is used to mean "walking". **Verbs** have no tenses either, the meaning being indicated either by the context, or by the use of "time" words such as *sedang*, *akan* and *sudah* for the present, future and past. **Sentence order** is the same as in English, though adjectives usually follow their corresponding nouns.

PRONUNCIATION

The **pronunciation** of *Bahasa Malaysia* is broadly the same as the English reading of Roman script, with a few exceptions:

VOWELS AND DIPTHONGS

a as in c**u**p
e as in **e**nd
i as in bout**i**que
o as in g**o**t
u as in b**oo**t
ai as in f**i**ne
au as in h**ow**
sy as in **sh**ut

CONSONANTS

c as in **ch**eap
g as in **g**irl
j as in **j**oy
k hard, as in English, except at the end of the word, when you should stop just short of pronouncing it. In writing, this is frequently indicated by an apostrophe at the end of the word; for example, *beso'* for *besok*.

COMMON WORDS AND PHRASES IN BAHASA MALAYSIA

CIVILITIES AND BASIC PHRASES

Selamat is the all-purpose greeting derived from Arabic, which communicates a general goodwill.

Good morning	*Selamat pagi*	Where are you from?	*Dari mana?*
Good afternoon	*Selamat petang*	I come from...	*Saya dari...*
Good evening	*Selamat malam*	England	*Inggris*
Good night	*Selamat tidur*	America	*Amerika*
Goodbye	*Selamat tinggal*	Australia	*Australia*
Bon Voyage	*Selamat jalan*	Canada	*Kanada*
Welcome	*Selamat datang*	New Zealand	*Zealandia Baru*
Bon Appetit	*Selamat makan*	Ireland	*Irlandia*
		Scotland	*Skotlandia*
How are you?	*Apa kabar?*	Do you speak English?	*Bisa bercakap bahasa*
Fine/OK	*Baik*		*Inggris?*
See you later	*Jumpa lagi*	I don't understand	*Saya tidak mengerti*
Please	*Tolong*	I want...	*Saya mahu...*
Thank you	*Terima kasih*	I like...	*Saya suka...*
You're welcome	*Sama sama*	What is this/that?	*Apa ini/itu?*
Sorry/excuse me	*Maaf*	Can you help me?	*Bolekah anda tolong*
No worries/never mind	*Tidak apa-apa*		*saya?*
Yes	*Ya*	What?	*Apa?*
No	*Tidak*	When?	*Bila?*
		Where?	*Dimana?*
What is your name?	*Siapa nama anda?*	Why?	*Mengapa?*
My name is...	*Nama saya...*	How?	*Berapa?*

GETTING AROUND AND DIRECTIONS

Where is the...?	*Dimana...?*	Front	*Hadapan*
I want to go to...	*Saya mahu naik ke...*	Behind	*Belakang*
How do I get there?	*Bagaimanakah saya*	North	*Utara*
	boleh ke sana?	South	*Selatan*
How far?	*Berapa jauh?*	East	*Timur*
How long will it	*Berapa lama?*	West	*Barat*
take?		Street	*Jalan*
When will the bus	*Bila bas berangkat?*	Train station	*Stesen keratapi*
leave?		Bus station	*Stesen bas*
What time does	*Jam berapa keratapi*	Airport	*Lapangan terbang*
the train arrive?	*sampai?*	Ticket	*Tiket*
Stop	*Berhenti*	Hotel	*Hotel/rumah*
Wait	*Tunggu*		*penginapan*
Go up	*Naik*	Post office	*Pejabat pos*
Go down	*Turun*	Restaurant	*Restoran*
Turn	*Belok*	Shop	*Kedai*
Right	*Kanan*	Market	*Pasar*
Left	*Kiri*	Taxi	*Teksi*
Straight	*Terus*	Trishaw	*Becak*

ACCOMMODATION

How much is...?	*Berapa...?*	Please clean my	*Tolong bersikan bilik*
I need a room.	*Saya perlu satu bilik.*	room.	*saya.*
Cheap/expensive	*Murah/mahal*	Can I store my	*Bisa titip barang?*
I'm staying for one	*Saya mahu tinggal satu*	luggage here?	
night.	*hari.*		

Common Words and Phrases in Bahasa Malaysia continued

SHOPPING

I want to buy...	Saya mahu beli...	I'll give you no	Saya bayar tidak
Can you reduce	Boleh kurang?	more than...	lebih dari...
the price?		I'm just looking	Saya hanya lihat-lihat

PERSONAL PRONOUNS AND TITLES

You'll often see the word *Dato'* placed before the name of a government official or some other worthy. It's an honorific title of distinction roughly equivalent to the British "Sir". Royalty are always addressed as *Tuanku*.

I/my	Saya	They	Mereka
You	Anda/awak	Mr	Encik
S/he	Dia	Mrs	Puan
We	Kami	Miss	Cik

USEFUL ADJECTIVES

Good	Bagus	Big	Besar
A Lot/very Much	Banyak	Small	Kecil
A Little	Sedikit	Enough	Cukup
Cold (Object)	Sejuk	Closed	Tutup
Cold (Person)	Dingin	Hungry	Laparad
Hot	Panas	Thirsty	Haus
Sweet	Manis	Tired	Lelah
Salty	Garam	Ill/sick	Sakit

USEFUL NOUNS

Entrance	Masuk	Food	Makan
Exit	Keluar	Drink	Minum
Toilet	Tandas	Boyfriend/girlfriend	Pacar
Man	Lelaki	Husband	Suami
Woman	Perempuan	Wife	Istri
Water	Air	Friend	Kawan
Money	Wang/duit		

USEFUL VERBS

Malay verbs do not conjugate, and often double as nouns or adjectives. Here, they are given in the form in which you'd use the verb, rather than in the strictly grammatical infinitive.

Come	Datang	Give	Beri
Go	Pergi	Take	Gambil
Do	Buat	Sit	Duduk
Have	Punya	Sleep	Tidur

NUMBERS

0	Nul	7	Tujuh	21	Dua puluh satu
1	Satu	8	Lapan	100	Seratus
2	Dua	9	Sembilan	143	Seratus empatpuluh tiga
3	Tiga	10	Sepuluh	200	Duaratus
4	Empat	11	Sebelas	1000	Seribu
5	Lima	12	Duabelas	1 Million	Sejuta
6	Enam	20	Duapuluh	A Half	Setengah

Common Words and Phrases in Bahasa Malaysia continued

NUMBERS

0	Nul	7	Tujuh	21	Dua puluh satu
1	Satu	8	Lapan	100	Seratus
2	Dua	9	Sembilan	143	Seratus empatpuluh tiga
3	Tiga	10	Sepuluh	200	Duaratus
4	Empat	11	Sebelas	1000	Seribu
5	Lima	12	Duabelas	1 Million	Sejuta
6	Enam	20	Duapuluh	A Half	Setengah

TIME AND DAYS OF THE WEEK

What time is it?	Jam berapa?	Year	Tahun
It's...		Today	Hari Ini
three o'clock	Jam tiga	Tomorrow	Besok
ten past four	Jam empat lewat sepuluh	Yesterday	Kemarin
quarter to five	Jam lima kurang seperempat	Now	Sekarang
		Ago	Yang Lalu
six-thirty	Jam setengah tujuh (lit. "half to seven")	Not Yet	Belum
		Never	Tidak Perna
7am	Tujuh pagi		
8pm	Lapan malam	Monday	Hari Isnin
Second	Detik	Tuesday	Hari Selasa
Minute	Menit	Wednesday	Hari Rabu
Hour	Jam	Thursday	Hari Kamis
Day	Hari	Friday	Hari Jumaat
Week	Minggu	Saturday	Hari Sabtu
Month	Bulan	Sunday	Hari Ahad/minggu

For more Malay words, see the glossary of words and terms in the next section.

A GLOSSARY OF WORDS AND TERMS

ATAP Palm thatch.
AIR PANAS Hot springs.
AIR TERJUN Waterfall.
BABA Straits-born Chinese (male).
BANDAR Town.
BATANG River system.
BATIK Wax and dye technique of cloth decoration.
BATU Rock/stone.
BOMOH Traditional healer.
BUKIT Hill.
BUMIPUTRA Indigenous Malay person (lit. "son of the soil").
DAULAT Divine force possessed by a ruler that commands unquestioning loyalty.
DERHAKA Treason; punished severely even in contemporary Malaysia.
EKSPRES Express (used for boats and buses).
GASING Spinning top.
GELANGGANG SENI Cultural Centre.
GEREJA Church.
GODOWN Warehouse.
GUA Cave.
GUNUNG Mountain.
HALAL Something that's permissible by Islam.
HUTAN Forest.
IKAT Woven fabric.
ISTANA Palace.
JALAN Road.
JAMBATAN Bridge.
KAMPUNG Village.
KEDAI KOPI Coffee shop.
KELONG Large marine fish trap.
KHALWAT Close proximity; forbidden between people of the opposite sex under Islamic law.
KONGSI Chinese clan house/temple.
KOTA Fort.
KRIS Wavy-bladed dagger.
KUALA River confluence or estuary.
LEBUH Street.
LORONG Lane.
MAK YONG Epic courtly dance drama.
MAKAM Grave or tomb.
MANDI Asian method of bathing by dousing with water from a tank using a small bucket.

MASJID Mosque.
MEDAN SELERA Food centre.
MENARA Minaret or tower.
MERDEKA Freedom (and therefore applied to Malaysian independence).
MINANGKABAU Matriarchal people from Sumatra.
MUZIUM Museum.
NEGARA National.
NIPAH Palm tree.
NONYA Straits-born Chinese (female); sometimes *Nyonya*.
ORANG ASLI Peninsular Malaysia aborigines (lit. "original people"); also *orang ulu* (upriver people) and *orang laut* (sea people).
PADANG Field/square; usually the main town square.
PANTAI Beach.
PARANG Machete.
PASAR Market (*pasar malam*, nightmarket).
PEJABAT DAERAH District office.
PEJABAT POS Post office.
PEKAN Town.
PELABUHAN Port/harbour.
PENGHULU Chief/leader.
PENGKALAN Port/harbour.
PERANAKAN Straits-born Chinese.
PERIGI Well.
PINTU Arch/gate.
PONDOK Hut/shelter; used as religious schools.
PULAU Island.
PUSAT BANDAR Town centre.
RAJAH Prince (often spelled Raja).
RAMADAN Muslim fasting month.
REBANA Drum.
ROTAN Rattan cane; used in the infliction of corporal punishment.
RUMAH PERSINGGAHAN Lodging house.
RUMAH REHAT Rest house (usually government-run).
SAREE Traditional Indian woman's garment, worn in conjunction with a *choli* (short-sleeved blouse).
SEKOLAH School.
SILAT Malay art of self-defence.
SONGKET Woven cloth.
STESEN BAS Bus station.
STESEN KERATAPI Train station.
SULTAN Ruler.
SUNGEI River.
TAI CHI Chinese martial art; commonly performed as an early morning exercise.

TAMAN Park.

TANJUNG Cape/headland.

TASIK (or Tasek) Lake.

TELAGA Freshwater spring or well.

TELUK Bay/inlet.

TOKONG Chinese temple.

TOWKAY Chinese merchant.

WAU Kite.

WAYANG KULIT Shadow puppet play.

ACRONYMS

KTM *Keretapi Tanah Melayu*, the Malaysian national railway compay.

MAS Malaysian national airline.

MCP Malayan Communist Party.

MRT Singapore's Mass Rapid Transit system.

PAS *Parti Islam Sa-Melayu*, the Pan-Malaysian Islamic Party.

PAP Singaporean People's Action Party.

UNMO United Malays National Organization.

INDEX

INDEX OF MAPS

HELP US UPDATE

We've gone to a lot of effort to ensure that the *Rough Guide to Malaysia, Singapore & Brunei* is thoroughly up-to-date and accurate. However, things do change – particularly in places like Singapore and Kuala Lumpur – and we would greatly appreciate any comments, corrections or additions you may have. For the best letters, we'll send a copy of the new edition (or any other *Rough Guide* if you prefer).

Please mark letters "Rough Guide to Malaysia & Singapore Update" and send to:

Rough Guides, 1 Mercer Street, London WC2H 9QJ
or Rough Guides, 375 Hudson Street, 4th Floor, New York NY 10014.

DIRECT ORDERS IN THE UK

Title	ISBN	Price
Amsterdam	1858280869	£7.99
Andalucia	185828094X	£8.99
Australia	1858280354	£12.99
Barcelona & Catalunya	1858281067	£8.99
Berlin	1858280338	£8.99
Brazil	1858281024	£9.99
Brittany & Normandy	1858280192	£7.99
Bulgaria	1858280478	£8.99
California	1858280907	£9.99
Canada	185828001X	£10.99
Classical Music on CD	185828113X	£12.99
Corsica	1858280893	£8.99
Crete	1858280494	£6.99
Cyprus	185828032X	£8.99
Czech & Slovak Republics	185828029X	£8.99
Egypt	1858280753	£10.99
England	1858280788	£9.99
Europe	185828077X	£14.99
Florida	1858280109	£8.99
France	1858280508	£9.99
Germany	1858280257	£11.99
Greece	1858280206	£9.99
Guatemala & Belize	1858280451	£9.99
Holland, Belgium & Luxembourg	1858280877	£9.99
Hong Kong & Macau	1858280664	£8.99
Hungary	1858280214	£7.99
India	1858281040	£13.99
Ireland	1858280958	£9.99
Italy	1858280311	£12.99
Kenya	1858280435	£9.99
Mediterranean Wildlife	0747100993	£7.95
Malaysia, Singapore & Brunei	1858281032	£9.9
Morocco	1858280400	£9.9
Nepal	185828046X	£8.9
New York	1858280583	£8.9
Nothing Ventured	0747102082	£7.9
Pacific Northwest	1858280923	£9.9
Paris	1858280389	£7.9
Poland	1858280346	£9.9
Portugal	1858280842	£9.9
Prague	185828015X	£7.9
Provence & the Côte d'Azur	1858280230	£8.9
Pyrenees	1858280931	£8.9
St Petersburg	1858280303	£8.9
San Francisco	1858280826	£8.9
Scandinavia	1858280397	£10
Scotland	1858280834	£8.9
Sicily	1858280370	£8.9
Spain	1858280818	£9.9
Thailand	1858280168	£8.9
Tunisia	1858280656	£8.9
Turkey	1858280885	£9.9
Tuscany & Umbria	1858280915	£8.9
USA	185828080X	£12
Venice	1858280362	£8.9
Wales	1858280966	£8.9
West Africa	1858280141	£12
Women Travel	1858280710	£7.9
World Music	1858280176	£14
Zimbabwe & Botswana	1858280419	£10

Rough Guides are available from all good bookstores, but can be obtained directly in the UK* from Penguin by contacting:

Penguin Direct, Penguin Books Ltd, Bath Road, Harmondsworth, West Drayton, Middlesex UB7 0DA; or telephone our credit line on 081-899 4036 (9am–5pm) and ask for Penguin Direct. Visa, Access and Amex accepted. Delivery will normally be within 14 working days. Penguin Direct ordering facilities are only available in the UK.

The availability and published prices quoted are correct at the time of going to press but are subject to alteration without prior notice.

* For USA and international orders, see separate price list

DIRECT ORDERS IN THE USA

	ISBN	Price		ISBN	Price
e			Italy	1858280311	$17.95
e to Travel	1858281105	$19.95	Kenya	1858280435	$15.95
sterdam	1858280869	$13.95	Malaysia, Singapore		
alucia	185828094X	$14.95	& Brunei	1858281032	$16.95
tralia	1858280354	$18.95	Mediterranean Wildlife	1858280699	$15.95
celona & Catalunya	1858281067	$13.95	Morocco	1858280400	$16.95
in	1858280338	$13.99	Nepal	185828046X	$13.95
zil	1858281024	$15.95	New York	1858280583	$13.95
tany & Normandy	1858280192	$14.95	Pacific Northwest	1858280923	$14.95
jaria	1858280478	$14.99	Paris	1858280389	$13.95
fornia	1858280907	$14.95	Poland	1858280346	$16.95
ada	185828001X	$14.95	Portugal	1858280842	$15.95
sical Music on CD	185828113X	$19.95	Prague	185828015X	$14.95
sica	1858280893	$14.95	Provence		
te	1858280494	$14.95	& the Côte d'Azur	1858280230	$14.95
rus	185828032X	$13.99	Pyrenees	1858280931	$15.95
ch & Slovak			St Petersburg	1858280303	$14.95
publics	185828029X	$14.95	San Francisco	1858280826	$13.95
pt	1858280753	$17.95	Scandinavia	1858280397	$16.99
land	1858280788	$16.95	Scotland	1858280834	$14.95
ope	185828077X	$18.95	Sicily	1858280370	$14.99
ida	1858280109	$14.95	Spain	1858280818	$16.95
nce	1858280508	$16.95	Thailand	1858280168	$15.95
many	1858280257	$17.95	Tunisia	1858280656	$15.95
ece	1858200206	$16.95	Turkey	1858280885	$16.95
temala & Belize	1858280451	$14.95	Tuscany & Umbria	1858280915	$15.95
land, Belgium			USA	185828080X	$18.95
Luxembourg	1858280877	$15.95	Venice	1858280362	$13.99
g Kong & Macau	1858280664	$13.95	Wales	1858280966	$14.95
gary	1858280214	$13.95	Women Travel	1858280710	$12.95
a	1858281040	$22.95	World Music	1858280176	$19.95
and	1858280958	$16.95	Zimbabwe & Botswana	1858280419	$16.95

gh Guides are available from all good bookstores, but can be obtained directly
e USA and Worldwide (except the UK*) from Penguin:

rge your order by Master Card or Visa (US$15.00 minimum order): call
0-255-6476; or send orders, with complete name, address and zip code, and list price,
$2.00 shipping and handling per order to: Consumer Sales, Penguin USA, PO Box
– Dept #17109, Bergenfield, NJ 07621. No COD. Prepay foreign orders by
rnational money order, a cheque drawn on a US bank, or US currency. No postage
nps are accepted. All orders are subject to stock availability at the time they are
cessed. Refunds will be made for books not available at that time. Please allow a
imum of four weeks for delivery.

availability and published prices quoted are correct at the time
oing to press but are subject to alteration without prior notice.
es currently not available outside the UK will be available by
1995. Call to check.

or UK orders, see separate price list

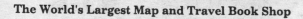

You are
A STUDENT

You travel
THE WORLD

You want TO SAVE MONEY

Here's how

The International Student Identity Card

Available at Student Travel Offices Worldwide.

Entitles you to discounts and special services worldwide.

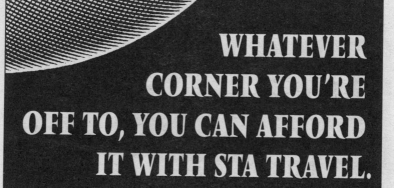